CRIMINAL INVESTIGATION

An Illustrated Case Study Approach

CRIMINAL INVESTIGATION

An Illustrated Case Study Approach

James Lasley

Nikos Guskos

**with
Randy A. Seymour**

PEARSON

Boston   Columbus   Indianapolis   New York   San Francisco   Upper Saddle River
Amsterdam   Cape Town   Dubai   London   Madrid   Milan   Munich   Paris   Montreal   Toronto
Delhi   Mexico City   São Paulo   Sydney   Hong Kong   Seoul   Singapore   Taipei   Tokyo

Editorial Director: Vernon Anthony
Acquisitions Editor: Sara Eilert
Assistant Editor: Megan Moffo
Editorial Assistant: Lynda Cramer
Director of Marketing: David Gesell
Senior Marketing Manager: Mary Salzman
Senior Marketing Coordinator: Alicia Wozniak
Senior Marketing Assistant: Les Roberts
Senior Managing Editor: JoEllen Gohr
Production Project Manager: Jessica H. Sykes
Senior Operations Supervisor: Pat Tonneman
Senior Art Director: Diane Ernsberger
Text and Cover Designer: Candace Rowley
Cover Art: ilbusca/iStockphoto
Lead Media Project Manager: Karen Bretz
Full-Service Project Management: Jogender Taneja/Aptara®, Inc.
Composition: Aptara®, Inc.
Printer/Binder: LSC Communications
Cover Printer: LSC Communications
Text Font: ITC Garamond Std Light

Library of Congress Cataloging-in-Publication Data
Lasley, James R.
   Criminal investigation: an illustrated case study approach/James R. Lasley, Nikos Guskos.
      p. cm.
   ISBN-13: 978-0-13-505749-0
   ISBN-10: 0-13-505749-3
   1. Criminal investigation—Pictorial works.   2. Criminal investigation—Case studies.   3. Crime scenes—Pictorial works.
4. Crime scenes—Case studies.   5. Legal photography—Case studies.   I. Guskos, Nikos.   II. Title.
   HV8073.L318 2014
   363.25--dc23   2012043165

ISBN 10:   0-13-505749-3
ISBN 13: 978-0-13-505749-0

Dedication

To the good, the bad and the ugly.

—James Lasley

I would like to dedicate this book to my lovely wife Renae and my four kids; Teddy, Sierra, Kayla, and Leah. Without their tireless dedication allowing me the time to write the book, it could not have been done. I would also like to thank my parents, Tony and Trudy Guskos, who gave me the guidance to maximize my achievements. I want to especially dedicate this book to my late sister Anna, whose brave and valiant fight against cancer ended too early. We all miss and love you.

—Nikos Guskos

I would like to dedicate this to my wife Veronica, my daughters Nicole and Kelsea, my step daughters Taviana and Felicity, my step son Ronald, and my grandchildren Jade, Jewel, Jasmine, Jillian, and Travis (two more on the way). A law Enforcement career is demanding of our time, and our family is what is left when we finally retire. I am truly blessed. I love you all.

—Randy A. Seymour

CONTENTS

Chapter 5   INVESTIGATIVE INTERVIEWING AND INTERROGATION   134

Chapter 7   DEVELOPING INVESTIGATIVE LEADS AND INTELLIGENCE   180

Chapter 10   SEXUAL ASSAULT SCENES   292

Chapter 19 TRANSNATIONAL, DOMESTIC, AND NARCO–TERROR SCENES 528

Chapter 20 FROM THE CRIME SCENE TO THE COURTROOM 554

PREFACE

Other criminal investigation texts *claim* to be different from all of the others, but this book *truly* is. In fact, from the moment we agreed to write this text during ongoing discussions with the editorial staff at Pearson, the general consensus was that our work *had* to stand apart from the countless criminal investigation books currently on the market, which have presented the same material the same way for years on end. Also, because we are not just authors, but also experienced first responders and investigators, our answer to the editors' question of how to create a criminal investigation book that "breaks away from the pack" was immediate and obvious: "Make crime scene photos a learning tool rather than just pictures as they are in *all* the existing texts!" Thus, *Criminal Investigation: An Illustrated Case Study Approach* was designed and written to bring this idea alive in the classroom.

INTRODUCING A NEW INVESTIGATIVE LEARNING TOOL

The Illustrated Case Study Approach

Our *Illustrated Case Study Approach* (ICSA) method is brought to life in several ways throughout the writing and design of this text. First, and most important, the ICSA method relies on presentations of related crime scene photos—from the same criminal incident—that illustrate the particular concept of criminal investigation being presented and discussed. The sequence begins with photo illustrations of views as they would appear to the first responders arriving at the scene. As the photo series continues, views as they appear to investigators actually processing the scene are presented to illustrate important learning points and promote discussions about specific methods and procedures of criminal investigation.

Second, the ICSA method is founded on the principle that the study of criminal investigation is a highly visual endeavor. After sifting through literally thousands of crime scene photos, we selected only those that best illustrate the investigative concepts presented in each chapter. Not only do these photos allow for instructing and learning applied investigative techniques, but they serve other instructional purposes as well. For example, the sequences illustrate various forensic photographic methods of producing visual evidence at the crime scene—which can additionally serve as an instructional tool for discussing issues relating to crime scene photography. We also prepared the photos for use in showing and discussing the actual pictorial record of a criminal incident that investigators consult for follow-up activities, lead development, and case preparation long after the crime scene has been released.

ORGANIZATION OF THE TEXT

Part I: Investigative Tools and Illustrated Cases

This first section of the text, chapters 1 through 8, presents a comprehensive discussion of both existing and state-of-the-art applied investigative techniques as well as the relevant legal, behavioral, and substantive information used to support the investigation process. In framing the information presented in this section, we attempt to strike a balance between the street and the classroom. That is to say, equal emphasis is given to experiential knowledge acquired at the crime scene and to research-based academic sources that view the investigative process through scientific methods. The ICSA method is introduced within the chapters in this section by the inclusion of brief **Illustrated Case Examples**. These crime scene photo sequences can be used as an instructional tool to apply various investigative concepts presented in a specific chapter. Additionally, students can reexamine all of the Illustrated Case Examples many times as they learn new investigative tools presented in subsequent chapters. The following specific topical material is presented in Part I:

CHAPTER 1 CRIMINAL INVESTIGATION: THEN AND NOW

- A comprehensive introductory chapter outlining the history and development of criminal investigation in the United States, and its roots in early European investigation including London's Bow Street Runners, Scotland Yard's CID, and the famous detective Vidocq in Paris. Present-day investigative agencies, including the Department of Homeland Security, also are discussed.

CHAPTER 2 INVESTIGATORS, INVESTIGATIONS , AND THE LAW

- The primary focus of this chapter is a thorough presentation of laws applicable to the investigative process, including those relating to search, seizure, and arrest. Special emphasis is given to explaining various types of warrants and the warrant acquisition process. An Illustrated Case Example of a firearm concealed within a vehicle is featured.

CHAPTER 3 THE PROCESS OF INVESTIGATING CRIME

- One of the core chapters of the text, introducing the major methods and techniques of investigation at the crime scene. The preliminary investigation is discussed from both the first responder's and the investigator's perspective. Special emphasis is given to crime scene sketching, photography, measurement, and search techniques. This chapter contains over 40 photos, diagrams, and figures, as well as a comprehensive Illustrated Case Example of a dead body outdoor crime scene.

CHAPTER 4 IDENTIFYING, COLLECTING, AND PRESERVING PHYSICAL EVIDENCE

- Another core chapter, providing a comprehensive overview of various types of evidence—trace, biological, firearms, documentary, and other crime scene evidence. Specific collection techniques are also presented for each evidence type. This chapter contains over 70 actual crime scene photos as well as images from tests used to examine evidence submitted to the crime lab for analysis. The Illustrated Case Example depicts a residential break-in containing nearly every possible type of physical evidence.

CHAPTER 5 INVESTIGATIVE INTERVIEWING AND INTERROGATION

- This chapter thoroughly discusses the "how-tos" of interviewing witnesses and interrogating suspects. Special attention is given to preinterview/interrogation behavioral assessments used to identify personality types and ways to use this information for selecting the most effective interview/interrogation method. Question construction methods, various interrogation techniques, and a detailed discussion of current Miranda laws are included along with an Illustrated Case Example involving a suspect interrogation.

CHAPTER 6 INVESTIGATIVE REPORT WRITING

- Although often overlooked by most criminal investigation texts, the process of investigative report writing is given "priority status" in this text as one of the most important aspects of conducting effective criminal investigations. In addition to presenting the basic format and construction of an incident investigation report, the FACCCT model of report writing also is described. An Illustrated Case Example of an officer-involved shooting is included to demonstrate how a report is generated following the crime scene investigation.

CHAPTER 7 DEVELOPING INVESTIGATIVE LEADS AND INTELLIGENCE

- The first half of this chapter deals with undercover work, surveillance, stings, use of informants, and other methods of developing leads and gathering information that can be used for criminal intelligence purposes later. The second half of the chapter explains methods and techniques used in the intelligence function. Special emphasis is given to transforming raw data sources to integrated sources of intelligence through link charts, net worth analysis, and other methods of analytic methods. An undercover operation used to bust an auto shop doubling as a drug lab is the Illustrated Case Example featured in this chapter.

CHAPTER 8 INVESTIGATION AND THE FORENSIC SCIENCES

- This chapter goes far beyond the discussion of crime lab functions included in most criminal investigation texts. Today's investigative environment—namely the C.S.I. effect—requires that investigators thoroughly understand how criminalists in the crime lab will examine and test evidence collected at the crime scene. This chapter provides this necessary higher level of information to contemporary students of criminal investigation. All major forensic areas, their examination procedures, and presumptive and confirmatory tests are discussed as well as illustrated with photos. Applied and clear examples of DNA profiling methods are also presented. A bound and gagged victim at a home invasion–style crime scene is the Illustrated Case Example in this chapter.

Part II: Crime Scenes and Illustrated Cases

The second half of the text discusses 12 specific types of criminal activities, laws relating to them, and specialized methods used in their investigation. This section also contains **Illustrated Case Examples** for each crime variety. These crime scene photo sequences are expanded and more detailed than those presented in Part I. Illustrated cases enable both students and instructors to apply not only the investigative methods learned in the earlier "Tools" section, but also the specific practices introduced in each chapter of Part II. Each case presented in Part II can be used as a self-contained learning example within each chapter or in conjunction with other crime scene case photos presented elsewhere for purposes of cross-comparison. The following chapters are included in Part II:

CHAPTER 9 HOMICIDE AND WOUNDING SCENES

- This chapter presents a detailed analysis and discussion of homicide crime scenes, including those caused by gunshot wounds, stabbings, blunt force trauma, asphyxiation, and poisoning. Descriptions of wounding characteristics and patterns used to investigate the likely cause and manner of death are presented in a step-by-step fashion. The Illustrated Case Examples include an indoor shooting victim at a crime scene staged by the offender, a body discovered in the trunk of an abandoned car, a victim of multiple stab wounds within a residence, and a premature burial victim excavated from a dirt grave. This core crime chapter includes over 60 crime scene photos.

CHAPTER 10   SEXUAL ASSAULT SCENES

- In this chapter, necessary procedures for first responders to and investigators of sexual assault scenes are outlined. In addition, methods for interviewing victims of sexual assault are also presented—along with suggestions for gaining their trust and cooperation in the investigation process. Detailed information is presented on the various types of biological evidence obtained from the sexual assault scene and the victim along with descriptions and functions of the physical evidence recovery kit (PERK). Other specialized discussions include psychological classifications of sexually deviant acts and sex crimes committed against children The Illustrated Case Examples include a public sexual assault and a domestic sexual assault.

CHAPTER 11   GANG CRIME SCENES

- To familiarize investigation students with the growing number of gang-related crimes, this specialized chapter on gang crime scenes has been included. This is the only chapter of its kind in a major criminal investigation text. Legal classifications of gangs and gang membership, gang typologies, characteristics of street gang behaviors, and specific investigative tools used to investigate street gang crimes are featured in this chapter. Also included is a special discussion on the investigation of gang crimes committed in prison and jail populations. Illustrated Case Examples in this chapter involve both vehicle and residential drive-by shootings.

CHAPTER 12   ROBBERY SCENES

- The legal and investigative foundations of street and commercial robbery are presented in this chapter, along with numerous types of robbery situations. In addition to ordinary street robberies, this chapter discusses robberies of banks, ATMs, armored cars, semi-trucks and trailers, motor homes, trailers, taxi cabs, convenience stores, and other commercial establishments. An illustrated case of a convenience store robbery is highlighted in this chapter.

CHAPTER 13   BURGLARY SCENES

- This chapter covers not only the various types of burglaries commonly encountered in the field, but also "new age" burglaries such as ATM Ramraids and Big Rig Heists. Behavioral profiles of burglars and fences are presented to show the *modus operandi* of these offender types. Stings, false store fronts, and other covert investigative techniques are presented to illustrate proactive investigative strategies for apprehending burglary suspects. An illustrated case of a residential burglary is featured in this chapter.

CHAPTER 14   LARCENY-THEFT SCENES

- A full range of thefts, schemes, swindles, and scams is presented in this chapter. Step-by-step illustrations of traditional white-collar crimes such as Ponzi and pyramid schemes are provided as well as discussion of newly emerging theft crimes involving identity theft, ATM tampering, romance scams, and telemarketing fraud. A special section on mortgage fraud is included due to the importance of understanding this offense for today's investigators of economic crimes. An Illustrated Case Example showing how ATM theft is carried out using a "Lebanese V" is given in this chapter.

CHAPTER 15   VEHICLE THEFT SCENES

- This chapter is a nontechnical explanation of the investigative tools used in vehicle theft and fraud-related crimes. All the vital components of vehicles that serve as identification points, such as the VIN, part IDs, and serial numbers, are shown in picture form so that students can gain a visual understanding of their function in the investigative process. Special attention is given to the investigation of automobile theft rings and to the identification and investigation of chop shops. Methods of vehicle theft and offender typologies are also presented. A large-scale chop shop is featured as the Illustrated Case Example in this chapter.

CHAPTER 16   COMPUTER CRIME SCENES

- The focus of this chapter is the investigation of electronic crime scenes. The various uses of computers, cellular phones, and other electronic devices to commit crimes such as tech-vandalism, cyber bullying, and international terrorism are explained. Types of cyber offenders, including novices, cyber punks, and information warriors, also are included. Evidence collection methods of electronic devices seized from residential and commercial crime scenes are presented in a step-by-step fashion. An Illustrated Case Example of a residential electronic crime scene in presented in this chapter

CHAPTER 17   ARSON AND EXPLOSION SCENES

- This chapter is divided into two sections: one covering the investigation of arson scenes, and the other examining the investigation of bombing and explosives crime scenes. Both chapters include rich crime scene photographs that illustrate the various investigative concepts related to fires and explosions necessary for the investigation of these crime scenes. This chapter also includes a unique discussion-photo series explaining the effects of high explosives used in terrorist attacks. Three Illustrated Case Examples are presented in this chapter.

CHAPTER 18   DRUG CRIME SCENES

- The design of this chapter was created (1) to familiarize students with drugs that are currently most often seen, sold, and trafficked through illegal street networks and (2) to present investigative methods most effective for detecting and apprehending drug offenders at both the individual and organized crime levels. Special attention is given to newly emerging varieties of street drugs used by emerging cultures in the United States and to the safe investigation of clandestine methamphetamine laboratories. This chapter features two Illustrated Case Examples: one scene showing a large marijuana grow house operation, and the other presenting a detailed clandestine meth lab crime scene.

CHAPTER 19   TRANSNATIONAL, DOMESTIC, AND NARCO–TERROR SCENES

- This chapter provides students with a broad overview of various forms of terrorism likely to be encountered by investigators within the United States. Various transnational terrorist groups active in the United States are presented from an investigative/culture perspective, along with a detailed discussion of their cellular organizational structure within major U.S. cities. Domestic terrorists, including hate groups, militias and lone wolf terrorists, are also presented. These forms of terrorism are also examined from a legal perspective within the context of the Patriot Act. A special section on narco–terrorism is featured, which addresses terrorist activities related to the illegal drug and human trafficking trades that currently target the U.S. border. This chapter includes an Illustrated Case Example featuring a simulated terror attack and response by the Los Angeles Sheriff's Department.

CHAPTER 20   FROM THE CRIME SCENE TO THE COURTROOM

- This chapter focuses on laws and practices related to the effective presentation of criminal cases by investigators in the courtroom. The material and discussions are practical in nature, showing various strategies employed by seasoned investigators for providing clear and convincing courtroom testimonies.

SPECIAL FEATURES

- *Hot Tips & Leads Boxes:* Each chapter presents at least one Hot Tips & Leads box in which special "how-to" information is provided for specific types of investigations and investigative problem solving.

- *Case Close-UPS:* Real cases from investigative agencies throughout the nation are provided in each chapter to illustrate specific types of investigations, investigative techniques, and lessons learned by investigators.
- *Summaries:* Each chapter includes a summary discussion of key learning objectives to provide students a quick reference to essential subject matter presented in the reading.
- *Key Terms:* Important investigative terminology is highlighted within each chapter, and is also presented at the chapter's end.
- *Review Questions:* Following the chapter readings are review questions on important investigative and legal concepts that both instructors and students can use for written assignments and in-class discussions of chapter material.
- *Applied Investigative Exercises:* Each chapter contains an investigative scenario—directly related to the Illustrated Case Examples—that challenges students to apply investigative techniques presented in the chapter readings to crime scene photos illustrating the case or cases featured in the chapter.
- *Internet Resources:* Web sites with more information about topics presented in the readings are included at the end of the chapter. Many of these sites provide links to professional investigative associations whose members have extensive knowledge, professional experience, and valuable employment information about the field of criminal investigation.

INSTRUCTOR SUPPLEMENTS

The following supplementary materials are available to support instructors' use of the main text:

eBooks. Criminal Justice is available in two eBook formats, CourseSmart and Adobe Reader. CourseSmart is an exciting new choice for students looking to save money. As an alternative to purchasing the printed textbook, students can purchase an electronic version of the same content. With a CourseSmart eTextbook, students can search the text, make notes online, print out reading assignments that incorporate lecture notes, and bookmark important passages for later review. For more information, or to purchase access to the CourseSmart eTextbook, visit www.coursesmart.com.

TestBank and MyTest. These supplements represent a new standard in testing material. Whether you use the basic Test Bank in the Instructor's Manual or generate questions electronically through MyTest, every question is linked to the text's learning objective, page number, and level of difficulty. This allows for quick reference in the text and an easy way to check the difficulty level and variety of your questions. MyTest can be accessed at www.PearsonMyTest.com.

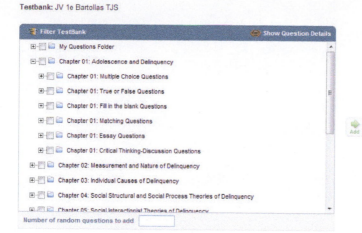

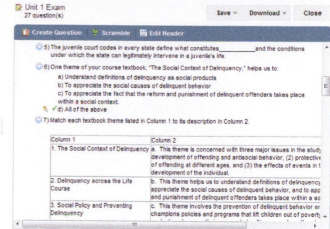

Interactive Lecture PowerPoint® Presentation. This supplement will enhance lectures like never before. Award-winning presentation designers worked with our authors to develop PowerPoint presentations that truly engage the student. Much like the text, the PowerPoint presentations are full of instructionally sound graphics, tables, charts, and photos that do what presentation software was meant to do: support and enhance your lecture. Data and difficult concepts are presented in a truly interactive way, helping students connect the dots and stay focused on the lecture.

The Pearson Criminal Justice Online Community. Available at www.mycriminaljusticecommunity.com, this site is a place for educators to connect and to exchange ideas and advice on courses, content, Criminal Justice, and so much more.

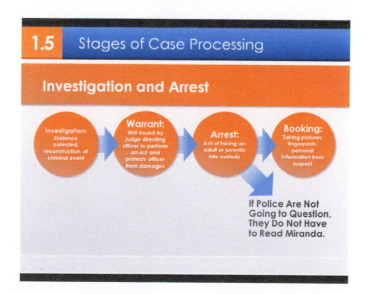

To access these supplementary materials online, instructors need to request an instructor access code at www.pearsonhighered.com/irc. Within 48 hours after registering, you will receive a confirmation e-mail that includes an instructor access code. When you receive your code, go to the site and log on for full instructions on downloading materials you wish to use.

Additional student and instructor resources can be accessed at www.pearsonhighered.com/Careers.

ABOUT THE AUTHORS

James Lasley

James Lasley, Ph.D., is Professor of Criminal Justice at California State University, Fullerton, and has held previous faculty appointments at Washington State University, Arizona State University, and The University of Southern California. His previous criminal justice agency experience includes prior work with United States Probation and Parole (Washington, D.C.), The Los Angeles Police Department, and California Commission on Police Officer Standards and Training (P.O.S.T.). He has also worked previously in the criminal justice private sector as a licensed Bail Bond Agent and Bounty Hunter (California) and has provided expert testimony on street gang matters in criminal trials, as well as in hearings conducted by the U.S. Congress. His published works include over 50 books and articles covering a variety of issues concerning policing, forensic science and investigation, which have been featured in a wide range of practitioner-, trade-, government-, and academic-oriented publications, including Muscle & Fitness Magazine, FBI Law Enforcement Bulletin, NIJ (National Institute of Justice) Research in Brief, and Justice Quarterly.

Nikos Guskos

Nikos Guskos is a Criminal Justice professor and lectures at various universities including California State University, Fullerton, where he is currently an Adjunct Professor of Criminal Justice. He holds a Master of Arts degree in Criminal Justice from Chapman University and is founder of the Guskos Institute—a criminal justice consulting firm located in Huntington Beach, CA. His teaching and research areas of expertise, in addition to criminal investigation, include street gangs, financial crimes, and homeland security. He is also presently an active member of law enforcement in Southern California and has several years of field experience in policing, which include patrol and specialized units focusing on gangs, financial crimes, and tactical training. Additionally, he is experienced as a first-responder to death scenes and has assisted in investigating several homicides.

Presently, he is assigned to the Homeland Security Division of his department. Previous to his current assignment, he spent five years at the highest soft risk threat target in the Southern California region area. Responsible for enforcement, investigations and threat assessments. On a national level, he also serves as a consultant to The National Institute of Justice (NIJ) for research issues concerning policing and criminal investigation and is a proud veteran of the United States Army.

Randy A. Seymour

Retired Sergeant Randy Seymour has over 25 years of law enforcement experience with a large metropolitan Sheriff's Department. His assignments included Custody, Patrol, Specialized Street Gang Patrol, Patrol Training Officer, and Patrol Sergeant. He also has seven years experience as a Street Gang Detective and more than nine years as a Homicide Investigator. He was the lead investigator in close to 100 homicides including stabbings, shootings, blunt force trauma, strangulation, rape, and poisoning. He assisted in more than 100 additional homicides during his career.

Sergeant Seymour was also the lead investigator in more than 30 deputy- and officer-involved shootings and has assisted in more than 30 additional shootings. He also investigated approximately 50 suicides from gunshot wounds, hangings, overdoses, bleeding to death from self-inflicted cuts, and stepping in front of trains or other vehicles. He also investigated more than 100 suspicious deaths where the cause of death was not initially known.

Sergeant Seymour personally responded to more than 250 death scenes and conducted the appropriate investigation. He also taught homicide scenes, homicides, suicides, sudden infant death syndrome and gang related homicides to local law enforcement and law enforcement personnel from across the country. Sergeant Seymour has a Bachelor of Science Degree in Occupational Studies- Vocational Arts from California State University Long Beach.

ACKNOWLEDGMENTS

First, the authors would like to express their extreme gratitude to the following municipal, county, state, federal and private law enforcement/investigative agencies for their assistance in providing information and/or advice used in the preparation of this text. Any agency not listed below that nonetheless assisted us in our endeavors was inadvertently excluded and we apologize, and thank you, for your time, effort and professional expertise.

	Municipal Agencies	County Agencies	State Agencies
AL	Birmingham Police	Jefferson County Sheriffs	Alabama Department of Public Safety
	Mobile Police		
AK	Anchorage Police		Alaska Department of Public Safety
AZ	Mesa Police	Maricopa County Sheriffs	Arizona Department of Public Safety
	Phoenix Police		Arizona Department of Corrections
	Tucson Police		
AR	Little Rock Police	Superior Court, Pulaski Co.	Arkansas State Police
CA	Anaheim Police	Los Angeles County Sheriffs	California Highway Patrol
	Chula Vista Police	Orange County Probation	California P.O.S.T
	Garden Grove Police	Orange County Sheriffs	CA Dept. of Corrections & Rehabilitation
	Los Angeles Police	San Diego County Sheriffs	CA State Dept. of Insurance
	National City Police	Superior Court, Los Angeles Co.	
	Riverside Police	LA County District Attorneys	
	Sacramento Police	Orange County District Attorneys	
	San Diego Police	Santa Clara County Sheriffs	
	San Francisco Police		
	San Jose Police		
	Santa Ana Police		
	Oakland Police		
CO	Denver Police	Denver County Sheriffs	Colorado Bureau of Investigation
	Vale Police		Colorado State Patrol
CT	New Haven Police		
DE	Delaware Police		Delaware Department of Justice
FL	Miami Police	Broward County Sheriffs	Florida Dept. of Law Enforcement
	Jacksonville Police	Miami-Dade County Sheriffs	Florida State Attorney's Office
	Tampa Police	Orange County Sheriffs	
	St. Petersburg Police	Miami District Attorneys	
	Gainesville Police		
GA	Atlanta Police	Fulton County Sheriffs	Georgia Dept. of Public Safety
	Augusta Police		
HI	Honolulu Police		Hawaii Dept. of Public Safety
ID	Boise Police		Idaho State Police
IL	Chicago Police	Cook County Sheriffs	Illinois State Police
	Fairview Police Department		Illinois Dept. of Corrections
IN	Indianapolis Police		Indiana State Police
IA		Jefferson County Sheriffs	
KS	Kansas City Police		
KY	Louisville Police		Kentucky State Police
LA	New Orleans Police	Jefferson Parish Sheriffs	Louisiana Dept. of Public Safety & Corrections
ME	Portland Police		Maine State Police
MD	Baltimore Police	Frederick County Sheriffs	Maryland State Police
			Maryland Dept. of Motor Vehicles
MA	Cambridge Police		Massachusetts State Police

MI	Detroit Police	Marion County Superior Court	Michigan State Police
	Grand Rapids Police		
	Ann Arbor Police		
MN	Minneapolis Police		Minnesota State Police
MS			Mississippi Department of Public Safety
MO	St. Louis Police	DA Office, St. Louis County	Missouri State Highway Patrol
	Kansas City Police		
MT	Billings Police		Montana Dept. of Justice
NE	Omaha Police	Polk County Sheriffs	Nebraska State Police/Patrol
	Lincoln Police		
NV	Las Vegas Metropolitan Police	Clark County Sheriffs	Nevada Department of Public Safety
	Reno Police		Nevada Gaming Control Board
NH			New Hampshire Dept. of Safety
NJ	Newark Police		New Jersey State Police
NM	Albuquerque Police		New Mexico Dept. of Public Safety
NY	New York City Police	Erie County Sheriffs	New York State Police
	New York City Transit Police	Suffolk County Sheriffs	New York State Division of Parole
	New York City Fire Department		New York State Attorney General's Office
	Albany Police		
	Buffalo Police		
	Rochester Police		
	Yonkers Police		
	New York City Probation Department		
NC	Charlotte Police		NC Dept. of Crime Control and Public Safety
ND	Fargo Police		North Dakota State Police
OH	Cleveland Police	Franklin County Sheriffs	Ohio State Highway Patrol
	Columbus Police		
	Cincinnati Police		
OK	Oklahoma City Police		Oklahoma Department of Public Safety
	Tulsa Police		
OR	Portland Police	Multnomah County Sheriffs	Oregon Dept. of Public Safety
	Eugene Police		
PA	Pittsburgh Police	Philadelphia District Attorneys	Pennsylvania State Police
	Philadelphia Police		
	Erie Police		
RI			Rhode Island State Police
SC	Columbia Police		SC Dept. of Public Safety
SD			SD Dept. of Public Safety
			SD Dept. of Game, Fish and Parks
TN	Nashville Police		Tennessee Dept. of Safety & Homeland Security
	Memphis Police		Tennessee Dept. of Human Services
	Knoxville Police		
TX	Dallas Police	Dallas County Courts	Texas Dept. of Public Safety
	Houston Police	Dallas County Sheriffs	DPS Texas Rangers
	Austin Police	Harris County Sheriffs	Texas Department of Criminal Justice
	Brownsville Police		
UT	Salt Lake City Police		Utah Dept. of Public Safety
	Ogden Police		
VT			Vermont State Police
VA	Virginia Beach Police		Virginia State Police
	Norfolk Police		
WA	Spokane Police	Kings County Sheriffs	Washington State Patrol
	Seattle Police		
	Tacoma Police		

DC	DC Metropolitan Police	
WV	Charleston Police	West Virginia State Police
WI	Madison Police	Wisconsin State Patrol
	Milwaukee Police	
	Eau Claire Police	
WY	Cheyenne Police	Wyoming Highway Patrol
		Wyoming Game and Fish

FEDERAL AGENCIES

Federal Bureau of Investigation

Bureau of Alcohol, Tobacco, Firearms & Explosives

U.S. Customs & Border Protection

U.S. Immigration & Customs Enforcement

The Department of Homeland Security

TSA Federal Air Marshal Service

United States Probation

National Institute of Justice

U.S. Coast Guard

U.S. Marshal's Service

U.S. Drug Enforcement Administration

U.S. Secret Service

Federal Bureau of Prisons

U.S. Naval Criminal Investigation Service

INTERPOL (U.S. & Abroad)

Office of Special Investigations

Bureau of Justice Statistics

United States Marine Corps

PRIVATE AGENCIES

National Insurance Crime Bureau

National Fraud Information Center

International Association of Marine Investigators

Cellmark Forensic Services

Pinkerton Consulting & Investigations

The National Center for Victims of Crime

Target Corporation Security Division

National Center for Missing & Exploited Children

Also, we express our extreme gratitude to the countless individuals who helped us in various ways to development, prepare and complete this book. In particular, we would like to thank Gerald Pittenger (Chief, Scotts Valley Police Department) for his assistance in preparing the historical aspects of criminal investigators presented in the text. James Farris, former Special Agent for the U.S. Office of Special Investigations (OSI) must also be thanked for his sharing countless hours of informative conversations regarding investigative field tactics that we ultimately used as "intelligence" in this book. We are also highly indebted to James Larson (San Diego, PD), James Guffey (Oakland, CA, PD) and Michael Hooper (LAPD and California P.O.S.T.) for their invaluable input regarding state-of-the-are first-responder and on-the-ground crime scene investigative duties. LeRoy A. Scheller USMC (Ret.) cannot be forgotten for his providing us with technical expertise regarding the subject areas of terrorism and counter-terrorism. Additionally a special thanks to Michael R. Havstad of the Los Angeles County Sheriff Crime lab whose expertise on crime scene photography was essential to the completion of the book. We would also like to thank Ken Talianko, Tom Wilford, Jaime Machuca, Eric Matias, and Chad Dowdy for their participation and input into various subject matters contained within. Last but not least, Judge Michael Harwin deserves a special thanks for allowing us into his courtroom and sharing with us his experience involving extreme "courage on the bench." Thanks to the following reviewers: Samuel Thomas, Hawaii Community College; Charles Kocher, Cumberland County College; Jim Newman, Rio Hondo College; Todd Lough, Western Ilinois University; Sarah Elhoffer, St. Louis Community College—Meramec; Jane Munley, Luzerne County Community College; Bert Ouderkirk, San Antonio College; Greg Osowski, Henry Ford Community College; and Richard J. Mangan, Florida Atlantic University.

Of course this book could not have been completed without the highly skilled and trained staff of Pearson Publishing (Jessica Sykes, Megan Moffo, and Sara Eilert). Thanks a bunch!!!!!!!

CRIMINAL INVESTIGATION

An Illustrated Case Study Approach

CHAPTER ONE

CRIMINAL INVESTIGATION: THEN AND NOW

Learning Objectives

After completing this chapter, you should be able to:

1. Outline the history of policing and criminal investigation.
2. Describe how developments in research and science have aided criminal investigation.
3. Discuss the three periods of American criminal investigation.
4. Discuss the origins of criminal investigative agencies in America.
5. Explain the organization, roles, and responsibilities of various police agencies.

Chapter Outline

Criminal Investigation and the Detective are Born
- The First Detectives: London's Bow Street Runners
- Eugène Vidocq: The Father of Criminal Investigation
- The First Police Detective Branch at London's Scotland Yard

Fictional Sleuths
- Sherlock Holmes Invents Crime Solving by Deduction

The First Scientific Investigators of Crime

American Criminal Investigation

The Prescientific Period
- The First Wave of American Investigators

The Scientific Period
- The First Investigative Crime Laboratory
- Calvin Goddard: The Study of Ballistics Goes to Trial
- The FBI Turns to Scientific Investigation
- The Academic Innovations of Investigative Science by Paul Kirk
- Criminalistics and the Forensic Sciences: Contributions of the Scientific Era to Today's Crime Lab

The Technological Period
- Suspect Information (NCIC) and Fingerprint (IAFIS) Databases
- The Pitchfork Case: Sir Alec Jeffreys Discovers DNA Fingerprinting
- Homeland Security and the War on Terror

A "Real World" Approach to the Study of Criminal Investigation

INTRODUCTION

IN A SECURE ROOM WITHIN a heavily guarded building, a group of investigators makes final plans to raid the residence of a middle-age male allegedly plotting to overthrow the U.S. government. At approximately 11:30 P.M., a confidential informant notifies the investigative team that the suspect is asleep in an upstairs bedroom of his home. Reacting quickly to this information, the investigators arm themselves with weapons, a battering ram, and a warrant for the suspect's arrest. At the suspect's home, they immediately serve the "no-knock" warrant, rushing upstairs and arresting their man without incident.

Upon first reading the incident just described, you might assume that it is the investigation and capture of a present-day "post-9/11" terrorist. In reality, however, this account is a report of the events in 1776 leading to the arrest of William Franklin, then-governor of Pennsylvania and the son of Benjamin Franklin—founder of the nation's first police department in the City of Philadelphia. William Franklin was arrested by a group of New Jersey rebels, who called themselves *U.S. Marshals,* after their investigation revealed that he was acting as a spy for the British government. Franklin is believed to have been the first prisoner taken in the name of the newly formed United States of America, making his arrest the nation's first investigation by the country's first investigators.

As you will discover in this chapter, the story of William Franklin is not an atypical one in the history of modern criminal investigation. The field of criminal investigation as it exists today has been shaped by several critical events and key individuals. For example, it was not until a handful of detectives from London's Scotland Yard tracked down a serial killer terrorizing England's countryside that citizens began to trust police officers called *detectives* who did not wear a uniform and strictly performed investigative tasks. Similarly, the birth of both public and private investigation can be traced back to the ideas and aspirations of one man, Allan Pinkerton. Pinkerton's life-long ambition to become an investigator led him to persuade the Chicago Police Department to appoint him the nation's first municipal detective in 1849. Just one year later, he left this post and created the first

U.S. private detective agency, which also formed the roots of governmental investigative agencies such as the U.S. Secret Service.

Complex fingerprinting methods, which replaced wanted posters as a means of tracking down offenders,were introduced by an ambitious new director of the FBI, J. Edgar Hoover, whose mission during the 1940s was to introduce scientific methods into the practice of criminal investigation. In the 1970s, computer databases further advanced the efficiency of investigators through the creation of automated fingerprint identification systems. Most recently, the terrorist attacks of September 11, 2001 prompted the U.S. government to perform its largest coordinated effort to improve the nation's investigative capabilities both domestically and internationally by creating the Department of Homeland Security in 2002.

As you read this chapter, constantly remind yourself of the various people and events that have made criminal investigation in the United States what it is today. By doing so, you will better understand not only the present-day methods of criminal investigation discussed in later chapters, but also the likely professional paths that investigators will follow in the future.

CRIMINAL INVESTIGATION AND THE DETECTIVE ARE BORN

The First Detectives: London's Bow Street Runners

As just discussed, the origins of criminal investigation can be traced back to many significant people and events throughout the history of crime detection. It is possible that formal investigations—separate from the regular police function—came into being with the advent of the detective. Unfortunately, pinpointing this event in history is difficult because many persons and groups lay claim to the title of "First Detective." The earliest of these may have been a small group of unpaid citizen volunteers, referred to as "thief takers," organized in the Bow Street area of London in 1748 by **Henry Fielding** (1707–1754).[1] Known for their fleetness of foot, thief takers tracked down property offenders and received rewards from crime victims upon return of the property—serving a function similar to that of modern-day bounty hunters. In 1754, the thief takers were transformed by Fielding and his half-brother **Sir John Fielding** (who was blind and noted for recognizing criminals by their voice) into what many believe to be the first organized nonmunicipal detectives—the **Bow Street Runners** (see Figure 1.1). The group's six to eight members—each armed with a truncheon, cutlass, and pistol—tracked offenders across all of England. Many police historians regard them as the first paid plainclothes investigators of suspected criminals.[2] The Bow Street Runners also had a sketchy history of professionalism, however, including accusations of corrupt practices—such as cooperating with criminals to steal property and then staging its recovery to gain cash bonuses from their victim clients.[3]

FIGURE 1.1 ▶ An artist's depiction of the Bow Street Runners breaking up a house party in London circa 1824. (Courtesy Getty Images USA, Inc.)

Eugène Vidocq: The Father of Criminal Investigation

In his book *The First Detective*,[4] Morton argues that **Eugène Vidocq** (1775–1857) should be fêted as the "father of criminal investigation." Vidocq (pronounced "Vee-Dok," and pictured in Figure 1.2), similar to many other pioneering

FIGURE 1.2 ▶ Eugène François Vidocq (1775–1857) is considered by many to be the father of criminal investigation. Vidocq is credited with the creation of many detective methods used today, including the use of disguises and costumes to perform undercover work. The fictional sleuth Sherlock Holmes was based on the casework of Vidocq. (Pantheon/SuperStock)

detectives, had a criminal past, which he relied upon as an investigator to "beat criminals at their own game." In 1811, Vidocq began his career as perhaps the world's first public detective with *La Sûreté* (French Undercover Police) in Paris. Upon rising to the rank of chief, he supervised a small group of four detectives who investigated cases ranging from common thefts to political espionage. Vidocq was best known for his use of disguises and trickery to infiltrate criminal gangs and elicit confessions from street thugs. According to Metzner:

> Detective Vidocq assumed the parts of women as well as men, foreigners as well as Frenchmen, older as well as younger people. He impersonated porters, craftsmen, soldiers, businessmen. And, of course, Vidocq continued to play thieves.[5]

After leaving public service in 1827, Vidocq founded France's first private investigative agency, *Le Bureau de Reassignments* (Office of Intelligence). This agency maintained the first comprehensive database of criminal identification, with information on some 30,000 known offenders throughout Europe.[6]

The First Police Detective Branch at London's Scotland Yard

Historically speaking, the most influential move toward creating a permanent criminal investigation function within municipal law enforcement agencies was the establishment in 1842 of London's **Scotland Yard Detective Branch**. Although Sir Robert Peel had founded the London Metropolitan Police in 1829, the London public took over a decade to warm to out-of-uniform police officers conducting investigations. The idea of establishing a permanent branch of detectives dressed like ordinary citizens (as shown in Figure 1.3) was fiercely opposed because people feared that police would overstep their authority and unnecessarily invade individuals' right to privacy.[7] Not until London was struck by the Daniel Good murder case did negative public attitudes begin to thaw regarding permanent plainclothes police detectives at Scotland Yard authorized to conduct covert criminal investigations. According to the case history:

> on the evening of Wednesday, April 6, 1842, a four-wheeled pony-chaise pulled up at a tailor's shop in Wandsworth High Street. The driver, Daniel Good, who had his small son with him, was a middle-aged Irishman and the servant of Mr. Shiell, a well-to-do retired West India merchant living at Roehampton. Good was known to Mr. Collingbourne, the tailor, who allowed him to take a pair of black knee-breeches on credit; but as he was leaving he was seen by the shop-assistant to slip a pair of trousers under his coat. Followed to his chaise by Collingbourne and the assistant, he indignantly denied the theft and drove off.
>
> A policeman was fetched, P.C. Gardner of V Division. Gardner went to Roehampton, then a small village a mile or two from Putney, and at Mr. Shiell's house was told that Good was probably at the stables. When found there Good again denied the theft, but offered to pay for the breeches.

This was a mistake, for it must have strengthened Gardner's determination to search the premises. He discovered nothing to concern him in the coach-house, where the pony-chaise was standing; when however, he proposed to look further Good raised objections. In the corner of the stall were some trusses of hay, which Good began to shift about; Gardner stopped him, removed a truss or two himself and by the light of a candle saw what at first he took for a plucked goose. One of the shop-boys thought it was a dead pig. Another candle was lighted, but before the object could be examined events took a new turn. Good rushed out of the stables and locked the door behind him.

> While attempts were being made to break it open Gardner cleared away more trusses and revealed the mutilated torso of a woman . . . [and also] noticed an obnoxious smell, and in the fireplace of the harness-room discovered the charred remains of a head and limbs.[8]

Daniel Good remained at large for nearly two weeks. During this time, newspaper reports of the horrific murder and a "madman on the loose" caused a wave of fear and panic throughout London. Good's highly publicized trial revealed that the uniformed police's lack of investigative ability led to unnecessary delay in the killer's capture. The resulting public demand to

FIGURE 1.3 ▶ Early plainclothes London detectives accompany uniformed police to conduct the search of a crime scene. The idea of a special nonuniformed squad of police that specialized in investigative work was not accepted at first by the public, who feared that police out of uniform could not be trusted. (Courtesy Library of Congress)

improve existing police investigative know-how brought about the creation of the Detective Branch at Scotland Yard. Initially staffed with six full-time police-detectives (later shortened to *detectives*)—who wore plainclothes when approved to do so by the Police Commissioner—this branch could be hired out to work private cases as well. Ultimately, in 1877, the Detective Branch was succeeded by the CID (Criminal Investigation Division), which is considered the world's first large-scale criminal investigative division with a municipal policing agency. Still in existence today, the Detective Branch at Scotland Yard is England's largest detective force.[9]

FICTIONAL SLEUTHS

Sherlock Holmes Invents Crime Solving by Deduction

The field of criminal investigation has many of its conceptual roots in early writings about fictional sleuths. Almost immediately after the first detectives were created, writers were publishing stories about them. These stories contained their fair share of embellishments, but were also grounded in reality. For example, The Bow Street Runners were featured in Charles Dickens' 1838 classic *Oliver Twist*.[10] In 1842, Dickens became a regular at Scotland Yard's new Detective Branch, where he studied the methods of investigators. He later used his research in writing his novel *Bleak House*[11] (1853), in which history's first fictional detective—Inspector Bucket—was introduced. Perhaps the most influential fictional sleuth to shape "real-life" criminal investigation—Auguste Dupin in Edgar Allan Poe's *The Murders in the Rue Morgue*[12] (1841)—was fashioned after the exploits and methods of Vidocq, who had published his personal memoirs in 1828. Moreover, 12 years after his death, Vidocq was immortalized as the famed **Sherlock Holmes** (see Figure 1.4) in Sir Arthur Conan Doyle's 1887 novel *A Study in Scarlet*.[13]

In *Scarlet,* Doyle for the first time introduces logic to the world of criminal investigation—a scientific method for solving crime that he referred to as *deduction*. In the following passage from this novel, Sherlock Holmes explains the concept of deductive logic as an investigative tool:

> Like all other arts the Science of Deduction and Analysis is one that can only be acquired by long and patient study . . . By a man's fingernails, by his coat-sleeve, by his boot, by his trouser knees, by the callosities on his forefinger and thumb, by his expression, by his shirt cuffs—by each of these things a man's calling is surely revealed.[14]

In addition to a keen eye for detail, as the above quote illustrates, Holmes' deductive process requires the ability to determine what does not exist from an analysis of what does exist. In other words, numerous observations aimed at explaining the "unknowns" surrounding a criminal event are tested one by one against known facts derived from available evidence. Observations not supported by the facts are excluded, leaving the remaining ones to pinpoint likely suspects and circumstances

FIGURE 1.4 ▶ Pictured above are Tony Howlett (left) and Maurice Campbell (right) portraying detective Sherlock Holmes and his investigative companion Dr. John Watson, respectively. Mr. Howlett and Dr. Campbell both are members of the Sherlock Holmes Society of London. The Sherlock Holmes Society has members throughout the world and is dedicated to preserving and revitalizing the image of Sherlock Homes in contemporary times. The Society, founded in 1951 in London, today has members throughout the world. Information about the Sherlock Holmes Society can be obtained at www.sherlock-holmes.org.uk/society/society.php. (Courtesy The Sherlock Holmes Society of London)

responsible for a particular crime. Ironically, the deductive method first introduced in Doyle's fictional detective novels has proven over time to be one of the most valuable investigative concepts for solving real-life criminal cases.

THE FIRST SCIENTIFIC INVESTIGATORS OF CRIME

Yet another possible origin of criminal investigation is the development of crime detection through scientific and laboratory analyses. Fingerprints were used for identification purposes in China as far back as the 700s, about the same time the Chinese invented gunpowder.[15] In the 1100s, England first established the national office of coroner, but not until the late 1500s were autopsies performed for the specific purpose of identifying wounds. Around 1600, chemists had invented invisible ink.[16] This perhaps led to the first application of science to a specific criminal activity—François Demelle's 1609 treatise on how to identify a forged document.[17]

The definite beginning of the scientific expert era in criminal investigation matters, however, is marked by the work of Spanish toxicologist **Mathieu Orfila**[18] (1787–1853). In 1813, he defined the study of **toxicology** in a book on the effects of various poisons as a cause of death. His investigative abilities became known to the general public in 1840, when he served as an expert witness in a high-profile criminal case where a woman was accused of killing her husband by sprinkling a white powder on his food. The available toxicological tests gave negative results for the presence of arsenic in the man's body. Applying his own toxicological methods in the case, Orfila proved that poisoning was indeed the cause of death, which ultimately led to the wife's conviction for murder.[19] Other pioneering investigative scientists

ABSTRACT OF

THE ANTHROPOMETRICAL SIGNALMENT

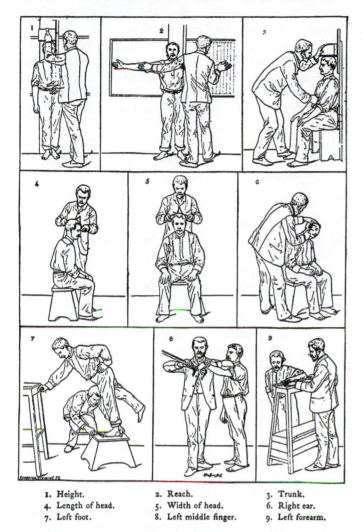

1. Height.
4. Length of head.
7. Left foot.

2. Reach.
5. Width of head.
8. Left middle finger.

3. Trunk.
6. Right ear.
9. Left forearm.

FIGURE 1.5 ▶ The Bertillon method of anthropometry was widely used in the early 1900s in the United States for identifying and classifying criminals by taking scientific measurements of their body including arm length, ear diameter, and head circumference. Because this method had numerous flaws, law enforcement agencies later replaced it with fingerprinting. (NLM/Science Source/Photo Researchers, Inc.)

include **Alphonse Bertillon** (1853–1914), who in 1883 developed a method of **anthropometry** in which features of the human body were measured and recorded for purposes of criminal identification[20] as illustrated in Figure 1.5. This method, however, was superseded by **Sir Francis Galton's** (1822–1911) work (*Fingerprints,* published in 1892) demonstrating how offenders could be identified more precisely through scientific analyses of fingerprints.[21]

Ironically, the term *criminal investigation* was coined by **Hans Gross** (1847–1915), an Austrian attorney interested in the application of science to crime. Gross's 1893 book *Criminal Investigation* is the first systematic treatise explaining how a wide range of available scientific methods could be used in the investigative process.[22] For example, with regard to employing the principles of geology in crime scene investigation, Gross wrote, "Dirt on shoes can often tell us more about where the wearer had last been than toilsome inquiries."[23] Gross also advocated the use of chemistry, photography, physics, fingerprinting, psychology, and numerous other existing academic and scientific methodologies in criminal investigation. Furthermore, he introduced the term **criminalistics** to describe the general process by which any science could be used as a criminal investigation tool.

AMERICAN CRIMINAL INVESTIGATION

The history of American criminal investigation can be divided into three distinct periods. The first can be called the *Prescientific Period.* At this time a nexus existed between the types of crimes, offenders, laws, and investigators that shaped the future of criminal investigation in the United States. The subsequent evolution took place, at different times and in different ways, throughout different regions of the nation. The predominant investigative methods used during the Prescientific Period included monetary incentives for the capture of fugitives by private citizens and the creation of public investigative agencies to hunt down specific "public enemies" by employing various intelligence gathering methods—and of course, keen intuition.

The second period of American investigative history—the *Scientific Period*—was ushered in by the creation of the modern crime lab. Physical evidence now became a hallmark of crime scene investigation and a necessity for proving guilt in a court of law. In this period there was a veritable explosion of crime scene investigation methods based on laboratory tests of both biological and nonbiological evidence. Blood stains, fingerprints, medical pathology, toxicology, lie detection—to name a few of these methods—came onto the investigative horizon in the Scientific Period. Within this era was born an ongoing partnership between criminal investigation in the field and evidence analysis in the laboratory.

The final, and present, period of criminal investigation can be called the *Technological Period.* This period's primary benchmark includes the advanced use of large-scale computer evidence databases and DNA for purposes of suspect identification. These technological investigative tools have either built upon innovations of the Scientific Period or rendered some of them obsolete. Overall, advanced technology applied to evidence processing, suspect identification, and crime scene reconstruction has greatly enhanced the overall effectiveness and efficiency of the criminal investigation process.

THE PRESCIENTIFIC PERIOD

The First Wave of American Investigators

The beginnings of the Prescientific Period can be traced back as far as the American Revolution. Shortly after Britain's surrender, private individuals and military operatives conducted scattered investigations concerning the unlawful activities as well as national loyalty of the new American citizenry. These informal investigative activities soon gave way to the formal establishment of state, local, and federal agencies as well as private detectives to detect, track, and arrest the growing number of offenders committing sophisticated criminal acts. The historical development of these investigative agencies is discussed in the following sections.

U.S. MARSHALS SERVICE

The **U.S. Marshals Service (USMS)** is the first and oldest federal law enforcement agency in the United States. It was created in 1789 by President George Washington to support federal courts, and to oversee the proper enforcement of laws within various jurisdictions. Early on, the Marshals Service's law enforcement activity consisted of handling suspected law violators on a case-by-case basis, preparing the cases for prosecution by the U.S. Attorney General's Office, also established in 1789. The agency also enforced laws and carried out legal orders issued by judges as well as Congress and the president. Persons serving as Marshals were appointed for a term of 4 years.[24] The present-day Marshals Service (as shown in Figure 1.6) still has a general mission to protect court officers and buildings and to ensure effective operation of the U.S. judicial system. In addition, U.S. Marshals assist with court security, transport prisoners, serve arrest warrants, and perform investigations leading to the capture of fugitives.

U.S. POSTAL INSPECTION SERVICE

The nation's first formal investigative branch, the Office of Instructions and Mail Depredations, was formed in 1830 by the U.S. Post Office Department. The agency was later to become

FIGURE 1.6 ▶ The U.S. Marshals Service is the nation's first and oldest federal law enforcement agency, established by President George Washington in 1789. Today, the U.S. Marshals Service engages in fugitive apprehension, asset seizure and forfeiture, witness protection, and various other vital investigative functions. (Courtesy U.S. Department of Justice)

the second oldest U.S. federal law enforcement organization, the **U.S. Postal Inspection Service (USPIS)**. Investigators, initially called *surveyors,* later had their title changed, becoming the first U.S. law enforcement officials known as *Special Agents.* By 1853, there were 18 full-time postal inspectors assigned to various duties, including reporting on the condition of steamboats, stagecoaches, railroads, and horses used to deliver the mail. In addition, the inspectors investigated all activities related to mail theft, for which an act of Congress in 1792 had authorized the death penalty.[25] Currently, the U.S. Postal Inspection Service continues to enforce the laws defending the nation's mail system from illegal or dangerous use, including mail fraud, mail theft, violent crimes, identity theft, bombings, child exploitation, and terrorism.

TEXAS RANGERS

The early to mid-1800s was also the starting point for many local and state investigative agencies. The **Texas Rangers**, founded in 1835, were the nation's first policing agency with statewide jurisdiction. Their primary function was to provide security for early Texas settlements, but many of the original 200–300 Rangers also investigated and apprehended outlaws "wanted dead or alive" for a cash bounty.[26] In 1934, Ranger Frank Hamer and his fellow investigators brought national acclaim to the Texas Rangers by ambushing and killing the infamous gangster couple, Bonnie and Clyde, in a hail of gunfire during morning hours in a remote location on a Louisiana highway (see Figure 1.7). The Texas Rangers still operate today as a major division within the Texas Department of Public Safety and are the primary investigators of major crime incidents, unsolved crimes, serial offending, public corruption, and officers involved in shootings. They also engage in border security operations.

MUNICIPAL DETECTIVES

There is considerable debate over which American city policing agency was the home of the first municipal detective and detective squad. In 1846, investigation as a means for solving major crimes was introduced in Boston by the city's marshal, **Francis Tukey**. Tukey also introduced a technique he called "the show-up of rogues," where he rounded up known burglars, pickpockets, and other criminals and presented them in person to Boston officers so that these offenders' activities could be more effectively monitored in the streets. Not until 1860, however, was the position of Captain of Detectives, formally in charge of a separate investigative branch, first created by the Boston Police Department. Many historical accounts suggest that the first official municipal plainclothes detective of record in the United States was **Allan Pinkerton**, appointed by the Chicago Police Department in 1849. Pinkerton stayed with the force only one year before leaving to start his own private detective agency.[27] Other police departments to establish some of America's first separate branches of municipal police detectives were the New York Police Department (in 1857) and the Philadelphia Police Department (in 1859). The NYPD Detective Bureau currently houses the nation's largest number of municipal investigators and has played a leading role in investigating crimes at both

(a)

(b)

FIGURE 1.7 ▶ Bonnie Parker and Clyde Barrow (a) and their gang were one of the many groups of notorious organized crime groups that terrorized the United States during the 1930s. "Bonnie and Clyde" were wanted for numerous violent crimes including murder, robbery, and kidnapping. They were ultimately killed in an ambush by the Texas Rangers and other law enforcement officials. In the hail of gunfire, over 100 bullets penetrated the Ford sedan they were driving (b) with 50 striking Parker and 27 hitting Barrow. (Courtesy Federal Bureau of Investigation and Library of Congress)

FIGURE 1.8 ▶ Allan Pinkerton (seated bottom row left) with original agents of the U.S. Secret Service Presidential Protective Branch (seated bottom row center and right; standing right) and President Abraham Lincoln (standing left). (Courtesy Library of Congress)

national and international levels, including the famed "French Connection" drug trafficking case and the terrorist attacks on New York City's World Trade Center Building.

PINKERTON DETECTIVES

After leaving his municipal detective position in Chicago, Allan Pinkerton in 1850 founded the nation's most private investigative agency—the **Pinkerton National Detective Agency**. Pinkerton detectives were noted for their work on many high-profile cases and clients (as shown in Figure 1.8 providing protection for President Abraham Lincoln). The agency's slogan "We never sleep" soon led to the appellation *private eye* for the detectives. Pinkerton detectives were hired as Abraham Lincoln's security force during the Civil War period and are credited with thwarting a would-be assassin's plot to kill the president. Famed outlaws such as Jesse James, Butch Cassidy, and John Younger were all tracked and apprehended by the Pinkerton National Detective Agency. Detective Kate Warne, believed to be the first full-time American female investigator, was employed with the Pinkerton National Detective Agency in 1856.[28] Other large U.S. cities to break ground in establishing separate investigative units staffed by nonuniformed detectives included Boston (in 1851) and New York (in 1857).[29] After over 150 years of operation, the Pinkerton National Detective Agency (now known as *Pinkerton's Government Services, Inc.,* or, simply, *the Pinkertons*) continues to provide worldwide private investigative and security services.

SECRET SERVICE

A wave of counterfeiting activity swept across the nation during the 1860s, which led to America's second "detective boom." Many types of currency circulated following the Civil War, and this situation together with the relatively few law enforcement entities available to police the burgeoning number of alleged offenses led to the formation of a third federal investigative agency in 1865—the **U.S. Secret Service (USSS)**.[30] Housed within the Department of Treasury, the Secret Service was initially commissioned to prevent acts of counterfeiting. The U.S. Marshals service assisted in this endeavor, who, with help from private detective agencies such as the Pinkerton National Detective Agency, had been attempting to stem the flow of counterfeit money. Secret Service agents also were "on loan" to investigate criminal cases prosecuted by the U.S. Department of Justice, which lacked its own investigative branch. In 1908, members of Congress alleged that Secret Service operatives were investigating their professional and private affairs for potential wrongdoing. As a result, legislation was passed limiting the enforcement powers of the Secret Service to investigating counterfeiting activities and to protecting the president. In addition, private detectives such as the Pinkertons no longer could be hired to assist federal agents in their duties. Thus, lending or hiring detectives to governmental agencies for investigative purposes effectively came to an end.[31] Today, Secret Service agents are charged with enforcement of counterfeiting statutes and investigation of crimes that involve financial institution fraud, computer and telecommunications fraud, false identification documents, access device fraud, advance fee fraud, electronic funds transfers, and money laundering.

FEDERAL BUREAU OF INVESTIGATION (FBI)

The Department of Justice's need of investigative powers was soon filled in 1908 when U.S. Attorney General Charles Bonaparte converted the Department's Attorney Examiners section into the Bureau of Investigation (later to become the FBI). The Bureau consisted of 34 investigators under the supervision of Chief Investigator, Stanley W. Fitch.[32] The crimes within the powers of this agency included those committed against the U.S. government, such as land fraud, moonshining, murder on federal property, and espionage. In the early 1900s, the Bureau's investigative jurisdiction was expanded by the passage of several new, strict federal laws such as the Mann Act (prohibiting the transportation of women across state lines for purposes of prostitution or immoral acts) and the Dyer Act (making transportation of a stolen vehicle from one state to another a federal offense). In 1936, the Bureau of Investigation became formally known as the **Federal Bureau of Investigation (FBI)**.[33] The duties of today's FBI have expanded greatly since the agency's founding days. These include the investigation of civil rights matters, counterterrorism, foreign counterintelligence, organized crime/drugs, and a range of violent and financial crimes.

BUREAU OF PROHIBITION

In 1920, Prohibition and its related laws essentially made liquor illegal in the United States, leading to the rise of organized crime activities within major U.S. cities. Chicago at this time became the nerve center for most of the nation's notorious mobsters and their criminal acts during the Prohibition era. Liquor production and distribution were the primary illegal activi-

FIGURE 1.9 ▶ Mug shot of infamous Chicago gangster Alphonse "Scarface" Capone after his arrest by U.S. Treasury Agents on tax evasion and Prohibition charges.
(Photo by Popperfoto/Getty Images)

ties fueling this unprecedented organized crime wave in the nation's "Second City." Among the most notorious gang leaders responsible for Chicago's liquor and vice activities was **Alphonse "Scarface" Capone**, head of the Chicago Mob, who ran most of the city's bootlegging, prostitution, and gambling rackets. Although Capone, whose arrest Mug Shot is shown in Figure 1.9, was listed as the Chicago Crime Commission's top "public enemy," he continued his illegal activities with impunity because many local authorities, including Chicago police and investigators, held corrupt ties with Capone and other organized crime groups. The only hope of stemming the tide of corruption in Chicago, and of bringing the likes of the Capone mob to justice, was federal law enforcement intervention.[34]

The **Bureau of Prohibition**, created in 1927 as part of the Department of Treasury to enforce liquor-related laws, was assigned this task. The agency directed Special Agent **Eliot Ness** to topple Capone's organized crime network. Ness and his group of agents became popularly known as the **Untouchables** because of their integrity and inability to be corrupted by mob influences. Their investigations of the Chicago Mob were conducted on two fronts. First, Ness and his men gathered evidence of Capone's illegal money laundering activities through a series of covert operations, including wiretaps of his brother's headquarters at a local café.[35] Second, they cut off Capone's flow of illegal money by raiding and shutting down his underworld businesses—often gaining entry with a steel ram attached to the front of a 10-ton flatbed truck. These and related efforts based on specialized enforcement tactics as shown in Figure 1.10 led to Capone's eventual indictment, conviction, and incarceration for federal income tax evasion and prohibition violations in 1931.[36] After the end of Prohibition in 1933, and following a series of legal and organizational changes in the decades to come, the Bureau of Prohibition evolved into the **Bureau of Alcohol, Tobacco, Firearms and Explosives (ATF)** in 1970. The ATF's current mission is to investigate violent criminals, criminal organizations, the illegal use and trafficking of

FIGURE 1.10 ▶ Early investigators engaged in specialized tactical training such as shooting on the move, or "shoot and scoot" tactics, as illustrated here. (Courtesy Federal Bureau of Investigation)

firearms, the illegal use and storage of explosives, acts of arson and bombings, acts of terrorism, and the illegal diversion of alcohol and tobacco products.

BUREAU OF NARCOTICS

Investigation of other illegal drugs began with the creation of the Federal Bureau of Narcotics in 1930 under the direction of Harry J. Anslinger within the Department of Treasury. This agency originally consisted of 17 investigators assigned to enforce the Harrison Narcotics Tax Act of 1914, which restricted the sale and distribution of opiates.[37] Eventually, the enforcement function of this agency evolved into that of the current federal **Drug Enforcement Agency (DEA)** established in 1973 within the U.S. Department of Justice by an Executive Order of President Richard Nixon. The general law enforcement mission of the DEA includes investigations of major violators of controlled substance laws at the interstate and international levels—criminals and drug gangs who perpetrate violence in communities and terrorize citizens through fear and intimidation.

THE SCIENTIFIC PERIOD

The First Investigative Crime Laboratory

The Scientific Period of criminal investigation began with the advent of the investigative crime laboratory during the early 1920s. It was then that the scientist and the investigator became partners in a search to discover systematic methods of identifying and processing criminal evidence. The world's first official crime lab was started by **Edmond Locard** in 1910 in Lyons, France[38], but not until over a decade later did American law enforcement agencies begin implementing the idea. The Los Angeles Police Department, under the direction of **August Vollmer**, instituted the nation's first municipal crime

laboratory within LAPD in 1923. The lab was run by officer Rex Welch, who had been trained as a dentist and was equipped with "an antiquated microscope and a handful of glassware and chemicals to form a makeshift lab." This lab, however, would provide a model for other future partnerships between scientists and criminal investigators.[39]

Calvin Goddard: The Study of Ballistics Goes to Trial

In 1927, **Calvin Goddard** in New York helped found one of the nation's earliest private crime labs, called the Bureau of Forensic Ballistics. The nation's first partnership between investigation and laboratory science was formed when Goddard served as a ballistics expert in the famed **Sacco-Vanzetti murder case**. Ultimately, the case's outcome hinged on Goddard's expert testimony regarding whether or not a bullet striking and killing a security guard during an armed robbery was indeed fired from the defendant's (Sacco's) gun. Using a comparison microscope, Goddard proved that markings on a test bullet fired from Sacco's Colt pistol were identical in all respects to those on the shell recovered from the robbery victim's dead body. Due largely to this unprecedented use of science in the investigative process, the court upheld the execution of Sacco and his crime partner, Vanzetti.[40]

Approximately two years later, Goddard had a second opportunity to prove the value of science to the legal and investigative world when he provided expert testimony during the **St. Valentine's Day Massacre** trial. Hired as an independent investigator, he analyzed and gathered physical evidence related to the brutal killing of seven gangsters associated with Chicago's Irish organized crime syndicate. From two distinct sets of markings on the 70 expended cartridge casings recovered at the crime scene, Goddard concluded that the killings were carried out with two separate murder weapons. Furthermore, he identified both weapons as .45 caliber Thompson submachine guns. Witnesses to the killings stated that some of the assailants were, in fact, uniformed Chicago police officers. This led Goddard to test fire all eight of the Thompson submachine guns at Chicago police headquarters. He found no similarities between cartridge markings left by the police weapons and those left by the murder weapons; thus, he ruled out the possibility that the killings were the result of law enforcement corruption. The only other likely suspects were none other than Alphonse Capone and his mob, who recently had been feuding with members of the victimized Irish mob. Capone denied his involvement in the murders, and his alibi was supported by his presence in Florida at the time the massacre took place. An investigation led by Goddard, however, recovered two tommy guns from the residence of known hit man Fred "Killer" Burke, who was associated with the Capone gang. This time, Goddard's ballistics tests provided identical matches between the cartridge casings removed from the crime scene and those from the guns at Burke's residence. Despite this compelling evidence, neither Burke nor the unidentified shooters responsible for the massacre were tried for the crime.[41]

The fame and national attention that Goddard gained from his participation in the Sacco-Vanzetti and St. Valentine's Day Massacre investigations led to his appointment as director of the nation's first large-scale private criminal laboratory in 1929. The lab, housed within the Law School of Northwestern University in Chicago, was supported by the school's chief administrator, Dean John H. Wigmore. Wigmore was an outspoken supporter of scientific testing in the investigative process and was also a proponent of Goddard's work during the Sacco-Vanzetti case investigation.[42]

The FBI Turns to Scientific Investigation

The public figure who perhaps can be credited with perpetuating the greatest expansion of scientific applications within the field of criminal investigation is former FBI director **J. Edgar Hoover**. Initially appointed in 1924 to lead and reform the Bureau of Investigation, Hoover produced a new mission and goals statement for the agency, including "the instruction and practice" of scientific investigation principles to solve crime.[43] His earliest effort to bring science to the crime-fighting arsenal of investigators was the creation of a national clearinghouse for fingerprints located at FBI headquarters. The project began with slightly over 800,000 prints gathered mainly by large local police agencies (in New York, Chicago, and Baltimore, to name a few). The persons represented were mainly arrestees and prisoners; however, some nonoffenders also were included, which led to criticisms that Hoover was secretly creating a means to spy on the general public. Each set of prints was contained on a standardized 8-inch square card and was manually classified by a numeric score for each individual, based on numbers assigned to characteristics of all the fingers (otherwise known as the Henry Method). The FBI's fingerprint repository became known as the **National Bureau of Criminal Identification** and was made available to assist investigators both domestically and abroad.[44]

Most of the early scientific innovations in criminal investigations, many of which are still used today, were discovered by FBI Special Agent **Charles Appel** and his staff during the 1930s. Appel, like many other Special Agents hired during the Hoover administration, was required to attend criminalistics training offered by independent scientific experts—one of whom was Calvin Goddard. As the result of his training experiences, Appel proposed to then-director Hoover that the FBI create its own state-of-the-art crime lab as a resource for state and local law enforcement agencies. The lab, originally named *The Criminology Laboratory,* was eventually opened in 1932 at FBI headquarters in Washington, DC, under Appel's direction. It was equipped with "an ultraviolet light machine, a microscope, a moulage kit (for impression casting), a wiretapping kit, photographic supplies, chemicals, a drawing board, and other office equipment. . . ." Although the lab had humble beginnings, it soon was recognized as the nation's center of creativity for the development of new scientific investigation methods.[45] From 1932 to 1935, the laboratory created numer-

(a)

(b)

FIGURE 1.11 ▶ (a) FBI Technical Crime Laboratory in the 1930s. (b) Advanced technology in today's FBI crime lab permits the specialized analysis of hazardous materials evidence. ((a) Courtesy Federal Bureau of Investigation)

ous collections of evidence reference resources, including the Typewriter Standards File, the National Fraudulent Check File, the Anonymous Letter File, the National Automotive Paint File, and the Reference Firearms Collection.[46] Some of the field investigative support functions of lab personnel included fingerprinting, handwriting analysis, and impression casting. The lab, shown in Figure 1.11, received national acclaim early on when it helped identify the kidnapper of famed pilot Charles Lindberg's infant son by matching handwriting in ransom notes with writing samples obtained from suspects.[47]

The Academic Innovations of Investigative Science by Paul Kirk

From the 1940s well into the 1950s, many other laboratory-based scientific innovations further defined criminal investigation. Among these were GSR (gunshot residue) testing procedures, improved microscopic and photographic capabilities, and advanced methods for identifying and classifying human biological evidence. Many of these scientific applications to criminal investigation were developed and pioneered by **Paul Kirk** at the University of California, Berkeley. Within the University's Department of "Technical Criminology," Kirk and his students engaged in many ground-breaking studies, which became the foundation for modern techniques used to trace microscopic crime scene evidence—such as glass fragments, soil, dust, pollen, fibers, hairs, and threads—to specific persons, places, and things (collectively referred to as *trace evidence*). Kirk also recognized that human blood at crime scenes could be used to identify things such as the type of weapon used to create a wound or the approximate location in a room where the offender wounded the victim. For this new field of forensic study he coined the term *blood spatter analysis*.[48]

Criminalistics and the Forensic Sciences: Contributions of the Scientific Era to Today's Crime Lab

Techniques developed during the scientific era, based on the principles of criminalistics and the forensic sciences, have formed the foundation of the various investigative techniques used in today's crime lab. Goddard in 1895 first defined criminalistics as "the use of the system to discover clues about crime."[49] Goddard's definition still stands today, but has evolved with the advent of modern crime-fighting technology. The **American Board of Criminalistics** now defines the field as "the professional and scientific discipline dedicated to the recognition, collection, identification and individualization of physical evidence and the application of natural sciences to matters of law."[50] In practice, criminalistics generally involves the application of all scientific principles that are appropriate to the investigation of any type of crime.

CRIMINALISTS

It is perhaps no surprise that the science of criminalistics is carried out by criminalists. Most criminalists employed by law enforcement agencies spend most of their time conducting scientific evaluations of evidence in crime labs. In most jurisdictions, only persons possessing a 4-year degree in the biological sciences, chemistry, or an equivalent "hard science" can be employed as a criminalist. Criminalists are usually civilian employees; but in some agencies, they are also sworn law enforcement officers. The term *scientific generalist* often is used to describe criminalists since they perform not only routine analyses—such as identification of fingerprints, DNA, blood, hairs, fibers, bullets, and controlled substances—but also specialized analyses of any materials that may provide evidence in a criminal case. Criminalists sometimes assist in the crime scene investigation process as well.

THE FORENSIC SCIENCES

The **forensic sciences**, on the other hand, can be defined as the application of any science to the law. Numerous fields of study and practice in the world of investigations are commonly referred to as *science*. For a particular forensic science to be used as evidence in court, however, specific judicial requirements must be met. The courts have accepted some sciences as meeting the legal forensic standard, including fingerprints, blood spatter analysis, firearms examination, and most recently DNA identification. *Junk sciences* are those that do not pass the legal standards to become viable forensic sciences, such as the polygraph ("lie detector") and graphology (the study of behavior through handwriting analysis).

Forensic scientists are most often civilians (i.e., nonsworn law enforcement officers) who are highly trained and educated in a specific scientific discipline and may or may not be employed by a law enforcement agency. For example, a chemist may be employed by a police agency to perform high-level tests on controlled substances or explosive materials. Other forensic scientists, however, may work independently of law enforcement agencies and as consultants for specialized cases. These individuals can represent virtually any scientific discipline. Physical scientists, such as engineers, may help investigate a plane crash to rule out terrorist activity. Psychologists, who are social scientists, often provide essential court testimony regarding the mental state of criminal defendants. Forensic scientists play a key role in noncriminal situations as well. Civil disputes involving paternity, for example, may require interpretation of DNA samples by an expert in genetics. The suitability of a couple seeking to adopt a child often is assessed by a behavioral scientist. Remember, however, that only forensic scientists who practice judicially approved sciences can provide evidence that is acceptable in a court of law.

THE TECHNOLOGICAL PERIOD

Suspect Information and Fingerprint Databases

The Technological Period commenced in the 1960s with the application of computers and large-scale databases to criminal investigation. The first major computerized system used by American investigators was the **National Crime Information Center (NCIC)**, created by the FBI in 1967. The system was designed as a national clearinghouse of crime-related information to assist local and state law enforcement agencies in apprehending fugitives and recovering stolen property. Information on vehicles, missing persons, gang members, and terrorists comprises some of the many separate records contained in the NCIC database.[51] In addition, computer applications for fingerprint identification were developed by the FBI with the creation of the world's first automated fingerprint database in 1977—originally referred to as AFIS and known today as **Integrated Automatic Fingerprint Identification System (IAFIS)**. The IAFIS system contains computerized fingerprint images derived from millions of offenders and crime scenes and can search its entire database in seconds. Investigations employing IAFIS fingerprint identifications have resulted in the arrest and conviction of countless criminals.[52]

CASE CLOSE-UP 1.1

"THE BELTWAY SNIPER"
IAFIS Breaks the Case

Among the high-profile cases in which IAFIS played a significant investigative role was that of "The Beltway Sniper." In what was referred to as "the 23 days of terror" in October 2002, ex-military sniper John Allen Muhammad, age 41, and his 17-year-old companion, Lee Boyd Malvo, embarked on a 3-week murder rampage throughout the Washington, DC, metro area, killing 10 persons and wounding 3 others. In all of the killings they employed the same modus operandi: killing their victim sniper style with a single shot fired from a high-power rifle. The duo were dubbed "The Beltway Sniper" by the media because of an erroneous profile by the FBI identifying the

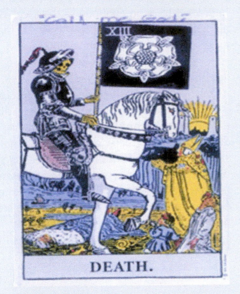
(a)

(b)

(c)

FIGURE 1.12 ▶ (a) Evidence in the Beltway Sniper Case: Tarot card with writing "Call me God"; (b) Blue Chevrolet sedan; (c) Tape recorder used to make extortion messages and rear seat of vehicle with access to trunk and a Bushmaster .223 assault rifle. (Courtesy Federal Bureau of Investigation)

two African-American killers as "a single white supremacist who traveled the Washington, DC, Beltway Interstate Freeway." The case investigation was headed by the Montgomery County Police in Maryland, in association with several other local police agencies and the FBI.[53]

Available evidence in the case included bullets and spent cartridge casings recovered from the crime scenes. Tarot cards also were left at the crime scene with cryptic messages such as "Mr. Policeman, I am God" scrawled on them along with handwritten notes demanding $10,000,000 in cash to stop the murder spree. Despite these clues, the investigators had no solid suspect leads until one of the snipers called a priest to boast about his earlier killing of a liquor store clerk in Alabama. After the taunting phone call,

investigators obtained physical evidence remaining from the unsolved liquor store murder, which included a gun magazine left behind at the crime scene. An IAFIS search on a fingerprint taken from the magazine yielded a positive match or *hit* with Lee Boyd Malvo, whose print had been entered into the system previously for prior criminal activities. This break in the case ultimately led to the identification of Malvo's co-conspirator, John Allen Muhammad, and to the suspects' vehicle, a blue 1990 Chevrolet Caprice. Subsequently, both of the killers were arrested on the basis of this vehicle description.[54] The suspects' vehicle crime scene photo along with investigative photos of other key criminal evidence in the Beltway Sniper case are presented in Figure 1.12.

The Pitchfork Case: Sir Alec Jeffreys Discovers DNA Fingerprinting

Perhaps nothing has advanced the field of criminal investigation more than the discovery and perfection of suspect identification through the use of **deoxyribonucleic acid (DNA)**. Although the foundation of DNA analysis as an investigative tool was established during the 1950s, when scientists Watson and Crick first identified its structure in the human cell, law enforcement did not employ the method to fight crime until well into the 1980s. The first recognized application of DNA to a criminal matter was by **Sir Alec Jeffreys** in England in an effort to help solve the famous 1986 **Pitchfork case**. In an effort to help investigators solve the sexual assault and murder of two women, Jeffreys applied his new DNA fingerprinting technique to blood and semen samples belonging to the killer, which were obtained from the crime scene. Jeffreys concluded that the two killings were carried out by the same perpetrator and was able to create a genetic fingerprint belonging to the killer. To identify the murderer, investigators attempted to collect blood or semen samples from thousands of men between the ages of 18 and 36 whom police believed to be most likely to commit a sexually related crime. Fearing detection, the killer—a baker named Colin Pitchfork—paid another man to provide a DNA sample to investigators under Pitchfork's name. Shortly thereafter, investigators learned that a man bragged at a local pub about the money he received from Pitchfork to give the false information and evidence. Using this lead, investigators arrested Pitchfork, and Jeffreys was able to make a positive match between Pitchfork's DNA and that obtained from the murder victims. This first attempt at DNA fingerprinting proved that the power of advanced investigative technology was a double-edge sword. While the DNA procedure resulted in the conviction of Pitchfork for the murders, it also proved the innocence of another man who was being held by authorities and was believed to be the real killer.[55]

Since the Pitchfork case, application of DNA fingerprinting technology to the investigative process has advanced rapidly. Today's methods of DNA analysis, as shown in Figure 1.13,

require much less biological evidence to process, take much less time to provide results, and cost agencies much less money to perform. As a direct result of improved DNA processing, computerized databases of genetic fingerprints were created to aid in criminal investigations. Beginning in the 1980s, many states began to collect DNA information on convicted offenders and to formulate their own automated DNA databases. In 1990, the FBI began **CODIS (Combined DNA Index System)**, a nationwide DNA database with the original purpose of housing genetic fingerprints obtained only from sex offenders. Although the federal government has placed restrictions on the type of DNA evidence that CODIS may include, emerging state legislation has expanded the DNA information that may be included in existing state law enforcement databases. Currently, DNA evidence gathered by individual states ranges from samples

FIGURE 1.13 ▶ The process of DNA extraction from crime scene evidence has been greatly streamlined with modern technology. Several years ago, weeks or months were required to complete a single DNA test. Now, most results can be obtained in 5–7 days or less.

TABLE 1.1 DEPARTMENT OF HOMELAND SECURITY INVESTIGATIVE AGENCIES

1. U.S. Customs and Border Protection (CBP) Keeps terrorists and their weapons out of the United States; is responsible for securing and facilitating trade and travel while enforcing hundreds of U.S. regulations, including immigration and drug laws.

2. Transportation Security Administration (TSA) Searches for bombs at checkpoints in airports, inspects rail cars, patrols subways, and investigates potential crimes committed against all other modes of transportation.

3. U.S. Coast Guard (USCG) Protects America's maritime borders from all intrusions by halting the flow of illegal drugs, aliens, and contraband into the United States through maritime routes; preventing illegal fishing; and suppressing violations of federal law in the maritime arena.

4. U.S. Secret Service (USSS) Enforces counterfeiting statutes and investigates crimes that involve financial institution fraud, computer and telecommunications fraud, false identification documents, access device fraud, advance fee fraud, electronic funds transfers, and money laundering.

5. Office of Inspector General (OIG) Inspects, audits, and investigates to promote effectiveness, efficiency, and economy in Department of Homeland Security programs and operations; and prevents and detects fraud, abuse, mismanagement, and waste in such programs and operations.

6. Federal Protective Service (FPS) Investigates crimes relating to the security of federally owned and leased buildings, courthouses, properties, and other federal assets and the personnel associated with those assets.

7. U.S. Immigration and Customs Enforcement (ICE) Investigates any crime with a connection to the U.S. border, including weapons trafficking, child pornography, human trafficking, and drug offenses.

collected only from sexual and violent offenders to samples collected from anyone convicted of a felony or certain classes of misdemeanor offenses.[56]

DNA technology has also helped exonerate the innocent. In 1992, attorneys Barry Scheck and Peter Neufeld initiated the Innocence Project with a mission to use DNA technology to reexamine criminal cases resulting in criminal convictions that took place before DNA evidence testing procedures were available. Thus far, the Innocence Project has helped release from custody over 200 persons—16 of whom were sentenced to death—who were falsely accused of crimes.[57] Inevitably, as the Technological Period continues to evolve, the detection of crime as well as the protection of the innocent will improve within the realm of criminal investigation.

Homeland Security and the War on Terror

The September 11, 2001, terrorist attack on the World Trade Center in New York City significantly changed the future direction of the Technological Period of criminal investigation. Before this event, terrorism and crime were considered to be separate phenomena: Acts of terror fell within the realm of political intelligence, and crimes within the field of criminal investigation. Nowadays, however, the lines between terrorists and criminals are no longer clearly drawn: Both domestic and international terrorism are considered to be crimes against humanity that must be addressed by criminal investigators as well. This recent change is clearly evident from the creation of the nation's newest investigative branch, the **U.S. Department of Homeland Security (DHS)**, in 2002. The DHS was the result of the largest reorganization of existing governmental investigative agencies in American history (see Table 1.1).

A "REAL WORLD" APPROACH TO THE STUDY OF CRIMINAL INVESTIGATION

As the historical timeline outlined in Table 1.2 clearly illustrates, the study of criminal investigation encompasses the combined contribution of forensic sciences, criminalistics, and numerous other academic and applied disciplines relevant to solving criminal cases. Thus, the nature of the information included in this text is as broad as the range of circumstances and acts that collectively fall within the sphere of criminal activity. Compared to other areas of study, criminal investigation is truly an academically eclectic discipline. It includes the precepts of physical sciences such as biology, chemistry, and physics as well as the findings of behavioral sciences, including psychology and sociology. The real-world application of criminal investigation has been aptly described as both an art and a science. In essence, the criminal investigative process is guided by scientific knowledge on whatever has been systematically tested, proven, and applied with a strong sense of logic, intuition, and common sense. This text is constructed and organized with the latter statement in mind. In Section I, you will be introduced to the various scientific tools and methods of the criminal investigation process. Section II presents a series of real-life cases involving specific criminal acts to provide you the opportunity to apply the techniques you have learned. This combined illustrated case study approach should help you gain the appropriate balance of academic and applied knowledge required to become a highly effective professional in the field of criminal investigation.

TABLE 1.2 HISTORICAL TIMELINE OF CRIMINAL INVESTIGATION

DATE	PERSON/AGENCY	INVESTIGATIVE MILESTONE
1748	Henry Fielding	Established first detectives in London, "Bow Street Runners"
1754	Sir John Fielding	Took over control of "Bow Street Runners"
1789	U.S. Congress	The U.S. Marshals Service is established
1789	U.S. Congress	U.S. Attorney General's Office established
1811	Eugène Vidocq	First public detective, *La Sûreté*, Paris, France
1830	U.S. Postal Office	U.S. Postal Inspection Service established
1835	State of Texas	Texas Rangers established
1842	Sir Robert Peel	"The Detective Branch" established at London's Scotland Yard
1846	Boston P.D.	Appointed Francis Tukey City Marshal
1849	Allan Pinkerton	Appointed first U.S. municipal detective Chicago Police Department
1850	Allan Pinkerton	Created the Pinkerton National Detective Agency
1851	Boston P.D.	Started the first nonuniformed detective branch
1856	Kate Warne	First female (private) detective hired by the Pinkerton National Detective Agency
1857	NYPD	Began nonuniformed detective bureau
1865	U.S. Treasury Dept.	U.S. Secret Service established
1870	U.S. Congress	U.S. Department of Justice created
1877	Scotland Yard	CID. Criminal Investigation Division formed
1887	A. Conan Doyle	Introduced Sherlock Holmes in *A Study in Scarlet*
1893	Hans Gross	Wrote the first book on the study of criminal investigation
1908	U.S. Attorney Gen.	U.S. Bureau of Investigation created (later renamed FBI)
1910	Edmond Locard	Established world's first crime lab in Lyons, France
1923	August Vollmer	Created first municipal crime lab at Los Angeles Police Dept.
1923	INTERPOL	Created world's largest international policing organization
1924	J. Edgar Hoover	Appointed director of the Federal Bureau of Investigation
1924	FBI	Created the National Bureau of Criminal Identification for fingerprints
1924	U.S.D.O.J.	Created the U.S. Border Patrol
1927	Calvin Goddard	Established nation's first private crime lab in New York
1927	U.S. Treasury Dept.	Created Bureau of Prohibition to enforce liquor laws (later ATF)

(Continued)

TABLE 1.2 (CONTINUED)

DATE	PERSON/AGENCY	INVESTIGATIVE MILESTONE
1930	U.S. Treasury Dept.	Federal Bureau of Narcotics established (later DEA)
1932	Charles Appel	Founded the FBI Crime Laboratory in Washington, DC
1947	U.S. Congress	Central Intelligence Agency (CIA) created
1952	U.S. Treasury Dept.	Internal Revenue Service creates Inspection Division
1955	Paul Kirk	Develops the study of trace evidence at U.C. Berkeley
1966	U.S. Navy	Naval Inspection Service (NIS) established
1967	FBI	Develops the National Crime Information Center (NCIC)
1970	U.S.D.O.J.	Bureau of Alcohol Tobacco and Firearms (ATF) established
1973	U.S.D.O.J.	Drug Enforcement Administration (DEA) established
1977	FBI	Creates the Automated Fingerprint Identification System (AFIS)
1979	U.S.D.O.J.	Creates the Office of Special Investigations (OSI)
1986	Alec Jeffreys	Develops DNA profiling methods
1990	FBI	Creates the Combined DNA Index System (CODIS)
1992	Barry Scheck	Began the Innocence Project sponsored by U.S.D.O.J.
1999	ATF	National Integrated Ballistics Information Network (NIBIN)
2001	U.S. Congress	Transportation Safety Administration (TSA) established
2002	U.S. Congress	Established The Department of Homeland Security
2003	U.S. Customs/Imm.	U.S. Immigration and Customs Enforcement (ICE) established

Summary

1. **The origins of criminal investigation.**

   The origins of criminal investigation can be traced back to the activities of several private individuals and groups, known as *thief-takers,* who offered their services to investigate and track down offenders for a fee. In 1748, Henry Fielding and his half-brother Sir John Fielding organized the first such group, the Bow Street Runners, in London. Another thief-taker, Eugène Vidocq, is credited as the world's first detective. He was hired in 1811 by *La Sûreté*, the investigative branch of the municipal police force of Paris, France—and was noted for his use of disguises to conduct undercover assignments.

2. **Creating the first public image of a detective.**

   Fictional accounts of detectives in early novels played a key role in defining the public's image of the detective. Most important among these was the portrayal of Sherlock Holmes by author Sir Arthur Conan Doyle in his 1887 book, *A Study in Scarlet.* In that novel, Doyle introduced the idea of deductive logic as a tool for detectives to use for solving cases.

3. **The first scientific applications to criminal investigation.**

   Although fingerprints were used for identification purposes as far back as the year 700 in China, not until 1840, when French toxicologist Mathieu Orfila testified as a forensic expert in a suspected murder by poisoning case, did the sciences become an established investigative tool. Other notable pioneering scientific contributions to the field of investigation include Bertillon's 1833 method of criminal identification by measurement (anthropometry) and Galton's 1892 method of fingerprint classification.

4. **The three evolutionary periods of criminal investigation.**

   The first period of American criminal investigation, referred to as the *Prescientific Period*, was characterized by information gathering techniques, including rewards offered to the public for revealing the whereabouts of suspected offenders. The second period, known as the *Scientific Period*, involved the use of newly developed criminal identification methods such as fingerprint classification, ballistics, blood spatter analysis, and trace evidence as investigative tools. Present-day investigations, in the *Technological Period*, involve the use of sophisticated high-tech innovations such as automated databases for fingerprints (IAFIS), ballistics evidence (NIBIN), and DNA profiles (CODIS).

5. **The origins of American criminal investigation.**

   The first investigative agency was the U.S. Marshals Service, formed at the federal level by President George Washington in 1789. The Texas Rangers, established in 1835, was the first state police force to incorporate investigative operations. Allan Pinkerton was appointed the first municipal detective at the Chicago Police Department in 1849, and a year later he founded the nation's first private detective agency—The Pinkerton National Detective Agency. The first detective branch was formed in 1851 within the Boston Police Department.

6. **Criminal investigation today.**

   The largest municipal police investigative force today is the Detective Bureau within the New York City Police Department. The Pinkerton National Detective Agency is still one of the largest private investigative agencies in the world. At the federal level, there are over 60 investigative agencies, the largest of which are the Federal Bureau of Investigation (FBI), the Central Intelligence Agency (CIA), and U.S. Customs and Border Protection (CBP). In 2002, the largest reorganization of investigative agencies in the United States took place with the creation of the Department of Homeland Security.

Key Terms

Henry Fielding
Sir John Fielding
Bow Street Runners
Eugène Vidocq
Scotland Yard Detective Branch
Sherlock Holmes
Mathieu Orfila
toxicology
Alphonse Bertillion
Sir Francis Gaulton
Alphonse "Scarface" Capone
Eliot Ness
The Untouchables
Hans Gross
criminalistics
U.S. Marshals Service (USMS)
U.S. Postal Inspection Service (USPIS)

Texas Rangers
Francis Tukey
Allan Pinkerton
Pinkerton detectives
U.S. Secret Service
Federal Bureau of Investigation (FBI)
Bureau of Alcohol, Tobacco, Firearms and Explosives (ATF)
Integrated Automated Fingerprint Identification System (IAFIS)
U.S. Department of Homeland Security (DHS)
Calvin Goddard
J. Edgar Hoover
forensic sciences
Sir Alec Jeffreys
Paul Kirk

Drug Enforcement Agency (DEA)
National Crime Information Center (NCIC)
CODIS (Combined DNA Index System)
deoxyribonucleic acid (DNA)
Pitchfork case
August Vollmer
Charles Appel
American Board of Criminalistics
anthropometry
Edmond Locard
National Bureau of Criminal Identification
Sacco-Vanzetti murder case
St. Valentine's Day Massacre
U.S. Immigration and Customs Enforcement (ICE)

Review Questions

1. What group of thief-takers is credited with being the first investigators in history?

2. Who is considered to be the world's first detective? Why does this individual deserve this title?

3. What happened in the Daniel Good case? Why was this investigation so important in the history of criminal investigation?

4. What is the investigative principle of logical deduction? By whom was it created, and when?

5. What were some of the earliest scientific contributions to the field of criminal investigation? Who were the scientists that created them?

6. What are some of the major contributions of the Prescientific Period of American criminal investigation? What investigative agencies were formed during this period? Who helped to form them?

7. What are some of the major events that occurred during the Scientific Period of American criminal

investigation? Who were the investigators and scientists that contributed to the development of this period?

8. Which investigative innovations were created during the Technological Period of American criminal investigation?

9. Who is Sir Alec Jeffreys and what was his contribution to the science of investigation? How does this relate to the Pitchfork case?

10. Which investigative agencies comprise the Department of Homeland Security? What are some of their specific investigative functions?

Internet Resources

Department of Homeland Security	www.dhs.gov/index.shtm
U.S. Department of Justice	www.justice.gov
U.S. Department of the Treasury	www.ustreas.gov
U.S. Postal Inspection Service	postalinspectors.uspis.gov
Central Intelligence Agency	www.cia.gov
Texas Rangers	www.txdps.state.tx.us/TexasRangers
Pinkerton, Inc.	www.securitas.com/pinkerton/en
NYPD Detective Bureau	www.homicidesquad.com
Vidocq Society	www.vidocq.org/vidocq.html
Sherlock Holmes Society	www.sherlock-holmes.org.uk
London Metropolitan Police	www.met.police.uk/history

Notes

[1] Gilbert Armitage, *The History of the Bow Street Runners: 1729–1829* (London: Wishart, 1932).

[2] Ibid.

[3] Samuel Hercules Taunton, "A Reminiscence of a Bow-Street Officer," *Harper's New Monthly Magazine*, Vol. 5, No. 28 (September, 1852).

[4] James Morton, *The First Detective: The Life and Revolutionary Times of Vidocq* (London: Ebury Press, 2005).

[5] Paul Metzner, *Crescendo of the Virtuoso: Spectacle, Skill, and Self-Promotion in Paris During the Age of Revolution* (Berkeley: University of California Press, 1998), 156.

[6] Ibid.

[7] Douglas G. Browne, *The Rise of Scotland Yard* (Westport, Conn.: Greenwood Press, 1956).

[8] Ibid., 122–123.

[9] Ibid.

[10] Charles Dickens, *The Adventures of Oliver Twist* (New York: Dorset Press, 1995).

[11] Charles Dickens, *Bleak House* (New York: Bantam Books, 1983).

[12] Edgar Allan Poe, *Murders in the Rue Morgue* (New York: Thompson, 1902).

[13] Sir Arthur Conan Doyle, *A Study in Scarlet* (Rockville, MD: Wildside Press, 2004).

[14] Ibid., 77.

[15] Richard Saferstein, *Forensic Science: An Introduction* (Upper Saddle River, NJ: Prentice-Hall, 2007).

[16] Ibid.

[17] Ibid.

[18] William Tilstone, *Forensic Science: An Encyclopedia of History, Methods and Techniques* (Santa Barbara, CA: ABC-CLIO, 2006).

[19] Ibid.

[20] Ibid.

[21] Ibid.

[22] Hans Gross, *Criminal Investigation* (London: Sweet and Maxwell, 1949).

[23] Ibid., 34.

[24] Fredrick S. Calhoun, *The Lawmen: United States Marshals and Their Deputies, 1789–1989* (Washington, DC: Smithsonian Press, 1989).

[25] United States Postal Inspection Service website, postalinspectors.uspis.gov. Accessed October 15, 2008.

[26] Steven Hardin, *The Texas Rangers* (Oxford, UK: Osprey Publishing, 1991).

[27] James D. Horan, *The Pinkertons: The Detective Dynasty That Made History* (New York: Crown Books, 1968).

[28] Ibid.

[29] Jack R. Greene (ed.), *The Encyclopedia of Police Science* (New York: Garland Publishing Co., 1996).

[30] Judson C. Welliver, *New Secret Service of the United States* (Charlottesville, VA: University of Virginia Library, 1994).

[31] Ibid.

[32] Rhodri Jeffreys-Jones, *The FBI: A History* (New Haven, CT: Yale University Press, 2007).

[33] Ibid.

[34] Laurence Frederick Schmeckebier, *The Bureau of Prohibition: Its History, Activities and Organization* (New York: AMS Press, 1972).

[35] Ibid.

[36] Ibid.

[37] Patricia Rachal, *Federal Narcotics Enforcement: Reorganization and Reform* (Boston, MA: Auburn House, 1982).

[38] Lisa Yount, *Forensic Science: From Fibers to Fingerprints* (New York: Chelsea House Publishers, 2006).

[39] Michele Kestler, *Scientific Investigation Division: Eight Decades of Fighting Crime Through Science* (Los Angeles, CA: Los Angeles Police Department, 2000).

[40] Colin Wilson and Damon Wilson, *Written in Blood: A History of Forensic Detection* (New York: Carroll and Graf Publishers, 2003).

[41] Ibid.

[42] Federal Bureau of Investigation, *The FBI: A Centennial History 1908–2008* (Washington, DC: USGPO, 2008).

[43] Ibid.

[44] Ibid.

[45] Federal Bureau of Investigation's website, www.fbi.gov/about-us/history/highlights-of-history/articles/laboratory. Accessed July 23, 2012; Kim Waggoner, *The FBI Laboratory: 75 Years of Forensic Science Service* (Washington, DC: Federal Bureau of Investigation, 2007).

[46] Kim Waggoner, *The FBI Laboratory: 75 Years of Forensic Science Service* (Washington, DC: Federal Bureau of Investigation, 2007).

[47] Ibid.

[48] Brian Lane, *The Encyclopedia of Forensic Science* (London: Headline Publishers, 1992).

[49] Keith Inman and Norah Rudin, *Principles and Practice of Criminalistics: The Profession of Forensic Science* (Boca Raton, FL: CRC, 2000).

[50] American Board of Criminalistics' website, www.criminalistics.com. Accessed September 12, 2008.

[51] Federal Bureau of Investigation's website, www.fbi.gov/about-us/cjis/ncic. Accessed July 23, 2012.

[52] Ibid.

[53] Federal Bureau of Investigation, *The Beltway Snipers Part I and II* (Washington, DC: U.S. Department of Justice, 2007).

[54] Ibid.

[55] John Sanders, *Forensic Casebook of Crime* (London: Forum Press, 2000).

[56] U.S. Department of Justice, *The Combined DNA Index System* (Washington, DC: USGOP, 2001).

[57] Innocence Project's website, www.innocenceproject.org. Accessed November 10, 2008.

CHAPTER TWO

INVESTIGATORS, INVESTIGATIONS, AND THE LAW

Learning Objectives

After completing this chapter, you should be able to:

1. Understand how a crime is legally established by a criminal investigation.
2. Summarize the legal guidelines that police must follow for searches, seizures, and arrests.
3. Describe the process of obtaining and executing a search warrant.
4. Explain when warrantless searches are authorized.
5. Define the term *exclusionary rule* and its relationship to illegal searches and seizures.
6. Outline the necessary investigative requirements for building a case for prosecution.

Chapter Outline

Establishing That a Crime has been Committed
- *Corpus Delicti*
- Elements of a Crime
- *Actus Reus* and *Mens Rea*

Gathering Evidence to Prove the Crime
- Reasonable Suspicion and Probable Cause
- Search Warrants
- Warrantless Searches
- Illegal Searches

Identifying and Arresting Suspects
- Consensual Encounter
- Detention
- Arrest

Building a Case for Trial

INTRODUCTION

IN HIS FAMOUS DUE PROCESS and Crime Control Model of Justice, legal scholar Herbert Packer[1] suggests that the American legal system is like a political pendulum, constantly swinging to the left to preserve the legal rights of persons accused of crimes, and to the right to neglect these same rights in an effort to arrest as many criminals as possible. Nowhere is this legal metaphor more appropriate to mention than in this chapter, which discusses the laws governing criminal investigations and investigators. As you will soon discover, the specific guarantees of the Fourth Amendment to the U.S. Constitution to protect citizens from unreasonable invasions of privacy in searches and seizures by police have been swinging back and forth between due process and crime control for decades, if not centuries. For example, in the early 1900s, investigators could search individuals and their homes in violation of the Fourth Amendment and still have evidence from the illegal search presented in court to obtain a conviction. From the 1940s to the1960s, a series of Supreme Court cases interpreting the Fourth Amendment barred any and all illegally seized evidence from all court proceedings to punish police who

unjustly invaded citizens' privacy. More recently, in the 1980s and 1990s, the Supreme Court reinterpreted the Fourth Amendment, providing several exceptions to enable some seized evidence illegally seized by police to be used for gaining criminal convictions. Most recently, after the 9/11 terrorist attacks, the pendulum swung farther in the crime control direction in the passing of the Patriot Act, which enables police to invade privacy under virtually any condition so long as the invasion is in the interest of national security. As is readily apparent from this short introduction, investigators need to keep a close eye on the direction in which the search-and-seizure pendulum is swinging—for it alone can make or break a case.

Regardless of the crime being investigated and the law enforcement officer acting as the investigator, all investigations must be carried out in a legal—*as well as moral and ethical*—manner. Laws that govern proper procedures for investigators in arresting suspects, searching crime scenes, and seizing property as evidence are referred to as **criminal procedural laws**. In addition, investigators must be mindful of **substantive criminal laws**, which define the legal requirements that have to be met to determine whether a crime has been committed, and whether a given suspect is guilty or innocent of a specific criminal act.[2] Although investigators must follow the same legal standards as any other law enforcement officer, certain aspects of the aforementioned criminal laws bear specific importance to the investigative process. Specifically, these legal requirements can be grouped within the four primary goals of carrying out a criminal investigation:

- To establish that a crime has been committed
- To gather evidence or proof of the crime
- To identify and arrest suspects
- To build a case for trial

ESTABLISHING THAT A CRIME HAS BEEN COMMITTED

Corpus Delicti

The first legal requirement that must be satisfied in order for a criminal investigation to proceed is determining the **corpus delicti** (Latin for "body of the crime") of a suspected criminal activity. In other words, an investigator must establish that a crime has indeed been committed before partaking in any further investigative efforts. On the surface, many situations appear to involve criminal conduct when, in reality, they do not, and vice versa. For example, a partially decomposed body discovered alongside an isolated hiking trail in the desert at first may appear to be a murderer's attempt to hide the victim from police in a deserted shallow grave site. Upon examination of the body, however, medical experts may rule that the death in fact was accidental—the fatal mistake of a hiker stranded in an uninhabitable environment. Likewise, arson may be suspected when the home of a prominent and controversial politician burns to the ground in the middle of the night; in reality, however, as the firefighters discover, the blaze was the result of a faulty electrical appliance. In both these cases, the legal standard of *corpus delicti* has not been met, and there is no need to expend additional investigative resources on the matter. In some instances, where actual physical evidence does not exist, the *corpus delicti* of a crime can be established by examining the circumstances surrounding the alleged criminal incident. For example, a murder case can be established—even without discovery of a dead body—based on facts surrounding the relationship between a suspected offender and the missing person presumed to have been murdered.[3] Figure 2.1 presents a crime scene where investigators must determine whether or not the *corpus delicti* for the crime of murder can be established by available physical evidence.

Elements of the Crime

After determining that a crime likely has been committed, investigators need to consider the specific **elements of the crime** outlined by criminal law. These are the factual legal requirements of a crime that must be demonstrated and supported by evidence obtained during the investigation. Every crime has its particular elements, which are usually outlined in the **statutes**, or written legal codes, of a particular jurisdiction. For example, the following is a generic description of the elements of burglary:

1. Breaking and entering into the dwelling of another;
2. In the nighttime;
3. With the intent to commit a felony therein.

To successfully prosecute a suspect for burglary according to the above elements of the crime, each separate element must

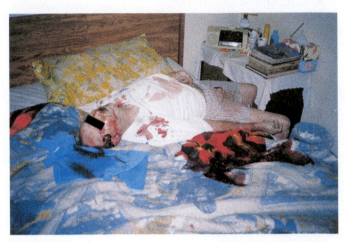

(a)

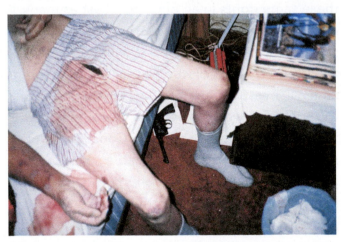

(b)

FIGURE 2.1 ▶ In the situation shown here, a murder seems to have taken place. If so, the *corpus delicti* for a wrongful killing would be established and homicide investigators would search for the shooter. Further investigation, however, reveals that the handgun used in the killing not only was registered to the decedent, but also contained his fingerprints. Gunpowder residue was also discovered on the victim's right hand. All of this evidence indicates that the death was a suicide rather than a murder. Thus, the *corpus delicti* of a crime was not established.

be supported by the facts of the case—which, in turn, are supported by the investigator's evidence and proof of the suspect's guilt. For example, a screwdriver containing the fingerprints of the suspect was found at the crime scene, which was a house belonging to the suspect's ex-wife. Furthermore, scratches and impressions on a broken window lock where the burglar entered the house matched the head of the screwdriver. Both the latter and former items of physical evidence would satisfy the first element. It is also known that the break-in occurred sometime between 9:00 PM and 4:00 AM while the woman occupying the house was away working the night shift—satisfying the second element. As for the last element, a matchbook discovered in the suspect's pants pocket after his arrest contained the access code to a wall safe containing valuable jewelry located within burglarized home—leading to the conclusion that felony grand theft was indeed the motive for the break-in. It is critical that investigators know the specific elements of the particular crime they are investigating, and that their search for evidence be guided by the need to provide adequate proof of each element of the crime.

Actus Reus and Mens Rea

As can be seen from the burglary example just presented, the crime elements require both an act on the part of the suspect (i.e., breaking and entering) and a mental state (i.e., intent to commit a felony). The act requirement is referred to in legal terms as **actus reus**. In reality, this requirement can be satisfied by either performing an act or failing to act when legally required to do so—for example, parents neglecting their child's safety needs. A suspected offender's action or inaction must be proven to be voluntary. For example, a person who injured or killed others by starting an apartment fire after suffering a heart attack while smoking in bed would not be held criminally accountable under the rule of actus reus.

It is much easier to obtain investigative proof of the act than of the suspect's mental state during the act, referred to as **mens rea**. In traffic violations or other minor offenses, only the act itself is required to imply guilt (known as **strict liability offenses**); most formally investigated crimes, however, will require evidence proving that the suspect possessed a guilty mind or criminal intent when the alleged criminal act was committed. If this evidence cannot be obtained, the particular act in question usually will be considered involuntary and the suspect will not be held legally accountable for the alleged criminal conduct. In most criminal investigations, an offender's guilty mind (or lack thereof) can be demonstrated through various means, including direct physical evidence as well as witness accounts. To meet the mens rea requirement of most offenses, however, investigators usually must demonstrate that the suspect's mental state at the time of the act somehow influenced his or her decision to carry out the alleged criminal act.

There are four levels of mental criminal responsibility that can be proven or disproven through investigative evidence. Table 2.1 provides a brief description and example of each:

TABLE 2.1

MENTAL STATE	DESCRIPTION	EXAMPLE
Purposeful	Mental desire for the act to produce a specific outcome	Shot fired with the hope that the bullet will result in death
Knowing	Mental awareness that the act most likely will produce a specific outcome	Shot fired while aware that there is a significant chance the bullet will result in death
Reckless	Committing the act while disregarding its potential to produce a specific outcome	Shot fired while ignoring thoughts that the bullet can result in death
Negligent	Committing the act while failing to foresee its potential to produce a specific outcome	Shot fired without giving thought to the fact the bullet can result in death

The legal states of mind presented in Table 2-1 can be further illustrated by applying them to real-life examples of gang crime. A drive-by shooting at a cemetery to kill rival gang members attending a funeral for one of their own is *purposeful* since it was planned and executed to kill as a means of payback. By comparison, a death resulting from spontaneous gunfire between two rival gangs after they "hit each other up" with "mad dog" stares and hand signs is *knowing*, despite its lack of planning, due to the highly anticipated deadly consequences. A street gang's initiation of newly recruited "B.G.s" (i.e., "baby gangsters") by requiring them to shoot out the lighted kitchen window of a home becomes *reckless* when a couple sitting at the kitchen table is struck and killed by the gangsters' stray bullets. In this case, although the window may have been covered by curtains, the shooters had reason to believe that a home with a lighted window might be occupied and that bullets aimed at the window could strike the occupants (as, in fact, they did). Nevertheless, such warning signs were ignored and the fatal shots were fired. Last, members of a street gang, while partying and showing off their new AK-47 rifles, fire numerous rounds into the air without the intention of harming anyone. When the bullets fell from the sky, however, they struck two pedestrians in the head—killing them instantly. The shooters charged with the crime were *negligent* in that their failure to anticipate the potentially deadly consequences of their actions could not be excused. Figure 2.2 shows a shooting crime scene involving a single female victim wherein the investigation must examine any and all available evidence that would prove the shooter's legal state of mind at the specific time this incident took place.

FIGURE 2.2 ▶ The woman pictured here was struck and killed by a single bullet while standing on the front porch of her residence. Upon identification and arrest, the man responsible for the shooting claimed that he and his friend were only shooting at streetlights at the time the victim was fatally wounded, and they had no intention of hurting anyone. In his defense, he claimed that the incident was an unfortunate accident.

GATHERING EVIDENCE TO PROVE THE CRIME

Reasonable Suspicion and Probable Cause

Perhaps the two most important legal standards applied to investigators pursuing evidence or attempting to provide legal proof of a crime are **reasonable suspicion** and **probable cause**. Each of these legal principles is derived from the Fourth Amendment to the United States, which guarantees a U.S. citizen's right to privacy as well as freedom from unreasonable searches and seizures. Furthermore, the U.S. Supreme Court's ongoing legal interpretations of the Fourth Amendment have held investigators to strict legal standards when conducting activities related to proving crimes. Foremost in these rulings is that an investigator must satisfy the requirements of reasonable suspicion to initiate the investigative process, and those of probable cause to conduct formal searches and arrests—barring exceptions established by the U.S. Supreme Court.

Reasonable suspicion exists when a particular situation would lead an officer to *suspect* that a crime is being committed, is about to be committed, or has already taken place. As will be discussed further in this chapter, reasonable suspicion is often a necessary first step for initiating the investigative process. Probable cause—which is necessary for nearly every investigation that could invade a person's constitutionally guaranteed privacy—can be defined as the legal standard to arrest when an officer has a reasonable belief a crime has occurred and the accused has violated the elements of a certain crime. Only under certain exceptional circumstances, which will be outlined later, does the Fourth Amendment allow investigators to legally search property, seize evidence, or even arrest suspects in the absence of reasonable suspicion or probable cause.[4]

Both reasonable suspicion and probable cause are established through a legal procedure known as the **totality of the circumstances** approach. In other words, officers may use any and all legally relevant facts and observations that they have gained (including hearsay from third parties) to justify their suspicions or beliefs regarding an alleged criminal offense or offender. This process is especially relevant for investigators because they are likely to collect bits and pieces of knowledge about a given crime over the course of an investigation.[5] For example, various eyewitness accounts of an auto theft suspect reveal that the offender wears an athletic suit, jogs along a roadway until spotting a vehicle he wants to steal, then breaks the driver's window and steals the car. Witnesses also reported seeing the man remove an object from his pocket that resembled a knife. Furthermore, examining footprints left at one of many crime scenes determined that the offender wears Nike cross-trainer tennis shoes. After briefly surveilling a college parking lot where several car thefts have recently occurred, an investigator notices a man in an athletic suit and Nike cross-trainer tennis shoes jogging along a walkway adjacent to the parking lot. The investigator also noticed an electrical wire with a switch extending from the pants pockets of the jogging suit. Detaining the man, the investigator conducted a routine pat-down search of his pockets and felt a weapon-like object, which turned out to be an ignition "punching" device used to start cars without a key. The suspect was arrested and searched at the scene, further revealing numerous small lock-picking devices within his pockets. At trial, the accused car thief's attorney argued that the investigator did not have reasonable suspicion to detain his client because it was unreasonable to believe that a man wearing an athletic suit, jogging on a college campus, with a wire in his pocket was involved in criminal activity. However, given the totality of the circumstances known only to the investigator— the unique combination of the offender's method of car theft, his apparel, and the high-frequency auto theft location—the court ruled that reasonable suspicion was established for the detention. This in turn permitted the determination of probable cause evidence (the wire) justifying the man's arrest. Additionally, as illustrated in Figure 2.3, the Supreme Court has allowed police officers to use various precautionary tactics during the detention and arrest of potentially dangerous suspects to enhance officer safety.

Search Warrants

There's an old saying in the world of investigation, "When in doubt, get a warrant!" In fact, a series of U.S. Supreme Court rulings suggests that all searches conducted without a warrant are in violation of the Fourth Amendment, until proven otherwise by a legal exception. Generally speaking, unless there is a medical emergency or a crime is in progress, it is always a good idea to obtain a warrant before conducting any type of search for criminal evidence. Numerous specific legal exceptions, however, have been outlined by the Supreme Court that waive

FIGURE 2.3 ▶ Police conduct a felony traffic stop on a vehicle related to a serious crime. Due to the increased danger of a potentially armed suspect (in this case, a felon), the officers require the detained suspect to place her hands on her head and kneel on the ground in a location that prevents her from reaching into the vehicle for a gun or other weapon. In such circumstances, the Fourth Amendment permits officers to take reasonable measures to ensure their personal safety before making contact with a suspect believed to be dangerous. (Photo courtesy of Fairview Heights, Ill., Police Department)

factual circumstances supporting the officer's belief that the person, place, or thing that is the target of the intended search is somehow related to a specific criminal activity. Information justifying probable cause for a search warrant includes direct observations of the investigating officer or other officers; surveillance information; offending profiles; confidential informant statements; and statements taken from third parties who have reliable knowledge about the criminal activity that is the subject of the warrant. This written portion of the warrant is called the **affidavit** (see Figure 2.5).

As shown in Figure 2.6, the completed affidavit is reviewed by a judge to determine whether it provides legally sufficient grounds to substantiate the existence of probable cause. Officers completing the affidavit must also swear under penalty of perjury that, to the best of their knowledge, all the document's contents are truthful and accurate. According to rules of law outlined in *Illinois v. Gates* (1983)[6], a search warrant can be issued only after a judge determine from the facts presented in the affidavit that the totality of the circumstances suggests the existence of probable cause. For hearsay evidence obtained from third parties, the judge must also be convinced that such information has been obtained from reliable sources. Including within the affidavit an informant's name, personal information, prior cooperation with authorities on other cases, relationship to the subject of the search, or any other personal stakes that the informant may have in the case (e.g., criminal charges lessened or dropped for providing information) can help demonstrate the adequacy of hearsay evidence to the warrant-issuing judge.

The search warrant itself must include information that specifies the location, persons, or vehicles to be searched. When describing a residence it is important to provide the entire address and describe the location in detail. For example:

the premise at 664 North Richard Street, Raleigh, North Carolina; further described as a single story dwelling house with a brown shingle roof and light green stucco exterior; including all rooms, attics, basements, and other parts therein, the surrounding grounds and any garages, storage areas, trash containers, and outbuildings of any kind located therein.

the requirement of a warrant to conduct a legal search for proof of criminal activity (discussed later in this section). Needless to say, it is essential for investigators to know the circumstances under which a search warrant is required and how to properly obtain valid warrants.

A search warrant is a written order, in the name of the people, signed by a magistrate, directed to a peace officer, commanding him or her to search for persons, things, or personal property. The search warrant is usually prepared by the law enforcement officer conducting the investigation. To justify the need for the warrant, the investigator must prepare a **statement of probable cause** (see Figure 2.4) outlining all the

---

STATEMENT OF PROBABLE CAUSE

The victim filed a report (09-7689-923) stating that person(s) unknown had obtained her personal information and used it without her permission to open an account with Daily First Card, Stances MasterCard, and a Discovery Card between the dates of January 1st, 2003 and April 13th, 2003. The victim also stated that she found fraudulent charges on her bank checking account.

On 04-14-03 I called the custodian of records, Tara Diamond, at Deceptive Checking, a web transaction service (WTS), who told me a person(s) using an e-mail address of Sampletime@email.com charged $49.95 to the victim's existing checking account at Bank of Blank. On 4/15/03 I contacted David Sternmen at an Internet dating service who told me the

person using the name of the victim applied for dating services by using the victim's checking account information. I called the Internet carrier and asked who the person was registered to the above e-mail address. The customer service representative told me she could not release any information without a search warrant.

Your Affiant believes a search of these records will result in the identification of the individual who applied for the Discover card, Daily First Card, and Stances Mastercard as well as the fraudulent use of her Bank account. This information will provide account information identifying the suspect and possibly additional victims.

FIGURE 2.4 ▶ This is a hypothetical example of a probable cause statement similar to one that would be prepared to obtain a search warrant to conduct a financial crimes investigation. The actual length of the probable cause statement will vary by type of incident.

(Exhibit A: Sample Affidavit)   SW NO. _____

SEARCH WARRANT AND AFFIDAVIT

(Affidavit)

Detective John Smith swears under oath that the facts expressed by him in this Search Warrant and Affidavit and the attached and incorporated **Statement of probable cause**, are true and that based thereon he has probable cause to believe and does believe that the property described below is lawfully seizable pursuant to Penal Code Section (Dependent upon State) as indicated below, and is now located at the locations set forth below. Wherefore, affiant requests that this Search Warrant be issued.

_____ , NIGHT SEARCH REQUESTED: YES [ ]   NO [X]

(Signature of Affiant)

(SEARCH WARRANT)

THE PEOPLE OF THE STATE OF TEXAS TO ANY SHERIFF, POLICEMAN OR PEACE OFFICER IN THE COUNTY OF GALVESTON: proof by affidavit having been made before me by Detective John Smith that there is probable cause to believe that the property described herein may be found at the locations set forth herein and that it is lawfully seizable pursuant to Penal Code Section (Depends on State) as indicated below by "X" (s) in that it:

__X_____ was stolen or embezzled,

_____ was used as the means of committing a felony,

__X_____ is possessed by a person with the intent to use it as a means of committing a public offense or is possessed by another to whom he or she may have delivered it for the purpose of concealing it or preventing its discovery,

__X_____ tends to show that a felony has been committed or that a particular person has committed a felony,

_____ tends to show that sexual exploitation of a child, in violation of P.C. Section 311.3, has occurred or is occurring

(Exhibit B: The Search Warrant)

YOU ARE THEREFORE COMMANDED TO SEARCH: (Premises, persons, vehicle)

(A)

The residence located at 5567 First Street, Galveston, Texas of Richard Diamond is a single story dwelling house with a brown shingle roof and light green stucco exterior; including all rooms, attics, basements, and other parts therein, the surrounding grounds and any garages, storage areas, trash containers, and outbuildings of any kind located therein.

(B)

Any and all vehicle parked at the location or on the street in front of the residence, as long as they are associated with the location being search:

For the Following:

1) Any article of personal property tending to establish the identity of person(s) who have dominion and control over the residential property located at 5567 First Street and any vehicles searched, which includes keys to the described location and vehicles, rent receipts, utility bills, telephone bills, addressed mail, purchase receipts, sales receipts, vehicle pink or registration slips.

2) Any and all financial records, including bank checking and savings account statements, canceled checks, credit card statements, receipts, balance sheets, money orders or bank drafts, safes, information regarding safe deposit boxes, safe deposit box keys, U.S. currency, tax records, certificates of deposit and investment accounts relative to Richard Diamond

3) Any and all credit cards, financial documents, credit reports, notes, journals, diaries and daily organizers; electronic or otherwise, containing other peoples' personal information not belonging to Richard Diamond including but not limited to any other potential victim of Identity or credit card theft.

4) Any and all computer hardware which consists of all equipment which can collect, analyze, create, display, convert, store, conceal, or transmit electronic, magnetic, optical, or similar computer impulses or data, including tower and desktop central processing units (CPU's), "laptop" or "notebook" styled computers and hand held "palm pilot" styled devices; as well as external hard drives and other memory storage devices; and any parts that can be used to restrict access to computer hardware, such as physical keys or locks.

5) Any and all computer software which consists of any digital information which can be executed by a computer and any of its related components to direct the way they work, including hard and floppy disks, CD roms, zip disks and DVD discs.

6) Any and all computer passwords and other data security devices designed to restrict access to or hide computer software, documentation, or data, consisting of hardware, software, or other programming code. Data security hardware may include encryption devices, chips, and circuit boards. Data security software or digital code may include programming code that creates "test" keys or "hot" keys, which perform certain preset security functions when touched. Data security software or code that may also encrypt, compress, hide, or "booby-trap" protected data to make it inaccessible or unusable, as well as reverse the process to restore it.

7) A forensic search of any data found on any computers, hardware and software found at the locations and it may be moved to a secondary location in order to allow forensic investigators to conduct such searches.

8) Any and all card reading machines, which can remove the information contained in any magnetic strip and place it on a credit card of similar make.

AND TO SEIZE IT IF FOUND and bring it forth before me, or this court, at the courthouse of this court. This Search Warrant and incorporated Affidavit was sworn to and subscribed before me this day of _____ at _____am/pm. Wherefore, I find probable cause for the issuance of this Search Warrant and do issue it.

_____ , **NIGHT SEARCH APPROVED: YES [ ]   NO [ ]**

(Signature of Magistrate)

Judge of the Superior Court, Northwest District

FIGURE 2.5 ▶ Examples of an affidavit and search warrant used by investigators. This affidavit (see Exhibit A) is prepared simultaneously with the search warrant, and together the documents are presented to the magistrate. Exhibit B shows the search warrant portion of the document listing specifically the location and items targeted in the search.

If the premise to be searched contains a suspected hiding place for evidence, a description of this hiding place should be included within that of the premises. For a vehicle search, details of the vehicle and various compartments in it where evidence is thought to be hidden should be provided; and the vehicle's identifying information (e.g., license plate or VIN number), if known, should be included in the warrant as well. When describing a person, include the name, sex, race, age, height, weight, eye color, and distinguishing marks to the extent they are known—as in the following example:

> the person known as "Doe, John" Male/White, approximately 25–30 years old, 5'11" 180 lbs. black hair and blue eyes, with a mustache, and believed to be residing at 664 North Richard Street, Raleigh, North Carolina.

For a suspect who has a record of prior criminal offenses, physical descriptive information can perhaps be drawn from existing local arrest files or state and national databases.

Search warrants issued for items that are technical in nature require specific details in their narrative descriptions. For example, when attempting to seize a controlled substance, the warrant description should specify the type of controlled substance, such as heroin, cocaine, marijuana, and so on. A general term such as *controlled substance* is often considered too vague to use in a warrant issued to search for specific drugs. As a general rule, descriptions in search warrants should provide enough detail to enable an officer with no knowledge of the case to effectively serve the warrant without encountering difficulties in locating the place(s), recognizing the vehicle(s), or identifying the person(s) to be searched.

A warrant generally is served as a **knock warrant**. In these situations, investigators inform the suspects named in the warrant that the premises are about to search by knocking first and presenting the warrant before entering. However, laws governing the issuing of search warrants do not require that persons be informed in advance of a search under all circumstances. Rather,

FIGURE 2.6 ▶ Detective Eric Matias presents a search warrant to Judge Michael Harwin. The judge will read the search warrant and determine whether probable cause exists to conduct a search or arrest. The detective is also placed under oath swearing to the truth and validity of the information presented.

if giving notice of a search demonstrably will result in adverse consequences—for example, danger to investigators conducting the search or the opportunity to destroy evidence—notice need not be given. In such instances, a **no-knock warrant**, by which investigators undertake a surprise entry (often defeating doors with a battering ram) to execute the warrant, is permitted. Figures 2.7 and 2.8 show the service of a no-knock warrant within a residential area by a specialized officer team organized for performing this type of enforcement.

After the search warrant has been executed, the investigator will prepare a **search warrant return**. In this final stage, investigator identifies and lists all the items seized during the search and presents those items before a judge. For purposes of convenience, large items (e.g., vehicles, numerous marijuana plants) are exempt from presentation requirements. Generally, the search

FIGURE 2.7 ▶ Officers prepare to execute a no-knock search warrant, which may require a battering ram to gain entry. (Photo courtesy of the Los Angeles Police Department)

ENTRY AND SEARCH WAIVER

File No. _____

I _____, having legal custody or

    (Last name)   (First Name)   (Middle name)

control or authority or personal ownership of the premises located at _____

_____

and described as _____

_____

_____

do hereby grant full and unconditional authority to the _____ to enter

                                      (Name of agency)

those premises to conduct a search for _____

_____

_____

and to conduct any related investigation in any related criminal or non-criminal law enforcement matter.

I will grant this consent freely, knowingly and intelligently with full knowledge that members of the Department will have free and unrestricted access to the premises until the investigation is completed

_____   _____   _____

           (Signature)   (Date)   (Time)

FIGURE 2.8 ▶ Example of the entry and search waiver form used by investigators to provide a written record of an authorized consent to conduct a warrantless search.

warrant return procedure for large items requires merely sufficient documentation of where and how the evidence was seized.

Other types of warrants utilized by investigators include **anticipatory warrants** and **sneak and peak warrants**. An anticipatory warrant is used when there is probable cause to believe that potential criminal evidence is on a sure course to a specific destination and will arrive at a specified date and time. For example, in the case of *U.S. v. Grubbs*[7], child pornography was legally seized as evidence upon delivery of the illegal contraband to the man identified in the warrant as the purchaser. Sneak and peak warrants authorize law enforcement officers to enter private property without the permission or knowledge of its occupants and to search for (but not seize) evidence, and afterwards return with a proper search warrant. Although not allowed to seize any items, law enforcement officers can use details from their observations to obtain a warrant that permits seizure of evidence. Sneak and peak warrants normally are used in lengthy high-risk drug investigations, but can be used for installing wiretaps and other surveillance equipment as well.

Warrantless Searches

As previously mentioned, the U.S. Supreme Court has ruled that the Fourth Amendment allows for warrantless searches by law enforcement officials in certain situations. These include the following:

- Voluntary consent to search provided by the suspect
- Exigent circumstances
- Stop-and-frisk searches
- Search incident to arrest
- "Special circumstances" searches

VOLUNTARY CONSENT

A law enforcement officer may without a warrant or probable cause conduct a search based on an individual's **voluntary consent**, and any evidence discovered during that search may be seized and admitted at trial. Should a legal issue arise on whether consent was given for a search, however, the burden of proof is on the officer. In criminal court proceedings, suspects often claim they never gave officers permission to search them or their property.[8] To avoid such problems, suspects can be required to sign a **consent to search form** after verbal approval for a search is given. Specific information on this form gives officers permission to search, and the document can be presented in court to counter claims that officers conducted an unlawful search. By giving officers consent to search, individuals in effect waive their Fourth Amendment right to privacy. This waiver must be voluntary and undertaken with rational judgment on the part of person providing the consent to search. Legal challenges to the voluntary nature of consent can occur when the suspect:

- is a juvenile, impaired by alcohol/drugs, or mentally disabled (psychological or developmentally);

- is hearing impaired, or cannot understand the language spoken to them by officers;
- does not appear to have authority to provide consent for the search (it usually is assumed that a person lives within the residence for which they are providing consent to search);
- is not in the process of facing a resisting arrest charge;
- is not subject to any form of coercion or trickery on the part of officers attempting to gain consent, referred to as **deceptive consent**.

Third parties may give consent to investigators for searching property that they own or occupy. (Note, however, that a landlord cannot provide consent for the search of property leased to the subject of the search.) Furthermore, if two persons disagree on whether consent should be given for a search, the search may not be carried out. Business owners and managers can consent to the search of their commercial establishments but not of a specific work area assigned to an employee. Investigators must always remember that persons giving consent to a search have the right to restrict the areas and items to be examined, and can withdraw their consent to end the search at any time (i.e., any time before discovery of any illegal evidence). The law does not require investigators to inform persons giving consent that they have the aforementioned rights.

EXIGENT CIRCUMSTANCES

Warrantless searches can be conducted in situations where **exigent circumstances** are present. For the most part, these are emergencies requiring immediate action by officers who do not have time to go through the formal warrant process. Imminent threats to public safety, the likely escape of a dangerous prisoner, and the removal or destruction of evidence are some of the more general situations that fall in the category of exigent circumstances.[9] More specifically, emergency warrantless searches can include the following:

1. Imminent threats of death or serious bodily harm.
2. Imminent threats of substantial property damage (e.g., fire, burglary).
3. Imminent possibility of destruction of evidence (provided that the officers do not create the situation to avoid the warrant requirement).
4. Immediate and continuous hot pursuit of a suspect from the scene of a serious crime to where the suspect is reasonably believed to be.
5. Imminent threat to public safety by dangerous instrumentalities or hazards (e.g., an explosive drug lab, as in *People v. Duncan*)
6. Preventing escape after lawfully attempting to detain or arrest while the suspect is in a public place. (Any offense can qualify; see, e.g., *People v. Lloyd*[10] involving the lawful pursuit of a traffic violator into a residence.)

The exigent circumstances rule can also be used in cases requiring an emergency search of an individual for as well as a specific location or premises. When applying this rule to individuals, there must be probable cause to believe that an immediate search will:

- uncover evidence concealed within (e.g., swallowed drugs or drugs located in a body cavity) or on the suspect's body, and;
- prevent the imminent destruction of evidence.

In addition to the above criteria, it must also be established (1) that the emergency nature of the situation did not allow time to obtain a warrant and (2) that the action taken was reasonable and necessary given the circumstances (e.g., preservation of evidence).[11]

STOP AND FRISK

The term **stop and frisk** refers to the authority of law enforcement officers to stop and conduct a warrantless cursory or pat-down search of a person for concealed weapons (for example, see Figure 2.9). The primary rationale that the Supreme Court provided for allowing these limited warrantless searches was to

FIGURE 2.9 ▶ Officers conduct a stop-and-frisk search of a suspect in cold weather. Heavy clothing worn by subjects of such searches in cold climates can be challenging to officers conducting the search as well as enable suspects to conceal weapons. Such searches, also known as *pat-down searches*, are authorized for purposes of officer safety—provided that they are conducted on the exterior of the clothing. Searches may extend to pockets and other interior clothing areas if officers believe that what they detect is either a weapon or contraband. (Photo courtesy of Vail, CO Police Department)

ensure officer safety. The investigative need to search a person in stop-and-frisk situations is often misunderstood in theory and sometimes misapplied in the field. Some officers believe that any person walking or driving on a public street is fair game and can be subject to a pat-down search; but nothing is further from the legal truth, according to Supreme Court rulings. Reasonable suspicion must be established before a stop-and-frisk search is conducted. As previously mentioned, this legal threshold is established by a totality of the circumstances approach, which includes any and all information drawn from sources including the officer's training, observations, sensory perceptions, or hearsay knowledge. It must also be remembered that the primary legal purpose of this type of search is officer safety, not suspicion alone.[12] Key questions that can assist in this process include the following:

1. What is the reason for the stop?
2. What were the person's activities and behaviors (verbal/nonverbal) at the time?
3. What is the location and time of the stop?
4. Did the individual fit the description of a suspect in a recent crime?
5. Was the location a high-crime area?
6. Was the person a known criminal who carries weapons?

After the frisk has been justified under probable cause standards, it is limited to the suspect's outer clothing areas, which can include jackets, hats, and other layers of apparel. At this preliminary stage, the inside of pockets cannot be searched; however, if during an external search the officer feels an object that—from his or her knowledge, training, and experience—resembles a weapon or illegal contraband, the interior of the pockets or clothing may be searched. Legally speaking, this rule is referred to as the **plain feel exception**.[13] When invoking this rule during a search, however, it is imperative that the identity of the object being seized beneath the suspect's clothing be immediately apparent to the investigator as a weapon or some other type of contraband. For example, if several small soft, pliable, balloon-like objects are felt above the surface of the suspect's pants pocket during the initial weapons search, they may be removed from the pockets if the officer trained in narcotics identification thinks that the objects are balloons or condoms, which commonly are used to transport heroine or other drugs. Conversely, if the officer cannot immediately conclude, based on his or her knowledge, that these objects are indeed a specific type of illegal contraband, removing the pocket contents to search for narcotics would be considered fishing for evidence or an illegal search. Removal of items from suspect's undergarments or other private areas (which may constitute a strip search) should be handled by investigators of the same gender, properly witnessed, and performed according to departmental protocol.

PLAIN VIEW

Law enforcement officers are permitted to search and seize illegal items that they observe in **plain view**[14] without a search warrant so long as they are legally authorized to be where the observations of the evidence took place. Plain view searches for evidence can be conducted in a variety of circumstances. Often, they take place during non–crime-related emergencies where entry is gained to private premises or locations under the rule of exigent circumstances. For example, a fire breaks out in a residence, and upon entry police discover that the source of the blaze was a meth lab explosion. In other situations, police may observe illegal contraband in plain view during the course of their routine duties. For example, investigators may be called to the residence of a suspected burglary. In the course of their burglary investigation, which involves an examination of a break-in to a storage unit, the investigators notice an open box in plain view containing several explosive devices—including timing devices, grenades, and mortars. After such items are determined indeed to be illegal contraband, and not merely unarmed collector's items, they can be legally seized as evidence. To legally apply the plain view doctrine, the following conditions must be observed:

- It must be immediately apparent that the item in plain view is illegal in nature.
- Items and property cannot be moved or removed in order to create a plain view of illegal evidence.
- Certain technology may not be used to enhance an officer's ability to conduct a plain view observation of illegal evidence.
- Although the observation of illegal evidence in plain view does not need to be inadvertent or accidental, it must occur without any trickery or deception of suspects, or any other activity designed to avoid seeking a search warrant.
- The seizure of illegal items following plain view must be founded on probable cause to believe the items are being, were, or are about to be used in the commission of a crime.

The plain view doctrine has been extended to various search situations. For example, as illustrated in Figure 2.10, observations made from an aircraft using binoculars and other visual magnification devices—for example, aerial surveillance revealing drug cultivation on rooftops—have been ruled permissible. Courts also have ruled, however, that certain technologies are not protected by the plain view doctrine. Recently, it was determined that using infrared heat-sensing and visualizing devices to discover marijuana grow houses from heat originating within a residence constitutes an illegal search. The reasoning here is that heat waves internal rather than external to the residence are not subject to public inspection and thus, according to the Fourth Amendment, a search warrant is required. The plain view doctrine, although it implies the use of sight only, has been extended to all the officer's senses—as in the previously mentioned plain feel exception or when an officer can plain "smell" smoke from crack cocaine. As a general rule, however, the use of any device that assists the senses (sight, taste, touch, smell, sound) to obtain evidence where there is a reasonable expectation of privacy (such as behind walls or closed doors) is not considered to be a legal search under the plain view doctrine.

FIGURE 2.10 ▶ Investigators seize marijuana plants from a grow field observed during an aerial surveillance. According to the plain view doctrine, warrantless searches like this one conducted via aircraft are permissible in situations where the contraband is readily observable and the method of observation used does not invade a person's reasonable expectation of privacy. (Photo courtesy of The Indiana State Police)

SEARCH INCIDENT TO ARREST

Once a legal arrest has taken place based on adequate probable cause (see the "Arrest" section later in the chapter for more detail), the law permits officers to conduct a warrantless search of the arrestees, items they are wearing or carrying, and the physical area within their immediate control. The purpose of a **search incident to arrest** is to ensure the officer's safety, to prevent the arrestee's possible escape, and to prevent the arrestee from destroying evidence. As is illustrated in Figure 2.11, the area of immediate control will depend on where the arrest is made.[15]

If the suspect is arrested while or after driving a motor vehicle, it is permissible to search the arrestee as well as the entire passenger compartment. The latter rule applies regardless of whether the suspect is arrested inside or outside the vehicle. All compartments and items, whether locked or not, can be searched so long as there is a logical connection between the items being searched for and the location of the search. For example, it would not be legal to search for an assault rifle inside a locked

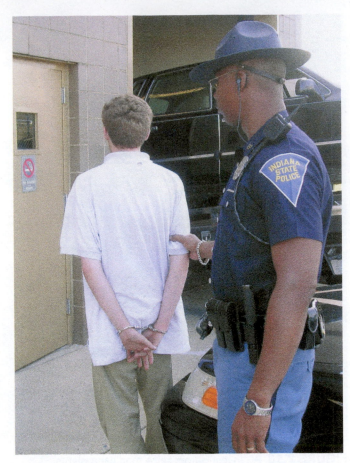

FIGURE 2.11 ▶ After arrest following the establishment of probable cause, a full search of the suspect's person and possessions can be legally conducted. In addition (as shown in the background of this photo), the suspect's vehicle is impounded and its contents are inventoried by police. If items are discovered during the inventory that suggest criminal activity (e.g., weapons or drugs), the arrestee will be charged with an additional crime. (Photo courtesy The Indiana State Police)

briefcase. If the suspect's vehicle is impounded, officers are permitted to inventory the entire contents of the vehicle both to protect the suspect's property as well as to search for items potentially dangerous to others. When conducting the inventory, all areas of the vehicle that might possibly contain valuables or dangerous items (including the trunk, locked compartments, and locked items) may be searched. It is vital that the officer note all items within the vehicle. If this is not done, the suspect can claim that money, jewelry, and other valuables inside the car are missing when the vehicle is returned. The suspect then may perhaps file a claim and even assert that an officer stole the items. During this search, if the officer locates weapons, drugs, or other contraband, the suspect will be charged an additional offense.

In general, the Supreme Court has ruled that virtually no expectation of privacy is afforded to search situations involving motor vehicles, a situation referred to in court rulings as the **motor vehicle exception**. Any motor vehicle can be searched if (1) probable cause exists to believe that evidence of crime is located on or in the vehicle, (2) the vehicle is located where it

is legally accessible to officers, and (3) the search is not conducted in a random manner—that is, it focuses on places where the illegal item searched for could be concealed. The latter search criteria extends to trucks, vans, motorcycles, trailers, motor homes, and water vessels such as house boats. Regardless of whether the vehicle to be searched is motorized or not, so long as that vehicle is considered mobile, it falls within the motor vehicle exception rule.[16]

For arrests that take place within a residential setting, the search of the area of the suspect's immediate control is usually limited to the specific room where the arrest is made. Extending the search to other rooms in the residence would usually be illegal. If the arrest transpires in large, open premises that are not defined by walls—such as an industrial building or warehouse setting—the area of immediate control governing the scope of the search is usually an imaginary perimeter within which the suspect could lunge for a weapon or for incriminating evidence.

SPECIAL CIRCUMSTANCES SEARCHES

Under special circumstances a warrantless search can be undertaken because there is no reasonable suspicion or probable cause, no reasonable expectation of privacy, or both. These special circumstances include:

- **Open Fields:** Searches can be conducted in open fields because there is no expectation of privacy in such locations—a legal concept referred to as the **open fields doctrine**. This rule also applies to all fields where crops are being cultivated, regardless of whether the crops are legal ones, such as corn, or illegal ones, such as marijuana. To apply this rule, however, open fields must be distinguished from areas that may be considered **curtilages**—which are legally protected against warrantless searches. Curtilages are any land areas, including structures on them, used exclusively by persons living on them. These can be backyards, fenced grounds, storage sheds, unattached garages, dog houses, horse stables, and even tree houses.[17]

- **Abandoned Property:** If there is a reasonable belief that individuals have surrendered their right to privacy as applied to a particular place or thing, search and seizure may take place without a warrant. The courts use a totality of the circumstances approach when determining whether some place or thing has been effectively abandoned. The abandonment of homes, vehicles, personal property, and temporary lodging areas (motels, campgrounds) allows for warrantless legal searches and seizures of evidence. Often, items discarded in garbage cans, ashtrays and other refuse receptacles are legally recovered for evidentiary purposes.[18]

- **Probation/Parole Searches:** Persons under active probation or parole supervision may themselves be searched without reasonable suspicion, probable cause, or obtaining a warrant. This includes their personal possessions, residence, vehicle, and other places and items to which they have access. Because such persons are technically incarcerated, but living in the community, they are still without the Fourth Amendment rights that they lost while under correctional supervision. In some instances, this type of warrantless search can be conducted even though an individual other than the probationer or parolee controls the area or item being searched. For example, persons who allow a parolee to reside in their personal residence may effectively give up their right to privacy, and common areas shared by them with probationers or parolees may be searched without a warrant at any time.[19] Conversely, areas or items not considered common or shared generally require a warrant before being searched.

- *School searches:* On school grounds, warrantless searches may be conducted of students' belongings in primary and secondary school environments, but only on the basis of reasonable suspicion.[20]

- *Patriot Act searches:* As the result of the Patriot Act passed after the 9/11 terrorist attacks, searches may be conducted and evidence seized without warrants if such searches are performed in the interest of national security. Specifically, e-mails, telephonic communications, medical records, financial records, and other usually privileged documents have been excluded from normal warrant requirements. Also, the Act allows for the use of special administrative subpoenas called National Security Letters, which require persons to provide private information for government investigations involving suspected terrorist activity. Furthermore, routine searches at or near the U.S. border do not require a warrant.[21]

Illegal Searches

Searches conducted without a proper warrant, or without a legally justified reason for not obtaining a warrant, will nearly always be considered illegal. Furthermore, any evidence obtained from an illegal search will most assuredly be declared **inadmissible evidence**—which cannot be used in a court proceeding to prove the guilt of an individual accused of criminal activity. The legal prohibition against illegally seized evidence is referred to as **the exclusionary rule**, and it is designed to enforce the Fourth Amendment guarantee against unreasonable searches and seizures. Essentially, the ruling states that evidence secured by illegal means and in bad faith cannot be introduced in a criminal trial. Bad faith occurs when law enforcement officers intentionally and knowingly search for and seize evidence by illegal means.[22]

An additional restriction on the use of illegally seized evidence during an investigation derives from a second landmark legal interpretation of the Fourth Amendment by the Supreme Court—the **fruit of the poisonous tree** doctrine. In effect, this ruling extended legal restrictions imposed by the exclusionary rule to all evidence originating from an illegal search. That is, if it can be proven that a case against a suspect was originally founded upon illegally obtained evidence, courts will declare all evidence subsequently gathered and collected in that case as tainted evidence—inadmissible in court for proving a suspect's guilt. In formulating the fruit of the poisonous tree doctrine, the Supreme Court relied on a simple analogy: If the roots of the tree are poisoned (the original illegal search), so too will the fruit that the tree bears (any additional tainted evidence). Both this ruling and the exclusionary rule, taken together, serve as a strong encouragement for investigators to abide by legal due process regulations ("follow the rules") when conducting searches and seizing evidence.[23] The search and seizure concepts discussed in the preceding sections can be applied to the actual crime scenes presented in Case Example 2A (see Figure 2.12) and Case Example 2B (see Figure 2.13)

CASE EXAMPLE 2A

Search and seizure involving a murder within a homeless camp

FIGURE 2.12 ▶ A homeless woman is found dead with multiple bleeding head wounds. She resides in a public park where many of the city's homeless have established makeshift housing. In most murder investigations involving the homeless, the suspect also is homeless. First responders and investigators conducted a warrantless search within the area of all legally permissible persons, places, and things to uncover possible evidence relating to the crime. Is the scope of this search limited by any laws entitling residents of the homeless encampment to a reasonable expectation of privacy?

CASE EXAMPLE 2B

Executing a technically invalid arrest warrant

FIGURE 2.13 ▶ Officers executing a no-knock arrest warrant (see Figure 2.8) gain entry into a suspect's residence at the address listed on the warrant. They observe drug manufacturing activities inside the home and arrest all suspects involved, but the man whose name is listed on the warrant cannot be found. If the search warrant was later determined to have the wrong address and so was executed at the wrong residence, are the arrests under this technically invalid warrant enforceable under any legal exceptions to searching and seizing people or property without a valid warrant? (Photo courtesy of the Los Angeles Police Department)

Under certain circumstances, however, law enforcement officers recover evidence in violation of the Fourth Amendment, yet the evidence can be used against the criminal defendant in a court of law. Most notable among these circumstances are the **doctrine of inevitable discovery** and the **good faith exception**. If evidence is obtained without a warrant and it is later determined that the evidence eventually would have been discovered as the result of a legal ongoing search, such evidence can be used in court against an accused suspect under the rule of **inevitable discovery**.[24] To invoke this rule, however, courts often require proof that the police were actively pursuing a lawful investigation that inevitably would have led to discovery of the evidence at the time that the evidence was obtained without a proper warrant.

Under the good faith exception, illegally obtained evidence can still be admissible if it can be shown that officers conducting the search were acting in good faith—in other words, they believed that they were legally justified to conduct the search. These situations include scenarios like the following:

- officers executing warrants that they believe to be valid at the time of the search, but judicial review later determines lack of sufficient probable cause;
- incomplete or mistaken property descriptions of evidence to be seized;
- entry into a search area based on consent given by a person believed to have—but who, in reality, does not have—the authority to do so.[25]

Good faith exceptions cannot be granted if officers improperly execute the search warrant, provide false information to the judge, or do not substantiate enough information on the search warrant to establish its legal validity.

IDENTIFYING AND ARRESTING SUSPECTS

When investigators encounter persons of interest who perhaps later become crime suspects, there are three progressive levels of legal contact that they can make with such individuals: consensual encounter, detention, or arrest.

Consensual Encounter

The first, and least legally intrusive level of contact between an investigator and a potential suspect is a **consensual encounter**. Consensual encounters involve casual, nonthreatening, yet perhaps slightly inquisitive conversations between officers and persons with whom they are making contact. Reasonable suspicion and probable cause are not necessary to initiate a consensual encounter with a suspect. To keep a consensual encounter out of the realm of Fourth Amendment protections, the officer's words and actions must not implicitly or explicitly restrict a person's freedom. Always remember that in these situations the individuals you are contacting are under no obligation to cooperate with you and are free to leave at any time. A law enforcement officer has no authority during a consensual contact to search the person they are speaking with, unless either reasonable suspicion or probable cause is established at some point during the discussion.

During a consensual encounter, the officer can ask the individual to voluntarily provide information or perhaps even to consent to a search. For example, questions such as "Would you be willing to answer some questions?" "Do you have any identification?" or "Do I have your permission to search you?" would all be within the legal realm of a consensual encounter. If the individual refuses to voluntarily comply with an investigator's requests, however, this refusal must be accepted and honored. Similarly, requests for information that the individual perceives as commands (e.g., "Show me your personal identification"), or actions such as displaying a weapon, physically touching the individual, calling in several other officers, or using a police vehicle to block the individual's car all may be legally construed as a more serious form of contact requiring Fourth Amendment restrictions. Generally speaking, investigators have the absolute right to make contact with any individual so long as they do not turn the consensual encounter into a detention by giving orders, making demands, or doing something that makes that person believe they are not free to leave.

Detention

The next, more serious level of contact beyond that of a consensual encounter is **detention**. Individuals are considered to be legally detained when the investigator's words or actions cause them to reasonably believe that they are not free to leave the officer's presence. For example, the commands "Stop! Police!" or "Hold it!" issued to an individual would constitute a detention. As previously discussed in relation to a stop-and-frisk search, any type of contact considered to be a detention requires that the officer have reasonable suspicion. The legal purpose of a detention is to provide the officer an opportunity to ensure his or her own safety (as in a stop and frisk) and to briefly investigate the circumstances to determine whether a crime has been committed and, if so, whether the individual detained is somehow involved in its commission. If the officer believes that the person detained has committed a crime, probable cause will be established for an arrest. On the other hand, if the investigation reveals no criminal conduct, the detained individual is released. Case Example 2C (see Figure 2.14) provides a "real world" scenario to which the concepts of suspect detention can be applied.

Arrest

An **arrest** occurs when a law enforcement officer takes a person into custody. Such action may follow a brief detention, or may be taken immediately without any prior contact—as when witnessing a crime in progress. Under the Fourth Amendment, arrest is classified as a seizure and is the most intrusive form of contact an officer can make with an individual. Therefore, arrest requires the establishment of probable cause, which is the highest level of an officer's certainty with regard to a suspect's criminal involvement. For an arrest to occur, suspects need not be informed that they are under arrest. Rather, if the attendant circumstances surrounding a detention are such that individuals

---

CASE EXAMPLE 2C

Detaining potentially dangerous suspects

FIGURE 2.14 ▶ Officers detain multiple suspects to determine whether they were involved in a crime that just occurred. Are their detention and manner of detention permissible under the laws of arrest? What information must the officers have before detaining individuals related to a crime that just occurred? (Photo courtesy of Fairview Heights, Ill., Police Department)

(a)

FIGURE 2.15A ▶ (a) Booking photo of notorious football legend O. J. Simpson, following his arrest for the brutal stabbing murders of his ex-wife, Nicole Simpson, and Ronald Goldman. His trial was later referred to in the media as "The Trial of the Century." (Courtesy of the Los Angeles Police Department)

feel as though they have been taken into custody—such as being placed in handcuffs—the legal requirements for arrest will have been satisfied. At this point, the arresting officer must respect various constitutional considerations and rights of the arrestee (such as Miranda warnings, discussed in Chapter 5 on interviews and interrogation).

An arrest may occur with or without a warrant. Investigators usually perform warrantless arrests if they have established probable cause through one or more of the following:

- Observing a crime in progress
- Eyewitness identification of a suspect at the scene of a crime
- Admissions and confessions provided by suspects

Most arrests of suspects, however, are made by investigators after an **arrest warrant** has been issued (see Figure 2.15). Briefly, the arrest warrant provides the basis for probable cause necessary to take an individual into legal custody to answer to criminal charges. Information contained in the warrant includes the suspect's personal information, specific criminal charges against the suspect, and evidence establishing probable cause for the arrest. Once a judge reviews, approves, and signs the arrest warrant, investigators or any other law enforcement officer may legally arrest the suspect. If the suspect can be located, investigators may serve the arrest warrant themselves or assign a patrol unit to conduct the arrest. The arrest warrant authorizes the arresting officers to enter a particular residence

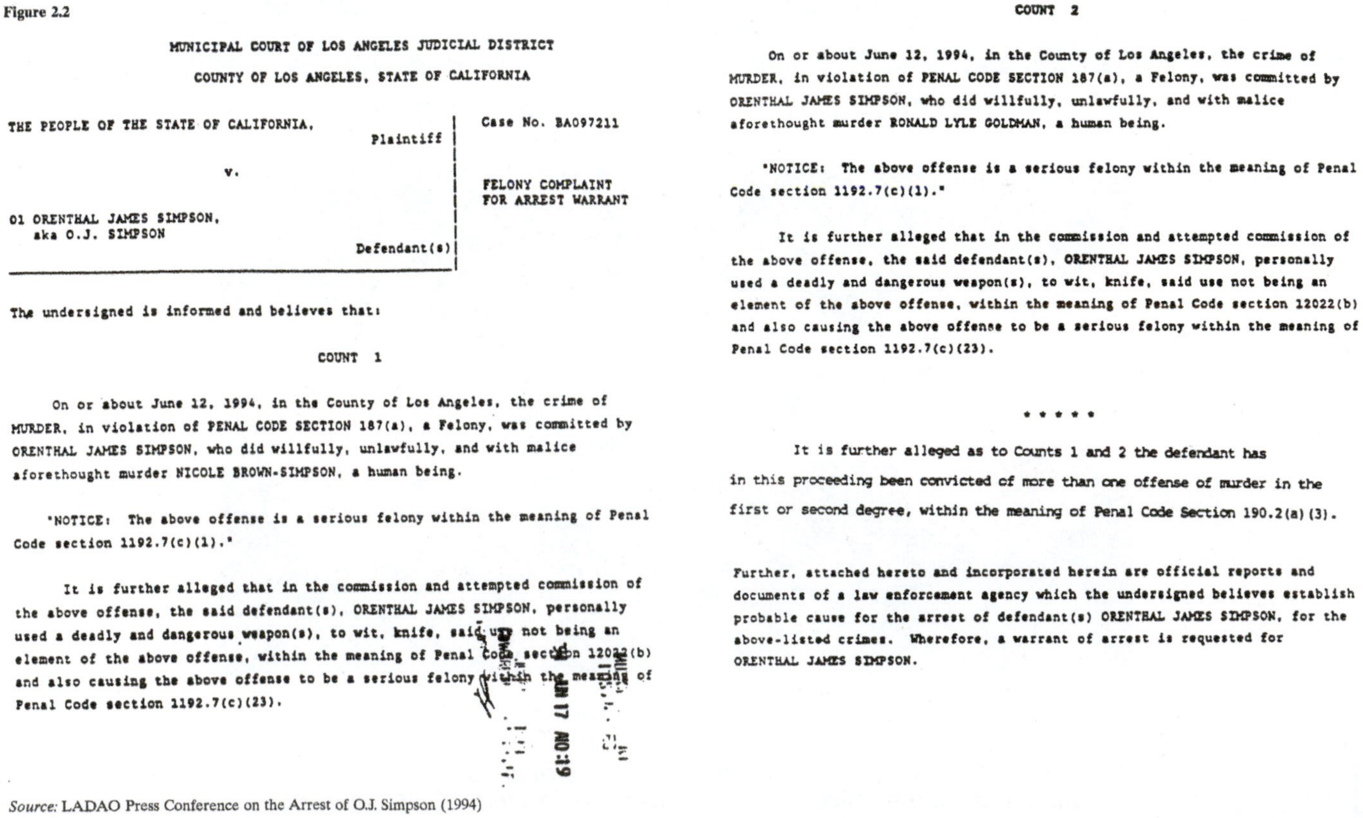

Figure 2.2

MUNICIPAL COURT OF LOS ANGELES JUDICIAL DISTRICT

COUNTY OF LOS ANGELES, STATE OF CALIFORNIA

THE PEOPLE OF THE STATE OF CALIFORNIA,
                                        Plaintiff

        v.

01 ORENTHAL JAMES SIMPSON,
   aka O.J. SIMPSON
                                        Defendant(s)

Case No. BA097211

FELONY COMPLAINT FOR ARREST WARRANT

The undersigned is informed and believes that:

COUNT 1

On or about June 12, 1994, in the County of Los Angeles, the crime of MURDER, in violation of PENAL CODE SECTION 187(a), a Felony, was committed by ORENTHAL JAMES SIMPSON, who did willfully, unlawfully, and with malice aforethought murder NICOLE BROWN-SIMPSON, a human being.

"NOTICE: The above offense is a serious felony within the meaning of Penal Code section 1192.7(c)(1)."

It is further alleged that in the commission and attempted commission of the above offense, the said defendant(s), ORENTHAL JAMES SIMPSON, personally used a deadly and dangerous weapon(s), to wit, knife, said use not being an element of the above offense, within the meaning of Penal Code section 12022(b) and also causing the above offense to be a serious felony within the meaning of Penal Code section 1192.7(c)(23).

COUNT 2

On or about June 12, 1994, in the County of Los Angeles, the crime of MURDER, in violation of PENAL CODE SECTION 187(a), a Felony, was committed by ORENTHAL JAMES SIMPSON, who did willfully, unlawfully, and with malice aforethought murder RONALD LYLE GOLDMAN, a human being.

"NOTICE: The above offense is a serious felony within the meaning of Penal Code section 1192.7(c)(1)."

It is further alleged that in the commission and attempted commission of the above offense, the said defendant(s), ORENTHAL JAMES SIMPSON, personally used a deadly and dangerous weapon(s), to wit, knife, said use not being an element of the above offense, within the meaning of Penal Code section 12022(b) and also causing the above offense to be a serious felony within the meaning of Penal Code section 1192.7(c)(23).

* * * * *

It is further alleged as to Counts 1 and 2 the defendant has in this proceeding been convicted of more than one offense of murder in the first or second degree, within the meaning of Penal Code Section 190.2(a)(3).

Further, attached hereto and incorporated herein are official reports and documents of a law enforcement agency which the undersigned believes establish probable cause for the arrest of defendant(s) ORENTHAL JAMES SIMPSON, for the above-listed crimes. Wherefore, a warrant of arrest is requested for ORENTHAL JAMES SIMPSON.

Source: LADAO Press Conference on the Arrest of O.J. Simpson (1994)

FIGURE 2.15B ▶ (b) The warrant for his arrest could arguably be referred to as "The Arrest Warrant of the Century." (Courtesy of the Los Angeles Police Department)

I DECLARE UNDER PENALTY OF PERJURY THAT THE FOREGOING IS TRUE AND CORRECT AND
THAT THIS COMPLAINT, CASE NUMBER BA097211 , CONSISTS OF 2 COUNT(S).

Executed at LOS ANGELES, County of Los Angeles, on June 17, 1994.

PHILLIP VANNATTER
DECLARANT AND COMPLAINANT

· ·

GIL GARCETTI, DISTRICT ATTORNEY

BY: MARCIA CLARK, DEPUTY

| AGENCY: LAPD RHD | I/O: VANNATTER | ID NO: | PHONE NO: 485-2531 |
| DR NO: 9408-17431 & 17432 | OPERATOR: | PRELIM.TIME EST.: | |

| DEFENDANT | CII NO. | DOB | BOOKING NO. | BAIL RECOM'D | CUSTODY R'TN DATE |
| SIMPSON, ORENTHAL JAMES | M92188176 | 7/09/47 | | NO BAIL | |

It appearing to the Court that probable cause exists for the issuance of a
warrant of arrest for the above named defendant(s), the warrant is so ordered.

Judge of the above entitled Court

FELONY COMPLAINT - ORDER HOLDING TO ANSWER - P.C. SECTION 872

It appearing to me from the evidence presented that the following offense(s)
has/have been committed and that there is sufficient cause to believe that the
following defendant(s) guilty thereof, to wit:

(Strike out or add as applicable)

ORENTHAL JAMES SIMPSON

Count No.	Charge	Charge Range	Special Allegation	Alleg. Effect
1	PC187(a)	Check Code	PC12022(b)	+1 YR
2	PC187(a)	Check Code	PC12022(b)	+1 YR

I order that defendant(s) be held to answer therefor and be admitted to bail in
the sum of:

ORENTHAL JAMES SIMPSON   Dollars

and be committed to the custody of the Sheriff of Los Angeles County until such
bail is given. Date of arraignment in Superior Court will be:

ORENTHAL JAMES SIMPSON   in Dept: ____

at: _____ A.M.

Date: _____   Committing Magistrate _____

FIGURE 2.15B ▶ (Continued)

or business when there is reason to believe that the suspect is present within. Thus, officers executing the warrant must have reasonable suspicion that the suspect is present at the time and within the place that the arrest warrant is served. Case Example 2D (see Figures 2.16 to 2.21) provides an extended illustrated search scene allowing the application of numerous search and seizure concepts discussed in this chapter.

BUILDING A CASE FOR TRIAL

Although most cases handled by investigators will never go to trial, the strongest case possible is essential to help prosecutors obtain a plea bargain from offenders contemplating exercising their right to a court hearing. The investigator's primary responsibility is to furnish prosecutors with sufficient evidence to show that the facts developed in a case prove **beyond a reasonable doubt** that the legal requirements of a particular crime have been met. Studies measuring the degree of mental certainty implied by the notion of reasonable doubt indicate that this standard is met in most people's minds when they are at least 90 percent certain that the case evidence proves the suspect's guilt. In most instances, when a case does go to trial, the individuals who must evaluate the adequacy of evidence relative to the fact, known as the **trier of fact**, are members of a jury. The judge's role in trial proceedings is to ensure that the law is properly applied during the trial—a role referred to as the **trier of law**. When suspects waive their right to a jury trial, a **bench hearing** is held, where the judge serves as the trier of both fact and law. Research studies indicate that the strength of evidence needed to prove case facts beyond a reasonable doubt is significantly higher for judges than it is for members of civilian juries.

Investigators can use various forms of evidence in the preparation of a case:

- **Physical or "real" evidence:** This includes tangible objects—both visible and microscopic—as well as anything that can be perceived by the senses. Examples include weapons, clothing items, fingerprints, microscopic shards of glass, laboratory test results for DNA and body fluids, and even demonstrations performed in court by experts—such as projecting blood on a surface to show the likely effects of weapon strikes on skin.

- **Documentary evidence:** Anything that exists in written, printed, reported, or recorded form can be classified as documentary evidence. Sources for this type of evidence can be mechanical (e.g., in handwriting) or electronic (e.g., graphs, printouts, etc.). Examples include forged signatures, handwritten notes, public documents, telephone records, computer usage data, and even ancient documents. A suicide note containing a fingerprint may serve as documentary evidence as well as physical or "real" evidence.

- **Testimonial Evidence:** This type of evidence includes spoken words as well as behaviors reasonably associated with the speaking of words. Common examples include testimony of eyewitnesses and crime experts during criminal trials. Also included in this category is the oral testimony obtained in a suspect interrogation, during which the suspect's nonverbal behavior while speaking (e.g., eye squinting, arm crossing, stammering) can be considered to be testimonial evidence as well.

Furthermore, each of these forms of evidence can prove the facts of a case in various ways. These include the following:

- **Direct evidence:** Evidence that directly proves a suspect's guilt; for example, surveillance camera photos showing the suspect robbing a bank.

- **Circumstantial evidence:** Evidence that provides indirect proof of a suspect's guilt; for example, a fiber from the victim's clothing found in the suspect's car.

- *Corroborative evidence:* Evidence that suggests the validity and reliability of other types of evidence. For example, a suspect claims that he was nowhere near the crime scene when a murder occurred. He provides a credit card receipt from a motel to corroborate his alibi that he was out of town during the date and time of the murder.

- *Cumulative evidence:* Various evidence of the same nature that provides additional strength to the proof of a case. For example, it is determined that a suspect's bloody footprints, tire tracks, and clothing are all found at the scene of a crime. This type of evidence may be necessary when specific types of direct evidence, such as eyewitness testimony or DNA, are unavailable.[26]

Subsequent chapters provide illustrated case study examples of actual criminal activity, discussing specific types of evidence in greater detail as they pertain to the legal requirements of proving a particular criminal act. At this point, however, the most important thing is to comprehend the rules of law and necessary procedures designed to ensure that the investigative process is carried out in a fair and just manner. This is especially

CASE EXAMPLE 2D

Search and Seizure during a Routine Traffic Stop

FIGURE 2.16 ▶ In a routine traffic stop of a vehicle containing one male driver, the officer, while asking for identification, noticed some 9mm cartridges in the center console next to the driver's seat.

FIGURE 2.17 ▶ After removing and securing the driver, the officer begins a search of the driver side compartment.

FIGURE 2.18 ▶ The officer's search extends to an unlocked glove compartment, which contains the magazine of a 9mm semiautomatic handgun.

FIGURE 2.19 ▶ The officer extends his search to the trunk.

FIGURE 2.20 ▶ The search reveals a 9mm handgun buried beneath various items contained in the trunk.

FIGURE 2.21 ▶ The final view of the weapon as seen by the officer after removing various items obscuring view of the handgun. Considering the sequence of events that has taken place here, is the officer's search legally justified under the search and seizure laws, based on the Fourth Amendment? Was the search conducted in a proper and legally acceptable manner? Can the officer legally seize that weapon and related items as evidence to be used in court against the vehicle's driver?

true with regard to the laws of search and seizure. At the very least, it should be realized that carrying out criminal investigations without proper knowledge or regard for these procedural rules will most likely result in the identification and collection of inadmissible, useless evidence. Thus, as each new concept of investigation is presented in the following chapters, always remember the legal foundation on which each investigative method and objective rests.

Summary

1. **Legal requirements for determining whether a crime has been committed.**

   First, available evidence must suggest that a crime has been committed—the *corpus delicti* of the crime. Second, sufficient evidence must be presented that satisfies the specific elements of a particular criminal activity proved within written codes or statutes. For most crimes that are the subject of investigation, a physical act (*actus reus*) as well as a criminal state of mind at the time of the act (*mens rea*) must be demonstrated by available evidence.

2. **Establishing reasonable suspicion and probable cause.**

   Reasonable suspicion occurs when officers have reason to suspect that a crime has been, or is about to be committed. It is the basic starting point of the investigative process, which allows suspects to be detained for purposes of additional investigation related to a suspected criminal activity. Probable cause is established when officers have reason to believe that a crime has been, or is about to be com-

   mitted. Probable cause is the necessary standard for conducting most searches and carrying out arrests.

3. **The Fourth Amendment requirements for searches and seizures.**

   The Fourth Amendment to the U.S. Constitution prohibits unreasonable searches and seizures. Any search or seizure without a warrant based on probable cause is assumed to be illegal and unconstitutional unless proven to be legal through demonstrating special circumstances that provide for a warrantless search. The Supreme Court has authorized warrantless searches and seizures in situations involving potential medical emergencies, threats to officers' safety, and the preservation of public safety.

4. **The exclusionary rule and the fruit of the poisonous tree doctrine.**

   The exclusionary rule states that evidence searched for and/or seized through illegal methods and means is inadmissible (or not allowable) in a court of law. This rule has been extended through the fruit of the poisonous tree doctrine to prohibit from court proceedings all evidence proven to have originated from an illegal search. According to the Supreme Court, after one item of evidence has become tainted, the entire body of evidence becomes tainted as well.

5. **Consensual encounter, detention, and arrest**

   Consensual encounter between an individual and an officer permits unrestricted casual conversation and perhaps some information gathering as long as the individual feels free to leave the officer's presence at any time. Detention occurs when individuals perceive the officer's actions or words as requiring them to remain in the officer's presence. Detention requires the establishment of reasonable suspicion. Arrest occurs when the individual is taken into cus-

tody and is placed in a situation that is the constructive equivalent of custodial confinement. Probable cause is necessary before carrying out an arrest.

6. **Building a case for successful prosecution.**

   For investigators building a case for successful prosecution, the primary goal is to gather evidence to prove beyond a reasonable doubt that a particular suspect has committed a specific crime. Investigators can rely on physical or "real" evidence, documentary evidence, and testimonial evidence to build their case. These forms of evidence can be presented in the form of direct evidence (directly proving the guilt of a suspect) or indirect evidence (indirectly proving the guilt of a suspect).

Key Terms

criminal procedural laws	no-knock warrant	bench hearing
substantive criminal laws	anticipatory warrant	search warrant return
corpus delicti	sneak and peak warrants	curtilages
elements of the crime	voluntary consent	inadmissible evidence
statutes	consent to search form	the exclusionary rule
actus reus	deceptive consent	fruit of the poisonous tree
mens rea	exigent circumstances	good faith exception
strict liability offenses	stop and frisk	inevitable discovery
reasonable suspicion	plain feel exception	consensual encounter
probable cause	plain view	detention
totality of the circumstances	search incident to arrest	arrest
statement of probable cause	motor vehicle exception	arrest warrant
affidavit	open fields doctrine	beyond a reasonable doubt
knock warrant	trier of fact	trier of law

Review Questions

1. Define the term *corpus delicti*.
2. What is the difference between substantive criminal law and procedural criminal law?
3. What are the elements of a crime? Of what importance are they to investigations?
4. Define the terms *mens rea* and *actus reus*? Provide an example of each.
5. How do the legal standards of reasonable suspicion and probable cause differ?
6. Define *totality of the circumstances*. Provide an example of how it is applied to criminal investigations.
7. Outline the process for obtaining and executing a search warrant. Discuss your answer in terms of a hypothetical criminal activity.
8. Name five situations in which a warrantless search may be conducted. Provide an example of each situation.
9. Define *exigent circumstances*.
10. What is the difference between a knock and a no-knock warrant.
12. Explain the plain view doctrine. Provide an example of how it is used in an investigation.
13. What is a stop-and-frisk search?
14. What is the motor vehicle exception?
15. Explain the exclusionary rule and how it differs from the fruit of the poisonous tree doctrine.
16. Describe and provide examples of the three levels of contact between an officer and a potential crime suspect.
17. Define and provide examples of the various forms and types of evidence that can be used by an investigator as proof to support a criminal case against a suspect.
18. Explain the doctrine of inevitable discovery and the good faith exception. How do they relate to the exclusionary rule?

Internet Resources

American Civil Liberties Union (ACLU)   www.aclu.org
Association of Federal Defense Attorneys   afda.org
NOLO Legal Information Resources   www.nolo.com
Cornell Legal Information Institute   www.law.cornell.edu/index.html
truTV Legal Case Collection   www.trutv.com/sitemap/index.html
Yale Law School Avalon Project   avalon.law.yale.edu/default.asp
United States Supreme Court   www.supremecourt.gov

Applied Investigative Exercise

Examine the various crime scene photos in Case Example 2D, while considering the specific laws that apply to handgun possession within your state. If you were the officer in this case example, what legal considerations would be on your mind before searching this vehicle? Are there legal grounds to search the passenger compartment and trunk of this vehicle? If not, why not? If so, under what circumstances would the search be legal and the evidence seized be admissible in court?

Notes

[1]Herbert Packer, *The Limits of the Criminal Sanction* (Stanford, CA: Stanford University Press, 1968).

[2]Michael F. Brown, *Criminal Investigation: Law and Practice* (Newton, MA: Butterworth-Heinemann, 1998), 16.

[3]Henry Campbell Black, Joseph R. Nolan, and Jacqueline M. Nolan-Haley, *Black's Law Dictionary*, 343.

[4]*Terry v. Ohio*, 392 U.S.1 (1968).

[5]Ibid. Also see *U.S. v. Cortez* 449 U.S. 411 (1981).

[6]*Illinois v. Gates*, 130 S.Ct. 2317 (1983).

[7]*U.S. v. Grubbs*, 547 U.S. 90 (2006).

[8]Charles R. Swanson, Neil Chamelin, Leonard Territo, and Robert Taylor, *Criminal Investigation*. 10th ed. (New York, NY: McGraw-Hill, 2009).

[9]*Mincey v. Arizona*, 437 U.S. 385, 392 (1978).

[10]*People v. Lloyd*, 17 Cal. 4th 658 (1998).

[11]*Warden v. Hayden*, 387 U.S. 294 (1967).

[12]*Minnesota v. Dickerson*, 113 S.Ct. 2130, 124 L.Ed. 2d 334 (1993).

[13]Ibid.

[14]*Harris v. U.S.*, 390 U.S. 234 (1968).

[15]*Chimel v. California*, 395 U.S. 752 (1969).

[16]Ibid.

[17]*Oliver v. U.S.*, 466 U.S., 170 (1984).

[18]Ibid.

[19]*Samson v. California*, 547 U.S. 843 (2006).

[20]*New Jersey v. T.L.O.*, 469 U.S. 325 (1985).

[21]U.S. Patriot Act (U.S. H.R. 3162, *Public Law* 107-56) Title X, Sec. 1011(a).

[22]*Weeks v. U.S.*, 232 U.S. 383 (1914).

[23]*Silverthorne Lumber Co. v. U.S.*, 251 U.S. 385 (1920).

[24]*Nix v. Williams*, 104 S.Ct. 2501 (1984).

[25]*U.S. v. Leon*, 468 U.S. 897 (1984).

[26]Brown, *Criminal Investigation: Law and Practice*, 39–40.

CHAPTER THREE

THE PROCESS OF INVESTIGATING CRIME

Learning Objectives

After completing this chapter, you should be able to:

1. Describe the preliminary investigation.
2. Describe the investigative process and the stages of criminal investigation.
3. Explain the first responder's duties during the preliminary investigation.
4. Identify the investigator's role during the preliminary investigation.
5. Explain the proper methods of crime scene photography and videography.
6. Explain the proper methods of crime scene sketching.
7. Describe the proper ways of conducting a crime scene search.

Chapter Outline

Criminal Investigators: The Specialists of Criminal Investigation
- Investigators, Detectives, Inspectors, and Special Agents
- Essential Traits of Investigators
- The Investigative Team
- The Goals and Objectives of Criminal Investigation

Hot, Warm, and Cold Cases

The Stages of Investigation
- Stage 1: Crime Detection
- Stage 2: The Preliminary Investigation
- Stage 3: The Follow-up Investigation
- Stage 4: Case Preparation and Prosecution

The Preliminary Investigation: The First Responder's Role

The Investigator's Arrival at the Crime Scene

Examining the Crime Scene

Processing the Crime Scene

Photographing the Crime Scene
- Initial Photographs: Capture the Crime Scene and Mark Evidence
- Photographic Equipment and Methods
- Telling the Crime Story with Photos
- Specialized Crime Scene Photographic Techniques
- Forensic Videography

Crime Scene Sketching

Taking Crime Scene Measurements
- Rectangular Coordinates
- Triangulation
- Baseline Coordinates
- Polar Coordinates
- The Total Station and Advanced Crime Scene Imagining

Searching the Crime Scene
- Objectives of the Search
- Search Strategies
- Crime Scene Search Methods

Completing the Preliminary Investigation

INTRODUCTION

AT FIRST, THE TITLE OF this chapter may be somewhat confusing because, as you will soon discover, there is no single "best process" of investigating crime. Rather, there are a multitude of investigative practices that criminal investigators can successfully employ. Identifying the best practice for investigating a specific criminal event will depend on many factors relating to both the investigator and the particular crime that has occurred. For example, the extent of an investigator's experience, education, and training as well as access to necessary resources are key in determining the approach taken to investigate a particular case. Likewise, crimes characterized by an abundance of physical evidence and eyewitness accounts will be investigated much differently from crimes committed with no witnesses and of which the victim cannot be found. After completing this chapter, however, you will understand and be aware of the many tools and methods currently available to perform a criminal investigation. Bearing in mind that no two offenses or offenders are exactly alike, it will be up to you to select and apply the best investigative practices given the unique circumstances of the case to be solved.

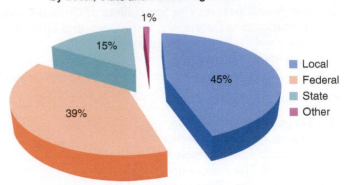

Investigators Employed in the United States by Local, State and Federal Agencies

- Local 45%
- Federal 39%
- State 15%
- Other 1%

FIGURE 3.1 ▶ The majority of investigators in the United States are employed by municipal and federal agencies, totaling approximately 84 percent of the investigative work force. *Source:* Bureau of Labor Statistics, Employment Data for Detectives Investigators, 2009, www.bls.gov/oes/current/oes333021.htm#nat

CRIMINAL INVESTIGATORS: THE SPECIALISTS OF CRIMINAL INVESTIGATION

Investigators, Detectives, Inspectors, and Special Agents

Criminal investigators are the specialists of the investigative process. That is, they focus on the specific aspects of evidence needed to establish whether or not a crime has been committed; and, if so, they discover the necessary evidence to prove that a particular suspect committed or did not commit the crime. In addition to identifying crimes and criminal suspects, investigators must gather sufficient evidence to build cases that can be successfully prosecuted in a court of law.[1]

The specific duties of investigators depend largely on the agency that employs them. The majority of the nation's criminal investigators work for municipal policing agencies serving cities and counties. They are typically referred to by titles such as "Investigator," "Detective," or "Inspector" and conduct probes into a wide variety of offenses. Smaller agencies may have only one or two officers who investigate offenses ranging from murder to vehicle thefts, while larger agencies have divisions or branches composed of numerous investigators who specialize in particular offenses including murder, sex crimes, identity theft, domestic violence, vice, narcotics, and gang crimes. Most investigators serving within municipal agencies have served as patrol officers or deputies before being assigned to an investigative position.[2]

Investigators at the state and federal level, often given the title of "Special Agent," usually handle cases dealing with violations of specific laws or codes regulating drug manufacturing/sales, gambling, taxation, insurance, fire arms production/sales, business practices, domestic security, wildlife management, and other specialized areas of law enforcement. Special Agents may assist in solving cases opened by city police and county sheriff's investigative units operating as a multijurisdictional taskforce. Such operations are often directed at cases involving large amounts of contraband, narcotics, illegally obtained money, or stolen property acquired by organized criminal operations. Upon solving such cases, local, state, and federal investigative multijurisdictional task forces frequently must decide how to split money and property seized from offenders that is returned to their respective jurisdictions under **asset forfeiture laws**.[3] Although many state and federal investigators have prior experience within a municipal policing agency, some have no law enforcement experience. Rather, they are hired as first-time investigators and become sworn peace officers through a combination of academy and on-the-job training. Figure 3.1 shows the estimated number of criminal investigators currently employed at the local, state, and federal level by public agencies in the United States.

The investigator's job often is challenging. The investigator must learn to multitask because there is seldom enough time to handle the many cases that must be worked simultaneously. In addition, extensive travel between various jurisdictions may be required when investigations focus upon highly mobile offenders. Danger is a part of the investigator's job as well. As nonuniformed, sworn peace officers, investigators carry firearms, make arrests, conduct surveillance activities, and sometimes work undercover assignments gathering proof of criminal activity conducted by extremely dangerous individuals connected to street gangs, drug cartels, organized crime groups, and terrorists. Perhaps most demanding of all are the time-related aspects of the investigator's job. Being on-call 24 hours a day, 7 days a week is the norm. Likewise, cases may last weeks, months, or even years in rare instances. Most discouraging, after an extensive amount of time has been spent investigating a particular crime or offender, a seemingly hot case can go cold, resulting in a suspect going free or a case never being solved. Most investigators feel, however, that the job's benefits far exceed its drawbacks.

Essential Traits of Investigators

Regardless of the agency they work for, all investigators share several essential traits. They must be able to understand and apply the following concepts:

- *Science:* Investigators do not have to be scientists in a professional sense, but they must be familiar with scientific principles, especially as they apply to the collection of evidence. For example, most investigators now are required to know the proper techniques for handling, collecting, and preserving DNA-bearing biological matter. Also, investigators will be called upon to review results obtained from autopsies and other medical examiner's reports.

- *Psychology:* Knowing how to deal with people under a variety of stressful circumstances is essential for investigators. Asking the proper questions at the right time to gain the cooperation of witnesses, victims, or suspects is an absolutely critical investigative skill. Pressing the right psychological buttons to get a guilty suspect to confess will save countless hours of investigative time and effort.

- *Communication:* Investigators must know how to communicate clearly to persons of all cultures and backgrounds. Perhaps the most important communicative skill utilized during an investigation is knowing when to talk and when to listen. Quite often, investigators miss important information by interrupting victims, witnesses, and suspects before they have had a chance to finish their thoughts. They must also perfect the skill of providing clear testimony and statements in legal proceedings.

- *Law:* It is often said that criminal investigators have a better understanding of applied criminal law than do lawyers. Whether or not this is true, it does suggest the high level of legal acumen that an investigator must attain to achieve a successful case outcome. Most important in this regard is having a solid understanding of the **legal elements** of specific crimes and the evidence that is required to prove them in a successful prosecution of a suspected offender. The investigator also must know how and when to secure a search or arrest warrant, and the proper procedures for legally executing such warrants to either prove that a crime has been committed or effect the arrest of a suspect. Investigators also assist prosecutors in case preparation, and are often called upon by the prosecution to provide testimony regarding their investigations at depositions and trials.

- *Ethics:* Investigators must always be aware that the consequences of their actions have life-changing consequences for the persons involved in the cases they investigate. For this reason, a case must be investigated with the highest level of ethical standards. This means that all evidence and matters relating to the case must be documented or stated in a truthful and accurate manner. Putting a spin on any investigative information to increase the odds of a favorable case outcome is unethical, and under many circumstances can be illegal. The aim of an ethical investigation is to spend just as much time and effort to confirm a suspect's guilt as to exonerate a suspect from guilt.

- *Economics:* Unlike television detectives, real-life investigators do not have unlimited financial resources at their disposal to pursue and solve every case that comes along. It is nearly always a rule that the decision regarding which cases to investigate and how to investigate them boils down to a cost-benefit analysis. Simply put, cases with the highest probability of being solved will be placed ahead of those with a lesser probability when the time comes to make investigative assignments. In addition, DNA analysis, fingerprint processing, and other expensive, labor-intensive laboratory procedures will have to be used judiciously and sparingly in cases involving large amounts of physical evidence.

The Investigative Team

Investigators can work alone or with partners when building and solving cases. Even when there is only one investigator assigned to a case, however, the investigative process still involves teamwork and the assistance of support staff and other related personnel. Think of this as the **investigative team**, which consists of the following:

1. *The Crime Scene Technician:* Civilian staff who are trained in evidence search and collection methods and assist in documenting and gathering physical evidence from the crime scene.

2. *The Crime Scene Photographer:* Photographers employed by law enforcement agencies at a variety of investigative crime scenes to take still photos or videos that document the position and location of physical evidence as well as the general setting in which the crime took place.

3. *The Dispatcher:* Communications personnel who receive incoming initial reports of criminal activity to be investigated. They can assist in the identification of victims, witnesses, suspects, and types of evidence located at the crime scene.

4. *The Patrol Officer:* Sworn police officers, often the first to respond to the crime scene, who are charged with securing the crime scene, gathering preliminary information about the alleged crime(s), providing notice of the crime to investigators, and briefing investigators about preliminary case-related matters that occurred at the crime scene.

5. *The Criminalist:* Criminalists are scientists trained in biology, chemistry, and other physical and natural sciences who work in crime labs analyzing physical crime scene evidence submitted to them by

FIGURE 3.2 ▶ Criminal investigation is a team effort involving many personnel and the use of specialized equipment. The investigators pictured here use a mobile crime lab and consult with a patrol officer at the crime scene.

investigators or crime scene technicians. They are usually employed in conjunction with municipal law enforcement agencies operating at the local, state, or federal level, but may also be employed by independent, privately operated crime labs.

6. ***The Forensic Scientist:*** The terms *forensic scientist* and *criminalist* are often used interchangeably, and in reality both can correctly refer to scientists who work full-time in crime labs analyzing physical crime scene evidence. Many forensic scientists, however, are experts specializing in a specific science and serve only as outside consultants on particular criminal matters; for example, a metallurgist (an engineer specializing in the study of metals) may be employed to inspect the destruction of steel beams within a building allegedly destroyed by a bomb. As you will soon discover, many branches of study fall within the investigative meaning of the term *forensic science.*

7. ***The Confidential Informant:*** Investigators form trustworthy relationships with confidential informants— persons who have inside knowledge of offenders and their criminal activities. Such information, obtained to secure search or arrest warrants, usually is provided in exchange for monetary compensation or, when a criminal informant is involved, reducing or dropping charges related to crimes he or she may have committed.

8. ***Other Team Members:*** Others playing a potential role on the investigative team include emergency response personnel (EMTs, firefighters), bomb disposal

technicians, hazardous waste removal experts (HAZMAT), canine units, air support, marine and diving units, crime scene clean-up crews, emergency room physicians, victim advocates, polygraph technicians, and community volunteers.

Figure 3.2 shows a mobile vehicular command post commonly as the central location for coordinating the activities of all investigative team members located at a crime scene.

The Goals and Objectives of Criminal Investigation

Most criminal investigators, when they first open a case on an alleged crime, have general intentions, or goals, which can be summed up in the simple acronym **C.I.A.** The specific investigative objectives for achieving each of these goals are as follows:

"C" for Crime: **Establish whether or not a crime has been committed.**

Objectives:
- *Discover the alleged victims of the crime.*
- *Determine whether the available evidence suggests criminal activity.*
- *Assess whether the evidence supports legal elements of a crime.*
- *Determine whether the evidence corroborates victim and witness accounts.*

"I" for Identification:	**Identify suspects involved in the crime.**

Objectives:

- *Arrest suspects at the crime scene.*
- *Develop suspect leads through available evidence.*
- *Use informants or other proactive measures to identify suspects.*

"A" for Association:	**Associate suspects, victims, and the crime scene.**

Objectives:

- *Use evidence to link suspects and the crime scene.*
- *Use evidence to link suspects to the victims at the crime scene.*
- *Use evidence to link the victims and the crime scene.*
- *Use evidence to link suspects and the means of victimization. (e.g., weapons).*

HOT, WARM, AND COLD CASES

When investigating crime, time is of the essence. As a general rule, the sooner a crime is discovered and investigated while evidence is fresh, the more likely it will be solved. If this rule is assumed to be true, all cases fall into one of the following three categories depending on how soon they are reported and investigated:

1. ***Hot Cases:*** These are cases in which offenders or victims are still at or very near the crime scene when the investigative process begins. Such cases usually are solved by arresting the suspect at or around the crime scene vicinity. The investigator's involvement is minimal in these cases and may entail only helping patrol officers prepare the supporting documentation and evidence necessary for the suspect's arrest and prosecution. Crimes that involve violent victimization (e.g., aggravated assaults, bank robberies, gang fights, and murders), are highly visible, and occur in a public setting commonly fall within the hot case category.

2. ***Warm Cases:*** In warm cases offenders have fled the crime scene and victims may or may not be present, but the scene still contains fresh or **smoking gun evidence** that can be used later to establish a suspect's or victim's identity and perhaps whereabouts. This type of evidence may include eyewitness accounts, and physical evidence. Depending on the strength and quality of the evidence discovered during the preliminary and (perhaps) follow-up investigations, a warm case most likely will be solved if it involves a crime of violence, but is less likely to be solved in

property crimes. Warm cases often occur because of the time lag that usually occurs between the commission of an offense is committed and its subsequent reporting or detection. Shock, embarrassment, fear, and a "don't tell" or "don't want to deal with the criminal justice system" attitude on the part of crime victims and witnesses all contribute to the cooling of a hot case down to a warm one.

3. ***Cold Cases:*** In these cases a crime has either (1) been reported or detected sometime after it has occurred (usually a year or more) or (2) been investigated for at least a year with no suspect leads. Such cases typically end up in a cold case file and will not be followed up on unless new suspect leads somehow materialize. Cases involving unsolved murders, sex crimes, and kidnappings often go cold. These cases usually go unsolved due to time's degrading of the physical evidence, missing witnesses, and general fading of memory among all parties involved. Only the most seasoned investigators work cold cases. Figures 3.3 and 3.4 show the estimated number of violent and property crimes that are cleared or solved compared to the estimated number of these crimes that law enforcement officials know have occurred.

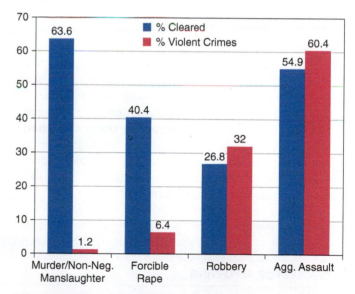

FIGURE 3.3 ▶ The odds of clearing or solving a violent crime case. Despite the fact that murders are the least common form of violent crime (1.2%), they are the most likely crime to be cleared through investigation (63.6%), followed by forcible rape (40.4%), aggravated assault (59.9%), and robbery (26.8%). Cleared crimes are ones that have been solved either by arrest or other means (referred to as *exceptionally cleared*—e.g., the suspect died, was arrested for another crime, or could not be located). *Source:* Federal Bureau of Investigation, Uniform Crime Reports, 2008, www.fbi.gov/ucr/cius2008/offenses/clearances/index.html#figure; www.fbi.gov/ucr/cius2008/data/table_01.html

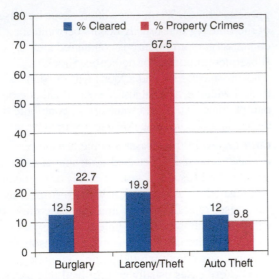

FIGURE 3.4 ▶ The odds of clearing or solving a property crime case. Property crimes, in general, are the least likely type to be cleared or solved. As the statistics here show, larceny/thefts comprise the majority of property offenses known to authorities—yet only about 20 percent are cleared or solved.

THE STAGES OF INVESTIGATION

Stage 1: Crime Detection

The criminal investigative process begins when a crime—being committed, already committed, or about to be committed—comes to the attention of police or other law enforcement authorities. Most offenses are reported by citizen complaints, a process known as **reactive crime detection**. Far fewer criminal activities are discovered by **proactive crime detection**, whereby law enforcement officials are the first to discover an offense or offender—for example, sting or undercover operations targeting covert illegal activities such as drug sales, human trafficking, or political espionage.

Stage 2: The Preliminary Investigation

Regardless of how a crime is discovered—through reactive or proactive means—the moment of its discovery marks the beginning of the investigative process. At this time, the **preliminary investigation** begins with duties and observations of the first responder to the crime scene, and may continue with the work of additional investigators and uniformed officers dispatched to the scene. In essence, preliminary investigations involve the initial collection of all information and evidence that is readily available following the discovery of a suspected criminal offense. The first concern in an investigation is to ascertain, through examining the circumstances surrounding an alleged offense, whether sufficient reason exists to believe that a crime has been committed. For example, discovery of a dead body or missing property without any other evidence to suggest foul play may not be sufficient to begin a homicide or theft investigation, respectively. It will be up to the investigator to establish the necessary proof of criminal conduct showing that the dead body resulted from a murder or that an allegedly stolen item was intentionally taken from its owner.

The primary objectives in conducting a preliminary investigation include identifying offenders; determining crimes that have occurred; locating available witnesses; and identifying, collecting, and packaging evidence—a process commonly known as **CSI** or **crime scene investigation**. If enough evidence is gathered at this phase to confirm that a particular suspect has committed a specific crime, the preliminary investigation may also mark the end of the investigative process. However, if more information and evidence are needed to prove that a crime has been committed or to strengthen a case against a suspected offender, investigators may have to proceed to the second phase of criminal investigation—the **follow-up investigation**.

Stage 3: The Follow-up Investigation

At this more advanced stage, investigators attempt to follow up, or act on clues and leads uncovered during the preliminary investigation. Potential suspects can be identified using state- and

TABLE 3.1	REASONS FOR REPORTING AND NOT REPORTING A VIOLENT CRIME TO POLICE		
REASON FOR REPORTING	**%**	**REASON FOR NOT REPORTING**	**%**
Prevent Future Violence	19%	Private/Personal Matter	20%
Stop the Offender	17%	Not Important Enough	17%
Protect Others	9%	Reported to Other Official	14%
Punish the Offender	8%	Fear of Reprisal	5%
Catch the Offender	5%	Protect the Offender	3%

Source: Bureau of Justice Statistics, *Reporting Crime to the Police 1992–2000* (Washington, DC: USGPO, March 2003).

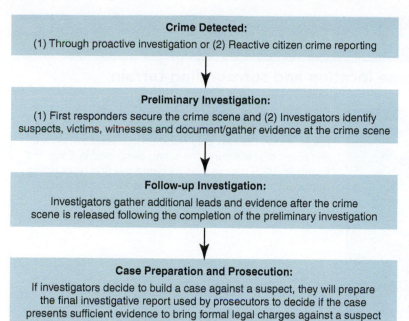

Crime Detected:
(1) Through proactive investigation or (2) Reactive citizen crime reporting

Preliminary Investigation:
(1) First responders secure the crime scene and (2) Investigators identify suspects, victims, witnesses and document/gather evidence at the crime scene

Follow-up Investigation:
Investigators gather additional leads and evidence after the crime scene is released following the completion of the preliminary investigation

Case Preparation and Prosecution:
If investigators decide to build a case against a suspect, they will prepare the final investigative report used by prosecutors to decide if the case presents sufficient evidence to bring formal legal charges against a suspect

FIGURE 3.5 ▶ Various stages of the investigative process.

nationwide offender fingerprint and firearms databases. New witnesses can be found by distributing fliers in the crime scene area containing victims' photographs or a composite picture of the suspected offender. Generally, the follow-up investigation continues until the case is either solved by an arrest or declared unsolved because all leads have gone cold.

Stage 4: Case Preparation and Prosecution

All available evidence—eyewitness testimony, physical evidence from the crime scene, results of any follow-up investigative efforts, and any other legally admissible information—will be assembled into a **report of investigation (ROI)**, which is submitted to prosecutors, who will decide whether the strength of the case merits an attempt to officially charge the suspect with the investigated crime. If the case should go to trial, the investigator may be called to testify on a range of matters concerning evidence recovered during the investigative process. Figure 3.5 summarizes the criminal investigation process.

THE PRELIMINARY INVESTIGATION: THE FIRST RESPONDER'S ROLE

As previously mentioned, the preliminary investigation is where the formal investigation of a crime begins. More often than not, it does not occur as the result of investigative efforts of plain clothes detectives or some other specialized investigative unit. Rather, the first response to a crime usually is prompted by a citizen's call for service, and the first individual to arrive at the

crime scene (otherwise referred to as the **first responder**) is a uniformed patrol officer. The particular duties of the first responder depends on many factors. For example, if the reported offense is not serious enough to warrant calling in investigators, the first responder will likely handle all necessary investigative work at the crime scene. Even hot or crime-in-progress calls resulting in the perpetrator's immediate arrest, and where no victims have been injured or property damaged, may require little if any formal investigation at the crime scene. However, if criminal activity of a significant nature has occurred at the crime scene where offenders have fled or are not readily identifiable, the first responder usually will perform a full range of duties in support of a comprehensive criminal investigation. In these cases, the actions and reactions of all first responders are critically important to the success of the preliminary investigation.

Before we look at specific duties often performed during the first response to offenses eventually leading to a full-scale investigation, note that no two first responses to any crime scene are ever alike. Therefore, the particular tactics that the first responder employs must be adapted to the constantly changing dynamics and variables of the specific situation or crime. The following list is a recommended sequence of events and related duties for first responders created, in part, by a working group of investigative experts from across the nation assembled by the U.S. Department of Justice.[4] This suggested approach may be adapted to fit a variety of first responses and to varying conditions encountered at crime scenes by first responders:

1. **Note/Log Preliminary Crime Call Information.** As a general rule, first responders can never produce enough documentation regarding their activities before, during, and after arriving at the crime scene. Noting/logging information should begin as soon as the first responder is aware of a suspected criminal activity or as soon as possible thereafter. Key information about the potential crime should be recorded as it is discovered—noting date, time, and type of call; parties and weapons involved; and ongoing/escalating violence. The same should be done for the crime scene by noting address, location specifics (e.g., storefront, second floor rear, garage, mile marker, and ongoing and/or dangerous situations). Any information or insights regarding the reported crime should be transmitted immediately to help develop a coordinated approach to the crime scene area. The first in a series of illustrated case photos for Case Example 3A.1 (see Figure 3.6) shows an aerial photo providing a bird's-eye view of the terrain in which a suspected crime scene is located. Such pictorial information, if available during the preliminary call stage of an investigation, greatly enhances the safety and efficiency of first responders dispatched to scenes encompassing large urban or rural landscapes.

CASE EXAMPLE 3A.1

Aerial view of crime scene location and surrounding terrain

FIGURE 3.6 ▶ Aerial photography is often used to portray the entire landscape of a crime scene. This photo shows the vast configuration of desert terrain and dirt roads that surround the scene described in Case Example 3A. Suppose that you were the first responding patrol unit to this call, and you had prior knowledge of this location. What would you do immediately after being deployed to this location?

2. **Watch for Vehicles and Persons within or Leaving the Crime Scene Area.**

   Pertinent information useful for the identification of persons (namely, victims, witnesses, suspects, persons of interest) should be observed and recorded, including height, weight, race, age, clothing, sex, and distinguishing features. The same should be done for vehicles that may be linked to suspects, witnesses, or victims of the suspected crime in and around the crime scene, noting their make, model, color, condition, license plate number, and age. This information should be broadcast in the form of a alert such as a BOLO (be on the lookout) or ATL (attempt to locate) so that other responding units can identify and detain suspects as well as stop suspicious vehicles. The primary responder to a crime scene should not be distracted and should remain on course—unless fired upon, having direct contact with a fleeing suspect, or encountering any situation requiring immediate action. The first responder should watch out for rare, but possible setups carried out by sophisticated offenders—false emergency situations staged to distract or even ambush officers responding to the crime scene.[5] Case Example 3A.2 depicts the vantage point of a first responder approaching the suspected crime scene in the illustrated case at hand. The patrol car view in Figure 3.7 shows the range of

CASE EXAMPLE 3A.2

View from inside first responding unit en route to crime scene

FIGURE 3.7 ▶ First responding units to crime scenes encounter many dangers—anticipated and unanticipated. Given the remote location of this particular scene, what precautions would you take while approaching this scene?

possible natural and unnatural hazards that may be confronted when first arriving at a geographically complex (in this case, rural) location.

3. **Scan, Assess, and Reassess for Officer Safety Issues.** Notification of arrival at the scene should be provided communications or other coordinating units, noting the time of arrival. Officer safety should always be given top priority during the first response to the crime scene, followed by that of the victim and others at the scene. A crime scene always poses potential safety issues to first responding officers, until available evidence at the scene proves otherwise. Don't rush into the scene. Before entering the area where the suspected crime has occurred, the scene should be assessed for ongoing dangerous individuals and situations. If persons need medical attention and/or offenders can be identified at the scene, an emergency situation can be assumed to exist, exempting the need for a search warrant before entry. However, if it cannot be reasonably assumed that emergency circumstances exist at the scene, a warrant must be obtained before entering the crime scene. When extreme dangers such as bombs, downed power lines, animals, or biohazards are observed, the scene should not be entered until specialized personnel have dealt with these situations. Once the decision to enter is made, entry should be approached tactically in a way that follows a "safety first and evidence preservation second" plan of action. All the senses (sight, smell, hearing, touch, taste) should be used when scanning and assessing the scene. Any entry and exit paths taken by victims or offenders should be identified, noting their locations and establishing an ingress/egress pathway to the crime scene and victim location

(if a body is present) that is away from these areas or other potential evidence. First responders should watch out for firearms lying around at the scene, which may spontaneously discharge when the ground or surface they are resting on is slightly jarred. Upon entering the scene, if there is even the slightest doubt that the situation cannot be immediately handled by one officer, the scene should be immediately vacated and a call issued for backup units or other necessary personnel. These first impressions and conditions of the crime scene should be noted, as well as any actions taken, upon first arrival.[6] Case Example 3A.3 (see Figure 3.8) provides an illustration of various observational factors that may be noted by first responders to the crime scene. These initial observations often translate into vital information for investigators and other personnel who must know about specific conditions of the crime scene before their arrival.

4. **Assess and Address Emergency Medical Care Issues.** This is perhaps one of the first responder's most difficult duties given that preserving human life takes priority over preserving crime scene evidence. These goals are not mutually exclusive, however, and can be achieved successfully by appropriate actions taken by the first responding officer. When officers are the first to arrive at a scene containing injured persons, the need for emergency medical care should be assessed while also ensuring that such individuals do not endanger the officers or others in the immediate vicinity. Persons who appear to be injured victims in fact may be offenders who are armed and dangerous. Injured persons should be approached using the path established upon entry or picking a new path of entry

---

CASE EXAMPLE 3A.3

First responder's initial view of the crime scene

FIGURE 3.8 ▶ The safety of the officer and those around the crime scene is given top priority by first responders. After safety concerns have been addressed, preservation of evidence and other secondary concerns arise. Suppose that the illustration here is your first view of the crime scene. What would you do? What would be your priorities in approaching this scene?

into the scene least likely to disturb potential crime scene evidence. Attempts should be made to follow this path when moving within, or to and from, the crime scene. If the officer administers first aid, actions and movements potentially destructive to physical evidence should be restricted. Conversely, when emergency medical technicians (EMTs) are the first to arrive, responding officers should note all EMT movements that have altered the original condition of the crime scene or crime scene evidence.[7]

When possible, officers should counsel and assist EMTs treating injured parties regarding potential evidence and how best to preserve it, given the emergency situation. They also should instruct EMTs not to clean up clothing or other items related to the suspected criminal activity. Document any statements made by the victim. If possible, an officer should accompany injured people being transported for emergency care to obtain any potential personal statements about the crime. In addition, a dying declaration may be needed from persons presumed to be near death during transport for treatment of injuries. The date, time, names, and contact information of all EMTs entering the scene should be documented. Their specific activities, comments, statements, and locations within the crime scene also should be noted.[8] The necessity of a first responder to make timely and informed decisions in a crime scene involving a victim who has suffered a serious injury is illustrated in Case Example 3A.4 (see Figure 3.9).

5. **Control, Identify, Secure, and Initially Interview Persons at the Crime Scene.**
Once initial safety and emergency issues have been addressed, the first responding officer may then take steps to control the crime scene. First, persons within the crime scene must be controlled so that their movements do not alter/destroy evidence or pose a safety threat. Some crime scenes can be emotionally charged, volatile situations that, if not controlled quickly, may erupt into a mob scene resulting in theft, property destruction, or even violence—some of it directed specifically at the first responding officer. If practical, given the circumstances, candid photos of crime scene on-lookers should be obtained (without being obvious).

Second, key individuals at the scene should be identified—suspects, witnesses, bystanders, victims, or family members of victims. Their names, addresses, date of birth, telephone numbers, and other personal identification information should be obtained. Suspects, victims, and witnesses must be secured and separated from bystanders or other unauthorized persons (who must be removed from the crime scene). If possible, suspects, victims, and witnesses should be briefly interviewed. The victim should be interviewed separately to obtain a description of the suspect; or, if the suspect is detained at the scene, a positive ID can be made on the suspect. Witnesses are to be physically separated and interviewed individually so that they cannot compare stories; they can provide suspect descriptions and, if possible, an ID of the suspect in

CASE EXAMPLE 3A.4

First responder's approach to assess victim's medical condition

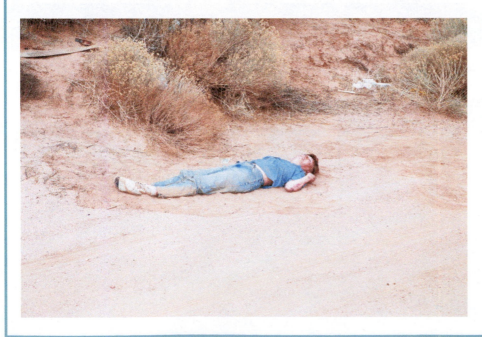

FIGURE 3.9 ▶ The medical needs of injured persons at the crime scene are of paramount importance to the first responder. How would you address this victim's medical needs?

custody. Also victims and witnesses should be asked about possible evidence at the crime scene and its location. This information can help establish separate crime scene locations and their approximate boundaries. Suspects can be arrested when identified by credible victims and/or witnesses as the perpetrator, or when there are other sources of probable cause for arrest. Miranda warnings should be provided to suspects following arrest. Any new information obtained about the crime should be broadcast as a bulletin if necessary—including suspect descriptions and possible whereabouts. If warranted, and available, supervisors should implement prearranged mobilization plans that perhaps use a mobile command post to coordinate uniformed officers' long-term presence and search activities in the crime scene area. Finally, document all statements made by suspects, victims, and witnesses and note any observations about their behavior at the crime scene.[9]

CASE CLOSE-UP 3.1

CRIME SCENE CHAOS AT WAL-MART

(Long Island, New York)

At approximately 5:00 A.M. on the morning of Black Friday (the day after Thanksgiving, traditionally the nation's busiest shopping day), over 2,000 shoppers rushed the entrance of a Wal-Mart store in anticipation of purchasing a limited number of low-priced plasma HDTVs, vacuum cleaners, and men's jeans. Upon crashing through the doorway, the out-of-control crowd trampled a store employee to death. First responding officers to the scene, attempting to attend to the deceased employee's body and control the crowd, were pushed, stepped on, and rendered helpless by the chaotic mob rushing around the employee's dead body. Eventually, a crime scene was established and the store was closed, only to reopen at 1:00 P.M.

---

6. **Establish Crime Scene Boundaries.**

Crime scene boundaries are to be established and secured by placing tape, cones, or other barrier-creating devices around the largest area that potentially contains most (if not all) of the physical evidence related to the criminal activities in question. When the central location of the crime can be identified, boundaries are best established by moving outward from this point to other points in all directions until locations are reached where no evidence is believed to exist. Although no hard-and-fast rule defines how large the boundaries of a crime scene must be, it is always best to err on the side of creating boundaries that are too large rather than too small. Areas believed to be suspects' entrances and exits to the crime scene and other locations believed to contain crime-related evidence that are adjacent to or separated from the main crime scene should be secured as well. When marking boundaries, existing structures (walls, doors, trees, etc.) that are not movable should be used, if possible, so as not to disrupt the original placement of objects within the crime scene. If necessary, vehicle and pedestrian traffic should be rerouted from areas rendered inaccessible by the scene, including roads, stairwells, and elevators.[10] Once the boundaries are established, all nonessential personnel are to be restricted from entering the crime scene—this includes curious police officers as well. A crime scene entry log should be started to document the names and contact information of all persons entering the crime scene as well as the times they entered and exited. Persons entering should be informed that they may be called as possible witnesses in the case. Illustrated Case Example 3A.5 shows the containment and control of our model crime scene. Figures 3.10 and 3.11 illustrate the creation of crime scene boundaries through the use of tape lines.

7. **Identify and Preserve Crime Scene Evidence.**

Before identifying or collecting any evidence at the crime scene, all legal conditions for a search must be met. If no dangerous conditions exist at the scene and the property belongs to someone other than the victim, the area is to be secured and legal assistance sought to determine whether a search warrant is needed. Personal observations and information obtained from victims and witnesses should be used to make a preliminary identification of key evidence and its location within the crime scene. This search should focus on **transient evidence** (e.g., evidence that is easily perishable or destroyed) and take measures to preserve it. Procedures of this sort are usually required at crime scenes in outdoor areas (e.g., blocking wind to prevent it from destroying impression evidence such as footprints or tire tracks in dirt, or shutting off sprinklers that could water down blood evidence contained on walkways). If necessary, items containing transient evidence should be moved from wet to dry areas. Gloves are to be worn at all times when handling evidence containing bodily fluids or other potentially hazardous substances. All evidence preservation efforts should be well documented because they will, in effect, alter the crime scene. The crime scene can be expanded, if necessary, to include locations of

CASE EXAMPLE 3A.5

First responder establishes tape line boundaries at the scene

FIGURE 3.10 ▶ Establishing control and identifying crime scene boundaries are important tasks for the first responder, once other priorities have addressed. What boundaries would you establish in this location? Where and how would you establish them?

FIGURE 3.11 ▶ Crimes often involve primary as well as secondary crime scenes. How many possible scenes does this particular offense involve?

new evidence discovered in the outer boundaries of the crime scene. Detailed notes should be taken regarding the location of key evidence and the general conditions of the crime scene including lighting, open or closed windows and doors, weather conditions, footprints, positioning of items, tire prints, footprints, smells, and anything else that may help investigators.[11] Continuing the investigation of our model case, Case Example 3A.6 illustrates the identification of potentially transient evidence at the outdoor crime scene (see Figure 3.12).

CASE EXAMPLE 3A.6

First responder identifies transient evidence: hair and blood

FIGURE 3.12 ▶ Identifying transient evidence immediately is an important task of the first responder. Consider the evidence shown here. Which is most important to preserve first? Given the wind, dust, rain, and other unpredictable weather elements of this outdoor crime scene, what emergency steps could you take to preserve this evidence?

CASE EXAMPLE 3A.7

First responder briefs arriving investigators at the crime scene

FIGURE 3.13 ▶ Notes, sketches, and other information are important for first responders briefing investigators at the crime scene. What would you tell investigators to brief them about this crime scene?

8. **Notify and Brief Investigator(s).**
Sometimes, the first responding officer will continue the preliminary investigation so as to act as primary investigator of the crime scene. Most often, and especially in response to serious crimes such as robbery, sexual assault cases, and homicide, plain clothes detectives or specialized crime scene investigators are dispatched to the scene to perform more detailed activities such as evidence collection and witness interviews. In these situations, the first-responding officer's duty is to brief the investigative staff on important activities and events that transpired before their arrival. These include (1) physical evidence locations in the crime scene, and any collection priorities needed to prevent evidence destruction or spoilage; (2) the boundaries of the crime scene and the selected entry and exit pathway(s); (3) parties identified as suspects, witnesses, or victims; (4) results of the officer's "look, listen, smell" observations; and (5) alterations to the crime scene made by the officer, EMTs, or others entering or leaving the scene, and other possible sources of civilian contamination. Investigators should be provided any rough sketches, documents, logs, notes, or other materials needed to continue the preliminary investigation.[12] As illustrated in Case Example 3A.7 (see Figure 3.13), it is the duty of the first responder(s) to provide arriving investigators with an initial orientation to the crime scene. This orientation must also include a briefing about any special circumstances at the crime scene such as key evidence locations or potential safety hazards.

9. **Review and Prepare Final Documentation.**
Immediately after relinquishing control of the crime scene, first responding officers should ensure that their documentation of observations and experiences spanning their entire time at the crime scene is complete and accurate. Recollections of locations, appearances, and conditions of specific persons, places, and things should be the central focus of this task. In addition, other insights potentially helpful to investigators reconstructing events before and after the crime—for example, neighbors present, music playing, vehicles running, weather conditions, doors and windows left open or closed, garbage collected, and so forth—need to be recorded in sufficient detail for easy recall by the officer and others, including investigators, prosecutors, and defense attorneys who may examine the first responding officer's crime scene documentation.[13]

THE INVESTIGATOR'S ARRIVAL AT THE CRIME SCENE

In situations involving misdemeanor offenses, and perhaps lower-level felonies, the investigator is not called to the crime scene; rather, first responding officers and civilian evidence technicians document and collect necessary evidence. Crimes resulting in serious personal injury or damage to property are those most likely to result in criminal investigators being dispatched to an already secured crime scene. When this occurs, the preliminary investigation continues into a much larger-scale, if not a full-scale investigative effort. The number of investigators and tactics employed during the investigation will depend on the type of crime committed, the size and geographic nature of the crime scene, the investigative personnel available, and numerous other factors—many of which remain unknown until the actual investigation is under way. At a minimum, investigators will examine and search the crime scene for physical evidence; collect and document evidence; and employ sketches, photos, diagrams, and measurements to document the entire scene to record locations of key evidence or other factors related to reconstructing the crime. In more complex criminal investigations, investigators may conduct detailed interviews of victims and witnesses; obtain search warrants; canvass neighborhoods for suspects or witnesses; coordinate uniformed officer search activities; handle media coverage at the crime scene; arrest suspects; and in some instances—fortunately rare—use deadly force.[14]

All investigators who become involved in a preliminary investigation start by obtaining as much information as possible from first responding officers and others who can provide fast and accurate details regarding the initial condition of the crime scene, possible types and locations of physical evidence, persons involved in or witnessing the crime, the nature of the crime committed, and other factors necessary to prepare the crime scene for a formal investigation. Every new crime scene presents a unique set of circumstances that investigators must deal with by quick and decisive thinking when they take control of the scene from first responders. The following is a sequence of investigative events and duties that investigators can adjust to meet the individual needs of their investigations and crime scenes upon arrival:

1. **Establish Division of Labor.**
   First, before arriving at the crime scene, the division of labor must be established for the investigation team. This initial step is not of concern for crime scenes where only one investigator is present. In such instances, the assigned investigator must perform all tasks at the scene. If multiple investigators are on the scene, however, clarity is needed regarding the specific duties of each investigator. Generally speaking, two separate investigative roles can be assigned—**principal investigator** and **lead investigator**—which carry out different duties at the crime scene. Principal investigators do the actual leg work of the investigation—establishing crime scene boundaries; performing a setup for the search; conducting evidence searches of the entire scene; and collecting, documenting, and packaging evidence for analysis at the crime lab. Lead investigators serve in supervisory, coordinator, and liaison roles. Their duties include providing media information, requesting assistance from specialized outside personnel, interacting with the coroner's office (if necessary), obtaining necessary search warrants, and making key decisions such as when to expand or conclude the investigation.

2. **Obtain Information from First Responders.**
   Upon arrival at the crime scene, first responding officers and their uniformed supervisor should be consulted in a private location away from other persons at the scene. First, and of most importance, the crime scene must be both secure and safe. If it is not, necessary adjustments should be made to secure the

scene before proceeding with the investigation. Next, pertinent information should be gathered from the first responders on all events that thus far have transpired within the crime scene area, especially those that require immediate investigative attention—such as preserving possible perishable evidence identified or collected by the first responder. Special personnel or units will be needed to deal with crime scene hazards and hazardous evidence such as chemicals or explosives. Additional investigators should be requested if needed and/or available. The general condition of the crime scene when first arriving should be noted as well as individuals present, the victim's or other person's injuries, weather, lighting, sights, and smells.[15]

3. **Interview Key Individuals.**
   It is advisable to postpone any detailed interrogation of suspects still at the scene, whether formally arrested or not, until after they have been properly advised of their rights and are within a more controlled setting. Basic information can be gathered from suspects for corroborating other accounts provided by victims or witnesses. Victims and witnesses at the scene should be interviewed as soon as possible. The order of interviews should begin with the victim and proceed to witnesses that have the most detailed first-hand accounts of the crime and/or suspect. Victims transported to an emergency room should be interviewed within the hospital setting as soon as possible. Background checks will be needed for the victims. Prior arrests for crimes similar to the one being investigated may indicate that the victim is engaged in a pattern of deception. Prior arrests in general may indicate that the immediate crime resulted from a criminal association between the victim and the offender.

   Timely interviews of witnesses may not only produce hot leads, but also prevent them from losing interest and leaving the scene. All interviews should be conducted individually, and all persons to be interviewed should remain separated. At this point, it is best to ask direct questions that will indicate possible locations of physical evidence such as hairs, fibers, or DNA; probable entry and exit routes taken by the suspect; or objects that have been touched that may contain fingerprints. Time should not be wasted by repeating questions, which can occur when several investigators interview the same witness. Transportation should be arranged for any key witnesses to an interviewing room to obtain written statements. Detailed documentation of all statements obtained from each person interviewed will be needed.[16]

4. **Conduct a Reassessment of the Crime Scene.**
   Based on information obtained from victims, witnesses, and other persons previously interviewed, a

reassessment should be conducted of the crime scene setup performed by the first responding officer(s). The scene is to be examined for adequate initial boundary establishment, exit/entry pathway creation, and overall safety concerns. Potential hazards and problems at the scene are to be noted, including unruly onlookers, damaged property that may injure or collapse, leaking water or gas pipes, stray animals, hazardous chemicals, volatile liquids, or biohazards such as shared objects containing blood or other bodily fluids. The crime scene should be expanded, if necessary. Also, locations other than where the primary criminal activity occurred should be identified. These additional locations must be secured and controlled if and when they are discovered. The necessary warrants need to be obtained before entering new crime scene areas.[17] Investigators handling the crime scene in Case Example 3A.8 are shown in Figure 3.14 assessing the central location (or core) of the crime scene before conducting a comprehensive search of the crime scene area.

5. **Canvass the Crime Scene Vicinity.**
   Canvassing an area involves a general search for additional witnesses and evidence related to the crime under investigation. An immediate canvass of the crime scene vicinity, if necessary and personnel are available, should be ordered while the crime scene is still hot or warm. Additional witnesses can be canvassed by identifying persons who may have been present before, during, or after the crime—residents, doormen, store keepers, delivery persons, taxi/bus drivers, crossing guards, coffee shop or restaurant patrons, and persons working in businesses in or near the crime scene. All persons within a particular location should be interviewed. They should be asked a short set of questions dealing with the crime; for example, whether they have observed any suspicious persons, vehicles, or activities; whether they have heard about the crime or have information about it; and whether they are familiar with the victim (without specifically revealing the victim's identity). Detailed information should be gathered from each person including name, address, date of birth, phone number, and place of employment. Also, vehicles parked in the area should be canvassed for their descriptions and license numbers. Items stolen or removed from the crime scene should also be the subject of a canvass focused along probable exits paths used by the suspect. Garbage cans, sewer outlets, rain gutters, trees, shrubs, and the underside of vehicles are some of the more common areas that may contain articles discarded by the offenders. Probable entry ways to the crime scene should also be canvassed for tissues, cigarette butts, footprints, fingerprints, chewing gum, soda cans, general litter, or any other evidence that could possibly be linked to the offender.[18]

CASE EXAMPLE 3A.8

Investigators examine the victim's body and reassess the scene

FIGURE 3.14 ▶ Investigators must reassess the crime scene after their arrival. What would you do or change upon arriving at this crime scene if you were the investigator?

EXAMINING THE CRIME SCENE

1. **Map out the Crime Scene.**
   It is always advisable to plan as much as possible before entering the crime scene to conduct a formal evidence search. The crime scene must be examined with the least amount of intrusion possible before entry so that an effective plan of action for searching the scene can be made. In fact, it is a good idea to create an approximate description of the crime scene and its boundaries using information from observers and person scans of the general area before physically setting foot inside the crime scene. Information obtained from officer, witness interviews, and prior personal scans of the scene can be used to create a rough sketch outlining key areas of the crime scene— known as a **logistics map**.

   This map contains the geographic locations of three main areas of the crime scene: the core, the inner area, and the outer area. First, the location and dimensions of the **crime scene core** are identified. This is the primary area where the crime was committed, and it contains the bulk of physical evidence directly related to the execution of the criminal offense. It can be depicted as any shape in the map, but is commonly drawn as a square area encompassing the body, room, vehicle, or other location where the crime is centered.

   Next, the area extending away from the core is mapped—referred to as the **peripheral crime scene** or *inner area*. This location may contain shell casings, footprints, fingerprints, or other evidence deposited before or after the crime was committed. Entry and exit paths to the crime scene core used by the offender and victim are useful indicators for determining likely locations and dimensions of the peripheral crime scene. As a rule of thumb, this area should extend in a circular fashion around the core and encompass roughly twice the area contained in the square depicting the core.

   The third and final logistics location, known as the **outer** or **extended area**, extends beyond the peripheral or inner area. This boundary is established to locate possible evidence that has not been previously discovered and to keep media and other onlookers away from the activity taking place in the crime scene and out of the sight and hearing of investigators. This area can be of any size or shape that is practical given the geographic limitation of the crime scene.[19]

   Further dimensions of the crime scene map can also be created by outlining the number of physical locations used to carry out the crime. The location where the criminal activity actually transpired is referred to and mapped as the **primary crime scene**. Additional locations that can be associated with the primary crime scene are referred to and mapped as **secondary crime scenes**—for example, when a driver of a car is killed in a drive-by shooting (the primary crime scene) and the shooter's car is later found in a remote location (the secondary crime scene). The primary and secondary crime scene locations relating to the same crime can be grouped together, in a conceptual sense, and referred to as the **macroscopic scene** of the crime. This is helpful for reconstructing the sequence of events occurring, for example, in a car-on-car drive-by shooting, where shots were exchanged at several areas on roadways and parking lots. Additionally, the **microscopic scene** refers to specific evidence found within a particular crime scene location—such as a cartridge casing, window glass, or blood stain found on the pavement where one of the drive-by shootings occurred.[20] The various components of a crime scene logistics map are illustrated in Figure 3.15.

2. **Perform a Walk-Through.**
   The main purpose of a **preliminary walk-through** is for investigators to learn the nature and quality of evidence to be collected and to develop a plan for searching the crime scene is as effective and expeditious a manner as possible. If crime scene technicians are to be utilized, they should be present on the walk-through. A walk-through is conducted primarily to determine the location and nature of

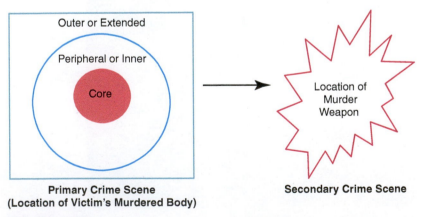

FIGURE 3.15 ▶ Components of the crime scene logistics map.

physical evidence at the crime scene. The collection of specific pieces of evidence can also be prioritized, with perishable items given first priority. Other specific tasks to be performed during this procedure include enlisting help from specialized units (e.g., hazardous waste disposal, explosives technicians), establishing safe paths to and from evidence locations, filling special evidence needs (i.e., preserving evidence from being destroyed or degraded), providing for special equipment requirements (e.g., an earth mover for a burial, or personal protection equipment (PPE) for investigating a clandestine laboratory), and identifying the need for special tools, lights, or cameras. Detailed notes should be taken documenting all observations during this procedure.

In addition, at the time of the walk-through, a location within the crime scene where investigators and other personnel can store equipment or gather for consultation without disrupting evidence—known as a staging area—can established at this time. A **crime scene storage area**, if needed, can also be created where evidence can be temporarily stored and preserved before being transported from the crime scene to other locations such as evidence lockers and crime labs. Also in this area, locations can be established for garbage disposal, storing hazardous materials, personnel decontamination (DCOM), and other activities that support crime scene processing. Generally, these specialized areas are located somewhere in the peripheral or inner crime scene area away from any sites containing physical evidence. Also, appropriate locations for a media center and mobile command post (if on the scene) should be determined and established. *Evidence should not be collected at this time; however, if valuable perishable evidence is discovered and in danger of immediate destruction, it should be preserved or collected immediately before the crime scene is formally processed.*

HOT TIPS AND LEADS 3.1

Media Relations at the Crime Scene

1. ***Provide information about the radio call:***
   The date, time, and location of occurrence; Information regarding crimes alleged or committed or any other incident investigated; Age of victim(s); Description of suspect(s); Description of vehicle(s); The factual circumstances of the incident; Any injuries, property damage, or weapons involved.

2. ***Unless doing so would adversely affect the investigation, release information about the arrestees:***
   Full name (do not release names of juvenile suspect); Area of residence; Occupation; Physical description; Age; Sex; Race/Ethnicity; Date and time of arrest; Location of arrest; Location held; Amount of bail; All charges including warrants; Parole or probation holds.

3. ***Release basic facts of the arrest:***
   Date, time, and location of arrest; Resistance by the suspect(s); Use of weapons by suspect(s); Use of force by officer(s); Identity of arresting/investigating officer(s); Limited description of evidence; The nature, substance, and text of charge; Any request for assistance from the public.

4. ***Don't release information about:***
   The identity of suspect(s) prior to arrest or results of investigative procedures prior to arrest unless it will aid in the investigation or warn the public of danger; Investigative proceedings involving officer-involved shootings or other personnel actions; Prior criminal record, reputation, or character of suspect(s); Personal information about juvenile arrestee(s) or suspect(s); Confessions or the existence of a confession; Officers' opinions; Any

photograph or mug shots, unless the information will aid in the investigation or warn the public of danger; Victim information regarding juveniles, deceased individuals (when family or next of kin have not yet been notified), persons placed on mental observational holds, persons whose personal reputation or personal safety would be compromised if identified (as in the case of a rape victim), or victims who explicitly request to remain anonymous; The identity, credibility, or testimony of prospective witnesses including:

   1. Any personal opinion as to the suspect's guilt or innocence, or the merits of the case

   2. Any information known not to be admissible in court

   3. References to investigative procedures such as fingerprints, polygraphs, or ballistic tests

5. ***In general:***
   The media has a legal right to be provided reasonable information about the criminal activity being investigated and reasonable physical access to the crime scene itself. Don't attempt to isolate the media from public areas around the crime scene. They are entitled to photograph, film, and interview persons in public around the crime scene. It is reasonable to restrict media vans and other vehicles from the crime scene, but entrance by foot should be permitted. Also, provide warning to media members regarding potential safety hazards within the crime scene.

Source: Courtesy Los Angeles Sheriff's Department, www.lasd.org.

PROCESSING THE CRIME SCENE

The primary collection of evidence occurs when investigators **process the crime scene**. The main goal of this stage of the preliminary investigation is to methodically identify, collect, and package physical evidence from the crime scene. In addition, the crime scene is thoroughly documented using photographic methods, sketching, and note taking. Large crime scenes often require **evidence collection teams** consisting of numerous investigative personnel, sometimes both sworn and nonsworn officers as well as citizen volunteers. If **crime scene technicians**—civilian staff trained in forensic science methods to identify, collect, and document crime scene evidence—are used, they should be provided a description of the crime, how it took place, and probable entry and exit points used by the suspect. Also they should be informed of specific evidence items and their probable locations within the crime scene. Key to processing the crime scene successfully is to foster constant and open communication between all members of the investigative search team.

CASE CLOSE-UP 3.2

BREAKING THE TAPE LINE
(Uptown Chicago, Ill.)

At approximately 8:00 P.M., crime scene investigators set up a tape line within an Uptown Chicago residential neighborhood where a near-fatal stabbing had taken place following an altercation between two males. After formal processing of the crime scene began about half an hour later, with 15–20 officers and investigators now on the scene, the driver of a stolen car came careening around a corner of the street on which the crime scene was located.

The driver, who had no idea that the crime scene processing was taking place, plowed the vehicle directly through the tape line, causing investigators to flee the scene. The stolen car, screeching tires and moving backward and forward across the tape line, smashed seven police vehicles before speeding away down a sidewalk, narrowly avoiding the use of deadly force by investigators who had the driver at gunpoint during the debacle.

As previously mentioned, crime scenes can be located virtually anywhere. When a house is broken into, a car is stolen, or a person is assaulted, there is usually a specific geographic location where criminal activity has taken place—and if discovered, it can be investigated as a crime scene. Situations such as these, usually encountered by criminal investigators, are known as **physical crime scenes**. Other types of crime scenes, however, are not so readily identifiable because they lack a well-defined physical location. One such situation is the mid-air explosion of an aircraft. Investigations of this "crime scene" may involve searching hundreds of miles of land or ocean for pieces of the aircraft to rule out a terrorist attack. Even more elusive to investigators attempting to identify a crime scene are crimes committed in cyber-space via computer technology such as the illegal transfer of funds, e-mail threats, or child pornography. These virtual locations where an offense is committed are referred to as **electronic crime scenes** and may require special investigative tools and methods different from those typically used in physical crime scene investigation. This section focuses on procedures used primarily for the processing of physical crime scenes, but the methods discussed here also apply to computers, digital memory systems, cellular phones, and other physical devices that can be associated with the electronic crime scene.[21]

Thus, there are many different types of crime scenes and approaches that can be taken to process them. The particular processing methods selected will depend largely on the physical and environmental factors specific to each individual location. The first critical processing step, however, is to thoroughly document the entire crime scene photographically, both inside and out, before collecting any evidence. Next, measurements are taken to record locations of evidence within the crime scene, which are then sketched by the investigator. Finally, the scene is completely searched for the presence of any evidence material to proving the crime at hand. Final photographs are taken documenting each piece of discovered evidence to show its context within the overall crime scene.

PHOTOGRAPHING THE CRIME SCENE

Before conducting any other crime scene processing activity—or in other words, before anything has been touched or moved—photographs must be taken to capture the scene *in situ*. Typically, this is done by the crime scene photographer (for example, see Figure 3.16), who accompanies the investigators both inside and outside the crime scene. The purpose of **crime scene photography**, or *forensic photography* as it is sometimes called, is to create a permanent visual documentation of the crime scene. Forensic photos are used after the preliminary investigation is complete as a resource for investigators and other concerned parties who want to "revisit" the crime scene after it has been closed. In addition, crime scene photographs may be a central source of evidence should a case

Initial Photographs: Capture the Crime Scene and Mark Evidence

The first round of crime scene photographs should be taken during the initial examination of the crime scene before any evidence has been moved or collected. At this point, the overall purpose is to photographically document the crime scene in its original condition. These photos should not show law enforcement personnel and equipment in the field of vision. If necessary, tape lines or vehicles may be removed from areas that are photographed. Any evidence removed from the crime scene before photographic documentation has begun, however, should not be placed back in its original location and photographed. In this situation, it is best to simply take a photo of the area where the evidence was located before its removal. A proxy for the evidence, such as an evidence marker, can be used to show the original placement of the evidence. Fragile and perishable evidence, such as fingerprints and other impressions, should be photographed immediately before it is degraded or destroyed.

FIGURE 3.16 ▶ Here a semiautomatic pistol and its magazine are marked and photographed from various angles to photographically document the crime scene.

go to trial. For crime scene photos to be admitted as evidence at trial, however, they must meet certain legal standards.

First, the photos must be **relevant and material** to the case at hand; that is, they must be able to prove or disprove any disputed fact and legal issue in the case. For example, photos showing a knife collection at a murder suspect's personal residence may be excluded from a trial for an alleged killing by strangulation. Second, crime scene photos must accurately portray the crime scene and physical evidence. Photos that contain unclear images, distorted perspectives, or unnecessary emotional flair will likely be excluded as evidence from legal proceedings. Therefore, certain established methods of crime scene photography must be followed to provide photos that are useful from both the investigative and legal perspectives.[22]

After the entire crime scene has been photographically documented in its untouched state, investigators and/or evidence technicians can place evidence markers in the crime scene. The evidence markers provide a numbering system for identifying specific items of physical evidence and referencing the numbers in photographs, sketches, notes, or other documentation. Many types of evidence markers are commercially available. Some varieties in popular use today are produced in the form of numbered or lettered stands, cones, markers, tapes, and flags. Additional evidence will be marked and photographed if, and when, it is discovered during the search phase of the crime scene processing. Returning to our model case, Case Example 3A.9 illustrates the photographic documentation process of physical evidence at the crime scene (see Figure 3.17).

CASE CLOSE-UP 3.3

CAUGHT "BY A HAIR"

(Helena, Montana)

The search of a residence where a female in her early 20s was found dead revealed a key piece of evidence resulting in the release of two suspects and the successful prosecution of a third suspect for the woman's murder. The evidence was a single reddish colored facial hair on the inside of a plastic toilet paper bag wrapped around the head of the victim, causing her to die by suffocation. Not only did the color and characteristics of the hair match hair samples taken from the convicted murderer, but so did DNA extracted from the single hair.

CASE EXAMPLE 3A.9

Physical evidence is marked and photographed

FIGURE 3.17 ▶ Transient evidence is photographed and marked before other less perishable types of evidence. What other evidence at this crime scene should be given high priority for marking and photographing?

Photographic Equipment and Methods

Most crime scene photos are still taken with 35mm conventional film cameras because they produce negatives, which can easily be enlarged to produce clear, high-contrast images. Also, original negatives provide sound evidence if the question is raised as to whether or not a photograph has been enhanced or altered. Recent advances in electronic imagery have produced digital cameras with nearly the same resolution as that of the standard film cameras. Therefore, many agencies now use digital cameras to document crime scenes. Some authenticity issues, however, have been raised regarding digital photos in some court proceedings in an effort to exclude these crime scene photos as evidence at trial. These challenges, some of which have been successful, are based on the assumption that without a true negative image there is no way to prove beyond a reasonable doubt that a photo in question has not been photoshopped or modified in some other way. To address these legal shortcomings, some companies have created digital cameras that produce a special encoded image for authentication purposes.

With notable exceptions, crime scenes should be photographed in color and at eye level. The particular time, place, location, and subject matter of each photo can be recorded in a **photo log** for purposes of later identification. The number of photos taken, the locations where they are taken, and how they are taken are left up to the discretion of the *crime scene photographer*. This individual may be (1) a civilian technician whose only job responsibility is taking crime scene photos or (2) a crime scene investigator who has received specialized photographic training.

Telling the Crime Story with Photos

Telling the story of the crime—documenting the crime from beginning, middle, to end—is a central goal to be achieved by all photographers of a crime scene. This is carried out by pho-

tographing evidence and other key areas of the crime scene so as to zoom in on the particular area or item of interest. To do so, photos are taken in a series that captures long-range, mid-range, and close-up images.

Long-range photos provide an overview of the crime scene, and are usually taken in outdoor locations. These may be the exterior of a building where a robbery or a murder took place, an intersection of streets leading to and from a parked vehicle targeted by a drive-by shooting, or an aerial view of mountainous terrain containing the location of an outdoor body dump site. Doors, windows, and other means of entering and exiting the crime scene used by the suspect(s) are key elements of the long-range photo. Once inside the crime scene, photos are taken from the point of entry and continue leading up to the central location where the crime occurred. If the crime setting is a residential dwelling, for example, photos are first taken of the doorway to show whether or not there are signs of forced entry. Next, photos from various angles are taken of the primary crime location to capture how it appears when viewed for the first time. Within a room, this would involve taking photos from all opposing walls and also from each of the four corners of the room. In an outdoor scene, photos are taken from all possible sides as well. Taking additional photos of areas and locations contiguous to the main crime area—other rooms, adjoining roadways, or outdoor landscape in nearby proximity—can also help to create a well-defined overview of the crime scene.[23] To illustrate the photo documentation of a crime scene, Case Example 3A.10 (see Figure 3.18) shows the first long-range photo in a sequence of photos designed to "tell the story" of the criminal incident examined in our model case.

Two photos, one at mid-range and one at close range, are typically taken of all important physical evidence. Showing the context of physical evidence within the crime scene is the function of a mid-range photo. In other words, this view shows

CASE EXAMPLE 3A.10

"Telling the Story"—Long-range photo of the core crime scene

FIGURE 3.18 ▶ Crime scene photographs are meant to "tell the story" of the crime. What part of the story does this full view of the victim's body tell you?

CASE CLOSE-UP 3-4

CRIME SCENE PHOTOS "BUG" SUSPECTED KILLER
(Bakersfield, California)

A 44-year-old man accused of fatally shooting and stabbing five members of his family was convicted when investigators proved his defense alibi untrue with evidence photos of a wasp and a cricket taken from a rental car driven by the suspect. In his defense, the suspect claimed that he had never driven the rental car outside Ohio when the murders took place out west in the California town of Bakersfield. An insect expert examining forensic photos of internal parts of the car, however, discovered recently deposited grasshopper legs and wasp wings belonging to species found only in western states, thus discrediting the accused offender's alibi that he had never left the Midwest and also corroborating the discovery of an excessive amount of mileage on the vehicle.

how the particular object within the photograph is related to its immediate setting. For example, a mid-range photo of a knife on the ground in a pool of blood next to the legs of a bar stool may help illustrate the fact that the stabbing victim was attacked while drinking at the bar. This photographic technique (i.e., moving from mid- to close-range shots) is illustrated in the following continued photographic documentation of our model crime scene in Case Example 3A.11 (see Figures 3.19, 3.20, and 3.21).

Close-range photos are then taken to show specific details of the evidence. In the latter example given above, an image of the knife and its bloody blade resting on top of a beer bottle with the victim's fingerprints could be used to further support the theory of a surprise deadly assault. Because close-up shots often make things look larger, longer, or more distant than they actually are, scaling devices are often included in the photo to show proper size and distance perspectives. Although various items have been and can be used for this purpose (coins, business cards, pencils, keys, flashlights, etc.), it is best to use either a flat or right-angled ruler placed beneath the evidence on a level surface. Specialized measuring devices have been designed specifically as evidence scales, such as the **ABFO#2** (American Board of Forensic Odontology), which was originally

CASE EXAMPLE 3A.11

"Telling the Story"—Mid-range photos of victim's body

FIGURE 3.19 ▶ As the investigator of this case, you tell the photographer that you want to get a mid-range shot of the victim's head and upper torso. The photographer replies, "Why?" What is your response to this question?

FIGURE 3.20 ▶ What part of this victim's crime story is told by this photo? How does the photo help you reconstruct the events that took place between the victim and her offender before her death?

FIGURE 3.21 ▶ Here, the photographer asks you, "Why do you want a picture of the victim's shoes?" What is your reply to this question?

fashioned as a scale for bite mark photos. In addition to measures at both straight and right angles, the ABFO#2 contains a series of circles, squares, and gray scales that indicate perspective and color distortion, should these problems occur. When photos are taken containing scales or other items such as evidence markers, it is recommended to take one separate shot containing these items and another that depicts the evidence item alone. This will guard against future claims that foreign objects placed in the photo are perhaps concealing evidence or distorting the visual quality of the crime scene. The investigative story told by the photographic sequence documenting our model crime scene also ends with close-range photos, shown in Case Example 3A.12, depicting perhaps the most vital evidence contained in the scene—suggesting the crime of murder and the manner in which the victim was assaulted by her attacker (see Figures 3.22 and 3.23).

Specialized Crime Scene Photographic Techniques

Many special circumstances encountered while photographing crime scenes require specialized photographic techniques. Most common among these is taking photographs of certain impression evidence; namely footprints and tire tracks in dirt, sand, mud, carpet, or dusty surfaces. These, and other 3-D impressions, do not photograph well using color film and standard lighting. Rather, for maximum image quality, they must be photographed using black-and-white film and **oblique lighting** (i.e., from the side of the object). This is because lighting placed at ground level from the side of the object will cast shadows across the raised portions of the 3-D impression,

which are captured in the detail of the high-contrast black and white image. Taking the photograph directly above the object (at a 90° angle) using a leveled tripod will produce the best possible image with the least possible distortion. All photographs should be taken before casts are made of the particular impression. Photographing fingerprints, which are essentially 3-D impressions, is similar to photographing other impression evidence. Although color film can be used, black-and-white film often provides the highest-contrast image of fingerprints. Photograph all fingerprints before they are lifted or any other procedure is performed that may alter their original appearance.[24] The techniques outlined here are illustrated in Case Example 3A.13 for the photographic documentation of tire tracks believed by investigators to have been produced by the murder suspect's vehicle at the model crime scene (see Figures 3.24 and 3.25).

Other specialized techniques include infrared methods, which produce an image based on the heat absorption qualities of the object being photographed. This may be useful when evidence cannot be readily seen because it does not contrast with (or is the same color as) the surface where it appears. For example, a greasy fingerprint could not be visualized on a black t-shirt. Because the fingerprint absorbs heat at a different rate than the shirt, however, the fingerprint would be readily visible in an infrared photograph. Specialized color filters and lighting often produce a similar effect to enhance contrast, and thus improve the photographic visualization of evidence. In addition, lasers, ultraviolet, and other alternate lighting sources used to enhance the visibility of evidence can help produce effective crime scene photos given proper photographic training and use of equipment.

CASE EXAMPLE 3A.12

"Telling the Story"—Close-up photos of victim's head wounds

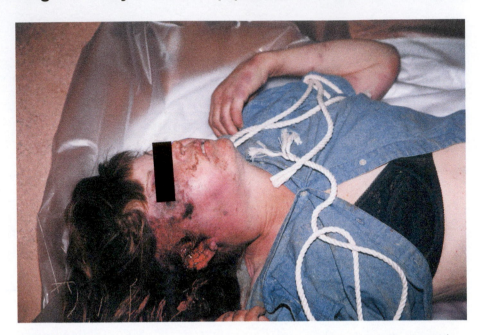

FIGURE 3.22 ▶ Close-up photos illustrate specific features about the crime that provide clues regarding how and perhaps why the crime was committed. What does this photo tell you about the killing and how it was carried out by the offender? (Note: The rope is not part of the crime scene. It is being used by the medical examiner's office to remove the body from the crime scene.)

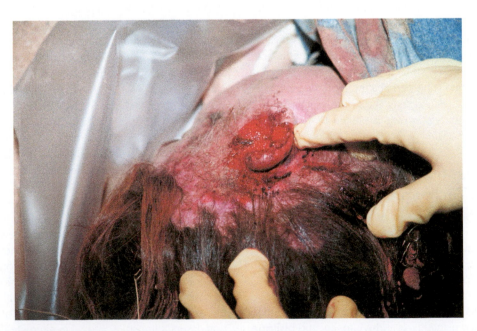

FIGURE 3.23 ▶ Of what value to your investigation is this close-up shot of the victim's head wound?

CASE EXAMPLE 3A.13

Black-and-white 90° photos with oblique lighting to capture impressions

FIGURE 3.24 ▶ Photos of tire tracks are taken at 90° angles, with oblique lighting. Why is this photographic method necessary for impression evidence?

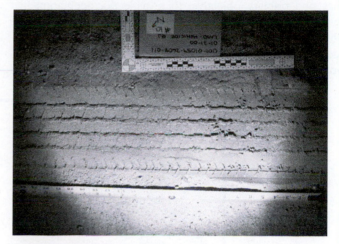

FIGURE 3.25 ▶ Impression evidence is usually photographed using black-and-white film. Why is this necessary? Of what use is this tire track photo to your investigation of this crime scene? (Note the ABFO ruler in the background. Why is this included in the picture?)

Forensic Videography

Adding motion to photographic documentation of the crime scene through the use of video cameras, otherwise known as **forensic videography**, has increased in popularity among investigators and inside the courtroom with the development of inexpensive, high-quality tape and digital recording formats. Although it is true that this method greatly increases the amount of photographic crime scene documentation, and can produce still photos as well, videographic evidence should be treated as only supplemental to still photography as a means of visually capturing the crime scene. Following are some general recommended guidelines for documenting the crime scene in video:

- Begin with an introduction performed by a member of the investigative staff and provide information regarding time, date, location, and type of scene; description of the rooms (if indoors) or terrain (if outdoors); and evidence to be viewed. Blueprints or diagrams of the crime scene may also be displayed to further clarify any of the introductory information.

- Record the scene from the outside to the inside. If the scene is indoors, start with the outside of the location (e.g., building, neighborhood) to develop an overview of the crime scene. If outdoors, begin recoding in locations where it is believed the crime began, such as an entry point to the crime scene. Turn off the audio to avoid distracting or perhaps unplanned audible statements.

- Move the camera steadily and slowly. Tripods are not necessary. Show all angles of the crime scene: right, left, up, down, corner-to-corner. When panning an area (for example, filming in a stationary position and moving the camera from one position to another), move the camera very slowly and deliberately to avoid producing an image that jerks or whizzes by.

- Use a zoom lens to provide close-ups on key pieces of evidence and crime scene locations. On extreme close-ups, a scaling device may be included in the image to add visual perspective.

- Never try to produce a video designed to exaggerate the crime scene content or to evoke emotional reactions from its viewers. These tapes will most likely not be admissible in court proceedings.[25]

- Never edit the original content. Editing of content will render the recording useless as courtroom evidence. Unlike other video production, the first take of a crime scene recording is also the final take.

CRIME SCENE SKETCHING

Photographs alone do not provide enough necessary documentation of the crime scene. This is because they tend to distort relational distances between physical objects. To overcome this problem, investigators must prepare sketches that portray the exact locations and distances of items photographed within the crime scene. The term **crime scene sketching**, however, is somewhat misleading nowadays because sketching with a pencil and paper has largely been replaced by computerized and automated methods of documenting the details of a crime scene. But regardless of how it is made, a crime scene sketch has one primary objective: to provide documentation that would allow anyone to return to the crime scene and determine the exact location and position of each piece of physical evidence. This is accomplished through the investigator's meticulous measurement and recording of locations, sizes, and

distances of pieces of evidence and other key components of the crime scene (discussed in the following section). Secondarily, yet equally important, this documentation is often essential for clarifying size and distance relationships contained within photos and videos taken so as to distort reality.

Before obtaining precise measurements of the crime scene, a **rough sketch** is prepared. Rough sketches are drawn in simple paper-and-pencil form while the crime scene remains undisturbed and in its original state. The size, shape, and location of key fixtures (e.g., furniture, windows, doorways) as well as

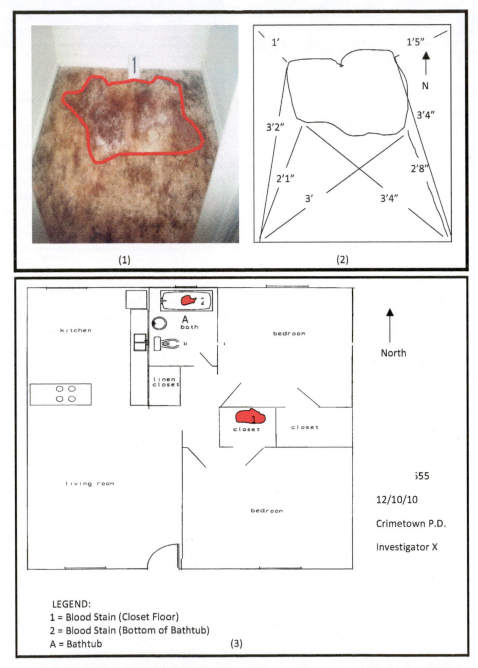

FIGURE 3.26 ▶ **Bird's-Eye Sketch:** (1) Photo of blood stain in closet; (2) rough sketch and measurement of closet and stain; and (3) finished sketch to scale of evidence locations within the crime scene, including a title block (bottom right) and a legend (bottom left) with numbers labeling evidence and letters labeling items.

physical evidence contained within the crime scene are included in the rough sketch. Usually one sketch is prepared for each specific room or location documented at the primary and/or secondary crime scene areas. For later identification purposes, each rough sketch must contain information about the crime scene location, case number, investigator's name, date and time completed, a legend defining each item contained in the sketch, and an arrow indicating the North direction of the crime scene.

Sketches can be created in a bird's-eye cross projection (or exploded), or **elevated perspective**. The bird's-eye perspective is used most commonly to depict ground-level areas such as flooring space and simply provides a two-dimensional view looking directly down from above the crime scene (see Figure 3.26). Conversely, crime scene sketches done from an elevated perspective provide a two-dimensional side view of a particular location (see Figure 3.27). Generally this method is used to show bullet holes or bloodstains on walls or other vertically oriented surfaces. Cross projections or exploded sketches show an entire structure or location in a flat two-dimensional view (see Figure 3.28). For example, in residential crime scenes, both floors and walls are depicted as flat surfaces. These types of sketches enable the examination of physical evidence locations

on the floor as well as on all walls in a room, or any other enclosed location. This enables the viewer to gain an overall perspective of how and where each piece of evidence is positioned as well as its relational distance from other physical features within the crime scene. Although each of these perspectives can be captured in three dimensions, via either simple drawings or computerized methods, the flat 2-dimensional picture is still the method of choice for crime scene sketching due to its simplicity and ease of interpretation. Precise distances between each of the items depicted in the rough sketch can later be included in the drawing after crime scene measurements have been taken.[26]

Later, within an office setting, the rough sketch will be converted to a **finished sketch** (for example, see #3 in Figure 3.26). This document is a refined and polished version of the rough sketch, which illustrates proper perspective of items photographed and observed at the crime scene. It is prepared by transferring information from the rough sketch to create a document that depicts the crime scene and evidence locations to scale; that is, exact locations of objects and relative distances are reflected in a standardized system of presentation and measurement. To do so, when computer technology is unavailable, hand

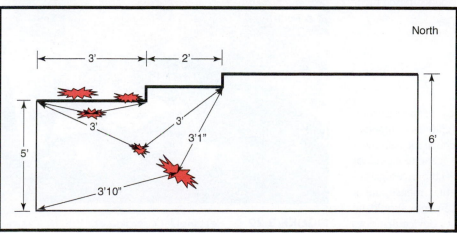

FIGURE 3.27 ▶ **Elevated Sketch**
This type of sketch depicts evidence locations and measurements of items located on vertical surfaces such as this wall. The bloody smears on the wall illustrate the path taken by a wounded suspect after climbing over from the opposite side.

FIGURE 3.28 ▶ **Cross Projection or Exploded Sketch.** This sketch is a view of the full crime scene in which the wall shown in Figure 3.27 (top square) was one of four enclosing a field. This perspective shows the offender's bloody path after climbing over and down the first wall, moving across a field (center square), and climbing up and over another opposing wall (bottom square). The purpose is to illustrate the locations of all evidence contained on both horizontal and vertical surfaces.

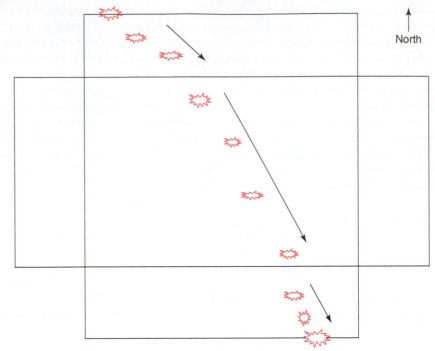

drawings on graph paper where each square represents a scaled-down version of the actual distance will suffice. Specialized templates are available to draw crime images of furniture, bodies, weapons, and other articles contained within the crime scene. The finished sketch will be utilized during later periods of the investigation to provide a technical illustration of the crime scene and ultimately may be used as an exhibit during trial.

The time and effort spent on the above manual sketching methods can be avoided, however, by using specialized crime scene mapping software. After fixed points and measures of the crime scene are inputted, these programs can create not only a professional appearing finished sketch, but also 3-D reconstructions of the crime scene through animations or by overlaying computer-generated distance measures on actual crime scene photographs. Another added feature to most of these new computer-generated methods is a crime scene reconstruction function that will create virtual images of likely movements and actions of offenders and victims based on evidence-based theories formulated by investigators.[27]

TAKING CRIME SCENE MEASUREMENTS

Many methods have been developed to provide the measurements necessary to prepare sketches and related documentation of the crime scene. The selection of a particular measurement method will depend on (1) the type of crime scene (e.g., indoor vs. outdoor); (2) the type of evidence; and (3) the investigator's knowledge of and experience with particular measurement methods. In general, crime scene measurements should be taken with a steel tape measure or some other device that does

not stretch or bend. Laser or infrared measuring devises are also excellent choices if used correctly and under the proper circumstances. Strings can be also be used along with tape measures to create straight lines or angles. Measurements can be taken by a single investigator, but are more quickly and effectively obtained by multiple investigators working in teams. This is usually the last step in the crime scene documentation process, and should be performed before collecting any physical evidence. Brief descriptions of each method, how it is carried out, and when it is most appropriate to use, follow.

Rectangular Coordinates

Figure 3.29 illustrates an example of the **rectangular coordinates** measurement method. This technique is very easy to interpret and perform, so it is commonly used by investigators to measure crime scenes. It is best used to document indoor

FIGURE 3.29 ▶ Rectangular coordinates.

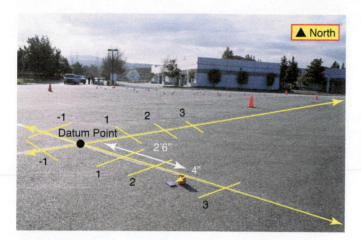

FIGURE 3.30 ▶ Grid evidence search method, using baseline coordinates measurement.

FIGURE 3.31 ▶ Triangulation.

crime scenes, but can be used for outdoor scenes as well. The method requires the identification of two fixed, adjacent points within the crime scene to create a horizontal and a vertical axis, or a rectangular area, within a given location. Typically, in a room, two adjacent walls (north and east, for example) are used. Outdoors, any surfaces or areas that form right angles can be used (e.g., divisions in roadways, curbs, partitions in driveways and sidewalks). Measurements are simply taken from both horizontal and vertical angles to the **center of mass** (the middle) of the object of interest, and the point of intersection is recorded as the location within the crime scene. A **grid system** of the rectangular coordinates method, as shown in Figure 3.30, is useful for large outdoor crime scenes and can be created by extending the horizontal and vertical axis lines so that they form a four-quadrant grid. One or more grids can be established covering crime scenes where evidence is located or scattered over large areas, such as in plane crashes, building explosions, separated body remains, or multiple burial sites. Grids of any size can be constructed, although it is best to create several smaller grids rather than one large one. All that is needed to construct the grid is a fixed center point marking the position where the horizontal and vertical axis intersect, and a series of markers placed at the outer boundaries of each of the four quadrants. Measurements are taken from the angles adjacent to the crime scene object of interest separately within each quadrant.[28]

Triangulation

Triangulation (see Figure 3.31) can be used anywhere, and is considered one of the most precise and flexible methods for performing crime scene measurements. The method begins by identifying two fixed points; for example, corners of buildings, trees, telephone poles, mailboxes, and curbs. These points should be permanent and have unique identifying characteristics (for example, a telephone pole marked with a serial number). Measurements are taken at angles from each of the fixed points until they intersect at the object within the crime scene. This method can be adapted further; for example, in a large outdoor area where the only two fixed points are located

some distance from the main crime scene, **secondary reference point coordinates** can be established. This involves using the triangulation method to establish the position of two new fixed points, which are closer to the crime scene. This makes taking measurements not only easier, but also more accurate. In addition, the triangulation method can be performed twice on one object to improve measurement accuracy. For example, if it is desired to show the exact position of a knife on a floor, one set of measurements can be taken at the handle and a second set at the tip of the blade.[29]

Baseline Coordinates

Baseline coordinates are performed first by establishing a straight line or baseline between two fixed points. Within indoor settings, a baseline could be created from one opposing wall to another; outdoor baselines can be formed from corners of two opposing structures such as houses or garages, or perhaps formulated from points identified though GPS technology. A single straight line measurement (right angle) or series of them is taken from the baseline to the object of interest in the crime scene. A second measure is then taken from one of the fixed points to each of the separate baseline measures. Baselines should be established relatively close to the desired objects in the crime scene to prevent measurement inaccuracies resulting from imprecise angles, which may occur when measuring over long distances and uneven terrain.[30] Figure 3.32 provides an illustrated example of the baseline coordinates method.

FIGURE 3.32 ▶ Baseline coordinates.

FIGURE 3.33 ▶ Polar coordinates.

Polar Coordinates

The **polar coordinates** method, although not used very often, is helpful for taking measures in large outdoor crime scenes that contain few fixed points of reference (for example, desert landscape). It is carried out by establishing one fixed point known as a **datum point** from which all measures are taken (see Figure 3.33). A datum point can be formed from a naturally occurring landmark such as a tree or immovable rock, or can be constructed by the investigator (driving a stake into the ground, after perhaps determining a location via GPS). Measures are taken from the datum point to desired crime scene objects of interest. The precise angle of the line of measure from the datum point to the object and its distance are recorded. The degree of angle can be determined using a handheld compass, protractor, or surveyor's transit.[31]

The Total Station and Advanced Crime Scene Imaging

Within the last decade, various technological advances have been made in crime scene imaging methods, and in the application of computer software using these methods to create state-of-the-art forensic maps. One such method involves the use of a **total station** approach. Used indoors or outdoors, the total station employs a surveyor's transit—which measures distances and elevations of selected objects and locations with a device known as an **electronic distance meter (EDM)**. Information collected from the total station can be interfaced with various computer programs and softwares. One such application is computer aided drafting (CAD) programs that can rapidly re-create 3-D images of the full crime scene, including locations and measurements of physical evidence.[32]

SEARCHING THE CRIME SCENE

Objectives of the Search

After the crime scene has been documented through photos, measurement, and sketching, it must be searched thoroughly and methodically to discover physical evidence that was not readily apparent during earlier stages of the investigation. The search should focus on the main objective of locating all evidence that will associate the suspect to the crime committed at the crime scene—referred to as **associative evidence**. Other objectives to bear in mind include the securing of evidence that may assist in:

- Reconstructing the crime
- Recovering missing property
- Discovering the location of a missing victim
- Revealing the identity of the suspect
- Pinpointing the whereabouts of a suspect who has fled the crime scene
- Uncovering the motive for the crime
- Providing leads for new witnesses to the crime
- Corroborating testimony obtained by the suspect, victim, and witnesses

Search Strategies

Always develop a plan before conducting the crime scene search. It is helpful to draw a diagram of the crime scene location depicting key physical features in the scene and probable locations of physical evidence. Although it may be useful to take the "collect everything" approach when searching smaller crime scenes, this strategy is not recommended in larger crime scenes containing hundreds or thousands of pieces of evidence. Time and money generally will not permit the collection and processing of such excessive amounts of physical evidence. In such situations, repetitive evidence should be identified and only an item or two that represents it collected; for example, if 100 cartridge casings have obviously been fired from the same gun, collecting one or two casings will do.

When searching rooms, enter and search one at a time. Start at the room or location that is from the doorway or entrance to the building being searched. Be sure to search ceilings and walls as well as floors. Remove ceiling panels and inspect attics and rafters. Start room searches in the corner or back area of rooms, and if necessary, move other articles in the room, such as furniture, to this previously inspected area as the search proceeds. Look under, over, and inside all objects to locate small pieces of evidence. Check pockets of clothing, inside books, and inside appliances—especially refrigerators and freezers. If conducting a search under a warrant yields additional evidence items that are not included in the affidavit, the warrant must be modified to include any new items seized before leaving the crime scene.

Crime Scene Search Methods

The particular method used to conduct a formal crime scene walk-through will depend largely on the nature of the crime scene. Some methods are best suited for searches indoors, outdoors, in water, on roadways, or in countless other characteristics of crime scenes encountered by investigators. Furthermore, some situations may not be optimal for any one search method; thus, a **hybrid search** consisting of two or more methods may be required to carry out the search of a single crime scene. The following are among the most commonly utilized crime scene search methods (see Figure 3.34 for illustrated examples):

1. **Line or Strip:** The crime scene is divided into a series of lanes or strips across the search area. The distance

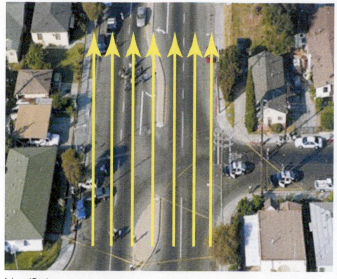

Line/Strip

Grid

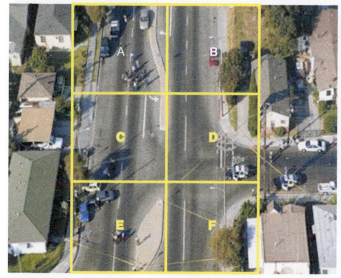

Zone

Link

Outward Spiral

Inward Spiral

FIGURE 3.34 ▶ Crime scene area search methods.

from each lane to the next is usually about an arm's length, or an area no wider than would permit searchers to clearly visualize evidence. The search is conducted by walking down each lane, looking ahead and from side to side attempting to locate physical evidence. Discovered evidence is marked or designated without disturbing its position. This method is best for searching large areas with large numbers of persons conducting the search. It is especially useful for conducting outdoor searches for small- or medium-size objects (such as cartridge casing and handguns). When used indoors, the method is easily adapted to building locations with large open floor plans—as in a warehouse or airport search.[33]

2. *Grid:* For the most part, the grid search is an extension of the line or strip method and is sometimes called the *double-strip technique*. It is performed by first conducting a standard line or strip search of the crime scene. Following this, a second set of lanes is searched, which are positioned perpendicular to the first set of lanes (forming the grid). This, in effect, results in a second search of the same area from a different position. This method is extremely useful when it is necessary to conduct an intensive search for small pieces of evidence that may be concealed within ground cover (weeds, grass, natural foliage), or beneath dirt and gravel within rocky terrain.[34]

3. *Spiral:* Evidence is searched for in a series of concentric circles or spirals that may begin from the inside of the crime scene and extend to the outer perimeter (known as an **outward spiral**) or from the outward perimeter to the innermost area of the crime scene (known as an **inward spiral**, considered by many investigators to be the best method). The distance of each concentric circle from the other is usually that which is optimal for visualizing evidence. This method is best applied to larger outdoor crime scenes, including those involving snow or water, where searches are focused on the discovery of bodies or other large sized evidence.[35]

4. *Link:* Searches are conducted along paths the most likely to contain evidence as indicated by existing physical evidence patterns in the crime scene. In other words, evidence search methods and locations are guided by the investigator's intuition and crime reconstruction theories regarding the linkage or association between the suspect, victim, physical evidence, and the crime scene.[36]

5. *Zone:* Distinct areas or zones—either artificially constructed (measured outdoor sections of terrain, for example) or naturally occurring (as in the rooms of a house)—are searched for evidence. Larger zones can be constructed, and then smaller zones can be constructed within the larger ones, as in a street area divided into separate addresses or blocks. Zones can be carried out indoors or outdoors, and can easily be combined with line, spiral, link, grid, or other search methods. They are extremely effective for searches in crime scenes where the same item of evidence has passed through several separate locations (or zones), such as trails of blood created by a fleeing suspect, or bullets passing through several walls of a building.[37]

CASE CLOSE-UP 3.5

JANE DOE IN THE SNOW
(Clackamas County, Oregon)

The nude body of an unidentified female in her early 20s was discovered lying face down in about 18 inches of snow near the side of a rural interstate highway. Around 10 A.M., crime scene investigators conducted a line search of the location around the body and discovered no blood, no signs of footprints, and no footprints or tire marks. Measurements revealed that the woman's body was lying in a position perpendicular to the highway in about 6 ft. of packed snow and was located approximately 14 feet from the roadway's edge. Weather reports indicated that it had been several days since there was new snowfall in the area, so any tracks in the snow should have remained intact and visible. The medical examiner's report indicated that the woman's blood alcohol level was .18 (.08 being the legal limit) and that she had had sexual intercourse sometime before her death. Her 5'3" 120 lb. body showed no signs of trauma indicating that she had been shot, beaten, strangled, or subject to any other means of physical assault. Two pieces of jewelry belonging to a necklace, a heart-shaped locket, and a silver letter "L" were discovered without the chain to which they were attached. Due to circumstances of the crime scene, irrespective of the lack of evidence, investigators believed the woman was murdered.

HOT TIPS AND LEADS 3.2

Health and Safety Hazards at the Crime Scene

Before entering the crime scene, assess and inquire to discover the existence of any health and safety hazard. Many of these situations are not so obvious, and can be deadly.

WATCH OUT FOR:

1. *Toxic or explosive chemicals.* Solvents and acids found in industrial manufacturing plants as well as in clandestine drug laboratories produce toxic vapors and can explode when mixed together. Toxic effects can be transmitted by inhalation, ingestion, or direct contact with the skin.

2. *Smoke.* Smoke at a fire scene may contain dangerous vapors from accelerants, plastics resins, lead, or other toxic substances. Even after a fire is extinguished, smoldering material may emit hazardous vapors.

3. *Agricultural materials.* Orchards, nurseries, farmland, and other agricultural areas can contain harmful pesticides, insecticides, fungicides, and other toxic poisons.

4. *Bloodborne pathogens.* Potentially fatal viruses such as human immunodeficiency virus (HIV), hepatitis B (HBV), and hepatitis C (HCV) are spread primarily through contact with blood and semen; however, they can also be transmitted through contact with bodily fluids and tissues that contain visible blood. Needle sticks; cuts; fluid splashes to the eyes, nose, and mouth; or exposure to breaks in the skin are possible sources of disease transmission. HIV virus dies upon exposure to light and air. HBV, however, can survive in dried blood up to 1 week.

5. *Airborne pathogens.* Many diseases can be contracted through breathing them in the air. Tuberculosis is among these. Infection usually takes place through inhalation in confined locations infected by diseased individuals through coughing, sneezing, or spitting.

6. *Forensic products.* Dust and chemicals used to visualize fingerprints are harmful to eyes and lungs—and some contain known carcinogens. Prolonged exposure to UV and laser light can cause damage to vision. Numerous chemicals used for forensic testing are toxic and/or fatal if inhaled, ingested, or absorbed by skin contact.

7. *Physical hazards.* Buildings that have been burned, or structures where an explosion has taken place may collapse when entered. Other locations such as mines, caves, sewers, and unsupported dirt ditches that can collapse and trap investigators should be thoroughly examined before entry.

WHAT TO DO: Use your PPE (Personal Protective Equipment). PPE is graded as A, B, C, or D. Level A guards against

FIGURE 3.35 ▶ Level D Personal Protective Equipment (PPE) used for the most severe health and safety hazards at a crime scene. In this case, the investigator is performing a walk-through of a meth lab.

the lightest or nuisance contaminants and involves the use of gloves, footwear covers, protective gowns, and other barrier protective devises. For the most serious contaminants, Level D PPEs are employed, which include the use of full-body chemical protective suits utilizing an air-purifying respirator (see Figure 3.35). If exposed to any potentially harmful agents by touch, bite, cut, needle stick, or otherwise, wash the affected area with water and soap, antiseptic cleanser, or other antibacterial agent; notify supervisors; and seek professional medical assistance immediately. Guard against smoke and vapor inhalation by standing downwind of potentially toxic airborne agents.

Sources: Based on information from Federal Bureau of Investigation, *FBI Handbook of Crime Scene Forensics*, Skyhorse Publishing, 2008; National Institute of Justice, *Guide for the Selection of Personal Protection Equipment for Emergency First Responders* (Washington, DC: USGPO, 2002).

COMPLETING THE PRELIMINARY INVESTIGATION

During the crime scene search, any evidence that is identified will be photographed, collected, packaged, labeled, logged, and placed in a secured evidence storage area or immediately transported to a crime laboratory for analysis. The specific procedures used following the identification of physical evidence at the crime scene are outlined and described in the Chapter 4, "Identifying, Collecting, and Processing Physical Evidence." Suffice it to say, the preliminary investigation will continue until either all necessary or possible evidence has been collected or it no longer is feasible to continue processing the crime scene. In the latter situation, possible scenarios include extreme weather conditions (rain, snow, wind, extreme heat), hazards to investigators (dangerous wildlife, chemicals, poisons, or other threats to human life), or time constraints (investigators are needed at another more serious crime scene, or extended crime scene processing will place an excess burden on business or transportation flow).

After all members of the crime scene search team have agreed that enough evidence has been gathered from the scene, the lead investigator will order a **release of the crime scene**. Before releasing the scene, however, the investigative team should conduct a **final walk-through** to make sure no evidence, tools, equipment, or other items involved in the crime scene search have been left behind. Usually a crime scene release form—including the time, date, scene location, and the persons present to whom the scene is released—is completed by the investigator initiating the release. Unfortunately, the burden of cleaning the scene after it has been released usually rests on private individuals who are in legal control of the location or property affected by the crime. Crime scene personnel should advise such persons in charge of cleaning a scene containing biological matter or bodily fluids such as blood to take health precautions while doing so. Private companies exist that specialize in the professional clean-up of crime scenes for a fee.

In many cases, the preliminary investigation is the last step in the investigator's search for case evidence. On the one hand, if the evidence obtained thus far is sufficient to prove an offense beyond a reasonable doubt, the case will proceed to prosecution without further investigation. In the event that evidence from the preliminary investigation proves that no crime was committed (perhaps due to victim or eyewitness error), the evidence available is too weak to build a case, or perhaps the crime was fabricated or staged by the victim (where the victim now becomes the perpetrator), the case may be dropped entirely as the result of the preliminary investigation. If, however, the investigator's review and analysis of all available evidence gathered during the preliminary investigation suggest new leads—additional witnesses or information to corroborate existing suspect, victim, or witness statements—a follow-up investigation may be ordered. The follow-up investigation is specifically presented and outlined in Chapter 7.

Summary

1. **The role of criminal investigators.**

   The primary role of criminal investigators is to focus on the specific aspects of evidence needed to establish whether or not a crime has been committed; and, if they do, to discover the necessary evidence to prove that a particular suspect committed or did not commit the crime. In addition to identifying crimes and criminal suspects, investigators must gather sufficient evidence to build cases that can be successfully prosecuted in a court of law.

2. **The investigative process and the stages of criminal investigation.**

   The first stage of the investigative process involves the detection of a crime. The second stage of the investigative process begins with the preliminary investigation, which is initiated at the time authorities begin their response to the crime. The preliminary investigation comes to a close when the initial search of the crime scene is concluded. The third stage is the follow-up investigation, where further evidence is gathered to build a case. The fourth and last stage requires the investigators to use available evidence to build a case for prosecution.

3. **The first responder's duties during the preliminary investigation.**

   First responders have the following primary duties during the preliminary investigation: 1. Approaching the Crime Scene, 2. Entering the Crime Scene, 3. Controlling and Securing the Crime Scene, 4. Establishing Crime Scene Boundaries, 5. Preserving Crime Scene Evidence, and 6. Briefing the Investigators and Documenting the Crime Scene.

4. **The investigator's role during the preliminary investigation.**

   The investigator's role at the crime scene is to facilitate and coordinate evidence gathering activities at the scene. This includes conducting a reassessment of the first responder's crime scene setup, interviewing witnesses, coordinating a canvass of the crime scene vicinity, performing a preliminary walk-through of the crime scene, as well as processing and documenting the crime scene for available evidence.

5. **Techniques of crime scene photography.**

   Photographs are taken to create a permanent record of the crime scene and crime scene evidence. Photos of individual pieces of evidence are taken in a series that captures long-range, mid-range, and close-up images to tell the story of the crime committed, and to show the evidence within the context of the entire crime scene. Photographs are taken in color, with the exception of black-and-white images combined with oblique lighting to create contrast to capture the 3-D aspects of impression evidence such as footprints and tire tracks.

6. **The principles of crime scene sketching and measurement.**

Crime scene sketching is used to document key characteristics of the crime scene and the exact location, physical dimensions, and distances of evidence and other key objects located within the crime scene. Methods of crimes scene measurement used to determine specific scales and measures in the sketch include the following: 1. Rectangular Coordinates, 2. Triangulation, 3. Baseline Coordinates, 4. Polar Coordinates, and 5. Total Station Method.

7. **Crime scene search methods.**

A full search of the crime scene is conducted using an appropriate method, given factors such as the physical and geographic nature of the crime scene, or available personnel on hand to conduct the search. Methods available include: 1. Line or Strip, 2. Grid, 3. Spiral, 4. Link, 5. Zone.

Key Terms

crime scene investigation
ABFO#2
criminal investigators
investigative team
oblique lighting
rectangular coordinates
smoking gun evidence
physical crime scenes
electronic crime scenes
reactive crime detection
proactive crime detection
preliminary investigation
secondary crime scene
crime scene sketch
center of mass
grid system
asset forfeiture laws
macroscopic scene
processing the crime scene
crime scene technician

first responder
baseline coordinates
electronic distance meter (EDM)
lead investigators
polar coordinates
relevant and material
triangulation
transient evidence
evidence collection teams
crime scene core
peripheral crime scene
primary crime scene
inward spiral
rough sketch
secondary reference point
    coordinates
total station
legal elements
microscopic scene
photo log

release of the crime scene
preliminary walk-through
C.I.A.
forensic videography
logistics map
principal investigators
report of investigation (ROI)
outer or extended area
staging area
crime scene storage area
hybrid search
outward spiral
follow-up investigation
finished sketch
elevated perspective
datum point
crime scene photography
associative evidence
final walk-through

Review Questions

1. What are the three types of evidence that are most important to criminal investigations? Provide an example of each.

2. Name some of the essential traits of investigators. Which ones do you think are most important and why?

3. Who are some of the members of the investigative team? What are their functions during an investigation?

4. What does the C.I.A. acronym stand for and how does it help explain the goals and objectives of criminal investigation?

5. What is the difference between a hot, a warm, and a cold case? Provide an example of each.

6. What are the main steps in the investigative process?

7. It is often argued that the first responder to a crime scene plays one of the most vital roles in determining the ultimate success or failure of an investigation. Do you feel this statement is true? Explain why.

8. What are some of the key functions performed by investigators during the preliminary investigation?

9. What is meant by the term *forensic photography*? Of what importance is it to crime scene investigation?

10. What is the difference between a rough and a final crime scene sketch? Why is crime scene measurement of importance to the creation of a crime scene sketch?

11. Which crime scene search method would you use to locate a handgun thrown by a fleeing offender along a hiking path located in a wooded mountainous area? Why is this method most appropriate?

Internet Resources

Association for Crime Scene Reconstruction	www.acsr.org
FBI Investigator Job Description	www.fbi.gov
International Crime Scene Investigators Association	www.icsia.org
High Technology Crime Investigation Association	www.htcia.org
International Association for Identification	www.theiai.org
Federal Law Enforcement Training Center	www.fletc.gov
Evidence Technology Magazine	www.evidencemagazine.com

Applied Investigative Exercise

Examine the various crime scene photos provided in Case Example 3A. Imagine yourself as the first responder or investigator on the scene. Discuss each step of the preliminary investigation process as it relates to the sequence of photos. How would you handle the scene? What are some of the most important factors to consider during your investigation? Try to reconstruct the crime to determine what exactly happened here.

Notes

[1] William Sanders, *Detective Work: A Study of Criminal Investigations* (Montclair, NJ: Patterson Smith, 1977).

[2] Jack Kuykendall, "The Municipal Police Detective," 88–91, in D. Kenney (Ed.) *Police and Policing* (New York: Praeger, 1989); Peter Greenwood., Jan Chaiken, and Joan Petersilia, *The Criminal Investigation Process* (Santa Monica, CA: Rand Institute, 1975).

[3] Ross M. Gardner, *Practical Crime Scene Processing and Investigation* (Boca Raton, FL: CRC Press, 2005).

[4] National Institute of Justice, *Crime Scene Investigation: A Reference for Law Enforcement Training* (Washington, DC: U.S. Government Printing Office, 2004).

[5] Ibid., 11.

[6] Ibid., 12.

[7] Ibid., 14.

[8] Ibid., 18.

[9] Ibid., 20.

[10] Ibid., 22.

[11] Ibid., 25.

[12] Ibid., 25–28.

[13] Olivier Ribaux, Amélie Baylon, Eric Lock, and Olivier Delémont, "Intelligence Led Crime Scene Processing," *Forensic Science International*. Vol. 199, No. 1–3 (June 15, 2010), 63.

[14] Barry A. J. Fisher, *Techniques of Crime Scene Investigation*, 7th ed. (Boca Raton, FL: CRC Press, 2005); Mike Byrd, *Duty Description for the Crime Scene Investigator*, posted at www.crime-scene-investigator.net/dutydescription.html; George Schiro, *Protecting the Crime Scene*, posted at www.crime-scene-investigator.net/evidenc1.html.

[15] Ibid.

[16] Vernon J. Geberth, *Practical Homicide Investigation Checklist and Field Guide* (New York: CRC Press, 1996).

[17] Center for Disease Control, *Guidelines for Prevention of Transmission of Human Immunodeficiency Virus and Hepatitis B Virus to Health-Care and Public-Safety Workers*, posted at wonder.cdc.gov/wonder/prevguid/p0000114/p0000114.asp; Mike Byrd, *Hazards and a Crime Scene*, posted at www.crime-scene-investigator.net/hazards.html; John W. Bond, Christine Hammond, "The Value of DNA Material Recovered from Crime Scenes," *Journal of Forensic Sciences*, Vol. 53, No. 4 (June, 2008), 79.

[18] John Horswell, *The Practice of Crime Scene Investigation* (Boca Raton, FL: CRC Press, 2004); Federal Bureau of Investigation, *FBI Handbook of Forensic Science, Collection, Identification and Shipping Index* (Washington, DC: Federal Bureau of Investigation, 2004).

[19] Paul L. Kirk, *Crime Investigation*, 2nd ed. (New York: John Wiley & Sons, 1974).

[20] Charles O'Hara and Gregory O'Hara, *Fundamentals of Criminal Investigation*, 7th ed. (Charles C. Thomas, Springfield, IL: 2003).

[21] Richard H. Fox and Carl L. Cunningham, *Crime Scene Search and Physical Evidence Handbook* (Washington, DC: U.S. Department of Justice, National Institute of Justice, 1973); Bureau of Alcohol, Tobacco and Firearms, *Crime Scene and Evidence Collection Handbook* (Washington, DC: U.S. Government Printing Office, 1999).

[22] International Association for Identification, *Crime Scene Photography Requirement for Criminal Investigative Analysis*, posted at www.iowaiai.org/crime_scene_photography_requirements_of_criminal_investigative_analysis.html.

[23] Ibid.

[24] Ibid.

[25] Ibid.

[26]Robert Ogle, *Crime Scene Investigation and Reconstruction* (Upper Saddle River, NJ: Prentice Hall, 2003).

[27]W. Jerry Chisum and Brent E. Turvey, *Crime Reconstruction* (San Diego, CA: Academic Press, 2007); Louis B. Schlesinger, "Psychological Profiling: Investigative Implications for Crime Scene Analysis," *Journal of Psychiatry & Law*, Vol. 37, No. 1 (Spring 2009), 7.

[28]Charles R. Swanson, Neil Chamelin, Leonard Territo, and Robert Taylor, *Criminal Investigation*, 10th ed. (New York: McGraw-Hill, 2009).

[29]Ibid., 81.

[30]Ibid., 82.

[31]Ibid., 83.

[32]Ibid., 84.

[33]Henry C. Lee, Timothy Palback, and Marilyn Miller, *Crime Scene Handbook* (San Diego, CA: Academic Press, 2001).

[34]Ibid., 122–123.

[35]Ibid., 124–125.

[36]Ibid., 126–127.

[37]Ibid., 128.

CHAPTER FOUR

IDENTIFYING, COLLECTING, AND PRESERVING PHYSICAL EVIDENCE

Learning Objectives

After completing this chapter, you should be able to:

1. Describe the various types and forms of physical evidence.
2. Distinguish between class and individual evidence.
3. Understand the essential tasks of physical evidence collection and preservation.
4. Describe the science of fingerprinting, the different types of fingerprint patterns, and how fingerprints are collected and developed.
5. Describe how firearms used in crimes are examined.
6. Describe how blood evidence is examined.
7. Summarize various other types of evidence and methods of identification.

Chapter Outline

Classifying Physical Evidence
- Types of Physical Evidence
- Class and Individual Characteristics
- Making an Identification

Obtaining Physical Evidence
- Locard's Exchange Principle
- Comparison Samples
- Chain of Custody
- The Evidence Collection Process
- Alternate Light Sources

Fingerprints
- Fingerprint Characteristics
- Categories of Prints
- Locating Prints
- Capturing Prints
- Hard and Nonporous Surfaces: Powder Developers
- Soft and Porous Surfaces: Chemical Developers
- Order of Applications
- Securing and Packaging Fingerprint Evidence

Object Print and Impression Evidence
- Photographic Techniques
- Evidence Collection and Preservation Methods
- Casting Impressions
- Tire Impressions
- Obtaining Matching Physical Evidence

Tool Mark Evidence

Firearms Evidence
- Handling Firearms
- Ammunition Evidence
- Gunshot Residue (GSR)
- Ballistics Evidence
- Classifying and Individualizing Firearms Evidence

Arson Evidence

Blood Evidence
- Identifying Blood Evidence
- Collecting Blood Evidence
- Testing for the Presence of Blood
- Blood Spatter
- Special Blood Spatter Indicators

Dental Evidence

Skeletal Remains

Soil, Dust, and Botanical Evidence
- Soil
- Dust and Botanicals

Glass Evidence
- Classifying Glass
- Individualizing Glass
- Origin and Direction of Fractures
- Cause of Breakage

- Order of Impact
- Vehicle Lamp Evidence
- Handling Glass Evidence

Hairs, Fibers, Cordage, and Tape

Paint Evidence

Abrasive evidence

Questioned Documents
- Handwriting Analysis and Comparisons
- Other Documents Examinations
- Analytical Techniques

INTRODUCTION

NOVELIST SIR ARTHUR CONAN DOYLE should perhaps be credited with first suggesting to investigators that physical objects present within a crime scene could be used to identify, exclude, and prove the guilt of suspected offenders. Doyle, a medical doctor whose practice was failing, decided to make a living writing about the imaginary detective Sherlock Holmes—who introduced the practice of solving crime by using scientific principles. Observations such as "the size and shape of shoe prints as well as the relatively long distance between them indicates the suspect is male, tall, and walks with a limp" and similar fictional ones by Holmes arguably laid the groundwork for modern-day use of physical evidence as an investigative tool. Ironically, the influence of make-believe stories focusing on physical evidence and crime scene investigations appears to be just as profound today as it was over 100 years ago when Sherlock Holmes was introduced. Specifically, media portrayals of modern investigators who employ laser lighting, computerized imaging devices, and other high-tech innovations have had profound effects on both the public and the practice of criminal investigation. Researchers studying this phenomenon call it the **C.S.I. Effect**, referring to the popular television show "Crime Scene Investigation." This theory argues that fictional stories of superhuman investigators using crime

analysis methods that resemble science fiction have created citizens who expect elaborate forms of physical evidence to be gathered at crime scenes and presented in court. This, in turn, has placed added pressure on investigators to not only uncover physical evidence at crime scenes, but also to present it in the courtroom in a way that satisfies juror demands and dispels many of the scientific myths perpetuated by the media. Perhaps now, more than ever before, it is critical for investigators to know both the facts and fallacies about physical evidence. This information is discussed in the following chapter, along with state-of-the art methods for identifying, collecting, and preserving physical evidence.

CLASSIFYING PHYSICAL EVIDENCE

Types of Physical Evidence

Physical evidence generally can be defined as anything with tangible qualities, no matter how small, that can be measured or visualized to provide information about an actual or suspected criminal activity. This definition includes not only material objects, but also fluids, gases, and even detectable electromagnetic waves like those transmitted to microchips located in medical devices, credit cards, tracking devices, and the like. There are several broad categories within which specific types and forms of physical evidence can be placed. (Note, however, that these categories are not necessarily mutually exclusive for all types of evidence.) These include the following:

- *Trace Evidence:* This category includes objects that are undetectable with the unaided eye, and usually must be visualized using some type of specialized lighting and/or magnification device. Hairs, fibers, dust, pollen, soil, glass fragments, wood chips, and gun powder particles are some of the more common forms of trace evidence. Paul Kirk (1902–1970), considered by many to be the father of modern criminalistics, pioneered many of the trace evidence procedures presently used in the practice of criminal investigation.

* *Impression Evidence:* Shoe prints, tire tracks, cloth, cordage, bite marks, and even fingerprints are common forms of **impression evidence**. Any object that causes an image of itself by penetrating another object or surface area qualifies as a form of impression evidence. Likely locations for discovering impression evidence outdoors include mud, snow, loose dirt, and sand. Indoors, shoe prints, and finger prints are often discovered on dusty surfaces such as floors, window sills, and chairs.

* *Biological Evidence:* Bodily fluids and tissues comprise most evidence that would be considered biological in nature. Blood, urine, semen, sweat, and mucus as well as bones, skin, and other soft tissues of the body are all examples of biological evidence. Besides being highly perishable and potentially hazardous to handle, the identification, collection, and preservation of this type of evidence is often considered by investigators to be of foremost importance because of its potential to provide an offender's DNA profile.

* *Firearms and Weapons Evidence:* Includes the identification of specific types of guns, rifles, shotguns, ammunition, knives, and specialized devices used as weapons.

* *Documents Evidence:* Includes documents in paper, electronic, or other physical form such as contracts, wills, checks or other currency, licenses, passports, and other official documentation.

Figure 4.1 shows documents evidence in the form of sports memorabilia. The baseball depicted contains a fraudulent signature of the legendary Babe Ruth and was sold to an unsuspecting collector who purchased it from thieves for thousands of dollars. Compare the fraudulent signature (see Figure 4.1(a)) to that of the real Babe Ruth's signature shown on the photograph in Figure 4.1(b).

Class and Individual Characteristics

It is further possible to group all types of physical evidence by class and individual characteristics. **Class characteristics** are simply what individual pieces of evidence have in common. Once these common traits are identified, general categories for identifying and grouping like forms of evidence can be

(a)

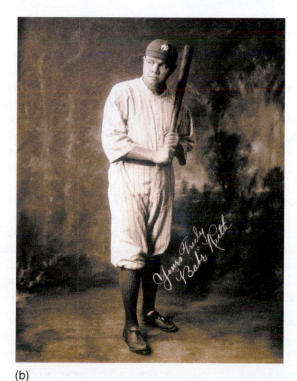

(b)

FIGURE 4.1 ▶ (a) Pictured to the left is a baseball allegedly signed by Babe Ruth, which sold for thousands of dollars at an antique auction. After the signature was determined to be a forgery, this baseball became key physical evidence in a criminal investigation resulting in the arrest and conviction of several individuals selling fraudulent sports memorabilia. (b) The photograph to the right bears Babe Ruth's real signature, showing that the signed baseball is clearly a fake. ((b) courtesy of © Everett Collection Inc / Alamy)

provided. For example, hairs can be classed by size, shape, color, or the body part from which they originated (e.g., head, beard, limb, etc.). Likewise, firearms can be classed by their type: pistol, rifle, or shotgun. Any type of physical evidence can be placed into a given class based on its characteristics. However, this type of evidence identification is limited in that it does not allow for the determination of the specific person, place, or thing from which it originated. In other words, knowing from a shoe print impression that a burglar was wearing a size 10 men's Nike cross-trainer tennis shoe does not permit the investigator to claim that this shoe belonged to a specific suspect.

On the other hand, **individual characteristics** do allow a specific piece of physical evidence to be identified as originating from a specific person, place, or thing. Not all types of physical evidence possess the uniqueness to be individualized. To meet this highest standard of identification, the claim that no two pieces of evidence are alike, or that there is an extremely low probability of two pieces of evidence being alike must be supported by facts. For example, it is argued that only one individual can possess a specific set of fingerprints. Conversely, there is always the chance that two individuals share the same DNA profile; however, depending on the analytical methods used, the probability of this occurring can be reduced to as little as 1 in 1 billion persons. As can be imagined, evidence possessing individual characteristics is the most sought after in any criminal investigation.

Making an Identification

The term **identification** refers to physical evidence's ability to prove beyond a reasonable doubt that a specific individual committed a specific criminal act. In other words, a judge or juror determining guilt or innocence in a criminal trial would be sufficiently convinced by the available evidence that the accused was indeed guilty as charged. An identification is extremely unlikely to be made when only one or two pieces of class evidence are presented in support of a case. Furthermore, reasonable doubt can be cast on a piece of individualized evidence used for an identification when defense counsel question the nature of its quality, its handling by investigators, and its analysis in the crime lab. However, combining class and individual evidence can be a potent method for overcoming reasonable doubts raised during the identification process. Therefore, at a minimum, the following formula is recommended for use when attempting to perform identification with physical evidence:

At Least 2 Pieces of Class Evidence + At Least 1 Piece of Individualized Evidence = Identification

OBTAINING PHYSICAL EVIDENCE

Locard's Exchange Principle

Locard's **exchange principle**[1] that every contact leaves a trace is deceptively simple. In reality, the latter proposition makes several important points regarding physical evidence and the

FIGURE 4.2 ▶ A criminalist examines the hood of a vehicle involved in a crime. Opaque lighting reveals several footprints from the suspect caused by residue from the shoes' contact with the hood's painted surface—demonstrating Locard's exchange principle. In addition, shoe type may be identified as a class characteristic, and distinct wear patterns evidenced in the print can be used to "individualize" the shoes as belonging to the suspect.

criminal investigation process. First, if contact or an exchange between two objects has taken place, there is at the very least a trace of evidence to be found on each object. Thus, if it can be established that offenders or their instruments of crime have made contact with anything or anyone, there is physical evidence to be discovered in the crime scene. Contact evidence in the form of a suspect's footprints left on the hood of a vehicle is shown in Figure 4.2.

Often, the manner in which two objects make contact will leave distinct patterns or makings that enable a physical match between materials that have been transferred to each object. For example, consider a screwdriver used by a burglar to pry open a window. According to the exchange principle, traces of the screwdriver in the form of scratches and other toolmarks will be found in the area where it made contact with the window. Likewise, traces of the window, perhaps consisting of miniscule paint chips, will be discovered on the screwdriver's blade upon microscopic examination. Furthermore, it may be possible to match the various shaped paint chip traces to the scratch patterns on the window in a jigsaw puzzle–like fashion to prove that the screwdriver was indeed used for purposes of burglary.

Another equally important investigative assumption drawn from the exchange principle is that a piece of evidence can become tainted by allowing it to make contact with some other physical material. This process involving an unwanted transfer of physical material to a piece of evidence is called **cross-contamination**. To avoid cross-contamination, evidence must be collected, packaged, and handled in such a way that it does not make contact with other items of evidence or foreign physical materials. Biological evidence is especially susceptible to the effects of cross-contamination. Bacteria can be introduced to blood and other bodily fluids through a variety of external sources, quickly rendering such evidence useless.

Comparison Samples

The primary purpose of comparison samples is to determine the origin of an unknown piece of evidence, referred to as **questioned evidence**, by matching it to other materials of known origin. This process, as illustrated below, allows for the identification of the unknown/questioned evidence's origin, which may be linked to a person, place, or thing related to the crime under investigation:

Evidence at Crime Scene	Evidence Discovered Outside of Crime Scene
Unknown/Questioned Origin ⟶	Known Origin
Known Origin ⟵	Unknown/Questioned Origin

Samples generally consist of a small amount of physical material, of a known or unknown/questioned origin, that is removed from the crime scene and stored for purposes of later comparison. Unknown/questioned comparison samples include the following:

- Materials/evidence at the crime scene that have an unknown origin, but may be matched later to sources related to the criminal act, such as offender and victims. Example: Carpet fibers found in a burglarized apartment will all tile flooring.
- Materials/evidence that may have been transferred to offenders and taken away with them from the crime scene. Example: Paint from the exterior of an ATM machine that has been robbed by ramming a vehicle into it.
- Materials/evidence of an unknown source obtained from several crime scenes used to associate two or more separate crimes that may have been committed by the same offender(s), tools, or weapons. Example: Soil samples taken from muddy shoe prints at multiple locations where it is believed that the same offender has carried out a series of aggravated sexual assaults.

Comparison samples involving materials/evidence of a known origin at the crime scene include the following:

- Standard or **reference samples** consist of materials taken from a verifiable source, which, when compared with evidence of an unknown source, show an association between the crime scene and/or the offender(s) and victim(s). For example, a sample of soil may be taken from where a body is dumped by a killer for the purpose of comparing it later with soil discovered in a suspect's shoes; similarly, a piece of carpet is removed from an apartment living room where a sexual assault has taken place to provide a comparison between carpet fibers in the room and fibers discovered on the pants of a suspected rapist that may have transferred to his clothing when the crime was committed.

- **Control samples** (or *blank samples*) are uncontaminated materials obtained from the same origin as that of crime scene evidence physically contaminated at the time the crime was committed. For example, a chip of paint may be taken from the hood of a car next to an area that was dented while striking a pedestrian. The crime lab will use the control sample to examine layers of paint and other qualities of the undamaged area of the hood to assess likely changes in the painted surface of the damaged area after striking the victim; also, a small section of linoleum flooring that has not been burned in a suspected arson fire may be removed as a control sample to compare with burnt sections of flooring that contain traces of gasoline used as an accelerant.

- **Elimination samples** are taken from known sources, usually individuals, that were not involved in the criminal activity being investigated but were lawfully present at the crime scene. The purpose of these samples is to help eliminate evidence left at crime scene that was the product of lawful activities. For example, the fingerprints of medical emergency personnel can be taken as elimination samples so that prints left at the scene by an offender can be isolated and identified; likewise, when a woman has had sexual intercourse with her partner and was raped a short time later by a stranger, an elimination sample of blood can be taken from her partner to eliminate his DNA as that of the rapist.

Chain of Custody

The **chain of custody** is a written record that documents the handling of any physical evidence (including that of an electronic origin) from the time it is collected at the crime scene. The purpose of this procedure is to provide a chain of persons possessing the evidence that ensures the following:

- The evidence presented in court is the evidence discovered at the crime scene.
- The evidence has not been subject to cross-contamination by coming into contact with other evidence or physical materials.
- The evidence has not been intentionally altered to suggest guilt of a suspect.

Once evidence has been identified, marked, and packaged at the crime scene, the investigator or technician initially handling the evidence will start the chain of custody. The documentation, printed on the outside of the package containing the evidence or somehow otherwise affixed to the evidence, contains information such as names of persons handling the evidence; times and dates, locations, and purposes for handling

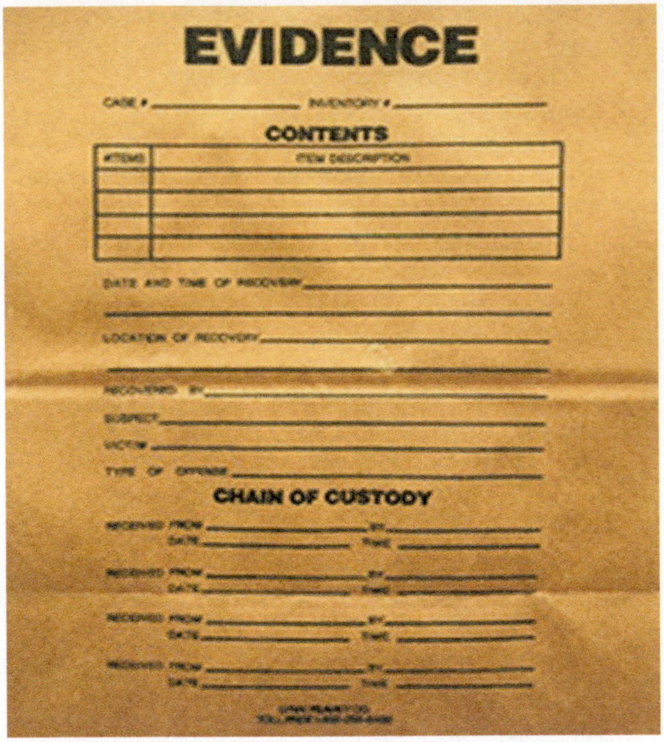

FIGURE 4.3 ▶ Paper evidence bag for containing case and evidence information; chain-of-custody information is noted on the outside. (Courtesy U.S. Department of Justice)

the evidence; the condition of the evidence and anything done to it; and the signature of the handler. This information is provided by each person thereafter who subsequently handles the evidence. Many evidence containers, such as the bag shown in Figure 4.3, have chain-of-custody logs printed directly on them to keep the log together with the container.

In general, the length of an evidence chain should be kept as short as possible. The fewer people who handle the evidence, the less likely claims can be raised that the chain has been broken—which likely will render the evidence inadmissible for presentation in court. Broken chains usually result when there were persons who handled that evidence who are not recorded in the chain of custody documentation or when periods of time in the history of handling the evidence cannot be accounted for. If the evidence is believed to have been contaminated, the chain of custody can be referenced to determine who contaminated the evidence, when, and how.

The Evidence Collection Process

As a general rule, different types of evidence require different handling methods to ensure proper preservation and documentation. It should be noted, however, that all evidence must be:

1. Collected from the crime scene in such a way that it is not contaminated or changed from its original condition;
2. Identified by tagging, marking, inscribing, or labeling;
3. Packaged in such a way that it is not damaged or contaminated;
4. Documented so that an unbroken chain of custody is established;
5. Transported safely to a crime lab or evidence storage facility; and
6. Stored within a secure location so that its legal integrity cannot be questioned.

Alternate Light Sources

When collecting physical evidence at the crime scene, it is often difficult to visualize trace evidence, fingerprints, and impressions made by objects such as shoes, tires, and tools. This is because standard lighting sources, including daylight, cause background surfaces to glow, making it difficult to visualize small or latent materials. Special light sources, operating at wavelengths that differ from standard lighting, have been developed that cause specific evidence items to glow rather than the backgrounds on which they are located. There are various forms of **alternate light sources (ALS)** including ultraviolet (UV), infrared, krypton, halogen, fluorescent, laser, and light emitting diodes (LED), which can be used along with highly specialized filter materials to make hidden evidence highly visible. For example, UV light applied to bodily fluids, including semen, saliva, urine, and blood, causes organic properties in these materials to **fluoresce** and produce a highly visible glow (see Figure 4.4). UV is also useful for the illumination of fingerprints, and its use is particularly effective to illuminate difficult-to-visualize evidence such as hairs, fibers, glass, paint, bone fragments, and bite marks. Blue UV light combined with an orange filter barrier (usually in the form of tinted goggles or lens filters for cameras) can make small fragments of bone and teeth highly visible as well. Infrared lighting often can be used to visualize objects that cannot be distinguished from the background or surface area in which they are located by detecting differing levels of heat absorbed by the evidence and background materials. For example, a greasy fingerprint on a black T-shirt, which would not be visible under standard light, would become highly visible under infrared lighting due to heat absorption differences in the grease and cloth surfaces.

Numerous other forms of light can be used to illuminate fingerprints invisible to the unaided eye, including UV, laser, blue, and green light, to name a few. Laser light can reveal fingerprints and different types of ink on paper and other documents that are over 40 years old. Specialized devices known as *forensic light sources (FLS)* have also been developed that provide a variety of ALS illumination wavelengths in a single unit used to detect various types of physical evidence that normally would require the use of several separate lighting mechanisms.

In the following sections, the specialized uses of ALS as well as other specific methods to identify, document, and generally process specific types of physical evidence encountered at crime scenes are discussed in detail.

(a)

(b)

FIGURE 4.4 ▶ (a) Photo showing the carpet in the back seat area of a rape suspect's vehicle under normal lighting. (b) The same carpet illuminated by ALS, enabling the visualization of fluorescing semen stains.

FINGERPRINTS

Fingerprints are one of the few types of evidence that can precisely identify an individual. It is often argued that fingerprints are the only type of evidence with true individual characteristics, a quality that cannot be claimed by DNA. In other words, everyone's fingerprints are unlike those of any other person. Identical twins possess different print characteristics, even though they have the same DNA profile. Not only are the unique patterns of each print an invaluable investigative resource, but the prints themselves may contain trace evidence such as hairs, fibers, glass fragments, soil, soot, blood, skin cells, and a host of other materials (discussed later in this chapter) that can provide additional investigative leads. For this reason, each fingerprint has to be identified, documented, collected, and preserved carefully and strategically to capture the potential multitude of evidence that it may contain.

Fingerprint Characteristics

It is often possible to learn a great deal about the individual leaving a fingerprint behind at a crime scene just by using sim-

ple common sense. For example, large prints are usually produced by an adult male whereas smaller ones are likely those of a female or child. Prints on handles or doors not only reveal the hand used to open them, but also may indicate whether an individual is left or right handed. Poorly defined or rough appearing prints with signs of scarring, calluses, or other damage may indicate advanced age or long-term employment involving manual labor. The height of prints located on a window, door, or cabinetry can indicate whether an individual is tall or short. By smelling prints, an investigator can sometimes determine the perfume or cologne worn by an offender or perhaps determine the petroleum product used by an arsonist.

Of greatest value to investigators, however, are the unique impressions—left by raised portions of skin on the palm side of the fingertip—called **friction ridges.** Friction ridges exist not only on tips of fingers, but also on the entire finger, palms, toes, and foot soles. The specific length, size, and patterns of these ridges, which differ among all persons, are referred to as **minutiae.** The minutiae, or combined patterns of each friction ridge on the fingertip, can be classified into one of three general types: the arch, loop, and whorl. Each finger can possess a different fingerprint type; for example, a person's thumb can be a loop and their forefinger a whorl. The general class characteristics of each fingerprint type are as follows:

- **Arches:** Recognized by the appearance of friction ridges that resemble rolling hills, without the presence of a defined center or core. Arches are the least common type of fingerprint pattern, occurring in only 5 percent of the population. They tend to be most prevalent among African-American individuals.

- **Loops:** Identified by a well-defined center or core formed by friction ridges that resemble a series of tightly wound loops. If the loops begin and end in the direction of the thumb, the print is referred to as a radial loop. Prints that begin and end in the direction of the little finger are referred to as an ulnar loop. Persons may possess varying combinations of these loop patterns on each hand. Loops are the most common fingerprint pattern, occurring in 65 percent of the population. They are most prevalent among Caucasian individuals.

- **Whorls:** Recognized by a series of round friction ridges, graduating from small to large, with a well-defined center or core that resembles the inside of an onion. There are numerous forms of whorls, some of which have highly irregular patterns that are easily distinguishable from arches and loops. Whorls are the second most common fingerprint pattern, occurring in 35 percent of the population. They are most prevalent among persons of Asian ancestry, including Latinos, Hispanics, and Native Americans.[2]

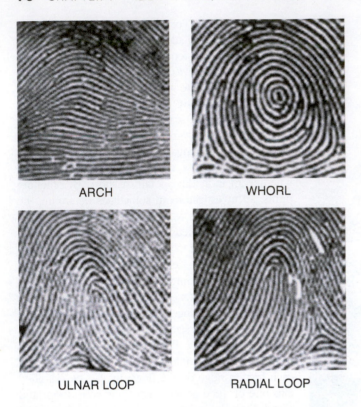

ARCH | WHORL

ULNAR LOOP | RADIAL LOOP

FIGURE 4.5 ▶ Examples of the major fingerprint patterns: Arches are characterized by a rolling "wave" or "hill" pattern; whorls are recognized by their well-defined core, somewhat resembling an onion; and loops possess a well-defined core formed by a series of friction ridges that sweep to the right or to the left. Loops with friction ridges forming the core that begin and end pointing toward the pinky finger are *ulnar loops*. Loops with friction ridges forming the core that begin and end pointing toward the thumb are *radial loops*. The example here assumes that both of the loop prints pictured are on fingers of the left hand with the palm facing upward. (Courtesy United States Department of Justice)

Whorl patterns along with other major general class characteristics of fingerprints are illustrated in Figure 4.5.

Once a fingerprint has been classified as one of the above three types, further identification of unique characteristics within the friction ridge pattern can lead to the individual's specific identity. This is the information used by computerized fingerprint analysis systems such as the FBI's AFIS (discussed in Chapter 7) to compare against databases of prints recovered from crime scenes and convicted offenders. Computer print recognition typically locates and counts the occurrence of two ridge characteristics—ridge endings and ridge bifurcations—in a digitized image of the print. However, different types and greater numbers of print identification points can be included in a fingerprint database search by customizing search settings and criteria. Sometimes only one partial print is needed to make a hit that can identify an offender existing in a computerized fingerprint database. Numerous identification points can be identified in a single fingerprint, in addition to other individualizing characteristics such as scars, creases, folds, warts, friction ridge shape, pore size, and so on. These are typically located and documented manually by a fingerprint examiner.

Categories of Prints

Fingerprints are composed of (1) residue such as dirt and oil that adheres to the friction ridges and (2) sweat released from pores located within the friction ridges. The composition of sweat is mostly water and salt. Depending upon their visibility and the nature of the surface to which they are applied, fingerprints discovered at a crime scene can be categorized as follows:

VISIBLE/CONTAMINATED PRINTS

Visible prints are visible to the unaided eye and results from the transfer to a surface of some foreign substance that has contaminated the fingers. Agents that typically cause visible prints include paint, oil, blood, dye, lipstick, cosmetics, dust, soot, and food residue (e.g., catsup, grease, chocolate).

PLASTIC PRINTS

Plastic prints are a form of visible fingerprint that is 3-dimensional in quality; that is, the fingerprint is created when pressure is applied by the finger to a soft surface. In effect, this creates an impression or mold of the finger and its surface area. Plastic prints are often found in soap, cosmetics, gum, putty, cement, and objects containing adhesives such as labels, stamps, or tape.

LATENT PRINTS

Latent prints are by far the most common at crime scenes. These prints are not visible to the unaided eye, and must be *developed* (or made visible), through the use of specialized devices, lighting, chemicals, or powders. They are produced by sweat emitted from pores within the friction ridges, mixed with body oils and other contaminants that transfer from the fingers to the object or surface. Latent prints can be found on a variety of surfaces, which are hard, soft, porous, or even wet. In rare instances, latent prints can be developed on the bodies of deceased individuals. Figure 4.6 illustrates the use of fingerprint dust to develop a latent print.

Locating Prints

An investigator, unless also acting as a first responder, is generally not the first person to arrive at a crime scene. This poses one of the most formidable problems for fingerprint recovery. Patrol officers who initially secure the crime scene, emergency medical technicians who provide aid to a victim or suspect, and other persons with prior access to the crime scene most likely will have deposited their prints as well. For this reason, the search for an identification of fingerprints must follow a targeted strategic approach such as the following:

1. ***Assess, Protect, and Collect:*** Before conducting an active search for prints, the entire situation should be assessed and a plan developed. First responders, witnesses, and other individuals who initially arrived at the scene or know about the criminal activity being investigated must be interviewed and try the areas in which they were most likely to leave their prints identified. Generally speaking, the best quality prints are found in locations least disturbed or traveled by

others. Crime scene sketches by first responders, if available, should be reviewed. In outdoor settings, prints that may be destroyed by water, rain, dew, wind, or other adverse environmental conditions are collected first. Sprinklers or any other water source that may activate and destroy prints are shut off. Prints on moveable objects are protected by placing them in a secured indoor location. Plastic or other weatherproof material should be used to cover prints located outdoors on immovable objects.

2. ***Elimination Prints:*** Elimination prints should be obtained from EMTs, first-responding officers, witnesses, or other individuals known to have touched surfaces in the crime scene before and during the first response period.

3. ***Crime Scene Reconstruction:*** The crime scene, and the likely movement of victims and offenders are reconstructed. First, the POE (point of entry) of the offender is identified, and the search for prints begins at that point before proceeding to the internal crime scene area. The POE is usually where the offender applied the most force on a surface. Door knobs and handles are probable POEs yielding prints, although their print quality is sometimes rather poor due to excessive use, smearing, and smudging. Other surfaces likely to contain usable prints include glass, aluminum foil, polished metals and wood, plastic bags, china, smooth painted surfaces, hard plastics, paper, and cardboard. In some instances, prints have been located on cigarettes, imitation leather products, fruit, and on the inside of latex or rubber coated gloves. Rarely are prints discovered on rough surfaces, unfinished wood, grainy leather, rusty or cold metal, or cloth or other absorbent materials. Surfaces covered with dust, dirt, or grease also are not likely to yield usable prints. For laboratory processing purposes, prints are generally considered old and subject to degrading 1 week after their deposit at the crime scene. However, prints on paper, cardboard, and unfinished wood have been known to last 40 years or more if they are not exposed to water or other forms of moisture.[3]

4. ***Photograph and Collect Prints:*** The primary rule to always remember when collecting fingerprint evidence is to *photograph before doing anything!* First, photograph and collect prints that are readily visible. Next, search for and photograph prints that are not visible using ALS or other vision enhancing methods. If only standard lighting is only available, reduce ambient lighting in the crime scene, and illuminate prints using a flashlight or other beam directed to the side of the suspected print location in an oblique fashion. When using ALS for identification and photographic purposes, the specific type of light best suited to a given set of prints will depend on the type of print to be visualized and the surface on which it is located. UV and blue lighting combined with red, yellow, or orange goggles

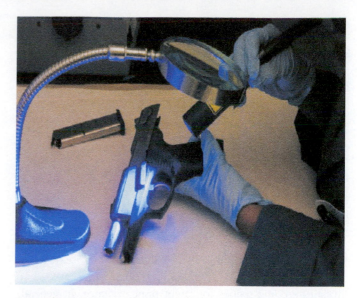

FIGURE 4.6 ▶ Possible latent prints are searched for using UV lighting.

or other filter barriers provide an excellent means for visualizing latent prints on a wide variety of surfaces and color backgrounds. Prints on paper and porous surfaces are best illuminated using a form of laser lighting. Heat applied by infrared methods to surfaces containing latent prints can often cause latent prints to be distinguished from backgrounds in which they have become hidden. It may be possible to visualize prints from fingers, palms, feet, and other body parts by using infrared thermal imaging that detects residual heat on various surface areas. This method, however, must be used relatively quickly (within 30 minutes or so) before heat contained within the print dissipates. As illustrated in Figure 4.6, when using any ALS method, the area to be visualized should be made as dark as possible and goggles or other safety eyewear worn to protect against the potentially harmful effects of ALS light rays.

Capturing Prints

If fingerprints are visible or plastic, they can be captured for analysis by physically removing the printed surface from the crime scene, or by photographing the printed surface. As previously discussed, latent fingerprints must be developed before they can be visualized and documented. Latent print development is very much a learned art perfected only by hours upon hours of practice. Specialists in fingerprint investigative methods usually attend numerous training sessions involving weeks, if not months, of formal training. Because fingerprints are often the most vital piece of evidence from a crime scene, only those investigators most experienced in fingerprinting methods and technologies should perform latent print development.

Many methods exist for developing latent fingerprints, and it is not necessary to know all of these techniques to effectively

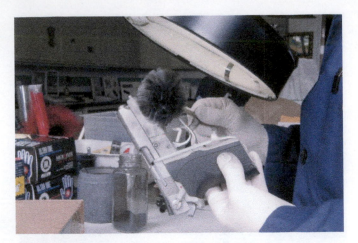

FIGURE 4.7 ▶ Latent prints are developed by dusting.

investigate crime scenes for latent print evidence. In general, the specific method selected for developing a latent print will depend on the characteristics of the surface containing the print (e.g., smooth, wet, etc.), and the nature of the residue transferred from the fingers to the surface (e.g., perspiration, oil, blood, etc.). Several of these methods, and their application to various scenarios likely encountered by investigators during a search for latent prints, are discussed below.

Hard and Nonporous Surfaces: Powder Developers

Usually, powder is used to develop latent prints on hard and nonporous (nonabsorbent) surfaces. Such surfaces include those made of metal, tile, glass, plastic, and treated wood. As illustrated in Figure 4.7, fingerprint dusting is ideal for developing latent prints on the smooth metal surfaces of a firearm. All powders have the consistency of dust, come in virtually all colors, and adhere to the perspiration and body oils composing the latent print. Most are made from carbon, charcoal, or aluminum particles and are applied with a brush containing camel's hair or fiberglass bristles. Although investigators tend to develop their own specialized techniques for dusting fingerprints, the following steps represent a basic process for using powder to develop latent prints:

1. Select the color of powder that contrasts best with the color of the surface where the latent print is located. Lighter colors are used with darker surfaces, and vice versa. This will provide the color contrast needed to clearly visualize and photograph the print. White or gray powder works best on a range of dark surfaces; for lighter surfaces, black powder is preferable. White or gray powder should also be used when processing prints on polished metal or mirrors because reflective surfaces will photograph as black in color.

2. Photograph the print surface before, during, and after the power application process. This will provide documentation of the print should the powdering process fail. At least one of these photos should include a scale.

3. Apply small quantities of powder in increments to the surface area, first by swirling the brush above the print and then lightly brushing in the direction of the friction ridges. Repeat this process until the print becomes fully visible. Carefully brush excess powder from the surface area. The application of too little powder will create an underdeveloped print that will not photograph well. Overpowdering a print will also result in a print that has poor reproductive quality.

   Specialized powders have also been created to improve the application and visualization process of latent print development. Magnetic-sensitive powder, applied with a magnetized instrument (known as a *Magna Brush*) rather than a brush with bristles, is deposited over a latent print without physical contact with the surface area. Fluorescent powders are also available that cause a latent print to glow or fluoresce in numerous colors when exposed to ultraviolet (UV), laser, and alternative light sources.

4. Preserve the print by lifting it from the surface on which it was developed. This is most often done by using clear fingerprint lifting tape. Place a section of the tape gently over the print, and roll the tape from the surface area immediately preceding the leading edge of the print. Make sure the tape is flat on all surface areas to avoid excessive bubbling of the tape. After the tape has been applied, with a small area at the end left unsecured for lifting purposes, scrape the top of the tape to remove any air bubbles. Lift the tape slowly and carefully using the unsecured tab created at the end of the strip. Secure the tape to a fingerprint backing card colored to provide the most contrast with the color of the developed print. Scrape the tape again to remove bubble areas. Mark the reverse side of the backing car with the investigator's name, case number, evidence location, evidence marker number, time, date, and other pertinent information about the print collection process. In situations where dusted prints must be lifted from irregular or curved surfaces, rough lifting tape specially designed for porous surfaces or gel lifters can be used instead of standard lifting tape.

Soft and Porous Surfaces: Chemical Developers

Chemical developers are usually employed for developing latent prints on surfaces that are soft and porous—most commonly cloth, paper, or cardboard. The development process involves either spraying or brushing liquid solutions directly on the print area, or exposing the printed surface to chemical vapors. Popular methods include the following:

1. **Iodine Fuming.** Vapor created by heating iodine crystals is absorbed by the oils and other constituents of the latent print, which causes it to gradually change

from its clear appearance to a visible brown image. Although iodine fuming can be used on virtually any surface, it works especially well on paper products. The process is usually carried out by placing the object containing the print within an enclosed laboratory device known as an *iodine fuming hood*; however, portable iodine fuming devices exist that can be used at the crime scene. It is necessary to photograph the latent print at the point at which it is fully developed by the iodine vapors because it will begin to fade back to its natural clear state when the fuming process ends. Fixatives can be applied to the print to prevent fading and create a permanent image. Unfortunately, this process will preclude the print from being developed by any other method. Iodine fumes are highly toxic and should never be inhaled; the fuming process should always take place in well-ventilated areas.

2. **Ninhydrin.** This chemical developer reacts with the traces of amino acids contained in perspirations and causes the latent print to turn a bluish-purple color in approximately 2 to 3 hours after application (heat speeds the process). Ninhydrin solution is applied to the latent print surface by either spaying, brushing, or dipping. The product works especially well on porous surfaces, including paper (see Figure 4.8) and finished wood. Documents should be carefully analyzed before applying ninhydrin because the chemical has been known to destroy certain ink and impression marks. The health dangers associated with ninhydrin exposure require that the wearing of protective garments and breathing apparatus at all times while handling this chemical. Another chemical with qualities similar to those of ninhydrin is *DFO (1,8-Diazafluoren-9-one)*— an excellent developer for prints on paper and other porous surfaces. DFO is applied in liquid form, and when it is dried with a heat application (oven or iron, or steam-type) for approximately 20 minutes it will produce a vivid red print that fluoresces in laser light or other ALS lighting. The chemical *zinc chloride* can also be applied after ninhydrin to increase print development on porous surfaces.

3. **Silver Nitrate:** If an attempt to develop a print with ninhydrin should fail, the chemical silver nitrate can be used. Silver nitrate reacts with chlorides (i.e., salts) in the sweat of a latent print. Treating the latent print area with the chemical, allowing the specimen to air dry, and exposing it for approximately 10 minutes to either sunlight or UV light will produce a yellowish, then gray/black visualized print. Silver nitrate is destructive to the print so it generally is used as a last resort when other developing agents have failed. Protective wear and splash goggles should be worn when using this method.

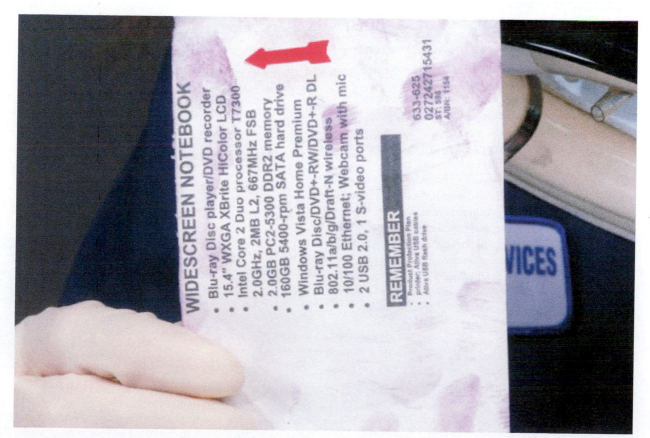

FIGURE 4.8 ▶ Latent prints developed on paper with ninhydrin.

FIGURE 4.9 ▶ Fuming chamber used to develop latent fingerprints on physical evidence with super glue developer. Vapors from the glue are heated and emitted upward, where they adhere to sweat, oils, and other residue composing the print—forming a visible white outline of the friction ridges. Iodine vapors can be similarly used to develop latent prints in fuming chambers.

4. ***Super Glue Fuming (Cyanoacrylate).*** The chemical components of ordinary super glue (cyanoacrylate), when heated, form a crystallizing gas that deposits on latent prints, causing them to have a white visible appearance that can be photographed. This process is relatively easy. It can be performed by placing latent prints in an airtight container such as a fuming chamber, as shown in Figure 4.9, where the heated super glue releases gases and then is deposited on the print surface, or it can be done at the crime scene with a super glue wand that emits super glue gas directly on any desired surface. The time needed to fully develop prints with super glue fuming varies greatly (from minutes to hours) depending on factors such as the technique used as well as the object to which it is applied. Prolonged exposure to super glue fumes can cause overdevelopment and destruction of latent prints. Make sure there is adequate ventilation before performing super glue fuming at indoor crime scenes to avoid inhaling toxic fumes. Many chemicals can be used to visually enhance the whitish developed print produced by the super glue. These include the following:

- ***Rhodamine 6G:*** produces bright luminescence under laser light and can be used as a stand-alone print developer for nonporous surfaces (see Figure 4.10).
- ***Androx Fluorescent Dye Spray:*** fluoresces yellow/green under UV light.
- ***Basic Yellow:*** fluoresces bright yellow/green under UV light and can be used to develop prints on a variety of multicolored surfaces.

Another highly effective device for visualizing prints that have been enhanced by chemical means (such as those listed above) is the Scene Scope, which operates with imaging technology referred to as *RUVIS (Reflected Ultra-Violet Imaging System)*. RUVIS operates by reflecting UV light from the surface of trace or other illuminated evidence back to a magnification device that greatly enhances the luminescent print so that it can be visualized as well as photographed. Prints will appear black, white, or green without background interference, depending on their qualities. Oily and sweaty prints on nonporous surfaces are best visualized by the RUVIS system. However, prints on porous surfaces such as textured wallboard and the adhesive side of tape can also be enhanced. Prints that cannot be readily visualized often can be developed by super glue fuming, as later visualized by a follow-up RUVIS application. Figure 4.11 illustrates the use of RUVIS to visualize fingerprints on a firearm, and Figure 4.12 shows the visualized print after it is transformed to a digital image.

Order of Applications

Because some chemical developing methods can be used together with others while others cannot without destroying the print, it is important to determine the proper order of their application. As a general rule, iodine fuming is used first because it does not permanently alter the print. If this fails, then

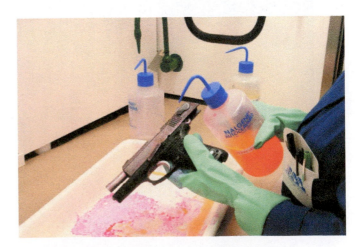

FIGURE 4.10 ▶ Here, surface areas of the firearm containing latent prints developed by super glue fuming are treated with the chemical enhancing agent Rhodamine 6G which will cause them to fluoresce yellow in color under ALS lighting.

FIGURE 4.11 ▶ The RUVIS imaging system is used to visualize latent prints and to digitally record their images.

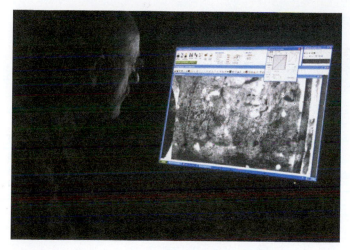

FIGURE 4.12 ▶ Digital photo images of fingerprints captured by the RUVIS system can be computer enhanced for detailed analysis and uploaded to databases used in worldwide searches for matching prints from known suspects or crime scenes.

ninhydrin can be applied and the print will develop normally. Silver nitrate or super glue fuming should be applied last, because after its use, the latent print will not be easily developed by other methods.

Other Surfaces and Methods:

- Wet Surfaces:

  Small-particle reagent: Solution capable of developing prints on wet surfaces. Prints are developed in gray color tones on surfaces covered by or immersed in fresh or salt water. Small-particle reagents can recover prints on surfaces that have come into contact with rain, dew, snow, or mud as well as those that have been lightly washed. Once dried, prints developed with small-particle reagent form a whitish colored print that can be lifted with tape and/or photographed.

- Waxy or Greasy Nonporous Surfaces:

  Sudan Black: Applying this chemical to nonporous waxy or greasy metal or glass surfaces, milk cartons, or the interior of latex gloves and candles will produce a dark blue/black print.

- Bloody Surfaces:

  Leuco Crystal Violet: Prints left in bloody surfaces or by bloody fingers on clean surfaces can be developed using Leuco Crystal Violet, which will produce a visible dark purple impression. This chemical can develop prints created by wet blood or blood that has dried on fingers. Similar results can also be obtained with ninhydrin.

  Luminol: Reacts with proteins in blood to produce a dim white fluorescence on prints that contain traces of blood—even when blood has been cleaned from a surface. However, reactions can be produced by agents other than blood, such as ones that contain vegetable proteins or bleach products.

  Fluorescein: Produces the same effect as Luminol, but can work much longer without a repeat application and can be visualized well with UV or other ALS lighting.

  Acid Fuchsin: Enhances bloody fingerprints and fluoresces in the presence of UV or ALS lighting.

- Sticky Surfaces:

  Sticky-side Powder: Latent prints on the sticky side of adhesive tape, labels, or stamps can be recovered using sticky-side powder. The process involves applying the developer, usually in paste form, to the adhesive surface and then rinsing the surface with water. Within minutes a dark image of the latent print appears.

  Crystal Violet: Can be applied to the adhesive side of all tapes to produce a developed bluish/purple print.

- Skin Surfaces:

  Iodine Fuming: Although it is often extremely difficult to recover latent prints from skin surfaces (e.g., living or dead human bodies), attempts can nonetheless be made. Iodine fuming the surface of the skin to identify the print and then capturing it by transferring the print to a chemically treated metal sheet (a process called iodine/silverplate transfer) is one method that has proven effective.

  Super Glue Fuming: Super glue fuming has also been proven to recover latent prints from skin or nonliving tissues.

  Amido Black: Can be applied in an attempt to develop latent fingerprints on skin (as well as other surfaces) containing traces of blood, leaving a dark blue/black developed print.

Securing and Packaging Fingerprint Evidence

Secure, package, and transport smaller items containing fingerprints for laboratory analysis. For larger items that cannot be

FIGURE 4.13 ▶ After a print match or "hit" is produced by an automated fingerprint identification system, the fingerprints must be examined manually for identification points before being presented as evidence in court.

transported to a laboratory, develop and document prints at the crime scene. Make sure to identify, document, and collect all other types of evidence that may be damaged by agents or chemicals used to develop fingerprints before beginning the final fingerprint development process at the crime scene. Ultimately, all fingerprint evidence used to positively identify crime suspects is scrutinized in a hands-on fingerprint examination such as that illustrated in Figure 4.13.

CASE CLOSE-UP 4.1
"FINGERED AT THE CRIME SCENE"
Gwinnett, Georgia

Donald Smith was arrested for carjacking and murder in what appeared to be a slam dunk case for police detectives. Not only was Smith witnessed committing the acts, but other evidence was gathered against the accused killer including his DNA at the crime scene as well as security camera footage positively identifying him as the offender. Despite the fact that all available evidence strongly suggested his guilt, Smith told authorities that he was innocent and that the real offender was his twin brother. His story was later confirmed when further examination of the crime scene evidence revealed that fingerprints found at the scene were indeed not his, but were a match to his twin brother Ronald—who was subsequently arrested and convicted for the crimes in question.

OBJECT PRINT AND IMPRESSION EVIDENCE

Evidence in the form of object prints and impressions can be extremely valuable because it can produce individualizing characteristics. For example, soles of shoes and tire treads often contain unique wear patterns that have the same identification qualities as a fingerprint. Two-dimensional print evidence is produced when residue is either applied to or removed from a given surface area by an object. First, **residue prints** can be created when dirt, dust, paint, oil, grease, or blood is transferred from an object such as a shoe to a floor, chair, counter, or other hard surface. Such prints can also be present in the form of lip, ear, or facial prints resulting from lipstick and cosmetics transferred to surfaces from the victim's skin. These types of prints are often discovered in sexual assault cases and the lipstick or cosmetic residue provide DNA evidence from the victim. Second, surfaces already covered with residue can produce **void prints**—for example, a footprint caused by the sole of a shoe removing dust from a floor. Impression evidence, which is three-dimensional in nature, can be found in snow, mud, dirt, sand, wet cement, and other soft surfaces where pressure has been applied by shoes,

tires, and other objects. Both print and impression evidence can be visualized by using an oblique lighting technique such as a flashlight projected to the side of a suspected evidence location, or an alternate lighting source such as UV, infrared, or laser light.[4]

Photographic Techniques

Photography is the best method for capturing print and impression evidence. Photos should be taken before chemically or otherwise visually enhancing the evidence, and it is necessary to use only those photographic methods that minimize possible distortion of the evidence image. Recommended photographic techniques include the following:

- Use a 35mm camera mounted on a tripod with a detachable strobe.
- Capture images in black-and-white film, although color images can also be taken to illustrate unique qualities of the print or impression.
- Include a scale or tape measure placed at the same depth as the impression, and identifying information including case number, item number, north arrow, and date, making sure these items do not interfere with the impression photo.

- Mount the camera on the tripod directly over and parallel to the evidence. If the evidence is on an incline, adjust the back of the camera to the same angle as the evidence. If in a lighted environment, create a shadow over the evidence.

- Take a minimum of four photos of each evidence location from different angles, lighting the evidence at a 45° angle or less until the greatest amount of contrast is attained.

- Tire impression photos should be taken in a series to capture the entire length of the tire's circumference (approximately 8 feet). Take separate photos capturing approximately 2 feet in length with a flat tape measure placed alongside the tire print or impression. There should be as much as 20 percent overlap between each frame of each photo.

- After taking an initial set of photos, remove any items that have fallen onto the print or impression after it was made (i.e., leaves, stones) and take a second set of photos.[5] *Do not remove any object that was present at the time the print or impression was made.*

Evidence Collection and Preservation Methods

COLLECTING PRINTS

When and where possible, collect print evidence by removing the physical object containing the print from the crime scene. Such items should be packaged in boxes and taped in position so that they cannot rub against any other object or surface area, damaging the print surface. If physical removal of the evidence is not possible, there are various means of lifting a print from a fixed surface. **Electrostatic dust print lifters (EDPL)** can lift dust prints from nearly any hard, flat surface as well as irregular soft surfaces such as carpet and fabric. The device is operated by first placing a dark-colored sheet of metallic film over the evidence to be captured. Then, an electronic charge is emitted through the film to the surface area containing the print, causing dust particles to magnetically adhere to the metallic film, creating a mirror image copy of the original print. Alternatively, similar results can be obtained by using a **gel print lifter**. This is simply a colored or clear sheet with a low-adhesive gelatin surface that adheres to dust particles or other trace materials composing foot, shoe, tire, or other prints. Similar results have been reported for using automobile window tinting film to lift dust prints from a variety of surfaces. The use of a gel print lifter for capturing footprints on a chair seized from a crime scene is illustrated in Figures 4.14 and 4.15.

Casting Impressions

Casts can be taken of nearly any impression; even puncture wounds in human flesh have been casted to produce a permanent likeness of a killer's knife. Typically, however, the casting of impression evidence is performed in outdoor crime scenes

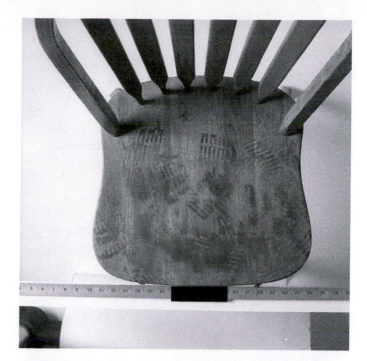

FIGURE 4.14 ▶ Black-and-white 90° image of a suspect's footwear prints on a wooden chair located at the crime scene of a residential burglary.

FIGURE 4.15 ▶ A black rubber gel lift creating a permanent mirror image of footwear impressions created by dust and residue deposited on the chair's surface.

to capture shoe or tire impressions left in ground surface areas—sometimes involving mud, water, or snow. Several commercial products are available for use as casting materials, including dental stone, Diecast, Traxtone, Bio-Foam, and liquid silicone agents. Among these products, dental stone is perhaps the one used most often due to its versatility in outdoor investigations and its relatively low cost. To make dental stone casts of impressions:

1. Photograph the impression before beginning the casting process.

2. Remove any debris that has fallen on the impression; leave debris that is contained within the impression or that would damage the imprint when removed.

3. Mix 1 lb. dental stone with 6 oz. water in a large plastic zip lock bag. (1 lb. quantities of dental stone can be premeasured and packaged to save time.)

4. Prepare the mixture by churning the closed bag or gently stirring until a milkshake consistency is attained.

5. Pour the mixture into the impression from a height of not more than 2–3 inches. (If the impression is located on an incline, place a pouring frame around the impression to prevent spillage.)

6. Include enough mixture to cover the entire impression and provide an overall thickness of about ¾ inch to prevent breakage.

7. After the cast has set, which occurs in about 20–30 minutes (longer setting time is required in cold weather conditions), include identifying information on its reverse side.

8. Package each cast individually in a sturdy box and cushion it with crumpled papers or bubble wrap packing material. Do not remove soil or other objects adhering to the cast.

Casting with dental stone can also be carried out when impression evidence is located in water- or snow-covered areas. If an impression contains water, as with a footprint

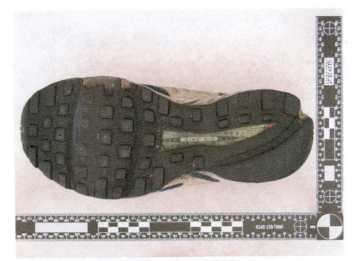

(a)

(b)

(c)

(d)

FIGURE 4.16 (a)–(d) ▶ (a) The sole of a suspect's shoe recovered as evidence; (b) a crime scene photo of a footwear impression believed to match the suspect's shoe; (c) investigators prepare a case of the footwear impression at the crime scene; (d) the finished cast as prepared for the crime lab.

made in mud or during rainfall, it can be captured by gently applying (sprinkling or sifting) the appropriate amount of dental stone directly into the water already present in the imprint. To complete the cast, apply additional amounts of mixed dental stone until the necessary size and thickness are achieved. Impression evidence can be captured in snow through the use of Snow Print Spray, a special colored spray-on wax that coats the surface of the impression and keeps it from melting down or deforming when casting materials are applied. When using Snow Print Spray, be sure to photograph the impression before applying the spray. Rephotograph the impression after applying the spray, which is colored to improve the photographic image of the evidence. Dental stone, silicone, or foam can be used to create the final cast. Figure 4.16 illustrates the casting process for a suspect's shoe-print impression in dirt at an outdoor crime scene.

Tire Impressions

Tires believed to have caused impression evidence should not be removed from the vehicle for lab testing. Rather, the entire vehicle should be trailed and transported to a laboratory garage where tire tread, track width, and wheelbase analyses can be conducted within a controlled setting. Exemplars or prints of the tire tread can be produced as follows:

1. Remove each tire from the vehicle and record its mounting location (front right/left; rear right/left).
2. Construct four sheets of drafting film (clear plastic)—one for each tire—1 feet wide × 8 feet long and attached to a cardboard backing.
3. Label the sidewalls of each tire into sections (1, 2, 3, 4, and so on), using locations of wear bars.
4. Using a gloved hand, cover the tread of the tire with a thin coat of petroleum jelly.
5. Slowly roll each tire on separate sheets of the drafting film, marking each section of the tire print on the cardboard surface that corresponds to the sections labeled on the side wall.
6. Sprinkle black magnetic fingerprint powder on the petroleum jelly prints to develop them and spray each with lacquer as a preservative.

Track width and wheelbase determination from tire tread impressions also can be helpful for identifying the size and type of vehicle. Track width is the distance between the middle of a tire on one side of the vehicle and the middle of the tire on the opposite side of the vehicle. It is best calculated by measuring the distance from the outside of the left front tire to the inside of the right front tire (same procedure for the rear tires, which may have a different track width). A vehicle's wheelbase is the distance between the middle of the vehicle front axle to the center of the vehicle's rear axle. This dimension is best calculated by measuring the distance between the leading edge of the front tire to the leading edge of the rear tire. Both the track width and the wheelbase measurement can

FIGURE 4.17 ▶ A length of tire tread impression evidence is photographed at a distance sufficient to capture the tire's full rotation—thus, documenting the entire tread pattern on the tire. Note tread cross-over patterns suggesting entry and exit paths of the vehicle. Photos and castings of the tire tread patterns can often provide individualized evidence used to positively identify a suspect's vehicle.

be used to exclude certain vehicle types from suspicion and perhaps identify a likely class of vehicle involved in the criminal activity based on the manufacturer's vehicle specifications as well as vehicle identification databases (see the discussion on TreadMate in the next section).[6] Figure 4.17 shows various tire tracks in soft dirt left by a suspect's vehicle at a crime scene. In addition to cross-over patterns in the tracks suggesting entry and exit paths, unique tread wear patterns obtained from these dirt impressions can be compared to lab exemplars taken from the actual tires of the suspect's vehicle. The tire tread impressions can also be used to establish the suspect vehicle's wheelbase and track width (see Figure 4.18) so that investigators can determine the likely size, make, and model of the vehicle.

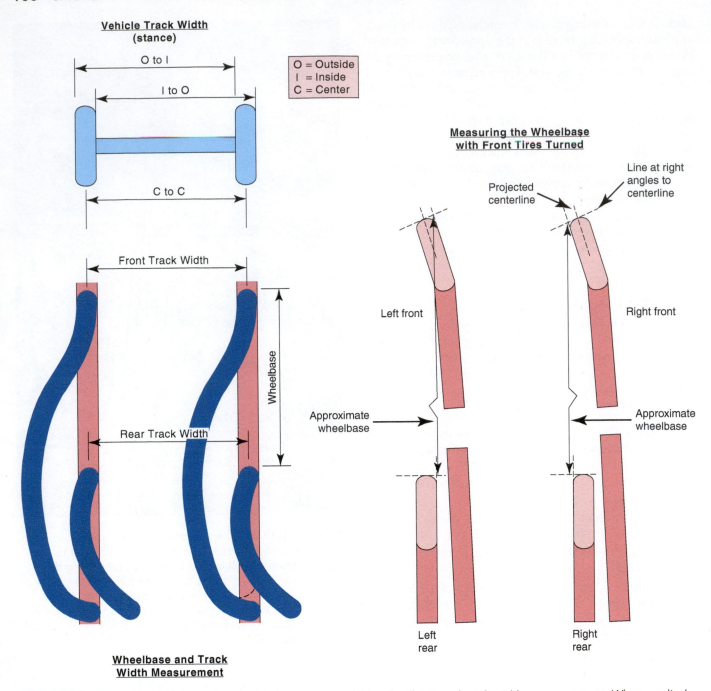

FIGURE 4.18 ▶ Suggested procedures for determining vehicle wheelbase and track width measurements. When applied to tire tread impression evidence, these measurements can provide valuable leads as to the make and model of a vehicle leaving tracks at a crime scene.

Obtaining Matching Physical Evidence

Matching physical evidence, or questioned objects believed to have created a print or impression at the crime scene, should be collected as soon as possible—if their whereabouts are known. Rapid identification and collection of these items is necessary because their continued used by victims or offenders may substantially change their print or impression characteris-

tics in a relatively short period of time. For example, the soles of shoes may become chipped or otherwise damaged by sudden exposure to abrasive surfaces; tires sometimes develop new wear patterns due to abnormal road conditions or mechanical failures of steering or braking systems. Several databases are available to provide investigative leads for shoe and tire tread impressions. Following the creation of a shoe-print impression (see Figure 4.19), the print image can be

FIGURE 4.19 ▶ A transparent lifter is used to reproduce a shoeprint impression of footwear recovered from a suspect, which is compared to photos and castings taken at the crime scene.

inputted into a database such as TreadMark, which contains data obtained from outer soles of shoes worn by crime suspects in custody and footwear evidence obtained from crime scenes. Another footwear database, SoleMate, provides information for over 12,000 shoe types and can provide details such as manufacturer, date, and location of market release. For tires, the TreadMate database has been created, which provides information to identify tread types and wear patterns for over 5,000 tire brands.

CASE CLOSE-UP 4.2

"THE BAREFOOT BANDIT"
Bonners Ferry, Idaho

While investigating the theft of a small airplane from a Northern Idaho airport, deputies discovered a set of large bare footprints on the dusty floor of the hangar where the plane was located. Authorities gave the moniker "Barefoot Bandit" to the thief, based on the assumption that the plane was indeed stolen by an offender who did not wear shoes. Later, at the scene of several other property crimes, including the theft of vehicles and a luxury yacht, footprint evidence was found linking the Barefoot Bandit to a series of criminal activities. At the site of a commercial store break-in, the now-notorious offender taunted authorities by drawing a series of chalk-outlined footprints on the store's floor leading to an exit where the letters "C.U." were written. After a two-year crime spree, the Barefoot Bandit—19-year-old Colton Harris-Moore, a resident of a group home in the Pacific Northwest region—was identified by print as well as DNA evidence and arrested in the Bahamas. One of his victims, whose muddy yard contained the Barefoot Bandit's footprints, attempted to sell a casting made of the infamous thief's print evidence on eBay. Bids for the casting started at $300; however, not a single bid for the item was received.

TOOL MARK EVIDENCE

Tools used for purposes of breaking into windows, doors, display cases, cash registers, safes, and other locked areas often leave **tool mark evidence** useful for classing or perhaps individualizing the instrument causing the physical intrusion. Pry bars, screwdrivers, chisels, and other tools with flat, sharp edges can scrap the surface of objects, leaving **striation marks** that reveal class characteristics such as the size and shape of the tool. Sometimes, these markings also show unique metal patterns on the surface of the tool, created during the manufacturing process, that can be used as individualizing evidence. Other types of tools used to grip and apply pressure to objects, such as vice grips, pliers, and wrenches, leave compression marks that provide mirror stamp-like images of their gripping surfaces. Also included among these are devices that employ scissor-style cutting mechanisms. Compression markings, too, can be used to class and sometimes individualize tools.

Tool mark evidence can be recovered from the crime scene in a variety of ways. First, photograph the object or area containing the tool mark. This will be useful for purposes of locating a particular piece of tool mark evidence within the crime scene, but photographs of tool marks have no value for identification purposes. Second, if possible, cut out or remove the object containing the tool mark. If the object is too large (e.g., a vehicle) or it is impractical to cut out the affected area, a cast of the mark should be made. Commercial casting putty and silicon compounds (Mikrosil, Silmark) can be used to make a permanent record of tool marks that can be used for microscopic laboratory analyses. These compounds take approximately 10 minutes to dry and can be applied to vertical surfaces by surrounding the tool mark impression with modeling clay to act as a dam for the liquid casting agents. Finished casts and actual objects containing tool mark impressions should be packaged in such a way that the surface containing the tool mark is protected from damage or contamination from other objects.

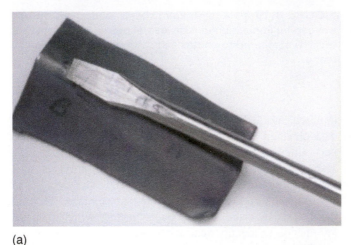

(a)

(b)

FIGURE 4.20 ▶ (a) A screwdriver seized as evidence in a larceny case and (b) comparison of striations from its blade to impressions left on the drawer of a cash register believed to have been pried open with the screwdriver.

Reference samples of paint and metal from the surfaces containing tool mark evidence should also be obtained and submitted with the evidence items. Figure 4.20 shows a screwdriver that was used to pry open a cash register. The drawer of the register (pictured with the screwdriver) shows tool mark impressions, or striations, that can be matched to the unique metallic features of the screwdriver's blade.

Offenders may break tools at the crime scene due to improper use or haste. Pieces of broken tools can be used not only to determine the type, model, and manufacturer of the tool, but also to construct a physical match with a questioned tool that is later recovered from the crime scene or from a suspect. Besides fingerprint evidence, recovered tools may also contain visible or trace evidence of paint, wood chips, metal chips, or other material from the surface to which they were applied. In some circumstances, microscopic physical matches can be performed between objects on a recovered tool and the surfaces from which they have been displaced. For example, a paint chip discovered on a screw driver can be matched in a

jig-saw fashion to a door jamb where it was originally located. Sometimes metal flakes chipping off a tool at the crime scene can also be later matched to the tool's gripping, grinding, or scraping surface. Metal chips can be searched for by sliding a magnet over the area containing the suspected tool mark. Recovered chips should be packaged and labeled in pill bottles, film canisters, or other airtight containers. Plastic bags should be taped around the end of tools to trap any loose trace evidence. The use of ALS lighting, especially UV light, can help in identifying trace evidence associated with tool marks as well as in visualizing actual tool mark impressions.[7]

FIREARMS EVIDENCE

Firearms evidence is best thought of as encompassing two distinct areas. First, there is the area of **firearms identification** which concerns the determination of weapon types, including the size, model, manufacturer, and other features of an actual firearm. This may include the identification of pistols, rifles, shotguns, cartridges, bullets, loading devices, and so on. **Ballistics evidence**, the second area, is generally concerned with the characteristics of weapons and cartridges once they have been fired. There are three specific areas of ballistics examination: internal (explosive discharge of the cartridge within the gun), external (the bullet leaving the gun barrel and its trajectory in space), and terminal characteristics (the bullet striking a surface and/or coming to a place of rest). The identification of residues such as soot, ash, and gun powder deposited on clothing and other surfaces also falls within the scope of ballistics evidence. Figures 4.21, 4.22, and 4.23 show a variety of firearms and ammunition commonly encountered by investigators as street weapons used to carry out criminal activities.

(a)

(b)

FIGURE 4.21 ▶ Popular street guns #1: (a) semiautomatic Kalashnikov (AK-47) type rifle, 7.62 × 39mm Soviet Caliber; (b) pump-action Ithaca shotgun, 12 gauge (with pistol grip).

(a)

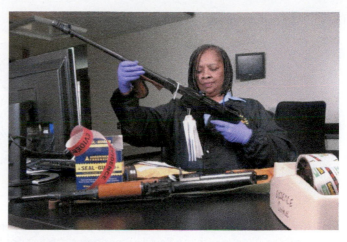

FIGURE 4.24 ▶ Firearms evidence being checked in and prepared for storage. (Note the Thompson "Tommy Gun" submachine gun being examined.)

(b)

FIGURE 4.22 ▶ Popular street guns #2: (a) semiautomatic AR-15 type rifle, 5.56 × 45mm NATO Caliber; (b) semiautomatic S.W.D. Inc. M-11 pistol, 9mm Luger Caliber.

(a)

(b)

FIGURE 4.23 ▶ Popular street guns #3: (a) semiautomatic Glock 19 pistol, 9mm Luger Caliber; (b) Smith & Wesson model 686 revolver, .357 Magnum Caliber.

Handling Firearms

First and foremost, investigators should ensure the safe handling of firearms evidence at any crime scene. Never second-guess a gun. Always assume that any weapon being handled is loaded and set to fire. Firearms that have modified actions such as a hair trigger for quick firing or that have been converted to discharge in a fully automatic mode are not uncommon, and are extremely dangerous. Never pick up a gun by inserting an object such as a probe or pencil into its barrel chamber or operating surfaces. This is not only dangerous, but may destroy valuable evidence such as blood, tissue, or other materials that may have been deposited within the weapon's barrel or firing mechanisms when the weapon was discharged. Firearms seized by investigators are stored as evidence in secure locations like that shown in Figure 4.24.

Before weapons are removed from the crime scene they should first be photographed. Removing the weapon immediately before a full documentation of the scene is not recommended, but may be necessary if conditions require such immediate action. Weather conditions that may destroy fingerprints persons reaching for a weapon to harm officers or others, and weapons that have a high probability of accidently firing (because they are placed a precarious position or have an apparent malfunction) are situations that require the prompt removal of weapons before completely processing the crime scene. After weapons are recovered they should be:

- Unloaded, labeled with evidence tags, wrapped in paper, and packed separately in an appropriate-size cardboard or wooden box. Take careful notes when removing cartridges. Be sure to note the order in which cartridges are removed from the weapon. If multiple weapons are present, be sure to document which cartridges belong to each weapon. When removing cartridges from the cylinder of a revolver, the cartridge aligned with the barrel is considered the first position, and subsequent rounds are numbered sequentially in a clockwise rotating

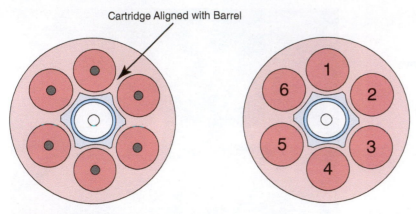

FIGURE 4.25 ▶ Proper method for recovering cartridges from a revolver. The Cartridge Aligned with the Barrel is considered the first position, and subsequent rounds are numbered sequentially in a clockwise rotating pattern.

pattern (see Figure 4.25). Magazines for semiautomatic weapons may remain loaded, but should be packaged separately from the weapon.

- Do not fire, clean, and take apart weapons before laboratory analysis.
- Wrap areas on weapon containing blood or other transfer evidence with paper.

Ammunition Evidence

Collect all fired and unfired bullets as well as cartridge cases from the crime scene. However, when time is limited and large numbers of bullets and cartridge cases have been produced by weapons with large ammunition capacities, collect at least five duplicative rounds representing each weapon fired. Floors, walls, ceilings, and furniture are some of the likely terminal locations for bullets. All fragments of bullets that have separated on impact, as happens with hollow-point rounds, should also be collected. Be sure to take thorough notes on the location of each bullet and cartridge casing recovered, especially noting the scatter patterns and direction of travel of multiple cartridge casings ejected from a moving weapon—as in a drive-by shooting. Bullets still remaining in bodies will be removed during medical examination, and should not be removed by the investigator at the crime scene. However, bullets sometimes fall from exit wounds on the victim's body. Careful attention should be directed to these wound areas and the surface area where bullets may have fallen from the body. Although recovered bullets often are highly deformed, measurements with calipers and weight determination methods performed in the crime lab may identify class characteristics, such as the caliber of the bullet and the type of weapon, as well as individual characteristics to identify the specific weapon from which a bullet was fired. Often a deformed bullet recovered from a crime scene can be measured with calipers (Figure 4.26) to determine its caliber and other original characteristics.

As a general rule, if the number of bullets fired exceeds the number of visible strikes (on a victim or other surface), additional stray bullets exist and should be searched for at the crime scene. Conversely, if the number of bullet strikes exceeds the number of cartridge casings recovered, these may indicate multiple shooters

or single bullets that may have fragmented causing additional strikes. For shotgun ammunition, plastic casings, pellets, buckshot, and wadding should be collected. The crime scene, as well as suspects, should be searched for unfired ammunition, which can be used as a comparison against that which has been fired. Objects containing bullet strikes should be recovered such as bedding, upholstery, sections of drywall, rugs, clothing, and so forth.

If bullets contain blood or other transfer evidence that is still wet, they should be air dried outside of direct sunlight, which can degrade DNA evidence. Handle this type of evidence with extreme care. Trace evidence such as glass, wood, wallboard, fibers, or other material may be embedded in the bullet surface and will provide valuable information on the order in which a bullet has hit multiple targets. When possible, try to avoid directly handling bullets and cartridge casings by scooping evidence from surfaces using coin envelopes or paper bindles. In general, bullets and other ammunition evidence should be wrapped in paper, packaged separately in a pill box, or enveloped and labeled appropriately (see Figure 4.27).[8]

Gunshot Residue (GSR)

Gunshot residue (GSR) is very delicate evidence, and should be handled in a timely and careful manner to ensure its preservation. It has the consistency of talcum powder and is dispersed from the barrel of a weapon in a conical pattern. Because of its extreme volatility, GSR should be gathered as soon as possible after it has been deposited by using the appropriate methods, including a GSR kit. Likely locations for GSR evidence include the suspect's hands (inner palm area, the web between thumb and forefinger) and clothing, the victim's body and clothing, vehicle interiors (especially headliner nearest to the shooter), and other areas within close range of the weapon's barrel (approximately 3 feet or less). As shown in Figure 4.28, guns fired within close range, approximately 1 foot or less, will leave entry holes surrounded by noticeable burn marks consisting of

FIGURE 4.26 ▶ Calipers used to measure the diameter of a bullet recovered from a crime scene. Although the bullet is deformed from striking a surface, scientific formulas can be used to estimate the bullet's original dimensions.

FIGURE 4.27 ▶ Fragmented bullet recovered from a crime scene, packaged as evidence.

soot and ash. As this distance increases by a matter of inches, the burn patterns will become noticeably less evident and random of pepperlike marks about the entry hole produced by burning gunpowder granules will become less frequent and increase in diameter about the bullet strike area as illustrated in Figure 4.28. After a distance of about 3 feet, gun powder residue is usually not evident on the bullet strike surface.

GSR evidence is most useful if collected within 3 hours after being discharged and deposited. In average conditions, GSR residue over 6 hours old will no longer be of value for laboratory analyses. Traces of GSR are also easily removed by water, and suspects who have washed their hands will test negative for GSR residue. In these situations, pocket areas of a suspect's clothing should be tested since GSR may have been deposited there before a hand washing. If GSR tests cannot be performed before the body is removed from the crime scene, the hands should be covered with paper bags to preserve GSR evidence for laboratory analysis. Clothing of persons suspected of shooting a firearm, or others in close proximity to the shooter, should be packaged separately in paper with identifying labels affixed to the exterior of the evidence item.[9] Figure 4.29(a) shows a color reaction indicating the presence of GSR on a swab taken from a suspected shooter's hand. Positive identification of GSR particles like that shown in Figure 4.29(b) is often done in a laboratory setting using specialized high-power microscopes.

Ballistics Evidence

It is useful to remember that a bullet always travels in a straight line before it strikes an object when retracing the path of a discharged bullet. After a bullet strikes an object, however, it may lose velocity and continue its path of travel or may imbed itself into the object. Larger-caliber, higher-velocity cartridges tend to create straighter, more predictable paths, as they have the power to continue their path as they pass through an object. Smaller-caliber, lower-velocity cartridges often travel on erratic paths after striking a surface, moving up, down, or sideways in a rather unpredictable fashion. There are documented instances where .22 caliber bullets initially struck a victim's leg

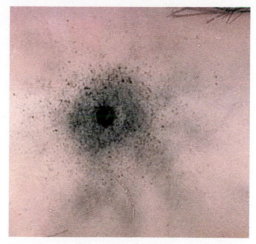

(a)

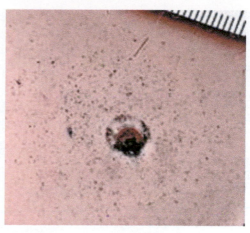

(b)

FIGURE 4.28 ▶ (a) Pattern of gunshot residue (GSR) from a shot taken 1 in. from the target. The pattern shown in (b)—with much less depositing of GSR—resulted from a shot taken 4 in. from the target. (United States Department of Justice)

bone and then traveled all the way up the bone to settle in the victim's upper torso. High-velocity bullets that strike and pass through an intermediate object before hitting a final target also may display similar unpredictable movement upon termination. Often, when two or more holes are created in objects by the same bullet, **trajectory rods** are placed through the holes to determine the bullet's path (see Figure 4.30). For long-distance trajectories, this process can be carried out using laser light photography to determine the likely angle and path of a bullet.

Classifying and Individualizing Firearms Evidence

If firearms are recovered from a crime scene, it may be possible to determine the manufacturer, model, and other classification details through simple visual examination. Rifles, pistols, shotguns, and other firearms from domestic as well as foreign arms manufacturers are well documented by appearance and serial numbers. The identification process becomes more challenging; however, when

(a)

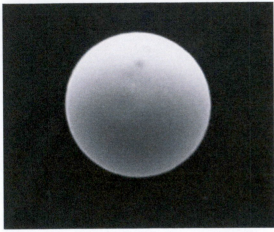

(b)

FIGURE 4.29 ▶ (a) Close-up of a swab taken from a person's hand after firing a handgun; it reacts positive for GSR by turning a reddish-brown after treatment with DPA (diphenylamine). Field test kits using this and other chemicals reacting to GSR can provide results in minutes; they provide more immediate results than older methods for GSR detection, which required sending swabs from shooting suspects' hands to a lab for analysis of gunpowder particles (b) under a high-power SEM microscope. (Courtesy U.S. Department of Energy)

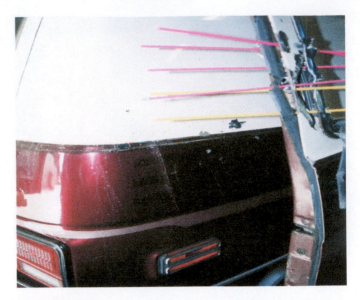

FIGURE 4.30 ▶ Trajectory rods used to determine the path of travel of bullets that have struck a suspected homicide victim's vehicle. Note different color rods used to show bullet strikes caused by two different weapons.

els. Longer barrels, with longer rifling, generally produce greater spin, resulting in the bullet traveling a greater distance.

At the very least, the weapon's rifling can be used for purposes of classification. Generally, different types of firearms produced by different manufacturers contain lands and grooves that vary in size, number, and direction of twist. Rifling that twists to the left will cause counterclockwise bullet spin, and rifling that twists to the right will produce clockwise spin. The specific characteristics of the lands and grooves are readily identified on the exterior surface of bullets that have been fired. Even severely disfigured bullets often contain sufficient rifling impression to classify a particular weapon.

It is the unique characteristics of rifling possessed by each weapon, however, that serves to individualize that particular firearm. During the manufacturing phase of the weapon's rifling, minute bits of metal inside the barrel as well as imperfections in the device used to form the rifling together produce random microscopic scratches known as **striation marks**, extending down the barrel's interior. Because striation marks are *negative impressions* (or indentations) on the barrel's surface, they result in *positive impressions* (or microscopic raised lines) on a bullet after it has been fired. Collectively, the striations on an expended bullet form an individual fingerprint of the barrel's interior that belongs to only one particular firearm. This fingerprint may be of limited use, however, if the weapon that fired a recovered bullet is not available. Individualizing a weapon relies on an examination in which a bullet recovered from the crime scene or a suspect's body is compared to a bullet test-fired from a suspect's weapon. After a bullet is test-fired into a **recovery tank** (see Figures 4.31 through 4.34 for an illustration of a bullet test fire and bullet recovery procedure), it is then placed in a **comparison microscope** that allows the firearms' examiner to compare striation marks on the sample and suspect bullets side by side as shown in Figure 4.35. Matching

an actual weapon is not recovered. A fired bullet, cartridge case, or shotgun shell case may provide enough evidence to determine factors such as the weapon's type, brand, and caliber.

Given the proper evidence, forensic scientists can individualize firearms as well. Key to determining the specific identity of a firearm lies in the detailed examination of its *rifling* characteristics. Most firearms (excluding shotguns) contain rifling, which is composed of raised and recessed surfaces inside the barrel known as **lands** and **grooves**, respectively. Collectively, the lands and grooves serve as tracks for the bullet as it travels down the barrel, causing it to spin either clockwise or counterclockwise before it exits the weapon. The spinning motion causes the bullet to remain straight and not tumble end-over-end as it trav-

FIGURE 4.31 ▶ Ballistics test-fire tank.

FIGURE 4.32 ▶ Suspect weapon is test fired into a water buffer inside the tank.

FIGURE 4.33 ▶ Test-fired bullet is siphoned from the tank.

FIGURE 4.34 ▶ Test-fired round is recovered from the collection basket, ready for analysis.

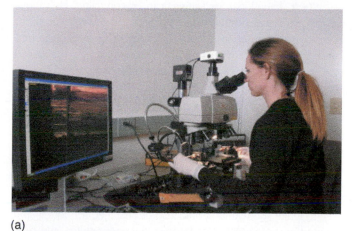

(a)

(b)

FIGURE 4.35 ▶ (a) Two bullets are examined for common striation patterns using a comparison microscope. (b) The magnified image shows matching striation patterns for the bullets.

striation marks confirm that the two bullets were fired from the same weapon. Advanced technologies are now available that allow this procedure to be performed in 3-D microscopic imaging as well. Such information can be inputted into firearms databases, most notably the ATF's NIBIN system (discussed in

Chapter 7), to determine matches with weapons used at other crime scenes and recovered from arrested offenders.

Tool marks on cartridge casings are individualized using a process very similar to that just described for striations. For example, a cartridge case may exhibit marks or scratches produced by the unique features of one particular weapon. For example, ammunition in a semiautomatic is first extracted from its magazine, and then fired and ejected from the weapon. This process can produce individualized **extractor marks** and **ejector marks** on the cartridge case. In addition, the weapon's **firing pin**, used to ignite the ammunition, also may leave similar impressions. Furthermore, scratches and indentations also may be evident as the result of the cartridge passing through its magazine, or being compressed in its chamber during firing. The general assumption here is that no two firearms are exactly alike and therefore will not produce identical marks. The NIBIN database can also be used to identify like individual characteristics of cartridge casings the same way it is used to individualize bullet evidence (see Chapter 7).[10]

ARSON EVIDENCE

Arson (e.g., intentional fire setting) can be committed for various reasons, including destruction of property for revenge, profit, or to cover up evidence from another crime. In cases of suspected arson, most evidence will usually be debris burnt by a fire ignited by a chemical agent referred to as an **accelerant**. Some accelerants may emit strong smells, while others may be odorless. Common accelerants include gasoline, kerosene, solvents, and other ignitable fluids. Residue from these agents is deposited on a variety of surfaces such as metal, wood, plastic, paper, glass, carpet, wallboards, mattresses, and cloth (including suspect's clothing). Residue also may be found below burnt surfaces in soil, below floorboards, or under baseboards and sills as the result of seeping through cracks or porous surfaces. Potential objects and sources used to ignite accelerants should also be searched for both in and around the crime scene. Matchbooks, lighters, candles, and cigarettes used to start a fire may contain valuable evidence revealing not only the method of ignition but also the identity of a suspect through the presence of DNA or fingerprints. Even though firefighters may have sprayed the arson debris with water or fire-extinguishing chemicals, accelerant residue, and other types of evidence often can still be recovered in laboratory analyses.

Arson evidence must be gathered in an effective and timely fashion because of its **volatility** (the propensity to be lost through evaporation). Packaging of this type of evidence should include the following:

- placing smaller solid debris evidence in airtight containers (filled about three-quarters full) such as metal paint cans or glass jars—never ordinary plastic or rubber containers;
- storing larger solid debris evidence in KAPAK plastic bags;
- putting liquid samples of accelerant in small glass screw-top vials (approximately 2 ml) by transferring samples from the original source with a disposable pipette.[11]

BLOOD EVIDENCE

The main value of blood evidence is that it often contains genetic markers in the DNA that can be used to positively identify individuals. In addition, blood has unique physical qualities that allow investigators to perform crime reconstruction by analyzing stains or patterns left on floors, walls, ceilings, and other surfaces from bleeding caused by stabbing, shooting, bludgeoning, and other traumas. First, blood is a viscous fluid that resists separation and flowing. It also possesses **surface tension**, which acts like a protective barrier surrounding blood droplets, helping them maintain their shape before striking a surface. These physical properties make a drop of blood behave very similar to a water balloon when it travels through space and strikes a surface; that is, the drop—like the water balloon—remains intact in flight and then bursts open and spills its contents when it strikes a surface. This creates relatively predictable sizes, shapes, and characteristics in blood droplets projected from certain types of wounds and striking specific types of surfaces. Using such information as crime scene evidence is referred to as blood spatter analysis (discussed in more detail later in this chapter).

Identifying Blood Evidence

Blood is often difficult to identify at the crime scene. It can leave a visible stain on virtually any surface—porous or nonporous. The color of the stain can vary from bright red to dark tones of brown or gray. Minute particles of blood may not even be visible to the naked eye. Besides the difficulty of its identification, blood evidence's extreme volatility presents specific challenges to the crime scene investigator. If collected too slowly or improperly, blood evidence can easily be destroyed.

If blood evidence is present at the crime scene, it should be collected immediately. This is especially true when it is contained within an outdoor crime scene. Prolonged exposure to sunlight, moisture, wind, and environmental contaminants may degrade blood evidence and render it useless for laboratory analysis. Blood is a biohazardous material, and should always be handled using gloves and other required protective clothing to protect against exposure to bloodborne diseases such as HIV and hepatitis.

Blood evidence is equally valuable in either a wet or a dry state. Wet blood emitted from a fresh wound appears bright red due to its initial exposure to oxygen in the air. Over time, after drying begins, the blood will gradually turn various shades of darker red to brown. In large quantities of blood, after approximately an hour, the fluid portion, called **serum**, will begin to turn yellow and gradually separate from the solid portion known as **plasma** as the blood begins to clot or **coagulate**. By comparison, blood that has totally dried often appears as a brown chip or flake on nonporous surfaces. On porous or absorbent surfaces such as cement, soil, carpet, or clothing, dried blood stains may not be visible and may be detectible only through special testing procedures.[12]

Collecting Blood Evidence

Blood evidence should be photographed and collected as soon as possible—usually before collecting all other types of evidence.

Depending on whether the blood is wet or dry, the collection process includes the following:

Wet Blood Collection:

- Use sterile absorbent material, such as cotton swabs or squares, to obtain samples of wet blood from pools or large immovable objects. Never handle sampling materials with bare hands. Always use gloves and tweezers or forceps. Refrigerate or freeze samples as soon as possible and transport them to a secure location to air dry. Use clean paper containers such as packets, envelopes, or bags—not plastic—to package blood samples. Loose trace evidence containing blood should be removed and packaged separately. Plastic containers used for temporary transportation purposes should be replaced by paper containers or the blood evidence will usually be destroyed in 1 to 2 hours.
- Wet blood stains on movable objects should be packaged in the manner outlined above and transported to a secure location to air dry. Entire items of clothing should be collected, wrapped in paper, and air dried so that blood stain patterns are not altered.

Dry Blood Collection:

- Scrape dry blood stains with a clean knife into paper packets. Clean the knife and use separate packets after obtaining each sample.
- Tape lift dried blood stains and place the tape containing the sample on a separate vinyl backing. Never place the tape on a paper or cardboard backing.
- Cut out areas on objects that contain blood evidence (see Figure 4.36). Also obtain a cut-out piece that does not contain blood for use as a control sample. Package samples in paper.
- Never place dry blood samples in plastic containers.

Blood evidence should be collected not only from the crime scene, but also from victims, suspects, and individuals in and around the crime scene whose blood may be present. Without these as reference samples, it is difficult to determine whether blood evidence at the crime scene belongs to suspects, victims, or bystanders. Medical examiners will provide reference samples of blood from deceased individuals, and similar samples from living persons are drawn by medical technicians. These samples can then be compared by investigators with known DNA genetic markers contained in blood evidence obtained from the crime scene.

Testing for the Presence of Blood

When it is uncertain whether or not a certain substance is indeed blood, a **presumptive test** is first performed. Such procedures provide a preliminary indication that a given substance is perhaps blood (or not), but are by no means legally conclusive. (Tests that provide legal confirmation that substances identified by presumptive procedures are truly blood and perhaps human blood are performed under controlled laboratory conditions and

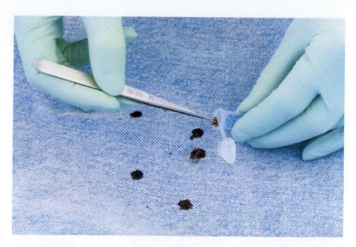

FIGURE 4.36 ▶ Blood evidence on hard surfaces, after air drying, should be removed by scraping it with a sterile instrument. On cloth surfaces (as pictured here), the area containing blood evidence should be removed by cutting it from the fabric.

are discussed in Chapter 8.) Two types of presumptive tests are generally available and can be applied to either wet or dry blood specimens. The first involves applying to the suspected evidence a chemical, known as a **chromogen**, that will change in color in the presence of blood. Most of these tests will not harm the blood sample and allow further testing either to confirm the existence of blood or to extract DNA. Specific presumptive tests for the presence of blood include the following:

- ***LMG (Leucomalachite Green) test:*** Also known under the commercial name of *Hemident,* this chromogen reacts by turning green when blood is present. For investigative field use, test strips that contain LMG, called *Hemastix,* are available. The suspected stain is sampled by a swab moistened with distilled water and then it is rubbed on the reactive surface of the test strip. The strip turns from yellow to green when blood is present. A word of caution: Swabs pretreated with cosmetic agents have been known to cause false positives with Hemastix.
- ***Kastle-Meyer (KM) test:*** This test is carried out in a manner similar to that described for the LMG test. However, the chromogen in this test (phenolphthalein) reacts with hemoglobin, turning a pink color when exposed to blood as shown in Figure 4.37.
- ***Leuco Crystal Violet:*** Previously mentioned as a method of enhancing blood fingerprints, this is an excellent chemical for determining the presence of blood transferred to a variety of surfaces, including bloody footprints on carpet, tile, wood, paper products, etc. The application of Leuco Crystal Violet to a bloody footprint on a tile at a crime scene is shown in Figure 4.38.

The second type of presumptive test for blood involves fluorescent light production chemicals. These are best used in areas where blood stains are not readily visible or have been washed away or perhaps covered with paint or some other surface coating. Most common among these are spray-on applications of

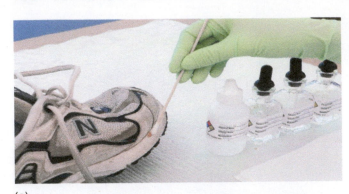

(a)

(b)

FIGURE 4.37 ▶ (a) Suspected blood deposit on a suspect's shoe is swabbed. (b) After subjecting the sample swab to Kastle-Meyer (KM) chemical reagent, the pink-colored reaction indicates the likely presence of blood.

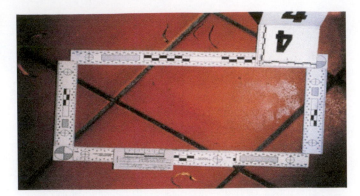

(a)

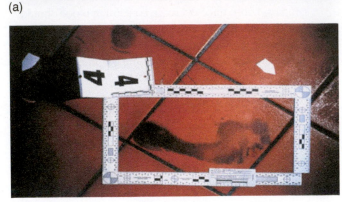

(b)

FIGURE 4.38 ▶ (a) Section of tile floor suspected of containing a bloody footprint; (b) the same section of floor displaying the bloody print after treatment with Leuco Crystal Violet.

the chemicals Luminol and Fluorescein. As discussed in the preceding section on fingerprint evidence, Luminol is a liquid chemical that causes blood to emit light or **fluoresce** as shown in Figure 4.39. It can be applied to virtually any surface, including those where blood evidence is not visible or has been covered up by washing or painting. Once in contact with blood, Luminol will begin to glow pale blue and requires nearly total darkness to be properly visualized. Its visual effects can also be enhanced by using UV light and other ALS sources. The illuminated blood evidence must be quickly photographed using

special light-sensitive techniques because the observable fluorescent effects of Luminol last only a matter of minutes. Fluorescein has blood detection abilities similar to those of Luminol, but its luminescent effects last much longer and it requires UV light or other ALS lighting to be visualized. The use of Luminol or other light reaction methods should be a last resort when attempting to identify blood evidence. This is because these tests can degrade blood evidence, rendering it useless for further testing, which includes attempts to extract DNA genetic markers.[13]

(a)

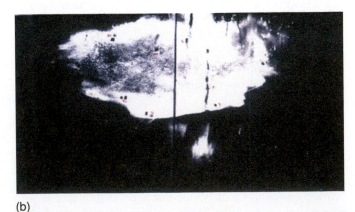

(b)

FIGURE 4.39 ▶ (a) A mattress believed to have been cleaned of blood stains after a shooting. (b) A large fluorescing blood stain is revealed after treating the mattress with Luminol.

Blood Spatter

Patterns of bloods stains, known as **blood spatter**, often are useful for reconstructing the events resulting in a crime, and for corroborating information about a criminal activity provided by suspects, victims, and witnesses. In particular, this type of evidence is useful for determining (1) the position and location of the offender relative to the victim; (2) the number of times the offender wounded the victim, and the method of attack—including any hesitation that occurred while the attack transpired. Blood spatter and its relative qualities can be categorized as follows:

LOW-VELOCITY SPATTER

This type of spatter is usually created by natural forces of gravity, and is usually evidenced as blood droplets falling to the ground from a dripping wound. Cuts or gashes created either offensively or defensively often create large quantities of low-velocity spatter, which form blood trails following the movements of a wounded individual. Investigators often find it useful to follow blood trails leading away from the crime scene to locate wounded suspects or victims and to discover exit points. The bleeding suspect's direction of travel is indicated by the edge of the drop that exhibits an irregular appearance. This edge typically will show spines (shape points radiating away from the drop), scallops (curving patterns at the drop's edge), or satellites (small droplets near the edge of the drop). Thus, if the bleeding individual is traveling from left to right, the irregular edge will be noticeable on the right edge of the droplet. In addition, as the bleeding person begins to move more quickly, the drop will appear less round and become increasingly elongated or angular. When the bleeding individual stops and becomes stationary, pools of blood are created by low-velocity droplets falling into other droplets, causing splashing that is evidenced by satellites surrounding a noticeably larger drop. Droplets falling from a wound that is directly perpendicular (or at a 90° angle) to a surface will be round in shape. Larger drops will generally be greater in size and display spines as well as satellites when falling greater distances to a surface area. Due to the unique physical qualities of blood, however, at heights greater than about 7 feet the size of blood droplets will remain the same regardless of how far they fall.

MEDIUM-VELOCITY SPATTER.

Wounds caused by blunt force trauma such as kicking, punching, striking, or stabbing are the situations most likely to leave behind this spatter pattern. In essence, these spatter patterns are the result of blood being projected from a wound vis-à-vis impact created by a weapon or other object striking the body's surface area, or perhaps a surface already containing blood. Another type of medium-velocity spatter is the arterial spurt. These blood patterns are often discovered at suicide scenes or where victim have endured major blood loss resulting from cut wounds to the neck, leg, and arm regions. Arterial spurts are easily recognized by the large pools of blood they create on surface areas and walls. On vertical surfaces, such as walls and furniture, they appear as a series of elongated splashes that taper off in the direction of gravity (usually toward the floor area). Also, a dense, highly concentrated area of blood in the stain will be located in the direction of gravity as well.

HIGH-VELOCITY SPATTER

Nearly always, this type of spatter is caused by a gunshot wound. It appears on surfaces as a fine mist of pinpoint-size blood droplets. **Backward spatter** results when blood is forced in the direction opposite to a bullet entering the body, and may be deposited on a shooter's skin, hair, wristwatch, shoes, clothes, or within the gun barrel when a shot is taken at close range to the victim. This type of spatter, because of its very small size, has a maximum travel of between 2 and 4 feet. **Forward spatters** are created by blood projected from wounds where bullets exit the body.[14] This type of spatter may also contain particles of skin and other tissue torn from the exit wound. The visual qualities of high-velocity spatter, compared to those of medium- and low-velocity spatter, are illustrated in Figure 4.40. More discussion on blood characteristics of gunshot wounds is presented in Chapter 9.

Special Blood Spatter Indicators
DIRECTION OF TRAVEL

The direction of travel for medium- and high-velocity spatter can be identified by observing the *tail* that extends from

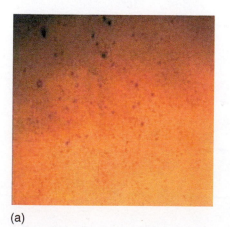

(a)

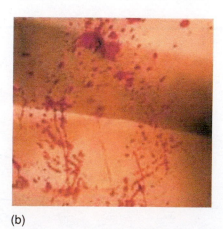

(b)

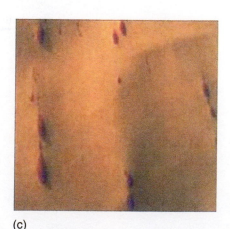

(c)

FIGURE 4.40 ▶ (a) High-velocity spatter, (b) medium-velocity spatter, and (c) low-velocity spatter.

the main body of the blood droplet as shown in Figure 4.41. The side of the droplet containing the tail also indicates the direction of travel. For example, a droplet with the tail located to the left indicates that blood was projected from the right to the left of the surface on which it landed.

POINT OF ORIGIN

One of the most useful interpretations of blood spatter at the crime scene is the determination of the **point of origin**—the approximate location within the crime scene where the bleeding injury took place. For low-velocity spatter, the point of origin is usually easily determined by a concentration of blood pooling about the area where the wounding occurred. Medium- and high-velocity spatter patterns are usually formed on walls a short distance from the impact of the wound, but are found on floors and ceilings (see Figure 4.42 for an illustrated example of the point of origin at a crime scene containing blood spatter).

WIPES, SWIPES AND VOIDS

Blood wipes appear as streaking marks on walls and other surfaces and are produced when an object containing wet blood comes into contact with a surface not containing blood. Common sources of swipes are bloody hair, clothing, hands, weapons, and shoes. Swipes appear as similar streaking patterns but are produced by an object moving through wet or partially dried blood that already exists on a surface. The direction of the feathering pattern usually exhibited at one end of the wipe or swipe streaking pattern denotes the direction of movement for the object making the mark. Swipes may also exhibit a skeleton image of dried blood around the perimeter of the blood marking, which outlines the original strain before it was disturbed. This can also be used to determine the direction of movement. Voids are caused when an object comes between a source of blood spatter and a surface. For example, blood from a shooting victim may be projected onto a shooter who blocks the spatter from reaching the wall behind him. In this case, a void would result in a bloody silhouette of the shooter's body on the wall.

CAST OFF

As illustrated in Figure 4.43, when a wound is created by a blunt force trauma, blood can be flung off the weapon, fist, or other

FIGURE 4.41 ▶ (a) Direction of travel for blood spatter is indicated by scalloped or spined edges for slower moving drops and by a tail for faster moving drops. (b) Blood spatters become more elliptical in shape as the angle of projection becomes more acute (less than 90°). (c) Wave cast off pattern produced by four separate strikes of a weapon (the first accumulates no blood).

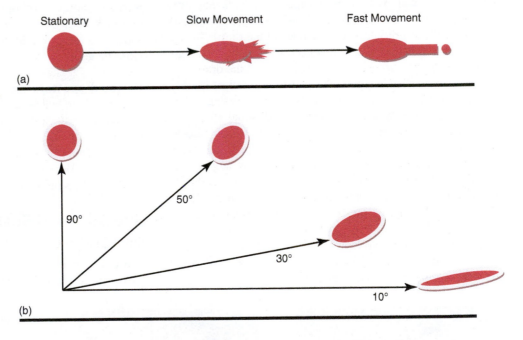

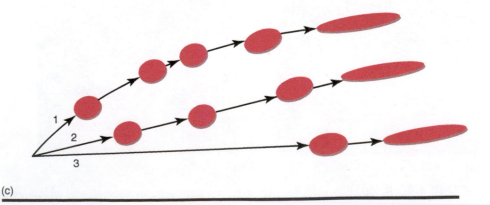

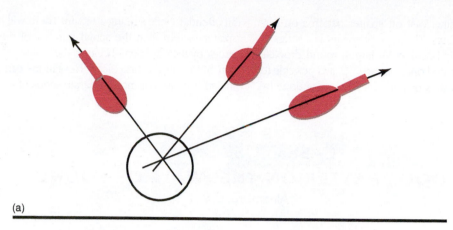

(a)

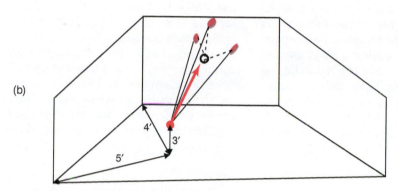

(b)

FIGURE 4.42 ▶ (a) The area of convergence in 2-D on a wall showing the axis or center of the conical pattern from which the blood spatter was projected. (b) The point of origin is the approximate location in 3-D space where the spatter originated. It is determined by estimating the angle from which several drops in the spatter pattern were projected and observing the point at which all droplet angles intersect. This can be done manually with strings or laser lights, or by using specialized computer programs.

FIGURE 4.43 ▶ High-velocity blood spatter patterns. What can be determined about the position of the shooter and victim from this photo? What blood spatter characteristics are present here?

object used and create distinct cast off spatter patterns on surfaces such as walls and ceilings. This type of spatter is a series of arc-like patterns that usually begins with larger, round droplets and ends with smaller elongated ones. Sometimes it is possible to determine the amount of strikes or perhaps hesitations done by an offender while striking a victim. There will be one less cast off spatter pattern than the actual number of times the victim was struck by the offender—because the striking object does not contain blood on the first blow. Hesitations can perhaps be determined from two or more separate series of cast off patterns.

CASE CLOSE-UP 4.3

"BLOOD SPATTER ON THE 'WALL OF SOUND'"
Alhambra, CA

Legendary rock music producer and creator of the "Wall of Sound," Phil Spector, depended on blood spatter evidence as a key factor in his legal defense when charged with the murder of a woman in his home. Prosecutors claimed that Spector had pulled the trigger on a handgun positioned in the victim's mouth, leaving a small amount of backward blood spatter on the sleeve of a jacket he was wearing at the time of the shooting. In his defense, Spector claimed that he was standing at a distance from the victim when she voluntarily decided to commit suicide by discharging the weapon in her mouth. Expert witnesses for the prosecution testified that the backward spatter could travel a distance of only 2 to 3 feet—implying that Spector was standing at arm's length of the victim and was indeed capable of pulling the trigger. Forensic experts testifying on Spector's behalf countered by stating that it was scientifically possible for the backward blood spatter produced by the shooting to have traveled up to 6 feet—supporting Spector's claim that the blood could have been deposited on his jacket sleeve when he was beyond arm's length from the victim when the fatal shot was fired. After two trials, Spector was convicted of second-degree murder.

DENTAL EVIDENCE

The practice of **forensic odontology** is primarily concerned with the classification and individualization of criminal evidence relating to human teeth and bite marks, although the analysis of impression evidence made by animal teeth may be included as well. Most persons working in this area of the forensic sciences are licensed dentists or oral surgeons. They are often used to provide personal identities of persons whose bodies have been destroyed or mutilated as the resulting of mass disasters, bombings, accidents, fires, and homicide. Because of their level of expertise with dental stone, forensic odontologists are also employed to form permanent casts of impressions made not only by teeth but also from various other sources such as shoes, tires, and tool marks.

Besides performing the routine classing of teeth based on size, shape, number, and eruption patterns, forensic odontologists often can establish an individual identity on the basis of dental features unique to each person, known as the **dental fingerprint**. This level of dental identification can be carried out by inspection of the following:

- Number and type of teeth present or absent
- Wear patterns and chipping of teeth
- Dental work compared to existing dental records
- Size and shape of the dental arcade
- Rotation and alignment of individual teeth

Taken together, all of these dental characteristics form a dental fingerprint that is so complex that it can be assumed that no two bite mark impressions are alike.

Of particular importance to criminal investigations is the analysis of bite mark evidence in homicides, sexual abuse, domestic violence, and assaults. The location of such evidence can often provide clues as to the type of attack and attacker. For example, multiple bite marks on the hands, arms, neck, and shoulder areas often reflect defense wounds administered to attackers by their victims. Conversely, single bite marks in isolated areas such as breasts, nipples, the back, buttocks, and inner thighs can often be linked to sexually assaultive activity. Bite marks can also indicate whether the victim was living or dead at the time of attack. Typically, when the victim is alive, bruising occurs around the wounded area (see Figure 4.44). Victims who are dead do not exhibit bruising around bite marks.

Bite marks can also be discovered on numerous objects; pencils, food items, Styrofoam cups, chewing gum, cigarette/cigar butts, and straws, to name a few. Areas on objects that have been bitten can often be identified by the use of ALS sources. In particular, UV light will illuminate bite marks, especially those containing bodily fluids such as blood and/or saliva. ALS illumination of bite mark evidence often can be used to detect areas on skin that are months old. Impressions not involving actual penetration of the skin by teeth (i.e., where there is only bruising) can be visualized as well.

Bite marks should be photographed in black and white and in color from a 90° angle as well as other angles with a scale for size and color (preferably ABFO) in the photo frame. This should be done within 8 hours after the bite because inflammation will likely obscure the surface of the wound after that time. After preliminary photographs are taken, the wound should be swabbed for bodily fluid evidence that perhaps may

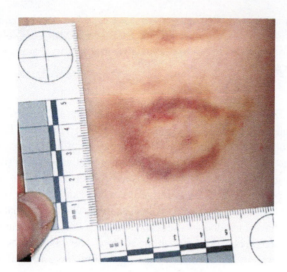

FIGURE 4.44 ▶ Bruising left from a bite mark on a sexual assault victim.

yield DNA evidence deposited by the offender. Bodily fluids such as saliva and blood, as well as hairs, present in the bite wound may also be collected and tested along with the bite mark impression. Appropriate medical personnel generally should be consulted before performing the swabbing procedure. Swabs taken from bite marks that are over 48 hours old or that have been washed most likely will not produce usable evidence. Sampled swabs should be air dried, labeled, and packaged separately in paper bags to avoid cross-contamination as well as spoilage due to bacterial growth. Casts of the bite mark impression may also be taken at this time if the wound is sufficiently deep. Casting materials are usually the same as those used to make standard dental impressions. After all evidence collection procedures are complete, a second round of photographs of the bite mark impressions should be taken.

After the victim's impression is documented, by photograph and/or casting, sample impressions are obtained from likely suspects. Measurement, photographic comparisons, and **bite exemplars**, made from casting the suspect's dental impressions, may all be used to compare bite marks obtained from suspects and victims. Sketches or specialized computer programs that produce transparent overlays of bite mark patterns can be used to perform this matching procedure. Some dental evidence on missing and unidentified dead persons is also available for computer matching on the National Crime Information

Center (NCIC) system. Once a match is identified, the forensic odontologist may perhaps be required to provide details of the bite mark comparison and match in a court of law.[15]

SKELETAL REMAINS

Skeletal remains (bones, skull, and teeth) may be discovered in various crime scene situations, including buried bodies, fires, and explosions. They may be located directly within the crime scene, as in a burial or fire, or at some distance from the primary location of the crime (for example, removal by animals, or scattering by explosion). Most often, buried bodies are discovered by hikers and hunters in remote areas. When found, skeletal remains may or may not have soft tissue (flesh). If soft tissue is present, the remains will likely be infested by insects—especially flies. Clothing items such as shoes, hats, or gloves may still be intact, and they should not be separated from the bone to which they are attached. Intact bodies of infants and small children can be placed in their entirety within body bags to avoid disturbing the anatomical position in which they were found. When handling entire adult bodies, anatomical position can be maintained by placing the torso and trousers as a single unit in a body bag. The remaining hands, feet, and skull can be bagged separately. Soil around the abdominal and torso area should be searched for bullets or other signs of weapons that may have been lodged in soft tissue before decomposition. If possible, a crime scene technician or forensic anthropologist specifically trained in handling skeletal remains should be consulted before removing bones from the crime scene. Specific methods of recovering skeletal remains evidence from crime scenes include the following:

- Never pulling bones from dirt, but rather removing them only after they have been fully exposed
- Cleaning remains with soft instruments (i.e., brushes) and air drying them before storage
- Immediate refrigeration of remains when soft tissue is present
- Placing dry remains in body bags or paper bags and wet remains in permeable plastic containers
- Wrapping fragile bones with acid-free tissue paper for padding
- Obtaining insect samples on and around the remains and packaging them in film canisters or pill bottles[16]

CASE CLOSE-UP 4.4

"INSIDE GACY'S BASEMENT"
Des Plaines, Ill.

After the arrest of notorious serial killer John Wayne Gacy, investigators had to perform the gruesome task of unearthing the skeletal remains of many of the 33 victims whose bodies had decomposed in the basement of the killer's home. To complicate matters, most of the soft tissue had been removed from the victims' bones by a flesh-decomposing chemical solution that Gacy had applied to the dead bodies, and most of the bones were stacked together in common graves. Many of the skeletons were eventually reconstructed by experts who matched bones by size and shape using x-rays and dental records of missing persons as well as personal identification material, such as driver's licenses, that Gacy had kept as souvenirs of the victims he had killed. Eventually, these skeletal reconstructions were key evidence leading to Gacy's murder conviction.

SOIL, DUST, AND BOTANICAL EVIDENCE

Soil

Soil is composed of various elements, including minerals, microorganisms, particles, fossils, and decayed plant matter. When these are visualized microscopically and tested through other means, different types of soils and their class characteristics can be differentiated. Generally, samples of earth cannot be individualized down to specific locations of origin. Rather, analyses of specific colors and particle sizes can be used to determine the approximate area from which a given piece of soil evidence likely originated. For example, it would be possible to claim that soil discovered in the tires of a suspect's vehicle did or did not originate from a field where a murder victim was buried; however, it would be highly improbable that the same soil evidence could be linked to the gravesite itself. Where soil contains traces of human or industrial activity, such as fibers, cinders, paint chips, glass fragments, and so forth, it may be possible to approach the level of individualization. For example, soil containing wood chips transferred to the suspect's shoe from a baseball bat used as a murder weapon might perhaps be treated as individualizing evidence. Similarly, soil obtained from packages, containers, and storage areas where illegal drugs have been seized—especially those containing marijuana plants or other illegal drugs grown in earth—may be useful for determining not only where the illegal substance originated but also trade routes through which it has been smuggled.

Trace soil evidence can be gathered from impressions, suspects, or as comparison samples. For impression evidence, take samples directly from contact points within the shoe print or tire track—but do so only after the impression has been photographed and/or a cast of it has been made. From subjects, obtain a tablespoon-size sample of soil. Do not remove mud or other soil adhering to shoes, clothes, or tools. Rather, these items should be air dried and packaged separately as one complete piece of evidence. Articles containing loose soil can be shaken over a clean piece of paper, which can be folded and packaged inside a plastic bag or container.

The number of comparison **soil samples** taken from a crime scene or other location will depend on factors such as its size and geography. Usually, the scene to be sampled will consist of the ground's surface area. For these locations, collect three separate samples of 1 tablespoon each from the top ¼ inch of the surface. Carry out this procedure in specific sections of soil where the crime scene and the suspect can be compared. If the suspect's soil-covered shoes or tires are discovered, attempt to locate matching impressions from the crime scene and take samples from areas of the impression directly corresponding to soil located within the shoe sole or tire tread. When impressions are not present, attempt to collect representative samples of soil from ground areas (including isolated flower beds) believed to have been used by the suspect to enter and exit the crime scene. It is especially important to collect samples from areas that suspects have included in their alibis, such as fields, recreational areas, yards, or work areas. If the scene is one where some type of excavation has occurred (e.g., a gravesite), take vertical samples at different depths and record each sample's location.

In general, all soil samples should be collected as soon as possible to avoid changes produced by weather and other sources of physical disruption. When feasible, a sampling of soil should be obtained from not only the crime scene but from areas surrounding the crime scene as well. Sample all locations where there are noticeable changes in color, text, and composition. Even where visible differences in soil are not readily apparent, different areas contiguous to the crime scene should still be sampled because the chemical structure of soil can change radically within a very short distance. To obtain a representative sample of large areas, approximately 50 random locations should be sampled as shown in Figure 4.45.

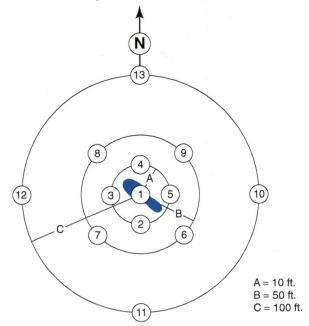

A = 10 ft.
B = 50 ft.
C = 100 ft.

FIGURE 4.45 ▶ Soil sample collection: Start at point #1 (the location of the print or body, or the central location of evidence within the core of the crime scene) and collect soil samples at each of the 13 points. Mark each sample with the number corresponding to its location in the scene. Note any unusual characteristics of the soil or terrain at each location.

identifying information. Note any unique characteristics of the area sampled (for example, wet, dry, oil-saturated soil). Be sure to air dry soil before packaging to avoid mold growth. Leave all clumps of soil intact and package to avoid breakage or separation from the item to which the clumped soil is affixed.[17]

Dust and Botanicals

Dust is another form of trace evidence providing information similar to that of soil. Fine particles of soil and stone are the major components of dust; however, particles of soot, plastic, and clothing fibers as well as deposits of substances such as cooking grease, vegetable oils, candle wax, and cleaning/polishing products can be discovered in dust. In cases of suspected arson, dust is often useful for identifying traces of accelerant settling on vehicles and clothing of suspects who claim that they were nowhere near the arson location. Dusts produced by grain and flour mills, lumber yards, and industrial manufacturing locations also can be used to indicate where, and possibly when, suspects, vehicles, or bodies were near the dust source.

Botanical evidence, or trace evidence produced by plants and trees, are often found in soil and dust. Pollen and spores produced by plants have unique sizes and shapes that can be traced to specific botanical species. Clumps of pollen are often dropped on ground areas near plants disturbed by the movements of offenders. For example, a burglar kicking over a flower pot would deposit pollen on the ground below the displaced plant as well as on the offend-

FIGURE 4.46 ▶ Recently the FBI has reopened the D. B. Cooper case, releasing to the public the evidence shown here in the hope of obtaining new leads. In 1971, after hijacking a Northwest Airlines flight and obtaining a parachute and $200,000 in ransom, Cooper jumped from the plane somewhere around Portland, Oregon, and was never found. The major case evidence recovered thus far is pictured here. New technology currently is being used to analyze pollen found on his tie and soil caked in the bills to discover the approximate location where he landed—in hopes that his remains can be discovered and the case finally closed. (Courtesy United States Department of Justice)

Autos used during the course of a criminal activity or involved in hit-and-runs often provide valuable evidence in the form of soil samples. Aside from tire treads, samples can be taken from the (1) inner and exterior surface areas of the front bumper, grill, and rear bumper; (2) wheel wells and tires; (3) engine compartment, and especially the air filter housing; (4) rock panels; (5) control arms/A-frames and leaf springs; (6) tops of mufflers and condensers; and (7) interior of the passenger compartment and trunk. Clothing items, especially socks, pant legs, and gloves, should also be inspected for possible dirt deposits that may match soil reference samples taken from autos and outdoor crime scenes.

Label and package all soil evidence in separate plastic bags, film canisters, pill bottles, or airtight containers (preferably nonglass or paper). Labeling should include location of sample, name of collecting officer, date, time, and other pertinent

er's shoes and perhaps other clothing items. Microscopic plant seeds or spores are another botanical released from plants that can be linked to specific species within certain locations. Leaves, stems, wood particles, bark, needles, and other botanical residue form plants and trees can also be identified as originating from specific areas and terrains. Figure 4.46 shows botanical evidence on money believed to have been in the possession of missing felon D. B. Cooper when he jumped from an aircraft at high altitude. The FBI hopes that this evidence will lead them to the place where Cooper landed.

Dust and dust-like particles perhaps containing pollen, spores, or trace botanical evidence can be collected using the following methods:

- Using adhesive tape to lift the dust and attaching it to a clear glass microscope slide (make sure the tape does not damage the surface to which it is applied)

- Wiping the dusty surface with a sterile cloth, swap, or filter paper and then packaging the sample in a clear plastic bag or other airtight container

- Vacuuming surfaces containing dust (be aware that certain filters may block larger particles from being collected by this method)

- Brushing dust from surfaces (synthetic bristles work best) and preserving the sample in a Glassine envelope or resealable plastic bag

- Scraping solidified dust from a surface area with a razor blade or scalpel and placing the chips as well as the blade into a plastic container

Because this type of trace evidence is highly susceptible to cross-contamination, extreme care should be taken to either discard disposable evidence collection tools after each use or to thoroughly clean any reusable tool with alcohol or disinfectant before using it to take multiple samples. As always, each evidence item must be labeled and documented before it is shipped to storage facilities or a crime laboratory.

CASE CLOSE-UP 4.5

"THE LINDBERG KIDNAPPING"
Hopewell, N.J.

When the 18-month-old child of famed aviator Charles Lindbergh was kidnapped from his home, the only solid clue at the crime scene was a wooden ladder that the offender used to climb through a second-story window into the room where the child was sleeping. The ladder was homemade, consisting of three separate sections each about 6 feet in length. Investigators assumed that the sections were assembled to form a single 18-feet ladder after being transported to the Lindbergh home inside the kidnapper's vehicle. An inspection of the ladder by a botanicals scientific expert revealed that it consisted of four specific types of wood and exhibited tool marks from a hand saw, chisel, and wood plane—causing investigators to conclude that the kidnapper was perhaps a carpenter. Some 2 years after the kidnapping, a carpenter named Bruno Hauptmann was arrested after spending marked bills contained in ransom money paid by Lindberg. An examination of the attic at Hauptmann's residence revealed numerous missing and cut floorboards as well as traces of sawdust. At trial, scientific experts demonstrated how the type of wood used to construct the ladder obtained from the crime scene was biologically identical to that discovered in floorboards found in Hauptmann's attic. In addition, microscopic analyses of saw, drill, and wood plane tool marks in the evidence precisely matched the cutting edges of Hauptmann's carpentry tools.[18]

GLASS EVIDENCE

Glass evidence has the potential to yield both class and individual characteristics. From glass samples, it is often possible to:

- classify or determine the type of object from which fragments of glass originated;
- individualize or identify the specific object from which fragments of glass originated;
- specify the cause of glass breakage;
- pinpoint the origin of a glass fracture, the direction of the projectile causing the fracture, and the order of impact of several objects causing multiple fractures.

Classifying Glass

Through simple observation, it is often possible for investigators to class a particular type of questioned glass fragment. Safety glass, the type most often used in car windshields, is manufactured so that it does not shatter. Establishing the origin of this glass type is usually never a problem because when it breaks it either remains intact within the windshield area of a vehicle or other frame where it is secured. Chunks of safety glass can be observed at some crime or accident scenes when sections of glass have been separated from the main sheet. It is highly unlikely that fragments would be found on the clothing of persons breaking this type of glass because small particles do not scatter upon impact. Another type of glass commonly used in vehicle side windows, rear windows, commercial buildings, shower doors, and other locations where safety is a concern is tempered glass. When tempered glass shatters (see Figure 4.47), it can be identified by fragments that resemble small cubes that are designed to reduce the likelihood of cutting. Loose particles of tempered glass can become lodged in clothing, tire treads, or shoe soles of offenders who have forced entry into automobiles or structures utilizing tempered glass. Common sheet glass, or float glass, found in residential structures, furniture, and other household or manufactured items, cracks into jagged pieces resembling jigsaw puzzle pieces upon impact. In addition, small shards of glass capable of cutting are projected both in the direction of the impact and backwards toward the source of impact. Blood is frequently found at the scenes of break-ins

FIGURE 4.47 ▶ Pieces of tempered glass magnified under a microscope for purposes of obtaining a physical match.

FIGURE 4.48 ▶ A physical match of glass fragments from an automobile windshield.

executed by fracturing common sheet glass. Particles of this glass type easily become imbedded in tools, clothing, shoes, bullets, or other objects associated with the offender—including the offender's hair and skin. Shards of sheet glass have been known to be projected 4 feet or more from the point of impact. When glass evidence cannot be readily identified by simple observation, specialized laboratory tests for its chemical composition, physical properties, and microscopic characteristics can be used for classification purposes. The Glass Evidence Reference Database has been constructed to identify over 700 types of glass and can provide leads regarding specific manufacturers and distributors.

Individualizing Glass

The most common technique for individualizing glass evidence is through a process referred to as physical matching. This method involves assembling the loose pieces of glass from any given source to determine which, if any, fit together in a jigsaw-like fashion as shown in Figure 4.48. Physical matches provide extremely convincing individualized evidence because of the fact that each fracture pattern in glass is as unique as a fingerprint; therefore, no two matching broken glass pieces are alike or can be artificially duplicated. For glass cut with a tool such as a glass cutter, laser light sources have proven successful in illuminating microscopic indicators of a physical match between two sections of cut glass. Safety glass and tempered glass, because of their specialized design, cannot be individualized by using a physical matching procedure.

Origin and Direction Fractures

When objects strike glass they commonly leave a hole, fracture lines, and a crater. When there is a well-defined hole within an intact sheet of glass, the point of origin of the breakage is without question. When there is a complete fracture of the entire glass sheet, however, or large sections of glass are missing (which is common in fractures of safety or tempered glass),

determining the origin of breakage can be difficult and perhaps impossible. In such instances, existing fracture lines in the glass should be examined to identify a point where they would likely have converged had the glass remained intact. The direction of fracture can usually be determined by locating which side of the glass contains a crater and which does not. Usually, the side without a crater indicates the initial strike (entry) and that with the crater (as shown in Figure 4.49) suggests the direction of travel (exit). In situations where well-defined craters are not visible, sections of glass can be examined for **Wallner lines or rib marks** that indicate the direction of impact. These markings can be seen on broken pieces of glass when viewed from the side where the breakage occurred. To use this type of analysis, however, it is imperative to determine whether the broken area being observed was the result of either a **radial fracture** or a **concentric fracture**. Radial fractures form in a spoke-like pattern extending away from the entry/exit hole or point of impact.

FIGURE 4.49 ▶ An exit hole produced by a bullet fired into ordinary sheet glass. Note the larger amounts of glass displaced around the hole produced by the exiting bullet, and the radial factures within the glass. (© Arunas Gabalis/Shutterstock)

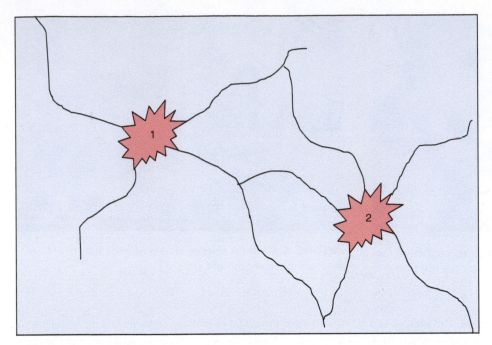

FIGURE 4.50 ▶ Radial fractures often can be used to determine the order of bullets shot into the same section of glass. In the case of the above example, the termination of the radial fractures from bullet hole #2 indicates that it was created after bullet hole #1.

Rib marks on fractured edges of these pieces will be noticeably perpendicular to the surface of the glass on the side opposite the point of impact (e.g., the exit point). Concentric fractures form in a circular pattern around the entry/exit hole or point of impact and exhibit perpendicular rib marks on the side of the glass where the entry or strike occurred.[19]

It is often possible to identify the trajectory of a bullet or other projectile striking glass by examining the angle of the hole caused by penetration. In addition, the crater on the reverse side, if present, will exhibit a shoulder that has increased size and glass flaking on the side representing the angle of travel. When multiple fractures exist in the same sheet of glass, it is usually possible to ascertain the order in which each projectile struck the surface. This is done by examining the configuration of radial fracture lines originating from each strike area. More specifically, lines that stop at the point of convergence with other lines indicate a strike that has followed one that has already taken place. Figure 4.50 illustrates a typical two-shot sequence as it would appear on a sheet glass window. (See also the Order of Impact section.)

Cause of Breakage

Technically speaking, glass breaks when pressure is applied to its surface, causing it to bend to the point where it fractures. Thus, any object that can stress glass to the point of fracturing can be identified as the cause of breakage. Such objects can be blunt and travel slowly, or sharp and move at a high velocity. When a large, slow-moving object, such as a brick, rock, or even a protected fist, is used as a breaking instrument, large sections of glass will be displaced, and the particular item

causing the breakage (unless removed by the offender) usually remains at the scene. Breakages caused by smaller, faster moving projectiles are often most problematic to investigators attempting to determine the cause of broken glass. These objects typically leave several telltale characteristics of investigative importance.

First, and most obvious, a bullet or another projectile causing the breakage may be located at the scene. Hollow-point bullets and other types of ammunition with limited jacketing, however, may simply be ground to dust as they travel through the glass—leaving no clue as to the cause of breakage. Generally, though, larger caliber high-velocity bullets leave well-defined round holes surrounded by minimal cracking in the glass they have penetrated. Visible round portions of missing glass or craters located on the reverse side of impact also become larger and begin to exhibit greater amounts of flaking glass as the velocity of the bullet decreases. (Glass fragments from caters can travel as far as 18 feet from the point of impact.) On the other hand, smaller caliber lower-velocity ammunition will leave large amounts of visible cracking around an irregular appearing hole at the point of impact. In some instances, a low-velocity bullet fired from a distance, or a high-velocity one fired at close range but striking an intermediate object, will move so slowly that it fails to penetrate the glass it strikes. Often in these instances all that can be seen is a crater on the glass surface opposite that of the impact. Pellets or BBs from air rifles and small pebbles thrown from moving vehicle tires are common causes of this type of breakage as well.

Order of Impact

When multiple gunshots and other high-velocity objects strike a single piece of glass, it is often possible to determine the order of impact. This is done by examining the fracture lines emerging away from strike points that are close to one another. The first strike point can be identified by continuous fracture lines that extend away from the point of impact (or bullet hole) in an uninterrupted fashion. The second strike point will exhibit radial fracture lines that terminate into fracture lines of the first strike. Additional strikes—third, fourth, and so on—can be determined in the same manner by inspecting the termination sequence of radial fracture lines. Figure 4.51 shows multiple gun shots into a safety glass automobile windshield. As this figure illustrates, it is often difficult to determine the order of impact from bullets fired into windshields because safety glass restricts the spread of fracture lines.

FIGURE 4.51 ▶ It is often difficult to determine the order of impact of bullets in glass where there are multiple scattered bullet holes—as in this windshield riddled with automatic gun fire.

(a)

Vehicle Lamp Evidence

When vehicles are involved in hit-and-runs or other criminal activity where there is breakage of headlights, taillights, and directional indicators, it is possible to obtain a physical match between pieces of broken headlight or other light lenses found on the victim's body and those still remaining intact on the vehicle. In these situations, it is necessary to remove the broken lens from the vehicle and collect all pieces of broken glass or plastic belonging to the affected lens. In addition, examination of the headlamp filament can suggest whether the light was on at the time of a crash. When the lights are on, the hot filament is flexible and generally will remain intact upon impact and bend in the direction of impact—a process referred to as **hot shock** (see Figure 4.52(a)). Thus, a rear-end collision will curve a filament toward the rear of the vehicle. Hot filaments will also show signs of oxidation in the form of white powder or dust located on the filament and within the headlight lens area. They may also collect glass shards and plastic residue from shattered lenses. Cold filaments, on the other hand, tend to break upon impact—known as **cold shock** (also shown in Figure 4.52(b)). Thus, broken filaments suggest that lights were indeed off at the time of a collision. Make sure that the filament is intact on the filament post; if not, attempt to locate the filament. Package the vehicle lens material in a firm container and cushion it with cotton or paper. Smaller fragmentary evidence should be similarly packaged and protected with gauze or tissue.[20]

Handling Glass Evidence

Larger pieces of glass can be collected by hand, using rubber or fabric gloves, forceps, tweezers, or other handheld collection devices. Vacuuming is recommended for very small or microscopic fragments, especially those located on clothing items. Typically, shards of glass become trapped within pockets, cuffs of pants, and shoes (both top and soles). Glass can also become

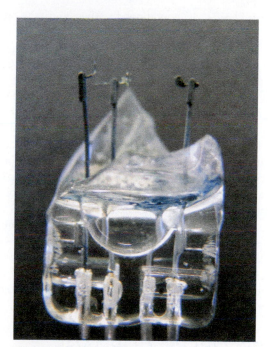

(b)

FIGURE 4.52 ▶ (a) Headlight filaments turned on during a collision exhibit *hot shock*, remaining intact and bent in the direction of impact. (b) Filaments turned off at the time of a collision are broken by *cold shock*.

lodged within head hairs and recovered by combing or shaking hair over a sterile sheet of paper. Tire treads of vehicles entering and exiting the crime scene may also contain traces of glass. When handling glass evidence, take care not to disturb possible transfer evidence located on the glass such as fingerprints, blood, dust, fibers, and the like. Guard against cross-contamination by sanitizing or disposing of tweezers or other collection implements that have possibly made contact with any transfer-type trace evidence located on glass fragments.

Collect as many pieces or fragments of glass as possible given the circumstances and time constraints of the crime scene. If multiple objects are broken, as happens with several window panes or vehicle windows, take samples from each area of breakage. Keep all samples of glass from separate objects or areas separated. If glass from various objects appears to be mixed together, try to separate them out based on differences in physical properties such as sizes, shapes, and colors. Broken windows or other objects from which physical matches can likely be made require the collection of most if not all fragments of glass that can be recovered from the location of breakage. Where possible, it is recommended that the entire frame of an affected window be removed so that a jig-saw puzzle physical matching procedure of all associated glass fragments can be performed. For structures that cannot be removed, take sections of glass from the frame and label both the inside and outside surfaces. It is useful to construct a diagram if multiple panes are involved.

Grease pencils, diamond-tipped scribes, and tape-on labels can be used to mark glass evidence. Larger pieces of glass should be marked on the surface that is facing up at the time of recovery and include the recovering officer's initials, in addition to the time and date of recovery. When a particular item of glass has been identified with an evidence marker, the number or letter of the marker should also be inscribed on the glass. Smaller fragments that cannot be individually labeled can be placed in pill bottles, film canisters, or other sealed containers and marked in an appropriate manner. Glass should be packaged so that it does not move or break. Crumpled paper or packing material can be used to secure larger pieces placed in containers such as cardboard boxes. Smaller pieces can be wrapped in paper and cushioned with cotton. Make sure, however, that the cotton or other materials containing fibers do not make direct contact with the evidence. Clothing items and tools containing glass fragments should be packaged and labeled separately. Be sure to air dry any items containing blood or other bodily fluids.[21]

HAIRS, FIBERS, CORDAGE, AND TAPE

Hairs and fibers from clothing, furniture, carpets, rope, and other woven materials are valuable sources of evidence because they are often *transferred* (or passed) from suspects to victims or to the crime scene. These include human and animal hairs, as well as natural and synthetic fibers. Generally speaking, loose hairs and fibers associated with the crime scene should be collected. Because this type of evidence is often quite small in size and difficult to visualize, ALS lighting is often required to locate hair and fiber evidence. In particular, UV lighting is effective because it causes hair and fibers to fluoresce. If ALS is not available, oblique lighting using a flashlight or other standard illumination device can provide satisfactory results.

Hair, in particular, has the unique quality of becoming embedded into certain objects and surfaces. In particular, hats, carpet, wool clothing, fabric-covered car seats, and material-upholstered furniture are likely places to discover embedded hairs. Objects containing hairs or fibers, even those in which the hair is simply attached with dried blood, should be gathered in their entirety without attempting to remove the hair or fiber. Hair evidence is particularly important in the investigation of sexual assault cases, especially forcible rape, where transfer can occur to undergarments, bite wounds, and existing hair within the head and pubic region.

When possible, for comparative purposes, hair samples should be gathered from the victim as well as the suspect(s). This procedure is normally carried out by medical personnel in the presence of an investigator who is the same gender as the person from whom the sample is taken, and requires a search warrant before being performed. Samples of **foreign hair** (loose or unattached) are collected by combing or brushing the head, pubic area, and other areas of the body. Fresh combs or brushes should be used for each separate region of the body and then submitted to the laboratory along with the sample they were used to obtain. Samples of living attached hair, in multiples of 25, are also collected by medical personnel by either plucking or tweezing (not cutting) from the desired location. Because the shape, size, and characteristics of hair are different in various locations of the head, separate samples should be taken from the top, side, and back of the head area. As a rule, the greater the number of hairs sampled from different regions of the body, the stronger the hair evidence will be in a court of law.[22]

Weave patterns produced by cloth from clothing, blankets and other woven materials can sometimes be detected (1) within bloody transfer prints on floors, walls, and objects, (2) as an impression on the skin after wounding or death (see Chapter 9 for more details) and (3) possibly as a print on surface areas covered with dust or other residue. In shootings, fibers from clothing or other materials through which a bullet passes sometimes are trapped on the projectile's surface area and can be used to identify the order in which certain objects were hit. Twine, shoelaces, rope, or other cordage-type materials used for victim restraint purposes or strangulation (as in ligatures) often leave impression patterns on skin where they have been applied with pressure. In any of the foregoing examples, it may be possible to match physical fibers from evidence items to those obtained from suspects or standard samples. It is also sometimes possible to match the cut ends of cordage with those of known standard samples or from primary pieces of rope or twine belonging to suspects.

Tape is often discovered at crime scenes. Most common is duct tape used for restraining victims, securing containers containing drugs, and perhaps as ligature material. Second most common is vinyl electrical tape, most frequently used to fashion explosive devices. As previously mentioned, most tape varieties can be developed for fingerprints and other impression

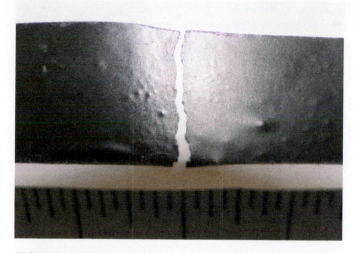

FIGURE 4.53 ▶ Physical match between electrical tape recovered from a crime scene and the original roll of tape from which it was removed.

evidence. As shown in Figure 4.53, ripped or torn edges of tape sections obtained in crime scenes can also be compared to standard samples or to full rolls of tape with torn edges possessed by suspects to perform a physical match. Many types of industrial use tape include fibrous materials to add strength. These fibers as well as adhesive products in the tape may become deposited on the hands, shoes, tools, weapons, and other objects handled by the offender. Microscopic analyses can be performed on such fiber evidence to determine the type and manufacture of the tape product as well as perhaps individualize matching fiber patterns between known and unknown evidence sources. The adhesive side of tape may

contain hairs, clothing fibers, skin cells, or sweat possibly containing DNA, glass fragments, and other valuable trace evidence.

Generally, the following methods can be used to recover hair and fiber evidence from a crime scene:

- Tweezing: using a pair of tweezers to pick up hairs or fibers and place them into paper bindles or wrapping them in clean paper.
- Taping: using a 5- or 6-inch piece of celluloid adhesive tape to collect hairs and fibers and then adhering the tape to a clear plastic sheet
- Vacuuming: using a vacuum to suction hairs and fibers from surfaces
- Picking: using your gloved fingers to recover hairs and fibers
- For tape evidence, do not remove tape from the evidence object if possible; rather submit entire taped object for analysis. If tape is removed, identify cut ends and package loosely in a box made from plastic or other materials that will not adhere to the tape. Do not expose tape to tissues, cotton, or other packing materials that will transfer to the tape. Do not attempt to unravel balled-up tape. Submit such evidence in the condition in which it was discovered.
- For cordage evidence, package in plastic bags, paper, or cardboard containers. When removing tied cordage from a victim or object, do not cut knotted areas. Perform a new cut away from knots and secure the loose ends of the cordage with string to form a complete loop and attach an evidence tag with appropriate identifying information.[23]

CASE CLOSE-UP 4.6

"THE UNABOMBER"
Lincoln, Montana

Ted Kaczynski, aka "The Unabomber," admitted to planting two human hairs that he found at a bus station into one of his homemade bombs in order to throw police off his trail. After confessing to the bombing sprees that left 3 people

dead and 23 injured, a search of Kaczynski's cabin in the rural hills of Montana revealed a pair a shoes that he had modified by covering the original soles with another set of soles that were smaller and different in design.

PAINT EVIDENCE

Wet or dry paint can be a potential source of evidence. Smears, palm prints, fingerprints, and footprints are often left on various surfaces within crime scenes where an offender has come into contact with wet paint. Hairs and fibers may also be stuck to freshly painted areas. Dry paint evidence is usually created when paint is transferred from one surface to another as the

result of a scraping motion or some other type of abrasive contact. For example, a vehicle involved in a hit-and-run with another vehicle (or even a person) will deposit paint residue on the object it strikes. **Cross-transfer** occurs when two painted objects strike and deposit residue on each other as, for example, when two vehicles collide. Other items with hard metallic surfaces such as firearms and tools are also likely to transfer paint evidence when used during criminal activities. Efforts

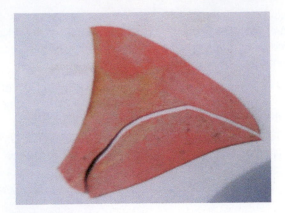

FIGURE 4.54 ▶ Physical match of two paint chips.

should be made to search for chips of dry paint that have broken away from the surface of a vehicle or weapon. Both large and small fragments may be discovered in and around the point of impact, or lodged within a victim's hair, skin, or clothing. As illustrated in Figure 4.54, unique jig-saw patterns of dried paint chips can be matched to locations from which they originated on a particular firearm, tool, or other instrument used in a crime. The following are important guidelines for collecting paint evidence:

- Entire clothing items containing paint evidence should be packaged separately.
- Paint chips should be placed within paper bindles, leakproof vials, or pillboxes.
- Entire objects containing transfer paint residue should be packaged separately, if possible.
- Areas containing paint residue on motor vehicles should be sampled by scoring the affected area with a clean knife and removing a full paint chip that extends to the bottom of the painted surface to capture all layers of the paint. Samples of the vehicle's original color should be taken as well in the same manner.
- Avoid placing paint evidence in plastic bags, envelopes, or within cotton; do not collect such items with adhesive tape.

It is often possible to obtain suspect and vehicle leads based on paint evidence through the use of available paint identification databases. The Royal Canadian Mounted Police (RCMP) maintains forensic data on the chemical composition of most paints used on domestic and foreign vehicles sold in North America since 1973. Likewise, the FBI houses a database that includes over 40,000 samples of auto paint provided by vehicle manufacturers.[24]

ABRASIVE EVIDENCE

Abrasives are either natural or synthetic substances that consist of coarse particles and are typically used to wear down hardened solid metal surfaces. In the past, the criminal use of abrasives has been mainly limited to persons seeking revenge by putting gritty compounds in the gas tank of their ex-lover's or employer's vehicle to cause mechanical and motor failure. Recently,

however, abrasives have been used in a growing number of crimes committed by domestic terror organizations (some of which have international ties) designed to sabotage machinery or vehicles belonging to governmental and private organizations. Sand, dirt, salt, and various forms of commercial grinding compounds are the abrasives of choice for most crimes. (Despite popular belief, sugar placed in gasoline tanks or other fuel supply locations will not cause permanent damage to internal combustion engines.) The sabotage of electrical motors is usually carried out by introducing the abrasive to the motor's bearings either directly or packed in grease. The abrasive substance, if present, will generally remain present in the bearing unit.

Attempts to destroy gasoline or diesel motors involve pouring the abrasive directly into either the oil or the fuel supply. Abrasive residue may be visible in and around the motor's gas or oil fill location, oil dipstick/dipstick holder, gas filter, and oil filter. Abrasives tend to settle within oil and gas. The crime scene area should be searched for gloves, funnels (used to pour), and plastic bottles (used to mix abrasives with oil or fuel). Persons purchasing or attempting to steal grinding compounds commonly called *grit* from either auto supply stores or gem shops (silicon carbonate—used to polish stones) may provide fruitful suspect leads. Sand or dirt abrasives usually can be traced to their original location by soil analyses, and often these locations are near the residence, workplace, or other area frequented by the offender.

Cranes, bulldozers, and other heavy construction equipment are popular targets for intentional destruction via abrasives. These crimes may be perpetrated against construction companies by vengeful ex-employees or business competitors as well as by environmental extremists attempting to foil property development—a practice termed **monkey wrenching**. Other related crimes may include the destruction of commercial machinery for purposes of insurance fraud, or as previously mentioned, simply the malicious destruction of a private vehicle for the purpose of payback. In general, when collecting evidence from a crime scene where abrasives may have been used:

- Consult with or hire trained mechanical personnel who are familiar with the particular machines/motors affected by the abrasive to remove specific parts for lab analysis;
- Obtain oil and gas samples. Filters, pumps, and oil pans provide the best source to locate evidence for laboratory analysis for internal combustion motors;
- Remove bearings from electrical motors;
- If sand or dirt is the suspected abrasive, obtain a soil sample in and around the crime scene area for comparative purposes;
- Package abrasive evidence in heat-sealed or resealable plastic bags or paint cans. Such evidence should not be placed in paper or glass containers.[25]

QUESTIONED DOCUMENTS

Questioned documents examinations of crimes for financial gain include the analysis of legal instruments such as checks, wills, deeds, medical records, income tax forms, and contracts for suspected forgery and counterfeiting activities. Crimes against persons such as those involving threatening letters, bank robbery notes, and gang graffiti also employ the skills of questioned documents examiners.

Handwriting Analysis and Comparison

To authenticate a signature, or to determine whether a particular individual wrote a note of legal importance, a handwriting analysis is usually performed. This method typically involves a **handwriting comparison.** The writing contained within the questioned document is compared with **exemplars**, which are original samples of handwriting from a known source such as a suspect or victim. Exemplars can be either *natural* or *collected*. Natural types are preferable to those that are collected because they are less subject to a person's efforts to distort or conceal their true handwriting qualities. Driver's licenses, booking cards, tax returns, letters, employment applications, and fingerprint signature cards are some popular sources for obtaining natural exemplars. If possible, it is best to obtain these comparison documents for the same time period as that of the questioned document. If exemplars are collected, the process should capture handwriting in a fashion that is as similar as possible to that evidence within the questioned document. For example, a document in the form of a handwritten letter with black ink, on white unlined paper, in cursive style writing would call for the exemplar to be collected in a manner which captured each of these specific features. In addition, the collection process should involve repetitive writings of signatures or statements identical to those within the questioned document. The content of collected exemplars should always be dictated rather than written, and when each writing sample is completed it should be removed from the writer's view to prevent intentionally distorted handwriting from being duplicated during subsequent collections.

Other Documents Examinations

In addition to handwriting analyses, questioned documents examinations can also lead to the identification of the following:

- **Inks:** Often, the specific type and brand of writing instrument, the ink color's manufacturer, and even the year in which a particular color of ink was produced can be identified. Such analyses enable the documents examiner to determine whether the ink composing a signature on a document is approximately the same age as the document itself. Newer inks on older documents would suggest a forged signature.
- **Typewriters:** Different brands of typewriters, and perhaps a specific typewriter, can be identified by an examination of the type contained in documents. Broken, missing, or poorly aligned typefaces may provide enough unique characteristics to match a typewritten exemplar obtained from a specific machine with a questioned document.
- **Photocopies and Laser Printers:** Photocopied documents and those produced by a laser printer are

extremely similar in appearance, and it is often difficult to discern one from the other. The particular photocopy machine used to produce a given questioned document may be identified if the machine produces unique markings in the print or on the paper's surface. These markings are most likely the product of parts on the machine that have become worn and produce distinct imperfections during the photocopying process. Laser printers, by comparison, leave very few distinguishing characteristics that can be used to either classify or individualize a specific machine.

- **Paper:** Analytic processes have been developed to determine the age of paper to authenticate the date when a document was produced or signed. Some higher quality papers bear water marks, which identify the paper's manufacturer and certain details such as the time, place, and date of manufacturing.

Analytical Techniques

Certain physical and chemical properties of questioned documents can be determined through the use of a **video spectral comparator (VSC)**. This device enables questioned documents examiners to employ both standard and alternate light sources, including ultraviolet and infrared types, so that alterations to both signatures and documents can be readily visualized and photographed. Identifying erasures, hidden security codes, signature overlays, as well as reassembling shredded documents are some of the various tasks that can be easily accomplished with the help of VSC visualization methods. Another device, the *electrostatic detection apparatus (ESDA)*, can be used to visualize indented writing on paper. This enables the recreation of documents from paper or other soft surfaces, which bear only the impressions or indentations created by pressure applied by a pen or pencil when the original document was written. In addition, various microscopic applications are employed during the document authentication process.[26]

CRIME SCENE RECONSTRUCTION THROUGH PHYSICAL EVIDENCE

In gathering various types of evidence from a crime scene one of the investigator's main goals is to use this evidence to reconstruct the criminal events that took place there. An investigator's greatest challenge, however, is to reconstruct a crime using only physical evidence available at the scene; that is, there are no offenders, no victims and no witnesses at a scene. Case Example 4A presents such a case. As the crime scene photos presented in Figures 4.55 through 4.64 illustrate, a violent crime most definitely has taken place and it is the investigator's task to gather the physical evidence needed to reconstruct the crime. When examining this case, put yourself in the investigator's shoes. In other words, it is your job to gather physical evidence from the scene in a timely manner so as to reconstruct the crime, develop suspect leads, and build a case against a suspect.

CASE EXAMPLE 4A

Kitchen Crime Scene

FIGURE 4.55 ▶ Patrol units responding to a disturbance call from neighbors discovered the scene shown here upon arriving at the residence. The home owners or residents were absent and could not be located. Noting the condition of the kitchen area, which contained blood and other signs of physical injury, the officers notified investigators, who approached the home as a possible crime scene. Is it necessary to obtain a search warrant before walking through this scene? What other preparations/precautions should be taken by the investigators responding to this scene?

FIGURE 4.56 ▶ Rear view of the kitchen area. How would you proceed in the evidence collection process? What types of physical evidence are present?

FIGURE 4.57 ▶ Blood-soaked articles, blood stains, and debris scattered across the kitchen floor. What does this physical evidence indicate about the criminal activities that likely took place here?

FIGURE 4.58 ▶ Close-up of large blood pool on the kitchen floor. What does this type of blood evidence, and the other physical evidence near it, indicate?

FIGURE 4.59 ▶ Broken knife and blood spatter on the kitchen floor. Is the blood on the floor a swipe or a wipe? What does this indicate about the movement of the person leaving these spatter stains on the floor? What other evidence can be collected here?

FIGURE 4.60 ▶ Bullet on the kitchen floor at the refrigerator's base. How would you handle collection of this ballistics evidence? What other ballistics or firearms information can be determined from this set of physical evidence?

FIGURE 4.61 ▶ Blood spatter on the kitchen wall. What type of spatter is this? Can direction or any other information be determined from this pattern?

FIGURE 4.62 ▶ Duct tape on the kitchen table. Of what value is this tape evidence? How should it be collected? What other evidence could be searched for in this area?

FIGURE 4.63 ▶ Broken door and hardware on the kitchen door. Of what value is the physical evidence in this breakage area? What types of evidence would you search for or collect here and how would you carry out the evidence collection process?

FIGURE 4.64 ▶ Bullet hole in the kitchen door window. What types of glass evidence might be present here? How would you go about identifying and collecting them?

Summary

1. Types and forms of physical evidence.

The general categories into which most forms of physical evidence fall include (1) trace, including hairs, fibers, glass, and soil; (2) impression, including prints left on and within objects from finger, palms, feet, tires, cloth, and footwear; (3) biological, including blood, teeth, and skeletal remains; (4) firearms and weapons, including guns, ammunition, knives, and specialized weapons; and (5) documents, including contracts, currency, passports, and other official documentation.

2. Class and individual evidence.

Class characteristics of evidence enable the identification of a specific type of evidence and the ability to differentiate it from other similar types of evidence. For example, a specific type of footwear can be classed as a tennis shoe versus a dress shoe. Individual characteristics of evidence enable the evidence item to be linked uniquely and directly as originating from a specific person, place, or thing. For example, the unique wear patterns on the sole of a shoe left as impression evidence in mud at a crime scene could be used to link the shoe to the individual wearing it.

3. Essential tasks of physical evidence collection and preservation.

All evidence should be photographed in its natural state at the crime scene before actual collection takes place. Marking and documenting physical evidence is necessary for later identification and comparisons with crime scene photographs. Evidence should be packaged in such a way as to guard against cross-contamination or other destruction. It is necessary to establish a chain of custody documenting all persons handling evidence from the moment the evidence is first collected until it is stored in a secure location.

4. Fingerprint evidence.

Fingerprint evidence is unique to each individual. There are three classifications of fingerprints: arches, loops, and whorls. Fingerprint evidence at crime scenes can be one of three types: (1) visible/contamination prints—such as observable prints made by transferring blood, paint, grease, or other materials from the print to a surface; (2) plastic prints, which are formed by a stamped-like impression of the print in a soft object or surface; and (3) latent prints, which are invisible to the unaided eye and must be developed to become visible or visualized by using an alternate light source (ALS).

5. Firearms identification and ballistics evidence.

Firearms identification involves the classification of firearms into specific makes, models, sizes, and so forth. It also involves the classification of various types of ammunition used in firearms. Ballistics evidence involves the analysis of firearms and ammunition during as well as after a bullet has been fired. Specific markings called *striations* left on bullets and tool marks left on cartridge casings are types of ballistic evidence that can be used to individualize a particular firearm. NIBIN is the primary database used for matching ballistics evidence with firearms collected from suspects and used to carry out crimes.

6. Blood, bite marks, and skeletal evidence.

Blood can provide DNA evidence as well as physical evidence in the form of blood spatter that can be used to determine how and where offenders have used weapons to wound victims. Bite marks left by offenders in the skin of their victims or other objects can also be used as a means to identify and exclude suspects by individualizing tooth patterns—sometimes referred to as a *dental fingerprinting*. Skeletal remains, including bones and teeth, can be used to determine the age, gender, ethnicity, and sometimes individual identity of a fully decomposed body.

7. Trace evidence.

Trace evidence is composed of physical objects that are not readily visible to the unaided eye. These include glass fragments, paint chips, pollen, soil, hair, fibers, and other microscopic materials. Trace evidence is generally collected through vacuuming, tweezing, or tape. Many forms can be visualized using alternate light sources (ALS).

Key Terms

physical evidence	cross-contamination	chain of custody
class characteristics	reference sample	alternate light source (ALS)
individual characteristics	control sample	friction ridges
exchange principle	elimination sample	visible prints

C.S.I. effect
cold shock
electrostatic dust print lifter (EDPL)
firing pin
foreign hair
identification
presumptive test
residue prints
void print
plastic prints
latent prints
impression evidence
tool mark evidence
striation marks
ballistics evidence
firearms identification
gunshot residue (GSR)

trajectory rods
lands/grooves
accelerant
blood spatter
chromogen
comparison microscope
exemplar
fluoresce
gel print lifter
minutiae
questioned evidence
serum
volatility
forward spatter
backward spatter
point of origin
dental fingerprinting

bite exemplars
soil/botanical evidence
concentric fracture
radial fracture
cross-transfer
monkey wrenching
handwriting comparison
video spectral comparator (VSC)
coagulate
ejector marks
extractor marks
forensic odontology
hot shock
plasma
recovery tank
surface tension
Wallner lines or rib marks

Review Questions

1. What is meant by the term *physical evidence*? List some examples of types of physical evidence.

2. What are some of the important methods used to identify, collect, and preserve physical evidence?

3. What is Locard's exchange principle and why is it important to the field of crime scene investigation?

4. Name and explain the various types of evidence sampling procedures undertaken in crime scene investigation. Under what circumstances would each method be used?

5. What is meant by the term *identification* and what is the identification formula?

6. What are the major forms of fingerprint evidence and how are they collected?

7. How is print/impression evidence identified and collected?

8. Discuss the types of evidence that would be classified as tool mark evidence and explain how they are collected.

9. How does firearms evidence differ from ballistics evidence?

10. Explain the proper procedure for identifying and collecting arson evidence?

11. What is blood spatter and how is it used as a form of physical evidence?

12. Identify the major types of blood spatter.

13. In which crime situations would the collection of bite mark evidence be of the greatest importance to investigators?

14. How are skeletal remains useful to investigators?

15. Describe how soil, dust, and botanicals can be used as physical evidence.

16. Imagine you are at a crime scene containing various forms of glass evidence. What possible characteristics contained within this glass evidence could you look for and what would these characteristics indicate?

17. Name three types of trace evidence and discuss the proper methods for collecting and packaging each type of evidence.

18. What is cold and hot shock, and how is it of use in the investigation of crimes involving vehicles?

19. What do hair, fiber, cordage, and paint evidence all have in common?

20. What are some of the methods used for questioned documents investigations?

Internet Resources

FBI Forensic Services Manual

Questioned Documents
Forensic Geology
Hair and Fiber Evidence

Glass

www.fbi.gov/about-us/lab/handbook-of-forensic-services-pdf/view
www.asqde.org
www.geoforensics.com/geoforensics/home.html
www.fbi.gov/about-us/lab/forensic-science-communications/fsc/july2000/index.htm/deedrick.htm
www.fbi.gov/about-us/lab/forensic-science-communications/fsc/jan2005/index.htm/standards/2005standards4.htm

Applied Investigative Exercise

Imagine that you are the investigator in Case Example 4A, the Kitchen Crime Scene. Detail how you would process this crime scene. Which types of evidence would you collect, and how would you collect them and package them? Based on the available physical evidence at the crime scene, what conclusions can you draw about the type of crime that occurred at this location? In other words, do your best to reconstruct the crime based on the evidence you gathered.

Notes

[1] Richard Saferstein, *Criminalistics: An Introduction to Forensic Science,* 10th ed. (NJ: Prentice-Hall, 2011), 8.

[2] Henry Lee and Robert Gaensslen, *Advances in Fingerprint Technology* (Boca Raton, FL: CRC Press, 2001), 35–98.

[3] Ibid.

[4] U.S. Department of Justice, *The Science of Fingerprints* (Washington, DC: U.S. Government Printing Office, 1990).

[5] California Department of Justice, *Preservation of Shoe, Tire, and Other Impression Evidence,* posted at www.cci.ca.gov/Reference/peb/peb.html.

[6] Ibid.

[7] California Department of Justice, *Toolmark Evidence Collection,* posted at www.cci.ca.gov/Reference/peb/peb.html; Jerry Miller and Michael McLean, "Criteria for Identification of Toolmarks," *AFTE Journal,* Vol. 30, No. 3, 15–61.

[8] Federal Bureau of Investigation, *Handbook of Forensic Services* (Quantico, VA: FBI Laboratory Division, 2007), 63–68.

[9] Edward Hueske, *Practical Analysis and Reconstruction of Shooting Incidents* (Boca Raton, FL: CRC Press, 2006), 139–150; Evan Thompson, "Stippling/Tattooing versus Powder Burning," *AFTE Journal,* Vol. 32, No. 4, 178–181.

[10] Saferstein, 419–425.

[11] U.S. Department of Justice, *Fire and Arson Scene Evidence: A Guide for Public Safety Personnel* (Washington, DC: National Institute of Justice); Bureau of Alcohol, Tobacco, Firearms and Explosives, *Arson Investigative Guide* (Washington, DC: ATF Publications, 1992).

[12] Federal Bureau of Investigation, *Handbook of Forensic Services* (Quantico, VA: FBI Laboratory Division, 2007), 45–50.

[13] California Department of Justice, *Collection of Evidence Blood & Other Body Fluid Stains & Reference Samples for Conventional Typing & DNA Analysis,* posted at www.cci.ca.gov/Reference/peb/peb.html.

[14] Stuart H. James, Erwin Kish, and Paulette Sutton, *Principles of Bloodstain Pattern Analysis,* 3rd ed. (Boca Raton: FL, 2005), 15–56; William Eckert and Stuart James, *Interpretation of Bloodstain Evidence at Crime Scenes* (New York, NY: Elsevier Press, 1989).

[15] Michael Bowers and Gary Bell, *Manual of Forensic Odontology,* 4th ed. (New York, NY: ASFO, 2011).

[16] Karen Burns, *The Forensic Anthropology Training Manual* (Upper Saddle River, NJ: Prentice Hall, 1999), 120–190; William Bass, *Death's Acre: Inside the Legendary Body Farm* (New York, NY: Putnam, 2003).

[17] Ray Murray, *Evidence from the Earth: Forensic Geology and Criminal Investigation* (Missoula, MT: Mountain Press, 2004); Ray Murray and John Tedrow, *Forensic Geology: Earth Sciences and Criminal Investigation* (New Brunswick, NJ: Rutgers University Press, 1975); Interpol, *Forensic Examination of Soil Evidence,* posted at www.interpol.int/public/Forensic/IFSS/meeting13/Reviews/Soil.pdf.

[18] Botanical Society of America, *Crime Scene Botanicals,* posted at www.botany.org/planttalkingpoints/crime.php.

[19] James Michael Curran, Tacha Natalie Hicks Champond, and John S. Buckleton, *Forensic Interpretation of Glass Evidence* (Boca Raton, FL: CRC Press, 2000); Federal Bureau of Investigation, *Handbook of Forensic Services* (Quantico, VA: FBI Laboratory Division, 2007), 69–71.

[20] California Department of Justice, *Automobile Lights,* posted at www.cci.ca.gov/Reference/peb/peb.html.

[21] Curran et al., 160–195.

[22] J. W. Hicks, *Microscopy of Hair: A Practical Guide and Manual* (Washington, DC: Federal Bureau of Investigation, 1977).

[23] Ibid.

[24]Brian Caddy, *Forensic Examination of Glass and Paint* (Boca Raton, FL: CRC Press, 2001); David Crown, *The Forensic Examination of Paint and Pigments* (Springfield, IL: Charles C. Thomas, 1968).

[25]Federal Bureau of Investigation, *Handbook of Forensic Services* (Quantico, VA: FBI Laboratory Division, 2007), 14.

[26]Ordway Hilton, *Scientific Examination of Questioned Documents* (Boca Raton, FL: CRC Press, 1992); Richard Brunelle and Robert Reed, *Forensic Examination of Ink and Papers* (Springfield, IL: Charles C. Thomas, 1984).

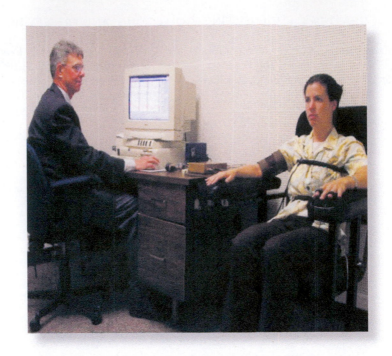

CHAPTER FIVE

INVESTIGATIVE INTERVIEWING AND INTERROGATION

Learning Objectives

After completing this chapter, you should be able to:

1. Differentiate between interviews and interrogations.
2. Describe effective interviewing and interrogation techniques.
3. Summarize the legal requirements of interviewing and interrogation, including Miranda rights.
4. Explain how to deal with special witnesses.
5. Identify how lying and deception are detected.
6. Explain why people confess and how confessions are documented.

Chapter Outline

INTRODUCTION

IN THE NOT-TOO-DISTANT past, investigators believed that the most effective way to obtain information about criminal activities was to subject individuals to what was referred to as **the third degree**. This was an arsenal of methods that often included the infliction of physical pain or psychological distress, or both. Stories of investigators extracting facts, admissions, and confessions from persons by exposing them for long periods to glaring hot lights, beating them with rubber hoses, and even dangling them by their feet from the windows of tall buildings were commonplace in the practice of American criminal investigation before the mid-1930s. Beginning with the landmark 1936 case *Brown v. Mississippi*, which essentially prohibited most third degree tactics, police began to rely on psychologically based procedures to "break" or "crack" persons who were withholding knowledge of crime-related matters. The polygraph and various other deception detection protocols were developed to replace past practices of beating, torture, and threats.

FIGURE 5.1 ▶ Teams consisting of male and female investigators can be a very effective means of conducting suspect interrogations and witness interviews.

Today, most investigators who are successful at interviewing and interrogation agree with the old adage, "You can catch more flies with honey than with vinegar." That is, they realize the benefits of using psychology over force when gathering information about crime and criminals. This is especially important considering that approximately 80 percent of all crimes are eventually resolved by a suspect's confession. In addition, about 50 percent of all crime suspects confess during interrogation. Thus, it can be argued that obtaining a truthful, legally admissible confession from a guilty suspect should be the primary goal of the criminal investigation process. Not only will such an admission of guilt save the time and money of a lengthy criminal trial, but it will also bring more rapid closure to crime victims and free investigators to pursue new cases.

In this chapter, various methods of interviewing and interrogation are presented. At the outset, it must be understood that one method is not always superior to any other for obtaining crime information and confessions; rather, the investigator's job is to decide which technique is best applied to a particular suspect or witness under a particular set of circumstances. Even then, the most experienced investigators using state-of-the-art fact gathering procedures sometimes fail. Occasionally, luck and timing are far more important than an investigator's skill and training in motivating a person to inform about or confess to criminal activity.

THE GOALS OF INTERVIEWING AND INTERROGATION

Both interviews and interrogations have the basic goal of gathering accurate information about criminal activities that can be used for investigative purposes. These two methods have separate goals, however, regarding the use of the information gathered. The general goal of an **interview** is to obtain insights and observations from persons who may have personally witnessed

or otherwise gained knowledge about criminal matters under investigation. Often, these witness accounts can be used for reconstructing a crime, identifying suspects and other witnesses, or perhaps proving a suspect's guilt. In addition, during an interview, it may be determined that a witness is actually involved in the crime under investigation and should be treated as a suspect. An **interrogation**, on the other hand, aims specifically at determining the guilt or innocence of persons suspected of involvement in criminal activities by using specialized information-gathering techniques and technology. Ultimately, the goal of both interviews and interrogations is to obtain a truthful and well documented confession from a crime suspect, thus avoiding a costly and lengthy court proceeding. When conducting both interviews and interrogations investigators can use various techniques (discussed later in this chapter) to improve the level of information they obtain, as illustrated by Figure 5.1, which shows the intentional use of a female investigator to interrogate a juvenile suspect.

INTERVIEWING WITNESSES

Preinterview Activities

Witness interviews are routinely conducted with witnesses or other persons who know about a particular criminal act, and with the victims of attempted or completed crimes. Interviews may be conducted by first responders or investigators shortly after an offense has occurred. Alternatively, they can be performed later in a neutral setting as part of a follow-up investigation. The first stage in the interview process consists of various preinterview activities to ensure that the most factual and valid information is gathered from witnesses:

- *Identifying Witnesses:* Identify witnesses at the crime scene by using names, physical descriptions, and other information provided by the initial dispatch, officers at the scene, or persons who present themselves as witnesses or victims. Additional witnesses can be identified by using a snowball method whereby a known witness is asked for the names of additional persons who may know of the crime or the suspects being investigated. This procedure can be repeated with each additional new witness interviewed.

- *Separating Witnesses:* Separate witnesses before they can discuss the details of the crime under investigation with each other. Tell witnesses not to discuss details of the crime with others who may have witnessed the crime. This will prevent witness contamination whereby less-confident witnesses change their accounts of a criminal activity to match those of other witnesses whom they believe to be more accurate. Place all witnesses in a secure area away from strangers and the media. The crime scene area can be canvassed for additional witnesses, if officers are available to do so. When single officers are working a scene with multiple witnesses, initial contact information should be obtained to forestall witness walk-aways from the crime scene before an interview can be conducted.

- *Gathering Background Information:* Never begin a witness interview without first gathering background information about the persons, events, and circumstances surrounding the incident being investigated. Admittedly, as a first-responder to the crime scene, this may be difficult. At a minimum, prepare for the interview by determining the nature of the offense, its time and location, and the particular witnesses with the most detailed knowledge of the crime and/or offender(s). If time and resources permit, more extensive pre-interview preparation can be conducted to ascertain the witness's background characteristics (especially prior contacts with law enforcement) and crime scene reconstruction facts—including any physical evidence or other witness statements that can be corroborated or disproven during the interview.

- *Selecting an Interview Location:* As a general rule, witness interviews should be conducted as soon as possible after a criminal event. Often, witnesses must be interviewed at the crime scene at a time when there is a great deal of noise, confusion, and other distracting elements. In such cases, do your best to find a location such as a patrol unit or other semisecluded area to conduct the interview. If witnesses are injured, confused, tired, emotionally distressed, or suffering from some other condition, it is best to conduct the interview at a later time when they are more composed and rational. If possible, interview witnesses within nonthreatening locations where they feel comfortable and relaxed. The interview location need not be in a police facility; however, if the witness could be targeted by potentially dangerous individuals, be discreet when selecting a public location to conduct the interview. For an interview conducted at the witness's home or business, always make an appointment at a time most convenient for the witness. Also, be sure to select

a time when chance distractions or interruptions from children, phone calls, pets, friends, employers, and so forth are minimal.

- *Considering Questions to be Asked:* Other than the standard questions of "who, what, why, when, where, and how," questions posed to witnesses will have to be tailored to their specific knowledge of the criminal event. Generally speaking, interview questions should tap into the witness's sensory awareness; that is, when appropriate, ask witnesses to describe specific things they have seen as well as heard, touched, smelled, or possibly even tasted (see Table 5.1).[1] Investigators must also know how to adjust their questions to special witnesses such as juveniles (see Figure 5.2) who may be unaware that they have witnessed a crime.

- *Identify the Type of Witness:* Perhaps the most important preinterview activity is identifying the type of witness being interviewed. Generally speaking, witnesses can be classified as friendly, neutral, or hostile. **Friendly witnesses** are easily recognized because they eagerly present themselves to known crime scene investigators as persons who can provide information regarding the crime. In addition to enthusiastic cooperation, the dialogue they provide about the crime will show a great concern for the well-being of the victim or the recovery of stolen property, and they may express outward disdain for the alleged offender. **Neutral witnesses**, in contrast, usually are cooperative; however, the information they provide likely will be limited to specific responses to questions they are asked about the crime situation. They will show little emotional reaction to the crime, and their statements will show neither support for the victim nor contempt for the offender. The most challenging of all witnesses to be interviewed are those classified as hostile. **Hostile witnesses** are not only uncooperative, but they will intentionally avoid or even openly express hostility toward investigators when approached for an interview. If indeed hostile witnesses are eventually interviewed, they may place unjustified blame on the victim or try to excuse the offender's actions in an effort to derail the investigation. The following sections present specific interview strategies for specific types of witnesses.

The Friendly Witness

Begin the interview by establishing rapport with the witness. This can be done by conversing casually about non–crime-related topics including the news, sporting events, or even the weather. Once rapport has been established, attempt to make a smooth transition into the fact gathering stage of the interview. A statement such as "Sorry, I like to talk and tend to get carried away at times . . . but getting back on track, let's talk about why you're here," should suffice. Start gathering information by asking general **open-ended questions** about the criminal event that allow friendly witnesses to recall information and details

TABLE 5.1	EXAMPLES OF SENSORY QUESTION TOPICS
SENSE	**EXAMPLE**
Sight:	
Persons	Physical Description, Behaviors, Victim, Witness, Suspect
Weapons	Firearm, Knife, Object, Size, Shape, Coloring, Use
Vehicles	Color, Make, Model, License Plate, Occupants
Sound:	
Voices	Gender, Age, Ethnicity, Tone, Pitch, Conversation
Firearms	Shots Fired: Number, Sequence, Loudness
Break-in	Alarms, Tool and Breaking Sounds, Footsteps
Smell:	
Smoke	Accelerant Use: Gasoline/Petroleum, Explosives
Offenders	Cologne/Perfume, Body Odor, Breath, Cigarettes
Drugs	Odor During and After Use, Production Labs
Taste:	
Toxins	Intentional and Accidental Poisonings
Drugs	Consumed by Sexual Assault Victims (e.g., Date Rape)
Offenders	Condom Lubricants, Lotions/Creams (e.g., Oral Sexual Assault)
Touch:	
Offenders	Hands, Beard, Hair, Clothing, Skin
Objects	Coarse, Smooth, Slick, Sharp, Hairy, Sweaty
Explosions	Shock Wave or No Shock Wave After Blast

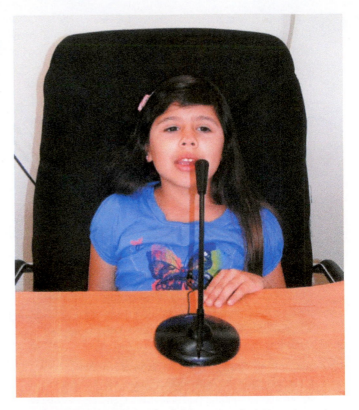

FIGURE 5.2 ▶ Although children are often interviewed as witnesses, investigators must always be aware that their recall of criminal events can be influenced by their age-related suggestibility.

about the offense and offender in an unstructured, free-flowing dialogue. This question can be something as simple as "Can you tell me what happened?" Let the witness continue talking and complete their entire thought process without interruption. Even if you think of a question that you fear will be forgotten if not asked immediately, write it down and ask it later. When the witness has finished talking, wait a while before asking a new question. Often, a witness will pause to ponder something that came up in the initial dialogue and will provide more detailed information in a secondary dialogue that follows the pause.

Next, some targeted **closed-ended questions** about details uncovered during the open-ended questioning phase can be asked. This line of questioning should aim primarily at verifying the truth of particular statements, obtaining more evidence in support of the case, and uncovering more potential witnesses to the crime. Closed-ended questions may either require a simple "yes/no" response or ask the witness to recall specific details of the crime. These questions, however, must not lead the witness into providing a particular answer or answering in a certain way. For example, when investigating a residential burglary it would be appropriate to ask, "What was the condition of the sliding door in the backyard area of the home?" to find out whether the witness observed that the glass on the door was broken. On the other hand, asking "Was the glass in the sliding door in the backyard area of the home broken?" would be inappropriate and perhaps lead the witness to recall an event that in reality had never occurred.

Last, the interview session should end by giving the witness a final chance to expound upon earlier thoughts by asking, "Is there anything else at all you'd like to tell me about what we've been talking about?" Surprisingly, this final question may cause the witness to recall important facts that have been suppressed or withheld. Even if the witness interview is audio or video recorded, it should be in written form as well. This is done by preparing a written victim statement containing and detailing important facts related to the case that were uncovered during the interview session. The statement is written in the first person, as if composed by the witness, and signed by the witness in the presence of a notary. This document will be an official record of the witness's account of the crime and can be presented as evidence later should the witness's story change. Also, a handwritten document, so long as the signatures are verified, can be prepared in situations where it is imperative that the witness statement be prepared and signed immediately.

The Neutral Witness

Because neutral witnesses do not take sides with either victims or offenders, they are often the best for providing an unbiased account of the crime under investigation. Should the case go to trial, they also are considered the best trial witnesses because of their impartiality. The techniques for interviewing neutral witnesses are similar to those used for friendly witnesses; however, because neutral witnesses have no emotional stake in the case's outcome, they may forget details they have observed faster than other witnesses. Therefore, this type of witness probably should be interviewed before any of the other types. Second, even though a particular witness appears neutral at the outset of the interview process, he or she might shift to a friendly or hostile position later. Soliciting information from neutral witnesses is best done using a questioning method that is somewhat more structured than an open-ended format and less rigid than closed-ended questions that require simple "yes-no" responses. Targeted questions that address the who, what, where, why, and how of the criminal activity appear to work best for the neutral witness. If a neutral witness turns either friendly or hostile, the interview tactic should also shift immediately to the one best suited to handle that particular type of witness.

The Hostile Witness

Hostile witnesses are frequently encountered in crime situations where the victim and offender are friends or family members—for example, an assault involving roommates or domestic violence between spouses. In these instances, the witness (who may be a victim as well) will downplay the offense as "just playing around" or even support the offender's actions as acting in self-defense. Witnesses to gang crimes also are characteristically hostile, either because they are trying to protect the offender (sometimes a fellow gang member) or because they fear retaliation from the offending gang.

Establishing rapport is the first step that should be taken when interviewing the hostile witness. This strategy may, in fact, cause the witness's attitude to shift to neutral or perhaps friendly. Often, hostile witnesses build barriers between themselves and the interviewer. If these barriers can be identified and lifted through rapport building early on, there is a good chance of gaining the hostile witness's cooperation. Some common sources of these barriers are fears related to the following:

- Job/income loss
- Retaliation
- Deportation
- Self-incrimination
- Child custody
- Marital discord
- Cultural customs
- Criticism from friends/family

If the witness softens to either neutral or friendly status after rapport building, then apply the appropriate interview technique as previously discussed. If the witness remains hostile, employ a technique that is the direct opposite of that recommended for the friendly witness. That is, begin the formal interview with targeted, closed-ended questions about various details of the criminal event that the witness probably has observed. It may be necessary to begin with questions requiring a "yes/no" answer format. Next, if the witness begins to cooperate, move to more general open-ended questions requiring more detailed responses. If the witness fails to cooperate at any stage of this process, the interview should stop. Never attempt to make hostile witnesses respond to questions by issuing threats or making promises. Have a second investigator witness statements made by the hostile interviewee because odds are they will be unwilling to sign any type of witness statement. Later in the investigation, it may be discovered that the hostile witness is indeed a suspect who should be interrogated rather than interviewed.[2] Table 5.2 summarizes

TABLE 5.2	WITNESS TYPES AND INTERVIEW STRATEGIES	
WITNESS TYPE	**QUESTION STRATEGY**	**APPLIED EXAMPLE**
Friendly	Open Then Closed	Q1: Can you tell me about the burglar?
		Q2: What color was his hair?
Neutral	5 Ws & H Then Closed	Q1: Who, What, When, Where, Why, & How?
		Q2: Did he have a gun . . . yes/no?
Hostile	Closed Then Open	Q1: Did he have a gun . . . yes/no?
		Q2: Can you tell me more about the gun?

specific interview question strategies for each type of witness discussed above.

COGNITIVE INTERVIEWING

Cognitive interviewing (CI), developed as an alternative to standard interview procedures, incorporates scientific research findings on memory recall from the field of cognitive psychology. After establishing rapport, the CI interview begins by asking the witness to recall all that can be remembered about the context of the crime scene. This can include details about the crime scene environment (weather conditions, sights, smells, sounds) as well as personal factors (clothes worn, mood, thoughts). This mental exercise may provide cues that trigger recall of specific crime scene information encoded or stored in the witness's mind along with general thoughts and observations at the time the crime occurred. Other tactics to refresh the witness's memory of the crime scene context also can be employed:

- Showing pictures of the crime area
- Returning to the physical location of the crime scene
- Asking specific questions about details of the crime scene
- Attempting to recreate the witness's mindset at the time of the crime

The second step in the CI process is to ask the witness to recall all details, no matter how trivial, about the crime itself. Refreshing the witness's memory though crime context cues in the first step should cause rich details of the offense and offender(s) to emerge. Next, additional information is probed for by asking the witness to put themselves in the role of another person present at the crime scene and then describe to the interviewer how this person might have felt during the commission of the offense. For example, the witness of a carjacking who attempts to recreate the victim's feelings and experiences may be able to recall specific details about the crime stored in the witness' memory by observing the victim before, during, and after the offense occurred. This step can be repeated to reenact the roles of various persons present at the crime. The final CI interview step involves having witnesses recall everything that they can remember about the crime in reverse order—from their last memory of the crime to their very first recollection of it. This process helps refresh lost memories about the crime, much in the same way a person jogs their memory by retracing the places they have been to find lost keys. The CI interview method is not recommended for use with very young children, uncooperative witnesses, and persons who have had a long period of time lapse since observing the criminal activity.[3]

EYEWITNESS ACCOUNTS

Eyewitness accounts have led to more convictions in U.S. courts than any other type of evidence. Unfortunately, researchers estimate that approximately 75 percent of wrongful convictions directly result from investigators and juries relying on inaccurate eyewitness information about criminal activity. Although eyewitnesses to a crime may appear confident and well-meaning when providing information during an interview, many factors should be considered in assessing the accuracy of their observations:

- **Age:** Young to middle-age adults provide the most accurate eyewitness accounts. Young children (13 years or younger) and older adults (over the age of 60) are less reliable, especially in facial recognition.
- **Gender:** In general, men can provide greater detail about people, places, and things associated with typical male interests. Examples include being able to identify and describe a type of vehicle or tool. Women, on the other hand, are better at identifying gender role–related things such as type of clothing, hair, and accessories, such as watches and jewelry.
- **Race:** Persons of the same race are better at recognizing each other's physical characteristics (especially facial features) due to the **cross-race effect**.
- **Drug/Alcohol Use:** The influence of drugs or alcohol when witnessing a crime can distort eyewitness accounts even after the effects of the mind-altering substance have worn off.
- **Type of Crime:** Persons who witness property crimes often recall the criminal event better than those who observe a crime of violence.
- **Frequency of Observation:** The more times an eyewitness has seen a particular person, place, or thing related to a criminal activity, the more accurate their account will be.
- **Weapon:** The presence of a weapon during the commission of a crime like that shown in Figure 5.3 causes eyewitnesses to focus on the weapon (especially a handgun) rather than other features of the offender

FIGURE 5.3 ▶ Detailed eyewitness accounts of robberies where the victims are held at gun point are often difficult for investigators to obtain because victims tend to focus on the weapon (referred to as *weapon focus*) rather than on the offender's facial features or clothing. (United States Department of Justice)

and the crime scene environment—a process known as **weapon focus**. Thus, more detailed accounts of criminal activities are provided by eyewitnesses to crimes in which a weapon is not present.

- *Illumination:* More accurate recall of criminal events is associated with better lighting of the crime scene. Observations made in full daylight tend to be much more reliable than those made during twilight.

- *Time Effects:* Most eyewitnesses overestimate the actual length of criminal events. In addition, the longer a crime takes, the more accurate and detailed the witnesses' information will be.

- *Witness Anxiety:* Witnesses who are extremely anxious at the time they observe a crime provide less reliable information than those who are less nervous.

- *Flashbulb Memory:* Criminal events that are extremely shocking or unexpected to the eyewitness may cause what is known as a **flashbulb memory**. This type of memory is very detailed and vivid, even though the witness may have been exposed to the criminal event for only a matter of seconds.[4]

INTERVIEWING SPECIAL WITNESSES

Occasionally, investigators interview witnesses with special emotional, physical, or legal needs. Never assume at the outset of an interview that individuals exhibiting one or more of the following special conditions automatically have testimony that is of lower value. Usually, from a legal standpoint, the testimony of witnesses deemed **mentally competent** at the time they made their observations is legally admissible. Common legal reasons for excluding a witness's testimony based on lack of mental competence include reduced mental functioning due to old age, mental illness, low IQ, and alcohol/drug intoxication. On the other hand, regardless of competence, a witness's **credibility** may be called into question based on perceived limitations due to age-related or physical factors. For example, an elderly individual who provides investigators with a positive identification of a suspect's photograph may have general vision problems under restricted lighting conditions. Thus, juries or other persons evaluating this evidence may have grounds to consider the identification less believable or credible than similar photographic identifications provided by younger witnesses.

Following are various types of special witnesses commonly encountered by investigators:

- *Mentally Impaired Witnesses:* Mentally challenged individuals or those suffering from a mental illness or disorder can be interviewed, but mental competence issues may limit the use of information they provide. Obviously, the individual investigator must decide whether or not interviewing such persons would be fruitful in developing a case. In making this decision, however, remember that a history of mental impairment does not automatically nullify such witnesses' statements or testimony. The legal issue, rather, is whether the statements or testimony were given while the witness was suffering active mental impairment or was experiencing a period of mental clarity. If the latter is true, any information obtained would be deemed admissible evidence in court.

- *Intoxicated Witnesses:* Witnesses who appear intoxicated, or have been arrested under the suspicion of alcohol or drug use, should not be interviewed until the effect of the intoxicating substances has dissipated to the point where the witness has regained their rational judgment. The primary danger here is that any legal affirmation of interview material (such as signatures) obtained from these individuals will be challenged on the legal basis of voluntariness and the ability of the witness to make an informed decision.

- *Elderly Witnesses:* All persons experience reductions in memory and physical functioning with advanced age. However, some experience these more than others. Before interviewing an elderly individual, the investigator must assess the prospective witness's age-related functions—namely, sight, hearing, and memory. First, look for obvious indicators of reduced function. Does the individual wear glasses or a hearing aid? If so, were these worn when the witness observed or heard information related to the criminal activity under investigation? Other indicators may include requesting increased light to examine photos or written materials, which suggests visual impairment; or, in the case of hearing impairment, asking for questions to be repeated or providing an inappropriate response. If the crime occurred recently, short-term memory skills will be an important factor. Indicators of poor short-term memory skills include forgetting recent events such as where one's car is parked, recent appointments that have been made, or even the investigator's name after an introduction. Alternatively, cases that are years old will require long-term memory abilities. Although an elderly witness may be able to recall details of a 20-year-old crime, it is always a good idea to test the accuracy of such accounts by asking related questions such as, "What type of car did you own back then?" or "What street did you live on at that time?" that can be corroborated later to assess the accuracy of the witness's overall long-term memory skills. When interviewing and assessing elderly witnesses, always treat them as you would any other younger, normal person. Don't rush them; listen to them, and never treat them as though they are not competent by talking loudly or in short words and sentences.

- *Physically Disabled Witnesses:* The assessment procedures outlined above for elderly persons are also applicable to witnesses suffering from physical disabilities affecting sight, hearing, and memory. In addition, the Americans with Disabilities Act requires that suitable accommodations be made for disabled persons who are victims of crime. For example, sign language interpreters must be provided for the hearing impaired who request them, and guide dogs allowed to be present when interviewing sight-impaired witnesses who rely on this method of assistance.

- *Juvenile Witnesses:* Generally, parental permission must be obtained or a parent or guardian must be notified before interviewing a juvenile as a witness to a criminal event. Questioning of a juvenile that can be legally construed as an interrogation, however, requires that Miranda warnings be issued for obtained information to be legally admissible (this topic is discussed in detail later in the chapter). Many juveniles, especially those under the age of 12, are highly suggestible and are likely to respond affirmatively to leading questions presented by investigators. Therefore, use open-ended questions when interviewing younger juveniles.

- *Confidential Informant (CI) Witnesses:* Informants are a special class of witnesses who are usually compensated in the form of money or judicial leniency for providing information about crimes and suspects to investigators. Sometimes CIs provide vague interview statements, make untruthful claims, or withhold information in hopes of increasing their payoff. Before conducting an interview session, investigators should make clear to CIs the conditions of their remuneration—providing specific, accurate details about the matter under investigation—and that they will receive no compensation until the information they provide can be independently verified. In addition, witness credibility is always a consideration when using interview material obtained from a CI witness. In particular, CIs who have participated in the criminal activity under investigation or who have an extensive criminal record will likely have credibility issues.

- *Gang and Drug Trade Witnesses:* Witnesses who belong to street gangs or are connected to the drug trade share some common traits in regard to their willingness to partake in a witness interview. First, both these types of individuals characteristically fabricate and are likely to tell investigators what they think they want to hear or inaccurate information to protect themselves or an associate. Those who may be labeled as "snitches" or "rats" for cooperating with authorities will adopt a "don't tell anything" stance and sometimes outright refuse being interviewed. In some instances, individuals who deal with higher-up members in gangs and drug sales networks jeopardize their personal safety by merely being seen in the presence of an investigator. Thus, subpoenas or other legal means often are needed to secure the cooperation of these witnesses.[5]

DOCUMENTING INTERVIEWS

Interviews are typically documented through audio recording, videotaping, or note taking. Of these three methods, videotaping provides the most thorough documentation of an interview because it not only enables investigators to transcribe the exact words spoken, but also allows them to visually analyze nonverbal behaviors. The only drawback to either videotaping or audio taping witness interviews is that some jurisdictions require transcriptions of all verbal content during the taping session for legal purposes. In lengthy and/or multiple interviews, this requirement can make audio taping and videotaping witness statements cost prohibitive.

Whichever method is used, it should be as unobtrusive as possible. Recording devices should be either small or hidden to avoid distraction during the interview session. Generally, it is legal to record any conversations and use the content as admissible evidence so long as one of the parties is aware that the conversation is being recorded. If note taking is the method of choice, the amount of time actually taking notes should be held to a minimum. In short, note taking can be a major distraction and impediment to the interview process. Some witnesses become nervous and refrain from expanding on key information when copious notes are taken. Also, excessive note taking can cause the investigator to miss key statements made by the witness. It is best to record only important points made by the witness during the interview, and then make more detailed notations expanding on this information once the session has ended.

Try to get witnesses to legally authenticate their words and observations spoken during the interview. This can be done with a written statement signed by the witness and containing the time, date, location, and signatures of the investigator and one other party serving as witness to the documentation process. Other methods include having the witness prepare a written statement in his or her own words, or having the witness sign and date the investigator's interview notes. If written documentation of the interview is not possible, at least review the witness' statements in the presence of at least two other parties (preferably police officers), who can later testify regarding the information obtained during the interview. Proper documentation of interviews is necessary to prevent reluctant witnesses from changing their stories later, and to preserve statements made by those who later refuse to cooperate or cannot be located.

CONDUCTING A SHOWUP

If one or more suspects have been detained shortly after a crime has occurred, and are in close proximity to the crime scene, it is often possible to have witnesses make an identification or nonidentification of such individuals by conducting a **showup**. This usually involves transporting witnesses to where suspected offenders are being held so they can briefly view them for identification purposes. Typically, this is done by slowly driving the witness in a squad car past the detained suspect or having the witness view the suspect while detained in a patrol unit. Positive identifications resulting from a showup serve as probable cause for arrest, and are admissible evidence at trial, so long as the totality of the circumstances suggests that the witness's identification was reliable—even though the showup procedure itself may have been suggestive of the suspect's guilt.

Before conducting a showup, obtain a description of the crime suspect(s) from the witness. If there are multiple witnesses, use only one witness for the showup and use the others to make a suspect identification through other means such as a line-up, composite photo, or mugbook (all discussed in Chapter 7). Before the witness views the suspect, inform him or her that the detained individual(s) may or may not be the perpetrator. Documentation of the showup should include the following:

- Name and other identifying information for the participating officer and witnesses as well as for suspects being viewed

- The circumstances warranting the showup: the suspects' matching descriptions provided by witnesses, possessing of items from the crime scene, exigent circumstances

- Description of the showup: lighting, positioning of the suspect, distance of suspect from the witness, detention characteristics of the suspects (e.g., wearing handcuffs, in patrol unit)

- Statements made by the witness and others during the showup

Regardless of whether a positive identification of the suspect is made, a written statement documenting the results of showup should be prepared and signed by both the officer conducting the procedure and the witness who viewed the suspect.

CASE CLOSE-UP 5-1
"DYING DECLARATION GONE WRONG"
Hohenwald, Tenn.

In 2009, near death in a hospital after suffering a major stroke, an elderly Tennessee man wanted to clear his conscience for a crime he had committed some 30 years earlier. In 1977, He allegedly shot and killed his neighbor, whom he suspected of having an affair with his wife. On his deathbed, the alleged shooter summoned local detectives to provide a confession for the murder—in the form of a dying declaration. After providing the confession, however, he miraculously recovered from his stroke and is now being prosecuted for first-degree murder, affording detectives with the honor of solving one of their oldest cold cases.

DYING DECLARATIONS

Dying declarations are a legal exception to the Fifth Amendment's right to confront one's accusers in a court of law. Courts make a special allowance to admit *ante mortem* statements of a deceased individual into evidence because a court appearance of such persons is not possible; however, it is not automatically assumed that a person making a statement before death is always telling the truth.

OBTAINING A DYING DECLARATION

In situations where victims, suspects, or witnesses have received serious injuries or are gravely ill, yet are conscious and talking about the circumstances or causes of their condition or the crime under investigation, attempts should be made to document their statements. If such persons are being transported to a hospital, an officer should accompany them in the ambulance to obtain any possible dying declaration. It is also advisable to have two officers witness all verbal statements and, if possible, obtain some type of signed statement. Dying declarations are considered legally relevant regardless of whether a person actually believes he or she is near death. If a person making a dying declaration lives, any statements obtained will likely be of no legal value (even if a suspect is appropriately Mirandized)—yet will perhaps provide a strong lead for further investigation.

INTERROGATING SUSPECTS

Interrogations are the most intense of all fact-finding procedures used during the investigation process. They are carried out on persons strongly suspected of assisting in or perpetrating a criminal act. The ultimate outcome of a successful interrogation is a truthful **confession** from a criminal suspect or the discovery that the individual being interrogated has no criminal involvement in the matter under investigation. Confessions are verbal and/or written statements in which a person states that they are guilty of a particular criminal act. Another type of information often revealed through the interrogation process is an **admission**. Admissions merely allow inferences of suspect's guilt to be made; that is, they fall short of a full confession of guilty conduct. For example, a suspect may admit to having thought about killing his wife, but does not confess to murdering her. Other information uncovered through the interrogation process may include the location of physical evidence, the identities of accomplices, or other crimes that may or may not be related to the one currently being investigated.

As previously mentioned, it is not legally permissible to use or threaten physical force as a means of carrying out an interrogation. Use of these and other physically coercive tactics (giving a suspect the third degree), will render any information gathered from the interrogation inadmissible and possibly subject the investigator to both civil and legal sanctions. Although techniques such as water boarding have been approved for use in military interrogations of suspected international terrorists, they are clearly not permissible in nonmilitary interrogations. Rather, as outlined in the following section, investigative interrogations now use a host of psychological methods designed to trigger emotional and cognitive functions of the mind that elicit truths about criminal conduct.

Preinterrogation Activities

As in the witness interviewing process, before interrogating a suspect investigators must make sure they are adequately prepared. Because of the intensity of this procedure, and the likelihood that there will be only one shot at interrogating any given suspect, the need for adequate preparation cannot be overemphasized. First, prepare by examining all available case information, including physical crime scene evidence and witness accounts. Use this factual material to construct lines of questioning useful for verifying or disproving claims made by the suspect during the interrogation session. Discover what you can about the suspect's personal background, including family, employment, education, connections to the victim, and crime scene, and prior contacts with law enforcement and offending history.

Conduct the interrogation in a room that provides optimum privacy and minimal distractions. The room may include a simple table (preferably round) and two chairs, although some investigators prefer to simply use two chairs without a table. The furniture and other objects in the room should be organized in such a way that physical barriers between the interrogating investigator and the suspect are minimized. Not only does this type of room design convey a psychological feeling of "no place to hide," but it also allows clearer observation of the suspect's body language. Figure 5.4 shows an interrogation observation room that investigators can use to covertly examine the behavior of suspects in real time while located in a separate physical location. Video or audio recording devices, if used, should be tested for proper functioning—visual and sound quality. In addition, make sure that all personal necessities (e.g., water, food, notepads, etc.) are readily available so that the session doesn't have to be interrupted by leaving the room to acquire them.

INTERROGATION TECHNIQUES

The following sections outline various interrogation techniques used in today's investigative community. Each has a unique psychological approach for gaining information, and no one method is superior to the others in all situations. Selecting the most effective means of interrogating a particular suspect is a process that is learned with experience. First and foremost, investigators should practice and perfect a range of interrogation strategies. After doing so, the appropriate investigative application of the following techniques will essentially come naturally.

The Reid Nine-Step Technique

One of the most widely used and effective interrogation techniques is the **Reid Nine-Step Technique**, initially developed in 1947 by John Reid and his associates as an alternative to the polygraph machine. The method relies on a combination of targeted statements, questioning, and analysis of verbal and physical reactions by the suspect at various stages of the interrogation process. The technique is typically carried out using the following nine-step approach:

1. ***The Direct Positive Confrontation:*** Tell the suspect, in an assertive and confident manner, that he or she is considered to be the person responsible for the crime. Strong statements such as "Our investigation reveals that you shot and killed the victim" or "We gathered evidence from the crime scene that leaves no doubt you broke into and stole the car" are typically used to begin the interrogation session. Less confrontational statements (for example, "We have no choice, given the available evidence, except to include you in our investigation of the auto theft") may be used when there is considerable doubt as to the suspect's guilt or when the suspect can invoke his or her *Miranda* rights to halt the interrogation. Figure 5.5 illustrates the typical body language of both the interrogator and the suspect during this preliminary stage of Step 1. Next, direct confrontation of the suspect is followed by a

FIGURE 5.4 ▶ Interrogation Observation Room (IOR) where interrogations in other locations can be recorded and observed in real time. (United States Department of Defense)

FIGURE 5.5 ▶ The beginning of an interrogation process requires the investigator to establish control over the situation, while acting in a confident and, when necessary, assertive manner.

brief behavioral pause lasting 3 to 5 seconds. The suspect's behaviors following this pause are then observed and analyzed. Indicators of guilt include verbal stalling (asking questions such as "I didn't quite understand you," or "What exactly do you mean?"); avoiding direct eye contact by looking at floors, walls, hands, or other objects; shifting body position; crossing legs; brushing clothing; slouching in the chair; moving the chair to create distance from the investigator; apparently fake gestures and verbalizations; or exhibiting a generally passive reaction to the direct confrontation. Signs of innocence include moving forward toward the investigator, direct response without verbal stalling, flushed face, maintaining eye-to-eye contact, appearing angry, responding in a blunt manner, firm denial, and aggressive reaction to the direct confrontation. Step 1 concludes with the investigator providing a transition statement, which functions to shift the overall accusatory tone of the interrogation to one that is more understanding or compassionate to the suspect. For example, an assault suspect may be told by the investigator, "Aside from the fact that you struck your spouse with your fist, tell me more about what led up to this incident so that I can understand why you were so angry."

2. **Theme Development:** Provide the suspect with a moral excuse for committing the crime without being morally judgmental. Try to identify themes in the offender's own rationalizations, excuses, and justifications for the crime. Develop these themes to engage in discourse with the offender that demonstrates understanding as to why the illegal behavior took place. For example, after detecting a family obligation theme, an investigator may tell an armed robbery suspect, "I

understand that you needed to hold up the liquor store just to support your family in these tough economic times." If the suspect becomes passive during this stage, such behavior is generally considered a sign of guilt.

3. **Handling Denials:** During this stage, the interrogator's job is to stop the suspect from repeating or elaborating claims of innocence. The minute a suspect says something like "Let me explain," do not listen to the explanation. Instead, redirect the interrogation back to the offending theme developed in Step 2. Innocent suspects usually will not tolerate being cut off from telling their story. Alternatively, guilty suspects will be more tolerant of having their story "stepped on" by the interrogator.

4. **Overcoming Excuses:** Next, suspects will attempt to offer various reasons why they could not possibly have committed the offense—"I'm a trusted businessman," "I'm afraid of guns," and so on. These excuses are usually given only by guilty persons and should be considered as a sign of progress in breaking the suspect down. Innocent persons, on the other hand, will continue in a manner that expresses absolute denial. When suspects begin to offer excuses, the interrogator should listen and act in an attentive manner.

5. **Keeping the Suspect's Attention:** Maintain the suspect's attention by continued listening to the suspect's excuses and showing outward signs of sincerity. At this time, the interrogator should move physically closer to the suspect (if possible, in a knee-to-knee position), establish eye contact, and use physical gestures that instill confidence and trust.

6. **Suspect Submission:** Reduced verbal resistance, body language such as tears, looking toward the floor, or covering one's face as illustrated in Figures 5.6 and 5.7

FIGURE 5.6 ▶ Reading body language is important for determining the course of an interrogation. Note the suspect's head-in-hands position, which, along with other indicators, suggests a breakdown in resistance to the investigator's questioning.

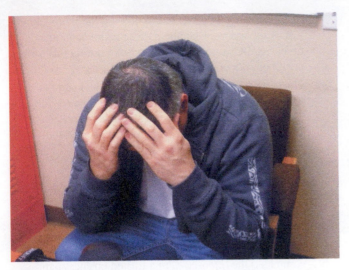

FIGURE 5.7 ▶ Detecting subtle body language changes is key to finding the "sweet spot" of an interrogation when the suspect is willing to give investigators the true facts of a case. Note that the suspect's fingers have moved from a closed (see previous photo) to an open position, which indicates submission to the investigator's further line of questioning.

should be taken as signs that the suspect is beginning to weaken. The interrogator, during this step, should continue to maintain eye contact and a sympathetic demeanor.

7. **Offering Choices:** Figure 5.8 illustrates the body language of a suspect who has accepted the fact that he must eventually admit his guilt. At this time, the interrogator provides an opportunity for the suspect to admit guilt. This is done by offering choices, in the form of questions, regarding the suspect's involvement in the offense. There should always be one choice that is far easier, and less accusatory, for the suspect to

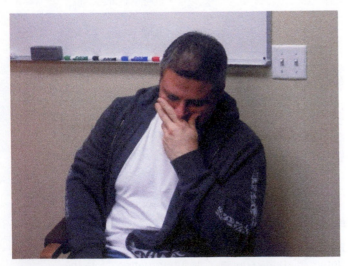

FIGURE 5.8 ▶ The suspect's body language now suggests acceptance and cooperation rather than excuses and denial.

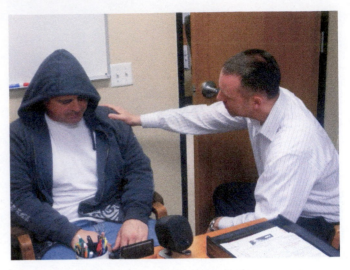

FIGURE 5.9 ▶ The investigator shifts the focus of the interrogation from an accusatory theme to that of offering choices to the suspect on how to tell his side of the story.

answer than others. For example, two questions may be posed: (1) "Did he confront you and make you angry before you stabbed him?" or (2) "Did you sneak up on him from behind to stab him?" The first question clearly puts the suspect in a more favorable scenario than does the second one. Any interest on the suspect's part in clarifying how one's choice is preferable to the other should be considered a tacit admission to the crime. In Figure 5.9, the suspect had admitted his guilt to the interrogator after receiving several verbal choices to promote his cooperation with the investigation.

8. **Obtaining Crime Details:** Next, suspects can be probed for details regarding their involvement in the crime. Locations of likely physical evidence, names of other suspects involved, motivations for carrying out the crime, and other details should be explored at this step. This process should be reinforced by letting suspects know that their cooperation with the investigation will be noted and relayed to prosecutorial staff.

9. **The Confession:** Once a verbal confession is obtained, a written confession should be obtained as well. As shown in Figure 5.10, confessions should always be obtained in writing, even if a verbal confession has been captured on audio or video tape.[6]

Good Cop/Bad Cop

Good cop/bad cop, a classic technique that has proven effective when used on youthful or inexperienced offenders, generally will fail if applied to sophisticated or experienced criminals. The process begins with the bad cop conducting the initial interrogation of the suspect. Here, the bad cop attempts to instill fear, intimidation, and general psychological discomfort in the suspect for not cooperating with specific lines of questioning about the offense. Loud vocal tones, angry physical gesturing, and denial

FIGURE 5.10 ▶ When, and if, the investigator is satisfied that the facts provided by the suspect are truthful and accurate, a signed confession is the final step of the interrogation process.

of simple privileges (use of bathroom, providing water) may be employed; violence or threats of violence can never be used—testimony obtained after a bad cop role has gone too far will not be admissible as evidence. After the negative emotional stage has been set, the bad cop exits the interrogation room and the good cop enters. The good cop's role is that of an understanding "negotiator" who will shield the suspect from further exposure to the bad cop if sufficient information about the crime is obtained. Interrogators who play the bad cop role should constantly monitor the good cop's progress (through audio/visual means) to know whether or when their assistance is again needed. Sometimes, the good cop/bad cop scenario has to be played out repeatedly before the suspect provides information or perhaps a confession. This method should be well rehearsed between two experienced investigators before attempting it on live suspects. Positive results are best obtained by exposing suspects to a strong contrast of good versus bad emotions rather than by merely building the suspect's trust in the good cop.

Neuro Linguistic Programming

Neuro linguistic programming (NLP) assumes that certain involuntary verbal reactions from suspects as well as body and eye movements can be used to identify when suspects are being deceptive during an interrogation session. In practice, it is carried out as follows:

1. *Identify the suspect's sensory modality.* The NLP interrogation begins by determining (in a nonaccusatory manner) the sensory modality dominant in the suspect's mental process of processing information. There are three possible modalities: visual (sight), auditory (sound), and kinesthetic (feeling). This can be done by asking the suspect any nonthreatening question before the formal interrogation and then assessing the

response. For example, during casual conversation, you ask the suspect about his or her favorite sporting events. The suspect's dominant modality can be determined by observing the following:

- *Speech Patterns:* Visual persons will respond in words that use sight descriptions. For example, in the above example, a response such as "I really like seeing the mixed martial arts fighters go at it" is a sight-oriented description indicating a dominant visual modality. Different answers to the same question, however, could indicate auditory and kinesthetic modalities: "The best thing you can hear is when the mixed martial arts referee announces the winner" (auditory) or "I can just feel how hard those mixed martial arts fighters hit" (kinesthetic).
- *Hand Gestures:* Fast, jerky hand gestures at the neck and head level are associated with a visually dominant modality. An auditory modality is reflected by more even, fluid hand movements in the shoulder and upper-torso area. Slow, methodical gesturing at the lower torso and waist areas are most frequent among persons with a dominant kinesthetic modality.
- *Eye Movements:* Various involuntary eye movements indicating modality include the following:
  a. *Visual:* movements to the upper right or left of center direction at a 45° angle when thinking and attempting to recall information.
  b. *Auditory:* movements straight across either right or left of center direction when thinking or recalling, or down and to the left of center when pausing to hear one's own voice, repeating mentally the question being asked.
  c. *Kinesthetic:* movements down and to the right of center during thought or recall, or in a centered up and down direction when attempting to recall information that is more difficult to recall.

Those who utilize the NLP method of interrogation claim that most suspects (45–60 percent) process information visually, followed by auditory means (20–45 percent) and kinesthetic means (10–15 percent).

2. *Establish Rapport.* Next, establish a relationship, or rapport, with the suspect using words or phrases that support their primary sensory modality—examples include "I see what you are saying" (visual), "I hear you loud and clear" (auditory), and "I can feel your stress" (kinesthetic). This process ideally makes suspects feel that they share things with the interrogator, which, in turn, will cause suspects to let down their guard or natural defenses to resist questioning.

3. *Analyze Baseline Movements:* Ask a series of nonaccusatory questions that the suspect can answer truthfully without stress (i.e., name, town of residence, etc.) so that a baseline of body movements for truthful responses can be established. This step is especially important for the analysis of eye movements. Look for

the suspect's natural direction of eye movement when telling the truth.

4. *Lie Detection.* NLP theory suggests that suspects who are not telling the truth move their eyes in a direction other than that observed during the baseline analysis. Once the formal interrogation starts, visual persons who naturally move their eyes to the upper right when telling the truth may move to the upper left or stare down or straight ahead when lying. Similarly, auditory persons whose eyes gaze to the right when being truthful may drift to the left or straight ahead when being deceptive. Persons with a kinesthetic modality who normally look down and to the right when telling the truth may look down and to the left, or stare straight or upwards when lying.[7]

The Behavioral Analysis Interview

The **behavioral analysis interview** is often referred to as the human lie detector method because it employs many of the same interrogation principles as the polygraph examination. It is relatively simple to carry out. First, the suspect is given a preinterrogation interview consisting of about 15 questions that range in content from general questions about the suspect's background to specific probes about the offense being investigated. The preinterrogation interview serves two purposes. First, the subject's verbal and behavioral reactions can be analyzed during truthful responses to background questions and then later used as a basis for comparison in situations where the suspect may be lying. Second, suspects who fail to display distinctive lying behaviors during the preinterrogation are let go. Behaviors associated with lying include verbal stalling, indirect or convoluted responses, confusion, laughter, misinterpretation, abrupt shifting of body position, and distractive activities such as looking at hands, fingernails, playing with pencils, twisting hair, and so forth. Innocent persons, by comparison, provide answers that are spontaneous, short, clear, and nonevasive without dramatic changes in nonverbal behavior. During the formal interrogation, these same behaviors are then analyzed as suspects respond to questions about their involvement in the offense.

Interrogation Profiling

Unlike other techniques that attempt to detect deception, **interrogation profiling** profiles the offender and then uses psychological manipulations based on that criminal profile to elicit a confession during the interrogation. Offenders can be profiled as one of the four following types:

- *Real need* offenders typically commit theft, robbery, arson for profit, embezzlement, and other crimes motivated by financial gain for purposes of survival or physical safety. The real need offender usually acts alone, is a first-time offender, and commits a spontaneous, opportunistic act.
- *Lifestyle* offenders are methodical and commit well-planned crimes that protect or support their social status. Embezzlement, fraud, con schemes, and other illicit acts

that result in a financial payoff are their crimes of choice. Lifestyle offenders do not have accomplices, they have outgoing personalities, and are well-liked and are seldom suspected by others as criminals.

- *Impulsive* offenders commit crimes of opportunity, are spontaneous, and usually lash out at their target in some type of emotional boilover. Their criminal activities could be of a property or violent nature, depending on the situations or individuals that provoke their criminal conduct. They usually have aggressive personalities and act alone.
- *Esteem* offenders commit crime as a psychological means of proving their self-worth. Esteem offenders can aim at persons or property, or both, as victims. Sexual predators, serial killers, and armed robbers are some of the many esteem offenders whose activities provide support for their sagging egos. In many cases, it is the fear they instill in their victims, rather than the crime itself, that motivates them to offend.

After the appropriate offender profile has been determined in a preinterrogation interview, the formal interrogation proceeds. At this time, the interrogator provides various psychological rationales to the offender that (1) focus on the particular motivation to offend and (2) minimize the offender's feelings of guilt. For example, real need offenders may believe that their theft of money was justified because, as they see it, it is the basic survival instinct of humans to do whatever it takes to preserve their own lives. Likewise, impulsive offenders who commit an assault may think that their crime was justified because they were actually provoked by the victim. Each of these psychological manipulations is designed to soften the offender's resistance during the interrogation process, which may eventually lead to an admission of guilt.[8]

Kinesics Analysis

Kinesics analysis—the analysis of body movements—is an essential element of many interrogation techniques. In particular, the interrogator can examine facial expressions, eye movements, body position, vocal tone, and gestures to detect whether or when a suspect is lying. Following are some of the various indicators of deception discovered by those who study and practice kinesics as an interrogation tool:

Face:
- Less eye contact
- Squinting
- Pupil dilation
- Blinking
- Closed eyes

Gestures:
- Frequent and rapid gesturing
- Rubbing hands together
- Rubbing arms together
- Putting hands over face, mouth, forehead, eyes
- Pulling ears
- Grooming behavior

Body Movement:

- Shifting in seat
- Angled body position
- Slumping
- Tucking feet under chair
- Creating interpersonal distance
- Crossing/uncrossing legs and arms

Voice:

- Higher vocal tones
- Talking longer
- Making more speech errors (noun–verb disagreements, confusing tenses)
- Greater speech hesitations
- Greater use of speech fillers (uhmm, ahh . . .)

Although the above examples are associated with deception in American culture, kinesics in general—and especially eye contact and gesturing—can differ between cultures. For example, in Southeast Asian culture, lack of eye contact is a sign of respect. Thus, interrogation of persons from this culture might suggest the suspect is lying when in fact they are showing respect for the law. Likewise, in Brazilian culture hand gesturing is considered an insult—yet would be an indicator of truthfulness in terms of interrogation kinesics. Thus, cultural differences must be taken into account when utilizing kinesics for lie-detection purposes.[9]

Baiting the Suspect

The importance of the interrogator's inventiveness and creativity cannot be overstated. Often, suspects confess their crimes to investigators skilled at the art of acting their part well rather than in the strict science of interrogation. Besides presenting an air of confidence and assertiveness when confronting the suspect (even when the case may, in fact, be a weak one), the use of psychological bait can help punch holes in what may appear to be an iron-clad alibi. **Baiting the suspect** can be any tactic, including props, questions, statements, or body language, that causes deceptive suspects to trip up when providing false information during an interrogation. Popular forms of baiting the suspect include the following:

- Bringing to the interrogation props such as a file folder loaded with papers—creating the appearance of extensive documentary evidence obtained on the case—or labeled, sealed boxes allegedly containing physical evidence.
- Asking questions that imply a witness to the crime, i.e., "Is there any reason why a person who saw you rob the liquor store would not be telling the truth?"
- Providing statements that imply the existence of strong physical evidence relating to the case, i.e., "It's good to know that DNA taken from the crime scene will be able to exclude you as a suspect!"
- Using a bait statement to see whether the suspect agrees or disagrees with false information provided about the case. For example, the statement "Our traffic officer

thinks he saw you on 12th Street at the time the robbery occurred on 15th Street. Was that you?" The suspect may agree to this statement and provide a story that falsely elaborates on the bait statement, suggesting guilt.

The number of enticements that can be used during the interrogation process is limited only by the investigator's imagination. Current constitutional rulings support the use of these tactics, as well as others designed to fool the suspect into confessing, so long as the methods are not employed forcefully to intentionally gain a false confession from an innocent person.

DOCUMENTING INTERROGATIONS

The documentation methods for witness interviews, discussed earlier this chapter, are generally the same as those used to document interrogations. Unlike interviews, however, interrogations will result in suspects providing admissions or confessions to the crime under investigation. Therefore, the entire interrogation session should be videotaped from beginning to end. This will document not only a spontaneous admission or confession, but also protect against suspects claiming later that they had not made certain statements of guilt or that they had been coerced into making certain incriminating statements. After a verbal confession is obtained from the suspect, immediately prepare a written document recounting the general confession as well as the statements that support each of the necessary legal elements of the crime. Have the suspects initial each crime element supported by their statements and have them sign and date the overall document in the presence of another investigator as witness. The written confession is complete after the interrogating officer(s) and all witnesses also have signed and dated the final document. As a potential legal resource, continue to videotape during the post-confession documentation process. This too, will provide protection against any future allegations made by a suspect that the signed confession was not provided in a voluntary manner.

FALSE CONFESSIONS

An estimated four out of every five crimes are solved by a suspect's confession to police; yet, there is no telling the percentage of these confessions that are actually false. Recent statistics from the Innocence Project, however, suggest that approximately 25 percent of their exonerated cases stem from incriminating statements, outright confessions, or guilty pleas made to authorities. They identify the following reasons for why a suspect may make a **false confession** to criminal activity:

- Duress
- Coercion
- Intoxication
- Diminished capacity
- Mental impairment
- Ignorance of the law
- Fear of violence

- Infliction of harm
- Threats of a harsh sentence
- Misunderstanding the situation

Furthermore, false confessions fall into three broad types based on the suspect's psychological needs and motives for providing false information:

1. *Voluntary False Confessions:* These involve a rational individual who elects to make a false confession to authorities without being interrogated or pressured in any way. Motives for this behavior include fame and recognition, protection of a friend or relative, and self-punishment of real or imagined feelings of guilt associated with past activities unrelated to the crime at hand.

2. *Coerced-Compliant False Confessions:* Even though they know they are innocent, suspects falsely confess primarily to avoid perceived or real threats of physical harm if they do not provide a confession.

3. *Coerced-Internalized False Confessions:* These confessions result when innocent suspects provide false confessions as the result of mental suggestibility or confusion and come to believe during the course of an interrogation that they are actually guilty. Young suspects, highly suggestible individuals, and mentally ill or disabled persons are most prone to engaging in this type of false confession.[10]

INTERROGATING SPECIAL SUSPECTS

Procedures recommended earlier in this chapter for interviewing juveniles and other persons with physical or mental disabilities should also be followed when interrogating them. A crucial difference between interviews and interrogation when dealing with special suspects, however, is the need to avoid violating constitutional guarantees (e.g., Miranda warnings; see "Legal Requirements" later in this chapter) of such individuals during the interrogation process. Such violations would render any statement made by them legally inadmissible. Investigators must make a special effort to identify and compensate for any condition that would prevent a person from fully understanding or comprehending their legal rights during an interrogation. These may include providing language interpreters, making sure hearing aids and eyeglasses are worn, making sure medication is or is not taken, and making general assessments of physical and mental well-being. Such considerations are especially important when interrogating juveniles or questioning them in a way that may be legally construed as interrogation. Laws regarding the interrogation of juveniles vary by jurisdiction. Most state laws governing these procedures, however, do not specify age limits or require that parents be present.

HOT TIPS AND LEADS 5.1

Detecting False Confessions

Throughout history, there have been countless famous false confessions:

The Charles Lindberg Baby Kidnapping (1932): Over 200 persons provided false confessions to this highly publicized crime.

The Black Dahlia (1947): Hundreds of individuals have confessed to the infamous slaying of would-be actress Elizabeth Short (aka "the Black Dahlia") whose mutilated body was found in a Los Angeles-area field.

The Central Park Jogger Murder (1989): Forty-eight hours after the discovery of a slain jogger in Central Park, NY, five teenage boys were arrested and interrogated, and they confessed to the murder. After serving between 7 and 13 years in prison for the offense, the boys were released after the true murderer voluntarily confessed in 2002, providing a match between his DNA and that found at the crime scene.

JonBenet Ramsey Murder (2006): John Mark Karr confessed to the unsolved murder of 6-year-old JonBenet Ramsey, leading to his arrest. Karr's false confession became known when his DNA did not match that of the killer, found at the crime scene.

Warning Signs of a False Confession:

1. The facts surrounding the confession do not provide details about the crime beyond what might be obtained from media sources. Persons who are truly guilty can provide far more detailed information about a crime than is reported in news and other public information sources about the crime.

2. The false confessor's story includes actions or details that do not match what is known about the crime as indicated by evidence gathered at the crime scene, eyewitness accounts, or other factual sources.

3. All of the pieces of the story told during a false confession do not make logical sense. There are inconsistencies in times and places, lack of specific physical descriptions and details of key events, and remarkable events that border on the impossible.

4. In general, persons who are young, appear mentally unstable, are under the influence of drugs or alcohol, or seem highly confused or suggestive should be considered high risks for providing false confessions.

OTHER DECEPTION DETECTION METHODS

The Polygraph

Polygraph examinations such as that illustrated by Figure 5.11 are often used during the investigative process to exclude innocent suspects, obtain confessions from guilty suspects, verify information obtained from witness interviews, and validate the credibility of confidential informants. The polygraph examination, in many ways, is similar to an interrogation—the main difference being that the questioning is being done by the polygraph examiner (PE). Specific questions contained in the exam, however, must be carefully crafted so that they are directly relevant to the suspect's involvement in the case or to some other set of facts related to the matter at hand. Consequently, the investigator must reveal all details of the case, no matter how minute, to the PE—that way, the most effective line of questioning can be prepared for the exam. It is always advisable for investigators to work with PEs in this process. This is why a basic understanding of the polygraph and its methodology is essential for investigators.

Polygraphs come in many forms. Older models were relatively large machines that produced a rolling paper graph marked (or "inked") by the PE during the examination. This paper graph was then analyzed by the PE later for locations indicating truth or deception. Modern polygraphs, however, are much smaller units, and many are simply laptop computers that have specialized attachments and lie detection software. Results from these newer devices are digitized and saved in files that can be downloaded for later use. In addition, sophisticated computer analysis applications that analyze polygraph exam results for deceptive answer patterns are also available for use on computer systems. These results also can be prepared and presented in digital form to prepare visual presentations to other investigators, or perhaps to suspects to help elicit a confession.

The usual polygraph procedure (there are many variations, depending on the PE's preferences and training) is carried out as follows:

1. ***The Pretest Interview:*** Before the exam begins, the PE meets with the suspect to discuss the examination procedure and to discuss the exact questions that will be asked. This is done to guard against subjects having a startle reaction to an unfamiliar or disturbing question. At this time, the subject signs a release agreeing to participate in the polygraph exam and perhaps to have the session recorded on audio/video tape. Written Miranda waivers can be obtained at this time; if not, Miranda rights should be read to the suspect before asking any questions about the case.

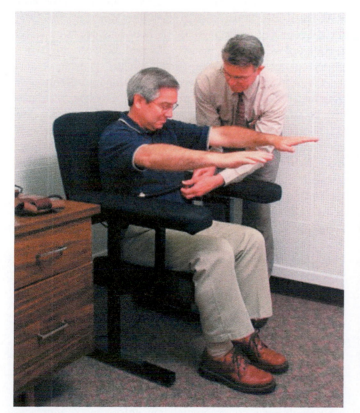

(a)

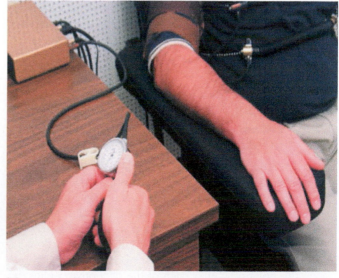

(b)

FIGURE 5.11 ▶ (a) A polygraph examiner prepares for test administration; (b) The blood pressure cuff is applied, along with other devices to monitor breathing and stress reactions.

2. ***The Pretest:*** At this point, various monitoring devices from the polygraph instrument are applied to the subject. Two hollow tubes, one placed around the abdomen and the other around the chest, are used to input information to the machine's *pneumograph,* which calibrates the subject's breathing patterns. Fingers on the subject's left hand are fitted with metal electrodes to capture the *Galvanic Skin Response (GSR),* which monitor perspiration by measuring the conductivity of a small electric charge passed through the skin. A third device known as the *cardiograph,* consisting of a cuff attached to the upper right arm region, monitors the suspect's blood pressure and pulse rate. After the machine hook-up is complete, the subject is asked some questions, known as *irrelevant questions,* that can easily be answered in a truthful manner (for example, "Are you wearing shoes?") and can be used as baseline measures of truthfulness. Involuntary physiological reactions related to lying behavior are then measured after each question. These include increases in heart rate, blood pressure, and perspiration coupled with more frequent shallow breathing. Each of these bodily reactions is detected and recorded by the polygraph and analyzed by the PE.

3. ***The Examination:*** In the formal examination, questions soliciting a "yes" or "no" response from the subject are asked in sets lasting 3 to 4 minutes each. One of the more popular methods of administering the exam is called the *control question technique (CQT).* This method involves having the subject answer two types of questions. *Relevant* questions are the first type, which directly ask subjects about their involvement in the crime being investigated. Responses to these questions are compared to replies given to *control* questions—the second type. These lines of inquiry, unrelated to the crime itself, are constructed to obtain a more general untruthful reply from the suspect that is a lesser stretch of the imagination than would be a direct lie denying involvement in the offense. Consider the following question set:

> ***Relevant Question:*** "Did you steal $10,000 from the U.S.A. Bank vault?"
>
> ***Control Question:*** "Have you ever stolen something in your lifetime?"

The guilty suspect, who in reality stole the money from U.S.A. Bank, will lie by responding "no" to the relevant question. In addition, the suspect will probably lie again on the second question to avoid being perceived as having a past criminal history of theft. The PE will look for physiological reactions of lying behavior in the subject's body as recorded by the polygraph after each of the deceptive replies. In the above example, the bodily changes recorded directly after the "big lie" answer to the relevant question (e.g., increased respiration, blood pressure) will be comparatively greater in magnitude than similar results displayed for the much less important smaller lie produced by the control question. Similar patterns for a significant number of relevant and control questions would lead the PE to conclude that the final polygraph test results suggest that the subject is lying—referred to as an *ID (Indicates Deception)* pattern. Also based on this method, however, are two possible alternative examination outcomes. If the overall polygraph results show that most of the subject's lie reactions are greater for the control questions than for the relevant questions, the PE will likely conclude that the test result was *NID (Not Indicate Deception),* which suggests that the subject was truthful. The third and last possible test outcome for the polygraph exam is an inconclusive result, which occurs when the suspect's physical response measures are roughly the same for both the control and relevant questions. This outcome occurs in approximately 10 percent of all first-time polygraph exams. When the same subject is given a second exam, however, either an ID or an NID outcome is discovered about 90 percent of the time.

All laws that apply to information gained from a suspect who is being interrogated apply to suspects undergoing a polygraph exam as well. Participation in the polygraph examination process must be strictly voluntary, and the exam process must stop immediately if subjects decide to assert their Miranda rights. Usually, the results of a polygraph test are not admissible as evidence in court unless there is a written agreement between the prosecution and defense that the results be admitted as evidence and there is judicial approval of this agreement. In jurisdictions operating under the Daubert standard of evidence, polygraph results may be admissible by judicial approval alone. In addition, the U.S. Supreme Court's ruling in *Garrity v. New Jersey*[11] has been interpreted to prohibit the use of polygraph results obtained from law enforcement officers and other governmental employees for administrative reasons in criminal investigations of such individuals. To curb potential abuses of polygraph examination results in noncriminal situations, Congress passed the Employee Polygraph Protection Act (EPPA) in 1988. This law prohibits employers (except those engaging in pharmaceutical or government work) from using the polygraph as a preemployment screening device. This law does allow employers to ask a current employee suspected of wrongdoing to take a polygraph exam, however. The law further stipulates that employees cannot be terminated solely on the basis of negative polygraph results or the refusal to submit to a polygraph examination.

Brain Fingerprinting

Brain fingerprinting, experimented with by the FBI, CIA, and other high-level governmental law enforcement agencies, involves monitoring a suspect's brain waves for what is known as the *P300 wave.* The P300 wave is a measurable spike in otherwise normal brainwave patterns that occurs about 300 milliseconds after a subject becomes aware of recognizable stimuli. As an investigative tool, brain fingerprinting has been to test a suspect's prior knowledge of crime victims or crime scene evidence. For example, a suspect in a rape case may claim during a routine interrogation that he has never before seen his alleged female rape victim. When shown a picture of the victim's face under brain fingerprint analysis, however, the electrical impulses in his brain may emit a P300 wave indicating that he indeed recognizes the facial features of the victimized female. Conversely, another suspect who has truly never seen the victim would continue to exhibit a normal brain wave pattern after viewing the same photo image.[12]

Voice Stress Analysis

Voice stress analysis (VSA) technology involves the analysis of specific voice patterns that occur when a person makes an untruthful reply, statement, or extended narrative explanation. The method is based on the same lie detection principles as the polygraph, yet does not involve hooking up a suspect to numerous attachments designed to monitor physical changes in the body. Rather, all that VSA needs is a microphone that feeds spoken words into a laptop computer with specialized software that can differentiate between truthful and deceptive voice patterns. Like the polygraph, the CQT questioning process is typically used when conducting the VSA interview. The theory underlying VSA is that when lies are told, the body reacts in a spontaneous and involuntary manner, causing the voice to tremor. These tremors (see Figure 5.12), called *voice marks*, are detected by the VCA method as indicators of potential lies. Research assessing the effectiveness of VCA ranges from conclusions that the method is 99 percent effective at pinpointing deception to more critical reviews that claim VCA is a flawed lie-detection technique with a success rate no better than chance. Despite uncertainty about its effectiveness, VCS continues to be a popular investigative tool used by thousands of law enforcement agencies, largely because it is less cumbersome and expensive to operate than the polygraph.[13]

Functional Magnetic Resonance Imaging

The **functional Magnetic Resonance Imaging (fMRI)** method assumes that a person's brain reacts in different recognizable patterns when telling the truth or being deceitful. When brain functions are visualized using an MRI machine such as that pictured in Figure 5.13, specific brain areas that are active when a lie is told appear as bright spots in MRI imagery. This is because the brain areas doing the most work during a cognitive function such as lying require more oxygen, which shows up in the MRI analysis as detectible patterns of higher blood flow throughout specific areas in the brain. These lie patterns of blood flow detected by the MRI are different for all individuals, however. Thus, the fMRI methods must first determine a consistent lie pattern for a given individual and then compare this to other patterns present when the subject is being truthful. Currently, courts are skeptical of the fMRI lie-detection technique, citing research that claims the method has at best a 60 percent accuracy rate.

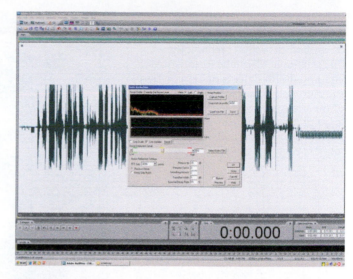

FIGURE 5.12 ▶ Results of a voice stress analysis (VSA) that shows changes in speech patterns associated with lying.

Clinical Hypnosis

During the 1960s the use of **clinical hypnosis** in criminal investigations was a readily accepted practice, but nowadays the idea of hypnotizing a suspect, witness, or victim of crime is seldom entertained. This is largely due to the many legal restrictions that limit the admissibility of statements made under hypnosis as courtroom evidence. Many jurisdictions adhere to the *per se rule* that automatically excludes as evidence any statement that is the product of hypnotically refreshed memory. Other states abide by the *totality of the circumstances rule* that requires a pretrial hearing to determine whether a particular statement made by a subject while under hypnosis is admissible, or is declared inadmissible because it is likely the untrue product of hypnotic suggestion. Case law concerning the use of hypnotically refreshed memory in court, as outlined in *People v. Shirley,* states that any memories that a subject has before undergoing a hypnotic session would be admissible; however, any information remembered during and after hypnosis would not be admissible. Thus, investigators must take care when contemplating the use of hypnosis for gaining case evidence rather than for investigative purposes only.[14]

Truth Serum

Many drugs have been tested as a **truth serum**, used to recall faded memories of witnesses or crime victims, and perhaps to gain truthful statements from crime suspects. Most popular among these is the drug sodium pentathol—a sedative that depresses the central nervous system's inhibitory mechanisms governing a person's ability to tell a lie. The use of truth drugs on crime victims, witnesses, and suspects is called *narcotherapy* and is carried out by a licensed psychiatrist. Narcotherapy can be used for investigative purposes such as helping a crime victim or witness recall details of an offense repressed as the result of psychological trauma (i.e., retrograde amnesia). Under ordinary circumstances, however, such recollections are rarely

FIGURE 5.13 ▶ (a) MRI brain scanning is the newest frontier of deception detection technology; (b) Functional Magnetic Resonance Imaging (fMRI) detects deception by showing color changes in specific areas of the brain that occur when a suspect is lying. (National Institute of Mental Health, Department of Health and Human Services)

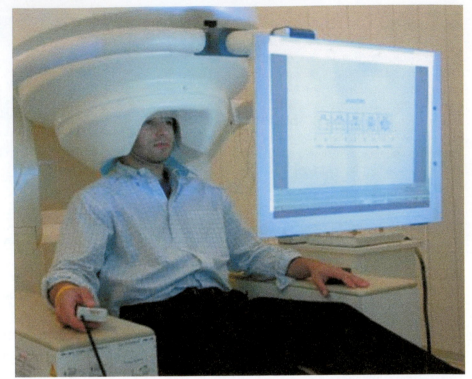

(a)

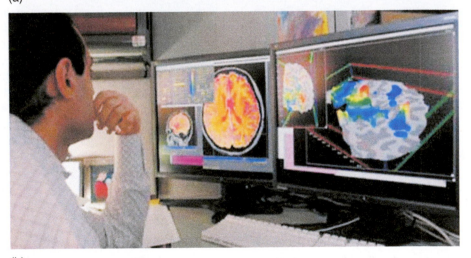

(b)

admitted as courtroom evidence. Current case law has ruled that any confession to a criminal activity obtained by narco-therapy is inadmissible.

LEGAL REQUIREMENTS

Miranda Warnings

Special care must be taken when issuing **Miranda warnings** before interviewing witnesses or interrogating suspects. As discussed earlier in Chapter 2, it usually is standard procedure to issue a Miranda warning to a crime suspect upon formal arrest. After the warning has been given, there is little doubt that the sus-

pect is now in custody. Officers may be equally aware that any questioning of the suspect from this time forward would fall within the legal parameters of an interrogation. In investigative situations, however, where information must be gathered from individuals who have not been formally arrested, knowing when and if Miranda warnings should be issued can make or break a case.

For purposes of review, recall that the intended purpose of Miranda warnings is to protect the suspect's Fifth Amendment right against self-incrimination. Since the Miranda case was first decided in 1966, countless court cases in virtually every jurisdiction have attempted to clarify the ruling's legal requirements as they apply to investigators who are either interviewing witnesses or interrogating suspects. The sum total of these cases, and their rulings, boils down to one basic rule: Once individuals are (1) in custody and (2) being interrogated by law enforcement officers, they must be advised of their Miranda rights before any of their statements or related behavior can be considered legally admissible in court. Consequently, the critical aspects of case law relating to Miranda and the investigative process involve how courts have legally defined the terms *in custody* and *interrogation*. For the investigator, it is imperative to know how to recognize the particular environment that, under Miranda rulings, would constitute placing a suspect in custody. Similarly, investigators must be aware of the point in time at which questions asked of suspects turn from a mere inquiry to an interrogation.

The U.S. Supreme Court's reasoning for establishing the necessity for suspects to be advised of their Miranda rights during custodial interrogation is that:

> without proper safeguards the process of in-custody interrogation of persons suspected or accused of crime contains inherently compelling pressures which work to undermine the individual's will to resist and to compel him to speak when he would not otherwise do so freely.

Furthermore, the Court has provided a specific definition of the term *custodial interrogation*:

> Custodial Interrogation is questioning initiated by law enforcement officers after a person has been taken into custody and otherwise deprived of his freedom of action in any significant way.

On a case-by-case basis, courts at all levels and within virtually every jurisdiction have grappled with these interpretations in an effort to provide investigators with a clear understanding of the specific environments, languages, and behaviors that satisfy the legal requirements of a custodial interrogation. Collectively, these rulings suggest that two questions need to be answered "yes" to determine whether a Miranda warning must be issued to ensure the legal admissibility of what a person says or does in the presence of investigators:

- Considering all the circumstances, would a reasonable person in the individual's position believe that he or she is in custody?
- Given the circumstances of the situation, would the particular environment that an individual is in coerce a reasonable person into saying things about their involvement in the crime?

To answer the first question, courts have considered a variety of circumstances, both in and out of custodial settings. Generally, the courts have ruled that persons are in custody when they have been formally arrested or have been subject to the functional equivalent of a formal arrest. In deciding what constitutes the functional equivalent of arrest, courts have relied on a totality of the circumstances approach. Factors typically considered include the following:

- Specific language that officers use to summons an individual
- Implied threats or actual use of physical restraint by officers
- Freedom of movement provided by the environment the individual is in

- The time when and location where officers approach an individual
- The number of officers present and their methods employed to confront the individual[15]

In more definite terms, nearly all courts have ruled that mere detention does not by itself qualify as placing a person in custody; however, most courts have concluded that it is reasonable for a person to assume that they are in custody at the time officers place them in handcuffs.

The answer to the second question, whether or not specific lines of questioning constitute an interrogation, lies in the way individuals perceive their environment at the time of questioning— not in the motives and thoughts of investigators for asking particular questions. According to most court rulings, a simple question-and-answer session can become an interrogation for the following legal purposes:

- If the express or implied purpose of questioning is to confer guilt on the individual
- When the physical setting of the questioning is threatening to or provokes fear in the individual
- The individual is confronted with evidence of guilt in an overly forceful manner
- The tone and method of questioning are intimidating to the individual[16]

Most courts have ruled that officers may question a person for purposes of obtaining personal identification, booking information while in custody, and information that establishes whether or not a crime has occurred; however, when investigators ask questions that are likely to elicit an incriminating response or confession in a particular place or with particular words or actions that are perceived by the individual as coercive in nature, the legal requirements of an interrogation will likely be satisfied. In such instances, then, a Miranda warning should be issued to suspects or witnesses if their responses are desired as evidence in a case.

Exceptions to Miranda Warnings

It is a common misconception that Miranda warnings must be given to a crime suspect at the time of arrest. It is up to the investigator when, or even if, a person should be Mirandized. In fact, many **post-Miranda exceptions** are provided by law to assist investigators who wish to present as legally admissible evidence self-incriminating statements made by individuals who have never been notified of their Miranda rights. These include the following:

- If a suspect states an alibi to their crime during questioning, information about that alibi can be admitted as evidence.
- Confessions or other self-incriminating statements made before a Miranda warning has been given can be used if repeated after a Miranda warning is issued.
- Statements given directly to officers working undercover or to informants can be admitted as evidence.

- Statements provided to officers regarding public safety issues—such as the presence of a bomb or weapon—that require immediate attention to prevent an imminently dangerous situation are exempt from Miranda requirements.
- Statements may be introduced at trial that prove the individual is lying under oath.[17]

Post-Miranda Warning Actions

Immediately following the issuance of a Miranda warning, investigators may legally begin questioning, or interrogating, the individual in custody about matters that may be self-incriminating. If, at this time, suspects offer replies to questions posed by officers, their words or actions will be admissible as evidence. According to the recent Supreme Court decision *Berghuis v. Thompkins*[18] (2010), suspects who speak voluntarily after being Mirandized have effectively waived their Miranda right to remain silent. In addition, failure to speak to officers alone is not legally sufficient to invoke the suspect's Miranda right to silence or to stop officers from continuing to ask questions and solicit replies. Suspects must clearly and unambiguously articulate to officers their wish to remain silent (e.g., "I wish to remain silent"). Equivocal statements such as "I think it would be a good idea for me to remain silent," are not sufficient to trigger a suspect's Miranda rights and replies made subsequently to these uncertain assertions will most likely remain admissible evidence. The same legal standard holds true for the Miranda right to counsel. If suspects unambiguously state that they wish to see an attorney (e.g., "I wish to see an attorney"), the interrogation must cease; however, suspects who fail to clearly request the assistance of counsel (e.g., "Maybe an attorney could help me out here") will enable officers to continue questioning. Furthermore, officers do not have to explicitly tell a suspect who is being interrogated that they have a right to a lawyer during the interrogation process. For suspects who have effectively invoked their Miranda rights to counsel, the Supreme Court has ruled that they have a right to have an attorney present during future interrogations, but the request for a lawyer is good for only 14 days after the suspect's release from custody. Suspects who freely and voluntarily begin to speak to investigators after they have requested either to remain silent or to be provided legal counsel have, if effect, waived the Miranda rights they have requested, and their statements will likely be admissible in court.

Miranda Waivers

Research suggests that about four out of five suspects will eventually waive their Miranda rights during an interrogation. In addition, similar study findings indicate that persons who are innocent are more likely to provide **Miranda waivers** than those who are either guilty of the immediate offense or have a prior record of felony offending. The actual waiver of Miranda rights, in particular the right to remain silent and to have assistance of legal counsel, can be executed as (1) a formal unambiguous statement made by the suspect after receiving a Miranda warning or (2) a formal written document stating the suspect's desire to waive his or her Miranda rights. Although either of these methods can be used to legally secure the waiver of rights by a suspect, a signed written statement provided by the suspect is recommended to prevent the suspect from legally disputing the waiver process later.

The U.S. Supreme Court has stipulated that, at the time suspects decide to waive their Miranda rights, the decision be voluntary as well as "knowing and intelligent." Waivers deemed to be the product of pressuring, coercing, or deceiving suspects will be ruled by courts as invalid—perhaps barring all of a suspect's self-incriminating testimony as evidence. In effect, suspects must be fully aware of the nature of the rights they are waiving and the potential consequences of waiving them. Thus, it is extremely important for the investigator to first assess the suspect's ability to fully understand the importance of giving up his or her Miranda right before obtaining a formal waiver. Cultural differences, language barriers, physical disabilities, mental illness, low I.Q., learning disabilities, and being under the influence of drugs or alcohol at the time of interrogation are some of the many conditions that can legally invalidate a Miranda waiver provided by a seemingly "knowing and intelligent" suspect.[19]

LEGAL REQUIREMENTS FOR JUVENILES

Juveniles must be issued Miranda warnings and afforded the same Fifth and Sixth Amendment safeguards as those extended to adults. Crime-related information obtained from juveniles by school personnel is legally admissible without Miranda warnings being issued as long as the school official questioning the child is not acting directly as an agent for police—involving themselves with police during a questioning session—and is not inducing the student to make an incriminating statement. As previously mentioned, only a minority of states require that a child be a certain age (usually 14 years), or have a parent or legal guardian present before he or she can be questioned about criminal matters. Furthermore, in most jurisdictions juveniles may waive their Miranda rights without a parent or other adult being present.

By far, the most important question investigators must answer while advising juveniles of their legal rights before questioning them about a crime is "Do they have the mental and logical capacity to clearly understand each right in the manner in which it is presented to them?" In answering this question, most courts have adopted a totality of the circumstances approach. That is, the courts will consider factors such as age, education, intelligence, emotional characteristics, time of day, presence or absence of a parent, and previous experience with the criminal justice system in determining whether juveniles have a clear understanding of their rights before or during a confession. To ensure that juveniles understand their rights, it is recommended that investigators have a juvenile suspect explain to them—in their own words—what is meant by each legal right they have heard. For example, a juvenile advised of his or her right to an attorney may be asked, "Can you tell me what an attorney does?" If the juvenile suspect cannot answer such basic questions in a cogent manner, chances are the court will rule that Miranda waivers or incriminating statements made by that youthful suspect are legally inadmissible.

APPLYING INTERVIEWING AND INTERROGATION TECHNIQUES

As previously mentioned, no method of conducting a witness interview or suspect interrogation fits every case encountered by an investigator. In fact, ultimately an interview's or interrogation's success will depend largely on the investigator's ability to "read" a situation or person and effectively execute a particular method believed to be most appropriate and effective for obtaining accurate information. Case Example 5A presents photos (see Figures 5.14 through 5.18) of a violent crime scene that poses many challenges to an investigator who must conduct witness interviews and perhaps interrogate possible crime suspects. When examining this case, pay careful attention to the crime scene evidence, attempt to reconstruct the crime, and develop a line of questioning for witnesses and suspects that is based on your overall assessment of the scene.

CASE EXAMPLE 5A

(a)

(b)

FIGURE 5.14 ▶ (a) Investigators arrive at the home of a suspected homicide following an initial survey of evidence at the scene by first responding officers and crime scene technicians; Many people (unpictured) located beyond the tape line set up by first responding officers have gathered in the street to view the crime scene. Some claim they are witnesses to the crime incident. How do you approach these and other individuals at the scene? What questions do you ask them and other officers at the scene? Where and when do you talk to the potential witnesses at the scene? (b) Investigators observe evidence items at the front gate as they proceed to the rear of the home. How would this and other types of evidence at the scene be useful in developing a line of questioning for potential witnesses and suspects?

(a)

(b)

FIGURE 5.15 ▶ (a) Investigators proceed to the rear patio area of the home; (b) Investigators continue their preliminary assessment of the scene by following a blood trail extending from the patio to the side of the home. Many of the witnesses later identified at this scene are friends, relatives and acquaintances of the victim. Some are believed to have been seated in the crime scene area shown in the above photos. What steps would you take in preparing to interview these witnesses? What methods would you use to gather information from them, bearing in mind some are children and others are quite elderly?

(a)

(b)

FIGURE 5.16 ▶ (a) Investigators follow a bloody path leading to the interior of the home; (b) Investigators enter the room to discover the core of the crime scene. Before the victim died at the scene he provided a dying declaration to officers stating that his killer was a member of a rival gang that had attacked him in the front of the home. This suspect is now in custody. What information, based on evidence at the scene, would you gather in order to make a pre-interrogation plan for this suspect?

(a)

(b)

FIGURE 5.17 ▶ (a) Investigators' full view of the crime scene; (b) Investigators move closer to the victim's body. While investigating the core of the crime scene, it has been discovered that a second person has also been taken into custody who has come forward to officers outside of the home and provided a verbal confession stating "I'm the killer." Furthermore, he is a family member of the victim. He claims that both he and the victim had a heated argument that "turned deadly" inside of this room where the victim's body was discovered. What questions, based on evidence at the scene can be used to develop a pre-interrogation plan for interrogating this suspect?

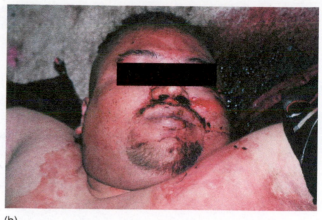

(a)   (b)

FIGURE 5.18 ▶ (a) Investigators note the toppled chairs, and a baseball cap located on top of a large blood stain; (b) Investigators examine the victim for facial wounds. After fully viewing the crime scene, and considering that there are two suspects and multiple witnesses to the crime, what method of interrogation would you use on each suspect? What evidence-based questions would you ask? What investigative means for obtaining truthful confessions other than interrogation might you use?

Summary

1. **The major differences between interviewing and interrogation.**

   Interviews are typically conducted with persons who are not suspects of crime, but who have witnessed or can provide information regarding a criminal activity. Interrogations are aimed at uncovering information from a crime suspect, or other persons who may have participated in a crime, to establish guilt or innocence. The physical settings, techniques, and laws involved in conducting interrogations are much more stringent than those relating to the interview process.

2. **Interviewing techniques and how they are used with witnesses.**

   The particular technique used to conduct an interview is generally adapted to the type of witness that is being interviewed. Friendly witnesses, those willing to cooperate with investigators, are asked open-ended questions followed by closed-ended questions. Neutral witnesses, those who neither volunteer nor refuse to cooperate, are best interviewed using a "who, what, where, when, why, and how" strategy. Hostile witnesses refusing to cooperate should first be approached with closed-ended questions and then, if they choose to cooperate, open-ended questions should be administered. Cognitive Interviewing (CI) can also be employed as a means of refreshing a witness's memory about a criminal event.

3. **How to deal with special witnesses.**

   Special witnesses are persons whose physical or mental condition or personal status may affect their com-

petence or the credibility of information they provide investigators about a crime. The investigator must perform a tactful assessment of special witness to determine whether their condition or status may negatively affect the value of the information they provide. For example, if it is clear during an interview that a witness is hard of hearing, were they wearing their hearing aid when they heard only two gunshots being fired?

4. **Interrogation techniques and how they are used with crime suspects.**

   Numerous methods have been developed for interrogation purposes: the Reid Nine-Step Technique, good cop/bad cop, interrogation profiling, and neuro linguistic programming, to name a few. Each of these methods relies on behavioral tactics, namely psychological persuasion and/or the analysis of nonverbal behavior. Practice and experience are key factors in developing the knowledge of determining which interrogation technique is best suited to a particular situation or individual.

5. **The polygraph and other deception detection methods.**

   The polygraph determines deception through analyzing changes in an individual's involuntary physiological functions as a reaction to being untruthful. Elevated breathing, blood pressure, and pulse rates are some of the reactions associated with being deceitful. Other methods aimed at determining deceit through physiological responses include changes in brain wave patterns (P300 Wave), changes in blood flow patterns in the brain (MRI analysis—fMRI), and changing vocal patterns (voice stress analysis—VSA). Clinical hypnosis and truth serum have also been used to lower a person's resistance to telling the truth.

6. **Legal requirements for conducting interviews and interrogations.**

In order for statements made during an interrogation to be legally admissible, Miranda warnings must be given to individuals who are being questioned in a custodial setting about their involvement in a crime. This rule applies to juveniles as well. On the other hand, Miranda warnings are not required for persons who are merely being interviewed as witnesses. For juveniles, parents or guardians may need to be present during interrogation or interview depending upon the specific jurisdiction. Self-incriminating statements also may be admissible in the absence of a Miranda warning if certain post-Miranda exceptions apply. Miranda rights may also be waived by a crime suspect, allowing for a full range of questioning during an interrogation.

Key Terms

interview
interrogation
friendly witness
neutral witness
hostile witness
open-ended questions
closed-ended questions
cognitive interviewing (CI)
eyewitness accounts
cross-race effect
weapon focus
flashbulb memory
mentally competent

credibility
showup
dying declaration
the third degree
confession
admission
Reid Nine-Step Technique
good cop/bad cop
interrogation profiling
Miranda warnings
post-Miranda exceptions
kinesics analysis
baiting the suspect

false confessions
polygraph
brain fingerprinting
voice stress analysis (VSA)
functional Magnetic Resonance
   Imaging (fMRI)
clinical hypnosis
truth serum
Miranda waiver
behavior analysis interview
neuro linguistic programming
   (NLP)

Review Questions

1. What are major differences between interviews and interrogations?
2. Identify and describe the various preinterview activities performed by investigators.
3. What is an open-ended interview question? Provide an example.
4. What is a closed-ended interview question? Provide an example.
5. Describe the different uses of open- and closed-ended questioning formats used for friendly, neutral, and hostile witnesses.
6. How is cognitive interviewing carried out?
7. What are some of the major concerns related to the use of eyewitness accounts of crime?
8. Define the terms *mental competence* and *witness credibility*.
9. What are some of the problems encountered when interviewing special witnesses?
10. How should a witness interview be properly documented?
11. What is a showup? How should it be carried out?
12. Of what use is a dying declaration?
13. How do admissions and confessions differ?
14. What are the nine steps involved in the Reid interrogation technique?
15. When is it most appropriate to use the good cop/bad cop interrogation method?
16. How is neuro linguistic programming carried out?
17. Provide an example of how you would conduct a behavioral analysis interview.
18. Describe how the interrogation profile technique is used as an interrogation tool.
19. What is baiting the suspect? Provide an example of how this method is used.
20. What types of behaviors suggest deception and truthfulness according to kinesics analysis?
21. What are the major reasons for a person making a false confession?
22. By what means does the polygraph detect deception?
23. What are some other means of truth determination, besides the polygraph?

24. Under what circumstances must a Miranda warning be given?
25. Of what importance are Miranda waivers and exceptions to the interrogation process?
26. What are the important legal issues to be considered when questioning or interrogating a juvenile?

Internet Resources

The 3rd Degree: Interview and Interrogation Research	the3rddegree.com/
The Lie Guy®: Interview and Interrogation Websites	www.kinesic.com/
John E. Reid & Associates, Inc.	www.reid.com
The Interview & Interrogation Group	www.igroops.com/members/lies
Advanced Interviewing Concepts	www.statementanalysis.com/
L.I.E.S.	www.truthsleuth.com/

Applied Investigative Exercise

Construct an investigative plan for interviewing witnesses and interrogating suspects who may have knowledge of the crime described in Case Example 5A. For your interviews, develop a question set geared toward friendly, neutral, and hostile witnesses. For your interrogation, select a specific technique and apply it by developing a line of questioning based on your reconstruction of the crime and the available physical evidence in the scene.

Notes

[1] John E. Hess, *Interviewing and Interrogation for Law Enforcement* (Cincinnati, OH: Anderson, 2010), 30–87.

[2] William M. Hart and Roderick D. Blanchard, *Litigation and Trial Practice*, 6th ed. (Clifton Park, NY: Thomson, 2007), 237–249.

[3] David E. Zulawski and Douglas E. Wicklander, *Practical Aspects of Interview and Interrogation*, 2nd ed. (Boca Raton, FL: CRC Press, 2002), 228–230.

[4] Elizabeth F. Loftus, *Eyewitness Testimony* (Cambridge, MA: Harvard University Press, 1979).

[5] Charles L. Yeschke, *The Art of Investigative Interviewing*, 2nd ed. (Boston, MA: Butterworth-Heinemann, 2003), 141–147.

[6] Fred E. Inbau, *Essentials of the Reid Technique: Criminal Interrogation and Confessions* (Sudbury, MA: Jones and Bartlett, 2004).

[7] Aldert Vrij and Shara K. Lochun, "Neuro-Linguistic Programming and the Police: Worthwhile or Not?" *Journal of Police and Criminal Psychology* 12, no. 1 (1997), 56–68.

[8] Richard A. Leo, "The Third Degree and the Origins of Psychological Interrogation in the United States," in G. D. Lassiter (Ed.), *Interrogations, confessions and entrapment* (pp. 37–82), New York: Kluwer Academic/Plenum, 2004.

[9] Judith A. Hall and Mark L. Knapp, *Nonverbal Communication in Human Interaction* (Fort Worth, TX: Harcourt Brace Jovanovich College Publishers, 1992).

[10] Richard P. Conti, "The Psychology of False Confessions," *The Journal of Credibility Assessment and Witness Psychology*, Vol. 2, No. 1 (1999), 14–36.

[11] *Garrity v. New Jersey*, 385 U.S. 493 (1967).

[12] Lawrence A. Farwell, *Brain Fingerprinting*, posted at www.forensic-evidence.com/site/Behv_Evid/Farwell_sum6_00.html.

[13] Darren Haddad et al., *Investigation and Evaluation of Voice Stress Analysis* (Washington, DC: U.S. Department of Justice, 2002), 33–49.

[14] Joe Niehaus, *Investigative Forensic Hypnosis* (Boca Raton, FL: CRC Press), 85–101.

[15] *Miranda v. Arizona*, 384 U.S. 436 (1966).

[16] Ibid.

[17] Ibid.

[18] *Berghuis v. Thompkins*, 547 F.3d 572, 576 (6th Cir. 2008).

[19] Devallis Rutledge, *Miranda Invocation and Waiver* posted at www.policemag.com/Channel/Patrol/Articles/2010/08/Miranda-Invocation-and-Waiver.aspx.

Courtesy of Vail Police Department, Vail, CO

CHAPTER SIX

INVESTIGATIVE REPORT WRITING

Learning Objectives

After completing this chapter, you should be able to:

1. Understand the importance of field notes and their use in incident/crime reports.
2. Explain the circumstances in which field notes are commonly taken.
3. Know the basic information contained in an incident/crime report.
4. Explain the required contents of incident/crime reports and the term *FACCCT*.
5. Know the different types of incident/crime reports.
6. Summarize how to take written and recorded statements.

Chapter Outline

Taking Field Notes
- Field Note Content
- Strategies for Taking Effective Field Notes

Writing Incident/Crime Reports
- Preparation of the Report
- General Report Writing Tips
- Specialized Crime Reporting Formats

Report Classifications

Supplemental Reports

Report Writing Technology

INTRODUCTION

LET'S START THIS CHAPTER WITH a quiz. Here's the question:

What is the most important aspect of investigative work, according to many seasoned investigators?
A. The reconstruction of crimes
B. The recognition of physical evidence
C. A keen sixth sense about a suspect's guilt or innocence
D. None of the above

As you know from previous chapters, answers A, B, and C are all important aspects of the investigative process. But what if the results of these investigative activities cannot be conveyed effectively in writing? The results of this scenario would be catastrophic not only to investigators, but also to all parties associated with an investigation. For this reason, and others that will be outlined in this chapter, the correct answer is D.

Missing from the above answer set is "Learning to effectively document investigative information in written form." An estimated 50 percent of an investigator's time is spent writing. This includes taking field notes about incidents or crimes under

investigation and then converting these notes into formal reports that may ultimately determine whether an offender is prosecuted, a trial is won, or a case is solved. Consider the following examples:

- Prosecutors rely on well-documented investigative reports to support their decision to file formal charges.
- Judges depend on details in the investigator's report to make sentencing decisions.
- Investigations of cold cases, serial crimes, and other crimes related to habitual offenders are often solved by comparing reports from different investigative jurisdictions.

These are just a few of the many reasons and justifications for learning how to write a good investigative report. As this chapter will show, good investigations go hand in hand with good report writing skills.

TAKING FIELD NOTES

The first step in the report writing process involves collecting accurate and detailed **field notes**. These notes provide a permanent record of the investigator's observations and interviews. They serve primarily as a reference tool for jogging officers' memory while preparing a formal incident or crime report. Field notes serve other important investigative functions as well, including documentation of the following:

- Persons involved in or with knowledge of a criminal matter
- Previous interviews conducted, preventing unnecessary reinterviews, and collection of redundant information
- Exact statements made by suspects, perpetrators, and witnesses
- Information that may provide future investigative leads
- References that can be compared to check for consistency with other investigators' notes/reports on the same incident/crime
- Items to refresh an investigator's memory when asked to testify about an incident or crime
- Crime scene sketches
- Notes, statements, and other content that can be treated as admissible evidence

Although automated note-taking aids are available, investigators still record field notes by hand in a **field notebook**. Some agencies provide a standard field notebook to all their officers, while others allow officers to select one based on their individual preferences. Loose-leaf notebooks allow pages to be inserted or removed—which makes adding or deleting materials convenient, yet may also allow defendants to claim that officers do this intentionally to alter recorded information. Questions about the original condition of field notes can be avoided by using spiral-bound field notebooks with pages that cannot be removed without tearing; remember, however, that others who gain legal access to this style of notebook may observe nonessential information or notes taken on other cases. Notes should be written in black ink because blue ink does not often reproduce well and pencil lead smudges and smears. Standard practice is to write all notes in printed capital letters so that they are legible to others who may need to review case materials. For the same reason, unfamiliar abbreviations or cryptic shorthand also should be avoided. Mistakes should not be erased, as this will cause notes to appear intentionally changed or fabricated; instead, a line should be drawn through the unwanted notes and their location on the page initialed. The overall appearance, organization, and clarity of notes taken in a given case convey an overall perception of the investigator's competence to those who review the field notebook.[1]

Available electronic methods of documenting the investigator's observations and interviews can be used to support note-taking efforts. These include in-car cameras and other audio/visual recording devices. One method recently gaining popularity is the **digital audio recorder (DAR)**. This small, inexpensive device, which can be concealed in a pocket or other unobtrusive location, provides a digital audio recording that can be downloaded on a personal or agency computer. Such electronic documentation provides an invaluable backup of investigator's field notes; however, neither this electronic recording method nor any other should supplant the traditional

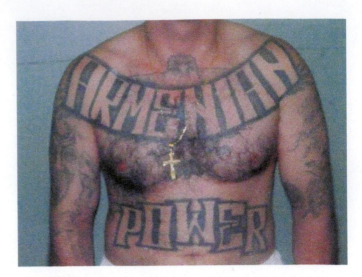

FIGURE 6.1 ▶ An arrested gang member who has several tattoos. These characteristics should always be noted in an officer's notebook. They not only aid in the current case, but may also help in identifying suspects in unsolved crimes.

field note-taking method. In short, the attention to detail that is a hallmark trait of handwritten field notes cannot yet be duplicated by modern technology.

Field Note Content

The content of field notes will depend largely on the incident or crime being investigated. For example, in the case of the gang crime suspect pictured in Figure 6.1, unique body characteristics such as gang tattoos should be noted in detail so they can be described adequately in a written formal report. Generally, however, the investigator's observations and personal interview materials—the foundation of all field notes taken—will be based on a series of questions gathering the **5 Ws & H** or the "Who, What, When, Where, Why, and How" of the matter or situation being investigated (see Figure 6.2). The following sections suggest lines of inquiry that may assist in this aspect of the note-taking process.

WHO

Notes on the "Who" aspects of an incident or crime invariably focus on persons and their knowledge, characteristics, and/or behaviors that are relevant to the investigation. These notes may determine the following:

- Victims
- Suspects/perpetrators
- Witnesses
- Informants
- Emergency medical personnel
- Other officers/personnel entering the crime scene

FIGURE 6.2 ▶ An investigator examines an incident report for the who, what, where, when, why, and how of a suspected crime to decide whether or not the case should be given priority status and receive a full-scale criminal investigation.

- Persons (e.g., neighbors, business associates) with special knowledge of victims, witnesses, suspects, and the crime scene
- Persons reporting the incident/crime
- Persons who may have been motivated to harm the victim or damage/steal the property
- Persons who have previously committed similar crimes in the area
- Persons handling physical evidence during a chain of custody
- Owners of property, either stolen or somehow involved in the incident/crime
- Persons at the scene before, during, or after the incident/crime
- Experts on technical matters, such as criminalists and forensic scientists

Information gathered about suspects can include race, sex, age, type of build (e.g., heavyset, medium, small frame), approximate weight and height, color of eyes and hair, hair style (e.g., long short, shaved, etc.), facial hair, clothing type (e.g., hats, jeans, jackets etc.), prior knowledge of name and street name, missing teeth, tattoos, scars, moles, and unusual odors. Victims sometimes can identify a suspect from unusual gestures, speech patterns, speech accents, what hand was used, and any gang affiliation. Victims, witnesses, and other persons providing suspect description and information useful for investigative purposes should be identified by documenting their full name, age, date of birth, race, sex, telephone numbers (home, cell, and work), addresses (home and work), e-mail addresses, and place to contact. This information, however, may be gathered following any initial witness statements on the suspect's description and whereabouts that can be used to issue or update a *BOLO* (be on the lookout) broadcast.

WHAT

The "What" of note taking primarily helps establish whether the incident being investigated is a crime; and if so, what type of crime it is. In addition, this line of information gathering includes the following:

- Items damaged or stolen, and their value
- Weather conditions at the incident/crime location
- The sensory perceptions (sights, sounds, smells, etc.) of the officer and others at the crime scene
- Unusual circumstances, conditions, situation, and behaviors observed
- Vehicles driven by suspects
- Weapons or tools used by the suspect
- Suspect's motives for carrying out the offense
- Specific statements made by victims, witnesses, and suspects
- Physical evidence items and materials available
- Actions and behaviors of parties involved in the incident/crime
- Other similar crimes previously committed in the crime scene area
- Victim's routine activities such as travel patterns, work, school, leisure activities, etc.

While taking notes on these subject areas and related ones, the investigator should develop theories regarding the specific type of crime which can be supported—or cannot be supported—by the information provided. Additional field notes should document the specific elements of such crimes.

WHERE

When focusing on the "Where" of a suspected criminal activity in note taking, documenting the physical location of primary and secondary crime scenes is a central concern. Other, relevant lines of inquiry include the following:

- Missing or stolen property items
- Perpetrators' entry and exit paths/points
- Suspects' places of residence, vehicles owned, places of employment, etc.
- Physical evidence inside or outside the crime scene(s)
- Surveillance cameras or other recording devices that may have captured the criminal incident
- Hiding places used by suspect(s)
- Places where weapons have been discarded or stashed
- Drugs or other contraband
- Places where the victim and offender may have crossed paths on prior occasions
- Hospitals or other locations to which victims or others were transported for treatment

WHEN

The "When" of field notes documents the time and date of events relating to the incident or crime under investigation. Accurate times and dates are very important to the investigation because they establish a timeline for the events. Among the first times and dates to be noted are those of the officer's arrival at the incident/crime. It is crucial that an accurate timeline of events be established when noting the "whens." If noted times do not follow a logical sequence starting from when a call was first reported, a case could be severely delayed or even dismissed. A note that incorrectly places the time of the incident/crime after the time an item of physical evidence was collected will enable case-damaging arguments to be made (for example, that the evidence in question could not have originated from the crime scene). Additionally, if the victim statement time is confused with the time of the incident, doubt about the suspect's presence could be raised in the suspect's defense. These are only a few examples of problems that could occur if the times are not duly documented. The best time to document times is when the officer becomes aware of them. Specific examples of common "When" notation include the following:

- The incident/crime was reported
- Suspects were detained or arrested
- The officer and other personnel arrived at and departed the crime scene
- The victim, witnesses, and suspects were interviewed
- Items of physical evidence were located or obtained
- Items of physical evidence were handled during a chain of custody
- Certain weather conditions (e.g., rain, snow) occurred

WHY

The particular victimology aspects of an incident/crime are the main focus of "Why" note taking. This involves documenting answers to questions underlying the suspect's motive to offend, the victim's attractiveness to the offender, and the specific circumstances that resulted in the offender's decision to carry out the criminal act against the victim or property. Specifically, information should be gathered as to why the following occurred:

- The offender was attracted to the victim or victimized property
- The offender was in the crime scene location (if not one where such crimes normally take place)
- The victim was in the crime scene location, if not his or her residence or place of work
- Witnesses were at the crime scene
- A particular type of weapon or tool was used or not used
- The incident/crime was not reported immediately
- Offenders took or did not take measures to hide their identity from witnesses and surveillance cameras

- Measures were taken or not taken to remove physical evidence from the crime scene
- Victims did or did not take precautions to protect themselves or their property
- Offenders used a particular method to enter or to escape the crime scene
- The victim himself or herself did or did not report the incident/crime
- Attempts were made or not made by the offender to remove physical evidence from the crime scene

HOW

For the most part, the "How" of note taking centers on aspects of the M.O. or the *modus operandi* of the incident/crime. Thus, to document the offender's method of operation, it is essential to gain information noting how the following occurred:

- Offenders carried out or attempted to carry out the incident/crime
- Victims crossed paths in time and in space with the offenders
- Suspects gained entry into the crime scene
- Suspects exited the crime scene
- Offenders prepared to commit the incident crime (e.g., either planned or spontaneous)
- Stolen property was disposed of or fenced
- Offenders obtained illegal items such as drug, guns, explosives, or other weapons
- Witnesses were able to see or hear criminal activities
- Offenders behaved in a strange or unique manner at the crime scene

Strategies for Taking Effective Field Notes

Good note taking involves many issues. The following sections discuss these.

ATTENTION TO DETAIL

Good note taking is grounded in an investigator's attention to detail. Simply put, field notes can never be too detailed! Detailed notes, however, need not delve into details of the incident or crime that are irrelevant to solving the case. Furthermore, it is vital that investigators know the specific legal elements required to prove specific criminal acts and how to write detailed field notes addressing these substantive areas. If sufficient detail cannot be documented because witnesses or victims claim that they don't know or can't recall, probes or memory cues can help uncover detailed information hidden within a cloudy memory. For example, victims who say they cannot recall a suspect's exact height can be asked, "Was the suspect taller or shorter than me?"; or, in the case of the suspect's weight, "Was the suspect heavier or lighter than you?" Relative comparison probes often spark the memory and provide a means for obtaining additional crime-related details from victims and witnesses. In short, don't just give up and mark "N/A" in your field notes when the initial response to your interview question is "I don't remember anything."

CONSISTENCY AND AN ORGANIZED FORMAT

In recording field notes, officers should use a consistent format. The note-taking process usually starts with stating simple facts and observations upon arriving at the scene of an incident/crime—time, date, and conditions at the crime scene. Most important, however, notes must be factual, clear, and concise. Field notes that are incomplete, difficult to read, or poorly organized will be of little use for report writing or other legal purposes. For example, at both preliminary hearings and trials, officers have to recall specifics about certain incidents. If the officer cannot recall certain details of the criminal investigation due to incomplete or poor note taking, a case may be easily lost. Officers are involved in numerous situations and write many reports, so it is easy to see how an officer's memory could fade. Unless something unusual occurs, the chance of remembering a past arrest or report months later is difficult at best.

ADOPT AN EFFICIENT RECORDING STYLE

Officers typically use abbreviations and abbreviated sentences to make notes recording the statements of victims, witnesses, and other persons about the crime under investigation. The mistake that many officers make is attempting to write down the interviewee's every word. Without a tape recorder, it is virtually impossible to record statements word for word. Perhaps most difficult, officers must (1) keep the interviewee's story focused and on track and (2) condense a multitude of words into legible notes from which a detailed and logical final incident report can be written.

HOT TIPS AND LEADS 6.1

Field Note Abbreviations

Officers commonly use abbreviations when note taking as a time-saving measure. The following is an example of an abbreviated statement taken during a domestic violence call:

01/12/08 1335 hrs, **Cntd** V/Smith, Jane **FW**/111271. Stated **Sus** is **Husb** of 3 yrs. **Sus** came home on 01/12/08 0800 and told **V** to make him food. **V** was tired and said "no." **Sus** walked up to **V** and punched her on her **Rt** eye area. **Obs** redness/**Bru** on **Rt** eye area of **V**.

Notice that the birth date is condensed: There is no need to put hyphen marks, as all officers should be able to recognize the birth date numbers. Abbreviations in the above example include: "Cntd" is short for contacted; "V" stands for victim; "FW" stands for Female White; "Sus" stands for suspect; "Husb" is short for husband; "Rt" is abbreviated for right; "Obs" stands for observed; and "Bru" is short for bruising.

There are many different abbreviation formats to choose from. Officers should select the format or style they are comfortable with; however, the particular notation and abbreviation must be intelligible to all persons who may read the officer's field notes later.

WRITING INCIDENT/ CRIME REPORTS

Officers write **incident/crime reports** to provide a permanent record of their investigative activities, which also is a duty mandated by law. Extreme care must be taken in preparing an incident/crime report because its quality directly reflects on the quality of the officer's investigative efforts. This aspect of report writing is especially important considering the many influential persons who could read the report. These include the following:

- **Supervisors:** Typically reports are submitted to supervisors for approval before becoming a formal record. The quality of the report will create a lasting impression of the officer's writing and investigative abilities.

- **Prosecutors:** The ability of a report to clearly spell out facts that support the required elements of a crime will determine whether or not a prosecutor decides to file formal charges against a suspect.

- **Judges:** An officer's report may be a critical piece of evidence that a judge uses in a decision regarding the existence of probable cause to hold a suspect to answer to criminal charges or whether a particular piece of physical evidence is legally admissible at trial.

- **Probation/Parole Officers:** Reports often assist probation and parole officers in deciding whether or not to recommend that a suspect/inmate participate in special programs that are alternatives to jail or prison time.

- **Defense Attorneys:** The suspect's defense strategy will rely heavily on what can or cannot be legally supported in the officer's report. In particular, the overall strength of the report may be key in the defense attorney's decision to accept a plea bargain or go to trial.

- *Insurance Agents:* When private insurance companies are required to make large payouts for death or damages, insurance investigators review incident/crime reports to determine whether compensation is justified. For example, if a report indicates that an insured building has burned as the result of arson rather than an accidental fire, not only will an insurance claim not be honored, but criminal charges will likely be filed as well.

- *Other Investigators:* Investigators and other specialized units performing follow-up and new investigations may rely upon and supplement reports prepared by first responding officers to an incident/crime.

- *Crime Analysts:* Accurate posting of crime trends, suspect bulletins, and other "intelligence-based" activities requires accurate incident/crime reports. Media accounts of police performance and public safety issues often are based directly on statistics made public by the FBI's Uniform Crime Reports and other data sources created from police reports.

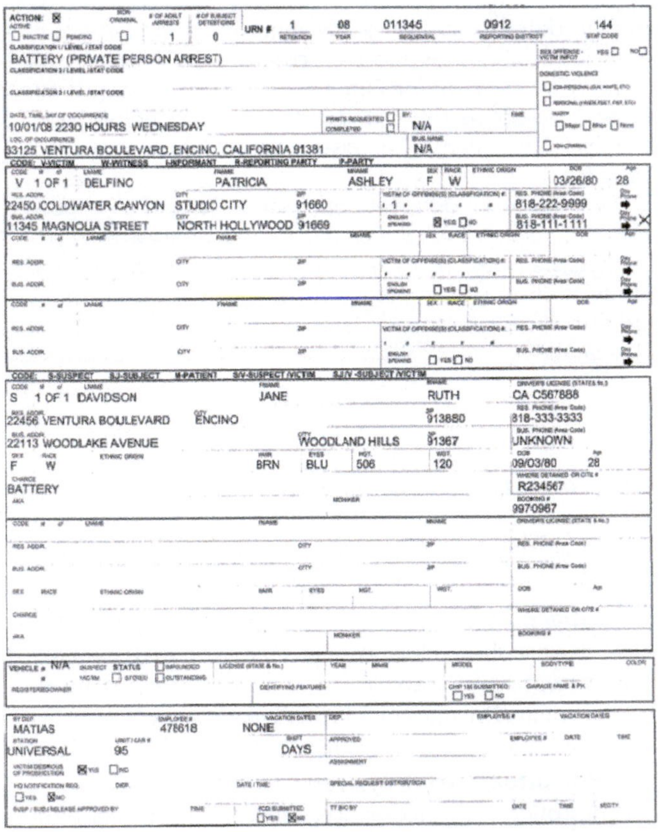

FIGURE 6.3 ▶ Face sheet of an incident report. The exact format varies by department, but most face sheets generally include the same crime and suspect identifying information. (All of the information contained in this example is fictitious.) See the second page of the face sheet in Figure 6.4.

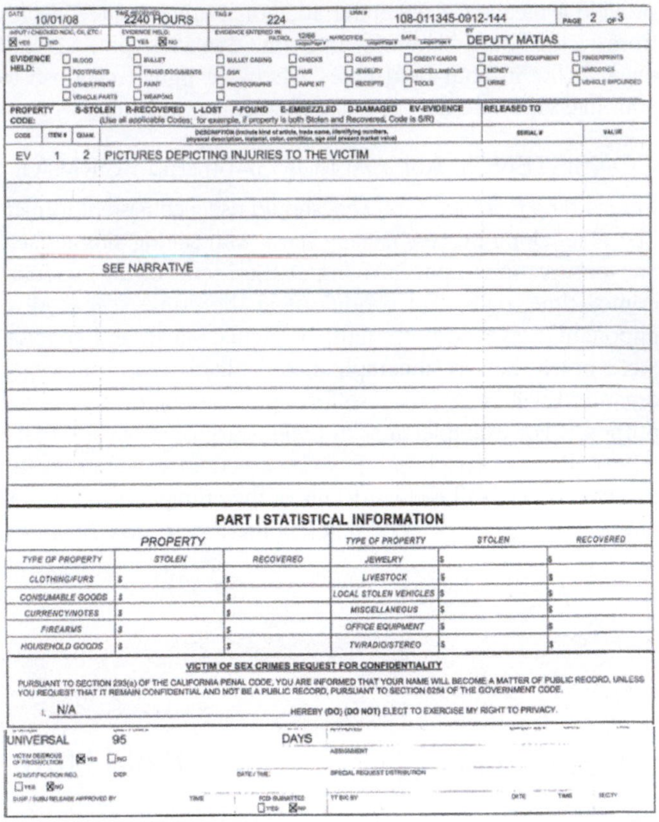

FIGURE 6.4 ▶ Second page of face sheet. Note the "EVIDENCE HELD" boxes at the top and the "PROPERTY" boxes at the bottom. These are used by investigators to perform a preliminary review of the incident for case assignment purposes.

Preparation of the Report

After notes are collected, a formal report of the crime or incident should be prepared immediately so that important facts and information obtained during the field note-taking process are not forgotten or confused. Each agency usually has its own standard format for report preparation, but there are several characteristics that all reports have in common:

THE FACE SHEET

Most reports begin with a **face sheet** (see Figures 6.3 and 6.4) that contains various fill-in lines and check boxes regarding key information:

- The time, date, and nature of the crime/incident
- The suspect(s)/victim(s)/subject(s)
- The reporting officer(s)
- Evidence obtain
- Property stolen and its estimated value
- Requests for special distribution to other units/investigators

Providing accurate and sufficient details on the face sheet is extremely important since the information provided is typically inputted into automated databases tracking crimes, victims, and offenders. In addition, it is a bad idea to leave spaces empty on the face sheet or fill them in with "N/A" (not available) or "UNK" (unknown) to reduce paperwork time; this also reduces the accuracy of databases, so it should be avoided.

THE NARRATIVE

Immediately following the face sheet is a page or more (commonly referred to as *continuations*) of the **report narrative**. This section provides detailed incident/crime information in the officer's own words. Some officers still prefer to prepare this portion of the report as a hand-written document; however, the bulk of today's narratives are word processed. The main purpose of the narrative is to tell a clear, logical, and accurate story of the persons and events involved in the incident/crime being reported. Good narratives are ones that enable readers to mentally visualize the details of what is being reported.[2]

Content in the report narrative can be organized in many ways, but usually a chronological approach is employed. Typically, the narrative begins with the first thing the officer did/observed and ends with the officer's last activity or observation. The following is an example of this style:

At approximately 1500 hours on October 15, 2010, I responded to disturbance at 122 W. Elm St., Bigtown. When I arrived at this location, I saw a man (later identified as Jason Jackson) lying in the street . . . *(the report continues in the chronological order of events)*

Jackson was examined at the scene by Bigtown City Fire Department Paramedics Smith #EMT111 and Jones #EMT222 and transported to Bigtown Hospital for further evaluation. *(the report ends with the final event)*

Most important, the narrative content provides a detailed account of the "Who, What, Where, When, Why, and How" documented in the investigator's field notes. Detailed information on the "5 Ws & H" should be presented accurately and objectively in the narrative section (see Figure 6.6). In a report geared toward substantiating an arrest or criminal activity, the facts supporting the elements of the crime in question are especially important. When discussing officers' actions—such as use of force—the narrative should support any legal or practical justifications for particular actions. Also to be included are descriptions of suspects, victims, witnesses, physical evidence, crime scene dimensions, sensory observations, and other similar details directly relevant to the case. If information is not available to support one of the "5 Ws & H," the narrative should say so. In such cases, it is helpful to briefly explain why such information was unattainable.

The California Commission on Peace Officer Standards and Training provides a useful acronym—**FACCCT**—for remembering the key components of report writing:

F (Factual): Include only facts that are objective and relevant.

A (Accurate): Avoid including information that is inconsistent or illogical.

C (Clear): Use words and terminology that are clear and unambiguous.

C (Concise): Don't be wordy and don't provide more information than is necessary.

C (Complete): Make sure all "5 Ws & H" are covered and factually supported.

T (Timely): Make sure the report is submitted within agency-required deadlines.[3]

CASE CLOSE-UP 6.1

"GATES-GATE: REPORT WRITING GONE HORRIBLY WRONG"

Cambridge, Mass.

Upon responding to a 911 call reporting a possible residential break-in, Sgt. James Crowley of the Cambridge Police Department observed a man attempting to open the front door of a home near the reported offense. Sgt. Crowley detained the man—who was Harvard Professor Louis Gates, Jr.—for questioning. According to Sgt. Crowley's police report, Professor Gates was uncooperative and became verbally abusive. In response to this behavior, the officer arrested Gates for disorderly conduct. The case received national attention as an example of police racial profiling when Gates claimed that his arrest and detention were motivated by the fact that he was African-American. Subsequently, the case received national attention as an example of police racial profiling run amok. In his defense, Sgt. Crowley pointed to his police report, which stated the following about his interview with the woman who placed the 911 call: "She went on to tell me that she observed what appeared to be 2 black males with backpacks on the porch." The woman reporting the crime denied that she made the comment to the officer, and the original 911 recording of her call revealed that she, in fact, said, "two large men, one

CAMBRIDGE POLICE DEPARTMENT
CAMBRIDGE, MA
Incident Report #9005127
Report Entered: 07/16/2009 13:21:34

Case Title	Location	Apt/Unit #
	● WARE ST	

Date/Time Reported
07/16/2009 12:44:00

Date/Time Occurred
to

Incident Type/Offense
1.) DISORDERLY CONDUCT c272 S53 —

Reporting Officer
CROWLEY, JAMES (467)

Approving Officer
WILSON III,JOSEPH (213)

Persons

Role	Name	Sex Race Age DOB	Phone	Address
WITNESS	WHALEN, LUCIA	40 ▬▬▬▬	H ▬▬▬▬	▬▬▬▬▬▬▬▬▬
			C ▬▬▬▬	▬ MA

Offenders

Status	Name	Sex	Race	Age DOB	Phone	Address
DEFENDANT	GATES, HENRY	MALE	BLACK	58 - ▬▬▬	H ▬▬▬	● WARE ST
					C	CAMBRIDGE, MA

Vehicles

Property

Class	Description	Make	Model	Serial #	Value

Narrative

On Thursday July 16, 2009, Henry Gates, Jr. (▬▬▬▬, of ● Ware Street, Cambridge, MA) was placed under arrest at ● Ware Street, after being observed exhibiting loud and tumultuous behavior, in a public place, directed at a uniformed police officer who was present investigating a report of a crime in progress. These actions on the behalf of Gates served no legitimate purpose and caused citizens passing by this location to stop and take notice while appearing surprised and alarmed.

On the above time and date, I was on uniformed duty in an unmarked police cruiser assigned to the Administration Section, working from 7:00 AM-3:30 PM. At approximately 12:44 PM, I was operating my cruiser on Harvard Street near Ware Street. At that time, I overheard an ECC broadcast for a possible break in progress at ● Ware Street. Due to my proximity, I responded.

When I arrived at ● Ware Street I radioed ECC and asked that they have the caller meet me at the front door to this residence. I was told that the caller was already outside. As I was getting this information, I climbed the porch stairs toward the front door. As I reached the door, a female voice called out to me. I turned and looked in the direction of the voice and observed a white female, later identified as Lucia Whalen. Whalen, who was standing on the sidewalk in front of the residence, held a wireless telephone in her hand and told me that it was she who called. She went on to tell me that she observed what appeared to be two black males with backpacks on the porch of ● Ware Street. She told me that her suspicions were aroused when she observed one of the men wedging his shoulder into the door as if he was trying to force entry. Since I was the only police officer on location and had my back to the front door as I spoke with her, I asked that she wait for other responding officers while I investigated further.

FIGURE 6.5 ▶ Incident report filed by Cambridge, MA, police after arresting Professor Henry Gates. (City of Cambridge, MA Police Department)

looked kind of Hispanic, but I'm not really sure—the other one entered, I didn't see what he looked like." Some speculated that Sgt. Crowley "enhanced" his police report adding the racial descriptor "Black" to substantiate his decision to detain Gates as a probable suspect in the break-in. Others contend that the error in the officer's report was a careless mistake. Controversy over the "Gates-gate" incident—based primarily on a police report that went horribly wrong—reached a fever pitch within the African-American community as a symbol of prejudicial treatment by police. Ultimately, President Obama stepped in to settle the matter by inviting both Gates and Sgt. Crowley to the White House to smooth things over while having a beer. Again, the power of the police report cannot be underestimated. As Figure 6.5 illustrates, an incident report often becomes the subject of significant media attention when it concerns a high-profile case such as this one.

I responded to 33125 Ventura Boulevard, in the city of Washoe, regarding a battery that just occurred call. Upon my arrival, I contacted V/ Doe, Jane who told me the following:

She was walking her dog westbound on Seter Boulevard, in the city of Washoe, when she saw a male white (later identified as S/Blank, John) who appeared to be a transient, sitting on the sidewalk impeding the victim's path to walk. The victim asked the suspect to please move and the suspect told the victim to walk around him. The victim stated she could not walk around him because the sidewalk was too narrow. The suspect stated he did not care and if the victim asked him to move again, he would hurt her. The victim asked the suspect a second time to move. The suspect stood up and came to within arm's reach of the victim and punched her three times on her right arm. The victim immediately stepped back, fearing further attack, and called the police.

I contacted the suspect and asked if he wanted to talk to me about what had occurred. The suspect stated he did not want to discuss the incident. I observed the victim to have bruising and swelling to her upper right arm area. I took two pictures of the injuries (EV1). The victim declined any medical attention.

I advised the victim of the private person's arrest procedure and she stated she understood them. The victim advised me she was desirous of private person's arrest for battery. The suspect was subsequently arrested and released in the field with a citation. Cite # 444444

FIGURE 6.6 ▶ Sample narrative, which follows the face sheets for the battery incident report example provided in Figures 6.3 and 6.4.

General Report Writing Tips

There are countless ways to write a good investigative report; however, the quality of a report can be diminished through improper content, incorrect word use, and inattention to detail. Some of the avoidable pitfalls of report writing are as follows:

1. ***Avoid imprecise or wordy forms of grammar:*** Certain forms of grammar, when combined, create a shorter, easier-to-read, and more understandable report. These include the following writing recommendations:

Write using:

- First Person: **I** saw the gun . . . Not: ***The arresting officer*** *saw the gun.*
- Full Names: **Hector Sanchez** is the victim . . . Not: **He** *is the victim.*
- Active Voice: **I searched** the car . . . Not: *The car* **had been searched**.
- Clear Words: I **warned** the suspect . . . Not: *I* ***provided a verbal admonition to*** *the suspect.*
- Correct Words: The drug had an immediate **effect**... Not: *The drug had an immediate* **affect**.

2. ***Avoid including personal opinions:*** Reports are factual documents and should not include the reporting officer's opinions. If it is necessary to state an opinion, state clearly that it is your opinion: *Jones was hitting his head against the brick wall and displayed no signs of pain. Therefore, in my opinion, Jones was under the influence of a pain-killing drug.*

3. ***Avoid misquoting statements:*** Quotations imply that the words were obtained verbatim from an interview with a victim, witness, suspect, or other party that may be included in the report. The number of direct quotes should be kept to a minimum, being used only when they provide information that specifically illustrates the person's motives, actions/omissions, and state of mind.

Also, any profanity included in the report should be in the form of a direct quote. Otherwise, statements heard or obtained during interviews should be paraphrased in sentences with quotation marks omitted. For example:

Direct Quote: Smith said, "If I have the chance, I'll kill my homeboy TWO TIMER. I'll fuck him up."

Paraphrased: Smith stated that he wanted to kill a member of his gang named TWO TIMER.

4. ***Avoid repeating information.*** Unless agency report writing guidelines require it, information contained in the face sheet or elsewhere in the report need not be repeated in the narrative section. Repeated content detracts from the main points raised in the report.

5. ***Avoid using excessive or unfamiliar abbreviations.*** The report must be intelligible to a variety of audiences—some with technical expertise in law enforcement and others without. To prepare a universally understandable report, only abbreviations easily identifiable in the written context should be used.[4]

Correct Use: The suspect was arrested for **DUI**.

Incorrect Use: The suspect failed the **FST** (referring to **Field Sobriety Test**).

6. ***Avoid overstating and overpunctuating.*** Write in short, clear sentences. Begin paragraphs with a topical sentence describing the primary subject to be discussed. Use sentences that follow to elaborate, describe, and support this topical area. Keep punctuation marks such as commas, colons, and semicolons to a minimum to avoid producing a document "peppered" by punctuation marks.

7. ***Avoid sloppy and careless work:*** Obviously, the entire report should be thoroughly checked for typographical errors, incomplete sentences, missing information, and proper formatting before its formal submission.[5]

Statement of Private Person's (Citizen) Arrest

File No:

Date:

As a private person, I, _____ have

(Last)   (First)   (Middle)

arrested_____

(Last)   (First)   (Middle)

for _____

(Indicate Violation)   (Penal Code Section or Ordinance)

I hereby request deputy(s) or Officer(s)_____

to take custody of the arrestee.

I agree to cooperate fully and appear when required at all stages of the proceedings. I understand that I may be liable for any false arrest action or civil liability that the person arrested may initiate as a result of this incident.

_____   _____

Signature of Person making arrest   Address

_____

Telephone Number

FIGURE 6.7 ▶ Blank private person's arrest form. The blanks can be filled in easily as needed.

Specialized Crime Reporting Formats

Various classifications of incident/crime reports exist in every law enforcement agency. Following are several specialized types of incident/crime reporting formats:

PRIVATE PERSON'S ARREST REPORT

Figure 6.7 shows an example of a **private person's arrest report**. A private person's arrest occurs when a citizen places another citizen under misdemeanor arrest. In general, police are not legally permitted to arrest a person for a misdemeanor that is not committed in their presence. Exceptions to this rule include (1) enforcing a fresh misdemeanor domestic violence charge and (2) enforcing a domestic violence restraining order violation. Normally, private person's arrests are executed in situations such as store shoplifting arrests where a loss prevention officer arrests a person for stealing a relatively small item. Private person's arrests are also used extensively in misdemeanor battery cases. These situations typically involve one person striking another without causing extensive injury. The example report in Figure 6.7 depicts how the crime of battery may look on a police report. With private person's arrest, the liability of false arrest falls upon the person pressing charges.

THE "WHO DONE IT?" REPORT

Another basic police report is one that contains no workable information—commonly referred to as a **"Who done it?"**

report (WDR). Workable information is that which could lead investigators to a possible suspect. Such information could be in the form of a brief suspect description or an ID left at the crime scene. In WDRs, the suspect information included in the report is represented by the term *1 of ?*. Often, investigators do not know how many suspects were responsible for the crime under investigation. The most common crimes involving reports with no suspect information are burglary or theft, since many burglaries are committed when the victim is not present. Although an officer may think that preparing WDRs is a waste of time, this attitude is unwarranted given the potential importance of these reports. For example, WDRs are vital for victims who cannot get financial reimbursement from an insurance company without presenting some form of police report. In addition, information from WDR reports is routinely placed into crime-mapping systems. After several reports relating to the same crime and/or offender are inputted, crime analysts often can identify common methods of operation, or *M.O.s*, and suspects leading to new investigative leads and strategies.

THE MISSING PERSON REPORT

Another report mandated by law to be taken when requested is a **missing person report** (see Figures 6.8 and 6.9). In the past, law enforcement agencies required that a person be missing for 24 hours before these reports could be taken. Today, however, most jurisdictions require that a missing

MISSING PERSON REPORT

☐ ACTIVE ☐ INACTIVE

| ☐ ADULT ☐ CHILD | DATE & TIME REPORTED | FILE NO. |
| | | ORI NO. |

☐ PRIOR MISSING ☐ FOUND ☐ AT RISK (IF AT RISK WHY?)

LAST NAME	FIRST	MIDDLE	AKA'S/MONIKER
MP/ ST. ADDRESS	CITY/STATE,ZIP	AREA/TELEPHONE	
EMPLOYED BY OR SCHOOL ATTENDED	CITY/STATE,ZIP	AREA/TELEPHONE	

GENDER	RACE	EYE COLOR	HAIR CLR/LTH	RECORD TYPE
☐ MALE	☐ W ☐ C	☐ BLK ☐ HAZ	☐ BLK ☐ RED	☐ RUNAWAY JUVENILE
☐ FEMALE	☐ H ☐ J	☐ BLU ☐ MAR	☐ BLN ☐ SDY	☐ VOLUNTARY MISSING ADULT
☐ UNKNOWN	☐ B ☐ F	☐ BRO ☐ PNK	☐ BRO ☐ WHT	☐ PARENTAL/FAMILY ABDUCTION
	☐ I ☐ O	☐ GRY ☐ MUL	☐ GRY ☐ UNK	☐ NON FAMILY ABDUCTION
	☐ UNKNOWN	☐ GRN ☐ UNK	☐ BLD ☐ BBF	☐ STRANGER ABDUCTION
			LTH	☐ DEPENDENT ADULT

☐ CATASTROPHE
☐ SEXUAL EXPLOITATION SUSPECTED
☐ LOST
☐ UNKNOWN CIRCUMSTANCES

| HT: | WT: | DOB: | GANG: |

NOTIFY MISSING PERSONS DETAIL ON ADULT AT RISK SITUATIONS ONLY.
DO NOT NOTIFY ON M/CHILDREN

| GLASSES WORN ☐ YES ☐ NO | CLOTHING DESCRIPTION/SIZE |
| CONTACT LENSES ☐ YES ☐ NO | |

MENTAL CONDITION	PROBABLE DESTINATION	SCARS' MARKS' TATTOOS
DATE/TIME LAST SEEN	LOCATION LAST SEEN	POSS. REASON FOR LEAVING
JEWELRY DESCRIPTION	M/P FINGERPRINTED ☐ YES ☐ NO	WHEN	WHERE

| REPORTING PARTY R/P NAME | RELATIONSHIP TO M/P | RES. PHONE/AREA CODE ☐ DAY |
| R/P STREET ADDRESS | CITY/STATE/ZIP | BUS. PHONE/AREA CODE ☐ DAY |

| VISIBLE DENTAL WORK | BROKEN BONES/MISSING ORGANS |
| DENTIST'S NAME | ADDRESS/CITY/ZIP | AREA CODE/TELEPHONE NO. |

SKELETAL X-RAYS ☐ YES ☐ NO	DENTAL X-RAYS ☐ YES ☐ NO	DENTURES: ☐ UPPER ☐ LOWER ☐ FULL ☐ PARTIAL BRACES: ☐ YES ☐ NO	
PROBATION/SOCIAL WORKER NAME & PHONE NO.	SOCIAL SECURITY NO.	DL NO./STATE CII NO. FBI NO.
VEHICLE INVOLVED ☐ YES ☐ NO	YEAR	MAKE	MODEL	COLOR(S)	LIC. NO./STATE
PHOTO AVAILABLE ☐ YES ☐ NO	PHOTO SUBMITTED ☐ YES ☐ NO	AGE IN PHOTO	PHOTO/X-RAY WAIVER RELEASE (SS 5567) SIGNED (CHILD ONLY): ☐ YES ☐ NO

| IF ABDUCTION DID IT INVOLVE MOVEMENT OF M/P DURING A CRIME? ☐ YES ☐ NO |
| SUSPECT NAME | RELATIONSHIP TO VICTIM | DOB: | WARRANT NO. |
| KNOWN ASSOCIATES TELEPHONE NOS. |

FIGURE 6.8 ▶ Typical missing person report form.

person report shall be taken upon notification of any person missing. Failure to take a missing person report can often delay investigation of crimes where time is of the essence—such as child abduction and murder. In addition, age is not a requirement for the initiation of these reports. The missing person report may also play a key role in determining the tactical response taken by a law enforcement agency. For example, a 19-year-old female who went out with her boyfriend the night before, and has not returned home, would be treated differently than a 5-year-old who wandered off from home. In the latter case, the young missing child is often referred to as *missing critical* and may garner immediate large-scale tactical responses including a command post, grid searches, and specialized investigative teams. Similar reaction will likely result from missing person reports concerning persons who are mentally disabled, suicidal, suffering from life-threatening medical conditions, possible victims of parental abduction, victims of foul play, or with no prior runaway/missing history.

Typically, a missing person report consists of up to four pages, counting the front and back of the form. The front of the form contains several descriptors of the missing person. The form also documents the mental condition and possible location of the missing person. Mental condition, for example, is usually recorded as fair, unstable, bipolar, schizophrenic, and so forth.[6] The investigator may also request information regarding dental records to include in the missing person report as shown in Figure 6.10. The following is the narrative section of a missing person report:

The reporting party (RP/Smith, Janice) is the mother of the missing person (MP/ Smith, Sandra FW/072393). RP/ Janice stated she has been fighting with MP/Sandra for the past week about the type of friends she has been hanging around with after school. On 08/09/2009 at approximately 1630 hours, MP/Sandra brought home her report card and had failed four classes and received a "D" in another. RP/Janice told her daughter she was grounded until she was able to improve her grades. MP/Sandra

INSTRUCTIONS FOR COMPLETING MISSING PERSON REPORT

RECORD TYPE:
RUNAWAY JUVENILE - MISSING JUVENILE (MJ) THAT HAS LEFT HOME WITHOUT THE KNOWLEDGE/PERMISSION OF PARENTS OR GUARDIAN.
VOLUNTARY MISSING ADULT - MISSING ADULT WHO HAS LEFT OF HIS/HER OWN FREE WILL.
PARENTAL/FAMILY ABDUCTION - CHILD TAKEN BY A PARENT/NON-PARENTAL FAMILY MEMBER.
NON-FAMILY ABDUCTION - CHILD TAKEN BY A KNOWN ABDUCTOR, BUT NOT A FAMILY MEMBER.
STRANGER ABDUCTION - CHILD TAKEN BY A STRANGER OR MISSING UNDER CIRCUMSTANCES THAT MAY INDICATE A STRANGER ABDUCTION.
DEPENDENT ADULT - M/A WHO IS BETWEEN THE AGES OF 18 OR OVER WHO HAS PHYSICAL OR MENTAL LIMITATION WHICH RESTRICTS HIS OR HER ABILITY TO CARRY OUT NORMAL ACTIVITIES (i.e., ALZHEIMER, MENTALLY HANDICAPPED).
LOST - ANY PERSON WHO HAS STRAYED AWAY OR WHOSE WHEREABOUTS ARE UNKNOWN.
CATASTROPHE - ANY PERSON WHO IS MISSING AFTER A CATASTROPHE (i.e., PLANE CRASH, BOATING ACCIDENT, FIRE, EARTHQUAKE, ETC.).
UNKNOWN CIRCUMSTANCES - WHEN CIRCUMSTANCES SURROUNDING MP'S DISAPPEARANCE ARE UNKNOWN.
CATEGORY:
AT RISK: AT RISK INCLUDES, BUT IS NOT LIMITED TO, EVIDENCE OR INDICATIONS THE MP IS/HAS:
    A) THE VICTIM OF A CRIME OR FOUL PLAY
    B) IN NEED OF MEDICAL ATTENTION
    C) NO PATTERN OF RUNNING AWAY OR DISAPPEARING
    D) THE VICTIM OF A PARENTAL ABDUCTION
    E) MENTALLY IMPAIRED
PRIOR MISSING - MP HAS BEEN REPORTED MISSING PRIOR TO THIS OCCURRENCE.
SEXUAL EXPLOITATION SUSPECTED - SEXUAL EXPLOITATION/ABUSE OF THE MP IS SUSPECTED.

MP'S RACE - CHECK ONE:

W-WHITE	J-JAPANESE	H-HISPANIC/MEXICAN/LATIN
F-FILIPINO	B-BLACK	O-ALL OTHER/MULTIRACE
C-CHINESE	I-AMERICAN INDIAN/ALASKAN NATIVE	X-UNKNOWN

MP'S EYE COLOR - CHECK ONE:

BLK-BLACK	HAZ-HAZEL	BLU-BLUE
MAR-MAROON	BRO-BROWN	PNK-PINK
GRY-GRAY	MUL-MULTI-COLOR	GRN-GREEN

HAIR COLOR/LENGTH - MP'S HAIR COLOR, CHECK ONE AND LENGTH, SPECIFY SHORT, MEDIUM, LONG OR ACTUAL LENGTH.

BLK - BLACK	RED-RED/AUBURN	BLN-BLOND/STRAWBERRY
SDY-SANDY	BRO-BROWN	WHI-WHITE
GRY-GRAY	XXX-UNKNOWN	SP-SALT & PEPPER
		BLD-BALD

MENTAL CONDITION - LIST ANY MENTAL CONDITION THE MP MAY HAVE, (i.e., STABLE, SUICIDAL, DEPRESSED).
PHOTO/X-RAY WAIVER RELEASE SIGNED - INDICATE WHETHER A RELEASE FORM (SSB67) HAS BEEN SIGNED BY REPORTING PARTY.
PHOTO SUBMITTED - WAS A PHOTO SUBMITTED WITH REPORT.
KNOWN ASSOCIATES - ANY KNOWN ASSOCIATES OF MP WHO MAY HAVE KNOWLEDGE WHERE THE MP IS OR WHO MAY BE ACCOMPANYING THE MP.

FIGURE 6.9 ▶ The second page of a typical missing person report. Note the narrative portion where the responding officer places information concerning the circumstances of the missing person.

became upset and ran out of the house. RP/Janice has not seen her daughter since.

The RP does not know where her daughter may have gone and as far as the RP knows, there has been no history of mental illness or drug use. According to the RP, this is the first time her daughter has run away and she is not aware of any suicidal thoughts.

REPORT CLASSIFICATIONS

After the incident/crime report is officially filed, it is classified within one of several categories:

1. **Closed:** Settled by the officer initially responding to the call for service and requiring no further investigation.
2. **Unfounded:** In the officer's opinion, stated in the report, the alleged crime was mistakenly reported, the result of a lie or fabrication, or otherwise did not really exist.
3. **Referred for Follow-up Investigation:** Uniformed or plainclothes investigators will review the initial report and decide whether or not to conduct further follow-up investigations.
4. **Inactive:** The reported incident/crime will not continue to be investigated due to lack of suspects or evidence, and factors that suggest a very small likelihood that the crime will be solved. Such cases may be reactivated upon the discovery of new evidence, however.

SUPPLEMENTAL REPORTS

If an initial incident/crime report is filed, and the case remains active, more information can be added to the case file in the form of a **supplemental report**. This report may include additional developments in the case from follow-up investigations revealing facts relating to new suspect leads, physical evidence, witness

**AUTHORIZATION TO RELEASE
DENTAL/SKELETAL X-RAYS**
(Missing Adults Only)

NAME OF MISSING ADULT	
REPORTING AGENCY AND CASE NUMBER	REPORTING PARTY

Under California Penal Code Section 14206, the family or next-of-kin of any person reported missing and not located within 30 days may authorize the release of the dental or skeletal X-rays, or both, of the person reported missing. *Dental X-rays are preferred. Skeletal X-rays should be sent only if dental X-rays are not available.* The executed authorization should be taken to the dentist(s), physician and surgeon, or medical facility of the missing person to obtain the release of the dental or skeletal X-rays. The dental or skeletal X-rays, or both, shall be released to the person presenting the request. The person to whom the records are released shall, within 10 days, bring those records to the police or sheriff's department or other law enforcement authority to which the missing person report was made.

If the missing adult is found, please notify the law enforcement agency *immediately.*

AUTHORIZATION

I am a family member or next-of-kin of the above-named missing adult and I hereby authorize the release of all dental or skeletal X-rays to assist law enforcement agencies in locating the missing adult.

NAME OF DENTIST			
ADDRESS			
CITY	STATE	ZIP	TELEPHONE NUMBER ( )
NAME OF PHYSICIAN, SURGEON OR MEDICAL FACILITY			
ADDRESS			
CITY	STATE	ZIP	TELEPHONE NUMBER ( )
SIGNATURE OF FAMILY MEMBER			
RELATIONSHIP TO MISSING ADULT		DATE	
ADDRESS			
CITY	STATE	ZIP	TELEPHONE NUMBER ( )

FIGURE 6.10 ▶ Form authorizing the release of dental/skeletal x-rays. This form generally accompanies the missing person report. Though this form is only for missing adults, the form for juveniles is very similar. These forms are needed in situations where skeletal remains are found and x-rays from the missing person's dentist will aid investigators in determining whether the discovered remains are those of the missing person.

interviews, or lab test results. (Calls resolved or completed at the scene that do not need follow-up investigations will not require supplemental reports.) In addition, information relevant to a particular case originating from sources such as official records maintained by outside law enforcement agencies, businesses, and governmental agencies are often included within supplemental reports. Also, supplemental reports are filed when a case is inactive due to lack of evidence or the death of suspects, witnesses, and other parties to the crime being investigated.

REPORT WRITING TECHNOLOGY

Numerous computerized report writing aids are available that provide automatic formatting, spell-check, sentence structure correction, and other functions. These computer applications, commonly referred to as **paperless reporting** software, are often made available on an agencywide basis through MDTs (Mobile Data Terminals) mounted in police vehicles. MDTs allow officers to prepare, share, submit, and access reports in the field in a real-time operating environment by accessing a central RMS (Records Management System). Information sources necessary for preparing reports, such as criminal records from state and federal databases (e.g., NCIC), also are readily accessible from the MDT unit. A growing trend among police agencies is to replace older centralized MDT units with notebook PCs and other laptop computers. In this setup, officers can install and remove their own laptop computers in patrol units by using a heavy-duty mounting system. Hand-held wireless systems that provide the same functions as in-car MDTs, called *H/MDTs* (Hand-held Mobile Data Terminals), have been recently developed for field use by foot, bike, mounted, and other patrols that do not use a motor vehicle or where the use of a full-size laptop computer would be impractical. These systems are compatible with Blackberry, iPhone, Palm, and other wireless digital technology.[7] Due to the small keyboards (i.e., "thumb pads") on these devices, however, paperless report writing is still not practical.

INVESTIGATIVE REPORT WRITING IN THE "REAL WORLD"

It is easy to provide textbook instructions on how to prepare the perfect investigative report (and there is nothing wrong with knowing the academics of report writing). In the field, however, preparing good reports takes much practice and patience. In fact, in the "real world" of investigation, there is no such thing as the perfect investigative report. Pressures to meet reporting deadlines on numerous cases at the same time often require investigators to produce a report that is imperfect, but the best that can be done by, say, Thursday at noon. This being said, investigators must learn to sift out the best and most relevant data from mountains of information that could possibly be included in the investigative report. Usually, crime scene photos are one of the most significant sources of information that investigators rely on when preparing reports. When learning the investigative report writing process, students should becoming skilled at assessing the importance of information contained in crime scene photos such as those presented for Case Example 6A (see Figures 6.11 to 6.19). The case provides not only the opportunity to practice various report writing methods presented in this chapter, but also an appreciation for the complexities of investigative report preparation and writing in the "real world."

CASE EXAMPLE 6A

FIGURE 6.11 ▶ This opening photo shows a crime scene in which an officer was fired upon while seated in the patrol unit. The driver of a vehicle, after the officer pulled the vehicle over for a traffic stop, immediately exited without warning, firing several shots from a hand gun at the seated officer. The officer, although injured by the gunfire, returned fire at the shooter, who later fled the crime scene in his vehicle. (The officer survived the assault. The suspect was apprehended later.)

FIGURE 6.12 ▶ Close-up view of bullet strikes in the driver's side of the patrol unit's windshield. What information should be recorded in an officer's field notes taken at this scene in preparation for completing a crime/incident report? When recording these notes, what questions should be answered by the information contained in the officer's field notebook?

FIGURE 6.13 ▶ Blood stain patterns on the inner driver-side door panel of the patrol unit.

FIGURE 6.14 ▶ Inside driver's-side dash area of the patrol unit, showing bullet strikes and the officer's blood-stained eyeglasses.

FIGURE 6.15 ▶ Large pool of blood located on the driver's seat.

FIGURE 6.16 ▶ Pool of blood from the driver's-side seat, which soaked through the seat and onto the floor below the seat.

FIGURE 6.17 ▶ Long-range view of the crime scene showing evidence markers placed at locations of fired cartridge casings from the weapons of both the officer and the suspect.

FIGURE 6.18 ▶ Close-up view of evidence markers showing the trail of gunfire from both the officer and the shooter.

FIGURE 6.19 ▶ The suspect's vehicle, later discovered abandoned in a parking lot some distance from the crime scene.

Summary

1. **Field notes and their use in incident/crime reports.**
   Field notes are the basis for the incident report. An investigative report often is written several hours after the investigation of a specific event or incident. Certain types of information such as statements, times, observations, addresses, and so on can be easily forgotten or confused with other information if not recorded while still fresh in the officer's mind. Noting times is very important to the crime because this establishes a timeline of events as they took place. Field notes are the first step in the investigative process and create a visual picture for those who need to further investigate the matter noted. The field notes are documented at the scene of the incident and afterward are transcribed to various parts of the incident report.

2. **Circumstances in which field notes are commonly taken.**
   Field notes should be taken at the scene of an event or incident or when interviewing persons (e.g., victims, witness, suspects). They should also be taken whenever an officer wishes to record specific facts for a crime report and any time the officer wishes to remember specific details later on. Notes documented at various crime scenes will enable those responsible for crimes to be prosecuted.

3. **Basic information contained in an incident/crime report.**
   Victims and witness information is to include full name, age, date of birth, race, sex, address, and both home and work phone numbers. This basic information will allow investigators to follow up as needed to further investigate the case. The same applies to any suspect information, with the addition of unusual gestures, speech, gang affiliation, and any information that may give more credibility to the suspect's whereabouts or arrest. The report should also include the type of crime, date and time of incident, handled physical evidence, suspect description, and information that can illustrate the location and occurrence of the crime.

4. **Contents of incident/crime reports and the term FACCCT.**
   FACCCT is an acronym describing the detail listed within an incident report. The first letter, "F", refers to *factual* information. The second letter, "A", refers to *accurate* information, as any report must provide accurate information to further investigations and prosecution. The three Cs stand for *clear*, *concise*, and *complete*. The last letter, "T", refers to *timely*. Crime reports have to be clearly written and concise in the information presented. The information noted has to be complete; otherwise, the case at hand could be lost.

5. **Different types of incident/crime reports.**
   Different types of crime reports exist, which would be classified under different categories within a law enforcement agency. There is a report taken with no workable information, which is a report that has no information for follow-up by investigators. Another report is one that does have workable information for follow-up by investigators. Another type of report is a missing person report. This report must be taken in person or over the phone.

6. **Various uses of incident/crime reports.**
   Incident reports assist with identifying, apprehending, and prosecuting criminals. They serve as source documents for filing criminal complaints and recording the entire investigation process, and they provide a basis for follow-up. In addition, these reports assist prosecutors, defense attorneys, and other law enforcement agencies by providing records of all investigations, serving as source documents for criminal prosecution or documenting agency actions.

Key Terms

field notes
field notebook
digital audio recorder (DAR)
5 Ws & H
incident/crime report

face sheet
report narrative
FACCCT
private person's arrest report
"Who done it?" report

missing person report
supplemental report
paperless reporting

Review Questions

1. Why are good report writing skills important for investigators to acquire?

2. What is the importance of taking field notes to the investigative process?

3. What are the 5 Ws & H and how do they relate to field note taking?
4. What are the similarities and differences between taking field notes and report writing?
5. Describe the steps taken in preparing an incident/crime report.
6. What are some characteristics of a well-written incident/crime report?
7. What are some types of specialized formats of incident/crime reports?
8. What is a supplemental report?

Internet Resources

Report Writing POST Library	www.post.ca.gov/post-library.aspx
Report Writing N.C.J.R.S. Library	www.ncjrs.gov/library.html
Grammar and Style	www.libraryspot.com/grammarstyle.htm
Elements of Style	www.bartleby.com/141

Applied Investigative Exercise

Imagine you are the investigator of Case Example 6A. After reviewing these crime scene photos, do the following:

1. Discuss what you would observe and whom you might interview to collect field notes on the incident.
2. Develop questions about this incident—based on the 5 Ws & H rule—that you would use to gather information for your field notes.
3. Make field note entries based on hypothetical responses to the questions constructed in question #2.
4. Prepare a hypothetical incident/crime report based on your Case Example 6A field notes.

Notes

[1] Michael Biggs, *Just the Facts: Investigative Report Writing*, 3rd ed. (Upper Saddle River, NJ: Prentice Hall, 2007), 15–53.
[2] James Guffey, *Report Writing Fundamentals for Police and Correctional Officers* (Upper Saddle River, NJ: Prentice Hall, 2004), 21–45.
[3] California Commission on Peace Officer Standards and Training (POST) 1-6 to 2-4 *Basic Workbook Series: Investigative Report Writing* (Sacramento, CA: POST). Several points have been taken and added to by the authors.
[4] Guffey, *Report Writing Fundamentals*, 55–74.
[5] Ibid.
[6] Los Angeles County Sheriff Department, *Interviewing and Interrogation Techniques* (Los Angeles, CA: LASD). The authors have added to some points, drawing from their numerous years of practical experience.
[7] *iPad in Law Enforcement Forum*, posted at www.ipadforums.net/ipad-general-discussions/13067-ipad-law-enforcement-2.html.

CHAPTER SEVEN

DEVELOPING INVESTIGATIVE LEADS AND INTELLIGENCE

Learning Objectives

After completing the chapter, you should be able to:

1. Describe the different types of leads and how they are used.
2. Be familiar with the various databases used in the investigative process.
3. Describe how surveillance and undercover operations are conducted.
4. Discuss photo and live lineups.
5. Outline the process of intelligence collection.
6. Describe the application of criminal profiling to criminal investigations.

Chapter Outline

INTRODUCTION

THE OLD TERM FOR a police detective, *gumshoe*, is believed to have originated from the soft gum-sole shoes worn by detectives when performing foot surveillance, allowing them to follow suspects without being given away by noisy hard-sole shoes. Despite the invention of electronic investigative sources, the good old-fashion surveillance, neighborhood canvasses, and undercover operations performed by gumshoes in the past are just as valid today for developing investigative leads and intelligence. The main difference between contemporary criminal investigators and yesteryear's gumshoes is that today's investigators are well versed in both traditional and high-tech information gathering methods. Some of the new lead and intelligence development tools include enhanced computer-aided database searching capabilities, various forms of crime analysis used to transform raw investigative data into criminal intelligence, the sharing of crime information through integrated data sharing networks like those operated within fusion centers, and the use of advanced social/behavioral techniques to generate descriptions of offenders' and victims' probable lifestyle characteristics and/or whereabouts. These modern investigative techniques are presented in this chapter, along with the more standard methods that have survived the test of time. Discussions and illustrations are also provided to show how these methods can be used in follow-up investigations, major case planning, crime pattern analyses, investigative decision making, intelligence processing, and related investigative activities.

INVESTIGATIVE LEADS VS. CRIMINAL INTELLIGENCE

An **investigative lead** is a form of information that can be obtained—persons, places, or things that may be of use for achieving investigative goals. For example, persons with knowledge of a murder victim's personal affairs may provide workable leads in the form of names and addresses of other persons with a possible motive for taking the victim's life. Likewise, places where the victim is known to have gone on a regular basis—bars or other entertainment venues—might provide additional leads such as parking lot surveillance video of the murder victim entering a stranger's vehicle. This information, in turn, may provide things such as a physical description of the suspect's vehicle and the vehicle's license numbers. On the other hand, **criminal intelligence** consists of raw information obtained from leads or other investigative sources that has been analyzed to provide specific knowledge about past, present, or future crime-related activities.

FIGURE 7.1 ▶ Emergency response centers, such as the one pictured here, combine the expertise of investigators representing numerous agencies and disciplines during mass disasters and terrorist threats. (Courtesy Federal Bureau of Investigation)

As the following discussion illustrates, both leads and intelligence can be used to support pre- and postcrime investigation efforts.

PROACTIVE INVESTIGATIVE INFORMATION

Information based on investigative methods is often thought to be useful only after a crime has been committed. There are many situations, however, where investigators can play a key role in addressing crime-related matters before they occur. Most notable among these are the areas of crime detection and prevention using investigative techniques, otherwise known as **proactive investigation**. Some of these operations involve developing leads and gathering intelligence on potential perpetrators and their possible targets. For example, identifying potential offenders is essential for security operations involving persons of notable status such as celebrities, political figures, or high-level business executives. In addition, location-specific protective efforts for businesses, exhibitions, sporting events, and even activist rallies rely on investigative methods to assess potential individual and group security/safety threats—a process referred to as **threat assessment**. Especially after the 9/11 terrorist attacks, the functions of preventative investigation have become increasingly important for ensuring national security. The collection and sharing of proactive investigative information by local, state, federal, and international military and law enforcement agencies has become an essential tool for combating terrorist activities.[1] The emergency response center shown in Figure 7.1 is one of many joint intelligence gathering efforts involving investigators form various agencies and jurisdictions.

Additionally, proactive investigations are conducted to expose offenders engaging in clandestine illegal activities that otherwise would go unreported. These crimes include the following:

- Drug sales, distribution, and trafficking
- High-level financial crimes
- Political corruption
- Organized crime

- Human trafficking
- Child predatory activities
- Vice crimes: gambling, prostitution, pornography
- Stolen property distribution networks
- Terrorist/gang/hate group crimes
- Illegal weapons trade/espionage

Most victims or witnesses of these types of crimes refuse to come forward to inform authorities due to fear of criminal retaliation or self-incrimination. Thus, investigations of these and related activities usually must rely on tactics that catch the offender in the act such as surveillance, undercover operations, stings, and confidential informants. On rare occasions, however, anonymous tips may provide investigative leads capable of bringing down the largest and most formidable offenders and criminal networks.

REACTIVE INVESTIGATIVE INFORMATION

Follow-up Investigations

After a crime has occurred and a preliminary investigation has been conducted, evidence may exist that enables a case to be immediately solved by a suspect's arrest or to be closed—inactivated for lack of evidence. For cases that remain open after the preliminary investigation, however, the decision must be made whether to continue to investigate the case by initiating a **follow-up investigation**. This decision may also help determine whether a case previously closed should be reopened in light of newly discovered evidence or witnesses. Normally, serious felonies (e.g., murder, sexual assault, domestic violence, significant financial loss), and politically sensitive crimes will by policy or law automatically receive a follow-up investigation. Crimes not involving serious personal injury or property loss, however, will routinely be screened for solvability factors before deciding to conduct a follow-up investigation. This decision-making process, or case flow, is as follows:

1. The preliminary incident/crime report is routed to a patrol supervisor or an investigative division, either in person or electronically, and is evaluated for a follow-up investigation.
2. A cost/benefit evaluation of the case is performed. This involves weighing the benefits of the case (solvability) against the costs of the investigation (resources, personnel hours). If the benefits outweigh the costs, generally a follow-up investigation will be authorized. If the reverse is true, or if there are no leads or evidence, the case will be classified as inactive and no further investigation of the incident/crime will be conducted.[2] Checklists such as that shown in Figure 7.2 are often used to keep track of the investigative progress made in a particular case.

The decision-making process just presented can be carried out on a subjective basis by having an investigative supervisor personally examine the merits of a particular case; or, the evaluation process can be carried out by a manual or computerized calculation of a numeric investigative decision-making formula. This formula assigns weights to salient factors of the case such as witness availability; types of physical evidence; victim cooperation; seriousness of the crime; whether or not there is a description of the suspects, vehicles, or property involved in the crime; and so forth.

The Follow-up Investigation Process

An affirmative decision to conduct a follow-up investigation will result in the case being assigned to an investigator, or perhaps an investigative team. Some or all of the following tasks will be performed by the investigator(s) receiving this case assignment. (The particular order of tasks presented in the following list is merely suggestive, and may differ based on departmental policies within various jurisdictions and/or agencies.)

1. Perform a thorough review of the incident/crime report. Examine it for all potential leads, including stated witnesses, victims, and suspects, as well as for other persons that may have seen or been involved in the criminal activity.
2. Review supplemental reports, if available, and discuss these and the full incident report with the original reporting officer(s). Before meeting, prepare questions based on key factors relating to the "who, what, where, when, why, and how" of the report.
3. View crime scene evidence/photographs/sketches and other available information from the preliminary investigation. Check other property items inventoried from suspects or vehicles by the arresting officer. (Before executing this step, check with prosecutors to see whether a warrant is required.)
4. Submit evidence (not already submitted) to the crime lab for analysis. Review results of evidence lab tests and discuss test results with criminalists if further clarification is needed.
5. Examine autopsy results/medical reports, if available.
6. Conduct or reconduct suspect interrogations, witness and victim interviews, neighborhood canvasses; and internal agency records checks for associated crimes/offenders.
7. Provide crime information to internal agency personnel/ divisions, the media, and other law enforcement agencies in outside jurisdictions as appropriate.
8. Visit/revisit the crime scene and perform crime scene reconstruction analyses.
9. Keep victims/key witnesses apprised of the investigative progress.
10. Develop and carry out an investigation plan that incorporates follow-up investigative tools for obtaining additional leads and intelligence.
11. Apply for and obtain necessary warrants for additional searches/arrests and for recovering stolen property.
12. Thoroughly document all activities. Submit regular supplemental reports based on investigative progress.
13. Consult with prosecutors and other investigators to prepare the case for trial.

FIGURE 7.2 ▶ A typical investigator's checklist, which accompanies a case file to provide a quick summary of activities that have or have not been carried out during an investigation.

INVESTIGATORS CASE FILE CHECKLIST

CASE NUMBER _____ DEPT. _____

INVESTIGATING OFFICER _____

DEFENDANT'S NAME _____

_____ INCIDENT REPORT

_____ VICTIM STATEMENT WRITTEN _____ TYPED _____

_____ WITNESS STATEMENT WRITTEN _____ TYPED _____

_____ ARREST WARRANT

_____ SEARCH WARRANT

_____ SUSPECT STATEMENT WRITTEN _____ TYPED _____

_____ SUSPECT MIRANDA WAIVER FORM

_____ SUSPECT ARREST BOOKING REPORT

_____ OFFENDER IDENTIFICATION DATA

_____ INVESTIGATOR'S REPORT

_____ EVIDENCE SLIPS

_____ PHOTOGRAPHS

_____ CRIME LAB REPORTS

_____ MEDICAL REPORTS

_____ WITNESS LIST

_____ OFFICER INPUT

_____ D.A. BOND FORM

_____ CRIMINAL HISTORY

_____ WEAPON IDENTIFICATION DATA

_____ CO-DEFENDANT INFORMATION

_____ DAMAGE/RESTITUTIONS FORMS

_____ MISC. INFORMATION

DATE CHECKED _____

CHECKED BY: _____

DATE CASE FILED SUBMITTED TO DISTRICT ATTORNEY'S OFFICE_____

Suggestions for carrying out Step 10 in the preceding list of follow-up investigation tasks are presented in the remaining sections of this chapter. In addition, many of these methods may be used for proactive investigative purposes as well as discussed earlier.[3]

DATABASE AND RECORDS CHECKS

The NCIC Database

All database searches to obtain investigative leads should begin with a query of the **NCIC (National Crime Information Center)** data system maintained and operated by the FBI. The NCIC database, which began in 1967, is the most comprehensive crime information source in the world. Currently, the system includes more than 15 million active records, which are assembled into the following 19 files (7 for persons; 12 for property):

- *Article File*—stolen articles and lost public safety, homeland security, and critical infrastructure identification.
- *Gun File*—stolen, lost, and recovered weapons, and weapons used in the commission of crimes that are designed to expel a projectile by air, carbon dioxide, or explosive action.
- *Boat File*—stolen boats.
- *Securities File*—serially numbered securities that have been stolen, embezzled, used for ransom, or are counterfeit.
- *Vehicle File*—stolen vehicles, vehicles involved in the commission of crimes, or vehicles that may be seized based on federally issued court order.

- *Vehicle and Boat Parts File*—serially numbered stolen vehicle or boat parts.
- *License Plate File*—stolen license plates.
- *Missing Persons File*—individuals, including children, who have been reported missing to law enforcement and for whose safety there is a reasonable concern.
- *Foreign Fugitive File*—persons wanted by another country for a crime that would be a felony if it were committed in the United States.
- *Identity Theft File*—descriptive and other information that law enforcement personnel can use to determine whether an individual is a victim of identity theft or might be using a false identity.
- *Immigration Violator File*—criminal aliens whom immigration authorities have deported and aliens with outstanding administrative warrants of removal.
- *Protection Order File*—individuals against whom protection orders have been issued.
- *Supervised Release File*—individuals on probation, parole, or supervised release or released on their own recognizance or during pretrial sentencing.
- *Unidentified Persons File*—unidentified deceased persons, living persons who are unable to verify their identities, unidentified victims of catastrophes, and recovered body parts. The file cross-references unidentified bodies against records in the Missing Persons File.
- *U.S. Secret Service Protective File*—names and other information on individuals believed to pose a threat to

the U.S. president and/or others afforded protection by the U.S. Secret Service.

- *Gang File*—violent gangs and their members.
- *Known or Appropriately Suspected Terrorist File*—known or appropriately suspected terrorists.
- *Wanted Persons File*—individuals (including juveniles who will be tried as adults) for whom a federal warrant or a felony or misdemeanor warrant is outstanding.
- *National Sex Offender Registry File*—individuals who are required to register in a jurisdiction's sex offender registry.[4]

NCIC data runs are restricted to law enforcement personnel, and are based on crime-related information assembled from local, state, federal, tribal, and international law enforcement agencies. From the time a data request is submitted, the NCIC system will return a report in less than one second. If a hit is reported, revealing likely criminal involvement relating to the individual or item searched for, this information alone is not grounds for establishing probable cause. Rather, NCIC policy requires that agencies conducting a search contact the agencies originally reporting the criminal information to the NCIC system to confirm the validity of the hit before making an arrest or taking other legal action.[5] Information on suspected offenders and crimes of the distant past often is accessible through an NCIC run, as demonstrated by the present-day report shown in Figure 7.3 for the notorious 1930s mobster Al Capone.

Other Public and Private Databases

Since the advent of the Internet, there has been a literal explosion of both public and private databases useful for developing investigative leads. Many of these sources, however, have significant data overlap with one another and contain repetitive information. In addition, many of the private databases are fee-based and can be quite costly when conducting a large number of runs on single- or multiple-case suspects and/or leads. Fortunately, many private databases allow free runs for law enforcement purposes. The following are just some of the many public and private sources and databases of potential value for developing investigative leads:

- *Bankruptcy and Other Financial Public Records:* Bankruptcies, IRS tax returns, credit reports, and other financial information can be obtained on many public and private databases. Bankruptcy filings are public record and contain an individual's entire financial history, including work history, income, mortgages, loans, creditors, debts owed, property addresses, phone numbers, etc. Similar, but less extensive, information can be obtained for persons not declaring bankruptcy in credit reports and IRS tax returns.
- *Real Estate Records:* Information on homes purchased, loans/mortgages, property liens, property taxes, home values, address history, phone numbers, relatives, neighbors, and e-mail addresses can often be obtained from a public records search at a county clerk's office.
- *Business Filings/Permits:* Records searches for business permits, building permits, fictitious business

MKE/IMAGE
IMR/
MIS:FOR TESTING ONLY
NAM:CAPONE, ALBERT B DOB: 19380415
RAC: U HGT: 507 WGT: 165 DOI: 20080000

FROM: NCIC1-14018038 20091210 09:23:41 23F2019408
1L0123F20194082ZP
MNBCA00C1
***MESSAGE KEY ZW SEARCHES WANTED PERSON FILE FELONY RECORDS REGARDLESS OF EXTRADITION AND MISDEMEANOR RECORDS INDICATING POSSIBLE EXTRADITION FROM THE INQUIRING AGENCY'S LOCATION. ALL OTHER NCIC PERSONS FILES ARE SEARCHED WITHOUT LIMITATIONS.
WARNING - THE IDENTITY OF THE SUBJECT IDENTIFIED IN THIS RECORD HAS BEEN REPORTED STOLEN. REVIEW THE VICTIM PROFILE AND USE CAUTION IN VERIFYING THE IDENTITY OF THIS PERSON. THE PASSWORD INCLUDED IN THIS RESPONSE HAS BEEN ASSIGNED TO THE IDENTITY THEFT VICTIM. VERIFY THAT THE SUBJECT OF INQUIRY CAN CONFIRM THE PASSWORD.
MKE/IDENTITY THEFT PERSON
ORI/MNBCA00C1 NAM/CAPONE, ALBERT B SEX/M RAC/U POB/MN
DOB/19380415
HGT/507 WGT/165 EYE/HAZ HAI/BRO CTZ/US SKN/RUD
SMT/TAT UL ARM
DOP/20141203 SOC/123443333
OCA/20091210TEST
NOA/Y
MIS/FOR TESTING PURPOSE ONLY * * MINNESOTA DL NUMBER X99999999 SEE ALSO IMAGE
MIS/I206096823 AND TATOO IMAGE I176094144 RECORD IS FOR TESTING ONLY * * * *
PWD/PEPSI2009- IDT/OTHR DOT/20080510
ORI IS MINN BUR CRIM APP ST PAUL 651 793-7000
AKA/CAPONE, AL
IMN/I206096823 IMT/I
IMN/I176094144 IMT/I
NIC/J660024827 DTE/20091203 1057 EST DLU/20091210 1022 EST
*****WARNING - STANDING ALONE, NCIC IDENTITY THEFT FILE INFORMATION DOES NOT FURNISH GROUNDS FOR THE SEARCH AND SEIZURE OF ANY INDIVIDUAL, VEHICLE OR DWELLING.*****

MKE/IMAGE
IMR/
MIS:FOR TESTING ONLY
NAM:CAPONE, ALBERT B DOB: 19380415
RAC: U HGT: 507 WGT: 165 DOI: 20080000

NAM:CAPONE, ALBERT B DOB: 19380415
RAC: U HGT: 507 WGT: 165 DOI: 20080000

FIGURE 7.3 ▶ An NCIC run for notorious gangster Al Capone, showing the modern suspect imaging capabilities of today's system. (Courtesy Getty Images USA, Inc.)

names, business licenses, incorporations, taxes, violations, or other business-related information are often readily obtainable at city, state, and local clerks' offices.

- *Court Records:* Births, deaths, marriages, divorces, civil legal judgments, mental health commitments, traffic violations, traffic accidents, court proceedings, license restrictions, and other personal information not contained within ordinary law enforcement data runs can be obtained through examination of civil and criminal court records.
- *Insurance Databases:* Items stolen, recovered, or reported missing/destroyed can often be accessed through private databases, including a variety of personal and business insurance claims.
- *Social Networking Databases:* Names, phone numbers, e-mail addresses, screen names, and URLs relating to social networking name searches are available through various on-line social networking sources.
- *Stolen Property Databases:* Various private databases are available where citizens have reported thefts of specialty items such as jewelry, laptops, cell phones, and even pets. Some of these items may or may not have been reported as officially stolen to police. Searches of eBay, Craigslist, and Pawnshop databases often can provide fruitful leads for the identification of stolen property.
- *Vehicle Databases:* Numerous private databases track vehicle histories, which are useful for accident records, odometer readings, and determining whether or not a vehicle has been previously salvaged.
- *International Databases:* Although frequently difficult to use and at times inoperable, databases originating from foreign countries are sometimes available for person or property searches. One example is the INTERPOL Stolen Motor Vehicle Database, which provides information on stolen vehicles from 126 nations, including 22 of the 27 member states comprising the European Union (EU).[6]
- *Victim Forums:* Families of missing persons, parents of abused and murdered children, victims of sexual assaults,

FIGURE 7.4 ▶ J. Edgar Hoover, described as the founder of the Federal Bureau of Investigation, was instrumental in the creation of numerous national crime information databases to assist federal, state and local investigators. (Courtesy FBI)

watchdog organizations for hate crimes, and animal rights advocates are a few of the many groups that have created Web-based search engines and databases useful for investigating citizen-based crime information. Much of this effort must be credited to the pioneering criminal awareness and apprehension efforts of John Walsh, who began the America's Most Wanted enterprise (AMW) in memory of his son Adam, who was abducted and murdered.

Internal Records Examinations

Other sources of potentially useful investigative information include the following:

1. *Booking Records:* When a suspect has been arrested, the following information/physical items are obtained:
   - *Personal Background Information:* Full name, birth date, address, phone number, employment, physical descriptors (including distinguishing marks, tattoos, scars, etc.), driver's license number, social security numbers, correctional department and FBI case numbers, emergency contact, doctor, attorney (if known).
   - *Criminal Information:* Arrest charge, arresting officer, location of arrest, booking number, bail information.
   - *Property Information:* Property/weapons taken from the arrestee's person and/or vehicle by the arresting officer and by custodial officers following a jail custody search. The arrestee's clothing also will be secured.
   - *Photographs:* Booking mug shots are taken.
   - *Fingerprints:* Full set of prints, and submitted through computerized fingerprint database. (It should be noted that former FBI Director J. Edgar Hoover, shown in Figure 7.4, is credited with originating this and other national-level automated fingerprint information made available to law enforcement officers.)
   - *Medical Information:* Medication taken/required, present/past illnesses.
   - *Other Information:* Some documents/receipts may contain the arrestee's signature (although they may refuse to sign). Postarrest phone calls made are recorded and the arrestee's behavior and statements during the booking are videotaped. If a vehicle is impounded, consult the towing service, impound lot supervisor, and impound inventory log for items that may have evidentiary value. (Consult a legal advisor; a warrant is usually necessary when performing postimpound vehicle investigations.)[7]
2. *F. I. Cards:* F. Is (Field Interviews) that contain basic information concerning the identification, location, and circumstances of suspicious persons, vehicles, and activities are often taken by patrol officers. These can provide leads for suspects who may have cased locations and/or persons before victimizing them. F. I. cards often are useful for identifying suspects involved in rapes, kidnappings, auto thefts, ATM

"SERIAL KILLER CAUGHT BY PARKING TICKET"
New York, NY

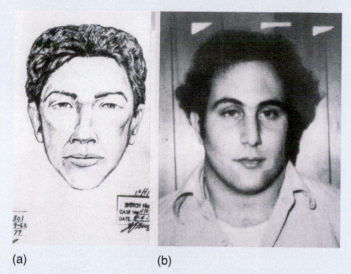

Infamous serial killer David Berkowitz, dubbed *The Son of Sam* by the media, was located and arrested by NYPD detectives using information from a parking ticket he received while his vehicle was parked near the murder scene of his two shooting victims. A records check of traffic citations issued at the time and place of the shooting revealed that a Ford Galaxy belonging to Berkowitz was cited for parking next to a fire hydrant. The killer's residential address and other personal information were obtained by running the license plate number listed on the ticket. Ironically, Berkowitz paid the citation, providing additional information to investigators about his identity and whereabouts.[8]

(a)   (b)

FIGURE 7.5 ▶ "Son of Sam" serial killer David Berkowitz's police composite drawing (a) and his booking photo (b) issued to the public by investigators. (Courtesy Corbis Images)

robberies, commercial robberies, burglaries, and serial crimes.

3. ***Citations:*** Citations for infractions such as traffic violations and municipal codes as well as misdemeanor offenses often provide leads regarding the travel patterns, vehicles, drug habits, hang-outs, and associates of suspects. Citations can often provide fruitful suspect leads, as is illustrated in Case Close-Up 7.1 discussing the capture of notorious serial killer David Berkowitz (see Figure 7.5).

FIGURE 7.6 ▶ A Customs and Border Protection agent controlling an unmanned aerial vehicle (UAV) used to conduct surveillance activities along the U.S. border. (Courtesy U.S. Customs and Border Protection Agency)

SURVEILLANCE

Surveillance can be a very time-consuming and resource-intensive way of gathering information during a follow-up investigation. Therefore, it is generally considered to be an investigative method of last resort—used only when other methods prove impractical or have failed. It can also be very dangerous for the investigator working any type of assignment, otherwise referred to as an **operative**. Obviously, assignments calling for the surveillance of high-profile offenders such as big-money drug dealers, hardcore street gang members, or organized crime figures involved in racketeering are risky business. But any suspect—even one being investigated for nonviolent fraudulent activities—who discovers that he or she is being followed or photographed covertly may unexpectedly place an investigator in harm's way.

As an investigative tool, conducting surveillance has one highly desired outcome: to make a first-hand observation of a suspect engaging in criminal activity. Other purposes of surveillance include (1) identifying suspects' associates, residences, places of business, or places where leisure time is spent; (2) identifying possible witnesses or potential confidential informants; (3) corroborating information provided by victims, witnesses, and suspects; (4) providing security back-up for ongoing undercover operations; and (5) establishing probable cause to obtain court orders and warrants.

The object of surveillance activity, referred to as the **target**, typically is a person, but also can be a place (e.g., a park frequented by drug dealers) or a thing (e.g., a stolen vehicle). Before conducting surveillance, investigators need to prepare thoroughly by gaining as much information as possible about the intended target. If a suspect is the target, intelligence information should be gathered detailing present and prior criminal activities; past experience with surveillance activities; possible crime associates; and personal characteristics and habits including physical description, residence, work/school location, vehicles owned, regular hang-outs, quirks such as hot temper, drug/alcohol use, athletic activities, possession and use of firearms, and so on. Similar detailed background information should be gathered for location and object surveillance activities as well.[9] Figure 7.6 shows state-of-the-art surveillance technology in the form of an unmanned drone.

Presurveillance Activities

Regardless of the intended target, best practice is to do some reconnaissance on the persons, places, and things to be placed under surveillance. This scouting can be performed by a single investigator unobtrusively walking or driving by the intended target(s). Aircraft equipped with surveillance cameras, or portable wireless webcams also can be used for reconnaissance (*recon*) activities. When conducting these preliminary observations it is especially important to avoid alerting suspects or others under observation. Taking photographs or notes, or other activities likely to raise suspicions need to be done sparingly and covertly. In addition, invasions of privacy without a proper warrant should be avoided. Information gathered during a surveillance recon investigation includes all factors of importance for establishing the best overall surveillance location, known as the **eye**, and features of the area that may present hazards to investigators conducting surveillance activities. The following are examples:

- Door and window locations in target buildings or residences
- Footpaths or roadways used by a subject to enter and exit the target area
- Vehicles used by the target subject and his or her associates, neighbors, etc.
- Physical structures and street configurations that may provide opportunities or pose dangers to investigators
- Checking motor vehicle and utility records
- Utilizing confidential source contacts

After conducting the recon, all available information should be assembled into a **surveillance plan**. This plan guides investigators in conducting the surveillance, and it includes all present and past case background information, procuring necessary equipment such as cameras and vehicles, surveillance objectives, warrants and other legal requirements, and intelligence gathered about the target (e.g., descriptions, photographs, cautionary measures to be taken, etc.). If a team approach is used, a presurveillance briefing should help acquaint all operatives with the surveillance plan and assign specific roles such as team lead and log keeper. The one member selected as log keeper documents and describes all major activities undertaken by the surveillance team. Individual investigators will initial the log next to each activity they have engaged and can also add personal observations to the log content. The log serves as an official file of the surveillance and can be used as evidence and for review in planning follow-up investigations.[10]

Conducting the Surveillance

Surveillance is generally carried out using one of the three following methods:

- **Static Surveillance:** This method, also known as a *stakeout,* involves observing the target from a fixed location. In this method the investigators initially situate themselves in a location (e.g., eye) that provides the optimum vantage point for viewing the target. All possible entrance and exit paths used by subjects should be clearly visible. In more elaborate operations, motel/hotel rooms or apartments can be rented. Any vehicles used should be parked and/or rotated so as not to raise suspicion. Park regularly staffed vehicles far enough away that they are not clearly visible to the target and do not raise neighbors' suspicions. In long-term static surveillance activities, it is always preferable to use specialty vehicles, such as vans or utility vehicles, equipped with closed circuit television, remote video, and basic necessities for the investigators, who must remain in them for extended periods. In these situations, progressive surveillance also can be used, whereby subjects who remain at work or another location for many hours are observed in a sequential manner on separate occasions (e.g., separate surveillance sessions on separate days covering the subject's arriving at the workplace, leaving for lunch, and leaving for home).

- **Mobile Surveillance:** Any means that provides mobility to investigators can be used to conduct this type of surveillance. Examples include shadowing the target on foot, using vehicles to tail a suspect vehicle, or placing tracking devices on subjects or their vehicles. Although mobile surveillance can be carried out by a single investigator, the team approach employing multiple investigators is always preferable because it adds different "faces" and more "eyes" to the operation. To avoid detection, the maximum amount of distance should be maintained from the target when in open spaces (referred to as *loose surveillance*); however, this distance should be narrowed (or *close surveillance*) when obstacles may obstruct viewing the subject's whereabouts. On foot, a distance of 100 yards or more is recommended when only a few people are between the investigator and the subject. When crowds are present, move in closer, perhaps separated by only a few persons. The same rule applies to vehicle surveillance operations: That is, traffic situations will require traveling a distance of no more than three vehicles behind the subject; on open roads or without traffic, however, trailing the subject by hundreds of yards is acceptable—as long as the subject's vehicle remains in clear view. When performing close vehicle surveillance, and more than one traffic lane is available, it is always best to travel within the subject vehicle's blind spot—usually the right rear of the vehicle. Bumper beepers, or mobile tracking devices, also can be placed on or inside the target vehicle so that it may be tracked from up to a 5-mile distance without making visual contact.

- *Combined Surveillance:* Static and mobile methods often are used together depending on the changing circumstances of a given surveillance operation.[11]

Countersurveillance

Investigators must always be aware of subjects' efforts to uncover surveillance operations, otherwise known as **countersurveillance**. If subjects do discover they are being observed, the investigators have been *burnt* and all surveillance activities should be abandoned if there is the slightest chance its continuance will jeopardize the safety of participating operatives. The only exception to this is situations where surveillance activities are intentionally revealed to targets so that they react by perhaps revealing additional information about their criminal conduct, such as warning a criminal associate or moving stolen property to new hiding places. The following are typical countersurveillance methods:

- *Making Sudden Moves:* Targets on foot or in vehicles often take unexpected sharp turns around corners or suddenly change direction. When this occurs, keep moving in the same direction being traveled and continue past the target. Do not attempt to follow the subject. Have another investigator pick up the subject's trail (if using a team approach) or try to continue the surveillance from a new location at a later time.

- *Traveling in Circles:* Mostly in vehicles, but sometimes on foot, subjects will travel in circles to see whether they are being followed. Commonly, this is done by taking three right turns from their immediate location to return

to the place or direction from which they originally started. This can also be done in parking lots/structures, on streets that make circular patterns, or by driving down dead-ends or cul-de-sacs. Knowledge of specific roadway patterns in the surveillance area is the best defense against this type of countermeasure.

- *Using Setups:* Suspects may intentionally drop a piece of paper or place an object into a trash can while looking back to see if the investigator stops to pick up the object. They may also try to lure a suspected operative into an area such as an open field where there is no cover. The rule here is that if the suspect's behavior seems the slightest bit strange, it is probably a setup.

- *Asking Questions:* Questions such as "Do you live in the area?" or "What type of work do you do?" may be asked by the suspect to see how the investigator reacts and perhaps to later verify the information provided. Thus, before conducting surveillance, a **cover story** should always be prepared to effectively answer such questions if posed by a suspecting target.

- *Having Decoys or Convoys:* **Decoys** are persons used to divert the investigator from the subject under surveillance. For example, a person pretending to have a heart attack and need immediate medical assistance, or an attractive woman seeking companionship with the investigator are just two of the countless decoys that can be employed. **Convoys** are individuals whose function is to detect surveillance measures directed toward the target. Typically, convoys follow behind the target on foot or in vehicles to detect investigators tailing their subject. In such instances, investigators must employ their own counter-countersurveillance measures to detect the presence of decoys and convoys.[12]

CASE CLOSE-UP 7.2

"THE FBI MIAMI FIREFIGHT"
Miami, Florida

On April 11, 1986, an FBI surveillance team consisting of 14 agents in 10 separate vehicles performed a combined stakeout and mobile surveillance operation focusing on two heavily armed suspects believed to have engaged in a year-long spree of armored car and bank holdups. At 9:00 A.M. on a Friday, one of the FBI surveillance units spotted the suspects' vehicle traveling down a local highway. After notifying other team members of the sighting, the single FBI operative unit began tailing the suspects until other FBI units could respond and provide assistance in the mobile surveillance. Shortly, three surveillance units were following behind the suspects, who had exited the highway and were traveling roadways in a semiresidential area. The suspects performed the classic countersurveillance measure of making three right turns to detect any tails. The FBI surveillance units followed the suspects while

making the turns and were immediately "burnt." Instead of fleeing, the suspects—who were armed with high-power pistols, an assault rifle, and a shotgun—confronted the agents head-on in a firefight. Both suspects were eventually killed by members of the surveillance team, although 6 FBI agents were injured and 2 killed by the suspects' gunfire. Not only was this incident the bloodiest firefight in FBI history, it also called into question the firepower of standard FBI weaponry. Later it was determined that the regular issue 9mm handgun carried by the operative agents should be replaced with a more potent semiautomatic pistol utilizing with a specially designed cartridge capable of penetrating at a distance the metal side panels and doors of passenger vehicles.[13] A sketch of the FBI Miami Firefight crime scene outlining the above sequence of events is shown in Figure 7.7.

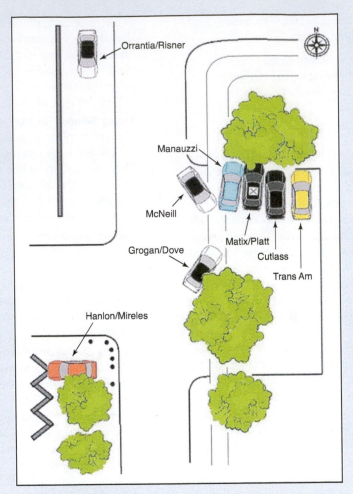

FIGURE 7.7 ▶ The final positioning of the FBI mobile surveillance team and the target suspect vehicle (designated as "X") at the time the shootout between agents and the suspects began.

ELECTRONIC SURVEILLANCE

Wiretapping

Wiretapping, otherwise known as *electronic eavesdropping*, involves covert interception of communication content in the furtherance of an investigative effort. Warrants based on probable cause must be obtained for most wiretaps. These warrants—often referred to as *super warrants* because of their difficulty to obtain—assume that countless unsuspecting persons could have their privacy invaded by a wiretap order. Even when wiretap warrants are properly obtained, investigators are not permitted to go on "fishing expeditions" to secure evidence through electronic eavesdropping. Wiretapping laws require that only conversations or communications that can be reasonably assumed to be made in the furtherance of criminal activity be monitored and/or recorded. In practice, these law require wiretap surveillance to cease if, at the beginning of a communication, there is no reason to believe the content is crime related—a process known as *minimizing*. Consequently, persons who suspect they are being wiretapped talk about the weather or other mundane topics at the beginning of their conversation—before discussing criminal activities—to use wiretap laws in their favor.

The content of all oral (e.g. face-to-face), wire (voice transmitted through phones, cellular networks, the Internet), or electronic (nonvoice, including e-mails, text messages, instant messages, digital faxes, etc.) communication is protected by law and a proper warrant must be obtained before conducting electronic surveillance of these types of communications. If at least one of the parties participating in an oral, wire, or electronic conversation consents to the surveillance, however, the content communicated by all parties involved may be intercepted without obtaining a wiretap order.

No warrant is required for surveillance of undercover investigators or informants who have consented to having their communications monitored by an audio or video surveillance device. In addition, warrants are not required to participate in any communication considered to be a public forum, such as a social networking website or chatroom. Thus, an investigator may post entries, enter threaded discussions, and engage in chats with individuals on social network websites such as Craigslist, Facebook, or others without first seeking a wiretap order. Most wiretap orders permit communication interception for 30 days and require the nature of the content intercepted to be reported to a judge and the targets of the wiretap to be notified when the surveillance ends. As will be discussed later in Chapter 19, warrantless investigations involving wiretapping are routinely conducted by the federal government in the interest of national security under the special provisions of the Patriot Act.[14]

Pen/Trap Devices

Pen registers and trap and trace devices (**pen/trap devices**) are used primarily to monitor incoming and outgoing communications made by telephones, cellular networks, and computer connections. Unlike wiretaps, surveillance made by these devices can be authorized by court order without establishing probable cause. Such orders are usually secured by investigators swearing under oath that the use of pen/trap surveillance methods would likely provide information material to an ongoing investigation. These orders allow for

60 days of continued surveillance activities. Information that it is permissible to obtain through pen/trap devices includes the following:

- Incoming calls
- Outgoing calls
- The time each call is made
- Whether a call is connected or goes to voicemail
- The length of a call
- E-mail addresses, size of e-mail files, time/date/location where messages are sent

Note that monitoring content of communications detected by pen/trap devices is strictly forbidden. If the preliminary pen/trap surveillance provides evidence for establishing probable cause, however, an emergency wiretap warrant may be secured to allow review of communication content.

When applied to field investigations, pen/trap devices can be a very useful tool. For example, suspects using a cell phone can often be located in minutes by a process known as *pinging* whereby phone connections to specific transmission towers can be identified and tracked in real time. Also, information on outgoing and incoming calls can be used to identify criminal associates and locate fugitives, missing persons, or stolen property. Many agencies do not have access to pen/trap technology, however, due to its current high cost.[15]

TABLE 7.1	SURVEILLANCE AND COUNTERSURVEILLANCE TECHNIQUES	
SURVEILLANCE TACTIC	**SURVEILLANCE**	**COUNTERSURVEILLANCE**
Foot Surveillance:		
Object Drop*	T-Discards/O-Secures	O-Discards/T-Secures
Crowded Area	Close-Surveillance	Enter Crowded Area
Open Areas	Loose Surveillance	Sudden Stop/Direction Change
Multiple Person	Shadow/Tail	Use of Convoy(s)
Vehicle Surveillance:	Single/Multiple Vehicle	Use any/all of the following: Sudden Rt., Lt., or U-Turn/3 Rt. Turns/Increase/Decrease Speed/Run Red Light at Intersection
Eavesdropping	Electronic Bug	Radio-wave sweep
Telephone	Pen/Trap Device	Install Tap Detector
Computer	E-mail/Text Interception	Encrypt Messages/Files

*Note: O = Operative; T = Target; Rt. = Right; Lt. = Left. Objects could be papers, receipts, or other decoys

FIGURE 7.8 ▶ Investigators often must stage the arrest of their informants, as depicted in the photo, so that the informant maintains credibility among criminal associates.

HOT TIPS AND LEADS 7.1

Conducting Cell Phone Tracking and Surveillance

Under the proper legal circumstances, missing persons, abductions, vehicle/property thefts, and crime suspects can be tracked or placed under surveillance using cell phone technology. Because all cell phones constantly transmit signals to *cell towers*, with which they communicate to place a call, and these signals are recorded by cell phone service providers, investigators can use a technique called *pinging* to track past movements of a particular phone by location—or, sometimes, to conduct a real-time surveillance of movements of a phone. Depending on the particular type of phone and where it is being used, pinging can reveal phones located within 50 feet of some towers (usually within urban, high-traffic areas) and in other instances 3 miles or more from towers located in remote locations. Phones without GPS capabilities must be activated in order for pinging activity to be recorded. Phones equipped with GPS (e.g., iPhones, Blackberry), however, will provide a pinging record from both cell towers and Wi-Fi locations even when they are turned off—and often can provide locations within 20 meters of the phone. ID numbers of cell towers, along with other information including outgoing phone calls and the times they were made, are included in reports issued by cellular service providers to investigators. A tower ID can be used to determine the tower's geographic location in Google Maps. Although cell phones communicate with towers every 7 seconds or so, complete data detailing every tower location with which the phone has communicated is generally not available after long time periods such as more than one week. Exigent circumstances will waive the requirement for a court order or search warrant to gain immediate access to pinging records if the investigator informs the cellular service provider that an emergency situation involving death or great bodily injury may be imminent. Otherwise, a *2703 (d) order* must be obtained based on the investigator's showing that reasonable grounds exist to believe that the contents of the desired phone record are relevant and material to an ongoing criminal investigation. Additional uses of cell phones for surveillance activities include remote activation of the phone (usually one with GPS) to serve as a listening device that can capture the conversations of those who possess it. This same surveillance method can also be used with vehicles equipped with ONSTAR communication systems.

INFORMANTS

Informants, or *CIs* (Confidential Informants) as they are often called, are persons with access to crime-related information that they are willing to provide to investigators. Persons are willing to serve as an informant for various reasons, including monetary compensation, reductions in criminal charges, fear, revenge, or perhaps being a "good citizen." In addition, there are the following different types of informants:

- The Anonymous Informant: Persons who provide tips and leads to investigators without revealing their identity or requesting compensation.
- The In-Custody Informant: Persons serving jail or prison terms who are willing to provide information in exchange for money, protection, or legal considerations.
- The Criminal Informant: Persons who are involved in, or know about criminal activities or criminal networks.

Informants can be walk-ins (persons who volunteer their services by initiating contact with investigators), or they can be developed by investigators who gain the confidence of individuals with criminal knowledge. The best informants are persons who possess the closest or most intimate contacts with targets—the persons, places, or things that are the focus of an investigation. If such persons do not initiate contact with authorities and must be recruited, there are several methods that investigators can use to identify potentially cooperative informants. First, existing agency files such as incident/crime reports, arrest records, F. I. (field interview) data, surveillance, and other intelligence reports can be examined to find possible persons associated with the investigative target. Public records and databases also are valuable sources. Vehicle registrations, property ownership documents, welfare and child protective services, civil judgments, utilities, marriage/divorce or death certificates, bankruptcies, and social networking databases are just some of the many possibilities for obtaining valuable informant leads. Other fruitful sources of informants may include persons acquainted with investigative targets such as fellow employees, bartenders, mechanics, parking lot attendants, doormen, or other individuals involved in the target's routine activities. Often, friend of a friend of an individual associated with an investigative target can be a valuable source of investigative information.

Perhaps the most important assessment of a potential informant that an investigator can make is a determination of why a particular person may be willing to provide authorities with information about criminal activities. Persons who approach investigators as volunteer informants must be especially scrutinized because they may use their informant role to subvert an investigation of their criminal associates. The same can be true, however, for recruited informants. Trustworthy informants have a specific motivation for wanting to provide information to authorities. It is up to the investigators to uncover this motivating factor—whether money, revenge, legal leniency, or protection—and use it as a bargaining chip to gain the confidence and cooperation of a would-be informant. One measure of an informant's trustworthiness may be his or her willingness to engage in enforcement related activities such as a mock arrest such as that illustrated in Figure 7.8.

Regardless of how informants make initial contact with investigators, a thorough background investigation is needed on these individuals and this investigation should continue until the investigator's relationship with the informant is terminated. A good general rule is to verify all information provided by an informant and practice counterintelligence measures whenever or wherever possible. An undue willingness on the part of informants to provide sensitive information that jeopardizes the informant's personal safety or appears as a goldmine for the investigator should be viewed as a potential setup until proven otherwise. Anytime there is reason to believe that a relationship with an informant has gone bad, it probably has, and association with the informant should be terminated at once.

Any and all information about the informant must be recorded in an *informant dossier*. This file includes reports of information about the informant including casual observations (e.g., methods of initial contact, assessments of willingness to cooperate); true name, cover names, photos, and personal information; records of contacts with investigators and criminal associates; financial or other compensation provided; legal documents and agreements; and other pertinent case activity information relating to the informant. Key portions of the informant dossier, such as the informant's true and assumed identities, investigator contact, type of information provided, and area assigned should be placed with similar information from other informants in a central *informant information file* housed within the agency's investigative intelligence unit. This file and all other informant data should be maintained at the highest security level.[16]

UNDERCOVER OPERATIONS

When all other methods of information gathering about criminal activities have failed or are deemed impractical, **undercover operations** can be used as a last resort. This is due largely to the inherent dangers of going undercover and to the high cost of funding an undercover operation. The decision to go undercover in an investigation is usually made by the agency's top command staff and is carried out as a carefully planned and tightly supervised field tactic. Once approved, the undercover assignment process begins with the construction of an undercover investigative plan. This plan includes information regarding the specific individuals/groups to be targeted; places and geographic areas where investigators will be operating; particular criminal activities that will be investigated; and the logistics of the operation, including the nature of supervision, time frames, costs, necessary equipment, required personnel, specialized training, and so forth.

One of the most critical decisions is the investigators most suitable to work the undercover assignment. Selection criteria for the best officer candidate to serve as an operative will depend on the characteristics of the targeted individuals/groups. Younger, less experienced officers are often the candidates of choice with targets who may recognize older, more experienced officers familiar to criminals in certain areas or locations. On the other hand, much older officers may assume the role of a more seasoned operative. The officer's race/ethnicity, ability to speak a foreign language, or specialized looks and skills may also influence the operative selection process. Additionally, selected officers with specialized training may be needed before the undercover operation begins. For example, officers attempting to infiltrate jewelry theft rings should know the specialized jargon of jewel thieves as well as the processes of identifying precious metals and gems. Operatives who have the most in common with their targets in all respects have the greatest potential for success as undercover investigators.

Developing a workable and believable cover is also extremely important to officers working undercover assignments. The officer's cover is an assumed identity conveyed to targets and others while serving as an operative on assignment. To be convincing, the cover must come second nature—especially when the investigator must answer questions under stressful situations. For this reason, the best cover is one based on prior real-life experiences or on the identity of a real-life person with whom the officer has been familiar with in the past. In particular, assuming the name of a real person—especially a dead person—helps greatly in creating a convincing cover. If this strategy is adopted, however, the person selected as a cover identity must possess shared characteristics such as age, ethnicity, height, weight, and eye color. Targets may search public records, and perhaps even police records, to gain intelligence information for purposes of checking out an undercover officer's cover.

The first, and most challenging, step in the undercover process is gaining access to the target individuals or groups under investigation. One method is to have the operative introduced or *sponsored* to the target by an informant. Here, the informant's credibility is central to establishing trust between the undercover officer and the target, who are complete strangers. This method can be dangerous, however, because the officer's cover can be blown at any time by an unscrupulous informant. Another, and perhaps safer, method to gain access to targets is simply by implementing an infiltration strategy. Commonly, this technique requires undercover officers to establish their presence and cover reputation among people with whom targets associate or within places where targets are known to frequently go. The latter may include bars, restaurants, adult stores, Internet sites, casinos, horse racing tracks, recreational areas, and so on.

When going undercover in the field, operatives should always work alone, stay within designated areas, and be closely monitored by another investigator. Only a few individuals, including top administration and other investigators working on the case, should know the particulars of the undercover assignment. Undercover officers must also refrain from engaging in criminal or unsafe activities with targets or entrapping targets by suggesting that they engage in a criminal act. When and if such situations arise, have a story or plan prepared that will provide a believable escape from the situation. In the event of an emergency, develop a means of communicating emergency codes with other investigators that signal when help is needed. Undercover operations are discussed further in Chapter 18 concerning covert methods used to detect illegal drug sales and trafficking activities.[17]

Sting Operations

Sting operations are a specialized form of undercover operations that involve enticing offenders to commit crimes in front of undercover operatives. This investigative method is used most often to target specific types of offenders and offenses, including political corruption, fencing stolen goods, drug sales/distribution, organized crime, alcohol sales to minors, auto theft, and a range of vice crimes. Some sting operations require investigators to wear disguises and learn the trades, mannerisms, and speech patterns of target offenders. Other operations may involve a confidential informant or surrogate, who may be a professional thief or juvenile fitting the part of an unsuspecting victim, client, or offender. The following are some popular sting techniques:

- *False Storefronts:* False stores, such as pawnshops, are set up to lure in burglars to sell or *fence* their stolen property. Undercover operatives may also pose as fences to sting criminal pawnbrokers.
- *Bait Cars:* High-theft model vehicles are used as places under surveillance and/or contain surveillance equipment to capture offenders who are lured to steal them.
- *False Advertising:* Adds are placed in newspapers and other media sources containing the names of wanted offenders and stating they have won a prize or the lottery. If the offenders appear to claim their prize, they are stung.
- *The Internet:* Ads are placed on eBay, Craigslist, or other Internet sites searching for/selling stolen property, providing fencing opportunities for burglars, and enticing child predators and participants in other illegal activities. Undercover operatives may hang out in juvenile chat rooms, providing opportunities for pedophiles to hook up for sexual activities with minors.[18]

PHOTO AND LIVE LINEUPS

Another follow-up investigative procedure useful for (1) identifying likely suspects not yet in custody or (2) positively identifying or exculpating suspects already in custody is the **lineup** (see Figure 7.9). Lineups can be carried out in several ways, all of which are acceptable under current legal standards. First, and used most often by investigators, is the *photo lineup*. In this procedure, the witness views a series of photographs, which typically include a suspect's photo presented in a uniform fashion with photos of other, similar looking individuals known as *fillers*. Simple methods include the use of a mug book containing pages of photographs of suspects and fillers. More technologically advanced procedures have been developed whereby digital photographs are presented on video monitors, laptop computers, or even handheld devices such as iPhones. Another alternative, used less often, is the *live lineup*. This method requires witnesses to view suspects and fillers both live and in person. Usually this is done in specially prepared police viewing rooms that have one-way glass or some other similar configuration that allows witnesses to view persons in the lineup

(a)

(b)

FIGURE 7.9 ▶ (a) View of a lineup room from the stage where suspects are located, looking out through a glass panel to where victims are seated during the identification process. (b) Suspects in a lineup.

and not vice versa. *Video lineups* also can be carried out by videotaping a live lineup and displaying it to a witness in either delayed or real time. Both photo and live lineups can be performed either simultaneously or sequentially. In *simultaneous lineups*, suspects and fillers are presented at the same time to witnesses—a process preferred by most investigators due to its ease and convenience. Alternatively, in *sequential lineups* suspects and fillers are presented one by one to witnesses.[19]

Eyewitness identifications made during lineups can be used to establish probable cause for arrest or as other forms of legally admissible evidence as long as the lineup is not considered to be unduly suggestive. This means that all photos, fillers, or other forms of visual identification examined by witnesses must be uniform in appearance and not cause a particular suspect or individual to stand out as different. For example, lineups using fillers with facial features, clothing, or other physical characteristics significantly different from the general appearance of the suspects would most likely be considered unduly suggestive if legally challenged. In addition to appearance considerations, a lineup's legal fairness can be challenged if investigators

administering the procedure say or do anything unduly suggestive before, during, or after the lineup. For these and related purposes, investigators preparing and conducting lineups must ensure that whatever method is employed conforms to current legally acceptable standards. The following are suggested protocols for conducting lineups, derived from guidelines prepared by the U.S. Department of Justice:

1. ***Provide witnesses with instructions before the lineup by informing them of the following:***
   - The procedure has two specific goals: (1) to determine who may be guilty and (2) to determine who may be innocent; thus, it is just as important to identify persons who may be guilty as well as those who may be innocent.
   - They will be viewing a group of individuals, which may or may not include the person they witnessed.
   - If the person they witnessed is included in the lineup, he or she may have a different physical appearance than what he or she had when first seen at the crime or other location (e.g., facial hair, clothing has possibly changed).
   - If the witness is not able to make a positive ID of a suspect, the investigation will still continue.
   - If a positive ID of a suspect is made, the witness needs to explain in their own words how certain they are that the person they are viewing is indeed the suspect.

2. ***Conducting the lineup:***
   - Double check to make sure the witness understands the instructions before beginning the lineup.
   - For photo lineups, use a minimum of six or more filler photos—for a total of seven photos including the suspect. For live lineups, use a minimum of four individual fillers—for a total of five live persons including the suspect.
   - Select fillers that have the same general physical appearance as the suspect; however, avoid selecting fillers that appear so similar to the suspect that the witness becomes confused. When using photos, try to select a picture that is similar in appearance to other photos (size, shape, background) and best depicts the suspect at the time of the crime.
   - Include only one suspect in each lineup. If there are multiple suspects, conduct a new lineup containing new fillers for each suspect viewed by the same witness. If there are multiple witnesses, have them view the lineup separately and do not allow them to talk to one another before or during the lineup procedure.
   - Place suspects at random within photo arrays or live lineups. Refer to them as numbers (i.e., Number 1, 2, 3, and so on).
   - Avoid saying anything that would bias the witness during the lineup procedure, such as "Are you sure about that?" when presented with a filler rather than the suspect being identified. If a positive ID of the suspect

is made, continue through the entire set of fillers without commenting on the witness's observations.

- If possible, use a *double-blind* procedure where neither the investigator administering the lineup nor the witness knows which individual is the suspect.
- Remember to have witnesses state how certain they are about their identification of a suspect, regardless of whether they identify a suspect or filler. Take thorough notes to document all witness comments during the lineup procedure. Prepare written statements summarizing these comments and the suspect ID, if it is made, and have them signed by the witness in the presence of at least two investigators.[20]

3. *Legal Issues:* Suspects who have not been arrested and who volunteer to participate in a live lineup are not protected by the Fifth Amendment right to remain silent or the Sixth Amendment right to representation by legal counsel. Suspects who have been arrested, however, are entitled to have their attorney present during a live lineup. The Supreme Court ruled in *Ash v. U.S.* that suspects do not have the right to legal counsel in photo lineups, regardless of whether they have been arrested or not. In addition, it is legally permissible to request suspects and fillers to talk, walk, or make specific movements during a live procedure—as long as such requests constitute a request of the suspect to provide testimony about his or her involvement in the crime being investigated. Threats or inappropriate comments made by a suspect to witnesses during a live lineup can be grounds for the suspect's arrest on witness intimidation charges. Finally, both photo and live lineups should be videotaped in the event that legal challenges allege undue suggestibility on the part of investigators during the procedure.[21]

CRIMINAL INTELLIGENCE

The term *intelligence*, as used within the context of investigation, is often interpreted incorrectly as simply *the collection of crime-related information through investigative efforts*. However, collecting information of potential use for preventing and solving crimes is only the first step in the intelligence process. To qualify as intelligence, information initially obtained through an investigation must also be analyzed and transformed into a product useful for guiding decision making, planning, strategic targeting, and crime prevention efforts as they relate to the investigative process. For example, data and records gathered from a suspected fraudulent business would not be considered intelligence until this information is subjected to an investigative analysis—perhaps using forensic accounting software to generate a statistical profile showing illegal bookkeeping and money laundering practices. Such intelligence information then could be used for many purposes: arresting corrupt business persons, planning future investigative strategies to gather additional evidence, implementing preemptive strategies for preventing similar illegal

business practices elsewhere, or perhaps sharing the information with outside law enforcement agencies to connect this illegal business with others operating illegally within an organized crime network. Thus, as the latter example illustrates, intelligence is much more than merely gathering information through investigation—it is an information-based process that can support numerous investigative functions.

A Brief History of Criminal Intelligence

The basic intelligence model used in investigation is derived from military and national security models, and has been implemented slowly within police agencies since the late 1940s. Not until the 1970s was the practice of creating specialized intelligence officers and units at the local, state, and federal levels recognized by U.S. law enforcement as a necessary tool for combating crime. Efforts to create a national police intelligence network were also forestalled in the late 1970s, however, by widespread public outcry over use of investigative procedures such as illegal surveillance and wiretapping to gather information on numerous social and ethnic groups deemed to be potentially criminal and a threat to national security. Although the use of intelligence in policing regained momentum during the 1980s and 1990s with the creation of specialized state and federal crime information centers, not until shortly after the 9/11 terrorist attacks did intelligence gathering procedures begin to flourish and develop as an accepted tactic within the field of investigation.[22]

Types of Intelligence

As applied to the practice of investigation, intelligence functions can be broken down into the following four categories:

1. *Tactical Intelligence:* Intelligence used to identify and solve an immediate crime or security problem. Under this method, information is gathered within a narrow time frame to identify offenders and their targets. Authorities use intelligence analyses to implement short-term tactical enforcement strategies for dealing with specific criminal threats. Intelligence is also used for postarrest activities, such as prosecuting and convicting offenders.

2. *Strategic Intelligence:* Developing a long-term big picture of a particular crime problem is the primary goal of this intelligence method. Analyses of general crime patterns and trends, and how they are changing over time, can provide investigators with intelligence insights regarding how to improve or change existing enforcement practices to most effectively cope with new and emerging varieties of offenses and offenders.

3. *Evidential Intelligence:* Gathering information derived from known specific pieces of evidence that may lead to the discovery of other new forms of evidence is the primary goal of this intelligence method. Evidence to be located can include physical objects, persons, or geographic locations.

4. *Operational Intelligence:* This method focuses on specific large-scale criminal activities over an extended time period for purposes of identifying and gathering more detailed intelligence on specific criminal activities, offenders, and their targets. It is often used to analyze organized crime networks

FIGURE 7.10 ▶ Patrol unit equipped with cameras and Automated License Plate Recognition (ALPR). Mobile ALPR consists of three cameras mounted adjacent to a radio car's emergency light bar. These cameras automatically scan nearby license plates and determine whether a vehicle is wanted or stolen. ALPR systems can scan up to 8,000 license plates during the course of a single shift. Fixed ALPR systems are mounted primarily atop intersection signal poles and parking lots. These fixed systems scan each vehicle as it passes through the intersection and notify the concerned station when a stolen or wanted vehicle is detected.

and terrorist groups and to reduce such criminal organizations to their basic membership structure or cells.[23]

Police Intelligence Units

Depending on their particular size and mission, law enforcement agencies maintain one or more specialized intelligence units. Within each unit, files of information are kept relating to activities and associations of individuals, businesses, organizations, and groups for which there is an established reasonable belief or *criminal predicate* of involvement in a definable criminal or enterprise. These activities typically include the following:

1. Narcotics manufacturing and/or trafficking;
2. Unlawful gambling;
3. Extortion;
4. Vice and pornography;
5. Infiltration of businesses for illegitimate purposes;
6. Bribery;
7. Major crime including homicide, burglary, auto theft, kidnapping, destruction of property, robbery, fraud, forgery, fencing of stolen property, and arson;
8. Manufacture, use, or possession of explosive devices for fraud, intimidation, or political reasons;
9. Organized crime;
10. Corruption of public officials;
11. Threats to public officials and private citizens;
12. Traveling criminals;
13. Gang activities;
14. Other designated multijurisdictional activities.

Specific types of information for individuals maintained in intelligence files include the following:

1. Full name;
2. Date of birth;
3. Address;
4. Aliases;
5. Social Security number;
6. Driver's license number;
7. Physical description (height, weight, eye and hair color);
8. Place of birth;
9. Citizenship (if alien, identification number)
10. Distinguishing scars, marks, or tattoos;
11. Violence potential;
12. Criminal identification number;
13. Criminal associates;
14. *Modus operandi.*

Any information included in an intelligence file, regardless of whether it is separated from public records, can be subject to subpoena and turned over to courts for examination. Decisions regarding the release of such information will generally be made by a judge. Information should never be included in an intelligence file solely on the basis of an individual's or organization's support for unpopular causes, ethnic identity, religious affiliations, political viewpoint, or any other factor unrelated to suspected criminal activities.[24] Technological advances in police intelligence gathering have even made it possible to transform today's modern patrol unit into a source for intelligence gathering (see Figure 7.10)

FUSION CENTERS

Following the 9/11 terrorist attacks in 2001, the International Association of Chiefs of Police (IACP) and various representatives from the Department of Homeland Security recommended that the role of police intelligence within the United States be revitalized and enhanced as a major countermeasure against future terrorist attacks. In addition, this improved intelligence function could be used as a crime fighting tool as well. In 2003, the National Criminal Intelligence Sharing Plan (NCISP) was developed to provide a blueprint for the nation's first and most comprehensive police intelligence network. The main thrust of this plan was to develop a data sharing network involving collaboration between law enforcement, public safety organizations, and the private sector. This data, in turn, could be blended, analyzed, and evaluated to create an intelligence function for preventing and responding to terrorist threats as well as ordinary criminal activities. Central to this plan was the development of regional **fusion centers** (see, for example, Figure 7.11) to serve as a clearinghouse to store, coordinate, analyze, and disseminate intelligence information.

According to the NCISP, a fusion center is defined as a "collaborative effort of two or more agencies that provide resources, expertise, and information to the center with the goal of maximizing their ability to detect, prevent, investigate, and respond to criminal and terrorist activity." Currently there are approximately

TABLE 7.2   U.S. INTELLIGENCE SYSTEM/NETWORKS

INTELLIGENCE	DESCRIPTION
Border Control	**El Paso Intelligence Center (EPIC)** assists law enforcement in issues concerning drug movement and immigration violations.
Financial Crimes	**Financial Crimes Enforcement Network (FinCEN)** provides intelligence on domestic and international financial crimes, and monitors national and worldwide money-laundering activities.
Drugs	**High Intensity Drug Trafficking Areas Centers (HIDTA)** provides support to law enforcement by tracking and analyzing drug flow along known drug corridors and other locations used to traffic illegal drugs.
High-Tech Crime	**National White Collar Crime Center (NWC3)** supports law enforcement efforts through intelligence efforts to prevent, investigate, and prosecute economic and high-tech crimes.
Organized Crime	**Law Enforcement Intelligence Unit (LEIU)** records and analyzes confidential information on organized crime activities.
International Crime	**International Criminal Police Organization (INTERPOL)** provides worldwide information exchange and analysis between law enforcement agencies regarding crimes/fugitives and stolen properties.[26]

75 fusion centers located in various regions across the nation. Each center functions in a slightly different way, yet is part of an interconnected network operated by the Department of Homeland Security, known as the HSND (The Department of Homeland Security Data Network).[25] Types of data housed by fusion centers include the following:

Agriculture, Food, Water, and the Environment
Banking and Finance
Chemical Industry and Hazardous Materials
Criminal Justice
Education
Emergency Services (non-law enforcement)
Energy
Government
Health and Public Health Services
Hospitality and Lodging
Information and Telecommunications
Military Facilities and Defense Industrial Base
Postal and Shipping
Private Security
Public Works
Real Estate
Retail
Social Services
Transportation

FIGURE 7.11 ▶ The interior of a large fusion center.
(Federal Bureau of Investigation)

INTELLIGENCE-LED POLICING

Also included in the NCISP was a recommendation that police agencies in the United States incorporate various components of a law enforcement model developed around the year 2000 in Great Britain to counter terrorism, known as *intelligence-led policing.* Key to implementing this model is the proper utilization of intelligence information to guide police in identifying and targeting criminal threats. The major operational component of intelligence-led policing is the creation of an agency-based information network based on the following six-step intelligence process known as the **Intelligence Cycle** (see Figure 7.12):

1. ***Planning and Direction:*** The process begins with the agency establishing plans for how and what data will be collected. Investigators work collaboratively

FIGURE 7.12 ▶ The "Intelligence Cycle." (Courtesy Precision Computing Intelligence)

with analysts to establish enforcement priorities and decide which type of data would be most beneficial for dealing with various crime problems.

2. **Collection:** Next, raw data is collected from public, private, and—if proper legal authorization is obtained—confidential sources. Raw data collection commonly includes information based on the following:
   - Physical surveillance
   - Electronic surveillance
   - Confidential informants
   - Undercover operators
   - Newspaper reports (now also Internet sources)
   - Public records (e.g., deeds, property tax records)

3. **Processing:** Raw data are assembled into logical formats and files that can be easily accessed through an index, searches, or a computer analytic software system. Perhaps most difficult in this stage is the creation of databases that are compatible with one another, thus enabling the cross-referencing and blending of different raw data sources.

4. **Analysis:** Raw data is converted into usable intelligence after being processed and analyzed. This can be done by subjecting data sources to specialized computer software or by using persons trained to perform customized analyses. The primary goal of this stage is to provide meaning to the raw data sources that can be used to:
   - provide further investigative leads;
   - determine offenders and associates related to specific criminal acts;
   - recognize future crime patterns and trends; and
   - identify potential criminal threats.

5. **Dissemination:** Following analysis, intelligence information is presented in reports or alterative user-friendly formats to investigators and all other authorized personnel whose law enforcement activities would be enhanced by access to such knowledge. Various sources of criminal intelligence sharing and

dissemination are currently available for all law enforcement agencies, including the following:
   - LEO (Law Enforcement On Line) providing discussion forums, threads, photographs, expert links, and other electronic means of sharing intelligence and crime-related information both nationally and internationally. This site was created and is maintained by the U.S. Department of Justice.
   - N-DEx, operated by the FBI, allows electronic sharing, searching, linking, and analyzing of crime-related information by all law enforcement agencies within the United States and has the capability to "connect the dots" or determine associations between crimes occurring in various jurisdictions. In addition, incident/case reports, parole/probation data, and jail records can also be posted and shared in the system.

6. **Reevaluation:** Finally, feedback should be solicited from investigators and other persons who have used intelligence information to determine its effectiveness and to ascertain how future intelligence resources can be improved to fit specific investigative missions.[27]

CRIMINAL INTELLIGENCE ANALYTIC METHODS

Geoprofiling

Geoprofiling utilizes GPS methodology (see Figure 7.13) to predict the likely location of an offender's base of operations (for example, residence, workplace, hang-outs) as well as other geographic locations regularly frequented by offenders and their targets/victims. It is based on a predictive formula that focuses on likely travel patterns that offenders follow while carrying out routine activities such as traveling from their home to work, leisure locations, and associates' residences. These routes travelled by the offender are assumed to represent a likely comfort zone wherein the offender feels most confident in seeking out and acting on criminal opportunities. The technique is best applied to a series of crimes that can be linked to the same offender(s), but can be applied to a single offender/offense situation. Geoprofiling can be useful for focusing investigative activities, such as surveillance or canvass operations, within certain physical locations or for narrowing the scope of records searches to specific areas. Various commercial software applications of this technique are available, including Rigel, CrimeStat, and Dragnet.[28]

Crime Pattern Analysis

Also utilizing GPS technology, **crime pattern analysis** produces geographic area maps illustrating patterns of criminal activity such as (1) crimes occurring in a series that possibly are being committed by the same individual(s), known as *common offenses*; and (2) *hot spot* locations where specific types of crime

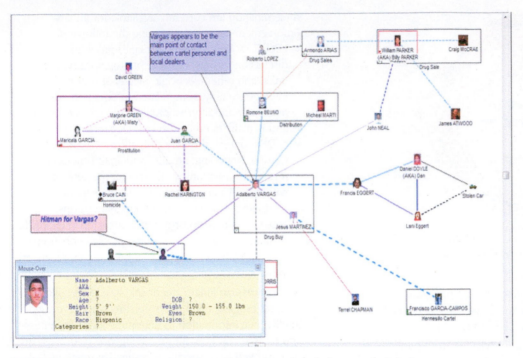

FIGURE 7.13 ▶ Linkage analysis performed on Crimlink Version 5 Software. (Courtesy Bill Jordan)

tax records, corporate banking accounts, purchase orders, accounts receivable, stock dividends paid or received, and so on, are investigated for financial discrepancies possibly linked to criminal associations and enterprises.[29]

Linkage Analysis

Linkage analysis, also referred to as *association* or *network analysis,* involves creating a chart to visualize associations among offenders and offense-related factors (see Figure 7.13). Graphic presentations employ photographs and symbols, which can be used to illustrate complex linkages between various crimes, individuals, groups/gangs, organizations, weapons, drugs, goods, money, and other subjects of investigative interest that are perhaps similar or related to one another. Link charts often are used to show the structure of criminal organizations, narcotics distribution networks, and terrorist groups and their cells.

are committed in high frequencies, determined by using *frequency distribution analysis* to identify areas where crimes happen most and least often. Many potential crime characteristics can be included or layered on GPS maps to determine likely crime patterns, including characteristics of crimes, offenders, vehicles, victims/targets, businesses, neighborhoods, weapons, witness accounts, and numerous other crime-related factors that can be linked to a series or pattern.

NET WORTH AND FINANCIAL ANALYSIS

This detailed financial accounting procedure has been used extensively in investigations of organized crime, tax evasion, fraud, money laundering, drug offenses, and other crimes in which illegal monetary profits are gained by offenders. It is performed by assessing an individual's or business entity's total known/declared financial intake for a fixed period of time (i.e., net worth) and then comparing these resources against the estimated costs of all purchases and financial expenditures during the same period. If an individual's net worth is less than that required to cover expenses for items purchased, mortgages/rent paid, auto/other loans, utility bills, and other miscellaneous costs, then there may be cause to believe that this financial discrepancy is the result of funds obtained illegally through criminal enterprises. Other forms of financial analysis include bank record analysis, which involves the inspection of bank statements, deposits, withdrawals, debit/credits, wire transfers, loan activities, and so on, to determine illegal money activities and perhaps likely associates or recipients involved in crime-related financial activities. Similar analyses can be conducted on business and corporate financial records, known as *corporate record analysis,* whereby accounting records, profit/loss statements,

TELEPHONE RECORD ANALYSIS

Data obtained from pen/trap devices can be analyzed to provide a wealth of investigative information, as well as probable cause evidence to support a wiretap order. The end result of telephone record analysis is charts and reports that draw investigative conclusions based on recorded telephone activity. Frequency of calling activity, times at which calls are placed, locations where calls are made, the durations of calls, and related telephone calling patterns can often be used for the following purposes:

- Identifying criminal associations and networks
- Potential victims/target of crime
- Potential crime witnesses
- Locations of criminal bases of operations
- Obtaining subpoenas of other suspects' phone records for comparative analyses

The basic principles outlined above for telephones can also be used to document similar use patterns and associations for e-mails, chats, text messages, and other forms of electronic communication.[30]

Event Flow Analysis

Event flow analysis is an appropriate method to document a crime or crime-related activity that is carried out in stages or

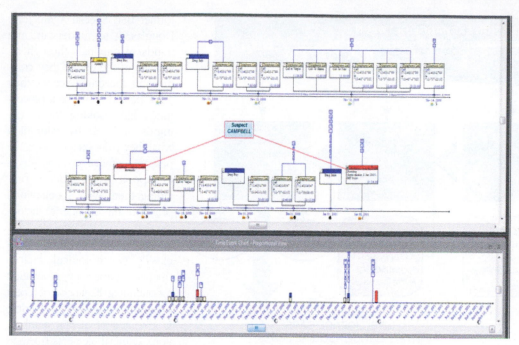

FIGURE 7.14 ▶ Time event analysis performed on Crimlink Version 5 Software. (Courtesy Bill Jordan)

this method is a time line analysis chart, which can include numerous suspects, victims, and evidence discovered on a single time line. Also, displaying investigative information in this manner often makes it easier to corroborate or question suspect alibis, witness accounts, or other time-related matters connected to case evidence. A related type of analysis, known as *activity flow analysis,* can be used in a similar manner to determine the chronological order of generic events such as criminal or behavioral patterns. For example, the M.O. (*modus operandi*) of a suspected serial killer may be charted over time to determine changes in methods used to attack victims or to predict when a future victimization may occur by studying time cycles of offending.[31]

is the product of sequential planning (see Figure 7.14). It is also useful for showing various individuals and activities that may be connected to multiple criminal acts over time. Simple event flow analyses are usually presented in chart form, known as an event flow chart, to illustrate a linear path of persons, places, or events in chronological order—as shown in Figure 7.15 for an event analysis of telephone use known as **telephone toll analysis**. More complex analyses may involve time sequences and paths. One common variety of

Commodity Flow Analysis

Commodity flow analysis is useful for documenting the flow of illegal goods to and from persons and/or places. Typically, charts show the illegal movement or networking of items such as laundered money, drugs, stolen goods, weapons, autos/auto parts, and related contraband. Human trafficking corridors have also been analyzed using commodity flow analysis.

Visual Investigative Analysis

For complex investigations, a detailed time line of activities carried out, including personnel and equipment requirements, is useful. Visual investigative analysis is a charting method (similar to that of a PERT or CPM chart used in industry) used to achieve this goal. In addition, a working visual investigation analysis chart can include outcomes and required changes introduced into an investigation plan as they occur in the field.[32]

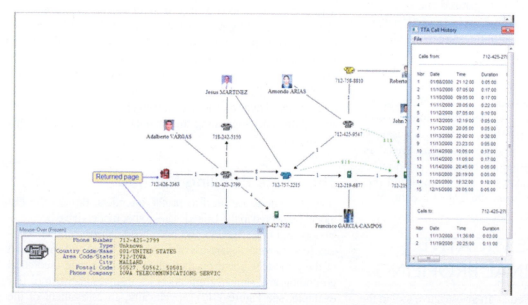

FIGURE 7.15 ▶ Telephone toll analysis from pen and register information performed on Crimlink Version 5 Software. (Courtesy Bill Jordan)

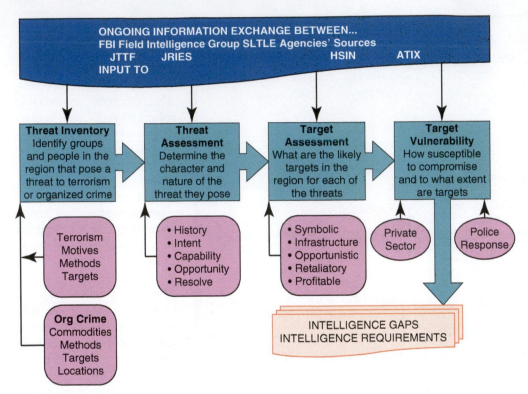

ONGOING INFORMATION EXCHANGE BETWEEN...
FBI Field Intelligence Group SLTLE Agencies' Sources
JTTF   JRIES   HSIN   ATIX
INPUT TO

Threat Inventory
Identify groups
and people in the
region that pose a
threat to terrorism
or organized crime

Threat Assessment
Determine the
character and
nature of the
threat they pose

Target Assessment
What are the likely
targets in the
region for each of
the threats

Target Vulnerability
How susceptible
to compromise
and to what extent
are targets

Terrorism
Motives
Methods
Targets

• History
• Intent
• Capability
• Opportunity
• Resolve

• Symbolic
• Infrastructure
• Opportunistic
• Retaliatory
• Profitable

Private
Sector

Police
Response

Org Crime
Commodities
Methods
Targets
Locations

INTELLIGENCE GAPS
INTELLIGENCE REQUIREMENTS

FIGURE 7.16 ▶ The flow of information during a threat assessment based on various intelligence sources. (Courtesy U.S. Department of Justice)

Threat and Vulnerability Analysis

Threat analysis is used quite often to determine the likelihood of criminal activities directed at governmental agencies, but can also be used in assess the possibility of illegal acts directed at private entities such as corporations, amusement/leisure locations, transportation systems, public utilities, and computer/electronic networks (see Figure 7.16). Organized crime, terrorist groups, street gangs, political extremists, and perhaps deranged lone offenders are often the subjects of threat analysis. The primary goal of this method is to produce an intelligence report that outlines a particular criminal's or criminal group's propensity for violence or other criminal behavior and the possibility that a specific target will be victimized. How and when the victimization will occur may also be included in the threat assessment report. Alternatively, vulnerability analysis focuses on assessing factors surrounding likely targets of criminal predators. The analytical focus is on determining criminal opportunities related to real or perceived weaknesses in the target and proposing ways to block them to increase the target's security.[33]

BEHAVIORAL INVESTIGATIVE METHODS: CRIMINAL PROFILING

Criminal profiling was conceived as an investigative tool in the United States during the 1970s by the FBI's Behavioral Science Unit (BSU). The theory behind this method, as explained by former BSU Special Agent John Douglas, is to "understand the minds of criminals through an analysis of the crimes they commit and the crime scenes they leave behind, which is a process much like looking inside the minds of artists by examining what they paint on a canvass." In practice, criminal profiling serves to support investigators by providing them with a behavioral profile of the offender(s) including demographics (age, ethnicity, gender, educational level, social class), psychological factors (mental competency, motivation for offending, likelihood of repeat offending, means by which crime is a source of mental gratification), criminal elements (method of committing crimes, selection of victim(s), future crime targets), and lifestyle (employment patterns, leisure activities, place of residence, mode of transportation, style of dress).[34]

The first major test of profiling was as an investigative support tool for the Atlanta Child Murder Case. From 1979 to 1981, at least 29 African-American children fell victim to a serial killer initially believed to be a white supremacist. Because investigative evidence indicated that the killer was able to openly abduct his victims within Atlanta's African-American communities without being noticed by residents, Douglas composed an offender profile of a young African-American male with a hot temper whose ethnicity allowed him to enter the crime scene completely unnoticed by potential witnesses. This profile, and the profiling method, was validated by the arrest and conviction of Wayne Williams for the murders. Williams, an African-American male whose background and behavior were almost an exact match to Douglas's profile, was ultimately convicted when his temper boiled over during trial, causing him to make uncontrollable statements suggesting the manner in which he killed his victims.

The Crime Profiling Method

Several methods are used to profile offenders. Besides the FBI model pioneered in the United States, other models have been created as well (e.g., Turvey) and have been utilized in other countries (e.g., Canter). Regardless of the specific origin and application of these models, however, they all share a common theoretical grounding and similar application as an investigative tool (for example, see Figure 7.17). Specifically, an assessment of the crime scene is used to determine the likely systematic and ongoing behavioral traits of the offender. This information, in turn, creates the basis for the criminal profile. The logic here is that persistent and ongoing behavioral traits specific to certain offenders are highly influential in determining who, what, where, when, why, and how offenders choose to strike particular targets, and how they live their day-to-day lives. This notion is based on the psychological principle of *adaptive behavior theory*, which assumes that many individual behaviors (i.e., choice of occupation, lifestyle habits) result from a person's attempt to adapt to their specific psychological orientation and needs—including personality types, traits, flaws, and so forth.

Generally, the first step in the criminal profiling process is to categorize the crime scene as *organized, disorganized, mixed,* or *atypical* with regard to available physical evidence. Organized crime scenes are those in which the physical evidence suggests planning and preparation for the crime on the part of the offender. Blood spatter, scattered cartridge casings, fingerprints, and other related forms of evidence are less likely to be discovered within these sites. When these are present, there will often be signs of the offender's attempts to destroy the evidence—such as wiping away fingerprints or bleaching bloody surfaces. Conversely, the disorganized crime scene is the direct opposite of the latter situation. In these scenes, physical evidence abounds. In addition, there are no signs of preparation, suggesting that the criminal act was spontaneous or opportunistic. When both organized and disorganized characteristics of physical evidence are present, the crime scene is best classified as mixed. An atypical crime scene is one that fails to exhibit any trait that allows it to be classified within any of the aforementioned categories.[35]

After the crime scene is categorized by type and related evidence has been collected, analyzed, and documented, the profiling process can begin. The primary basis for constructing a particular profile is the assumption that organized crime scenes are produced by **organized offenders** and disorganized ones by **disorganized offenders**. Organized offenders share in common a personality type that is shallow, manipulative, impulsive, thrill seeking, self-serving, and generally lacking in the ability to react emotionally to others' misfortunes. These abnormal personality traits enable organized offenders to rationally plan and commit criminal acts without regard for the harm inflicted on others by their actions. Moreover, because these individuals are driven by a warped desire to satisfy their lust for criminal activity, they usually organize their personal relationships, travel, occupation endeavors, and other lifestyle patterns to accommodate the successful completion of a crime. This balancing act between living life and committing crime forms the basis for creating a predictive profile of organized offenders. These people often possess the following criminal and behavioral traits:

- Basically a loner, but forms superficial relationships with others
- Has stable employment
- Maintains a personal residence and is considered a good neighbor
- Selects victims who are strangers but fulfill preconceived fantasy or criminal desire
- Travels to and from crime scene using a personal vehicle
- Chooses targets of least resistance and avoids physical confrontation
- Commits crimes in familiar areas—ones that are safe zones
- Crimes of violence tend to include multiple crime scenes
- Uses preplanned weapons/devices to carry out crimes

Whereas the organized offender carries out crime in a rational manner, selecting targets that provide the best chance for a successful outcome, the disorganized offender is not rational and may lack the mental ability to carry out a planned criminal act. Most often, disorganized offenders suffer from a temporary or ongoing behavioral disorder that renders them out of touch with reality, which also produces uncontrollable **delusions** (thinking things that have no basis in fact) and/or **hallucinations** (false sensory perceptions, usually hearing voices or seeing images). During these events—often triggered by prolonged exposure to a stressful situation—disorganized offenders may act out in a criminal manner toward persons or things they believe to be the primary source of the stress that they are feeling. Profiles of disorganized offenders include the following characteristics:

- Basically a loner, not by choice but because considered by others as "strange"
- Is either unemployed or has sporadic employment patterns
- May live with friends or family members, or in a shelter residence
- Does not own vehicle; uses public transportation
- Lives near the crime scene
- Uses a weapon of opportunity, often something readily available at the crime scene
- Attacks victim by direct physical confrontation, or in a "blitz" fashion
- In cases of homicide, signs of overkill may be present
- Usually not more than one primary crime scene
- Possible history of suicide attempts or attacks against family members
- May be taking or have taken prescription drugs (psychiatric medications) for psychiatric illness[36]

Profiling Serial Offenders

The term **serial offender** describes persons who commit related crimes (in other words, crimes in a series). Although the label *serial killer* has been popularized by the media to describe repetitive murders linked to the same individual, offenses, and offenders targeting persons or property can be classified as serial as well. For example, there are well-known serial cases involving rapists, arsonists, sex offenders, burglars, and even white-collar offenders. For investigators, recognizing serial

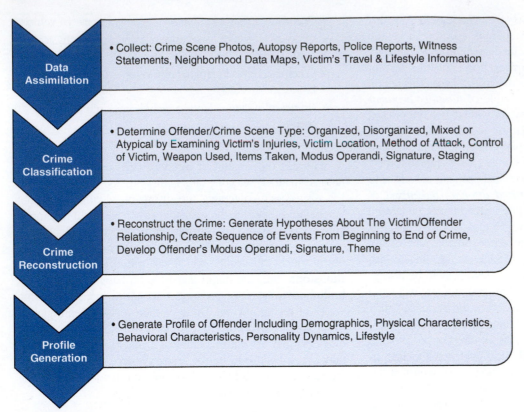

FIGURE 7.17 ▶ Sequential steps used in the criminal profiling process.

crimes is especially important because these perpetrators can commit many illegal acts over long periods of time, the majority of which are directed at random targets. Not only are these cases more difficult to solve, largely because of insufficient evidence, they also instill great fear in communities where they occur. Perhaps the most important aspect in the investigation of serial crimes is the fact that they are **instrumental offenses**. That is, they are committed for reasons directly related to the offender's need for psychological gratification. Because of this, the crime scene includes physical evidence that is a "fingerprint" of the offender, reflecting the psychological motivations underlying the criminal act. These behavioral indicators, which can remain remarkably similar each time an offender strikes, can be linked from one crime scene to another to identify likely serial offending activity. Following are some key elements of the crime scene that are used by investigators to identify serial crimes:

1. *Modus Operandi (M.O.).* An offender's **modus operandi** or M.O. is formally referred to as the *method of operation*. From an investigative standpoint, the offender's M.O. is a critical first step in identifying a potential serial crime. All crimes have an M.O., and it is best defined as the specific means by which an offender is able to carry out and complete a particular criminal activity. For example, in a suspected serial arson, investigations reveal that several building fires were started using a similar crude timing device fashioned from cigarettes placed in matchbooks near furniture soaked in kerosene. This M.O., like all others, represents the means by which an offender was physically and psychologically capable of starting and finishing the desired crime

at the time during which it was committed. The precise nature of an M.O., however, is very much a product of the learning process and will evolve to more effective and efficient means as the offender becomes more experienced. Therefore, the investigation of a potential serial offense should never require that M.O.s from separate crime scenes show exactly the same means of completing a crime. Rather, the investigation should focus on general rather than specific similarities in the M.O. to establish a serial crime linkage.[37]

2. *Signature.* Although unintentional and perhaps uncontrollable, the placement of a **signature** by a serial offender at the crime scene is almost inevitable and should be a central focus of a potential serial crime investigation. The signature, also known as the offender's *calling card*, is any offender behavior carried out before, during, and after a crime that is not directly necessary for successfully committing the crime. Signatures can be expressed directly in the form of written notes, spoken words, or specific actions. They also can be implied through what an offender does or does not do at the crime scene. It is the signature that is the specific source of the offender's psychological gratification above and beyond that of merely committing the crime. In essence, the signature can be identified through the determination of any offender behavior apart from the M.O. that relates to the specific criminal activity. For example, four separate female murder victims, discovered in different cities, have been killed by strangulation using a makeshift garrote made from a rope placed around the victim's neck and tightened by twisting the two ends with a wooden stick. In addition, the autopsy results revealed that the victims' bodies each displayed common nonfatal puncture wounds in their right breast. The puncture wounds, not essential for the commission of the murder, are potential signatures of the offender. In fact, they may be the result of *piquerism*, a form of sadomasochistic sexual satisfaction derived from the piecing of skin with a sharp object. Perhaps it is from the latter act, and not the actual murder, that the offender derived fulfillment of his or her psychological needs. The signature, unlike the M.O., remains much the same over time and is expressed in such a manner that it represents the same meaning or psychological needs from one crime to the next.[38]

3. *Theme.* One consistent behavioral indicator of serial offending—discovered through examination of multiple crime scenes—is the perpetrator's offending **theme**. Themes are dis-

covered by examining two or more signatures left by the same offender and determining what behavioral message, if any, is similar and consistent between each signature. For example, investigators may conclude that a series of armed bank robberies is being committed by a serial offender who has left similar signatures. At one of the bank robberies, the offender was caught on surveillance tape yelling "Death to capitalists" as he fled from the crime scene. At another robbery location, the armed gunman passed a note to a teller reading "Give me all of the bank's dirty money earned by sucking blood from the poor or you're dead." At a third site, the offender entered the bank wearing an "Uncle Sam" Halloween mask. Each of these situations clearly contains a signature, or an action on the part of the offender that is not necessary to complete the desired criminal act. Although each of the signatures is different, there is a common theme among them: The act of bank robbery, in addition to providing the offender money, is perhaps also fulfilling a psychological need to seek payback or vengeance against profit-making enterprises. Although signatures may change, the offender's theme generally will remain consistent over time.[39] Figure 7.18 illustrates the relationship between each of the above

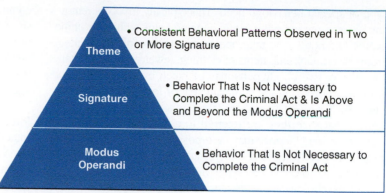

FIGURE 7.18 ▶ Relationship between behavioral traits of offending.

behavior traits as applied to the investigation of a serial offender.

Altered Crime Scenes

While most offenders commit their crime and immediately leave the crime scene, this is not the case for many serial offenders. The crime scene is a source of emotional gratification for them, so alteration of the crime scene may be necessary to fulfill some

TABLE 7.3	PROFILES OF ORGANIZED AND DISORGANIZED SERIAL KILLERS	
PROFILE FACTOR	**ED GEIN (DISORGANIZED)**	**RICHARD KUKLINSKI (ORGANIZED)**
Occupation	Handyman	Mob hit man
Psychiatric Diagnosis	Schizophrenic	Psychopath
Social Abilities	Limited/inadequate	Adequate/deceptive
Victim Focus	Female acquaintances	Male strangers
Modus Operandi	Spontaneous kill	Planned kill
Motivation	Delusion/fantasy	Money/hatred
Home Life	Unmarried/lived with mother	Married/domestic violence
Postmortem Activity	Necrophilia	Dismemberment
Trophy/Souvenir	Body parts	None
Signature	Killed in hunting style	Used cologne at crime scene
Theme	Disdain for females	Payback/vengeance
Staging	None	"Iced" bodies to hide time of death
Travel	None—crime near home	Extensive travel
Vehicles	Old pickup truck	Many—motorcycle, expensive cars

type of special behavioral need. This typically involves removing items, moving bodies, or rearranging items within the crime scene. Offenders may take one or more **souvenirs** with them from the crime scene. Items of clothing, jewelry, pieces of hair, pictures, or even body parts may be taken by the offender for purposes of reliving the criminal event or formulating fantasies later. Such items may also be taken as a symbol of conquest, and in that case they are referred to as **trophies**. Bodies or other physical evidence may be repositioned (known as **staging**) not only to try to fool investigators, but also to provide shock value, to convey a cryptic message, or to satisfy a deep-seated psychological desire. **Undoing**, a form of staging, may be performed, whereby the offender feels remorse after completing the crime and attempts to "make amends" for the harm that he or she has done. This phenomenon may be evident in a murder where the offender cleans the blood from the victim's face and places a blanket over the body as if to provide comfort.[40]

Criminal Profiling Assistance Provided by the FBI

Law enforcement agencies can seek criminal profiling assistance or the creation of a criminal profile for a specific investigation from the Behavioral Analysis Unit (BAU) of the FBI. The BAU is a division of the Bureau's National Center for the Analysis of Violent Crime (NCAVC) at FBI headquarters in Quantico, Virginia. It is composed of the following units designed to provide investigative assistance to local, state, federal, and international law enforcement agencies:

- Behavioral Analysis Unit 1: Counterterrorism and Threat Assessment—specializing in the investigation of terrorism, threats, arson, bombings, stalking, cyber-related violations, and anticipated or active crisis situations.
- Behavioral Analysis Unit 2: Crimes Against Adults—specializing in serial, spree, mass, and other murders; sexual assaults; kidnappings; missing person cases; and other violent crimes targeting adult victims, white-collar crime, public corruption, organized crime, and civil rights matters.
- Behavioral Analysis Unit 3: Crimes Against Children—specializing in crimes perpetrated against child victims, including abductions, mysterious disappearances of children, homicides, and sexual victimization.
- Also maintained within the NVAVC is the Violent Criminal Apprehension Program (VICAP).

Once contacted for assistance, the BAU performs a criminal investigative analysis of available evidence relating to the case under investigation. This process involves examining both the behavioral and physical evidence aspects of a criminal act. Investigative support in the form of criminal profiles, case management suggestions, crime analysis search warrant assistance, and prosecution advice can be provided to the agency requesting assistance. BAU agents communicate their investigative findings to law enforcement agencies via tele-communication conferencing or, in more complex cases, on-site visitation. Although serial crimes and terrorism are the primary cases handled by the BAU, other crime-related activities such as bombings/arson, communicated threats, corruption, and sexual assault also are frequently investigated by agents assigned to the unit.[41]

Much of the research conducted on violent offenders that forms the basis of BAU criminal profiles is based on data submitted by law enforcement agencies. This data is included in the VICAP database, a Web-based investigative tool providing various search and cross-referencing functions for purposes of investigating homicides, sexual assaults, missing persons, and other violent crimes involving unidentified dead bodies. The VICAP database[42] includes over 82,000 major crime cases and the following specific information:

1. Victim/Offender Information
   - Physical description
   - Scars and/or birthmarks
   - Identification
2. Offense M.O. (*Modus Operandi*)
   - Offender's approach to the victim
   - Body recovery site
   - Murder site
   - Offender's writing or carving on victim's body
   - Symbolic artifacts at the crime scene
3. Condition of Victim's Body When Found
   - Body disposition
   - Restraints used
   - Clothing and/or property
4. Cause of Death and/or Trauma
   - Cause of death
   - Trauma
   - Bite marks
   - Elements of torture or unusual assault
   - Sexual assault
5. Forensic Evidence
   - Weapons
   - Blood

In 2006, the Highway Serial Killings Initiative was created using VICAP information to assist law enforcement investigations of violent crimes along the nation's highways. The specific investigative focus of this program is on identifying suspected serial killers who target their victims on highways and in locations near highways. Specific VICAP information collected by a special team of investigators includes the following:

1. The remains of murdered persons discovered along highways, or at locations near highways such as rest stops, gas stations, or truck stops.
2. Kidnapped or missing persons who were last seen along highways.
3. Persons who have been the victims of sexual assault along highways or within highway locations.

FIGURE 7.19 ▶ Locations where human bodies or remains have been found along highways in the last 30 years, which are now under investigation by the FBI as part of the Highway Serial Killings Initiative. (Courtesy Federal Bureau of Investigation)

4. Truck drivers or other persons associated with or under investigation for murdering, kidnapping, or assaulting persons along highways or in highway locations.

Thus far, as shown in Figure 7.19, approximately 500 murder victims and 200 potential suspects have been identified in connection with the VICAP highway serial killer identification program.[43]

VICTIMOLOGY AND LIFESTYLE/ ROUTINES ANALYSIS

Victimology, the study of crime victims, attempts to explain the causes of crime from the victim's perspective. Of particular importance to investigators is the use of victimology to predict the relationship between victims and offenders, which falls within an area of study known as **lifestyle/routine activity analysis (LRA)**. LRA is particularly useful in many criminal investigations because it applies to crimes against persons as well as those against property. The overall goal of LRA is to determine likely demographic and behavioral characteristics of unknown offenders by examining the lifestyle and routine activities of persons, places, or things they have victimized. According to LRA, victimization is most likely to take place when the following three elements meet at the same time and in the same location:

- **Attractive Target:** The potential victim displays some favorable characteristic to the offender. For persons, this may include wealth, weakness, intoxication, gender, age, ethnicity, political orientation, etc. Property targets may be affluent homes, commercial businesses housing cash or selling valuables, certain makes and models of automobiles, etc.

- **Motivated Offender:** Offenders must be motivated to commit crime at the time contact is made with the person, place, or thing that they ultimately victimize. Psychologically speaking, would-be offenders are not constantly motivated to commit crime. Rather, their motivation for offending occurs in cycles of periods of high probability for criminal activity followed by emotional cooling off periods. For example, a substance abuser who burglarizes houses to obtain money for drugs will be less likely to offend after successful break-ins, when drugs and money are more plentiful.

- **Lack of Capable Guardianship:** The catalyst for motivated offenders to strike their attractive victim targets is the perceived opportunity to get away with the crime. This perception of criminal opportunity usually occurs in situations where the offender believes that there is a lack of capable guardianship. Guardianship for persons can include any means of self-defense (security guards, weapons, physical stature) and devices (cell phones, surveillance cameras, lighted structures, etc.). Gated properties, cars with alarms, or houses with security doors are examples of capable guardianship against property crimes.[44]

When applying LRA, note that most criminal victimizations occur when the three elements just described converge in time and space because of lifestyle and routine activity patterns common to both the victim and the offender. Past investigative applications of LRA reveal that it is during day-to-day lifestyle and routines activities—such as going to and from school, work, markets, and shopping areas—that victims and offenders are most likely to meet, and victimization is most likely to occur. Moreover, ALR assumes that the latter situation results because offenders also live in the same area as their victims and have routines that frequently cross paths with those travelled by victims. In the case of property crimes, victimized homes, cars, or businesses usually are located in areas well-travelled by offenders. Thus, for the investigator, discovery of victim lifestyles and routines through ALR often provides a mirror image of the offender from which numerous investigative leads can be drawn. The following list includes suggested LRA lines of questioning regarding crime victims:

- What are/were their specific lifestyle habits?
- Where were they employed and what did their job entail?
- How is their personality best described?
- How many friends did they have and how would you describe them?
- What were their spending habits? Did they live within or beyond their means?
- Were they drug or alcohol abusers?
- What was their normal type of dress?
- Did they have any physical handicaps?
- What types of transportation did they use?
- What was their reputation with others—their fears, their likes, their dislikes?

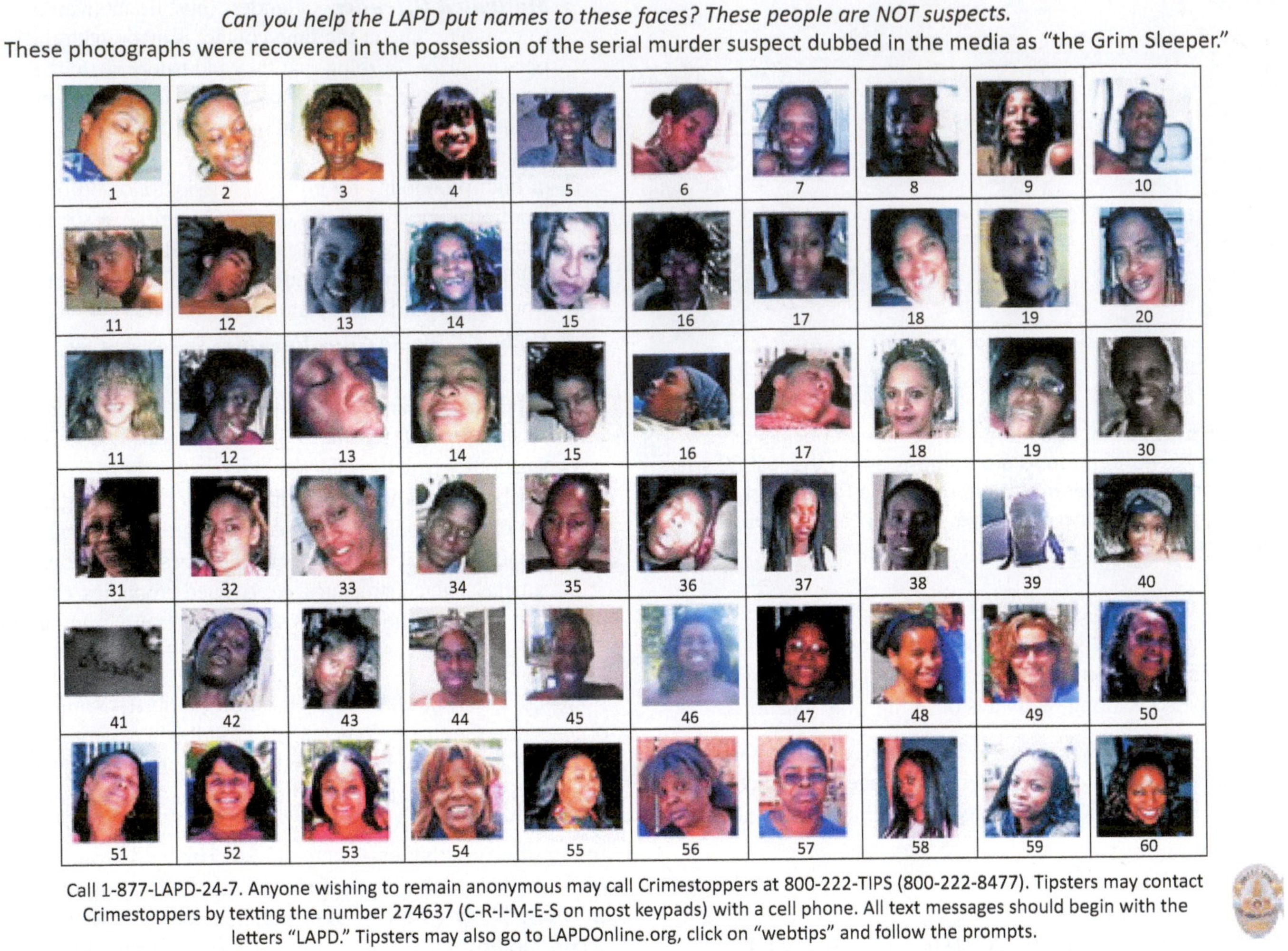
Can you help the LAPD put names to these faces? These people are NOT suspects.
These photographs were recovered in the possession of the serial murder suspect dubbed in the media as "the Grim Sleeper."
1 2 3 4 5 6 7 8 9 10
11 12 13 14 15 16 17 18 19 20
11 12 13 14 15 16 17 18 19 30
31 32 33 34 35 36 37 38 39 40
41 42 43 44 45 46 47 48 49 50
51 52 53 54 55 56 57 58 59 60
Call 1-877-LAPD-24-7. Anyone wishing to remain anonymous may call Crimestoppers at 800-222-TIPS (800-222-8477). Tipsters may contact Crimestoppers by texting the number 274637 (C-R-I-M-E-S on most keypads) with a cell phone. All text messages should begin with the letters "LAPD." Tipsters may also go to LAPDOnline.org, click on "webtips" and follow the prompts.

FIGURE 7.20 ▶ Faces of persons believed to be victims of "The Grim Sleeper" serial killer, released by the Los Angeles Police Department to the media to help provide investigative leads in the case. The Grim Sleeper is also perhaps the nation's most prolific serial killer, estimated to have murdered about 160 individuals over two decades. (Courtesy Los Angeles Police Department)

- What were their marital status/dating habits?
- What were their leisure activities?
- What were their activities immediately before the crime?[45]

In processing and analyzing information gathered from the above questions, investigators should search for victim's routines/activities involving regular travel patterns, places frequently visited, and day-to-day activities that would suggest criminal opportunity to would-be offenders. This information can help picture how the offender and victim met at the crime scene and perhaps guide investigators to the offender's routine physical or geographic zone of operation. This discovery, in turn, will enable proactive investigative efforts such as criminal records checks, surveillance, undercover operations, or the use of confidential informants in areas where a specific perpetrator most likely offended in the past or will offend in the near future.

PLANNING AND EXECUTING AN UNDERCOVER STING OPERATION

Case Example 7A shows photos (see Figures 7.21 to 7.25) of an auto repair establishment believed to be a front for various criminal activities, including fencing stolen property, money laundering, and the manufacturing/distribution of drugs. Due to the size, complexity, and sophistication of this illegal enterprise, a well-planned undercover investigation of the site and its occupants must be carried out before any suspects are arrested. The investigators in this case are being called upon to plan and carry out an undercover sting operation using all available intelligence gathering methods. The photos shown here, provided to the investigators by a confidential informant (CI), will be used to outline the investigative plan culminating in the execution of the sting operation.

CASE EXAMPLE 7A

Undercover Sting Operation

(a)

(b)

FIGURE 7.21 ▶ Exterior (a) and interior (b) views of the location targeted for an undercover investigation. A confidential informant (CI), who was a former employee at this auto repair facility, informed investigators that the shop was being used to conduct various illegal activities, including drug manufacturing and distribution, firearms smuggling, auto theft, fencing of stolen property and money laundering. Furthermore, the informant claimed the owners of the facility had ties to organized crime networks. Due to the size and complexity of this illegal operation, investigators decided to conduct an undercover sting operation at the site. How should investigators conduct reconnaissance and surveillance activities at this location to gather information and intelligence in preparation for the sting?

(a)

FIGURE 7.22 ▶ Interior views of the target location. What type of information should be gathered by an undercover operative at this scene to assist in preparation for a full scale sting?

(b)

FIGURE 7.22 ▶ (*Continued*) What types of databases or other crime information sources might be of use in developing intelligence on the shop owner, workers or other likely crime suspects at this location?

(a)

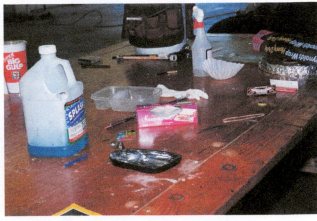

(b)

FIGURE 7.23 ▶ Mid-range (a) and close-up (b) views of a work table inside the auto shop. Can investigators perform electronic surveillance at this location? If so, what type would be most appropriate given the nature of the crime and the evidence available to investigators?

(a)

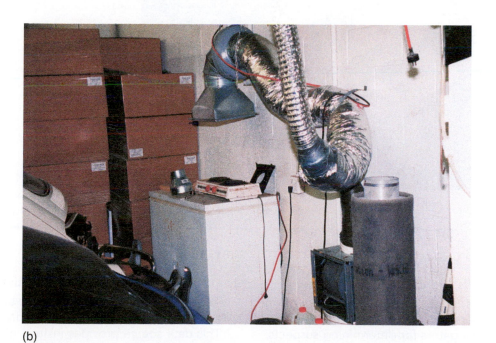

(b)

FIGURE 7.24 ▶ Mid-range (a) and close-up (b) views of objects behind dismantled vehicles. What type of sting operation would be most appropriate to conduct at this location, and have the least risk of having the undercover investigator's cover "blown."

(a)

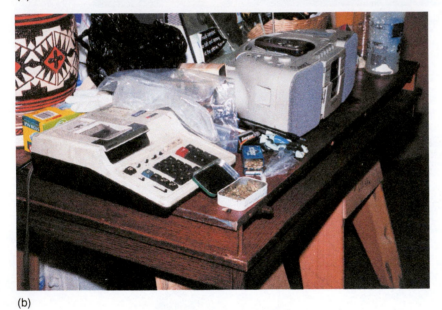

(b)

FIGURE 7.25 ▶ Mid-range (a) and close-up (b) views of objects located in the office area of the auto shop. After conducting the sting operation, and arresting suspects at the scene, what types of follow-up investigative activities could be conducted in this case? Which types of crime analysis and intelligence gathering methods would be most appropriate for investigators to use in order to discover how crimes and offenders at this location may be linked to those in other locations?

Summary

1. **Investigative leads and criminal intelligence.**

   Investigative leads consist of raw information obtained from persons, places, or things that may be of use to investigators for determining suspects, obtaining witnesses, gathering evidence, and investigating case related matters. Many investigative tools can be used to develop investigative leads, including the use of confidential informants, undercover operations, surveillance, and data record checks. Criminal intelligence consists of raw information processed through analytical methods into knowledge that can be used to focus investigative efforts on specific crime-related matters, including those of a clandestine high-level nature (involving organized crime or terrorism, for example).

2. **Databases used in the investigative process.**

   The most comprehensive database available to investigators is the NCIC database maintained by the FBI. This data source provides instant information to law enforcement queries regarding 19 criminal background factors (7 for persons; 12 for property). Other databases useful for investigative purposes include jail booking records, F. I. (field interview) cards, vehicle impound inventory records, and non–law-enforcement-related public or private records containing financial and personal background information.

3. **Surveillance methods.**

   There are many forms of surveillance. Static methods involve conducting observations of a target from a stationary location. Commonly referred as a *stakeout*, this form of surveillance is often carried out from a parked vehicle close to the target being observed. In rarer instances, it can also be done from buildings or other fixed locations with telescopic surveillance cameras and other specialized devices. Mobile surveillance can be done on foot and in vehicles. Usually, it is conducted by tailing a walking or driving target. Mobile surveillance is best conducted by coordinating the movement of three or more investigators who are on foot or in vehicles.

4. Photo and live lineups.

Lineups, in general, are used to make eyewitness identifications of potential suspects. They are just as important, however, for the exclusion of nonsuspects as for making positive identifications of suspects. Photo lineups are conducted by showing the witness seven or more photos, one of which is of the suspect. Live lineups, used less often, are performed by having the witness view at least five individuals, including one suspect. Photo and live lineups can be conducted either simultaneously (presenting all photos/individuals at once) or sequentially (presenting all photos/individuals one at a time).

5. The criminal intelligence function.

Most of the methods used to create criminal intelligence involve applying crime analysis techniques to raw information or data. Examples include *geoprofiling,* used to predict the physical zone of operation used by offenders; *linkage analysis,* allowing for the determination of crime and/or criminals somehow associated with each other; and *threat and vulnerability analysis,* which identifies potential crime targets, criminal opportunities, and crime prevention strategies.

6. Criminal profiling.

The primary objective of criminal profiling is to assist law enforcement in locating and apprehending individuals who have already committed an offense by creating a behavioral profile of the offender based on analysis of crime scene information. In FBI profiling methods, most offenders are profiled as either organized or disorganized criminal types. Organized offenders carry out crimes in a highly planned and organized fashion, leaving behind very little crime scene evidence. Alternatively, crime scenes created by disorganized offenders usually contain a wealth of physical evidence due to the crime being committed in an unplanned and chaotic manner. The criminal profile contains various background and lifestyle patterns characteristic of these offender types, who attempt to cope with or adapt to particular psychological disabilities and/or uncontrollable urges to commit crime.

Key Terms

investigative lead	pen/trap device	delusion
criminal intelligence	informant	hallucination
proactive investigation	undercover operative	*modus operandi*
threat assessment	sting operation	theme
follow-up investigation	lineup	signature
NCIC (National Crime Information Center)	tactical intelligence	trophy
	strategic intelligence	souvenir
surveillance	operative intelligence	evidential intelligence staging
operative	fusion center	undoing
target	geoprofiling	victimology
eye	crime pattern analysis	lifestyle/routine activity analysis (LRA)
surveillance plan	linkage analysis	
countersurveillance	event flow analysis	instrumental offenses
cover story	commodity flow analysis	serial offender
decoy	criminal profiling	intelligence cycle
convoy	organized offender	telephone toll analysis
wiretapping	disorganized offender	

Review Questions

1. What is the difference between an investigative lead and criminal intelligence?

2. How do proactive and reactive investigations differ? Give an example of each.

3. What is a follow-up investigation? Name the various steps taken to carry one out.

4. What type of information is contained in the NCIC database?

5. What type of information can be obtained from public and private databases to assist in criminal investigations?

6. What are the various methods by which surveillance can be conducted?

7. Name some of the terms used to identify the persons involved in a surveillance operation.

8. What are the various methods by which a sting operation can be carried out?

9. Name the various types of criminal intelligence.

10. What is meant by the term *countersurveillance*? Provide two examples of this method.

11. How can electronic eavesdropping be carried out? What are the legal concerns when conducting this type of investigation?

12. How are photo and live lineups carried out?

13. What are some of the crime analysis methods used to transform raw data into criminal intelligence? Give an example of how you would apply two of these methods to a real-life crime situation.

14. What is the basic technique used to carry out criminal profiling?

15. What are the key differences between organized and disorganized offenders?

16. Define the term *M.O. (modus operandi)*. Provide an example of a criminal M.O.

17. What is meant by the term *signature*? How does the signature differ from an M.O.?

18. What are some of the methods by which a crime scene can be altered?

19. What is meant by the term *victimology*?

20. How can lifestyle/routine activity analysis be applied to a criminal investigation?

Internet Resources

International Association of Crime Analysts (IACA)	www.iaca.net
International Association of Law Enforcement Intelligence Analysts (IALEIA)	www.ialeia.org
National Crime Information Center	www.fbi.gov/hq/cjisd/ncic.htm
International Crime Police Organization (INTERPOL)	www.interpol.int
Terrorism Research Center	www.terrorism.com
Justice Information Privacy Guideline	www.ncja.org/sites/default/files/documents/Justice-Information-Privacy-Guideline.pdf

Applied Investigative Exercise

Carefully examine the sequence of events, surroundings, and activities illustrated in Case Example 7A. Imagine that you are the lead investigator in this case and you must gather information to develop investigative leads and criminal intelligence. First, devise a plan outlining specific activities that you (and your co-investigators) would engage in to obtain potential leads in this case (hint, surveillance activities, informant development, undercover operations, etc.). Second, how could you transform the lead information into workable criminal intelligence? What crime analysis methods might you use? Provide examples.

Notes

[1] National Institute of Justice, *Threat Assessment: An Approach to Prevent Targeted Violence* (Washington, DC: National Institute of Justice, July 1995), 1–7.

[2] Jack R. Greene, *The Encyclopedia of Police Science* (Boca Raton, FL: CRC Press, 2007), 257–258.

[3] This section is based on the authors' practical experience in conducting follow-up investigation of violent, vice, and property crimes.

[4] Federal Bureau of Investigation, "NCIC Files," located at www.fbi.gov/about-us/cjis/ncic/ncic_files.

[5] Federal Bureau of Investigation, "National Crime Information Center," located at www.fbi.gov/about-us/cjis/ncic/ncic.

[6] U.S. Department of Justice, "U.S. National Central Bureau of INTERPOL," located at www.justice.gov/interpol-washington/index.html.

[7] This listing of information was drawn from several jail booking report databases, and in particular that for the Broward County, FL Sheriff's Office website located at bookingregister.sheriff.org.

[8]Owen Moritz, "Son of Sam: New York's Summer of Terror: 30 Years Later," New York Daily News, located at www.nydailynews.com/features/sonofsam/capture.html.

[9]Peter Jenkins, *Advanced Surveillance: The Complete Manual of Surveillance Training* (UK: Intel Publications, 2003), 25–58.

[10]Ibid., 67–123.

[11]Ibid., 145–151.

[12]Greg Hauser, *Techniques of Countersurveillance* (Boulder, CO: Paldin Press, 2003), 12–28.

[13]The Gun Zone, *An Unvarnished and Illustrated Forensic Examination of the FBI's Devastating Firefight in South Florida,* located at www.thegunzone.com/11april86.html.

[14]U.S. Department of Justice, *Search and Seizing Computers and Obtaining Electronic Evidence in Criminal Investigations* (Washington, DC: USDOJ, 2009), 166–170.

[15]Ibid., 159.

[16]Graeme R. Newman, *Sting Operations* (Washington, DC: USDOJ, 2007), 7.

[17]Ibid.

[18]Ibid., 11.

[19]Steven Sporer, "Eyewitness Identification Accuracy, Confidence, and Decision Times in Simultaneous and Sequential Lineups," *Journal of Applied Psychology, 78,* 22–33.

[20]U.S. Department of Justice, *Eyewitness Evidence: A Guide for Law Enforcement* (Washington, DC: USDOJ, 1999).

[21]*United States v. Ash,* 413, U.S. 300 (1973).

[22]U.S. Department of Justice, *Intelligence-Led Policing: The New Intelligence Architecture* (Washington, DC: 2005), 5.

[23]Ibid., 12–13.

[24]Ibid., 15–16.

[25]U.S. Department of Justice, *Fusion Center Guidelines: Developing and Sharing Intelligence in a New Era* (Washington, DC: USDOJ, 2006), 2.

[26]Ibid., 34.

[27]U.S. Department of Justice, *Intelligence-Led Policing,* 9.

[28]Kim Rossmo, *Geographic Profiling* (Boca Raton, FL: CRC Press, 2000).

[29]International Association of Law Enforcement Intelligence Analysts, Inc., *Successful Law Enforcement Using Analytic Methods* (Alexandria, VA: IALEIA, 1996), 3–4.

[30]Ibid., 5–6.

[31]Ibid., 7–8.

[32]Ibid., 9–11.

[33]Ibid., 12.

[34]John Douglas and Mark Olshaker, *Mindhunter: Inside the FBI's Elite Serial Crime Unit* (New York, NY: Scribner, 1995), 45–78.

[35]Ibid.

[36]John Douglas, Ann Burgess, Allen Burgess, and Robert Ressler, *Crime Classification Manual* (San Francisco, CA: Jossey-Bass, 1997), 260.

[37]Ibid., 261.

[38]Ibid., 262.

[39]Ibid., 263.

[40]Ibid., 251.

[41]Ibid., 355.

[42]Ibid., Appendix D.

[43]Federal Bureau of Investigation, *Highway Serial Killings: New Initiative on an Emerging Trend,* located at www.fbi.gov/news/stories/2009/april/highwayserial_040609.

[44]This method was constructed by the authors and is based on routine/activities theory; see Lawrence Cohen and Marcus Felson, "Social Change and Crime Rate Trends: A Routine Activity Approach," *American Sociological Review,* Vol. 44, 588–591.

[45]*Crime Classification Manual,* 12, with adaptations made by the authors.

CHAPTER EIGHT

INVESTIGATION AND THE FORENSIC SCIENCES

Learning Objectives

After completing this chapter, you should be able to:

1. Explain what is meant by the term *forensic sciences.*
2. Describe the role of the crime laboratory.
3. Describe the various sections making up a crime laboratory.
4. Describe how DNA analysis is used in criminal investigation.
5. Be familiar with types of forensic sciences used outside the crime lab.

Chapter Outline

INTRODUCTION

THROUGHOUT THE HISTORY OF FORENSIC science, most evidence testing procedures have been developed to help detect and prosecute offenders—and not to exclude the innocent. For example, during the late 1800s and early 1900s, questioned documents analyses were used to identify forgeries; toxicological tests became the primary means for determining murders committed by poisoning; and ballistics was used to link criminals with their weapons. Success stories of forensic science used as a prosecution tool soon led to the creation of local, state, and federal forensic laboratories working under the direct control of law enforcement agencies. Most forensic scientists within these facilities were police officers reassigned from patrol or other duties to work in the crime lab. Evidence was tested, results of scientific analyses were reported, and courtroom testimony on lab results was provided by police personnel without formal training or education in chemistry, biology, or any other science discipline.

Over time, individuals concerned with fair justice began to question the integrity and impartiality of evidence analyses prepared by crime labs staffed and managed by police. Specifically, concern arose regarding a possible conflict of interest between the police mission to prosecute offenders and that of the police crime lab—to test the evidence that the police collected. In the late 1990s, these issues were addressed by Frederic Whitehurst, Supervising Special Agent of the FBI Crime Laboratory. Specifically, Whitehurst publicly accused scientists within the FBI crime lab (mostly FBI agents assigned to lab testing duties) of intentionally misrepresenting forensic evidence analyses to help prosecutors convict persons arrested by local, state, and federal law enforcement agencies. Stories of crime lab corruption like that revealed by Whitehurst portray a not-too-distant past when investigators could approach lab technicians with mishandled crime scene evidence and suggestively ask, "Could you find proof from this evidence showing the suspect was present at the scene? You and I both know he's guilty, right?" Within hours or perhaps minutes, the investigator would receive a lab report declaring that hairs or fibers within the crime scene evidence were identical matches to the suspect's hair. Because of numerous scandals involving evidence misrepresentation and fabrication in both large and small police agencies, crime labs have increasingly been professionalized through external accreditation and hiring qualified scientists to perform testing procedures.

Even now, investigators are tempted to dismiss the new generation of highly trained forensic scientists as "eggheads" lacking knowledge of true police work when, after evidence is submitted for analysis, the lab report produced states ". . . the test results are inconclusive because there is not enough good evidence to complete the analysis procedure correctly." Investigators must appreciate, however, how they too have benefited from the great strides recently made in ensuring that crime labs examine evidence ethically and legally. Investigators also must understand the nature of specific forensic tests, their strengths, and their limitations—the goal of presenting specific information in this chapter. Forensic scientists must be permitted to conduct independent analyses of evidence, free from undue investigative influence and pressure to find evidence of guilt.

DEFINING FORENSIC SCIENCE

By definition, **forensic science** is the application of any science to the law.[1] Therefore, virtually any scientific undertaking, when applied to a legal issue, could be considered a forensic science. For a particular forensic science to be recognized by a court of law, however, it must pass a legal test. Depending on the jurisdiction in which the case is heard, the nature of this legal test may differ. In the United States there are two prominent tests or standards, or variations thereof, that all courts rely upon: the Frye test and the Daubert test.

Frye and Daubert Tests

Currently, most states operate under the **Frye test**, or a modified version of it, to determine whether a specific forensic science will be permitted in the courtroom and its resulting evidence heard by a jury. The original case upon which this test was created, *Frye v. U.S.* (1923),[2] involved the question of whether or not polygraph results showing that the defendant Frye, accused of robbery and murder, was innocent should be admitted as trial evidence. The trial judge ruled against admitting the polygraph results on the basis that such evidence had been validated only by experimental tests and was not the product of well-recognized scientific methods. This landmark case not only established the idea of judicial review for establishing a legally recognized forensic science, but also delineated the Frye test criteria—which are still used today; that is, for any science to be recognized by a court as a legitimate forensic science it must be generally accepted by a relevant scientific discipline. This is also known as the *general acceptance standard*.

More recently, as the result of a 1993 civil case, the rival **Daubert test** was created.[3] This test is followed by federal courts, but has been adopted by many state courts as a more stringent alternative to the Frye test. Under Daubert guidelines, for any given forensic science to be recognized as valid by the court it must be based on scientific evidence that (1) is testable, (2) is able to establish error rates, (3) has been peer reviewed and published in scientific journals, and (4) is generally accepted by experts who have training needed to evaluate the particular science in question. This test is often referred to as *scientific evidence standard*.

A specific forensic science that has an established legal track record in a particular court's jurisdiction generally will be recognized as legitimate and its results heard by a jury. Otherwise, special pretrial hearings will be conducted perhaps involving the introduction of expert testimony and published scientific evidence by the proponent (either defense or prosecution) of the new scientific method. The validity of results from new scientific methods is determined by the court in the judge's final ruling. Forensic sciences not passing either the Frye or Daubert tests will be excluded on the grounds that they are novel or, in terms used by harsher critics, are "junk" sciences.[4]

Although courts may consider a particular forensic test or method "junk" and disallow presentation of its results to a jury, investigators are permitted to use such legally inadmissible techniques. For example, polygraph results are generally barred from court proceedings, but they are used routinely during investigations as an interrogation tool. Moreover, a forensic science considered to be "junk" in one jurisdiction may be acceptable in others. For example, fingerprints and DNA are universally accepted as valid scientific evidence in all courts, while other established techniques such as ballistics, tool mark impressions, and blood spatter analysis are not. Also, even if a specific forensic method currently does not pass either a Frye or Daubert test, that does not mean that it will fail such tests in the future. Again, consider the polygraph. In its present form, with its current capabilities, it is not legally accepted as a valid evidentiary tool. Nevertheless, further refinements and testing of new polygraph devices may prove that the technique is worthy of being reclassified as a valid forensic science. Thus, under the law, what is not considered a forensic science today may be considered one tomorrow, and vice versa.[5]

Currently, 12 subdisciplines of forensic science are recognized by the National Institute of Justice, the research branch of the U.S. Department of Justice:

1. *General Toxicology:* The detection and identification of poisonous substances.
2. *Firearms/Tool Marks:* Identifying firearms and impressions made on surfaces by weapons, tools, and other objects.
3. *Questioned Documents:* Examining and restoring documentary evidence related to suspected criminal activity.
4. *Trace Evidence:* Identifying and examining hairs, fibers, paint, glass, and other evidence that is typically invisible to the unaided eye.
5. *Controlled Substances:* Analysis of drugs, including alcohol.
6. *Fire Debris/Arson:* Examining evidence from fires and explosions.
7. *Impression Evidence:* Examining prints left by the human body (finger/hand) and physical objects (footwear, tires).
8. *Biological/Serological Screening:* Analysis of blood and other bodily fluids.
9. *Blood Pattern Analysis:* Analysis of blood spatter.
10. *Crime Scene Investigation (CSI):* Examination/collection of physical evidence at crime scenes.
11. *Medico-Legal Death Investigation:* Autopsies and other postmortem investigative activities.
12. *Digital Evidence:* Analysis of evidence obtained from electronic devices/transmissions.[6]

FORENSIC SCIENTISTS

As previously mentioned in Chapter 1, the scientific analysis of physical evidence is carried out by either forensic scientists or criminalists. As a matter of definition, distinctions can be drawn between the titles *forensic scientist* and *criminalist*; in practice, however, these titles are used rather inter-changeably as a matter of personal preference and generally refer to individuals who perform similar duties. (Therefore, in this chapter, the terms *forensic science/scientist* will be used to represent *criminalistics/criminalist* as well.) Although many forensic scientists in crime labs perform analyses of crime scene evidence, some work as independent consultants performing specialized examinations for both defense and prosecution. Preparing reports of test outcomes and presenting the results of analyses as an expert witness in court proceedings are also common duties of the forensic scientist. Practitioners of forensic science often differ greatly in their training and experience. For example, some forensic scientists are highly trained (e.g., medical doctors, PhDs) and professionally certified in their specific area of expertise. Alternatively, other persons conducting forensic science analyses have received only on-the-job-training and have no formal training or certification.

Physical evidence usually is tested in the controlled environment of a crime lab, although forensic scientists sometimes examine physical evidence in various settings outside the crime lab. Most forensic scientists (60 percent or more) working for U.S. crime labs, however, do not collect evidence at crime scenes; rather, such duties are left to specialized technicians and officers trained in evidence collection methods. When specialized testing is required, university or industrial laboratories may be used—as when examining skeletal remains (see Case Close-up 8.2, The Body Farm). If a medical issue is relevant to a case outcome, forensic science in the form of an autopsy will take place in a medical examiner's or coroner's office. Although most forensic scientists work in public agencies, many are employed by private labs to conduct specialized analyses. Private

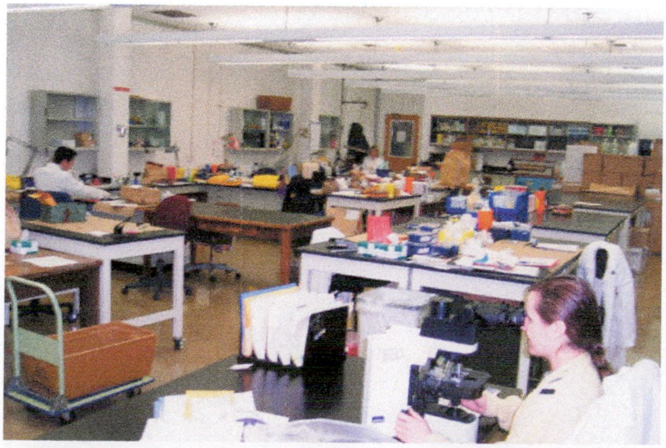

FIGURE 8.1 ▶ The evidence lay-out room of a typical crime lab. In this location, the first examinations of suspected evidence are performed to determine its quality and to assess the need for additional, more specialized testing.

FIGURE 8.2 ▶ State-of-the art technology used to extract DNA samples from oral swabs and various other DNA sources. This testing device also includes sophisticated robotics for sterile, controlled movement of the DNA specimens.

laboratories also are used to support investigative efforts, especially when there is a backlog of DNA analyses in police crime labs. An example is Cellmark, which contracts with local, state, and federal law enforcement agencies to conduct thousands of DNA tests each year. Also, defense teams hire forensic scientists working in private labs to perform DNA, toxicology, ballistics, and many other analyses to impeach findings from crime labs testing evidence for the prosecution.[7]

CRIME LABS

Currently, nearly 400 publicly organized and funded crime labs operate in the United States. About half of these facilities operate at the state or regional level, with the other half being run as federal, county, or city facilities. In all, the nation's crime labs receive and process evidence for nearly 3 million cases each year and employ about 12,000 individuals. The largest crime labs, usually at the federal and state levels, have state-of-the-art equipment and employ hundreds of technicians and forensic scientists. The average-size crime lab, however, has a staff of about 20 scientists and is located within a law enforcement agency. At the other end of the spectrum are the smallest municipal police agencies without crime labs, which must send forensic evidence to federal or regional laboratories for analysis. Nearly all crime labs, regardless of size, can perform controlled substance analyses. DNA, fingerprints, and trace evidence analyses are performed by about 50 to 60 percent of existing labs. Less than 20 percent of labs can perform questioned documents or computer/digital evidence examinations.[8]

Examination and Testing Procedures

The primary goals of all crime labs are (1) to identify physical evidence and (2) to determine its origin. The procedures used to carry out these goals usually involve the following:

1. Searching for and locating the evidence to be analyzed; for example, striations on a bullet or a blood stain on clothing. Some labs have a specialized location known as an "evidence lay-out" room where the evidence search begins.

2. Performing a presumptive test: A preliminary test is performed on the evidence item to determine its identity. For example, a chemical that provides a color reaction to a narcotics may be placed on a substance believed to be an illegal drug. Such tests are called *presumptive* because they may react positively to substances other than those for which the test is specifically being conducted.

3. Performing a confirmatory test: Usually a higher-level specialized test, such as DNA (for example, see Figure 8.2), is applied to the evidence in question and provides results indicating the exact nature and perhaps the origin of the evidence being tested.

4. Reporting the results: Test results are documented in a lab report that is used for investigative and legal purposes.

Case Example 8A (see Figures 8.3 to 8.9) shows a typical laboratory testing sequence involving presumptive and confirmatory testing in a sexual assault case.

CASE EXAMPLE 8A

Laboratory Test for Semen in Sexual Assault Case

FIGURE 8.3 ▶ Clothing evidence obtained from a sexual assault victim is inspected for semen stains under UV light.

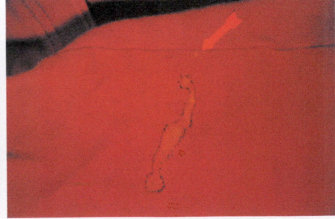

FIGURE 8.4 ▶ A fluorescing stain, possibly caused by semen, is observed and marked.

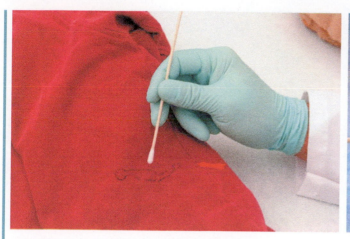

FIGURE 8.5 ▶ A sample of the stained area is swabbed in preparation for a presumptive test for semen.

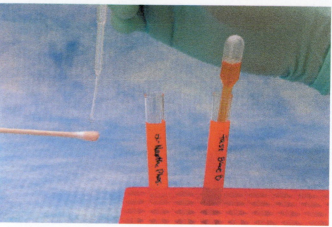

FIGURE 8.6 ▶ An acid phosphate test is conducted, which shows a color reaction for the likely presence of semen.

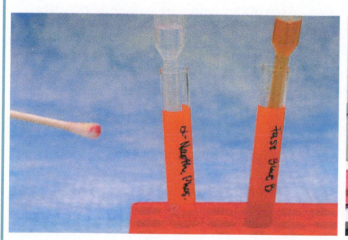

FIGURE 8.7 ▶ The swab's reddish color indicates a positive test reaction for semen.

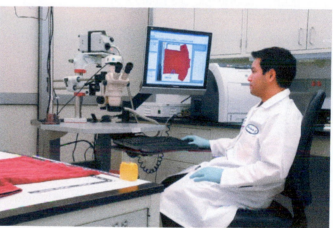

FIGURE 8.8 ▶ The presumptive test results are documented by computer in digital form.

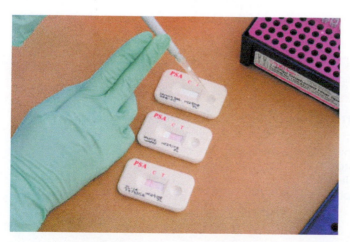

FIGURE 8.9 ▶ A confirmatory P-30 test is conducted to verify the presence of semen. The test detects PSA (Prostate Specific Antigen), which is contained in semen. Positive tests will show red bands under the "C" and "T" areas of the test cassette within 10 to 20 minutes if semen is present. As the investigator in this case, could you suggest other tests that the crime lab might perform on the victim's clothing to (1) provide further evidence in support of identifying the suspect, (2) search for additional evidence to support the charge of sexual assault and (3) discover additional crimes committed against the victim.

Tests/Analytical Methods

The following list, by no means exhaustive, describes some of the tests/analytical methods used most frequently in crime labs to examine physical evidence. These techniques, as well as many others not listed, can be used for both presumptive and confirmatory tests. In addition, some of these methods are extremely versatile and can be used to test various types of physical evidence (as will be noted in the following section, Laboratory Sections).

1. *Microscopic Analysis:* Various microscopes differing in magnification and lighting capacities are used to identify, sort, classify, and perhaps individualize evidence items. Depending on the particular application, microscopic analysis can provide either presumptive or confirmatory test results.

2. *Color Tests:* Chemical reagents are applied to suspected evidence items and provide results by changing color. Most color tests are presumptive in nature (for example, see Figure 8.10).

3. *Chromatography:* Used for various purposes, this technique targets a particular substance of interest and separates it out from other substances with which it is combined. For example, a specific drug can be isolated and separated from a blood or urine sample. Various types of chromatography—gas, liquid, thin-layer, and high-performance liquid—are used to isolate physical properties of evidentiary importance in liquids, gases, and solids. The most common is gas chromatography (referred to as *GC*). For numerous substances, this testing method can provide confirmatory results.

4. *Mass Spectrometry:* This technique is primarily used together with gas chromatography—a procedure referred to as *GC-MS*. After a substance is isolated with GC, spectrometry then identifies it by creating a *mass spectrum*—a graphic display representing the molecular structures in the substance being tested. A computerized database containing the molecular structures of all known compounds is then searched for a match to the newly identified substance. Other

FIGURE 8.10 ▶ A color test for the presence of gunshot residue being conducted in the crime lab's assessioning room, where evidence is first taken to determine whether it has qualities or characteristics of an illegal nature.

forms of spectrometry are available for examining specific types of substances: *infrared spectrometry (IS)* for inorganic chemicals and substances—most often used as a breath test method for determining blood alcohol levels; *visible spectrometry (VS)* for identifying and examining coloring agents; and *atomic absorption spectrometry (AAS),* which can be used to identify metals, hazardous waste, and other solid compounds. All methods of spectrometry can be used as confirmatory tests for the particular physical evidence items to which they are correctly applied.

5. *Biological Tests:* Certain biological agents and properties can be tested for in physical evidence. For example, bodily fluids can be identified by testing for the presence of certain proteins and enzymes. Immunoassay techniques bind antibodies found in blood and other bodily fluids with certain drugs for purposes of identification. Of course, biological matter containing DNA can be used to create human genetic fingerprints. Many, but not all, biological tests can be used to produce confirmatory results.[9]

HOT TIPS AND LEADS 8.1

Federal Crime Labs and the FBI Crime Laboratory

The FBI Crime Laboratory, established in 1932, is the nation's largest forensic testing and analysis center. Approximately 700 persons, both civilians and special agents, staff the lab. The following specific forensic examination sections comprise the lab:

chemistry

cryptanalysis and racketeering records

DNA analysis

explosives

evidence response

firearms-tool marks

hazardous materials

investigative and prosecutive graphics

(continued)

latent prints

photographic operations and imaging services

questioned documents

structural design

trace evidence

specialty units

The lab handles case evidence referrals from the FBI and all other federal, state, and local law enforcement agencies requesting forensic analysis assistance. It also maintains the world's largest criminal databases and is a repository for the most comprehensive crime evidence reference file libraries. Databases include IAFIS, CODIS, Expert Reference Tools database (EXPeRT), and the National Automotive Paint File. Reference libraries include the Explosives Reference File, with information on thousands of explosive materials and manufacturers of explosives and incendiary devices; the Reference Firearms Collection, including some 5,500 handguns and shoulder firearms; and the Standard Ammunition File, containing 15,000 types of ammunition produced by domestic and foreign manufacturers.[10]

Other Federal Crime Labs

U.S. Secret Service Forensic Services: Now a division of the Department of Homeland Security, the Secret Service maintains a full-service crime lab assisting federal, state, and local law enforcement agencies. The lab maintains the world's largest forensic ink collection and library to assist in counterfeit detection and other cases requiring questioned documents analysis—one of the lab's forensic specialty areas. As a result of the Amber Alert Bill authorized in 1993, the lab also serves as the nation's center for forensic assistance in investigations involving missing and/or exploited children.

Bureau of Alcohol, Tobacco, Firearms & Explosives Laboratories: Part of the Department of Justice, the ATF maintains four regional laboratories through the United States. The central ATF lab facility, located in Maryland, houses NIBIN as well as a specialized fire testing facility used to support fire investigations. The ATF also maintains mobile crime lab capabilities, enabling on-site evidence collection at fire and explosion sites.

Department of Defense Forensic Laboratory: The DOD forensic laboratory conducts traditional crime scene evidence analyses, primarily in support of military-related criminal matter, but also to support intelligence and counterintelligence casework. Specialized functions of the lab include the identification and sampling of DNA and fingerprints from military personnel as well as known and suspected terrorists. The lab also coordinates training and forensic testing conducted in all branches of the military.

National Bioforensic Analysis Center: Supports the FBI in the analysis of biological materials and biotoxins, many of which could be related to terrorist activities and other homeland security issues.

National Counterproliferation Center: Conducts research for the development, assessment, and validation of methods related to microbial forensics, a new area of biological analysis created to support intelligence and counterintelligence efforts concerned with biological warfare and bioterrorism.[11]

CRIME LAB SECTIONS

Full service crime labs, most of which are medium to large in size, usually are divided into sections that analyze specific types of physical evidence. The following sections are typical.

Toxicology

Toxicology sections are concerned with the various effects, both physical and behavioral, that poisons have on the body. Toxicologists usually are persons with advanced education in a science such as chemistry or biology, or they may be trained physicians. Professional standards and certification for the practice of forensic toxicology are established by the American Board of Forensic Toxicology. Toxicological examinations on dead persons are primarily performed in conjunction with autopsies and involve the detection and analysis of poisons in tissues and bodily fluids sent to the crime lab from the medical examiner's or coroner's office. These poisons include pesticides, prescription drugs, industrial chemicals, organic compounds, poisonous gases, illegal drugs, and alcohol. On living persons, toxicological tests for drugs and alcohol are routinely performed to prove or disprove the contributing effects of mind-altering substances during criminal activities or automobile accidents. Testing in support of DUI cases is one of the most common functions performed in the toxicology lab. Because of its drug and alcohol testing responsibilities, the toxicology section routinely performs more forensic examinations than all other laboratory sections—with the exception of the one that handles fingerprint analysis.[12]

If poisoning is suspected, the most valuable information that an investigator can provide to the toxicological lab is the type of poison that an individual is believed to have ingested. In such instances, the toxicology exam is rather straightforward—a direct test for the specific poison type. When such information is not available, toxicologists must test for a variety of possible poisonous agents. The most common poisonings often are either accidental or suicidal. Children who are the victims of accidental poisoning usually consume household cleaning products, detergents, weed killers, pesticides, or prescription drugs at home. Adults, on the other hand, usually experience accidental poisonings from drugs and/or alcohol overdoses. The most common types of drugs tested for in these situations are cocaine, heroin, or other morphine derivatives. Accidental death by alcohol poisoning is not commonly discovered in toxicological examinations because unconsciousness normally precedes consumption of a lethal quantity; the combined use of alcohol and prescription drugs, however, is a common cause of accidental death encountered by toxicologists today.

Although many suicides by poison are attempted or committed by inhaling carbon monoxide from automobile exhaust or by intentionally consuming products containing cyanide, arsenic, or commercial poisons, most suicides result from overdosing on prescription medications such as depressants and sleep aids. Suicides usually involve consumption of multiple drugs at the same time, so toxicologists must test suicide victims for the number of drugs as well as the quantity taken. Abnormal quantities of various prescription medications suggest suicide because such lethal combinations of drugs certainly could not be taken accidentally. Homicidal poisonings (see Chapter 9 for more detail) are rare. These are difficult to detect through toxicological analyses when little or no information is available regarding the likely poison used to commit the murder and how it was administered.[13]

Because poisons break down rapidly in the body after ingestion, evidence of suspected poisonings should be submitted to the toxicology lab as soon as possible. Color tests can be used to detect certain poisons. GC-MS analysis is used in most cases to make a positive confirmatory identification of a particular substance. Limitations of this testing method include the inability to detect alcohol use as well as the quantity of illegal drug use. Additionally, drug and alcohol identification tests must be performed on wet blood samples. The following are other means of detecting the presence of poisons, including drugs and/or alcohol:

- Analysis of breath, urine, perspiration, and other bodily fluids
- Testing of gastrointestinal contents for agents taken orally
- Examination of well-preserved tissue samples taken from the kidneys and liver for toxic agents taken orally; the brain, for psychoactive agents; the lungs, for inhaled or smoked agents; and the skin in and around injection points, for agents administered by hypodermic needles
- Analysis of hair and nail clippings for *metabolites,* which are deposited after certain toxins are ingested. This method can be employed to detect illicit drug use when wet blood, tissue, or other testing methods cannot be used. Cocaine, methamphetamines, opiates, marijuana, and PCP are detectable in all body hairs, fingernails, and toe nails approximately 5 days or more after use—as are certain poisons, including cyanide and arsenic.

As shown in Figure 8.11, drug identification is another major function of the toxicology lab. Whether the evidence is a minute quantity or a massive amount of drugs, all suspected illicit substances must be identified, weighed, and analyzed for chemical composition, strength, and purity. These lab results help determine how to charge a suspect for possessing, manufacturing, or trafficking drugs. This is because most of today's drug laws specify punishments based on the type as well as the amount and purity of the drug possessed.[14]

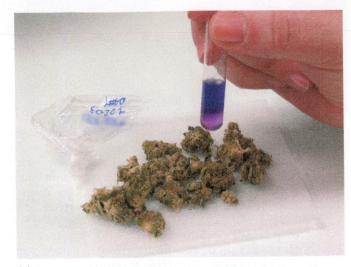

(a)

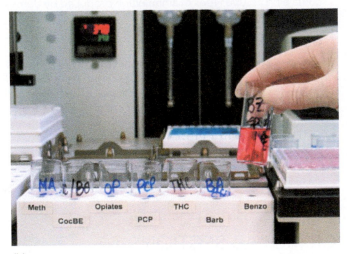

(b)

FIGURE 8.11 ▶ (a) Color tests used for marijuana identification and (b) the identification of drug traces in urine (testing positive for benzodiazephines, or "BENZO," commonly found in rohypnol "roofies" and other illegal or prescription sedatives).

Fingerprint Identification

The fingerprint identification section is probably the busiest section of any forensic laboratory. Forensic examiners working in this section may be civilians trained in fingerprint analysis or sworn officers who perform lab duties as well as field investigations. There are no set standards of training or experience for being a fingerprint examiner. Some individuals may receive as little as a week's training before performing fingerprint lab work. The most comprehensive training in fingerprint analysis is administered by the FBI crime lab, where potential examiners must undergo 2 years of formal training and an apprenticeship. The largest crime labs also may have a separate unit

FIGURE 8.12 ▶ A latent fingerprint is digitized for input into AFIS and IAFIS databases for a search against known offenders.

dedicated solely to the examination of latent print evidence as shown in Figure 8.12—often called an *LPU* (Latent Fingerprint Unit).

Hand processing of fingerprints has given way to automated fingerprint databases for purposes of identification. **AFIS** (Automated Fingerprint Identification System) was initiated in the 1970s by the FBI as the nation's first computerized fingerprint database with search capabilities. Today, AFIS systems have been created by and are housed in various local and state police agencies. Many of these systems are stand-alone databases that contain prints of local and regional felons only. Larger national fingerprint searches must be conducted on the FBI's **IAFIS** (Integrated Automated Fingerprint Identification System), which replaced the older AFIS system in 1999.[15]

Most AFIS searches begin by inputting digitized fingerprint information into the system, which can be either complete 10-print sets or single full or partial prints. Live scan terminals can be used to instantly upload a digital print image to the system, or print images obtained from photos, ink rolls, and other graphic sources can be digitized before uploading to the system.

After a print is entered into AFIS, it is assigned a mathematical code based on the computer's evaluation of identification points contained in the print. Usually, the computer scans for the number and locations of ridge endings and bifurcations in the prints. Operators of the AFIS system can control various functions relating to the sensitivity of the search, known as *search thresholds*. For example, the type, location, and number of identification points evaluated can be selected; poor-quality prints can be computer enhanced; and the number of likely print matches or hits returned by the system can be increased or decreased depending on the degree of detail desired to conduct the search. In most cases, examiners will request the return of a top-three candidate's prints. The term *candidate* refers to prints determined by the system to be most like those submitted as reference samples.[16]

Most print searches begin with runs against arrestees and convicted offenders at the local level, and then proceed to the state and national levels, if necessary. Depending on the particular jurisdiction, AFIS files may contain additional information in the form of palm prints, missing persons prints, prints from unsolved crimes, and prints of gang members and juvenile arrestees. Full 10-print runs and latent print runs can be executed, depending on print evidence available. For partial or incomplete prints, the AFIS operator can restrict the search to ridge characteristics located within the clearest and best defined areas of the print evidence. AFIS can also be used to run prints for the identification of dead persons or bodies damaged by extreme decomposition, burning, natural disasters, or terrorist activities. AFIS runs can return results in minutes or hours depending on the particular system's capabilities and traffic flow.

If local and state AFIS searches fail to provide a suitable candidate list, a national search (which also contains some international print data) can be executed through the F.B.I.'s Criminal Justice Information Services Division (CJIS), which maintains the IAFIS system—the world's largest and most comprehensive fingerprint database. It maintains palm print search capabilities as well. IAFIS houses nearly 70 million fingerprints in its criminal database, including prints collected from arrestees, convicted felons, and crime scenes of unsolved cases. It also contains some 25 million civil prints, largely those of U.S. government workers and military personnel. Also included are nearly 100,000 prints obtained from known or suspected terrorists. Along with fingerprint search capabilities, the IAFIS system contains criminal histories, mug shots, and information regarding each candidate's identifying marks such as scars and tattoos, height, weight, eye/hair color, and aliases. All data contained in the IAFIS database is submitted voluntarily by law enforcement agencies and is uploaded through electronic submissions of digitized print information—usually captured at the booking stage through live scan terminals. The IAFIS system is usually a stand-alone terminal that must be accessed independently of local and regional AFIS systems.[17]

Before a latent print match identified by an automated search is presented as evidence, the fingerprint examiner must visually examine the computer-generated points of identification to confirm that each point identified by the software is accurate. Most examiners use the **ACE-V** method to perform this task. This involves first performing an *analysis* ("A") of the print for general characteristics such as size, condition, and amount of usable print area. No further analysis will be performed after this stage for prints deemed to have an insufficient amount of detail. In the second stage ("C"), the examiner *compares* the latent print to the known one based on a visual inspection of identification points. Next, the examiner *evaluates* ("E") the print as (1) an identification, or a positive match; (2) an exclusion, or a negative match; or (3) an inconclusive, where not enough information is present for either a positive or a negative determination. Although other countries have specific criteria governing the number of points required for a positive match (for example, Australia requires 16 points; South Africa

FIGURE 8.13 ▶ Impressions examinations are often performed by lab sections that conduct fingerprint analyses as well. In this picture, random individualized wear patterns are labeled on a photograph of tire tread impressions taken at a crime scene.

requires 7), the United States does not specify a minimum number of points for fingerprint identification. The final step, *verification* ("V"), involves a second fingerprint examiner repeating the ACE-V process for the print to discover if a similar evaluation is determined.[18]

Personnel with the fingerprint lab section may also examine shoe and tire impressions, although large labs commonly have a separate impressions evidence section (for example, see Figure 8.13). The primary goal of scientists in these procedures is to determine the specific source of the impression evidence. The first step in the examination process is to determine the class characteristics of the evidence. Specific sizes, model lines, styles, and perhaps unique manufacturing details may be observed to determine when, where, and by whom a product was made or purchased. Second, the impression evidence is examined for individual characteristics. These include random or accidental wear patterns of tire treads and the outsoles of shoes.

Serology

The **serology** lab section analyzes blood stains and performs blood testing. It also performs examinations of bodily fluids such as semen, sweat, and saliva. DNA testing (discussed later in this section) is also routinely carried out by the serology section, although larger labs generally have a separate DNA section with scientists specifically trained in and dedicated to DNA testing techniques. Persons performing blood and bodily fluid analyses usually are trained in the biological sciences.

After blood evidence is brought from the crime scene to the laboratory, a presumptive test is performed. As previously discussed in Chapter 4, many testing agents are available to determine whether a substance or stain is indeed blood (Kastle-Meyer, Luminal, Leuco Crystal Violet, to name a few). These tests, however, do not distinguish human blood from that of other species. If a positive result is obtained from the presumptive test, confirmatory tests are administered to verify that the substance is blood and that it is of human origin. DNA testing will be performed if the blood sample contains enough usable genetic material. Otherwise, other less discriminatory tests can be performed. For example, an immunological test for human hemoglobin, called a *precipitin test,* can identify specific proteins contained only in human blood. In addition, ABO classification tests can be performed, which class the blood into one of four categories:

- **"O":** Comprising 45 percent of the U.S. population, and most common among persons of Native American or Latin descent;
- **"A":** Comprising 40 percent of the U.S. population, and most common among persons of Caucasians and European descent;
- **"B":** Comprising 11 percent of the U.S. population, and most common among persons of African-American descent;
- **"AB":** Comprising 4 percent of the U.S. population, and most common among persons of Asian descent.

Tests may be performed on bodily fluids as well to determine ABO blood types. This is because approximately 80 percent of all persons (known as *secretors*) secrete antigens and antibodies, enabling blood type to be determined from bodily fluids such as semen, sweat, saliva, urine, and vaginal fluid. Use of ABO classification testing for blood, however, has largely been replaced by DNA tests, which provide much more detailed results. Although ABO classification cannot be used to identify a specific individual, it nonetheless can exclude suspects who possess blood types different from those found on crime scene evidence.

Specific tests are also available to detect the presence of semen and saliva. The search for these and other bodily fluid stains initially can be carried out with ALS techniques. Both semen and saliva have luminescent visual qualities when subjected to UV and other ALS illumination. If sperm are still present, simple microscopic analysis can confirm the presence of semen. The PSA or p30 tests are mostly used to detect semen stains containing no sperm (because of sample degradation or a vasectomy). These tests provide a positive result by turning red after exposure to certain proteins and antigens contained in semen samples—wet or dried—on surfaces such as cloth, leather, carpet, and even skin. Similarly, saliva can be detected using a chemical test for amylase, an enzyme found in high concentration in saliva. Amylase is found in other types of tissue and feces, however, so the test is not considered confirmatory.[19]

CASE CLOSE-UP 8.1

"SWAPPING SPIT"
Grenada

A man was charged with attempted fraud during an investigation when he tried to fool forensic scientists by swapping spit during a saliva test for his DNA. After the first swab of saliva was obtained from the man's mouth, test results indicated the presence of two different DNA profiles. Because such a finding is practically impossible (although rarely persons can have two distinct genetic fingerprints—a condition known as *chimera*), a second DNA test was administered. The results of the second test, performed after the man washed his mouth out with water, revealed only a single DNA profile. When the man was confronted with the prospect of serious fraud charges for tampering with the forensic testing process, he confessed that he carried a small container of someone else's saliva to the exam and placed the contents in his mouth before the DNA test was administered.

Arson and Explosives

Lab sections that handle fire and explosives evidence examine (1) materials/objects burnt by fire or destroyed in explosions; control samples of materials/objects near, but unaffected by, fires and explosions; samples of flammable or explosive agents discovered at the crime scene, which may include liquids, powders, and slurries (i.e., liquid/solid mixtures); ignition or other devices associated with causing a fire or explosion; and clothing, shoes, and other personal items of persons suspected of setting a fire or causing an explosion. The primary goal of the arson and explosives lab section is to identify the particular material used to start a fire or explosion. Persons working in this section are among the most highly trained in chemistry and other physical sciences.

As expected, the analysis of explosives can be highly hazardous. Labs will not accept explosives crime scene evidence until it has been rendered safe to handle. Generally speaking, two types of examinations are performed on explosive materials: (1) preblast analyses, involving intact explosive materials; and (2) postblast analyses, involving fragments of intact explosive materials or explosive residue contained on materials affected by a blast. Both of these analytical procedures are concerned with identifying the components and construction of the explosive device as well as the explosive materials the device contained.

Preblast testing begins with a visual and microscopic examination of the device and/or explosive materials recovered from the crime scene. Before this initial evaluation stage, however, bomb squads or other experts may be called in to defuse a device before it is submitted for lab analysis. Likewise, raw explosive materials must be identified and rendered safe before submission to the lab. Following visual examination, the explosive agent may be subjected to a burn test. In effect, these tests allow forensic scientists to study the agent's explosive qualities when subjected to ignition by heat. The final analytic stage involves using sophisticated analytical methods (GC-MS, among others) to determine the explosive's molecular structure so that it can be compared to reference samples of known explosive agents. Postblast lab examinations are carried out in a similar fashion if unexploded materials can be discovered at the crime scene. If such evidence is unavailable, explosive residues must be extracted from materials on which they have been deposited before the examination begins. Final reports of results from an explosives analysis are summarized as one of the following:

- The explosives evidence is consistent with an explosive material, which is the highest level of identification.
- The explosives evidence is indicative of an explosive material, which suggests a moderate level of identification.
- The explosives evidence contains no explosive residue, indicating a negative finding.[20]

Lab exams for suspected arson fires focus primarily on identifying accelerants—whether discovered intact at the crime scene, or in the possession of a suspect, or within burned materials. Charred wood, burnt carpet, furniture, vehicle remains, and other materials collected from a fire scene are examined for the presence of volatile liquids, gases, or solids. Objects used to ignite a blaze—such as matches, cigarettes, streamers, and timing devices—also are examined. The GC-MS technique usually is used to identify flammable agents and residues located at the fire's point of origin. Common accelerants such as gasoline, kerosene, turpentine, and diesel are easily identified by this analytical method.

Because some established methods of visually identifying arson fires (e.g., cement spalling, wood alligatoring, furniture/mattress coil melting points, etc.) recently have been called into question, arson lab sections have conducted experiments to prove that accelerants were used to start a fire. This technique involves starting a fire on materials similar to those discovered at a suspected arson fire with an accelerant identified on physical evidence by lab analyses. This experimental fire evidence is then compared to control evidence, which consists of the same material burnt by igniting it without an accelerant. This not only allows comparisons between the experimental and control burns, but also enables investigators to show how burn patterns on fire scene evidence resemble those reproduced by the lab in the experimental burn.[21]

Firearms and Tool Marks

This lab section performs examinations to determine class and individual characteristics of tools and firearms. As previously discussed in Chapter 4, chemical color reagents can be applied to gunpowder and primer residues as a presumptive test, and SEM (scanning electron microscope) examination can be used as a confirmatory test for the presence of gunpowder molecules on clothing, automobile interiors, suspects' hands, or other surfaces that have been exposed to gunfire. The laboratory testing procedures for firearms and tool marks are quite similar. First, physical examinations are performed on the evidence to determine class characteristics. For example, a gun is classed by type, manufacturer, caliber, and so forth. The gun may also be test-fired to obtain known comparison samples and it may also be examined for a hair trigger or other operational quirks or insufficiencies that lead to accidental discharge. Tools, such as screwdrivers, can be classed on the basis of blade width, size, thickness, and length. Subclass characteristics—unique features possessed by a smaller subgroup of firearms or tools that usually result from a manufacturing error—also can be identified. Niches, gouges, or other uniform imperfections in the surface area of tool blades or gun frames are often recognized as subclass characteristics.[22]

Following class determination, both firearms and tools are examined microscopically for individual characteristics. This is usually done by comparing unknown samples recovered from crime scenes with known samples created from recovered guns or tools. Sample comparisons generally are carried out by using a comparison microscope to visually compare known and unknown samples for unique markings and wear patterns. These microscopes allow the examiner to view each piece of evidence at the same time and to superimpose the images to determine matching striations or other unique individualizing features. Individual characteristics in tool blades—including those made by knifes, screwdrivers, wire cutters, pliers, and bolt cutters—can be tested for by applying the tool's blade or cutting surface to a soft lead surface. The lead impressions can then be compared with tool marks from evidence or casts of impressions taken from the crime scene.

One investigative capability often used by the firearms and tool marks section is evidence analysis through the **NIBIN** (National Integrated Ballistic Information Network) system operated by the ATF. NIBIN is the world's most comprehensive database for the identification of firearms and their tool marks. It was created in 1999 by merging the FBI's ballistics database, Drugfire (which contained only cartridge case information), with a similar database, IBIS (Integrated Ballistic Information Network) which contained only bullet information), maintained by the ATF. The system works by providing computerized matches between digital photographs of tool marks on cartridge cases and striations on bullets fired from firearms suspected to have been involved in criminal activities.

Matches or hits can be made with guns that have been confiscated from known offenders, discovered at scenes of unsolved crimes, or recovered by police through investigative or other means. Numerous bullets and cases can be compared at the same time and hits can be cross-referenced to different guns and crime locations. The top candidates or likely matches between submitted photos and those within the database are generated and then analyzed microscopically for similarities by a firearms/tool mark examiner. As with fingerprints and impression evidence, there are no set standards for how many shared characteristics between two samples must be found to declare an identification of a bullet or cartridge casing. Executing a run in the NIBIN system can take minutes or hours depending on the amount of information submitted and the amount of system traffic (weekend nights are among the heaviest usage times).[23]

Newer versions of NIBIN software produce 3-D comparisons of surface images and measure the depth of striations and other marks. Thus far, over 1,500,000 pieces of evidence have been entered into the NIBIN system and approximately 35,000 hits have been obtained by law enforcement agencies using the system to make firearms identifications. BrassTRAX, a new software application made available by ATF, now permits partner agencies to access NIBIN through portable computer applications. NIBIN is currently expanding its network to include many countries outside the United States including Canada, France, and Thailand.[24] Case Example 8B (see Figures 8.14 to 8.18) shows the typical process used to perform a ballistics examination of firearms evidence using the NIBIN system.

Trace Evidence

Hairs, fibers, glass fragments, paint chips, and other materials in minute sizes are typically analyzed in the trace evidence section. The specific identifying aspects of common trace evidence found at crime scenes are outlined in Chapter 4. It should be reiterated, however, that many trace evidence examinations are living proof of Locard's exchange principle—that is, every contact leaves a trace. For example, if a person/object has come into contact with another person/object, scientists must search for trace evidence that has been transferred at the point of contact. The trace evidence analysis begins with a visual examination of the evidence item or location in which trace evidence may have been deposited. This often requires use of a low-power microscope. Other types of microscopes will be used depending on the type of evidence being visualized. Higher-power comparison microscopes may be used to compare known and unknown samples of hair, fibers, glass fragments, and other trace materials side by side. Sources of DNA contained within items (e.g., hairs) or transferred to items (e.g., blood on glass) also may be identified.[25]

Jigsaw-style physical matches of two evidence items broken, torn, or otherwise separated from each other also can be performed by this method of microscopic analysis. Polarizing-light microscopes are also utilized to study the physical features and structures of certain trace evidence (e.g., pigment patterns contained within a hair shaft). Chemical analyses such as GC-MS

Laboratory NIBIN Ballistics Exam

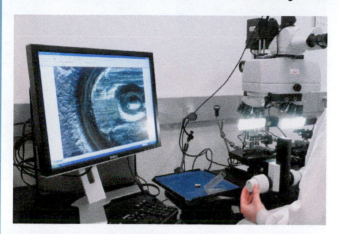

FIGURE 8.14 ▶ Ballistics evidence from a shooting scene is digitized at a workstation, where it will be entered into the NIBIN database.

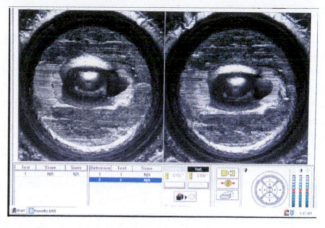

FIGURE 8.15 ▶ NIBIN allows side-by-side comparisons of potential matches. Pictured here is a match between firing pin impressions on a cartridge casing in the NIBIN database and those of a casing recovered from the shooting scene.

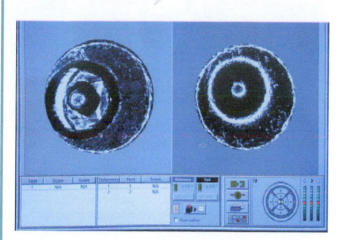

FIGURE 8.16 ▶ Images of a potential matching bullet contained in the NIBIN database and of a bullet test fired from a pistol recovered from the crime scene. NIBIN has both 2D and 3D view capabilities that allow images to be rotated for more detailed visual comparisons.

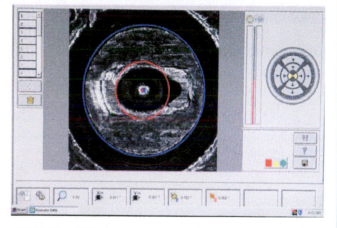

FIGURE 8.17 ▶ NIBIN can identify specific regions for focused comparisons. In this picture, the test-fired bullet from the shooting crime scene is analyzed for striations in and around the front hollow-point regions (circled in red and blue, respectively).

FIGURE 8.18 ▶ Visual results of four candidates in the NIBIN database that are probable matches with crime scene ballistics evidence (left side). Assuming that all 4 of the candidates in this NIBIN analysis are "hits," how could this information be used by investigators (1) if a suspect possessing the gun being tested is in custody or (2) if the gun being tested was recovered from a crime scene where no suspect has been identified?

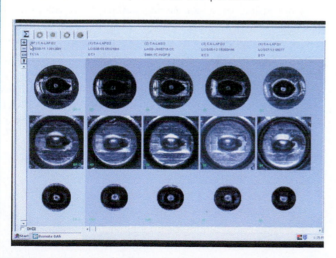

can be used to identify the chemical composition of dyes in fibers or specialized treatments of fibers with soaps and other agents. Absent the presence of DNA or a physical match, trace evidence will at best be considered to reveal class characteristics only.

The analysis of paint is a specialized task performed by trace evidence lab sections. Crime scene evidence often consists of objects that have been repainted to hide their original appearance. Vehicles, tools, bicycles, and other stolen items are commonly repainted by persons trying to sell them. Analyses of repainted evidence involve an examination of the color, texture, type, application method, paint layer sequence, and various chemical properties of the paint or coating applied over the original surface. In addition, analyses are performed on each paint layer. In doing so, it may be possible not only to identify the type of paint used by an offender, but also to match the painted surface of the evidence to paint found on the offender's hands, clothes, or vehicle, or from the location where the painting occurred. All paint matches are generally considered class evidence, with the exception of ones of a physical nature that exhibit unique individualized traits—such as two chips with joining edges, common brush stroke patterns, scratches, and so on.[26]

Questioned Documents

Many larger labs contain specialized personnel that perform questioned documents examinations to support investigations of various types of financially motivated crimes (e.g., contract fraud, check forgery, currency counterfeiting, identity theft, welfare fraud) and other crimes involving false documents that have consequences beyond financial gain (e.g., false security identifications to enable terrorist activities). Some of the primary functions of this lab section include:

- Determining how the questioned item was produced: by hand, photocopied, scanned, electronically generated
- Identifying inks, papers, writing styles, writing instruments, and other material used in creating the questioned item
- Restoring damaged, or altered questioned items to their original condition
- Assessing the questioned item's history and age, the steps taken in its production, its relationship to other questioned items, and modifications/alterations made to its original content
- Examining the questioned item for other evidence it may contain: DNA, fingerprints, arson accelerants, trace evidence[27]

As discussed in Chapter 4, specialized optical and lighting methods as shown in Figure 8.19 are used to examine questioned documents evidence. In most cases, examination of a questioned item begins with an overall search for the presence of class and individual evidence. ALS sources such as UV lighting can be used to detect differences in impressions left in paper as the result of using ball point, coarse tip, roller type, or

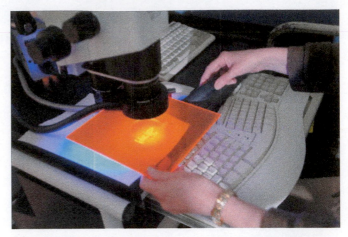

(a)

(b)

FIGURE 8.19 ▶ (a) A video spectral comparator (VSC) is used to visualize a latent invisible handwriting message. The device is also used to make ink comparisons and visualize alterations in documents. (b) An electrostatic detection apparatus (ESDA) is used to make visible handwriting impressions in paper or other surfaces that have been overwritten.

fountain pens. Laser lighting often will reveal a latent fingerprint not visible on a document's surface by developing the image of body oils that have soaked into paper or cardboard. Infrared lighting may show subtle differences in heat absorption of inks, revealing color differences not readily visible to the unaided eye.

More advanced testing (e.g., chemical agents, GC-MS) often can be used to determine the actual chemical composition of the inks/materials, which can be used to answer the following questions:

- Are the inks/materials used in one part of a questioned item the same as those used in other parts?
- Is the stated age of the questioned item consistent with the estimated age of the ink/materials?
- Was the same writing or printing method used throughout the entire questioned item?

- If the questioned item contains multiple written entries or is composed of various paper/parts compiled over time, can the age sequence of the entries/parts be verified? If not, were all writings or components of the item fraudulently prepared at the same time?

DNA LABORATORY ANALYSIS

DNA analysis may be performed within a dedicated section in large- and medium-size crime labs, but smaller labs that do not have the personnel or resources to do DNA testing will send evidence containing genetic material to regional, state, federal, or private laboratories.

It is an understatement to say that DNA testing is a revolutionary development in crime scene investigation. While fingerprints continue to be the only true biological measure of absolute difference between two human beings, the probability of two persons sharing the same genetic profile is so minute that DNA evidence used to establish an individual's identity is seldom called into question.

There are many methods of DNA analysis, and they continue to evolve in complexity and precision. Most of these, however, are based on the same biological premise: All humans possess unique genetic markers; and when they are isolated, identified, and calibrated, they provide a consistent DNA fingerprint that can be matched with other DNA evidence from a crime scene. DNA evidence is rarely uncovered by investigations, however; in fact, DNA evidence is only available in 5 to 10 percent of all criminal cases. Two types of DNA (deoxyribonucleic acid) are used in forensic analysis: nucleic DNA, or **nDNA**, which is derived from a cell containing a nucleus and can be used as individualized evidence; and mitochondrial DNA, or **mtDNA**, which is generally considered as class evidence and is most useful for the exclusion of suspects.[28] Figure 8.20 shows the cellular locations of both nDNA and mtDNA.

The nDNA Genetic Fingerprint

nDNA, hereafter simply called *DNA*, is often referred to as a person's *genetic fingerprint* and it contains the specific genetic instructions or codes used by the human body to create and sustain itself. These codes produce physical individuality—for example, eye and hair color, height, facial features, and so forth. One set of genetic codes is inherited from each parent. Therefore, a given individual's DNA profile consists of two separate sets of codes, one contributed by the father and the other by the mother. These codes are located on strands of DNA contained within the body's cells, which are the same regardless of the type of cell (e.g., blood or skin) or the location of the cell (e.g., exterior skin, interior organs). It is this cellular material, collected either directly from the person via laboratory procedures or from biological evidence at the crime scene, that provides the DNA samples necessary for forensic analysis. The relationship between the cell nucleus, chromosome and DNA strand containing an individual's genetic fingerprint is shown in Figure 8.21.

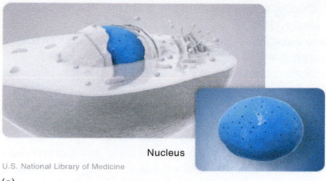

U.S. National Library of Medicine

(a)

Nucleus

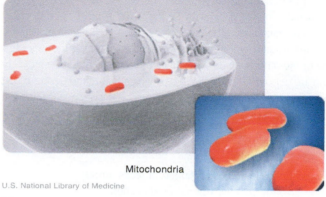

Mitochondria

U.S. National Library of Medicine

(b)

FIGURE 8.20 ▶ (a) Nuclear DNA (nDNA) is individualizable DNA within the cell's nucleus. (b) mtDNA is class-level DNA contained within the cell's mitochondria. (Courtesy of The National Institute of Health)

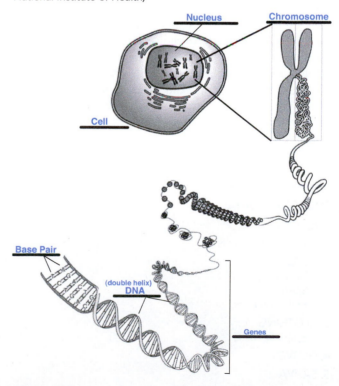

FIGURE 8.21 ▶ Various components of DNA. (Courtesy of The National Institute of Health.)

Usually, where there is a blood sample, there is also DNA evidence. This allows the blood evidence to move beyond mere classification into the realm of individualization. DNA is contained within the nucleus of white blood cells. It is much more abundant in wet blood than in dried blood, but the latter is preferable because the chances of bacterial contamination are greatly decreased. A simple procedure is performed in the laboratory to separate out white blood cells via centrifuge. These cells are then subjected to an extraction procedure that releases the DNA strands within the nuclei and recovers them for analysis. Generally, a blood sample visible to the unaided eye probably will yield enough DNA for tests to determine a person's genetic identity.

Besides blood, DNA can be extracted from tissues or other sources containing cells. The most frequent sources are **epithelial tissues** located within mucus membranes (forming the inner lining of the mouth, nose, and other bodily cavities) that break away and are deposited in bodily fluids—which in turn are deposited on persons, surfaces, and objects recovered as evidence. Following are sources containing DNA evidence:

1. White blood cells
2. Sperm cells
3. Epithelial cells contained in feces, urine, sweat, saliva, vomit, mucus, vaginal fluid, semen
4. Bone marrow
5. Tooth pulp
6. Follicle tags (on hair roots that have been forcibly removed)[29]

To perform a successful DNA analysis, approximately 30 to 50 cells are needed. The cells are extracted from the particular crime scene evidence with which they have come into contact. Whether or not a particular piece of evidence positively determines an individual's genetic markers depends on factors such as how many cells are present and the extent to which the DNA has been preserved or degraded. The various sources of DNA that can be used to generate a suspect's genetic fingerprint are summarized in Figure 8.22.

nDNA Analysis Methods

A full technical discussion of each of the many methods of DNA analysis is not necessary to gain an applied understanding of DNA testing. As previously mentioned, most DNA testing techniques rely on the same basic principle of identifying unique genetic markers contained within each DNA strand contributed by both parents. In most of today's crime labs, **PCR** (polymerase chain reaction) is the method of choice because it is not only accurate for a small number of cells, but it is also less time consuming and expensive compared to other DNA testing procedures.

The PCR process begins with the removal of DNA strands from cells contained within biological samples or crime scene evidence. Only a minute quantity of biological matter—perhaps a small drop of blood, saliva, or other bodily fluid containing intact cells—is necessary for PCR. Once the strands are isolated from the cell, the codes along the strand are copied and amplified by PCR. PCR can copy a single strand of DNA over a million times, thus eliminating the need for large original DNA samples. It also can be performed on DNA strands that are incomplete or fragmented due to degradation by copying only the specific areas of the DNA strand that are still intact.

Identifying the nDNA Fingerprint

After PCR has been used to create DNA strands with readable genetic coding patterns, many methods are available for unlocking the genetic fingerprint contained within the DNA strands. These rely on the discovery that only four individual codes or *acid bases*, in combination, create the entire set of codes contained within the DNA strand. These codes and their related symbols follow:

Adenine or "A"

Thymine or "T"

Guanine or "G"

Cytosine or "C"

SOURCES OF DNA:

1. BLOOD
   – White blood cells
2. SEMEN
   – Semen
   – Sperm cells
   – Epithelial cells
3. CLOTHING
   – Epithelial cells
4. GLOVES
5. SALIVA

– Cigarette butts, drinking glasses, soda cans, skin surfaces, and hair
– Epithelial cells
6. OTHER BODILY FLUIDS
   – Surfaces containing urine, feces, vomit, sweat, mucus, breast milk
   – Epithelial cells
6. CONDOMS
7. SECONDARY SOURCES
   – Hair brush/Comb
   – Tooth brush/Eyeglasses

FIGURE 8.22 ▶ Investigative sources of DNA.

Furthermore, each base combines with another, forming a single DNA strand known as a *double helix*, which is composed of two separate strands created by pairs of bases that are bound together. Because "A" bases pair only with "T" bases, and "G" bases pair only with "C" bases, each side of the DNA helix is composed of these complementary **base pairs**. Thus, the entire DNA strand is similar to a chain, where each link is composed of one base pair. The length of the entire DNA strand is the number of individual base pairs it contains. As will be described next, it is analysis of the size and number of base pairs at specific locations on the DNA strand that ultimately reveals a person's unique genetic fingerprint.[30]

nDNA Analysis Methods

Various methods are used to identify specific sequences of base pairs at specific locations on the DNA strand. One of these—which is used most often—is the STR method (Short Tandem Repeats). This method relies on the identification of base pair sequences that repeat themselves at a known *locus* (or location) on the DNA strand. For example, at one known location the sequence AACCT may be repeated from six to 20 times. The number of times the sequence repeats varies between individuals. The number of times the STR sequence repeats itself at a particular locus on the DNA is determined through the PCR process. The number of repeating sequences is then recorded and used to generate the genetic fingerprint ultimately used by investigators.[31]

Creating the nDNA Fingerprint

Typically, a specific location or locus on the DNA strand possessing STR repeating sequences—known collectively as an **allele**—is identified and assessed to determine the number of times a particular STR repeats itself. As shown in Figure 8.23, two alleles are analyzed for each location—one on the father's DNA strand and the other in the same location on the mother's DNA strand. Thus, each location on the DNA strand that is analyzed generates two pieces of information: (1) the father's allele and the number of STRs it contains and (2) the mother's allele and the number of STRs it contains. Occasionally, only one measurement is produced in cases where both the father's and mother's alleles contain the same number of STR repeating sequences. To visualize these DNA fingerprint results, a computerized graph of the two alleles showing the number of STRs present on each—known as an **electropherogram** (see Figure 8.24)—is generated, showing the number of times an STR repeats itself on the alleles for each parent. An older version of this method, known as an *autoradiogram,* is shown in Figure 8.25; it generates an x-ray-type visual print of the two alleles in the form of two dark bands in different vertical positions that indicate the relative size of each allele. Results from one test that show no matches may be enough to exclude a particular suspect. If results from a single test indicate a match, however (that is, the two alleles created from crime scene DNA are the same size as the alleles obtained from the DNA of a known suspect), subsequent tests on additional locations of DNA strands will determine whether alleles from those locations match as well.

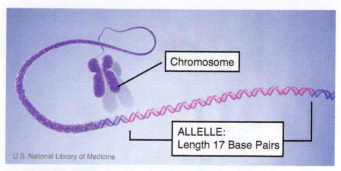

(a) Father's DNA strand

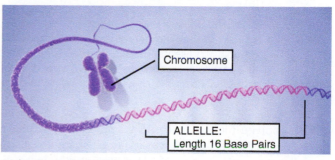

(b) Mother's DNA strand

FIGURE 8.23 ▶ One strand of DNA is removed from each side (or pair) of chromosomes. (a) One strand carries the father's genetic information and (b) the other carries the mother's. For the same location on each strand, the number of STRs occurring is determined through computer analysis. The length (or number of STRs) discovered on the DNA strands is represented graphically in an autoradiogram (i.e., older x-ray-style method) or by a computer-generated electropherogram. (Courtesy of The National Institute of Health.)

The combined results of these additional tests reduce the likelihood or probability that another person could share the same DNA fingerprint. For example, one test may be known to yield two alleles of a certain size from a specific DNA location in 1 out of every 100 persons (or .01 odds). By performing a second test from a second DNA location producing the same odds, the probability of another person sharing the same DNA profile is reduced to 1 out of every 10,000 persons (or .01 × .01 odds). Theoretically speaking, the odds of another person sharing the same exact DNA fingerprint produced by 13 of these tests (the number used to create the DNA fingerprint inputted into the FBI's CODIS system) could be less than 1 out of the entire world's population. At this point a true identification through individualized evidence is made.[32]

mtDNA Analysis

When standard nDNA profiling methods cannot be used, mtDNA analysis sometimes can be employed to generate a genetic fingerprint. This method is used most often when (1) there is not enough nDNA evidence to analyze, (2) nDNA evidence has become degraded, or (3) the type of DNA evidence

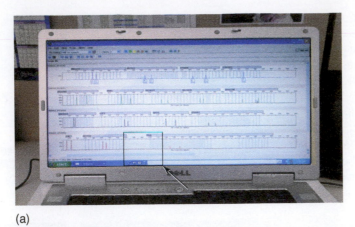

(a)

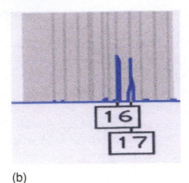

(b)

FIGURE 8.24 ▶ (a) Electropherogram results for PCR results displayed on a laptop. Each set of spikes represents different locations on the DNA strands tested. (b) The close-up box shows the graphic representation of the genetic fingerprint, which is the number of times an STR repeats itself at a particular location on the DNA strand. In this analysis, the suspect has 16 STRs on one strand and 17 STRs on the other—which relate to the example provided in Figure 8.23.

is inappropriate for standard nDNA analysis. For example, bones and teeth destroyed by age or fire often are tested successfully using mtDNA methods. Most importantly, however, the shaft region of all body hairs can be tested and yield results without any skin cells attached to the root area. Nail clippings

FIGURE 8.25 ▶ Old-style autoradiogram. Note that there are two bands representing the relative sizes of the father's and mother's alleles. The continuous bands are measurement scales referred to as *ladders*. The larger the DNA segment, the higher the band will be located on the ladder. Bands that are located in equal positions indicate a DNA match, as illustrated by the two red arrows.

as of yet have not proven to be amenable to the mtDNA testing process. Also, because mitochondria are found in every cell of the body, mtDNA testing can be performed as a backup procedure on nDNA cells that have become degraded or are otherwise untestable.

The greater versatility of mtDNA testing derives from its reliance on DNA contained in the *mitochondria* of a cell. One to thousands of mitochondria are found in cells throughout the body, and each may contain thousands of copies of mtDNA. This DNA, however, represents only the maternal contribution to a person's genetic make-up because mtDNA is transmitted only by the mother to her offspring. Therefore, mtDNA analyses provide only half the profile obtained through standard DNA testing. This limitation makes it impossible to use mtDNA techniques to discriminate between maternal relatives such as grandmothers, their daughters, and their daughter's sons. Even unrelated persons may share the same mtDNA profile because they have a common relative in the far-distant past. Despite these apparent weaknesses, mtDNA testing has proven to be a useful tool for (1) the creation of class evidence used in suspect identifications, (2) the exclusion of suspects, and (3) the identification of bodies suspected to be those of missing persons.[33]

CODIS AND THE FUTURE OF DNA

Beginning in the late 1990s, the FBI instituted a nationwide DNA database referred to as **CODIS** (Combined DNA Index System) that houses DNA profiles submitted by local, state, and federal crime labs. The system, depending on the state referenced, now includes DNA profiles for both adults and juveniles convicted or arrested for felony and (in some cases) felony-level offenses. It also includes missing and unidentified persons and DNA evidence from unsolved crimes. CODIS employs STR DNA testing results and generally requires similarities between 13 specific genetic marker locations before identifying a match between an offender and an arrestee. Matches generated by the CODIS system must be confirmed through first-hand examination by a certified DNA examiner.

At present, DNA technology can also make class distinctions based on genetic characteristics. Gender determination is possible through an examination of the sex chromosomes. In addition, ongoing research suggests that certain regularities in genetic markers among persons of the same ancestry can be used to predict a person's race. The future prospects of DNA profiling for use in the forensic sciences are seemingly endless. Since DNA contains the codes necessary to create an entire individual, perhaps investigators one day could use the DNA fingerprint to develop an offender's physical profile from head to toe.[34]

The Innocence Project

In 1992, the **Innocence Project (IP)** was initiated by civil rights attorneys Barry Scheck and Peter Neufeld. The program's primary mission is to assist prisoners who could be proven innocent through DNA testing. Since its inception, IP has resulted in the release of approximately 250 persons from prison (16 of whom were sentenced to death) by using DNA results that show that these individuals were falsely convicted. According to IP statistics, over 50 percent of these postconviction releases can be attributed to negligence, misconduct, and poor training in forensic laboratories. Most of these wrongful convictions were based on the presentation of forensic evidence using techniques other than DNA testing. Prevalent among these were serology results based on blood typing (without DNA testing), hair analysis, and bite mark impression comparisons. On the other hand, DNA testing performed by the IP staff on persons asserting their innocence has also confirmed guilt previously established through non-DNA forensic methods.[35]

OTHER FORENSIC SCIENCES

Besides the evidence testing performed by personnel directly employed by law enforcement agencies, specialized analyses in particular types of forensic science can be carried out by individuals outside a police crime lab. Among these individuals are university professors and researchers, industry experts, and professionals such as medical doctors, engineers, and computer scientists qualified to analyze physical evidence and provide expert testimony on the results of forensic examinations. Following are the forensic science fields in which they work.

Forensic Pathology

After all investigative evidence pertaining to a dead body has been gathered and documented at the crime scene; the body is bagged and transported to a morgue or other holding facility. Depending on the jurisdiction, the postmortem medical examination may fall within the power of the coroner and/or the medical examiner. Coroners are elected officials, usually without any medical training, who oversee the legal aspects of medical death investigations. Medical examiners, on the other hand, are certified medical doctors who actually perform autopsies and other medical investigative procedures. Some are specialists in forensic pathology, which deals with the medical investigation of death by criminal means.

Forensic pathology is performed by specialized medical doctors who investigate the cause of deaths. The college education requirements to become a forensic pathologist can involve 10 or more years of formal study. Most forensic pathologists are employed by governmental agencies and perform their work under the title of "Medical Examiner," although some are private consultants who assist in the investigation of suspicious or unexplained deaths. Besides performing postmortem examination of dead bodies, they may also assist investigators in situations involving living persons who may have fallen ill or been injured through the harmful actions of others (e.g., elder and child abuse cases). If needed, the forensic pathologist will appear in court proceedings to report and present evidence and to serve as an expert witness.

All deaths considered to have occurred under violent or suspicious circumstances are subjected to further medical investigation in an autopsy. These include sudden deaths where no medical explanations are readily apparent. Where there is a medical history of disease or illness that can explain a person's death and that person has recently been under the care of a medical doctor, an autopsy usually is not performed. In addition, absent any signs of criminal circumstances, autopsies are not performed on persons who have prepared a letter of religious objection stating that being subjected to an autopsy violates their religious beliefs. Investigators must work cooperatively as a team with those performing postmortem medical investigations to maximize the chances of a successful outcome. During the autopsy, investigators are present and play a key procedural role.

Before the autopsy begins, the investigator prepares preliminary documentation—including where and when the autopsy is held and the persons in attendance and performing the procedure. The medical examiner begins the autopsy by providing a general external description of the body, noting anatomical conditions, present and past injuries, and any type of trace evidence (e.g., glass fragments, paint chips, fibers, etc.). X-rays are taken to determine the presence of bullets or other metallic fragments in the body. Finally, the body is examined internally by making a full body incision from below the neck to the lower pelvic area. In addition, the brain is exposed for examination, and various bodily fluids as well as stomach contents may be sampled for later toxicological and DNA analyses. The medical examiner documents and often photographs each step and collects evidence from within the body. As the autopsy proceeds, investigators should dialogue with the medical examiner to answer questions arising from the crime scene:

- What is the estimated time of death?
- What type of weapon produced which type of wound?
- Was the death the result of a specific wound?
- Is there evidence of past wounding that may relate to the present death?

- Is there evidence of sexual assault?
- Are bullet holes or stab wounds consistent with the body's position at crime scene?
- Did the victim suffer from preexisting illnesses or diseases?
- Does the body show signs of ongoing substance abuse?[36]

The final result of all postmortem investigations is an autopsy report by the medical examiner. Briefly, the report attempts to identify both the medical cause and the specific manner of death. The terms *manner* and *cause* of death are often used interchangeably, but in an investigative sense, they have different meanings. The physiological and medical reasons for why a death occurred are referred to as the cause of death. In contrast, **manner of death** refers to the circumstances under which the death occurred and is classified as one of the following:

Natural: Resulting from naturally occurring circumstances such as old age, illness, or disease. Most deaths are classified as natural;

Accidental: Resulting from unintended or unavoidable circumstances that cannot be classified as natural, suicidal, or homicidal;

Suicidal: Death intentionally caused by oneself;

Homicidal: Death caused by another human;

Undetermined: Not enough evidence available to determine the manner of death. Sudden Infant Death Syndrome (SIDS) cases generally fall within this classification.

Ultimately, the medical examiner's job is to determine whether a death should be classified as a homicide. Investigators, however, can play a key role in this process by providing insights and information from the crime scene that can help the medical examiner make these determinations. When the final autopsy report submitted by the medical examiner concludes that a death was indeed a homicide, investigations likely will continue to focus on identifying, arresting, and/or prosecuting a murder suspect. If the medical examination fails to conclude that homicide was the manner of death, however, the case likely will be closed.[37]

Forensic Anthropology

Forensic anthropology is performed by anthropologists who have extensive training in physical anthropology and archaeology (for example see Case Close-Up 8.2 and related Figure 8.26). They routinely help investigators identify human remains that are decomposed, burned, or dismembered. Homicides and mass disasters are common investigative situations requiring the assistance of a forensic anthropologist. Depending on the nature of the evidence, there are several classifications of human skeletal evidence:

AGE

Age is best determined by examining teeth, if present. The fully developed dentition of an adult male consists of 32 teeth, and that of a child is 20 teeth. All childhood deciduous teeth (with the exception of third molars or wisdom teeth) are replaced by adult permanent teeth by the age of 12 years. Wisdom teeth, if fully erupted, are present by the age of 18 to 20 years. Missing or excessively worn teeth suggest advanced age in adults. Certain skeletal bone features can be used to determine the body's age, but are best used to corroborate estimates derived from teeth. Obviously, the skeletons of young children as noticeably smaller than those of adolescents and adults. Laboratory analyses of arm and leg bones, however, can distinguish adolescents aged 13 to 18 years from both children and adults. Other bones useful for determining an adult's age include the pelvic bone for persons under 40 years, rib bones for persons over 40 years, and the skull for persons 50 years and under.

- **Gender:** The teeth and bones of males tend to be, on average, larger than those of females. Precise mathematical formulas are used for determining gender based on bone size and length. These tests can be applied to virtually any bone from the hand, foot, arm, leg, skull, or spine areas. Examining bone size alone, however, may be misleading because the skeletal dimensions of adolescent males may be very similar to those of adult females. The pelvis is the most important skeletal part for gender identification. Besides the fact that a female's pelvic bones are much broader than a male's, laboratory examination of the full pelvic region can definitively determine the body's gender.

- **Ethnicity:** Most experts agree that determining race through skeletal remains is a rough approximation, at best. Skin may differ in color, but skeletons do not—except when they are exposed to environmental and other elements. A skull containing the facial bones is of the greatest use for determining ethnicity. In particular, the eyes, cheeks, nose, and jaw are used by experts to classify remains as Caucasian, African-American, Asian, or Latino. Although not as useful, bones of the pelvis and extremities also have been used for ethnic classification.

- **Appearance:** Faces and skeletons can be reconstructed by various means. Photographs or x-rays can be superimposed over the skull or skeleton. Sculptures of soft tissue covering the contours of facial bones are used to create a 3D personal image. Computer software is now available that applies complex formulas to digital images of skeletal remains to provide an animated reconstruction of personal appearance.

The most powerful evidence available to forensic anthropologists is DNA that can be extracted from bones, teeth, hair, soft tissue remains, and dried blood or other bodily fluids. With such evidence, a positive individualized personal identity is perhaps possible provided that there is a match to an existing DNA profile of a likely victim or suspect. In the absence of DNA or its match to a person of interest, some of the following characteristics can help individualize human skeletal remains:

1. **Dentistry:** Documentation including records and x-rays of implants, bridgework, fillings, and missing or extracted teeth can be matched to dental remains.
2. **Disease:** Cancer, tumors, and certain infectious diseases leave permanent lesions on the bone.
3. **Surgery:** Prosthetic devices such as hip or knee replacements, artificial heart valves, surgical pins and screws, or metal sutures will remain in the bone.
4. **Trauma:** Breaks and fractures leave heal lines where the trauma occurred.
5. **Use Patterns:** Bones in areas of the body that have been used more than others often have slightly larger features and show signs of arthritis in joints caused by stress and wear. This information can help determine left versus right handedness, an athletic or sedentary lifestyle, or an occupation involving manual labor.[38]

CASE CLOSE-UP 8.2

"THE BODY FARM"

Knoxville, Tenn.

When a local police officer suspected the murder of his older sister, despite an autopsy report from the medical examiner's office that declared the death accidental, he consulted Dr. Bill Bass at the University of Tennessee's "Body Farm." At the age of 16, in 1978, the officer's sister allegedly fell from a high cliff to her death. The autopsy, however, failed to discover any bone fractures consistent with such a fall. The officer always suspected that his sister was really murdered and the killer staged her body to look like she fell—to throw investigators off track. He always wondered, "How could a person could fall from such a high place, land on a hard surface, and not break any bones?" To answer this question, the officer consulted the expertise of Dr. Bill Bass and his team of forensic anthropologists at the Body Farm located at the University of Tennessee, Knoxville.

The Body Farm was founded by Dr. Bass, a physical anthropologist, as a research facility to study the characteristics of decaying human bodies and develop a body of research to help law enforcement solve cases involving highly decomposed bodies. The 3-acre facility houses multiple human bodies in various stages of decay that are studied to determine time and cause of death using indicators such as insect activity, soil characteristics, exposure to fire, temperature, and many other variables. Dr. Bass and his team have helped solve many crimes that have baffled investigators, including the one presented here concerning the mysterious cliff fall. After the Body Farm

staff examined the skeletal remains of the officer's sister—which were decades old—they discovered numerous bone fractures and cracked teeth in the woman's skull that suggested the impact of a fall from a high place. Although this evidence was not discovered during autopsy, it remained as a permanent record in the woman's skeleton—raising serious doubt that she was murdered as her brother suspected.[39]

FIGURE 8.26 ▶ FBI agents engage in specialized training at the Body Farm, part of the Forensic Anthropology Center at the University of Tennessee. (Courtesy Federal Bureau of Investigation)

Forensic Entomology

Forensic entomology is the study of insects as applied to criminal matters. It is based on the notion that scientific qualities of certain insects and their habitats can be used to help solve crimes. The most popular application of forensic entomology to crime scene evidence is the use of an insect's life cycle to find approximate time of death. This is made possible by studying the growth and reproductive habits of carrion insects, which feed on dead and decaying flesh. One such species routinely used by forensic entomologists is the *blow fly*. Blow flies are found in great abundance in warm weather climates and resemble ordinary house flies. In particular, they undergo a relatively predicable metamorphosis that allows the approximate determination of how long the insect and its offspring have been present at a crime scene. The typical female blow fly, with her keen sense of smell, can locate a dead body within minutes of death. She then lays eggs in natural openings such as the eyes and mouth. In normal weather conditions, the eggs hatch 24 to 48 hours after they have been deposited, and it is then possible to assess time of death by subtracting 1 or 2 days from the number of days representing the stage of maturation of the flies discovered on the body. For example, 6-day-old larvae would suggest that the death occurred approximately 4 to 5 days earlier. These estimates are highly variable, however, depending on the existing temperatures and weather conditions in and around the crime scene.

Forensic entomology can also determine whether or not persons or objects have been in certain geographic regions. For example, a car's windshield or radiator may pick up insects known to exist only in a certain locality. This determination may prove fruitful for corroborating or refuting a suspect's claims that they did or did not drive a car in a place where the insects are indigenous. Cases of abuse and neglect also can be revealed by insect evidence. In particular, children or adults who are injured or suffering from bed sores and left immobile for long periods of time may have signs of insect activity in their wounds.[40]

Forensic Psychology and Psychiatry

Forensic psychologists—who have a PhD degree in psychology—employ various techniques and testing methods to assess mental abilities and personality traits. Many are also licensed to provide counseling and therapy for persons suffering from behavioral disorders. Forensic psychiatrists, on the other hand, are medical doctors (i.e., MDs) who specialize in the diagnosis of behavioral abnormalities and their treatment through surgery, drugs, and other clinical and nonclinical therapeutic means. The following are examples of how persons working in the fields of **forensic psychology and psychiatry** can assist criminal investigators:

- *Criminal Profiling:* Predicting criminal and lifestyle patterns of offenders to help identify and apprehend first-time and repeat criminals.
- *Competency Assessment:* Performing tests to determine whether witnesses, suspects, or victims are mentally competent to provide testimony or confessions.
- *Eyewitness Identification & Recall:* Using memory refreshing techniques, including hypnosis, to help victims and witnesses retrieve lost memories of criminal events.
- *Interviewing Techniques:* Providing consultation regarding the most effective ways to obtain accurate

FIGURE 8.27 ▶ Evidence from electronic crime scenes awaiting analysis in one of the FBI's RCFLs (Regional Computer Forensics Laboratories). (Courtesy Federal Bureau of Investigation)

voluntary statements from witnesses, suspects, and other informants.[41]

Digital Forensic Science

Electronic crime scenes are becoming commonplace in the field of investigation, and evidence collected from them is analyzed in the field of **digital forensic science** (see Figure 8.27). Currently, most crime labs do not have a formal section dedicated to this type of examination. (The FBI crime lab is a notable exception.) Rather, expert consultants in fields such as computer application and electronic data transfer evaluate digital evidence. Most digital analyses consist of decoding, extracting, or restoring electronic documents and information contained within devices such as computers, cell phones, GPS systems, PDAs (personal data assistants), servers, video game consoles, and portable media players. Types of digital storage from which data are obtained for forensic analysis include magnetic (e.g., hard drives, tapes, floppy disks), optical (e.g., DVDs and CDs), and magnetic (flash drives, memory cards, and microchips). Files are copied from their original storage source to a hard drive, where they are examined as logical files in the form of pictures, e-mails, chat messages, tweets, texts, or other digitally transferred information to be examined as digital evidence. MD5 Hash software, which copies and extracts computer files through a mathematical coding system, is commonly used to perform this task. Similarly, other files deleted from electronic storage areas, considered to be latent digital evidence, can be copied and developed from file information retained in a computer's operating system. See Chapter 14 for a more detailed discussion on this and other topics related to the investigation of computer crime and electronic crime scenes.[42]

New Forensic Testing Methods on the Horizon

Fingerprint Testing for Lifestyle: New chemicals are currently being developed that can be applied to fingerprints to detect the presence of (1) nicotine, to reveal smokers versus nonsmokers; (2) excessive salts, which indicate a heavy diet of processed fast food and perhaps excessive body weight; and (3) alcohol and drugs, which perhaps could be used as a field presumptive test for DUI and being under the influence of controlled substances.

Fired Cartridge Casings: Criminal investigation courses have long taught that once a cartridge has been fired, extreme heat from the discharge obliterates possible fingerprints—and there is no way to recover any print evidence from the expended casing. Forensic scientists in England are now perfecting a breakthrough method to recover prints from fired cartridge casings and also prints that have been wiped off metallic surfaces. The researchers discovered that sweat coming into contact with certain metals, including the brass from which bullet cases are made, leaves a permanent impression in the metal that can be recovered using a process of heat and humidity.

Virtual Autopsies: Computed tomography (CT) scanning, a radiological technique used by physicians to look inside the body for such things as bone fractures, recently has been applied in the forensic sciences as a method for performing virtual autopsies. The method allows pathologists to view postmortem signs of crime-related blunt force trauma, bullet wounds, and bone fractures through x-ray-type images rather than by

surgically opening the body or peeling skin back from the skull. This technique also enables examination of persons on whom traditional autopsies cannot be performed due to religious objections.

Microstamping: This method involves etching or engraving minute codes on firearm parts that create a stamped tool mark impression on fired ammunition that can be used to track the weapon as well as its owner. Microstamps can also be placed on the ammunition itself to serve the same purpose. Currently, microstamping is mandated by law on all new semiautomatic handguns sold in California.

Blood Age Identification: The analysis of T-cells in blood spatter at crime scenes has proven useful as an indicator of a victim's or offender's age. Forensic scientists have developed certain testing procedures for wet or dried blood that provide an estimation of age accurate within $+\backslash-9$ years of the person's true age. This type of testing is appropriate for determining what particular generation (i.e., youth, parent, grandparent) a person may belong to, within 20-year intervals.

Blinking Evidence: Forensic scientists are now working on an ALS method that visualizes organic crime scene evidence, such as fingerprints and bodily fluids, as blinking light rather than a steady glow as they now appear under UV light and other traditional ALS sources. The blinking is created by special lighting methods that detect the low-level natural fluorescent qualities of sweat, saliva, semen, and blood.

CRITICISMS OF THE FORENSIC SCIENCES

Before the growth of forensic science disciplines and their use in analyzing physical evidence in support of criminal investigations, the primary evidentiary means available for proving or disproving a suspect's guilt in was eyewitness testimony. The Innocent Project's postconviction DNA analyses, however—resulting in the release of a staggering number of persons falsely convicted by eyewitness evidence—have demonstrated the superiority of forensic science to the human memory. Results of the Innocence Project have also identified the shortcomings of many forensic science applications, however. Postconviction DNA testing has resulted in the release of persons convicted by traditional forensic examination methods including hair analysis, serology, bite make analysis, soil analysis, and

even improper DNA analysis. Critics of the forensic sciences contend that many problems within the nation's current crime lab and evidence testing systems lead to miscarriages of justice—of which the Innocence Project provides tip-of-the-iceberg examples. These problems indicate the need for improvements in the following areas:

- ***Training:*** Although some persons working in crime labs possess extensive education and experience specific to the nature of the examinations being performed, others do not. Civilian and sworn personnel without formal education may be enlisted to conduct sophisticated and sensitive forensic examinations that result in invalid or misinterpreted results.

- ***Oversight:*** Usually, forensic science labs police themselves, so there is no mandated external oversight or means of quality control to examine their testing procedures and methods. Some labs, however, voluntarily seek out accreditation from agencies and comply with accreditation standards designed to ensure that proper testing procedures and techniques are applied to crime scene evidence. One accreditation agency is the **American Society of Crime Laboratory Directors (ASCLD)**, which performs site inspections of their accredited crime labs. Most of the nation's crime labs, however, are not accredited by the ASCLD or any other such organization, so they receive no external oversight of their forensic science equipment, testing procedures, or scientific competency.

- *Uniformity:* Surveys of forensic laboratories across the nation reveal significant variation in the laboratory procedures used to examine physical evidence. This is not to say that testing methods are being applied improperly, but rather that labs lack uniformity or standardization regarding test techniques, technology, and other functions utilized in the evidence examination process. Many of these differences, however, are due to financial constraints that limit advanced training and the purchase of cutting-edge technology.

- *Independence:* Most crime labs operate under the control of the law enforcement agency with which they are affiliated. Their personnel and budget issues must be handled by the chief of police or sheriff, who oversees general law enforcement operations. Some argue that crime labs should operate independently, in both a financial and a management capacity, because of the specialized nature of their work. Complete independence also means that forensic scientists would be free from pressures by law enforcement to process evidence in ways that may compromise the quality of evidence testing procedures.

- *Test Results:* Currently, the results of many forensic science testing procedures are presented as "identification/ no identification" or "match/no match." Also, the specific criteria and methods used to determine whether or not physical evidence can be individualized to confirm identification of a suspect or evidence samples often differ significantly from one examination to another. Critics recommend that a uniform system for evaluating and presenting evidence of testing results be developed—especially in the areas of firearms identification, ballistics, blood spatter analysis, and impressions evidence analyses.[43]

- *Backlogs:* Most, if not all of the nation's crime labs suffer from a backlog of cases. Even the nation's largest crime lab, the FBI Crime Laboratory, has thousands of backlogged cases—most of which perform latent fingerprint examination. Evidence submitted to the FBI lab now has a turnaround time of 30 days or more. DNA testing also is another major source of case backlogs, due to the time and money required to conduct genetic fingerprint analyses. Some crime labs report backlogs of 6 months or more of DNA cases, many of which must be outsourced to private labs for testing.

CASE CLOSE-UP 8.3

"SCANDALS IN THE CRIME LAB"

Crime labs have a tremendous responsibility to provide accurate and truthful scientific findings. As the Innocence Project has demonstrated, poorly executed or deceptive forensic science examinations of physical evidence have had devastating consequences on persons for whom such evidence has resulted in wrongful conviction. Listed here are some of the crime labs that have been exposed for either intentionally or mistakenly providing misleading forensic evidence.

FBI Crime Lab: In 1995, Special Agent Frederic Whitehurst blew the whistle on the FBI Crime Lab, contending that, among other things, the lab had released inaccurate or false results from evidence tests that had made their way throughout the court system. Whitehurst also claimed that evidence test outcomes had been slanted to facilitate successful prosecution of persons charged with criminal activity. Internal inquiries into Whitehurst's allegations sparked numerous scandals affecting the lab's credibility, such as false/inaccurate DNA results (entered into the DNA database), false/ misleading expert testimony by lab workers, and reports including results of evidence tests that were either not performed or performed improperly by persons without the necessary credentials to conduce scientific examinations. As a result of Whitehurst's allegation, over 40 major reforms have been instituted by the FBI crime lab, including accreditation and review by the ASCLD. In addition, some 3,000 cases potentially affected by tainted evidence have been reexamined.

Houston PD Crime Lab: The DNA section of the Houston Police Department's crime lab was shut down between 2002 and 2006 as the result of an audit showing that hundreds of DNA test results were potentially inaccurate due to poor testing methods and handling. Most notable among those falsely accused by tainted DNA from the Houston PD crime lab was a man convicted on a rape charge and sentenced to a 25-year prison term—who was later proven innocent by postconviction DNA testing performed under the auspices of the Innocence Project.

West Virginia State Crime Lab: Crime evidence affecting over 100 cases was discovered to have been falsified, fabricated, or omitted by a key member of the West Virginia State Crime Lab's serology testing unit.

Other Crime Labs: Crime labs representing the Chicago Police Department, San Francisco Police Department,

and the state of North Carolina are some of the more notable facilities that have had forensic evidence scandals. As the direct result of these and other situations questioning the quality of forensic lab results, many states have instituted their own version of the Innocence Project to reexamine questionable forensic evidence that may have resulted in false convictions. Moreover, in 2004, the Justice For All Act was signed into law, which provides all federal inmates the right to petition for DNA tests to determine their innocence. The law also provides financial incentives to states to preserve and store physical evidence and perform postconviction DNA testing for inmates.

FROM THE CRIME SCENE TO THE CRIME LAB

Case Example 8C presents a detailed set of crime scene photos (see Figures 8.28 to 8.45) that include numerous forms of physical evidence that will ultimately be collected from the scene and submitted to the crime lab for analysis. While processing this crime scene, it is important for investigators to bear in mind the type, nature, and quantity of evidence present so that it can

be collected in such a way that will maximize it potential to be successfully tested through laboratory analyses. In addition, after the scene has been processed, it is important for investigators in this case to submit the collected evidence to the appropriate crime lab section. Perhaps the most important consideration to investigators is determining and anticipating what laboratory results on which pieces of evidence will be most useful for solving this case.

CASE EXAMPLE 8C

Bound and Gagged Murder

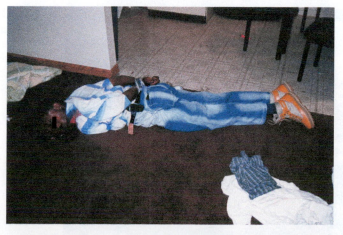

FIGURE 8.28 ▶ Assuming there are no witnesses to assist in the investigation of the above murder, what physical evidence can be gathered at this scene and tested in the crime lab to provide possible suspect leads?

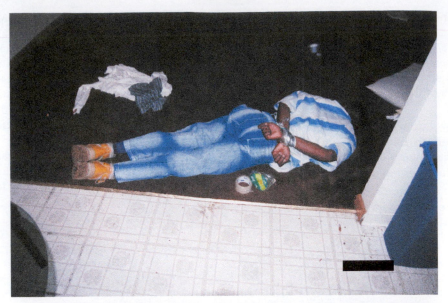

FIGURE 8.29 ▶ Surrounding the body are used rolls of duct tape, clothing items and a pillow. Of what significance are these items as potential sources of evidence? How should the evidence be collected? To which section of the crime lab should the items be submitted? What tests, if any, could be used on each item to provide possible suspect leads?

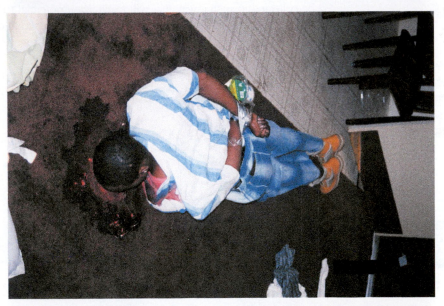

FIGURE 8.30 ▶ Blood and other biological matter surround the victim's head and facial area which provide a visible carpet stain. Of what significance is this evidence? How should it be collected? To which section of the crime lab should this evidence be submitted for testing and what tests should be performed?

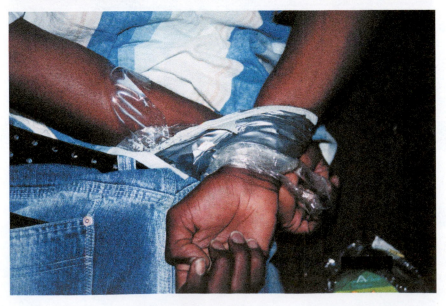

FIGURE 8.31 ▶ Cellophane wrap and duct tape have been used to bind the victim's hands together. Is this evidence of value to the investigation? Why or why not?

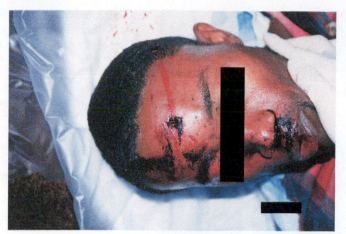

FIGURE 8.32 ▶ An examination of the victim's face shows what appears to be a single bullet wound, various lacerations, numerous dried blood stains and possible trauma to the nose and mouth region. Are any of these observations important to the investigation of this case? If so, what area(s) of forensic science/criminalistics would be used to evaluate this evidence?

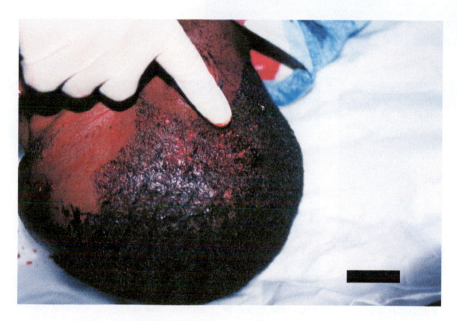

FIGURE 8.33 ▶ There is an area discovered on the side of the victim's head which exhibits what appears to be a large trauma or abrasion. Of what importance is this finding to the investigation and how might it relate to observations made in Figure 8.32?

FIGURE 8.34 ▶ A bloody cartridge casing is discovered near the victim's head. What procedures should be used in the crime lab to examine this casing and develop possible case leads?

FIGURE 8.35 ▶ A large blood stain is discovered on the bottom sleeve area of one of the clothing items on the floor, shown earlier in Figure 8.29. How should this evidence item be handled and collected? To which section of the the crime lab should this evidence be submitted? What questions about the the crime could be answered from lab tests conducted on this clothing item?

FIGURE 8.36 ▶ To which section of the crime lab should this tape evidence be submitted? What test could be performed on this evidence and what could possibly be discovered about the crime in the results of these tests?

FIGURE 8.37 ▶ Can the tape evidence and the cell phone evidence be somehow linked together by laboratory testing procedures to develop a suspect lead? Which section(s) of the crime lab would perform tests to accomplish this task and which tests would be performed?.

FIGURE 8.38 ▶ What is the significance of the multiple roles of tape evidence discovered at this scene? What tests could be performed on each roll to determine how and by whom they were used? Also, are the shoes of possible value as evidence in this case? If so, why?

FIGURE 8.39 ▶ The kitchen area of the victim's apartment appears to have been ransacked. Is there possible physical evidence located here? What is it? How should it be identified and collected? Which areas of the crime lab would be concerned with evidence obtained from the kitchen?

FIGURE 8.40 ▶ A remote land-line phone, a cutting devise, cellophane as well as unknown substances appearing to be some form of illegal drug are discovered at the scene. How should these items of evidence be analyzed/tested by the crime lab?

FIGURE 8.41 ▶ After locating the victim's vehicle, it was seized and transported to the crime lab. What areas of the vehicle's exterior should be examined/tested and for what possible types of evidence?

FIGURE 8.42 ▶ What type of evidence may be located in the driver's area of the vehicle's interior and how should it be identified and collected?

FIGURE 8.43 ▶ A white powder wrapped in cellophane is located beneath the driver's seat. Which test(s) might be performed on this substance to determine what it is or its "chemical" identity?

FIGURE 8.44 ▶ Papers found in the glove compartment of the victim's vehicle. Of what value is this set of papers as evidence to the present investigation? To which section of the crime lab could they be submitted for analysis? What might lab tests discover?

FIGURE 8.45 ▶ This partially smoked cigarette was discovered in the vehicles center console. Should it be analyzed as possible evidence in the case? if so, by which lab section and for what type of evidence?

Summary

1. **Explain what is meant by the term *forensic sciences*.**

   Forensic science is the application of science to the law. Although virtually any forensic science can be applied to the practice of investigation, the law dictates which forensic sciences can be used to present evidence in a legal proceeding. Two legal tests, the Frye and Daubert tests, are used to determine whether or not a particular science is considered to be a forensic science under the law. To satisfy the Frye test, a would-be forensic science must be generally accepted by a relevant scientific discipline. To pass the Daubert test, a particular science must be supported by valid external scientific research.

2. **The function of a crime lab.**

   Crime labs conduct scientific analyses on physical evidence obtained from crime scenes, victims, and suspects. Many of the functions carried out by crime labs include performing presumptive and confirmatory testing of suspected, yet unknown, illegal substances and materials. Specialized testing is also conducted to class and individualize evidence in support of investigations, legal proceedings, and trials.

3. **Sections making up a crime laboratory.**

   Crime labs are typically divided into sections that specialize in the testing and examination of specific types of evidence. These sections include toxicology, fingerprint ID, serology, arson and explosives, firearms and tool marks, trace evidence, questioned documents, and DNA analysis.

4. **DNA and the human genetic fingerprint.**

   DNA can be acquired from a variety of sources within the human body, including white blood cells, skin cells (nDNA), and hair (mtDNA). In the analysis of nDNA, which can be individualized in the form of a human genetic fingerprint, specific characteristics of locations on DNA strands are compared for differences. This generates a DNA profile, which can be used to positively identify offenders or exclude suspects. mDNA, which is obtained from hair or the mitochondria of cells, cannot be used to positively identify offenders, but is useful for excluding suspects.

5. **Forensic sciences used outside the crime lab.**

   Branches of the forensic sciences practiced by experts outside the crime lab include forensic pathology, forensic anthropology, forensic psychology and psychiatry, forensic entomology, and digital forensic science. Forensic pathology, which is practiced by medical doctors, is conducted within the medical examiner's/coroner's office and supports death investigations by determining whether the manner of death was natural, suicidal, accidental, homicidal, or undetermined in nature.

Key Terms

forensic science
Frye test
Daubert test
toxicology
AFIS/
IAFIS
ACE-V
serology
NIBIN (National Integrated Ballistic Information Network)

nDNA
epithelial tissues
PCR (polymerase chain reaction)
base pairs
mtDNA
allele
autoradiograph
CODIS
Innocence Project (IP)
forensic pathology

manner of death
forensic anthropology
forensic entomology
digital forensic science
American Society of Crime Laboratory Directors (ASCLD)
forensic psychology and psychiatry
electropherogram
STR (short tandem repeats)

Review Questions

1. Define the term *forensic science*.
2. What are the Frye and Daubert tests and how do they differ?
3. Describe three of the analytical and/or testing procedures used by crime labs.
4. What is meant by the term *presumptive test*?
5. What is meant by the term *confirmatory test*?
6. Describe the primary functions of the toxicology lab section.
7. Explain the procedures used to examine a fingerprint using an automated fingerprint database.

8. What is IAFIS?

9. Describe the steps used to carry out an ACE-V fingerprint examination.

10. Describe the primary functions of the serology lab section.

11. Can the presence of saliva and semen be detected through lab tests? If so, explain how.

12. Describe the primary functions of the arson and explosives lab section.

13. What are the primary duties of the trace evidence lab section?

14. What are the differences between nDNA and mtDNA?

15. Define the term *DNA fingerprint*.

16. What procedures are used to determine a person's DNA fingerprint?

17. What is CODIS?

18. What is the Innocence Project, and how has its work impacted the forensic sciences?

19. Name and describe three forensic sciences practiced outside the crime lab.

20. Identify three major criticisms of today's crime labs.

Internet Resources

International Association for Identification (IAI)	www.theiai.org
Crime Lab Census	bjs.ojp.usdoj.gov/content/pub/pdf/cpffcl05.pdf.
Innocence Project Fact Sheet	www.innocenceproject.org/Content/351.php.
California Association of Criminalists News	www.cacnews.org/news/4thq08.pdf
IAFIS Facts	www.fbi.gov/hq/cjisd/iafis.htm.
CODIS Database Information	www.fbi.gov/about-us/lab/codis
NIBIN Facts	www.atf.gov/publications/factsheets/factsheet-nibin.html
American Society of Crime Laboratory Directors (ASCLD)	www.ascld.org/
FBI Crime Laboratory	www.fbi.gov/about-us/lab
Body Farm	www.fbi.gov/news/stories/2009/july/bodyfarm_070709
Science Daily News	www.sciencedaily.com/news/matter_energy/forensics/headlines/
DNA Initiative	www.ojp.usdoj.gov/nij/welcome.html
DNA Guidebook for Law Enforcement	www.ncjrs.gov/pdffiles1/nij/bc000614.pdf

Applied Investigative Exercise

Carefully examine the crime scene photos for Case Example 8C, Bound and Gagged Murder. Imagine that you are the investigator of this crime and that you have collected each of the items of evidence marked in the crime scene photos. Identify the crime lab section where you would send each item of physical evidence. Explain why you would send that particular piece of evidence there. Also, indicate what types of test results you might expect to obtain from the crime lab examinations.

Notes

[1] William Eckert, *Introduction to the Forensic Sciences*, 2nd ed. (Boca Raton, FL: CRC Press, 1997), 23.

[2] *Frye v. United States*, 54 App. D.C. 46, 293 F. 1013 (1923).

[3] *Daubert v. Merrell Dow Pharm., Inc.*, 509 U.S. (1993).

[4] Peter W. Huber, *Galileo's Revenge: Junk Science in the Courtroom* (New York: Basic Books, 1991), 45.

[5] Ibid., 78.

[6] National Institute of Justice. 2006. *Status and Needs of Forensic Science Service Providers: A Report to Congress*, posted at www.ojp.usdoj.gov/nij/pubs-sum/213420.htm.

[7] U.S. Department of Justice, Office of Justice Programs, National Institute of Justice. *Death Investigation: A Guide for the Scene Investigator*, posted at www.ojp.usdoj.gov.

[8] Eckert, *Forensic Sciences*, 33–40.

[9] Ibid.

[10] Federal Bureau of Investigation, *The FBI Crime Laboratory*, posted at www.fbi.gov/hq/lab/html/ipgu1.htm.

[11]National Research Council, *Strengthening Forensic Science in the United States: A Path Forward* (Washington, DC: USGPO, 2009), 67–72.

[12]National Research Council, *DNA Technology in Forensic Science* (Washington, DC: National Academy Press, 1996).

[13]Eckert, *Forensic Sciences*, 107–111.

[14]Ibid., 121–126.

[15]Peter Komarinski, *Automated Fingerprint Identification Systems* (Boston, MA: Elsevier Academic Press, 2005), 120–135.

[16]Ibid.

[17]Federal Bureau of Identification, *Integrated Automated Fingerprint Identification System*, posted at www.fbi.gov/about-us/cjis/fingerprints_biometrics/iafis/iafis.

[18]John Vanderkolk, "ACE-V: A Model," *Journal of Forensic Identification*, 2004, Vol. 54(1), 45–52.

[19]Richard Saferstein, *Criminalistics: An Introduction to Forensic Science*, 4th ed. (Upper Saddle River, NJ: Prentice Hall, 2011), 242–245.

[20]Ibid., 365–369.

[21]Ibid., 380.

[22]Ibid., 435–437.

[23]Bureau of Alcohol, Tobacco, Firearms and Explosives, *NIBIN*, posted at www.nibin.gov.

[24]Ibid.

[25]Saferstein, *Criminalistics*, 329–347.

[26]Ibid.

[27]Saferstein, *Criminalistics*, 457–468.

[28]National Institute of Justice, *DNA Initiative: Advancing Criminal Justice Through DNA Technology*, posted at www.dna.gov.

[29]Ibid.

[30]Ibid.

[31]Ibid.

[32]Ibid.

[33]Ibid.

[34]Federal Bureau of Investigation, *Combined DNA Index System (CODIS)*, posted at www.fbi.gov/about-us/lab/codis.

[35]Benjamin Cardozo School of Law, *Innocence Project*, posted at www.innocenceproject.org.

[36]Eckert, *Forensic Sciences*, 93–98.

[37]Ibid.

[38]Ibid., 343–355.

[39]University of Tennessee, Knoxville, *Forensic Anthropology Center*, posted at web.utk.edu/~fac.

[40]Jason H. Byrd, *Forensic Entomology: Insects in Legal Investigations*, posted at www.forensic-entomology.com.

[41]Eckert, *Forensic Sciences*, 57–65.

[42]Casey Eoghan, *Digital Evidence and Computer Crime* (San Diego, CA: Academic Press, 2004).

[43]National Research Council, *Strengthening Forensic Science in the United States*, 183–192.

CHAPTER NINE

HOMICIDE AND WOUNDING SCENES

Learning Objectives

After completing this chapter, you should be able to:

1. Differentiate between the types of homicide, murder, and wrongful death.
2. Describe how a homicide investigation is conducted.
3. Summarize how time of death is estimated.
4. Explain the use of evidence in death investigations.
5. Explain the various types of gunshot wounds.
6. Identify stabbing wounds and the sharp objects used to inflict them.
7. Describe other types of death investigations.

Chapter Outline

Homicide Investigation
- The Legal Definition of Homicide
- Murder vs. Manslaughter
- Justified or Excusable Homicides
- Nonhomicides

Classifying Homicides

Characteristics of Homicide

The First Response Homicide Scenes

Opening Homicide Cases

Postmortem Indicators
- *Livor Mortis* (Lividity)
- *Rigor Mortis*
- *Algor Mortis*

Decomposed Bodies

Skeletal Remains

Gunshot Scenes
- Entry Wounds
- Exit Wounds
- Shooting Distance
- Type of Weapon
- Shooting Trajectory
- Reentry Wounds
- Multiple Shots
- Shooting Behavior

Reconstructing a Shooting Scene

Shotgun Shootings
- Contact Wounds
- Close Wounds
- Intermediate Wounds
- Distant Wounds
- Shotgun Choke
- Creating Shotgun Distance Standards

Suicide Shootings

Reconstructing a Suspicious Death Scene

Stabbing Scenes
- Stab Wound Characteristics
- Wound Marginals
- Wound Length
- Wound Width
- Wound Depth

Suicide by Sharp Objects

Reconstructing a Stabbing Death Scene

Blunt Force Trauma Scenes

Asphyxiation Scenes

Suffocation
- Smothering
- Choking
- Drowning

Chemical Asphyxiation

Strangulation
- Manual Strangulation
- Ligature Strangulation
- Hanging Strangulation

Poisoning Scenes

Homicide Typologies

INTRODUCTION

WHEN FIRST EXAMINING THE CRIME SCENE photo shown here, you might immediately conclude that this woman was murdered. Your assumption would probably be based on the many signs of murder present: an apparent dead body, a gun that appears to have been fired, and several cartridge casings strewn on the floor. So, how would you proceed to investigate this apparent murder? What evidence would you collect and not collect? What information would you see seek from first responders to the scene? What questions would you ask possible witnesses? As in most investigations of this nature, there will be limited time and resources available. You will have one shot at processing this crime scene—so you must do it as efficiently as possible.

To confirm your suspicions that the woman has indeed been murdered, you will have to focus your investigation on specific items of evidence that matter most for proving the crime of murder as it is defined by law. This is why investigators must have a solid understanding of all legal elements that must be satisfied to prove the commission of any particular crime being investigated. During the course of your investigation, you may discover evidence that suggests that your suspicions of murder are legally unfounded. Alternatively, evidence you collect may suggest the death was an accident, a suicide, or a shooting carried out in self-defense. At this point, you probably realize that the law must be the focus factor while conducting an investigation of the case at hand, or any other case for that matter.

Thus, this chapter appropriately begins with a discussion of the various legal definitions that can be applied to death investigations. In addition, material is presented in this chapter within the context of homicide investigation in relation to crimes that may involve nonfatal injuries.

HOMICIDE INVESTIGATION

The Legal Definition of Homicide

Lay persons and the media often use the term **homicide** to describe deaths occurring under a variety of circumstances; within the context of criminal investigation, however, the word has a very specific meaning. To the investigator, homicide includes all deaths that involve the *killing of one human being by the act or omission of another.*[1] All other forms of death falling outside this legal definition are not considered homicides (e.g., deaths resulting from natural causes, accidents, or suicide). Thus, just one piece of evidence at the crime scene suggesting another person's involvement in an individual's death will make the case a homicide. Depending on the exact circumstances surrounding the death of the victim, however, the homicide may be legally classified as either a criminal or a noncriminal act. Criminal homicides encountered most often by investigators include the legal categories of **murder** and **manslaughter**. Those of a noncriminal variety include killings that are *justified* or *excused* under the law. Other deaths may be classified as *nonhomicides* because the deaths are brought about solely by the victim's actions.[2]

Murder vs. Manslaughter

The act of murder, as commonly defined in U.S. legal codes, is the unlawful killing of a human being with malice aforethought. Simply put, murder is a form of homicide where a deliberate and specific intent (malice) to kill can be proven by available evidence. Results of the homicide investigation are vital for

(a)

(b)

FIGURE 9.1 ▶ (a) Overkill, as displayed in this photo of a revenge killing, leaves little doubt that a homicide should be treated as a murder case. (b) The remains of the victim's charred head, discovered in a fireplace in a room adjoining the crime scene.

determining the *degree* of murder with which a criminal defendant will ultimately be charged. In first-degree murder, evidence will reveal that death resulted from deliberate, intentional, and premeditated (or planned) killing. For example, when called to a death scene such as that illustrated in Figure 9.1 containing various signs of "overkill," the investigator should no problem concluding that a willful murder has taken place. Typically, this type of homicide provides some form of psychological and/or actual benefits to the killer. Other examples of potential first-degree murder situations include the following:

- Drive-by, ride-by, or walk-by shootings involving rival street gangs
- Killing for revenge or jealousy
- Serial and cult murders
- Murder for hire, or contract killings
- Killing for insurance money

- Hate crime murders
- Lover's triangle killings
- Killing for political convictions (terrorism)
- Killing during the commission of a robbery or carjacking

Successful prosecution of these cases will result in the most severe criminal sanctions, including life in prison and, depending on the state, the death penalty. If the death is caused by deliberate and intentional killing, yet premeditation cannot be demonstrated by the investigative evidence, a criminal defendant will likely be charged with *second-degree murder*—which is punishable by less severe criminal sanctions. Most murders fall within the legal realm of second-degree. Examples include the following:

- Bar fights
- Domestic violence
- Spontaneous encounters between rival gang killings
- Aggravated disputes between family members or acquaintances
- Drug deals gone bad

Manslaughter, also a form of criminal homicide, is generally defined as the unlawful killing of a human being without malice aforethought. Unlike murder, manslaughter does not evidence advanced planning; however, it may or may not involve the intent to kill. Intentional killings that result from some form of provocation on the part of the victim are classified as *voluntary manslaughter*. Examples of these homicides are (1) a father who spontaneously kills the person who sexually abused his child, or (2) a wife who in the heat of passion kills her husband and his lover upon discovering them in her bedroom. *Involuntary manslaughter*, the least serious form of criminal homicide, involves neither planning nor intent. The act resulting in death is so careless or negligent, however, that it cannot be considered a mere accident. Investigations of deaths that appear to be accidental such as shootings, poisonings, vehicular collisions, industrial injuries, mechanical malfunctions, or simple human error may in fact legally qualify as cases of involuntary manslaughter.[3]

Justified or Excusable Homicides

Homicides can be noncriminal as well. The deaths of persons killed as the result of their own intentions or carelessness, yet at the hands of another, are classified as either *justified* or *excusable* homicide. Justified homicides usually involve the claim of self-defense, where it can be proven that deadly force was necessary to avoid death or great bodily injury to the person or a third party. These include situations in which civilians kill persons while committing a felony and law enforcement officers kill felons in the line of duty. Excusable homicides usually involve accidents where either (1) victims are responsible for their own death or (2) a person is killed under legal and unavoidable circumstances. As an example of the former, a person may be killed by oncoming traffic while attempting to cross a busy freeway; in the latter situation, a pedestrian may be struck and killed by an emergency vehicle as the result of failing to observe its lights and siren. Common to both of these situations

TABLE 9.1 SUMMARY OF HOMICIDE TYPES AND EVIDENCE REQUIREMENTS

	OTHER'S ACT/OMISSION		MALICE		INTENT		PLANNING	
					Evidence Suggesting:			
Legal Classification	Yes	No	Yes	No	Yes	No	Yes	No
Illegal Homicide:								
Murder, First Degree	x		x		x		x	
Murder, Second Degree	x		x		x			x
Voluntary Manslaughter	x			x	x			x
Involuntary Manslaughter	x			x		x		x
Legal Homicide:								
Justified/Excused	x			x	x			x
Nonhomicide*		x			x	x	x	

*In the case of suicide and other planned nonhomicides.

is a lack of intent on the part of the person(s) responsible for the victim's death.[4]

Nonhomicides

A case will be ruled a **nonhomicide** when (1) it cannot be proven that the killing resulted from the act or omission of another, as with death by natural causes; or (2) suicide is proven by evidence demonstrating that the victim intended to take his or her own life without the help/assistance of another person. Table 9-1 summarizes various types of homicides and the evidence necessary to prove them.[5]

CASE CLOSE-UP 9.1

"THE SEAN BELL SHOOTING"
(Queens, New York)

Acquittal on the grounds of self-defense is often controversial in trials where the matter at hand is an officer's shooting of a crime suspect. Recently, this fact was demonstrated in the highly publicized trial of three New York City Police Detectives charged with manslaughter for the shooting death of Sean Bell. Bell, who was at a club attending his bachelor party, was killed when five detectives working a vice undercover assignment fired 50 rounds into the passenger compartment of a vehicle where Bell and two friends were seated. In their defense, the officers claimed they had overheard Bell and his friends talking about possessing a handgun and possibly using it to carry out an assault. Furthermore, the detectives claimed the decision to use deadly force came after one of the officers observed the vehicle's driver reaching for what he believed to be a handgun—and alerted the other officers on the scene by yelling "Gun!" In response, the detectives opened fire on the vehicle, killing Bell and wounding his two friends. Investigations conducted after the shooting revealed that all three men were unarmed at the time of the shooting. At trial, various items of evidence were presented to suggest the officers had acted in a reckless manner—including ballistics examinations indicating that one of the officers fired 31 rounds into the vehicle, reloading once. The detectives, claiming self-defense, were acquitted by a judge conducting a bench hearing of all charges related to the shooting incident. Following the trial, public outcry over this verdict as an example of racism, police brutality, and injustice was heard in New York City and throughout the nation. A civil law suit for wrongful death later resulted in the award of over $7 million dollars paid by the City to Sean Bell's estate.

CLASSIFYING HOMICIDES

There are various methods of classifying homicides. Of these, the FBI's homicide classification model constructed by Hazelwood and Douglas has achieved widespread acceptance and use in the media and by the law enforcement community. The following six categories of homicide are outlined by the FBI:

1. Single Homicide: One victim killed at one time in one location.

2. Double Homicide: Two victims killed at one time in one location.

3. Triple Homicide: Three victims killed at one time in one location.

4. Mass Murder: Four or more victims killed at one time in one location. Furthermore, two subcategories of **mass murder** can be identified. Classic mass murder is the killing of four or more people in one place in one length of time, no matter how much time is spent by the killer. The second, family mass murder, involves the killing of four or more family members. If four or more family members are killed and the killer takes his or her own life, this is referred to as a *mass murder/suicide*.

5. Spree Murder: A single homicidal event involving two or more locations and no emotional cooling-off period between the murders classifies as a **spree murder**.

6. Serial Murder: Three or more separate homicidal events committed in three or more separate locations by the same killer who experiences an emotional cooling-off period between each event are classified as a **serial murder**.[6]

CHARACTERISTICS OF HOMICIDE

Sometimes, it is useful to go with the averages when trying to identify the perpetrators or victims of a homicide; that is, there are certain known characteristics of homicide that give investigators the best chances of predicting who is most likely to become involved in a homicidal encounter. Based on known statistical averages derived from murder arrest/investigation data, the following is known regarding homicides:

- 77 percent are committed by males
- 48 percent are classified as single homicides
- 90 percent of all victims are males

- 51 percent of perpetrators are African-American, 46 percent are Caucasian, and less than 3 percent represent other races/ethnicities
- 88 percent of victims are 18 years or older, with 40 percent between the ages of 20–34
- 87 percent of offenders are 18 years or older, with 75 percent between the ages of 17–14
- 94 percent of African-American victims are killed by an African-American perpetrator; 85 percent of Caucasian victims are killed by Caucasian perpetrators
- 47 percent are carried out using a handgun
- 54 percent are committed by someone known by the victim (e.g., acquaintance, neighbor, friend) and 24 percent are committed by family members
- 35 percent of female victims with prior knowledge of the perpetrator were killed by their husband or boyfriend
- 41 percent occurred during an argument (which may have been precipitated by the victim's actions), and 23 percent during the commission of a felony (rape, robbery, burglary, etc.)
- Some independent sources indicate that many homicide offenders have prior arrest histories for assault and other violent offenses, are unmarried/divorced, have prior histories using/selling drugs, work in labor-type occupations, or are unemployed.[7]

THE FIRST RESPONSE TO HOMICIDE SCENES

Homicide investigations are often triggered by 911 calls involving crimes in progress such as assaults, domestic quarrels, and robberies. In these instances, a witness may have heard gunshots or observed an actual homicide before calling police to respond to the location. In situations where a death has already

FIGURE 9.2 ▶ Privacy curtains, such as the one pictured here, are used to encircle the core of the crime scene to protect evidence and block the view of onlookers.

occurred, a citizen may report discovering a dead body, or an informant may provide the whereabouts of a murder victim's body. When a prospective homicide call is received, both police and EMTs/fire personnel typically are notified and dispatched to the scene. With rare exceptions, most crimes that are potential homicides are treated by first responding officers as hot call emergencies and responded to with lights and siren by patrol units. First responders to suspected homicides must exert their best physical and mental efforts to make split-second decisions

and to prepare for the countless unpredictable events that may lie ahead. Specific duties of the homicide first responder include the following:

- Keeping in contact with dispatch to receive updates regarding the crime scene
- Ascertaining any suspect information
- Coordinating the activities of responding police units, EMTs, and other emergency personnel

HOT TIPS AND LEADS 9.1

The Mindset Variable

According to one of this text's authors, who has extensive experience as a first responder to homicide scenes, it is important for officers responding to possible murder situations to develop a *mindset variable*. This is a state of mind that is free of all thoughts except those focusing on the

problem at hand. Successfully applying the mindset variable requires the ability to neutralize all mental distractions, such as those originating from work or family problems. Usually, this mental skill develops with experience in responding to homicide crime scenes.

Field tactics used in response to homicide calls are similar to those outlined in the Chapter 3 discussion of first responder duties at the crime scene. In situations where homicides are actively in progress, however, officers must respond so as to ensure the safety of everyone at the scene and gather the maximum amount of information about the crime in a very short period of time. One method to accomplish this involves a multiunit response. In this tactic, a single first responding unit, commonly referred to as the *handling unit*, takes a lead role in coordinating assisting units and their positions around the crime scene. The plan of action for determining units' positions upon their arrival should aim both at safety and preserving the possible crime scene. Good positioning around the scene also will provide officers a clear field of vision to observe and apprehend possible suspects attempting to leave the call location either by car or on foot. In multistreet residential and commercial areas, the handling unit usually is positioned west of the call location, a second unit takes a position to the east, and a third unit is located directly behind the scene. In rural areas with limited roadways and backup units, a single handling unit could be located where roadways to and from the scene can be viewed simultaneously. Emergency personnel should be positioned far enough from the scene to avoid exposure to ongoing criminal activity and should enter the scene only when law enforcement clears them to do so.

Upon arriving at the scene, the handling unit should quickly (less than 30 seconds) search for anything out of the ordinary. Identifying possible ongoing criminal activity, potential safety hazards, the victim's body location, and possible suspects should be given priority. If a wounded victim is apparent, note the location and advise emergency medical units. Have them stand by at their staging location until the scene is cleared as safe to enter. Also, at possible homicide scenes, the handling

unit may provide further investigative leads by noting one or more of the following initial observations:

- Persons running or walking away from the scene (often a suspect will walk to avoid attention)
- Vehicles leaving the scene at high or low rates of speed (again, suspects often drive so as not to alert police)
- Persons entering stores, businesses, vehicles, and alleyways; also, pedestrians making sudden moves or changes in direction
- Sounds of screeching tires, loud engine acceleration, or doors or windows slamming
- Lights being turned on or off in residences or business establishments

When the initial examination of the scene is complete, the handling unit must devise an approach to the location—subject to change at any time, of course, depending on any pressing issues present or materializing at the scene. These issues may include sudden notification of a suspect's whereabouts, gunfire, unruly crowds, and other spontaneous possible threats to officer safety. Should these situations arise or any others where officer safety becomes an immediate issue, a tandem approach to the scene—usually three or more officers approaching the scene in unison—is advisable.

When officer safety issues are not readily apparent, the crime scene approach can be made by the handling officer (alone, or assisted by another officer) while other responding units remain on the crime scene perimeter. If the officer(s) entering the scene discover a possible homicide victim, the EMTs/fire department should be notified immediately to enter the location to administer first aid. Normally, victims showing any signs of life (or the potential to respond to lifesaving efforts)

(a)

(b)

FIGURE 9.3   (a) First responder's view of a suspected gang-related shooting involving a large amount of blood and biological matter. (b) The victim's extensive head wound is a sign of certain death that will require first responders to call investigators to the crime scene.

will be transported to the nearest hospital or medical facility. If personnel are available, an officer should accompany the victim to the hospital to obtain further information about the incident—and perhaps a dying declaration, if the victim's death appears imminent.

Alternatively, victims exhibiting signs of certain death as illustrated by the shooting victim shown in Figure 9.3 usually are pronounced dead at the scene. In either situation, after all emergency medical issues have been handled, the handling officer must begin securing the crime scene. At this time, several other units—together with a field supervisor—may show up or be called to the scene. After briefing the supervisor on first-response activities and observations, the handling unit must start a major incident log and begin securing the crime scene (as discussed in Chapter 3). In most cases, the attending supervisor will determine whether or not to dispatch homicide investigators to the scene. In some jurisdictions, homicide investigators will be notified directly by the handling unit at the scene.

OPENING HOMICIDE CASES

Most homicide investigations involve death-related crimes, although officer shootings and missing persons also may fall under the purview of homicide investigators. The homicide investigation process typically begins with discovery of a death resulting from criminal or suspicious circumstances. Dead bodies displaying outward signs of gunshot, stabbing, and other wounds inflicted by a weapon often leave little to the imagination regarding the cause and circumstances of death and nearly always automatically trigger a homicide investigation. In these situations, the homicide investigator normally conducts an on-site investigation of the body at the scene; then a representative from the coroner/medical examiner's office takes possession of the body and transports it to a county morgue or other postmortem storage facility. All items found on the body and not considered to be evidence are inventoried and stored as property. Where and when possible, attempts should be made to shield the activities of investigators, coroners and other personnel at the death scene from unauthorized onlookers. In outdoor scenes, this can be done by using a privacy curtain (see Figure 9.2) or some other means to restrict unwanted viewing of the on-going investigation.

In contrast to the scenario just presented, however, sometimes the need for a homicide investigation is not immediately evident—death has occurred under suspicious circumstances. For the most part, a suspicious death is one where a person has died unexpectedly or while not under the immediate care of a physician. Deaths are also generally considered suspicious when they occur while a medical patient is under anesthesia or has died within a legally specified period following surgery. Of course, any person (e.g., family of the deceased, first responding patrol officer, EMT, physician) who provides reasonable grounds for believing that a death has occurred under suspicious circumstances may cause a homicide case to be opened. There are various settings in which homicide investigators may be required to investigate a suspicious death:

- Persons who die at home of apparent natural causes such as old age or sickness, yet foul play or criminal responsibility is suspected
- Workers who die in apparent on-the-job accidents where underlying causes of death may be related to criminal circumstances
- Victims of apparent suicides
- Persons killed in situations involving self-defense or occurring during the apparent course of a serious crime (committed by either an officer or a civilian)

In all of these cases, investigators need to work closely with the coroner/medical examiner to determine whether the available evidence—obtained from autopsy results, crime scenes, victims/witnesses, and other sources—suggests that a person's manner of death should be classified as homicide or reclassified as such (if previously proclaimed natural, accidental, or undetermined).

Following the medical and legal discovery that a death likely occurred at the hands of another person, homicide investigators work the case from the initial gathering of crime scene evidence all the way to the final stage—an offender's conviction. During this time—which can be as short as a few days, or as long as many years—investigators form cooperative working relationships with the crime lab, prosecutors, and the coroner/medical examiner's office to review crime scene photos, autopsy reports, lab test results, and other relevant case evidence. Much of this evidence will concern examination of injuries or other biological factors believed to have caused the homicide victim's death. The investigator's job is to identify and interpret this evidence to answer key questions necessary for proving a homicide case:

- What was the type of weapon or other cause of death? Can it be traced back to the offender?
- With multiple injuries or causes of death, were they produced by a lone offender or multiple offenders?
- Which injuries or other potentially lethal factors present were the specific cause of death (e.g., out of multiple gunshot wounds, which one from which weapon was the first to produce the fatality)?
- What was the approximate time and date of death? Does this time frame corroborate or fail to corroborate offender alibis/witness statements?
- What situational factors occurred before, during, and after the death, including defensive measures taken by the victim, original positioning of the body at the time of death, and moving of the body by the offender after death?
- What was the offender's mental intent when the injury or other cause of death occurred (e.g., are signs of overkill present, suggesting that the victim's death was intentional and the desired outcome of the offender's action)?
- In what way did the offender voluntarily act or fail to act that directly or indirectly resulted in injury or death (e.g., was the killing produced by an action, such as a stabbing, or by an inaction, such as the neglect of protection/care that occurs when workers die because their employers fail to take legally required safety precautions)?

The sections that follow present various investigative tools and strategies that provide answers to these questions as well as others that arise in homicide investigations.

POSTMORTEM INDICATORS

There are various indicators of certain death, some of which are more reliable than others. One of the earliest indications of immediate death, although viewed as unreliable in all cases, is **corneal clouding**. If the victim's eyes remain open after death, mainly due to the gravity and positioning of the body, a thin film appears over the external area of the eyes, producing a cloudy or glazed appearance. Corneal clouding can appear as little as an hour after death, but is usually fully present within 3 hours. Pressure when placed on fingernails will often fail to produce signs of *blanching* (or a white discoloration of the otherwise pink colored nail bed). Urine and feces also may be expelled by dead persons, and the hands may curve tightly inward toward the body at the wrist. Other indi-

cators of certain death have a slower onset and more predictable outcome, however, and are more reliable for investigative purposes.[8] These are discussed in the following sections.

Livor Mortis (Lividity)

Livor mortis, commonly referred to as *lividity,* is discoloration of the skin that begins immediately after death. It is produced when noncirculating blood settles to the lowest points in the body. When using lividity as an investigative tool, it is important to note the areas of the body where discoloration appears and does not appear. This will provide a preliminary determination of the body's likely position following death. The color of the lividity can also be useful for determining the approximate time of death. Shortly after death, lividity begins to develop as faint pink blotches. Several hours later, these change into readily observable solid red patterns, which gradually turn purple approximately 12 hours following death.[9]

Further insights into time of death can be gained by determining whether the lividity has fully set, meaning that its appearance is fixed and will not change. This can be done by simply applying pressure to the discolored tissue. If the skin turns a lighter tone (or *blanches*) from the pressure, the lividity has not fully set. On the other hand, no change in color tone is a good indicator that the setting process is complete. In most cases, lividity is fully set 12 hours after death.[10]

Detailed lividity analyses help in crime scene reconstruction as well. For example, the question of whether or not a body has been repositioned after death is readily answered by carefully examining lividity pattern consistency. If the victim's original postmortem position was lying on the back on a flat surface with arms and legs extended, consistent lividity patterns should reveal discoloration in the lower portion of the entire body's trunk and extremities. If inconsistent lividity patterns, such as discoloration of the chest back regions, appear, however, the investigator should suspect that the body was repositioned after death.

In other types of death, such as suicide by hanging, lividity patterns can prove the existence of foul play. "Swingers," or those who hang themselves from a rope or some other sort of suspension method, usually evidence lividity in their feet and hands. Obviously, a body hanging from a rope with lividity evident in the chest region and absent in the feet or hands must be investigated as a homicide rather than suicide. Additional attempts to cover up a homicide, betrayed by lividity, include situations that appear at first to be an accidental death. For example, a dead hiker lying face down at the bottom of a cliff should evidence lividity patterns consistent with the position of the body where it came to rest. Absence of lividity in the facial area and the body's other low points would suggest that death occurred before the fall rather than afterward, or the body was repositioned for some reason.

Finally, various investigative clues can be found by looking for changes in lividity that may have occurred before the lividity had completely set. Until the setting process is complete, lividity patterns can be created, changed, or altered. For example, moving a dead body will cause lividity to form in new areas as the result of repositioning. It may be possible to distinguish between preexisting and newly created lividity patterns by examining color tone. As

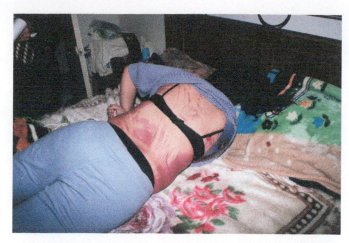

FIGURE 9.4 ▶ Well-developed lividity is shown on this murder victim's back and side torso area. The lividity patterns in the lower middle back region reveal the cloth patterns of the victim's shirt.

TABLE 9.2		TIME OF DEATH INDICATORS	
TIME OF DEATH	RIGOR MORTIS	ALGOR MORTIS	LIVOR MORTIS
3 to 6 hrs.	Not Stiff	Warm	Pink/Red
6 to 12 hrs.	Stiff	Warm	Red/Purple
12 to 36 hrs.	Stiff	Cool	Purple
> 36 hrs.	Not Stiff	Cool	Purple/Green/Black

a general rule, the longer an area has set in the same position, the darker or more purplish the discoloration will be. Another interesting feature of lividity is its ability to show impressions of objects that apply pressure during the setting phase. Clothing, rocks, furniture, and flooring features are some of the more common pressure impressions discovered in lividity. Figure 9.4 shows a shooting victim with fully developed lividity, which includes clothing impressions. Again, the impression found in lividity must be consistent with the position and location of the dead body.[11]

Rigor Mortis

Rigor mortis is the stiffening of the body for a brief time period following death. This results from postmortem biochemical changes that cause muscles to stiffen and lock joints in place. Because of its rather predictable qualities, *rigor mortis* can help determine time of death and provide rich investigative clues. When applying *rigor mortis* to time of death, the following timeline, based on the body's temperature and rigidity, is useful:

- If the body is warm and not stiff, time of death is approximately 3–6 hours.
- If the body is warm and stiff, time of death is approximately 6–12 hours.
- If the body is cool and stiff, time of death is approximately 12–36 hours.
- If the body is cool and not stiff, time of death is usually greater than 36 hours.[12]

Of course, the timeline just presented should be considered a rough means, at best, for determining time of death. Many factors have been proven to accelerate as well as inhibit the onset and resistance of *rigor mortis*. Specifically, warmer temperatures, larger body mass, and certain activities directly preceding death have been shown to speed up the *rigor mortis* process. A more detailed presentation of these factors can be found in Table 9.2.

Of additional benefit to the crime scene investigator is an understanding of the manner in which *rigor mortis* begins and

ends. The stiffening effects of *rigor mortis* consistently start in the body's smallest muscles and finish in the largest ones. Thus, the earliest stages of *rigor mortis* will affect the facial region (e.g., eyelids, jaw), fingers, and toes. For example, Figure 9.5 illustrates the beginning stages of *rigor mortis* in the fingers of a shooting victim. Last to be affected will be areas such as upper thighs and arms. When *rigor mortis* subsides, the same rule applies: smaller muscles relax before larger ones.

When examining a body in a state of *rigor mortis*, investigators must make sure that the position of the body's extremities is consistent with other crime scene indicators. In particular, any body part frozen in a position contrary to the forces of gravity should be considered a suspicious circumstance. Also, of potential benefit to the investigator is the discovery of *rigor mortis* that has been broken; that is, a stiffened muscle has been moved, breaking the *rigor mortis*. Once *rigor mortis* has been broken, it will not recur. Efforts to reposition a body in *rigor mortis* can easily be detected, when the stiffness in the large muscles of the arms or legs is broken, but smaller muscles such as those in fingers and toes remain stiff. Likewise, a gun found in the nonstiff hand of a suspected suicide victim must

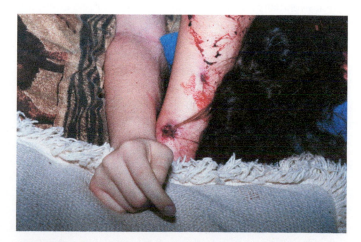

FIGURE 9.5 This shooting victim's fingers show the beginning stages of *rigor mortis*, which first affects the small muscles in the hands, feet, and facial areas and then spreads to larger muscles of the arms and legs.

be considered suspicious when the fingers on the victim's other hand and the toes remain in a state of rigor.[13]

Algor Mortis

Cooling (or warming) of the body following death is generally referred to as **algor mortis**. It begins the moment circulation stops and continues until the dead body reaches the ambient temperature of its immediate surroundings. Through various temperature comparisons associated with the *algor mortis* biological process, it is possible to estimate time of death. Studies show that, on average, a dead body cools 1.5° to 2° per hour if the ambient temperature of the crime scene area is between 70° and 75° Fahrenheit. Thus, a body with a living temperature of 98.6° Fahrenheit fully cools to the ambient temperature of its surroundings in approximately 12 hours. It must be recognized, however, that in locations where ambient temperatures are above 98.6°, the core temperature of a dead body will increase rather than decrease.[14]

DECOMPOSED BODIES

External decomposition of the body's soft tissue, referred to as **putrefaction**, begins approximately 36 hours after death. Bodies first discovered at this and later times are commonly referred to as *decomps*. They present particular challenges to homicide investigation because the rich clues preserved by the skin and other soft tissue may no longer be present. Depending on the stage of decomposition, and the location of the crime scene, it may be difficult to determine time and cause of death or even the victim's identity.[15]

Bodies entering the earliest stage of decomposition, at around 36 hours following death, turn various colors (orange, red, blue, green) beginning with the lower abdominal region. At about the same time, areas affected by lividity will turn from purple hues to a greenish/black tint. As time progresses, the multicolor flesh becomes evident in the thighs and upper torso until it eventually covers the entire body. In 36 to 48 hours, the body begins to show outward signs of bloating, especially in areas of the body where the skin is loose. This change is produced by the body's natural bacteria after death, which begin to break down the body's soft tissue into gas and liquid. At 72 hours the entire body will show signs of decomposition and emit a very strong odor often described as similar to rotting meat. This is the result of internal gasses seeping through the body and the decaying flesh.

Within 4 to 10 days, the body will appear fully bloated— sometimes appearing twice its original size. After 10 days black putrefaction takes place, which is best characterized as the body melting down (see Figure 9.6). During this phase, black patches appear on the body, and the flesh above them appears creamy in texture. Eventually, the entire body will turn black. In addition, it will start to flatten out and seep fluids from the skin and orifices. From 20 to 50 days, the body will dry and become totally flat as it begins to ferment. Finally, in 50 days to approximately one

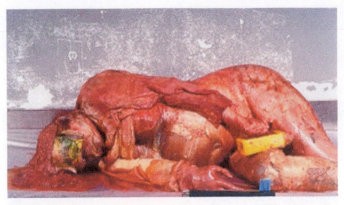

(a)

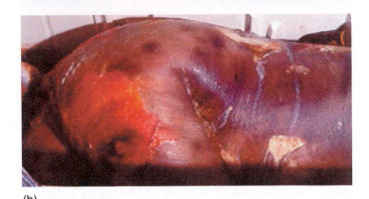

(b)

FIGURE 9.6 ▶ (a) Murder victim showing signs of advanced putrefaction; (b) close-up view.

year after death, the body undergoes dry decay until it is devoid of all soft tissue, leaving only skeletal remains.[16]

When using the data in Table 9.2 in actual homicide investigations, one must bear in mind that it is, at best, an approximation of actual time of death. No two bodies will decompose exactly alike. This is because many variables at crime scenes function to either slow down or speed up the decomposition process. Bodies decompose faster, for example, when exposed to warmer temperatures, parasitic bacteria, environmental contaminants, carrion insects, and carnivorous animals. Conversely, slower decomposition may be expected when such factors are absent at a crime scene. Cool temperatures, especially, have a strong effect in slowing the bacterial activity responsible for the body's internal breakdown. To totally stop the decomposition process, the body must be completely frozen; but a body frozen any time after death will show signs of decomposition.

In situations where death occurs outdoors, significant insect and carnivore activity may affect the body. As previously mentioned (in Chapter 8), the female blow fly may lay eggs within exposed natural body openings—namely the eyes and mouth. This can occur as soon as 10 minutes after death. Depending on the ambient outdoor temperature ranges, the eggs will hatch and go through their metamorphosis cycle, passing through the maggot, pupa, and adult fly stages at fairly predictable times—which can be used to determine the approximate time of death. Flies and insects will also infest bleeding open wounds created by injuries related to criminal activities, such as defense wounds in the victim's arms. Occasionally, fly larvae in the digestive tract, feeding on the body during their maggot phase, can be analyzed in the crime lab for the presence of certain drugs to determine whether the victim used illegal substances before death.[17]

SKELETAL REMAINS

Perhaps the most challenging crime scene for homicide investigators is one where only skeletal remains are discovered in crime scenes such as that illustrated in Figure 9.7. This situation typically arises when cold cases have been re-opened or the crime scene is located in a hot, dry, desert-type landscape. In the best scenario, investigators work with an undisturbed gravesite containing the victim's fully intact skeleton, clothing items, and perhaps personal belongings. Under the worst circumstances, however, the only evidence available may be a few scattered bones or teeth. Without the help of experts, it may even be difficult to determine whether the remains are those of an animal or a human being.

Fortunately, research in the field of forensic anthropology has provided invaluable information to assist investigators handling cases involving a fully decomposed human body. Investigators should be cognizant of the fact that DNA often can be extracted from bone or teeth to provide a positive personal identity if there is a match to an existing DNA profile of a likely victim. In the absence of DNA evidence, skeletal remains can be examined to determine the following:

- *AGE:* Age is best determined by examining teeth, if present. The fully developed dentition of an adult male consists of 32 teeth and that of a child is 20 teeth. All childhood deciduous teeth (with the exception of third molars or wisdom teeth) are replaced by adult permanent teeth by the age of 12 years. Wisdom teeth, if fully erupted, are present by the age of 18 to 20 years. Missing or excessively worn teeth in adults suggest advanced age. Certain skeletal bone features can be used to determine a

victim's age, but are best used to corroborate estimates derived from teeth. Obviously, the skeletons of young children are noticeably smaller than those of adolescents and adults. Laboratory analyses of arm and leg bones, however, can be used to distinguish adolescents aged 13 to 18 years from both children and adults. Other bones useful for determining an adult's age include the pelvic bone for persons under 40 years, rib bones for person over 40 years, and the skull for persons 50 years and under.[18]

- *GENDER:* The teeth and bones of males tend to be larger, on average, than those for females. There are precise mathematical formulas for determining gender based on the measurement of bone size and length. These tests can be applied to virtually any bone from the hand, foot, arm, leg, skull, or spine. The examination of bone size alone, however, may be misleading because the skeletal dimensions of adolescent males may be very similar to those of adult females. The pelvis is the most important skeletal remain for gender identification. Besides the fact that a female's pelvic bone appears much broader than that belonging to a male, examining the full pelvic region can provide a definitive determination of the body's gender.[19]

- *ETHNICITY:* Most experts agree that determining race through skeletal remains is a rough approximation, at best. While skin may differ in color, skeletons do not— except for color changes resulting from their exposure to environmental and other elements. A skull containing facial bones is of the greatest use for determining ethnicity. In particular, the eyes, cheeks, nose, and jaw are used by experts to classify remains as Caucasian, African-American, Asian, or Latino. While not as useful, bones of the pelvis and extremities also have been used for ethnic classifications.[20]

- *IDENTITY:* Rather than determining whether bones or teeth belong to a particular class of individuals, such as adult versus child or male versus female, the skeletal remains may be *individualized* to establish a homicide victim's personal identity by examining the signs of:

1. Dentistry:	Documentation including records and x-rays of implants, bridgework, fillings, and missing or extracted teeth can be matched to dental remains.
2. Disease:	Cancer, tumors, and certain infectious diseases leave permanent lesions on the bone.
3. Surgery:	Prosthetic devices such as hip or knee replacements, artificial heart valves, surgical pins and screws, or metal sutures remain in the bone.
4. Trauma:	Breaks and fractures leave heal lines where the trauma occurred.
5. Use/Wear:	Bones in areas of the body that have been used more than others often have slightly larger features and show signs

FIGURE 9.7 ▶ Skeletal remains discovered in a remote desert location.

of arthritis in joints caused by stress and wear. This information can be useful for determining left versus right handedness, an athletic or sedentary lifestyle, or an occupation involving manual labor.[21]

- ***APPEARANCE:*** Facial and skeletal reconstruction can be carried out by various means. Photographs or x-rays can be superimposed over the skull or skeleton. Sculptures of soft tissue covering the contours of facial bones are used to create a 3D personal image. Computer software is now available that applies complex formulas to digital images of skeletal remains to provide an animated reconstruction of personal appearance.[22]

- ***CAUSE OF DEATH:*** Bullets may be lodged in bones, or produce smooth entry holes and jagged, torn exit holes. Beveling of entry and exit points may suggest the trajectory of the bullet's travel, whereas the size of the hole indicates the type of weapon and caliber of ammunition. The presence of pellets combined with large, ripped-away sections of bone are typical of shotgun blasts. Hammers, knives, clubs, and other objects used to inflict wounds can mark bones with their unique impressions. Traces of lead, brass, or other metals left by a bullet or weapon may be deposited in or around suspected trauma areas.[23]

GUNSHOT SCENES

Death by gunfire is a generic term that describes lethal shooting injuries produced by seemingly countless varieties of firearms and their ammunition. Thus, the assumption that no two homicides are alike especially applies to shooting deaths. These cases pose many questions for the homicide investigator to answer. Foremost among these are the following:

- Was the shooter the victim or another person?
- Was the shooting purposeful or accidental?
- What was the circumstance that led up to the shooting?
- If evidence suggests more than one shooter, how many were there?
- Does the physical evidence paint a picture that is consistent with the crime scene?

Gunshot wounds are produced by bullets originating from either handguns or rifles (hereafter referred to as *firearms*), and they are characteristically different from those created by pellets or other projectiles fired from shotguns (discussed later in this section). After a firearm is discharged, gunshot residue is expelled from the muzzle along with the bullet and travels through space in a relatively straight trajectory. If the bullet hits a human body, it will produce an **entry wound** by piercing and stretching the skin where it first strikes. Gunshot residue consisting of shoot, ash, and unburned powder particles may or may not be present at the entry wound site depending on how far away from the body the shot was taken, the type of ammunition used, whether there was an intermediate target, or the type of clothing worn by the gunshot victim.

After entering the body, the bullet produces a path of travel known as the **bullet track**. The bullet track may extend straight from the entry wound, through the body, to a point where it exits, producing an **exit wound**. The bullet may strike bones or other bodily obstructions, however, producing an irregular-shape track traveling in various directions and perhaps blocking the bullet from exiting the body and producing an exit wound. These and other characteristics evidenced in the investigation of homicides produced by gunshot wounds are as follows.

Entry Wounds

The location of an entry wound is often readily observed by examining the victim's clothing for holes, torn or burnt fabric, gunshot residue deposits, and blood. Beneath the clothing exhibiting these external signs is likely a physical entry wound on the victim's body. Each strike to the body produced by a bullet leaves an entry wound that varies in size and shape depending on the caliber of the weapon used, the distance from which the weapon was fired, the type of ammunition used, and the bullet's trajectory. Because of these variables and others, the size of the entry wound does not reliably indicate the caliber (or size) of the bullet causing the wound. On average, however, an entry wound usually can be said to be smaller and more regularly round in shape than an exit wound.[24]

Skin immediately surrounding the bullet entry hole will often appear abraded (or ripped) and bruised. This characteristic, known as the **abrasion ring**, is caused by the stretching of the skin around the bullet's point of entry. In some case, abrasion rings can be used to estimate the trajectory of a bullet. If the ring is round in shape, this usually indicates the bullet was fired at a relatively straight angle. On the other hand, oval shaped rings suggest that the bullet was fired at an angle. Abrasion rings are often not evident in entry wounds of the hands and feet, or wounds caused by high-power firearms such as .357 Magnum handguns or .308 caliber rifles. Additionally, gunpowder residue commonly appears in and around the entry wound—depending largely on the distance of the firearm from the body when discharged. Figure 9.8 illustrates the large amount of gunshot residue that typically surrounds an entry wound from a bullet fired at close range. **Stippling/tattooing** also may be present around the entry wound. This appears as small pepperlike spots randomly dispersed in a circular pattern on skin around the wound, caused by small particles of foreign matter and/or gunpowder projected onto the skin by forces produced by the shooting.[25]

In some cases, the entry wound exhibits **bullet wipe**, a small dark ring appearing on tissue directly around the bullet entry hole. This is caused by deposits of lead, oils, and other residues transferred from the bullet to the skin's surface area. Bullet entry areas in large bones and the skull generally have fracture lines (similar to those produced in glass) radiating away from the wound location. In some cases, a slow-travelling or malformed bullet may lodge where it comes in contact with a bone. In rare instances, multiple entry wounds can be produced by a single bullet. This occurs when parts of the whole bullet separate into smaller pieces before entering the body,

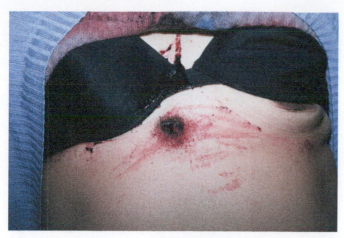

(a)

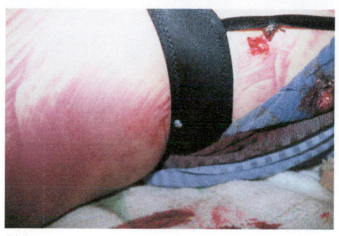

(b)

FIGURE 9.8 ▶ (a) Close-range gunshot entry wound in the victim's chest. (b) Exit wound in the victim's back—note that the bullet is trapped in the clothing strap above the wound.

usually as the result of passing through intermediate objects such as glass or doors before striking the body.[26]

Exit Wounds

Bullets may or may not pass entirely through the body to produce an exit wound, depending on many factors. One such factor is the type of ammunition used. Solid or fully jacketed bullets (e.g., lead covered by copper) are more likely to exit the body than semi-jacketed or hollow-point bullets. Bullets that strike bone and become immobilized or fragment inside the body also fail to produce an exit wound. Absent an exit wound, bleeding from the shooting victim's body may not be immediately present, creating the illusion that the death is perhaps not the result of gunfire. Bodies that do contain exit wounds, however (especially those facing in the direction of gravity), often have profuse pooling of blood beneath the wound.

As previously mentioned, exit wounds are usually larger and more irregular in appearance than entry wounds. They also do not display signs of gunshot residue or an abrasion ring, as found in entrance wounds. Another common indicator of a bullet's exit

area is tissue and other biological matter projected from the exit area. Skin still attached to the wound area may consist of numerous torn flaps that, when pressed together, fit together in a jigsaw-like fashion. Bullets passing through body areas pressed against a firm surface will occasionally produce a *shored* exit wound, which exhibits raised sections of skin surrounding the bullet entry hole. At time, these may be mistaken for entry wounds with an abrasion collar; however, these wounds do not show power residue and, on average, are larger than a typical entry wound.[27]

When the exit wound is located, it should be inspected for the expended bullet. In victims shot while lying on floors or other hard surfaces or wearing thick clothing, bullets or bullet fragments may be discovered within or directly beneath the exit wound. Separation or fracturing of a single bullet while traveling through the body can create the appearance of multiple exit wounds. In this situation, there is usually one larger exit location surrounded by several smaller wounds caused by exiting fragments. Exit wounds in the skull are typically identified by beveling on the bone surfaces broken by the bullet's impact.

Shooting Distance

The shooter's distance from the victim's body is best determined through an examination of the entry wound. The relationship between gunshot wounds and shooting distance is commonly classified in four categories: contact, close, intermediate, and distant. **Contact wounds** are produced by a gun muzzle placed directly on the body at the time the bullet is discharged. The extreme heat and force of gases produced by the gunfire and the bullet it propels permeate the skin, leaving behind a large gaping wound. If clothing is the first point of contact, it displays large amounts of soot, ash, and burning from the high concentration of gunpowder/shot residue. Also, the explosive gases travel inside the wound, producing a *stellate* (or star-shaped) entry wound.[28]

Care should be taken not to confuse contact entry wounds with exit wounds. At first glance their size and shape may look similar, but the entry wound displays interior charring from gunshot residue, whereas the exit wound does not. Also, the contact wound may display an imprint of the gun's muzzle, otherwise known as a **muzzle contusion** (see Figure 9.9). Not to be confused with an abrasion ring, the muzzle contusion is an impression left by the gun barrel's end in the skin near the contact wound. This is caused by the muzzle forcefully pushing into the skin, which leaves an imprint in the form of bruised tissue. The firearm's recoil or the aggression of the offender's acts may produce muzzle contusions.[29]

Wounds classified as close are those produced by guns 6–8 inches from the body. Large circular deposits of gunpowder residue surrounding the bullet entry hole are discovered most often in wounds produced at this shooting distance. Stippling/tattooing also may be present in a tight pattern around the outer edges of the wound. Intermediate-distance wounds, made by guns 8 inches to 3 feet from the body, are characterized by stippling/tattooing scattered around the entry wound, produced by unburned and partially burned gunpowder deposited in the

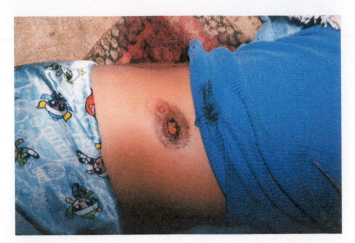

FIGURE 9.9 ▶ Close-range entry wound displaying a muzzle contusion produced by the weapon's recoil after the shot.

(a)

(b)

FIGURE 9.10 ▶ (a and b) Two views of a head wound produced by a high-power rifle.

skin. The farther the shooter's distance, the less concentrated the pattern of stippling/tattooing will appear around the perimeter of the wound. Distant wounds, or those made by gunshots from beyond 3 feet, do not characteristically show stippling/tattooing. Because of the distance between the victim and the shooter, heat and gasses expelled from the gun's muzzle do not produce a large, torn, or frayed entry hole; rather, a smaller, smoother hole is produced by a puncture motion of the bullet. These wounds do display well-formed abrasion rings, however, and visible signs of bullet wipe around the inner edges of the hole caused by the bullet's entry. Close or intermediate-distance wounds can appear as though they are of the distant type if the victim's clothing blocks gunpowder residue from the surface of the victim's skin. Thus, before a shooting distance classification is made, it should always be determined whether the skin area exhibiting a gunshot wound was covered by clothing or openly exposed at the time of the shooting.[30]

Type of Weapon

Higher-power handguns and rifles often produce large, ragged, stellate entry wounds at contact, close, and sometimes even intermediate shooting distances. Smaller, less powerful firearms tend to create rounder and more regular looking entry wounds. Shots made at contact or close ranges by high-power rifles produce large stellate wounds with heavy burning and soot deposits. At intermediate and distant ranges, shots are likely to produce much smaller entry wounds. High-power rifle shots at these distances that produce wounds to the head are likely to cause the skull to burst at the bullet's entry point or dislodge the brain as illustrated in Figure 9.10.

Shooting Trajectory

Several characteristics of gunshot wounds allow the angle or trajectory of the bullet's travel to be estimated. First, when shots are taken at a straight (or 90°) angle to the body's surface, round abrasion rings are produced. More oval-shape abrasion rings suggest a steeper or more angular shooting trajectory. Second, the bullet's

entry hole is often *shouldered* or angled in the direction of the bullet's travel. As a general rule, bullets travel in a straight path from the point at which they are fired. When a bullet hits an intermediary target, however, there can be radical changes in the bullet's path. Therefore, bullets that have not passed through an intermediary target (a window or door, for example) often are the best indicators of shooting trajectory.[31]

Reentry Wounds

Reentry wounds are created when a bullet enters one part of the body and then passes through another area of the body, forming a second entry wound. This usually occurs when the original entry wound is located on the outside of an arm or leg. For example, when shooting victims make defensive moves with their arms, the bullet passes through the forearm and reenters into the torso. Reentry wounds are noticeably larger than normal entry wounds because the bullet may become malformed and lose velocity. These wounds often are confused with regular exit wounds, but are readily identified by tracing the bullet's path from its initial point of entry. Bullets passing through intermediate targets, such as glass windows, wooden doors, or another human body, will likely pick up fragments of the objects they pass through, enabling microscopic analyses to reveal which objects were struck first, second, third, and so on.[32]

Multiple Shots

When multiple shots are evident within a body, it becomes necessary to determine whether all of the bullets came from the same firearm. It may also be possible to ascertain which of the bullet strikes caused the victim's death. In most instances, these questions can only be answered by a medical examiner conducting an autopsy. The examination of stippling/tattooing characteristics and the abrasion collar, however, may provide preliminary insights into whether the victim was alive or dead when particular individual shots were made. If victims were alive at the time a bullet wound was incurred, reddish stippling/tattooing will appear around the wound. This is because stippling/tattooing is a live body reaction to the foreign and/or hot powder particles touching the skin. Victims who are already dead when they are shot will likely exhibit yellowish or gray stippling/tattooing around the bullet entry wound. Similarly, bruising is also a live body reaction. Thus, large, well-developed bruising patterns form in the abrasion collar of wounds incurred by live victims. Bruising does not occur after death, so an abrasion collar without raised bruising around the entry wound may suggest that the shot causing the wound came after the victim's death from another bullet wound or some other cause.[33]

Shooting Behavior

A popular myth is that a person when shot falls instantly in their tracks or is propelled a great distance in the air. Clearly, these are media portrayals of shooting with no basis in reality. Studies of shooting victim's behaviors have consistently revealed that most persons continue walking, running, or moving for a brief or sometimes extended period of time after being shot. This occurs even when the victim is shot numerous times, resulting in a fatality. Many shooting victims claim that they were not even aware of having been hit by a bullet. Only when a bullet causes massive head trauma, hits the spinal cord, or ruptures a major blood source causing extensive bleeding will the shooting victim be stopped in their tracks and become immediately immobilized. Thus, probable postmortem movements of the victim should be considered when reconstructing a shooting incident.

RECONSTRUCTING A SHOOTING SCENE

Case Example 9A presents an indoor shooting scene involving one female victim with multiple gunshot wounds. The series of crime scene photos shown in Figures 9.11 through 9.20 illustrate the investigation, which requires the investigator to use many of the principles and concepts presented so far in this chapter to reconstruct the shooting incident. The first and most vital question to be answered when investigating this crime scene is whether or not the case should be considered a murder. In other words, does the shooting evidence suggest foul play at the hands of another person with an intent to kill the victim? Alternatively, does the evidence suggest that the shooting was accidental or suicidal in nature? The answers to these questions and others vital to the reconstruction of this death scene are contained within the crime scene photos.

CASE EXAMPLE 9A

Indoor Shooting

(a)

(b)

FIGURE 9.11 ▶ After a "shots fired" call, first responders discover the woman pictured here dead in her apartment. A suspect was later identified and apprehended by investigators. Notice the weapon between the victim's legs. Is this a suicide or accidental shooting scene? Or might the suspect have staged this shooting to look like a suicide to cover up a murder? (Courtesy of The National Institute of Health.)

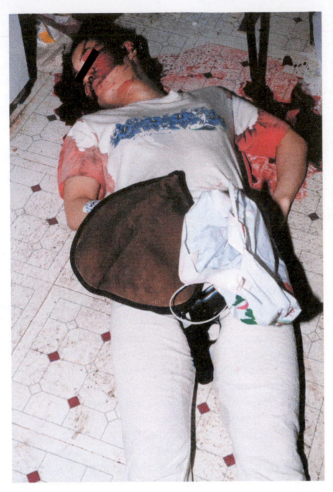

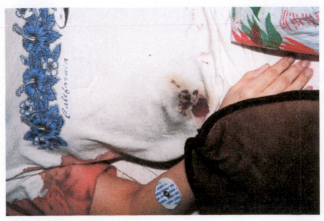

(a)

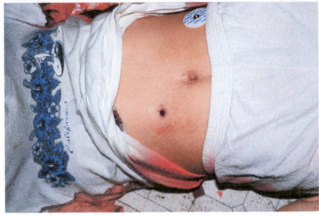

(b)

FIGURE 9.12 ▶ Full view of the victim's body on the kitchen floor after EMTs attempted to revive her. What directions would you have provided to emergency medical personnel attending to this shooting victim?

FIGURE 9.13 ▶ (a) Blood stain and gunshot residue on the exterior of the victim's shirt. (b) Bullet wound located underneath the blood-soaked area on the shirt. What conclusions can you draw about this bullet wound based on observing the victims shirt as well as the wound itself?

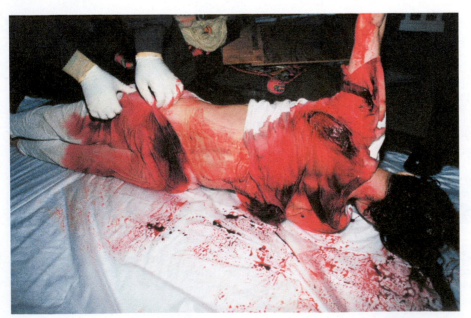

(a)

FIGURE 9.14 ▶ (a) The victim's body is placed on a plastic sheet, where it is positioned so the back region can be examined. Does this examination of the victim's lower back region, and the appearance of the victim's body when moved provide any indication of the likely time of death? (b) A bullet wound discovered in the victim's lower back. Of what significance are the appearance and positioning of this bullet wound to the crime scene investigation?

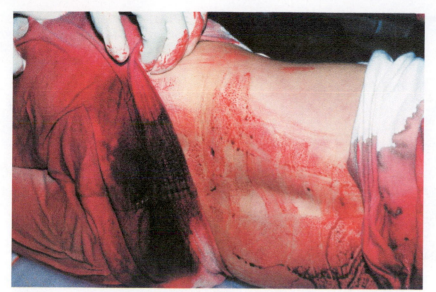

FIGURE 9.14 ▶ *(Continued)*

(b)

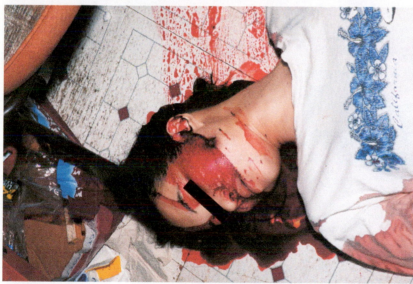

(a)

FIGURE 9.15 ▶ (a and b) Two views of a single bullet wound to the victim's face. What does the exterior appearance of this bullet wound suggest about the position of the victim and shooter when this shot was taken? Does this suggest anything regarding the order of the shots taken?

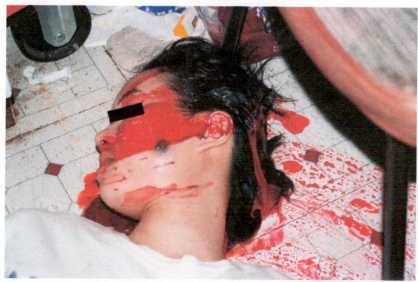

(b)

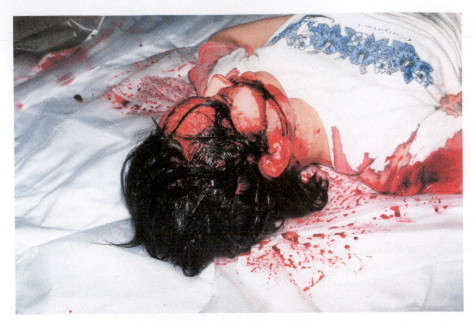

(a)

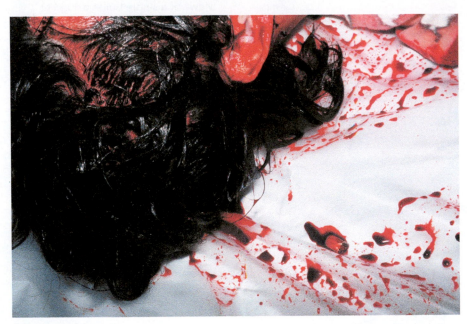

(b)

FIGURE 9.16 ▶ (a) When the victim is placed in a horizontal position on the plastic sheet, (b) a bullet falls from the rear area of her head (bottom right-hand side). Does the discovery of the bullet suggest anything of a physical nature regarding the victim' body at the time of the shooting?

FIGURE 9.17 ▶ Loaded gun lodged between the victim's legs. How should this firearm evidence be handled at the scene and utilized in the investigation? Has this gun been staged by the shooter or did if fall into this position after being handled by the victim? Of what significance is this evidence for the shooter who claims that he or she shot the victim in self-defense?

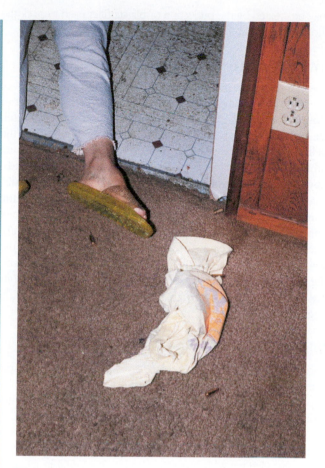

FIGURE 9.18 Unfired cartridges located on the floor below the victim's feet. Of what significance are these and their positioning in the core of the crime scene to the investigation? Are they of any use as evidence for proving a murder case?

(a)

(b)

FIGURE 9.20 ▶ (a) Bullet strike passing through the kitchen wall and (b) then through the exterior of the apartment building. How are these holes in the interior and exterior walls important to the investigation?

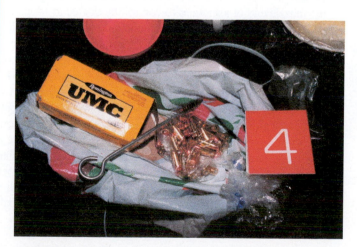

FIGURE 9.19 ▶ Cartridges and gun cleaning tool discovered in a plastic bag at the scene. Is this discovery of any use as evidence in the investigation from? Is this evidence of any use to prove a murder case?

SHOTGUN SHOOTINGS

Generally, wounds produced by shotguns are evaluated in the same manner as those resulting from pistols and rifles. Shotgun wounds, however, vary greatly in appearance due to differences in the type of gun and ammunition used. The following sections present general indicators useful for investigating shootings involving shotguns.

Contact Wounds

Most contact shotgun wounds appear in the mouth and upper-head region. Blasts to the skull produce massive displacement of bone and brain tissue, which often is projected some distance from the victim's body. Contact entry wounds to skin areas, such as the chest and thorax, usually produce a torn, square-shaped entry wound somewhat larger than the gun's muzzle. Large amounts of soot and gun powder often are found with the track of the shot used to produce the entry wound. Both the shot pellets and the wadding contained in the shotgun shell are deposited inside the wound. Muzzle impressions also may be observable on the skin's surface. Stippling/tattooing will not be present. Very seldom is an exit wound produced by shotgun pellets fired into the torso region. Shotguns armed with slugs, however, generally produce a large, torn appearing exit wound.[34]

Close Wounds

Close-distance shotgun wounds are those made from a distance 5 feet or less from the victim, but not making direct contact with the skin's surface area. These wounds consist of a large central wound, produced by the main pellet mass, surrounded by a tight grouping of satellite pellets creating smaller wounds, as illustrated in Figure 9.21. More satellite pellets will be evident when birdshot rather than buckshot is fired. The wadding also will be inserted inside the entry wound. Stippling/tattooing is usually present, as is an abrasion ring. If buckshot ammo is used, stippling/tattooing

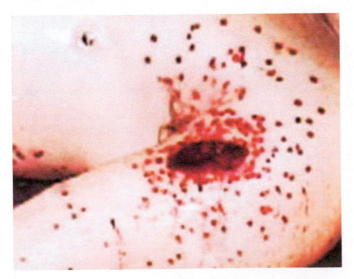

FIGURE 9.21 ▶ Close-range shotgun wound produced by bird shot.

may be created by the projection of plastic filler used to pack the shot pellets within the shotgun shell.[35]

Intermediate Wounds

These wounds are produced by shotgun blasts originating 5–10 feet from the victim's body. They appear somewhat similar to close-distance wounds, but there is a far greater spread of satellite pellet wounds around a smaller entry wound created by the pellet mass. Stippling/tattooing and an abrasion ring may be present. Most characteristic of intermediate-distance wounds, however, is the separation of the wadding from the pellets discharged. In some cases, the wadding becomes lodged in the entry wound, but before doing so it leaves a cross-shaped impression on the skin directly outside the wound. This is produced by the four petals of plastic formed by slits cut in the wadding that spread out due to air resistance. In other cases, the wadding completely separates from the pellet mass and hits the skin's surface away from the main entry area, leaving a large abrasion or bruise.[36]

Distant Wounds

Distant wounds are those produced by shotguns beyond 10 feet from the victim's body. Typically, these wounds do not exhibit stippling/tattooing and may or may not have a central entry wound created by the pellet mass. Rather, a scattered grouping of pellet wounds will be observed on the skin's surface. Depending on the distance, only a few pellets may actually strike the victim—with the other pellets recoverable at other locations at the crime scene. At a range of 20 feet, the wadding usually falls completely to the ground.

Shotgun Choke

Also of importance for wound identification is the **shotgun choke**. In brief, the term *choke* refers to a constriction placed at the muzzle end of a shotgun to control the degree to which the pellet mass spreads or scatters when it is projected. Full chokes provide maximum constraint on pellets, causing them to travel a greater distance before scattering. Less restrictive chokes, on the other hand, allow the pellet mass to spread out more quickly over a relatively shorter distance. Shotguns that have more choke produce a smaller, more concentrated wound pattern surrounded by few satellite entry holes. By comparison, the wound produced by weapons with less choke will have a spread-out appearance and perhaps consist solely of satellite holes without a main entry hole. In addition, random scrapes and markings produced on the wadding as it passes through a choking mechanism in the shotgun's muzzle may produce ballistics evidence useful for individualizing the weapon.[37]

Creating Shotgun Distance Standards

As previously mentioned, shotgun wounds can be highly irregular and variable—even when the same shotgun and ammo are used to produce two separate wounds. Therefore, the only certain way to determine the distance from which a particular wound was created is to create shotgun distance standards by test firing the same shotgun containing the same type of ammo used to produce the victim's wound. Test fires should be taken from minimum and maximum distances to create several standards. Each standard can then be compared to the wound for similar patterns of gunshot residue deposits and pellet spread. Thus, recovering the exact shotgun involved in the production of a victim's wound provides an essential piece of investigative evidence. If the shotgun cannot be recovered, information contained on the wadding regarding the gauge and ammunition type can be used to execute test fires from a shotgun similar to that used in the actual shooting.[38]

SUICIDE SHOOTINGS

Gunfire is a leading cause of death among male suicide victims, and is rarely the method of choice among female suicide victims. In Table 9.3, a percentage breakdown of suicide firearms deaths, by the type of firearm and location of the wound, is presented.

As the data in Table 9.3 suggest, a rather predictable statistical profile can be constructed for persons committing suicide with firearms. This profile includes the following:

- Approximately 50 percent of suicides are committed by revolvers, 20 percent by semiautomatic pistols, and 30 percent by rifles and shotguns.

- The vast majority of suicide wound locations are in the head region (83 percent), followed by the chest area (14 percent) and abdomen (2 percent).

- Between 95 percent and 98 percent of all wounds discovered among victims committing suicide by gunfire are of the contact variety.[39]

Regardless of whether a given suicide victim falls within the average statistical profile of suicides committed by firearms, investigators should treat a shooting crime scene as a homicide until medical examinations of the body and other evidence suggest a suicide. Common crime scene indicators of suicide include a single contact gunshot wound to the head region as illustrated in Figure 9.22; however, multiple gunshot wounds have been discovered in suicide cases where the victim's initial shot was not incapacitating or a semiautomatic pistol had a hair

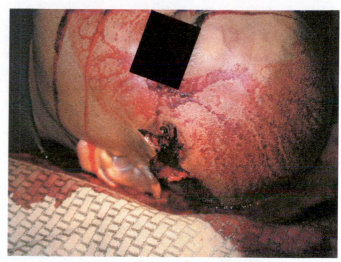

(a)

(b)

FIGURE 9.22 ▶ (a) Suicide shooting with contact shot entry wound and (b) the weapon producing the wound found at the victim's feet.

TABLE 9.3	SUMMARY STATISTICS FOR SUICIDE FIREARMS DEATHS		
	Suicidal Firearms Deaths		
SITE	HANDGUN (%)	RIFLE (%)	SHOTGUN (%)
Right temple	50.0	22.9	9.3
Left temple	5.8	3.3	3.7
Mouth	14.5	24.3	31.7
Forehead	5.9	15.7	8.1
Under chin	2.4	9.1	10.6
Back of head	3.6	3.8	1.2
Chest	13.2	15.7	19.9
Abdomen	1.4	1.9	5.6
Other	3.2	3.3	9.0

trigger, releasing several rounds consecutively. In rare cases, suicide victims can carry out close or intermediate-distance shots. When a pistol is used, the most telling evidence of suicide is perhaps gunshot residue on the hand used to hold the firearm (for GRS collection methods at the crime scene, see Chapter 4). GSR tests should reveal heavy deposits of residue on not only the palm, but also the web and forefinger of the victim's hand.

Sometimes, offenders stage a crime scene to present the appearance that their victim has committed suicide with a firearm. The fact that a particular suicide victim's wounds are not consistent with the average statistical profile of suicide victims should raise a red flag that a homicide may have taken place—but this observation by itself should not be used to entirely rule out the possibility of suicide. Where staging is suspected, make sure that the gun's position at the time it was discharged is not inconsistent with the gunshot wound evidence on the victim. As previously mentioned, most suicide shootings for pistols, rifles, and shotguns involve contact wounds. Therefore, stellate wounding and muzzle contusions should be present in suspected contact wound situations. In wounds caused by close or intermediate-distance shots, the entry hole and the abrasion ring usually are both round, indicating a relatively straight path for the bullet. Wounds resulting from shots extending beyond arm's length of the victim (where the victim is the presumed shooter) or within the reach of a trigger (where rifles and shotguns are involved) suggest homicide rather than suicide.

In addition, the firearm itself should be examined for fingerprints, bodily fluids, and other evidence linking it to the victim or a suspected homicide offender. Gunshot residue discovered on the suicide victim's hand should correspond to the hand normally used to hold the firearm (e.g., are they right- or left-handed?). Suicide notes should be submitted to the crime lab's questioned documents section for analysis of the victim's handwriting, as well as examined for fingerprints of the victim or of other persons who may have assisted in the victim's suicide or staged the scene to cover up a homicide.

RECONSTRUCTING A SUSPICIOUS DEATH SCENE

Case Example 9B illustrates a suspicious death scene involving an adult male discovered in the trunk of an abandoned vehicle. The crime scene photos in Figures 9.23 to 9.32 depict a complex case that contains virtually every type of physical evidence discussed up to this point in our discussion of death investigation. Key factors to be considered during the investigation of this scene include not only evidence necessary to reconstruct how the death occurred but also when and where the victim died.

CASE EXAMPLE 9B

Suspicious Death

FIGURE 9.23 ▶ A car that was missing for few days was found abandoned in a parking lot. When the car was returned, the owner noticed an unexplained heaviness and sagging in the trunk area of the vehicle. Upon looking in the trunk, he discovered a body and drove immediately to the local police station.

FIGURE 9.24 ▶ Investigators' first view of contents within the vehicle's trunk.

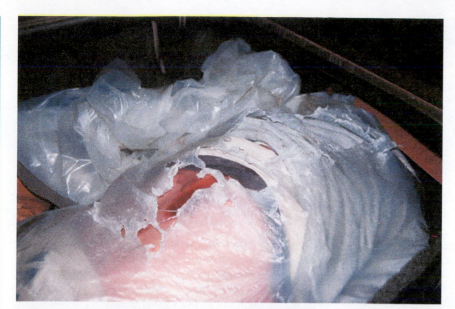

FIGURE 9.25 ▶ Investigators' close-up view of contents reveals a body. At this point of the investigation, what preparations of the crime scene should be made? Is there a need to notify any other personnel to assist in the investigation?

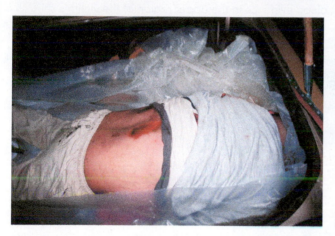

FIGURE 9.26 ▶ Unwrapping the body to reveal the victim's back.

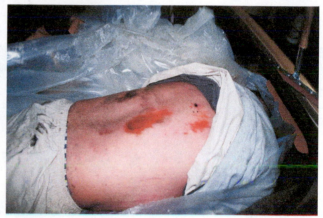

FIGURE 9.27 ▶ Lifting the victim's shirt reveals wounding and signs of putrefaction. At a time of death estimate be made from the inspection of this body decomposition evidence?

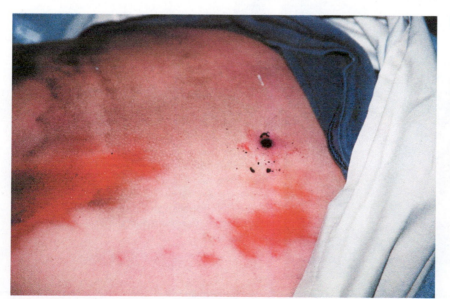

FIGURE 9.28 ▶ Close-up of the victim's back reveals a gunshot wound and some scattered signs of lividity. What does the shape, size and general characteristics of this wound suggest regarding the positioning of the victim and shooter at the time the shot was fired? Of what significance are the signs of lividity on the victim's back given the position of the body in the trunk?

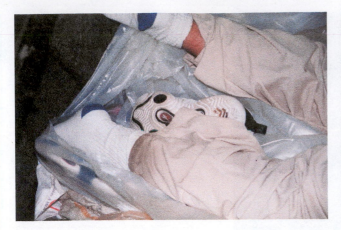

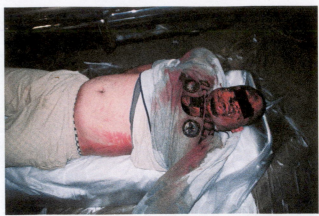

FIGURE 9.29 ▶ The victim's shoe, containing a blood stain on the sole. If this is the victim's blood, what is the importance of this discovery?

FIGURE 9.30 ▶ Front view of the victim showing lividity in the torso, a bloody t-shirt, and the victim's bloated and bloodied face. What does the location of the lividity suggest? There also appears to be limited pooling of blood beneath the victim's body with most of the blood evidence in the upper region of the victim's shirt. What does this suggest?

FIGURE 9.31 ▶ Close-up of the victim's face showing signs of significant bleeding and disfigured nose and other facial features. Of what significance are these signs of possible facial trauma?

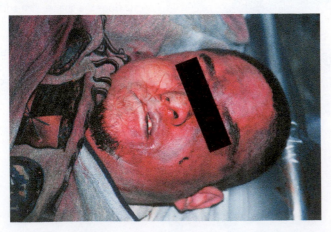

FIGURE 9.32 ▶ Close-up of the victim's face after removal of excess blood to examine for wounds or other evidence of trauma. Overall, given the evidence presented here, what conclusions can be drawn regarding how, where and when the victim was killed? What evidence is most useful for determining the appropriate murder charge for suspects, if they are located?

STABBING SCENES

Most stabbings cause excessive bleeding resulting from either **incision wounds** or **puncture wounds**. Incision wounds are produced when flesh is penetrated or sliced by an object with a sharpened edge. Puncture wounds, on the other hand, almost always involve the forceful penetration of the skin with an object sharpened only on its tip (e.g., an ice pick). To determine whether or not a death by sharp object is indeed a homicide, the investigator must be able to recognize various incision wound patterns and to identify the type of weapon and how it was used.[40]

Most homicidal stabbings are localized to the torso, neck, upper arms, or head. The number and location of these wounds also clearly rules out the possibility that the stabbing was either suicidal or accidental. (Stabbing deaths resulting from an accident or suicide are extremely rare, and when discovered tend to be in the form of a single stab wound to the heart or abdominal area.) Close wound patterns are also evident in victims who have been stabbed by surprise, or in their sleep, or while under the extreme influence of alcohol or drugs.

The stabbing victim's arms and hands may reveal **defense wounds**. These consist mostly of shallow cutting-type incisions on the fingers, the palms of the hands, and the underside of the forearms. They result from the victim's reacting to the attack in an attempt to block or grab the weapon. This is a characteristic of stabbing victims, who are either immobilized or in some other condition where they cannot defend themselves. Typically, stabbing victims who know they are about to be attacked exhibit defense wounds.

Stab Wound Characteristics

The investigation of stab wounds can be more perplexing than those involving gunshot wounds because, unlike guns, a knife or other sharp instrument only rarely can be linked to a particular wound with 100 percent accuracy. Whereas test-fired bullets from a suspect's gun can be used to match a bullet found at a crime scene, there is no equivalent test for stabbings. Unlike firearms, stabbing instruments neither contain nor leave consistent markings. Only when a piece of the stabbing weapon is left in a wound or the weapon contains evidence that can be traced back to the victim and offender (for example, a knife containing DNA, blood, hair, or fingerprints) can investigators assume that they have a definite match between a specific stab wound and a weapon of interest. Although limited in their matching abilities, stab wounds can and should be used whenever possible to exclude various types of sharp objects as a likely murder weapon.

The first step in the investigation of a suspected stabbing is to perform a general assessment of the stab wounds. Officially defined, stab wounds are those in which the depth of the wound is greater than its length; conversely, a slash or cutting wound has a length greater than its width. The next investigative step is to perform a detailed analysis of each individual stab wound. This can provide investigators with clues regarding the type, size, and shape of the murder weapon as well as the manner in which the weapon was used to carry out the homicide. The following are key areas that should be examined.

Wound Marginals

While many sharp objects can produce a stab wound, the most common is a knife with a single-edge blade. A comparison of the **wound marginal**, or edges of skin surrounding the opening of the wound, can help distinguish stabbings produced by single-edge knives from those by other types of knives and sharp objects. Whether a hunting knife or a common kitchen variety, single-edge blades produce a smooth, oval-shape wound marginal that appears slightly wider at the end produced by the unsharpened edge and narrower at the opposite end produced by the sharpened edge. By comparison, stab wounds produced by double-edge knives (such as a dagger) appear very similar in shape at both ends. Knives with duller and blunter edges, such as those with a serrated blade, produce a rough and/or torn appearing wound marginal.[41] As Figure 9.33 illustrates, wound marginals can vary greatly in size based on the size of the weapon and other factors such as movement of the victim and offender during a stabbing attack.

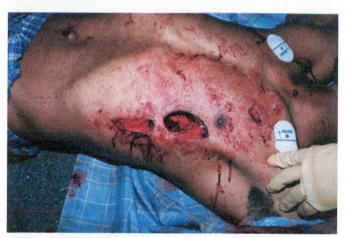

(a)

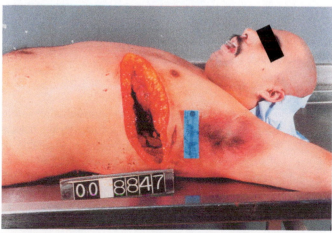

(b)

FIGURE 9.33 ▶ The size of stabbing wounds often can be deceptive if used as an indicator of the weapon's size and cutting surface. Ripping, tearing, and twisting motions of the knife can produce excessively large and irregular wounds, as illustrated by these photos (a and b).

Wound Length

The primary clues provided by wound length are an estimate of the stabbing weapon's width and perhaps the number of stabbing weapons used. Generally speaking, the wider the weapon's surface area, the longer the wound's vertical length. Wider knife blades, for example, produce longer wounds. This knowledge is important when attempting to link a particular stabbing instrument to a specific wound. The discovery of a stabbing victim with several wounds of varying lengths raises the question, "Were the wounds produced by more than one knife, perhaps suggesting that the victim was stabbed by multiple assailants?"

Before attempting to answer this question, the investigator must remember that the same stabbing instrument almost never produces two wounds of exactly the same length. Therefore, where there are multiple stabbings, it is best to compare the length of the wounds that are well formed rather than irregular in shape.[42]

Well defined wounds that appear to be approximately the same length suggest that they were produced by the same weapon. The actual blade length of the knife used to produce a wound will be slightly larger than the length of the wound itself. This is because once the victim's skin is expanded by the initial puncture of the knife, its elastic quality causes the wound opening to contract after the knife is removed. Smaller-length wounds on a stabbing victim's body along with larger length wounds may be from the same knife or by a knife with a narrower blade. Where the same knife is used to create both large and small stab wounds, the smaller wounds can be created by the narrower front portion of a knife with a tapered blade. Had the full length of the knife penetrated the skin, the smaller wound would perhaps be almost as long as the others. In addition, certain articles of clothing, including materials such as elastic, denim, rubber, or metals, can significantly decrease the degree to which a knife penetrates the skin, creating smaller wounds from larger knives. Besides blade taper, the up-and-down motion of the victim's body or vertical rocking of the knife by the assailant at the time of the attack can produce a deceptively long wound, especially if a double-edge blade is used.[43]

Wound Width

The width of the wound can provide some insights regarding the overall thickness of the weapon. As a rule, thicker objects leave wider wounds. For knife stabbings, the examination of regular oval-shape wounds is best for gaining a relative idea of the blade's width. The width of the wound itself, however, will always be greater than that of the knife creating the wound. This is due to several factors. First, the width of stab wound produced by the same weapon varies depending on where the wound is located and how it reacts with the body's **lines of cleavage**. These are the directions, either vertically or horizontally, in which the muscles flow throughout the body. The more a stabbing goes against the grain or natural direction of muscles, the more the muscles will pull the opening of the wound apart. This may cause the investigator to exaggerate the width of a knife blade or to falsely conclude that more than one stabbing weapon was used.[44]

For example, although two wounds are produced by the same knife, one may appear larger than the other due to line of cleavage effects. This is especially true for chest wounds because more muscle resistance is produced in the victim's chest area than in other regions such as the back and abdomen. Second, abnormally wide wounds can be produced by a twisting motion of the knife blade at the time of attack. This generally produces a torn looking, V-shaped opening, which can be produced by knives with blades both thin and thick.

Wound Depth

Wound depth can be of use for estimating the length of a stabbing weapon. The wound depth, however, is ultimately determined by the coroner or medical examiner, and even under these controlled conditions it is difficult to accurately assess. This is especially true for stabbings in areas, such as the abdominal region, where the skin is more elastic and can allow the object to stretch to depths much longer than its true length. In some cases, the investigator may be able to visually determine the depth of a wound if **hilt marks** are present. These are bruises surrounding the wound that are caused by striking of the skin by the *hilt* of the knife, or the area where the blade connects to the handle. Although most knives used in homicides do not have large hilts or handle guards, sometimes handle impressions are visible around the wound. This would suggest that the blade has reached full penetration. If the knife blade is tapered, wounds with hilt marks will show not only the deepest point of penetration but also the widest point of the blade.[45]

SUICIDE BY SHARP OBJECTS

Most suicides by sharp objects are carried out using a razor blade, knife, glass, or other sharp utensil to slice or sever major veins in the arm or neck as illustrated in Figure 9.34. Death is caused by rapid excessive bleeding, producing arterial spurt blood spatter patterns. Hesitation marks created by the selected cutting instrument in the general area of the fatal wound are common in suicides involving sharp objects. In these cases, the victim makes preliminary incomplete attempts to cut the selected location on the body before fully committing to the act of suicide. Right-handed individuals usually cut the left side of the neck in a downward motion. Conversely, left-handed suicide victims create an incision directed downward on the right side of the neck. Rarely is a suicide committed by making a straight cut across the throat. This is usually an indication of homicide committed by an offender attacking from behind the victim. In most cases, the suicide victim is found with the sharp object that produced the wound clenched in their hand or somewhere beneath their body. If the object that produced the wound is not in or around the body, the victim may have stayed alive long enough to hide the cutting instrument, or a family member in denial of the event may have removed the cutting object from the scene.

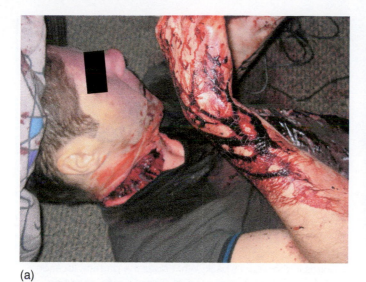

(a)

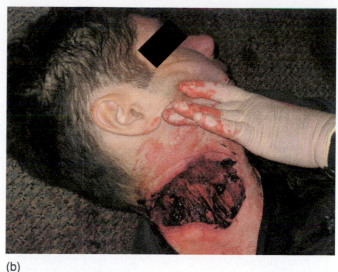

(b)

FIGURE 9.34 ▶ (a) This photo shows a suicide victim's neck wound and blood stains on the arm from arterial spurting (note the *rigor mortis*). (b) The depth of the wound extending into muscle tissue.

RECONSTRUCTING A STABBING DEATH SCENE

Case Example 9C (see Figures 9.35 to 9.41) illustrates a stabbing death scene involving an a adult female found dead inside her residence. This is a rare scene in that the victim's body was discovered with signs of certain death, so the death investigation takes place at a location left undisturbed by EMTs or other first responders. As with all death investigations, the investigator's primary goal is to locate (if possible) the weapon or instrument used to inflict the fatal wounds. In the case at hand, the chances of locating the knife that created the victim's wounds at the crime scene can be improved greatly by assessing the characteristics of the stab wounds. Reconstructing the crime also can help locate the knife and determine how and perhaps why the stabbing took place.

CASE EXAMPLE 9C

Stabbing Death

FIGURE 9.35 ▶ Investigators were called to this residence by patrol officers who entered the home after responding to a call for service from neighbors who reported hearing a woman screaming.

FIGURE 9.36 ▶ When the patrol officers searched the home, they discovered a dead woman wrapped in several blankets on the floor at the foot of a bed (lower left). Portions of the home appeared ransacked, with drawers opened and clothes strewn about; however, investigators found no signs of forcible entry on the doors and windows of the home.

FIGURE 9.37 ▶ Close-up of the victim wrapped in blankets. Does the condition and position of the victim's body suggest anything regarding the time of death? Did the crime take place at this location? How should an evidence search at this scene be conducted?

FIGURE 9.38 ▶ After removing the victim from the blankets, investigators discovered numerous stabbing wounds in the victim's back. What does the pattern, location and size of these wounds suggest regarding the condition and position of the victim at the time of the stabbing?

FIGURE 9.39 ▶ Side view of the victim's back and torso, revealing stab wounds and lividity. What characteristics of the murder weapon can be determined from these wounds? Was there more than one weapon or attacker involved here? Note the *rigor mortis* of the victim's fingers, which may be due to cadaver spasm—a condition that causes immediate *rigor mortis* of parts of the body where muscles become extremely tense or fatigued at the time of death.

FIGURE 9.40 ▶ View of kitchen drawers as they were discovered at the scene. Note the broken drawer and the open drawer containing various kitchen utensils and one large kitchen knife. Of what significance is the broken drawer, and what evidence should be searched for at this location?

FIGURE 9.41 ▶ All of the knives in the kitchen were removed and assembled to determine whether any could be the murder weapon. Which of these might have been the murder weapon? If a likely weapon is identified, how can it be proved or disproved that this is the weapon? Is this a case of murder or manslaughter given the evidence presented?

BLUNT FORCE TRAUMA SCENES

Deaths caused by blunt force trauma are usually the result of excessive bleeding caused by rupturing of the skull, skin, or vital organs. Typically, the victim is rendered unconscious by blunt force to the head from fists, feet, or an object and then succumbs due to complications related to a hemorrhaging wound. Although single traumatic wounds can be accidental, multiple wounds are highly suggestive of an intentional assault. Variations of blunt force trauma wounds include the following:

- *Contusions:* Bruising of the skin in areas where force is applied.
- *Avulsions:* Ripping or tearing of the skin produced by the impact of the trauma.
- *Artifacts:* Portions of skin torn from the body by the force of the trauma.

One or all of the conditions just described can be produced by blunt force trauma depending on the victim's body position at the time of the trauma, the force applied by the offender, and the object used to produce the wound. Contusions, or bruises, are evident in almost all cases. Bruising is a live body reaction, so swelling of skin tissues in areas affected by force suggests that the victim was alive at the time the wounds were inflicted. Fresh bruises appear reddish in color and turn purple to black

24–48 hours after death. Areas of the body that appear to have been affected by force (e.g., torn skin) but do not exhibit swelling or other bruising characteristics suggest that the wound was created after the victim's death.

It is often possible to identify the object responsible for a blunt force trauma by examining the shape and size of the wound. When bruising occurs, an impression of the object may be formed in the skin. For example, a victim who has been pistol whipped may exhibit bruising impressions of the gun's grip, magazine, and components making contact with the skin. Tearing wounds causing indentation in the skin can also leave three-dimensional impressions of the particular object penetrating the skin. If skin is torn away from the body in a blunt force trauma attack, as happens with an artifact, the skin section removed should be recovered and preserved to test for a physical match of the artifact with the wound. Attacks to the skull and other areas with thin skin covering bone will cause extensive bleeding through small traumatic wounds. In these situations, blood probably will be transferred not only to the object used to produce the wound, but also to the offender's hands, clothing, and shoes. Recovery of the trauma-producing object can help in obtaining physical matches to the wound and individualizing DNA evidence from blood and other bodily fluids transferred from the victim to the object and offender.

HOT TIPS AND LEADS 9.2

The Bruising Lifecycle

Bruising is caused by the leakage of blood beneath the skin's surface in reaction to some type of striking action or trauma. Discoloration and puffing of the skin is caused by the accumulation of blood beneath the wound. Although bruising does not occur after death, victims of homicide often have bruises in various stages of healing as the result of attacks they experienced while still alive—perhaps by the same offender who caused their death. This is especially true in ongoing domestic abuse situations involving spouses and children. Investigators should understand the lifecycle of bruising to estimate the times at which prior violent encounters between homicide victims and their offenders likely occurred. The following are general guidelines for determining the length of time since a bruising has occurred, based on color changes occurring in the bruise itself.

COLOR	AGE
Red	Less than 24 hours old
Blue-Purple to Black	1 to 2 days old
Green to Yellow	5–10 days old
Yellow/Brown to Brown	10–14 days old
Normal Skin Color	After 12 weeks

Generally, the greater the force applied to the surface of the skin, the larger and more pronounced the bruise will appear. Fingers tightly gripping the skin may cause **pattern bruising** (see Figure 9.42) showing where the offender's hand has made contact with the victim's body. Elderly persons bruise more easily and recover more slowly than do children and younger adults. Women bruise more easily than do men.[46]

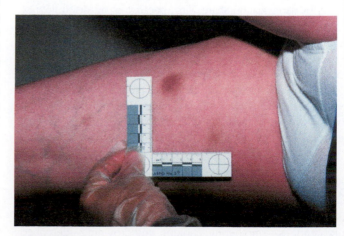

FIGURE 9.42 ▶ Pattern bruising.

ASPHYXIATION SCENES

Asphyxia is a condition where the body is deprived of the amount of oxygen necessary to sustain life, leading to unconsciousness and/or death. Death by asphyxia can come about either intentionally or accidentally, with the latter situation most frequently encountered by investigators. Thus, most deaths caused by asphyxia ultimately are not treated as homicides. Nevertheless, these cases should be treated as potential homicides until the medical examination can confirm that a death by asphyxia was not the product of foul play.

Death by asphyxiation can come about in numerous ways, but all of these can be classified into three categories: suffocation, chemical asphyxiation, and strangulation. Suffocation occurs when air passages necessary for respiration are obstructed, preventing the blood from being replenished with oxygen. Included in this form of asphyxia are deaths by smothering, choking, and drowning. Gases and other deleterious foreign agents entering the bloodstream prevent oxygen from being absorbed into the bloodstream when death occurs by chemical asphyxiation. Most common among these situations are deaths caused by the inhalation of automobile exhaust fumes resulting in carbon monoxide poisoning. Strangulation involves the physical restriction of flow of oxygenated blood to the brain, vital organs, and extremities—as occurs in hanging.

Determining the exact cause of death resulting from asphyxia often involves numerous complicated tests performed by forensic pathologists and toxicologists. Regardless of how the asphyxiation comes about, however, the process by which death occurs in these situations is basically the same. First, after initiation of the asphyxia event, the victim loses consciousness due to reduced oxygen in the bloodstream (known as *hypoxia*). Next, if the oxygen continues to be cut off following loss of consciousness, death will most likely ensue as the result of blood that contains little or no oxygen (known as *anoxia*). Determining time of death in homicide by asphyxia can be complicated and dependent on the consideration of many variables such as the victim's physical condition, the method of asphyxiation, and certain environmental factors at the crime scene.

There are several postmortem physical characteristics that all deaths by asphyxiation share. First, because of restricted flow of replenished (red) oxygen throughout the bloodstream, victims of death by asphyxia exhibit a telltale plum-blue color on the skin over most of their body—a condition referred to as *cyanosis*. Cyanosis may be especially evident in the lips, eyelids, and nail beds of the fingers and toes. Also, petechiae often are evident on the eyes, facial region, scalp, neck, and chest. The exact size, location, and distribution of these small hemorrhages depend on the particular method of asphyxiation responsible for the victim's death.[47]

SUFFOCATION

Asphyxiation by suffocation can be broken down into three subcategories—smothering, choking, and drowning—described as follows.

Smothering

Similar to the cause of death in the case just described, and a somewhat infamous legend in crime scene investigation folklore, is a method called *Burking* that combines mechanical asphyxiation and smothering. In the early 1800s, William Burke became known for his unique killing method whereby he killed public inebriants by sitting on their chest and simultaneously smothering them by blocking their nose and mouth with his hands. He would then sell the bodies for use as medical cadavers at a high premium because his killing method left no signs of visible trauma.

In general, smothering is a form of suffocation whereby air passages—namely, the nose and mouth—are externally blocked. This form of homicide by asphyxiation is rare, however. When it does happen, homicidal smothering usually involves the killing of (1) infants by distraught parents and (2) elderly persons by relatives and care providers in the name of mercy. Hands, pillows, plastic, or other soft material-type objects are often used to smother the victim while asleep or in some sort of incapacitated physical state. Crime victims with tight gags or hoods placed around their mouth and head region also may die from smothering, although the result was unintended by the offender. By comparison, suicidal smothering utilizing manual pressure over the nose and mouth are nearly impossible because persons invariably release the smothering object and continue to breathe once they become unconscious. Typically, suicides by smothering are executed by persons placing plastic or other airtight objects over their mouth, nose, and head to obstruct normal breathing.[48]

Choking

Death by choking occurs when the internal airway to the lungs (the trachea) is blocked, which prevents oxygen from reaching the lungs. Homicidal deaths by choking are extremely rare. Deaths of small children by choking typically are accidental and result from swallowing small foreign objects, such as toys, that block the airway. Most adult choking deaths are accidental as well and involve air blockages caused by excessive food intake; also, following excessive alcohol intake, choking death sometimes occurs when airways are blocked by vomit. Homicides caused by choking, when they do happen, are usually secondary to some other crime activity and result from attempts to silence the victim by forcing a foreign object (sock or other material item) into the victim's mouth. The unintended result is that the object slides down the victim's throat, totally blocking the airway and leading to death.

Drowning

Death by drowning, sometimes called *liquid asphyxia*, results when fluid, usually water, enters the lungs. This, in turn, causes an inability to breath. While most drowning deaths are either accidental or suicidal, the prospects of homicide always exist until evidence proves otherwise. Most important to homicide investigators are physical characteristics in the victims that suggest whether or not death occurred before or after exposure to the source of drowning.

Generally speaking, the odds of homicide are decreased when autopsy results reveal that the victim's lungs and air passages are filled to capacity with water or some other liquid causing the drowning. Simply put, this finding suggests that victim was alive and breathing before the drowning took place. On the other hand, less than full liquid saturation of the lungs generally is associated with victims who were dead and not breathing before exposure to the source of drowning. This situation is most common when the victim is killed and there is a body dump in a river, lake, or the ocean in an attempt to create the appearance of a suicide. Other evidence, although by no means absolutely conclusive, that can distinguish between homicidal and nonhomicidal drowning includes the following:

- Froth or foam in and around the mouth indicates that the victim may have been alive and breathing before death by drowning. Froth or foam is associated with many other causes of death, however, including poisoning, electrocution, and drug overdoses. Foam will not be present when the body has been submerged for a week or longer.

- Foreign objects such as grass, dirt, or gravel clenched within the victim's fist might perhaps reflect an attempt by the living victim to grab onto something before drowning. This process is the result of a cadaver spasm that causes the hand and wrist muscles to contract before death.

- Exterior skin wounds that can be positively linked to gunshots, knives, blunt force trauma, or self-defense should be considered obvious signs of foul play. On the other hand, wounds resembling those inflicted by other persons may be the result of marine life or the body striking objects while moving within water currents.[49]

HOT TIPS AND LEADS 9.3

Using Hands to Determine Time Since Drowning

It is relatively straightforward for investigators to determine how long a body has been submerged in water. Wrinkles on the finger pads indicate that the drowning took place approximately 3 hours ago or less. Wrinkled fingers and pads, referred to as *washerwoman fingers*, are typical of drownings that take place within a 12-hour period. Wrinkled palms usually befall the victim 2 days after drowning, and wrinkled feet indicate a 3-day time frame. Drowning victims submerged for 1 week or more usually display what is known as *degloving*, or skin separating from the hands.[50]

CHEMICAL ASPHYXIATION

Death by chemical asphyxiation is the result of chemicals, typically in gas form, that replace oxygen in, or block it from the bloodstream. Although this type of asphyxia is usually employed in suicides, it can also be used in homicides. The most common type of chemical asphyxiation encountered by homicide investigators is performed by carbon monoxide poisoning. Carbon monoxide is an invisible, tasteless, odorless gas emitted when fuels such as wood, natural gas, coal, gasoline, and propane are burned. It causes death by preventing oxygen from being absorbed into the body's bloodstream. Often, victims succumbing to carbon monoxide poisoning can be recognized by the cherry-red coloring of their skin. This skin coloring may not be present in victims of advanced age, however, or where the body is exposed to extremely cold ambient temperatures.

Generally, homicide investigators encounter carbon monoxide deaths resulting from (1) accidental overexposure to the gas in poorly ventilated areas and (2) intentional exposure to the gas to commit suicide. Piping exhaust from a running vehicle into the vehicle compartment or running a vehicle in a closed garage are two of the M.O.s more commonly employed by suicide victims. Although rare, some deaths that appear to be suicides by carbon monoxide or other gas poisoning in fact could be crime scenes staged in an attempt to cover up an earlier homicide. Absent lethal wounds or other signs of external trauma to the body, a toxicological medical examination will be necessary to confirm whether or not chemical asphyxia was the primary cause of death. In cases of true suicide, toxic levels of carbon monoxide will be discovered in the bloodstream due to the living victim's inhalation of the poisonous gases. Conversely, such lethal gas toxins will be absent from the blood of homicide victims who were already dead and not breathing when their body was placed in a staged suicidal setting (such as a running car or a burning house).[51]

STRANGULATION

There are three subclassifications of asphyxiation by strangulation: manual, ligature, and hanging strangulation.

Manual Strangulation

Victims of this variety of strangulation typically are females involved in domestic disputes; however, manual strangulation can also be the method of choice for combative men attempting to subdue a male opponent. Most manual strangulation cases are homicidal rather than suicidal in nature. Typically, manual strangulation is a spontaneous rather than a planned act. It is usually carried out by compressing the victim's neck and throat area with the hands and fingers, although other extremities such as wrists, forearms, and legs can be used (as in martial arts choke holds or scissor-type body holds). Usually, death by manual strangulation results from compression of arteries and veins in the neck rather than restriction of air flow through the throat. This is because the pressure needed to restrict blood flow in the neck region (10 lbs. or less) is significantly less than that needed to block the airway (or trachea) within the throat (30 lbs. or more). If the offender's grip is sufficient to block blood flow to the brain, the strangulation victim will be rendered unconscious in approximately 10 seconds. Unconscious victims released from a strangle hold generally regain consciousness in 10 seconds as well; however, if pressure from strangulation continues, the victim usually dies within 4 to 5 minutes after losing consciousness.[52] Common physical signs and symptoms exhibited by manual strangulation victims include the following:

- Scrapes and abrasions about the face, chin, and neck area
- Pattern bruising—finger tips and thumbs on the throat, neck, or behind the ears
- Petechiae

Ligature Strangulation

Ropes, wires, cords, clothing, or any other flexible object that can fully encircle and tighten around the neck can be used as a ligature to carry out a strangulation (see Figure 9.43). Nearly all cases of ligature strangulation are homicides, although suicide is possible if the method involves elaborate means such as sophisticated knotting or the use of some external apparatus. The outward signs of ligature strangulation are similar to those of manual strangulation and hanging, with the major exception being evidence of wounding to the skin produced by the ligature. If the ligature is a soft material such as a towel, faint markings or bruising may appear within the neck region.

Hard ligatures, on the other hand, produce a brown horizontal indentation encircling the neck. The shape and depth of the groove left in the skin by the ligature will depend on several factors including the nature of the ligature itself, the amount of force applied by the assailant, and the resistance offered by the victim. In some cases, distinctive markings left on the neck by a ligature can be matched to a rope, belt, string,

(a)

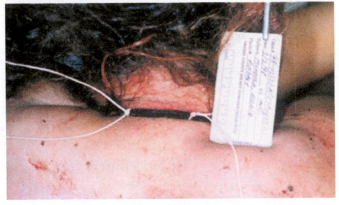

(b)

FIGURE 9.43 ▶ Victim of ligature strangulation with a shoestring.

or other object suspected as the murder weapon used in a ligature strangulation.[53]

Hanging Strangulation

Most hangings are suicidal in nature, but they can also be accidental or homicidal. Hangings involve constriction of the neck with a rope, belt, bed sheet, or some other tethering object through the gravitational force of one's own body weight. Hanging can be carried out in many positions, ranging from full body suspension (i.e., swingers) to kneeling or nearly prone positions. In most cases, death is caused when pressure to the neck blocks main veins and arteries that supply oxygen to the brain. In seconds, the victim is rendered unconscious, with complete death occurring anytime from 3 to 10 minutes afterwards. The victim's lips, eyelids, fingernails, and toenails will appear deep blue due to the failure of oxygenated blood to reach these tissue areas. If the neck is tightly constricted, the face will be pale white and swollen due to complete blockage of blood flow to the head. Petechiae (see Figure 9.44) may be present in the sclera (white area of the eye) and the surface of the face as well. Ligature marks above the Adam's apple, caused by the upward thrusting of the rope or constriction apparatus,

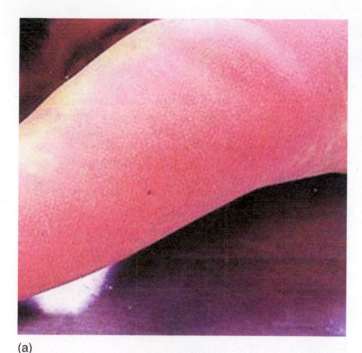

(a)

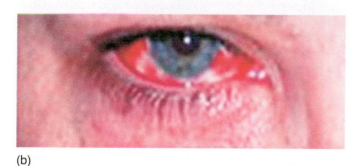

(b)

FIGURE 9.44 ▶ (a) Cherry-red skin resulting from carbon monoxide poisoning. (b) Petechiae of the eye resulting from strangulation.

FIGURE 9.45 ▶ Hanging victim after cutting the suspension rope from the tree.

discovering a nude autoerotic victim dress the body before notifying authorities.) Although rare, a hanging may be staged to look like a suicide or autoerotic session to cover up a homicide. Weak or absent ligature marks may suggest this situation, but can also result from low-pressure neck constriction like that produced by a soft fabric such as a bed sheet. Any of the symptoms just described, if present in the hanging victim, should be recorded in detail for future reference.[54]

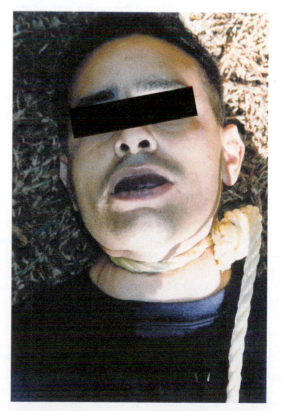

FIGURE 9.46 ▶ Hanging victim showing the location of the noose above the Adam's apple.

usually are discovered in cases of intentional suicide (see Figures 9.45 and 9.46).

Marks below the Adam's apple are more frequent among accidental suicides in which victims purposefully restrict blood flow to the brain to heighten sexual sensations while masturbating—known as *autoerotic asphyxiation*. These victims typically are found nude or partially dressed, whereas the victim of intentional suicidal hanging is fully clothed. Perhaps most important from an investigative standpoint is to examine the victim's body position and make sure that it is consistent with postmortem indicators such as lividity and rigor. For example, bodies that are fully suspended off the ground will have "stocking and glove" *livor mortis*; that is, a purplish-blue coloring concentrated in the hands and feet. Inconsistent lividity patterns can suggest either homicide, or that the body was moved by someone after being discovered. (Sometimes family or friends

CASE CLOSE-UP 9.2

"PREMATURE BURIAL"

The term premature burial *quite simply means being buried alive. In the following case description, investigators were challenged not only to locate the gravesite of a possible homicide victim, but also to determine whether the deceased individual was the victim of a premature burial.*

Locating the Body

The case began with a missing persons notification to investigators from the wife of a man who had not returned home from work as usual. According to the woman's statement, her husband always came home "right on time" at 5:30 P.M. every evening after work "without fail." She also stated that he was worried lately because "he owed $10,000 to some guys at work" and she suspected his life might be in danger. The only immediate case lead came from the construction company where the man worked, which revealed the location of some remote work sites to which the missing man had been traveling.

After focusing on the top three most likely locations where the victim last worked, investigators discovered the missing man's truck abandoned on a remote dirt road. Also present were tire tracks on the road leading from the site; after the investigators followed the tracks a short distance, however, the trail ended abruptly due to high winds that had recently obscured the tracks. The investigators returned to the abandoned truck and discovered that the man's tool box in the truck's bed had been pried open. After the contents of the toolbox were inventoried, the man's wife verified that at least one shovel and pick were missing. This caused the investigators to believe that if the man had been murdered in the area, his body might be in a makeshift gravesite.

Acting on their burial theory, the investigators used numerous tactics to aid their search for the man's potentially buried body. The investigators used infrared vision and photography in both ground and aerial searches in a circular pattern extending out from the truck's location. The infrared visualizing methods used in the investigative search can detect places that emit heat, and locations where bodies are buried sometimes appear visually different from places where they are not. Recent burials may emit retained body heat. In reviewing the aerial search results, the case investigators saw a small rectangular point in one set of infrared photos that was markedly different, brighter in color and tone than the surrounding area.

Once traveling to and physically examining the spot identified by the infrared visualization, it was evident that the soil had been loosened and replaced. This explained the infrared photo results revealing that this location absorbed and emitted heat at much different rates than those observed in the surrounding packed and untouched soil. Although not used in this case, more complex x-ray and sonar echo sound technology could have created a digital image of the shape and size of objects beneath the ground at the suspected burial site. Also, specially trained canines with a keen nose for decomposing human bodies—known as *cadaver dogs*—could also have been used to sniff out the possible burial location.

Moreover, without the assistance of advanced technology, the investigators in this case could have relied on simple physical indicators to locate the burial site. Patches of dirt with broken, thin, or absent trees, weeds, and other vegetation may suggest burial locations. Also visible may be signs of scavenging animals or birds, burrowing rodents, or flesh-eating insects. If the grave is shallow enough, the tell-tale smell of decomposition may be evident, as well as oozing liquids resulting from an advanced stage of decay.

Excavating the Body

Once located, the body was excavated and removed in a systematic fashion. This involved removing dirt in layers from depths of 6 inches to 1 foot and carefully documenting and photographing each stage of the excavation. This process continued until the body was removed, preserving its position in the soil until investigation of the grave was complete. From the surface of the burial site, excavation continued downward and around the body until it rested on what resembles a dirt pedestal. The excavation area was wide enough to uncover possible evidence, such as weapons or personal items that may have belonged to the victim or offender. After the body was removed from the burial site, the remaining dirt below the victim was thoroughly examined for articles thrown or falling into the grave before it was covered. Insect and/or rodent activity above, around, and below the body was documented as well.

Any heavy machinery (e.g., a backhoe) used in the excavation, such as that described in this case, must not strike the body. Generally only the top level of soil in a suspected grave site should be removed by heavy machinery. Sometimes living victims of premature burials have been killed, or severely disfigured after death by force applied from power-assisted excavation devices. Where financial resources permit, trained specialists can be called in to assist investigators in excavating and recovering the body. These include forensic archaeologists—experts in the scientific and methodical removal of human remains; forensic botanists—who can identify changes in vegetation in and around the grave site that may suggest when the body was buried and whether it was moved from a primary killing location; and forensic entomologists—who study insect lifecycles, which also can help determine time and location of death.[55] Case Example 9D (see Figures 9.47 to 9.54) illustrates the above investigative scenario describing the death investigation of a premature burial victim.

CASE EXAMPLE 9D

Burial Death

FIGURE 9.47 ▶ Case Example 9D, Burial Death, crime scene location (see Case Close-Up 9.1, Premature Burial, for the full case description).

FIGURE 9.48 ▶ Removal of surface dirt reveals the burial victim. What has caused the lividity in the victim's head and facial area? Does this support the case for a premature burial of the victim?

FIGURE 9.49 ▶ Early stages of excavating the body. What facts should be noted by investigators during the body excavation process?

FIGURE 9.50 ▶ Dirt is strategically removed around the body. What sources of evidence should be looked for during the body excavation process?

FIGURE 9.51 ▶ Straps are tied around the victim's body to expedite removal. Does the condition and positioning of the victim's body within the burial location provide evidence of a premature burial?

FIGURE 9.52 ▶ There are signs of dirt deposits in and around the victim's mouth and nose area. Of what significance is this discovery?

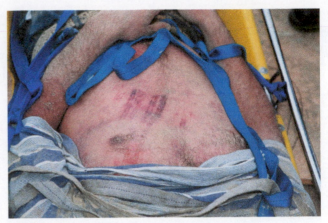

FIGURE 9.53 ▶ The victim's chest and abdomen showing signs of abrasions. Such abrasions are often found on burial victims, who voluntarily or involuntarily scratch themselves with their own fingernails.

FIGURE 9.54 ▶ Persons of interest interviewed in this case claim that the victim was killed while working on his own in an trench that caved in because it was not properly reinforced. The victim's family claims that the burial was the product of foul play. Is this final piece of evidence, showing lividity and abrasions on the victim's back, of any use in validating either of these claims? Should a murder investigation be opened in this case?

POISONING SCENES

The number of substances that can be used to carry out a homicidal poisoning is vast. No scientist, let alone a criminal investigator, can learn all there is to be known about the subject area. Complicating matters, substances considered nonpoisonous still can produce death when used improperly or to excess; for example, excessive water consumption can cause a chemical imbalance in the body, resulting in death. Fortunately, poisoning homicides are extremely rare, and most fall in the category of suicide or accidental death. Although toxico-logical examinations are necessary to confirm death by poisoning, the criminal investigation plays a key role in establishing whether a poison was self-administered or was given by another person with the intent to kill. Often, toxicological examinations reveal large doses of multiple drugs in the victim's system, indicating suicide rather than homicide or death by accidental overdose.

Unlike homicides committed in the heat of passion, homicidal poisonings usually are carefully planned and executed over a long time period. Formerly, intentional killings by poison were believed to be most prevalent among feuding family members, love triangles, and care providers who would "mercy kill" terminal patients. Recent research contradicts these claims and indicates that poisoning homicides claim many victims, most of whom are not related, are usually male, and often terminally ill or elderly.

As mentioned previously in Chapter 8, seemingly countless poisons can be used for homicidal purposes. This extensive list can be reduced significantly, however, to include only those substances most often encountered by homicide investigators:

- **Drugs/Narcotics/Alcohol:** By far, the most lethal combination used in most suicidal, accidental, and homicidal deaths involves popular prescription and street drugs used alone or with alcohol.

- **Arsenic:** A common ingredient in insecticides, arsenic can cause instant death with a single concentrated dosage, or prolonged death with numerous small doses over time. Predeath symptoms include headaches; nausea; vomiting; numbness in the arms, hands, and feet; and delusional thoughts and hallucinations.

- **Cyanide:** Generally found in insecticides, this substance produces predeath symptoms similar to those of suffocation—shortness of breath, dizziness, and confusion. In about 60 percent of cases, the victim's breath smells like bitter almonds.

- **Thallium:** Most often found in rat poison, thallium produces a general failure of the vital organs and nervous system. Predeath symptoms include vomiting, diarrhea, and temporary hair loss.

- **Aconitine:** Used as a main ingredient in rat poison and in ancient Chinese medicines. Predeath symptoms are similar to those of a major heart attack—chest pains, numbness in the shoulder/left extremity, and irregular heartbeat.

- **Atropine:** Commonly used in liquid form by eye doctors to dilate pupils for an eye examination, and known to be used by Native Americans as a medicine. Predeath symptoms resemble those of alcohol intoxication—loss of balance, double vision, staggering, and loss of consciousness.

- **Ricin:** A popular terrorist poison, ricin most commonly is a white powder, but can be administered as a mist or in pill form. Predeath symptoms include difficulty breathing, coughing, heavy sweating, and a bluish color in the skin.

Drug paraphernalia, pill bottles, containers, or other objects containing substances or residue suspected of causing poisoning in a victim's death should be collected at the crime scene. Toxicological and other evidence from such items may help determine the cause and manner of death. Also, tests of the victim's blood, urine, hair, and nails may provide information on the nature and extent of the poisoning.[56]

HOMICIDE TYPOLOGIES

Several typologies of homicide have been suggested. These attempt to classify homicides based on factors such as the offender's motivations and the particular methods by which the victim is killed. These typologies include the following:

1. **Contract Homicide:** Involves a quick killing of the victim with a high-power pistol or rifle. The firearm often is left at the crime scene and is stolen and/or unregistered. Limited shots are fired (perhaps in a blitz-style attack) that produce wounds in vital organs and the head area. Shooting victims' bodies may be burned to eliminate forensic clues.

2. **Gang Homicide:** Usually carried out with assault rifles, automatic rifles (e.g., AK47), semiautomatic handguns, and shotguns. Killings may occur in drive-by shootings, ride-up shootings (on bicycle), or walk-up shootings (on foot). Shots are aimed primarily at the victim's head and chest, but preliminary ritualistic shots may first be fired into the victim's arms, legs, knees, and groin. Excessive shooting of the body (overkill) is done to make an example of the victim, showing the shooting gang's superiority over its rivals. Knives are not used as often as firearms in gang murders.

3. **Kidnap Homicide:** After abducting an individual, the killer usually attempts to communicate with family, friends, and associates of the kidnap victim to make monetary or other demands in return for the victim. Victims not freed by captors are usually murdered by contact or near-contact gunshot wounds to the head or other vital organs.

4. **Drug-Related Homicide:** These killings usually result from drug deals gone bad between criminal partners and associates. The killing often takes place in a public location for high-profile shock appeal to instill fear in rival drug traders. Weapons commonly used are high-caliber semiautomatic pistols. Overkill involving numerous stab wounds and blunt force trauma wounds may also be used as a display of payback violence.

5. **Insurance/Inheritance Homicide:** This form of killing is carried out by relatives, business associates, care providers, and others who stand to profit from the legal death of a particular individual. Various methods of killing are used to avoid the impression of homicide, including poisons and chemical agents, asphyxiation, arson, and perhaps shootings related to a staged burglary or robbery of the victim.

6. **Erotomania Homicide:** In these murders a psychologically imbalanced individual kills a person on whom they have become mentally fixated. The killer's fixation is usually organized around a romantic fantasy about the victim. Stalking and other harassing behaviors eventually culminate in the victim's murder in a public place. Intermediate or distant shoots are

usually taken by the killer with a handgun aimed toward the victim's chest and head. Stabbing also may be used as a method of murder.

7. **Domestic Homicide:** The offender and victim are usually romantic partners or family members involved in some type of emotional turmoil or stressful event. Drugs and alcohol are commonly involved in the criminal event. Gunshot wounds, blunt force trauma, and battering of the face are some of the injuries inflicted on the domestic murder victim's body. The killer may attempt to stage the murder scene to make it seem that the violent attack on the victim was performed in self-defense.

8. **Authority Homicide:** In these murders, killers feel that their victims have wronged them in some way. The killer is often armed with one or more pistols of various calibers and/or rifles as well as a large supply of ammunition and perhaps protective body armor. Overkill is usually present, with the authority figure suffering numerous gunshot wounds in various areas of the body. Unintended targets also may be shot at the killing scene. The killer may shoot himself or be shot by police at the scene.

9. **Extremist Homicide:** The killer in this type of homicide is motivated by extremist thoughts focusing on political, economic, religious, or social ideologies. Prominent figures or groups representing a particular ideology with which the killer is obsessed usually become the victims of extremist murderers. The weapon of choice for these killings is usually a firearm or knife, although blunt-force trauma also may be used. Extremist killers also have been known to ambush victims or use long-distance sniper-style attacks.

10. **Serial Homicide:** Serial murders, or those related in a series, have several motives. One involves a killer who murders repeatedly in a spontaneous, blitz-style manner—referred to as a *visionary* serial killer. Usually this offender suffers from several psychological illnesses and kills by stabbing or bludgeoning victims with improvised weapons existing at the crime scene. The *mission* serial killer targets victims based on the belief that the victims' death will improve society. This offender usually employs a firearm to quickly kill the victim. Abortion doctors, lawyers, and victims of hate crimes are common targets of this killer type. Repeated murders carried out to fulfill fantasies and selfish desires are the motive of the third type of serial killer—the *hedonistic* killer. The fourth type—the *power-control* killer—kills in a slow process to fulfill sexual desires though torturing and controlling victims. Both hedonistic and power-control type killers rarely use firearms to kill their victims. Manual and ligature strangulation are the methods preferred by these killers because they are more personally gratifying than causing death by gunfire.[57]

Summary

1. **Homicide, murder, and manslaughter.**

   Homicide is the killing of one human being by the act or omission of another. Murder and manslaughter are illegal forms of homicide, whereas self-defense is a legal form of homicide. Murder is the act of killing with intent and a criminal state of mind known as *malice aforethought*, which is the desire to inflict death or great bodily harm. Murder is usually classified as either first-degree (premeditated) or second-degree (not premeditated) in seriousness under the law. Manslaughter is homicide that is not committed with malice aforethought, but rather through neglectful or reckless behavior.

2. **Postmortem indicators in the investigative process.**

   Postmortem indicators include *livor mortis* (lividity), *rigor mortis*, and *algor mortis*. They generally are used to determine certain death of an individual and can be useful for reconstructing homicides. Lividity is a purple color of the skin that occurs after death and is evident in areas of the body facing toward gravity. It can be used to determine body position after death, time of death, and other postmortem factors. *Rigor mortis* is stiffening of the muscles after death and can also be used to determine postmortem body position and time of death. *Algor mortis* is the cooling (or warming) of the body after death to the ambient temperature of its location; it is another time-of-death determination tool.

3. **Types of gunshot wounds.**

   Gunshot wounds can be produced by rifles, pistols, and shotguns. Firearms expelling bullets produce fairly recognizable wound patterns when fired at various distances from the shooting victim. The estimated distance from which a bullet is fired is classified in one of four categories: contact, close, intermediate, and distant. Contact shots produce torn appearing, stellate entry wounds and result from a firearm's muzzle being placed directly on the skin. Close and intermediate shots show heavy and lighter gunshot residue, respectively, on the outside of the entry wound. Distant shots show no gunshot residue on the entry wound. Shotgun wounds are similarly identified, but when these shots are taken at greater distances they usually have larger entry wounds with signs of pellets entering the skin around the main entry wound.

4. **Types of stabbing wounds.**

Stabbing wounds are usually classified as incisions (caused by a knife or similar object) and punctures (resulting from a long, thin, sharp object such as an ice pick). Most homicidal stabbings are localized to the torso, neck, upper arms, or head. The exact type of instrument used in a stabbing can be determined by examining the wound's width, length, and depth. These characteristics of stab wounds can also be used to determine whether one or more different stabbing instruments were used in an attack—suggesting multiple attackers assaulting a homicide victim.

5. **Types of asphyxia.**

Death by asphyxiation can come about in numerous ways, but all of these can be classified into three categories: suffocation, chemical asphyxiation, and strangulation. Suffocation occurs when air passages necessary for respiration are obstructed, preventing the blood from being replenished with oxygen. Included in this form of asphyxia are deaths by smothering, choking, and drowning. When death occurs by chemical asphyxiation, gases and other deleterious foreign agents entering the bloodstream prevent oxygen from being absorbed into the bloodstream. Most common among these situations are deaths caused by the inhalation of automobile exhaust fumes, resulting in carbon monoxide poisoning. Strangulation involves physically restricting flow of oxygen-carrying blood to the brain, vital organs, and extremities—as occurs in hanging.

Key Terms

homicide	*algor mortis*	shotgun choke
murder	putrefaction	incision wound
manslaughter	entry wound	puncture wound
nonhomicide	bullet track	defense wound
mass murder	exit wound	wound marginal
spree murder	abrasion ring	lines of cleavage
serial murder	stippling/tattooing	hilt marks
rigor mortis	bullet wipe	pattern bruising
corneal clouding	contact wounds	asphyxia
livor mortis	muzzle contusion	

Review Questions

1. What is the legal definition of *homicide*?
2. What are the legal differences between murder and manslaughter?
3. Name the various classifications of homicide.
4. What are the typical statistical profiles of homicide offenders and victims?
5. How is *livor mortis* (lividity) identified and used in homicide investigations?
6. What are the various stages of *rigor mortis* and how are they recognized?
7. How is *algor mortis* used in the investigative process?
8. Which characteristics are used to identify contact, close, intermediate, and distant wounds?
9. How can shooting trajectory be determined through an examination of a gunshot wound?
10. How do entry wounds and exit wounds produced by bullets differ?
11. What characteristics of shotgun wounds are not present in bullet wounds?
12. How can the type of weapon used in a stabbing be identified by an examination of wounding patterns?
13. What are some key differences between intentional shootings and stabbings and those related to self-inflicted wounds by suicide victims?
14. How is a wound produced by blunt force trauma identified?
15. How is death produced by asphyxiation?
16. What are the various forms of suffocation?
17. Under what circumstances does death result from chemical asphyxiation?
18. What are the various forms of strangulation?
19. Name and describe the victim effects of four poisons known to cause death.
20. What typologies are used to describe specific types of homicide?

Internet Sources

NIJ Death Investigation Guide	www.ncjrs.gov/txtfiles/167568.txt
FBI National Center for Analysis of Violent Crime	www.fbi.gov/about-us/cirg/investigations-and-operations-support
Mercer School of Medicine	library.med.utah.edu/WebPath/webpath.html#MENU
Explore Forensics	www.exploreforensics.co.uk/entrance-and-exit-wounds.html
Poisoning Deaths	www.rightdiagnosis.com/p/poisoning/deaths.htm
Stab Wounds	www.forensicmed.co.uk/wounds/sharp-force-trauma/stab-wounds

Applied Investigative Exercise

Select any of the illustrated cases in this chapter and describe how you would investigate the incident. If and where appropriate, discuss your first response to the scene, analysis of the victim's wounds, examination of the crime scene for physical evidence, and reconstruction of the crime. Also, draw conclusions about the weapon used, how it was used, and (if applicable) what wounds produced the victim's death. Determine whether the case should be treated as a homicide or a suicide (if the victim's death is presumed). If homicide is determined, should a murder or manslaughter case be pursued?

Notes

[1] Bryan A. Garner, ed., *Black's Law Dictionary*, 9th ed. (St. Paul, MN: West Group, 2009), 184.

[2] Ibid., 184–188.

[3] Ibid.

[4] Ibid.

[5] Ibid., 190.

[6] John Douglas, Ann W. Burgess, Allen G. Burgess, and Robert Ressler, *Crime Classification Manual* (San Francisco, CA: Jossey-Bass, 1992), 20–21.

[7] FBI, *Uniform Crime Reports 2009*, posted at www2.fbi.gov/ucr/cius2009/offenses/violent_crime/index.html.

[8] William Eckert, ed., *Introduction to the Forensic Sciences*, 2nd ed. (Boca Raton, FL: CRC Press, 1997), 97.

[9] Calixto Machado, *Brain Death: A Reappraisal* (New York, NY: Springer, 2007), 74–83.

[10] Ibid.

[11] Ibid.

[12] Robert G. Mayer, *Embalming: History, Theory, and Practice* (New York, NY: McGraw-Hill Professional, 2005), 203–212.

[13] Ibid.

[14] Ibid.

[15] Ibid.

[16] Ibid.

[17] Ibid.

[18] Steven Byers, *Introduction to Forensic Anthropology*, 3rd. ed. (Upper Saddle River, NJ: Pearson, 2005), 98–120.

[19] Ibid.

[20] Ibid.

[21] Ibid.

[22] Ibid., 125.

[23] Ibid., 122.

[24] Jason Payne-James, Anthony Busuttil, and William S. Smock, *Forensic Medicine: Forensic and Clinical Aspects* (London: Greenwich Medical Media, 2003), 166.

[25] Ibid.

[26] Ibid., 167.

[27] Ibid

[28] Ibid.

[29] Ibid., 165.

[30] Ibid.

[31] Ibid., 164.

[32] Ibid.

[33] Ibid.

[34] Mercer University School of Medicine, *Firearms Tutorial*, posted at library.med.utah.edu/WebPath/TUTORIAL/GUNS/GUNINTRO.html.

[35] Ibid.

[36] Ibid.

[37] Ibid.

[38] Ibid.

[39] Ibid.

[40]William J. Tilstone, Kathleen A. Savage, and Leigh A. Clark, *Forensic Science: An Encyclopedia of History, Methods and Techniques* (Santa Barbara, CA: ABC-CLIO, 2006), 212–218.

[41]Ibid.

[42]Ibid.

[43]Ibid.

[44]Ibid.

[45]Ibid.

[46]F. D. Dunstan, et al., *A Scoring System for Bruise Patterns: A Tool for Identifying Abuse* (London: BMJ Publishing Group, 2002), 330–333.

[47]Vincent DiMaio and Dominick DiMaio, *Forensic Pathology*, 2nd ed. (Boca Raton, FL: CRC Press, 2003), 256–277.

[48]Ibid.

[49]Ibid.

[50]Ibid.

[51]Ibid.

[52]Ibid.

[53]Ibid.

[54]Ibid.

[55]Byers, *Introduction to Forensic Anthropology*, 213.

[56]Eckert, *Introduction to the Forensic Sciences*, 110.

[57]Douglas et al., *Crime Classification Manual*, 23.

CHAPTER TEN

SEXUAL ASSAULT SCENES

Learning Objectives

After completing this chapter, you should be able to:

1. Define and provide examples of the term *sexual assault*.
2. Describe how sexual assault investigations are conducted.
3. Explain the importance of biological evidence in sexual assault cases.
4. Summarize the types of sexual assault offenses.
5. Identify the various types of paraphilias and deviant sexual acts.

Chapter Outline

Legal Definitions of Rape and Sexual Assaults
- Megan's Law

Typologies of Rape

Characteristics of Rape Offenders and Victims

First Response to the Sexual Assault Scene
- Victims
- Suspects
- Witnesses

Beginning the Sexual Assault Investigation
- Rape Trauma Syndrome (RTS)

Handling Sexual Assault Hot Cases

Special Considerations at the Sexual Assault Crime Scene

The Follow-Up Investigative Interview

Conducting the Sexual Assault Victim Interview
- Physical Characteristics of the Suspect's Body
- Details of the Sexual Attack

Biological Evidence of Sexual Assault

The Sexual Assault Examination

Victims Who Refuse Medical Treatment

False Rape Accusations

Criminal Investigative Analysis of Rapists
- Rape Classifications
- Development of the Analysis

Paraphilias and Deviant Sex Acts
- Fetishism
- Exhibitionism
- Voyeurism
- Telephone Scatologia
- Frotteurism
- Necrophilia
- Technophilia
- Sado-Masochism
- Partialism
- Hypoxyphilia

Sex Crimes Against Children
- The Inductive Pedophile
- The Fixated Pedophile
- The Regressed Pedophile
- The Exploitative Pedophile
- The Aggressive Pedophile

Reconstructing a Suspected Serial Rape Scene

INTRODUCTION

THE FORMS OF SEXUAL ASSAULT and the types of offenders who commit these crimes are many. Traditionally, the crime of forcible rape committed by a male perpetrator against a female victim was synonymous with the term *sexual assault.* As will be discovered in this chapter, forcible rape is but one of numerous sex crimes that fall within the investigative scope of sexual assaults. This fact is exemplified by the sex offender's conduct in the case photo shown here, captured by a night vision closed-circuit surveillance camera. (The case is presented later in the chapter.) Here, the offender can be seen exposing and rubbing his genitalia on unsuspecting persons, believing he is obscured in the darkness of a theater. This type of sexual assault is referred to as *frotteurism,* a form of deviant illegal activity typically carried out by males in crowded public places such as theaters, shopping centers, and elevators. Such acts fall within the general classification of *paraphilia,* a psychological condition in which predatory sex acts are committed against men, women, and children (e.g., pedophilia). These types of sexual assaults and others are presented in this chapter, along with the specific methods most useful in investigating sexually motivated crimes and criminals.

attempted rape, incest, molestation, and fondling as well as varieties of noncontact sexually motivated acts such as sexual threats, pornography, and indecent exposure. Most of these laws are also gender neutral, holding males and females equally responsible as perpetrators of sexual offending activities. In addition, laws governing offenses requiring sexual penetration can be satisfied by insertion of the offender's genitalia and other body parts or by material objects held by or in the control of the offender. In the sections that follow, the terms *rape* and *sexual assault* are used somewhat interchangeably, as they are in the U.S. legal system. Discussions specifically using the term *rape,* however, refer to sexual assaults that involve nonconsensual intercourse or its equivalent.

The exact legal definition of sexual assault is jurisdiction specific, but most prosecuting agencies break down the offense into degrees of seriousness based on the sexual force used by the offender, the amount of physical or psychological harm done to the victim, and the victim's age relative to that of the offender. The following examples reflect sexual assault categories common to many jurisdictions:

1. ***First-Degree Sexual Assault:*** Physically or psychologically forced vaginal, oral, or anal penetration with the addition of at least one of the following: great bodily harm (GBH) to the victim, the threat or use of a weapon, the assistance of one or more persons, or causing the victim's pregnancy. In the most extreme cases of sexual assault, such as that illustrated in Figure 10.1, the victim may exhibit wounds to the face, chest, buttocks, and genital regions.

2. ***Second-Degree Sexual Assault:*** Physically or psychologically forced vaginal, oral, or anal penetration with the addition of at least one of the following: use of the threat of violence; causing injury, illness, disease,

LEGAL DEFINITIONS OF RAPE AND SEXUAL ASSAULT

The FBI defines **forcible rape** as "the carnal knowledge (i.e., sexual intercourse) of a female forcibly and against her will."[1] Unfortunately, this generic definition captures only a limited range of sex-related offending activities. It excludes such acts as (1) oral and anal intercourse (i.e., sodomy); (2) forced sexual intercourse/contact with a male by a female, or a female by a female; or (3) numerous sexually motivated illegal activities produced by victim coercion or other nonconsensual means. To capture a much broader range of sex crime activities, offenders, and victims, most jurisdictions now place sexual offenses under the general category of **sexual assault** rather than rape or some other legal label implying only intercourse between a man and woman without consent. Most sexual assault laws encompass numerous contact sex crimes including rape,

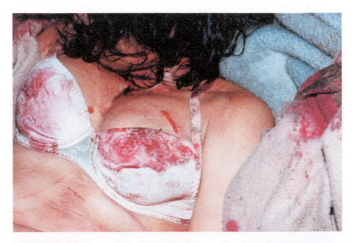

FIGURE 10.1 ▶ Sexual assault victim whose breasts were intentionally slashed by her attacker's knife. Such signatures are often associated with a type of sex offender known as a *sadistic rapist.*

or psychological impairment; or inflicted on a person who is unconscious, drugged/alcohol impaired, mentally ill, mentally deficient, or under the belief of undergoing a medical procedure.

3. ***Third-Degree Sexual Assault:*** Physically or psychologically forced vaginal, oral, or anal penetration.

4. ***Fourth-Degree Sexual Assault:*** Improper touching, attempted sexual contact, lewd and lascivious behavior, and other sexually motivated acts not involving intercourse, carried out without the consent or positive cooperation of the victim.[2]

In addition to the above classifications, many jurisdictions have special category offenses for sexual assaults of children and minors. Usually, these codes classify forceful sexual assaults or abuse committed against children under the age of 13 years at the first-degree level. In contrast, **statutory rape** involving adults having sex with a minor under the legal age of consent is considered a lower-level felony or perhaps a misdemeanor depending on the age difference between the victim and offender. In most jurisdictions, the legal age of sexual consent is 16 years—the nation's lowest and highest ages of consent are 14 and 18 years, respectively. Persons whose legal spouses are below the age of consent usually are legally exempt from statutory rape laws.

Megans's Law

Beginning in 1994, Congress passed a series of laws, collectively referred to as **Megan's Law**, requiring states to register and disseminate information to the public about persons deemed to be sexual predators. Sexual predators, as distinguished from persons committing a sexual offense, are individuals who habitually seek out victims for purposes of sexual exploitation. At present, persons committing any of the following sex offenses fall within the scope of Megan's Law:

- Aggravated sexual assault
- Sexual assault
- Aggravated criminal sexual contact
- Endangering the welfare of a child by engaging in sexual conduct that would impair or debauch the morals of the child
- Luring or enticing
- Kidnapping (if the victim is a minor and the offender is not a parent)
- Criminal restraint
- False imprisonment

Convicted sex offenders are required to register with law enforcement agencies within the community where they reside. Although the laws and registry information differ by jurisdiction, offender information commonly includes the sex offenders' names, descriptions and photographs, addresses, places of employment or school (if applicable), descriptions of the offenders' vehicles and license plate numbers, and brief descriptions of the offenses for which the sex offender was convicted. Most states have publicly accessible sex offender databases that allow searches for registered offenders by name and zip code.[3]

TYPOLOGIES OF RAPE

Efforts have been made to create typologies based on differences in victim/offender relationships and circumstances under which rape occurs. These typologies are as follows:

1. ***Date Rape:*** Occurring most often between offenders who are casually familiar with their victims before the offense. In addition to dating the offender, the victim may also be acquainted with the offender through work, school, friendship networks, on-line social networking, or some other method of personal introduction. The majority of rapes reported to authorities fall into this category. In 80 percent of date rape cases, one of the parties involved is under the influence of alcohol or drugs; in 50 percent of cases, both the victim and offender are alcohol or drug impaired. Popular date rape drugs used to seduce victims include Rohypnol (ruffies), Ketamine, and GHB. Intentional use of these drugs for purposes of seducing the victim carries harsh legal penalties.

2. ***Stranger Rape:*** Occurring between an offender with no prior knowledge of the victim, and usually involving the use of force and/or a weapon. Between 25 and 35 percent of all rapes fall into this category.

3. ***Spousal or Marital Rape:*** Occurring between persons who are legally married, or in a legal union. All states now have laws prohibiting nonconsensual sexual relations between spouses.

4. ***Child Rape:*** Occurring between a legal adult and a minor child. When the offender is a parent of close relative of the child, the crime is referred to as incest. These offenses are often carried out by aunts, uncles, and grandparents as well. Other nonrelatives likely to engage in this act are schoolteachers, care providers, neighbors, religious figures, and others to whom the child's care has been entrusted.

5. ***Prison Rape:*** Occurring between persons who are in custody within a penal institution. This act is most often brutal, resulting in serious physical injury or perhaps death to the victim. It may be perpetrated against weak inmates as a display of dominance by other inmates, but it is also used as a form of payback to victims who have not paid gambling or drug debts.

6. ***Serial Rape:*** Occurring as an ongoing, habitual predatory act by an offender who preys on four or more separate victims on separate occasions. This act should be distinguished from multiple rape, where the offender repeatedly victimizes the same individual. Serial rape consists of any one or combination of the above classifications.[4]

CHARACTERISTICS OF RAPE OFFENDERS AND VICTIMS

- About 88,000 cases of rape are reported each year in the United States, of which 41 percent are cleared by arrest or other means.
- Approximately 94 percent of rape victims are female and 99 percent of offenders are male.
- Most rape victims (about 65 percent) have prior knowledge of their offender. Of the offenders, 38 percent are friends or acquaintances, 28 percent are prior intimate partners, and 7 percent are family members.
- Most rapes (43 percent) occur between 6 PM and midnight, 33 percent between 6 AM and 6 PM, and 24 percent between midnight and 6 AM.
- The location of most rapes (50 percent) is inside or within 1 mile of the victim's place of residence, with an additional 20 percent taking place at the home of a friend, neighbor, or relative.
- Most rapes are committed by single offenders (93 percent), who are Caucasian (52 percent), approximately 31 years old, and may be married at the time of the attack (22 percent).
- Most rapists are generalist offenders who have a history of committing various other crimes, including public order crimes (20.5 percent), other violent crimes (18.6 percent), property crimes (14.8 percent), and drug-related crimes (11.2 percent).
- Approximately 11 percent of rapes involve the use of a weapon. Of these, 3 percent are committed with guns, 6 percent with knives, and 2 percent with other weapons.
- About 39 percent of attempted rapes and 17 percent of sexual assaults against females result in injury.
- Most persons who are injured during a rape do not seek medical treatment.
- Only 35 percent of all rape victims report their victimization to police.[5]

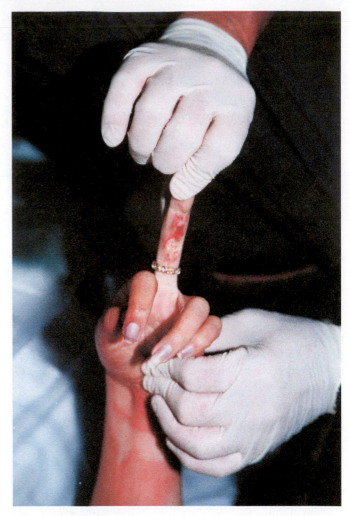

FIGURE 10.2 ▶ Defense wound on the finger of a sexual assault victim. This type of wounding is also commonly found on the hands and forearms of sexual assault victims who suffer physical attacks.

FIRST RESPONSE TO THE SEXUAL ASSAULT SCENE

The manner in which the first responding officer attends to the sexual assault crime scene is extremely important in obtaining victim cooperation, evidence, and other factors necessary for identifying and convicting the victim's offender through follow-up investigations. Following are various suggested lines of action to be taken by first responders when dealing with sexual assault victims, suspects, and witnesses:

Victims

- Upon arrival, document the victim's location.
- If the victim is injured, seek first-aid assistance if EMTs have not already been notified. Some injuries may be beneath clothing or not readily visible, as in the case of bruises or strangulation marks, or defense wounds (see Figure 10.2) which may take 3 or 4 days to appear on the victim's skin.
- Document statements made by the victim. Record each statement in the exact words used by the victim. Let the victim tell his or her story before asking any specific questions. Be a good listener. If the victim begins to provide rambling descriptions, ask specific questions about the incident.
- Describe the victim's emotional condition. The victim will likely be traumatized and appear anxious, but may act depressed or withdrawn.
- Document the victim's injuries. Take photographs of specific injuries as well as a photo of the victim's face for future identification purposes.
- If the suspected offender is still on the scene, detain the offender and interview the victim out of the sight and hearing of the suspect. If the victim provides a description of the offender, and the offender is believed to still be

in the vicinity of the crime scene, issue a bulletin to responding units providing suspect ID information.

- Note the victim's relationship to the suspect, document any history of prior abuse with the suspect or other persons, and note any temporary restraining or other court orders. Inquire about the victim's drug or alcohol use with the offender. If the use of date rape drugs is suspected, attempt to locate the drink containing the drug.

- Be sympathetic to the victim: Do not act judgmental in response to the victim's statements; use eye contact and body language that conveys concern and understanding to the victim; and explain to the victim that the assault is not his or her fault and medical assistance and other help options are available.

- Photograph the room or scene where the alleged sexual assault took place. Look for signs of displaced items such as bed sheets, furniture, or other items that show signs of a struggle between the offender and victim.

- Document any temporary address or telephone number of the victim.

Suspects

- Describe the suspect's location upon arrival.
- Administer first aid to the suspect if he or she is injured.
- Document any statements or admissions made by the suspect.
- Describe the suspect's emotional condition.
- Describe the suspect's physical condition.
- Document the suspect's injuries in detail. Attempt to identify specific defensive wounds, such as bites or scratches, that appear on the suspect's body.
- Document evidence of substance or chemical abuse by the suspect.
- Interview the suspect in a separate area from the victim. The suspect may appear calm, but may suddenly turn violent and attempt to attack. As a precaution against suspect violence, seat the suspect (or apply handcuffs, if legally warranted by the situation) before starting the interview.
- Obtain a photograph of the suspect from the victim (if available), if the suspect is not present at the scene.

Witnesses

- Interview the reporting party, if other than the victim.
- Identify all witnesses and interview them separately.
- List names and ages of children, if present at the scene.
- Interview the children, if present. Conduct the interview at a comfortable location away from parents. Be seated or assume another type of nonintimidating physical position or position when conducting the interview. Use open-ended questions, rather than specific questions that may cause the child to respond in a misleading manner.

- Document names and addresses of emergency personnel.
- Document the name of the treating physician in the emergency room, if the suspect received emergency medical treatment.[6]

BEGINNING THE SEXUAL ASSAULT INVESTIGATION

It is difficult to predict how sexual assault victims will react when first approached by investigators. Some are eager to talk about every detail of their attack and attacker. Others have little to say about their victim experience, and their silence often is inaccurately interpreted as a failure to cooperate with the investigation. Regardless of the victim's initial reaction, all individuals who have endured this crime are trying to cope with the emotional and physical aftermath of a life-changing experience. Investigators must be aware of these coping mechanisms, be able to recognize and understand them, and develop strategies to overcome the obstacles they pose when gathering information about the victim's sexual assault experience. These obstacles include the following:

1. ***Rage:*** Enraged victims are usually eager to provide information as a means of expressing and alleviating pent-up hostility. The victimization details they initially provide, however, often contain inconsistencies due to a highly adrenalized state of mind. These victims may later generalize their anger toward all males, resulting in an unwillingness to cooperate with male investigators.

2. ***Fear:*** Fearful victims tend to withhold information because of concerns for their personal safety. Common fears including being killed, seeing the rapist again, suffering another rape, and having a negative experience in the criminal justice system.

3. ***Worthlessness:*** Low self-esteem following a rape may cause the victim to withdraw emotionally. Victims typically attempt to distance themselves from investigators by remaining silent. Uncontrollable sobbing and emotional outbursts are also common reactions.

4. ***Guilt/Blame:*** These victims, in some way, blame themselves for their own sexual assault. They may feel guilty because their choice of clothing attracted the offender, or blame themselves for not heeding warnings from friends and family about going to dangerous places or dating certain individuals. Such feelings often cause victims to withhold or distort facts of the victimization. This is because they often believe the investigation will result in nothing more than the legal system ultimately holding them accountable for their own sexual assault.[7]

Rape Trauma Syndrome

In situations involving rape, mental health professionals have recognized that the victims often have a prolonged and psychologically debilitating reaction known as **rape trauma syndrome**

(RTS), a form of post-traumatic stress disorder (PSD) specific to sexual assault experiences. Victims of RTS pass through three distinct stages. The first, referred to as the *acute stage*, is evidenced by symptoms such as reduced alertness, disorganized thinking, nausea, and hypersensitivity to stress. During the second or *outward adjustment stage*, rape victims may outwardly appear to be normal, yet experience insomnia, flashbacks of their victimization, phobias, and mood swings, and may readjust their lifestyle to accommodate fears of a repeat attack. Victims entering the third and final *renormalization stage* come to grips with their victimization by shedding many of the defensive behaviors they have exhibited in the past. They exhibit greater normality in their lifestyle and a psychological acceptance of the fact that they have lived through a sexual assault.[8]

HANDLING SEXUAL ASSAULT HOT CASES

Sexual assaults that are reported immediately after they have occurred are referred to as sexual assault *hot cases*. In these cases the preliminary interview of the victim will most likely be done at the crime scene by the first responding patrol officer (see the earlier section, First Response at the Sexual Assault Scene). Investigators should not attempt, however, to interview victims in unsafe conditions or in need of immediate medical attention until these situational factors have been adequately addressed. The primary purpose of the preliminary interview is to quickly gather enough information from the victim to determine whether the crime of rape has taken place. In most situations, the time that investigators take to complete this interview is a matter of minutes rather than hours. A second, more detailed follow-up interview usually is later conducted in a location other than the crime scene, after the victims have regained their composure or received medical attention.

Any first attempt to interview sexual assault victims should not be demeaning or offensive. Rather, a sympathetic, optimistic, yet professional tone works best to gain the victim's confidence and cooperation. Time is of the essence, however, and targeted questions must be asked that require the victim to provide a specific answer. The first line of inquiry should concern legal requirements for establishing the sex crime suspected to have occurred. If the facts provided by the victim suggest that a sexual assault crime indeed has occurred, further targeted questioning about the offender's identity and sexual conduct is necessary. If the offender's identity is revealed by the victim, and adequate evidence supports probable cause that he or she committed the act, appropriate steps should be taken to locate and arrest the suspect. If only a description of the suspect is obtained, this information should be made immediately available to all patrol units around the crime scene.

Perhaps the most difficult aspect of conducting preliminary interviews of rape victims is asking about potentially troublesome and embarrassing details of the offender's contact with the victim's body and other sex-related conduct at the crime scene. Essential questions along these lines include the following: (1) "Did the offender ejaculate? If so, was it on your clothing, body, or other specific location?" (2) "Did the offender wear a condom? If so, where was it discarded?" (3) "Did the offender wipe bodily fluids (for example, blood, semen or saliva) on tissues, sheets, or any other object?" To preserve potential evidence, the first responder must also advise rape victims to refrain from brushing their teeth, using mouthwash, bathing, douching, changing or washing their clothing, disturbing their bedding, flushing toilets, or otherwise disturbing the location where the assault took place. As a follow-up to the presentation of sensitive subject matter or embarrassing questions, the interviewer should remind victims that providing this type of information is of the utmost importance for convicting the person who victimized them.

Sometimes, the preliminary interview takes place in an ambulance while the victim is in transit to the hospital or sometime after arrival. In these situations the questioning about the rape incident must be completed before the victim's formal sexual assault medical examination. Specifically, it is most important at this time to identify locations on the victim's body that may contain traces of the offender's bodily fluids. For example, the offender may have ejaculated on the victim's chest, back, buttocks, legs, arm, or hair, or have licked the victim's skin in specific locations. If this information is provided to medical personnel before the examination, specific clinical searches can be conducted and swabs taken of these bodily areas for evidence collection purposes. Soil, hairs, fibers, grass stains, rug burns, and other physical evidence from the crime scene location may also be identified on the victim's body during the sexual assault medical examination. Last, investigators should always respect privacy considerations while in a hospital setting and reassure victims that questioning will cease and the questioners will not be in the room when the exam takes place.[9]

SPECIAL CONSIDERATIONS AT THE SEXUAL ASSAULT CRIME SCENE

After the victim's initial interview, several special investigative considerations must be taken into account when investigators process the sexual assault crime scene. These are in addition to those used at the scenes of other crimes and include the following:

1. ***Extending the Crime Scene Perimeter:*** Do not restrict the search for physical evidence to the immediate area of the assault. Confer with the victims (ask where they first saw the offender), witnesses, or just use common sense to locate the point farthest away from the assault location where the offender began stalking the victim or prepared for the assault. Often remote locations and objects along the victim's path leading up to the primary crime scene contain the offender's fingerprints. These places and objects include elevators, drinking fountains, park benches, handrails, doors, windows, and surfaces on parked cars. Similarly, the search should also look for discarded soda cans, clothing items, weapons, chewing gum, cigarette butts,

condoms, condom wrappers, and tissues possibly containing the offender's DNA. If the offender was wearing a condom, specialized tests can be conducted for the presence of lubricant or spermicidal residue on the condom's exterior, which may have been deposited in or on the victim's body and clothing. Footprints on walkways and stairwells along with tire tracks on roadways leading to and from the victim's residence also may be recovered. Similar search strategies should be employed along routes possibly used by the offender to flee from the assault location, looking especially for any item taken from the crime scene. Sewer drains, garbage cans, bushes and shrubs, space under vehicles, and all other likely hiding places should be searched.

2. *Visualizing Trace Evidence:* Oblique lighting can be used to detect hairs and fibers on bedding, floors, car seats furniture, and other areas where the offender's hairs and fibers may be found. Suspected locations for the suspect's bodily fluids can be examined with ultraviolent (UV) light and the areas outlined or marked for more extensive confirmatory analysis. Semen, blood, urine, vaginal secretions, sweat, and saliva all fluoresce when exposed to UV lighting. This method of examination can detect wet or dried bodily fluids in virtually any location, including the victim's hair and clothing—especially on white cotton undergarments, where semen stains are difficult to visualize. Vaginal secretion stains have a much weaker glow under fluorescent lighting than do stains produced by semen. Stains from grass and most other green plants produce a UV glow as well. Many substances fluoresce under UV light, however, including oils in make-up, certain food residue, toothpaste, bleached hair, and certain soaps. Bodily fluid stains cannot be visualized on clothing that has been washed. A suspected semen stain needs to be confirmed using an appropriate test such as an APT (Acid Phosphate Test).

3. *Recalling Smells:* Because of the close contact between the offender and the victim, smells are an important form of crime scene evidence in sexual assaults. Suspects with poor hygiene have a distinct body odor, and others may wear a tell-tale cologne or have a soap smell on their body or clothing. In some cases, the scent of the victim's perfume rubs off on the offender's body or clothing. In some instances canines may be used on crime scene evidence to detect body odors of the offender or the victim on clothing and objects.

4. *Preserving Biological Evidence:* Most of the key evidence in a sexual assault crime scene is of a biological nature and highly perishable, so first responding officers and investigators must guard against its destruction by weather or other potentially destructive circumstances. Sunlight, heat, wind, rain, dew, sprinklers, splashing cars, smoke, and chemical agents are some of the many elements that destroy biological evidence. Other scenarios involve victims who demand to wash their mouths or bodies after being assaulted, despite investigators' demands not to do so. The general rule here is that some evidence is better than none. When textbook rules of evidence collection can't be followed, it may be necessary to improvise—and fast! Evidence must be covered before it gets wet and, if need be, moved from its crime scene location to a place where it can be preserved (preferably after photographing it). Rubbing cotton or a Q-tip inside the victim's mouth may be the only way to capture some of the offender's semen left by a forced oral copulation before the victim rinses their mouth or brushes their teeth. As illustrated in Figure 10.3, bodily fluids located on undergarments and other clothing items may be swabbed for laboratory analysis.

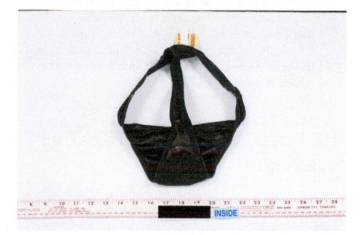

(a)

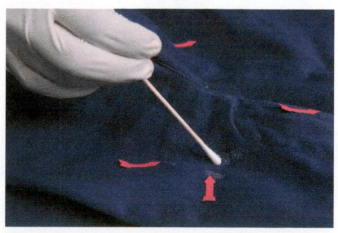

(b)

FIGURE 10.3 ▶ (a) Undergarment recovered from a rape victim, containing semen and other bodily fluid evidence from the offender and victim. (b) Dried semen being extracted from the zipper area of the rape suspect's pants, recovered as evidence after the suspect was booked on sexual assault charges. Laboratory analyses will determine whether this sample matches that found in the victim's undergarment.

5. ***Managing the Media:*** The media can both help and hinder investigation of a sexual assault. On the one hand, the news media should avoid intentionally or unintentionally revealing confidential information about assault victims such as name, place of work, vehicle make and model, or residential address. Too often, camera crews at the scene of a sexual assault accidentally film apartment buildings, businesses, road signs, and familiar landmarks that allow virtually anyone, including the offender, to get too much information about the sexual assault victim. On the other hand, the media can be very helpful in broadcasting physical descriptions, locations of attacks, artist sketches and composite images, still photos, surveillance videos, and other information about the suspect that the public can use to protect itself and to provide suspect leads to investigators. It is also imperative that any media story on a sexual assault provide the investigating unit's contact information for any citizens wishing to assist in the investigation. Generally speaking, it is the duty of investigators to ensure that media coverage of a sexual assault crime is in the best interest of the victim and of investigative efforts to solve the case.[10]

THE FOLLOW-UP INVESTIGATIVE INTERVIEW

A detailed follow-up interview with sexual assault victims should be carried out as soon as possible after the assault to identify and exclude suspects, secure additional witnesses, collect new evidence, and avoid forgetting of details of the crime. This interview can be short or long, but it needs to be long enough to capture every nuance of the crime. In addition to providing facts, the second interview enables investigators to determine other case-related factors such as the chances of a successful prosecution, the victim's credibility, and, most important, whether or not the victim is falsely alleging sexual victimization.

The physical setting for the follow-up is important. The meeting should be held in a room that creates a comfortable and uplifting feeling for the victim. The victim should not be interviewed in a public location where there are distractions and the conversation can be overheard; or in a stark, intimidating interrogation room. If possible, arrangements should be made to conduct the interview with a partner. Two investigators are better than one in sexual assault interviews due to the intimate questions being asked and possible later accusations that investigators acted unprofessionally or in a sexually harassing manner in soliciting answers from the victim. Furthermore, it has been demonstrated repeatedly that the investigator's gender is not a factor in conducting a successful victim interview; that is, mixing or matching the gender of investigators and victim provides no advantages in the information gathering process. What matters most is that investigators, regardless of their gender, treat the victim with compassion. There are some basic rules and suggestions for investigators, however, that will help ensure the success of a follow-up interview:

- Never be judgmental of the victim or the victim's behavior—no matter how morally offensive or deviant it may appear from a personal perspective.
- Show the victim respect and refer to them by their title (Mr., Ms., or Mrs.) or a particular name they like to be called.
- Refrain from touching the victim after their criminal ordeal; they may perceive touching as a physical intrusion of their personal space.
- Don't try to be a counselor to the victim. Be sympathetic when necessary, but also be professional.
- Expect the victim to fabricate certain stories, especially those that may suggest sexually provocative or deviant behavior that the victim is ashamed to admit having engaged in.
- Expect the victim's accounts of the sexual assault to be inconsistent due to their confused emotional state at the time of the offense.
- Let the victim speak freely while telling their stories and answering questions. Too often, investigators interrupt victims in mid-speech and miss valuable information that would have been disclosed had the interruption not occurred.
- Attempt to interview the victim alone. Friends, family, or other support persons present during the interview often try to support the victim by intentionally or unintentionally discouraging investigators from probing too deeply into sexually explicit details of the assault.
- If at any time the victim appears emotionally overwhelmed or becomes socially withdrawn (which happens quite often), stop the questioning immediately. Reassure the victim that you are on their side, and that you feel for them and the trauma they have endured. Also, inform them that the more detail they can provide regarding the offender and the assault, the more likely the case will have a successful outcome.[11]

CONDUCTING THE SEXUAL ASSAULT VICTIM INTERVIEW

To start the interview, the investigator should provide the victim a brief personal introduction and explain how the interview will proceed and the general nature of the questions that will be asked. At this time, while gathering basic personal background information, rapport should be established by showing interest in certain positive aspects of the victim's life—such as their work or educational accomplishments, hobbies, specialized knowledge, and so forth. Use this time to make the victim feel at ease and to show that you have a compassionate side that is both sympathetic and supportive.

After establishing rapport with the victim, slowly make a transition into questioning about the sequence of events that transpired before the rape. If the offender was a stranger, discover when and where the victim first noticed the suspect and use this as a starting point. This information may also help in uncovering additional evidence such as fingerprints, condom wrappers, surveillance camera photos, chewing gum, cigarette butts, soda cans, or other items discarded by the offender while approaching the victim. Also, inquire about the victim's actions and behavior during the time preceding the attack. The victim may twist or distort the facts relating to these questions if they believe the investigator will construe their personal conduct as sexually or morally inappropriate, or as leading on the attacker to engage in sexual relations.

Next comes the most difficult line of questioning for both the investigator and the victim—which focuses on the sexual attack itself. The victim should be told of the graphic nature of the forthcoming interview questions and that they should strive to provide candid, detailed responses. Also, victims should be allowed to describe sexually explicit details in their own particular way, using any slang or other jargon with which they are familiar. If they cannot provide a verbal description, have them draw a picture of the object or event that they are unable to describe. Specific topical areas included in this questioning segment include (1) any unique physical features of the suspect's body and (2) a detailed account of the sexual assault. The following sections discuss these topical areas.[12]

Physical Characteristics of the Suspect's Body

Besides providing a general physical description of the suspect, the victim will perhaps be able to describe physical features of the suspect's body that ordinarily would be covered by clothing. These may include generalized characteristics such as tattoos, body piercings, birthmarks, cuts, scratches, warts, moles, and scars. In addition, if the victim can do so, the offender's genitalia should be described in detail including size, shape, color, identifying marks, and circumcised or uncircumcised penis.[13] Figure 10.4 illustrates a specialized medical form that is used to describe the nature and location of wounds and other physical evidence discovered during an examination of a female sexual assault victim.

Details of the Sexual Attack

Answers to these questions can inform investigators regarding the offender's M.O. (*modus operandi*) and crime signature. Linking two or more rape cases with similar M.O.s and signatures may allow investigators to identify a serial rapist. On the other hand, two or more victims who describe a similar signature, yet a different M.O. may also indicate a single serial rapist who changes his method of attack over time. At a minimum, details of the sexual attack provided by the victim will explain the offender's motive. Before questioning begins, victims should

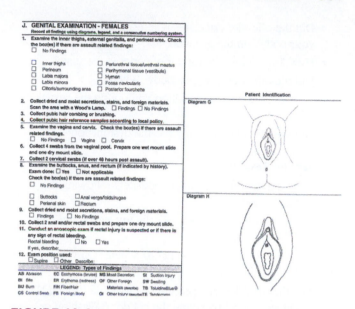

FIGURE 10.4 ▶ Sexual assault victim medical examination form completed by medical professionals who examine victims within 72 hours after sexual contact with the offender.

be reminded to recall memories using all their senses—that is, to remember what they saw, heard, smelled, tasted, or felt. Specific questions should focus on details and events occurring before, during, and after the sexual assault. Examples include, but are not limited to the following:

Before the Assault:

- What was the offender wearing?
- Did the offender wear a mask or disguise, or do anything else to avoid identification?
- How was the offender acting?
- How would you describe the offender's personal hygiene?
- How did the offender initially approach you?
- What did the offender specifically say to you before the assault?

During the Assault:

- How did the offender first gain control over you?
- How did the offender continue to maintain control over you?
- How did the offender remove your clothing?
- What did the offender specifically say to you during the assault?
- Did the offender ask you to say or repeat specific things?
- What did the offender do to you sexually? In what order were these acts performed?
- Did the offender's attitude change at any point during the assault?
- Did the offender demand that you perform a specific sexual act?
- Did the offender wear a condom? How was it applied? Where was it discarded?

- Did the offender ejaculate? Where? In the condom? On your body? On the ground?
- How long did it take for the offender to ejaculate?
- Did the offender lick your body? Where?
- How did the offender position you during the sexual assault?
- Did the offender have any erectile dysfunction?

After the Assault:

- How did the offender act immediately following the sexual assault?
- What did the offender specifically say to you after the assault was over?
- Did the offender wipe his penis? Where? On what? Was the object discarded or taken by the offender?
- Did the offender take precautions to avoid leaving DNA evidence behind by taking the condom? Washing or cleaning up semen?
- Did the offender attempt to wipe fingerprints or footprints from any surfaces or objects?
- Did the offender steal any personal belongings from you? Items of value (i.e., money, credit cards)?

Items not of value (i.e., jewelry, panties, personal identification)?

- How did the offender leave the crime scene?[14]

The final line of questioning in the follow-up interview focuses on the victim's sexual activity before the attack. The victim must be urged, tactfully, to provide a truthful account of their sexual activity, including how frequently they engage in sex. Furthermore, the victim must describe in detail any sexual activity they engaged in 72 hours before their assault. If they have had consensual sex, their partner's blood or other elimination samples will have to be taken to identify bodily fluids that can be individualized to the offender. If the victim has a history of consensual sexual behavior with the offender (e.g., spouse/lover, ex-spouse/ex-lover), details of this relationship should be obtained, especially regarding when and how often they have had sex. Victims should also be asked to divulge any prior sex-related crimes they have experienced, regardless of whether they have been reported to police. Any reported crimes should be verified through a background check. Although the investigator's first inclination might be to discredit the claims of a rape victim with an extensive record of reporting sex victimizations to authorities, such prior incidents may have been unsuccessful prior attempts by the same offender who committed the sexual assault under investigation.

CASE CLOSE-UP 10.1

"DOMESTIC VIOLENCE, SEXUAL ASSAULT, AND STALKING"

Domestic violence (also referred to as *intimate partner violence*) is the willful intimidation, physical assault, battery, sexual assault, and/or other abusive behavior perpetrated by an intimate partner against another. For domestic violence laws to apply to a particular situation, most jurisdictions require that the perpetrator and victim be current or former spouses, be living together, or have a child in common. In addition, some states include current or former dating relationships as well as same-sex relationships within the purview of domestic violence laws.

The first response and investigation of domestic violence cases is very similar to those generally described for sexual assault. The primary differences in handling and investigating these cases stem from the fact that the victims and offenders always have been intimate partners. These prior relationships, many of which involve children, can endanger not only the domestic violence victim but also the officers and investigators handling the case. It is not unusual for fighting couples to misdirect aggression toward law enforcement personnel attempting to control or investigate a suspected domestic violence incident.

About 85 percent of domestic violence victims are women, with the remainder being men. Females between the ages of 20 and 24 years represent the highest concentration of domestic violence victims. Sexual assault or forced sex occurs in about 40 to 45 percent of intimate partner violence situations. Furthermore, approximately one-third of all female homicide victims are killed by intimate partner violence. In 70 to 80 percent of intimate partner homicides, no matter which partner is killed, the man has physically abused the women before the murder. Children also may become a target of a quarrelling couple, with anywhere between 30 and 60 percent of domestic abusers being physically abusive to children in their household as well. Stalking is also related to domestic violence and sexual abuse. Women who are stalked by a current or former intimate partner have an 80 percent greater chance of being physically assaulted and a 31 percent chance of suffering sexual assault by that partner compared to women who are not the target of stalking. About two-thirds of all domestic violence perpetrators are under restraining orders at the time they rape or sexually assault their victim.[15]

Case Example 10A, illustrated in Figures 10.5 to 10.14, shows crime scene photos of a domestic violent/sexual assault incident that also involves a shooting and death. It is not uncommon in the most serious sexual assault or domestic violence cases for victims and/or offenders to be discovered dead at the scene. In this case, the female assault victim alleges that she shot her assailant in self-defense. She told investigators that the man was grabbing, punching and hitting her with a stick in such a forceful manner that she felt he was going to not only sexually assault her, but take her life as well.

CASE EXAMPLE 10A

Domestic Violence/Sexual Assault Incident

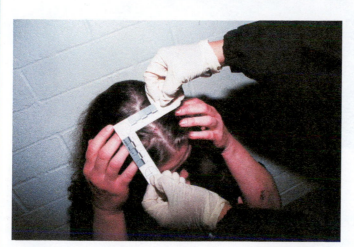

FIGURE 10.5 ▶ Investigators respond to the scene of a domestic violence-turned-homicide scene, discovering a woman who has suffered a severe physical assault and a dead male shooting victim in a bathroom at the residence. In the possible domestic violence defense scenario, does a previous history of violence by one individual against another take precedence in determining what charges, if any, are filed? What type of steps would an investigator take to investigate a scene of this type?

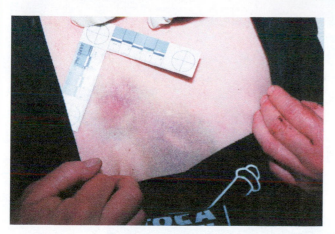

FIGURE 10.6 ▶ Large contusion in the rape victim's mid-chest area. Are the size and color of this bruise consistent with the victim's claims of an immediate attack?

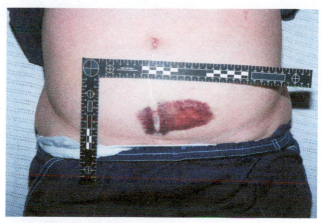

FIGURE 10.7 ▶ Wounding in the abdomen area. Is this abrasion consistent with the victim's claim of being attacked with the stick pictured below (see Figure 10.10).

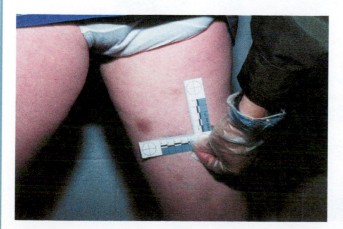

FIGURE 10.8 ▶ Leg bruising. Can it be concluded that these bruises are related to the domestic violence incident?

FIGURE 10.9 ▶ The pistol used in the shooting. What questions might be asked of the victim regarding this firearm and its use at the crime scene?

FIGURE 10.10 ▶ The victim stated that she was beaten with the stick pictured here. Is the available evidence at this scene consistent with the victim's claim of being attacked with this stick?

FIGURE 10.11 ▶ The victim claimed that after she shot her attacker, he died in this position on the bathtub. Does the blood evidence support this claim?

FIGURE 10.12 ▶ Blood pooling and patterns on the bathroom floor. Is the blood spatter evidence here, including the presence of pooling, satellites and a wipe stain, consistent with the victim's account of the incident?

FIGURE 10.13 ▶ Inspection of the fatal gunshot wound. Is there any other evidence in this view of the victim's body that is useful in the investigation?

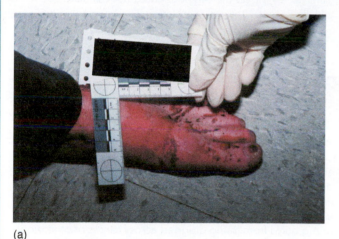

(a)

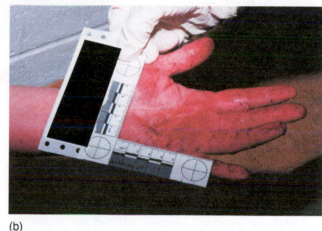

(b)

FIGURE 10.14 ▶ (a and b) Blood-covered foot and hand of the woman at the scene. What questions must be asked of the victim in order to the determine the origin of these blood stains? What must the answers to these questions be in order to support the victim's claim of self-defense?

BIOLOGICAL EVIDENCE OF SEXUAL ASSAULT

If it is determined through the victim interview or otherwise that the only biological evidence of a sexual assault is the offender's semen within an orifice of the victim's body (i.e., vagina, rectum, mouth), a medical examination for evidence identification purposes must be conducted as soon as possible after the attack. This is because semen and sperm degrade very rapidly when contained within the victim's living body. For example, within 6 hours after the assault, sperm typically is degraded to the point where it becomes useless for identifying the suspect's DNA. In general, much of the valuable forensic information provided by

semen and sperm samples is lost in living victims if a medical exam is conducted later than 72 hours after the attack.

Of particular investigative importance for a timely medical exam of the victim is the analysis of motile (living and moving) and nonmotile (not moving, dead, or degraded) sperm cells, which can be observed through microscopic analyses of seminal fluid recovered from the victim's body. In particular, sperm motility can help roughly approximate when the sexual assault occurred and whether it took place while the victim was alive or dead. These and related analyses are based on the length of time that sperm remain motile in different parts of living and nonliving bodies. In a living body, numerous motile sperm can be observed in the vagina 3–6 hours after intercourse. The number of motile sperm observed will diminish markedly after 12 hours in the same body, and they will rarely be seen in the vagina after 24 hours. Motile sperm usually can be observed in a living person's mouth up to 6 hours following fellatio, and up to 8 hours in the rectum after anal intercourse. Nonmotile sperm in living bodies can remain in the vagina for 6 to 7 days, in the rectum for 2 to 3 days, and in the mouth for less than 24 hours.

In dead bodies, sperm cells remain motile significantly longer because the biological conditions within living bodies that serve to degrade semen and sperm are not present. Sperm deposited in nonliving bodies can remain motile for up to 2 days in the vagina, rectum, or mouth, and nonmotile sperm can be found up to 2 weeks in these locations following intercourse. Applying this information to a sexual assault investigation is rather straightforward. For example, if a victim claims to have been vaginally raped within hours of a medical examination, the story can easily be corroborated though the observation that most of the sperm in the vagina are still motile. If the victim is dead, a vaginal exam revealing the presence of motile sperm coupled with the determination that the victim was murdered within the last 12 hours or less would suggest that the offender committed a simultaneous rape-homicide. On the other hand, motile sperm in the vagina of a victim who was determined to be dead for at least 36 hours would clearly indicate that the offender had engaged in postmortem sex with the corpse (i.e., necrophilia).

Tests for semen can also be conducted to help verify a sexual assault where sperm is not observable. In such instances, sperm may be so highly degraded that it disintegrates or the offender may have had a vasectomy. Semen deposited within the vagina or rectum generally can be detected for up to 72 hours in a living victim. Two separate tests can be performed: one for the semen-specific protein p-13, and another that reacts to high levels of the enzyme acid phosphatase (the p-30 test discussed in Chapter 8) contained within seminal fluid. In contrast, semen that has dried on clothing or other locations outside the body can react to such tests and provide sperm cells useful for DNA profiling many years after being deposited.

Investigators should not immediately conclude that victims are lying about suffering a sexual assault if semen or sperm cannot be detected on the victim or at the crime scene. Plausible reasons for this discovery include (1) the offender was wearing a condom when assaulting their victim (some 40 percent do so), or (2) the offender could not ejaculate due to sexual dysfunction before completion of the assault (this occurs about 35 percent of the time).[16]

HOT TIPS AND LEADS 10.1

Offensive and Defensive Injury Analysis

Examining the victim's and offender's injuries is often a key factor in determining blame in sexual assault and domestic violence situations involving couples who both claim to be the victim. Examine both parties for defensive and offensive injuries. Defensive injuries commonly inflicted by victims on offenders are scratches to the arms, neck, and face; bruising of the legs and shins produced by kicking; and bite marks on the hands, arms, shoulders, and neck. Signs of defensive action taken by the victim may include broken fingernails, bruising, and cutting of the hands and forearms. Offensive injuries produced by the offender include pattern bruising of the forearms, arms, and neck (from grabbing); petechiae of the face and whites of the eyes (from strangulation); and red abrasions or rug burns from being dragged across carpet or other flooring. Many bruises are not visible for 48 hours after the assault, so revisiting the victim 2 days after the incident may uncover observable bruising of the victim. Faded and healing bruises could suggest that the victim delayed reporting the attack.

THE SEXUAL ASSAULT EXAMINATION

Hospital emergency rooms and some clinics are staffed and equipped to perform specialized medical examinations of sexual assault victims for purposes of documenting and collecting forensic evidence. In fact, many larger hospitals have **SANE (Sexual Assault Nurse Examiner)** nursing professionals trained specifically to not only examine victims of sexually related crimes, but also perform other investigative support functions such as follow-up counseling for victims and court testimony procedures. Victims cannot be forced to undergo a sexual assault examination, but they should be urged to do so for numerous reasons (in addition to the collection of forensic evidence); these include general treatment of injuries and testing for pregnancy and sexually transmitted diseases. If victims consent to an exam, investigators need to ensure that they are transported to the proper medical testing facility and that somebody (a friend, counselor, or victim services volunteer) is available to assist them in the hospital waiting room before the exam takes place. Often, victims left to wait alone change their minds about having the exam and ultimately decide not to cooperate further with the investigation.

Before the exam begins, investigators need to inform the medical practitioner of likely locations of any trace and biological evidence in or on the victim's clothing and body. Not doing

FIGURE 10.15 ▶ Contents of a physical evidence recovery kit (PERK) or rape kit.

so will likely cause the doctor or nurse performing the exam to overlook valuable forensic evidence. All evidence that could corroborate (or perhaps refute) the victim's account of the assault must be obtained during the medical examination. Victims should have the utmost privacy during the exam; therefore, investigators should never be in the victim's presence during the actual sexual assault examination procedure. Once the exam begins, victims have the right to deny completing any medical procedure requested of them, and are free to leave the examination room any time they wish.

The procedures for completing a standard sexual assault examination have been standardized within the medical profession. Hospitals and clinics use what is known as a *physical evidence recovery kit* (PERK), also referred to as a **rape kit**, to document, collect, and preserve evidence recovered from the victim's exam. The kit, as shown in Figure 10.15, contains everything needed for collecting biological as well as trace evidence related to the assault, and includes separate envelopes and containers for each type of evidence collected. The contents of the kit are in a sterile package, and each kit is documented and controlled to establish a legal chain of custody for the evidence it contains. The exam itself is usually carried out in the following sequence of events:

1. Photographs are taken of victim while clothed, showing any tears in the clothing and exterior bodily injuries. Most common are bruises, abrasions, bite marks, or lacerations on the mouth, throat, wrists, arms, breasts, and thighs.

2. The victim is asked to undress over a large sterile sheet of paper designed to collect any trace evidence that falls from the victim's body or clothing while disrobing. The clothing (handled only by the victim) is collected and placed in separate evidence bags.

3. The victim's fingernails are scraped for possible blood or skin evidence from the offender. Broken fingernails can be cut and later compared for physical matches to nail fragments contained in the offender's clothing or wounds. A head hair sample of approximately 20 hairs from the front, side, and back regions is taken by plucking or cutting each hair. Any matted hair containing the offender's bodily fluids can be cut away, or dried substances contained in the hair can be flaked off. In the case of male victims, any facial hair should be inspected for signs of dried semen or other biological residue.

4. Oral swabs are taken from the victim's mouth for traces of the offender's semen and sperm (in cases of forced oral copulation). Dental floss can be used to dislodge the offender's pubic hairs from between the victim's teeth.

5. Swabs are done on the victim's body in locations likely containing dried bodily fluids where the offender may have ejaculated, spat, bled, or sweated on the victim. Large amounts of dried semen can be flaked away from skin where it is located.

6. The victim's pubic area is combed for the offender's pubic hairs, which may have comingled with those of the victim during the assault. Evidence of semen, sperm, blood, or saliva deposited in the victim's pubic hair is often also visualized and collected. A sample of

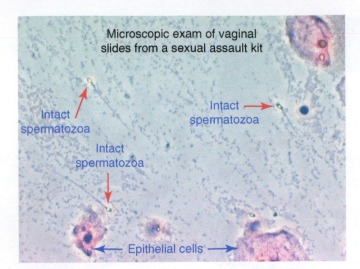

Microscopic exam of vaginal slides from a sexual assault kit

Intact spermatozoa

Intact spermatozoa

Intact spermatozoa

Epithelial cells

FIGURE 10.16 ▶ Microscopic view of sperm and epithelial cells (from the vagina) recovered from a rape victim who underwent a sexual assault medical examination.

approximately 10 pubic hairs is taken from the victim by either plucking or cutting.

7. Genital swabs and smears are taken from the victim's vaginal and rectal areas. Penal swabs will be performed on male victims. Magnified examination may also be performed on the victim's vaginal or rectal areas for signs of skin tearing. Magnification, as illustrated in Figure 10.16, can also be used to examine genital swabs of bodily fluids for the presence of sperm, epithelial cells and other biological matter that may contain valuable DNA evidence.

8. Blood samples are drawn and other medical tests are performed to establish the victim's DNA profile, pregnancy, and exposure to sexually transmitted diseases, including the HIV virus. If the victim has been impregnated by the offender, which occurs in roughly 5 percent of all rape cases, a morning-after pill (effective only during the first 72 hours following intercourse) or other pregnancy prevention procedures can be administered. Documentation of external wounds is also performed, including taking bite mark impressions. Toxicological tests should be requested if it is suspected that the offender used any type of illegal drug, such as ruffies or GHB, to subdue the victim. Drugs usually can be detected in the victim's system up to 12 hours after being taken.

9. Any other physical evidence, such as a loose condom, will be collected, documented, and packaged in the sexual assault kit.[17]

In 2005, Congress passed the Violence Against Women and Department of Justice Reauthorization Act (VAWA) guaranteeing that sexual assault victims receive free forensic medical examinations, whether or not they cooperate with law enforcement officials. Under this law, any person suspecting that they have been sexually assaulted may obtain a free medical examination, regardless of whether they have reported the suspected crime to police. In addition, after the results and evidence of the medical examination have been contained in the rape kit, the victim must sign a release to request that the evidence be processed by authorities. Many jurisdictions provide the victim up to 6 months to make this decision, after which the medical evidence collected from the sexual assault will perhaps never be processed.

VICTIMS WHO REFUSE MEDICAL TREATMENT

If a victim does not wish to have a sexual assault medical examination, investigators have no choice but to honor the victim's wishes. Attempting to threaten or coerce the victim into taking a medical examination will result not only in the victim's lack of cooperation with the investigation, but perhaps also in sanctions imposed by courts on investigators who use illegal methods to obtain evidence. Investigators may, however, attempt to collect limited medically related evidence themselves, after obtaining written permission from the victim. Photographs can document external wounds on the victim's body. Photographing areas beneath the clothing, such as breasts or other private bodily locations, should be done in a secured, private setting by persons who are investigators or authorized personnel of the same gender as the victim. Photos of bite marks and specific injuries should contain a measurement scale. If the victim's clothing is secured, each item should be placed in a separate paper bag and appropriately labeled. Clothing items containing bodily fluids should never be placed in plastic bags because this promotes bacteria that degrade biological evidence such as sperm, semen, and blood. Makeshift swabs can even be taken from the victim's mouth by vigorously rubbing cotton, cloth, or a paper napkin inside of the victim's mouth. It is also possible to use these and other absorbent objects to soak up suspected bodily fluids left by the offender. Wet objects collected as evidence should be placed in a clean paper envelope and then sealed and labeled once they have air dried. Never lick the envelope to seal it (leaving your saliva and DNA)! Rather, use a moistened gauze pad or paper towel. Remember that these improvised sexual evidence collection methods are used only as a means of enforcing the old adage "Some evidence is better than none." In other words, these techniques are a last resort for investigators who have practically no chance of using proper procedures before biological evidence has been contaminated or is spoiled.[18]

FALSE RAPE ACCUSATIONS

All victims who claim to have been raped should be considered to be telling the truth until facts become known to investigators that suggest otherwise. Of all crimes, rape and other types of sexual assault are the most likely to be fabricated by the victim. False rape accusations reported to police by alleged victims are estimated to compose from 25 percent to 40 percent of all reported rapes. Most studies, however, and practical investigator accounts suggest that 1 in 4 victims file a false rape report with authorities.

As previously mentioned, victims often fabricate facts of a sexual assault if the true account somehow suggests that they were responsible in some way for their own victimization. In these situations, the victims are telling the truth about being assaulted, yet are trying to preserve their personal reputation. It is critically important for investigators to distinguish between this type of victim and other victims who outright lie about their entire victimization. Some red flags associated with totally fabricated rape claims include the following:

- Late reporting of the offense
- Lack of evidence to corroborate the victim's story
- The victim's (or witnesses') lack of cooperation with investigators
- Refusing a sexual assault medical examination
- Filing reports of the crime in the wrong jurisdiction
- Discrepancies and vagueness in the victim's story and description of the offender
- The victim providing investigators with a wrong home address
- Prior histories of the victim's mental illness, alcoholism, or drug abuse
- Prior arrests for vice crimes, including prostitution
- A history of filing sexual abuse reports with police, especially if the accusations were unfounded
- Ongoing domestic disputes such as divorce and child custody issues

A key question that investigators must ask themselves when confronted with a possible false rape allegation is "What is the victim's possible motive for lying?" In searching for this motive, the victim's possible relationship with the person claimed to be the offender must be explored. Often, the motives for lying about a rape are quite different for alleged offenders who are acquaintances of the victim compared to those who are strangers. The most common motives for filing a false rape report are as follows:

1. ***Creating a False Alibi:*** An estimated 50 percent of false rape claims are motivated by a victim's desire or need to create a false alibi about an act they have committed, yet are ashamed to admit to others. The false alibi motive is used quite often by teenage girls who become pregnant from consensual sex with their boyfriends and attempt to blame their pregnancy on a stranger rape. Adults, on the other hand, tend to lie about being raped to cover up embarrassing or illegal activities they have voluntarily engaged in such as physical fighting with lovers, drug or alcohol binges, or sexually promiscuous situations including prostitution. In most cases, the false alibi motivation involves the victim falsely reporting that they have been raped by a stranger.

2. ***Revenge:*** False rape accusations often are motivated by revenge against a current or former acquaintance. The scenario reported to authorities may be spousal rape or date rape, but it is very seldom stranger rape. Those seeking to support a false allegation of suffering an aggravated rape may even batter themselves to substantiate their story. In most cases, the alleged victim has been emotionally rejected by the person they claim assaulted them. Ongoing domestic disputes, financial gain, or child custody battles are also common motivations associated with victims who lie for revenge purposes.

3. ***Attention/Sympathy:*** Victims may lie about being raped to gain attention and/or sympathy from others. This type of false allegation can be directed at strangers as well as acquaintances. For example, victims may lie about being raped by a celebrity or other person of high social status in search of ill-gotten fame. Other victims may enjoy attention and sympathy they receive from friends, family members, law enforcement, and the medical community after falsely posing as a rape victim.[19]

CRIMINAL INVESTIGATIVE ANALYSIS OF RAPISTS

Criminal investigative analysis (CIA) has been used by the FBI to profile unidentified rapists. The technique can be applied to a single rape incident; however, it appears to be most effective in identifying individuals who have raped on repeated occasions (i.e., serial rapists). The first step in conducting a CIA for rape crimes is to obtain a detailed statement from the victim regarding the offender's verbal, sexual, and physical behavior during the assault. Second, this information is used to determine the type of rapist responsible for the crime. According to the FBI method, there are two broad typologies within which a rapist can be classified:

1. ***The Pseudo-Unselfish Rapist:*** These individuals commit rape primarily to obtain power over their victim, which, in turn, helps them overcome feelings of personal and sexual inadequacy they experience in their normal, everyday interactions with women. In general, this type of rapist shows concern for the victim's well-being and does not intend to cause physical harm beyond the rape itself. Verbal, sexual, and physical indicators of the pseudo-unselfish rapist include the following:
   - ***Verbal:*** Comments made to the victim tend to be reassuring, complementary, and show concern for the victim. For example, an offender may say, "You are so beautiful I won't hurt you . . . if you show me you love me." These offender types are also noted for making self-demeaning, apologetic, and personally disclosing statements, such as "I'm sorry we had to meet this way . . . I know somebody like you would never want to be with a person who looks like me."
   - ***Sexual:*** For these offenders, rape is a means of acting out their sexual fantasy. If at any time the victim is verbally or physically resistant, the fantasy may be broken and the rapist most likely will cease any further sexual activity or aggressive behavior directed toward the victim. With compliant victims, this rapist type may engage in criminal foreplay, which typically

involves fondling the victim's breasts or buttocks and inserting fingers into the vagina. Offenders may also demand that the victim kiss them. Fellatio, anal sex, and the insertion of foreign objects may be carried out in addition to vaginal sex by offenders who are allowed to act out their sexual fantasies.

- *Physical:* As previously mentioned, these rapists do not obtain gratification from inflicting injurious physical harm on their victim. They will use verbal threats, or perhaps a weapon, to control their victim. If a weapon is involved, chances are it will not be used and may even be set aside when the sexual assault begins.

2. *The Selfish Rapist:* Anger toward women is the basic motivating factor for this type of rapist. They are dubbed selfish because their method and style of sexual assault tends to be all about satisfying their personal needs in a brutal sexual manner with a conscious disregard for the victim's well-being. Behavioral indicators of the selfish rapist are as follows:

- *Verbal:* Comments made to the victim are offensive, abusive, threatening, profane, demeaning, descriptive, humiliating, nonpersonal, and sexually explicit. Statements such as "Fuck me, you piece-of-shit whore," which are extremely offensive to the average individual, provide emotional gratification to the selfish rapist.
- *Sexual:* To this type of rapist, the victim is merely a sex object rather than a person. Kissing, fondling, and other forms of personal sexual contact are avoided. Victims are often bitten or pinched during sex. The victim may also be forced to engage in anal sex, fellatio, and masturbation. Any resistance on the victim's part will have no effect on the offender's desire to continue with the sexual assault.
- *Physical:* Selfish rapists use any type of physical force to dominate their victims, including extreme injurious brutality. Punching, kicking, and strangulation are commonly used by this rapist. If a weapon is present, it will perhaps be used to control as well as injure the victim. The extent of physical injury suffered by the victim tends to have no relationship to the amount of resistance against the offender's assault.

Rape Classifications

After rapists are identified as either pseudo-selfish or selfish, they can be assigned a classification based on their particular motivation for raping the victim. As will be noted in the following section, only one of offender classes is based on the pseudo-selfish profile. Six rape classifications, and their general offending characteristics, are identified by the FBI:

The Power Reassurance Rapist (Pseudo-Selfish)

- Rape is motivated by the offender's feelings of inadequacy and low self-esteem in situations and relationships with women. Sexual assault is a means of overcoming these feeling and confirming the rapist's sense of masculinity.
- Referred to as a *gentleman rapist.* Uses minimal force against victims and has no desire to inflict injurious physical harm. Will remove or have victim remove clothing, without engaging in ripping or tearing activity.
- Surprises victims in their residence during late night or early morning hours by gaining entry through unlocked door or window.
- Victims are strangers, living alone or with small children, who are roughly the same age as the offender.
- Engages in surveillance of victims through window peeking or other means before the attack and will repeat offend in the same geographic area.
- Attacks during periods when feelings of personal inadequacy peak, which may occur in regular cycles or time frames.

The Power Assertive Rapist (Selfish)

- An inflated masculine self-concept and the desire to dominate women are the main motivating factors for committing rape.
- Victims include strangers as well as friends, spouses, or other acquaintances usually of a similar age to the offender.
- Cons victims into compliance by using charm or personal appeal and then changes to threatening and aggressive demeanor after gaining the victim's confidence.
- Inflicts moderate to high levels of physical injury on victims, primarily by punching with fists. Often rips off or tears the victim's clothing.
- Carries out rapes in familiar areas, and strikes in an irregular opportunistic manner.

The Anger Retaliatory Rapist (Selfish)

- Openly hates and despises women and is motivated by rape as a means of demeaning women and inflicting punishment on them.
- Uses extreme injurious physical force, usually punching victim with fists or kicking victim with feet. Also tears or rips off victim's clothing.
- Attacks are spontaneous and unplanned in a blitz fashion, which usually result when the offender has an outburst at a particular victim that triggers pent-up anger.
- Selects victims of roughly the same age or somewhat older.
- Does not restrict offending activity to particular geographic areas or time periods.
- Targeted victims may be persons who cause the offender to be angry or resemble a person in the offender's past who has caused them anger.

The Anger Excitement Rapist (Selfish)

- This type of rapist is also known as a *sexual sadist,* and is motivated by the desire to achieve sexual satisfaction by causing pain and suffering to the victim.
- Victims are of both genders (although females are prevalent), all races, and all ages. They are usually total strangers to the offender.
- Infliction of injurious physical injury is usually extreme.
- Attacks are carried out by conning the victim into a position of trust and then unleashing an extremely violent and bizarre sexual attack on the victim, which often includes abduction and transportation to a location for purposes of torture.
- Extreme preplanning of the criminal event along the lines of the offender's bizarre sexual fantasies. Restraints, torture devices, transportation methods, instruments, and other items necessary to carry out a prolonged sexual assault session with the victim are brought to the crime scene by the offender.
- Sex rituals based on the offender's fantasies may include inserting foreign objects into the buttocks and vagina, accompanied by bondage, fetish, and masturbatory behavior on the part of the offender.

The Opportunistic Rapist (Selfish)

- Rape is motivated by sexual desire, and is usually an unplanned offense committed as a secondary crime following a planned robbery or burglary.

- Offenders may be under the influence of drugs or alcohol at the time of the offense.
- Minimal physical force is used, although the victim may be left bound and gagged at the crime scene.

The Gang Rape (Selfish)

- These rapes involve three or more persons (usually males) and are motivated by sexual desire as well as a warped variety of peer pressure to seek recognition and status by collectively raping a victim.
- Leaders of the gang rape typically emerge and should be a primary focus of investigation and analysis.
- Weak links, or persons who are hesitant to participate in the group rape, should be identified and analyzed.
- Force used can range from minimal to extremely brutal.

Development of the Analysis

The final step in the CIA process is to develop an analysis of the unknown rapist that paints a picture so vivid that investigators and other persons such as family, friends, or acquaintances who have had contact with the offender can provide leads to, or an identification of the rapist. It is beyond the scope of the present discussion to provide a comprehensive of the complete CIA profile development procedure. Investigators can use the typologies just described, however, as a starting point to build their own analysis of a given rape situation that predicts the rapist's personality and demographic traits.[20]

HOT TIPS AND LEADS 10.2

Interrogating the Suspected Rapist

Interrogating rape suspects is likely to elicit many justifications and excuses to persuade investigators of their innocence. The following are the most common among these:

1. **The Seduction Theme:** Many rape suspects will deny their guilt by claiming that the victim was the initial sexual aggressor and willingly participated in the alleged illegal sexual activity. They may also suggest that the victim offered to exchange sex for alcohol, drugs, or money.

2. **The "No Means Yes" Theme:** Rape suspects may claim that the victim at first acted like a somewhat unwilling participant, but really enjoyed having sex with the offender after the incident began. Suspects may also claim that the victim was playing games with them and sending mixed signals of encouragement for sex, and never offered any resistance to the suspect's sexual advances.

3. **The "Nice People Don't Get Raped" Theme:** Suspects attempt to discredit victims by asserting that they have a reputation for being "loose" or work as a prostitute.

They may also claim that the victim is a drug addict or alcoholic who sells sex to support their habit.

4. **The "Only a Minor Offense" Theme:** Suspects may admit that they are not totally innocent, but they do not accept full responsibility for their actions. They may claim to have gotten carried away, been high or drunk, or to have misread the situation, but never intended to sexually assault the victim. Suspects may also suggest that the victim's behavior somehow contributed to their sexually aggressive behavior, resulting in the general claim, "It's the victim's fault as much as it is mine."

At the beginning of the interrogation process, most rape suspects are clearly in denial that they are a rapist. As the interview progresses, many suspects will lower their defenses if the interrogating investigator is sympathetic to the theme that is presented as an excuse or justification. Agreeing with the suspect's self-justification theme and convincing him or her that they are really not a rapist but rather a good person who did a bad thing often can lead to a confession.[21]

PARAPHILIAS AND DEVIANT SEX ACTS

Paraphiliacs are individuals who are sexually aroused by deviant, and sometimes criminal, acts. **Paraphilias** are characterized by fantasies, behaviors, or sexual urges focusing on unusual objects, activities, or situations. These disorders are mostly evidenced in males, and usually begin in adolescence and continue through adulthood. The paraphiliac's compulsion to engage in abnormal sex patterns varies in intensity depending on the individual's life circumstances. At one end of the spectrum are persons who suffer from a minor form of paraphilia. These individuals can control their deviant sexual urges and satisfy them through legitimate outlets such as legal pornography and consenting sexual partners. Extreme paraphiliacs, on the other hand, are persons who organize their entire lifestyle around satisfying their abnormal sexual urges. Some are so driven by their sexual obsessions and compulsions that they will victimize others to satisfy their fantasies and sexually warped desires. Various types of paraphilias can be encountered during the investigation of sex offenders and their related offending activities.

Fetishism

Fetishism is a sexual attraction to objects. Shoes and underwear are common items of interest to those with fetishes. Persons with an underwear fetish may stage a residential burglary to conceal the fact they targeted and stole a victim's undergarment from their home. These types of fetishists are known to frequent Laundromats to steal soiled clothing. Fetishists can also be prolific shoplifters of items that are the focus of their sexual interest.

Exhibitionism

In this type of paraphilia offenders experience intense sexual arousal from exposing their genitals to strangers. **Exhibitionism** accounts for one-third of all arrests for sexually deviant activities. These offenders typically suffer from erectile dysfunction and they achieve sexual gratification through witnessing the fear they arouse in their victims. Victims typically are at no risk of rape by the offender, who has no desire to engage in sexual intercourse. The recidivism rate for this offense is extremely high.

Voyeurism

Voyeurism is the condition of seeking sexual arousal from observing unsuspecting persons undressing or engaging in sexual activity. These offenders, commonly known as *peeping Toms,* use various means to view their victims. Some view persons they target by close-range peering through bedroom windows (often while masturbating and leaving DNA at the scene), while others view their victims from a distance using telescopes, binoculars, or similar devices. Cell phone cameras often are used to capture images beneath women's skirts while the offender stands at the bottom of a stairwell. These offenders are also known to frequent restrooms, dressing rooms, and other locations where they can view or photograph persons in various stages of undress.

Telephone Scatologia

This act is otherwise known as *obscene phone calling.* The offender becomes sexually aroused when listening to the fear in the victim's voice, and often masturbates during the obscene call. Caller ID has severely reduced the incidence of this paraphilia.

Frotteurism

Frotteurism involves touching and rubbing against an unsuspecting person in a sexual manner. These paraphiliacs are known to frequent crowded public locations where they can anonymously rub, grab, or bump into their victims in a manner that appears accidental. One of the most common locations for frotteurism is in elevators. In addition to touching the victim's buttocks, breasts, and other intimate body parts, these offenders also are known to rub their genitals against the unsuspecting victim's body. The most daring offenders engage in frotteurism by unobtrusively removing and exposing their genitalia in public places. Case Example 10B presented in Figures 10.17 to 10.26 illustrates a suspected case of sexual assault involving a single male believed to be engaging in the act of frotteurism with unsuspecting females in the confines of a dark theater. The offender is unaware of the night vision surveillance video that is capturing his activities. When questioned by investigators about his involvement in this incident, the suspect claimed that his genitals were exposed as the result of forgetting to zip up his pants after using the restroom. Furthermore, in his statement to investigators, he claimed to be unaware that his genitals had touched anyone while he was in the theater, and if such touching had occurred, it was not intentional.

Necrophilia

People with the condition of **necrophilia** become sexually aroused by a corpse. Necrophiliacs often are serial killers who kill to have postmortem sex with their victims. Infamous offenders noted for this paraphilia include Jeffrey Dahmer, John Wayne Gacy, and Andrei Chikatilo. This type of offender may seek work in funeral homes, or they may solicit prostitutes for "ice down" sessions, which involve placing the sexual partner in ice (usually in a bathtub) to create a body temperature resembling that of a corpse. The partner's body also may be covered with talcum powder or another white substance to further enhance the illusion of death before engaging in sex.

CASE EXAMPLE 10B

Frotteurism Sexual Assault Case

FIGURE 10.17 ▶ The crime scene shown is a theater where patrons are allowed to go back stage before a performance to get a closer look at stage props used in the play and to have a "meet and greet" with actors. The stage area is very dimly lit but is equipped with surveillance cameras with night vision capabilities that capture the sexually deviant activities of the suspect (identified by the red arrow), who believes that he cannot be seen by others in the theater.

FIGURE 10.18 ▶ Suspect walking up the stairs behind three girls.

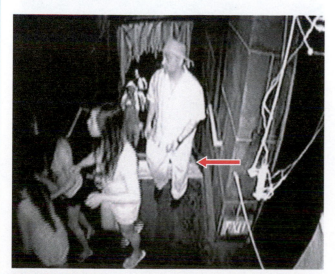

FIGURE 10.19 ▶ Suspect has removed his genitals from his pants.

FIGURE 10.20 ▶ Suspect is walking to the next room, masturbating.

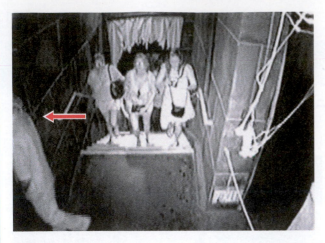

FIGURE 10.21 ▶ Suspect is entering the next room.

FIGURE 10.22 ▶ Suspect enters the room with his hands holding his genitals. The suspect passes the witness (actor, identified by green arrow). Notice that the witness immediately follows behind the suspect. The suspect continues to masturbate.

FIGURE 10.23 ▶ The suspect is caught masturbating by the witness. Notice the witness looking down at the suspect.

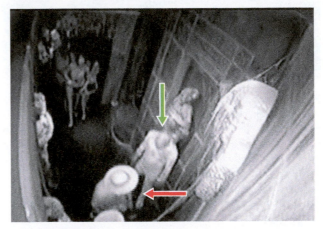

FIGURE 10.24 ▶ The suspect, realizing he has been caught, places his genitals back in his pants and walks away.

FIGURE 10.25 ▶ The witness immediately turns toward his phone to call for assistance. The suspect turns his head to see where the witness is going.

FIGURE 10.26 ▶ The witness calls management and security. The suspect is later apprehended upon exiting the premises. After agreeing to answer questions from investigators regarding the incident, the suspect claims that he had no knowledge that his genitals were exposed and blamed the incident on a wardrobe malfunction. In addition to the surveillance photos, what other information could be gathered to investigate this incident as a possible sexual assault? Are the surveillance photos alone strong enough evidence to arrest the suspect for committing a sex-related crime?

Technophilia

In **technophilia** the offender engages in computer-related sexual activities. Cybersex with minors is the most common variety of technophilia. These offenders typically are pedophiles (discussed later) who live a socially isolated lifestyle, and usually are males of a broad range of ages. They usually masturbate while communicating with their victims and are unable to have normal sexual relations. In extreme cases, technophiliacs use social networking to lure their victims to locations for purposes of sexual assault or perhaps abducting and killing them.

Sado-Masochism

Sado-masochists seek sexual pleasure by having pain inflicted on themselves or inflicting pain on someone else. Varieties of **sado-masochism** include (1) sadism, which involves sexual arousal achieved by infliction of pain or watching another in pain, and (2) masochism, characterized by sexual arousal through being controlled by bondage, regulation, or commands. In sado-masochism, individuals usually begin in the role of masochist and slowly progress to dominating others through sadistic acts. Popular forms of these paraphilias include the following:

1. Excrement (enemas) expelled, retained, ingested, smelled, buried
2. Burning, branding, hot wax
3. Stomping with high heels
4. Infantilism, diapering, cuddling, bottle feeding
5. Bootlicking (asphyxiation) using masks, hoses, nylons
6. Clamping body parts with clothes pins
7. Fisting, placing or receiving a person's fist in the anus

Partialism

These individuals are sexually aroused by specific body parts, for example, feet or hands. In most cases, **partialism** is not the motivation of violent acts against others. In rare exceptions, however, this paraphilia can be the driving force for criminal conduct—as in the case of serial killer Jerry Brudos. Brudos suffered from an extreme shoe fetish causing him to abduct and kill female victims to satisfy his twisted fantasies about their shoes. Combined with this fetish was his fixation on women's feet, which caused him to remove the foot of one of his victims to model shoes he had obtained through acts of killing and theft.

Hypoxyphilia

These offenders achieve sexual arousal through a physiological condition known as *hypoxia*—the reduction of oxygen to the brain. This condition can cause an accidental death that may resemble either suicide or homicide. Persons typically engage in hypoxyphilia through strangulation, smothering, and inhaling volatile substances while masturbating alone or having sex with a partner. Reductions in oxygen caused by these acts are used to enhance sexual sensations and orgasm. Death may occur when persons use self-strangulation as a means to achieve hypoxia—which is referred to as **autoerotic death**. Under these circumstances, the individual is accidentally rendered unconscious, and the strangulation device continues to restrict blood flow causing brain death. Hypoxyphilia can result in homicide at the hands of a sex partner who performs strangulation or some other means of hypoxia on the victim.[22]

SEX CRIMES AGAINST CHILDREN

Sexually abused, murdered, missing, or abducted children often are the victims of **pedophiles**, who are among the worst child predators. These offenders usually are selective about the children they target based on the child's age. Some sexually desire only prepubescent children (usually under 13 years of age), while others (technically referred to as *hebephiliacs*) exclusively desire adolescents who have achieved puberty. Other pedophiles are nonexclusive in selecting their victims and sexually target children of all ages. Depending on their sexual behaviors and offending patterns, pedophiles can be categorized in the following four categories.

The Inductive Pedophile

These offenders are almost exclusively male and usually target female children as victims. They tend to limit their offending behavior to fondling and touching the child's body in a sexual manner. Sexual penetration of the victim by the inductive pedophile is extremely rare. Most offenders are friends, family, caregivers, or others who have an established familiarity with the child victim. The use of physical force or violence against children by these pedophiles is observed in less than 10 percent of known cases. The average age of the inductive pedophile is from 36 to 40 years. Those under the age of 40 are more likely to target 12- to 15-year-old girls. Background characteristics of these offenders include the following:

- No history of other psychological problems or illness
- Use drugs/alcohol
- History of poor school performance
- Unstable work habits
- Low socio-economic status
- Unskilled or semiskilled labor employment

The Fixated Pedophile

These offenders appear childlike and act immature, often showing an age-inappropriate desire to engage in play or activities that usually are only of interest to children. They mask their sexual desires by conveying the image of simply being interested in entertaining and befriending children. The fixated pedophile is usually an unmarried male who has virtually no history of normal dating behavior. They also are noted for being very timid in their behavior patterns. Their offending behavior is usually restricted to sexual fondling without penetration. They are usually of average intelligence, have steady work skills, and possess somewhat normal social skills. These pedophiles often use toys, video games, and other play items of interest to children to lure their victims to private locations, such as their home, where they carry out illegal sexual activity with the child. They may also attempt to use drugs, alcohol, or pornography as an inducement for sexual activity.

The Regressed Pedophile

These pedophiles begin their lives with a normal adolescent sexual history, but in the teenage and early adulthood periods develop strong feelings of sexual inadequacy with adult females. They often are made fun of and/or labeled as sexually inadequate by their peers and female acquaintances. The victims of choice for these offenders are female children and adolescents primarily targeted in locations and neighborhoods outside the offender's place of residence. The regressed pedophile usually seeks out troubled youths who are runaways, have drug habits, or are alcoholics. They are also known to prey on children of friends and family. Usually, these offenders engage in genital sex with their victims and are seldom satisfied by merely touching or fondling the child.

The Exploitative Pedophile

These offenders utilize trickery or deception to lure their victim into illegal sexual activities. They often are strangers to their victims. After luring the child into a location perceived as a safe zone for sexual conduct, these pedophiles often become highly aggressive and sexually attack their child victim in a manner causing physical injury. Psychologically, the exploitative pedophile objectifies the child victim to carry out a range of illegal sexual acts including oral copulation and genital sex. Background characteristics of this offender type include the following:

- An extensive criminal record
- Explosive personality traits
- Very bad interpersonal skills
- A very unpleasant personality and demeanor

The Aggressive Pedophile

This individual is extremely dangerous to children, and is the most aggressive and violent of all pedophiles. Typically, these offenders possess a long criminal record, which includes lewd and lascivious acts against children. They are exclusive in their targeting of children, nearly always selecting victims of the same sex. The more harm they can inflict on their victims, the more sexual pleasure they experience. Often, the aggressive pedophile has an established record of mental illness and often has been intermittently institutionalized in a mental health facility or has received similar treatment on an outpatient basis. This offender's typical *modus operandi* is committing child abduction before engaging in sadistic sexual acts. Unfortunately, the aggressive pedophile often murders the victim as part of a sexual fantasy or to prevent the victim from revealing the offender's identity to authorities.[23]

RECONSTRUCTING A SUSPECTED SERIAL RAPE SCENE

Case Example 10C shows photos of various crime scene evidence (see Figures 10.27 to 10.36) used to investigate the activities of a serial rapist with the *modus operandi* of raping his victims while wearing a condom and then leaving his condom at the location of the sexual assault. DNA evidence is obtained from a condom left at one crime scene, allowing the investigators

---

CASE EXAMPLE 10C

Serial Rapist Case

FIGURE 10.27 ▶ The used condom pictured here was recovered by investigators in a trash can close to where a woman was raped by a stranger she claimed was "wearing a condom." Although the suspect was not apprehended, the main lead in the case is the prospect of obtaining the suspect's DNA from the condom and perhaps making a CODIS "hit" against the DNA of known sexual predators.

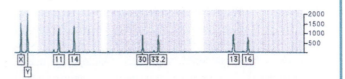

FIGURE 10.28 ▶ After recovering the condom, crime lab analyses of semen contained in the condom resulted in the electropherogram shown here revealing the suspect's DNA fingerprint. The first set of peaks verify that the DNA is from a male (e.g., X,Y), and the following sets of peaks show the suspect's unique genetic traits (e.g., alleles) for three separate loci used to develop a CODIS profile. For example, the first set of peaks show that for this particular loci, the suspect has an 11 and a 14 allele. The heights of the peaks indicate that sufficient DNA material was present to gain reliable results from this test.

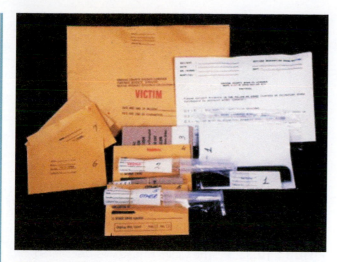

FIGURE 10.29 ▶ In addition to the condom evidence, investigators persuaded the victim to undergo a sexual assault examination within 8 hours after the assault.

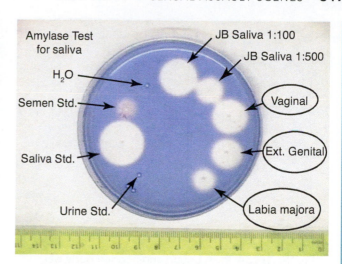

FIGURE 10.30 ▶ Results of an amylase test for the presence of saliva tested positive for the victim, suggesting that the offender's saliva was found in her vaginal area. (Positive results are circled.)

FIGURE 10.31 ▶ After a year of no leads on the sexual assault case, investigators were forced to place it in the cold case file. Shortly afterward, investigators received notification from the Homicide Bureau that the victim's family had recently filed a missing person report stating that "she had not been seen or heard from for several weeks straight." When an unidentified body was discovered in the desert region pictured here, investigators went to the scene to possible identify it as the missing sexual assault victim.

FIGURE 10.32 ▶ The body was discovered wrapped in garbage bags.

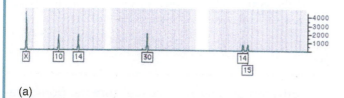

(a)

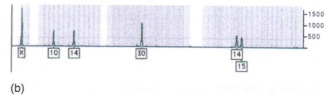

(b)

FIGURE 10.33 ▶ (a) DNA from the unidentified decomposing victim's body found in the desert was used to generate the electropherogram shown here. The first peak (X) verifies the victim as female and the remaining peaks show the DNA fingerprint. (b) Results from a second DNA test on the victim's epithelial cells found on the condom located at the crime scene a year earlier revealed the above DNA fingerprint.

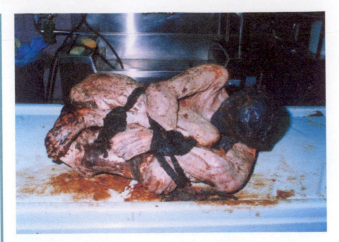

FIGURE 10.34 ▶ A bound and hooded body was discovered when unwrapped from the garbage bags.

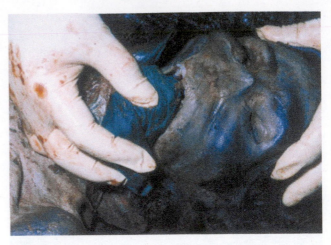

FIGURE 10.35 ▶ The victim's head was discovered beneath the hood.

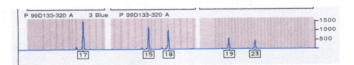

(a) DNA Fingerprint: Suspect #1

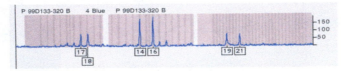

(b) DNA Fingerprint: Suspect #2

FIGURE 10.36 ▶ After the hood covering the victim's head was examined, skin cells from the hood were used to generate the electropherogram showing a DNA profile for a suspect in the serial rape and killing case. (b) More DNA evidence was also discovered on the gag recovered from the victim's mouth, which generated a second suspect DNA profile shown here as Suspect #2. What should investigators do with this DNA evidence? What conclusions can be drawn regarding the relationships between the victims and suspects in this case using the available DNA profiles?

to obtain the suspect's DNA profile. One of the rape victims later becomes a missing person, and her dead body is believed to have been found in a remote desert location near a city where other serial rapes with a similar *modus operandi* have been reported. Investigators use DNA evidence to determine if the body is indeed that of the missing victim. In addition, DNA evidence of suspected offenders is also found at the scene. In examining this case, the available DNA profiles must be used to link the victim to any known or unknown sexual assault offenders.

Summary

1. Defining the term *sexual assault.*

Most offenses categorized as sexual assaults encompass numerous contact sex crimes including rape, attempted rape, incest, molestation, and fondling as well as varieties of noncontact sexually motivated acts such as sexual threats, pornography, and indecent exposure. In addition to these classifications, many jurisdictions have special category offenses for sexual assaults of children and minors.

2. **Conducting a sexual assault victim interview.**

   Investigators should be prepared to face formidable emotional obstacles while attempting to interview victims of sexual assault. Fear, rage, guilt, and self-blame are often some of the reactions of victims of sex crimes at the time of initial contact. It is best to interview the sexual assault victim in two stages. First, conduct a quick interview to obtain the most important details of the incident to establish that a crime was committed, where it was committed, and possibly by whom it was committed. Second, after the victim has dealt with the trauma of the situation, begin a more detailed interview, probing for specific details of the sexual assault such as (1) a physical description of the suspect's body and (2) details of the attack.

3. **Biological evidence in sexual assault cases.**

   Obtaining biological evidence from the victim's body and from the crime scene is key to demonstrating that a sexual assault crime has taken place and for providing evidence of a suspect's guilt as the perpetrator of the alleged sex crime. Bodily fluids containing DNA such as sperm, saliva, and semen are highly perishable biological evidence and must be obtained from the victim through a sexual assault medical examination within 72 hours of the attack—otherwise such evidence will be destroyed. Specially trained medical personnel (SANEs) use a rape kit to extract and preserve evidence from the sexual assault victim's body.

4. **Special methods of sexual assault investigation.**

   Various typologies of sexual assault offenders have been created that are useful for conducting and profiling perpetrators of sex crimes. For example, the FBI has developed a method known as *criminal investigative analysis (CIA)* for classifying rapists based on factors such as their behavior with victims at the crime scene and the M.O. they use to carry out a sexual assault. There are also various typologies of rape victims who provide investigators with false rape accusations. Estimates of false rape accusations reported to police by alleged victims are estimated to be from a low of 25 percent to a high of 40 percent.

5. **Paraphilias and deviant sexual acts.**

   In addition to rapists, there are various types of deviant sexual offenders known as *paraphiliacs*. These offenders commit various sex crimes from noncontact acts such as exhibitionism to aggressive predatory attacks on children. Some of these offenders engage in occasional criminality, while others live a lifestyle of habitual sexual offending. Hypoxyphilia is one form of this sexual disorder commonly encountered by investigators, which sometimes results in what is known as *autoerotic death*.

Key Terms

forcible rape	statutory rape	rape trauma syndrome (RTS)
domestic violence	rape kit	paraphilias
fetishism	voyeurism	autoerotic death
serial rape	child rape	stranger rape
sexual assault	Megan's Law	frotteurism
SANE (Sexual Assault Nurse Examiner)	CIA	necrophilia
exhibitionism	pedophile	partialism
spousal rape	prison rape	technophilia

Review Questions

1. What is the difference between *forcible rape* and *sexual assault*?

2. How do the various degrees of sexual assault offenses differ? Provide one example of each.

3. What is Megan's Law and of what significance is it to the prevention of sexual assault?

4. Provide a profile of the typical characteristics of sexual assault offenders and victims.

5. What are some of the special considerations in processing a sexual assault crime scene?

6. What are the various duties of a first responder to a sexual assault incident?

7. How should investigators conduct interviews with sexual assault victims?

8. What types of questions should be asked of the sexual assault victim during an interview?

9. How is the sexual assault medical exam conducted? What types of evidence are collected?

10. What are some of the warning signs of a false rape accusation?

11. How is criminal investigative analysis (CIA) for rapists carried out?

12. In your opinion, which types of paraphiliacs are most dangerous, and why?

13. What are the various types of pedophiles and how do they prey on children?

Internet Resources

National Center for Victims of Crime	victimsofcrime.org
National Coalition Against Domestic Violence	www.ncadv.org/
Stalking Resource Center	victimsofcrime.org/our-programs/stalking-resource-center
Victim's Law Database	www.victimlaw.info/victimlaw/
VINE Offender Database	www.vinelink.com/vinelink/initMap.do

Applied Investigative Exercise

Select any of the illustrated cases presented in this chapter (10A, 10B, or 10C) and explain how you would investigate it. Start with your initial contact of the victim, discussing how you would establish rapport with the victim and gather information about the sexual assault. Be specific about the types of questions you would ask about the suspect and the sexual assault attack. Discuss the types of evidence that could be gathered from the crime scene to determine the suspect's guilt.

Notes

[1] Federal Bureau of Investigation, *Uniform Crime Reports 2009*, posted at www.fbi.gov/stats-services/publications.

[2] This section was adapted from sexual assault legal codes representing various states in the United States.

[3] Jill S. Levenson and Leo P. Cotter, "The Effect of Megan's Law on Sex Offender Reintegration," *Journal of Contemporary Criminal Justice*, 2005, 21 (1), 49–66.

[4] Jacqueline B. Helfgott, *Criminal Behavior: Theories, Typologies and Criminal Justice* (Newbury Park, CA: Sage, 2008), 79–84.

[5] National Center For Victims of Crime, *Facts About Sexual Assault Victims and Offenders* posted at victimsofcrime.org.

[6] This section was adapted from Connecticut Sexual Assault Crisis Services, Inc., *Police Response to Crimes of Sexual Assault Training Manual* (East Hartford, CT, 1997).

[7] Thomas P. Carney, *Practical Investigation of Sex Crimes: A Strategic and Operational Approach* (Boca Raton, FL: CRC Press, 2004), 135–140.

[8] Ibid.

[9] P. Frazier and J. Burnet, "Immediate Coping Strategies among Rape Victims," *Journal of Counseling Development*, 1994, 72(6), 633–639.

[10] Ibid.

[11] Vernon Geberth, *Practical Homicide Investigation: Tactics, Procedures, and Forensic Techniques*, 3rd ed. (Boca Raton, FL: CRC Press, 1996).

[12] Carney, *Practical Investigation of Sex Crimes*, 155–167.

[13] Ibid.

[14] Ibid.

[15] National Coalition Against Domestic Violence, *Domestic Violence Facts*, posted at victimsofcrime.org.

[16]Carney, *Practical Investigation of Sex Crimes*, 121–130.

[17]United States Department of Justice, *A National Protocol for Sexual Assault Forensic Medical Examinations* (Washington, DC: USGPO, 2004).

[18]Carney, *Practical Investigation of Sex Crimes*, 202–212.

[19]The False Rape Society, *Giving Voice to Men and Women Charged With False Rape Accusations*, posted at falserapesociety.blogspot.com.

[20]John Douglas et al., *Crime Classification Manual* (San Francisco, CA: Jossey-Bass, 1992), 191–207.

[21]Adapted from Paul Cromwell, *In Their Own Words: Criminals On Crime*, 5th ed. (New York, NY: Oxford Press USA, 2005).

[22]Ronald J. Comer, *Abnormal Psychology* (New York, NY: Macmillan, 2010), 435–446.

[23]Ibid.

CHAPTER ELEVEN

GANG CRIME SCENES

Learning Objectives

After completing this chapter, you should be able to:

1. Explain the relationship between street gangs and the law.
2. Be familiar with the investigative indicators of street gangs.
3. Be able to distinguish between street gangs of various races/ethnicities.
4. Be familiar with Midwest and East Coast street gangs.
5. Understand how prison gangs differ from street gangs.

Chapter Outline

Street Gangs and the Law
- Identifying Street Gangs
- Validation of Street Gang Membership
- Recognizing Gang Crimes

The Gang Investigator's Role

The Nature of Street Gang Crime

Drive-by Shootings
- The Planned Drive-by
- The Spontaneous Drive-by

First Response to the Gang Crime Scene

Street Gang Investigative Indicators
- Weapons
- Firearms
- Weapon(s) Discovery
- Ballistics Evidence
- Graffiti
- Hand Signs and Verbalization

Street Gang Organizational Structure
- Peripherals or Wannabes
- Associate or Affiliate Members
- Hard Core Members
- Cliques

Female Gang Members

Race/Ethnicity

West Coast Street Gangs
- Latino Street Gangs
- African-American Street Gangs
- Asian Street Gangs
- Caucasian Street Gangs

Midwest and East Coast Street Gangs

Prison Gangs

Race and Prison Gangs

Organizational Structure and Leadership of Prison Gangs

Recognition of Prison Gangs

Modes of Communication

Relations with Street Gangs

Relations with Police

Reconstructing a Gang Crime Scene

INTRODUCTION

THE OPENING CASE PHOTO PRESENTED here (see the entire case in this chapter) illustrates what a gang drive-by shooting looks like. In this instance, the target was a vehicle—but private dwellings, businesses, and individuals are just as likely to be the object of similar street gang violence. This photo also shows the complex nature of ballistics evidence typically processed at these scenes—namely, a lot of bullet strikes, cartridge casings, broken glass, and spent bullets. Additionally investigators attending to this type of gang crime frequently encounter extensive blood evidence from fatal high-power gunshot wounds. The frustrations that the gang associates pictured here feel when witnessing the crime scene will most likely compel them to lash out at or "do payback" on other gangs. Chances are, members of the victimized gang know street names and locations of the shooters who carried out this drive-by shooting. This is because the victimized gang likely has engaged in some type of earlier assaultive behavior against the perpetrators. Although crimes such as the drive-by portrayed here—and other gang crimes presented in this chapter—are exceedingly violent to witness, they often provide a wealth of suspect leads due to the predictable nature of gang-on-gang warfare.

STREET GANGS AND THE LAW

Identifying Street Gangs

To investigate gang crimes, investigators first must know the specific legal criteria in their respective jurisdictions that are used to make positive identifications of street gangs. Specific words and phrases used to legally describe a street gang often differ among the many jurisdictions possessing such legal definitions. Currently, 39 states, including the District of Columbia and the federal government, define by law the characteristics of a street gang. Common to all of these definitions is the general notion that a street gang is recognizable by the following three criteria:

1. *Size of Membership:* A group consisting of three or more persons (39 states).

2. *Common Identity:* Having a common name, identifying sign, or symbol as an identifier (24 states).

3. *Criminal Behavior:* Engaging in one of numerous criminal acts typically associated with furthering a criminal group or group enterprise (24 states).

Street gang definitions in the legal codes for the states of California and Alabama, as well as the federal government, are provided below:

California:

An ongoing organization, association, or group of three or more persons whose primary activities include the commission of one or more serious or violent criminal acts; that has a common name or identifying sign or symbol; and whose members individually or collectively . . . have engaged in a pattern of criminal gang activity.[1]

Alabama:

Any combination, confederation, alliance, network, conspiracy, understanding, or similar arrangement in law or in fact, of three or more persons that, through its membership or through the agency of any member, engages in a course or pattern of criminal activity. Ala. Code § 13A-6-26 (2002).[2]

Federal Government:

An ongoing group, club, organization, or association of five or more persons: (A) that has as one of its primary purposes the commission of one or more of the criminal offenses described in subsection (c); (B) the members of which engage, or have engaged within the past five years, in a continuing series of offenses described in subsection (c); and (C) the activities of which affect interstate or foreign commerce.[3] *18 USC § 521(a).*

Many law enforcement agencies formulate a general definition of a street gang that is based on street behavior rather than legal principles. For example, a police agency may define a street gang as, "three or more persons who commit crimes in furtherance of the gang itself and its reputation." This simple working definition can be used to clearly identify many criminal behaviors unique to street gangs, including drive-by shootings. In a drive-by shooting, it is common for several gang members to act as shooters at the same scene and to yell out their gang affiliation as they kill their enemies.

HOT TIPS AND LEADS 11.1

Prosecution of Gang Members

Because gang crime is characteristically group crime involving multiple offenders, the following legal remedies are often available for investigators:

1. **Aiding and Abetting**: Gang members who advise, counsel, encourage, support, or similarly assist another gang member who is actively committing a criminal act can be charged with aiding and abetting. In many jurisdictions, the punishments for this act are similar, if not the same, as those for the individual actually carrying out the gang crime. Typical acts of aiding and abetting gang crime include driving a car; supplying weapons or ammunition; or pointing, shouting, holding, or otherwise setting up a victim.

> 2. **Conspiracy**: If gang members agree or make plans to commit a criminal act, and they engage in some sort of conduct that furthers their offending objectives, conspiracy charges are an option—although the planned crime never took place. For example, one gang member calls another to tell him he wishes to kill a rival in an enemy gang. Both discuss the best way to carry out the murder. In addition, each gang member puts the word out on the street that they would like to buy a stolen gun to "take care of business." Although the plan is never carried out, both gang members could be charged with conspiracy to commit murder for planning the murder and attempting to buy "hot" guns—presumably to commit the murder.

Validation of Street Gang Membership

Identifying individual gang members by systematic and legal means, a process known as **validation**, is necessary not only for investigating attempted or completed gang crimes, but also for starting legal actions directly aimed at curbing and/or prosecuting street gang activity. Merely belonging to a street gang is not illegal; nonetheless, establishing street gang membership is a viable investigative tool and under some instances can procure enhanced punishments for suspects legally identified as gang members. Most jurisdictions have specific criteria that must be met in order for an individual to be legally classified as a gang member. The number of these criteria varies by state, but they usually include the following:

- Self-admission as a gang member
- Identification as a gang member by a family member, informant, known gang member, or other reliable source
- Residing in or frequenting known gang locations and neighborhoods
- Personal appearance and behavior consistent with that of gang membership, including style of dress, use of hand signs, tattoos, vocabulary, etc.
- Associating with known gang members
- Physical evidence suggesting gang membership, photographs, letters, e-mail, texts, rags, drawings, symbolic objects/items
- Having been arrested in the presence of known gang members or for crimes typically committed by street gangs

Some states do not specify the number of criteria that must be met for positive identification. Most, however, require two or more—as in the case of the following criteria used in Florida:

- Admits to criminal gang membership
- Is identified as a criminal gang member by a parent or guardian
- Is identified as a criminal gang member by a documented reliable informant
- Adopts the style of dress of a criminal gang
- Adopts the use of a hand sign identified as used by a criminal gang
- Has a tattoo identified as used by a criminal gang
- Associates with one or more known criminal gang members

- Is identified as a criminal gang member by an informant of previously untested reliability and such identification is corroborated by independent information
- Is identified as a criminal gang member by physical evidence
- Has been observed in the company of one or more known criminal gang members four or more times. Observation in a custodial setting requires a willful association. It is the intent of the legislature to allow this criterion to be used to identify gang members who recruit and organize in jails, prisons, and other detention settings
- Has authored any communication indicating responsibility for the commission of any crime by the criminal gang[4]

The more criteria that can be satisfied for a particular individual, the stronger the case that can be made for the individual's membership in a street gang. The reasonable suspicion that is legally required for certain methods of gathering gang intelligence (e.g., taking photographs of the suspect, entering the suspect in a gang member database) can also be established when the appropriate gang member criteria are demonstrated for a particular suspect.

Recognizing Gang Crimes

The term **gang crime** refers to a rather elusive concept, which can and has been conceived in many ways. Some agencies recognize gang crimes as only those offenses that can be linked (1) to illegal acts of street gangs directed against other street gangs or (2) to crimes carried out by street gangs for the specific purpose of enhancing the gang's reputation or financial status. This method of recognizing gang crime focuses on *gang motivated* criminal activities. Another, more widely used method concentrates on what are called *gang related* criminal activities. Under this classification method, any crimes connected to the gang operating either as a group or individually are recognized as gang crimes. Furthermore, crimes involving known gang members who are the suspects or the victims of criminal activity also will be classified as gang related crimes. Most states that provide legal definitions of gang crimes do so by describing illegal activities associated with street gangs, as in the following example representing the state of Kansas:

[Gang crimes are] the commission or attempted commission of, or solicitation or conspiracy to commit, one or more person felonies, person misdemeanors, felony violations of the uniform controlled substances act, or the comparable juvenile offenses, which if committed by an adult would constitute the commission of such felonies or misdemeanors on separate occasions.[5]

In contrast, other states provide general definitions of street gang crime as well as a laundry list of specific crimes that legally determine the offenses recognized as gang crimes. The most comprehensive of these lists is for the state of California:

- Assault with a deadly weapon or by means of force likely to produce great bodily injury
- Robbery
- Unlawful homicide or manslaughter
- Sale, possession for sale, transportation, manufacture, offer for sale, or offer to manufacture controlled substances
- Shooting at an inhabited dwelling or occupied motor vehicle
- Discharging or permitting the discharge of a firearm from a motor vehicle
- Arson
- Intimidation of witnesses and victims
- Grand theft
- Grand theft of any firearm, vehicle, trailer, or vessel
- Burglary
- Rape
- Looting
- Money laundering
- Kidnapping
- Mayhem
- Aggravated mayhem
- Torture
- Felony extortion
- Felony vandalism
- Carjacking
- Sale, delivery, or transfer of a firearm
- Possession of a pistol revolver or other firearm
- Threats to commit crimes resulting in death or great bodily injury
- Theft or unlawful taking or driving of a vehicle[6]

THE GANG INVESTIGATOR'S ROLE

The process of investigating crimes committed by street gangs is similar to that used for other crimes. The unique aspect of street gang investigation, however, is that gang crime enforcement tactics focus on both individual and group offenders, who often commit a wide range of offenses. For example, gang investigators may work a case involving a series of street robberies carried out by a single gang member only to discover later that the same suspect is but one of several shooters involved in an armed assault on a rival gang. Another special facet of gang investiga-

FIGURE 11.1 ▶ Gang graffiti is often referred to as "the gang member's cell phone" in that it is a potent form of communication within and between street gangs. The message illustrated here states that the area is a "tax free" location—referring to the fact that this street gang will not pay "tax" or extortion money to prison gangs. (Courtesy of The Los Angeles Police Department)

tion is the nature of victim and offender relationships. In gang crime situations, the lines between those who victimize and those who have been victimized often are unclear. A common example of this is the discovery during an investigation of a gang-related shooting that the victim is also responsible for earlier unsolved gang murders. Gang members often refer to their graffiti as "their telephone message" to rival gangs. Oftentimes, graffiti messages such as those illustrated in Figure 11.1 will contain names and other information that can be used by investigators to develop leads in cases involving gang-on-gang crimes.

Gang investigators may work in specialized units, commonly referred to as *GUs* or *Gang Units,* which are solely dedicated to investigating gang crimes and gang related activities. Agencies without specialized gang units usually assign investigators to gang crimes on an as-needed basis. In addition to their own cases, gang investigators handle various cases referred to them from other investigative units and patrol divisions. Typical crimes investigated include gang related assaults, robberies, drug sales and trafficking, and sex crimes committed by both adults and juveniles. Gang investigators usually assist homicide units who take charge of homicides committed by gang members—due to the extreme time and effort required to solve these cases. They also investigate gang crimes in schools, provide expert court testimony about gang related crimes, perform training on gang issues, and maintain intelligence sources on gang activity.

Teams of gang investigators may work with other officers or investigators to target specific gang members, gang activities, or entire street gangs. This team approach is often used in multi-jurisdictional task forces to carry out crackdowns on numerous high-profile gangs and their members. These operations typically involve coordinated raids of gang locations by teams of officers from numerous law enforcement agencies at the local, state, and federal levels. Both uniformed and undercover officers participate in these operations to conduct surprise searches and arrests of specific gang targets.

Perhaps the most valuable skill that gang investigators must attain is the ability to gather street-level intelligence about gang members and their criminal activities. Gang intelligence is crucial to the successful investigation of gang related crimes. Therefore, gang investigators must be proactive in their gathering of information concerning the following:

- The types and numbers of gangs existing within specific locations
- The size and structure of individual gangs
- Members of specific gangs and their criminal behavior
- Gang allies and enemies
- Graffiti writing as a form of gang communication
- The types of weapons, drugs, and violence associated with specific gangs
- Gang dress, symbols, language, rituals, and culture

Local, state, and federal databases exist in many jurisdictions that contain this and other intelligence information about criminal street gangs throughout the nation.

In addition to the types of intelligence just listed, gang investigators must attempt to discover which known gang members are in and out of prison—and which are ready to become **drop-outs**. Drop-outs are great source of information for investigators. In street terms, a drop-out is a gang member who is technically no longer active in the gang, but still has ties to

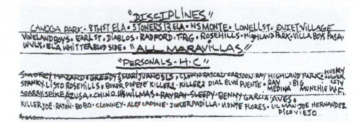

FIGURE 11.2 ▶ A green light list or hit list containing the names of street gangs and individual street gang members, authorizing violence to be used against them within a jail setting. Such lists are smuggled into detention facilities and when intercepted by authorities can provide detailed information regarding ongoing gang rivalries and homicides or other intergang violent crimes.

the gang. In general, drop-outs are quite aware of recent criminal activities carried out by their former gang. For the most part, drop-outs are placed on a hit list and are marked for death by the gang they left behind. Figure 11.2 shows what gang members refer to as a *green light list* that contains the names of persons in a jail population that have been identified by their gang rivals to be "hit" while in custody. Obtaining such a list can provide a wealth of intelligence information for gang investigations; on the other hand, the lives of persons who carry and lose a green light list to investigators will be in immediate danger—which often provides an opportunity for investigators to gain more information from such individuals in exchange for personal protection.

CASE CLOSE-UP 11.1
"ON-LINE GANG INVESTIGATION"
Cincinnati, OH; Lee County, FL

The newest trend in gang investigation is using social networking websites such as MySpace, Facebook, and Twitter to validate street gang members and build cases with photo evidence. For example, investigators in Cincinnati used MySpace and Facebook pages to arrest more than 20 members of one of the city's most notorious street gangs. The gang posted not only numerous pictures of themselves and their associates wearing gang colors, flashing hand signs, and carrying weapons, but also information about numerous felony offenses they had committed. Despite such risks, street gangs continue to post pictures and information about gang membership on social networking sites. The state of Florida has now made it a felony to use electronic media to promote gang activity. As a result, two men charged with violating the law by posting pictures of themselves "flashing" gang hand signs currently face up to 5 years in prison.[7]

THE NATURE OF STREET GANG CRIME

The old saying "actions speak louder than words" is especially true when it comes to the investigation of street gang crime. That is, the nature of the crime being investigated may perhaps be the strongest indicator of whether or not a criminal activity is gang-related. Most crimes committed by street gang members are motivated by the desire for economic gain, establishment of reputation, or revenge against enemies.

Street gang crimes can be committed by single members acting alone, but normally they involve several members acting

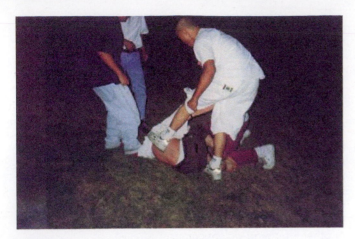

FIGURE 11.3 ▶ Gang members jumping-in a new member.

together in either a planned or a spontaneous manner. Next to physical assaults of other gang members and the sale of narcotics, robberies targeting citizens and businesses are one of the most common serious gang crimes. In addition, many gang initiations require **associate** members to carry out robberies to become full-fledged members. Associates are individuals who desiring to become a member of a gang, and spend much of their time with the gang. Typically, they conduct a robbery to show allegiance to a specific gang. This criminal act, coupled with a **jumping in** (see Figure 11.3), will almost guarantee membership. *Jumping in* is a term used to describe a gang initiation process. The would-be member allows himself or herself to be beaten by four or five fellow gang members. In prison, much more violent crimes are usually required to become indoctrinated into the prison gang. This is due to the special social environment created in prison.

DRIVE-BY SHOOTINGS

The Planned Drive-by

In a **planned drive-by**, street gangs generally attack their enemies or rivals at a time and in a location that (1) provide the most opportunity to cause damage and/or injury and (2) the least opportunity for apprehension by law enforcement or self-defense by the victimized street gang. In other words, this type of drive-by shooting is a planned rational criminal act whereby offending street gangs members weigh both the costs and benefits of their actions before proceeding. It is generally preceded by a significant event or motivating factor that can often be discovered through victim informant interviews or reviewing the victimized gang's recent criminal activities.

More rarely, yet a distinct possibility, planned drive-by shootings result from conflicts between individual gang members of opposing gangs over trivial, non–gang-related situations such as a lost fight at school or competition over a female. By and large, most gangs that are repeat victims of planned drive-bys are undergoing an ongoing cycle of payback for prior acts

of violence that the victimized gang perpetrated against the offending gang. Common to all planned-drive by shootings is that they are usually *victim precipitated crimes;* that is, the victimized gang or gang member has played some role in bringing about their own victimization.

Disputes between street gangs over territorial claims, drug sales, **state prison orders**, and actions perceived as disrespectful to the street gang's reputation are common precipitating events for planned drive-bys. State prison orders are those in which a prison gang issues an order to a street gang to commit a drive-by or a murder. The connection here is quite simple. Prison gangs are aligned with the races and territories of their respective street gangs. The street gang members often get caught and end up going to state prison. If the gang or a specific member does not comply with orders from the respective state prison gang aligned to them, they usually have a **hit** placed on them—commonly referred to in prison slang as "being put in the hat." This type of hit mandates an attack on that individual or that gang once they are in arm's reach of other inmates.

The Spontaneous Drive-by

The **spontaneous drive-by** attack is less common than the planned drive-by, but can be just as lethal. As the name implies, a spontaneous drive-by shooting typically involves a chance encounter between two opposing street gangs, resulting in a combative situation leading to the exchange of gunfire. Investigators have discovered that this type of inter-gang violence usually begins with an offensive verbal challenge known in street vernacular as the "mad dog" or "hit up." This process is illustrated in the following example:

STAGE ONE:	DISCOVERY OF CONFLICT:
GANG 1:	Flashes hand signs representing the street name of the "claimed location" or "turf" and/or shouts "Where you from?"
GANG 2:	Responds by flashing hand signs and/or shouting response identifying the street name of their "claimed location" or "turf."
RESULT:	If the gangs conclude that they are not rivals, the challenge will end; the perception of rivalry will result in elevation to Stage 2.
STAGE TWO:	OFFER AND ACCEPTANCE OF CHALLENGE:
GANG 1:	Counter-responds by "disrespecting" Gang 2 with hand signs or verbal comments to Gang 2, such as "***** your hood!"
GANG 2:	Counter-responds with a similar actions and statements
RESULT:	The exchange of spontaneous gunfire.

This above exchange can take place on foot, in vehicles, in public places, in residential locations, or any combination thereof. The gangs involved may or may not know each other, or have prior histories of conflict.

FIRST RESPONSE TO THE GANG CRIME SCENE

First responders attempting to obtain suspect descriptions and other information from witnesses are likely to encounter the same response from everybody at the scene: "No, Officer, I didn't see or hear a thing." This lack of cooperation in identifying likely suspects is often encountered during the investigation of gang crime. Most gang-infested neighborhoods have a "no tell" attitude when it comes to providing information on gangs to police. This stems from another street adage causing eyewitness intimidation: "Snitches get stitches" (implying that if you tell, you get hurt).

On rare occasions victims or other individuals assist first responders by providing information about gang crimes they have witnessed. Usually, however, any information provided at the crime scene marks the end of the witness's or victim's assistance in the gang case investigation. In most cases, sources providing information at the crime scene will refuse to provide additional details during follow-up investigations. More troublesome, they also often refuse to show up at court proceedings when requested—even if the investigator has a **body attachment** signed by a judge. A body attachment is used when a person ordered to testify in court refuses to appear. In a gang crime case, a body attachment gives law enforcement the authority to take a potential witness into custody.

In gang-related crimes, especially those involving murder, jail time for not testifying is not as bad as the alternative; that is, supplying information about a gang crime to police or testifying against a gang member may result in personal injury or death at the hands of a retaliating gang member. Usually, interviewing efforts directed at both victims and witnesses of gang related crime are stifled by the unwritten rule within gang culture that calls for **retaliation** against persons inside or outside the gang who provide information (or "snitch") to law enforcement officials. This gang practice has severely hampered and tainted the efforts of community policing. Thus, developing suspect leads generally does not depend on first-responder information obtained at the gang crime scene. Rather, it hinges on the investigator's ability to pierce the veil of secrecy that shrouds the identities of specific criminal members within street gangs and to link those offenders with physical evidence obtained at the crime scene. Case Example 11A illustrates a vehicle drive-by shooting case. The crime scene photos shown in Figures 11.4 to 11.13 also illustrate the complexities of processing an outdoor drive-by shooting crime scene. As in the immediate case, containing the scene requires securing a large geographic area and includes the closure of several main streets for an extended period of time to process the scene. When examining these crime scene photos, it is important to consider not only the logistical issues that are present (e.g., containing and processing the crime scene) but also the relevant evidence that must be examined in order to reconstruct the drive-by shooting incident from beginning to end.

CASE EXAMPLE 11A

Vehicle Drive-by Shooting Case

(a)

(b)

FIGURE 11.4 ▶ (a) A patrol unit observes a vehicle crashed into a black gate. Upon driving closer to the vehicle, officers also notice the shattered passenger side window. The shattered window would be a sign of a shooting. In addition, there are bullet holes on the driver's-side door. (b) The view as officers make their approach to the vehicle. Because this is a known gang neighborhood and this appears to be a drive-by shooting, what special precautions should first-responding officers take when beginning their investigation of this crime scene?

(a)

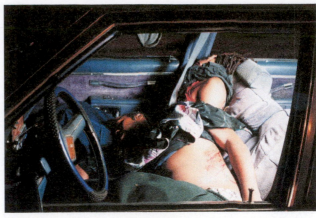

(b)

FIGURE 11.5 ▶ (a) As the officers approach the car, they observe two males shot inside the driver's compartment. (b) Upon closer inspection, it is apparent that both are deceased. Note: The driver's body is laid on the lap of the passenger. The passenger's head is facing away. Based on the positioning, the driver was attempting to distance himself from the bullets by leaning toward the passenger. The passenger was turning himself away from the line of fire. In addition, are there any characteristics of the vehicle that should be noted by officers?

(a)

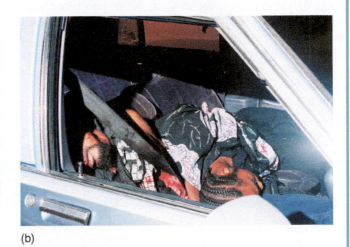

(b)

FIGURE 11.6 ▶ (a) A search of the passenger side of the vehicle reveals no bullet holes. (b) The bodies as observed from the passenger side of the vehicle. What information should first-responding officers gather at this scene that will be of importance to gang investigators? What are some of the special concerns to officers who must secure this crime scene?

(a)

(b)

FIGURE 11.7 ▶ (a) After the scene has been secured, gang investigators begin to identify evidence. A search of the street reveals multiple casings in a long sporadic pattern. (b) A close-up of two spent cartridge casings. Do the casing patterns on the street suggest how the drive-by shooting took place?

FIGURE 11.8 ▶ View showing the opposite end of the crime scene containment. Because of the pattern length of the casings, the crime scene is an entire block. Based on the pattern and location of the cartridge casings, can it be determined if this was a spontaneous or planned drive-by shooting? Where the shooters in a vehicle or on foot outside of a vehicle at the time of the shooting? What other types of evidence or information might be gathered by investigators at this scene now or during a follow-up investigation in order to provide suspect leads?

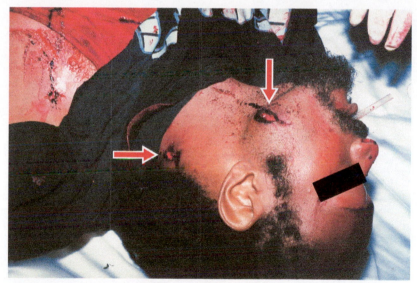

FIGURE 11.9 ▶ (a) Once the bodies were removed from the car, investigators determined where each victim was shot. This victim sustained two gunshot wounds on his face and neck. (b) The same victim also sustained a gunshot wound to his left shoulder.

(a)

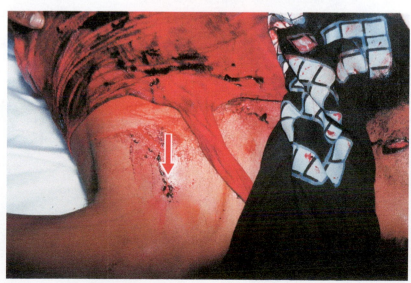

(b)

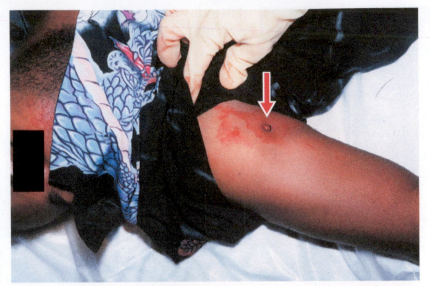

(a)

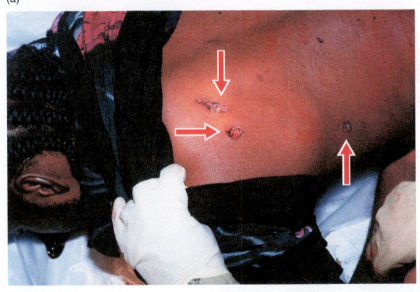

(b)

FIGURE 11.10 ▶ (a) The second victim sustained a gunshot wound to his right arm. (b) The second victim also sustained gunshot wounds to his back. Do the characteristics and positions of the bullet wounds indicate how the victims were approached by the shooter, how many shooters were at the scene, the type of weapon that was used, or other situational factors that may be related to a gang style attack?

(a)

FIGURE 11.11A ▶ (a) Blood and bullet holes in the driver's area of the vehicle. How should investigators proceed in their search of the vehicle's interior. What evidence should be gathered and how should it be collected? What type of evidence would be important to establish a gang-related motive for this crime?

(b)

FIGURE 11.11B ▶ (b) Trajectory rods placed through the bullet holes. Do the number and trajectory of bullet strikes further suggest the number of shooters participating in this drive-by, or the shooter's position at the time the shots were taken? Of what significance is the glass evidence in the rear passenger windows?

(a)

FIGURE 11.12A ▶ (a) Trajectory rods used inside the vehicle to determine bullet paths.

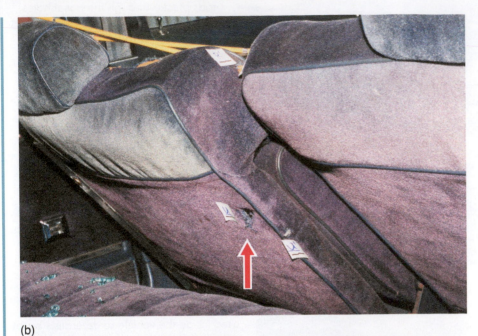

(b)

FIGURE 11.12B ▶ (b) View from behind the front driver side seats showing bullet holes.

FIGURE 11.13 ▶ Trajectory rods showing bullet paths through the passenger seat. If more than one suspect is arrest in this can, can the ballistics evidence presented here be used to determine which shooter was responsible for the death of which passenger in this vehicle? Overall, does the evidence in this case suggest a possible motive for this gang related crime?

STREET GANG INVESTIGATIVE INDICATORS

In a broader sense, gang investigators must understand each gang and gang member as the product of a unique subculture. Because gangs are a subculture, they socialize their members into unique behaviors and lifestyles that the investigator can translate into rather predictable patterns of criminal conduct. Specifically, the group to which gang members belong may systematically influence how they select victims, carry out crimes, and leave evidence at the crime scene. Investigators who recognize the various cultural nuances of specific gangs, such as monikers, jargon, tattoos, and hand signs, have distinct advantages when processing crime scene evidence and later using that evidence to solve a gang crime.

One of the most challenging and frustrating problems encountered by gang investigators is assembling the overwhelming amount of case material on street gangs, their membership, and specific crimes under investigation. No two gangs or their crimes are exactly alike. As will soon be shown, street gangs differ in many characteristics, including ethnicity, size, structure, sophistication, territorial habits, and criminality. Thus, the discussion that follows cannot comprehensively examine how gang culture relates to all criminal conduct. Rather, the intent here is to provide a detailed discussion of the relevant information most useful for investigators confronted with a crime scene that is the product of gang activity or gang-affiliated offenders.[8]

Weapons

Theoretically, no weapon or type of weaponry is off limits to street gangs. Stories abound about gang members using exotic weapons such as cross-bows, rocket launchers, or blow-guns during the commission of crimes. In fact, however, firearms are the weapon of choice of most criminal street gangs. This is perhaps the result of the changing nature of inter-gang rivalries, which have moved from the face-to-face "rumble" style of fighting of the 1950s to today's "hit-and-run" fighting method. The likely catalyst for this change was the infusion of illicit drug money into the gang culture and the proliferation of illegal rifles and handguns on the streets beginning in the early 1970s.

The increasingly impersonal combat style coupled with readily available high-tech firearms are a lethal combination on the battlegrounds of modern street gangs. The primary objective in investigations of suspected street gang crimes in which weapons have been used is to (1) discover the weapon(s) or type of weapon(s) used, (2) determine the number of persons involved in a particular weapon assault, (3) identify the location and position from which the weapon assault was carried out, and (4) link specific damages or injuries to a specific weapon, and if possible to a specific suspect.

Most firearms used in gang assaults are stolen and/or unregistered. Registered firearms will likely be traceable to their original purchaser and place of purchase. Often, identifying information such as make, model, and serial number typically is altered or destroyed. Crime lab methods are available, however, to restore pressure stamped serial numbers that have been filed down. The weapon may also be a hybrid or "mix-and-match" gun composed of several interchangeable parts taken from other firearms. Street gang members' efforts to alter firearms for enhanced performance or to stymie the firearms identification process pose special safety concerns to crime scene investigators and crime lab personnel. For example, pistols converted from semiautomatic to fully automatic firing or containing a "hair trigger" are common modifications—requiring extra caution by first responders securing crime scenes or criminal investigators removing crime scene evidence. In addition, suspected ill-performing firearms should always be thoroughly examined before test firings are conducted.[9]

Firearms

Unsurprisingly, automated firearms identification databases often reveal that a particular firearm used in a street gang assault has been used in numerous other crimes. Street gang members are notorious for "recycling" their weapons. Not only is the same firearm often used in numerous crimes, but it may also be used by generations of the same gang or even by different gangs over several years.

Because of the hit-and-run style of modern gang warfare, one of the most informative pieces of evidence for investigating street gang assaults is expended cartridge casings. Various cartridge casings belonging to multiple weapons point to multiple shooters at the crime scene. Seldom does a lone gang member bear and fire multiple weapons during a single street assault. If shots are fired in succession, the "scatter pattern" of expended cartridge casings can be used to assess the shooter's movement relative to the intended target. All things being equal, the greater the distance separating each casing fired in sequence, the faster the shooters were moving while firing their weapons. This information may help determine whether a hit-and-run assault was carried out while running on foot (**walk-by**), riding a bicycle (**ride-by**), or riding on a motorcycle or in a car (**drive-by**). If shots are fired from an offensive gang and the victimized gang returns fire, the scatter pattern of expended cartridges for both sets of shooters should be roughly equivalent. In the case of ICI 3, there was only one set of casings.[10]

Weapon(s) Discovery

In cases involving non-firearms weapons—knives, clubs, chains, or baseball bats—both the primary and secondary crime scene areas should be searched carefully for weapons. This is because most gang offenders immediately flee the crime and dispose of their weapon either at the crime scene or somewhere on their escape route, in case they are stopped by police. The same can be true for crimes involving handguns and compact rifles or sawed-off shotguns; however, gang members may be loath to part with expensive and hard-to-obtain weapons such as automatic rifles. Interestingly, street gangs often have a strange relationship with their firearms that they don't have with other weapons. In gang culture, it is generally considered cowardly and dishonorable to merely throw the weapon away after committing a crime. Dropping a smoking gun into a body of water or down a street gutter is considered a last resort. The more respected alternative, and a testimonial to a gang member's planning of an assault, is to place the firearm where it can later be recovered by the shooter or other members of the gang. For this reason, potential hiding locations for firearms, either whole or in parts, should be especially targeted during a crime scene weapons search. These places include rooftops, trees, trash cans, bushes, and other permanent fixtures.[11]

Ballistics Evidence

External ballistics are important when investigating street gang crimes involving weapons fired from inside a vehicle. If a vehicle is suspected to have been used in a drive-by shooting, inspection and testing for gunshot residue should be carried out in the passenger compartment area. Because gunshot residue is emitted in an aerosol pattern, cone-shaped spray patterns of GSR are often detectible in and around the vehicle's windows, seats, dash, and headliner. In addition to performing standard GRS tests on suspected shooters, the skin and clothing of other occupants in the vehicle should also be tested for GSR spray. Second, from a terminal ballistics standpoint, it is important that many if not all expended bullets fired from suspect's weapons are recovered from within and around the primary crime scene. The number and location of these bullets can sometimes be estimated by examining the amount and positioning of expended cartridge casings. If the gunfire's likely point of origin can be established, trajectory rods (for short distance) or a laser light beam (for long distance) can be used to plot the bullet's path of trajectory and discover where it came to rest.[12]

Graffiti

One informant, when asked about the significance of **graffiti** to life in the gang, remarked, "Graffiti is a gang member's telephone to the enemy." This statement—which suggests that graffiti provides a means of communications between gangs and/or gang members—suggests how graffiti interpretation can be a valuable tool in the gang crime investigative process. Gang graffiti usually is a brief set of block-style letters spray painted on curbs, walls, or fixed objects such as benches, fountains, and statues in public areas. Graffiti can also be scribed onto wooden or metallic surfaces or etched into glass with a glass cutter, diamond-tipped tool, or jewelry item. Gang members usually write graffiti to mark or "claim" their territory—or to send a message challenging a rival gang. Seldom will gang graffiti be artistically elaborate or placed in hard-to-reach locations such as freeway overpasses or building rooftops—graffiti styles more associated with "taggers" than street gang members.

Graffiti often can indicate a street gang's turf, size, organizational structure, and enemies. In general, gangs establish their turf by marking some type of geographic perimeter in which they operate. These markings range from simple (the name of a single gang and/or gang member) to complex (a graffiti "roster" defining various aspects of the gang and its entire membership). Generally, large gangs mark large geographic areas, and small gangs mark smaller areas.

One unwritten code of gang warfare is that a gang should never mark an area larger than it can "back up" or control. Enemies of a particular gang or ongoing gang rivalries can often be revealed by graffiti strike outs. Strike outs, such as those illustrated in Figure 11.14, occur when one gang defaces or crosses out (usually with spray painted lines) the graffiti of another gang—the ultimate form of disrespect in gang culture. Often, the opposing gang place its name and membership monikers in new graffiti next to their strike out of the original graffiti writing. Graffiti from gangs that does not contain strike outs should be noted. This suggests that a particular gang is too intimidating or

powerful for other gangs to challenge or simply is the only one to claim a particular area and does not yet have any rivals.

Rival gangs who want to send a death threat to another gang normally spray paint a line through that gang's name or certain members' names. The line is drawn in the color of the threatening gang. For example, bloods, known nationwide, use the color red to draw a line. The line signifies a possible war brewing between both gangs, or sometimes simple disrespect. Either way, a clash between both gangs is almost assured. These are the things that good gang investigators look for when conducting investigations—the *encyclopedia of the street*. This encyclopedia lets gang investigators know who may be responsible for certain gang-related crimes.[13]

Hand Signs and Verbalization

Nearly all street gangs communicate via hand signs, sometimes backing up their hand signs by shouting out the name of their gang. Often street gangs throw hand signs and verbalize their monikers—or **set**—sometime before, during, or after an assault on their enemy. For this reason, witnesses and victims of street gang crimes should always be questioned to discover anything said or heard, no matter how esoteric or incomprehensible it may seem. Although the average citizen who has witnessed a gang assault usually cannot recall visual clues such as gang hand signs, street gang members often can, providing strong suspect leads.[14]

STREET GANG ORGANIZATIONAL STRUCTURE

Not all members of a street gang have an equal propensity for committing crime, especially when it comes to acts of violence. The average street gang, which ranges in size between less than 10 to 20 members, can be broken down into three distinct categories with regard to the criminal roles of its members:

Peripherals or Wannabes

Wannabes usually are the least likely to commit serious crimes with a street gang and comprise approximately 20 to 30 percent of the total gang membership. They are generally not considered to be active members, but they still enjoy the social aspects, status, and reputation of being part of the gang. They tend to separate themselves from the gang in times of trouble with authorities or conflict with other gangs. Peripherals, especially if they are youthful, can cross the line into more active gang roles, however.

Associate or Affiliate Members

Associate/affiliate members comprise the largest subgroup of a street gang, from 40 to 50 percent. They often are considered "partial" members of the gang who have not yet proven themselves worthy of full membership status. In many respects, associate/affiliate members consider the gang to be their family and will commit crimes when higher ranking members direct them to do so. These criminal activities may also be an attempt to prove loyalty to the gang to gain full membership status.

FIGURE 11.14 ▶ Gang graffiti showing strike outs, or puto marks, suggesting that one gang is challenging another gang's territorial boundaries and street reputation.

Hard-Core Members

The members that commit the most crimes, and the worst crimes, in the gang's name are the **hard-core** members. They make up between 10 and 20 percent of the gang's membership but are responsible for 60 to 80 percent of their gang's criminal activity. They not only are full gang members, but are considered the most streetwise, respected, and violent individuals in the gang. Generally, the street gang's status and its reputation for violence are established by the hard-core gang member.

Of all the classifications and criminal roles just described, the hard-core street gang member by far is most likely to be involved in planning and/or participating in a street gang crime. This is especially the case if the crime is a violent one. Early in the gang crime investigation, efforts should be made to identify hard-core members and to target investigative efforts on these individuals. One absolute about hard-core gang members is that they have been in state prison at some point. Many of them are members of, or associates to their respective prison gang.[15] Figure 11.15 shows the relationships between each of the three subclasses of gang members just discussed.

Cliques

The structure of most street gangs consists of layers of membership, or **cliques**. Cliques are formed by gang members of roughly the same age (2 to 3 years apart) who have an identity affiliated with, yet distinct from the parent gang. The larger the gang's membership, the more cliques it will have. Names used by cliques—nearly always evident in gang graffiti—reflect the age differences of the members. For example, the 13th Street Locos may consist of "Pee-Wee," "Sharky," and "Veterano" cliques—ranging from younger to older members, respectively. Although each clique can have its own distinct leadership, cliques consisting of the oldest members usually have the most influence over all other members in the gang.

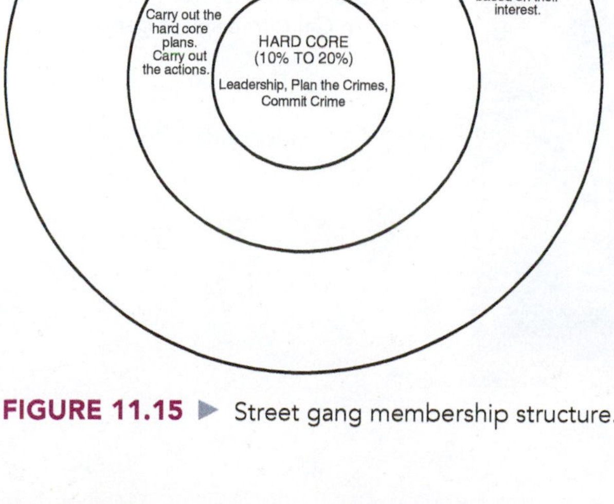

FEMALE GANG MEMBERS

Female gang members usually provide support to male members of the gang. In some instances, all-female street gangs have acted autonomously in committing crimes, including violent ones such as drive-by shootings. This type of behavior, however, is by far the exception to the rule. Most female gangs are heavily reliant on and influenced by their male street gang counterparts. This fact is reflected in their monikers, street gang names, and criminal activities. For example, a female street gang named the "Frog Town Girls" most likely will be modeled after an all-male gang named "Frog Town." Individual members of female gangs often receive their monikers from male gang members, and these may reflect relationships that they have with male members (for example, "Party Girl"). The crimes of female street gang members, for the most part, are committed in concert with male street gang members. Females usually perform a support function for the males, who take a lead role in a particular criminal activity. In this capacity, female street gang members are noted for holding guns or drugs, driving a getaway car, or acting as a decoy to create a criminal opportunity.

RACE/ETHNICITY

The ethnicity of most street gangs is homogeneous, meaning that all members come from a similar racial/ethnic background. Recently, however, **hybrid gangs** with ethnically diverse members have begun to emerge. Attempts have been made to classify the behavior of street gangs based on ethnic differences. The following sections present some of the classifications that may be relevant to street gang investigations.

WEST COAST STREET GANGS

Most, if not all, street gangs established in the west coast region of the United States pattern their behavior after styles and customs first established by early Latino street gangs from Mexico and dating as far back as the 1920s. Particularly in the Los Angeles, California area, Latino street gangs came into prominence as a criminal subculture during the 1940s and 1950s. During this time period, many of the features that street gangs use today to recognize and validate members were created by pioneering Latino street gangs. These included the following:

- A unique style of gang dress, evidenced by the creation of "zoot suits"—loose-fitting, baggy two-piece suits accompanied by a wide-brimmed hat

GANG MAKEUP

ASSOCIATES AND/OR PEEWEES
(20% TO 30%)

REGULAR MEMBERS
ACTIVE/PERIPHERAL
(40% TO 50%)

Usually the best informants. Participate in gang activity based on their interest.

Carry out the hard core plans. Carry out the actions.

HARD CORE
(10% TO 20%)
Leadership, Plan the Crimes, Commit Crime

FIGURE 11.15 ▶ Street gang membership structure.

- A specialized gang language, known as "Calo" and composed of words and phrases created by the gang by combining Spanish and English
- An appreciation for drug use and sales, involving the use of pills (mainly barbiturates/depressants) rather than alcohol for a clean high
- Use of graffiti—known as *placas*—to mark the gang's territory and as a form of street communication
- Use of tattoos and colors to distinguish members of the same gang who were of the same race/ethnicity
- Use of a hit-and-run style of fighting known as *japing* (named for the Japanese attack on Pearl Harbor), carried out in the form of surprise attacks on rival gangs
- The establishment of prison gangs, which are still in existence today and coordinate various illegal activities with street gangs

As this brief history suggests, the early roots of the west coast street gang subculture are well established. The following sections, which describe identifying characteristics of various contemporary west coast street gangs, suggest that the traits of the early Latino gangs of California and other western states have been contagious. Not only have today's west coast street gangs—of all racial/ethnic backgrounds—modeled their behavior after those originally created by Latino gangs, but the influence of gangs representing the west has spread to virtually every state in the nation—and throughout county, state, and federal correctional institutions as well. This has occurred largely due to the "transplanting" of western gangs—families with gang-involved youths relocating from Los Angeles to other locales. In addition, the nationwide spread of west coast gangs has been fueled by their increasing presence within the federal prison system. Thus, gang investigators in all jurisdictions must have a working familiarity with west coast gangs and the various aspects of their criminal subculture.

Latino Street Gangs

As previously mentioned, Latino street gangs primarily originate from Mexico and display one or more of the following behavioral/criminal characteristics[16]:

- ***Protection of Turf:*** Many view themselves as soldiers protecting their turf or the neighborhood that they "claim." This is not always the case nowadays, however, since many gang members victimize persons in their neighborhood—especially Mexican-American immigrants who have recently located to the United States or are undocumented aliens.
- ***Lifelong Loyalty:*** Having a lifelong allegiance to a particular gang in a particular location is not unusual. Hard-core members return to their gang as runaways from their parents if relocated away from their original gang neighborhood. Less dedicated members seek out other Latino gang members who have been relocated to other neighborhoods and states, and form a common gang bond—referring to themselves generically as **Surenos** (predominantly from Southern California) or **Nortenos** (predominantly from Northern California). Many established Latino gangs are multigenerational, with the expectation that family will become members.
- ***Drug Use/Sales:*** Methamphetamine is the drug of choice for use and sales, mainly due to its easy availability and cheap cost. Other popular drugs used/sold include black tar heroin, crack cocaine, marijuana, and inhalants. Drugs are commonly referred to as *clavos*.
- ***Named for a Location:*** Most identify with streets, parks, neighborhoods ("varrio" or *barrio*), and geographic characteristics in establishing their gang name and identity; for example, 18th Street Gang (one of the nation's largest street gangs), Frogtown (near a swamp inhabited by frogs), and Varrio Sur Trece (S. 13th Street neighborhood). Figure 11.16 shows a Latino gang

(a)

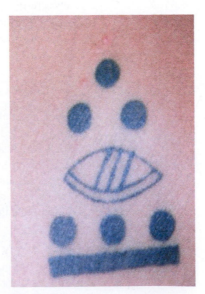

(b)

FIGURE 11.16 ▶ (a) Latino gang member posting (or standing guard) outside a "crashpad" where fellow gang members are gathering for a party. (b) The number "13" tattoo in the Aztec numeral system, signifying a Southern California street gang.

member "posting" or guarding his "varrio" in a typical soldier-type fashion.

- **Member Monikers:** Ironically, and useful as an investigative tool, many members receive a street name or *moniker* based on their personal habits or appearance. For example, "Melon" (referring to the fruit) may be a moniker for a large, round person, or "Dopey" (adapted from the 7 Dwarfs) for a gang member who is a heavy narcotics user. Often, members of the same gang do not know each other's real name, but only each other's moniker.

- **Dress:** Can vary, but often is khaki-colored pants with sharp creases running down each leg, with a white t-shirt worn underneath a flannel shirt buttoned only at the collar—known as the "Cholo" look. Shorts may be worn in warmer weather with high white crew socks extending upward almost to the knees (considered an "old-school" look in certain areas). The "Sports Look" is also popular in some locations, with attire including athletic jerseys, very baggy Levi jeans, baseball-style sports caps, and military-style sliding belts with buckles showing an identifying symbol of the gang or gang member.

- Leadership is situational and is not structured or permanent. Specific members will emerge as leaders in situations where they demonstrate a necessary expertise. For example, the best fighter will lead in a physical confrontation with another gang or the best communicator with females will lead in a party situation.

- **Cliques or "Klikas":** These subsets of the main gang have their own names, members, and identity. Klikas consisting of younger members have names such as "Cherries" or "Pee Wees," and older-member klikas are often referred to as "Veteranos" or "Winos." In short, the name often identifies their age structure. Because many gangs are multigenerational, gang members can belong to several or all of a particular gang's klikas throughout their lifetimes.

- **Tattoos:** Usually of the gang name, dead gang affiliates, the gang member's mother or daughter, three dots signifying "La Vida Loca" (the crazy life), Aztec numerals (composed of dots and lines), or symbols (see Figure 11.16).

- **Clean Graffiti:** Latino gang members are noted and respected for their clean and often artistic graffiti style; so much so, that gangs of other races enlist them to do their graffiti and tattoos. "Puto" (meaning male whore) marks, or the crossing out of rival gang graffiti, is symbolic of a challenge that can lead to physical confrontation or death. The numbers "13" and "14" are usually written to represent gangs from Southern and Northern regions, respectively.

- **Females:** Female involvement is usually restricted to supporting activities of male gang members, through either sexual or criminal means. "Hienas" (female partners of male gang members) may carry guns or drugs given to them by males trying to avoid arrest. Although very rare, some Latino female gang members form their own all-female gangs, which operate independently of male gangs.

African-American Street Gangs

Most African-American west coast gangs affiliate with either **Crips** or **Bloods**. The Crips and Bloods have their origins in Los Angeles area cities, namely Compton and South Central Los Angeles. The Crips emerged first, during the late 1960s, as an offensive gang that pressured many unaffiliated African-American neighborhood gangs, known collectively as the Watts Gangs, to join the Crips franchise under the threat of physical violence. While many joined under the pressure of fear and intimidation, others did not. Especially vigilant in maintaining their independence were gang members residing in the Piru Street area of Compton. They later became their own defensive gang franchise in opposition to the Crips, known at first as "Pirus" and later as "Bloods." Crips and Bloods have similar gang characteristics, but also a few notable differences[17]:

- **Protection of Turf:** Today's African-American gang members are very turf oriented, as opposed to those of the past. Their turf is usually a neighborhood or "hood" in which they grew up as a child and/or use for illegal drug sales activity.

- **Gang Identity:** They are proud of their "gangster" identity, and fellow gang members or *homies* often are viewed as members of their gang family. Many have grown up in the same neighborhoods and have attended the same schools. Younger, less committed members often lead dual lives: as a gangster when around their gang, and as a nongangster in family or school settings.

- **Jumping In/Out:** To join the gang, members often must be "jumped in," where they have to fight a group of other members for a specified period of time (usually one hour or less). Members leaving the gang are sometimes forced to "jump out"—engage in a similar fighting situation—before being allowed to give up their active gang membership. "Jumping out" is not always required, and leaving the gang without violence can occur when a member gets married, joins the military, or has some other legitimate reason for giving up the gang lifestyle.

- **Dress:** African-American gang members are noted for their use of color, especially blue for Crips and red for Bloods. Although some gang members still sport colors, this trait is not always a reliable indicator of today's African-American gang affiliation. Many colors are now worn, including green, purple, brown, and black. Athletic suits, sports jerseys, and baseball caps with oversize jeans worn below the waist (or "sagging") are common attire. Gang names and affiliations are often written or embroidered on their hats and clothing.

- **Language:** Words and phrases used are often derived from rap music lyrics popular at the time. As a result, street jargon used by these gangs changes very rapidly, with members separated in age by only a few years perhaps not speaking the same gang language. Language is also used as a form of challenge to other gangs. Crips and Bloods formulate words and phrases in their everyday speech that are a product of their hatred toward each other. For example, Bloods often substitute the C for B in words they speak and write—e.g., "cup" becomes "bup."

- *Graffiti:* African-American gang graffiti is much less carefully written and placed that of Latino gangs. Usually, its sole function is to mark territory and to create challenges (crossing out rival gang's graffiti with strike outs). The letters "B/K" (Blood Killer) or "C/K" (Crip Killer) often are present.

- *Sets:* Individual street gangs aligning with the Crip and Blood organizations are referred to as *sets* and are usually identified by the area or street where they are located— for example, the "10th Street Crips." In addition, larger sets can have smaller sets as well—for example, spinning off the "10th Street Crips" may be the "Mid-Block 10th Street Crips" or the "Jackson Park 10th Street Crips."

- *Leadership:* Unstructured and not permanent, similar to that of the Latino gang. Situational leaders are often referred to as *shot callers* and attain status in their gang for reputations of brutality against enemies and wealth from drug sales. Shot callers may also have served "state time" in prison, further adding to their street reputations.

- *Membership:* Some sets have as few as three members while others have thousands. Within larger sets are subsets or cliques that represent different age groupings. Designations such as "BGs" (Baby Gangsters), "Gs" (Gangsters), and "OGs" (Original Gangsters) can be used to determine the low-, mid-, and older-age members within a single gang set. Most persons first joining African-American gangs are usually in their early teens. Some gang members, however, may raise their children from a young age to become gang members. At the other extreme, persons in their 30s or older may join a gang for the first time to sell narcotics or profit in other ways from gang membership.

- *Rivalries:* Crips tend to fight other Crip sets, whereas this fighting pattern is not nearly as prevalent among Bloods. Crips and Bloods have been known to call truces, or "tie their rags," however, to engage in joint business ventures—namely drug sales. In terms of fighting capabilities, many claim that Bloods fight in a more violent manner than do Crips—perhaps because they are greatly outnumbered in terms of gang membership. Shooting may be carried out on foot (walk-bys), on bicycles (ride-bys), and in vehicles (drive-bys). War can be carried out with Latino gangs over turf and drug sales.

- *Drugs:* Crack cocaine is clearly the drug of choice for use and sales, although other drugs such as marijuana and methamphetamines also are popular. More organized gangs have begun investing their drug sales profits in legitimate enterprises, such as businesses and real estate. One gang can control several drug distribution networks and street sales operations.

- *Tattoos:* Most are of the gang name, dead gang associates (usually signified by "RIP"), and girlfriends and are located on the head, neck, arms, and chest.

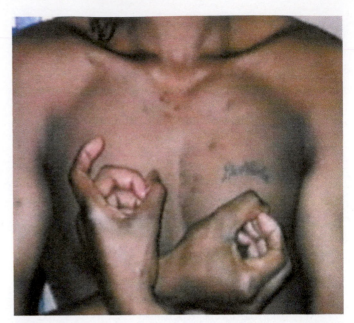

(a)

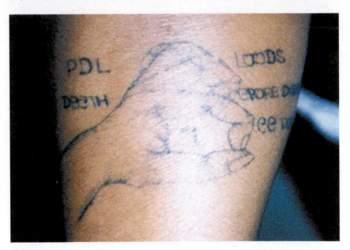

(b)

FIGURE 11.17 ▶ (a) Crip gang member shows hand signs. (b) Blood gang member shows hand sign in the form of a tattoo.

- *Hand Signs:* "Flashing" with hand signs as illustrated in Figure 11.17 can be used to identify gang affiliation to allies or to challenge enemies. Each gang has its own hand sign.

- *Females:* Females affiliated with the Crips are referred to as *Cripletts*, and those aligned with Bloods are called *Bloodletts*. They usually have sets that are off-shoots of, and named for male sets. For example, females aligned with the "Orange Street Bloods" would be the "Orange Street Bloodletts." Their behavior is usually restricted to supporting male gang members in sexual and criminal activities, but some are noted for engaging in violence such as drive-by shootings and robberies.

Asian Street Gangs

There are many varieties of Asian street gangs representing numerous cultures and countries. Therefore, it is very difficult to categorize these groups based on common characteristics and behaviors. Generally speaking, however, Asian gangs possess some of the following traits[18]:

- *Turf/Territoriality:* For the most part, there is no designated turf that is protected. Turf is only viewed in terms of locations of neighborhoods and businesses where illegal activities are conducted. While the gangs may victimize persons within areas assumed to be their territory, they will outwardly "claim" it as do Latino gangs. In addition, many Asian gangs operate in a variety of territories while carrying out their illegal financial activities.

- *Gang Loyalty:* There is no loyalty to a specific gang. Gang membership tends to shift, and a gang member may belong to several different gangs depending on which ones provide the greatest financial opportunities.

- *Dress:* Asian gang members dress in two styles, depending on the occasion. They wear normal dress when engaging in nongang activities such as going to work or school. They wear gang attire, or "play clothes," when they are with the gang. This style of dress includes colored head rags or bandanas, baseball caps, Dickie-style pants, colored T-shirts, and football or other athletic jerseys.

- *Tattoos:* A triangular pattern of three dots on the hand between the thumb and forefinger, signifying "My Crazy Life," is a common Asian gang tattoo. Also common is the five dots or 5 Ts tattoo created by ink or cigarette burn marks (to show toughness), signifying Love, Money, Prison, Crime/Sin, and Revenge (see Figure 11.18).

- *Leadership:* There may be strong leadership in the form of a centralized leader called a **Dai Lo**. These individuals usually have ties to international organized crime and have prior military experience in an Asian country.

- *Organization:* The gang structure is similar to that of the cliques of the Latino gang, and commonly has four distinct levels of membership organization: Associates (friends and girlfriends), Junior (pee-wees or wannabes about to be jumped in), Regulars (making up the bulk of jumped-in gang members), and Hard-cores (less than 5 percent of members carry out the majority of the gang's criminal activities).

- *Crimes:* Usually target residences and businesses of other Asians. Commercial robbery, business extortion, identity theft, and home invasion robbery are common. Organized trafficking of drugs and stolen goods are also carried out by larger, more sophisticated gangs.

- *Names/Signs:* Asian gangs usually name themselves for the area or territory from which they originate, for example, "The Centerville Boyz." They use hand signs as a means of gang identification and communication.

- *Rivals/Enemies:* As a rule, Asians gangs get along with each other and are respectful of each other's turf

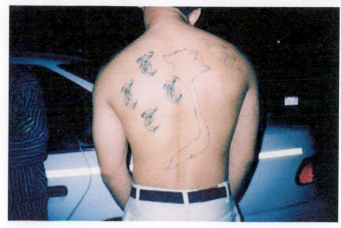

(a)

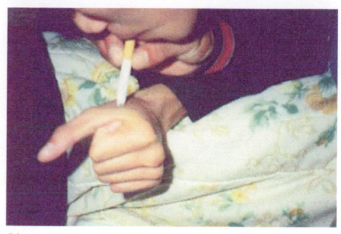

(b)

FIGURE 11.18 ▶ (a) Asian gang member displays a "T T T T" tattoo (or 4 Ts), which stands for "Love," "Money," "Prison," and "Crime/Sin," (sometimes there are 5 Ts, which add the term "Revenge"). (b) An Asian gang member makes a burn mark on his hand to show his strength, courage, and loyalty as a gang member.

and illegal enterprises. Violence is used only when it is necessary to defend the gang's economic interests.

- *Graffiti:* Rarely, if ever, is graffiti used. Asian gangs prefer to remain "beneath the radar" and not have their identities or activities known by other gangs—and especially not by law enforcement.

- *Females:* Although females did form their own separate Asian gangs, this is no longer a trend. Most female gangs are branches of male gangs with which they are affiliated. The adopt their names from the male gang—for example, females associated with "The Centerville Boyz" would name themselves "The Centerville Girlz."

- *Other Asian Gangs:* Filipino gangs are generally not as financially motivated as other Asian gangs. They tend to focus on violence merely to defend their gang's name and reputation. Their membership consists largely of brothers, cousins, and other blood relatives. Filipino gangs usually fight with other gangs of the same ethnicity as well as Latino gangs. Samoan gangs are another prevalent Asian gang. Most often these gang members behave in a manner similar to that of African-American gangs and can align themselves with either Crips or Bloods.

Caucasian Street Gangs

Most Caucasians involved in gang activity are affiliated with Neo-Nazi type organizations, while a very small portion may participate in hybrid gangs of mixed ethnicities that emulate either African-American or Latino street gangs. A detailed description of Neo-Nazi and other organized hate groups is given in Chapter 20 as a form of domestic terrorism. Some identifying characteristics of these hate-oriented groups are as follows[19]:

- *Territory/Turf:* These groups do not claim turf as the other gangs do; however, they will mark territory with graffiti to let others know they are present in a particular area as a form of challenge or intimidation.

- *Membership:* Teenagers with troubled family lives often are recruited for membership in white supremacist organizations. Runaways, drug addicts, and incorrigible youths often seek refuge in the homes of older persons who accept them and provide shelter in exchange for adopting neo-Nazi ideologies. Other members may include youths that have been the target of physical violence committed against them by members of other races. Members of white supremacist groups often refer to their groups as *crews,* or to themselves as **Peckerwoods**.

- *Criminal Activity:* Most crimes involve threats and intimidation of racial minorities. Acts of violence such as shootings, stabbings, and physical assaults directed at persons of specific colors, religions, and sexual orientations do occur, but are far less frequent than similar acts committed by traditional street gangs.

Vandalism of property by destructive means is far more prevalent among the crimes committed by these groups. Drive-by shootings and other typical methods of intergang violence are not used.

- *Head Shaving:* Most members shave their heads, or become "skins," to guard against having their hair pulled during a fight. Head shaving is more symbolic now than a means of protection. Skinheads may let their hair grow as a means of camouflaging their true identity.

- *Organization:* There are three levels of group organization, differentiated by the level of the members' dedication to white supremacy. *White Pride* members are largely independents who sometimes affiliate with an organized neo-Nazi group. *White Power* members are the second most dedicated in their beliefs of white supremacy and will resort to violence, when provoked, to protect their honor. *White Supremacists* are the most dedicated and most violent of all neo-Nazi groups and consider themselves gang members in support of the white race.

- *Dress:* White polo shirts (Fred Perry brand), tank tops or T-shirts worn with red suspenders ("braces"), and "Dickie"-style pants are usually the attire of choice. Black steel-tip boots, known as "Doc" (Doc Marten brand), are also worn with colored shoe laces (usually white or red). These boots are the primary weapon used for assaulting others, referred to as a "boot party."

- *Language:* Perhaps the most used phase is "14" or "the 14 words": "We must secure the existence of our people and a future for white children." The term "Oi" (pronounced oyee) is used often to show agreement or excitement (similar to "Wow").

- *Hand Signs:* Most popular is the Nazi salute, with the right arm raised about head level. Individual hand signs with fingers forming a W and P are also used to show group affiliation.

HOT TIPS AND LEADS 11.2

Asking Gang Members Questions

Information can be obtained from even the most hard-core gang members if questions are asked the right way. Here are some pointers:

1. Always talk to gang members one-on-one and in places where other gang members cannot see or hear you. Even being seen near a uniformed or plain-clothed officer can be grounds for being labeled a "snitch."

2. Kindness is weakness to the gang member. Be firm when asking questions, but don't be confrontational.

3. When asking about a crime incident, try to get information from the time leading up to the incident. The more background information that can be obtained, the greater the chance other persons involved, motives for the crime,

and additional crime-related information can be obtained. Gaps in time or other inconsistent times and places may suggest that the gang member's story is deceptive.

4. If gang members deny gang membership, ask them, for example, "OK, what did the gang call you when you used to gang bang?" Cooperation is often obtained when casting questions in the past, making the gang members feel as though you believe they are no longer active in the gang.

5. Be sympathetic if one of the gang member's friends or family was hurt in a gang assault. Their emotional reaction over the event often results in feelings of revenge and a willingness to provide information regarding a suspect's identity.

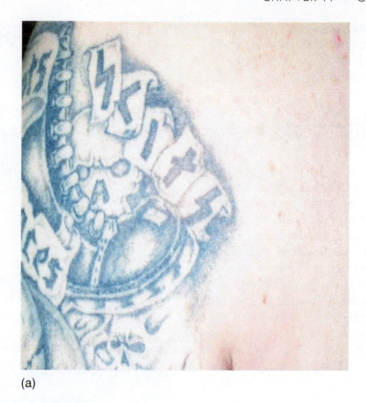

(a)

Younger Futhork
This version of the runic alphabet was used sporadically in Scandinavia, in particular in Denmark and Sweden, until about the 17th century

(b)

FIGURE 11.19 ▶ (a) An Aryan gang member tattoo in the Runic alphabet, which is used by Aryan gangs as a universal code. (b) One of many Runic alphabets. This one can be used to translate the above gang tattoo, which spells (in English) "Skins," in reference to skinhead gang members.

- *Monikers:* Names are given after acceptance or "jumping in" by the group. As with other gangs, these monikers may reflect physical appearance or attitude, or—in these groups—political or hate preferences.
- *Tattoos:* Most commonly swastikas, 88 (signifying "Adolph Hitler," since "H" is the eighth letter of the alphabet), W.P. "White Power," or SWP "Supreme White Power," lightning bolts, the German Eagle and Iron Cross, Boot Power, Skins, Oi, or cobwebs on the elbow indicating that the member has committed a homicide in the name of the group. Tattoos may also contain cryptic symbols representing names and

messages in the ancient Runic alphabet as illustrated in Figure 11.19.
- *Music:* Neo-Nazi groups produce their own music and have heavy metal-style rock groups that compose and perform songs with racist hate lyrics and themes that support white supremacy. Albums and recordings of this music often are found in the possession of suspected neo-Nazi gang members.
- *Graffiti:* Graffiti is used to define territory as well as to identify groups, their members, and to challenge rivals. It most often appears on public areas, but can be written on personal items to show pride or to intimidate others.

- *Females:* Also known as **Featherwoods** or *Skinbyrds,* dress in a similar style as males but, if not wearing pants, may wear skirts with fishnet stockings. They mainly engage in social/hate activities with males.

MIDWEST AND EAST COAST STREET GANGS

As in the west, there is a long established street gang network in the mid-western and eastern states. The racial/ethnic composition of these gangs is mostly African-American and Puerto Rican; but persons from other Latin countries—namely Panama, The Dominican Republic, El Salvador, Honduras, and Mexico—also are represented among these groups. The major concentrations of east coast gangs are in Chicago and New York, where they have roots dating back to the 1960s—and in some cases much earlier. In addition to their presence in the streets, these groups also maintain a presence in many prisons in the east and mid-west, and federal prison systems. They are also noted for maintaining ties and control with street gangs with which they are affiliated. Often, the prison gang factions serve as advisors to their street gang affiliates in matters such as narcotics sales, trafficking stolen goods, and intergang rivalries. They are also known to impose "taxes" on street gang drug profits.

The two largest organizations of affiliated street gangs in Eastern and Midwestern locations are the People and Folk Nations. Both of these groups, which war with each other, have common identifying mannerisms and characteristics. Members of the **People Nation** are recognized by the following[20]:

- *Manner of Dress:* Often called an "up-left" style. This is evidenced by their wearing of clothing and/or jewelry items that emphasize the left side of their body. This is commonly seen in the form of wearing baseball hats tilted to the left; pant legs rolled up on the left leg; double shoe laces of gang colors in the left shoe; body rings on the left ear, eyebrow, nose, or lip, etc.
- *Colors:* People identify with the color red or tones of red.
- *Graffiti/Tattoos:* A five-point star (see Figure 11.20), pyramid and eye, five-point crown, five dots, five dots in dice, and Playboy-style rabbit with straight ears. May also use numeric codes based on the position of letters in the alphabet (a = 1, b = 2, and so on).

Members of the **Folk Nation** have similar identifying symbols and characteristics, with most being the direct opposite of those used by the People Nation, including the following[21]:

- *Manner of Dress:* An "up-right" style. Baseball hats, jewelry, shoe laces, and other clothing and/or accessories worn on or tilted to the right side of the body.
- *Colors:* Folk identify with the color blue and tones of blue.
- *Graffiti/Tattoos:* A six-point star (see Figure 11.20), pitchforks, heart with wings, the number 6, six dots, dice with six dots, and Playboy-style rabbit with bent ears.

(a) People Nation

(a) Folk Nation

FIGURE 11.20 ▶ (a) The five-point star (sometimes accompanied by a crescent moon) is typical of the midwestern gangs aligned with the People Nation. (b) A six-point star, a pitchfork, and the number 6 are seen in the symbols and graffiti of gangs associated with the Folk Nation.

May also use numeric codes based on letter positions in the alphabet.

Both the People and Folk Nations present symbolic challenges, often leading to physical confrontations by "dissing" each other's reputation through "upside down" hand signs and graffiti. Examples of such challenges include writing the opposing gang name or graffiti symbol upside down, flashing the opposing gang's hand sign upside down. In general, the People and Folk gangs seem to have a stronger organizational structure than the more loosely structured western gangs. They are noted for having a centralized leader and requiring that members of the gang have a thorough knowledge of the gang's history and rules—which often includes written codes in book form. Members of the gang may be expelled for not possessing adequate knowledge of the group to which they belong. Allegedly, the People Nation has a street alliance with Blood gangs, and the Folks Nation aligns with the Crips. Many western gangs do not observe these alliances, however, and victimize People and Folk gang members in Los Angeles jail settings.

PRISON GANGS

Prison gangs are best defined as gangs that are formed in state- or federal-level penal institutions, which are composed of members who are serving or have served sentences in such institutions. These groups, unlike street gangs, are highly organized and clandestine. Rarely, unless a member is attempting to drop out of the gang, does a witness or suspect provide information to investigators about criminal acts committed by a prison gang. For example, any inmate witnessing a murder taking place and revealing the killer to correctional officers would be labeled a snitch. Snitches are in the lowest echelon and are the most highly despised inmates[22].

Most persons even rumored to be snitches must be removed to protective custody units or invariably they will be killed by other inmates. There is no doubt that the effects of prison gang culture can be a significant impediment to criminal investigation efforts. Knowledge of the rules or "codes" and inner-workings of prison gangs, however, can be an invaluable investigative tool when attempting to crack these difficult cases. The various aspects of prison gangs that are most useful in investigating prison gang crime are presented in the following sections.

RACE AND PRISON GANGS

Prison gangs are not equal opportunity employers. In nearly every respect, the prison gang is a product of racist ideals and practices. Race plays a key role in the success of prison gangs for two reasons. First, it can serve as a means of instantly recognizing an enemy based on skin color and other readily observable racial differences. Second, persons from the same racial or ethnic background may share similar cultural practices, originate from the same geographic area, and communicate in the same language. For these and related reasons, prison gangs are formed along racial boundaries. The primary racial groupings of prison gang members include African-Americans, Latino/Hispanics, and Caucasians. Hybrid prison gangs with members from different races are extremely rare.

Race is also a key factor in the creation of allies and enemies of prison gangs, but it can be an inconsistent investigative tool. Developing suspect leads by determining which races of prison gangs are at peace or at war with each other may be effective in certain situations where the patterns and past history of gang warfare are relatively straightforward. For example, determining strong suspect leads in the case of a Latino prison gang member may be quite straightforward when there is knowledge that his gang has an ongoing feud

with another specific gang of a different race. On the other hand, playing the race card alone in the latter investigation may easily create false suspect leads because the relationship between the victim and offender can be inter- (between) or intra-racial (within) in nature. For example, it is just as likely that the murder victim was killed by an opposing gang for "payback" as it is that members of his own gang killed him for breaking the rules.[23]

ORGANIZATIONAL STRUCTURE AND LEADERSHIP OF PRISON GANGS

Prison gangs are highly organized. They have a pyramid structure similar to that of a military organization. There is a recognized leader who is the primary "shot caller" for the entire group. This individual issues commands to subordinates, who have defined roles in the organization and must carry out the directives of their superiors or face dire consequences. Most prison gangs have formalized written rules in the form of a constitution. Membership is achieved through sponsorship by an established member of the gang. There are many potential consequences of sponsoring a new member into the gang. The most serious of these is making sure that the person recruited will live up to the gang's expectations. Should the new member fail to perform as required by the gang, it is up to the sponsor to remove their protégé from the gang—usually through some form of violent death. The sponsor, too, faces death if he does not carry out this directive. This is but one of the many ways that the prison gang fosters membership loyalty by creating an organizational atmosphere of fear and intimidation. Hence, another possibility for explaining a prison gang member's death is that he was killed by his own gang for not living up to the acceptable standards of a respected prison gang member.

Regardless of the specific reasons underlying an act of deadly violence committed by and against prison gang members, such an activity almost certainly is a planned rather than a spontaneous act. Prison gang crimes nearly always have a purpose, and that purpose is established and approved by the gang leader. This is true regardless of whether the crime is perpetrated against one of the gang's own members or members of an opposing gang. In cases of murder, the killing of a prison gang member usually results from a rational choice made by many of the offending gang's members to put a **green light** or hit on the victim. The final authorization for the victim's execution is most often given by the gang's **shot caller** or leader. Figures 11.21 to 11.23 illustrate a typical green light execution crime scene as it may be discovered by investigators in a jail or prison setting. Every county jail and state prison in the United States has a person deemed a representative for the respective gangs inside the facility. The representative is known to have the **keys** or control for that gang inside that facility. If something

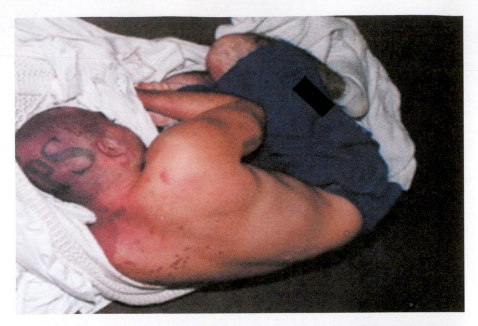

FIGURE 11.21 ▶ An inmate killed as the result of being placed on a green light list by rival gang members. Note the extensive puncture wounds produced by a shank or a prison knife. Puncture wounds are most typical of prison-style gang killings.

FIGURE 11.22 ▶ Puncture wounds can be seen on the victim's arm and face. The number of puncture wounds is often symbolic of payback by one gang against another. For example, if a gang executes a hit involving the stabbing of an inmate 150 times, the payback hit, such as the above case, will involve stabbing the rival gang victim 151 times.

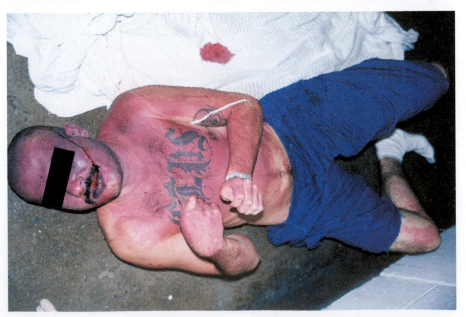

FIGURE 11.23 ▶ *Rigor mortis* and lividity are evident in the above stabbing victim's body. In addition, note the victim's clinched fists. This is a condition known as *cadaver spasm*, which results in the hands (and other parts of the body) tensing during violent encounters before death. In this case, the victim was likely fighting at the time of his death, which is reflected in the positioning of his fists.

happens inside the jail or prison, they are the ones who usually sanction it. Each prison gang has one overall leader, who for the most part is usually locked down in a maximum security prison.[24]

RECOGNITION OF PRISON GANGS

Unlike their street gang counterparts, prison gang members rarely identify themselves through graffiti or hand signs. They do, however; have distinct symbols and tattoos that may indicate their affiliation with, and their rank in a particular prison gang. These methods of immediate external identification are especially important in distinguishing between members of opposing gangs of the same race. For example, Latino gangs at war with each other in California prisons have used various items of color (bed sheets, headbands, handkerchiefs) for recognition purposes. In recent years, however, the use of identifying signs and symbols among prison gangs has waned greatly. This is due in large part to harsh sanctions imposed on individuals identified or "validated" as prison gang members by their distinctive tattoos, clothing items, or other means of symbolic identification. In fact, younger prison gang members may not even have body tattoos representing their affiliation or rank to avoid detection by correctional authorities.[25]

MODES OF COMMUNICATION

Prison gang members seldom carry out a criminal act without first communicating a plan of action to other members. Communication may take place both within the confines of a correctional institution and/or outside the prison to members on the street. Many gangs have their own cryptic communication codes, which are both verbal and written in nature. Inside correctional institutions, criminal communiqués often take place during inmate phone calls or visits. Often conversations containing many words, numbers, names, or phrases that seem illogical or out of context are in reality a means of sending criminal messages. Written communication between prison gangs is done with the use of *kites*. Kites may take the form of a standard letter containing cryptic symbols or languages. Because it is against the law in most states for one inmate to communicate with another, most kites mailed from correctional institutions are mailed to a neutral party who later delivers the kite to its intended prison gang member recipient. Kites may also be used to create hit lists of persons whom the prison gang has given a green light to other members to assault or kill. These lists typically contain numerous names written in very small lettering on a single piece of paper. These lists are smuggled into and out of correctional institutions (usually by **keestering**, or concealing within the rectum) for approval and execution by the appropriate prison gangs. Discovery of a kite containing the name of a victimized individual would strongly suggest that his assault or kill-

ing was a prison gang hit, and perhaps indicate which opposing gang had approved the illegal activity.[26]

RELATIONS WITH STREET GANGS

Prison gangs operate in jails, prisons, and in the general public. Within correctional settings, they are far superior in power and status to members of street gangs. Their power comes from their ability to control the underground economy (consisting mainly of money and drugs) of any given institution. If street gang members are recruited for membership by the prison gang, they must disavow their prior affiliation with the street gang. This is necessary because members from different street gangs at war on the streets will bring disorder to the prison gang if they continue their preexisting rivalries within jail or prison.

When prison gangs operate outside the institution they usually do so through members who have been released on probation or parole into the community. One key enterprise of these "free" members is to act as "tax collectors" for the sale of illegal drugs by street gangs. Typically, "orders" are given by prison gang leaders from inside of an institution to outside gang operatives to collect a certain percentage of money from specific street gangs controlling the drug trade in a specific area or community. Street gangs feel pressured to pay the tax because they know that soon or later they may end up in a correctional environment controlled by the street gang. If the taxes are paid, an incarcerated street gang member will receive a "free ticket" and be left alone by the prison gang. Street gangs owing or refusing to pay taxes will be placed on a "green light" list, which gives prison gang members the authority to assault or kill to them. It is rare for a street gang to effectively carry out an act of violence against members of a prison gang.[27]

RELATIONS WITH POLICE

There are marked differences between how members of street gangs and prison gangs react to police and law enforcement in general. Whereas the hallmark of street gangs is to show maximum disrespect to authorities, quite the opposite is true with prison gangs. Prison gang members are very experienced with the criminal justice system and know how to "play the game." Generally, prison gang members are respectful and compliant when interacting with law enforcement; however, officers should never let their guard down. Prison gang members will play by the rules of the institution, unless it interferes with their business. The business of the prison gang could be monies owed, drug sales, murder, and war with other gangs. Many hard-core prison gang members are doing consecutive life terms, and for them, getting caught doing another murder is trivial. As one prison gang member said in an interview, "If we have to go to the warden's office to kill someone, we will. If the warden gets in the way, we will kill him too. It just doesn't matter."

The relationship is almost an ironic one. When a prison gang member has had enough or has been placed in bad light with the gang (being put in the hat), they will turn to prison officials to help them. The prison gang member will tell prison officials that they are ready to drop out—that is, they are ready to leave the gang. This drop-out period can last up to a year. The inmate is required to discuss his past gang membership and all the crimes they and others have committed. In turn, the inmate will be taken into protective custody and placed on a soft needs yard for the rest of his sentence. This is a death sentence for that inmate. The prison gang they have decided to leave will send anybody they can to kill them.

The inmate is left on a drop-out cell block for a period of up to a year. Prison officials want to make the sure the gang member is not trying to go after another drop-out. Recently, prison gangs have allowed certain members to drop out, in an attempt to kill other drop-outs, who have caused the gang severe problems. Severe problems could be ratting or snitching on others, money profits, and telling police about past crimes.

As previously mentioned, street gangs are composed of various ranks. Some are relatively new to the lifestyle (Associates or Wannabes) and are attempting to make a name for themselves. These individuals tend to be very disrespectful to police as they have not been indoctrinated into the world of gangs and crime. By comparison, others have had a few stints in the local county jail (first timers), but have not yet gone to state prison. At this stage of involvement with the criminal justice system, gang members usually must make the choice of staying in or leaving a gang. It is here that if they decide to stay in or "live the life," they will then usually graduate up to a state prison sentence. Many prison gang members have stated that this is where the point of no return from turning to a gang lifestyle occurs.

Street gang members who rise to the ranks of state prison become much smarter and more elusive criminals as the result of their incarceration in what they call "The University." In other words, a first-time street gang member who goes to state prison creates stronger ties to the prison gang and to hard-core gang members. They will then begin the transformation into a hardened gang member. Until they are fully transformed, these gang members will commit the most crimes and have the most strained relationships with police on the street. Once they reenter prison, possibly one or many more times, they will perhaps achieve the status of a hard-core prison gang member. At this stage, they usually avoid frivolous confrontations with police because they have learned "how to play the game" on the street.[28]

RECONSTRUCTING A GANG CRIME SCENE

Case Example 11B illustrates a case involving a residential drive-by shooting. Factors such as the neighborhood in which the crime occurred, the known gang affiliation of the crime victims, and the manner in which the shooting assault took place all suggest that the incident shown in Figures 11.24 to 11.32 is gang related. The crime scene photos presented in this case include various types of physical evidence that can be used to reconstruct the crime itself and to develop possible suspect leads by using the information on street gangs and gang investigation presented in this chapter.

CASE EXAMPLE 11B

Residential Drive-by Shooting Case

FIGURE 11.24 ▶ Investigators were called to the above location to investigate a possible gang-involved drive-by shooting. Victims living in the home told investigators they were not gang members and were not aware of anyone who would want to harm them. Interviews with neighbors were inconclusive regarding the gang status of residents living at this address. The only witness information obtained was that "lots of loud popping" was heard outside the residence. Suspect or vehicle descriptions were not provided by any of the witnesses who were interviewed.

FIGURE 11.25 ▶ Car parked in front of the shooting location. After noticing a bullet strike in the rear window of this vehicle, which is parked in the driveway of the victimized home, what steps must investigators take prior to examining this vehicle for evidence? How should this and other vehicles parked in and around the shooting scene be utilized by gang investigators for developing case leads?

FIGURE 11.26 ▶ Spent shell casing discovered at the scene. What evidence could possibly be obtained from this cigarette butt and cartridge case, and how could it be utilized by gang investigators?

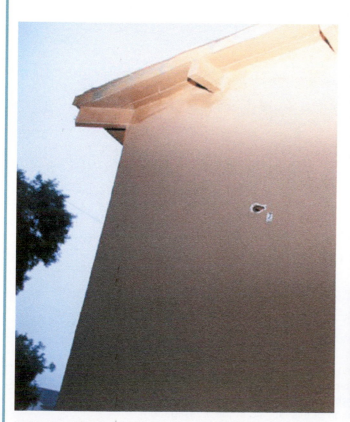

FIGURE 11.27 ▶ Exterior view of the residence shows a bullet hole. After determining the direction of travel of this bullet, of what importance is this discovery to the investigation?

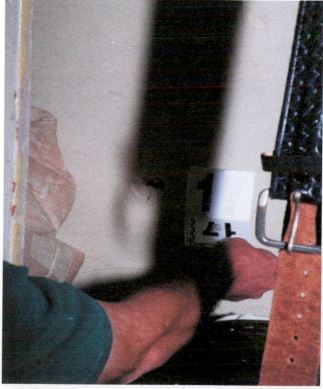

FIGURE 11.28 ▶ Investigator discovers a bullet hole within the interior of the home. How is this bullet strike related to that in Figure 11.27 and of what importance is this relationship to the search for evidence at the crime scene?

(a)

(b)

FIGURE 11.29 ▶ (a) Exterior of metal security door of the home showing a bullet strike. (b) Interior of the same metal security door showing a bullet strike. Was the shooter close or distant from the security door? How could this knowledge be of use for gang investigators processing the crime scene?

(a)

(b)

FIGURE 11.30 ▶ (a) Bullet strikes in a car parked in the driveway of the residence. (b) Close-up of bullet strikes in the car hood and windshield. Judging from the size and shape of the bullet strike in the vehicle's hood, how was the shooter positioned when this shot was taken? How can the determination of this fact aid in the investigation?

(a)

(b)

FIGURE 11.31 ▶ (a) Investigators examine the car's interior for further evidence. (b) Cartridge casing discovered as evidence in the driver's seat. Of what significance is the discovery of this cartridge case? Can it help to establish a gang related motive for the crime that is being investigated? What questions should be asked of the vehicle's owner? If a decision is made to search this vehicle, will a warrant have to be obtained?

FIGURE 11.32 ▶ Investigators observe graffiti writing on a partition wall directly in front of the victimized residence. Of what possible importance is this graffiti to the investigation? What other types of evidence/information should investigators search for as they canvass this neighborhood? After releasing the crime scene, what steps could investigators take to develop suspect leads during a follow-up investigation of this crime?

Summary

1. Relationships between street gangs and the law.

In most jurisdictions, the law provides criteria for the identification of street gangs, street gang members, and street gang crimes. Street gangs are usually legally defined as a group of two or more individuals having a common identifying name, sign, or symbol who engage in a type of criminal activity typically classified as a *gang crime*. Anti-gang laws also typically include criteria for the validation of street gang members. These criteria include self-identification, tattoos, photographs, and so one. Common street gang crimes under the law include assault with a deadly weapon (ADW), robbery, extortion, etc.

2. Investigative indicators of street gangs.

Some of the investigative indicators of street gangs include the types of weapons they use, their internal leadership and organizational structure, and their methods of communication. When fighting, gang members use a hit-and-run style involving one or more members. When firearms are used, gang members often use the walk-by, ride-by, or drive-by methods of assaulting their enemies. Most gangs are age-graded with several sublayers (known as *cliques*) that represent various age groups of membership within the same gang. There is usually no designated permanent leader of a street gang. Gangs communicate with each other through graffiti and hand signs, and they often use one of these forms of communication to identify themselves when they conduct a street assault.

3. **Street gangs of various races/ethnicities.**

Street gangs are primarily represented by persons of African-American, Latino, and Asian races/ethnicities; however, Caucasians are also known to become involved in traditional street gangs, but most belong to groups organized around philosophies of white supremacy and the commission of hate crimes. African-American gangs are territorial, proud of their "gangster" reputation, and are motivated by violence and economic gain. Latino gangs also are territorial and possess a high degree of loyalty to the gang and its lifestyle. Comparatively speaking, Asian gangs are more secretive than other street gangs and commit crimes of violence only when such activities will help further their illegal economic enterprises.

4. **Midwest and East Coast street gangs.**

Midwest and East Coast street gangs are mostly represented by the People and Folk Nations. The race/ethnicity of these gangs is predominantly African-American and Puerto Rican. Members of the People Nation are at war with those of the Folk Nation. Each gang can be recognized by its unique style of dress and symbolism. Folk gang members employ an "up-right" style whereby clothes and jewelry are worn so that they emphasize the right portion of their body (e.g., wearing a baseball cap tilted to the right, an ear ring in the right ear). People gang members identify themselves in a similar manner, but it is an "up-left" method.

5. **Difference between prison gangs and street gangs.**

Compared to street gangs, prison gangs are much more secretive, organized, and violent. There is usually a designated leader of a prison gang, and the structure of the gang and the role of gang members are designated within a gang constitution. Prison gangs exert control over street gangs, and particularly over their drug sales activities. Often, street gangs are required to pay "tax" to prison gang members (representing a portion of their drug sales profits) to avoid becoming victimized in jail and prison settings.

Key Terms

validation	ride-by	Bloods
aiding and abetting	graffiti	Dai Lo
conspiracy	set	prison gang
gang crime	wannabe	Peckerwoods
drop-outs	associate	Featherwoods
jumping-in	hit	People Nation
planned drive-by	hard-core	Folk Nation
spontaneous drive-by	cliques	green light
drive-by	hybrid gang	shot caller
body attachment	Sureno	keys
retaliation	Norteno	keestering
walk-by	Crips	state prison order

Review Questions

1. How does the law define *street gang*?
2. What are the legal criteria for validating a street gang member?
3. What types of crimes are typically classified as street gang crimes?
4. Describe some of the specialized functions of investigators assigned to a Gang Unit.
5. What are the differences between planned and spontaneous drive-by shootings?
6. What are some types of physical evidence that can be found at the scene of a gang crime?
7. How is a typical gang crime structured?
8. What type of leadership is present in a street gang?
9. What is meant by the terms *clique* and *set*?
10. Name some of the identifying characteristics of African-American gangs.
11. What are some of the identifying characteristics of Latino gangs?
12. How do Asian gangs differ from other street gangs?
13. What are the common traits of Caucasian gang members?
14. What are the People and Folk Nations and how do they differ?
15. How do prison gangs differ from street gangs?

Internet Resources

National Alliance of Gang Investigators' Associations (NAGIA)	www.nagia.org
National Gang Crime Research Center (NGCRC)	www.ngcrc.com
StreetGangs.com	www.streetgangs.com
Gangs OR Us	gangsorus.com
NCJRS Gang Resources	www.ncjrs.gov

Applied Investigative Exercise

Select either Illustrated Case 11A or 11B and explain how, as a gang investigator, you would go about building a case for this crime. In doing so, be sure to examine each of the crime scene photos for physical evidence that would suggest gang crime activity. In addition, identify other sources of potential information and leads (witnesses, other gang members, surveillance video, cell phone records, graffiti, hand signs, etc.) about the crime and possible gang-involved suspects. Describe how you would go about securing information from each source. Finally, attempt to reconstruct the events leading up to the crime.

Notes

[1] Robert Walker, *Gangs OR Us*, posted at www.nationalgangcenter.gov/Content/Documents/Definitions.pdf.

[2] Ibid.

[3] Ibid.

[4] Ibid.

[5] Ibid.

[6] Ibid.

[7] Fla. Stat. 874.11 (2008).

[8] This section, and those that follow, are based on the authors' extensive experience investigating gang crimes in Los Angeles Co., especially in the city of Compton, CA.

[9] Ibid.

[10] Ibid.

[11] Ibid.

[12] Ibid.

[13] Ibid.

[14] Ibid.

[15] Arlen Egley et al., *The Modern Gang Reader*, 3rd ed. (New York, NY: Oxford USA, 2007), 87–92.

[16] Portions of this section were adapted from *The Modern Gang Reader* as well as the authors' experience with the investigation of homicide and other crimes committed by Latino, African-American, Asian, and Caucasian gangs.

[17] Ibid.

[18] Ibid.

[19] Ibid.

[20] Chicago Gangs, posted at www.chicagogangs.org.

[21] Ibid.

[22] This section is based on information gathered by the authors while interviewing and/or interrogating members of prison gang members within the LA County and CDCR (CA) correctional systems.

[23] Ibid.

[24] Ibid

[25] Ibid.

[26] Ibid.

[27] Ibid.

[28] Ibid.

CHAPTER TWELVE

ROBBERY SCENES

Learning Objectives

After completing this chapter, you should be able to:

1. Summarize the trends and elements of robbery.
2. Differentiate between the types of robbery.
3. Identify robber types and characteristics.
4. Describe common victims and targets of robbery.
5. Explain how a robbery investigation is conducted.
6. Describe the use of evidence and witnesses in robbery investigations.

Chapter Outline

INTRODUCTION

THIS OPENING CASE PHOTO SHOWS the crime scene of a robbery that has gone horribly wrong. Although most robberies do not end in injury or death to either the perpetrator or the victim, robberies of convenience stores—such as the one pictured here—are an exception to this rule. Convenience store robberies (also called **"C store" robberies**), which comprise only 6 percent of all reported robberies, are the most lethal variety of hold-ups, second only to those carried out against taxi drivers. They are especially deadly when the victim displays some form of resistance during the robbery. Many robbers are aware that clerks of smaller, owner-operated convenience stores usually have a firearm hidden within reach in anticipation of a robbery. This is why experienced "C store" robbers are often extremely violent in their approach to the victim, sometimes shooting the clerk in the arm or leg to prevent them from reaching for a gun or alarm. When both the victim and offender are armed during a robbery (such as the one pictured here), however, the chances of serious injury or death at the scene greatly increase. As you will learn in this chapter, robberies like the one shown here are relatively rare compared to the many others types that investigators commonly encounter. Most occur in streets, parking lots, and other public locations, and they do not involve injuries to either the victim or the offender. In addition, the average "take" from these crimes is less than $1,000 in money or items of value. Another unfortunate fact that investigators must confront, however, is that the clearance rate for robbery is the lowest among all major categories of violent crimes. Despite recent advances in crime scene investigation methods and technology, three out of four robbery cases still go unsolved.

ROBBERY CHARACTERISTICS

The Crime of Robbery

Robbery is the taking or attempting to take anything of value from the care, custody, or control of a person or persons by force or by threat of force or violence and/or by putting the victim in fear. Thus, the law considers a robbery complete when property is taken from an individual by means involving even the slightest force or threat of force. Robbery is a unique crime in that it includes the elements of both a property crime and one of violence; that is, the act is motivated by property theft and is carried out by violent means. There are various legal classifications or *degrees* of robbery based on victimization characteristics and the type of force employed by the offender. For example, many jurisdictions legally define robbery in the first degree (the most serious form) as involving a deadly weapon or serious injury to a victim. In second-degree robbery, considered less serious, the offender works with accomplices or merely displays any type of weapon—even a replica or toy weapon. Unarmed robbers comprise the least serious legal classification of robbery—robbery in the third degree.[1]

Robbery Offenders

Robbery comprises about 10 percent of all violent crimes that come to the attention of authorities, being the second most reported crime of violence following aggravated assault. Most robbers (about 95 percent) are male, and approximately 75 percent of these individuals are 25 years of age or less. The primary motivation for robbery appears to be greed; however, several studies based on first-hand interviews with robbers suggest that a "rush" or "thrill" is many younger offenders' sole motive for engaging in the criminal act. In addition, most robberies have the following characteristics:

- Committed by amateurs, who engage in various other offending activities in addition to robbery

- Carried out in public locations such as streets, parks, fields, playgrounds, or parking areas
- Attacks by offenders who are strangers to the victim in approximately three out of four incidents
- Disorganized, unplanned events that involve little if any preparation
- Brazen acts where the offender(s) rob their victim(s) with little concern for being recorded by CCTV cameras or other security devices
- Situations in which the victim(s) most likely will endure some type of physical harm, especially when the offender uses a weapon
- Executed by offenders who behave irrationally or carelessly because they are under the influence of drugs and/or alcohol at the time the crime is committed[2]

In general, robbery is the act of an offender who wants or needs a quick payoff with little criminal planning or effort. This is especially true when carried out by persons with an immediate need for money to purchase drugs to avoid or alleviate painful withdrawal symptoms. By comparison, other property crimes such as burglary require much more time and effort—for example, breaking into a residence, stealing property, and then selling the property to obtain cash.

Armed and Strong Arm Robbery

Robberies are typically classified according to the type of force the perpetrator uses to carry out the act. Approximately 50 percent of all robberies are executed by an offender armed with a weapon—a crime classified as **armed robbery**. Handguns are the weapon of choice in about half of all armed robberies; furthermore, one out of every 100 persons robbed at gunpoint is murdered by the assailant. Other types of offensive weapons, namely knives and clubs, are used in the remaining portion of armed robberies.[3] Illustrated Case 12A (see Figures 12.1 to 12.3)

ILLUSTRATED CASE 12A

Convenience Store Robbery

FIGURE 12.1 ▶ A robbery suspect enters a market and looks behind him as he removes a weapon from his hooded sweatshirt. Note the large baggy clothing worn by the suspect to conceal his weapon and shield his identity from witnesses.

FIGURE 12.2 ▶ The offender carries out the robbery by thrusting his weapon through a protective barrier and pointing it directly at the clerk while demanding money.

FIGURE 12.3 ▶ The suspect exits the scene with his weapon still exposed.

shows surveillance photos of an armed robbery carried out in a convenience store. As discussed later in this chapter, proprietors of convenience and liquor stores and taxi drivers run the highest risk of being targeted for an armed robbery.

Alternatively, robbery committed by either using or threatening to use physical force is classified as **strong arm robbery**. These acts, commonly referred to as *muggings,* can involve one or many offenders who use tactics such as punching and/or kicking to complete a theft of property from their victim. Other forms of strong arm robbery include "snatch and grab" thefts. When items of any value are taken from an individual's possession (for example, a cell phone is snatched from a person's pocket, or a purse beneath someone's arm), and the victim becomes aware of the force used, a strong arm robbery has taken place. Crimes that employ this type of force, without the aid of a weapon, make up the other 50 percent of all robberies. All in all, about 25 percent of all robbery victims suffer at least minor injuries at the hands of their assailants. Of all violent crimes, robbery has one of the lowest clearance rates—ranging from 25 to 30 percent of all incidents reported to police. This is because robbery is the only type of major violent crime where most (about 80 percent) of victims and perpetrators are total strangers to each other.[4]

INVESTIGATIVE TACTICS

After the robbery crime scene has been secured, the investigation should proceed immediately. In robberies, the greater the amount of time that passes without apprehending the suspect, the less likely the suspect will ever be apprehended. Statistics suggest that if a robbery is not cleared within 30 days of its occurrence, it most likely will go unsolved. Also, for safety purposes, the crime scene should not be processed until it is absolutely clear that the offender(s) are not hiding in or around the area to be searched. If available, canine units should be used to help clear the crime scene of possible lingering suspects.

1. ***Interview Victims and Witnesses:*** Any and all witnesses, including the victim, need to be quickly identified, separated, and interviewed to discover the details of the robbery and the robbery suspect(s). If the victims are in a physical and/or mental condition to be interviewed, they should be taken to a calm secure area and interviewed immediately. Because of the emotional turmoil they have just endured, victims should not be pressured to provide responses if they are not in the state of mind to do so. Some victims who refuse to cooperate may know their assailant and so fear retaliation resulting from cooperating with the robbery investigation. Uncooperative victims may themselves be involved in some sort of illegal conduct, or conduct that may have precipitated the robbery. For example, individuals may start fights with others, leading to being not only physically assaulted but robbed as well. This is especially true for victims under the influence of alcohol or drugs before the robbery.

2. ***Obtain a Physical Description of the Suspect(s):*** As soon as possible, the preliminary investigation should attempt to obtain a physical description of the suspect(s). Surveillance photos or other security imaging devices may provide an exact image of the robbery and the suspect(s). The victim or other eyewitnesses can make positive identifications of the suspect(s) in photo images, but only after verbal descriptions are obtained during the interview. In addition to a general physical description of the suspect(s), other preliminary pertinent information should be gathered from witnesses to conduct an immediate search for the suspect(s):
   a. Whether or not a weapon was used, and if so, what type?
   b. Where did the suspect(s) enter and exit the crime scene?

c. How did they escape the crime—on foot, bicycle, or in a vehicle?

d. If a vehicle was used, what was the color, make, model, or other identifying characteristics?

Caution should be exercised when interviewing victims or witnesses recounting the physical features of armed robbery suspects, particularly in crimes involving use of a firearm. These individuals may provide inaccurate or distorted descriptions of the assailant due to **weapon focus**. Weapon focus can cause eyewitnesses of armed robbery to focus on details of the weapon that the offender is holding and thereby block out all other details of the robbery event.

If actual photos cannot be obtained, forensic artists' sketches and/or computer imaging based on eyewitness accounts can be used to create a composite image of the robbery suspects.

3. ***Canvass the Crime Scene Vicinity:*** After issuing a bulletin to patrol units that provides a general description of the suspect, the general vicinity in and around the robbery scene should be canvassed. In addition, flyers containing the suspect photo and physical description, brief information about the robbery, and contact information for the investigator should be posted and distributed around the crime scene area.

HOT TIPS AND LEADS 12.1

Assessing an Armed Robber's Unique Traits

Not all armed robbers use the same *modus operandi* (M.O.) on all occasions. As previously mentioned, an offender's M.O. may stay the same for a short while and then change over time as easier, more proficient methods of carrying out desired criminal activities are learned. The sequence of events used to complete most armed robberies, however, can be quite similar among offenders. The specific words used by, and mannerisms of the armed robbers committing these crimes often can be used as *unique traits* that provide leads for identifying specific suspects. Thus, when interviewing armed robbery victims it is important to note these traits by asking the following targeted questions:

1. What type of approach did the offender use?
   Armed robbers typically use two methods to approach their victims: (1) catching the victim off guard by sneaking up on the unsuspecting victim (most often from behind) or (2) approaching the victim for a legitimate purpose (e.g., asking for directions or the time).

2. How did the offender announce the crime?
   After the approach, the armed robber attempts to instill instant fear to gain control over the situation and total compliance from the victim. Most create the illusion of impending death by words spoken in tones intended to make the victim feel they will die if they attempt to resist the robber's demands. Many armed robbers stick with a dialogue that has worked for them in the past—using the same words and delivery in the same way each time they announce the crime. For example, victims may be told, "You're getting' robbed you piece of shit motherfucker." "Don't make me kill you, so do whatever the fuck I tell you to do, cocksucker!" Then, the robber may attempt to calm the victim somewhat so that they can comprehend and

comply with their demands. This is a trait of more experienced robbers.

3. How were the goods transferred?
   Armed robbers either take the goods themselves from the victim or have the victim hand the goods over to them. When the victim hands over the goods, the offender may take what is given to them without further action (done mostly by amateurs) or may use more intimidating words and perhaps physical violence to make sure the victim has given them all the goods and is not holding out on them (done mostly by experienced or professional robbers). Most armed robbers who take the goods themselves from victims do so to make sure all money or other property is obtained or to guard against resistance or use of a weapon by the victim.

4. How was the offender's escape made?
   Offenders can either leave the scene of the robbery or force the victim to leave the scene. Most prefer to leave the scene and will attempt to ensure they are not followed by the victim or the victim does not alert police by making further verbal threats of physical injury or death. Some offenders place a time limit on victims such as "Don't leave here for 5 minutes—if me or my friends see you outside a minute sooner, we'll kill your ass!" Other will present an open threat to the victim by saying, "I'll know if you ever call the cops, and when I find out, I'm gonna hunt you down and put you in a box!" In more extreme cases, armed robbers restrain their victims before leaving the scene by tying them up or perhaps injuring them by breaking bones or shooting them in bodily areas that will not produce a lethal injury.[5]

BANK ROBBERIES

Although bank robberies appear quite often in the media, in reality they comprise only 2 percent of all robbery victimizations and 10 percent of all robberies involving commercial establishments. Of all forms of robbery, bank robberies are most likely to be solved through the investigative process. In all, approximately three out of five bank robberies are eventually solved. In those cases, about 50 percent of all suspects are arrested either at the scene or at another location on the day of the robbery. Many factors explain why the clearance rate for bank robbery is so much greater than that for other forms of robbery:

- **Timing:** Because banks are usually open only during daytime hours, most bank robberies are committed in daylight settings, providing maximum visibility of offenders and their crime-related activities.
- **Security:** Banks employ numerous security measures to identify and thwart robbery suspects, including video surveillance, armed/unarmed security personnel, and special antitheft devices.
- **Witnesses:** There are many potential witnesses to bank robberies, including banking customers, passers-by, and tellers trained in suspect recognition methods.
- **Reporting:** There is seldom a bank robbery that goes unreported; the reporting of most robberies takes place only minutes after the crime has occurred.[6]

It is difficult, however, to generalize one particular profile or set of information to all bank robberies and robbery suspects. This is largely due to the various settings in which banking establishments are targeted (freestanding banks, drive-through depositories, banking counters within malls or superstores), their locations (isolated, urban, suburban, rural locals), and the nature of the offense (armed or unarmed; amateur or professional). With respect to these and other related variables, one bank robbery can be very different from another. Thus, the investigation of a particular bank robbery must be specifically oriented toward the particular nuances of the offense and the offender that can be gleaned from all available sources of evidence.

Bank Robbery Methods

Most bank robberies are passive rather than violent in nature, involve single rather than multiple suspects, and are relatively spontaneous rather than well-planned acts. On rare occasions, however, bank robberies employ overtly violent means or can turn violent if certain situational factors go wrong, such as customers or security personnel attempting to apprehend an armed offender. Following are the most common types of robberies encountered in banking settings:

1. **The Note Pass Robbery:** This is by far the most common type of bank robbery. Usually, a lone offender enters a bank during normal operating hours, dressed in normal clothing without a facial disguise.

The suspect then progresses through the line to the teller station, where a threatening note is passed unobtrusively to the teller. The note may have been prepared by the suspect before arriving at the bank, or it may have been written on a deposit slip after entering the bank. The note is usually handwritten in block lettering and states a monetary demand such as "Give me all the cash in your drawer" along with a threat to the effect of ". . . or everybody will get killed," "I have a gun and I'll use it," or "I have a bomb and I'll blow everyone up." More sophisticated offenders include in their note some reference to not setting off alarms or providing money that has been marked or rigged with a security device. After obtaining the cash, the offender walks calmly from the premises to avoid alerting other customers or banking personnel to the fact that a robbery has just occurred.[7] Figure 12.4 shows a sequence of events illustrating a note pass bank robbery where the teller gives the robber currency loaded with a **dye pack**. Dye packs create a time-delayed explosion, spraying ink over the stolen money and other nearby objects. Also illustrated in Figure 12.4, objects belonging to the robber and the stolen money recovered near the crime scene show the red ink deposited on them by the dye pack.

2. **The Traditional Stick-up Robbery:** The stick-up basically follows the same M.O. as the note pass robbery, but with one main exception: The suspect confronts the teller with a weapon (usually a handgun or knife), or something resembling a weapon (a toy or makeshift handgun, or simply a hand concealed beneath clothing to fake gun possession). Offenders often make a verbal demand for cash while brandishing the weapon in the teller's presence, or may flash the weapon tucked in their waistband or concealed within an object such as a satchel or large envelope.[8]

3. **The Morning Glory Robbery:** This type of robbery usually occurs in small- to medium-size banking locations staffed by very few employees. The robber's primary goal is to enter the bank and obtain cash during early morning hours before it is open to the general public. That can be done in several ways. In a very direct approach, the robber waits in hiding outside the bank (e.g., behind shrubs, walls, garbage dumpsters, or perhaps in a vehicle), makes an armed approach to an employee attempting to open the bank, and then makes cash demands once inside the building. A second approach involves offenders who attract the attention of bank personnel preparing to open for business. The robber, usually located outside a glass door or display window, pretends to be a regular customer in a hurry with a special banking need or a personal emergency and requests to be let into the bank immediately. Upon unlocking the bank's

(a)

(b)   (c)

FIGURE 12.4 ▶ (a) Surveillance photo of a robber carrying out a note pass robbery. (b) Items possessed by the robber, recovered outside the bank after the robbery. Note the red stains left on the bottom of the bag by the exploding dye pack contained in the stolen money. (c) Money stained by ink from the dye pack, recovered from the robbery suspect.

front door, the usually armed suspect storms into the establishment making cash demands and threats in the absence of regular customers or security staff who have yet to arrive. A third, and much more daring approach is when the robber somehow enters the bank before it opens and overpowers employees arriving for work during morning hours. In these instances, the robber may have broken into the bank, had a corrupt employee provide entry, or hidden in the bank before closing, spending the night in anticipation of committing robbery the next morning. Regardless of the particular method used, the morning glory robbery provides the robber a low-risk situation where

employees are caught off guard, alarms are not yet armed, relatively few witnesses are present, and a stockpile of cash is present from overnight deliveries and cash deposits.[9]

4. ***The Closing-Time Robbery:*** Closing time is another opportunistic period for bank robbery. Typically, this type of offense is carried out by a lone suspect who enters the bank just before closing time and lingers until becoming the last customer of the day. After all other customers have gone and the bank doors have been locked to prevent more customers from entering after hours, the robbery takes place behind closed doors. In these robberies, the offender's preferred

target is a small branch location where one or two employees conduct the bank's closing procedures.[10]

5. ***The Take-Over Robbery:*** This is the most daring, violent, and dangerous form of bank robbery. Take-overs are usually carried out by multiple offenders who have planned their individual roles in the robbery and their means of escape. In most cases, an overtly violent direct approach is used to intimidate customers and employees inside the bank. Many, if not all of the assailants may be armed with various firearms ranging from small-bore pistols to shotguns. Shots may be fired into objects, walls, or ceilings or at victims to gain immediate compliance and to discourage any type of resistance. Persons in the bank frequently are forced to the floor and told to remain still under the threat of being shot. After going behind the partition or counter separating customers from tellers, the offender usually removes all cash from the tellers' stations and may take a manager hostage while demanding that the bank's vault and/or ATM machines be opened. Wallets, purses, cash jewelry, watches, and other personal effects of value may be removed from customers as well. Suspects may also taunt their victims, making violent threats or sexual overtures. In these types of robberies, the offenders are well aware of the amount of time they have before first responding police will arrive, and they may use this time to fulfill a warped egotistical desire to display their dominance over their captives. Recently, many take-over robberies have been linked to the growing economic enterprise of street gangs, drug gangs, and organized crime.[11]

Amateur and Professional Bank Robbers

Bank robbers can be classified as either **amateur robbers** or **professional robbers**, based largely on how they carry out their criminal acts. By far, the most often encountered bank robber is an amateur; or, in other words, an offender who has very limited experience in robbing financial institutions and does not specialize in the act. Approximately 80 percent of persons taken into custody for bank robbery have no prior record of committing the crime. These offenders also tend to exhibit certain characteristics during the commission of their crimes that distinguish them from most experienced professional offenders:

- Working alone without the help of other offenders
- Failing to wear a disguise or alter physical appearance
- Having a history of abusing drugs and/or alcohol, and perhaps are under the influence of such during the commission of the crime
- Using a passive method of force or fear, such as note passing instead of a weapon
- Employing a "wait in line" approach to victimize a single teller

- Committing the crime during heavy customer traffic hours, such as middays or Fridays before closing
- Obtaining a relatively low sum of money from the crime, on average between 4,000 and 5,000 dollars
- Completing the actual robbery and leaving the scene in a very short period of time, usually 5 minutes or less[12]

In addition to the factors just listed, amateur bank robbers usually attempt to make their getaway on foot or using a bicycle. Vehicles are not used for several reasons, including possible identification of the vehicle by security personnel or cameras, traffic delays upon exiting the crime scene, and the offender's lack of ownership of, or access to a vehicle. Due to this limited geographic mobility, most amateur bank robbers live within walking distance of the crime scene and will select high-traffic pedestrian routes to blend into the crowd while making their escape. They also walk rather than run from the scene and follow a path that avoids open spaces such as parking lots, parks, and fields.

In most respects, professional bank robbers are the mirror image of their amateur counterparts. These offenders perform much more sophisticated, larger-scale robberies not only because they possess prior experience, but also because their prior experience has made them confident enough to orchestrate the violent behavior that crime of this nature requires to be successful. Similar to all robbers, professional types are noted for committing a wide range of criminal activities (e.g., drug sales/trafficking, burglary, auto theft, murder), but they also engage in repeated bank robberies to supplement their need for fast cash. Their style of offending is easily identified by the methods they employ at the time of the robbery:

- Using masks or other methods to disguise physical appearance
- Deactivating alarms or disabling surveillance cameras
- Working with multiple offenders
- Using a take-over robbery technique
- Carrying and/or using weapons
- Entering the bank at times when relatively few customers are present
- Taking hostages to enforce demands
- Robbing multiple teller stations and attempting entry into the bank's vault
- Verbalizing loudly, making threats to instill fear and intimidate onlookers
- Obtaining large amounts of cash, usually $40,000 or more[13]

The escape strategy for professional bank robbers is unlike that of the amateurs in that it appears to be more planned out and depends on a vehicle for a quick getaway. Typically, the getaway vehicle is stolen before the robbery and may be **cold plated** (equipped with stolen license plates from a similar appearing vehicle) to avoid detection by police. The vehicle used to flee the scene may be abandoned at a remote location within the general proximity of the robbery. There, the suspects may also have parked secondary vehicles (that have not been identified by witnesses) for use in completing their escape. Usually, professional bank robbers subscribe to the NIMBY (Not In My Back Yard) strategy of offending; that is, they travel outside their primary residence to select bank targets that provide the most opportunities for profit and escaping without apprehension.

ATM ROBBERIES

The advent of ATM cash machines has created an entirely new opportunity for both street and commercial robbers. Although statistics are not specifically gathered on **ATM robberies**, many facts can be derived about these crimes from studying the growing number of violent criminal encounters between robbers, ATM customers, and ATM service/banking personnel. These can be used to group ATM robberies into the following general categories of offending patterns:

1. *Street ATM Robberies:* These situations involve a relatively straightforward violent attack on an ATM customer who is usually using a machine in a remote location that enables the offender to catch the victim by surprise. Typically, the robber hides near an ATM machine and waits for a lone victim to withdraw cash. After the withdrawal, the offender quickly approaches the victim from behind with a real or fake weapon and demand the cash and perhaps the victim's ATM card. Some offenders do not wait for a withdrawal to take place, but rather use force or fear to make the victim perform an ATM transaction. In either case, the offender may make a getaway in the victim's car to escape the area. If the ATM card is taken, it usually is used only hours after the robbery, before the victim can cancel future ATM transactions. The offender may sell the card to more sophisticated computer criminals with knowledge of how to hack into the victim's bank account through security information contained on the card's magnetic strip. The PIN also may have been obtained by a second offender who "shoulder surfed" the victim (i.e., stood behind the victim to view and record or memorize the PIN) at the ATM machine before the robbery. In these cases, the offenders usually make additional withdrawals with the card from an ATM machine near the crime scene as soon as possible after the robbery.

2. *Commercial ATM Robberies:* This type of robbery is directed at either banking or security personnel who maintain and service ATM machines. Typically, the offender strikes when ATM machines are opened for repair or to replenish the machine's supply of cash. Armed robbers will attempt to overpower persons attending to the machine and steal the money being loaded into the machine or the cassettes inside of the machine that contain cash to be dispensed. This type of robbery, unlike other more spontaneous street versions, may require planning on the part of the offender(s). For example, would-be robbers must know times when and places where ATM machines are serviced or restocked with funds. More-spontaneous robberies of ATM machines occur during servicing or money loading times, in which the robbers seem to just happen to be in the right place at the right time. These crimes may be based on inside information on ATM machine activities provided to robbers by corrupt employees or other individuals who know ATM security practices.[14]

TAXI CAB ROBBERIES

Because of physical harm to drivers caused by robberies, taxi cabs are rated as the number-one most hazardous place for job-related homicides and assaults. As with most other robbery situations, the **taxi-cab robbery** is primarily motivated by money. Drivers often carry large amounts of cash from fares, and to provide change to customers. This is especially true on weekends and holidays in large cities during popular periods of tourist travel—a time when taxi robberies are most likely to occur. Taxi robberies usually occur in the late evening hours, and the offender(s) typically employ one or more of the following tactics:

- Hailing a taxi at a roadside taxi stand and then robbing the driver immediately upon stopping the vehicle
- Entering the cab as a client and sitting in the front passenger seat; then asking the driver if the shift has been busy (to assess the driver's cash on-hand) and, if so, holding up the driver with a handgun
- Having a woman decoy call for a cab to pick her up at a remote location and then having the cab driver victimized upon arrival by a male robber
- Ordering the driver at gunpoint to a remote location, robbing the driver, and then locking the driver in the trunk of the vehicle
- Robbing the driver, dropping the driver in a remote location, and carjacking the taxi
- Asking the driver to change course or make an unplanned stop to a location where the robbery executes the robbery or has accomplices waiting to assist in the robbery

Some taxi cabs are equipped with security cameras to obtain photographs of robbers and robbery events. In addition, many taxi cab companies have GPS records of the times and routes that their taxies have travelled. Physical evidence in the form of hairs, fibers, fingerprints, and bodily fluids such as sweat may be left by the robber both inside and outside the taxi cab. Victims of taxi cab robberies are often hesitant to provide investigators information about their victimization. This may be due to their immigrant status and fears that their dealings with authorities will lead to their deportation. Also, some taxi drivers themselves are involved in illegal dealings such as drug sales, property fencing, or other crimes, leading to their fear of investigative inquiries. In these situations, the driver's robbery may in fact be payback for an illegal business relationship that has gone bad.[15]

CONVENIENCE STORE ROBBERIES

Overall, approximately 6 percent of all robberies are carried out against convenience stores and their operators. Additionally, these robberies can be very violent. In support of this claim, statistics show that clerks of convenience stores are second only to taxi drivers for being at risk of becoming the victim of a homicide during a robbery. Most "C store" robbers, as they refer to themselves on the streets, are males under the age of 25 years who are amateur thieves. They do not plan, or they do very little planning before committing a robbery, and are likely to use a gun or other weapon to intimidate their victim. Also, they are typically motivated to gain quick cash to support a drug or alcohol habit, and about half of these offenders are under the influence when they carry out their crimes. Most professional convenience store robbers exclusively use guns, wear disguises, are more apt to injure employees, and have perhaps done prison time for past robberies. In addition, these more experienced offenders typically engage in serial robberies of convenience stores, performing them at regular times and within distinct geographic patterns.

Robbers of convenience stores take two distinct types of approaches. The first is the **straight approach**, where the offender bursts into the store in a grand intimidating fashion and immediately demands money from the clerk—usually by pushing the weapon close to the clerk's face. Offenders employing this method either demand that the clerk empty the register, or may themselves empty the register by reaching in or jumping over a counter to do so. Offenders using this style typically run as they exit the robbery scene. Offenders may also employ what is known as the **customer approach**. In these situations, the offender enters the store pretending to be a customer and then sometime later makes either an overt command (similar to that used in the straight approach) or a covert demand (e.g., talking calmly, pretending to pay for an item at the checkout area) for money from the clerk. Usually, offenders using this style exit the store walking so as not to attract attention.

Most convenience store robberies do not result in injuries to the victimized clerk. Injury is likely to occur during a robbery, however, if the clerk's behavior is interpreted by offenders as resistant to their demands. Sudden moves, extreme nervousness, or extended eye contact are some of the more common clerk behaviors likely to provoke physical attacks by offenders during the course of a robbery. Some offenders, usually the more professional ones, are noted for engaging in unprovoked blitz attacks on clerks at the outset of a robbery just to show them who is "in charge" of the situation. Interestingly, approximately 6 percent of all convenience stores account for 65 percent of all convenience store robberies. Thus, certain stores are undeniably much more at risk of robbery than are others. Following are some store characteristics associated with a higher risk of being targeted by robbers:

- Located in isolated industrial or commercial areas away from shopping centers or strip malls
- A large amount of obstructions inside or outside the store, and in particular windows covered with advertisements that block persons on the outside from seeing into the store's interior
- Staffing only one employee during overnight graveyard shifts
- Allowing persons to loiter in the store's parking lot or in front of the store
- Inadequate lighting or security technology, including CCTVs, security cameras, or alarm systems
- Having large amounts of money on hand, and not using drop safes or other methods to limit cash in registers
- An internal store layout that enables persons to hide out of sight from the clerk and also provides multiple entrance and exit locations

Available crime statistics also indicate that most robbers prefer to victimize convenience stores located within the general proximity of where they live, allowing for an easy escape from the scene to their residence. The peak hours of "C store" robberies are between 10 PM and 12 AM, with about 60 percent being carried out on Friday, Saturday, and Sunday nights. One in every two convenience store robberies is carried out during the months of November and February, a finding consistent with the general fact that most property crimes are committed during winter months. Interestingly, many convenience stores are victimized repeatedly by the same offender or different offenders. If this occurs, it usually happens within a three-week period from the date of the initial robbery.[16] Illustrated Case 12B illustrates a convenience store robbery that went terribly wrong for the offender. In a small percentage of "C store" robberies, the store clerk is armed and provides defense against the assailant, as did the clerk in this case. The crime scene photos shown in Figures 12.5 to 12.14 show evidence that investigators discovered concerning the store clerk's shooting of the robber. Although the robber was not discovered at the scene, ample physical evidence exists to reconstruct this crime and perhaps identify the offender.

ILLUSTRATED CASE 12B

Robbery Gone Wrong for the Offender

FIGURE 12.5 ▶ Tape line establishing a crime scene perimeter in the parking lot of a gas station where an armed robber held up a convenience store clerk. Both the perpetrator and the clerk were armed with a semiautomatic handgun, which resulted in the robbery-injury scene shown in the following figures.

FIGURE 12.6 ▶ Investigators arrive to discover blood droplets and spatter at the entrance of the store.

FIGURE 12.7 ▶ Blood transfer finger and hand prints on the exterior door handle. Blood spatter can be seen on the glass door interior.

FIGURE 12.8 ▶ The interior of the store showing blood spatter patterns on the cement floor and the victim's pants.

FIGURE 12.9 ▶ Bloody print on the interior door handle.

FIGURE 12.10 ▶ Bloody print on the door's interior panel.

FIGURE 12.11 ▶ Semiautomatic handgun and two magazines located on top of a tool chest in the garage area adjacent to the convenience store.

FIGURE 12.13 ▶ Blood trail leading from the entrance to the garage area. The tool chest containing the gun is situated (out of the picture) next to the left inside wall after passing through the doorway.

FIGURE 12.12 ▶ Close-up of the pistol and magazines, showing blood stains.

FIGURE 12.14 ▶ Concentration of blood droplets at the end of the blood trail. In a case such as this, where the robbery suspect is either injured or killed during the robbery attempt, how should investigators proceed in their investigation? What information and evidence should be gathered from the scene? What information and evidence should be gathered in a follow-up investigation of this incident? What questions should be asked of the store attendant who shot the robber? If the robbery suspect survives the shooting, what questions should be asked of the suspect?

HOME INVASION ROBBERIES

Known in most jurisdictions as simply *residential robbery*, the **home invasion robbery** is a crime of opportunity created by victims who store large amounts of money or valuables in their homes rather than in a more secure location such as a bank or safety deposit box. This type of robbery, created by Asian gangs, is now committed by gangs and persons of other races/ethnicities. In the Asian culture, a distrust of U.S. banks, possession of expensive jewelry, gambling money, and elaborate gifts make Asian households depositories for large sums of wealth; consequently, they are disproportionately targeted for this type of robbery.

Most home invasion robberies are carried out by gangs or organized groups who make extensive plans for how to enter the home, take the goods, and exit the crime scene. Typically, a juvenile male family member of the targeted home provides information to the would-be robbers in exchange for a split of any profits obtained from the robbery. Most Asians plan these robberies at meetings in cafes—a popular meeting place for Asian gang members. A typical home invasion robbery usually takes place in the following sequence of events:

1. Detailed plans are made between robbery suspects and a juvenile male informant with extensive knowledge of the residence to be robbed. Information is provided on valuables in the home and their locations.

2. The robbery suspects pick up weapons (usually hand guns), duct tape, wire ties, and other items used to restrain, gag, and perhaps blindfold their victims. Walkie-talkies or Nextel-type phone communications are used to coordinate pre- and postrobbery activities.

3. One or two cars are stolen—one to drive to the residence, and a second vehicle (if used) to switch cars after the robbery. Each of the stolen cars is cold plated with plates stolen from vehicles matching in color, make, and style.

4. Usually one or two girls are enlisted as decoys for the robbery.

5. The robbery usually takes place when an older family member or adult female is at the home alone or is taking care of infants or younger children. The decoy girls knock on the door, pretending to have been hurt in an accident or the victim of some other type of emergency situation. Once residents open the door (believing the girl is injured and in need of assistance), the male robbers rush into the home and begin the robbery.

6. Screaming and gun-wielding robbers tie their victims' hands and feet using duct tape and wire ties and may also pistol whip them to show "they mean business." Demands are made of the victims to reveal alarm and safe codes, hiding places, keys for locks, and any other obstacle hindering the robbers' securing of money or other valuables. If children are present, and adult victims are uncooperative in meeting the robbers' demands, threats to kill the child generally are made. A popular threat is executed by putting a young child's face in a toilet to simulate drowning.

7. After the stolen items are secured, the robbers exit the home—leaving the residents restrained and gagged. Hours may pass before other family members return to the residence to witness what has taken place and notify authorities.

8. The robbers exit the crime scene in either the first or a second stolen vehicle, perhaps driven by one of their female associates. The offenders leave the area of the victimized home immediately, and they will change their clothes to avoid identification.[17]

DRUG ROBBERIES

Although dealers of illegal drugs traditionally are targets of robbers who steal their money and narcotics, there is now a new breed of street and commercial robber that targets legal prescription drugs. The street robbery version of this crime, known as a **drug robbery**, targets persons leaving pharmacies after picking up pain killers and other prescription drugs used for illicit purposes. These crimes are usually carried out by young amateur robbers, usually addicts, who target their victims by gaining inside information about the type of prescription being filled. Much more serious are commercial takeover robberies of pharmacies to steal large quantities of pain killers and other prescription drugs with a high street value. In these crimes, the robber usually enters the pharmacy during late evening or early morning hours and, using a handgun or other weapon, compels pharmacy personnel to open safes or other secured areas where large quantities of drugs are stored. If a robbery of this type is committed when fresh shipments of certain drugs (e.g., pain killers) arrive, the offender probably was informed by a pharmacy insider of the type, time, and place of the drug delivery. These offenses can also be staged robberies (this topic is discussed later in the chapter) in which corrupt pharmacy employees work with the offenders to plan their own victimization and, by doing so, receive a split of the stolen profits.

FREIGHT ROBBERIES

Freight robbery has become one of the fastest growing and costliest crimes in the United States over the past decade. In 2010, there were 899 robberies, compared to 672 reported during 2007—a 34 percent increase in offenses in just 3 years. In addition, the average loss per robbery incident is $471,000, with the highest single-incident losses being for pharmaceuticals ($3.78 million) and tobacco products ($1.26 million). Most of these robberies, constituting approximately 81 percent, involve stealing fully loaded tractor-trailer rigs or loaded containers unattached to tractor trucks. The items most frequently stolen are food and drink items (21 percent), consisting mostly of raw products such as sugar, rice, tea, coffee, meats, and canned/bottled drinks. The second and third most frequently stolen items are electronics and clothing products—19 percent and 11 percent of all freight robberies, respectively. Among electronics products, televisions and laptop computers are the most popular items targeted by freight robbers.

Freight robbers use several M.O.s. Some resort to violence to hijack a truck and loaded trailer from its rightful driver. In this situation, the robber usually targets a truck parked at a truck stop or alongside the highway while the unsuspecting driver is resting. The robbery is then executed by forcing the driver from the rig at gunpoint, then driving the truck and its load to another location for unloading. A robber who is unable to operate a truck may force the driver at gunpoint to drive the rig to the desired unloading location. Offenders who use weapons or violence against drivers to secure a truck and its load are usually experienced professional robbers.

Most freight robberies, however, are performed in a nonviolent manner, whereby the robber takes the entire tractor-trailer or an unattached loaded trailer at a location where it has been parked and left unattended by the driver. This usually occurs when (1) drivers park their rigs in truck stop parking areas and leave them to shower, eat, or rest; or (2) they leave their trailer in a drop lot after unhitching it and using the tractor portion to drive to other locations. In the former situation, the thief obtains the keys by either passively stealing the truck's keys from the driver's clothing or other location—or, in more extreme cases, using weapons or physical force to make drivers surrender their keys. In the latter situation, robbers hitch up their own tractor (rented or stolen) to the parked and loaded trailer. Often, multiple trucks or trailers are stolen during one criminal event by freight robbery teams. Amateur robbers are more likely than professionals to use nonviolent means to rob loaded trucks and trailers.

Most freight thefts occur in unsecured locations such as truck stops, public access parking areas, roadsides, and unsecured parking lots such as those in large shopping centers. About one of every three truck robberies, however, occurs in secured parking areas in and around warehouses and freight yards. In rare cases, truck drivers are the victims of "last mile robberies." Robbers in these situations are noted to commandeer trucks in traffic or at staged road blocks a short distance (i.e., 1 mile) from their delivery destination. Loads of pharmaceuticals, alcohol, and tobacco are most frequently stolen using this method. Nonetheless, most big rigs targeted by freight robbers are on long hauls either within or between states, with very few operating as local delivery trucks. Approximately 60 percent of all freight thefts occur on Saturday or Sunday, when the driver has parked the truck for the weekend. Unfortunately, hours or perhaps days pass before the driver returns from a weekend trip and discovers the truck is missing and reports its theft to investigators. Most offenders abandon the stolen tractor portion a close distance from the crime scene. Trailers, on the other hand, are usually discovered miles away from the robbery scene, where their contents are offloaded into another tractor trailer or into several smaller trucks and transported to warehouses, trains, planes, or perhaps directly to cargo ships destined for other countries. Abandoned trailers may be repainted or reworked to avoid recognition.[18]

ARMORED TRUCK ROBBERIES

Known to robbers as *money magnets*, armored trucks are the target of robbery less often than are banks; but when they are robbed, the scene is often much more violent than that of the average bank robbery. This is largely because both the victims and offenders at a typical armored truck heist are both armed. In 2009, according to FBI statistics, 79 armored trucks were robbed while picking up and delivering money from banks alone. This statistic does not take into account the hundreds of other armored truck hold-ups occurring across the nation at shopping malls, grocery stores, and other private and public establishments.

Unfortunately, very little is known about the dynamics of armored truck robberies except that they are usually planned incidents involving two or more offenders who usually wear ski masks or other disguises. Other than the latter generic profile, however, it is very difficult to identify a "typical" armored truck robbery scenario. Some robberies are carried out while the truck is parked at a location where money is being picked up or delivered. In this type of robbery, the offenders often are staked out at a parking lot or other location in a stolen vehicle near a parked armored truck. When security personnel exit from or return to the truck, the robbers rush the armored truck and perhaps exchange gunfire with its guards. Another common scenario is known as the *highway hijacking*. Here, the robbers either (1) construct a roadblock on a remote highway location or road to stop an armored vehicle in transit or (2) use a stolen vehicle to overtake the truck by running it off the road. After the armored truck is immobilized and its drivers are incapacitated, the robbers move money and other contents in the truck's storage area to another vehicle (usually stolen) for transportation away from the scene.

Other robbery scenarios involve outright theft of the entire truck and its contents, using tear gas or pepper spray to overpower guards and enable the theft or blowing open trucks with high explosives to access their contents. As many as 90 percent of armored car robberies are an **inside job** planned and/or executed by persons with knowledge of alarms, delivery routes, and other information concerning when or where armored trucks are carrying the most money and are most vulnerable to attack. Red flags of an inside job include robbery of money bags and trucks containing large amounts of cash where it appears the robbers were just lucky in picking the right armored car target. Contrary to popular belief, only trucks making money pickups and/or deliveries on particular routes, at certain times, and in specific places contain the high-denomination bills that are the desired target of a seemingly well-planned heist. Usually robbers without armored truck security information end up stealing money bags containing nothing more than stacks of checks and deposit receipts, or several thousand dollars in dimes and nickels.[19]

FALSE ROBBERY CLAIMS

Creating a **false robbery report** is a crime in most states. Usually, to arrest and charge a person suspected of filing a false robbery report the bogus claim must be made (1) to a law enforcement official, (2) by the person claiming to be the victim or witness of the robbery, and (3) with the knowledge that the robbery incident was fabricated. False robbery claims can be made for various reasons:

- **Workplace Robberies:** In these inside jobs, corrupt employees either fake their own robbery to steal money or merchandise from their workplace, or work as a team with outsiders to arrange a staged robbery in which they or other employees are the victims of a real or fake hold-up. This type of false robbery ranges in sophistication from single employees who fake victimization for a small amount of money, drugs, or other items, to elaborate crimes involving well-coordinated teams of robbers targeting money or property worth millions of dollars, such as big-rig drug heists or armored car robberies.
- **Insurance Fraud:** Private individuals or business owners file a false robbery claim of money, jewelry, or other valuables to obtain cash reimbursements for the stolen items from insurance companies.
- **Revenge:** Jealous lovers, angry friends, or feuding family members may claim that they have been robbed by persons whom they seek to hurt or get even with.
- **Attention:** Some persons, many of whom may be suffering from some form of mental instability, fake becoming a robbery victim to gain sympathy or notoriety from law enforcement officials, family members, friends, and other individuals from whom they seek attention.
- **Cover-ups:** Persons engaged in illegal, deviant, or socially disapproved behaviors, they may fake a robbery to cover up their involvement in such activities.

Various obvious warning signs during a robbery investigation suggest that a supposed robbery victim is filing a false claim. First, and foremost, the victim either cannot provide a suspect description or provides vague details about the perpetrator's physical characteristics. Likewise, if a weapon is involved, the victim is unable to describe it. If there are two robbery victims or witnesses, they should be separated to determine whether their stories are consistent. In situations where the robbery has been faked, even if persons have practiced getting their stories straight ahead of time, there will be glaring inconsistencies in their recall of fine details of the event—such as the words allegedly spoken by the offender or the offender's tone of voice. Second, the victim will not appear to be as emotionally "rattled" by the robbery as one would expect. Real robbery victims are usually extremely excited and shaken when interviewed and often do not gain their composure until hours after the event. Third, the victim claims to have resisted the perpetrator, yet they were not injured or the injuries they sustained are in inappropriate locations or seem self-inflicted (as may be confirmed by a medical examination). Last, and most important, the circumstances of the robbery event appear too good to be true. Large sums of money or high-value items taken at times and in locations where the robber appears to have randomly chosen the victim or victimized establishment should be huge red flags to investigators that the robbery perhaps may have been staged.

In these and other cases of suspected false robbery claims, investigators should (1) do background checks on the victims to possibly reveal a past history of similar claims; (2) interview persons associated with the alleged victim to help reveal a motive for faking the robbery, such as revenge; (3) check surveillance photos, if available, to confirm the victim's story; (4) check to see whether any allegedly missing credit cards were used by the victim after the time and date of the alleged robbery; and (4) obtain and serve search warrants on the victim's residence to discover property allegedly taken during the robbery. Unfortunately, some persons filing false robbery claims go to extreme measures to make investigators believe their fabricated stories, including providing a false identification of persons they claim to be the robber(s) from photo and live lineups.[20]

CASE CLOSE-UP 12.1
FALSE ROBBERY REPORTS

As the following cases clearly illustrate, false robbery reports can be provided to investigators for various motives—many of which appear frivolous and selfish on the part of the alleged victims:

Needed a Ride Home (Waldorf, MD): Sheriff's deputies received a call at 1:47 am from a man claiming to have been robbed of his watch and money by a lone assailant who approached him in a car while he was walking along a roadway. After canvassing the area of the alleged robbery and noticing inconsistencies in the victim's account of the incident, the man confessed that he dialed 911 and made the fake robbery claim to get a ride home from deputies.

Avoided Getting in Trouble at Work (Parsippany, NJ): A city employee filed a false robbery report claiming that he had been robbed by two Hispanic men and had suffered a head injury during the incident. He later confessed that he had fallen and struck his head while performing a work assignment and conjured up the story to avoid getting in trouble for not following proper safety procedures on the job.

Revenge against Boyfriend (Gainesville, FL): A woman falsely accused three men of a snatch-and-grab robbery of her cell phone. She provided investigators with street names and a mugbook identification of one of the alleged robbers. Investigators later discovered that the victim had been romantically involved with one of her alleged attackers, prompting a confession that she faked the robbery to seek revenge against one of the men for choosing to watch football rather than spend time with her.

Wanting to Look Tough (Starkville, MS): Two Mississippi State University students, one male and the other female, claimed to have been victims of an attempted robbery by a man wielding a knife and demanding money. The two victims each suffered gashes on their upper arms, which they claimed were caused by the assailant when they struggled with him in an attempt to resist his attack. The students' wounds allegedly produced by their attacker's knife were later discovered to have been self-inflicted. The students confessed to investigators that they faked their story and their injuries so that they would "look tough" to others.

RECONSTRUCTING A ROBBERY CRIME SCENE

Illustrated Case 12C illustrates a "questionable" crime scene that may or may not be classified by investigators as a robbery. After the evidence presented and the behavior of the robber and store clerk are examined, the incident may even be classified as a false robbery claim. As previously mentioned, investigators must be aware that in some cases a robbery may be staged by corrupt employees who use false robbery claims as a means to steal from their employer. When reconstructing this crime scene from the photos shown in Figures 12.15 to 12.19, the investigators must ascertain (1) whether the crime shown in the photos can be legally classified as a robbery and (2) whether this situation could be a false robbery claim.

ILLUSTRATED CASE 12C

A Questionable Robbery

FIGURE 12.15 ▶ Surveillance footage of a convenience store robbery. The suspect enters the store and approaches the cash register, pretending to be a legitimate customer while casing the location.

(a)

FIGURE 12.16A ▶ (a) The suspect makes a small purchase and reaches for a gun concealed in his waistband while the clerk rings up the purchase on the register.

(b)

FIGURE 12.16B ▶ (b) When the clerk looks down at the cash drawer, the suspect removes his weapon.

(a)

FIGURE 12.17 ▶ (a) The suspect makes a demand for money.

(b)

FIGURE 12.17B ▶ (b) The clerk complies with the suspect's demands.

FIGURE 12.18 ▶ The clerk opens the cash drawer while the suspect watches the store entrance.

FIGURE 12.19 ▶ For some unexplained reason, the suspect puts his pistol back into his pants and pretends to make a legitimate purchase before walking out of the store without taking any money or merchandise. In the above "C" store robbery, what are some of the unique traits of the robbery suspect? Does he appear to be an amateur or a professional robbery? Does he use the straight or customer approach? What are some of the questions that might be asked of the clerk or other witnesses to this crime regarding the unique traits of this offender? What are some of the ways that these surveillance images of the robbery can be used by investigators to develop suspect leads?

Summary

1. The legal definition of robbery.

Robbery is the taking or attempting to take anything of value from the care, custody, or control of a person or persons by force or threat of force or violence and/or by putting the victim in fear. Most jurisdictions have first-, second-, and third-degree classes of robbery. Robbery in the first degree is most serious and usually involves use of a weapon and/or injury to the robbery victim.

2. Typologies of persons committing robberies.

Approximately 50 percent of all robberies are executed by an offender armed with a weapon, which classifies the crime as an armed robbery. Alternatively, robbery committed by either using or threatening to use physical force is classified as strong arm robbery. These acts are commonly referred to as *muggings* and can involve one or many offenders who use tactics such as punching and/or kicking to complete a theft of property from their victim. Bank robbers can be classified as either amateurs or professionals, based largely on how they carry out their criminal acts. Amateurs are less likely to plan out their crimes or hide their identities at the time of the robbery. Professionals are more likely to plan their entrance into, and escape from the robbery scene; to wear disguises; and to use a weapon.

3. **Types and methods of bank robbery.**

Most bank robberies can be classified as one of several types, based on the offender's method of execution. First, and most common, is the note pass robbery, where the offender simply passes a note to the bank telling demanding money. Second, the traditional stick-up involves the use of a weapon (usually a handgun) to gain compliance of bank personnel during the robbery. Third, the morning glory robbery is carried out when the robber enters the bank before opening hours by using some form of trickery. Fourth, the closing-time robbery occurs when the bank has locked its doors for the day, serving the remaining customers in the building—the last of which is the robber. Last is the most daring, violent, and dangerous form of bank robbery—take-over robberies. These are usually carried out by multiple offenders who have planned their individual roles in the robbery and their means of escape.

4. **Common victims and targets of robbery.**

Perhaps the most dangerous workplace robbery, where homicide is most likely to result, takes place in taxi cabs. Second most dangerous are robberies taking place in convenience stores. Other popular targets for robbery include persons at ATM machines, persons storing large amounts of cash and valuables in their homes, big rigs and armored trucks that carry cash and property with a high black-market value, and pharmacies for their prescription drugs.

Key Terms

robbery	stick-up robbery	straight approach
armed robbery	morning glory robbery	home invasion robbery
strong arm robbery	closing time robbery	drug robbery
weapon focus	amateur robber	freight robbery
note pass robbery	cold plated	armored car robbery
professional robber	ATM robbery	inside job
customer approach	taxi cab robbery	false robbery report
"C store" robbery	take-over robbery	dye pack

Review Questions

1. How is the crime of robbery legally defined?
2. What are the differences between an armed robbery and a strong arm robbery?
3. What are the major types of bank robberies and how are they carried out?
4. How do amateur and professional robbers differ in their approach to bank robbery?
5. What are some of the common characteristics of an ATM robbery?
6. Describe the difference between robberies executed by a straight approach and a customer approach.
7. How are taxi cab robberies typically carried out?
8. Describe a home invasion robbery. Who are the likely perpetrators and victims involved?
9. What is a freight robbery?
10. What is meant by the term *inside job*?
11. How can a false robbery report be identified?

Internet Resources

Bank Robbery Resources	www.bankersonline.com
FBI Bank Robbery Statistics	www.fbi.gov/stats-services/publications/bank-crime-statistics-2009/bank-crime-statistics-2009-q3
Robbery Research (POP Center Library)	www.popcenter.org/library
Freightwatch (Truck Robbery)	www.freightwatchintl.com
Armored Car Robbery	www.armoredpro.com

Applied Investigative Exercise

Select either Illustrated Case 12A or 12B and imagine that you have been assigned to investigate this robbery. Explain the procedures you would perform with issues that must be addressed at the crime scene such as collection of physical evidence, identifying and interviewing witnesses, and release of the scene. Based on the available evidence, attempt to ascertain whether the robbery is the work of an amateur or a professional offender.

Notes

[1] Legal definitions of robbery provided in this section were derived from CAL. PEN. CODE § 211 and similar sections of penal codes from the states of Florida, Washington, Georgia, and New York, in addition to the legal definition of robbery provided in Black's Law Dictionary [see Bryan A. Garner (ed.), *Black's Law Dictionary*, 9th ed. (Eagan, MN: West Publishing, 2010)].

[2] Federal Bureau of Investigation, *Uniform Crime Reports 2009*, posted at www.fbi.gov/stats-services/publications/bank-crime-statistics-2009/bank-crime-statistics-2009; Deborah Lamm Weisel, *Bank Robbery* (Washington, DC: Center For Problem Oriented Policing, 2007), 20–23.

[3] Rosemary Erickson, *Armed Robbers and Their Crimes* (Seattle, WA: Athena Research Corporation, 1996), 45.

[4] Ibid., 45–51.

[5] This section was derived from material appearing in Richard T. Wright and Scott Decker, "Creating the Illusion of Impending Death: Armed Robbers in Action," *The HFG Review*, Vol. 2, 1997, 10–19.

[6] Timothy Hannan, "Bank Robberies and Bank Security Precautions," *Journal of Legal Studies*, Vol. 1, 1982, 83–92.

[7] Deborah Lamm Weisel, *Bank Robbery* (Washington, DC: Center For Problem Oriented Policing, 2007).

[8] Ibid.

[9] Ibid.

[10] Ibid.

[11] Ibid.

[12] S. Morrison and I. O'Donnell, *Armed Robbery: A Study in London* (Oxford, UK: Centre for Criminological Research, 1994), 68–87.

[13] Ibid.

[14] Michael S. Scott, *Robbery at Automated Teller Machines* (Washington, DC: Center for Problem Oriented Policing, 2002), 35–56.

[15] Martha J. Smith, *Robbery of Taxi Drivers* (Washington, DC: Center for Problem Oriented Policing, 2005), 12–23.

[16] Alicia Altizio and Diana York, *Robbery of Convenience Stores* (Washington, DC: Center for Problem Oriented Policing, 2007), 9–35.

[17] This section was derived from information provided to the authors by Master Officer Timothy Kovacks of the Garden Grove Police Department, August 2008.

[18] FreightWatch International, posted at www.freightwatchintl.com.

[19] Information in the section was derived from Armored Pro, posted at www.armoredpro.com.

[20] Conclusions presented here are based on the authors' investigative experience.

CHAPTER THIRTEEN

BURGLARY SCENES

Learning Objectives

After completing this chapter, you should be able to:

1. Summarize the trends and elements of burglary.
2. Be familiar with the various typologies of persons committing burglaries.
3. Describe the types of burglaries and types of burglars.
4. Describe how burglary investigations are conducted.
5. Describe the illegal markets used to distribute and sell stolen property.

Chapter Outline

INTRODUCTION

ALTHOUGH BURGLARY RATES IN THE United States have significantly declined over the past several decades, burglary is still the second most frequently reported felony offense (behind larceny-theft) and comprises approximately 18 percent of all serious criminal activities. Of all property crimes, burglary is perhaps the most alluring to offenders because it tends to be a crime with a low risk of apprehension that also has a relatively high monetary pay off. The average clearance rate (i.e., suspects identified and/or apprehended) of burglary cases ranges between 8 and 14 percent, meaning that about 9 out of every 10 burglaries go unsolved. Furthermore, the average take in terms of dollar value of money and property in residential burglaries hovers around $2,000, and that from a commercial establishment can be many times more.[1]

BURGLARY AND THE LAW

Burglary is a common law offense dating back many centuries. Today's legal definition of burglary, as written in modern codes and statutes, maintains many of its original common law characteristics and is defined in a rather similar fashion from one jurisdiction to the next. The offense of burglary, according to most state laws, is proven when available evidence can demonstrate that the following elements have been met:

- ***Breaking:*** The offender's actions have resulted in a "break" or the opening of an inhabited location that was intended to remain closed from intrusion to preserve privacy or security. Breaking can occur regardless of whether the item being "broken" is locked or not. Merely pushing open a closed gate can satisfy the element of breaking.
- ***Entering:*** The moment any portion of the offender's body (or an extension thereof) crosses into the dwelling's physical area or space, entering has occurred. A finger passing through the frame of an open window, a pry bar extending across the threshold of a doorway, or even a rock hurled through a glass window can all constitute a completed element of entering.

- ***The Dwelling of Another:*** The dwelling must, in most cases, belong to someone other than the offender. In situations where the victims and offenders share a common interest in property (e.g., husband and wife or cohabitants), the victim must show that the offender's legal right to access the property no long exists in order to satisfy this element of burglary.

- ***Intent to Commit a Crime:*** Evidence must show that the offender had formulated the mental intent to commit a felony (or in some jurisdictions, a misdemeanor) before entering the location of the alleged burglary. Most often, the intended crime is some form of larceny-theft. The offender's possession of tools (pry bar, screwdriver, glass cutter), location of entry (a secluded area of the dwelling), or preparations to carry stolen goods (having empty cases or bags on hand) are all types of evidence from which the assumption of criminal intent prior to entry may be made.

Depending on the particular jurisdiction, the crime of burglary is broken down into degrees based on the relative seriousness of the offender's actions. Burglaries involving assaultive behavior on the part of the offender toward a victim during the commission of the crime are usually classified as *first degree.* *Second-degree* burglaries are usually reserved for situations in which offenders carry a weapon to the scene of the crime. Most

burglaries, however, fall within the category of *third degree* or *common* burglaries, where the offender neither injures a victim nor possesses any type of weapon.[2]

RESIDENTIAL BURGLARY

Residential burglaries—comprising about 70 percent of all burglaries—are carried out against residents of private dwellings including single-family homes, apartments, condominiums, duplexes, and temporary places of habitation such as hotel rooms and cruise ship cabins. Most of these burglaries happen during late morning and early afternoon hours when residents are not home. In contrast, only some 35 percent of known residential burglaries occur after dark, when there is a higher probability of a home being occupied. For the investigator, burglary can often present a frustrating situation because the victims usually cannot provide information about the suspect, there are no eyewitnesses to the crime, and little or no physical evidence is present at the crime scene. Burglary victims, too, are equally frustrated not only by the offender's intrusion of their personal space, but also by the realization that the odds of recovering their stolen property are definitely not in their favor. Timely and targeted investigative methods, however, can greatly increase the chances of suspect identification and property recovery.[3]

TABLE 13.1	BURGLARY CHARACTERISTICS	
CHARACTERISTIC	**MAJORITY OF BURGLARIES**	**PERCENTAGE/RATE**
Location	Occurring In Homes/Private Dwellings	72.6%
Time: Residential	Occurring During Daytime Hours	64.8%**
Time: Nonresidential	Occurring During Nighttime Hours	55.9%**
Entry Method	Forcible Entry	62.4%
City Size	Highest: 500,000 to 999,999 Population	1,166.4 per 100,000
National Area	Highest in the West	114.5 per 100,000
Offender Age	Over 18 Years	75.3%
Offender Race	Caucasian	66.5%
Offender Gender	Male	84.2%

Source: FBI Uniform Crime Reports 2009, posted at www.fbi.gov/about-us/cjis/ucr/crime-in-the-u.s/2009/crime2009

**Estimates based on burglaries with known times of occurrence only. In approximately 1 out of every 4 burglaries reported to police, the time of occurrence is unknown.

Targeted Households

Burglary is and always has been a crime of opportunity. This fact is best supported by an examination of burglary trends from the 1930s until present. Although burglary rates have been declining since the early 1970s, residential burglary statistics before this time show an overall upward trend that lasted for nearly four decades. This steady increase has been explained, more so than for any other crime, as a function of social change in the United States during this time period that provided greater opportunities for offenders to carry out residential burglaries. Most significant among these changes is perhaps the greater number of females in the workforce, lessening the number of stay-at-home moms in their residences during daytime hours. Over time, this trend has created more empty homes to target for burglaries, as well as fewer eyes and ears of neighbors to observe break-ins on their street. In addition, growing divorce rates have fueled burglary by not only creating more homes left unguarded, but also increasing the number of households to burglarize and the amount of durable goods within them to steal.

As opportunists, burglars take a rational approach to selecting their targets. An empty home is the first prerequisite, and second is the opportunity to steal the most valuables, with the least effort, while having the lowest chances of getting caught. To determine whether a home is empty, burglars may use several approaches. Typically, they simply examine the outside of the home for absence of activity, indicated by accumulating mail/newspapers, overgrown lawns, absence of vehicles, no interior noise or lighting, and other signs of inactivity. To confirm their suspicions, most burglars use the simple and unsophisticated method of knocking on the front door or ringing the doorbell. If there is no answer, no sounds of children or dogs, or no movement within the residence, the next step is gaining entry. If by chance a person does answer the door, the would-be burglar usually has a cover story prepared, such as, "I'm sorry, I have the wrong address." Sometimes they may brazenly pose as salesmen to get a short glimpse of the home's interior through the doorway, or they may ask to enter the home to demonstrate a cleaning product or other items they are allegedly selling. Other less creative strategies include asking to use a telephone to report an accident or sexual assault. Therefore, while investigating completed or attempted burglaries, the burglary victim as well as the neighbors should be interviewed to determine if any persons—regardless of their intent—had approached them or their homes in the days preceding the criminal event.

Some burglars are very creative in how they pick their targets. In effect, they perform extensive intelligence gathering on their prospective victims. Again, in keeping with their goal of discovering a location that contains suitable wealth and provides an easy/low-risk means of entry, offenders often use external indicators. Large homes; expensive vehicles parked in driveways (which may themselves be targets); open garages

FIGURE 13.1 ▶ Often the targets of burglary are not high-end residences but rather easy-opportunity locations, like this storage area where the door lock was simply kicked in.

containing quads, motorcycles, tools, or other valuables; deliveries of goods; or even garbage containing bills, receipts, or other documentation suggesting items of value in the home are some of the outward signs of wealth burglars may employ to select their targets. External indicators of easy, low-risk entry include no alarm systems, no dogs present, open doors and/or windows on a first-floor level, unreinforced locks and door frames, bushes and shrubs that provide cover, and the absence of neighbors with a clear vision of the target residence. As shown in Figure 13.1, an unreinforced locked door is easily defeated by a burglar who merely punches or kicks out the locking mechanism.

Direct information about valuables contained within a residence and the time and dates when the owners will be away can be provided to well-connected burglars through various sources. For example, information about items of value and their whereabouts is usually obtained from persons with legitimate access to details regarding the burglary target's value and location. Such persons include corrupt service workers, realtors, insurance agents, appraisers, salespersons, ex-boyfriends/girlfriends/spouses, former roommates, and even spiteful relatives. Burglars also seek opportunities by combing newspapers and the Internet for information about estate sales and items to be sold at them; wedding announcements suggesting the presence of money and gifts; obituaries indicating empty homes; news articles detailing persons who have purchased valuable jewelry, antiques, and collectibles; and social network postings detailing vacation plans, job routines, and possessions owned. Garage sales also provide burglars with a legitimate opportunity to go undetected by posing as a potential customer while studying a home's entrances, exits, alarm systems, occupant characteristics, and the like.[4]

CASE CLOSE-UP 13.1
MTV'S "BURGLARIZED" CRIBS
(Las Vegas, NV)

When boxing champion Floyd Mayweather, Jr., appeared on the television show MTV Cribs to show off his lavish Las Vegas mansion and the various high-priced items in it, he never imagined that professional burglars would use the show to case his home. About 1 year after the episode aired, burglars broke in to Mayweather's residence early one morning at a location that provided direct access to a bathroom adjoining his master bedroom. In his Cribs episode, Mayweather showed various pieces of expensive jewelry on display in this same bathroom, including a Rolex watch and a gold medallion that he stated were worth $500,000 and $275,000, respectively. In all, investigators speculate that the burglary heist of Mayweather's house was the largest in Las Vegas history, netting the offenders an estimated $7 million in jewelry and other valuables. Although the image of one thief was caught on surveillance cameras at the burglarized home, no arrests have been made in the case.

First Response to the Burglary Scene

There are several ways in which residential burglaries are first discovered, ultimately prompting a first response to the crime scene. Most common is the situation where residents of the burglarized dwelling notice that their house has been broken into either by (1) observing some exterior breakage to doors or windows or (2) noticing items missing inside the home. Neighbors, passers-by, or triggered alarm systems are other means by which a residential burglary is often initially identified and brought to the attention of the first responder. When responding to a residential burglary, the scene care should approached as quietly as possible—without compromising the safety of others—so as not to alert the burglar of an approaching police vehicle. Once at the location of the call, the scene should be treated as an "in progress" call, always assuming that the burglar is still on the premises, and armed and dangerous. This is especially important with silent alarms where the burglar, if present, has no idea that police are responding. At locations known for frequent false alarms, first responders should never automatically assume that the call is just another bogus one—this time, it may be a "live" one.

When approaching the scene, responding units should make careful observations of persons or vehicles in and around the call location. Burglars working alone often park their vehicles, which may be stolen and cold plated, a distance away from the residence they target. Those working with others in a team usually have a second vehicle in the area, either parked or circling, to pick up the burglar from the scene. This pick-up vehicle may be stolen as well and is perhaps a truck, van, or larger passenger car capable of carrying large items from the target residence. Burglars working in teams also may have spotters or persons on the lookout for police vehicles approaching the scene. The spotters usually warn the burglar by using walkie-talkies, cell phone calls, horn honking, whistling, or yelling. Burglars who exit the scene may run if startled, but many walk slowly away so as not to attract attention. Often, they carry some type of bag or a bed or pillow case stuffed with stolen items beneath their clothing. When walking from the scene, many burglars act as if they belong in the neighborhood by faking entry into a parked vehicle, going to a neighboring home and acting as if they belonged there, entering a car with an accomplice, or sitting on a bus bench. In short, many burglars will remain at the scene and lay low, trying to fit in with their surroundings to avoid recognition by police or others.

Ideally, two or more units should respond to the burglary call. The strategic location of each unit should allow officers to observe all sides of the residence as well as streets and walkways coming and going from the call location. The scene should be approached simultaneously from the front, back, and sides. Single officers responding to a burglary scene should remain outside the location and examine the exterior of the residence for a possible place of entry. Windows, doors, and walls should be examined for points of entry; and attic and basement areas, and especially roofs, for cut holes and broken skylights. Actual entry into the residence should be done using a sequential method whereby each room, beginning with the front door, is cleared before proceeding to the next. Persons present in the home should be asked to exit to the exterior of the premises before the search is conducted. When available, a canine unit provides the most certain method for clearing the location of possible hidden burglary suspects before entry. If alarms are activated, notify the owner or the alarm company to deactivate the system.[5]

PRELIMINARY BURGLARY INVESTIGATION

Depending upon the size and policies of the particular agency where a residential burglary has occurred, the initial investigation may be performed by personnel assigned to specialized burglary investigative units or may be handled entirely by the first responding patrol officer who is trained in burglary investigation techniques. Once the residence is deemed secure and safe for entry, a walk-through of the burglarized premises must be undertaken by the investigator(s) to identify the following key behavioral elements and physical evidence of the burglary crime scene:

- Point of entry
- Point of exit
- Items stolen and offender behavior
- Evidence collection and documentation
- *Modus operandi* and signature
- Potential suspect profile/leads
- Preventative victim education

THE BURGLARY WALK-THROUGH

The burglary walk-through should focus on identifying the offender's point of entry and exit, *modus operandi*, items stolen, signature behaviors, and the collection and documentation of crime scene evidence. When and where possible, the walk-through should enlist the help of either the burglary victim or, if the victim is unavailable, another person who has knowledge of the victimized premises. Quite frequently, burglary victims or witnesses are the first to discover the points of entry and exit. Thus, they can lead the investigator to these locations, saving considerable investigative time and effort. (In these situations, however, other possible undiscovered points of entry or exit should still be searched for both outside and inside the victimized residence to validate any victim or witness observations.) The burglary victim's assistance is also essential for identifying specific stolen items and for determining their approximate value. In addition, victims will perhaps recognize **extra-burglary factors**—behaviors unrelated to the actual taking of property that are carried out at the crime scene. Examples include moving furniture and other household goods, turning lights on or off, eating food, watching television, or other offender actions above and beyond those needed to actually carry out the burglary.

Before commencing the walk-through, victims should provide information regarding any items touched, doors closed, surfaces cleaned, or other changes and possible alterations made to the crime scene before the walk-through. In addition, victims should be advised to avoid disturbing any potential evidence by (1) watching where they walk on floors or pathways and (2) not using their hands to make physical contact with anything in the crime scene area. Any pets present should be secured in areas away from potential sources of physical evidence.

Point of Entry

The investigation should start with a detailed examination of the burglarized residence for the likely **point of entry**—simply put, a location used by the offender(s) to enter the residence. Generally, only one point of entry will be evident even if two or more burglars have victimized a single home. When force is used to enter a home, which occurs in roughly 70 percent of all burglaries, the point of entry is quite easily determined. Most forced entries are carried out by unsophisticated methods such as (1) pushing open an unlocked door or window, or (2) using a screwdriver or pry bar to jam open a door or window that has a weak or malfunctioning locking mechanism. More aggressive entries, which are less frequent, are even more easily identified because they usually leave behind broken glass windows or kicked-in doors in what is known as a **smash and grab** burglary. If there is no sign of forced entry, the point of entry is almost invariably a door or window that has simply been left open. It is also possible that a person possessing a copied key, entry code, or electronic garage door opener simply opened a locked access area. Specialized burglary tools also may have been used to pick a lock. On rare occasions, a burglar may remove a window air conditioner to crawl through the open space where it was located, or have a child crawl through a pet-door to gain entry and then open a locked door from inside the home. Popular point of entry locations include garage doors (when left open); doors and windows obscured from view by walls, partitions, or overgrown landscape; doors and windows located on the side or rear of a home; sliding glass doors; and basement doors or windows. Exotic points of entry such as broken rooftop skylights, holes cut in structures, or punched-out walls are infrequent and are usually the work of an experienced professional burglar.

HOT TIPS AND LEADS 13.1

Methods of Entry

Many methods of entry are used by burglars. Some leave obvious signs indicating a point of entry, while others do not. These include the following:

METHOD OF ENTRY	EXAMPLE
Signs of Entry:	
1. Shouldering/Kick-in:	Smash in door with shoulder or kick door with foot
2. Breaking Small Door Windows:	Break glass, reach through window, and unlock door
3. Use of Glass Cutter:	Cut glass in glass door/window near lock with tool
4. Smash and Grab:	Throw brick, rock, or other object through window
5. Prying:	Use screwdriver or pry bar to force open door/window
6. Transom Entry:	Remove air conditioning unit and enter through hole/duct

(Continued)

METHOD OF ENTRY	EXAMPLE
No Signs of Entry:	
1. "Beeping":	Open garage door after cloning garage door opener code
2. Alarm Bypass:	Defeat alarm system before entering door or window
3. Lock-in:	Hide inside building until locked in after closing time
4. Picking:	Use burglary tools to unlock door through key opening
5. Key Entry:	Use stolen or discovered key to unlock door
4. Door Knob Check:	Go through apartment complex looking for unlocked door[6]

Point of Exit

The **point of exit**, or the location from which the burglar(s) permanently flee(s) the crime scene, may or may not be the same location as the point of entry. This location is usually a door or window opened by the offender from the home's interior without use of force. Typically, burglars who enter through windows exit through doorways because they may provide easy access to hidden alleyways as well as more sizeable openings through which larger stolen goods can be passed. Absence of such a second exit route usually indicates that the entry and exit points are one and the same. This usually occurs when burglaries involve a large door, such as an attached garage door or a rear sliding door, as a point of entry. Victims should be asked to recall whether or not specific doors or windows were locked before the burglary just in case the offenders obscured their exit point by closing a door or window upon leaving the residence.

ITEMS STOLEN AND OFFENDER BEHAVIOR

From the point of entry, a detailed room-by-room search should be conducted to determine specific stolen items and to identify out-of-the-ordinary circumstances that suggest the offender's behavioral patterns. The victim should also take informal notes on which items were stolen to help compile a formal **stolen property list** to be provided at a later date to police and insurance agencies. A **sequential search** approach is preferable if the burglar seems to have entered many rooms and opened drawers or ransacked the premises. This technique first involves a cursory search of all areas of the home for openly visible items that have been stolen, without disturbing the existing order of the crime scene. Second, a more detailed search for evidence may then involve moving furniture, opening drawers and closets, or removing room fixtures from their original locations. Last, a most detailed search can be performed by carefully and methodically removing contents within drawers, cupboards, toolboxes, shelves, and storage locations. Field notes, evidence markers, and photographs should be taken at each stage of the sequential search.

Offenders' movement patterns vary markedly depending on the offender's sophistication and the architectural design of the burglarized residence. Most burglars, however, attempt to steal the greatest number of items of the highest street value, while expending the least amount of time and effort. Offenders often avoid utility and children's rooms, moving directly to the master bedroom in search of jewelry, guns, and money as illustrated by the crime scene photo of a residential burglary presented in Figure 13.2. They know that many people still hide money and other valuables under mattresses, in underwear drawers, or beneath objects on shelves in clothes closets. Guns also may be hidden in this bedroom for protection purposes. Often, kitchens are the second most favorite target of burglars. Again, burglars know that many people hide money and other valuable small items in freezers, refrigerators, or food pantries within security containers that look like drink cans, food packages, or frozen food containers. Home offices are targets primarily because they may contain items related to the personal identity or finances of the persons living in the home. Passports, cell phones, laptops, personal IDs, credit cards, bank statements, keys, safe deposit box information, telephone lists, and addresses are just some of the many specific items that make home offices an attractive target for burglars. Bathrooms also may be secondary targets because of medicine cabinets containing prescription medications.

FIGURE 13.2 ▶ Often, personal documents are just as valuable to the burglar as money, jewelry, and electronics.

TABLE 13.2 BURGLARY OFFENDER AND VICTIM BEHAVIORS

OFFENDER/VICTIM BEHAVIOR	PERCENTAGE OF CASES
Offender Forcible Entry:	
Door	73.4%
Window	48.8%
Offender Unlawful Entry:	
Unlocked door/window	39.5%
Open door or window	17.2%
Had key	7.9%
Picked lock	4.1%
Victim Activity at Time of Break-in:	
Working or on duty	25.1%
Leisure activity	23.3%
Shopping/errands	6.7%
Sleeping	5.5%
Victim's Property Stolen by Offender:	
Electronics	32.6%
Personal items	30.7%
Purse, wallet, credit cards	28.8%
No items taken	25.2%
Household items	22.2%
Jewelry, watches, keys	13.2%
Cash	5.5%
Firearms	3.5%
Food/liquor	3.4%
Victim's Reasons for Not Reporting:	
Minor crime	29.5%
Police could not solve case	17.9%
Police would not bother with case	14.6%
Protection of the offender	2.3%

Source: Bureau of Justice Statistics (2010), *Victimization During Household Burglary* posted at bjs.ojp.usdoj.gov/content/pub/pdf/vdhb.pdf

Most burglars spend 10 minutes or less in any particular residence, and they focus their behavior on the task of stealing. Some offenders, however, appear to spend much more time in the execution of their burglaries and engage in behaviors seemingly unrelated to the act of stealing. Some of these behaviors that may be evident at the crime scene include drinking water or other beverages, eating food, using telephones, watching television, using the toilet, wiping hands on cloth or paper towels, using writing utensils, and acts of vandalism. Also, discarded litter from the offender containing biological evidence, such as saliva in chewing gum or mucus in toilet tissues, has been found at crime scenes and has been used successfully to prosecute offenders.

EVIDENCE SEARCH AND COLLECTION

The basic methods used to collect and document evidence in a burglary crime scene are similar to those used for other crimes where a distinct location of the criminal activity can be identified. A burglarized residence, however, may not have a well-defined primary crime scene where the bulk of physical evidence is centrally located. Typically, the search for and collection of evidence begins at the designated point of entry. It is there that the burglar must have made some type of physical contact, leaving, at the very least, trace evidence. The exact type of evidence to be found, however, will depend largely on the method of entry used by the offender.

Entry points showing no signs of force should be examined for fingerprints in areas where contact was required to open or move an object such as a handle or lock. Areas around the point of entry should also be careful inspected where the offender may have applied leverage to an object such as a wall or doorjamb to slide through high windows or restrictive openings. Hairs; clothing fibers; bodily fluids; footwear impressions; dirty handprints; and even personal items such as matches, keys, coins, and papers may have been unwittingly left behind by the offender while attempting to enter the residence.

Figure 13.3 represents a crime scene photo of a burglary involving tools to carry out a forcible entry. In scenes such as this one, tool marks often are identifiable when force has been applied by hammers, screwdrivers, or pry bars to break open a lock. Channel locks (pliers) and pipe wrenches used to "twist" open a lock by applying force to a door knob usually leave impressions of the tool's gripping surfaces on the knob itself. Photographs of these marks and perhaps even castings made from dental stone or gel could help identify tools used in a burglary. These tools could be recovered from suspects later, or perhaps from other persons and locations identified through a follow-up investigation or other law enforcement action. In a smash and grab, the burglar, by using a hand to break a pane of glass, may deposit blood on surfaces or glass fragments in the area of the breakage. These areas should also be examined for such evidence and for fibers from clothing or other material

FIGURE 13.3 ► Broken lock and metal door displaying various tool marks.

objects used to shield hands and arms from cuts when the glass was broken.

Entry areas where doors have been kicked in or broken in by **shouldering** (see Figure 13.4) should be examined for shoe impressions on the door's exterior surface and on the ground area below the door. The approach to the point of entry on the exterior of the residence also should be examined for footprints and other signs of physical evidence. Often an offender will test several doors and windows before finding the one that provides the easiest and safest place for entry. Neighbors should be interviewed to determine whether they saw any persons entering the burglarized residence or heard sounds produced by the break-in.

From the point of entry, the evidence search and collection process should proceed along the likely path taken by the offender during the burglary. In the obvious case, this path will be quite visible by observing the sequence of items stolen, the rooms entered, or furniture and other household items that have been disturbed, broken, or misplaced. The steps and movements of the offender should be carefully retraced, and the victim consulted to uncover locations and items of potential physical evidence. Latent fingerprints are often discovered in places that show signs of touching, and those that do not. Often, the offender attempts to open a locked drawer or to remove and replace an item—leaving fingerprint evidence in locations that otherwise appear to be undisturbed. Sketches should be made of the burglar's likely path of travel and of the particular evidence located and collected during the preliminary investigation. Any photograph obtained from the victim of the stolen items or of the home before it was damaged will prove invaluable for reconstructing the crime and for identifying items taken during the burglary.

At the point of exit, additional evidence may be discovered—for example, marks on the flooring from heavy items wheeled or dragged from their original locations to the exit area. Scuffs and other footwear impressions may be evident in the flooring, indicating the particular type of sole on the offender's shoes. Varying footprint patterns may also suggest that multiple persons carried out the burglary. The burglar's likely pathway when exiting the residence should be inspected for possible evidence. Sometimes burglars discard their break-in tools when leaving the crime scene so that they will not be found in their possession if they are stopped by police, as illustrated by the burglary crime scene shown in Figure 13.5. Neighbors or other persons within sight or sound of the offender's exit route should be interviewed to determine whether they noticed any suspicious persons, activities, or vehicles around the time of the burglary.[7]

FIGURE 13.4 ► Split door panel resulting from a forceful break-in.

FIGURE 13.5 ▶ Most burglars who use tools to gain entry carry nothing more than a single screwdriver, often leaving it at the scene to avoid detection if searched by police outside the crime scene.

NONRESIDENTIAL BURGLARIES

Approximately 30 percent of all burglaries are nonresidential. This type of burglary has many crime scene characteristics distinct from those discovered at the scenes of residential burglaries. Although the primary motive for these crimes is money, the methods that nonresidential burglars use to gain entry and transport goods are often much more sophisticated and better planned than those used by residential burglars. In addition, numerous targets and situations can be classified as a nonresidential burglary. Some of the more common types are discussed in the following sections.

Commercial Burglaries

Most jurisdictions legally define **commercial burglary** as "entry into a nonresidential structure to commit theft or any felony." This offense is generally considered a second-degree burglary and is punished less severely than similar acts committed against personal residences. Popular targets of commercial burglaries include stores and other retail establishments as well as warehouses. About 60 percent of these crimes, unlike those of a residential type, usually occur at night, when stores are closed or warehouses are unoccupied. Popular days and times to commit commercial burglary are between 12 AM and 4 AM on weekends and holidays when police may be distracted by a high volume of calls for service. Frequently stolen goods are ones that are small, valuable, and easily sold on the black market—such as electronics products, cigarettes, and drugs.

Commercial burglars can operate alone and make virtually no plans before striking. These spontaneous burglaries may simply involve a lone offender breaking a display window to do a smash-and-grab burglary. At these scenes, the victim's fingerprints and blood may be found and secured as physical evidence. Other less well-planned operations may employ a crude ram-raid break whereby a stolen car or truck is used to crash into front or rear doors to gain entry. These situations usually involve two offenders at the minimum, with one offender outside the location acting as a lookout and the second offender carrying out the actual break-in. More sophisticated, well planned burglaries may involve teams of five or more offenders who act as **frontmen**, who execute the break-in and theft of the good; **wheelmen**, who smash stolen vehicles into the target and transport goods away from the scene; and **spotters** posted outside the break-in location to watch for police or other persons responding to the crime.[8]

Typical tools used by commercial burglars include bolt cutters, wire cutters, tin snips, pry bars, screwdrivers, sledge hammers, drills, and sometimes welding torches. More professional offenders are undeterred by alarms and will either trip them (knowing that they have a limited amount of time before police arrive) or defeat them. Warehouses or electronics superstores in isolated areas or on the outskirts of cities are popular targets because offenders know that the police response time to a burglar alarm is often 10 minutes or longer. Offenders sometimes plan their burglaries by first taking pictures of the interior and alarm systems of the targeted commercial establishment. Thus, surveillance video should be examined for persons taking pictures throughout victimized locations. Occasionally, offenders photograph alarms or security cages that they are unable to defeat while carrying out a robbery as information for planning a second, more successful attack on the same premises later.

In most jurisdictions, shoplifting, credit card fraud, and other forms of larceny can be treated as a commercial burglary if an intent to commit a felony can be proven to exist at the time the offenders entered the establishment targeted for crime. Intent often can be proven by showing that the offenders worked as a team; possessed some type of tools, bag, or other apparatus to conceal stolen goods; or simply entered the store with no money, credit cards, or other means to make a purchase. In addition, the intent must be to commit any felony; thus, in the case of stolen property, the item(s) must have enough value to classify the crime as felony theft.

Safe, ATM, and Machine Burglaries

Countless machines and devices hold and dispense money and valuables that are targets of burglary. In the past, before automated teller and vending machines were common, safes were the primary targets of burglars with the intent of scoring large profits at one location. Safecracking is not as popular as it once was, however. In 2009, for the entire nation, the FBI reported only 29 offenses against banks where the M.O. was "cracking" a bank's vault or safe. Common methods of **safe burglary** include the following:

- **Punching:** The safe's dial is knocked off using a sledge hammer or hammer/chisel combination, and a punch is driven into the safe's locking device, causing it to fail.
- **Pulling:** A device is used to pull the combination dial away from the safe and expose the safe's locking mechanism.

- *Peeling:* Involves removing the exterior of the safe's door to access and defeat the safe' locking mechanism.
- *Ripping:* A chisel or other metal cutting device is used to "rip into" the safe's metal exterior.
- *Drilling:* Holes are drilled into the safe's dial to set the locking mechanism to open.
- *Burning:* A welding torch is used to cut into the safe's door and/or metal casing.
- *Blasting:* Explosives are used to blow open the safe's door or metal casing.
- *Carrying:* The safe is dislocated from its position, carried away, and opened at a different location.[9]

Ostensibly, the modern version of safecracking is **ATM burglary**. Many jurisdictions have passed laws making most attacks on ATM machines a specific form of burglary that carries punishments comparable to those for other commercial burglaries. ATM machines weigh between 300 and 800 pounds and can hold up to $200,000 in unmarked bills—although most carry about $35,000 in cash at any given time. Most ATM robberies are carried out by teams of two or more offenders who target freestanding units in convenience stores or gas stations. Wall-mounted bank ATM units are not targeted as often because they are more difficult to defeat or dislodge from their secured locations. Typically, ATM burglaries are executed using a ram-raid technique. This usually involves backing a stolen truck—either a flat-bed or a box style with a hydraulic lift—to the front door of the targeted establishment. Then, one of the offenders smashes the glass windows of the store, gains entry, and attaches chains to the ATM machine. Within minutes or even seconds, the truck is accelerated, ripping the machine from the floor where it is bolted and dragging it—and any other object in the way—to the front of the store. It then is lifted into the truck and transported to another location where it will be opened by force, perhaps with explosives or cutting tools such as a rotary saw, blowtorch, thermal lance, or diamond-tipped drill. Many ATMs are now equipped with GPS tracking devices, sensors that sound loud alarms when the machine is tampered with, and exploding dye packs that leave stains on bills when the machine's money cassette is forcibly removed. Passive ATM burglaries also have been encountered by investigators, in which the offenders pose as technicians and simply remove the machine from its location, wheeling it away in the presence of public bystanders.

Other types of money and vending machines are targeted for burglary as well. These include soda, change, product vending, ticket dispensing, and other machines holding cash and/or merchandise. Burglaries executed against these types of machines are usually the work of lone offenders using unsophisticated forced entry methods—cutting locks with bolt cutters, smashing-and-grabbing glass or plastic doors, or prying doors open with crowbars. Some higher-end machines are equipped with alarm systems and security cameras that trigger when a rattling, tipping, or attempted break-in occurs.

Vehicle Burglaries

Theft of money or property from any vehicle is classified as a **vehicle burglary** when the offender formulates the criminal intent to commit a felony (usually grand theft) at the time an object is removed or taken from the vehicle's interior or trunk. Most jurisdictions require that the vehicle be locked to constitute the crime of burglary; otherwise, if unlocked, the crime would be a lesser charge such as trespassing or vehicle tampering. Many vehicle burglaries are executed by smashing out windows with rocks, tools, porcelain tops of spark plugs, or any other hard object located at the scene to gain entry. Figure 13.6 represents a crime scene photo of an auto burglary where window smashing was used to gain entry into the vehicle. Other offenders use more passive approaches like using a stolen key, a Slim Jim, or reaching into an open window to unlock a door—all of which satisfy the "break-in" requirement of most vehicle burglary laws.

Cars are the most common target of vehicle burglars. Many of these offenders are groups of amateur juveniles who target CD/DVD players, MP3 players, iPads, Smart Phones, wallets, purses, change,

FIGURE 13.6 ▶ A shattered window on a vehicle, as pictured here, is often the first piece of evidence needed to turn a simple theft charge into the more serious offense of auto burglary.

and other property that they can steal for personal use. Other car burglars are adults who target high-value items such as GPS devices, laptops, and dash-mounted entertainment systems. Often these individuals are high-rate offenders committing multiple car burglaries per day and targeting specific types of vehicles. Their motivation for theft may be money to help fuel their drug or alcohol addiction, gambling habits, or perhaps lavish street lifestyle. Popular locations for car burglaries include parking lots in shopping centers where recently purchased items are stored in vehicles; streets and lots near nightclubs where patrons may leave their wallets or purses in their vehicles before entering an establishment; parking areas in airports, train stations, and cruise terminals where travelers park for extended time periods; and parking areas where persons attending sporting events, theaters, and college classes leave their vehicles for a fixed amount of time.

Recreational vehicles and trailers also have become a growing target for vehicle burglars. Because these vehicles are a "home away from home" for many people, **RV burglaries** involve many of the same items that are stolen during residential burglaries. In particular, flat-screen TVs appear to be a very popular target for offenders striking RVs and trailers. Other items typically stolen from these vehicles include GPS tracking systems, back-up cameras, DVD/CD players, surround sound speakers, LP gas propane tanks, and money and valuables. Interestingly, persons operating methamphetamine laboratories have been linked to the purchase of stolen RV back-up cameras for spotting intruders around the lab's perimeter and propane tanks for storing gases needed to "cook" a batch of meth.

When new RVs are the target, offenders typically strike while the vehicles are parked in retail lots. They may case out the vehicles they intend to strike during the day when the lot is open. Some act as though they are potential purchasers of the units, entering the vehicles and leaving doors or window unlocked in anticipation of returning later at night to steal items from them. Also, while acting like legitimate shoppers, they may disconnect wires and mounting devices to make removal of anchored-down objects much easier and faster upon returning to burglarize the vehicle. RV and trailer parks, repair and accessory installation facilities, and public storage areas also are popular burglary locations for new and used recreational vehicles. Most of these offenses take place during nights and weekends, when lots and other places where vehicles are parked are either unattended or closed.

As mentioned in Chapter 12, big-rig trucks carrying trailers loaded with merchandise have been the object of armed robbers; however, when more passive methods short of hijacking the entire truck are used, the theft of loads from trailers is often classified as vehicle robbery. When truckers leave their loaded trailer unhitched in truck stop lots or other commercial parking areas, offenders may off load the trailers by breaking into their locked compartments and transferring the goods to another big rig or to several smaller trucks for transportation away from the burglary scene. In more daring crime situations, offenders hitch up tractors (sometimes stolen) to the parked trailers and drive them away to another location where the stolen goods are off loaded and shipped to other locations or perhaps stored. When the goods stolen are refrigerated perishable items, a vehicle burglary can turn into a homicide. For example, offenders who steal products such as food or drugs that can become tainted with deadly bacteria without proper handling will be held responsible for the deaths of persons who later consume the illegal goods.

Several investigative methods have proven effective at detecting and arresting vehicle burglars. First, simple surveillance of high-theft lots and other areas where car break-ins are prevalent can be implemented without high-cost equipment or detailed planning. If the appropriate technology is available, bait vehicles equipped with video surveillance and items to entice offenders, such as laptop computers, can also be used. Locations where offenders store stolen property, fences conduct operations, or trade routes of illegal property begin and end often are determined by delaying arrest of the vehicle burglary suspect who has stolen bait property containing a GPS tracking device. The property then can be tracked to various locations and persons conducting illegal activity. Unfortunately, vehicle burglaries, especially those from new cars and RVs, may in fact be inside jobs committed with the help of present or past employees working at the location of the theft. If this is suspected, in addition to doing background checks on employees, suggest to the owner that all employees be fingerprinted as a security measure. These prints can then be run through fingerprint databases, and the act of fingerprinting alone sometimes results in one or more employees quitting out of fear of being identified as the culprit.[10]

BURGLAR TYPOLOGIES

Investigative interviews conducted with convicted burglars have revealed that certain aspects of the crime scene may help determine the type of burglar who has committed a particular offense. In general, most burglary typologies include the following categories of criminals:

1. *The Professional Burglar:* These offenders tend to make their living primarily from money and valuables obtained from burglaries. They are older than other types of burglars, generally in their late twenties to early forties—although some have been known to be active into their sixties and beyond. The professional burglar's most notable characteristic is a relatively extensive planning of the burglary event and detailed knowledge of their criminal target or mark. Before committing a burglary, professional burglars gain information on the items to be stolen and their whereabouts at the location to be entered. Specific targeted items, such as large sums of cash, vehicles, electronic equipment, expensive jewelry, rare coins, stamps, antiques, or other collectibles, are high in value; other targeted items that are potentially high in value include credit cards; checks; information used for identity theft; and keys to safe deposit boxes, storage units, safes, other homes, and vehicles. The preferred method of entry for professional burglars is surreptitious in nature (i.e., neither forceful nor noticeable).

These offenders seldom use a ransacking technique, and days, weeks, or months may pass before the victim has even noticed that a burglary has taken place. For example, if jewelry is taken from a box, the box will be left in its original location so as not to raise suspicion; likewise, a few checks will be taken rather than the entire checkbook, or selected credit cards will be taken and not the entire wallet or purse they are contained in. Professional burglars are undeterred by reinforced locks, security doors, or alarm systems and may have prior experience as alarm installation technicians. These offenders commit crimes day or night depending on when they perceive the time is right to strike. They tend to commit only a few high-take burglaries per year, work alone to avoid partners who may inform police, use the same M.O. in all of their crimes, and have wide geographic distances between their targets—often travelling to different states or countries.

2. *The Semiprofessional Burglar:* These offenders attempt to make a living through committing burglaries, yet are not nearly as successful or skilled as professional burglars and may even be known by police for prior offending activity. Typically, they are older offenders, in their late twenties and beyond, and have acquired rather extensive criminal records of prior burglaries and other crimes—typically shoplifting, drug offenses, and arson. The semiprofessional typically uses a straightforward and obvious method of entry that could take the form of breaking small glass panes to access and open locks or prying open locked doors and windows with screwdrivers or other tools. Once the M.O. is established for this offender type, criminal record checks should be performed for prior crimes and arrestees matching the same M.O. within geographical areas in and around the burglary scene. Checks should also be made to determine whether older burglars with specific M.O.s similar to that discovered at the crime scene are currently on probation, parole, or have recently been released from a correctional institution.

3. *The Young Amateur Burglar:* This type of offender is usually in their late teens to early twenties and is often associated with a semiprofessional or professional burglar. In many respects, they are learning the trade to eventually become a professional who makes a living from committing burglaries. Older street gang members who are actively committing burglaries often enlist younger gang members as apprentices to perform break-ins for them. This is because the punishments for juveniles caught committing burglary are far less severe than those for an adult.

4. *The Juvenile Amateur Burglar:* These offenders are 16 years of age or less. They commit daytime burglaries for the most part, usually after school or on school holidays. They primarily enter through unlocked doors and windows, or perhaps with a key taken from the premises while visiting another adolescent who resides at the burglarized premises. Often, adolescent burglars operate in groups to target property of personal interest such as computers, cell phones, electronic games, CD/DVD players, and iPods. They also steal alcoholic beverages from refrigerators and other storage locations as well as

FIGURE 13.7 ▶ Amateur burglars, especially those that are drug addicted, are most likely to use crude forms of entry involving force such as kicking or shouldering open a door.

prescription drugs from medicine cabinets. Juvenile burglars usually live close to the locations they victimize and either use or store stolen items at their home.

5. *The Addicted Amateur Burglar:* This burglar type is addicted to alcohol and/or drugs. Typical drugs that they are addicted to include opiates, methamphetamine, and cocaine (especially rock cocaine). The addicted burglar is the least sophisticated of all burglar types. The burglaries are committed strictly for acquiring quick money to support addictions. Their method of entry is usually smashing in windows or kicking in and shouldering doors. As illustrated in Figure 13.7, broken locks or other securing devices at the point of entry often are discovered at the scene because addicted amateur burglars seldom attempt to conceal or destroy physical evidence left at the crime scene. If the target is a store or other commercial establishment, these burglars typically use a smash-and-grab technique, breaking a display window with a stone or other object to gain access to and steal the item of interest. When committing residential burglaries, the addicted burglar ransacks the premises and often steals change or other items of minimal value. Offenders stealing large quantities of change often use Coinstar and similar machines to convert the stolen coins to dollar bills. These offenders tend to operate in cycles, usually committing a series of burglaries in the same geographic area within a span of one to several days. As their addiction worsens, requiring stronger and more expensive doses of drugs, these burglars will increase their burglary activity and perhaps engage in street robberies as well.[11]

MARKETING STOLEN PROPERTY

Most thieves do not keep what they steal. In fact, most of them seek fast cash turnarounds for stolen goods in their possession. The average burglar holds illegally obtained property for no more than 1 to 2 hours after completing a theft, with most getting rid of their hot items in about 30 minutes. Approximately one out of every three burglars is drug dependent and in need of a quick fix (i.e., heroin and cocaine addicts) and need to convert their stolen property to cash because it will not usually be traded for drugs by dealers—most of whom operate on a cash-only basis. To facilitate a quick transaction, most burglars do not travel far from the scene before unloading their stolen property. In fact, clusters of burglaries in any area are a good indicator that the illegal market for the burglarized goods is in the same area.

Fences and Stolen Property

There are several means and markets by which burglars dispose of illegally obtained items. Most popular among these is the use of a **fence**, an individual who specializes in buying and selling stolen property. In effect, fences act as middlemen between burglars and other persons who purchase the illegal goods for personal use or perhaps to resell them through a legitimate market. Some fences deal only with persons with whom they have established trustworthy relationships to avoid being sold out by a client becoming a police informant. Some of these illegal marketing friendship networks are established within trades; for example, carpenters, plumbers, electricians who buy and exchange stolen tools and supplies; service industries, such as barbershops, beauty salons, nail parlors, small retail stores, restaurants, gymnasiums, parking lots, casinos, bars, and nightclubs, where business proprietors become familiar with regular clientele; and social organizations consisting of sporting teams, fraternities, sororities, car clubs, on-line social networks, and even charitable organizations. Other fences take a riskier approach and attempt to sell their stolen property to complete strangers. Most popular among these outlets are on-line sources such as e-Bay, Craigslist, Yahoo, and other Web-based classified advertising providers. At the street level, swap meets and taxi drivers are common fences for burglarized property. Fences tend to buy and sell items currently popular among average retail consumers, which can be sold fast and at a good price. They typically rely on the burglars' ability to spot, steal, and supply them with the "right" popular items, but they may also place orders with burglars to target specific items for which they have lined up buyers in advance. Fences can be classified as operating on one of three levels:

- **Level-1 Fence:** Thieves sell their property directly to a level-1 fence, who is often the owner of a pawnshop, jewelry store, or other seemingly legitimate business. The goods are then sold from the store, often mingled with legitimately purchased goods. They can also be resold to another fence. Level-1 fences may sell the goods at standard retail prices, or may sell them at considerably lower than retail prices to undercut their competitors.

- **Level-2 Fence:** Level-2 fences buy from level-1 fences, and operate more or less as wholesalers of the stolen goods. Then often launder the stolen goods by cleaning and/or repackaging them to make them look like they came directly from the manufacturer. Stolen car rings

often supply vehicles to level-2 fences for resale. In addition, rings involved in the theft of large quantities of electronics or even raw material may enlist the services of level-2 fences. These operations are very secretive and are rarely exposed through informants or other street-level law enforcement investigative efforts. Usually, they are discovered after detecting and gathering information from level-3 fences.

- **Level-3 Fence:** Level-3 fences act as distributers of stolen goods that they acquire from level-2 fences. They may attempt to market the stolen goods through black market avenues either domestically or internationally, but are just as likely to sell the stolen goods to legitimate retail establishments—including large chain stores and franchises. This type of fence may even attempt to sell property back to stores where the items were originally stolen. Stolen auto parts, personal care products, and even medications are some of the many illegally distributed items originating from level-3 fences that have resurfaced in legitimate establishments.[12]

Illegal Markets

Various illegal markets distribute and sell stolen goods for both fences and burglars who operate without fences or other criminal intermediaries. These are as follows:

1. **Commercial Fence Supplies:** Legitimate business owners are approached directly by fences who supply stolen goods that can be resold in their establishments. These shops include pawnshops, jewelry stores, and second-hand stores. They may also include on-line retailers who operate Web pages and action sites on e-Bay and related electronic sales networks.

2. **Commercial Sales:** Fences operate seemingly legitimate businesses as a front to sell stolen goods to consumers unaware that the products they are purchasing were obtained illegally. In other instances, items that fences are unable to sell in their retail establishments may be sold to other retailers or through other marketing outlets.

3. **Residential Fence Supplies:** Fences sell stolen goods directly from their residence. This method commonly involves high-volume sales of products such as electronics and tools at lower-than-market prices at shops set up in garages or other easily accessible residential locations. Many work trucks and cars coming and going from a specific residence often indicate a residential fence. Fences may also use homes as warehouses for stolen goods distributed via the Internet.

4. **Network Selling:** Stolen products are passed through a network of individuals, perhaps working in a ring, whereby each person taking possession of stolen items increases their purchase price before handing them off to the next buyer.

5. **Hawking:** Burglars sell stolen products directly without a fence or other middleman. This typically involves selling the items to friends, at clubs, to drug dealers, to strangers on the street, or, in rare cases, on the Internet.

6. **e-Fencing:** Stolen goods are sold through Internet sources such as e-Bay and Craigslist, or they may be sold to another party, who later places the stolen goods for sale on the Internet. Some e-fencing is conducted by individuals who begin by selling legitimate products, then become hooked on the Internet sales process and inadvertently become full-fledged fences. This occurs when persons eventually run out of legitimate products to sell and then enlist the help of boosters (shoplifters) or burglars to provide them with illegal products to keep their business operational.[13]

Investigative Tactics

Nearly all jurisdictions have laws specifically prohibiting professional fencing activities, or at the very least statutes making it illegal to knowingly, buy, sell, possess, receive, or conceal any stolen goods or property. To invoke such laws against fences, burglars, and others suspected of peddling stolen property, the following must be proven:

- The stolen goods were received and controlled by the person(s);
- The illegal merchandise was stolen at the time it was received by the person(s), and;
- The person(s) knew at the time they received the property that it was stolen.

Surveillance, informants, baiting, electronic tracking, false store front operations, and undercover buys and sells are often productive investigative methods for establishing these legal requirements. In addition, various databases are available to perform background checks on persons and property suspected of involvement in fencing or other illegal property activities. Many jurisdictions have pawnshop and secondhand store databases with information about items sold and persons selling them—sometimes including fingerprints of the selling individual(s). Texas and Florida also have public databases including information on possible stolen property listed through on-line websites. Other red flags that a person may be selling or receiving stolen property include the following:

- Property is sold for prices far below fair market value.
- Serial numbers on products have been removed, changed, or scratched out.
- Original paperwork, instructions, or owner's manuals are missing.
- The item is repackaged, repainted, or otherwise altered from its original appearance.

- Sellers or buyers appear nervous and are not able to clearly state where or from whom they purchased a suspected stolen item.
- Persons selling or purchasing property do not offer or ask for a sales receipt.
- Property is purchased from strangers selling on the street, door-to-door, or from roving vehicles.

BURGLARY PREVENTATIVE MEASURES

Most burglary victims make changes in their homes, businesses, and lifestyles to avoid becoming revictimized. Occasionally, victims do not learn from past mistakes and become multiple victims of burglary. For these individuals, investigators must provide information on preventative measures that can be taken to avoid future victimization. Because burglary is largely a crime of opportunity, there are various ways of "opportunity blocking" would-be burglars by increasing the effort and risks, and reducing the rewards that they would receive by targeting a specific residence or business location:

1. Increasing the Burglar's Effort:
   - **Target Hardening:** This involves making it more difficult for targeted stolen items to be taken from their physical locations. Bolting down safes, placing security chains on the bottom of ATM machines, locking up valuables in secure locations, and placing steel poles in paths leading to front doors to prevent ram-raids are examples of hardening soft targets.
   - **Access Control:** Making it harder for burglars to access targeted stolen items is the point of access control. For example, persons entering parking facilities for loaded big rigs are screened by ID badges, PIN-controlled access gates, and similar means of identification. Likewise, security cages can be installed within stores to protect targeted items such as expensive electronics and drugs.
   - **Controlling the Facilitators:** Facilitators are weapons, tools, or other devices that make stealing property easy and should be removed. For example, ladders should be removed from the outside of houses with second-story windows. Similarly, loose bricks and stones should be removed from the front of stores with window displays.

2. Increasing the Burglar's Risks:
   - **Improving Security Systems:** It is well known that burglars select residences and businesses with either poorly constructed security systems or none at all. Silent and audible alarms, CCTV, pressure pads, and infrared motion detection devices are security improvements that can be made at reasonable cost to home or business owners.

- *Improving Natural Guardianship:* This involves making changes to improve the natural "eyes and ears" of physical locations targeted by burglars because they feel others will not see or hear them when they conduct a break-in. Improving lighting, removing large shrubs and trees blocking views of doors and/or windows, and conducting neighborhood watches are some examples of this opportunity blocking technique.

3. Reduce the Burglar's Rewards

- *Reducing the Value:* Items not readily identifiable as stolen properties have the most value to burglars and fences when resold through illegal markets. Marking personal items with names, numbers, or other IDs using etching devices or permanent ink greatly reduces their street value and may cause thieves to think twice before taking such items in a burglary.

- *Removing the Inducements:* Certain forms of property are attractive targets to burglars. These include particular makes of vehicles, vehicle accessories, types of watches and jewelry, and electronics. Removing or securing these highly desirable items may change a situation that

otherwise would attract a burglar to a given location. For example, car thieves may be attracted to a specific residence that has an RV filled with electronics parked in its driveway. The burglars sometimes not only victimize the RV, but also break into houses in the same neighborhood after noticing other opportunities. Thus, high-profile single inducements such as the RV should be removed to a secured storage area to prevent burglaries of the entire neighborhood.[14]

RECONSTRUCTING A RESIDENTIAL BURGLARY CRIME SCENE

Case Example 13A illustrates a residential burglary scene in Figures 13.8 to 13.18. Reconstructing this crime scene will require an investigation that identifies the burglar's entry and exit points and the stolen property, and processes the scene for physical evidence. In addition, the investigation will require the identification of witnesses, who may have observed or heard suspicious activities before, during, or after the burglary.

CASE EXAMPLE 13A

Residential Burglary Crime Scene

FIGURE 13.8 ▶ Residents of the home shown here left a second-story window open during the day while at work, believing that the window was out of the reach of potential burglars. What initial steps should first responders to this suspected burglary incident take to secure the crime scene? If the residents of this home are at the scene, what should they be instructed to do?

FIGURE 13.9 ▶ In the initial stages of inspecting the scene, investigators discover the open window with a ladder beneath it. Of what significance is this discovery to the investigation? What, if any, evidence should be collected from this location?

FIGURE 13.10 ▶ Room A: Ransacked bedroom area #1. Investigators conduct a sequential search of the home, beginning in this room. How should the search proceed?

FIGURE 13.11 ▶ Room A: Ransacked bedroom area #2. As the search continues to the other side of the room, investigators observe what appears to be an open jewelry box on the bed. What should be done by investigators to determine if this box is of value for evidence purposes?

FIGURE 13.12 ▶ Room A: Ransacked bedroom area #3. Continuing the sequential search to a large dresser in the room, how should the search proceed to gather any possible evidence from this location?

FIGURE 13.13 ▶ Room B: Ransacked bedroom area. After comparing the scenes in rooms A and B, does there appear to be a clear modus operandi of the offender? Has the offender left any type of behavioral signature? Does the offender appear to be a professional or amateur burglar?

FIGURE 13.14 ▶ The sliding glass door was discovered closed, but unlocked. The residents informed the investigators that they had locked it before leaving home. As a probably point of exit, how should investigators process this area for possible evidence?

FIGURE 13.15 ▶ Alleyway directly behind the burglarized residence. A package of cigarettes is discovered on a possible exit path taken by the burglar. What should be examined or search for at this location?

FIGURE 13.16 ▶ Close-up of cigarettes located next to the trash cans. Of what use is this package of cigarettes as potential evidence for developing a suspect lead?

FIGURE 13.17 ▶ Gloves discovered in the alleyway. What possible evidence could be obtained from these gloves if, in fact, they were used to carry out the burglary?

FIGURE 13.18 ▶ Screwdriver discovered beside the gloves in the alleyway. Can this screwdriver be used in the investigation of the burglary? What final steps should be taken by investigators before releasing this crime scene? In a follow-up investigation of this burglary, what steps can be taken to possibly identify the whereabouts or to recover any of the stolen property?

Summary

1. **The legal definition of burglary.**

   The offense of burglary, according to most state laws, is proven when available evidence can demonstrate that the following elements have been met: (1) breaking or opening of an inhabited location intended to remain closed from intrusion to preserve privacy or security, and (2) entering a physical area or space of a another person's dwelling with the intent to commit any felony (grand theft, in most cases).

2. **Burglar typologies.**

   There are five typologies of burglars: (1) the professional burglar, recognized by a well-planned break-in, surreptitious entry, and the theft of large-value items; (2) the semiprofessional burglar, an older offender conducting less well-planned burglaries than the professional type, and perhaps known to police; (3) the youthful amateur burglar, who often serves as an apprentice to professional and semiprofessional burglars; (4) the juvenile amateur burglar, usually under the age of 16, who targets households in his or her own neighborhood; and (5) the addicted amateur burglar, who performs crude break-ins to steal property to buy drugs or alcohol to support an addiction.

3. **Types and methods of burglary.**

   Residential burglaries involve either forcible or unlawful entries into homes, apartments, and other personal dwellings. Varieties of nonresidential burglaries are break-ins of commercial establishments, stores, ATM machines, safes, vehicles, banks, and other buildings where money, goods, and valuables are stored. Aggressive entries to homes or businesses characterized by broken glass windows or kicked-in doors are known as *smash-and-grab burglaries*.

4. **Illegal markets used to distribute and sell stolen property.**

   Six primary markets are used to sell and distribute stolen property: (1) commercial fence supplies, where a *fence* buys stolen goods from burglars and sells them to stores and other outlets; (2) commercial sales, where the fence sells stolen goods directly from a retail outlet; (3) residential fence supplies, where the fence sells stolen items from his or her personal residence; (4) network selling, where the fence sell stolen property through a network of friends or associates; (5) hawking, where the burglar sells stolen goods directly without the use of a fence; and (6) e-fencing, where Internet sources such as eBay and Craigslist are used to sell stolen property.

Key Terms

residential burglary
extra-burglary factors
smash and grab
point of entry
point of exit
sequential search
shouldering
burglary

frontmen
wheelmen
spotters
ATM burglary
vehicle burglary
RV burglary
safe burglary
commercial burglary

professional burglar
semiprofessional burglar
young amateur burglar
juvenile amateur burglar
addicted amateur burglar
fence
hawking
stolen property list

Review Questions

1. How is the crime of burglary defined by law?

2. What are the differences between first- and second-degree burglary?

3. What are the general characteristics of a residential burglary?

4. How should the walk-through of a burglary scene be conducted?

5. What types of physical evidence should be looked for at a residential burglary scene?

6. Describe the various methods of entry used by burglars in residential burglaries.

7. What are the various typologies of burglars?

8. How does nonresidential burglary differ from residential burglary?

9. What are some of the various forms of nonresidential burglary?

10. What is a fence? What are the various levels of fences?

11. Name the various illegal markets used to sell and distribute stolen goods.

12. What measures can be taken to prevent burglaries for occurring?

Internet Resources

Center for Problem-Oriented Policing
Situational Crime Prevention
NCVS Burglary Statistics
Property Crime Investigators (NAPRI)

www.popcenter.org
www.popcenter.org/25techniques
bjs.ojp.usdoj.gov/index.cfm?ty=pbtp&tid=321&iid=1
www.napri.org/alliances.php

Applied Investigative Exercise

Imagine that you have been assigned to investigate the burglary in Illustrated Case 12A. Explain the procedures you would take to identify the burglar's entry and exit points at this scene. In addition, explain the special investigative procedures you would perform when processing the burglary crime scene. Based on the available evidence, attempt to ascertain whether the burglary is the work of an amateur or a professional offender.

Notes

[1] Federal Bureau of Investigation, *Uniform Crime Reports 2009*, posted at www.fbi.gov/stats-services/publications.

[2] Legal definitions of robbery provided in this section were derived from CAL. PEN. CODE § 459 and similar sections of penal codes from the states of Flor-ida, Washington, Georgia, and New York, in addition to the legal definition of robbery provided in Black's Law Dictionary [see Bryan A. Garner (ed.), *Black's Law Dictionary*, 9th ed. (Eagan, MN: West Publishing, 2010)].

[3]Federal Bureau of Investigation, *Uniform Crime Reports 2009.*

[4]Investigative procedures appearing in this section are based on the authors' field experiences.

[5]Ibid.

[6]Joseph Petrocelli, "Burglaries," *Police Magazine,* posted at www.policemag.com/Channel/Patrol/Articles/Print/Story/2010/01/Burglaries.aspx.

[7]Investigative procedures appearing in this section are based on the authors' field experiences.

[8]Ronald V. Clarke, *Burglary of Retail Establishments* (Washington, DC: Center for Problem Oriented Policing, 2002), 2–25.

[9]Charles R. Swanson, Neil Chamelin, Leonard Territo, and Robert Taylor, *Criminal Investigation,* 10th ed. (New York, NY: McGraw-Hill, 2009), 434–435.

[10]Investigative procedures appearing in this section are based on the authors' field experiences.

[11]This typology was created by the authors, but it is derived from Marilyn Walsh, *The Fence: A New Look at the World of Property Crime* (Santa Barbara, CA: Greenwood Press, 1977), 117–130.

[12]Michael Sutton, *Stolen Goods Markets* (Washington, DC: Center for Problem Oriented Policing, 2002), 1–18.

[13]Ibid.

[14]Suggested strategies in this section were derived from Ronald V. Clarke, *The Theory and Practice of Situational Crime Prevention,* posted at badlandsmm.files.wordpress.com/2011/06/clarke_theory-and-practice-of-situational-crime-prevention.pdf.

CHAPTER FOURTEEN

LARCENY-THEFT SCENES

Learning Objectives

After completing this chapter, you should be able to:

1. Summarize the trends and types of larceny theft.
2. Describe how larceny-theft investigations are conducted.
3. Describe the different types of fraud and how fraud investigations are conducted.
4. Know how cons, scams, and schemes are carried out and investigated.

Chapter Outline

INTRODUCTION

IN THIS CRIME SCENE—fully described in Case Example 14A later in this chapter—the offender appears to be a normal customer at an ATM machine. In reality, however, he is committing an act of larceny-theft known as **card trapping**. First, he will remove a customer's ATM card that is apparently stuck inside the machine—but really has been intentionally trapped by the offender, who has inserted a crude handmade device into the ATM card slot known as a *Lebanese loop*. Then, he will use the card immediately, perhaps at a nearby ATM, and draw out the card's cash limit; or even worse, take the card to another

more sophisticated offender, who will read financial information from the card's magnetic strip to drain the victim's entire bank account. This is only one of the many crimes classified as larceny-theft that will be discussed in this chapter. Although these crimes do not have the raw appeal of the "kick in the door" type of offenses discussed in earlier chapters, they are nonetheless a form of crime that many investigators believe to be the most harmful to victims and society. Billions of dollars are lost each year to frauds, scams, schemes, and other financial crimes. The potential criminal magnitude of one man employing a relatively simple con game is best illustrated by the so-called "fraud of the century" committed by Bernie Madoff, who bilked investors out of an estimated $60 billion dollars. Schemes such as Madoff's can be just as, or perhaps more devastating to victims than ordinary street crimes. The loss of lifetime savings, homes, credit ratings, retirement pensions, and even lives are just a few of the many catastrophic results in the lives of those targeted by financial thefts. Information presented in this chapter will assist investigators in detecting larceny-thefts and gathering key evidence to convict offenders who perpetrate these acts of financial greed.

THE CRIME OF LARCENY-THEFT

Legal Definitions

Crimes involving the taking of anything of value without the consent of its owner, with the intent to permanently deprive him or her of the value of the property taken, are classified as *larceny* or *theft*, or are referred to by a hybrid term such as **larceny-theft**, depending on the legal codes of a particular jurisdiction. The item of value can be tangible property, such as a stolen vehicle, or it can be intangible, such as an electronic transmission used to wire funds. When the crime is referred to as *theft*, as it is in most states, laws usually specify the nature and type of stealing activity, as the following examples illustrate:

- Theft of Services, e.g., pirating cable TV, phone, or other utilities
- Theft by Check, e.g., writing bad or forged checks for purchases
- Theft by Deception, e.g., making a false insurance claim[1]

States that employ the term *larceny* typically group crimes of stealing into broad categories based on how a particular item of value was stolen as follows:

- Larceny by Theft, e.g., taking and carrying away someone's property, as in the case of shoplifting
- Larceny by Trickery, e.g., posing as a salesman and conning someone to give you their property
- Larceny by Fraud, e.g., using a stolen credit card to make purchases, and other forms of identity theft[2]

In addition, the federal government has over 100 codes constructed for the enforcement of theft-related crimes, most of which fall within the general category commonly known as *white-collar crimes*. These include the following:

- Health Care Fraud, e.g., doctors charging insurance companies for medical procedures that they did not perform
- Theft of Trade Secrets, e.g., corrupt employees or organizations who sell product formulas, chemical compounds, plans for devices, or other proprietary information belonging to manufacturers, businesses, and corporations
- Anti-Trust/Price Fixing, e.g., individuals or businesses that work as a team to illegally inflate or deflate prices for products, thereby limiting competition in the open market for products and services

As the FBI has noted—providing a blanket definition of theft-related offenses that the agency investigates—criminal acts at the federal level commonly classified as larceny-theft are best described as criminal activities involving "lying, cheating and stealing."[3]

The Elements of Larceny-Theft

The crime of larceny-theft (with the term *theft* used hereafter to generically describe crimes of theft) is often confused with other property crimes, especially robbery and burglary. Unlike robbery, however, in larceny-theft no force or fear is used by the offender at the time the property is stolen. Similarly, unlike burglary, the offender does not have to break into or otherwise enter a location belonging to another individual with the intent to commit a theft. These legal distinctions between robbery and burglary are clear when considering the following three elements required for proving the crime of larceny-theft in most jurisdictions:

1. ***Taking:*** This element is proven by the removal of the property from its original location, usually in a manner that demonstrates the offender's control over the stolen item(s). Merely moving or resituating an item without removing it from where it is situated would not constitute the legal "taking" element of larceny. For example, a jewel thief who unfastens the clasp on a victim's diamond bracelet would not have completed the "taking" requirement until the bracelet is fully removed from the victim's wrist. In addition, offenders need not physically touch the property to meet the "taking" requirement—for example, money stolen by wiring funds from one account to another. Additionally, the offenders *in absentia* can enlist the help of a third party (who may or may not be aware of the criminal activity) to carry out a larceny-theft. Some jurisdictions require that the offender "carry away" stolen property in order for the crime of theft to be complete.

2. ***The Intent to Permanently Deprive:*** Intent is required for larceny-theft crimes, but the offender's mental state at the time of the act must be to permanently deprive the owner of the property taken. A common defense

used by persons accused of larceny-theft is that they were only borrowing the items taken. If it can be proven that the offender indeed intended to return the property taken, this crime becomes a form of theft legally referred to as *conversion* in most jurisdictions.

3. ***Having a Sufficient Value:*** The seriousness of a particular larceny-theft crime is usually determined by the value of the item stolen. This value is typically not the original purchase value, but rather the appraised value at the time of the theft. Some jurisdictions specify a two-level system for determining the seriousness of larceny-theft crimes. The most popular designations are the following:

   1. **Petty or "Petit" Theft/Larceny:** The taking of money and/or property of a nominal value—in many states below $400—which is considered a misdemeanor offense.

   2. **Grand Theft/Larceny:** The taking of money and/or property of a significant value—in many states above $400—which is considered a felony.[4]

Other jurisdictions create degrees of larceny-theft based on the specified value of the stolen items.[5] For example, Table 14.1 presents the state of Connecticut's degree-based legal code for the crime of larceny.

Nature and Extent of Larceny-Theft Crimes

In 2009, larceny-theft crimes comprised 67.9 percent of all property crimes. The average value of property stolen was $864 per offense, and the annual loss for all larceny-theft victims combined was nearly $5.5 billion. Similar to other property crimes,

larceny-thefts usually occur during the winter, especially in the months of November and December when more durable goods are sold and juveniles are on vacation for school holidays. The most prevalent forms of larceny-theft are thefts of property from motor vehicles (27 percent) and shoplifting (18 percent). The typical offender is White (70 percent), male (57 percent) and about the age of 18 years (76 percent). Approximately 1 out of 5 (or 21 percent of) larceny-theft offenses is cleared by arrest or by other means. Comparisons of crime rates between 2000 and the 2009 show that the overall level of larceny-theft offenses has been declining—roughly a 33 percent drop during this 9-year time period.[6] The statistical characteristics of larceny-theft offenses and offenders are presented in Table 14.2.

Larceny-theft is usually a crime of opportunity committed by amateur offenders. Most amateur property offenders begin their criminal activity at an early age, sometime in their early to mid-teens. They start by stealing items for personal use that they are unable to purchase due to their lack of income. Working alone

TABLE 14.1	STATE OF CONNECTICUT: DEGREES OF LARCENY	
DEGREE OF LARCENY	**AMOUNT OF PROPERTY INVOLVED**	**CLASSIFICATION**
First Degree	Over $10,000	Class B felony
Second Degree	Over $5,000	Class C felony
Third Degree	Over $1,000	Class D felony
Fourth Degree	Over $500	Class A misdemeanor
Fifth Degree	Over $250	Class B misdemeanor
Sixth Degree	$250 or less	Class C misdemeanor

Source: State of Connecticut Criminal Code, posted at www.cga.ct.gov/2012/rpt/2012-R-0134.htm.

TABLE 14.2	CHARACTERISTICS OF LARCENY-THEFT OFFENSES AND OFFENDERS				

Offenders:

RACE:		GENDER:		AGE:	
White	70%	Male	57%	Under 18	24%
Black	28%	Female	43%	18 and over	76%
Other	2%				

Offenses:

TYPE:		LOSS:	
Pick-pocketing	<1%	Over $200	45%
Purse-snatch	<1%	$50 to $200	23%
Shoplifting	18%	Under $50	32%
Theft from motor vehicle	27%		
Theft of motor vehicle accessories	9%		
Theft from buildings	11%		
Theft of bicycles	3%		
Other theft	31%		

Source: FBI, Crime in the United States, 2009. *All percentages are rounded to the nearest nondecimal value.*

and stealing a limited number of items per criminal incident are the earmarks of amateur thieves. Other, older amateurs may steal any items of value that are "easy takes" to support drug habits and other street lifestyles. Professional thieves, on the other hand, may work in teams and target specific items that are not for personal use but rather can be easily sold through illegal markets. They tend to concentrate their criminal efforts on high payoff/low risk of apprehension situations. Some very sophisticated thieves engage in high-level white-collar crime activities that require a thorough knowledge of intricate business practices such as stock trades, bank loan underwriting, and insurance claim procedures. Specialized investigative task forces who consult with industry insiders are usually assigned to handle such cases.

SHOPLIFTING

Shoplifting and Financial Losses

The crime of **shoplifting** typically involves offenders who enter a retail establishment, hide some type of property on their person, and leave the establishment with the property without paying the merchant as illustrated in Figure 14.1. There are other varieties of shoplifting, however. For example, most jurisdictions include the intentional failure to pay less than full price for an item by removing, altering, or switching price tags on property as a shoplifting offense. In food stores and retail outlets, shoplifting can occur when a patron eats or drinks products in the establishment and leaves without paying for them—an offense known as *dine and dash*. Also included within the realm of shoplifting are similar failures to pay hotels for rooms, bars for tabs, theaters for tickets, gas stations for gas, and so on. These are only a few of the many situations in which

FIGURE 14.1 ▶ A surveillance photo showing a suspect stealing electronics items. This image is one of many that can be found on police websites as part of a growing trend by law enforcement to enlist the public's help in identifying persons who commit crimes against retail stores. (Courtesy Los Angeles Police Department)

a merchant is not paid full price for products or services by shoplifting offenders. Shoplifting losses to merchants are approximately $33 billion per year, making this offense the most costly of all property crimes. Furthermore, this type of crime accounts for an estimated 30 to 40 percent of retail "shrinkage" or property losses—and in some cases forces the victimized retailer out of business.[7]

Shoplifting Offender Characteristics

As with nearly all crimes involving property, most shoplifters are amateurs and not professionals. About one out of every four thieves are between the ages of 13 and 17 years, with the bulk of shoplifting incidents (75 percent) being carried out by adults over the age of 18 years. Just about as many men as women are arrested for shoplifting offenses, although some statistics suggest that girl shoplifters outnumber boy shoplifters (55 versus 45 percent, respectively) at the juvenile age level. Most shoplifters strike their targets on either Fridays or Saturdays during the afternoon and early evening hours. The specific types of items targeted by shoplifters within specific types of retail establishments are presented in Table 14.3. Although many shoplifters cannot be placed into a specific group based on their offending behavior, some consistent qualities of many retail thieves enable them to be classified as follows.

Amateurs: Sometimes referred to by the term **snitch** (not to be confused with the *snitch* who informs police about others' criminal behavior), these offenders shoplift on impulse and steal items primarily for thrills and/or personal use. Specific classes of amateur shoplifters include the following:

- Juveniles who steal because of boredom or peer pressure to acquire items that will increase their status and popularity. Clothing, shoes, electronics, cosmetics, cigarettes, condoms, alcohol, and pornographic magazines are popular theft targets of juvenile shoplifters.
- Kleptomaniacs who steal because of a psychological compulsion to do so. Many target lingerie and men's and women's undergarments.
- Drug addicts who shoplift items to support a narcotics habit. These offenders are often noted for aggressive theft methods and violent reactions when approached or apprehended during their crimes.
- Vagrants who steal basic necessities for survival, such as food, alcohol, cigarettes, toiletries, etc. These types of shoplifters are commonly under the influence of alcohol during the commission of their crimes.[8]

Professionals: These shoplifters, also known as **boosters** or **heels**, tend to dress and talk in a manner that blends in with other patrons of establishments they target. Items they prefer to steal are high in cost and small in size. Multiple professional shoplifters may operate in rings and converge on individual stores or shopping areas. They often know how to defeat antitheft devices such as electronic labeling systems that trigger alarms when stolen property passes through theft detection gates at store entrances and exits.

TABLE 14.3 TYPE OF MERCHANDISE SHOPLIFTED, BY TYPE OF RETAILER

TYPE OF RETAILER	MERCHANDISE
AUTO PARTS	HARD PARTS
BOOKSTORES	ELECTRONICS, CDs, CASSETTE TAPES, VIDEOS
CONSUMER ELECTRONICS/COMPUTERS	PORTABLE CD PLAYERS, CAR ALARMS, CORDLESS PHONES
DEPARTMENT STORES	CLOTHING: SHIRTS
DISCOUNT STORES	CLOTHING: UNDERGARMENTS, COMPACT DISCS
DRUG STORES/PHARMACIES	CIGARETTES, BATTERIES, OVER-THE-COUNTER REMEDIES
FASHION MERCHANDISE	SNEAKERS
GENERAL MERCHANDISE STORES	EARRINGS
GROCERY STORES/SUPERMARKETS	OVER-THE-COUNTER REMEDIES, HEALTH AND BEAUTY AIDS, CIGARETTES
HOME CENTERS/HARDWARE STORES	ASSORTED HAND TOOLS
MUSIC	COMPACT DISCS
SHOES	SNEAKERS
SPECIALTY STORES	BED SHEETS
SPECIALTY APPAREL STORES	ASSORTED CLOTHES, SHOES
SPORTING GOODS	NIKE SHOES
THEME PARKS	KEY CHAINS, JEWELRY
TOYS	ACTION FIGURES
VIDEO STORES	VIDEO GAMES
WAREHOUSE	PENS, MOVIE VIDEOS

Source: Chamard, Sharon and Marcus Felson. 2011. Business Crime Prevention, San Marcos, TX: Texas State University, School of Criminal Justice. For further information, see Ronald V. Clarke, 1999. Hot Products. London: British Home Office, Police Research Series Paper 112. Reprinted by permission.

Shoplifting Investigative Methods

Most major retailers have either CCTV image recording cameras or private security personnel, or both, to combat shoplifters, which can provide investigative information on specific cases. Unfortunately, smaller establishments often do not have such devices to assist investigators in developing leads on possible shoplifting suspects. Consequently, most of these cases have to be solved by catching the thief in the act. When time and resources are available, a single investigator or an investigative team often can conduct surveillance or undercover activities in stores where shoplifting is frequent. Following are some of the more salient indicators to look for when attempting to identify potential shoplifting suspects:

- An umbrella, carried over the individual's arm, which is used to catch and conceal items dropped into them, or an arm sling used to store stolen items. Generally, any item carried by an individual can be used to conceal stolen property; for example, a shoplifter can drop stolen jewelry into a milkshake cup.

TABLE 14.4	SHOPLIFTING INVESTIGATIVE OUTCOMES, 2009
	2009
Apprehensions	1,014,817
Recoveries	$111,776,369
Avg. Case Value	$110.14
Hours Per Apprehension* (*12 companies reporting)	43.78
Recoveries (No Apprehensions Made)	$29,266,930

Source: Adapted with permission from Jack L. Hayes International, Inc., http://www.hayesinternational.com.

- Folded-up or rolled newspapers/magazines carried to conceal items placed within or beneath them
- Strollers and diaper bags used to conceal items beneath toys and other child care items they may normally contain.
- Large coats with holes cut through the pocket linings in which the shoplifter's hand can reach through the pocket, grab an item, and then pull it back and conceal it within the inner area of the coat. The offender often does this with one hand while the other holds a product to create the appearance of contemplating a purchase.
- Shopping bags from other stores used to store stolen items, often pushed below the surface of items legitimately purchased from other establishments.
- Entering fitting rooms or bathrooms with merchandise and leaving them without the items being present
- Stores with one employee who is asked by the offenders to look for merchandise in a store room or other out-of-sight area while the shoplifter steals items and leaves the store
- Persons who appear nervous and engage in a series of short conversations with other individuals in the store

- Wearing oversize clothing to perhaps conceal items or to go into fitting rooms or bathrooms to put stolen clothing on under the baggy outer clothing
- Persons placing large numbers of the same items in shopping carts, particularly ones that are small and expensive, or picking up and putting back a large number of items while pretending to be confused
- Strange behavior such as walking in an unusual manner (women may place items up their dress between their thighs—known as the **crotch walk**); abnormal rubbing of sleeves, neck, or legs; walking aimlessly around the same areas; or looking at the sales staff more often than at merchandise[9]

When fearing apprehension, shoplifters may drop the stolen items before leaving the store. Shoplifting laws in some jurisdictions allow such offenders to be arrested because all that is needed to complete the shoplifting crime is to carry the stolen items away from the original merchandising area. In other jurisdictions, the shoplifter may not be arrested until he or she leaves the store. Table 14.4 presents selected information on shoplifting investigative outcomes.

Employee Theft

Employees often are entrusted with the care of money or property in the establishments where they work, so they generally cannot be charged with shoplifting after stealing property in their workplace. Rather, they are charged with the crime of **embezzlement**, which is the use of money or property by the employee in a manner inconsistent with that specified by the employer; in other words, the employee violated the financial trust relationship established with his or her employer. Generally, the only thing needed to prove that embezzlement has occurred is evidence that the employee used or profited from mishandling items placed in his or her trust. Under some codes, embezzlement is restricted to the misappropriation of money, whereas the mishandling of property is considered **pilfering**. Employee theft and fraud result in approximately $50 billion in revenue losses among businesses nationally each year. Studies show that approximately 75 percent of all employees admit to stealing from their workplace at least once during their time on the job. Half of those employees who admit to stealing once claim to have stolen multiple times from their employer.[10]

HOT TIPS AND LEADS 14.1

Identifying Workplace Theft

Many theft cases are generated by employers filing criminal charges against employees suspected of stealing cash or merchandise on the job. When building a criminal case against suspected workplace offenders, investigators may observe various "red flags" during the investigative process that are suggestive of theft, fraud, embezzlement, or other financially motivated offending behavior:

- Sudden or unexplained changes in lifestyle; for example, an out-of-character purchase of new cars, boats, houses, jewelry, or clothing
- Evidence of increased personal debt and credit problems such as repossessions, bankruptcies, evictions, or creditors visiting the workplace

(continued)

- Behavioral changes: defensiveness, fear of job loss, isolation, secrecy
- Refusal to take vacation or sick leave
- Borrowing money from co-workers
- Easily annoyed at questioning; providing convoluted, illogical answers to job-related questions
- Bad credit rating due to late payments, unpaid bills, or excessive credit card and loan applications
- Regularly changing addresses, phone numbers, bank accounts, and other personal information provided to creditors and employers
- Social and/or workplace isolation from friends and co-workers

Generally speaking, the reasons underlying workplace theft involve one of three financial dilemmas faced by the employee:

1. *Extravagant Lifestyle:* Employees who live beyond their means may use theft as a means of making ends meet. Performing a net worth analysis to compare the suspect's expenses to his or her income generally reveals this type of motivation for workplace theft.

2. *Lifestyle Problems:* These are typically evidenced by some addiction in the employee suspected of theft. In short, workplace theft is a means of supporting the employee's addiction. Common lifestyle problems include alcoholism, drug abuse, and gambling. Employees usually do not communicate about their addictions with others, even with intimate friends and family members.

3. *Financial Problems:* Reductions in the employee's disposable income due to the following causes may serve as a motivation for workplace theft:
   - Divorce
   - Child support
   - Furloughs/pay cuts due to bad economic times
   - Car repairs
   - Family obligations
   - Spouse's job loss
   - Medical bills

IDENTITY THEFT

The altered birth certificate shown in Figure 14.2 is just one of the seemingly countless examples of how offenders carry out identify theft. Over 10 million persons become the victims of **identity (ID) theft** each year. The average amount of financial loss varies depending on how soon the ID theft is reported by the victim and how the offender uses the stolen ID. Before examining the specific crimes associated with ID theft, however, it is useful to understand the methods by which an identity thief illegally procures an individual's ID. Foremost among these methods are the following:

1. *Mail Theft:* Offenders (1) submit change-of-address forms to divert victim's mail containing financial information to new addresses; (2) steal credit card bills, prepaid credit offers, bank checks, and other financial information from incoming and outgoing mail; (3) steal mail from work in and out boxes or other business mail locations; (4) gather old bills and other financially oriented mail discarded in both indoor and outdoor trash receptacles, known as **dumpster diving**.

2. *Public ID Theft:* Offenders steal the victim's personal ID information in public places by (1) lifting names and social security numbers from employee badges, copying student IDs from examination/grade reports, recording personal information contained on checks, or using medical information provided by patients at doctors' or dentists' offices; (2) watching in on, listening to, or recording cell phone calls of persons providing security information during financial transactions such as retail purchases, billing disputes, or ATM transactions—referred to as **shoulder surfing**;

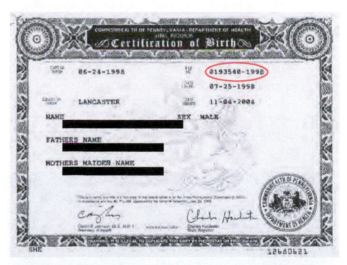

FIGURE 14.2 ▶ The starting point for many offenders attempting to assume a fraudulent identity is obtaining a fake birth certificate such as the one pictured here. Various standardized security features are built into real birth certificates that can be used to authenticate them. For example, most authentic U.S. birth certificates issued after 1948 contain a *state* or *area code* (in the area highlighted by the circle above) assembled in the following fashion: **123-95-789243** where the first three numbers ("123") are a code for the issuing state; the second two numbers ("95") are the year of birth; and the last six numbers ("789243") are the document's registration number. As this example shows, the creator of this fake birth certificate, similar to most other thieves, did not bother to follow the proper rules of certification, hoping that such mistakes would be overlooked by officials reviewing the document.

(3) using books and media that provide biographical and financial information.

3. ***Personal ID Theft:*** Offenders with access to personal records of individuals execute ID theft by (1) stealing co-workers' financial/human resource information; (2) taking personal information such as social security numbers, checking account statements, and other financial documents during a burglary; (3) obtaining children's social security numbers from school records, day care, and emergency medical information; (4) lifting personal information when invited into homes as visitors, or using financial information of friends and relatives; (5) pretending to be a government official or other legitimate party who needs financial information to process taxes, bank accounts, or credit; (6) stealing electronic devices containing personal information such as laptops, cell phones, iPads, and so on.

4. ***Electronic ID Theft:*** Offenders use computers, cell phones, and other electronic devices to steal personal IDs by (1) hacking into computers, cell phones, and other electronic personal storage areas; (2) sending legitimate-appearing e-mails directing users to phony web sites that ask for personal and financial information—known as **phishing**; (3) sending spam e-mails that promise prizes or cash rewards for providing financial/personal information; (4) sending fake IRS or other government forms via e-mail (the government does not request personal information via e-mail); (5) using a **pharm** technique in which an entire computer domain location is hijacked and used to gather information from users who believe they are communicating with their legitimate Internet service provider; (6) **skimming** information from the magnetic strip of credit cards, ATM cards, ID cards, driver's

licenses, and other items—usually carried out by corrupt merchants or other seemingly legitimate employees.[11]

Crimes Related to ID Theft

Usually, ID theft is only an initial crime that leads to many more offenses committed by the offender who stole the identification materials. Approximately 85 percent of the time, ID thieves will go on to commit additional financial crimes:

- Gaining access to existing credit card accounts: Use of stolen credit cards and associated identification materials represents the most prevalent type of crime committed following an ID theft. Approximately 60 percent of all ID theft offenders use stolen identification materials (including credit cards) to access existing credit card accounts. This is also the most costly form of ID theft, resulting in approximately $50 million in losses from the illegal theft of money and goods. The average loss per victim—about $4,800 per incident—is also the greatest among all types of ID theft.

- Opening new accounts in the victim's name: About 20 percent of all ID thefts result in the offender opening new credit accounts in the victim's name to obtain money loans and cash advances and to purchase goods. Approximately $33 billion per year is lost by offenders committing this type of crime following an ID theft. This illegal use of stolen IDs is also the most costly to victims, averaging $10,200 per incident.

- Other common forms of financial loss after an initial ID theft, according to the percentage of time they occur, include access to the victim's bank account (19 percent), access to the victim's telephone accounts (10 percent), and establishing real estate or auto loans (4 percent).[12]

(a)

(b)

FIGURE 14.3 ▶ (a) Real social security card under ultraviolet light. The center seal fluoresces along with random identifying marks called *planchettes* (as indicated by the arrows). (b) Fake social security card under ultraviolet light, without a fluorescing central seal or planchettes.

Following an ID theft, the stolen identification materials are used and often altered, such as the fake social security card illustrated in Figure 14.3, to commit crimes of a nonfinancial nature 15 percent of the time. This type of offense can be committed separately or in combination with the IDs used for financial gain. Following are common nonfinancial uses of stolen IDs:

- For illegal immigration purposes, e.g., false citizenship claims, obtaining medical or social assistance, applying for employment
- Obtaining government licenses, e.g., obtaining a fraudulent driver's license, vehicle registration, professional/employment certification
- Terrorism, e.g., purchasing firearms, obtaining passports, acquiring student visas, purchasing items used to create explosives or aid in terrorist attacks. Figure 14.4 illustrates how ALS (Alternate Light Source) is used to visualize an address markover on a mailing envelope containing contraband that was sent to a correctional facility.

In 1998, the Identity Theft Act[13] was passed, making identity theft a federal offense in cases where an individual:

knowingly transfers or uses, without lawful authority, a means of identification of another person with the intent to commit, or to aid or abet, any unlawful activity that constitutes a violation of Federal law, or that constitutes a felony under any applicable State or local law[14].

The Act was enhanced in 2004 to include enhanced penalties for acts of "Aggressive Identity Theft," which include the intentional theft and use of stolen IDs for acts of terrorism. ID theft investigations can be aided through access to the Federal Trade Commission's (FTC) Identity Theft Data Clearinghouse database, which houses case information on over 800,000 incidents of identity theft. Victim, offender, crime, and financial loss information is accessible and can be cross referenced by investigators who include their own cases for comparison. Unfortunately, however, only about 25 percent of all ID theft victims report their losses to police. To increase the percentage of incidents reported, investigators can assist ID theft victims in completing an Identification Theft Report (similar to a police report) provided by the FTC. This report, when presented by the victim, requires credit and financial institutions by federal law to immediately act to aid the victim. In addition, investigators can obtain the victim's identity theft–related financial records from creditors without a subpoena simply by proper authorization from the victim.[15]

CREDIT CARD AND CHECK FRAUD

Credit Card Fraud

Credit card fraud not only involves the illegal use of another person's credit card or credit card information, but also can be carried out by any person who fraudulently acquires a credit card. This type of larceny-theft is one of the simplest and most widespread forms of financial crimes. Following are M.O.s frequently used by offenders who commit credit card thefts:

- **Application Fraud:** This crime can be carried out in one of two ways. First, the offender can assume someone else's identity and simply apply for a new credit card, requesting that it be sent to a temporary, untraceable address. Persons who have recently moved are prime targets for offenders committing application fraud because banks cannot verify permanent addresses through voter registration records, utility bills, or other public records verifying mailing locations. Friends and family also may be used as assumed identities by persons committing application fraud. The second method, referred to as *financial fraud*, is committed by individuals who apply for credit cards under their own name and gain credit, or more credit than they are entitled to, by providing false pay stubs or other financial information that makes them appear highly creditworthy.
- **Interception:** This method is carried out by simply intercepting a credit card before the rightful owner can receive it, who may have applied for a new card or is receiving a replacement for a lost or expired card. Typically, offenders intercept credit cards in the mail but can also acquire them from corrupt bank or postal employees.
- **Lost or Stolen Cards:** This is by far the most common way in which thieves get their hands on credit cards to commit fraud. Most offenders will use the cards immediately to obtain cash advances and buy goods. They may also enlist the help of corrupt merchants to run the cards through their credit systems to assess credit limits and acquire cash.
- **Altered or Counterfeit Cards:** After acquiring a stolen credit card, the offender can destroy information contained on the magnetic strip by exposing it to

FIGURE 14.4 ▶ ALS lighting used to visualize a packaging label marked over with black ink.

a strong magnetic field, which forces the cashier to perform a transaction by using the card's numbers, which may be altered. Totally fake counterfeit cards also can be produced and used by employing this method.

- *Skimming:* Skimming involves using a battery-operated electronic device to read and record the electronic information contained on the card's magnetic strip. Corrupt cashiers can skim by pretending to swipe a customer's card to conduct a transaction. Skimming can also be performed to carry out an electronic pick pocket, whereby the offender waves the portable electronic card reader (concealed in a bag or carrying case) near the victim's wallet or purse to obtain the card's credit information. New smart chip technology also can be read with skimming devices, which can also reprogram the information on the credit card's information chip. In sophisticated cases, information from the magnetic strip on the card can be cloned and used to make counterfeit credit cards. One new technique, referred to as **synthetic cloning**, may mix the characteristics of several cards together to form one card representing the credit profile of a person who does not even exist.

- *Illegitimate Computer Applications:* Web pages sometimes are used to acquire a victim's credit card number and other information under the guise of selling the victim a legitimate product or service. By using a *false merchant site*, the offender acquires the victim's credit information and uses it to obtain money or purchase property. Pornographic Internet sites are common false merchant sites. A technique called **triangulation** can also be used in which the offender uses the illegally obtained financial information to purchase stolen products in the victim's name, causing investigators to focus their case on the victim rather than the offender. Another highly sophisticated method is executed using a computer credit card number generator. This software enables the computer-savvy offender to create thousands of legitimate working credit card numbers and expiration dates derived from just a single valid account number. This technology is most prevalent among highly organized transnational credit card fraud rings.[16]

Check Fraud

Check fraud can be carried out by multiple means, but usually by manufacturing fake checks, altering real checks, forging signatures and check information, and writing bad checks for

FIGURE 14.5 ▶ (a) Forged check with the dollar amount altered from $100/One Hundred Dollars to $700/ Seven Hundred Dollars. (b) The original amount written on the check can be clearly distinguished from the overwritten amount under ALS lighting.

(a)

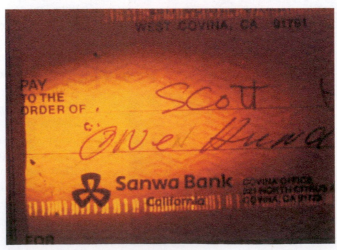

(b)

which insufficient or no funds are available. Following are some of the more frequent methods of check fraud:

- ***Forgery:*** Usually the offender steals a check, endorses it with a forged signature, and presents it at retailer establishments or banks to obtain goods and/or money—and perhaps also uses a fake ID to execute the financial transaction. When a business is the victim, a corrupt employee issues a check without proper authorization.

- ***Fake and Altered Checks:*** Fake checks can be produced quite easily by using scanners, digital imaging software, high-quality laser printers, or simply a color photocopy machine. These checks may be detected, however, by the lack of reflective appearance of the MICR line that contains the bank and customer account information. This line, at the bottom of the check, is encoded with magnetic ink that reflects light for automated devices that read the financial information on the check. Regular toner ink used to produce fake checks does not have the same qualities, and offenders rarely produce the MICR line with magnetic ink. Checks can also be altered using certain chemicals. Acetone, brake fluid, and bleach can be used to remove handwriting and modify information written on the check. Discoloration in areas of checks containing the dollar amount to be paid, called *spot alteration*, may be present. In other instances, all the information on a check can be obliterated with chemicals—referred to as *check washing*. Instead of using these sophisticated chemical methods, offenders may simply alter the original written information on the check using pens or other writing instruments, as illustrated in Figure 14.5. These types of simple alterations can easily be detected using ALS procedures.

- ***Paperhanging:*** Writing checks on closed accounts or reordering checks on closed accounts for future use are the most common methods of this check fraud technique. Checks may be issued in the offender's name or that of an innocent third party.

- ***Check Kiting:*** The offender opens checking accounts in two or more banks and writes a bad check on one account to deposit in another to create fraudulent balances. The offender draws money from the fraudulent funds before the bank can determine that the account balance was created with a check written against another account with insufficient funds.[17]

ATM SCAMS

ATM machine scammers usually operate in teams of two or more, with one thief acting as a front man to obtain PIN numbers or cards from victims (often referred to as *chumps*) and the others acting as spotters who look out for police, bank security, or other persons who may witness or interrupt the scam. ATM machines also contain internal software that captures the customer's card information. This ATM software, however, usually

requires additional translation from more sophisticated bank software to make the card information usable by offenders. As the offending techniques presented here clearly demonstrate, most offenders prefer a more direct approach when pulling off an ATM scam:

- ***Card Skimming:*** Magnetic strip details and the access PIN number are captured from the victim's ATM card by using a device known as a *skimmer*. This information is subsequently used to produce counterfeit cards.

- ***Spy Camera:*** A tiny camera and a PIN pad overlay (a fake PIN pad) transmit the victim's ATM card information via Bluetooth technology to the offender's laptop computer at a nearby location. The victim's ATM security information is then sent to other offenders, sometimes all around the world.

- ***Fake ATM:*** Fake ATM machines capture the victim's card information or perhaps physically trap the victim's card.

- ***Card Trapping:*** The offender fits a loop of tape, wire, or strong thread over the ATM card reader so that when the victim places an ATM card in the machine it is trapped and not returned. The trapping device is known as a *Lebanese loop* or *Algerian V*. The offender then returns to the ATM machine posing as another customer who assists the victim by suggesting something like, "If I press Return at the same time you enter your PIN, the card will come out." After obtaining the victim's PIN, the offender removes the card and drains the victim's bank account.

- ***Distraction Theft:*** Also known as *manual skimming*, this technique involves the offender distracting the victim whose card and PIN have already been entered into the ATM machine, then pressing the Cancel button and taking the card after telling the victim, "The ATM must be broken." A popular distraction method is to drop money on the ground and ask victims whether it is theirs. The card's PIN number is usually obtained through shoulder surfing.

- ***Shoulder Surfing:*** The offender looks over the shoulder of the victim, or in more sophisticated cases uses a telescopic device, and memorizes, writes down, or enters the victim's PIN into a cell phone.

- ***Leaving Live Transactions:*** The offender makes the victim believe the ATM is out of order after the card and PIN have been entered in the machine, then lures or scares the victim away before the transaction can be canceled. The offender may withdraw money from the ATM after the victim has left the scene, or steal the card and use it at a nearby ATM machine before the victim can report the theft.

- ***Cash Trapping:*** The offender inserts a device into the ATM machine's money dispenser that either covers or blocks bills as they are dispensed. After the owner leaves the machine, believing it is broken, the offender returns to remove the hidden bills.

- **Network Attacks:** In this sophisticated method, usually carried out by professional computer hackers, a computer program (malware) is used to attack the ATM's information retrieval system to access users' card information and PIN numbers. After obtaining this information, thieves create and distribute new ATM cards that sometimes are used throughout the world.

Besides witness and victim information, the investigation of ATM scammers usually employs surveillance video capturing the thieves' identities. Some ATM machines have built-in surveillance cameras that take still or time-sequenced photos of persons carrying out transactions. Machines without this technology may be within view of outside lobby or store surveillance cameras, which may record the parties involved in an ATM scam. In addition, new anti-skimming technology for ATMs is available that triggers surveillance and alarm systems when the machine's card reading or money-dispensing devices are tampered with.[18]

HEALTH CARE FRAUD

The primary targets of individuals committing health care fraud are private and public insurance providers. Private insurance companies pay out most of the funds spent for health care claims each year in the United States, covering approximately 70 percent of citizens requesting medical assistance. The remaining 30 percent are covered by governmental insurance providers, the largest of which are Medicare (available to persons over the age of 65, regardless of income) and Medicaid (provided to persons of all ages, based on income) administered at the federal level. Currently, total health care expenditures in the United States each year average $2.3 trillion. An estimated $51 to $85 billion of this total is illegally obtained by individuals and business entities through acts of health care fraud.

Health care fraud takes on many forms, and it is not restricted to a particular region of the country or to specialized types of offenders and victims. The FBI considers it to be most serious form of white-collar crime affecting U.S. citizens, second only to public corruption and corporate fraud. Following are some of the more popular health care frauds and scams encountered by investigators:

- **Billing for services not rendered:** Health care professionals bill insurance companies for unperformed services, which involves billing for (1) the same medical procedure multiple times, known as *duplicate claims fraud;* (2) a more expensive procedure than was actually performed; or (3) a procedure that was not performed at all.

- **Upcoding:** Health care providers are required to provide insurance companies specific computer database codes to receive payment for the procedures they perform. This type of fraud involves intentionally inputting a code for a procedure costlier than the one actually performed, resulting in an illegal higher payment

for medical services (office visits, surgery) or items purchased (wheelchairs, prosthetic devices).

- **Unbundling:** Payments for certain tests and other services related to the same medical condition often are *bundled,* or billed together, resulting in the health care professional receiving one flat payment for services. When services are *unbundled,* however, they are charged to the insurance company as separate tests and services, resulting in higher, yet fraudulent, payments to doctors or other health care providers.

- **Excessive and unnecessary services:** Medical professionals may perform unnecessary tests or procedures, prescribe drugs that are not needed, or require patients to use expensive medical equipment that they don't need. This allows medical professionals to bill insurance companies for these excessive and unnecessary services and for related costs such as the purchase of hospital time and medical devices.

- **Kickbacks:** This fraud involves illegal payments, or *kickbacks,* that health professionals make to each other for referral of patients and other persons requiring medically related services. For example, a doctor

FIGURE 14.6 ▶ Physician's prescription pad with latent handwriting impressions produced below the original prescription. This visualization is performed using techniques such as Electrostatic Detection Apparatus (ESDA), ALS, and other methods.

may refer a patient in need of testing to a particular clinic where the owner provides money, jewelry, paid vacations, or other items of value to the doctor in return for referring the patient Evidence of illegal activities by health care providers, such as that shown in Figure 14.6 for a prescription kickback case, may often be uncovered through document examination procedures in the crime lab.

Each year, health care fraud in the United States continues to increase and is expected to grow exponentially in coming years as the number of aging American citizens continues to grow. In addition, the extension of health care benefits to an additional 32 million Americans by the 2010 Healthcare Reform Bill will be the largest expansion of health care costs in U.S. history. Unfortunately, this in turn will lead to even greater opportunities for health care fraud.[19]

MORTGAGE FRAUD

Mortgage fraud typically is committed when loans for the purchase of property are illegally obtained from banks or other lending sources by intentionally misstating, forging, falsifying, or otherwise being untruthful in the loan acquisition process. Many forms of mortgage fraud and many of the scams connected with this particular offending activity are exceedingly complex. In general, offenders committing mortgage fraud fall into two categories. The first category is persons committing *fraud for housing*, which entails borrowing money under false pretenses to purchase and maintain a home. Most offenders committing this variety of mortgage fraud are single home buyers and their family members. The second offender type commits what is known as *industry insider fraud*, which is motivated by the sole aim of illegal profit. These scams are perpetrated by corrupt industry insiders such as real estate agents, loan brokers, title/escrow officers, attorneys, and bankers who collaborate to create bogus documentation to illegally secure money from lenders and property owners.

Mortgage fraud has always existed in the world of banking and money lending, but recently this type of white-collar crime has reached epidemic proportions. Loose credit and unregulated lending standards by financial institutions during the early to mid-2000s led to the widespread issuance of countless bad or "toxic" loans. In 2006, persons paying (or defaulting) on these loans triggered the largest meltdown of the U.S. economy since the Great Depression. Foremost among these bad debts were subprime home mortgages, loans given to borrowers who do not meet standard loan requirements due to poor credit, lack of income, sketchy employment history, and so forth. Before the financial meltdown, virtually anyone could obtain a subprime loan for hundreds of thousands of dollars. To secure a sizable home mortgage, all that prospective buyers had to do was to provide lenders little more than a stated income (i.e., just tell the bank how much you earn, without any verification or documentation). Although subprime lending is not an illegal

practice, there are many loopholes in the subprime loan application process that are conducive to white-collar crime. Following are some of the many scams and frauds that affected the mortgage industry as the result of the boom in money lending during the subprime loan era:

- *Illegal Property Flipping:* Typically, a loan is obtained for a low-value home at a purchase price double or triple the actual value of the property. This overinflated loan is usually given to the borrower based on a fraudulent appraisal of the property, which states that its value is equal to or exceeds the loan amount. The same property may then be quickly sold or "flipped" many times to different individuals performing the same inflated appraisal scam. After several "flips," when the bank lends, say, $400,000 for the purchase of a home that is really worth $80,000, the final buyer defaults on the loan and keeps leftover profits.

- *Straw Buyers:* A **straw buyer** is a person who purchases a home with someone else's identity or with a false identification. The person purchasing the home for the straw buyer never intends to live in the home or to make any loan payments. Often a straw buyer pays a person for purchasing them a home, and then becomes the legal owner of the property at a later date. After obtaining legal ownership, the straw buyer may engage in rent scams or loan fraud.

- *Equity Theft:* Offenders take over ownership of a home by filing fraudulent deeds and then obtain the existing equity by selling or refinancing the home. Home owners may not know that they have been the victim of equity theft until they receive eviction papers ordering them to leave the property they no longer own.

- *Chunking:* The scammer usually persuades a group of investors to purchase multiple properties; however, using the investors' finances and credit, the offender purchases many more properties than promised. The properties are usually purchased at inflated prices, and the scammer pockets the proceeds from overvalued loans. In the end, the investors are left with properties that are worth far less than their original investment.

- *Churning:* The offender, who is a loan broker or serves in a similar capacity, fraudulently earns excessive fees and commissions by engaging in repeated unnecessary lending services or transactions for a client. For example, a loan may be refinanced for a customer several times instead of once to obtain a reduced interest rate. The broker then collects three fees instead of just one.

- *Illegal Short Selling:* The owner of a home colludes with an individual to sell their home to the bank on a *short sale,* and then the purchaser of the home sells it back to the original owner at a lower price. Short selling is a legal real estate practice, which involves selling a home at a price less than what is owed on the mortgage. This home sales method has gained popularity during the recent downturn in property values. Short selling becomes illegal, however, when done for fraudulent purposes; for example, home buyers or owners who take advantage of banks for their own financial benefit.

Besides these mortgage scams, which target money lenders, there are other fraudulent practices in the money lending industry that aim at legitimate home buyers and existing home owners:

- *Mortgage Debt and Foreclosure Elimination Schemes:* Because of rapidly falling property values, many home owners have found themselves "upside down" on their mortgages—that is, they owe much more to the bank than their home is worth on the open market. Recognizing this trend, various unscrupulous companies target financially desperate home owners, promising to reduce or wipe out their mortgage debt and/or prevent the loss of their home through foreclosure. The solutions proposed often involve large up-front service fees and sometimes signing away any existing equity in the home to fraudulent financial advisors, who provide no services and simply abscond with any funds received from struggling home owners.
- *Predatory Lending Practices:* Loans are made to home buyers with hidden or special conditions that pay lenders unjustified profits and charge the owner exorbitant fees and interest rates—perhaps eventually causing the owner to lose the home. Recently passed truth-in-lending laws require transparency from lenders in mortgage transactions and seek to deter predatory lending practices.[20]

INSURANCE FRAUD

Insurance fraud is the intentional act of lying or falsifying a claim to an insurance provider for purposes of illegal gain. Taking advantage of an opportunity, such as a personal injury or auto accident, to lie or exaggerate the amount of damage to get greater insurance payoffs is referred to as *soft insurance fraud.* Conversely, intentionally staging a car theft, a slip-and-fall injury, or some other entirely false damage situation is considered *hard insurance fraud.* Insurance fraud is more prevalent during hard economic times, and has become more difficult to investigate as the insurance industry has become an international business. There are various types of insurance fraud, but those aimed at exploiting automobile insurers (see Figure 14.7) are among the ones most frequently encountered by investigators. Persons who no longer can make payments on their vehicle or who own more on their auto loan than the car is worth often commit soft auto insurance fraud by either (1) having their car intentionally stolen and sent to a chop shop or (2) contributing to the car's theft by placing it with keys in the ignition in a high-auto-theft location. Common scenarios involving hard auto insurance fraud are the following:

- *The Swoop and Squat:* A "swoop car" driven by one offender pulls quickly in front of a "squat car," driven by a second offender, which responds by slamming on the brakes—causing the victim's car to collide with the squat car.
- *Sudden Stop:* A squat car pulls in front of the victim's vehicle and suddenly brakes, causing the victim to collide with the squat car.

FIGURE 14.7 ▶ Fully parted-out stolen vehicles, such as that pictured here in a chop shop, are used to conduct auto repair insurance scams.

- *Backing:* The victim backs into the suspect's vehicle, which is strategically positioned behind the victim's car.
- *Paper Collisions:* Two or more offenders using predamaged vehicles or staging vehicle damage to fake an accident that the police are never called to investigate.
- *Phantom Car:* Accident involving damage to a lone suspect vehicle, allegedly caused by a hit-and-run "phantom car" driver.[21]

TELEPHONE AND TELEMARKETING FRAUD

Listed here are numerous forms of financial fraud typically carried out over the telephone and by offenders posing as telemarketers. Although anyone is a potential victim of these fraudulent calls, most successful frauds of this type are carried out against the elderly.

Fake Check Scams: Scammers make calls typically requesting to buy items the victim is selling, to pay the victim for work performed, or to pay an "advance" fee to the victim on prize winnings or investment payoffs that supposedly will be provided at a later date. Usually, a fake check (often so realistic that banks don't immediately know that it's phony) is sent to the victim in excess of the amount owed to them. After the victim deposits the check, the offenders ask the victim to wire the excess funds back to them. The bank often takes weeks to determine that the check is fake, and when it does, the victim is responsible for the funds withdrawn. Sources indicate that this is perhaps the most frequent form of telemarketing fraud, comprising 58 percent of reported cases and averaging $3,854 in financial loss per victim.

Prize/Sweepstakes Scams: Victims receive calls from scammers claiming that the victim has won a prize or sweepstakes contest (that they may have or have not entered) and must provide a deposit or advance fee in order to receive the full payoff (which never materializes). Sources indicate that the average monetary loss to victims of this scam is $6,601 per case.

Other Scams: Other popular telemarketing scams include telephonic requests for up-front fees for low-interest or bad credit loans, credit cards, credit repair, false magazine subscriptions, job search services, academic scholarships, vacations, charities, and Nigerian money offers.

Denial-of-Service Attacks: Scammers obtain financial information about the victim, primarily checking and savings account numbers with their access codes, and use automated dialing technology to tie up their victims' phone lines while attacking their bank accounts. The typical sequence of events carried out by perpetrators of this scam is as follows:

1. Offenders acquire vital financial information about the victim through legitimate means—such as social networking sites and public records—and illegal means, including deceptive calls, e-mails, and letters that trick the victim into providing PIN numbers, on-line banking passwords, and other security codes.
2. The victim receives a constant flood of automated phone calls, commonly consisting of recorded advertisements, solicitations, or perhaps just a dead line.
3. While the victim's phone line is tied up, the offenders make illegal money transfers or contact banks pretending to be the victim attempting to make a money transfer. When the financial institution calls to obtain personal verification of the money transfer request, the victim's phone line is tied up, making telephonic contact impossible. During this time, the offenders will call the financial institution or be called (after providing their contact number) and pose as the victim approving the money transfer.

Cramming: Charges for additional goods and services—established through unauthorized, misleading, or deceptive means—are "crammed" onto the victim's phone bill. This scam can be done by trickery, whereby coupons, checks, sweepstakes entries, and other financially related offers are approved by the victim, yet contain hidden additional charges for other unauthorized purchases. Another popular cramming method includes taping the victim's voice over the phone saying "yes" in response to questions unrelated to the purchasing of a particular good or service. Then the victim's statement of approval is used out of context as proof that a purchase charged to their phone bill was verbally authorized. Many cramming scams take the form of an initial offer to the victim of a free, no-obligation benefit such as no-cost advertising for businesses, free gifts, free Internet service, or free 30-day trials of products and services. Certain websites, including those hosting gambling, pornography, and other adult enterprises, often add an automatic acceptance of additional charges that later are crammed onto the user's phone bill.[22]

SCAMS, SCHEMES, AND CONS
419 Advance Fee Fraud

Each year hundreds of thousands of messages, sent by e-mail, letter, phone, or fax from West African countries (usually Nigeria), are received by persons throughout the world, who are promised millions of dollars if they furnish up-front money or an advance fee before receiving the entire fortune. Classic **419 advance fee** scams involve a company or individual who claims to have acquired large sums of money from an illicit business deal, often involving overbilling for crude oil supplies, and requests assistance in transferring the funds out of the country. The scammers also claim, however, that they need money wired to them to carry out the transfer of funds. They further promise that they will give a generous payout to the advance fee provider in exchange for providing them with the requested funds.

In addition to pocketing the advance fee, the offenders use the victim's personal financial information to carry out additional crimes involving identity theft. Money wired by the victim to the offender initially may be deposited into the bank account of a third party, known as a *money mule*, which lets offenders use their account for a small fee. Money that is supposedly owed from unclaimed lottery winnings, or willed from a long-lost relative, or even in need of cleaning to remove coloring agents or toxic substances with special chemicals that the victim pays for before use (known as a *black money wash*) are other classic forms of 419s. It is practically incomprehensible that these schemes—named after Section 419 of the Nigerian Criminal Code, which prohibits such fraudulent activities—could lure unwitting victims to surrender their money. Yet, 419 scams have already netted offenders an estimated $41 billion and approximately $9.3 billion in 2009 alone.[23]

CASE CLOSE-UP 14.1

419 SCAM LETTER

The following 419 scam letter was received by one of the authors via the Internet and is provided as an example of this type of fraud. The grammatical and spelling errors it contains are not typographical errors, but appeared in the original e-mailed letter.

Dear Friend In The Lord,

I am Mrs Phils Adams a former muslem and been converted to Christian alongside my Late Husband, I am 54 Years Old Woman and we have became more devoted in christianity for quite good number of years now but I am at this moment suffering with (Esophageal Cancer) breast and fibroid of the womb which has affected my health and after taking all type of medical treatment in other to find my self survives it still defiling that I will be only having some few Months to live, according to what the medical experts has observed in me.

My Husband who is now Late was killed during the September 19th 2002 political crisis. My late Husband was the Chairman of the Contract Awarding Committee under Budgeting and Planning of our Country.

Throughout the period of my marriage with him, all efforts to bear Children with him proved abortive because of my poor state of health and after his death issues, I inherited all his wealth, with our adopted son by name (Timothy) since he has no other next of kin but it is now obvious that I may not survive my poor state of health. I have deemed it necessary to leave a legacy on Earth and give a positive account and justification of the life I lived on Earth before the Almighty God.

This is what I want to achieve by committing this wealth in all Christian Societies or orphanages Homes/widows and the less privileged peoples around the Globe. I am meditating what may happen after death that is why I am taking this decision by giving this Money out to be use to accomplish the Almighty God's Divine Marvelous work around the Globe because I highly believed that I will be with Him in his most perfect and the most peacefully place.

Note that this sum (US$ 12 Million) was secured and Deposited in Central Bank of West African States - Benin Region with my name by my Late Husband and all the related Documentation covering the funds are Highly intact with me as the Co-beneficiary of the Treasure.

So on the receipt of your immediate response to me I will forward all the necessary Documents covering the funds were the Money is been packaged and sealed in the Treasure Box before Depositing it in the bank as to enable you open up your communication with them for the releasing of the Treasure Box to you as I cannot follow it up right now because of my illness condition. Please Religion doesn't matter in this divine project henceforth I put all my trust in you but do actualize my dreams with this Money for the sake of the Almighty God because My happiness is that I lived a life of a true devoted life worthy of emulation.

Lastly, I honestly pray that when releasing the funds to you by the bank were the Money is been packaged and sealed it will be well judiciously used for the said purpose as the Almighty god has reviewed for humanitarian services and you should be aware that whoever that wants to serve Him must serve him in truth and in fairness.

So Please always be prayerful all through your life in this Divine marvelous Work of the Almighty God. I wait to hear from you and be sure that all my dreams will rest squarely on your shoulders to be accomplish so that I can give you further details. Also provide me your direct tel/fax numbers to reach you.

Finally, 50% of this money will be for the work of God, while 35% will be for our adopted son which you will also help him to invest in your country, while 15% will be for you for your assistance.

Thanks once again.

Regards,
Mrs Phils Adams.

Ponzi Schemes

The **Ponzi scheme**, named for its creator Carlo Ponzi, pays investors dividends (periodic interest payments) on cash they have entrusted with an offender posing as a businessman who can make legitimate investments yielding extremely high profits. In reality, however, the offender never invests the victim's money but rather uses it to pay dividends to earlier investors, who are under the same false impression that their money is safely invested. Although this method of using money illegally obtained from later investors to pay earlier investors is deceptively simple, Ponzi schemes have robbed billions of dollars from victims in all walks of life—including some of the world's most educated and investment-savvy individuals. The allure of this scam is a "too good to be true" return on an initial investment—often 10 to 30 percent within a matter of months, or in the case of the original scheme carried out by Carlo Ponzi, 50 percent within 45 days and 100 percent in just 3 months. Victims usually receive payments as promised, along with phony financial statements, until the offenders are unable to keep up paying dividends due to an insufficient pool of new investor victims to fund the fake dividend payouts. Early indications of a failing Ponzi scheme include reduced or delayed regular payments to victims, accompanied by excuses such as "dips in the stock market" or "delays in funds provided by banks." When these scams begin to fail, victims suspecting fraud often inform authorities, which prompts an investigation. Although most victims of Ponzi schemes lose most, if not all of their initial investment, many are partially reimbursed for their losses through seizures and forfeitures of the offender's remaining finances and property.[24] "Scammer of the Century," Bernie Madoff (see Figure 14.8), is credited with carrying out the largest Ponzi scheme in history.

Pyramid Schemes

A **pyramid scheme**, also referred to as a *franchise fraud*, operates like a Ponzi scheme; that is, earlier investors are rewarded out of funds from later investors under the false impression that these profits are generated by legitimate investments. Pyramid schemes, however, require each new member of the scam to recruit new members, from which they will recoup their initial investment and gain a percentage of profits from persons who are "recruits of their recruits" and so on. Pyramids ultimately collapse when they grow so large the offender can no longer make payments to earlier victims at the top after failing to recruit enough new victims at the bottom to "pay the bills." These scams take many forms, but frequently involve the purchase of franchises for the distribution rights (not sale) of products—real or nonexistent—that carry bonuses or kickbacks for enlisting others to purchase similar franchises. For example, Victim X pays $5,000 to the offender at the top of the pyramid for the rights to distribute Lucky Brand Motor Oil. Then, Victim X sells a new motor oil franchise to Victim Y for $5,000 (which goes to the offender at the top), but receives a bonus of $200 for doing so. Next, Victim Y sells a franchise to Victim Z for another $5,000, from which Victim X receives a cut of $100 and Victim Y is given a $200 bonus. What makes these transactions part of an illegal pyramid scheme is that the bonus money paid to the victims comes not from commissions for the actual sale of goods, but only from the recruitment of new members. Other popular pyramids include chain letters and clubs targeting victims who are friends and family members.[25]

Pump and Dump Scams

A **pump and dump** is a stock market scam in which assets (stocks) are artificially inflated in value (pumped) and then deflated in value (dumped), resulting in profits to the offenders manipulating the stocks—and losses to the victims who purchased the assets at their peak value. This scam can be complicated in design, but generally involves the following steps:

1. Penny stocks (those selling for less than $5.00 per share) sold to the public as investments in unknown or little-known companies.
2. False press releases are sent to the media that hype the development of "hot" innovations or products soon to be marketed by the company and draw huge, fast profits.
3. Stock brokerage firms, Internet investment sites, and financial advisement networks add legitimacy to false media reports by spreading information to investors about the company's potential earnings.
4. Large quantities of the company's stock are purchased by offending "insiders" to increase the volume of stocks sold, which in turn increases the price of the stock shares to new investors.
5. New investors purchase the company's stock after it has risen in value (i.e., the pump), causing it to rise even more in value.
6. The offending "insiders" sell off their stocks at the peak artificially inflated value (i.e., the dump), gaining huge profits and driving down the price of the remaining stocks still held by the legitimate investors. In some cases, the offenders file for bankruptcy, causing unsuspecting investors to lose their entire stock investment.[26]

Romance Cons

A **romance con** scam is typically executed by a con who strikes up a friendship or romantic relationship with an individual residing in a foreign country. Many romance scams begin through e-mails and Internet sites, while others are formed through telephone calls and letters. Usually, the victim is lured in by offenders professing love and friendship shortly after an initial online meeting or personal correspondence. To create the illusion that their romantic intentions are genuine, offenders often send the victim a small gift in the form of costume jewelry or a seductive (yet false) picture of themselves. Once victims believe that they are in a viable relationship, they are inundated with requests from their supposed partner for money and favors. Often, victims are asked to receive parcels containing property purchased by their romantic partner under the guise that they are not allowed to send and receive shipped items in their native country. Victims of this scam will be asked to readdress and send the packages to their partner's alleged friends and family. Unbeknownst to the victim, all of the packages contain illegal property such as drugs, weapons, laundered money, forged documents, or at the very least items purchased with stolen credit information.[27]

CASE CLOSE-UP 14.2

TOP WHITE COLLAR FRAUD OFFENDERS OF RECENT HISTORY

Offender	Theft (in $)	Crime	Sentence	Year
1. Bernie Madoff	$60 Billion	Ponzi Scheme	150 years	2009
2. Bernard Ebbers	$11 Billion	Corporate Fraud	25 years	2005
3. Jeffrey Skilling	$50 Million–$1 Billion	Corporate Fraud	24 years	2006
4. Dennis Kozlowski	$100 Million	Corporate Fraud	8–25 years	2005

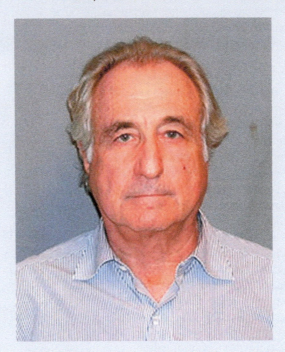

FIGURE 14.8 ▶ Mugshot of modern-day Ponzi scheme "Scammer of the Century," Bernard Madoff. (Federal Bureau of Investigation)

COUNTERFEITING

Counterfeiting is the fraudulent manufacturing, altering, or distributing of a product that is of lesser value than the original product. This offense is also referred to as *pirating,* especially when the fraudulent practices focus on electronically reproducible goods such as computer software, movies, music downloads, and so on. An important element of proving a counterfeiting offense is the intent to defraud. Generally, this is quite easy to establish for offenders who manufacture and distribute counterfeit items; however, persons selling such goods at the wholesale or retail level often claim they did not know the products were fraudulent. Persons possessing any tools or products used to carry out the counterfeiting process also are guilty of criminal acts under the laws of most jurisdictions. For example, the illegal production of currency may involve inks, paper, master plates, molds, or altered bills as well as electronic images (e.g., computer files containing scanned digital money images). Anticounterfeiting laws exist at both the state and federal levels. Some laws specify that when a copy of an original

product can be readily identified as a fake by a reasonable person, and is not sold under the guise of being genuine, no counterfeiting offense has taken place.

Usually, when one thinks of counterfeiting, the illegal production of money comes to mind. Counterfeit currency, however, includes not only fake bills and coins, but also the illegal manufacturing, altering, and distribution of anything legitimately used as a form of financial obligation. This includes checks, money orders, traveler's checks, promissory notes, certificates of deposit (CDs), and the like. This type of counterfeiting, often referred to as *paper operations*, can also involve the production of false identification and other documents used for identification purposes, such as social security cards, driver's licenses, marriage/death certificates, press passes, and so on. Paper operations can be unsophisticated crimes using a photocopy machine to print fake currency or highly organized transnational crimes that produce counterfeit money using expensive professional devices similar to those the U.S. government uses to print currency.

Most counterfeiting investigations involving fake currency generally begin with the complaint of a bank, retailer, or consumer who has been paid with phony bills. Usually, these are in denominations of $20, $50, or $100. Small retail establishments selling jewelry, electronics, tobacco products, liquor, or other higher-end items generally are targeted as victims for the distribution of counterfeit money—although larger superstore retail stores also can be hit. Counterfeiters also like to enjoy a lavish lifestyle with their phony money. They often pass bad bills at restaurants, casinos, and nightclubs where the establishments generally do not question the customer's integrity. Also, the saying "there is no honor among thieves" especially applies to counterfeiters, who also pay prostitutes and drug dealers with fake currency. Mapping the physical locations of personal victims and establishments is often helpful for determining the area of operation used by a counterfeiter or counterfeiting ring. Often, a particular location is flooded with phony bills to make illegal purchases so as to avoid detection through investigative efforts that follow a victim's reporting of the crime. Future times and places, developed from existing patterns of money distribution, may emerge from mapping "blitz spending" crime areas targeted by offenders. Surveillance camera images, the development of information from persons who have been "burned," victim/witness interviews, and undercover operations are other often fruitful methods of developing suspect leads.

Counterfeit "knockoffs," or illegal imitations of legitimate products, are perhaps even more widespread than crimes focused on fake currency. They may be even more financially lucrative to offenders and the most costly to victims, with an estimated $200–$250 billion in criminal losses each year. Generally speaking, this type of counterfeiting can be categorized as focusing on either tangible or intangible goods. Tangible goods include physical items that are usually not reproduced through electronic means. It would be impossible to list all of the counterfeited goods that fall within this criminal category. The most popular items targeted by offenders, however, are apparel and clothing items, electrical/machinery equipment, handbags, footwear, and tobacco products. This type of counterfeiting is extremely dangerous when it involves food and other items designed for human consumption. For example, as the U.S. population begins to age, commercial pharmaceutical drugs increasingly are being counterfeited and sold in the open market to pharmacies, clinics, and hospitals. These fraudulent medications often provide weak or insufficient treatment for serious medical conditions and result in harm or death to unsuspecting users.

Counterfeit intangible goods include, for the most part, illegally copied electronic images that are protected by copyrights or patents and are classified as intellectual property. Music, movies (see Figure 14.9), and computer software are among the most popular items targeted and sold as counterfeit intangible goods. Unlike tangible goods, the illegal production and distribution of digital products is not always done for profit. Rather, some offenders engage in this activity merely to beat the system (as in the case of illegal music downloads) and to gain popularity from others for supplying something of value for free.

Investigations of counterfeit goods can involve single offenders conducting small-time operations or multijurisdictional task forces that focus on highly organized international offending

FIGURE 14.9 ▶ Shown here is a counterfeit movie (left) as it looks when sold on the street for $5 or less in violation of copyright laws. The authentic legal version of the movie, sold in retail stores for $25 dollars or more, is pictured on the right.

rings. In the latter, illegal products are manufactured in countries such as China, South Korea, Taiwan, and Mexico and then shipped to the United States for distribution and sales. To avoid detection of stolen goods by customs officials, smugglers often place the illegal products in the back shipping containers behind legitimate products. After passing inspection, the goods are transported to warehouses, where they are stored until they are sold to wholesalers or retailers—or perhaps directly to consumers. Many of these organized counterfeiting rings, similar to terrorists, are organized in cells so that if one operation is detected, others will continue the illegal enterprise. They also have been known to use street gangs as spotters in street sales area, and to use gang members as sales agents for the counterfeit goods. Some offenders go so far as to employ counterintelligence efforts such as attempting to discover the identity of investigators and others who may uncover their illegal operations.[28]

RECONSTRUCTING A LARCENY THEFT CRIME SCENE

Case Example 14A (see Figures 14.10 to 14.17) illustrates a type of credit card larceny theft crime known as "card trapping." In this case, the offender prepares an ATM machine to trap and not return a credit card after an unsuspecting victim has inserted it into the machine's card slot. The card is trapped in the machine by a makeshift device called a *Lebanese loop*. After the victim leaves the machine to seek help, the offender removes the trapped card from the machine and may use it for a variety of larceny theft crimes. Reconstruction of this crime is made possible by the presence of surveillance technology at the scene. The surveillance photos taken provide abundant investigative information in this larceny theft case.

CASE EXAMPLE 14A

ATM Theft Crime Scene

FIGURE 14.10 Investigators have recovered the surveillance video shown here from a bank ATM lobby. Several customers have complained to the bank of stolen bank cards being used for fraudulent transactions and ATM withdrawals. An ATM card theft ring is believed to be operating in the area and to have targeted this ATM machine and numerous others in the area.

FIGURE 14.11 Another man is seen in the surveillance video outside the doorway of the ATM lobby.

FIGURE 14.12 The suspect has left the lobby, and a customer inserts his bank card into the ATM machine.

FIGURE 14.13 The suspect returns and interacts with the customer in a nonconfrontational manner.

FIGURE 14.14 The suspect returns after the customer leaves the lobby and appears to be tampering with the card slot of the ATM machine.

FIGURE 14.15 The suspect removes an object inserted into the card slot of the ATM machine that has captured the customer's bank card.

FIGURE 14.16 The object is a V-shaped piece of x-ray film cut with catch grooves on both sides (see arrows) that trap the card in the machine so it cannot be returned to the customer.

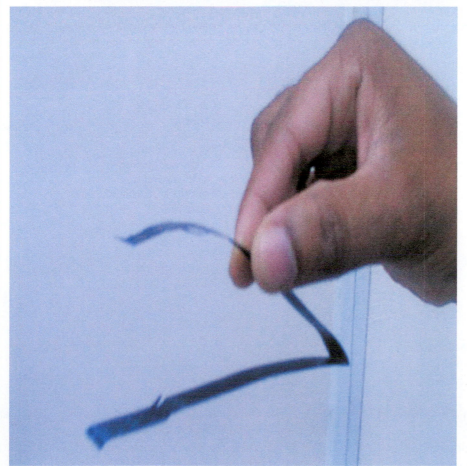

FIGURE 14.17 ▶ The suspect removes the bank card from the trapping mechanism and leaves the bank lobby. After viewing the surveillance photos of the card trapping theft, what information contained here is of value to investigators who must work this case? How should this information be used to help identify the theft suspects or victims? What additional financial crimes might be carried out by the suspects after trapping bank cards? Are there financial institutions or financial theft databases that may be of assistance in investigating this case? If victims are available for interviews, how can investigators best utilize these victims in their financial crimes investigation?

Summary

1. Larceny-theft and its legal definition.

Crimes involving the taking of anything of value without the owner's consent, with the intent to permanently deprive him or her of the value of the property taken are referred to under the law as *larceny-theft*. The item of value can be tangible property, like a stolen vehicle, or it can be intangible, such as an electronic transmission used to wire funds. Popular forms of larceny-theft include fraud, forgery, and counterfeiting. Victims of these types of crimes can be individuals, corporations, businesses, or government entities.

2. Shoplifting and similar acts of theft.

The crime of shoplifting typically involves offenders who enter a retail establishment, hide some type of property on their person, and leave the establishment with the property without paying the merchant. Most shoplifters are amateurs, referred to as *snitches*, who steal products for personal use or for personal thrills. A few shoplifters are professionals who steal small items of high value to sell for a profit. These offenders, also known as *boosters* or *heels*, also make their living by illegal proceeds from items they have shoplifted. Most other acts of theft committed against retailers for financial gain are committed by amateur rather than professional offenders.

3. Fraud and fraud investigation.

Popular forms of fraud include credit card fraud, health care fraud, insurance fraud, mortgage fraud, and various forms of fraudulent activities associated with identity theft. Typically, these crimes are investigated by subpoenaing financial records of offenders and their victims. In addition, interviews with witnesses and victims and the interrogation of suspects are just as likely to produce solid case leads as sophisticated investigations focusing on examinations of spreadsheets and accounting data.

4. Cons, scams, and schemes.

Some of the more widely used cons, scams, and schemes include Ponzi and pyramid schemes. Both of these methods involve collection of funds from victims by fraudulent means and payment of funds acquired from later victims to earlier victims—both of whom believe that they are involved in a legitimate investment. The main difference between these scams is that persons involved in Ponzi schemes receive a dividend payment as a return on their fraudulent investment, whereas victims of pyramid schemes are promised a commission for obtaining money from new victims they recruit to the investment pyramid. Both Ponzi and pyramid schemes typically collapse when too few new investors are drawn in to support fraudulent payments to earlier investors.

Key Terms

shoplifting	phishing	card trapping
larceny-theft	pharm	churning
snitch	skimming	pump and dump
booster	chunking	counterfeiting
heel	419 advance fee	shoulder surfing
crotch walk	romance con	cash trapping
straw buyer	mortgage fraud	network attacks
cramming	identity (ID) theft	upcoding
pyramid scheme	synthetic cloning	unbundling
insurance fraud	triangulation	property flipping
embezzlement	paperhanging	swoop and squat
pilfering	check kiting	Ponzi scheme
dumpster diving		

Review Questions

1. What is the legal definition of *larceny-theft*? How does it differ among jurisdictions?
2. Describe the various techniques used by shoplifters.
3. What is the difference between a booster and a snitch?
4. How does the crime of embezzlement differ from other forms of theft?
5. What are some common methods used to commit identity theft?
6. What types of crimes are committed by persons who have committed ID theft?
7. Describe what is meant by the term *credit card fraud*? How is it carried out?
8. What are some of the various methods by which an offender can commit check fraud?
9. Describe some popular techniques of thefts from ATM machines.
10. What types of criminal activities are considered to be health care fraud?

11. How is mortgage fraud carried out? Provide an example.

12. What are some common telemarketing scams?

13. What is the difference between a Ponzi scheme and a pyramid scheme?

14. How do offenders carry out a pump and dump scheme?

15. What is meant by the terms *tangible* and *intangible* counterfeited goods? Give examples of each.

Internet Resources

White-Collar Crime	www.fbi.gov/about-us/investigate/white_collar/whitecollarcrime
Internet Fraud	www.usa.gov/Citizen/Topics/Internet_Fraud.shtml
National Consumers League	fraud.org/fraudcenter.htm
Federal Trade Commission	www.ftc.gov/bcp/edu/microsites/idtheft
International AntiCounterfeiting Coalition (IACC)	www.iacc.org/about-counterfeiting

Applied Investigative Exercise

After examining the crime scene photos presented in Case Example 14A, imagine that you are the investigator of this case. You have acquired these photos from a surveillance camera in the lobby where the ATM machine is located. Describe the steps you would take to gather evidence. In doing so, describe the persons, places, and things that your investigation would focus on to develop suspect leads. Provide a personal assessment of the offender, addressing whether he is an amateur or professional. Support your investigative conclusions with information presented in this chapter.

Notes

[1] This discussion is based on information drawn from Chapter 31, Title 7, "Offenses Against Property," of the Texas Penal Code.

[2] This discussion is based on information drawn from Chapter 5, Sections 484-502.9 of the California Penal Code defining the crime of larceny.

[3] Federal Bureau of investigation, *White Collar Crime*, posted at www.fbi.gov/about-us/investigate/white_collar/whitecollarcrime.

[4] This discussion is based on information drawn from Chapter 5, Sections 484-502.9 of the California Penal Code defining the crimes of petty and grand larceny.

[5] Derived from a general discussion of Connecticut Penal Code Section 53a, posted at www.cga.ct.gov/2005/rpt/2005-R-0192.htm.

[6] Federal Bureau of Investigation, *Crime in the United States 2009*, posted at www.fbi.gov/stats-services/crimestats.

[7] Bureau of Justice Statistics, *Property Crime*, posted at bjs.ojp.usdoj.gov/index.cfm?ty=tp&tid=32.

[8] Kansas Bureau of Investigation, *Shoplifting: Another Word For Stealing, posted at* www.accesskansas.org/kbi/info/docs/pdf/Shoplifting.pdf.

[9] Ibid.

[10] U.S. Chamber of Commerce, *Who Is an Employee*, posted at www.uschambersmallbusinessnation.com/toolkits/guide/P05_0120.

[11] Federal Trade Commission, *Fighting Back Against Identity Theft*, posted at www.ftc.gov/bcp/edu/microsites/idtheft.

[12] Ibid.

[13] 18 U.S.C. Section 1028a.

[14] Ibid.

[15] Identity Theft Resource Center, *Working Together to Resolve Identity Theft*, posted at www.idtheftcenter.org.

[16] Oliver Sylvester, *Transnational Credit Card Fraud*, posted at people.exeter.ac.uk/watupman/undergrad/owsylves/index.html.

[17] National Check Fraud Center, *Check Fraud Prevention*, posted at www.ckfraud.org/ckfraud.html.

[18] Bankers on Line, *Increased Sophistication of ATM Crimes*, posted at www.bankersonline.com/articles/bhv13n01/bhv13n01a6.html.

[19] Federal Bureau of Investigation, *White-Collar Crime*, posted at www.fbi.gov/about-us/investigate/white_collar/whitecollarcrime.

[20] Ibid.

[21] Ibid.

[22] National Fraud Information Center, *2007 Top 10 Telemarketing Scams*, posted at www.fraud.org/telemarketing/2007telemarketing.pdf.

[23] National Consumer League Fraud Center, *419 Advance Fee Scams*, posted at www.fraud.org.

[24] Federal Bureau of Investigation, *White-Collar Crime*, posted at www.fbi.gov/about-us/investigate/white_collar/whitecollarcrime.

[25] Ibid.

[26] Ibid.

[27] National Consumers League's Fraud Center, *Romance Fraud*, posted at www.fraud.org.

[28] Piotr Stryszowski, *The Economic Impacts of Counterfeiting and Piracy*, posted at www.worldcommercereview.com/publications/article_pdf/152.

CHAPTER FIFTEEN

VEHICLE THEFT SCENES

Learning Objectives

After completing this chapter, you should be able to:

1. Describe the crime of motor vehicle theft and how motor vehicle theft investigations are conducted.
2. Be familiar with the various reasons for committing vehicle theft.
3. Know the methods of vehicle break-ins and thefts.
4. Know common types of vehicle fraud and how they are carried out.

Chapter Outline

INTRODUCTION

SHOWN IN THIS OPENING CASE photo is a bait car used by investigators to lure an auto thief into stealing the vehicle. Once the vehicle is stolen, not only is the offender caught in the act, but the vehicle's on-board digital video recorder captures the thief's illegal activities as evidence for use in court. Bait cars and other high-tech means of detecting auto theft are part of a growing effort by investigators to proactively counter thefts of auto and other vehicles. Many states have developed local and regional task forces that specifically target vehicle-related crimes. For example, 13 states now have Auto Prevention Authority Groups (Arizona, California, Colorado, Florida, Illinois, Maryland, Michigan, Minnesota, New York, Pennsylvania, Rhode Island, Texas, and Virginia), which focus on creating laws and enforcement strategies to prevent auto theft. Much of the recent growing concern over vehicle theft is related to the increasing professionalism of auto thieves. Unlike those of the past, today's auto thieves tend to be highly organized and steal cars for profit, dismantling them in minutes for parts that are sold through the illegal auto parts black market. Cars that are not dismantled are exported through ports of call to foreign countries, where they are sold for double or triple their value in the United States. Detecting and preventing auto theft has also become a concern for the Department of Homeland Security, and specifically CBP and ICE agencies, because of the increased use of stolen vehicles by terrorists to transport operatives and to make car bombs. These and other issues related to auto theft are discussed in this chapter.

GRAND THEFT AUTO AND RELATED VEHICLE THEFT LAWS

Vehicle Theft and the Law

Depending on the jurisdiction, the theft of cars and other motor vehicles may fall under theft or larceny codes for all types of property, or codes that specifically address the stealing of cars versus other types of vehicles. Some states have passed **grand theft auto** (GTA) laws that make auto theft an offense distinct from thefts of other types of property. Generally speaking, individuals who remove, steal, or drive a vehicle without first obtaining the owner's permission have committed motor vehicle theft. Whether this unauthorized taking is considered a misdemeanor or felony will depend largely on the vehicle's value at the time of the offense. Some state laws specify that the vehicle's value must exceed $1,000; others require

a $400 limit; and still other states have no value limit for felony classification when the vehicle stolen is an automobile. Intent also may be a factor in determining the seriousness of a particular auto theft. Some jurisdictions treat an auto theft as less serious if the thief's intent is to take the vehicle for a joyride rather than to permanently steal it for purposes of "parting it out" in a chop shop.[1]

In addition, the circumstances surrounding a particular vehicle theft may result in more legal charges against the offender. For example, breaking into a car before stealing it often results in the additional charge of auto burglary. Similarly, stealing a vehicle from a garage or other storage location may be classified as a residential or commercial burglary. Borrowing a work truck without an employer's permission might result in a charge of embezzlement. Finally, using force or fear in the act of stealing a vehicle would be classified as one of the most serious forms of robbery—carjacking.

Recent State and Federal Laws Related to Stolen Vehicles

Various laws have been passed at the state and federal levels to criminalize many activities related to motor vehicle theft. Examples of these are described here.

State Laws:

- Vehicle Chop Shop and Altered Property Laws: prohibit the operation of a chop shop or other facility that engages in the dismantling of stolen vehicles or the alteration of stolen vehicles or their parts.
- Salvage Certificate Fraud Laws: prohibit junk yards, salvagers, or other vehicle recyclers from creating fake or fraudulent titles on vehicles declared a "total loss" by insurance companies—which are often later used by thieves who sell stolen cars or misrepresent junked vehicles as undamaged vehicles.
- Vehicle Owner Fraud Laws: prohibit vehicle owners from filing false theft reports or engaging in other activities classified as insurance fraud to obtain monetary settlements for vehicles they cannot sell or otherwise cannot afford.[2]

Federal Laws:

Since 1984, the federal government has passed numerous laws specifically aimed at curbing motor vehicle theft. These legal enhancements began with Congress's passing of the Motor Vehicle Theft Law Enforcement Act of 1984. Since then additional laws have been passed—the Anti-Car Theft Act in 1992, the Motor Vehicle Theft Prevention Act in 1994, and the Anti-Car Theft Improvements Act in 1996—increasing federal legal oversight over motor vehicle thefts to stem the tide of professionals and terrorists committing these crimes. Key provisions of these laws include the following:

- Making it a federal offense to carjack a vehicle; to own, operate, maintain, or control a chop shop; to alter or remove motor vehicle identification numbers; to deal in stolen marked parts; to conduct interstate trafficking of stolen vehicles and parts (made illegal under federal RICO racketeering statutes); and to counterfeit or forge motor vehicle title certificates

- Requiring state DMVs to check VINs of out-of-state cars before issuing titles to new owners, and requiring auto recyclers and repair shops that sell or install used parts to check VINs against the FBI's stolen-car database

- Requiring manufacturers of certain high-theft passenger cars to put the identification numbers (i.e., VIN numbers) on the engine, the transmission, and 12 major body parts

- Allowing for the seizure and forfeiture of vehicles or components with falsified or removed identification numbers

- Requiring that exporters of used motor vehicles submit a proof of ownership containing the vehicle's identification number to the customs and border officials before exporting the vehicle

- Upgrading state motor-vehicle department databases containing title information, enabling federal and state law enforcement officials to rapidly determine whether a motor vehicle is stolen

- Providing immunity for persons furnishing knowledge to police about auto theft law violators[3]

VEHICLE THEFT TRENDS AND CHARACTERISTICS

In recent years, the number of vehicle thefts occurring in the United States has been declining. In just one year—between 2008 and 2009—there was a 17 percent decrease in the number of vehicles reported stolen to police. This is perhaps due, in part, to the increased sophistication of auto theft databases and to the increased enforcement tools available to investigators to detect and apprehend vehicle thieves. Nevertheless, vehicle thefts result in $5.2 billion of losses annually to victims, which include owners, dealers, manufacturers, and insurance companies. The average value per vehicle stolen is approximately $6,500. In terms of time, thieves steal one vehicle every 40 seconds and the majority of these vehicles are later stripped for their parts which are sold on the black market, as shown in Figure 15.1. The greatest percentage of vehicles are stolen in the South (37.8 percent) followed by states located in the West (34.2 percent). In 2010, the number-one hot spot, accounting for more auto thefts than any other U.S. city, was Laredo, Texas. Demographic profiles of auto thieves indicate that they are usually males, over the age of 18 years, who carry out their thefts in predominantly urban settings. Although the majority of these thieves are White (56.9 percent), the significant number of vehicle thefts committed by African-Americans (40.5 percent) makes this offense the most prevalent property crime committed by persons of this particular race/ethnicity.[4]

(a)

FIGURE 15.1A ▶ (a) Once stolen and brought to the chop shop, an entire vehicle can be dismantled into its component parts in a matter of minutes.

(b)

FIGURE 15.1B ▶ (b) As the name *chop shop* implies, vehicles are chopped into pieces, and metallic saws quickly remove engines and other large parts with a high street value.

REASONS FOR VEHICLE THEFT

There are various reasons why offenders steal autos and other vehicles. Often, investigators gain valuable insights regarding a thief's rationales and motives for stealing a particular vehicle if, and when, the stolen vehicle is eventually recovered. These reasons and their investigative indicators include the following:

Joyriding

Stealing a car or other vehicle for "fun" is what the term **joyriding** implies, but this form of theft can have very serious outcomes leading to death or injury. It is usually carried out opportunistically and is not done for profit. Cars may be taken from family and friends, or from total strangers. Joyriding typically takes place on weekends and holidays. Typical offenders include teenagers who do not own a car and seek the thrill of stealing and driving one. Joyriders are known for showing off to their friends, and sometimes invite them to ride in the car they have stolen to gain status within their delinquent peer networks. They are also noted for driving under the influence of drugs or alcohol and having hit-and-run accidents. Cars stolen for purposes of joyriding usually are recovered 24 to 48 hours after their initial theft. When recovered, these vehicles typically are found abandoned in secluded or remote areas in the city from which they were stolen or in neighboring communities. Signs of collision damage and vandalism often are present. Theft of major auto parts from stolen vehicles or the

auto's total destruction are not typical signatures of the joyrider; for some teenagers, however, joyriding may be a gateway crime that eventually leads to becoming a full-fledged auto thief for profit.[5]

Short-Term Transportation

Some offenders, who have no other means of short-term transportation, steal a vehicle simply to get from one place to another. These crimes of opportunity, like joyriding, are not for profit and seldom lead to the vehicle's recovery in a seriously damaged condition. Usually, cars stolen for purposes of short-term transportation are found in areas close to their initial location of theft. In other cases, however, offenders drive the stolen car as far as the existing fuel in the vehicle will take them. Then, they may attempt to refuel the car by stealing gasoline or simply steal another car to continue to their final destination. In the latter situation, the stolen vehicle will be recovered in a location that is a significant distance from the original theft location.[6]

Long-Term Transportation

Long-term transportation–type vehicle theft is motivated primarily by the offender's desire to obtain a particular type of vehicle and treat it as their own for months or even years. These thieves typically are older individuals in their twenties and thirties and are from economically deprived backgrounds. They attempt to radically alter the appearance of their stolen vehicle by changing its original color, applying accessories, or even chopping up the exterior to create a totally customized auto bearing little resemblance to the original. Some thieves sell or trade their stolen vehicle after fraudulently obtaining a legal title.[7]

Profit

Profit theft of a vehicle is usually the trademark of a professional thief, but can also be the work of amateurs trying to sell stolen vehicle parts to their friends. Autos stolen by true professionals for profit are almost never recovered because of the thief's elaborate connections to fences capable of disposing of the stolen vehicle and its parts hours after it is stolen. (For a more detailed discussion of this offender type, see the section titled Professional Vehicle Theft later in the chapter.[8])

Insurance Fraud

Persons who are financially upside-down on their vehicle (owe much more money than it is worth) may commit **insurance fraud** by faking or arranging a theft of an auto or other type of vehicle to claim insurance money—a scam known as *selling the car to the insurance company*. See the later section titled Vehicle Insurance Fraud for more discussion on this subject.[9]

Committing a Crime

Persons committing robberies, drive-by shootings, burglaries, drug transactions, and other crimes in public places prefer to steal cars or other vehicles for use in their criminal acts rather than to use vehicles that could be traced back to them. In effect, the vehicle theft merely facilitates a more serious secondary criminal activity. Other examples include commercial burglars who steal a large truck, which they later crash through security doors in a warehouse—in what is known as a *ram raid*—to enter the facility and steal merchandise; or "coyotes" who steal a large truck or van to smuggle undocumented immigrants across border crossings. More sophisticated criminals **cold plate** the cars they steal before committing a second crime. This process involves stealing a license plate from another vehicle of the same year, color, model, and manufacturer. Cold plating is intended to prevent officers from finding out that the car is stolen when they run the vehicle's license plate number through a stolen vehicles database. The most violent of these offenders resort to carjacking a vehicle for later use in an armed robbery (see the Carjacking section later in the chapter for more details).[10]

Trade for Drugs

To avoid forfeiture of their vehicle if apprehended, persons involved in drug sales and trafficking have recently adopted the practice of trading drugs to addicted clients in exchange for borrowing their vehicles to do drug deals. This is a win-win situation for both parties involved: The drug dealer runs no risk of losing a personal car to authorities if a drug deal ends up a bust; and if the drug dealer fails to return the vehicle, the drug addict can obtain more money for drugs by submitting an insurance claim for the stolen vehicle. This type of auto theft is also referred to as *crack for cars* because it attracts a high number of crack cocaine addicts.[11]

HOT TIPS AND LEADS 15.1

Cold Plating

Cold plating is the stealing of a license plate from a legally registered vehicle and applying it to a stolen vehicle of the same make, model, and color. Offenders often cold plate stolen vehicles before using them in bank robberies, burglaries, or drive-by shootings to avoid detection by police while traveling to and from a crime scene. The following are indicators often associated with cold plating:

1. The vehicle has only one plate in the rear and is missing the front plate, or the front plate does not match the rear one.

2. The rear plate appears dirty and the vehicle appears clean, or vice versa. Dusty plates may have clean spots where they have been handled. Clean plates may have dirty fingerprints.

3. The rear plate does not have registration tags, or the tags appear torn or removed from another plate.

4. Running the plate reveals that the features of the car (make, model, year, color) do not match those described for the plate number.

5. The car's VIN, license plate serial number, insurance information, or other title material does not match similar information associated with the plate number or the drivers of the vehicle.

One important investigative tip regarding a potentially cold plated vehicle is the report of a stolen license plate from a citizen. In such cases, the stolen plate number along with a detailed description of the victim's vehicle should be obtained. This information then can be compared to hot sheets or other stolen vehicle records to determine a possible make and model match. Patrol and investigative units can be provided the potentially cold plated vehicle's description in the event that it is used for criminal purposes.

MOTIVES FOR VEHICLE BREAK-INS

An auto or other enclosed vehicle can be broken into for various reasons. Shattered windows and broken door locks may be the product of intentional vandalism perpetrated as payback by a jealous lover or another person with a score to settle. Another motive could be responsible for theft of parts from, or contents within a vehicle. Usually, theft of property from the driver's compartment is committed by an opportunistic offender who has chanced upon a vehicle with an open window or unlocked door.

Less common, but still frequent, a forcible break-in is committed to steal property from within the vehicle. Such offenses are typically classified as auto burglaries and carry much harsher penalties than those given for the theft of items outside the vehicle. Purses, wallets, cell phones, auto registration/insurance information (for ID theft purposes), satellite radios, stereo systems, GPS devices, garage door openers, and loose change are some of the items usually stolen by ordinary offenders opportunistically targeting vehicles for theft. In other instances, however, the vehicle owner may be directly or indirectly involved in the theft; for example, the vehicle's financially stressed owner may stage a vehicle break-in to fraudulently claim insurance money for items allegedly stolen by a car burglar. Likewise, drugs, guns, or other illegal contraband inside the vehicle and belonging to its owner may be the motivation for an auto burglary carried out by an offender with knowledge of the illegal item's whereabouts inside the car. Unusual or out-of-the-ordinary circumstances surrounding a vehicle break-in such as (1) an offender breaking into a vehicle that has little target appeal or is a seldom stolen model and (2) forcible entry of vehicles in low-risk theft locations should raise a red flag to investigators that the vehicle's owner may have orchestrated the break-in or perhaps can provide inside knowledge of likely suspects.

Recently, auto burglaries have been linked to subsequent burglaries of residences. In this scenario, offenders break into vehicles located in parking areas adjacent to theaters, sporting events, concerts, and other events that occupy the vehicle owner for a lengthy and predictable time. In particular, vehicles with visible garage door openers and dash- or windshield-mounted GPA systems are targeted. The perpetrators know that the owners of the vehicle are away from home at the time of the event, so they locate the vehicle owner's home through information stored on the GPS device (or perhaps through a vehicle registration in the glove box) and use the garage door opener to enter the residence and commit burglary.

Finally, auto break-ins are also a necessary first step to the more serious offense of auto theft. Although auto thieves, like car burglars, usually employ forcible entry methods, the purpose for the vehicle break-in is clear since only fragments of glass or perhaps nothing at all remains where the stolen vehicle was last seen. On average, auto thieves enter the vehicle within 20 seconds or less and have completed the car theft in less than 3 minutes. Occasionally, however, what appears to be an ordinary car burglary is actually an attempted car theft gone bad. The unplanned return of the vehicle's owner, an alarm that cannot be quieted, a vehicle security system that could not be defeated, or any other unplanned occurrence that can startle would-be car thieves may result in a decision to abort the car theft. In such situations, the vehicle shows external damage related to the break-in, but few if any items are stolen from the interior. Furthermore, there may be damage to the vehicle's ignition, steering column, or dashboard.[12]

VEHICLE BREAK-IN METHODS

Offenders use perhaps as many vehicle break-in methods as there are different types of vehicles for them to break into. Listed here are some of the methods encountered most often during the investigation of car burglaries and auto thefts:

- *Ninja Rocks:* The offender throws almond-size bits of porcelain from the tops of engine spark plugs (known among auto thieves as **ninja rocks**) at the driver's-side window of a vehicle. With relatively little force and only a slight popping sound, the safety glass in the entire window shatters into small square-shape bits. A *spring-loaded center punch*—a construction tool used to make holes in wooden and metal surfaces—also is commonly used in the same fashion as ninja rocks.

- *Bricking or Stoning:* Bricks or rocks are often used by unsophisticated offenders to break vehicle windows when carrying out spontaneous auto break-ins.

- *Slim Jims:* A **Slim Jim** is a commercially produced device commonly used by police and tow truck drivers to open a locked vehicle without damaging windows, doors, or locks (see Figure 15.2). The Slim Jim is a thin, flat, ruler-shaped metal object that is slipped down between the window glass and car door to release the door locking mechanism. Makeshift Slim Jims can be made from metallic rulers used for construction and drafting purposes. There will be no signs of forced entry on locked vehicles opened with a Slim Jim. Some newer vehicles have door locks that cannot be opened using a Slim Jim.

- *Door Wedging:* Wooden wedges or tools like flat-end screwdrivers can be used to pry open a small space between the vehicle's door and door frame post. The vehicle's inside door locking button, switch, or handle then can be released with a wire, stick, or other object.

- *Master Keying:* Many car manufacturers provide information to locksmiths, dealers, and other authorized auto repair personnel regarding how to make a master key that fits the doors of all similar model lines. Nearly all towing companies possess books containing the formulas for master keys.

- *Lock Punching:* Door locks typically are made from metal, but are housed in plastic door handle frames. A common flat-head screwdriver is used to punch the lock from its plastic frame to the inside of the door, enabling the offender to manually manipulate the door lock; or

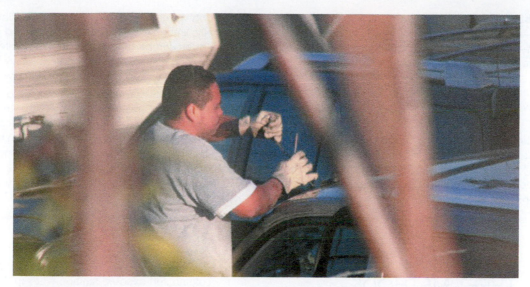

FIGURE 15.2 ▶ An auto thief under surveillance is photographed attempting to use a Slim Jim device to unlock the vehicle's door.

the screwdriver is merely pushed into the lock like an ordinary key and twisted to defeat the lock. The same method can be used on trunks with exposed key locks.

- **Code Grabbing:** Many newer vehicles have *remote keyless entry (RKE)* systems that enable owners to automatically open door and trunk locks remotely—outside of, and far from the vehicle. These devices send electronic encrypted signals to the vehicle's RKE system that are decoded into commands to engage or disengage door locks and the car's general security system. Rumors abound that thieves can use laptop computer software to easily receive and clone the signals for a vehicle's RKE codes when activated by the owner's remote control. The RKE, however, contains over 18 billion rolling encrypted codes that are virtually impossible to capture and decode; so, at this point, auto break-in technology does not allow offenders to enter a vehicle by cloning an RKE device.

- **Key Theft:** **Key theft** is perhaps the most common method for breaking into newer, higher-tech vehicles while leaving no damage from an external break-in. Typically, the offender somehow obtains the original key or a spare, which enables a quick and simple entry to the vehicle. Keys can be acquired illegally by stealing them in a residential burglary, or legitimately by receiving them on trust from the vehicle's owner (e.g., as a friend, family, neighbor, valet, auto repair person, or parking lot attendant).[13]

HOT TIPS AND LEADS 15.2

Predicting Higher Level Crimes from Vehicle Theft

When a vehicle is stolen, investigators may conclude that it is just another ordinary theft for profit; however, this may not necessarily be the situation at hand—especially if the factors surrounding the vehicle theft are unusual. It is a well-known fact that vehicle theft, like ID theft, is the first step taken by many offenders who intend to carry out a second, more serious crime. These crimes and some of their vehicle theft–related warning signs are as follows:

1. **Burglary:** Trucks, vans, and large passenger vehicles are often stolen by burglars to transport large goods removed from dwellings, warehouses, and businesses. In most jurisdictions, these types of vehicles are not prime targets for theft—with most thieves preferring imports and other compact passenger vehicles. In particular, commercial burglars intent on stealing pallets of merchandise or an ATM machine may steal a truck with a hydraulic lift. Larger, older trucks that are rarely stolen for a profit may also be stolen for use in a ram-raid style burglary.

2. **Drive-by Shootings:** Street gang members nearly always use stolen cars when "riding up" on their rivals to carry out a drive-by shooting. Mid- to large-size American passenger model cars are the vehicles of choice for these crimes because they provide more protection from return gunfire and can hold a greater number of shooters with access to large window openings. Before the drive-by, the gang members sometimes try to cold plate the vehicle.

(continued)

3. *Bank Robberies:* When a vehicle is used in a bank robbery—as happens in most professional take-over style robberies—it usually is stolen sometime immediately before the robbery. Two cars may be stolen in a relatively short time at the same general location to serve as a primary getaway car, which will be abandoned at a location where a secondary get-away car is parked. Both vehicles may be cold plated.

4. *Immigration and Smuggling:* Cargo trucks, vans, and large passenger vehicle may be stolen to support "coyotes" who smuggle undocumented persons across U.S. border check points. Smugglers also may use similar stolen vehicles to transport illegal goods and narcotics from ports of entry and across border crossings. Typically, smugglers steal older vehicles and equip them with hidden compartments to sequester stolen goods and modify the suspension to prevent heavy loads from causing the vehicle to appear weighted down.

5. *Terrorism:* Terrorists use stolen vehicles to do reconnaissance of areas that they intend to strike, or to make a rolling bomb (i.e., car bomb) to attack a desired target. Vans and large passenger vehicles can be filled with explosives or, as in the World Trade Center and the Oklahoma City bombings, stolen cargo trucks can be filled with explosive materials. Terrorists may steal a truck or car by first renting it with a stolen credit card and identification.

VEHICLE THEFT METHODS

The specific method used to commit a vehicle theft depends largely on three factors: (1) the type of vehicle, (2) the age of the vehicle, and (3) the offender's knowledge, experience, and expertise in defeating vehicle security systems. Over the past several decades, the world of auto thievery has changed dramatically as has the technology of security devices installed by vehicle manufacturers. Before the mid-1980s, most autos were stolen using simple tools like scissors, screwdrivers, and vise grips. Easy access to wiring inside the vehicle and the engine compartment enabled offenders to start the vehicle's engine with little electronics knowhow. From the late 1980s to the present day, advances in vehicle security technology have forced auto thieves to abandon the simple mechanical tricks of yesteryear and devise new methods that can beat today's high-tech auto theft prevention. Following are some of the more common auto theft methods encountered during the investigation of both late and older model stolen vehicles:

1. *Ignition Punching:* The perpetrator forcibly pushes or hammers a flathead screwdriver or similar-shape metal object into the car's ignition switch, twisting it like a key to make electrical contact and start the vehicle's engine (see Figure 15.3). This also may release a locked steering column; if not, a pair of vise grips can be used to forcibly break loose the locking mechanism on the steering wheel. This method is used primarily on vehicles manufactured before the mid-1980s, although it also works on some American vehicles produced up until the mid-2000s that were not equipped with modern security systems.

2. *Hot Wiring:* This method is used on vehicles of the same vintage as those stolen by ignition punching (i.e., predominantly older models). The thief starts the car's engine by bypassing the normal key-operated electrical system through a simple cross-wiring procedure. This can be done by accessing the engine's electrical system under the car's hood or within its interior. Obvious signs of hot wiring include breakage of the steering column and exposed ignition wires in the driver's compartment area—although hot wiring can be done under the hood by simply touching a screwdriver, wire, or other metal object between two electrical points in the engine area. Figure 15.4 shows evidence of hot wiring that was discovered and documented during a stolen vehicle investigation.

3. *Keys Stolen in Burglary:* The most common method of auto theft, especially for modern and expensive luxury models, is **key burglary**—stealing the vehicle's keys in a residential burglary. In these instances, the perpetrator performs a simple break-in and steals, among other items, the keys to the target vehicle, which usually are easily found in kitchen drawers, on countertops, or hanging on a wall. The vehicle may then be stolen immediately after the burglary and used to transport stolen goods from the crime scene, or the perpetrator may return later to steal the car from a

FIGURE 15.3 ▶ Some vehicles not equipped with modern antitheft devices can be stolen by merely punching the ignition with a screwdriver and hammer, as shown here.

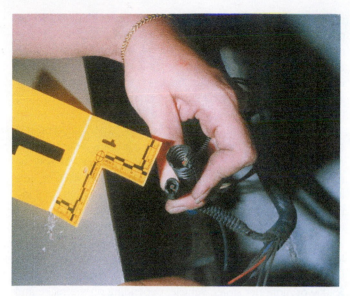

FIGURE 15.4 ▶ Wires cut from the ignition system of a stolen vehicle that was hotwired. These wires may be useful in making a physical match between the cut ends and wire cutting tools recovered from car thieves.

driveway, parking lot, or other location of opportunity. During the mid- to late-1990s, using the vehicle's key became necessary for most car thieves when auto security systems began to incorporate immobilizers controlled with transponder keys. Transponder keys contain a small computer chip that, when placed in the ignition, sends a signal to the auto's computer system to activate or deactivate (hence, immobilize) the engine and other mechanical components necessary for the vehicle to operate. This system made older car theft methods such as ignition punching and hot wiring virtually obsolete overnight for various reasons. First, the system is wireless, so there are no ignition wires to hot wire; second, punching or forcibly twisting the ignition will not activate the vehicle; and most important, defeating the ignition system by any forceful means will not cause the vehicle computer to activate necessary vital functions of the vehicle's engine such as starter activation and control of the fuel flow. Without the proper transponder key and its coded chip, chances are slim that even the most technologically savvy auto thief can steal the car by overriding its computerized security system.

4. ***Keys Stolen in Robberies:*** Less-patient auto thieves, frustrated with transponder key technology, may take the most direct route to auto theft—**key robbery**—by simply robbing the owner's key using physical force or fear. Keys may be stolen directly from the victim outside the vehicle or while the victim is operating it—commonly known as a *carjacking* (discussed in more detail later). Other personal belongings (e.g., purses, wallets, backpacks) robbed from the owner in an attempt to obtain money may later be discovered to contain car keys that the offender can use or trade off to an experienced auto thief to steal the robbery victim's car.

5. ***Keys Left in the Vehicle:*** The second most common method used by thieves is simply to locate a vehicle with the keys left in the ignition. Offenders commonly steal cars with keys in the ignition that are parked in driveways at residential locations. Often, however, thieves happen to locate a vehicle with keys in its ignition that is still running. To discover these opportunities, offenders linger in parking lots containing outdoor ATM machines, dry cleaners, convenience stores, video stores, postal mailing services, and other locations where individuals make quick deliveries or pickups without shutting off or locking their vehicle. More subtle tactics are also used to steal a running car, such as getting a driver to momentarily exit a vehicle to render help during a staged emergency, signaling to the driver that the vehicle has a flat tire, or bumping the vehicle from behind so that the driver steps out to check for damage.

6. ***Key Cloning:*** For certain transponder keys manufactured for specific car models, the encrypted computer chip code can be decoded and duplicated in a new key containing a blank computer chip. This is done with a **key cloning** machine, which sometimes can be purchased on-line for $200 or less. Certain locksmiths and hardware stores also can make duplicate transponder keys by using a cloning device. A key can cloned, however, only by duplicating an original vehicle key containing the transponder code—not another key that has been already cloned. Therefore, the offender must somehow secure the original vehicle key to perform the cloning process. This may involve parking lot attendants, valets, or auto shop personnel who acquire an original vehicle key for a short period of time, during which a key clone can be created that can be used to steal the car after it has been returned to its owner.

7. ***Taken Without Consent:*** These situations may involve (1) the taking of a vehicle from a person or place of business by an individual authorized to do so, but then never returning the vehicle; or (2) the unauthorized use, and subsequent stealing, of a car by a person familiar with its owner (e.g., a friend, family member, or business associate). Common to both these theft approaches is the fact that auto thieves take advantage of personal relationships to gain easy access to the vehicle. In some instances, the vehicle may be taken for a short period of time without the owner's consent and used to commit a criminal activity such as a burglary, robbery, drive-by shooting, street race, or illegal drug transaction. In addition, because of an existing relationship between the offender and the auto

theft victim, the owner of the missing vehicle may not necessarily immediately notify the police.

8. ***Identity Theft, Fraud, and Forgery:*** Increases in the incidence of identity theft have recently spilled over into the world of auto theft. False IDs or stolen legitimate IDs can be used in numerous ways to commit auto theft. For one, thieves posing as potential customers may enter a car dealership and secure a test drive of a vehicle by leaving a driver's license with the salesperson as security. The car is driven off and never returned, however, leaving the dealership with nothing more than a false identification of the offender. Another, and more involved scam is to steal a vehicle from a dealership by conducting a false purchase transaction, such as a vehicle sale or lease. Here, the thief provides false documentation to gain loan approval for the vehicle based on address, social security number, credit score, and other information that is the product of identity theft. Similarly, theft of vehicles from personal parties is carried out by offenders who respond to ads posted in newspapers or on websites such as Craigslist and either (1) test drive the vehicle and never return it, or (2) purchase the vehicle using counterfeit money, a bad check, a forged check, or an invalid cashier's check. The latter method is usually employed when banks are closed (i.e., nights, weekends, and holidays) and the funds secured by a cashier's check cannot be verified by the issuing bank.

9. ***Towing:*** This method is not routinely used, but is occasionally employed to steal high-profile sports cars or luxury vehicles that are of significant value and are equipped with a security system that is extremely difficult to defeat. Typically, the offender employs either stolen tow trucks or corrupt tow truck drivers to steal the target vehicle by pretending to tow the vehicle for purposes of repair, repossession, or enforcing a traffic violation.[14]

PROFESSIONAL VEHICLE THEFT

Although it is commonly believed that most auto thefts are committed by teenagers and other persons who target vehicles for their own personal gain, in reality most vehicle thefts—including cars, motorcycles, boats, and heavy equipment—are the work of professional thieves. Professional auto theft is carried out strictly for profit and appears to be a growing trend in today's weak economy. It not only affects the victims, but also contributes to rising insurance rates, which are passed on to consumers.

Professional auto thieves can operate either individually or in auto theft rings (see the Vehicle Theft Rings section later in the chapter). They do not target flashy new cars of high value, as portrayed in the media, but rather older vehicles that have high resale value for their parts. Parted-out stolen vehicles can

provide thieves four to five times the profit that would be obtained for the legitimate sale of the intact vehicles. Sometimes professionals are opportunists, stealing cars in high demand for their parts when they are left running or with keys in the ignition. In these cases, the car is merely driven away to a location where it may be stripped or stored temporarily until transported to a new location.

More often than not, however, the most experienced professionals begin their day by looking over a list of top-choice vehicles to steal and pay incentives for quick delivery of specific models. Parking lots, auto distribution centers, and even car lots are not off limits for this type of preselected auto theft. In addition, sophisticated surveillance and alarm systems do not deter these thieves once they have spotted the target vehicle. Professionals often blitz an area, stealing numerous cars from one location—for example, several of the same model of vehicle from a retail car lot. They can be paid anywhere from $500 to $5,000 or more per stolen vehicle, depending on the make and model. Prolific professional thieves can steal 5 to 10 cars per day. A vehicle purchased from these thieves is typically handed off to a second level of professionals, who perform one of the following illegal activities.

Chopping for Parts and Scrap Metal

The stolen vehicle may be taken to a **chop shop** where it will be dismantled for its parts, accessories, and metal components. These illegal operations are conducted in clandestine facilities specifically constructed for parting out vehicles or in legitimate auto repair facilities that operate an illegal side business. Welding torches are used to cut the car into sections, as are sawing mechanisms with metal cutting blades. Parts with identifying VIN numbers are separated from those without such numbers—the majority of the parts removed from the vehicle's chassis. Unmarked parts are then sold to corrupt auto parts dealers and repair shops that often fraudulently sell them as "new" to unsuspecting consumers. Airbags are among the most sought-after stolen auto parts because they are routinely replaced after auto collisions. Thieves are paid upwards of $300 for stolen airbags, which are later installed during a legitimate accident repair job—for which insurance companies or consumers are billed $1,500 to $2,000 for installing the stolen airbag. Marked parts and larger components of the car are fed into a shredder and turned into fist-size chunks of recycled metal. These are sold to countries such as China where metal is a rare commodity. Thus, as the foregoing discussion suggests, one vehicle with a street retail value of approximately $6,000 can quickly (sometimes within hours) be turned into a $25,000 (or more) profit via the chop shop.[15]

Strip and Run

In a **strip and run** all valuable accessories, including wheels, seats, DVD/entertainment systems, GPS navigation systems, and so forth, are stripped from the vehicle immediately after it is stolen. Depending on the thief's motives, the stolen parts may be sold or kept in storage. In cases where the accessories are not sold, the thief will attempt to buy the stripped car at a low price from police or insurance auto auctions after it has been recovered. After making the purchase, they will reassemble the vehicle and sell it for full profit. In addition, the vehicle is no longer considered stolen because it has formally been recovered by police.[16]

VIN Switching

Every automobile and motorcycle produced from 1981 to present has a unique 17-digit **VIN (vehicle identification number)** used not only to identify the vehicle, but also to authenticate the vehicle's legal title, registration, and other legal documentation used to prove ownership. **VIN switching**, also referred to as **vehicle cloning**, involves switching the stolen vehicle's identification information with that of an unstolen vehicle of the same make, model, and other design features. Installation of false VIN plates, fraudulent titles, and fake registrations are some of the ways thieves make stolen vehicles appear legitimate. These vehicles can be sold domestically or transported to Mexico, Central and South America, China, or Middle Eastern and Eastern European countries where they will sell for prices that may be double the vehicle's value in the United States. One clear sign of VIN switching is a VIN number that appears to have been replaced or tampered with, or an inconsistency between the vehicle's VIN and other official ownership documentation. For more information on the VIN and its use, see the Vehicle Identification Number and Reading the Vehicle Identification Number sections later in the chapter.[17] Crime scene evidence of VIN switching is illustrated in Figure 15.5.

Salvage Switching

In **salvage switching**, thieves use fake or stolen identities to purchase a car that has been deemed beyond repair, or *salvaged,* to obtain the vehicle's VIN plate and title. They subsequently obtain a stolen car essentially the same as the salvaged one, and then switch VIN plates between the two vehicles. After claiming to have legitimately rebuilt the salvaged vehicle, the thieves use the same fake or stolen identities used to initially purchase the vehicle to reregister it and gain a clear title so that the vehicle can be sold.

Counterfeit VIN

Counterfeit VIN plates of high quality are manufactured and used to replace VIN plates on stolen vehicles. Sometimes, thieves steal specific makes and models of cars and use the same counterfeit VIN on numerous stolen vehicles.[18]

Body Switching

In **body switching**, the entire body of a vehicle can be removed from one vehicle and placed on the chassis of another. If the body of an unstolen vehicle is placed on the chassis of a stolen vehicle, there will be inconsistencies between, or alternations of VIN numbers in the vehicle compartment, frame, and motor areas.[19]

(a)

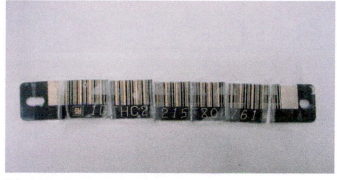

(b)

FIGURE 15.5 ▶ (a) Bar used to pry loose a VIN plate from the dash of a new car—resulting in breaking of the windshield. (b) The VIN was reassembled by mixing parts of VIN numbers from other vehicles to clone a stolen vehicle.

Vehicle Exporting

Up to 15 percent of all vehicles exported from the United States to other countries are thought to be stolen. Most of these illegal exports are the work of international vehicle trafficking rings that not only prepare and ship the stolen vehicle, but also have connections with criminal associates in the country where the vehicle is received and later sold. In the United States, it is the jurisdiction of the Customs and Border Patrol (CBP) to oversee the logistics of vehicle transportation from ports of entry. To have a vehicle authorized for shipment, exporters provide agents with proof of ownership, consisting largely of certificates of title, manufacturers' statements of origin, or bills of sale. Watercraft, including jet skis, are excluded from this requirement. Although CBP does not maintain a list of all vehicles exported from the United States, they are alerted by the National Insurance Crime Bureau (NICB) of stolen vehicles and have access to their stolen vehicle database to check the status of an exported vehicle. In addition, the identification materials for exported vehicles must be presented to CBP at least 72 hours before the vehicle's scheduled time of departure for port. Suspicious vehicle shipments typically are those in which the exporter provides last-minute documentation to CBP that just meets the

72-hour time deadline. In addition, vehicles not declared to CBP that are hidden as contraband beneath other cargo usually are identified by their shipping characteristics, which are (1) unusual products being shipped to unusual places and (2) containers that weigh much more (due to inclusions of vehicles) than they should, given the nature of the product being shipped. In the latter instance, inspectors require an open-container search to inspect contents at the bottom or end of the container, where the vehicles are likely to be hidden. The estimated cost to thieves of stealing and shipping stolen vehicles is only 10 percent of the price that will be received when the vehicle is sold in its country of destination. Popular countries of destination include those where American vehicles sell at a premium price due to differences in currency exchange rates, including European countries where the euro overvalues the U.S. dollar.[20]

VEHICLE THEFT RINGS

Vehicle theft rings are organized groups who steal large numbers of vehicles for a profit. Their membership nearly always consists of professional auto thieves. The following are some offense and offender characteristics typically linked to auto theft rings:

- Concentrate high-frequency theft in specific locations
- An organized group structure, with identifiable leadership (larger groups may be organized in a cell structure)
- Have a group size of 10 members or less (although some international rings may have a considerably larger membership, with combined cell memberships of 50 or more persons)
- Rarely use force to acquire a vehicle

- Target newer model cars
- Target cars with valuables in them
- Steal cars at all times of the day
- Have a centralized chop shop location
- Target cars with unique features/options
- Recruit males under the age of 30 years, of various racial backgrounds

Investigations of vehicle theft rings require a much more coordinated and methodical approach than those involving single professional or amateur thieves. This is because the slightest detection of law enforcement activities by even a single auto ring member causes a rapid-fire tipoff to the entire offender group. If this occurs, future investigative efforts will likely fail, which may pose an increased danger for investigators. Therefore, bringing down an auto theft ring requires a detailed investigative plan that will undoubtedly incorporate various tactics and strategies for gathering evidence as well as making arrests. Obtaining as much background knowledge as possible about the ring itself, including membership size, organizational structure, and *modus operandi*, is a vital starting point in this process. Following are some of the various information gathering techniques proven effective in auto theft ring investigations:

1. ***Parking Lot/Structure Surveillance:*** Specific areas (e.g., parking lots/structures) where auto theft rings have operated with high frequency can be placed under surveillance to obtain information about potential suspects and their methods of operation. Suspects can be photographed engaging in theft-related activities from a surveillance van or other location.

2. ***Car Buy/Traffic Stops:*** Undercover officers or informants purchase a stolen vehicle from various auto theft ring suspects. Then, after leaving the location in a vehicle, the suspects are stopped by traffic officers for an alleged violation, at which time a field interview is conducted to gain additional information about the suspects.

3. ***Controlled Buys of Parts:*** Multiple purchases of parts can be made from one or more suspects involved in the auto theft ring. Special orders for parts from suspects may lead to the discovery of a chop shop location like that shown in Figure 15.6 where large amounts of stolen parts are warehoused.

4. ***Undercover House:*** A specific location, usually a residential home, may be secured for conducting undercover buys of stolen cars and parts from auto theft rings. The undercover house may be outfitted with surveillance video equipment, a

FIGURE 15.6 ▶ Motors at a chop shop on their way to be sold on the black market to auto repair shops and perhaps exporters.

surveillance van, or undercover officers wearing body wires to document illegal sales transactions with suspects.

5. ***Bait Cars:*** High-theft model vehicles are parked in strategic locations in an opportunistic manner for auto thieves (windows down, keys in the ignition, or left running) to bait thieves to steal them. These vehicles are typically equipped with video recording devices in the passenger compartments to capture the thief's image and actions. GPS tracking is also commonly employed to map the vehicle's location. Electronic kill switches are also used to stop the vehicle when an arrest is made.[21]

During the information gathering phase, the decision on whether undercover buy operations should be carried out using an officer or an informant may have to be made. As a general rule, an informant is preferable to an officer if there is any doubt that suspects will feel uncomfortable doing illegal transactions with a stranger. After sufficient information has been gathered and proper warrants have been secured, suspected members of the auto theft ring should be arrested using a sweep/round up method. In other words, all identified suspects should be arrested simultaneously so that suspects served with warrants will not be able to notify those who have not yet been served.

CARJACKING

Carjacking is defined by the U.S. Department of Justice as the "completed or attempted robbery of a motor vehicle by a stranger to the victim." This violent form of auto theft is believed to have originated in Detroit sometime in the early 1980s, and it gained popularity by auto theft copycats throughout the nation during the 1990s. According to a U.S. Bureau of Justice Statistics study, approximately 49,000 carjacking incidents occurred nationwide from 1992 to 1996. The growing use of carjacking as a preferred means of auto theft is perhaps the result of average car thieves being unable to defeat the high-tech immobilizer security systems on newer vehicles through ordinary vehicle theft techniques. Growing numbers of violent incidents across the nation, resulting in injuries and killings of motorists for their autos, prompted Congress to pass the 1992 Federal Anti-Car Theft Act (FACTA). Among other things, the following section of FACTA made carjacking a federal offense and created harsh penalties for offenders engaging in the violent takeover of vehicles:

Whoever, possessing a firearm, as defined in section 921 of this title, takes a motor vehicle that has been transported, shipped or received in interstate or foreign commerce from the person or presence of another by force and violence or by intimidation, or attempts to do so, shall—1) be fined under this title or imprisoned not more than 15 years, or both. 2) If serious bodily injury . . . results, be fined under this title or be imprisoned not more than 25 years, or both, and 3) if death results, be fined under this title or imprisoned for any number of years up to life, or both.[22]

Currently, an estimated 25,000 carjacking crimes take place in the United States each year. Studies on the carjacking problem

conducted by the FBI have revealed the following information about carjacking incidents and offenders:

- It usually takes no more than 15 seconds for a carjacking suspect to overpower a victim and take possession of a stolen auto.
- If a weapon is used, it will be a handgun 90 percent of the time. Knives are the second weapon of choice of carjackers.
- Most carjacking incidents take place approximately 5 miles from the victim's home.
- The most popular location for a carjacking is a parking lot, followed by city streets, residential driveways, car dealerships, and gas stations. Persons stopped in traffic (parked at traffic lights, going to drive-up windows) or exiting their vehicles (at ATM machines or convenience stores) also are likely targets.
- Most victims of a carjacking are lone males (92 percent) who live in urban locations.
- There is no specific type of vehicle targeted by a carjacker; older, less expensive as well as new luxury models are both at risk.
- About half of all carjacking attempts are successful.
- Carjackers usually strike on weekends at night between the hours of 8 PM and 11 PM.
- Most carjackers operate alone, but sometimes in pairs when using a "bump and jack" technique. This involves two offenders in a car, sometimes stolen, who bump the victim's vehicle from behind. When the victim exits the targeted car to inspect likely damage, one of the carjackers approaches and carjacks the running vehicle. The other carjacker then drives away in his vehicle, following the stolen car.[23]

FIGURE 15.7 ▶ Often, license plates are cut and spliced together to change the registration of a stolen or salvaged vehicle to that of one with a clear title and no history of damage.

CASE CLOSE-UP 15.1

KATRINA CAR FRAUD
New Orleans, LA

In 2005, Hurricane Katrina damaged almost 500,000 vehicles by flood water and other extreme weather conditions. Although many of these vehicles were declared a total loss by the companies insuring them, thieves managed to restore and fraudulently resell them to unsuspecting buyers led to believe that the vehicle they purchased had never been damaged. This scam was enabled, in large part, by lax vehicle branding laws in Louisiana and other states that did not require a vehicle's title to be changed to salvage or another status indicating that it had been damaged by flood water. Thieves transported these vehicles throughout the nation, where there were sold with a new "clean" title. Tens of thousands of the Katrina flood-damaged vehicles are estimated to have been sold. Many of the owners have since discovered that their vehicle's motor and transmission fail after a few months of driving, the cloth interior smells of growing mold and mildew, and the trunk and passenger compartment are infested with numerous species of insects.

VEHICLE INSURANCE FRAUD

Insurance money for allegedly stolen or damaged cars is collected by countless fraudulent schemes and scams, usually carried out by the vehicle's legal owner, who perhaps is colluding with other criminal parties. Conversely, other frauds are executed by unscrupulous auto repair shops that target vehicle owners and insurance companies. The primary motives for these acts are greed and easy profit, although some fraudulent insurance claims are made to cover up other crimes committed involving the insured vehicle. These and other motives are evident in the following list of popular scams used to commit vehicle insurance fraud:

- *The Owner Give-Up:* In an **owner give-up** scam, owners who cannot sell or can no longer afford their vehicle report that it has been stolen to escape their liability to the bank that financed the vehicle. In most cases, the owner is upside-down on the vehicle, meaning that more is owed on the vehicle that it is worth on the open market. This scam usually involves the destruction of the vehicle by its owner or by another person whom the owner has hired to perform the staged theft. Often the same individual uses an owner give-up scam multiple times. Persons suspected of this criminal activity, therefore, should be investigated for having filed previous vehicle theft reports.

- *30-Day Special:* This is a variant of the owner give-up scam; however, the vehicle is usually very high mileage and/or needs extensive repairs. The owner files a false theft report on the vehicle and hides the car for 30 days or so until the insurance company settles the claim and issues a payment. After that time, the car will be discovered abandoned and perhaps stripped or destroyed.

- *Export Scam:* Shortly after a vehicle is purchased, leased, or rented, the owner makes a false theft report after giving or selling the vehicle to an auto theft ring, who exports the vehicle to a foreign country. A related version of the scam involves delivering the vehicle to a chop shop, where it is dismantled or given a new identity through the use of fraudulent license plates (see Figure 15.7) and titles of ownership. In either the export

or chop shop version of this fraud method, the owner stands to make a double profit from both the insurance settlement and the illegal sale of the vehicle to thieves.

- *Phantom Car Scheme:* A fake title and registration are used to secure insurance on a car that does not exist. In this scheme, the insurance company will be required to compensate the fraudulent owner because the allegedly stolen vehicle was never recovered. Phantom car perpetrators often insure expensive antique or luxury cars to maximize their payoff. This scheme works only on insurance companies that do not require a visual inspection of the vehicle before writing insurance on it.

- *Scapegoat Theft:* This scam is generally not for profit, but is executed to enable the vehicle's owner to avoid detection by authorities for committing another crime in which the vehicle was involved. Often, hit-and-run crimes are covered up by intoxicated drivers who claim that they had nothing to do with the incident, but rather the real guilty party was a thief who had stolen their car. In these situations, there is usually a significant lag time between the estimated time of the accident and the filing of the false theft report.

- *Auto Arson:* Vehicles may be intentionally torched to fraudulently obtain insurance money or cover up crimes. Car fires are relatively rare, especially when the entire vehicle has been affected by the fire. It is often a very difficult and tedious task for investigators to prove that a vehicle fire was deliberately set, absent other factors signaling intentional vehicle destruction such as accessories missing from the burnt vehicle. Most unintentional vehicle fires begin in the engine compartment and are the product of faulty fuel and ignition systems. The subject of vehicle fires is further examined in Chapter 17.

- *Inflated Costs:* In these swindles, the owner and/or a repair facility makes claims of inflated costs or values to secure a larger insurance settlement for a stolen or damaged vehicle. This scam differs from others previously discussed in that the vehicle does exist and is owned by the individual making the insurance claim. In addition, the vehicle in fact may have been

FIGURE 15.8 ▶ Vehicle manufacturers place various labels on parts throughout the vehicle for identification purposes. Pictured above is a vehicle parts identification label (left), which is placed on new and replacement parts; also pictured (right) is a vehicle load label indicating the amount of weight the vehicle can hold. Car thieves often use counterfeit or improperly placed labels when assembling a vehicle from stolen parts, as with the example shown here, where the labels are fake. Manufacturers provide reference sources for investigators to authenticate the appearance and position of parts and labels placed throughout the vehicle.

stolen, damaged, and repaired. The fraud is carried out by owners who lie about the vehicle's value or otherwise intentionally misstate their losses to gain a larger insurance payout. Likewise, repair shops submit fraudulently inflated repair bills to insurance companies, overcharging for services such as additional labor time, parts, towing, storage, and other repair billing items that may or may not have been provided.[24]

ODOMETER ROLLBACKS

Despite computerized databases containing vehicle odometer readings, the practice of **odometer rollbacks** is still alive and well. Some estimates suggest that millions of vehicles sold each year have been subject to odometer changes that underestimate their true mileage. Listed here are some key indicators that can be used to investigate vehicles for odometer rollbacks:

1. Loose screws or scratch marks around the dashboard where the odometer is located.
2. Fingerprints or debris located on the inner side of the clear plastic covering of the instrument panel where the odometer is located.
3. Numbers that do not appear straight or line up correctly, especially at the 10,000 mark.
4. Sticking of the odometer when the vehicle is driven.
5. Stickers on doors, windshields, or under the hood that indicate mileage at which services such as oil changes were performed. These may exceed the number showing on the odometer.
6. Perform computer checks on vehicle databases.
7. Altered sections of the original title where the vehicle's mileage was written by its previous owner.

8. Wear of brakes, tires, seats, or other vehicle components that is inconsistent with the wear expected for the stated odometer reading.
9. The vehicle is being sold shortly after a new title has been issued. A new title may have been created to cover up mileage stated on a previous title.
10. Many odometers contain security tags and clips where they are attached to the vehicle. These are broken when the odometer is either disconnected or replaced.[25]

VEHICLE IDENTIFICATION NUMBER

Knowledge of the VIN (Vehicle Identification Number) and how it can be used to identify vehicles and their histories is essential for conducting investigations of vehicle-related crimes. The VIN is a coded series of numbers and letters that serves as a unique identification for a specific vehicle. The particular location and type of coding sequence used to create the VIN can depend on many factors, including when, when, and by which manufacturer the vehicle was produced (for example, see Figure 15.8). For vehicles produced before 1950, a VIN was not required by law. Usually these vehicles were identified only by a serial number created by the manufacturer that identified the make, model, and year of production. From 1958 to 1970, nearly all vehicles were assigned a VIN consisting of 11 characters or less; however, the information contained in the ID codes was not necessarily consistent from one manufacturer to the next. To remedy this problem, the U.S. National Highway Traffic Safety Administration (NHTSA) passed legislation requiring that all road vehicles, beginning with models produced in 1981, be identified with a fixed, standardized 17-character VIN providing that same specific information for each vehicle. This law applied to automobiles, trailers, motorcycles, and mopeds. Beginning with the 1987 model year, this law was later amended to require that VIN numbers be used to mark 12 or 14 major components of passenger vehicles that were designated as "high-risk" for theft (see Figure 15.9). Some thieves may take extreme measures to ensure that VIN numbers on the various components of a stolen vehicle remain consistent, as in the case of the "body swap" method illustrated in Figure 15.10 In 1994, multipurpose vehicles (e.g., SUVs) and light-duty trucks were added to this list, and the following specific components were required to be identified with the vehicle's VIN:

- Transmission
- Front and rear bumpers
- Engine
- Hood
- Right and left doors
- Sliding cargo door
- Right and left quarter panels and side assembly
- Pickup/cargo box
- Rear doors and hatchback/deck lid/tailgate[26]

FIGURE 15.9 ▶ A VIN (circled above) is a 17-digit number placed in various locations and on numerous parts throughout the vehicle.

READING THE VEHICLE IDENTIFICATION NUMBER

In all vehicles, model years 1981 to present, the 17 characters of the VIN are defined as follows:

Position 1:   Country where the vehicle was manufactured. Examples: USA (1), Canada (2), Mexico (3), Japan (J), Germany (W)

Position 2:   Vehicle Manufacturer. Examples: Chevrolet (C), General Motors (G), Toyota (T)

Positions 3–8:   These positions provide a general description of the vehicle and its various features. Example: 1986 Honda Accord (MAD771)— where "M" = Passenger Car; "AD" = Accord model; "7" = 4-speed automatic transmission; "7" = 2-Door; "1" = Basic, nonluxury model.

Position 9:   The VIN's **check digit**. This is a single-digit number, or the letter "X", placed in the VIN's 9th position, created by performing a mathematical calculation that takes into consideration all of the other characters contained in the VIN. The purpose of the check digit is to provide a logical number based on the other VIN characters that can be used to identify false VINs on stolen vehicles or possible mistakes in the documentation of the vehicle's real VIN when it has been officially registered. (Note that the letters I, O, and Q are not included in any VIN to avoid confusing them with the numbers 1 and 0.) As you can see from examining the check digit calculation method, it would be very difficult to simply make up a false VIN that contains the proper check digit. To manually calculate the check digit for any given VIN, you can use the formula provided; however, various on-line VIN check digit calculators are available that can perform this task more quickly and with much less effort!

HOT TIPS AND LEADS 15.3

VIN Check Digit Formula

1. *Convert Vin Letters to Numbers:* Using the following hypothetical 17-character VIN = 2HKYF18636H529972, first substitute the following assigned values for each of the letters appearing in the VIN:

Assigned Values

A = 1	J = 1	T = 3
B = 2	K = 2	U = 4
C = 3	L = 3	V = 5
D = 4	M = 4	W = 6
E = 5	N = 5	X = 7
F = 6	P = 7	Y = 8
G = 7	R = 9	Z = 9
H = 8	S = 2	

This would result in the following converted VIN that excludes all letters and consists of only numeric values:

a. Original VIN: 2 H K Y F 1 8 6 3 6 H 5 2 9 9 7 2

b. Converted VIN: 2 **8 2 8 6** 1 8 6 3 6 **8** 5 2 9 9 7 2

2. *Multiply Each Vin Number by Its Weighting Factor:* Below is a list of numbers or *weighting factors* corresponding to each of the 17 VIN number positions. For each specific position in the VIN, multiply the VIN number by its corresponding weighting factor number.

Weighting Factors
Position

1st	= 8	9th	= 0 (Check Digit)
2nd	= 7	10th	= 9

(continued)

3rd	= 6	11th	= 8
4th	= 5	12th	= 7
5th	= 4	13th	= 6
6th	= 3	14th	= 5
7th	= 2	15th	= 4
8th	= 10	16th	= 3
		17th	= 2

a. Converted VIN: 2 8 2 8 6 1 8 6 3 6 8 5 2 9 9 7 2

b. Weighting Factor: 8 7 6 5 4 3 2 10 0 9 8 7 6 5 4 3 2

c. Multiply (A) × (B)   16 56 12 40 24 3 16 60 0 54 64 35 12 45 36 21 4

3. *Calculate Check Digit:* The check digit is calculated by adding all 17 of the multiplied number values (line "C" in step #2) and then dividing this sum total by 11. The remainder of this number is then rounded to the nearest whole number, which is the check digit. If the remainder is 10, the check digit is symbolized by the letter "X" in the original VIN. This final calculation for the hypothetical VIN is as follows:

$$16+56+12+40+24+3+16+60+0+54+64+35+12+45+36+21+4=498$$

$$
\begin{array}{r}
45.3 \\
11\overline{)498} \\
\underline{44} \\
58 \\
\underline{55} \\
3
\end{array}
$$

Remainder .3 is the check digit "3" in the 9th position of the VIN.

Position 10:   Year vehicle was manufactured. Example: 9 = 2009, A = 2010.

Position 11:   The final assembly plant for the vehicle. Example: "T" = Tennessee.

Positions 12–17: The vehicle's unique serial number. Example: In the above hypothetical VIN check digit example, "529972" in positions 12–17 would be the specific serial number given to that particular vehicle by its manufacturer; this number, for some vehicles, can also be used to determine the exact order the vehicle left the assembly line.[27]

CASE CLOSE-UP 15.2

VINS PROVIDE CLUES TO TERRORIST BOMBINGS
(New York, NY, and Oklahoma City, OK)

Vehicle VIN numbers thus far have provided key pieces of evidence for investigators in two terrorist bombings and one similar bombing attempt. In the 1993 World Trade Center bombing, which killed six and injured more than 1,000 persons, an axle from a rented van containing the bomb was recovered and its stamped VIN number was used to eventually identify the terrorists who perpetrated the crime. In 1995, the bombing of the Murrah Federal Building, which killed 168 persons, was solved using a similar investigative method. After the bomb blast, a VIN was recovered from an axle blown blocks away from the vehicle housing the bomb, resulting in the arrest of domestic terrorist Timothy McVeigh (known as the "Oklahoma Bomber"). Most recently, in 2010, a vehicle VIN provided a key piece of evidence in the investigation of an attempted terrorist attack known as the *Times Square Bombing*. In this case, an SUV containing an explosive device was abandoned in New York's Time Square during a time when it was heavily populated by pedestrian traffic. Fortunately, the bomb failed to detonate and was later disarmed. The SUV, apparently planted by terrorists, had had its VIN removed from the dash and was cold plated using a license plate registered to a junked Ford truck. The vehicle's VIN, however, was recovered from its motor and currently is being used as a key investigative lead in the case.

VEHICLE DATABASES AND INFORMATION SOURCES

Databases

Databases that contain information about vehicle histories, particularly on whether they have been reported as stolen, are invaluable tools to vehicle theft investigators. Within the last several years, numerous organizations—both public and private—have developed such databases for law enforcement use:

1. **The National Motor Vehicle Title Information System (NMVTIS):** This database, put into service in 2009, is the most comprehensive source of vehicle information available. Created and operated through a partnership among various federal agencies, including

the FBI, the NMVTIS currently contains information on 27.4 million vehicles. Specific types of vehicles included in the database are automobiles, buses, trucks, motorcycles, recreational vehicles, motor homes, and tractors. Passage of the Anti-Car Theft Act in 1992, which authorized the creation of the NMVTIS, mandated reporting of vehicle information to the database by various entities including state departments of motor vehicles, insurance agencies, and junk/salvage yards. The NMVTIS report contains five key areas of a vehicle's history:

- *Title Information:* Indicating whether titles are valid or fictitious through data showing the states in which a vehicle has been issued a title, has been registered, and a VIN number has been issued or registered.
- *Brand History:* Indicating whether the vehicle has been declared as junked, salvaged, or flood damaged by a particular state's titling agencies including junk yards, salvage yards, auto recyclers, and insurance centers. VIN numbers associated with brand histories are also included for each issuing of a change in title.
- *Odometer Readings:* Indicating whether the current odometer readings are accurate or have been rolled back or misrepresented, as suggested by database information showing mileage reported by states each time the vehicle has been sold or retitled.
- *Total Loss History:* Indicating whether an insurance company has ever declared a vehicle a total loss.
- *Salvage History:* Indicating whether, when, and how many times a vehicle has received a salvage title.
- *Law Enforcement Specific Information:* Indicating whether the vehicle has been reported by law enforcement agencies as having been used in a violent crime, smuggling operations, or associated with weapons, drugs, immigration, gangs, or other criminal activity, including past fraud cases associated with the vehicle. Also available are names of organizations reporting data to the system; individuals owning, supplying, purchasing, or receiving such vehicles (if available); and export information.[28]

2. *Insurance Service Office (ISO) Database:* The **ISO** database is privately operated and contains information similar to that presented in an NMVTIS report. Special features include a comprehensive file containing a detailed history of insurance claims that have been made against a particular vehicle. Specific information included in the database files is derived from information gathered by the National Insurance Crime Bureau (**NICB**), which has been gathering and disseminating data on vehicle thefts for nearly a century. Recent ISO database applications have been applied internationally in Venezuela, Tokyo, England, and Israel. ISO also operates the National Equipment Register (NER), which is the primary database source for information pertaining to equipment theft and ownership records.

FIGURE 15.10 ▶ The frame of this vehicle is being prepared for a body swap, in which the original body is removed from the frame and is replaced with that of another vehicle—usually a technique to give the stolen vehicle a new identity.

3. *National Crime Information Center (NCIC):* As previously mentioned, the NCIC database contains information on vehicles known to law enforcement to be stolen and/or involved in criminal activities. NCIC information is also included in the NMVTIS and ISO databases.[29]

Other Sources

All states have departments of motor vehicles that maintain information on vehicles registered in their jurisdiction, and some store this information in computerized databases accessible to investigators. Manufacturers of vehicles, parts, and accessories also maintain records on their products, which are often useful for investigative purposes. International information on vehicle crimes is accessible through Interpol's Automated Search Facility-Stolen Motor Vehicle (ASF-SMV) database. This database includes stolen vehicle data from over 130 countries, and in 2010 more than 34,000 vehicles were identified worldwide by the system. Other countries, including Canada (Canadian Police Information Center, CPIC) and Mexico (OCRA), which play a major role in U.S. international auto theft, also maintain specific information about stolen vehicle trafficking—much of which is accessible through the Interpol consolidated database.

NONAUTOMOTIVE VEHICLE THEFT

Motorcycle Theft

As with auto theft, motorcycle theft has been decreasing in recent years. Approximately 56,000 motorcycles were stolen in 2009, representing about a 13 percent decline from the previous year. Stolen motorcycles, however, unlike cars, have a very low recovery rate—somewhere around 30 percent. This is because most motorcycle thieves do not leave the bike intact, but rather subject it to a chop shop parting out process. Motorcycle frames are easily altered into new shapes, and parts can be interchanged between models. Most motorcycle thefts take place in the summer season and peak in the months of July and August. After the illegal sale of stolen parts, the sale of clone bikes is one of the most popular means by which motorcycle thieves profit from their criminal activities. Clone bikes are constructed of aftermarket and stolen parts and are sold fraudulently as original new motorcycles. The construction of custom bikes is another popular means by which thieves launder their stolen parts.

The most obvious way to determine whether a motorcycle has been stolen is through an examination of its VIN. Models produced before 1980 have variable-length VIN numbers that differ by manufacturer and require specific knowledge regarding make and model to authenticate them. From 1981 to the present, motorcycles have had standardized 17-digit VINs like those used on automobiles, and they can be interpreted in the manner described in the general discussion of VINs earlier. Motorcycle VIN numbers are found in two locations: on or near the steering head, and in the lower portion of the engine case. Checking that these numbers match ensures (if they have not been altered) that the motorcycle has its original frame and engine. Serial numbers are also located on some of the major parts for identification purposes. Motorcycle title and theft histories are available through the NMVTIS, ISO, and NCIC databases.[30]

Marine Theft

Approximately 30,000 known marine vessel thefts, including boats and jet skis, occur each year. This figure, however, may represent only 10 percent of the actual number of marine thefts because (1) many stolen boats go unreported and (2) statistical methods for tabulating boat thefts are flawed and greatly underreport the incidence of crimes against watercraft. From the crimes that are known, marine theft results in an estimated $20 billion in losses to victims yearly. The recovery rate for stolen boats and related marine vehicles is between 10 and 15 percent—far below the 30 and 60 percent rates for motorcycles and automobiles, respectively.

Most marine vehicles stolen are small crafts under 20 feet in length. Most of these crimes are carried out by professionals who supply marine chop shops that dismantle the stolen vessels to obtain motors and other valuable parts. Jet skis, on the other hand, usually are stolen by juveniles for personal use. The theft of luxury boats and yachts is rare, comprising less than 5 percent of all stolen marine vessels. Thieves of this type of craft usually do not part them out, but rather sell them intact to persons in countries where stolen boats can be used or sold without detection. The following specific methods are used to commit marine theft:

- **Dry theft:** Thieves hitch up the boats on trailers located in dry storage areas and simply drive them away.
- **Wet theft:** Thieves start the boat and drive it away, or use a boat to tow the stolen boat from its location in a marina slip or mooring.

- **Cut and grab:** Thieves use a saw or other cutting device to remove the rear section of the boat containing the motor and drive.

In addition to actually stealing a vessel, marine theft can involve fraud. Just as with automobiles and motorcycles, stolen boats can be cloned by VIN switching and other false identification scams. Insurance fraud can be committed by creating "paper boats" that do not exist but are insured based on phony titles and registration documents. These craft are then reported as stolen, and the thieves collect the insurance money. Owners of larger boats that they can no longer afford also may commit insurance fraud by arranging for their vessel to be stolen and sunk. Likewise, cash-strapped owners may set intentional fires on their boats—which, when discovered by investigators, can result in charges of insurance fraud and arson.

Fortunately for thieves, and unfortunately for investigators, the identification method for watercrafts is far from foolproof. By federal law, all crafts built after 1984 are required to have a **Hull Identification Number (HIN)** affixed to their transom (the flat area at the back of the vessel, e.g., its stern, where its motor is located). Another HIN is placed in a hidden location within the boat's interior (usually beneath a fixture or hardware item). Boats produced before 1984 were not bound by these requirements and have various serial numbers provided by manufacturers only for purposes of product and model identification. The present-day HIN consists of 12 characters without a check digit rather than the standard 17 characters with a check digit used for other vehicles. The methods by which the HIN can be placed on the boat's hull include stamping, gluing, and riveting. The lack of internal security checks of the HIN coupled with the various placement methods on the boat's hull provide thieves numerous opportunities to create fake and altered NINs.[31]

Heavy Equipment Theft

Approximately 1,000 pieces of heavy equipment are stolen each month in the United States. Tractors, loaders, bulldozers, forklifts, and other large machines used for construction and farming are the primary targets of theft. The estimated average yearly losses related to heavy equipment theft are between $300 million and $1 billion. The recovery rate for this type of stolen equipment is less than 20 percent. Some known characteristics of heavy equipment theft include the following:

- Most thefts take place after hours at construction sites.
- Most thieves are professionals who operate in organized rings.
- Newer and more valuable equipment in better condition is targeted.
- Theft involves loading the equipment on a trailer and hauling it off, renting equipment and never returning it, fraudulent theft claims by owners, cloning, and phantom or paper scams.
- Equipment is dismantled, or parts are cloned and sold.

- Many pieces of equipment are exported to foreign countries and shipped from ports closest to the location of the theft.
- Thieves are often given a "shopping list" of equipment to target and steal.

Unlike other vehicles, not all heavy equipment has a standardized identification numbering process. Serial numbers and other numbers used to identify specific pieces of equipment range from 4 to 17 digits. Beginning in the 2000 model year, however, over 200 manufacturers (including the world's largest companies) started placing a standardized 17-digit Product Identification Number **(PIN)** on their equipment, similar to a vehicle's VIN. There is no uniform placement method or location of the PIN on the equipment item, however, and the PIN is not tracked in a government database to identify stolen vehicles. The primary existing database used for the investigation of stolen heavy equipment is the ISO database, which includes a range of insurance, title, salvage, and other information files.[32]

RECONSTRUCTING AN AUTO THEFT CRIME SCENE

Case Example 15A illustrates a case involving simple auto theft that eventually leads to the investigation of a large stolen vehicle chop shop operation. As shown in Figure 15.11, the investigation begins with surveillance of a suspect who has been observed making frequent visits to a key shop. This suspect has been linked through additional surveillance to another suspect (shown in Figure 15.12), who while under surveillance steals a bait car placed in an outdoor parking lot by investigators. The bait car suspect then leads undercover investigators to various locations believed to be operated by a large vehicle theft ring. After assessing the evidence and suspected criminal activity illustrated in the crime scene photos (see Figures 15.13 to 15.21), develop an investigative plan that will help build the strongest case possible against members of this vehicle theft ring.

CASE EXAMPLE 15A

Vehicle Theft Crime Scene

FIGURE 15.11 ▶ An auto theft suspect under surveillance by investigators is observed entering a key shop and requesting to have keys made. He appears to be well acquainted with the locksmith. What observations could possibly be made during this surveillance that would be of importance to the investigation of the suspect and his auto theft activities? Should the locksmith and the key shop be included in the investigation? If so, how and when should this aspect of the investigation take place?

FIGURE 15.12 ▶ After leaving the key shop, the suspect is followed to a parking lot where he and a criminal associate use a key to enter and steal the vehicle. While under observation by investigators tailing the stolen vehicle, the driver is observed making a phone call. While tailing the suspects, what should investigators do? Thus far, what activities of the suspects viewed here will be of future use for building a case against them?

FIGURE 15.13 ▶ Investigators follow the stolen vehicle to a location that appears to be a large auto repair facility. Outside the facility two men are observed apparently stripping parts from a pickup truck. At this point in time, what should investigators do? What information about this scene should be noted for investigative purposes?

(a)

(b)

FIGURE 15.14 ▶ (a) Investigators follow a large tow truck loaded with auto parts to a nearby storage facility. (b) They observe a group of male subjects unloading the parts from the truck and placing them within several storage units. What should investigators do at this second location? Should the suspects be approached and detained at this time? Do investigators have probable cause to arrest the suspects?

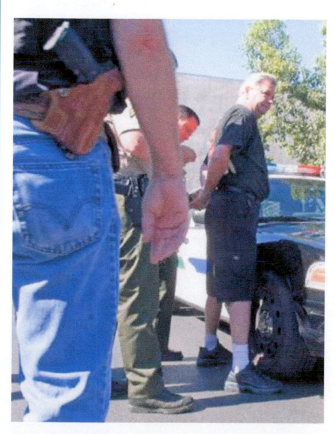

FIGURE 15.15 ▶ Search warrants are obtained for both facilities and arrests are made. What information and possible evidence from the earlier surveillance of suspects and facilities could have been used to obtain search and arrest warrants?

FIGURE 15.16 ▶ A team of investigators begins the crime scene search from the exterior of the auto repair facility and proceeds to the interior. How should investigators conduct the search of this facility? What specific types of auto theft related evidence should be searched for?

(a)

(b)

FIGURE 15.17 ▶ After a quick search of the facility's interior, it soon became evident to the investigators that the location was a chop shop for stolen vehicles. In conducting a more detailed search of these locations, what types of investigative discoveries would be of use for determining if this facility was associated with a large-scale professional auto theft ring?

FIGURE 15.18 ▶ Newer vehicles as well as older classic cars were the target of theft and restoration by the shop's owners. What vehicle and parts identification numbers would be of use for determining whether or not these cars have been stolen? What automotive databases could be used to help accomplish this task?

(a)

(b)

FIGURE 15.19 ▶ (a) Repainted classic Ford Thunderbird body. (b) Thunderbird chassis built from parts of stolen vehicles. What could investigators do at this scene to determine if the classic vehicle was being used in a VIN switch, salvage switch, body switch and/or other form of motor vehicle fraud?

(a)

(b)

FIGURE 15.20 ▶ (a) Tool kit containing rivets and other items taken from VIN plates and other car parts. (b) Sectioned license plate. Of what use are these pieces of evidence to proving a case against the auto theft suspects?

FIGURE 15-21 ▶ Miscellaneous weapons discovered within the chop shop facility. What should investigators do with these weapons seized from the scene? Can they be used as evidence to possibly increase the seriousness of charges against the auto theft suspects? If so, what might these enhanced criminal charges be?

Summary

1. Laws relating to vehicle theft.

Generally speaking, individuals who remove, steal, or drive a vehicle without first obtaining the owner's permission have committed motor vehicle theft. Some jurisdictions have laws specifying felony vehicle theft, otherwise referred to as *Grand Theft Auto (GTA)*, as thefts involving an automobile or other vehicle of a certain value (usually ranging from $400 to $1,000). Various laws have been passed at the state and federal levels prohibiting theft of an auto by force or fear (i.e., carjacking), operating chop shops, attempting to sell or distribute stolen autos or auto parts, exporting stolen vehicles to foreign countries, and so on. Many current vehicle anti-theft regulations exist at the federal level as the result of recent laws passed by Congress to curb the growing numbers of professional auto thieves.

2. Reasons for committing vehicle theft.

There are various reasons for committing vehicle theft including (1) joyriding, which is stealing a car or other vehicle to have "fun" with; (2) short-term transportation, which is stealing a vehicle simply to get from one place to another because there are no other available means of transportation; (3) long-term transportation, which is stealing for the purpose of acquiring a desired type of vehicle; (4) profit, which is stealing a vehicle to sell it or its parts for profit; (5) insurance fraud, which involves making fraudulent claims of theft of, or damage to a vehicle for purposes of obtaining an insurance settlement; (6) committing a crime, where a vehicle is stolen for transportation to and from a crime scene or for other means of facilitating a crime; and (7) trade for drugs, where a stolen vehicle is stolen and exchanged for drugs or money to buy drugs.

3. **Methods of vehicle break-ins and thefts.**

Most vehicle break-ins are carried out by techniques used to break windows, called *ninja rocking* and *bricking* or *stoning*, and to force doors open, called *door wedging*; lock punching; using devices called *Slim Jims*; methods involving electronic key code identification called *code grabbing*; or simple key theft from a residence. Vehicle theft methods include using force to break an ignition lock (ignition punching); hot wiring; using a key stolen in a burglary or robbery, or that has been left in the vehicle; using an electronic device called a *key cloner*; taking a car without consent; using a false ID to purchase or obtain use of a vehicle; or towing the vehicle away.

4. **Vehicle fraud.**

Vehicle fraud can be carried out to (1) sell a car that has been stolen or is of less value than the buyer believes it to be or (2) obtain an insurance settlement for a vehicle under false pretenses. Vehicle cloning is a popular method used to sell a salvaged or stolen car under the guise that it has never been damaged or stolen. In these cases, the VIN of a legitimate vehicle is switched with that of the fraudulent vehicle—which allows the vehicle title information to be switched as well. In insurance fraud, usually a vehicle owner who can no longer afford the vehicle makes a fraudulent claim to an insurance company that it has been stolen to obtain a monetary settlement.

Key Terms

grand theft auto
joyriding
profit theft
insurance fraud
cold plate
ninja rocks
bricking or stoning
Slim Jim
door wedging
master keying
lock punching
code grabbing
key theft
ignition punching

hot wiring
key burglary
key robbery
key cloning
chop shop
strip and run
VIN switching
vehicle cloning
salvage switching
counterfeit VIN
body switch
check digit
undercover house
bait car

carjacking
owner give-up
30-day special
phantom car
scapegoat theft
odometer rollback
VIN (vehicle identification number)
export scam
National Motor Vehicle Title Information System (NMVTIS)
ISO/NICB
Hull Identification Number (HIN)
PIN

Review Questions

1. What are some of the laws that have been passed concerning vehicle theft?
2. Describe the various reasons for which a vehicle is stolen.
3. How are vehicle break-ins typically carried out?
4. What are some of the motives for vehicle break-ins?
5. What are some of the techniques used to steal a car or other type of vehicle?
6. What are some of the characteristics of a professional auto theft?
7. What is an auto theft ring and how can it be detected and investigated?
8. Define the term *cold plating* and describe how it is used by auto thieves.
9. Name some of the ways in which vehicle fraud is carried out.
10. What are some of the investigative methods that can be used to detect and apprehend auto thieves?
11. Describe the function of a VIN and how it can be used to detect auto theft.
12. What is carjacking and what are some of the methods used to carry it out?
13. What is an odometer rollback and how can it be detected?
14. Name and describe some of the vehicle databases that are available to investigators.
15. How do motorcycle, marine, and heavy equipment thefts differ from auto thefts?

Internet Resources

National Insurance Crime Bureau (NICB)	www.nicb.org/theft_and_fraud_awareness/fact_sheets
International Association of Marine Investigators (IAMI)	www.iamimarine.org/iami
International Association of Auto Theft Investigators (IAATI)	www.iaati.org/Default.asp
International Association of Insurance Fraud Agencies (IAIFA)	www.iaifa.org
National Motor Vehicle Title Information System (NMVTIS)	www.nmvtis.gov

Applied Investigative Exercise

Examine the crime scene photos in Case Example 15A. Identify the most important aspects of this case for purposes of investigating the vehicle theft that has taken place here. In other words, what types of evidence would you gather to build your case (e.g., intent, method of break-in, and so forth)? What evidence exists in this case to suggest that the auto theft was the work of an amateur, a professional, or perhaps an auto theft ring? What steps might you take in conducting a follow-up investigation to determine whether more crimes and offenders can be associated with this vehicle theft incident?

Notes

1. Discussions of vehicle theft in this section are based on vehicle theft laws from various states, including those from California Vehicle Code Section 10851 VC and California Penal Code Section 487 (d) (1) PC.
2. Insurance Information Institute, *Auto Theft*, posted at www.iii.org/media/hottopics/insurance/test4.
3. Ibid.
4. Federal Bureau of Investigation, *Uniform Crime Reports*, posted at www.fbi.gov/about-us/cjis/ucr/ucr.
5. Jacqueline Helfgott, *Criminal Behavior: Theories, Typologies and Criminal Justice* (Thousand Oaks, CA: Sage, 2008) 256–270.
6. Ibid.
7. Ibid.
8. Ibid.
9. Ibid.
10. Ibid.
11. Ibid.
12. Investigative insights and discussions in the section are based on the authors' experiences in handling vehicle theft incidents.
13. Car Theft.Org UK, *Stop Car Theft*, posted at www.car-theft.org/theft-methods.
14. Ibid.
15. City of Pittsburgh Police Dept., *Types of Car Theft*, posted at www.city.pittsburgh.pa.us/bat/html/types_of_car_theft.html.
16. Ibid.
17. Ibid.
18. Ibid.
19. Ibid.
20. Ibid.
21. Government Technology, *Police Use GPS-Equipped Bait Car to Catch Car Thieves*, posted at www.govtech. com/public-safety/Police-Use-GPS-Equipped-Bait-Car-to.html?topic=117680.
22. Anti-Car Theft Act of 1992, 18 U.S.C.A. Section 2119.
23. David C. Bodette, "The Sixth Circuit Interprets the 'Person or Presence' Requirement of the Federal Carjacking Statute." *The University of Memphis Law Review, 2001*, 32 (Fall), 197–209.
24. National Insurance Crime Bureau (NICB), *Insurance Fraud*, posted at www.nicb.org/theft_and_fraud_awareness/fact_sheets.
25. Police Chief Magazine, *Vehicle Theft Investigation Is about—Looking beyond the Traffic Stop*, posted at www.policechiefonline.net/magazine/index.cfm?fuseaction=display_arch&article_id=739&issue_id=112005.
26. Auto-Theft.info, *VIN*, posted at www.auto-theft.info.
27. Ibid.
28. U.S. Department of Justice, *National Motor Vehicle Title Information System*, posted at www.vehiclehistory.gov.
29. ISO, *Information About Property/Causality Insurance Risk*, posted at www.iso.com/Products/A-PLUS/A-PLUS-the-Automobile-Property-Loss-Underwriting-Service.html.
30. National Insurance Crime Bureau (NICB), *Motorcycle Theft and Fraud*, posted at www.nicb.org/theft_and_fraud_awareness/fact_sheets.
31. International Association of Marine Investigators (IAMI), *Introduction to Marine Identification*, posted at nasbla.org/files/public/Enf%20&%20Training/IAMI%20HIN%20PPT.pdf.
32. National Insurance Crime Bureau (NICB), *Heavy Equipment*, posted at www.nicb.org/theft_and_fraud_awareness/fact_sheets.

CHAPTER SIXTEEN

COMPUTER CRIME SCENES

Learning Objectives

After completing this chapter, you should be able to:

1. Identify the different types of computer crime.
2. Describe characteristics of computer crime suspects.
3. Describe how computer crime investigations are conducted.
4. Understand the relationship between investigation and digital forensics.

Chapter Outline

INTRODUCTION

FIFTY YEARS AGO, WHEN a bank was robbed, the suspects used a gun. Nowadays, it can be done with just a keyboard. Utilizing computers and databases, suspects from all over the world have been able to access accounts and effectively withdraw millions of dollars. The money is then transmitted via computer into accounts that are not accessible by law enforcement. This is just one of the many crimes done from the comfort of home or a makeshift office with a computer and keyboard such as that shown here in the crime scene photo (see Case Example 16A presented later in this chapter). In these types of cases, investigators are called upon to process an electronic crime scene and gather digital evidence.

As computers and the Internet continue to become part of our daily lives, the potential for harm from computer crime increases dramatically. In turn, this trend has prompted law enforcement to form specialized investigative units to combat computer crimes. These units are trained to investigate electronic crime scenes using tactics developed within the newly emerging fields of computer forensics. From an investigative standpoint, computer forensics can be defined as the application of computer science to the practice of criminal investigation. The focal point of this chapter is examining the means by which computer forensics and other newly emerging technology are used as tools by investigators to fight the electronic war on crime.

In addition, various types of computer crimes and profiles of computer crime offenders are presented.

TYPES OF COMPUTER CRIMES

Computer crime, or as many refer to it, **cyber-crime**, is any crime that involves a computer and a network. Some of the more prevalent types of computer crimes encountered by investigators are presented below:

Computer as the target is the first of several general classifications of computer crime. These crimes include theft of intellectual property (e.g., customer list, or pricing data) or blackmail based on information gained from computerized files (e.g., personal history data or medical information). They can also involve acts such as sabotage of intellectual property, pricing data, or personnel data with the full intent to impede a business or cause chaos in business operations. This crime covers changing a criminal history; modifying information; and creating a driver's license, passport information, or any other document for identification purposes. A widely discussed crime targeting computers involves unleashing a virus through e-mail. A **virus** is a computer program that disrupts or destroys existing computer systems. A virus can spread rapidly around the world, annihilating computer files and costing companies and individuals millions of dollars in downtime.[1]

Theft of intellectual properties is a term referring to multiple distinct types of creations of the mind for which a set of exclusive rights is recognized—and the corresponding fields of law.[2] The two forms of IP most frequently involved in cyber-crime are copyrighted material and trade secrets.[3] Copyrighted material on the computer extends to computer software and material deemed to have been created by the person who copyrights the material. Trade secrets deal with a computer transmission and how it is involved in the transfer or destruction of corporate data from a computer whose use in some way affects interstate commerce.[4]

Techno-vandalism is another crime that uses the computer as a target. This occurs when there is unauthorized access to a computer that results in damage to files or programs. Interestingly, the damage is not necessarily so much for profit as for the challenge. Another crime in this category is **techno-trespass**, which refers to the intentional intrusion into a computer to view files or programs. In all these crimes the offender uses the computer to obtain information or damage operating programs.[5] One of the best examples of a crime in which the computer is the target can be found in the book *The Cuckoo's Egg* by Cliff Stroll. This book recounts the true story of a hacker from Germany, who infiltrated a number of computers in the United States. Many of the systems infiltrated were from the military, universities, and government contractors. The hacker attempted to locate and steal national security information to sell it to foreign governments.

The second general type of computer crime is the **computer as the instrumentality of the crime**. In basic terms of law, *instrumentality* refers to the diversion of a lawfully possessed item—that is, an instrument—to facilitate the committing of a crime. In this general category the computer's processes, not its actual contents, commit the crime.[6] Essentially, the criminal introduces new computer code (programming instructions) to manipulate the computer's analytical process, thus using the computer to commit the crime. Another more common method involves converting legitimate computer processes for illegitimate purposes. Crimes in this category include fraudulent use of automated teller machine (ATM) cards and accounts; theft of money from accrual, conversion, or transfer accounts; credit card fraud; fraud from computer transactions (stock transfers, sales, or billings); and telecommunication fraud.[7]

An automated teller machine has a computerized telecommunication device that allows a client of a certain bank to deposit and withdraw money. The most prevalent way a customer is identified is by the use of an ATM card. This card normally is composed of plastic, with the name of the account holder and several numbers embedded on the front. On the back side of the ATM card is a magnetic strip. This magnetic strip contains all the account holder's personal information.

There are several different scams that use the ATM; a common one is the stolen ATM or credit card. An individual gains possession of another's ATM or credit card and has access to the secret pin number. The suspect continues withdrawing funds until the victim notifies the bank of the theft. Another scam is the counterfeit ATM card, which is becoming a more rampant crime. In these offenses, the suspect uses a skimming device to attain the victim's personal information and creates a counterfeit card. The suspect would then use the counterfeit card to withdraw money or obtain services.

Other crimes include the fraudulent withdrawal of money at various ATM machines. This occurs when the suspect looks to find offline ATM machines where transactions are not processed in real time. In this situation, the suspect can remove more money than allotted by each bank's daily limit. As with withdrawals, fraudulent deposits occur when a suspect deposits a counterfeit check and falsely removes those funds.[8] A common crime in all states is credit card fraud. This is essentially committed when the suspect uses a credit card as a fraudulent source of funds in the transaction. The purpose of using the credit card could be to obtain goods, services, or unauthorized funds from an account. This crime is also coupled with identity theft. To use the fraudulent credit card, the suspect must assume the identity of that person, thus committing the crime of identity theft.

Another common crime facilitated by the use of a computer is the growing problem of **cellular phone fraud**. The offender uses a cellular phone and electronically bills charges to other customers. The offender obtains cellular billing identification codes by using scanning devices, which are small, parabolic (curve-shaped) antennae connected to portable computers. When activated, these scanners hone in and capture account numbers transmitted by other cellular phones. The offenders in these circumstances operate near highways and businesses because unsuspecting victims use their cell phones more frequently in these areas. Once a computerized billing code is captured, the offender programs this code into other cellular phones simply by hooking up the phone to the personal computer. This requires certain software, which is readily available in all black markets.[9]

The third general category of cyber-crime is the use of a **computer incidental to other crimes**. In this category, the computer is not essentially needed for the crime to occur, but it relates to the criminal act itself. What this means is that the actual crime could still occur without the computer; however, the use of this technology helps the crime occur faster. The computer allows for greater processing of large amounts of information, thus making the crime more difficult to detect and trace. Crimes in this category include money laundering, unlawful business transactions, organized crime records, and, in rare instances, murder. Money laundering is engaging in several financial transactions in an attempt to conceal the true ownership, source, control, or destination of illegally gained money. Essentially, it is the process by which proceeds from crime are made to have legitimate means.[10] An example would be an organized crime group or drug cartel funneling money into a business that has no high volume of sales corresponding to the money on its books.

Money laundering has increasingly become a worldwide problem, and its financial aspect has become increasingly complex. This is due in part to the rapid evolution in technology. Modern financial systems are all computerized, and this globalization of financial information permits criminals to transfer millions of dollars instantly through personal computers and satellite dishes. The money is laundered through currency dealers, casinos, automobile dealerships, insurance companies, trading companies, and other sophisticated systems. The basic question in money laundering is determining which money is clean and which is dirty. With the use of a computer, money laundering is done in several ways. The most common types of criminals who launder money are drug traffickers, embezzlers, corrupt politicians, mobsters, and terrorists. The process of cyber-crime laundering normally begins with millions of dollars. In the United States, this money would catch the eye of federal authorities if deposited within U.S. financial institutions. Consequently, the money is deposited into banks outside the United States. Normally, these foreign banks agree to keep the money in secrecy. The offender would then create fictitious businesses and bank accounts inside the United States. Once they are created, the offender uses a computer to transfer smaller amounts of money into these fictitious businesses and accounts.

Criminals also use technology to further their own illegal activities such as child pornography. With the rapid advancement of technology, pedophiles use computers to store, send, and save pictures of children in compromising positions. Child pornography with respect to computers deals mainly with storage of pictures, transmitting pictures to others, viewing and creating child pornography videos, and soliciting minors for sex.[11] MSNBC regularly displays on television ongoing investigations into soliciting minors. In these investigations, usually an adult who appears young pretends to be a minor and engages a predator in a chat room exchange of sexually provocative meanings. The entire exchange is monitored by law enforcement, and the predator, upon arranging a meeting place and time, is arrested.

CASE CLOSE-UP 16.1

CHILD PORNOGRAPHY

Ronald Riggs, 64, of Bel Air was sentenced to five years in prison for distributing child pornography. An undercover agent downloaded 11 files from a file-sharing program in December 2008. A computer and other electronic equipment confiscated from his home also turned up 88 images and 12 videos of minors being sexually abused.

John Joseph Kovach Jr., 53, of Resisterstown, was sentenced to five years in prison for sexually exploiting a minor to produce child pornography. Police seized his computers and found 252 images and nine videos of child pornography.

The last general category in cyber-crime is **crimes associated with the prevalence of computers**. As technology grows, it creates new crime targets and crime properties. Software piracy and counterfeiting, copyright violations of computer programs, black market computer equipment, and theft of technological equipment fall into this category.[12] The act of software piracy is sustained when copies of licensed software are produced so as to look authentic. Counterfeiting the software can include the copying and distributing of licensed software. A key study sponsored by Microsoft in 2006 showed that one in four websites offering counterfeit software attempted to install unwanted or malicious code upon download. This rate is rising, as found by Media Surveillance, an antipiracy solutions company, when it recently downloaded several hundred pirated copies of Windows and hacks found that 32 percent of them contained malicious code.[13]

TOOLS USED IN COMPUTER CRIMES

Those who commit computer crime, whether child pornography or hacking, share one thing in common—the computer. Each computer crime is specific as to what needs to be done to complete the crime. These crimes fall into one of four categories: crimes against an individual, crimes against property, crimes against organization, and crimes against society.

Crimes using a computer against an individual include **e-mail spoofing**, **spamming**, **cyber defamation**, harassment, and **cyber stalking**. A spoofed e-mail is one in which the header is forged so that the mail appears to originate from one source but actually has been sent from another. Essentially, the individual who spoofs an e-mail simply sets the display of the "from" field of outgoing messages to show a name or address other than the actual one from which the message is sent. Most POP e-mail clients allow you to change the text displayed in this field. The below pictorial is an example of how e-mail is spoofed.

Generally, spoofing an e-mail is not illegal unless it involves a direct threat of violence or death. Spamming is sending multiple copies of unsolicited mails or mass e-mails such as chain letters. One of the biggest problems associated with computers is cyber defamation. This occurs when defamation takes place with the help of computers and/or the Internet (e.g., someone publishes defamatory matter about an individual on a website or sends an e-mail containing some kind of defamatory information). The 2003 Can-Spam act[14] laid out multiple consequences for anyone found guilty of sending spam e-mails. The act allows up to $11,000 in fines per e-mail sent. Harassment and cyber stalking is what it sounds like: following an individual's activity over the Internet. It can be done through several protocols such as e-mail, chat rooms, and user net groups. There is a difference between harassment and stalking as each relates to the computer. All fifty states have enacted cyber stalking or cyber harassment laws, and recent concerns over protecting minors have led states to enact cyber bullying laws. Cyber stalking differs from harassment in that it refers to some form of threatening or malicious behavior, whereas cyber harassment does not have to pose a credible threat. Cyber bullying and harassment are used interchangeably; the difference is that bullying occurs among minors within a school context. One of the most recent cases of cyber bullying is that of Phoebe Prince.

CASE CLOSE-UP 16.2

THE CASE OF PHOEBE PRINCE

Phoebe Prince had been taunted and cyber bullied for several months by at least two separate groups of students at South Hadley High School, in South Hadley, Massachusetts. The taunting was done reportedly because of disputes with other girls over her brief relationship with a senior high school football player and a second male student. On January 14, 2010, after a day of harassment and taunting, followed by a final incident in which a student threw a can at her from a passing car as she walked home from school, Prince committed suicide by hanging herself in the stairwell leading to the second floor of her family's apartment. Her body was discovered by her 12-year-old sister.

There are also phishing e-mails, which are attempts to acquire sensitive information concerning an individual's account. The information could be a username, password, bank account information, and credit card information. Normally phishing is done through e-mail or instant messaging.[15] The following email content is an example of phishing which was carried out to entice recipients of the message to provide vital personal information to cyber identity thieves:

You have received this e-mail because of the launching of the State Vaccination H1N1 program. You need to create your personal H1N1 (swine flu) Vaccination Profile on the cdc.gov site. This profile has to be created both for the vaccinated people and those nonvaccinated. This profile is used for the registering of vaccinated and nonvaccinated people.
Create your Personal H1N1 Vaccination profile using the below link:
Create your personal profile.

The above phishing example was e-mailed throughout various states, and on face value unsuspecting victims would think that, when they clicked on the link, they would automatically be transferred to the listed website. In reality the victims will be transferred to the suspect's website and unknowingly fill out name, address, social security number, date of birth, and other damaging personal information. The suspect would then use that information to commit identity theft.

The use of computers to facilitate crime against property is widely touted as the most sophisticated crime to commit. These

(a)

(b)

FIGURE 16.1 ▶ (a) A PIN pad skimmer located at a local convenience store. Unsuspecting victims have their credit information swiped and transmitted to a skimming device. (b) This device is removed and the information downloaded into a computer database for illegal use.

crimes consist of credit card fraud, intellectual property crimes, and Internet time theft. Credit card fraud is committed using a credit card or any similar mechanism as a fraudulent source of funds in a transaction. The transaction could be performed to obtain goods without paying or to obtain unauthorized funds from an account. These transactions are done using a computer. One rapidly expanding fraud consists of obtaining account information from unsuspecting victims and transferring that information onto the magnetic strip of a credit card in the suspect's name. To do this, the suspect has to use a computer. In this situation the suspect uses a preexisting credit card with their name on it or makes a card. Each card will have the same back magnetic strip. The suspect will already have obtained several victims' identification and account information. Normally, this is done by hiding card skimmers in an area where credit cards are used extensively. Figure 16.1 shows an ATM card reader modified into a device used to illegally capture or "skim" PIN numbers, as well as personal and account information from the magnetic strip of ATM cards used by unsuspecting customers of retail stores.

A gas station is a common area where skimmers are hidden. The skimmer scans your account information just like a card reader would. With the help of a small camera attached to the terminal, the apparatus can also capture your PIN as you type it. The suspect afterward removes the skimmer and downloads the information to a database. The suspect then takes a fraudulent credit card and downloads the account information of an unsuspecting victim to it. When the suspect enters a store and makes a purchase, the card is used. The machine reads the card through the magnetic strip, and the information presents as a good account. The credit card itself appears on its face to be valid, with the suspect's name and the victim's account information being transmitted via computer.

Intellectual property crimes include software piracy: illegal copying of programs, distribution of copies of software, copyright

infringement, trademark violations, and theft of computer source code—programming instructions compiled into the executable files sold by software development companies.[16] In this situation, the suspect (usually an employee) steals the source code and could sell it to a rival company for profit. The suspect could also use the information to make their own version of the software.

Internet time theft is the usage by an unauthorized person of Internet hours paid for by another person. This form of computer crime is becoming increasingly prevalent in areas where there are wireless connections.

Crimes against organizations are becoming the most common form of cyber-crime, as corporations are losing billions of dollars through cyber-crime yearly. There are different types of crimes wherein an organization is the victim. One of these, *unauthorized accessing of a computer,* is defined as accessing a computer network without permission from the owner. This occurs in two forms: (1) unauthorized changing and deleting of data, and (2) computer voyeurism, where the criminal reads or copies confidential or proprietary information, but neither deletes nor changes the data.

Another computer crime is **denial of service** (see Figure 16.2), which basically entails flooding the Internet with several, continuous bogus requests so as to deny legitimate users access to the server or to crash the server. Perpetrators of these attacks typically target sites or services hosted on high-profile web servers such as banks and credit card payment gateways. A denial of service attack can be done in several ways. The five basic attacks are as follows:

- Consumption of computer resources, such as bandwidth and disk space
- Disruption of configuration information, such as routing information

Denial of Service

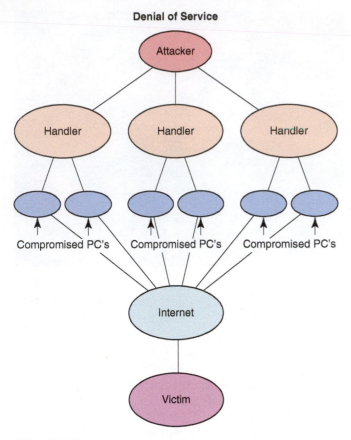

FIGURE 16.2 ▶ An illustrative drawing of what a denial of service would look like if it were an image. Note how a server can be flooded, thereby preventing legitimate users from accessing the system.

- Disruption of state information, such as unsolicited resetting of TCP sessions
- Disruption of physical network components
- Obstructing the communication media between the intended users and the victim

During the 2009 Iranian election protest, foreign activists seeking to help the opposition engaged in denial of service attacks against Iran's government. The official website of the Iranian government (ahmedinejad.ir) was rendered inaccessible on several occasions.[17]

Virus attacks employ computer programs (called *viruses*) that can infect other computer programs by modifying them so as to include a (possibly evolved) copy of the virus. Viruses can infect or affect the boot sector of the computer. Basically, a virus is a small piece of software that piggybacks on real programs. Each time that the infected program runs, the virus does too, essentially getting a chance to reproduce itself. Worms, unlike viruses, do not need to attach themselves to the host server. E-mail bombing is sending large numbers of e-mails to individuals, companies, or mail servers, thereby ultimately crashing their systems. Two common methods are used in committing an e-mail bomb. The first is *mass mailing*, which consists of sending numerous duplicate e-mails to the same e-mail

address. The second type of bombing is called a *zip bomb*. A zip bomb is an offshoot of a mail bombing, designed to crash or render useless the program or system reading it.

A *salami attack* occurs when negligible amounts are removed from a file and are accumulated into something larger. This attack on a bank's computer network involves the intruder siphoning off small amounts of money from a file (account) and placing them into another file that the suspect can access. In 2008, a man was arrested for fraudulently creating 58,000 accounts, which he used to collect money through verification deposits from online brokerage firms a few cents at a time.[18] These attacks are used to commit financial crimes. A **logic bomb** is an event-dependent program; as soon as the designated event occurs, it crashes the computer, releasing a virus. A very common virus, known as a **Trojan horse**, is an unauthorized program that functions inside what seems to be an authorized program, thereby concealing what it is actually doing.

The use of the computer in crimes against society encompasses forgery of currency notes, revenue stamps, and mark sheets using high-quality scanners and printers. A crime becoming increasingly rampant here in the United States and abroad is cyber terrorism. **Cyber terrorism** is the use of computer resources to intimidate or coerce others. This is especially prevalent with terrorist groups, such as al-Qaeda. This topic will be discussed later in the chapter. **Web jacking** involves hackers gaining access to and control over another's website. The Pentagon logs well over a thousand attacks a day on their computer systems.

PROFILING THE COMPUTER CRIMINAL

Profiling criminals in general is a very useful tool; unfortunately, profiling is of limited use in computer crimes. The issue comes about because the computer criminal's profile is not much different from that of the public. In a report covering hundreds of cases over a 10-year period, 75 percent of the perpetrators were men and 25 percent were women. Most are first-time perpetrators, having no previous criminal record. The report included the following educational information on computer criminals: 42 percent were high school graduates, 45 percent were college graduates, and 13 percent had college postgraduate work.[19]

Currently, the term **hacker** has many different definitions. The term was derived from a computer class at Massachusetts Institute of Technology in the 1960s. The most common description of a hacker is someone who uses flaws and oversights in a computer's security system to break into the system. Hackers are driven by the intellectual pursuit and curiosity about the system and its workings.

A leading authority, Marcus Rogers from Purdue University, who investigated computer crime as a police detective in Canada, has identified eight types of cyber-criminal. Each type is distinguished by its respective skill levels and motivations.

Novice

This type has limited computer and programming skills. Much of the novice's ability relies upon the execution of toolkits that can conduct the attack. Novices' attacks can cause extensive damage to systems, though they don't understand how the attack works. Many novice computer criminals are seeking media attention.

Cyber-Punks

These cyber-criminals are a bit more intelligent than novices; they can write their own software. They have a thorough understanding of the system they are attacking, and they engage in credit card number theft and telecommunication fraud to financially contribute to their cause. Many of these cyber-criminals get caught due to their extensive bragging about their exploits.

Internals

This term refers to the typical disgruntled employee or ex-employee. This cyber-criminal normally is already working in a technology-related job. These individuals are aided by the privileges afforded to them by the company they work with. These privileges include passwords and company-secured websites. This type of cyber-criminal poses the largest security problem to organizations. Additionally, employees, contractors, and consultants become opportunistic and take advantage of the poor Internet security that a company presents. Many internals are motivated by greed and financial difficulties, which lead to theft of various services.

Coders

These individuals write, test, and design computer programs. More experienced coders tend to act as mentors to the younger, newer coders. They write the script and automated tolls that others use to commit the crime. Many of these coders are motivated by a sense of power and prestige. They are very dangerous criminals in that they have hidden agendas and use viruses to destroy entire systems.

Old Guard Hackers

This hacker is what many think a hacker is—a person who does it for the sheer intellectual challenge. Many of these individuals appear to have no criminal intent, but do have an alarming disrespect for personal property.

Professional Criminals

Professional cyber-criminals have a specific intent and tend to specialize in corporate espionage. They are guns for hire who infiltrate corporations and seize assets, steal money, or destroy networks. They are highly trained, highly motivated, and have access to the most current state-of-the-art equipment.

Information Warriors and Cyber Terrorists

Since the fall of Eastern bloc intelligence agencies, many have scrambled to attain valuable information to sell it on the black market. These cyber-criminals are well funded and tend to mix political rhetoric with criminal activity. This is an emerging category of criminal that has only become stronger since the 9/11 attacks on the United States in 2001.[20]

CASE CLOSE-UP 16.3
CYBER-ATTACK

On March 7, 2011, hackers, in one of the most sophisticated cyber-attacks ever, broke into the French finance ministry computers in an effort to collect sensitive information relating to France's presidency of the Group of 20 industrialized nations. This attack caused the finance ministry to make changes to 10,000 computers over the weekend. Hackers also tried to access the computers of senior officials and French president Nicolas Sarkozy. French officials called this "pure espionage." The hackers are believed to have used a "Trojan horse" e-mail, which seems to have come from a known source. It was concealed in a PDF file.

RESPONDING TO COMPUTER CRIMES

Analyzing the aftermath of a computer crime takes far longer than a perpetrator takes to commit the crime. The speed of the response often determines the outcome, and the more prepared an investigator is when an incident first occurs, the quicker it can respond in the incident's wake. With the ever-increasing use of information technology (IT), organizations around the globe are facing the challenge of protecting valuable resources from a never-ending onslaught of threats. Computers and the networks that connect them process, store, and transmit information crucial for successful day-to-day operations, thus making them inviting targets for hackers and malicious code. The protection of critical IT resources requires not only reasonable precautions for securing these systems and networks, but also the ability to respond quickly and efficiently when system and network security defenses have been breached. Unfortunately, responding to computer security incidents is generally not easy. Proper incident response requires technical knowledge, communication, and coordination among the personnel in charge of the response process. In information technology, *incident* refers to an adverse event in an information system and/or network or to the threat of the occurrence of such an event.[21]

In any computer crime, the first responder normally is the individual who determines whether a crime occurred and, more specifically, what the crime is. Depending on the severity of the computer crime, the first responder does two things. First, they make observations of what occurred, document the entire crime scene, and interview victims, witnesses, and possible suspects. Once this process is completed, they seize the evidence.

If the first responder determines that the crime scene is very complex, a computer crimes investigator may be called in to assume the handle. First responders must use caution when they seize electronic devices. Improperly accessing data stored on electronic devices may violate federal laws, including the Electronic Communications Privacy Act of 1986 and the Privacy Protection Act of 1980.[22]

When responding to any crime scene, but especially a computer crime scene, one has to know what to look for. The initial responder has to react with knowledge of what they are potentially looking at. First and foremost, the utmost priority is to ensure the safety of officers and others. Once the scene is clear of all potential physical dangers, the first responder, depending on the type of computer crime, must perform five basic steps:

1. Recognize the investigative value of digital evidence.
2. Assess available resources.
3. Identify the equipment and supplies that should be taken to electronic crime scenes.
4. Assess the crime scene and the digital evidence present.
5. Designate the assignments, roles, and responsibilities of personnel involved in the investigation.

There are various types of electronic and storage devices that could be potential evidence. This five-step process will ensure that all possible evidence has been accounted for and a complete investigation into the cyber-crime will be conducted. To understand a computer crime scene, an investigator must understand the various pieces of electronic evidence that are involved in a computer crime.

Computer System

A computer system (see Figure 16.3) consists of hardware and software that process data. Typically, it includes a hard shell-like case containing circuit boards, microprocessors, hard

FIGURE 16.3 ▶ Computer systems and information processing devices range in size and technological complexity, which adds to the challenge of investigating an electronic crime scene.

drives, memory, and interface connections. Each system also has a monitor, keyboard, mouse, and peripheral drives, devices, and components. The externally connected devices are printers, modems, routers, and docking stations.

Storage Devices

Storage devices vary in size and in the manner in which they store and retain data. Regardless of their size, all first responders to computer crime must understand that these devices may contain information of value to any investigation and prosecution. The following sections present the different types of storage devices.

HARD DRIVES

Hard drives are data storage devices that consist of an external circuit board. First responders may also find hard drives that are not connected to or installed on a computer. These loose hard drives—which may contain valuable evidence—are very popular among serial pedophiliacs. Child predators know they are being watched, thus they constantly change hard drives to reduce the chance of being caught.

THUMB DRIVES, MEMORY CARDS, AND REMOVABLE MEDIA

Thumb drives are small, lightweight, removable data storage devices with USB connections. These devices—also referred to as *flash drives*—are easy to conceal and transport. Often, an individual with something to hide will attempt to disguise flash drives in watches and cell phones. *Memory cards* are small data storage devices commonly used with digital cameras and computers. *Removable media* are cartridges and disk-based data storage devices. Common digital information storage devices likely to be found at an electronics crime scene are shown in Figure 16.4.

(a)

(b)

(c)

(d)

FIGURE 16.4 ▶ Common digital information storage devices: (a) hard drive, (b) thumb drive, (c) compact disc (CD), (d) floppy disc.

Once the potential evidence has been located, the crime scene should be secured. Digital evidence on computers can be altered, deleted, or destroyed as illustrated in Figure 16.5. To allow for the best possible situation, all persons not directly related to the investigation should be removed from the crime scene. Document the scene by taking photographs of the computer items as they were originally viewed. Once accounted for, the items should be secured. There are a few ways to secure the items. It can be done with individual items or, if the crime scene is complex, crime scene tape can be used to contain the whole area, pending the arrival of an investigator. The investigator will determine what items should be seized and appropriately secure them for further processing.

Computer Evidence Collection and Preservation

In today's society, people employ electronic media and computers in various aspects of their daily lives. Criminals also use multiple electronic media and computers to perform their unlawful activities. Modern technology allows suspects to commit computer crimes remotely and internationally, obtain intelligence, and conduct counterintelligence with near-anonymity.[23]

A first responder or investigator responding to a computer crime scene must first have the legal standing and ground to be there. For first responders, often this will be a dispatch call, and for an investigator it will be by either direction from the first responder or follow-up from a first report. Computer crime evidence, referred to as *digital evidence*, must be handled carefully to preserve the integrity of the physical device as well as the data that it contains.[24]

Each piece of equipment related to the specific computer crime has its own method of collection. The items are unique in size and relevance to the scene. The investigator should document any activity on the computer, components, or devices. The power supply should be checked to ascertain whether the computer is powered on, and the monitor observed to determine if it is in sleep mode or off. After assessing the computer's power situation, an investigator should perform the steps outlined in the following sections to preserve the evidence.

FIGURE 16.5 ▶ Offenders often attempt to destroy evidence associated with computer crimes by dismantling or physically damaging hardware as pictured here. Investigators can use both traditional and electronic investigative methods to recover such evidence. For example, traditional tool mark analysis, fingerprints, and even DNA analysis can be used in the situation shown here to link a specific offender to the damaged computer. In addition, new technological advances have enabled the recovery of electronic information from damaged hardware.

Stand-Alone Home Personal Computer

1. Do not use the computer or attempt to search for evidence.
2. Photograph the computer's front and back as well as any cords and connected devices. Photograph the surrounding area before moving any evidence.
3. If the computer is off, do not turn it on.
4. If the computer is on and something is displayed on the monitor, photograph the screen.
5. If the computer is on and the screen is blank, move the mouse or press the space bar to display the active image on the monitor. After the image appears, photograph it.
6. Unplug the power cord from the back of the tower.

Network Home Personal Computer

The first six steps are similar to those just described for the stand-alone home personal computer. The difference is that after those six steps, the investigator should do the following:

7. Diagram and label cords to later identify connect devices.
8. Disconnect all cords and devices from the tower.
9. Package components and store them as fragile cargo.
10. Keep all media, including the tower, away from magnets, radio transmitters, and other potentially damaging elements.
11. Document all steps involved.

Storage Media Devices

1. Collect instruction manuals, documentation, and notes.
2. Document all steps and keep the devices away from magnets, radio transmitters, and other potentially dangerous devices.

As discussed thoroughly in an earlier chapter, the authority to seize evidence is no different in computer crimes than it is with other types of crimes. An investigator who is conducting a computer crimes investigation should get the potential suspect to sign consent to search each piece of computer equipment. This will ultimately prevent the suspect, if charged, from stating in court, "I never gave them permission." Once implicated, defendants almost always lie if they think it will get the charges dropped or lessened.

Packaging, Transportation, and Storage

Computers are fragile electronic instruments that are sensitive to temperature, humidity, physical shock, static electricity, and magnetic sources. Therefore, special precautions should be taken. When evidence is collected at a crime scene, its packaging, transport, and storage are equally important. In computer crimes, not taking care of the equipment can cause severe damage to it, thereby destroying evidence.

PACKAGING PROCEDURE

1. Ensure that all collected evidence is properly labeled.
2. Pay attention to latent or trace evidence and take actions to preserve it.
3. Pack magnetic media in antistatic packaging. Avoid material that can produce static electricity, such as standard plastic bags.
4. Do not fold, bend, or scratch computer media devices.
5. Ensure that all containers used to hold evidence are labeled properly.

TRANSPORTATION PROCEDURE

1. Keep electronic evidence away from magnetic sources.
2. Avoid storing electronic evidence in vehicles for prolonged periods of time.
3. Ensure that all containers holding electronic evidence are secured inside vehicles to avoid shock and excessive vibrations.
4. Always maintain the chain of custody.

STORAGE PROCEDURES

1. Ensure that all evidence is inventoried in accordance with the respective department's policy.
2. Store evidence in a secure area away from temperature and humidity extremes. Protect it from magnetic sources, moisture, dust, and other harmful particles.

Investigative Laws and Computer Crimes

As mentioned extensively in this chapter, the Internet and the computer have spawned new forms of crimes and made old crimes easier to commit—identity theft, child pornography, fraud, copyright violations, hacking, intellectual property theft—and the list can go on. Every state has laws to deal with computer crime and various aspects of it. Since these crimes usually cross state lines, the federal government bears much of the burden of prosecuting computer crimes.

A law used to prosecute computer criminals in the United States is the **wire fraud** statute,[25] which prohibits the use of communication wires in interstate or international commerce to commit fraud. This statute is used very effectively by federal prosecutors to prosecute computer crimes. This law requires intent to defraud the victim out of money or property and use of interstate or international wires during the commission of the crime. The problem with this law is it was not written for computer crimes. Not every crime committed with a computer is done intentionally to commit a fraud, and not all computer crimes cross state or international lines. In 1984, the Computer Fraud and Abuse Act was passed by Congress. Originally the Act had major limitations because it required proof that the person accessed the computer without authorization.[26] The statute excludes any crimes committed by an insider,[27] and it forbids prosecution in situations where intrusion into a computer without any gain is not a crime. In 1986 and 1994, the Computer Fraud and Abuse Act was modified to incorporate the problem of malicious code such as viruses, worms, and other programs, discussed previously in this chapter. This allowed for prosecution of those who transmit a program, information, code, or command to a computer or system with the intent to cause damage or prevent usage of the system.

In 1986, Congress passed the Electronic Communications Privacy Act, an amendment to the federal wiretap law. This act made it illegal to intercept stored or transmitted electronic communication without authorization. In 1998, the Digital Millennium Copyright Act was enacted. This act prohibits a person from bypassing technological measures meant to protect a copyright. A person found attempting to disable such technological measures would be in violation of this act. Additionally, this act prohibits the removal or alteration of information identifying the author and copyright holder.

In 2002, coupled with the passage of the Homeland Security Act, the Cyber Security Enhancement Act was enacted. This act gave law enforcement organizations and private companies authority to hand over documentation and information on anybody. If the reason for the exchange is deemed a national threat, then there is no accountability. The issue with this Act is that it does not define what a national threat is and who can make that determination. It is vague and allows for untrained individuals to possibly compromise a person's safety.

Digital Forensics

The skillful investigation of computer crimes rests on the recovery of information contained within pieces of electronic equipment. **Digital forensics** encompasses the recovery and

FIGURE 16.6 ▶ Investigators can use specialized forensic file retrieval software such as Cellbrite or EnCase to carry out "file dumps" of the entire digital contents of computers, cell phones, flash cards, and other electronic devices suspected to contain information on illegal activities.

investigation of information found in storage devices, usually in the context of computer crimes.[28] The term covers all devices capable of storing data. Several different types of software (for example, see Figure 16.6) and hardware on the market aid in the process of unveiling information contained in computers. Each tool is designed to serve specific functions, which are categorized into five areas: acquisition, validation and discrimination, extraction, reconstruction, and reporting.[29]

Acquisition

Acquisition is creating a bit-by-bit perfect copy of the digital media evidence. This is done by connecting the media to a write blocking device, which will essentially save an exact duplicate of the information contained on the computer being investigated. **Write blockers** are devices that acquire data on a drive without the possibility of accidentally damaging the drive's content. They do this by passing read commands but blocking write commands. The reason for making changes on a copy is to leave the original evidence intact. This prevents mistakes that could destroy evidence related to a case.[30]

The subfunctions of acquisition are physical and logical data copies, data acquisition format, command-line format, remote acquisition, and verification.[31] All of these subfunctions have data attached to them, and acquisition allows for the removal of that information.

Validation and Discrimination

Validation and discrimination is the process of ensuring and maintaining the integrity of the data acquired. The process of validating the data ensures the integrity of what is being transmitted. The discrimination of the data involves sorting and searching through all investigation-related data. Essentially, the process of validating the data is what allows discrimination of data.

There are three methods for discriminating data values. The first method is obtaining a hash value or **hashing**. This is a mathematical function that converts a large amount of data into a small datum. This function compares data and looks for specific information in a database. A hash value is comparable to a fingerprint. A fingerprint relative to the scale of a crime scene is very small, but it can identify a suspect. The same rule applies to hashing: A hash value is smaller than the file it is in, but it can readily identify the file from which it was created.[32] The second method of discriminating data value is referred to as *filtering*, or deciding which data packets are allowed to be sent and which are not. The last method is analyzing file headers values for known file types. Similar to hash values of known files, many computer forensic programs include a list of common header values. These header values allow for the identification of various file types related to the criminal investigation.[33]

Extraction

This function is the recovery task in the computer investigation and is by far the most difficult to complete. The subfunctions of extraction are data viewing, keyword searching, decompressing, carving, decrypting, and bookmarking. In any computer investigation, when information is extracted, depending on the type of tool used, the viewing mechanism displays file data and unallocated disk space.

Reconstruction

The purpose of a reconstruction is to re-create the pattern of activity in a suspect drive to show what happened during a crime. This reconstruction gives the investigator and court the step-by-step process by which a computer crime was committed. There are four sub-functions of reconstruction:

- Disk-to-disk copy
- Image-to-disk copy
- Partition-to-partition copy
- Image-to-partition copy

Reconstruction is relevant and needed in any criminal investigation. In computer crimes, reconstructing the pattern of how a file was created enables a successful investigation. Figure 16.7 shows a typical report generated for investigators following a digital forensic analysis of a crime suspect's computer.

Reporting

One important aspect of digital forensics is keeping track of the investigative work. This work is often long and tedious and, as

---

COMPUTER FORENSICS REPORT: SUSPECTED COMPUTER CRIME

(1) I conducted an exterior examination of the computer: Dell Tower Model, SN: 55555

(2) I disconnected and removed the hard drive from the suspect's computer. I connected the suspect's hard drive to my lab computer using a "write and protecting" device. This device permits data to be copied from a hard drive while preventing any data being written on to it. I then started the lab computer with Windows 7 Pro. I made an image of the computer's hard drive using EnCase , Version 6. I checked the data and time in the CMOS (Complementary Metal Oxide Semiconductor) and noted that the data was accurate and the time was one hour fast. Upon completion I verified the images. The hard drive was found to be partitioned into the following partitions:

ID	Type	Start Sector	Total Sectors	Size
de	Unknown	0	96,390	47.1MB
07	NTFS	96,390	150,386,400	71.7GB
db	CP/M	150,464.700	5,767,335	3.8GB

(3) I placed the hard drive back into the computer.

Results:

I ran a comparison of known hash values for child pornography provided by the National Center For Missing and Exploited Children. I found (9) matches. I then did a manual search for all images and videos. I found an additional 20 nude images of children. These records were captured on CD for the I/O to review.

FIGURE 16.7 ▶ Sample report generated for forensic analysis of a computer believed to contain child pornography.

time progresses, the investigators work on other cases and their memory fades. Computer crimes are intellectually taxing to investigators. Documentation of the investigation should be contemporaneous with the examination. Investigators should do the following:

- Take notes when consulting with the prosecutor
- Maintain a copy of the search authority with the case notes
- Maintain the initial request for assistance with the case file
- Maintain a copy of chain-of-custody documentation

- Include in the notes dates, times, and descriptions and results of actions taken
- Document irregularities encountered and any actions taken
- Include additional information, such as network typology, list of authorized users, user agreements, and passwords
- Document remote storage, remote user access, and offsite back-ups

Never underestimate the importance of documentation. Not being thorough in the task of reporting will only cause unnecessary work later and, worst of all, cases to be dismissed.

HOT TIPS AND LEADS 16.1

Utilizing Exigent Circumstance in Electronic Crime Scenes

When handling and packaging electronic devices and other electronic evidence, certain precautions should be taken to prevent loss of data and information contained in them. These devices require special handling instructions.

Computer Evidence and Exigent Circumstances

Exigent circumstances are an often-used justification for conducting warrantless searches and seizures involving physical evidence. Additionally, this exception, granted to investigators for obtaining a warrant, is also extended to electronic devices and crime scenes. Just as it is applied to physical crime scenes, the exigent circumstances rule may be invoked in electronic crime scenes when investigators are confronted with an emergency situation. Although it is well known that potential loss of life or possible destruction of evidence are typical emergencies justifying warrantless searches and seizures in ordinary crime scenes, what constitutes an electronic crime scene emergency situation? Instead of an imminent loss of life or destruction of evidence, these situations involve an imminent loss of electronic information or the destruction of data stored in devices such as computers and cell phones. In other words, exigent circumstances justify a warrantless search if it can be reasonably assumed that electronic evidence would be lost or destroyed if investigators had to obtain a warrant to seize the device and search its data storage areas. Some electronic exigent circumstances include the following:

- Battery-operated devices with a rapidly depleting power source that, when fully depleted, will cause

permanent loss of information contained within the device. This can occur when notebook computers enter power-saving mode or automatically turn themselves off when battery power is insufficient to power the device.
- Automatic or timed overwriting programs can destroy existing data files. This function is common on iPhones and iPads when they are linked to computer systems.
- Computer files can be deleted instantly from remote locations.
- Destruction of data by exposure to viruses.
- Suspects who destroy data on their computer or other device by overwriting it with as little as one key stroke.

These are just some of the many circumstances in which computer data could be destroyed, either intentionally or accidentally, requiring investigators to seize an electronic device under an exigent circumstances rationale. Care must be taken, however, to obtain a proper warrant to search the device's data files or other electronically stored content if—after the device's seizure—exigent circumstances no longer exist; that is, power has been restored or other potential threats to data or information on the device that initially justified the seizure are no longer imminent.

Cyber Terrorism

Since 9/11, cyber-attacks have not only destroyed life and property, but also crippled the government's electronic defenses. The phrase *cyber terrorism* is used to describe these Internet-based attacks. Law enforcement defines terrorism as the unlawful use

of force or violence against property or persons in an attempt to intimidate or coerce.[34]

Cyber terrorism would be the convergence of terrorism and cyberspace. It is generally understood to mean unlawful attacks and threats of attack against computers, networks, and the information stored therein when done to intimidate or coerce a government or its people in furtherance of political or social objectives.[35]

The number of ways in which terrorists can use computers as a tool is almost innumerable. Identity theft, computer viruses, hacking destruction of data, and malware all fall under this category. Yonah Alexander, an expert in terrorism research, had stated in a December 2001 announcement the idea of an Iraq net. This supposed network was the combination of more than one hundred websites across the globe to perform denial-of-service attacks against companies affiliated with the United States.[36]

Terrorist groups use the Internet to spread propaganda. In February 1998, Hizbollah was operating three websites: one for the central press office, another to describe its attacks on Israeli targets, and the third for news and information.[37]

One of the most common forms of communication by terrorist groups on the Web is the encryption of messages within the United States. These codes are hidden inside sport websites, chat rooms, and several pornographic websites. The codes, decipherable only by the members, are in places where many who investigate this crime don't go. Hamas and al-Qaeda use money from Muslim sympathizers to purchase computers from stores or by mail. Bin Laden's followers downloaded easy-to-use encryption programs from the Web. Wadih El Hage, one of the suspects in the 1998 bombing of two U.S. embassies in East Africa, sent encrypted e-mails under various names, including "Norman" and "Abdus Sabbur," to associates in al-Qaeda, according to the October 25, 1998, indictment against him.[38]

Each image, whether a picture or map, is created by a series of dots. Inside the dots are strings of letters and numbers that computers read to create the image. A coded message or another image can be hidden in those letters and numbers. The recent arrest of Army doctor Nidal Malik Hasan is another example of terrorism stretching through our computers. The army doctor had many e-mail exchanges with a known terrorist outside the United States.

Abroad or domestically, terrorism is a very real threat for the United States. Based on current patterns of activity in terrorist groups, terrorists clearly will use all means necessary to send their message into the United States. The computer as a tool and target expedites their message, and one could only speculate how many people in this country ingest the message and agree with it. Law enforcement investigators must stay on top of terrorist groups and monitor their behaviors in an attempt to thwart any future attacks on our soil.

RECONSTRUCTING A COMPUTER CRIME SCENE

Case Example 16A presents a residential electronic crime scene. In this case, the suspect is believed to have acquired and stored large amounts of digital photographs, videos, and information files that are illegal under current child pornography and exploitation laws. The investigation of this case requires the processing of both physical and digital evidence at the crime scene. The photo documentation of the scene is presented in Figures 16.8 through 16.13.

CASE EXAMPLE 16A

Residential Electronic Crime Scene

FIGURE 16.8 ► Front view of electronic crime scene at the suspect's residence. What initial steps should investigators take before processing this scene for suspected cyber crimes related to child pornography? Is a warrant necessary before processing this scene? What notes should be taken at this point in the investigation? What should be done if a suspect is at the scene?

FIGURE 16.9 ▶ Rear view of the electronic crime scene. What steps should be taken in processing this scene if it is a stand-alone system? What if it is a network system? Aside from the computer system, are there other types of electronic or data storage devices at this scene that should be treated as potential evidence in the investigation?

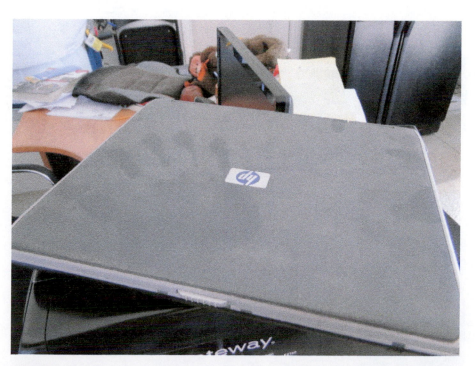

FIGURE 16.10 ▶ Close-up of laptop computer resting on desktop computer. Are there types of physical evidence (trace, fingerprint, DNA, etc.) at this scene that should be identified and collected? If so, how should it be collected if it is contained on or within the computer system and other electronic devices?

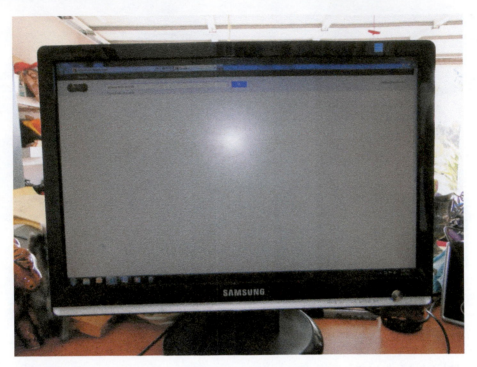

FIGURE 16.11 ▶ Computer monitor attached to suspect's desktop system. What steps should be taken to prepare this computer system for collection, packaging, and transportation as case evidence?

FIGURE 16.12 ▶ Close-up of suspect's computer monitor. What steps should be taken in securing the computer's monitor as evidence?

FIGURE 16.13 ▶ Rear view of wiring attached to suspect's desktop computer. How should the computer's power source, cords and other connective devices be disconnected, documented, collected and transported as evidence? What types of forensic analyses could be performed on the computer's data storage and media recording devices to discover digital evidence of illegal activity? How could this electronic evidence be used to prove the owner of the computer should be considered a suspect in this child pornography case?

Summary

1. The definition of computer crime.

Computer crime, or as many refer to it, *cyber-crime*, refers to any crime that involves a computer and network. Each computer crime is specific as to what needs to be done to complete the crime. These crimes fall into four categories: crimes against an individual, crimes against property, crimes against organizations, and crimes against society.

2. Varieties of computer crime.

There are numerous varieties of computer crimes, including e-mail spoofing, spamming, cyber defamation, harassment, and cyber stalking. A spoofed e-mail is one in which the e-mail header is forged so that mail appears to originate from one source but actually has been sent from another. Essentially, the individual who spoofs an e-mail simply sets the "from" field of outgoing messages to show a name or address other than the actual one from which the message is sent. Most POP e-mail clients allow you to change the text displayed in this field. Other forms of computer crimes are denial of service and Internet time theft.

3. Characteristics of computer crime suspects.

Computer crime suspects come from myriad backgrounds. In a report covering hundreds of cases over a 10-year period, 75 percent of the perpetrators were men and 25 percent were women. Most are first-time perpetrators, having no previous criminal record. The term *hacking* is used to describe the actual intrusion into a computer. Computer crime suspects are subdivided into several different categories. They are novice, cyber-punks, internals, old guard hackers, information warriors, and cyber terrorists.

4. Computer crime is investigation.

Initial responders have to react with knowledge of what they are potentially looking at. First and foremost, the utmost priority is to ensure the safety of officers and others. Once the scene is clear of all potential physical dangers, the first responder, depending on the type of computer crime, must perform five basic steps:

1. Recognize the investigative value of digital evidence.
2. Assess available resources.
3. Identify the equipment and supplies that should be taken to electronic crime scenes.
4. Assess the crime scene and the digital evidence present.
5. Designate the assignments, roles, and responsibilities of personnel involved in the investigation.

From here, the crime is investigated by the use of digital forensics.

5. **Digital forensics.**

   Digital forensics encompasses recovery and investigation of material found in storage devices. There are several different ways in which forensics is utilized. The term covers all devices capable of storing data. Several different types of software and hardware on the market aid in the process of unveiling information contained in computers. Each tool is designed to serve specific functions. The functions are categorized into five areas: acquisition, validation and discrimination, extraction, reconstruction, and reporting.

Key Terms

cyber-crime	denial of service	spamming
computer as the target	trojan horse	cyber defamation
virus	digital forensics	hacker
theft of intellectual properties	computer as the instrumentality of the crime	cyber stalking
techno-vandalism	computer incidental to other crimes	virus attacks
techno-trespass	crimes associated with prevalence of computers	hashing
cyber terrorism		logic bomb
web jacking	e-mail spoofing	write blockers
cellular phone fraud		wire fraud

Review Questions

1. What is cyber-crime? Provide some examples?
2. What are the two most common forms of intellectual property theft? List some recent cases.
3. What is a virus?
4. How does spamming work?
5. Define denial of service and list some recent examples of it in present society?
6. What is cyber-stalking and how is it relevant to computer crime?
7. What are the five areas of digital forensics?
8. What types of groups are affiliated with cyber terrorism?
9. Describe techno-vandalism. Give an example of how one would commit it.
10. Define the different federal laws applicable to computer crime investigations.

Internet Resources

Federal Bureau of Investigations	www.fbi.gov
United Nations Crime and Justice Information Network	www.uncjin.org
Computer Crime & Intellectual Property Section, United States DOJ	www.justice.gov/criminal/cybercrime
United States Department of State	www.state.gov
High Technology Crime Investigation Association	www.htcia.org

Applied Investigative Exercise

You are assigned by your law enforcement agency to investigate the case illustrated in Case Example 16A. Outline an investigative plan and procedure for this case, and in doing so, specifically address the following questions:

1. What evidence would you collect at the scene, and how would you collect it?
2. What type of questions would you ask the suspect following an examination of the digital (and perhaps physical) evidence?
3. What forensic tools would you use to remove data that has been stored on the computer and other digital storage devices?

Notes

[1] *FBI Law Bulletin*, 2008.

[2] Richard Raysman, Edward A. Pisacreta, and Kenneth A. Adler, *Intellectual Property Licensing: Forms and Analysis*. Law Journal Press, 1999–2008.

[3] Ibid.

[4] Ibid.

[5] Ibid.

[6] *FBI Law Bulletin*, 2005.

[7] Ibid.

[8] Based on the author's extensive experience in white-collar crime.

[9] Ibid.

[10] Financial Action Task Force, "Money Laundering," March 2, 2011.

[11] Based on the authors' extensive experience in the field of law enforcement and direct personal knowledge of investigations.

[12] *FBI Law Bulletin*, 2005.

[13] "The Risk of Obtaining and Using Pirated Software," IDC sponsored by Microsoft, Doc #WP1006GRO, October 2006.

[14] Bureau of Consumer protection center.

[15] www.reportcybercrime.com.

[16] www.cyberlawdb.com.

[17] Noah Shachtman (2009-06-15), "Activists Launch Hack Attacks on Tehran Regime"

[18] "Hacker Takes $50,000 a Few Cents at a Time," *PC Pro*, 2008-05-28.

[19] "Report to the Nation on Occupational Fraud and Abuse," prepared by the Association of Certified Fraud Examiners (ACFE).

[20] Dr. Marcus Rogers, "Psychological Crimes Scene Analysis," 2006.

[21] Ibid.

[22] NIJ, "Electronic Crime Scene Investigation" guideline for first responder.

[23] Secret Service, "Guidelines for Seizing Electronic Evidence," 2010.

[24] Ibid.

[25] Title 18 USC 1343, www.justice.gov.

[26] Computer Fraud and Abuse Act 1986 (US) 18 USC 1030.

[27] Electronic Communications Privacy Act.

[28] B. Carrier, "Defining Digital Forensic Examination and Analysis Tools," Digital Research Workshop, 2001.

[29] B. Nelson, "Field Manual for Collecting, Examining, and Preserving Evidence of Computer Crimes," 2008.

[30] Ibid.

[31] Ibid.

[32] Ibid.

[33] Ibid.

[34] Based on the authors' experience working within homeland security.

[35] D. Denning, "Cyberterrorism." Testimony before the special oversight panel of terrorism on Armed Services committee.

[36] Gabriel Weimann, "Cyberterrorism: How Real Is the Threat?" United States Institute of Peace, 2004.

[37] John Arquilla, "Networks, Netwar, and Information-Age Terrorism," Rand, 1999.

[38] Ibid.

CHAPTER SEVENTEEN

ARSON AND EXPLOSION SCENES

Learning Objectives

After completing this chapter, you should be able to:

1. Summarize the trends and elements of arson.
2. Summarize the motivations and characteristics of arsonists.
3. Describe how arson investigations are conducted.
4. Describe the investigation of bombings and bomb threats.

Chapter Outline

The Crime of Arson
- Arson Laws

Investigating Arson
- Legal Concerns

The Anatomy of Fire

Investigating the Burn Site
- The Point of Origin
- The Overhaul
- Multiple Points of Origin
- Accelerants

Indicators of Accelerant Use
- Inverted "V" Burn Patterns
- Floor and Rundown Burning
- Streamers/Trailers
- Early Smoke Color
- Alligatoring of Wood
- Melted Metals

Situational Indicators of Arson
- Target Location
- Target Preparation
- Ignition Devices
- Calling 911
- Fire Watching

The Great Arson Impersonator: Flashover

Arsonist Profiles

Vehicle Fires

Dead Bodies at the Fire Scene

Bomb and Explosions Investigation

Mechanical Explosions

Chemical Explosions

Explosives and Bombs
- High Explosives
- Low Explosives

Preblast Investigations

Postblast Investigations
- Preliminary Assessment of the Fire Scene
- Establish the Perimeters
- Determine the Search Method
- Examine the Epicenter
- Assess the Type of Explosion
- Determine the Type of Explosive
- Collect the Evidence

Vehicle Bombings

INTRODUCTION

FIRES SUCH AS THE ONE pictured here are among the most perplexing situations encountered by investigators, who must determine whether the fire was unintentionally set or was the work of an arsonist. Arson investigation is not only time consuming but potentially dangerous due to unforeseen toxic hazards, sharp broken objects, volatile or explosive materials, and unstable building structures at the fire scene. Arson is also one of the costliest property crimes in terms of monetary damage and is extremely difficult to prove through available physical evidence. When flammable liquids have not been discovered as the possible fire-setting agency used by an arsonist, searching for evidence to rule out natural or accidental causes as the fire's origin can be painstakingly difficult—to say the least. As in the present case, the discovery of a dead body at the suspected arson scene further complicates the investigator's work. Medical examinations of the body and other evidence gathered at the scene will be needed to determine whether the victim was alive before exposure to the deadly smoke and heat presumed to be the cause of death. If alive, was the victim intentionally prevented from escaping the fire location so as to kill him or her? If the victim was dead, was the fire intentionally set to destroy forensic clues at the scene and to prevent investigators from treating the crime as a homicide? Answers to these and related questions surrounding the case illustrated here come through an understanding of the principles of arson and explosions investigation presented in this chapter.

THE CRIME OF ARSON

Specific laws created to curb the dangers of fire setting can be traced back to medieval times; for example, French citizens were not allowed to have open fires after a certain time at night known as the *couvre feu* (the origin of the English word "curfew"). The crime of intentionally setting a fire for purposes of destruction, otherwise known as arson, has historical roots dating as far back as the Roman Empire. Such acts were typically punished by death. Today, however, the crime of arson is no less a threat to public safety than it was in ancient societies. An estimated 500,000 arson fires occur in the United States each year, claiming more than 700 lives and causing approximately $2 billion in property loss. Unfortunately, arson is one of the nation's costliest crimes and one of the most difficult to investigate and prosecute. Only 16 percent of all suspected arson fires lead to the arrest of a suspect. Even more discouraging, only 2 percent of persons arrested under suspicion of arson are eventually convicted of the crime.[1]

Arson Laws

In a general sense, arson can be defined as "any willing or malicious burning or attempt to burn, with or without intent to defraud, a dwelling house, public building, motor vehicle or aircraft, personal property of another."[2] Arson laws within most jurisdictions, although perhaps differing in their statutory wording, specify that a fire must be deliberately set with malicious intent. Some statutes require that a dwelling or other structure is somehow damaged by fire. Others specify that the burning of open land or personal property (e.g., clothing, documents) satisfies the legal requirements for arson. In addition, there are states with arson laws that simply require proof of criminal fire setting irrespective of structural or property damage.[3]

Under most laws, the act of arson is considered complete merely by the presence of some sort of burning, regardless of how serious or slight the fire damage may be. Many laws have extended the meaning of damage by burning to include evidence of surface charring, the presence of soot deposits, or destruction caused by explosive devices. Arson is usually categorized in terms of degrees that reflect the seriousness of a particular fire-setting activity. First-degree arson typically involves situations where fire has resulted in the injury or death of a human being and can be punishable by life imprisonment or death. Lesser degrees of arson tend to be based on factors such as the financial loss, extent of damage, and nature of intent associated with a particular offense.

INVESTIGATING ARSON

Arson is considered one of the most difficult crimes to investigate. Not only does fire destroy many articles of physical evidence, but establishing and proving an arson case by using unburned evidence can be extremely difficult. For the most part, arson fires are proven through the process of elimination; that is, other potential causes of a fire must be ruled out by available physical evidence before it can be argued that an intentional burning has taken place. There are four classifications of fire causation:

- *Incendiary:* This is a fire that has been intentionally set, and is legally defined as an arson fire.

- *Natural:* These fires are caused by acts of nature such as lightning, earthquakes, wind, or spontaneous combustion.
- *Accidental:* Such fires are started by misplaced cigarettes, defective appliances, chimney sparks, and other legitimate uses of a potential fire-causing device or agent.
- *Undetermined:* The cause of these fires cannot be determined through an investigation. Future investigative efforts, however, may later determine a specific cause, resulting in an undetermined fire's reclassification as natural, accidental, or incendiary.

Therefore, the investigator's primary mission in a suspected arson crime scene is to gather physical evidence that (1) supports the claim that an incendiary fire has taken place and (2) rules out the possibility that the fire was the product of either natural or accidental causes. To do so, the investigator must understand the process by which fire is created and sustained.[4]

Legal Concerns

Investigating a fire scene, from a legal perspective, is no different than investigating any other type of crime scene. All legal rights and expectations of fire investigators are covered under Fourth Amendment search-and-seizure case law. Two U.S. Supreme court cases—*Michigan v. Tyler*[5] and *Michigan v. Clifford*[6]—deal specifically with the investigation of fire scenes. In general, they specify that investigation of a fire scene is justified without a search warrant under the rule of exigent circumstances; however, the search must be conducted within a "reasonable time" after the fire has been extinguished. The Court has ruled that waiting until sunrise before investigating a fire extinguished at night is acceptable within the legal requirements of exigent circumstances.

THE ANATOMY OF FIRE

Basically, fire is produced by a combination of oxygen, fuel, and heat known as the **fire triangle**. The oxygen usually comes from air, but can also be from other oxidizing sources including various chemical agents. Fuels can be in solid, liquid, or gas form; for example, wood is the most common solid fuel involved in a structure fire; gasoline and natural gas are common liquid and gas fuels, respectively. When heat is applied to a mixture of oxygen and fuel, ignition of the fire is achieved. Fire burns continuously, or is sustained, as the result of a domino-like effect or chain reaction between fuel, oxygen, and heat. When one of the aforementioned components of fire dissipates or is removed from the others, the fire is extinguished. Typically, most fires begin in a three-stage process. First is the **incipient stage**, during which the fuel is preheated by the ignition source. The second, or **smoldering stage**, is evidenced by smoke and gas particles emitted from the fuel. The **flaming stage** marks the completion of the process when a visible flame erupts from the smoldering fuel.

As previously mentioned, the arson investigation must focus on proving the existence of an incendiary fire while simultaneously ruling out other causes. Bearing in mind the interactive process by which a fire is created, the investigator must seek out physical evidence indicating that human intervention has intentionally altered one or more of the essential components of fire starting. In other words, the key question that the investigation of a suspected arson crime scene must answer is, "Has either the oxygen, fuel, or heat source been artificially modified to assist in the production of fire?" If the physical evidence suggests that the answer is "yes," then the fire likely is incendiary and arson related. Conversely, the answer "no" suggests that the fire originated from accidental or natural causes.[7]

INVESTIGATING THE BURN SITE

The Point of Origin

Whether the fire is located outdoors or indoors, investigation of a burn site should begin at the outermost locations of the fire-involved area and proceed inward. The primary goal of this "outward-in" search method is to identify the location(s) where the fire originated, known as the fire's **point of origin**. In a typical outdoor fire involving grass or other wild vegetation during low wind conditions, the fire burns in a concentric circle pattern with the point of origin directly in the middle of the fire circle. When high wind conditions are present, an outdoor wildfire burns in an inverted triangular pattern with the point of origin located at the apex or top of the triangle. Trees and shrubs will also burn on the side facing any oncoming wind. Rocks, vehicles, structures, and other objects will show similar evidence of burning, smoke, and soot deposits on surfaces located in the direction of wind travel.

In structure fires, the primary indicator of the point of origin is the location at which the fire damage is greatest. This area may be quite evident in fires that have been extinguished early on or contained to an isolated portion of the structure. In a structure's total loss by fire, however, locating the point of origin may be extremely difficult. Often, these investigations must be conducted on the charred and water- and foam-soaked remains of a structure that has totally collapsed. Perhaps the best indicator of a fire's point of origin in these extreme situations is the relative amount of charring present on wooden structural components such as wall studs (boards running vertically inside walls), ceiling rafters (boards forming the roof and attic areas), and floor joists (boards supporting the floor in a house that has a basement). Charring most deeply penetrates wooden objects located within the point of origin (see Figure 17.1) because this is where fire burns most intensely. The relative depth of charring can be determined by pushing a small sharp probe such as a knife or screwdriver into the soft charred area until it stops at the hard inner surface of the unburned wood. Wooden structural components in walls, ceilings, or floors that have the deepest charring penetration are generally suggestive of the point of origin.

FIGURE 17.1 ▶ The point of origin of an arson fire showing the severest and most concentrated charring of wood.

In many cases, investigators are called to the fire scene long after the blaze has been extinguished. This time delay may cause many disruptions in the investigation process. First, witnesses present when the fire began most likely will have left the scene. Therefore, it is essential that the names and contact information of such persons be obtained by first responders and the individuals be contacted during the follow-up investigation. These witnesses can provide information not only about arson suspect leads during the outset of the blaze, but also about the early characteristics of the fire—for example, how it smelled, how it looked, the level of heat emitted, or suspicious sounds originating from the burn site.[8]

The Overhaul

In most cases the investigation proceeds at the point of origin, which is where most evidence of an intentionally set arson fire is typically found. Sometimes, however, it is difficult or impossible to locate the fire's true point of origin due to earlier firefighting activity related to extinguishing the blaze. For example, firefighters routinely conduct an **overhaul** of the scene after dowsing the fire with water and ostensibly putting it out. This process involves moving burnt articles from their original positions to inspect for burning embers that could cause the fire to reignite. In smaller fires, this postfire movement can cause some difficulty and confusion for investigators since specific charred articles indicating the point of origin have been moved from their original position. In such situations, the first responding firefighters should be interviewed to determine the nature and extent of the overhaul, as well as the original position of displaced pieces of evidence.

Multiple Points of Origin

Another situation that may cause investigators difficulty is the presence of multiple possible locations for the fire's origin. Most fires, whether arson or not, have one point of origin. Multiple points of origin, however, are not normal and are sometimes suggestive of foul play. Arsonists may set fires in multiple locations to make sure that an area or structure is more quickly fully engulfed in flames to ensure maximum destruction. Care should be taken in applying this principle to all fire crime scenes, however. Some fires appear to have multiple points of origin because of erratic burn patterns or multiple sources of ignition stemming from a single point of origin.[9]

Accelerants

The most certain indicator of an arson is the discovery of accelerant use at the fire scene—in particular, at the fire's point of origin. **Accelerants** are any substances used to speed the fire starting process. Although they can be in solid or gas form, accelerants used for purposes of arson are usually volatile liquids. Gasoline is by far the accelerant of choice used by most arsonists, largely because it is readily accessible and difficult to trace back to a particular point of purchase. Other liquid accelerants include kerosene, charcoal lighter, turpentine, acetone, and other mineral spirits. Used less often are solid accelerants such as camping fuels (e.g., sterno cans), explosive compounds (e.g., gunpowder), or gas accelerants such as natural gas, propane, butane, and aerosol propellants.[10]

INDICATORS OF ACCELERANT USE

Inverted "V" Burn Patterns

A fire started without the use of an accelerant leaves a characteristic **"V" burn pattern** on walls or other vertical surfaces closest to its origin. This is the result of a progressive build-up of heat and smoke expanding up and outward from the fire's base. Fires that build more slowly in intensity exhibit a wider "V" than those progressing more rapidly. In contrast, fires set with the aid of an accelerant exhibit a tell-tale **inverted "V" burn pattern** as shown in Figure 17.2. Wider at the bottom

FIGURE 17.2 ▶ An arson fire set with accelerant leaves a characteristic inverted "V" pattern (highlighted in red) whereas a normal fire leaves a normal "V" pattern (illustrated in black) due to the gradual build-up of heat and flames moving upward.

and tapering to a narrow apex at the top, these patterns are created when accelerant at the base of a fire ignites and causes a rapidly expanding horizontal burning effect. Wider patterns at the base of the inverted "V" generally indicate the presence of a greater concentration of accelerant at a given location.[11]

Floor and Rundown Burning

Anytime evidence indicates that a fire has started directly on the floor of a structure or on an object, the use of an accelerant for purposes of arson should be suspected. Telltale signs include more intense burning in floor areas caused by concentrated amounts of accelerant leaving unique **pour patterns**. This is especially noticeable when flammable liquids have been used on noncarpeted surfaces. Dips or uneven areas that allow pools of accelerant to collect (known as **puddling**) show darker, more pronounced burn characteristics. In addition, seams, cracks, gaps, and chips in flooring materials will similarly serve as collection areas for accelerant—thus, displaying similar burn patterns.[12]

Suspicion of arson is even more justified when the fire has burned below the flooring surface in what is known as a **rundown burn** pattern. Fires rarely start at floor level, so they are equally unlikely to burn in a downward direction without the aid of an accelerant. Figure 17.3 illustrates a rundown burn pattern on a wall when accelerant was applied by an arsonist to the roof of a structure. Accelerants pool on floor areas, even when applied to a wall or other horizontal surface, and in sufficient quantities they seep below locations where they are initially applied. Burned furnishings, automobiles, or other property that rests above ground level should be examined for burning in a downward direction. Floors or surfaces directly below these objects should be investigated for burn evidence as well. When structures are the intended target, floor coverings such as carpet, tile, linoleum, or wood veneers should be removed and inspected for burning that has penetrated below the surface area. Heat-induced chipping or flaking of concrete below floor coverings, referred to as **spalling**, may indicate accelerant use as well. It should be noted, however, that heat is only one of many potential causes of spalling in concrete.[13]

Streamers/Trailers

Arsonists may spread flammable liquids or objects, referred to as **streamers** or **trailers**, throughout areas and structures so that the fire will reach intended targets. Typical streamers/trailers include wood, paper, or rope that has been soaked in accelerant to increase combustibility. These objects create a wick-like effect useful for igniting fires from distances and in multiple locations. They also can be used to stage fires to appear to have been started by means other than arson; for example, an arsonist may place a streamer/trailer to link an electrical outlet to foam padding on a sofa in an attempt to mislead investigators into concluding that the fire was accidental. Streamers/trailers are often identified by the continuous

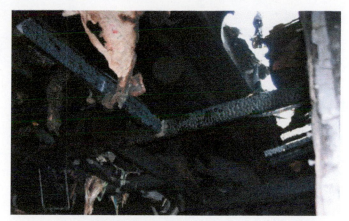

(a)

(b)

FIGURE 17.3 ▶ (a) The blistered or scaled appearance across the surface of charred wood is referred to as *alligatoring*. (b) Rundown burning on a wall where accelerant was poured on the building's roof by an arsonist, causing the fire to move downward.

burn lines that they leave behind. If fires are extinguished early on, unburned streamers/trailers may be still present at the crime scene.[14]

Early Smoke Color

Most burning fuels that have not been treated with an accelerant emit white or gray smoke. Such is the case for outdoor fires fueled by natural vegetation or structure fires fueled by wood. Dark brown or black smoke during the early stages of a fire, on the other hand, usually indicates use of an accelerant. Any witnesses who saw the fire in its early stages should be asked an open-ended question regarding the smoke's color during this stage of the fire (i.e., don't ask whether it was black or white) and also whether any petroleum-type smells were evident.[15]

Alligatoring of Wood

Alligatoring is charring that produces large shiny blisters on the surface of burnt wood as shown in Figure 17.3a. In general, alligator char indicates a fire that perhaps moved rapidly and

FIGURE 17.4 ▶ The amount of heat generated by a fire often can be determined by examining the melting characteristics of various metals at the scene.

burnt with intense heat. Although alligatoring can be produced on wooden surfaces by contact with accelerants, it can also be caused by many other factors resulting in increased fire temperatures. Thus, the discovery of alligator char (without other corroborative evidence) is not sufficient to support the assumption that arson has taken place.[16]

Melted Metals

A particular type of metal that shows signs of melting can provide an estimate of the fire's temperature and perhaps suggests the use of an accelerant. Typical structural fires reach about 1,900°F, which can melt a variety of metals; for example, aluminum melts at 1,220°F, gold at 1,945°F, and copper at 1,981°F. Iron, on the other hand, melts at 2,781°F, well beyond the melting point of most other metals. Disfigured objects located on or near floor areas and made from metals with relatively high melting temperatures (for example, copper coins, gold jewelry) may indicate the use of an accelerant. This is because accelerants placed on floors or lower levels of a structure produce intense heat, reaching temperatures capable of melting such metals. Without the presence of accelerants, such metals are less likely to melt because floors and lower structural areas tend to burn at cooler temperatures ranging from 1,400°F to 1,600°F.[17] The vehicle shown in Figure 17.4 contains various metals melted after exposure to extreme heat from a fire started by an accelerant.

SITUATIONAL INDICATORS OF ARSON

Besides accelerant use, there are other indicators that a particular fire was started by an arsonist. These include strategic location of the point of origin, preparation of the fire target to ensure that the blaze ignites and spreads, and use of ignition devices to delay triggering of the accelerant until after the arsonist has left the scene.

Target Location

Most arson fires are set in locations that (1) best conceal criminal activity from the eyes and ears of others and (2) most ensure the maximum amount of fire damage. In dwellings, the location that best satisfies these requirements is the basement. Basements are one of the most popular areas for starting arson fires because they usually have doors and windows for entry that are not readily visible and they allow upward movement of flames to ignite the underside of a structure's flooring components (usually made of wood). These fires, in comparison to those originating in other locations, spread most rapidly and cause the most damage. Other rooms that are likely targets of arson include living or leisure rooms containing ignitable furnishings, draperies, wood paneling, or exposed wooden structures such as open beam ceilings. Attics are the least preferable locations for arson because fire reaching upward likely will burn, at most, only the roof area before it is extinguished. Because most accidental fires start with the careless dropping of a cigarette by a person who has fallen asleep, some arsonists ignite couches or beds to make investigators believe this typical scenario has occurred. Kitchens also are a frequent target for arsonists, who make it look as though an electrical fire has started by the spontaneous ignition of a faulty appliance.

Target Preparation

Arsonists may need to prepare their targets in advance to ensure that the fire they set has enough fuel and oxygen to continue burning. To do so, holes may be punched in walls and ceilings to expose wooden beams and supports located beneath fire-retardant wallboard. In addition, windows and doors may be propped open to help spread the fire or to create cross-ventilation. Furniture also may be moved under low hanging drapes surrounding a window, which provides ventilation.

Ignition Devices

An **ignition device** is used to produce the heat needed to convert fuel and oxygen into fire. Most arson fires are not started with elaborate ignition devices but rather by simple heat sources such as matches or cigarette lighters. When ignition devices are used, they usually are constructed so as to cause a time-delayed fire that allows the arsonist to flee the crime scene before the fire begins. Such devices need not be sophisticated and are typically fashioned from household products such as matches attached to candles or cigarettes. More elaborate methods may include electric timers or cell phones that provide an electric circuit to a fuse-type ignition apparatus. Ignition devices do not require an accelerant and are rarely used with one.

Typically, the device is placed in or near easily combustible materials—for example, a cigarette and match mechanism on the surface of flammable furniture cushions or inside a trash can filled with paper. Certain accelerants, especially those emitting flammable vapors, are ignited with more careful preparation when used with a make-shift time delay device. To guard against premature combustion, most arsonists place the accelerant in an airtight container to separate gases or fumes from the source of ignition. Plastic containers, water bottles, balloons, garbage bags, and other meltable receptacles may be used for this purpose. Burnt remains of such objects discovered in locations where accelerant has been detected provide physical evidence of this fire ignition method.

Calling 911

Most arsonists, especially experienced ones, plan the timing and spread of their fires to avoid causing excessive damage as well as injury or death to humans (unless intended). Specifically, they do not want fires to spread from the intended target structure to other structures where persons may be killed—turning their act of arson into murder. If, and when, arsonists believe that their fires may have unanticipated dangerous consequences they may call 911 and report the blaze to prevent extreme destruction or loss of life.

Fire Watching

Many arsonists enjoy watching the fires they set. Therefore, during the first response to a fire the person responsible for the blaze sometimes acts like a witness, walking near the scene or sitting in a car parked close by. Arsonists are also noted for taking pictures or videos of their fires. Searches of suspected arsonists' homes should include looking for photographs, videos, DVDs, cell phones, computers, and other media sources capable of capturing permanent images of arson scenes. Diaries, personal notes, and other written materials are possible arsonists' mementos as well.

THE GREAT ARSON IMPERSONATOR: FLASHOVER

Flashover is an extremely dangerous situation during which entire rooms or enclosed areas burst into flames, causing total destruction and the absolute loss of human life. It occurs when hot smoke and gases from a fire rise upward, collect at ceiling level, and then are pushed downward, causing the ignition of combustible objects. When flashover occurs, a wall of fire rapidly consumes an entire room or area and depletes all available oxygen. In other words, at this point instead of there being a fire in a room, the entire room is now on fire. If the fire continues to burn, it may cause a **backdraft** whereby oxygen necessary to feed the blaze is drawn inward from external openings such as doors and windows.

From an investigative standpoint, it is important to understand the fire damage done by flashover because the extreme heat that it produces can leave burn indicators closely resembling those of arson. Classic signs of accelerant use such as extreme charring, alligatoring, collapsed furniture springs, burnt metal objects, multiple points of origin, crazed glass, and even apparent pour patterns can be imitated by flashover. The discovery of one or more of the following signs, however, indicates flashover rather than accelerant use:

- Burning on the top surfaces of materials
- Lack of normal fire spread from the point of origin
- Lack of accelerant residue
- Demarcation lines on walls and within the fire-involved area[18]

HOT TIPS AND LEADS 17.1

Developing Arson Suspect Leads

The best predictor of future criminal behavior is past criminal behavior. This is especially true with arson. Unlike most other crimes, the compulsion to intentionally set fires usually starts at a very early age—typically during the teenage years, but even as early as preschool. Major arson investigations have revealed that many, if not most arsonists are 18 years of age or younger. Their primary targets are schools they attend, with an average of 20 school fires being set in the United States each week. In addition, adult arsonists often have histories of setting fires as juveniles. When vandalism appears to be the motive for a fire, and the arsonist has not been identified, efforts to develop suspect leads should focus on juveniles who have an established history of fire setting recorded by child protective services or probation divisions, or who are enrolled in "Young Fire Starters" anti-arson intervention programs for juveniles considered at risk for future arson activity. Because many adult arsonists merely extend their juvenile compulsions for fire setting to a more mature age, inspecting the aforementioned youthful arson records may also provide fruitful investigative leads for tracking down adult arsonists unable to shake the "fire bug" habits of their childhood.

VEHICLE FIRES

Most vehicles are set on fire by owners who can no longer afford to pay for them to collect insurance money. Other motivations include getting rid of vehicles that have excessive mileage, are in need of costly repairs, are undesirable models and cannot be sold on the open market, or are worth less than the money owed on them. In rarer instances, a vehicle is intentionally set on fire to cover up forensic clues related to a criminal activity such as fingerprints, DNA, hairs/fibers, or bodies of murder victims who have been shot, stabbed, or strangled.

As previously mentioned in Chapter 15 concerning vehicle crimes, most accidental vehicle fires start in the engine compartment and sometimes spread to the passenger area depending on various circumstances including wind direction, dry brush or other combustibles surrounding the vehicle, the amount of fuel in the vehicle's tank, and oil or greasy residue deposit on or beneath the vehicle. With vehicle fires, as with other arson fires, the investigation begins with locating the fire's point of origin. This normally is the area with the most fire damage. Signs of intentionally set vehicle fires include the following:

- Missing parts or accessories (DVD stereo/entertainment system, speakers, GPS)
- Personal items missing from the vehicle (purse, wallet in the glove box or console)
- Tool marks on broken or leaking sources of fuel (gas lines, gas tank, gas cap)
- All windows completely rolled down or rolled down in abnormal patterns
- Multiple points of origin, e.g., extensive concentrated burning in both the engine and passenger compartments
- The hood is raised and the doors are opened
- Containers, matches, hoses, or other means of accelerant use at the scene
- Vehicle owner was present when the fire began and has burns or smells of smoke
- Pour patterns on the vehicle showing the placement of accelerant
- Downward or drip-down burning in areas such as the tires, the trunk, and passenger compartment where fuel sources are not present[19]

DEAD BODIES AT THE FIRE SCENE

Arson may be a primary crime or a secondary one related to murder. In the former situation, the arsonists set a fire in a house or other location where the victim is sleeping, drugged, intoxicated, bound, or otherwise incapacitated and cannot escape. In a secondary arson, the arsonist incinerates an already-dead body at the location of a murder or elsewhere away from the murder scene. In both situations, the body will evidence fourth-degree burns, which include extensive charring of the flesh, fracturing of the skull, and splitting and cracking of major bones—especially those of the arms and legs. Typically, facial features are burned beyond recognition.

Despite the extensive bone and tissue damage caused by fourth-degree burns, medical examiners can determine whether the victim's death occurred before or after the fire. Usually, examinations of blood and internal lung tissues reveal carbon monoxide inhaled by the victims before death, indicating that the victims were still alive at the time of the fire. In addition, bullet entry and exit points, stabbing wounds, and ligature marks resulting from strangulation also may be evident despite fourth-degree burns.

Besides medical examinations, investigators often can use the burn victim's body position to determine if the victim may have died as the result of exposure to a fire. This simple examination inspects the burn victim's body for what is referred to as the **pugilist posture**. Usually, the bodies of individuals who are alive before they die in a fire exhibit this condition in which the victim's arms are locked at the elbows with fists clenched and pointing inward toward the face in a fashion that resembles a boxing (i.e., pugilist) position. The victim's legs are bent at the knees are drawn inward toward the body as well. This positioning may be due to a live body reaction in which muscles contract from exposure to the fire and may also cause the victim's mouth to tense in a "smiling" position. However, investigators must apply this rule with caution because if the body has been dead for only a short period of time and *rigor mortis* has not yet set in, the pugilist position may be observed as well. The pugilist posture will generally not be observed in burn victims exposed to fire after being dead for a time—usually when and after *rigor mortis* has set in. In the latter case, the victim's body will be found in the position that it was in before it was burnt. Case Example 17A presents a vehicle fire involving two fourth-degree burn victims declared dead at the scene by first responders. This case, illustrated in Figures 17.5 to 17.12, provides many indicators that can help determine whether the vehicle fire and loss of life shown is the result of arson.

ARSONIST PROFILES

Of all major criminal offenders, the arsonist is by far the most youthful. More than half of all arson fires (approximately 55 percent) are set by persons less than 18 years of age. In addition, the typical arsonist is a Caucasian male (approximately 80 percent) with a history of prior offending, troubled family relations, and poor school performance. Contrary to popular belief, most arson fires are set by amateurs. Professional arsonists known as **torches**, who engage in fire setting for monetary gain, are rare. Less than 5 percent of all arson cases can be attributed to the work of a torch.

CASE EXAMPLE 17A

Vehicle Fire Scene

(a)

(b)

FIGURE 17.5 ▶ (a) Police are dispatched to a vehicle fire call. (b) The vehicle as it appeared when approached by first responding officers.

FIGURE 17.6 ▶ A charred body is discovered in the front passenger seat of the vehicle. What evidence is present within the burnt remains of this passenger compartment that suggests the use of an accelerant?

FIGURE 17.7A ▶ Investigators and the coroner are called to the scene. The body is removed from the vehicle. From an investigative standpoint, what does the position of the burn victim's body suggest?

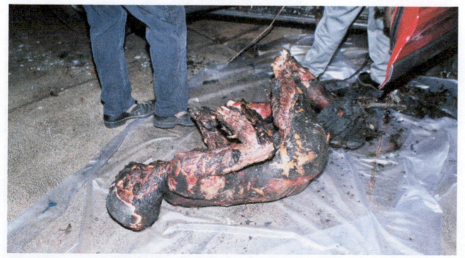

(a)

17.7B ▶ Close-up of the victim's facial area showing signs of fourth-degree burns.

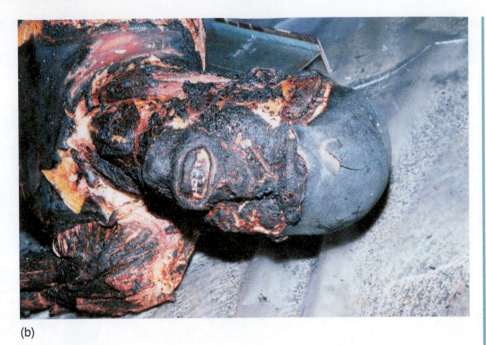

(b)

FIGURE 17.8 ▶ Examination of the rear passenger seat revealed the charred remains of a second victim. (Note the burn victim's leg and tennis shoe in the bottom right side of the photo.) Is there any evidence to suggest the use of accelerant in the rear passenger area of the vehicle?

(a)

(b)

FIGURE 17.9 ▶ (a) The second victim is removed from the vehicle. (b) Close-up of the second victim's face. What evidence is presented here to suggest that the victim died either before or after exposure to the fire?

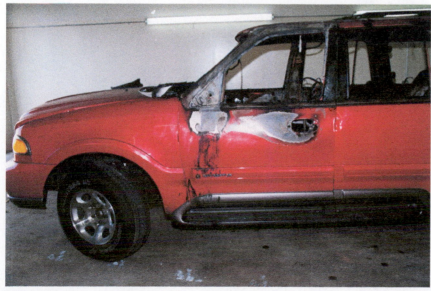

(a)

FIGURE 17.10A ▶ Examination of the arson vehicle's front left (a) and right rear. Do the burn patterns on the vehicle's exterior suggest the use of an accelerant?

17.10B ▶ Exterior panels. Does the appearance of the vehicle's exterior panels suggest an arson fire?

(b)

(a)

(b)

FIGURE 17.11 ▶ (a) Examination of the vehicle's interior and (b) floorboard within the vehicle. Can the point of origin of this vehicle fire be determined?

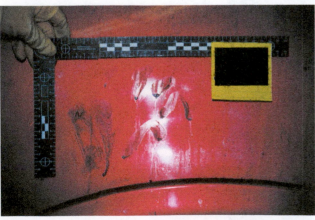

(a)

(b)

FIGURE 17.12 ▶ (a) Stains discovered on the exterior of the vehicle and (b) a drop of blood found on the curb at the crime scene. Of what use is this evidence to the investigation of the fire scene as a possible double homicide?

Many studies have attempted to uncover the "criminal mind" of an arsonist. These efforts have focused on creating a typology of psychological motives that explain why a particular arson fire was set by a particular individual. Many "types" of arsonists have been uncovered by various experts and law enforcement personnel, including the FBI and ATF. Following are some of the most common motives identified for setting an arson fire:

Revenge: Revenge is the most common motivating factor among adults who set arson fires. Vengeful ex-employees, estranged lovers, feuding family members, disgruntled friends or neighbors, and other individuals harboring resentment toward past associates may be motivated to start fires. The target for revenge arsonists nearly always is the property of someone who has caused, or is perceived to have caused them stress in their life. These acts are usually premeditated, with little or no effort to conceal the use of accelerants or other indicators of arson. About half of all arson fires are set for purposes of revenge against a person, organization, institution, group, or society in general.

Vandalism: Vandalism is the main motive for juveniles who commit arson. These fires are typically set on school grounds, involving recreation fields with dry vegetation, school lockers, and trash cans or garbage dumpsters. They also may involve abandoned buildings and vehicles. Relief of boredom appears to be a central underlying motivation for this type of juvenile fire setter. Fires motivated by vandalism are usually started with simple ignition devices such as matches and lighters; rarely are sophisticated methods, such as the use of accelerants or time delay devices, found at these burn sites.

Excitement: Persons who achieve excitement through arson are thrill seekers who set fires to fulfill a psychological pleasure or need. These types of arsonists are also referred as *pyromaniacs*. Psychologically speaking, they suffer from behavioral conditions relating to impulse control in which fire setting is a deviant means of relieving stress, satisfying curiosity, or acting out aggression. Excitement arson is usually committed by children and adolescents rather than adults. Because most of these offenders are still living with and financially dependent upon their parents or other family members, their targets tend to be close to home. Investigators usually can identify persons who set fires for excitement because they often return to the scene of the crime. This is because many of these arsonists have an uncontrollable obsession to witness the destruction they have caused.

For Profit: Arson for profit can be committed for either direct or indirect monetary gain. Direct gains include payoffs to alleged victims of arson fire committed in insurance fraud for property and real estate that has little or no value to its owner(s) or has been artificially inflated in value by its owner(s) to gain a higher monetary settlement. Likely suspects in this category include those who are "upside-down" (i.e., owe more money than the property's value) on homes, vehicles, or personal property that has been financed and/or insured. Arson that provides indirect profit benefits includes fires started to fraudulently obtain insurance money for remodeling old or outdated structures, to liquidate retail inventory that cannot be sold, or to remove a business competitor. Most arsonists motivated by profit are the owners of the property destroyed by fire. More rarely, a professional working as either an independent or an organized crime associate is contracted by a property owner to perform arson for profit. Personal financial indicators of arson for profit include the following:

- Businesses exhibiting decreasing revenue, increasing competition, high rental agreements, business losses, large depreciations listed on income taxes, excessive produce spoilage or loss, late vendor payments, closed bank accounts, bank overdrafts, bounced checks, bankruptcy, prior insurance claims, large numbers of lines of credit
- Persons exhibiting unsold homes listed for sale for long periods, costly monthly mortgage payments, recent loss of income, recent divorce, bounced checks, missed or late credit card payments, unpaid utilities, recent vehicle repossessions

Extremist: Extremist arsonists set fires primarily to make statements about social, political, or religious issues or causes. These fires commonly are set by multiple offenders. Housing developments and "gas-guzzling" vehicles have been burned by environmental extremists, as have abortion clinics by religious extremists. These arsonists often claim responsibility for their actions. Messages left at the fire scene and communications with police and the media often reveal the purpose and/or identity of the particular group claiming responsibility for the destruction of property. Extremist arson is also a popular tool that hate groups use to promote fear and intimidation among ethnic minorities and homosexuals. Churches, community gathering centers, and private residences are among the locations targeted by these arsonists.

Compulsive: Compulsive fire setting can be categorized as mass, spree, or serial arson. Each of these classifications involves the setting of three or more fires. Mass arsons, however, are fires set at the same location during a limited time period; spree arsons are fires set in separate locations without an emotional cooling-off period; and serial arsons are fires set in separate locations each time after the offender has had an emotional cooling-off period. Any amount of time, ranging from hours to years, could pass between these cooling-off periods. Serial arsonists are perhaps the most dangerous types of fire setters because they select their targets at random and do not have a readily identifiable motive. Most enjoy personally seeing their fires and often can be identified by examining crowds at multiple fire scenes for a "common face."

Crime Concealment: Some arson is committed as a secondary act to conceal another crime that has already been committed. The main motivation in these fires is to destroy evidence relating to the primary crime. Also, fire setting may be the offender's elaborate effort to stage a crime scene to make prior destruction of property or loss of life appear to be the result of an accidental blaze rather than an intentional criminal act. For example, a dead body in a burned home or car initially may appear to have resulted from a fire caused by a misplaced cigarette or an electrical malfunction. Forensic testing, however, may later reveal that the victim's bodily tissues and fluids showed no signs of smoke inhalation or carbon monoxide poisoning, thus suggesting that the victim's breathing had ceased before the fire was set and the death was perhaps a murder followed by arson.[20]

CASE CLOSE-UP 17.1

THE PILLOW PYRO
(Glendale, CA)

During the 1980s and 1990s a rash of fires occurred up and down the state of California, destroying numerous commercial establishments and causing millions of dollars in damages. Investigators suspected that these fires were caused by a serial arsonist because their geographic locations revealed a systematic pattern and they all shared a common *modus operandi*—an ignition device consisting of matches wrapped around a cigarette with a rubber band and covered with writing paper. Unlike most arson fires, liquid accelerants were not discovered at the fire scenes; rather, the arsonist ignited foam materials containing flammable petroleum products that were used as padding in pillows and furniture cushions (thus inspiring the criminal moniker "Pillow Pyro"). At one of the points of origin, a partially burned piece of paper from the ignition device revealed a fingerprint when developed with Ninhydrin. The print was run through a series of fingerprint databases, which included police and firefighters, and was identified as belonging to Captain John Orr, a veteran arson inspector for the Glendale, CA, Fire Department. Based on this initial evidence finding, investigators later pieced together the trail of known arson fires from one California city to the next. This trail aligned almost perfectly with Orr's travel patterns when he had attended various firefighting conventions and seminars throughout the state. Orr was convicted of arson in 1998, as well as the murder of four persons who died in one of his intentionally set fires. He is currently serving a life sentence in prison. He is believed to be responsible for almost 2,000 intentionally set building fires and wildfires.

RECONSTRUCTING AN ARSON CRIME SCENE

Case Example 17B (see Figures 17.13 to 17.22) presents the investigation of a fire started in a motel room, which may have killed a person discovered with fourth-degree burns in the room after the fire was extinguished. This investigation must use all available physical evidence in reconstructing this potential arson scene (1) to determine if the fire was indeed started accidentally by the room's occupant or intentionally by an arsonist and (2) if the intentionally, whether the burn victim was dead or alive before the fire erupted.

BOMB AND EXPLOSIONS INVESTIGATION

The investigation of criminal activities relating to bombs and explosives is extremely specialized and, to say the least, dangerous. Under normal circumstances, bomb disposal technicians, forensic engineers, military ordnance experts, and other persons specially trained in the handling and examination of explosive evidence are called upon to handle these cases. A general familiarity with the crime scene investigative techniques used in these situations, however, is essential given today's rising threat of political terror both in the United States and abroad. It is a sad yet undeniable fact that explosive devices are the weapon of choice among terrorists, foreign and domestic, and will perhaps be used more frequently for criminal purposes in the not-too-distant future.

According to the U.S. Bomb Data Center, a branch of the ATF that gathers data on bombing incidents, approximately 3,500 explosive incidents occur each year in the United States. On average, approximately 200 injuries and 20 deaths are caused yearly by a crime-related explosion. These averages, however, do not take into account isolated mass bombing and explosive incidents. For example, in 1993, the World Trade Center bombing resulted in 1,040 injuries and took the lives of 6 persons. Even more devastating was the Oklahoma City bombing, which injured 1,259 persons and killed 168 others. Unfortunately, like arsonists, it is very difficult to bring bombers to justice. Suspects are identified and prosecuted in only 1 out

CASE EXAMPLE 17B

Motel Fire Crime Scene

FIGURE 17.13 ▶ Residents in the motel pictured here awoke in the early morning to the smell of smoke and the sound of fire alarms, which alerted them to evacuate their rooms to escape an out-of-control blaze in an adjoining room. After the fire had burned for a few minutes, a loud explosion erupted from the burning room. In determining whether or not this fire was intentionally set by an arsonist, what should investigators respond to this scene do or not do?

FIGURE 17.14 ▶

View from the second-story balcony approaching the burnt-out doorway and window of the room where the fire was located. Do the burn patterns on the building's exterior appear to be the result of a natural (or perhaps accidental) or an incendiary fire?

FIGURE 17.15 ▶ The remains of a mattress extending from the room's main window, with the air conditioning unit below. Does the condition of the metal in this mattress indicate a likely arson fire?

FIGURE 17.16 ▶ Investigator's view of the room from the inside out.

FIGURE 17.17 ▶ Examination of the inside wall closest to the window.

(a)

FIGURE 17.18A ▶ The sink area at the rear of the room.

(b)

FIGURE 17.18B ▶ (b) Floor area directly below the sink. After examining each of the interview views shown in Figures 17.16, 17.17, 17.18(A & B), is it possible to determine the fire's likely point of origin?

(a)

FIGURE 17.19 ▶ After the blaze was extinguished, a burnt body was discovered in the room by firefighters. What investigative conclusions can be drawn from condition and posture of the body?

(b)

(a)

(b)

FIGURE 17.20 ▶ (a) Close-up of the fire victim's head and neck area. (b) Object falling from the body while being transported from the room by coroner staff. Was this fire set intentionally to cover up evidence of a ligature strangulation of the victim?

FIGURE 17.21 ▶ Posterior view of the burn victim's body.

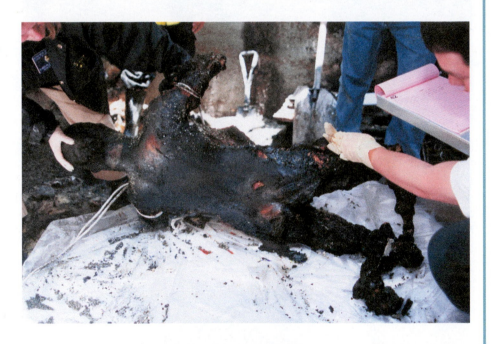

FIGURE 17.22 ▶ Close-up posterior view of the victim's head and upper back region. Do the burn marks on the victim's body suggest the victim's position during exposure to the fire? Do the victim's fourth-degree burns appear to have been caused by exposure to an accelerant?

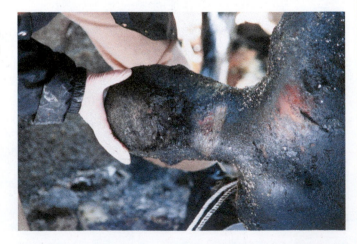

of every 5 criminal bombing incidents. Of course, no greater destruction of life and property caused by explosive means has occurred than the collapse of the 110-story World Trade Center buildings on September 11, 2001. That horrific act of terror caused 6,291 injuries and 2,747 deaths.[21]

MECHANICAL EXPLOSIVES

Mechanical explosions are usually caused when a vessel or container bursts as the result of internal pressure from expanding gases. A common form of these explosions is referred to as a **BLEVE (Boiling Liquid Expanding Vapor Explosion)** and can happen to an object as small as a spray can or as large as an industrial petroleum holding tank. In residential settings, BLEVEs typically occur in water heaters and furnace boilers. Regardless of the type of container involved in these explosions, the point of origin is fairly easy to detect. Large holes or broken seams are readily apparent in the exploded object. The most destructive and dangerous form of BLEVE, however, occurs when the bursting container holds flammable liquids and gases. Even the explosion of a container as small as a butane lighter can result in structure fires or wildfires. Massive blasts and huge, rapidly spreading fires are the product of BLEVEs affecting large fuel holding tanks like those used to store gasoline at service stations and oil refineries. Another type of mechanical explosion is produced by a pipe bomb, the most common explosive device found at crime scenes (see Figure 17.23). The destruction caused by this device results simply from the pressure of expanding gases (usually produced by igniting gunpowder) trapped within the pipe's interior.

Fires may erupt during and after a mechanical explosion. These blazes may burn intensely long after the initial blast because they continue to be fed by open lines supplying flammable gas or fuel to the broken holding tank. Even if no fire is present, and there is no petroleum product or odor, any open source of gas or fuel in or around a suspected BLEVE or other mechanical explosion must be identified and closed before the crime scene is searched.[22]

CHEMICAL EXPLOSIONS

Chemical explosions are caused by high-pressure gases produced by chemical reactions involving liquid or solid fuels. They usually involve an explosive mixture of air and a fuel derived from a petroleum product (e.g., gasoline, diesel, oil) or natural gas. Such blasts are commonplace in clandestine drug laboratories, especially meth labs (see Figure 17.24), where numerous highly

(a)

(a)

(b)

(b)

FIGURE 17.23 ▶ Variations of pipe bombs.

FIGURE 17.24 ▶ (a) Chemical explosion of a methamphetamine laboratory in a trailer. (b) Investigators in PPE suits examine and gather evidence at the explosion site.

combustible chemicals and gases are used to manufacture the drug. In rarer instances, chemical explosions occur when dusts from grains, plastics, metals, and other materials are mixed with air and ignited by a heat source. In all of these situations, one or more blasts result when chemical gases are produced at a rate faster than they can be vented from a particular area, causing a pressure build-up of gas that explodes upon contact with fire, friction, sparks, or other heat sources. In addition, all chemical explosions result from combustion or burning. The intensity of a particular explosion, however, depends on how rapidly the combustion takes place. **Detonation** is the most rapid form of combustion, and it produces the most dramatic explosive effects. For example, when dynamite is detonated, the chemical gases combust almost instantaneously. Detonations produce destruction accompanied by extreme heat, light, shock waves, and a loud "boom." Other types of chemical explosions triggered by **deflagration** (slower, burning combustion) do not produce such dramatic effects. An example of this is a Molotov cocktail, which explodes without sound or shock waves when its gasoline or flammable liquid contents are combined with air and ignited by a wick.[23]

EXPLOSIVES AND BOMBS

Explosives are substances that produce explosions through chemical reactions. They are referred to as **bombs or IEDs** (Improvised Explosive Devices) when used for illegal purposes. Although most explosives are composed of solid combustible chemical agents such as dynamite, others may be in liquid or gas form. Based on the type of blast pattern they create, and on the method by which they are ignited, explosives are classified as either **high explosives** or **low explosives**.

High Explosives

High explosives usually are detonated by a smaller primary explosive (e.g., blasting cap), causing heat and shock that, in turn, cause a larger secondary explosive (e.g., dynamite) to explode. This process does not require any confinement of gases to produce combustion. The blast pattern produced by high explosives is a characteristic crushing, shattering, and tearing of objects, including those made of hard metals. In addition, a crater is generally found in the ground or other surface where the bomb exploded. The high intensity of these explosions also produces what is known as a **blast pressure wave**. This not only projects large amounts of debris long distances from the blast site, but also produces a pressure vacuum that sucks a significant amount of this debris back to the bomb's point of origination. Loud noises, intense heat, light flashes, and shock waves are usually noted by nearby observers of high explosive bombings. The damage produced tends to be localized near the center of the explosion. Commonly, devices consisting of timers, wires, and batteries are used to carry out the detonation of high explosives.[24]

Low Explosives

Low explosives typically consist of bombs fashioned from petroleum products, smokeless gunpowder, black powder, or some

(a)

(b)

FIGURE 17.25 ▶ (a) The result of a car bombed with high explosives. (b) A car bombed with low explosives.

other chemical agents that are combustible through the process of deflagration (the rapid expansion of gas by burning). These explosives must also be confined within some particular area in order for an explosion to occur. This may be a large space such as a room or basement; or, as in the case of a pipe bomb, the inside of a small tube. Low explosives can do great damage, which tends to be widespread from the point of the initial blast. The damage pattern is created by a pushing motion of objects away from the point of explosion. Objects affected by the blast tend to appear burnt, scorched, or blistered by fire. Metal objects may be bent or melted by the extreme heat produced by low explosives. The point of origination of the blast itself will not be localized or show telltale signs such as a crater. Rather, areas surrounding the blast point that contain explosive gases will be noticeably damaged—as when entire walls in a room are pushed down and away from the blast rather than being shattered to bits.[25] Figure 17.25 illustrates the differences between high and low explosives used in a car bombing.

PREBLAST INVESTIGATIONS

Most preblast investigations involve bomb threats. Most threats are made by a letter or telephone call, although e-mail threats are gaining popularity. However unsophisticated the threat delivery process may be, all bomb threats should be taken seriously and responded to as if real. If available, specialized bomb threat units should be notified and activated to process the location of a suspected explosive device.

The initial stages of investigation should evaluate all information available from all available witnesses, and in particular the person(s) receiving the threat. If the threat is made by phone, answers to the following questions should be solicited from anyone who knows or is in contact with the caller:

- When is the bomb going to explode?
- Where is the bomb right now?
- What does the bomb look like?
- What kind of bomb is it?
- What will cause it to explode?
- Did you place the explosives?
- Why did you place the explosives?
- What is the caller's name and address?

After all available evidence regarding the threat is collected, an assessment of the threat's validity can be made. The following questions need to be answered in assessing the threat's validity:

- Does the caller have an accent?
- Are there any current international or national political, religious, or other activities going on that could be related to the threat?
- Does the caller appear to have knowledge about bombs and their construction?
- Does the caller seem nervous, angry, or confused?
- Does the caller seem to be merely creating a hoax to disrupt some type of normal activity at the suspected bomb location?

If the threat is deemed valid, the suspected location should be evacuated and searched immediately. Search thoroughly both indoors and outdoors. Indoor searches should be conducted room by room, preferably by officers familiar with each room's contents and design. Begin the search of each room by standing quietly and listening for any noises prior to entering the doorway. After entry, conduct the search on the lower, middle, and upper levels of the room. Never touch or move any suspicious object, backpack, package, or other item large enough to contain an explosive device. Canine units trained in detecting explosives, if available, should be employed to assist in the location of these objects. For the safety of the canine and its handler, however, sniffing for explosives should be used only for identifying the location of suspect bombs—not for determining whether or not a particular object or substance is an explosive! Any item suspected of being or containing explosives should be removed by a **Bomb Disposal Unit**. These specially trained and equipped teams can use a **containment vessel** (bomb truck, or other apparatus used to contain a bomb), portable x-ray machines, and robotic extraction devices to safely identify, remove, transport, and, if necessary, detonate explosive devices.[26]

POSTBLAST INVESTIGATIONS

Preliminary Assessment of the Explosion Scene

Searches of suspected explosion crime scenes (for example, see Figure 17.26) begin and proceed in a manner very similar to that utilized for arson investigation. First, a preliminary assessment is made of the entire area affected by the blast. Review all available information provided by first responders, witnesses, and technical experts. Before focusing on any other aspect of investigation, determine all safety or health hazards in and around the scene before entering the blast area. Some common hazards include the following:

- Blood sprayed by the explosion possibly containing bloodborne pathogens
- Dangerous metal and glass debris
- Ongoing fires or locations for potential fires
- Poor structural integrity of structures
- Damaged utilities: gas, water, electrical
- Hazardous materials (HAZMAT) in air, water, soil, or within structures or vehicles
- Potential for secondary explosions, either natural or mine-style traps
- Dangerous persons such as snipers or suicide bombers

If available, and time permits, use thermal imaging video to search the scene for **heat signatures** of metal objects either (1) used to construct the bomb or (2) affected by the blast. When in doubt regarding safety at the scene, do not enter the scene until it has been deemed safe by an expert with knowledge of the suspected hazard.

Enter and begin assessment of the scene at the outermost area of the explosion site. This area is the one containing debris that is located farthest away from the blast. Although debris from explosions often is projected in a circular fashion, wind and other factors may produce a rather sporadic and

FIGURE 17.26 ▶ The remains of a building bombed with high explosives. Examination of such a crime scene can be extremely time consuming and hazardous for investigators.

irregular spread pattern. These locations should be located with markers because they will be used later to create permanent barriers establishing the crime scene perimeter. Continue assessing by progressing inward toward the location in the crime scene containing the most damage. This area, known as the **epicenter**, is where the blast likely originated. It also likely contains the most physical evidence relating to what and/or who caused the explosion. Again, throughout the entire preliminary assessment process, be mindful of health and safety hazards as well as the preservation of evidence when selecting a path throughout the scene. Take notes, and log and photograph important items of evidence, including those that could be moved or destroyed by any postblast emergency activities.[27]

Establish the Perimeters

Due to the often large-scale scatter of debris produced by explosions, investigators need to modify the initial perimeters of the crime scene established by first responders. In most bombing investigations, both inner and outer perimeters must be created. The boundaries of the inner perimeters should cover an area 1.5 times the distance from the epicenter to the piece(s) of debris farthest away from this location. With indoor bombings, this may involve cordoning off several rooms connected to the room where the blast took place. In outdoor settings, sometimes too large for traditional tape lines, strategically placed temporary barriers of barricades, chalk lines, or other boundary markers may be employed. The outer boundaries are then marked at a distance from the inner boundaries that prevents persons uninvolved in the investigation from viewing or hearing activities at the crime scene. In marking outer boundaries, attempt to use existing structural and landscape features such as walls, trees, and fences.[28]

Determine the Search Method

The amount of physical evidence contained within an explosion crime scene often can be overwhelming. Especially in large, powerful blasts, seemingly countless articles of debris, referred to as **missiles**, project from the blast and spread over great distances. In these cases, the best strategy is to engage in a focused search for specific pieces of physical evidence that provide information regarding the following:

- Whether the blast was an intentional bombing or an accidental explosion
- What type of explosion caused the blast
- Which type of explosive was used

Any of the methods discussed previously (i.e., line, grid, etc.) are amenable to explosion searches. The best search method is the one appropriate for the particular geographic or structural characteristics of the site and also best suited to the number of personnel available to conduct the search. If persons

at the scene are either killed or injured by the blast, x-rays should be used to check for missiles lodged in the body. Such debris may contain residue or other physical evidence suggesting the type of materials used to create a particular bombing device.[29]

Examine the Epicenter

Often, evidence at the explosion's epicenter helps determine whether the blast was accidental or intentional. For example, if the epicenter contains a boiler furnace with a hole torn along a seam on its side, then the blast probably originated from an accidental mechanical explosion. Similarly, a broken natural gas line or damaged connection to a propane tank may indicate that these or similar malfunctioning fuel sources caused an unintentional chemical explosion. Any evidence in the epicenter of a timing apparatus or other ignition device, however, such as clock pieces, wires, batteries, or foreign metals, almost always indicates an intentional chemical explosion. Absent any legitimate and legal purpose for the presence of a high explosive, an epicenter containing evidence of solid explosives and/or detonators is a certain indicator of an intentional bombing.[30]

Assess the Type of Explosion

Further analysis of the epicenter and its immediate surroundings also provides the most valuable clues regarding the type of explosion that occurred. BLEVEs and other types of mechanical explosions typically thrust shrapnel in all directions from the exploding container. If the container holds a flammable material, a fireball may hurtle from the epicenter, causing fire damage to outlying areas. The direction of the fire path normally corresponds to the location in the container where the initial burst occurred. Because mechanical explosions are caused by malfunctions of containers or vessels at specific locations they usually are identifiable without an extensive investigation.

Once the prospect of a mechanical explosion is ruled out, a *de facto* assumption can be made that the explosion is of a chemical variety. As previously mentioned, chemical explosions are caused either by the combination of air, fuel, and heat that combusts in an enclosed area or by detonation of a solid chemical. These explosions produce numerous indicators in and around the epicenter and often are readily identified by the distinct odors they produce. The primary investigative task with a suspected chemical explosion is to determine the specific type of explosive causing the blast.[31]

Determine the Type of Explosive

Although sophisticated laboratory analyses are needed to determine the exact type of chemical explosive, the blast area can be physically examined to determine the presence of high or low explosives. The epicenter of a blast caused by low

FIGURE 17.27 ▶ The epicenter of a low explosive after detonation. Note the lack of a crater and the dispersion of burnt material.

explosives typically displays one or more of the following characteristics:

- The absence of a crater in the surface where the explosion occurred combined with significant burning in the explosion's epicenter (see Figure 17.27)
- The presence of some sort of fuel
- Noticeable odors of gas in soil, air, or debris
- No evidence of a detonation device
- Widespread, uniform fire damage in a specific direction
- Destruction caused by melting or bending
- Pushing or heaving of large objects and other debris away from the epicenter
- Scorching or blistering of burnt objects
- Evidence of a confined area, such as a room, fully affected by the blast

High-explosive blast sites exhibit many characteristics quite different from those just given for low-explosive blast sites:

- A defined crater where the explosion occurred (see Figure 17.28)
- Localized damage, with or without fire
- Objects and debris that appear cut, shredded, or crushed
- The presence of bomb construction components, including those used for detonation
- Explosive residue on debris
- Intact explosive material
- No source of fuel
- Nonuniform patterns of damage or debris scatter
- Fire damage localized around the epicenter

FIGURE 17.28 ▶ The epicenter of a high-explosive bomb after detonation. Note the crater and lack of surface burning.

In addition to these distinguishing characteristics, witness accounts of the blast can provide additional clues regarding the type of explosive used. When high explosives are used, witnesses often notice a bright flash preceding any explosion sounds and shock waves in water, air, or soil. Witnesses of low-explosive blasts may note the odor of gas in the air and notice smoke from fire at the same time they hear the explosion.[32] The discovery of a detonation device, such as that shown in Figure 17.29, is also a strong indicator of high explosive use.

FIGURE 17.29 ▶ A crude detonation device used for a high-explosive bomb.

Collect the Evidence

Small explosions may produce small amounts of debris and other evidence that may be collected relatively easily and quickly. Larger blasts, however, may produce so much debris that it would be impossible to mark, document, and collect every piece of potential evidence at the bomb crime scene. In these situations, focused evidence collection methods must be employed to save time and effort. For example, evidence suspected of containing explosive residue may be subject to a presumptive or field test before it is submitted to the laboratory for more elaborate testing. This can be done using mobile trace explosives detectors or a liquid color test such as **EXSPRAY** or DropEX.

The grid search method is recommended for the actual evidence search and collection process at larger crime scenes. Each grid can be marked with its own individual number or letter, allowing several items of evidence to be collected at the same time and in the same location. Smaller movable evidence should be collected at the same time within each grid and packaged in an appropriate container bearing the proper identifying information (grid number or letter, investigator's name, type of evidence, etc.). Photographs need not be taken of all evidence, but rather should be restricted to the most important items or those that are transient and may be destroyed. Larger immovable objects should be photographed in place and swabbed for explosive residue analysis, if necessary. In addition to explosive evidence, investigators need to be aware of any other physical evidence, trace or otherwise, that is relevant to the case at hand—including hair, fibers, tool marks, and so on.

If the area affected by fire has been watered down by fire crews, samples of water may be collected and analyzed for explosive residue. Many explosives do not break down in water and can be detected through laboratory analyses. In addition, explosive residue is detectable in clothing and hair and remains present for days, weeks, months, or even years. Comparison samples—or standards of objects not believed to be related to the explosion, yet found in and around the blast area—should be taken as well. These will help to differentiate materials such as metal, wire, or switches perhaps used in bomb construction from those at the scene before the explosion occurred.

Often a sifting process is useful for uncovering small pieces of debris evidence in piles of rubble composed of soil, glass, wood, or other particulate matter. Sieves can be used to separate larger from small evidence items in a relatively short time. Magnets also can be used to detect metal objects used in the construction of an explosive device. Specialized vacuums can locate trace explosive evidence and other debris embedded within carpet, clothing, furniture, and other areas following the blast.

Cross-contamination is always a serious threat posed to explosive evidence during the collection process. This is because explosive residue can be transferred with ease from one object to another. Persons conducting evidence searches must make sure that their clothing is free of all preexisting explosive residues before entering the crime scene. Clean clothing prepared especially for the explosive evidence search should be worn; for example, Tyvek coveralls with hood, booties, and gloves. Tools and other utensils used should be clean and sterile, and recleaned or discarded after touching evidence suspected of containing explosive residue. Immediately after use, clothing worn at the crime scene should be packaged in plastic bags or other airtight sealed containers and professionally laundered or discarded because they may contain pathogens or other biohazards.

Care should be taken to follow the appropriate directions for packaging and transporting collected explosive evidence to crime laboratories for analysis. Items suspected of containing explosive residue should be packaged in sealable metal cans, glass containers, or special forensic-grade nylon bags. (Sharp objects should be covered with sterile padding before being placed in nylon bags.) These containers will prevent possible cross-contamination of explosive evidence. Other evidence not suspected of containing explosive residue can be packaged in polyethylene plastic zip-top bags. Biohazard evidence should be packaged in specialized marked containers. As a rule, explosive material that is intact or perhaps "live" requires examination by bomb technicians to determine the safest method of packaging and transportation.[33]

HOT TIPS AND LEADS 17.2

Types of Bombs and Explosives

TRUCK BOMB: Large moving trucks are rented or stolen and used to house bomb materials in their cargo area. Typically, a truck bomb is parked in an underground parking area beneath a building targeted for destruction. This was the M.O. used in both the 1993 World Trade Center and the 1995 Oklahoma City bombings. In the latter case,

the bomb was constructed from ammonium nitrate fertilizer mixed with diesel fuel and packed in large plastic barrels located in the back rear compartment area. In total, the explosive mixture weighed more than 2½ tons. Fuses were used to ignite a primary explosive to cause a "shock" detonation of the secondary bomb mixture.

(continued)

SUICIDE BOMB: Suicide bombs are the most common form of terrorist explosive device. They are typically worn beneath the clothing of the suicide bomber, who positions himself or herself in the middle of a crowded area before detonating the bomb. Clothing is the key camouflaging agent in this type of bombing, with the explosives usually being sewn into a vest or belt worn by the bomber. Common explosive agents used in these attacks are TNT or C-4 plastic explosive obtained from military explosive devices. Common household chemicals, such as agents containing acetone peroxide, also can be used to create explosive compounds. The suicide bomb usually is detonated by a handheld switch connected to a battery. The electric current activates the filament of a light bulb, which ignites a small blasting cap, causing the larger bomb to explode.

PARCEL BOMB: Parcel bombs are disguised as packages, and they can be either sent through the mail or hand delivered by the bomber. Concealing explosive material within a computer print ink toner cartridge is a popular method of disguising a parcel bomb sent through the mail. Common explosives used to make these devices include PETN (a military explosive that will not ignite when handled, but can ignite when shot with a bullet) or household chemicals. The latter method often is selected because bomb dogs trained to detect explosives generally are not able to detect bombs made from household chemical agents. The package can be detonated by a tripping device that explodes the bomb when opened by its intended receiver, or a controlled detonation can be performed by a modified cell phone detonator called by the bomber. An alarm clock can also be used to create a "timed explosive" version of the parcel bomb.

PIPE BOMB: Pipe bombs are the most common explosive device made by amateurs. They can be fashioned from a variety of items that are not pipes, but are usually made from a section of pipe capped at both ends by screw-on caps (thus, the name *pipe bomb*). The inner area of the pipe is filled with black powder or other types of gunpowder taken from ammunition such as shotgun shells. The bomb typically is detonated by a burning wick, which can be fashioned out of many slow-burning combustibles such as match heads or a linked series of wicks taken from fireworks. The bomb explodes, projecting metal shrapnel at various angles over a distance that can be small or large depending on the size of the bomb.

VEHICLE BOMBINGS

Vehicles, especially cars, may be the object of an accidental or intentional explosion. Accidental explosions are usually of a chemical type, resulting from the combustion of gases or vapors created by a malfunction or leakage in the vehicle's fuel system. The intentional bombing of aircraft and marine vessels is extremely rare and normally requires the consultation of engineers and specialized technicians to be properly investigated. The suspected bombing of cars, on the other hand, is more commonly encountered by investigators. The intended target of these attacks, in most instances, is the owner of the vehicle. This is reflected in the typical placement of the bomb, usually under the driver's seat either outside or inside the vehicle. The initial location of the bomb can be determined by examining the direction of torn metal fragments inside the crater created by the explosion, known as **petaling**. Fragments pointing inward toward the driver's area indicate that the bomb was placed outside the vehicle beneath its floorboard. Bombs placed in the car's interior under the driver's seat create a crater with petaling pointing out toward the street's surface, which also may contain a crater and explosive residue.

Three possible scenarios explain the reasons underlying any vehicle bombing. First, as previously discussed, the bomb may have been placed in the vehicle with the specific intent of killing its owner or occupant. In these cases, the explosive device is placed to do the most harm to the person who is the intended target. Another possibility is that the vehicle was being used to transport the explosive material to some other location for some purpose other than killing the driver, and so the blast was unintentional. Damage to the vehicle in the trunk area or areas other than the driver's compartment often indicates this scenario. Last, and most deadly, is the situation in which the car is used to deliver the explosion to an intended target—otherwise known as a **car bomb**. There is little doubt regarding the intention of this type of bombing when, and if, the act is completed. An intended car bomb that explodes prematurely, however, will likely be evidenced by a massive explosion while the vehicle is in motion. Any type of vehicle can be used in a car bombing, but large sedans, cargo vans, and delivery trucks with a high storage capacity are the models of choice.[34]

RECONSTRUCTING AN EXPLOSION CRIME SCENE

Case Example 17C illustrates a crime scene involving the investigation of several pipe bomb explosions which occurred inside of a structure as well as within a vehicle. The weapon of choice in both of these seemingly related explosion scenes is a pipe bomb. The investigation of these scenes requires the identification and documentation of any postblast explosives evidence, as shown in Figures 17.30 through 17.38.

Pipe Bomb Crime Scene

FIGURE 17.30 ▶ Investigators were called to the location shown here to investigate fire damage to the interior of the building. The damage occurred the evening after construction workers renovating the home noticed burnt material on the floor when they arrived to work in the morning. While canvassing the area nearby the scene, investigators were told by one resident that he heard several loud explosions during the night.

FIGURE 17.31 ▶ Floor area inside the building with concentration of fire debris. Is this the possible epicenter of an explosion?

FIGURE 17.32 ▶ Burnt pieces of wood surrounding the fire debris.

(a)

(b)

FIGURE 17.33 ▶ (a) Burnt and broken wood fragments. (b) Close-up view of wood with charred edges. Has an explosive devise been used at this location?

FIGURE 17.34 ▶ Torn and melted plastic bucket. What does this burnt post-blast evidence suggest regarding type of explosives used here?

FIGURE 17.35 ▶ Unidentified objects discovered within the same room as the fire damage. Are these objects evidence of IED used at the scene?

FIGURE 17.37 ▶ The vehicle's interior, showing the ignition and steering column.

FIGURE 17.36 ▶ After checking on other arson-type incidents occurring near the residential fire scene, investigators discovered that a fire-damaged vehicle incident near the burnt residence had been reported two weeks earlier. They traveled to the insurance yard where the vehicle was being stored and examined it.

FIGURE 17.38 ▶ The vehicle's passenger compartment showing displaced accessories and other items. Does this vehicle appear to damaged by an IED similar to that discovered in the residential bombing investigation?

Summary

1. The nature and extent of arson crimes.

In a general sense, arson can be defined as "any willing or malicious burning or attempt to burn, with or without intent to defraud, a dwelling house, public building, motor vehicle or aircraft, personal property of another." Under most laws, the act of arson is considered complete merely by the presence of some sort of burning, regardless of how serious or slight the fire damage may be. Many laws have extended the meaning of damage by burning to include evidence of surface charring, the presence of soot deposits, or destruction caused by explosive devices. Arson is usually categorized in terms of degrees that reflect the seriousness of a particular fire-setting activity.

2. The investigation of arson fires.

Whether the fire is located outdoors or indoors, the investigation of a burn site should begin at the outermost locations of the fire-involved area and proceed inward. The primary goal of this "outward-in" search method is to identify the location(s) where the fire originated, known as the fire's point of origin. The point of origin is generally the location in a fire scene with the most damage as evidenced by the most extreme charring of burnt wood or other combustible materials. The discovery of accelerants and items used to ignite accelerants, such as matches, lighters, cigarettes, and timing devices, are often clear indicators that a particular fire is an arson.

3. **Types of explosions and explosives.**

Mechanical explosions usually occur when a vessel or container bursts as the result of internal pressure from expanding gases. A common form of these explosions, referred to as a *BLEVE (Boiling Liquid Expanding Vapor Explosion),* can happen with an object as small as a spray can or as large as an industrial petroleum holding tank. Chemical explosions occur as the result of high-pressure gasses produced by chemical reactions involving liquid or solid fuels. Explosives are substances that produce explosions through chemical reactions. They are referred to as a *bomb* or *IED (Improvised Explosive Device)* when used for illegal purposes. Although most explosives are composed of solid combustible chemical agents such as dynamite, others may be in liquid or gas form. Based on the type of blast pattern they create and on the method by which they are ignited, explosives are classified as either high explosives or low explosives.

4. **Investigative techniques used at bombing sites.**

Most preblast investigations involve bomb threats. Most threats are made by a letter or telephone call, although e-mail threats are gaining popularity. The initial stages of investigation should evaluate all information available from all available witnesses, and in particular the person(s) receiving the threat. Before focusing on any other aspect of investigation, determine all safety or health hazards in and around the scene before entering the blast area. Enter and begin assessment of the scene at the outermost area of the explosion site. Determine the epicenter of the explosion by finding where the most damage has been done, often a tell-tale crater blown in the ground where the bomb was detonated. Gather materials that may have been used to construct and detonate the bomb.

Key Terms

fire triangle	alligatoring	blast pressure wave
incipient stage	ignition device	Bomb Disposal Unit
smoldering stage	backdraft	containment vessel
flaming stage	torches	heat signatures
point of origin	pugilist posture	epicenter
overhaul	mechanical explosions	missiles
accelerants	BLEVE (Boiling Liquid Expanding	"V" burn pattern
inverted "V" pattern	Vapor Explosion)	petaling
pour patterns	chemical explosions	car bomb
puddling	detonation	flashover
rundown burns	deflagration	bomb/IED
spalling	explosives	EXSPRAY
streamers	high explosives	
trailers	low explosives	

Review Questions

1. What is the general legal definition of arson, and how does this definition differ across various jurisdictions?

2. What is the fire triangle and of what significance is it to understanding how an arson fire is set?

3. Why is the point of origin significant to arson investigators?

4. Why is overhaul of a fire scene problematic to arson investigations?

5. What are accelerants? Provide some examples.

6. What are some of the burn patterns associated with the use of an accelerant?

7. What is meant by the terms *pour patterns* and *puddling*?

8. Describe some of the characteristics of wood and cement that are noticed in cases of arson.

9. What are some of the situational indicators of arson?

10. What is flashover? Why is it important to recognize in arson investigations?

11. How can one tell if a person was alive or dead before being exposed to a deadly fire?

12. What are the differences between mechanical and chemical explosions?

13. How can one tell if a bomb was constructed from high or low explosives?

14. What steps should be taken when conducting a preblast investigation?

15. Describe the steps carried out when performing a postblast investigation.

Internet Resources

International Association of Arson Investigators (IAAI)	firearson.com
International Association of Bomb Technicians and Investigators	www.iabti.org
FEMA Learning Resource Center	www.lrc.fema.gov
National Institute of Standards and Training (NIST) Fire Research	fire.nist.gov
Bureau of Alcohol, Tobacco, Firearms and Explosives	www.atf.gov
InterFire Online	www.interfire.org

Applied Investigative Exercise

Select Case Examples 17A, 17B, or 17C and construct a plan for the investigation of this arson or explosion scene. Describe how you would approach the site; discover the point of origin/epicenter, and what evidence present at the scene you would use to determine whether the fire/explosion was accidental or intentional. Describe any other factors present or not present at the scene that should be considered when developing your case and supporting your conclusions.

Notes

[1] U.S. Department of Justice, *Fire and Arson Evidence: A Guide for Public Service Personnel* (Washington, DC: Office of Justice Programs, 2000), 1–2.

[2] Federal Bureau of Investigation, *Crime in the United States* posted at www2.fbi.gov/ucr/cius2009/offenses/property_crime/index.html.

[3] This discussion is based on laws from various states concerning arson and intentional fire-setting activities, and especially Sections 451 and 452 California PC, Article 150 Section 150 of New York Law, and Florida Statute Title XLVI Crimes Section 806.01.

[4] National Fire Protection Association. *NFPA 921: Guide for Fire and Explosion Investigations* (Quincy, Massachusetts: National Fire Protection Association, 2011), 34–42; James G. Quintiere, *Principles of Fire Behavior* (Albany, New York: Delmar Publishers, 1997).

[5] 436 U.S. 499.

[6] 464 U.S. 287.

[7] InterFire Online, posted at www.interfire.org.

[8] Ibid.

[9] Ibid.

[10] Ibid.

[11] Ibid.

[12] National Fire Protection Association. *NFPA 921: Guide for Fire and Explosion Investigations*, 85–101.

[13] Ibid.

[14] Ibid.

[15] Ibid., 134–155.

[16] Ibid.

[17] Ibid.

[18] InterFire Online, posted at www.interfire.org.

[19] Ibid.

[20] Ibid.

[21] National Fire Protection Association. *NFPA 921: Guide for Fire and Explosion Investigations*, 112.

[22] Ibid., 124–130.

[23] Ibid.

[24] Ibid.

[25] Ibid., 165–171.

[26] Ibid.

[27] National Institute of Justice, *A Guide for Investigating Bomb and Explosion Scenes*, posted at www.ojp.usdoj.gov/nij/topics/law-enforcement/investigations/crime-scene/guides/explosion-bombing/evaluate.htm.

[28] Ibid.

[29] Ibid.

[30] Ibid.

[31] John D. DeHaan, *Kirk's Fire Investigation*, 4th ed. (Indianapolis, IN: Brady Publishing/Prentice Hall, 1997).

[32] Ibid.

[33] National Institute of Justice, *A Guide for Investigating Bomb and Explosion Scenes*, posted at www.ojp.usdoj.gov/nij/topics/law-enforcement/investigations/crime-scene/guides/explosion-bombing/evaluate.htm.

[34] Ibid.

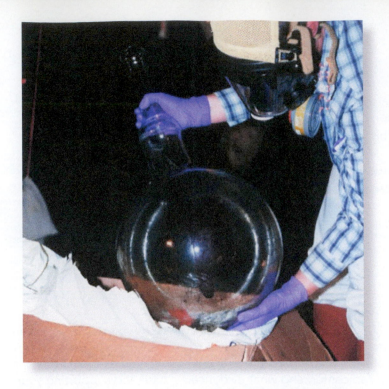

CHAPTER EIGHTEEN

DRUG CRIME SCENES

Learning Objectives

After completing this chapter, you should be able to:

1. Know and identify types of illegal and dangerous drugs.
2. Summarize the structure of drug laws.
3. Be familiar with common drug production and manufacturing locations.
4. Describe how drug investigations are conducted.

Chapter Outline

Drug Classifications
- Narcotics
- Stimulants
- Depressants
- Hallucinogens
- Inhalants

The Controlled Substances Act

Schedule I Drugs

Schedule II Drugs

Schedule III Drugs

Schedule IV Drugs

Schedule V Drugs

Nonscheduled Inhalants

Drug Production and Manufacturing Locations
- Grow Houses
- Grow Fields
- Rock Houses
- Clandestine Laboratories

Specialized Drug Crime Investigation Methods
- Undercover Drug Operations
- Buy Operations
- Drug Raids

Collection and Storage of Drug Evidence

INTRODUCTION

THE OPENING CRIME SCENE PHOTO for this chapter shows a bust of a clandestine laboratory or *clan lab* used to produce methamphetamine. This case, and any other type of drug raid situation, poses numerous potential hazards and risks to investigators. For example, in the present case, featured later in this chapter, the investigators must make detailed plans for how to handle multiple suspects, possible gunfire, innocent by-standers or perhaps children of the offenders, and drugs and other hazardous materials at the crime scene. In addition, the timing of a drug raid is essential. If the raid portrayed here were to be conducted too early, investigators would be forced to seize batches of chemicals not yet been transformed into completely manufactured illicit drugs—known as *drug precursors*. Possession of these base chemical agents generally carries a penalty lesser than that for possessing the compounds already mixed to manufacture an illegal drug. On the other hand, if investigators were to conduct the raid too late, this crime scene would perhaps be discovered abandoned by investigators—and without any signs of drugs or drug manufacturing materials. Thus, as will be discovered after examining this drug crime scene and other similar scenes presented in the sections that follow, drug investigations require a thorough understanding of illicit substances, their effects on users, and the illegal means by which they are sold and distributed.

DRUG CLASSIFICATIONS

Most drugs used for illegal purposes that are of concern to investigators fall within six broad categories: narcotics, stimulants, depressants, hallucinogens, and inhalants. Each category is based on common psychological and biological effects that the drug produces on its user. Investigators must learn not only how to recognize and identify these drugs, but also the specific role they play in the street drug culture and the various patterns of criminal behavior associated with their use.

Narcotics

The category of **narcotics** includes drugs used primarily as pain killers or for anesthetic purposes. Opium or its derivatives and synthetic substitutes generally fall within the legal definition of a narcotic drug. In its natural pure form, as shown in Figure 18.1, opium is extracted from opium poppies as either a milky substance from the seedpods of an immature plant or a fine brownish powder (referred to as *poppy straw*) from dried mature plants. Raw opium, sometimes used recreationally by Middle-Eastern and Asian people, appears as brown chunks or

(a)

(b)

FIGURE 18.1 ▶ (a) Raw opium poppy. (b) Opium as a street drug.

powder that is either smoked or eaten. Most narcotic drugs, however, consist of opium that has been processed into derivative forms (see, for example, Figure 18.1(b)). Some of these controlled substances, such as morphine and codeine, are legally produced for legitimate medical purposes but are illegally obtained and sold as street drugs. These include opium derivatives, either semisynthetic (oxycodone/oxycontin, a general medical-use pain killer) or fully synthetic (methadone, used medically to ease heroin withdrawal symptoms). Other forms of opium, namely heroin, are produced exclusively for illegal street sales.

Narcotics use results in distinct physiological and behavioral symptoms, many of which are clearly observable to investigators:

- Analgesia (inability to feel pain)
- Extremely relaxed, almost sleep-like state of awareness
- Feelings of euphoria
- Shallow breathing
- Constricted pupils
- Bloodshot eyes
- Confusion, poor judgment
- Slow, slurred speech patterns
- Possible needle marks in arms, legs, other extremities of the body
- Constipation
- Skin infections
- Seizures
- Jaundice or yellow skin due to reduced liver function

Narcotics can be taken orally in pill form, injected, snorted, smoked, or absorbed through the mucous membranes. The most notable side-effect of longer-term narcotics usage is its propensity to cause psychological and physiological addiction. **Habituation**, or the body's ability to develop a tolerance to a drug, is major problem encountered by narcotics users. For users in this condition, greater and more frequent dosages of the drug are needed to achieve the same high experienced during early stages of narcotics use and to fend off extremely painful withdrawal symptoms. Symptoms of narcotics withdrawal are generally more serious as the dosage of the drug increases. Pain, nausea, vomiting, and other symptoms opposite those experienced while under the influence of the drug are common during withdrawals. Heroin withdrawal, considered to have the most severe symptoms, has an onset 12–14 hours after the last dosage and peaks within 36–72 hours. Withdrawal symptoms may continue for one or two weeks, yet are not life threatening unless the addict has a serious underlying medical condition.[1]

Stimulants

Stimulants are commonly referred to as *uppers* because persons who use them experience temporary feelings of increased physical stamina and enhanced mental awareness. The legal

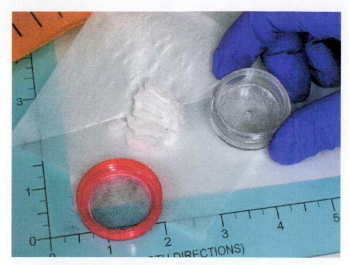

FIGURE 18.2 ▶ "Ice" methamphetamine crystals being assessed in the crime lab to determine the appropriate charges for the suspect arrested for possession of the illegal drug.

production and use of stimulants ranges from caffeine in soft drinks to stronger prescription drugs such as Ritalin or Dexedrine, used to counter the symptoms of attention deficit hyperactive disorder (ADHD), fatigue, depression, and other disorders. Although these prescription drugs are often sold on the street, their illicit use, distribution, and addictive qualities pale in comparison to those of illegally produced stimulants. Examples of such controlled substances include *cocaine,* which is naturally produced from coca leaves; *crack,* which is synthetically manufactured cocaine; and *methamphetamine,* which is a processed concoction of various chemical agents. In recent years, however, no illegal drug has gained more widespread popularity and use than methamphetamine. Produced in clandestine laboratories, this substance is not only easy and inexpensive to manufacture, it also has a potent stimulant effect that is linked to chronic addiction and serious criminal behavior. Figure 18.2 shows a form of methamphetamine referred to on the street as *ice* because of its clear crystal-like appearance.

Stimulants can be ingested orally, snorted, injected, smoked, or absorbed through mucous membranes. Users typically display the following symptoms:

- Dilated pupils, with very little color of the eye showing
- Suppressed appetite
- Dry mouth
- Excessive thirst
- Difficulty sitting still
- Hands, feet, and body shaking
- Thin, emaciated appearance
- Rapid speech accompanied by difficulty listening and answering questions
- Poor hygiene
- Running or bleeding nose

- Irritable, argumentative, nervous behavior
- Dizziness
- Paranoia

Abusers of stimulants may take excessive amounts of the drug over several days to keep experiencing the high or rush that the drug provides. During this time, the user will have no other desire except to continue taking the stimulant. Paranoid thoughts, hearing voices, and feeling sensations of cold bugs running over one's body are some of the common symptoms associated with **amphetamine psychosis**, which may also be triggered by prolonged stimulant use. After this binging period, however, the user typically experiences a "crash," extreme fatigue followed by deep sleep for an extended length of time—24 to 48 hours or more. Stimulants are addictive and do cause withdrawal symptoms lasting from several days for lighter, short-term users to several weeks for heavy users. Although stimulant withdrawal by itself is not life threatening, it is often characterized by overwhelming feelings of depression and anger. In some extreme instances, these feelings have been linked to suicidal and homicidal behavior.[2]

Depressants

Depressants, commonly known as *downers,* slow down mind and body functioning. The legitimate use of this drug type involves the treatment of disorders such as insomnia, anxiety, and stress. By far, the most widely used depressant is alcohol. Depressants sold for illicit use are overwhelmingly prescription drugs that have been diverted to street sales, with one primary exception being the clandestine laboratory production of GHB (gamma hydroxybutyric acid). Often referred to as the *date rape drug,* GHB has gained mainstream notoriety as a sedative enabling sexual assaults. It is also used for recreational purposes.

Most depressants are ingested orally in either liquid or pill form. Their observable symptoms of abuse include the following:

- Recognizable odor (alcohol)
- No recognizable odor, but drunken behavior (pills)
- Difficulty concentrating
- Clumsiness
- Poor judgment
- Slurred speech
- Sleepiness
- Contracted pupils

Depressant abuse may occur in combination with abuse of other drugs. Most notably, abusers of stimulants use depressants to help them "come down" from the effects of being high. The most negative aspect of depressant abuse, however, is the relatively rapid tolerance developed by users. Regular users often take 20 to 30 times their original dosage of depressants to achieve the same effects obtained when first taking the drug. This, in turn, leads to a heightened risk of death by overdose. Also, unlike other drugs, withdrawal from depressants can be potentially life threatening. Heavy and prolonged use of these drugs may cause deadly convulsions, psychotic episodes, and other serious mental and physical reactions for 6 months to a year, or longer.[3]

Hallucinogens

The term **hallucinogen** is derived from the word *hallucination,* which refers to an altered sensory state in which things that do not exist in reality may be seen, felt, heard, tasted, or smelled. Some hallucinogens can produce such mind-altering effects, but others do not. Generally speaking, all hallucinogens distort normal thought patterns and impair rational decision-making abilities. These experiences may be pleasurable or disturbing, depending on the mood of the user and the specific dosage taken.

Hallucinogens have been used for centuries, and have historical roots in various cultures and religions. Today, however, most hallucinogens have been outlawed—with the exception of peyote, used in Native American religious rituals; ketamine for general anesthesia; and medical marijuana. Outside of laboratory research, very few legitimate uses exist for hallucinogenic drugs. Most hallucinogens are either illegally manufactured or grown for sale to recreational users. Common symptoms exhibited by users are:

- Hallucinations
- Reduced perceptual reality, sensory confusion, e.g., hearing or seeing colors
- Tremors
- Paranoia
- Anxiety
- Reduced inhibitions
- Enhanced or reduced sensations of sight, sound, and taste
- Depression
- Aggressive or violent outbursts
- Distortion of time, direction, and distance
- Dilated pupils
- Nausea, vomiting

Hallucinogens can be administered in a variety of various ways, including snorting, injecting, smoking, swallowing, drinking, cooking into food, and chewing. One major drawback of long-term or heavy use is **flashbacks**, which are the reoccurrence of hallucinogenic effects at unplanned times during which the drug has not been taken. These episodes typically occur during periods of stress, and have an onset of weeks, months, or years after a planned hallucinogenic session. Although abusers of hallucinogens do not appear to suffer from withdrawal symptoms, the extreme mind-altering effects experienced by users have led to deaths from suicide, homicide, and accidents.

With the exception of marijuana, the use of hallucinogens for recreational purposes has both risen and fallen over time. Hallucinogens gained popularity from the psychedelic era of the 1960s to the 1970s, two decades marked by extensive use of LSD. In the 1980s, hallucinogenic drug use noticeably declined. The advent of MDMA (or *ecstasy*), however, led to resurgence in the use of hallucinogens during the 1990s. Older drugs such as LSD regained popularity as well. This increasing trend in the usage of hallucinogenic drugs continues to gain momentum throughout the 2000s.[4]

Inhalants

Inhalants are the drug of choice among adolescents and those with limited means to purchase other types of intoxicants. No one particular drug is classified as an inhalant; rather, inhalants are created from thousands of legal liquids, gases, and compounds readily available to consumers. Gasoline, butane, model glue, spray can propellant, paint, household cleansers, and even felt-tip markers are just some of the more common things that can be used. Currently, inhalants are not regulated by laws governing the use, sale, and distribution of controlled substances.

Most inhalants affect users similarly to alcohol or other depressants that produce feelings of relaxation and inhibition. The main exception to this is the effect produced by popular club inhalants, such as amyl or butyl nitrate, which produce a rush of dizziness accompanied by an overall body sensation and increased awareness. The following are common symptoms associated with inhalant use:

- Slurred speech
- Disorientation
- Lack of physical coordination
- Headaches
- Nausea and vomiting
- Lack of inhibition
- Coughing
- Running or bleeding nose
- Difficulty breathing
- A chemical smell on clothes, skin, and breath
- Sores or rash around mouth and nose area

Inhalants are breathed in through the nose and mouth in many ways. Fumes may be sniffed or snorted directly from open or aerosol containers. Alternatively, chemical substances can be transferred to rags and **huffed**, which involves sniffing inhalant vapors directly from the rag while covering the mouth and nose. Another popular method is **bagging**, in which the user inhales fumes directly from a paper or plastic bag containing the inhalant. Balloons, soda cans, discarded surgical masks, or virtually any object in which fumes can be contained and breathed is likely to be employed by inhalant users.

Long-term use of inhalants can produce withdrawal symptoms, including sweating, rapid pulse, hand tremors, insomnia, nausea or vomiting, hallucinations, and, in severe cases, seizures. Also, permanent damage to body functions involving the heart, liver, kidneys, lungs, and brain has been linked to inhalant use. Slurred speech, reduced memory function, learning difficulties, and personality changes are a few of the many permanent physiological changes observed in chronic inhalant users. Perhaps the most dangerous aspect of inhalant use is the prospect of **SSD** or Sudden Sniffing Death. SSD can strike first-time users as well as long-time users, causing sudden death by cardiac arrest minutes after breathing an inhalant. Asphyxiation, suffocation, and accidents from impaired judgment caused by inhalant use can also result in serious injury or death.[5]

(a)

THE CONTROLLED SUBSTANCES ACT

The **Controlled Substances Act (CSA)**, passed in 1970, established federal laws regulating the manufacture and distribution of drugs in the United States. The CSA was aimed particularly at curbing the street sales and use of illicit drugs. In 1973, President Richard Nixon established the DEA (Drug Enforcement Administration) through an executive order to provide a unified law enforcement agency charged with the sole mission of enforcing federal drug laws, and in particular the legal mandates of the CSA. One of the DEA's primary duties in an ongoing effort to stem illegal drug trade is to administer and oversee the DEA **drug schedules**. All recognized drugs, both prescription and illegal, are classified as Schedule I, II, III, IV, or V. An explanation of each schedule and the particular drugs of potential abuse it includes is presented in the following section.

(b)

SCHEDULE I DRUGS

- The drug or other substance has a high potential for abuse.
- The drug or other substance has no currently accepted medical use in treatment in the United States.
- There is a lack of accepted safety for use of the drug or other substance under medical supervision.

These are the criteria for DEA **Schedule I** drugs. In other words, Schedule I drugs are manufactured, distributed, and sold exclusively as illicit controlled substances. Because Schedule I drugs are considered the most illicit of all scheduled substances, they carry the most severe penalties for persons violating laws governing their control. Special provisions of the CSA allow the DEA to temporarily (for up to one and a half years) place newly emerging street drugs that have not yet been scheduled as Schedule I drugs. This emergency classification process allows the DEA to investigate whether or not a suspected illicit substance poses an imminent hazard to public safety and to determine the drug's proper placement on the drug schedule. The following are common Schedule I drugs of abuse encountered by investigators:

Heroin *(Narcotic)*

Street names: dope, smack, junk, H, horse, chiva, hell dust, thunder.

(c)

FIGURE 18.3 ▶ (a) Mexican brown heroin in powder form (left) and black tar heroin (right). (b) Black tar heroin as it appears for street sale packaged in cellophane and (c) tied and rolled heroin balloons used for selling and smuggling the drug in powder form.

Heroin, shown in various street forms in Figure 18.3, is a highly addictive narcotic created by chemically processing morphine derived from natural opium. It has no legal medical use and is sold exclusively as an illicit drug. Common street varieties of heroin include white, brown, or tan powder, and a black or brown substance known as *black tar heroin*, which may have either a sticky or a hard, chunky consistency. Pill and capsule versions, although less common, are also available. Heroin can be taken orally, snorted, or smoked, but injection is most users' preferred method because it produces the fastest and most intense effects. The drug produces a short period of euphoria, sometimes lasting only a few minutes, followed by a period of sedation lasting several hours. The strength of a single dose of heroin varies greatly depending on how and with what the pure version of the drug has been diluted or *cut*. Cutting agents include quinine, sugar, starch, powdered milk, and poisons such as strychnine. One dose or a bag of heroin can sell for as little as $50 or for more than $300 depending on the quality and purity. Deadly diseases such as HIV/AIDS contracted through intravenous use of heroin have led to an increase in smoking and snorting the drug. Death among heroin users can result from (1) overdose stemming from the increase dosages needed to overcome tolerance, (2) toxic substances used in the cutting process, and (3) excessive purity causing cardiac arrest and/or respiratory failure. Heroin withdrawal is usually not fatal; however, it is extremely painful to the addict, causing vomiting, goose bumps, extreme muscle fatigue, and other physical symptoms lasting up to 1 week after going "cold turkey" (i.e., immediately stopping use of the drug).[6]

LSD *(Hallucinogen)*

Street names: acid, blotter (on paper), window pane, L, cid, tabs (on paper), micro dots (small tablets), dots, mellow yellow.

LSD is a potent hallucinogenic drug that produces mind-altering experiences among those who use it. The exact nature of the drug's effects, either positive or negative, is unpredictable and relies greatly on the individual dose taken and the user's psychological state. In general, an LSD trip exaggerates sensations, resulting in distorted perception of colors, sounds, and feelings accompanied by irrational thought patterns. Usually, a hit of LSD is ingested orally in the form of either pills or capsules, or the liquid drug is placed on blotter paper (see Figure 18.4), on sugar cubes, or in gelatin (known as *window panes*). One hit of LSD is very inexpensive, ranging from five to ten dollars. After orally ingesting the drug, the user begins to experience its effects in less than half an hour, and these effects will continue for approximately 12 hours. Flashbacks—recurrences of an LSD trip without taking the drug—are noted among longer-term users. LSD today appears to be much less

popular as a recreational drug than it was during the 1960s and 1970s, and its current use is minimal compared to other illicit drugs.[7]

Marijuana *(Hallucinogen)*

Street names: pot, weed, grass, mota (Spanish), dope, bud, ganja, hash, doobie, blunt, spliff.

The term *marijuana* is slang for a drug made from the flowers, buds, and leaves of the cannabis plant. The cannabis plant is also the source of *hemp*—its roots, stalks, and stems, which are not considered illegal and are used to produce rope, cloth, and paper products. For decades, marijuana has been used and sold as an illicit drug to persons of all ages and backgrounds. Today, the drug is legal for medical use in some locations within the United States. Its active hallucinogenic ingredients, including **THC** and other psychoactives known as **cannabinoids**, can be extracted from the plant's leaves and buds to create many drug varieties including **hashish** (a concentrated resinous form) and **hash oil**, a sticky black liquid. Although marijuana is usually smoked, it can also be eaten or its psychoactive ingredients extracted and mixed with fluids such as alcohol to form a drinkable liquid. Users may experience mixed effects from the drug ranging from euphoria to paranoia, as well as mental distortions in time and space accompanied by hallucinations. These effects last anywhere from 3 to 9 hours or more, depending on the amount and strength of the drug consumed. Marijuana is typically sold on the street in one-quarter-ounce quantities for anywhere between $25–$150 depending on its quality and place of sale.[8] Estimating the quantity and examining the packaging of marijuana seized as evidence, as shown in Figure 18.5, is essential step for determining the charges to be filed against an individual arrested for illegally possession of the drug.

GHB *(Depressant)*

Street names: Georgia homeboy, G, liquid X, G-ing, gamma-oh, blue verve, liquid ecstasy.

GHB, produced illegally as a powder, is usually mixed with water or some other liquid to form a concentrate, which is then consumed either directly or mixed with a beverage for recreational use. The effects of GHB are very similar to those produced by alcohol, including dizziness, loss of coordination, slurred speech, and, in cases of extreme abuse, coma, or death. In addition to bars, raves, and nightclubs, places of likely illegal sale for GHB include gymnasiums because of its believed body-building qualities. More overdoses are associated with GHB than with other depressants because it is very difficult for users to assess the strength of street-level dosages. GHB has gained notoriety as a date rape drug because of its use by sexual predators to sedate their victims before assaulting them. The effects of an average GHB dose, which sells for five to ten dollars, last for approximately 3 hours, and chemical traces are difficult to detect through toxicological tests because the drug is quickly eliminated from the body.[9]

FIGURE 18.4 ▶ LSD blotter is sold as a "hit," which is contained in one postage stamp sized tear-away section of the sheet shown here. (Courtesy U.S. Department of Justice)

(a)

(b)

FIGURE 18.5 ▶ (a) Raw marijuana before it is packaged for street sale (Courtesy U.S. Drug Enforcement Agency). (b) Dime bags of marijuana packaged to be sold illegally ((a) United States Department of Justice).

MDMA *(Stimulant)*

Street names: ecstasy, X, E, XTC, Adam, go, hug drug, disco biscuit.

The stimulant **MDMA**, usually referred to as *ecstasy*, has become very popular as a club drug used by patrons of bars

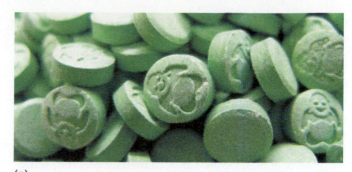

(a)

(b)

FIGURE 18.6 ▶ MDMA or ecstasy is manufactured in numerous shapes, colors, and sizes, but is often recognized by a "happy" character imprinted on its surface.

and nightclubs. It is also used frequently by persons attending raves, which are organized dance parties where MDMA is a substitute for the alcohol served at commercial dance clubs. In addition to the usual effects of a stimulant, MDMA users claim that the drug heightens sensual awareness and their ability to open up to others in a less inhibited manner. It is usually taken in pill or capsule form (see Figure 18.6), but can be snorted as a white, crystalline powder. An average dose, usually one pill, sells on the street for $10–$30. The effects of MDMA last from 3–5 hours per dose.[10]

Peyote and Mescaline *(Hallucinogens)*

Street names: buttons, mescal, big chief, mescalito.

Peyote is a small round cactus native to Mexico and Southwest regions of the United States (see Figure 18.7). The

(a)

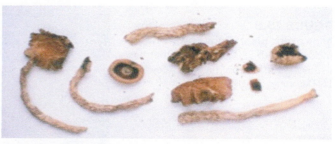

(b)

FIGURE 18.7 ▶ (a) Peyote, referred to as *buttons* on the street. (b) Psilocybin, or *shrooms* as they are known to users of the drug.

drug is formed from harvesting and drying button-shaped growths on the tops of mature cactus plants. Peyote is usually ingested orally by chewing the buttons and swallowing the liquid they produce. It also can be made into a potent tea made by dissolving the button in hot water. The primary natural psychoactive ingredient in peyote is **mescaline**, which causes its users to experience mind- and body-altering experiences—including visual hallucinations lasting up to 12 hours. Users characteristically become nauseous and/or vomit before the onset of effects. Peyote has been used for centuries within the Native-American culture for various religious and ceremonial purposes.[11]

Psilocybin *(Hallucinogen)*

Street names: magic mushrooms, shrooms, mushies, boomers.

Mushrooms containing the psychoactive ingredient **psilocybin** resemble ordinary mushrooms (shown in Figure 18.7(b)), which are brown or tan in appearance, and grow wild in subtropical locations. Magic mushrooms are native to Central and South America but are easily cultivated in natural or artificial environments within the United States. Despite their generic appearance, mushrooms containing psilocybin turn a distinctive blue color in areas where they have been bruised or broken. The effects of an average dosage are very similar to, yet less intense than those of a similar dosage of LSD. Symptoms include pupil dilation, confusion, elation, fear, and visual hallucinations, which last 4–6 hours. The drug is usually dried and taken orally in raw, capsule, or brewed liquid form.[12]

Khat *(Stimulant)*

Street names: kat, graba, African salad, bushman's tea, chat, graba, oat, Somali tea.

Khat (pronounced "cot") is derived from a shrub-like plant that is grown primarily in East Africa and the Arabian Peninsula. Its shoots and leaves, which are leathery in texture and yellow-green in color, are typically sold on the street in plastic bags or are wrapped in small bundles with banana leaves. The drug can also be sold in the form of dried, crushed leaves or powder. Single-use doses sell for $30–$50 and larger amounts used for trafficking and distribution sell for $300–$400 per kilo. Because the drug is a stimulant, it causes users to experience increased energy, an elevated mood, extreme talkativeness, and increased alertness. These effects have been described as a high somewhere between those of strong caffeine and a low dose of cocaine. Users typically chew khat plant products for 10 minutes or more, swallow the intoxicating juices, and then spit out the used leaves and shoots. Chewing sessions may last hours on end, with one dose of khat being ingested after another; the stimulant effects, however, tend to peak after 2 hours of continued use. Khat users usually emit a strong, sharp odor and show signs of extreme thirst. The drug is extremely popular among persons from Yemen, Somalia, Ethiopia, and other East African nations. In the Muslim community, it is considered an accepted alternative to alcohol. Because khat's intoxicating effects are greatly reduced 48 hours after harvesting, it must be transported and sold quickly in raw form. Leaves over 48 hours old, without being refrigerated, likely will be classified as a Schedule IV drug due to their loss of potency (i.e., their more potent ingredient, the drug **cathine**, will diminish). Popular sales locations include restaurants, bars, and stores that specialize in goods and services for Africans and Yeminis. Typically, the drug is transported from Kenya, Egypt, or Saudi Arabia by plane for arrival in the United States on Thursdays, Fridays, and Saturdays for weekend use.[13] Khat as packaged and sold on the street is shown in Figure 18.8.

Additional Schedule I Drugs:

Methcathinone (Stimulant): Produced exclusively in clandestine laboratories, methcathinone affects users in the same manner as methamphetamine. It appears as a salt-like crystalline powder that can be consumed in beverages, snorted, injected, or swallowed. *Street names: cat, gaggers, goob, stat, oat, tweeker.*

Fentanyl (Narcotic): Commercially produced as a pain killer and anesthetic, this drug mimics the effects of morphine, heroin, and other opiates—but may be many times stronger. Aside from diversion of prescription forms to the street, various forms of Fentanyl are produced in clandestine drug labs. When used illegally, the drug is a powder that can be snorted or a liquid that can be injected. *Street names: Apache, China girl, drop dead, jackpot, incredible hulk, lollipop (prescription form taken orally).*

FIGURE 18.8 ▶ Khat is one of the many exotic plant drugs now being imported to the United States that has a stimulant effect on its users. (Courtesy U.S. Department of Justice)

SCHEDULE II DRUGS

- The drug or other substance has a high potential for abuse.
- The drug or other substance has a currently accepted medical use in treatment in the United States or a currently accepted medical use with severe restrictions.
- Abuse of the drug or other substance may lead to severe psychological or physical dependence.

Perhaps the largest number of illicit drugs sold at the street level fall within the **Schedule II** classification. Many of these drugs rival Schedule I drugs in potency and potential for abuse, yet are considered less hazardous to society only because of their legal medical applications. Of the Schedule II drugs listed here, some are mainly prescription drugs diverted to street sales, and others are primarily produced by clandestine laboratories:

Hydrocodone *(Narcotic)*
Street names: vikes, hydro, norco.

Hydrocodone, more commonly known by its commercial name *Vicodin*, is a semisynthetic opiate used for the medically legitimate purposes of cough suppression and pain management. Users of the drug experience drowsiness, mental clouding, lightheadedness, sedation, and other morphine-like effects. Hydrocodone is not produced in clandestine labs, but rather reaches the street drug market by illicit means such as doctor or pharmacist diversion, doctor shopping, Internet drug sales networks, false or altered prescriptions, and theft from legitimate users. It is usually encountered in pill form, but has been trafficked illegally in capsules and as a liquid.[14]

Methamphetamine *(Stimulant)*

Street names: meth, crystal meth, speed, ice, cran, tweek, glass, uppers, yaba (pill), shabu shabu (pill).

Methamphetamine (see Figure 18.9) is primarily sold as an illegal street drug, but also is a legal prescription drug (*Desoxyn*) used in the treatment of ADHD (attention deficit hyperactive disorder). As a street drug, it usually is sold in small plastic zip-lock bags in the form of a bitter-tasting white or off-white powder. Other forms include pills, capsules, and large crystals known as *crystal meth* or *ice*. The drug can also be flavored and produced in red, green, purple, and various other colors. It is usually snorted, but it can also be taken orally, injected, or smoked. Users typically snort small piles of powder (about the size of a match head) known as *bumps* from the tip of keys or from pen caps until desired level of effect is achieved. Besides increased energy and alertness, meth users also can exhibit an extremely emaciated physical appearance, paranoia, hallucinations, "meth mouth" (loss of teeth), involuntary body movements, and aggressive behavior. Extreme depression and lack of physical energy are char-

(a)

(b)

FIGURE 18.9 ▶ (a) Methamphetamine can be manufactured in virtually any form, but powder meth is popular for street sale and is typically packaged in foil or plastic bags. (b) Crystal meth is typically smoked in a pipe similar to that pictured here. (Courtesy U.S. Department of Justice)

acteristic symptoms of withdrawal. The production of methamphetamine is relatively simple and can be executed using various household chemicals and over-the-counter drugs. In particular, the legal drug pseudoephedrine, used in various cold remedies, is a key component of methamphetamine production.[15]

PCP *(Narcotic)*

Street names: angel dust, crystal, rocket fuel, embalming fluid, hog, wack.

PCP was originally manufactured as an anesthetic for animals, but is no longer produced for legitimate purposes in the United States and is now solely manufactured in clandestine laboratories. It appears as a white, tan, or brownish crystalline powder and can be mixed with many substances so that the drug can be smoked, injected, snorted, or swallowed. Users of PCP experience numbness, rapid eye movements, slurred speech, paranoia, enhanced aggressive behavior and physical strength, and hallucinations. Leafy substances such as mint, parley, oregano, and tobacco may be found in the possession of PCP users, who mix them with the drug so that it can be smoked.[16]

Morphine *(Narcotic)*

Street names: dreamer, first line, Miss Emma, morpho, Mister Blue.

Morphine, a derivative of opium, is the most effective and powerful painkiller known to the medical profession. In the past, it was produced nearly exclusively in liquid form as a pain killer for surgical procedures and for treating painful diseases such as cancer. The drug, being an opiate, is highly addictive and produces severe withdrawals. Its effects are similar to those of heroin. Street use of morphine has been on the rise, since it is now produced in pill form for general pain killing applications. Users can take the pills orally or grind them to powder for snorting, smoking, or injection. Morphine is also used to produce **codeine**, a less powerful prescription analgesic used to manage low to moderate pain. Codeine, also used as a cough suppressant and a supplement to aspirin and Tylenol, often is diverted to street sales and is commonly purchased by opiate abusers.[17]

Cocaine *(Stimulant)*

Street names: blow, crack (smokable version), nose candy, snowball, tornado, wicky stick, perico (Spanish), snow, toot, white lady.

Cocaine is predominantly an illicit recreational drug, but is still used as a topical anesthetic for some surgical procedures (including dentistry). It is derived from the leaves of coca plants, which are native to South America. The drug is usually sold in two forms: (1) as a fine white powder with a bitter, numbing taste that is snorted as shown in Figure 18.10, or (2) as **crack** or *freebase cocaine,* small white or off-white rocks processed for purposes of smoking (see Figure 18.11). In either form, cocaine is highly addictive and produces feelings of stimulation and well-being for 5 to 15 minutes if smoked, and 20 to 40 minutes if snorted. The powder may also be converted into liquid form

(a)

(b)

FIGURE 18.11 ▶ (a) Rock or crack cocaine before packaging. (b) Individual rocks packaged in cellophane for street sale.

for heightened effects by injecting the drug together with heroin or morphine, a process referred to as **speedballing**. Tolerance to cocaine develops quickly, causing the user to crave greater quantities of the drug and greater frequencies of use. The street cost of powdered cocaine usually ranges from $80–$100 per gram, and a rock of crack typically sells for $25–$50.[18]

Oxycodone *(Narcotic)*

Street names: kicker, OC, oxy, ox, bue, oxycotton, hillbilly heroin, perks, roxies.

Oxycodone, a prescription pain killer, is similar to morphine in its chemical composition and the effects that it produces in its users. Commercial brands of the drug include Percocet and OxyContin. Although the drug is produced in pill form, it can be abused by grinding it to a powder and snorting it for a stronger effect. Generally, users experience a numbing sensation of the entire body, and exhibit "drunk-like" behavior lasting approximately 6 hours or up to 12 hours for time-release versions. All forms of oxycodone are highly addictive, and tolerance to its effects builds extremely quickly. It is not uncommon for a user to triple or quadruple dosages within weeks after first

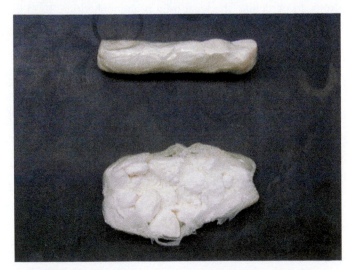

FIGURE 18.10 ▶ Cocaine, when sold on the street, can be packaged in various ways, including in cellophane rolls as pictured here, or in paper bindles, glassine bags, or foil. (Courtesy U.S. Department of Justice)

taking the drug. One dose (40 mg pill) has a prescription cost of $4–$7; and on the street, the same pill costs $20–$40.

Additional Schedule II Drugs:

Amphetamines (Stimulant): Mainly in prescription tablet or capsule form, but can be made into a powder for snorting, smoking, or mixing with liquids for purposes of swallowing. Effects are similar to, yet milder than those of methamphetamine. *Street names: speed, dex, bennies, black beauty, cross tops.*

Meperedine (Narcotic): Produced commercially under various names, but most commonly as *Demerol.* Usually sold on the street in pill form, yet could be a liquid. Effects are those of a general pain reliever. *Street names: demmies and new heroin (for the drug MPTP, which is similar in chemical form (i.e., is a drug analog) to meperedine).*

Methylphenidate (Stimulant): A prescription medication used primarily to combat drowsiness in patients who complain of excessive fatigue and to counter the effect of ADHD among children (under the name *Ritalin*), this drug is currently also popular among street users. It is usually ground to a powder from its original pill form and mixed with a liquid substance that can be injected. The high produced is similar to that of methamphetamine. *Street names: West Coast, vitamin R, crackers (when mixed with the narcotic drug Talwin).*

Methadone (Narcotic): Available in liquid or tablets, methadone is used primarily as a prescription drug to treat heroin and other forms of opiate addiction. Its primary purpose is to wean opiate abusers from drug cravings as well as painful withdrawal symptoms. The drug has been diverted to illegal street sales networks as a heroin substitute. *Street names: fizzies, chocolate chip cookies (when mixed with ecstasy/MDMA).*[19]

SCHEDULE III DRUGS

- The drug or other substance has less potential for abuse than the drugs or other substances in Schedules I and II.
- The drug or other substance has a currently accepted medical use in treatment in the United States.
- Abuse of the drug or other substance may lead to moderate or low physical dependence or high psychological dependence.

Generally, **Schedule III** drugs have a lower potential for physical addiction than do Schedules I or II drugs; nonetheless, they may be just as psychologically addictive. Most Schedule III drugs and their derivatives are also currently used for medical purposes and are less likely than those classified at higher levels to be diverted to the street. Popular Schedule III drugs of abuse include the following:

Ketamine *(Depressant)*

Street names: K, "special K," cat valium, vitamin K, honey oil, kit kat, purple, ket, super acid.

Ketamine, commercially marketed under the brand name *Ketaset*, is generally used as an animal tranquilizer—but is also approved for human use as an anesthetic. It is sold as a colorless, odorless liquid, a white or off-white powder, or in tablet form costing $10 to $20 on the street for one hit. Users typically mix the drug in liquid form with other beverages, but it can also be snorted, smoked, or injected. Effects last up to 24 hours and include distortion of sight and sound, loss of control, lack of coordination, and extreme confusion referred to by users as a being stuck in a **K-hole**. During the first 45 to 90 minutes of use, hallucinations may occur. Teenagers and young adults comprise 75 percent of ketamine users. Criminal activity associated with the drug includes its use by sexual predators to drug their victims and the sexual assault of intentional users who are unfamiliar with its sedative effects.[20]

Barbiturates and Benzodiazepines *(Depressants)*

Street names: barbies, blue bullets, downer, goofies, reds, strawberries, libs (Librium).

Barbiturates are one of the oldest forms of prescription depressants, and are used much less frequently nowadays because of their inherent long-term dangers, including high levels of tolerance leading to overdose and death. Depending on the type of drug, the effects range from minor relaxation to complete unconsciousness (when used as a general anesthetic). Street users will appear as if they are drunk, but not have an odor of alcohol. Barbiturates are usually taken in pill form, but can be a liquid or powder as well. The majority of street sales consist of diverted prescription drugs going by the commercial names of Amyta, Nembutal, Seconal, and Tuinal. Benzodiazepines were created as a safer alternative to barbiturates and affect the user in much the same way without many of the health risks and dangerous side effects. Common illegal street uses involve the commercial drugs Alprazolam and Diazepam. Most notorious of this drug class, however, is the powerful date rape drug Rohypnol, commonly known as *roofies, rophies,* and *roach.* This drug is not produced legally in the United States, but is smuggled in from other countries where it is legally produced. It is popular among sexual predators because it can be added to beverages, causing the victim to experience temporary amnesia, sedation, and unconsciousness.[21]

Anabolic Steroids *(Androgenic):*

Street names: Arnolds, roids, gym candy, pumpers, stackers, juice.

Anabolic steroids are classified as androgenics—basically drugs used for building tissue and muscle mass. Steroids may also be used together with the depressant date rape drug, GHB—also believed to possess body-building qualities. Depending on the particular type and quantity of steroid, the hormone testosterone is dramatically increased in the user's bloodstream and body tissues, causing not only rapid muscle growth but also acne, loss of hair, and a dental diastema or large gap between the two upper front teeth. Steroids are used by both males and females involved in competitive sports and body building. Aside from changes in physical appearance, steroid use can cause mood swings involving violent behavior known as **roid rage**. For illegal use, the drug either is a diverted prescription medication, smuggled to the United States from Mexico, where a prescription is not needed to acquire steroids; or it is produced in a clandestine laboratory. Steroids are most often in liquid form and injected, but they can also be taken orally as tablets or capsules. The drug is commonly taken in cycles, where the user takes a sequence of graduated doses over an extended period of time (usually 4 to 6 weeks), after which the effects of the drug will diminish. Long-term steroid users, who may experience serious physical problems including brain tumors, paralysis, and death, usually take the drug on a continuing basis and must administer increasingly stronger dosages to achieve the desired effect.[22]

SCHEDULE IV DRUGS

- The drug or other substance has a low potential for abuse relative to the drugs or other substances in Schedule III.
- The drug or other substance has a currently accepted medical use in treatment in the United States.
- Abuse of the drug or other substance may lead to limited physical dependence or psychological dependence relative to the drugs or other substances in Schedule III.

The vast majority of **Schedule IV** drugs used for illicit purposes are either prescription narcotics or depressants, which produce milder mental and physiological effects than drugs listed at higher schedule levels. These drugs appear in pills or capsules of various colors and shapes, and may also bear an identifying symbol impressed on their surface by the pharmaceutical manufacturer. These drugs are usually swallowed by abusers, but they can also be smoked, injected, or snorted by grinding pills and capsules to a water-soluble powder. They are often used in combination with other, stronger drugs. Common Schedule IV drugs discovered for street sale include:

Darvon *(Narcotic):*

General pain killing effects. *Street names: pinks, footballs, pink footballs, yellow footballs, 65's.*

Talwin *(Narcotic):*

General pain killing effects, but is frequently mixed with the stimulant Ritalin and injected to produce effect similar to that of a speedball mixture of cocaine and heroin. *Street names: T's & R's, T's & Rits, crackers, set (when mixed with Ritalin).*

Equanil *(Depressant):*

General sedative effects; also goes by the trade name Miltown. *Street names: Uncle Miltie.*

Valium *(Depressant):*

General sedative effects; by far the most available Schedule IV drug on the street. *Street names: blues, vallies.*

Xanax *(Depressant):*

General sedative effects; often used to combat anxiety disorder symptoms. *Street names: zanies, zanie bars, totem poles.*[23]

SCHEDULE V DRUGS

- The drug or other substance has a low potential for abuse relative to the drugs or other substances in Schedule IV.
- The drug or other substance has a currently accepted medical use in treatment in the United States.
- Abuse of the drug or other substances may lead to limited physical dependence or psychological dependence relative to the drugs or other substances in Schedule IV.

Relatively few **Schedule V** drugs are sold on the street due to their lack of potency. Quite often, these drugs are used by teenagers for experimental purposes. They may be used by seasoned abusers as a last resort when their drug of choice is unavailable. Commonly, these substances are taken for the secondary pharmaceuticals they contain; for example, cough syrups or mild pain relief formulas containing the narcotic Codeine or its chemical derivative, or the stimulant pseudoephedrine. Street names referring to abused prescription or over-the-counter cough suppressants include *triple-C, robo,* and *school boy.*[24]

NONSCHEDULED INHALANTS

Currently, inhalants are not considered a drug and are not scheduled by the DEA. Many States, however, have passed laws against the use of inhalants (referred to as *Glading*) as well as the illicit use of the chemicals they contain. These include gasoline, acetone, mineral spirits, Freon, computer duster, scented sprays, and commercially produced stimulant substances capable of producing intoxicating effects. Street names include *poppers, boppers (amyl nitrite), whippets, buzz bombs (nitrous oxide),* and *snappers (isobutyl nitrite).*

DRUG PRODUCTION AND MANUFACTURING LOCATIONS

Grow Houses

Indoor cultivation of illegal marijuana plants, once restricted to rural locations, now is commonplace in suburban neighborhoods through the use of **grow houses**. Grow houses can be established in virtually any indoor setting, but require many changes and additions to existing structures to ensure proper plant growth and drug quality. They range from simple one- or two-person operations set up to grow less than 50 plants in one room (known as a **grow room**) to elaborate organized growing schemes involving large numbers of workers who cultivate thousands of plants in the entire living space of one or more homes. Typically, grow houses are used only for growing plants and drying them in preparation for distribution. Street sales of marijuana from grow houses are extremely rare because such activities may bring unwanted attention to their clandestine growing activities, which yield much greater profits.

Investigators usually discover grow houses from suspicious activities associated with the specific conditions needed to grow marijuana plants within a residential dwelling. Among these are proper watering methods, temperature control, fertilizers, and lighting. Plants can be grown in either soil or hydroponic containers, where the plant roots are nourished in water and liquid nutrients rather than in soil. Marijuana, in particular, requires a hot (up to 95°F) and moist environment. To create such an environment, the walls of grow rooms are generally sealed with plastic sheets to lock in heat provided by 1,000-watt horticultural or aquarium lights, and windows may also be covered with plastic, paper, or tin foil. Extreme temperatures produced by these lights are cooled to the appropriate growing range with oscillating fans and air conditioning units. If grown in soil, plants are placed on tables elevated for protection from the coolness of floors, and watered through a drip system, which also drains excess water. Charcoal air filtration units cover up the potent smell of marijuana that may emanate from these rooms.

Usually persons working in and operating larger-scale grow houses are not the owners or renters of the residence. Rather, these houses are usually purchased by outside investors or by organized crime syndicates for cash—and perhaps with assistance from unscrupulous real estate agents. Although grow house proprietors attempt to keep a low profile, their illicit activities are often hard to mask from neighbors and investigators. First, the tremendous amount of electricity that the lighting and equipment need to grow plants indoors requires that the house's electrical system be rewired to provide higher electrical output in the growing rooms. Also, rooms must be modified to increase ventilation, and plumbing must be altered to provide additional water. Utility companies noticing excessive or unusual electric and water usage that sometimes signals the presence of a grow house may notify authorities. Efforts to hide telltale utility use may involve the pirating of electricity from transformers or electrical grids or the damaging of mechanisms used to monitor water usage. Neighbors may complain about excessive noise from electrical generators used to supplement existing electricity sources, and they may also notice late-night deliveries involving large numbers of bags (containing fertilizers and other plant foods) being brought from trucks into the house.

Larger grow houses are commonly staffed by workers smuggled illegally into the United States and forced to cultivate marijuana to repay their debt to human traffickers. Also possibly present is a heavily armed security staff. Although there may be many persons inside a grow house, their presence is often undetectable to neighbors and other outside observers. What is often detectible, however, is the extreme heat generated within the house by growing bulbs. Thermal imaging devices utilizing infrared technology help identify grow houses by visualizing the excessive heat they generate from walls and attic areas. Processing a grow house as a crime scene is illustrated in Case Example 18A (see Figures 18.12 to 18.19).

Interestingly, many states have passed laws legalizing marijuana cultivation and sale for medical purposes. Such acts are still considered illegal under current federal laws, however. In addition, most states that have legalized medical marijuana have not legalized transportation of the drug from its place of manufacture to its place of sale. Clearly, the enforcement status of marijuana as an illegal drug is constantly evolving and currently exists in a legal quandary.[25]

CASE EXAMPLE 18A

Grow House Crime Scene

FIGURE 18.12 ▶ Neighbors reported to police that "suspicious activities" have been going on at the residence shown here ever since it was purchased from its previous owners. They reported never seeing or hearing the new owners during the daytime, and that the residents come and go only in the middle of the night. In addition, the neighbors claim that they never see a light on inside the home or hear noises coming from inside the home. Occasionally, they claim, "a strange odor" can be smelled outside the residence on hot days. Narcotics investigators suspect this is a marijuana grow house. What information and evidence should be gathered in order to obtain a search warrant for this residence? What investigative techniques should be used? Should the premises be entered using a "raid" approach or would a more passive entry method be a better investigative plan?

FIGURE 18.13 ▶ Investigators at the scene decide to do a knock-and-talk inspection of the home. When one of the residents cracks open the front door, the investigators see the kitchen area as shown here. Does this view of the home enable investigators to immediately enter the home without a warrant? If so, should they enter the home at this time or enter the home later using a more planned out investigative approach?

FIGURE 18.14 ▶ After securing a search warrant for the home, investigators perform a drug raid. How should the search of this home be conducted?

FIGURE 18.15 ▶ Specialized lighting and fans are required to create a greenhouse effect.

FIGURE 18.16 ▶ Young plants are grown to replace older plants that are harvested.

FIGURE 18.17 ▶ High-output electrical circuits installed to handle the lighting and fans.

FIGURE 18.18 ▶ The room has been highly modified, with new wiring and walls removed, to accommodate the growing operation.

FIGURE 18.19 ▶ Additional heavy-duty electrical circuitry is required to power all of the growing. After performing a walk through of the grow house, what evidence at this scene should be collected, and how should it be collected? During a follow-up investigation of this scene, what possible information could be gathered from witnesses, suspects, informants, the property owner and other persons with knowledge of the grow house? What possible investigative leads could narcotics investigators discover from interviewing or (if suspects) interrogating these individuals?

Grow Fields

Although most plants containing substances used for illicit drug purposes are grown outside the United States, marijuana is cultivated domestically in many remote locations throughout America. Areas used are for illegal growing activities, known as **grow fields** or pot plantations, are usually located in forested or agricultural settings. Occasionally grow fields are discovered accidentally by hikers and campers, but more frequently they are revealed by aerial surveillance methods. Some growers attempt to avoid these detection efforts by interspersing marijuana plants with legitimate crops such as corn. Likely indicators of grow field include the following:

- Wooded property containing a tent or trailer with no evidence of recreational activities
- Vehicles seen in the same isolated area on a regular basis
- Barns or greenhouses on property where they have no apparent use
- Purchases of large amounts of fertilizer, hoses, PVC pipe, chicken wire, and pots
- Numerous PRIVATE and KEEP OUT signs posted on seemingly unoccupied land
- Guard dogs and alarm systems in locations where they don't appear to be necessary
- Cultivation or soil disturbance in area created within clearings of trees or foliage
- Purchase or presence of large amounts of pesticide or rat poison

Grow fields present certain dangers that must be anticipated before they are approached or entered by investigators.

Most persons operating such locations may be armed and willing to use firepower to protect their crops and may have trained guard dogs to attack trespassers; but most dangerous of all, they may have placed booby traps in and around the marijuana field. For example, investigators in drug eradication operations have reported the presence of makeshift devices to injure intruders such as poisonous snakes strategically placed in walking paths, land mine–type bombs, and guns set to discharge by trip cords attached to their trigger—to name a few.[26]

Rock Houses

Rock houses, also called *crack houses,* are used primarily for the street sales of crack cocaine, but can also serve as a manufacturing location and a safe location for users to smoke, snort, or inject the drug. Typically, rock houses are fashioned from burnt, abandoned, decaying, or otherwise highly undesirable dwellings in locations known for drug use and sales. They are noted, and readily observed, for their fortress-like external appearance resulting from the crude placement of iron bars and sheet metals over walls, windows, and doors. Internally, rock houses are commonly guarded by several heavily armed persons with a cache of high-power weapons. High security is essential due to the large amounts of drugs and cash inside the house. Booby traps also may be located near areas where valuable items are stored.

Large numbers of crack users are seen in and around crack houses, where they usually purchase the drug by depositing money in a small slot or shoot in a back or side door of the house. Video surveillance cameras, persons on the roof of the house, or spotters located in street areas typically provide advance warnings of potential dangers such as law enforcement activity. Rock houses are seldom independently operated, but rather are affiliated with numerous other member houses in other locations (referred to as *cells*). Other drugs in addition to crack cocaine may be sold from rock houses, and organized prostitution in exchange for drugs occurs quite frequently inside the premises.[27]

Clandestine Laboratories

Clandestine laboratories, or **clan labs**, produce many forms of drugs, but about 80 percent of this production involves the "cooking" of methamphetamine. Clan labs can be located virtually anywhere and in any place, including homes, apartments, commercial offices, storage units, motel rooms, trailers, boats, and even automobiles. Most of the labs are small in size, known as *mom and pop labs,* and produce less than 10 ounces of methamphetamine per production cycle. A larger, rarer type of lab, referred to as a *super lab,* can produce up to 10 pounds of the drug per production cycle. Super labs are responsible for an estimated 80 percent of methamphetamine produced for street sales.

Regardless of its size, any clan lab presents a significant danger to those operating it and to investigators seizing these illegal operations and their inhabitants. Because methamphetamine is prepared by heating numerous toxic and potentially explosive chemicals, various health and safety hazards accompany the investigation and seizure of these clandestine establishments:

- Fire and explosions resulting from the ignition of volatile chemical fumes either accidentally by existing sources, such as faulty wiring, or purposefully to create a booby trap for persons entering the lab
- Asphyxiation and breathing disorders produced by the inhalation of toxic vapors and gases
- Toxic poisoning from the absorption of poisonous chemicals through surface areas of the skin

In addition to these hazards, lab seizures often involve shootouts with armed persons operating the lab who may have their children at the site as well.

Clan labs should be investigated only after specially trained personnel have cleared the location of all existing safety hazards. **PPC (Personal Protective Clothing)** should be worn when investigating areas containing active hazardous materials and chemicals. The large amount of toxic waste associated with the manufacture of methamphetamine, usually 6 to 10 pounds for every pound of drug produced, may produce several dumping areas of toxic material outside the lab. Toxic substances may be buried in dirt near the lab, dumped in trash cans, stored in airtight containers, sealed in chemical storage barrels, flushed down sinks and toilets, pumped from recreational vehicle holding tanks, or poured into natural water sources such as rivers or lakes.

Often, clan labs are identified and reported by persons living around them because of the strong chemical odor they emit resembling that of ammonia. Their location can also identified by shipments of **precursor** chemicals (those used to manufacture the drug) interdicted by law enforcement. Ephedrine and pseudoephedrine are two such chemicals that are common mainstays of methamphetamine production. Neither is currently manufactured in the United States, so they are usually imported in bulk from other countries, including Germany, India, and China, by illicit drug distributors. Many other chemicals used by clan lab "cookers" (i.e., persons who make meth), however, are legal for commercial use and are sometimes contained in common household items. Excessive possession or purchasing of any of the following chemicals should alert investigators of possible production of methamphetamine and/ or the presence of a clan lab:

- Cold and allergy medications
- Lye
- Rock salt
- Battery acid
- Lithium batteries
- Pool cleaner

Many of these chemicals are acquired through illegal diversion processes:

- Stealing
- Smuggling across international borders
- Fraudulent labeling
- Bribing government officials, chemical manufacturers and distributors, deliverers
- Creating complex transaction chains so that tracking chemicals is difficult
- Purchasing chemicals from unscrupulous legitimate chemical suppliers
- Using undocumented cash transactions
- Converting unregulated chemicals into the desired illicit chemicals
- Storing chemicals in warehouses until officials lose track of them
- "Smurfing," or purchasing drugs in small quantities that do not require tracking[28]

SPECIALIZED DRUG CRIME INVESTIGATION METHODS

Undercover Drug Operations

Undercover drug operations are covert investigations of individuals, circumstances, and activities believed to be contributing to the spread of illegal drugs. These include drug sales, trafficking, distribution, manufacturing, and diversion activities.

Such operations can be extremely dangerous for undercover investigators because of the many unforeseen and uncontrollable circumstances that may occur when dealing with suspects. Effective planning, safety precautions, and information gathering are all key elements to carrying out a successful and safe undercover drug operation.

Like most other types of undercover investigations, those focusing on illicit drugs usually begin with the identification of suspects, organizations, or other targets suspected to be engaging in some aspect of the illegal drug trade. These initial leads can be produced by reactive means such as anonymous tips, information provided by informants, surveillance activities, or perhaps direct observation by patrol officers. Leads can also be procured through proactive measures, namely the undercover buying and selling of drugs to suspects by investigators. After a likely drug-related target has been identified, a decision may be made to immediately arrest a suspect or to raid a location believed to be linked to illegal drugs. On the other hand, it may be decided to postpone the arrest of drug operatives so that intelligence can be gathered on possible higher-level "players" engaging in organized drug distribution networks. In these cases, the goal of the undercover investigator is to infiltrate an illegal organization by establishing a relationship of trust with persons who can provide information about the nature and scope of the organization's illegal drug operations.[29]

Buy Operations

Perhaps the riskiest aspect of any undercover investigator's drug work is engaging in *buy operations* of controlled substances. The buy may be a one-time event where the undercover investigator purchases illegal drugs and then immediately arrests the suspect, referred to as a **buy-bust**. This method can be useful as an information gathering tool if deals can be made with an arrestee to provide information about other illegal drug-related persons, places, and activities in exchange for a reduction in charges or some other form of legal leniency. One potential negative aspect of a buy-bust is a blown cover, in which that investigator's identity is revealed to the suspect and perhaps other potential suspects where undercover drug operations are being conducted.

Conversely, a decision might be made to perform a **buy-walk** in which the investigator makes a drug purchase without an immediate arrest in hopes that the unwitting suspect will provide additional information leading to the identification and arrest of more suspects. This method is quite appropriate for attempting to identify persons at higher levels within larger-scale drug organizations. For example, the initial purchase of drugs on the street can create a snowball lead when investigators persuade dealers to connect them with the persons from whom they obtain illegal drugs. Larger buy-walks conducted with suppliers at secondary levels beyond the street may lead to more powerful figures at even higher levels, and so on. This process usually culminates with a large-scale buy-bust sting designed to provide a coordinated mass arrest of as many suspects in as many places as possible. As can be imagined, undercover operations such as these involving multiple drug buys are exceedingly dangerous and require the utmost detailed planning and information gathering.

In conducting any buy situation, the investigator should remember several basic rules. First, take charge of the buy location. That is, the investigator should always decide where the buy is going to take place and should never let the seller plan or change a buy location. Sellers demanding a particular buy location are perhaps planning to set up the officers for a money rip off. In addition, outdoor buy locations are always preferable to those indoor locations. Quick back-up responses and surveillance activities are more difficult when a buy takes place in a room or some other enclosed area. Second, take special precautions when using an informant. Make sure the informant's information is accurate by corroborating it with existing intelligence sources. If informants are conducting a drug buy, make sure that they are examined thoroughly immediately afterward to ensure that all of the drugs purchased are accounted for and not pocketed by the informant. The serial numbers of any money given to informants for purchasing drugs should be recorded as well. Third, always be aware of any counterintelligence activities (i.e., suspects conducting surveillance on investigators) being conducted by persons to whom the drugs are sold. Counterintelligence on the part of potential sellers is to be expected in larger buy situations, and may also be a signal that some form of foul play could occur before, during, or after the buy. Last, and foremost, all buy activities should be recorded by wiring the undercover officer with a concealed recording device and/or by undercover surveillance videotaping of the buy event. This documentation will prove invaluable for follow-up investigations, legal proceedings, and perhaps for securing confessions from suspects.

In addition to buy operations, investigators can also assume the role of a drug salesperson—a procedure often referred to as a **reverse-buy**. This method, however, can present both logistical and legal challenges. For example, drugs presented for sale by the investigator may be stolen by the prospective buyer. The theft can occur by forceful means, such as a planned hold-up, or by a passive technique whereby the buy presents the investigator with a dummy bag—a package believed to contain money, but that instead contains worthless items such as towels, paper, or sheets. In addition, the arrest of suspects under reverse-buy conditions always begs the legal question of entrapment. Suspects are likely to assert in their defense that the undercover officers entrapped them by somehow illegally encouraging the sale of the illegal drugs rather than merely providing an opportunity to purchase the drugs. Suspects may claim that the investigator "made me feel sorry for him," or that "she promised me sexual favors in return for the drug purchase," both of which are rationales that would likely support the legal claim of entrapment.[30]

HOT TIPS AND LEADS 18.1

Conducting Controlled Drug Buys

Controlled drug buys are often used to corroborate information provided to investigators by a confidential informant (CI) regarding the location of suspected drug activities, and details of the buy are commonly used to show probable cause in an affidavit to obtain a search warrant for the suspected drug location. Even though using a CI to conduct a controlled buy is standard practice in many narcotics investigations, nevertheless there are special precautions that investigators should take when conducting this type of an operation:

1. First, and foremost, never trust informants. They will burn investigators if they see that doing so will be to their personal or financial benefit.

2. Thoroughly document the informant. Perform a detailed background check on new informants and make files on them including personal identifying information, code names, and payments made to them. Keep the file in a secure location accessible only to supervisors or other restricted personnel.

3. Debrief the informant: Gather as much information as possible from the informant about the target and target location where the controlled by is going to take place. If possible, gather mug shots, driver's license photos, or other photos of the target and have the informant identify them. Conduct surveillance of the target and target location to corroborate debriefing information provided by the informant. Assess the informant's motivation for participating in the buy operation as well as other reasons for becoming a CI. During all contact times with the CI, have a second investigator present to serve as a witness.

4. Search the informant and the informant's vehicle before the buy. This is the only way that investigators can ensure that any drugs presented after the buy were not supplied by the informants themselves.

5. Document the buy money. Have the informant sign for the money upon receipt (with a second investigator present), and record serial numbers from or make photocopies of the bills. Recorded bills found at the buy location or on the target provides investigators with strong evidence for prosecution. Any buy money robbed from the CI during the operation can possibly be recovered later from the offender or another location.

6. If practical, have the informant wear a recording device or body wire. This will serve to document the buy operation.

7. Observe the informant entering and exiting the buy location. Surveillance of the informant should be continued from the point of departure to the buy location until the informant arrives to meet with investigators at a predetermined place after the buy. It is necessary to instruct the informant that no stops be made en route. After the buy, when the informant has left the target location, a member of the surveillance team should continue to watch the location for other persons arriving or suspicious activities.

8. Conduct a postbuy search of the informant and the informant's vehicle. Informants may attempt to steal money or drugs obtained in the buy. Submit drugs or other physical evidence for laboratory analysis. Arrangements can also be made to have the CI call the target after the buy to recount the events of the meeting, which is recorded for evidence.

9. Conduct a postbuy debriefing of the informant. Obtain detailed information about what transpired between the CI and the target during the buy. If required, prepare a statement containing the information provided and have it signed by the CI and witnessed by a second investigator.

10. Make cash payment to the informant. Document and make all agreed-upon payments in the presence of a second investigator so that the CI cannot allege any financial wrongdoing on the part of investigators later.

Source: From "Wrong-Door Raids, Phantom Informants and the Controlled Buy," by Dennis G. Fitzgerald, THE CHAMPION, November 2009, p. 36. © 2009 National Association of Criminal Defense Lawyers, www.nacdl.org. Reprinted by permission.

Drug Raids

Drug raids involve coordinated assault-style search-and-seizure operations directed at both indoor and outdoor locations where suspected illegal drug activities are, in most cases, currently taking place. The danger involved in conducting a raid cannot be overstated. Stories about lawsuits against investigative agencies who have raided a residence at the wrong address or, even worse, injured innocent by-standers or their own officers as the result of an ill-planned raid. If done correctly, however, a drug raid can result in the safe and immediate legal closure of even the most sophisticated drug operation.

The essential element of any successful drug raid is the element of surprise. This, however, requires the coordination of planned movements by highly trained officers comprising a raid team. Specialized personnel comprised of 5 to 7 SWAT members often form the drug raid team. Preraid planning will necessarily include the acquisition of search warrants naming locations, suspects, drugs, drug manufacturing items, and other things to be searched for and ultimately seized. Evidence in support of preraid warrants can be provided through sworn informant statements, surveillance, wire taps, undercover buys/ sells of drugs, or patrol arrests of suspects holding/using drugs in and around the intended drug-raid location. Attempts should not be made to gain entry to perform a raid, without a warrant, under the guise of performing health and safety inspections or some other false pretense. Other recommended preraid activities include the following:

1. ***Gather Intelligence:*** Identify and examine likely suspects, associates, the location or structure to be raided, and the neighborhood or geographic setting to be raided.

2. ***Conduct Reconnaissance:*** Use maps, aerial photos, Google satellite imaging, undercover operatives, and so on to conduct reconnaissance of the raid location to determine street/trail configurations, entrances/exits to the location or of a dwelling, traffic or road obstacles, and other features.

3. ***Pictorial Layout:*** Create a pictorial layout of the raid area depicting locations of key suspects/evidence to be identified or collected and illustrate the movements and locations of personnel participating in the raid.

4. ***Logistics:*** Outline a detailed plan of the separate activities of personnel conducting the raid, equipment they will be using, the sequence of events/duties to be accomplished by each person/team, and contingency plans in the event certain aspects of the plan are not or cannot be accomplished.

5. ***Communications:*** Determine methods of communication (radio, verbal, nonverbal), frequencies used for radio communication, and lead contacts for unit-to-unit communication if a task force operation involving multiple agencies is ordered.

6. ***Emergency Response:*** Devise primary and backup plans for coordinating emergency personnel responses (fire, hazardous materials, EMTs, SWAT, etc.) to the raid.

7. ***Crime Lab Personnel:*** Consult with crime lab scientists, inform them of the nature of drugs located at the site, and make arrangement for safe collection and handling of chemical or other evidence that must be secured and removed from the raid site.

8. ***Postraid Activities:*** Create a debriefing plan to gather important on-site information and evidence resulting from the raid. Arrange for safe transportation of drugs, firearms, and other evidence from the site to secure storage locations. Postraid activities may also involve press conferences requiring the display of confiscated drugs, as shown in Figure 18.20. Determine whether and how personnel should be used to maintain the raid site after it has been initially cleared in the event that further follow-up investigative activities must be carried out.

To maximize the element of surprise, most raids begin with some form of unanticipated entry into the suspected illicit drug location using a no-knock warrant. When raiding indoor drug

(a)

(b)

FIGURE 18.20 ▶ (a) Evidence from a large-scale bulk cocaine drug bust. (b) A cocaine brick or *kilo* with a street value of between $40,000 and $50,000. The drug trafficker's name is stamped on its surface.

labs, crack houses, or other secured buildings, it is common to use battering rams, sledgehammers, armored vehicles, or even tractors to displace walls and doors. If flash-bang grenades or other incendiary devices are employed, care should be taken to ignite them where there is minimal risk of starting a fire or creating an explosion. Raids of outdoor drug operations, such as grow fields, require careful inspection of roads or paths traveled by raid teams to make sure that they are free of surveillance cameras, spotters, booby traps, and snipers. Before executing the raid, any information specifically relating to the location to be raided such as physical layout, number of persons present (including minor children), presence of weapons, type of drugs produced, or health and safety hazards present will prove invaluable for planning. When a drug manufacturing site is the target, it is especially important to determine the timing of drug production cycles; that is, it is best to perform a raid when a sufficient quantity of finished drugs is produced. This will result in the maximum penalty for manufacture of a scheduled drug rather than a lesser penalty for a scheduled drug's precursor agents. Once entry is made, the raid typically is carried out in a rapid three-part sequence of events: (1) securing suspects, (2) sweeping for hazards, and (3) searching

---

INFORMATION TO BE COLLECTED DURING CLAN LAB INVESTIGATIONS

1. Make drawings of the clan lab site.
2. Take photographs.
   - General overviews.
   - Close-ups.
   - Specific items during inventory.
   - Evidentiary samples and original containers.
   - Visible contamination.
   - Photograph site after removal of bulk materials.
3. Inventory.
   - Inventory all equipment and paraphernalia present in terms of quantity, size, manufacturer's serial number, condition and location
   - Inventory all chemical present for type, concentration and quantity
   - Describe unknown and unlabeled materials in terms of phase (solid, liquid, gas), color, volume/mass and appearance
   - Describe the type, size, condition and labeling of all containers

    a. Plastic, glass, metal
    b. Five-gallon, 2-ounce, etc.
    c. Punctured, rusty, leaking, corroded, damaged, uncapped, bulging.
   - Identify the location of leaking or broken containers
    a. Describe spilled solids or liquids, specifying odor, color, appearance, location, size of spill, etc.
   - Identify the leaking compressed-gas cylinders
   - Identify unstable container storage
   - Identify other concerns
4. Samples.
   - Take samples of appropriate items for evidence
   - One-ounce sample size usually is sufficient
   - Photograph samples and original containers with identifying labels
   - Maintain chain of custody

FIGURE 18.21 ▶ Investigative procedures used in a clan lab seizure. (Source: U.S. Drug Enforcement Administration posted at http://www.justice.gov/dea/resources/redbook.pdf)

for contraband.[31] Recommended procedures for conducting investigative activities at methamphetamine production sites are presented in Figure 18.21.

COLLECTION AND STORAGE OF DRUG EVIDENCE

The proper method for collecting and storing drug evidence depends on the type and amount of drug evidence seized. Most drug evidence is in the form of powders, liquids, tablets, invisible powders, or residues of plant/vegetable materials. In addition, items such as money, scales, manufacturing apparatus, packaging products, paraphernalia, and even vehicles may also be confiscated as drug-related evidence. Before beginning the drug evidence collection procedure, the first and primary consideration is the safety of personnel who must work the drug crime scene. Many drugs and their precursors are inherently dangerous biohazards, which when handled incorrectly can cause toxic reactions, fires, and perhaps explosions. This is especially the case when the crime scene is a clandestine methamphetamine laboratory, which will require evidence collection personnel handling chemicals at the scene to wear proper HAZMAT-approved personal protective gear. At the very least, gloves and protective breathing apparatus should be worn when dealing with drugs of an unknown nature. For example, certain liquid drugs can be absorbed through the skin when touched, and minute amounts of invisible powders from specific drugs can be inadvertently inhaled or ingested.

After safety concerns have been addressed, perform an appropriate presumptive color test on suspected drug materials. Positive results will constitute probable cause for arrest and seizure. As a general rule, never use more than one-tenth of all the drug evidence for color testing. When dealing with minute quantities of drugs or drug residues where the color test would involve using more than one-tenth of the evidence, skip the color test and submit the entire sample for testing at the crime lab.

Most solid drugs can be packaged as evidence in heat-sealed Kapak pouches. Small amounts of powders and drugs that are still in a fresh vegetative condition (e.g., freshly cultivated marijuana plants), however, are the exception to this rule. Because small powder particles will stick to the interior of Kapak pouches, this type of material should be packaged in leakproof paper envelopes or glass vials. If marijuana and other drugs in plant form have been dried, they can be placed in Kapak pouches without destroying the evidence. This procedure also applies to other vegetable drugs such as peyote, psilocybin, and opium poppies. If still moist, air dry these and any other drugs in plant form by placing them on sterile paper in a secure location until all moisture has been removed. If air drying cannot be executed, either package moist drug plants in paper envelopes/containers or freeze them until they can be handled in an appropriate manner later.

Liquid drugs, such as GHB and PCP, are often illegally transported in glass containers. These original glass containers can be packaged directly as evidence by placing them in an outer breakproof evidence container. Otherwise, the liquid drug can be transferred from its original container to a glass vial with a Teflon lining and a screw top that is stored in a plastic outer tube or other breakproof container. Liquid drugs contained within syringes should be collected and packaged using the latter method as well. Many crime labs will not accept syringes containing needles for testing. If a syringe is submitted, however, it must be packaged in a plastic or other container with a hard punctureproof exterior. Often, drug evidence contains fingerprint and DNA evidence as well. In these situations, the drug evidence should be separated from the packaging or other materials where it is suspected to be located. Separate evidence containers should be used for drug and fingerprint or DNA materials.

In cases involving large bulk seizures of drugs, it will be necessary to arrange for safe and secure transportation of the drug evidence away from the crime scene to an evidence storage facility. Regional drug task forces and the DEA's Drug Transportation Team usually can be contacted for assistance in these specialized transportation efforts. Care should be taken not to break the chain of custody when transporting evidence from a bulk drug seizure. Photographs should be taken at the crime scene and at all stages of the evidence transfer. It is advisable to have a supervising officer at the scene and to videotape the entire movement of all drugs to the containers and/or vehicles in which they will be transported. Once the evidence is at the storage facility, supervision by the same agent and videotaping should continue during the weighing and further processing procedures. Depending on existing policy, most jurisdictions require that samples be taken and tested from each drug package or container confiscated during the bulk seizure. After the samples are taken, and the evidence is no longer needed for legal purposes, it most likely will be destroyed by incineration, chemical neutralization, or an appropriate biohazard waste disposal method.[32]

RECONSTRUCTING A DRUG CRIME SCENE

Case Example 18B presents what is perhaps one of the most difficult crime scenes to investigate and process: a clan lab producing methamphetamine. As previously discussed in this chapter, these crime scenes pose many physical dangers to investigators who must secure and process them. Foremost among these hazards is the presence of dangerous and often volatile chemicals. The investigation of the case illustrated in Figures 18.22 to 18.34 requires detailed coordination of personnel at the scene to search for, collect, document, and package drug-related evidence at the scene.

CASE EXAMPLE 18B

Clan Lab Crime Scene

FIGURE 18.22 ▶ Outside overall view of house containing a clan lab, where drug raid operation was carried out. What preparations should be made by narcotics investigators prior to re-entering the lab to process the crime scene?

FIGURE 18.23 ▶ Crime scene perimeter with tape line attached to HAZMAT vehicle. What safety precautions should be employed at this scene?

FIGURE 18.24 ▶ Equipment and lighting set up to begin processing evidence. What special equipment or knowledge is required by narcotics investigators who are processing this scene?

FIGURE 18.25 ▶ Evidence collection begins with the removal of a box containing an item wrapped in paper. How should this and other evidence items at this scene be handled, packaged and transported?

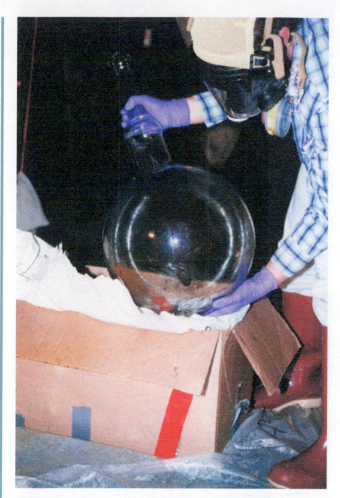

FIGURE 18.26 ▶ An investigator unwraps the contents to reveal a large "cooker."

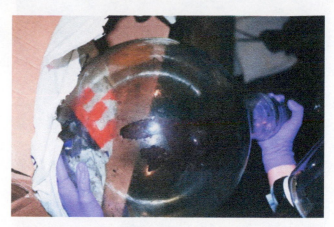

FIGURE 18.27 ▶ Close-up view of the "cooker" showing chemical residue. Of what value to the investigation is the cooker and the drug residue it contains?

FIGURE 18.28 ▶ Evidence collection staging area. What must be considered when setting up a staging area for the potentially volatile and dangerous chemicals at this scene?

FIGURE 18.29 ▶ Evidence labeling and inventory. Many of these items are legal household chemicals, but are they still considered evidence of illegal drug production in this case?

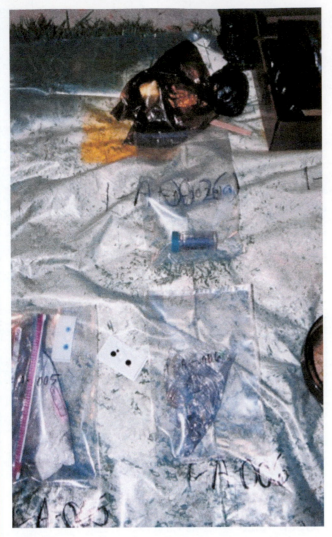

FIGURE 18.30 ▶ Specific evidence items being inventoried. Among these items there are numerous broken batteries packaged in the center evidence bag (containing lithium strips used for meth production).

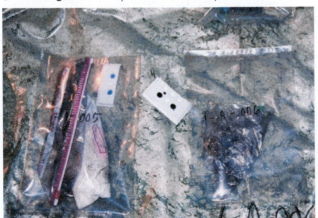

FIGURE 18.31 ▶ Evidence with results of presumptive field drug test. These tests, when positive, turn various colors depending upon the type of chemical substance being tested for. Assuming the bright blue color suggests that the white powder in the evidence bag (bottom left) is completely "cooked" meth, of what significance is this test result to the present investigation? What does the test result suggest regarding the production cycle of the drugs found at this scene?

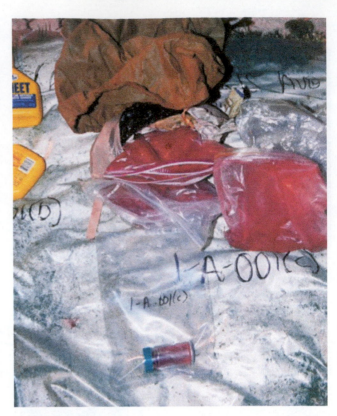

FIGURE 18.32 ▶ Chemicals in their original packaging repackaged in evidence bags. Pictures here is red phosphorus in powder form (bottom center evidence bag) and mixed with acid (center right plastic bags). Both are known chemical precursors of meth production.

FIGURE 18.33 ▶ Large quantity of capsules and tablets. Are factors such as the amount, manufacturer, and method of obtaining these pills important to the investigation?

FIGURE 18.34 ▶ Large glass "cooker" as originally packaged when seized during the raid. After making an overall assessment of the evidence at this scene, do the investigation suggest that this location is a "super" or a "mom and pop" lab? What other information and/or evidence could be gathered at this scene or in a follow-up investigation to make this determination?

Summary

1. **Classifications of illegal drugs.**

   Most drugs used for illegal purposes of concern to investigators fall within six broad categories: narcotics, stimulants, depressants, hallucinogens, and inhalants. Included within the general category of narcotics are drugs that are primarily used as pain killers or for anesthetic purposes. Stimulants are commonly referred to as *uppers* because persons who use them experience temporary feelings of increased physical stamina and enhanced mental awareness. Depressants, commonly known as *downers*, slowing down mind and body functions. The term *hallucinogenic drug* is derived from the word *hallucination*, which refers to an altered sensory state wherein things that do not exist in reality may be seen, felt, heard, tasted, or smelled. The term *inhalant* is used as a generic description for various chemical substances inhaled to produce a rush, or euphoric sensation.

2. **DEA Federal Drug Schedule system.**

   All recognized drugs, both prescription and illegal, are classified as Schedule I, II, III, IV, or V according to the DEA Federal Drug Schedule. Schedule I drugs are those such as heroin and LSD that have no accepted medical use. Schedule II drugs do have a current medical use but are severely restricted in their application because of their highly addictive qualities (for example, oxycodone and cocaine). Schedule III drugs, such as steroids and barbiturates, have medical applications but are less severely addictive than Schedule II drugs. Schedule IV drugs are used for medical purposes and have low potential for abuse compared to Schedule III drugs (for example, Xanax and Valium). Schedule V drugs have a medical use and are the least at-risk

   for abuse (for example, cough syrup containing codeine).

3. **Drug production and manufacturing locations.**

   Indoor cultivation of illegal marijuana plants, once restricted to rural locations, now is commonplace in suburban neighborhoods through the use of grow houses. Areas used for large-scale illegal marijuana or other organic drug growing activities, known as *grow fields* or *pot plantations*, are usually located within forested or agricultural settings. Rock houses, also called *crack houses*, are used primarily for the street sales of crack cocaine, but can also serve as a manufacturing location and a safe location for users to smoke, snort, or inject the drug. Clandestine laboratories, or *clan labs*, produce many forms of drugs, but about 80 percent of this production involves the "cooking" of methamphetamine.

4. **Specialized drug crime investigation methods.**

   The *buy bust* is a one-time event where the undercover investigator purchases illegal drugs and then immediately arrests the suspect. When the investigator makes a drug purchase without an immediate arrest in hopes that the unwitting suspect will provide additional information leading to the identification and arrest of more suspects, this technique is known as a *buy walk*. In cases where the investigator assumes the role of a drug salesperson, this method is called a *reverse-buy*. Drug raids involve coordinated assault-style search and seizure operations directed at both indoor and outdoor locations where suspected illegal drug activities are, in most cases, currently taking place.

Key Terms

narcotics	Schedule III	oxycodone
habituation	Schedule IV	ketamine
stimulants	Schedule V	mescaline
cocaine	THC	K-hole
crack	cannabinoids	barbiturates
methamphetamine	hashish	anabolic steroids
depressants	hash oil	roid rage
hallucinogens	cathine	grow house
flashbacks	GHB	grow field
inhalants	MDMA	rock house
huffed	peyote	clan lab
bagging	psilocybin	PPC (Personal Protective Clothing)
amphetamine psychosis	khat	precursor
SSD	hydrocodone	buy-bust
Controlled Substances Act (CSA)	PCP	buy-walk
drug schedule	morphine	reverse-buy
Schedule I	codeine	
Schedule II	speedballing	

Review Questions

1. What is a narcotic drug? Provide some examples and symptoms.
2. Identify some major street drugs that are classified as stimulants.
3. What are depressants and what behavioral effects can be noticed among people who abuse them?
4. What is an inhalant and how is it used?
5. What is the legal definition of a Schedule I drug? Provide some examples.
6. How do Schedule II drugs differ from those classified as Schedule I?
7. What is the legal definition of a Schedule III drug? Provide some examples.
8. What are Schedule IV and V drugs and how do they differ from each other?
9. What is a grow house and how can it be recognized?
10. Name some of the various types of clan labs and how they are identified.
11. What are some of the precautions that must be taken when investigating clan labs?
12. How does a buy-bust differ from a walk-bust?
13. What is a reverse-buy?
14. What is a drug raid and how should it be carried out?
15. Identify some of the important steps that should be taken when collecting drug evidence.

Internet Resources

U.S. Drug Enforcement Administration	www.justice.gov/dea/index.htm
Street Drug Identification	www.streetdrugs.org
Office of National Drug Control Policy	www.whitehousedrugpolicy.gov/streetterms

Applied Investigative Exercise

Select either Case Example 18A or 18B and discuss how you would conduct the following:

1. Preinvestigative intelligence gathering activities (e.g., reconnaissance) of the drug crime scene.
2. Undercover activities, surveillance, informant development, securing of warrants, and other preparations for a drug raid.
3. A drug raid of the premises, including providing for an adequate number of first responding personnel and necessary equipment.
4. Collection of the drug evidence, including identification, packaging, and transportation from the scene.

International Narcotic Enforcement Officers
   Association (INEOF)

www.ineoa.org/about/leadership.cfm

Ident-A-Drug (Online Drug Reference Guide)

intranet.trsecure.com/(S(221cbvjwmwlsdzyumgow2h45))/
home.aspx?cs=&s=ID

Notes

[1]U.S. Drug Enforcement Administration, posted at www.deadiversion.usdoj.gov/schedules/index.html.

[2]Ibid.

[3]Ibid.

[4]Ibid.

[5]U.S. Drug Enforcement Administration, *Drugs of Abuse*, posted at www.justice.gov/dea/pubs/abuse/doa-p.pdf.

[6]Ibid.

[7]Ibid.

[8]United Nations, *Bulletin on Narcotics*, posted at www.unodc.org/documents/data-and-analysis/bulletin/2006/Bulletin_on_Narcotics_2006_En.pdf.

[9]Ibid.

[10]Street Drugs.Org, *Streetdrugs*, posted at www.streetdrugs.org.

[11]Ibid.

[12]Ibid.

[13]Ibid.

[14]Ibid.

[15]Office of National Drug Control Policy, *Street Terms*, posted at www.whitehousedrugpolicy.gov/streetterms.

[16]Ibid.

[17]Ibid.

[18]Ibid.

[19]U.S. Drug Enforcement Administration, posted at www.deadiversion.usdoj.gov/schedules/index.html.

[20]National Drug Intelligence Center, *Ketamine Fast Facts*, posted at www.justice.gov/archive/ndic.

[21]U.S. Drug Enforcement Administration, *Drugs of Abuse*, posted at www.justice.gov/dea/pubs/drugs_of_abuse.pdf.

[22]U.S. Department of Justice, *Steroid Use in Today's Society*, posted at www.deadiversion.usdoj.gov/pubs/brochures/steroids/professionals/professionals.pdf.

[23]Office of National Drug Control Policy, *Prescription Drugs*, posted at www.whitehousedrugpolicy.gov/drugfact/prescrptn_drgs/index.html.

[24]U.S. Drug Enforcement Administration, *Drugs of Abuse*, posted at www.justice.gov/dea/pubs/drugs_of_abuse.pdf.

[25]U.S. Drug Enforcement Administration, *Press Release: 35 Charged, 28 Arrested in Connection with Port St. Lucy Marijuana Grow Houses*, posted at www.justice.gov/dea/pubs/states/newsrel/mia092006.html.

[26]U.S. Drug Enforcement Administration, *Press Release: DEA Task Force Eradicates $20 Million Marijuana Grow in CA National Forest*, posted at www.justice.gov/dea/pubs/states/newsrel/sd071408.html.

[27]U.S. Drug Enforcement Administration, *Cocaine*, posted at www.justice.gov/dea/concern/cocaine.html.

[28]Michael S. Scott and Kelly Dedel, *Clandestine Methamphetamine Labs*, 2nd ed. (Washington, DC: Office of Problem Oriented Policing, 2006), 14–35.

[29]Michael S. Lyman, *Practical Drug Enforcement* (Boca Raton, FL: CRC Press, 2002), 30–33.

[30]Ibid., 33.

[31]Ibid., 34.

[32]Ibid., 175–183.

TRANSNATIONAL, DOMESTIC, AND NARCO–TERROR SCENES

Learning Objectives

After completing the chapter, you should be able to:

1. Know the major forms of terrorist groups.
2. Discuss the various transnational terrorist organizations.
3. Explain domestic terrorism and domestic terrorist groups.
4. Understand the meaning and practice of narco–terrorism.
5. Summarize the acts and types of terrorism.

Chapter Outline

Defining Terrorism
- Past Political Definitions
- The Patriot Act Redefines Terrorism

Types of Terrorism

Transnational Terrorism
- Al-Qaeda
- Taliban
- Hezbollah
- HAMAS
- Other Terrorist Organizations

Transnational Terrorist Cell Structure

Motivations for Transnational Terrorism

Characteristics of Transnational Terror Attacks
- Methods of Attack
- Weapons, Injuries, and Deaths
- Victims of Terrorism
- Locations of Terror Attacks

Domestic Terrorism

Extremist Domestic Terror Groups
- Socio-political Terrorist Groups
- Special Cause Terrorist Groups
- Lone Wolf Terrorists

Narco–Terrorism

Mexican Narco–Terrorism
- Human Trafficking
- Transnational Terrorist Connections

Indicators of Terrorism and Initial Contact Questions
- General Indicators
- Initial Contact Questions

Special Terrorism Crime Scene Safety Concerns

Common Factors Among Terrorists

INTRODUCTION

TERRORISM IS THE NEW FRONTIER of American investigation. No longer can investigators isolate themselves within the boundaries of the cities, counties, states, or nations in which they investigate crimes. The case photo presented here (drawn from Case Example 19A later in this chapter) is a clear example of this fact. As the photo illustrates, scenes of suspected terrorist activities must be responded to and investigated in a highly specialized tactical manner in order to preserve human life as well as to preserve evidence at the scene. Whether terrorist acts are carried out by extremist groups from foreign nations or are committed by homegrown U.S. terrorists, investigators must be prepared for the challenges that terrorism poses to the practice of crime scene investigation.

DEFINING TERRORISM

Past Political Definitions

The act of terrorism has been defined in many ways historically, and its precise meaning continues to evolve today. Regardless of how terrorism is defined, the effects of terrorist activities can be overwhelming to the investigative mission, as illustrated in Figure 19.1, which shows the aftermath of catastrophic events transpiring at ground zero of the New York Trade Center on September 11, 2001 (hereafter simply referred to as *9/11*). Before this tragic event, terrorism was defined as a politically motivated act rather than a criminal act. This is evidenced by the longstanding FBI definition of terrorism as "the unlawful use of force or violence against persons or property to intimidate or coerce a government, the civilian population, or any segment thereof, in furtherance of political or social objectives."[1] The limited scope of this definition led to a rather narrow legal interpretation of which agencies should take the lead in investigating terrorist activities and what techniques should be employed in this investigative process. Thus, until issues surrounding the investigation of terrorism were put on the public's radar by 9/11, the CIA, FBI, U.S. Diplomatic Security Service (DSS), and other politically oriented intelligence gathering agencies performed terrorism investigations. All of this changed, however, when the public became keenly aware of the growing threat of both transnational and domestic terror on American soil. Before 9/11, several high-profile events of mass destruction caused the American public to rethink the longstanding politically oriented definition of terrorism:

- *The Lockerbie Bombing*—Abdelbaset al-Megrahi, a Libyan national, was convicted in Scottish courts of bombing Pan Am flight 103, which killed 270 persons. The doomed flight departed from London and was to arrive in New York City, but exploded in mid-air over Lockerbie, Scotland when a bomb was detonated in a suitcase within the aircraft's luggage hold. Physical evidence including an intact portion of the bomb's timing device and clothes wrapping the bomb inside the suitcase provided investigative leads culminating in the arrest and conviction of al-Megrahi. Although the exact motivations and terrorist groups responsible for the bombing remain unknown, the late Libyan dictator Muammar Gaddafi is believed to have personally ordered al-Megrahi to carry out the bombing as revenge against the United States for its military support of Israel.[2]

- *The 1993 World Trade Center Bombing*—Ramzi Yousef, a self-admitted terrorist with ties to al-Qaeda in Afghanistan, constructed and detonated a half-ton bomb that caused damaged the World Trade Center and killed seven and injured 1,047 persons.[3]

- *The 1995 Oklahoma City Bombing*—Timothy McVeigh, a U.S. citizen who sought revenge against the U.S. federal government, planned and executed an act of domestic terror second only to 9/11 for causing the most destruction in America. His bombing of the Murrah Federal Building in Oklahoma City resulted in 168 deaths and injuries to 680 persons.[4]

The Patriot Act Redefines Terrorism

The high-profile terrorism occurring during the late 1980s and 1990s increased awareness among American citizens and law enforcement that terrorist activities resulting in death and injury can rival, if not exceed, similar acts carried out by ordinary criminals. It was the U.S. Congressional response to 9/11, however, that initiated formal substantive and legal changes in the definition of terrorism with the passage of the **Patriot Act** (formally, USA Patriot Act) signed into law by President George W. Bush in October 2001. In signing the act, President Bush articulated the need to redefine terrorism as a legal offense of a criminal nature as opposed to a political concern. This was made clear when the president, during his endorsement of the Patriot Act, drew a direct analogy between terrorism and organized crime,

FIGURE 19.1 ▶ Aerial view of the transnational terrorist crime scene at New York City's World Trade Center following September 11, 2001. (Chao Soi Cheong/Associated Press)

stating "al Qaeda is to terror what the Mafia is to crime." This new view of terror as a crime is expressed in Title 18 of the U.S. Code, which generally defines terrorism as:

> violent acts or acts dangerous to human life that are a violation of the criminal laws of the United States or of any State, or that would be a criminal violation if committed within the jurisdiction of the United States or of any State [which] appear to be intended to intimidate of coerce a civilian population, to influence the policy of government by intimidation or coercion, or to affect the conduct of government by mass destruction, assassination, or kidnapping.[5]

Furthermore, the Patriot Act clearly distinguishes between acts of (1) "international terrorism," violations of the law that occur outside the territorial boundaries of the United States, and (2) "domestic terrorism," terror activities occurring within U.S. borders or territories. The creation of a separate legal classification for domestic terrorism has broadened antiterrorism enforcement powers to include the following:

1. Openly representing or seeking support for the acts of terrorist groups, regardless of membership status in a terrorist organization.

2. Raising money for or giving money to a terrorist group to support an act of terrorism, provided that funds are used to plan or conduct an act of terrorism.

3. Providing services to or assisting terrorists with knowledge that such funds will be used to promote terrorism.

4. Knowingly providing a hideout, transportation, training, firearms, or other goods and services to terrorists.

5. Being an immediate family member of a terrorist and also being openly aware of the relative's terrorist activities.

6. Being a spouse or child of a terrorist who has not renounced their husband's or father's involvement in terrorism.

In addition to these illegal associational aspects of terrorism, several specific criminal activities are identified as potential acts of terror under the Patriot Act:

1. Threatening, conspiring, or attempting to hijack airplanes, boats, buses, or other vehicles.

2. Threatening, conspiring, or attempting to commit acts of violence on protected persons, e.g., government officials.

3. Committing any crime (excluding those for mere personal monetary gain) with any weapon or dangerous device and intending to endanger public safety or commit substantial property damage.[6]

TYPES OF TERRORISM

Numerous classifications of terrorist groups are available, but for investigators working inside the United States the primary types of terrorism are transnational, domestic, and narco–terrorism.

Transnational terrorism, otherwise referred to as *international terrorism,* involves persons from one country perpetrating acts of terror against citizens, governments, institutions, or other entities of another country. Clearly, the 9/11 incident is defined as an act of transnational terror based on various factors. For example, the al-Qaeda terrorists responsible for the World Trade Center bombing had their roots in Middle Eastern countries and targeted their attack on the United States. Also, the large number of foreign nationals killed by the bombing could also quality the attack as a transnational act of terror. From an investigative standpoint, it is essential that both domestic and foreign investigators share intelligence information on transnational terror incidents to apprehend offenders and curb future terrorist activities.

In contrast, domestic or homegrown terrorism is restricted to acts where the offenders and victims all are of the same country. In the United States, many acts of domestic terror have been perpetrated by both lone offenders (for example, Timothy McVeigh in the Oklahoma City bombing) and organized groups. Among organized U.S. domestic terror groups, the FBI has identified the Earth Liberation Front (E.L.F) as a top concern due to E.L.F's recent arson attacks on construction sites, which have cost insurance companies millions of dollars in reparation costs. Hate crimes are also a common form of domestic terror, often involving physical assaults on persons and/or property for reasons of race, religion, or sexual orientation. Investigating these crimes requires local, state, and federal law agencies to share information due to the expanding inter-state networks of domestic terrorists.

Finally, narco–terrorism is yet another major concern for investigators both domestically and abroad. Narco–terrorists use violence, fear, and intimidation to further illegal drug sales activities that provide personal profits and fund their continuing criminal enterprises. Narco–terrorists could be said to be merely a subclass of transnational terrorists because they typically smuggle drugs from another country to other countries—especially across the U.S. border. In comparison to traditional transnational terror groups, however, narco–terrorists are much more motivated to commit crimes out of personal financial greed rather than for social or political causes. Nonetheless, narco–terrorist tactics are just as ruthless, violent, and dangerous to human life as those used by any other terrorist. Thus far, domestic narco–terrorism investigations have relied greatly on the ability of local law enforcement and U.S. antidrug agencies to interdict drug shipments and traffickers when they arrive in American ports of entry. Human trafficking, extortion, money laundering, and murder are just some of the many other criminal activities carried out by narco–terrorists.

TRANSNATIONAL TERRORISM

Transnational terrorism can originate from virtually any country, but the largest and most sophisticated terror organizations posing the greatest threat to U.S. security are of Islamic background originating from Iraq, Afghanistan, Pakistan, and

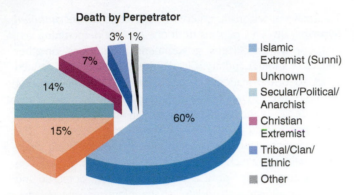

Death by Perpetrator

- Islamic Extremist (Sunni)
- Unknown
- Secular/Political/Anarchist
- Christian Extremist
- Tribal/Clan/Ethnic
- Other

FIGURE 19.2 ▶ Of all deaths attributed to terrorist activities in 2009, the majority (60%) were perpetrated by Islamic extremist (Sunni) groups. (Source: National Counter Terrorism Center, 2011)

various Arabic nations. In 2009, as shown in Figure 19.2, approximately 60 percent of all transnational terror attacks were carried out by Sunni Islamic extremists.[7] These individuals belong to a radical splinter group that broke away from mainstream Muslims to practice what they believe to be a purer form of Islam. They also believe that international alliances blending religious ideologies, and especially that between the United States and Israel, are conspiracies to destroy Muslims and must be dealt with by violence and terror. Other groups responsible for terrorist attacks include secular/political anarchists and Christian extremist groups, which carried out 14 percent and 7 percent of reported transnational terrorist incidents, respectively. The following sections describe organizations most likely to be encountered during the course of investigating acts of transnational terrorism.

Al-Qaeda

Al-Qaeda, also known as *the base,* is now considered one of the most dangerous and potent terrorist groups in the world. The group, founded during the mid-1980s, consisted of loosely knit rebels fighting in resistance to the Soviet Army's invasion of Afghanistan. Members of al-Qaeda are militant Sunni rebels who believe in the expulsion of Western influence from Muslim nations by means of violence and terror. Their motivation is purely religious in nature, unlike many other terrorist groups, which are motivated by political conflict. A driving force for al-Qaeda's terrorist activities is their concept of a holy war, or **jihad** against foreign influences in the Muslim world that are perceived to be a direct threat to their Islamic faith.[8]

Considerable debate exists regarding the size and organizational structure of today's al-Qaeda. Some intelligence experts contend that the group is highly organized and centralized with a defined leadership structure. Other sources of intelligence suggest that the group's core membership consists of only 20 to 30 members who serve as figureheads and advisors to fringe terrorist organizations with weak or nonexistent ties to the central al-Qaeda organization. After the Soviet war in Afghanistan

over two decades ago, Osama bin Laden served as a central leader of al-Qaeda's field operations until he was killed by U.S. Navy SEALs on May 1, 2011 at his compound near Islamabad, Pakistan. Before his demise, FBI investigators attempted to locate bin Laden by placing him on their 10 Most Wanted List of criminals and offering a $25 million dollar reward for information leading to his capture.

Besides 9/11, many of the most recent destructive terrorist acts targeting western countries have been associated with al-Qaeda operatives. For example, Moroccan terrorists claiming to be al-Qaeda associates perpetrated the 2004 Madrid Bombing, killing 202 persons and injuring 1,400 by detonating a bomb at a Madrid railway station—believed to be the worst terrorist incident in Spain's history. Similarly, perpetrators claiming ties to al-Qaeda were responsible for bomb blasts in a London subway in 2005, resulting in 52 deaths and about 700 injuries. The following are other, less recent terrorist attacks by al-Qaeda:

- 1998—The U.S. Embassies in Nairobi, Kenya, and Dar es Salaam, Tanzania were struck nearly simultaneously by truck bombs driven by an al-Qaeda suicide operative, causing an explosion that killed 216 and injured nearly 5,000 others in Nairobi; 11 persons were killed and over 100 were injured in Dar es Salaam.

- 2000—The naval ship U.S.S. *Cole* was struck by a small craft driven by a suicide bomber carrying some 700 pounds of high explosives, killing 17 U.S. sailors. The terrorists claiming responsibility for the attack claimed they were operating under direct orders from Osama bin Laden.[9]

These terrorist acts and crimes of terror targeting the West are believed to have been motivated by the participation of western nations and the United States in military activities within the Middle East—specifically, in Iraq and Afghanistan. It is not known, however, whether al-Qaeda operatives are directly responsible for these and similar terrorist activities or whether smaller, less known groups are merely claiming al-Qaeda affiliation in admiration of the group's religious mission and status as a terrorist organization. Besides western nations and other influences believed to be destructive to Islam, the country of Israel and Israeli nationals living abroad are central targets of militant Muslim extremists claiming ties to al-Qaeda. The most recent and serious attack against the United States since 9/11 for which al-Qaeda claims responsibility was in 2009, when a suicide bomber struck a military base in Afghanistan, killing eight Americans, seven of whom were CIA agents.

Taliban

The **Taliban** are a group of Sunni fundamentalists formed in the early 1990s following the Soviet-Afghan War, over a decade after the formation of al-Qaeda. The group is considered an Islamic religious sect as well as the legitimate political arm of al-Qaeda extremist ideologies. Beginning in 1996, the Taliban were established as rulers of the Afghanistan government and are noted for their offering of sanctuary to terrorists, including bin Laden following the 9/11 attacks. The Taliban are now believed to be providing a home base for operations and training of al-Qaeda operatives and many other affiliated terrorist groups in Afghanistan and/or in locations of Taliban allies such as the Pakistan Federally Administered Tribal Areas (FATA). Afghanistan, under the political control of the Taliban, produces much of the world's illicit heroin supply, cultivated from state-supported opium poppy farms spread across the country. Money obtained from illicit heroin sales is used to support terrorist operations sponsored by the Taliban.[10]

Hezbollah

Hezbollah, aka *the party of God,* is composed of Muslim Shi'ite militants operating mainly from Lebanon, but with cells in Europe, Africa, South America, North America, and Asia. They were formed in the early 1980s as a rebel fighting force to counter the invasion of Lebanon by Israeli troops. During this time, they were heavily influenced by Iranian Shi'ites, who aided them in their fight against Israel and developed their current extremist ideology that calls for the destruction of the state of Israel and other countries that support the Israeli cause—including the United States. Specific acts of terror orchestrated by Hezbollah against the United States include the 1984 suicide bombing of two U.S. marine bases in Beirut, which killed over 300 persons, many of whom were Marine and Navy personnel; the bombing of the U.S. Embassy in Beirut, also in 1984, killing 14 people; and the hijacking of TWA flight 847 involving the death of a U.S. Navy diver and holding the plane's passengers hostage for 2 weeks. Although Hezbollah is now a legitimate political influence in the Lebanese government, intelligence sources have revealed that the group is still involved in planning and executing terrorism in conjunction with Iranian Shi'ite militants, the Taliban, and al-Qaeda.[11]

HAMAS

HAMAS, also known as the Palestinian Islamic Resistance Movement, was founded in 1987 as an extension of the long-standing Muslim Brotherhood group centered in Palestine. They combine politics with terror, calling for jihad against Israel and its people. Their ultimate goal is to destroy Israel and convert the nation into an Islamic Palestinian state. Although HAMAS has not thus far targeted U.S. interests for terrorist attacks, the group has a violent history involving kid- napping and armed assaults against Israelis and other persons they call "the enemy." HAMAS members have been known to kill their own with friendly gunfire during armed encounters with their adversaries. Besides conducting terror activities, they operate as a legitimate political force recruiting members from mosques, raising and soliciting funds, and distributing propaganda materials.[12]

Other Terrorist Organizations

Most of the terrorist organizations posing the greatest immediate threat within U.S. borders are either associated with al-Qaeda or are somehow aligned with Muslim extremists fighting for an Islamic state. Currently, the U.S. State Department has a list of 45 designated terrorist organizations throughout the world. Most of these groups have base operations in Middle Eastern countries but increasingly are either radical Islamists or secular terrorists with an established presence in countries outside the Middle East. Some of these include Al Shabaab, aka *al-Qaeda in Somalia* or *The Youth* (Somalia); The Movement for the Emancipation of the Niger Delta, aka *MEND* (Nigeria); Abu Sayyaf Group (Philippines); Revolutionary Armed Forces of Columbia, aka *FARC* (Columbia); and the Irish Republican Army, aka *IRA* (Ireland).[13]

TRANSNATIONAL TERRORIST CELL STRUCTURE

Terrorist groups, especially the larger and more organized ones, operate in a **terrorist cell** organizational structure similar to that shown in Figure 19.3. Typically, there are 3–10 persons per cell. The cells are organized in a decentralized fashion, each with its own individual leader. Usually, each cell has a specialized function such as intelligence, sniping, bombings, robberies, or kidnapping. Very rarely does one cell know about the activities of other cells. This loose organization and communication style is devised intentionally for security reasons: If one cell is detected and caught by law enforcement, the cell members cannot provide information on the activities and locations of other cells. Typically, only one or a few individuals known as *planners* know about the coordinated activities of all cells during a terrorist attack. Therefore, the only effective means of thwarting terrorist actions is to identify and

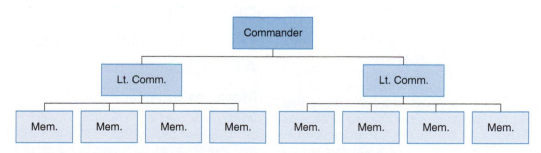

FIGURE 19.3 ▶ The organizational structure of a typical terrorist cell.

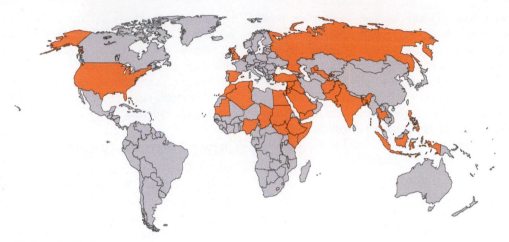

FIGURE 19.4 ▶ Countries in which Islamist terrorist attacks have occurred on or after September 11, 2001.

gain intelligence from planners before an attack has been set into motion. For example, in 9/11, each cell carrying out the coordinated bombing of the World Trade Center, the Pentagon, and the hijacking of an additional jetliner that never reached its bombing destination had little knowledge of the overall terror plan.

Of specific concern to investigators in the United States is terrorist *sleeper cells*—small groups of terrorists that are dormant or on stand-by, ready to execute orders from the main terrorist organization's leaders. In the United States, sleeper cells are located in various cities and rural venues. Their members are a mixture of persons smuggled from other countries, students attending college on visas, native-born individuals of foreign parents, or persons otherwise living in the United States with legitimate immigration status. Most members of sleeper cells are young, single males, but women and children also can play an active role because they are less likely to attract the attention of law enforcement. Children may serve as curriers of information, documents, weapons, and other items necessary to plan or initiate a terror strike. Women can be fighters, but typically serve in a support role by acting as couriers, gathering intelligence, operating safe houses, securing and organizing funds, acquiring weapons, and preparing/delivering documents. The socio-economic background of sleeper cell members also is mixed. Some are lower-class urban youths, while others—particularly in larger, more sophisticated organizations—are older, well-educated middle- and upper-class professionals. Although many members of sleeper cells live within the United States, many live in towns directly outside the U.S. border in Canada and Mexico to avoid detection by American law enforcement. If called to duty, these sleeper cell members may simply cross the U.S. border to carry out attacks on American soil and then retreat across the border to their permanent Canadian or Mexican residences.[14] As Figure 19.4 illustrates for Islamic terrorist attacks, countries throughout the entire world may already have sleeper cells in place to carry out acts of terrorism.

MOTIVATIONS FOR TRANSNATIONAL TERRORISM

Terrorists differ most from conventional criminal groups in regard to their motivations for committing violent acts. Street gangs, for example, direct violence at specific individuals or targets for purposes of personal revenge. Conversely, terrorists use generalized violence on random targets to maximize shock value and draw the greatest amount of attention to their cause. When the terrorists' attacks are not random, however, they focus on persons, places, or things that will draw the most attention if victimized. The primary motivation behind terrorist acts to cause governments or other groups to (1) take actions that further the terrorists' interests or (2) terminate actions contrary to their interests. These goals are further accomplished by garnering the most media attention possible. If the media become complacent about covering a particular terrorist group's acts of terror, the group often changes attack strategies from bombing, to armed assaults, to kidnapping, and so on to renew media interest. Terrorist groups' primary motivating interests include politics, economics, religion, and special causes.

CHARACTERISTICS OF TRANSNATIONAL TERROR ATTACKS

Methods of Attack

Investigators need to be familiar with the standard methods of attack used by terrorists to identify various M.O.s associated with terrorism. As shown in Figure 19.5, the most common method is bombing—used in approximately 61 percent

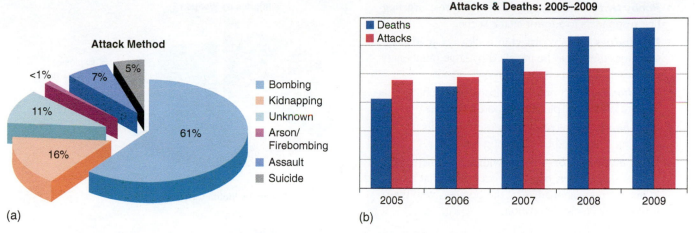

FIGURE 19.5 ▶   (a) Bombing is by far the most frequently used method of attack by Transnational Terrorists. (b) As this chart indicates, the number of terrorist attacks has appeared to stabilize; however, they have become increasingly lethal (Source: National Counter Terrorism Center, 2011)

of known terror attacks. Consequently, it is essential for investigators to know the specific bombing styles used by terrorists:

- ***Car bombs and truck bombs***—the vehicle is filled with explosives and may contain a booby trap under a seat, the hood, or the main body. Figure 19.6 shows many of the typical areas in a vehicle that will be used by terrorists to conceal a bomb.
- ***Motorcycle bomb***—the motorcycle contains saddle bags filled with explosives.
- ***Individual suicide bomb***—the bomber wears a self-detonating explosive vest.

- ***Postal bombs***—delivered and disguised as letters or packages.
- ***Grenades***—placed in containers that detonate when opened, or just simply thrown at targets.
- ***Road bombs***—bombs placed in roadways to destroy vehicles.
- ***Trashcan and mailbox bombs***—explosives that detonate when the object is opened.
- ***Firebombs***—often time-delayed bombs that start arson fires after exploding.
- ***Bicycle bombs***—ridden by suicide bombers into their targets.

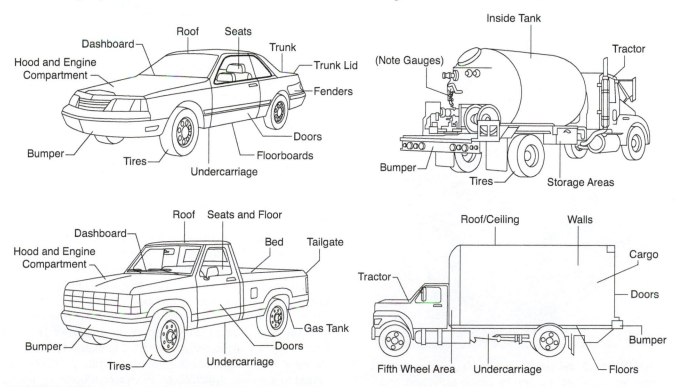

FIGURE 19.6 ▶   Popular locations for vehicle bomb placement and concealment.

- **Booby traps**—often triggered by trip wires, targeting first responders to a terror attack scene.
- **Landmines**—bombs placed in walkways, roadways, and areas thought to be travelled by large numbers of persons or first responders.
- **Nail bombs**—high or low explosives containing nails that are capable of piercing armored surfaces.
- **Wall bombs**—explosives hidden inside walls that may have been disguised by plastering over them.
- **Walk-away bombs**—bombs within containers such as suitcases, briefcases, bags, and backpacks that are placed in heavily populated areas by the bomber, who then walks away before detonation.[15]

Many of these bombing methods, particularly those using cars, trucks, and bicycles, can be used in a suicide mission. In these instances, the bombers are men, women, or children who sacrifice their lives to advance the terrorist cause. If the particular bomb used by the terrorists does not rely on suicide detonation, it typically will be detonated by (1) remote activation using radio signals, electronic lead wires, pull wires attached to mechanical strikers, or electronic signals from cell phones or microwave devices; (2) target activation, including trip wires, pressure/movement sensors, or an electronic triggering mechanism such as a switch or key; or (3) timed activation whereby clocks, fuses, or atmospheric, weight, or chemical changes are used to trigger a physical detonator. Certain types of explosives used by terrorists can be detonated by simply firing a bullet into them or exposing them to fire. Figure 19.7 shows a suicide bomber's vest-type explosive device that enables the bomber to arm and detonate an explosion manually through hand-held switches.

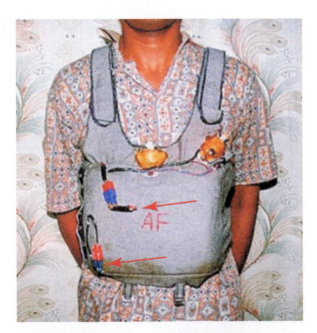

FIGURE 19.7 ▶ Suicide bomber's vest. Note that there are two switches: one for bomb activation, and the other for bomb detonation.

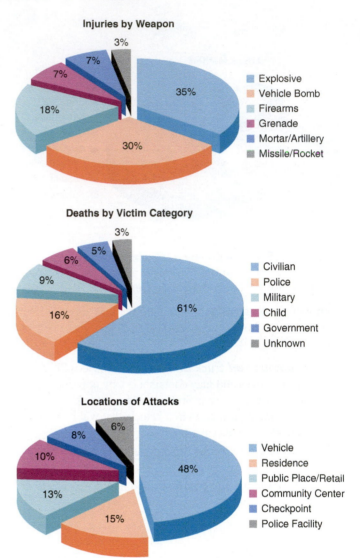

FIGURE 19.8 ▶ Percentage breakdown of weapons used, deaths by victim categories, and locations of known terrorist attacks. (Source: National Counter Terrorism Center, 2011)

Weapons, Injuries, and Deaths

Figure 19.8 provides a breakdown of popular weapons used by terrorists that have resulted in injuries, in addition to victim deaths and locations of terrorist attacks.

Explosives not involving vehicles account for about one-third of all injuries produced by terrorist acts. Nearly as many injuries (30 percent) are caused by explosives contained in some type of vehicle—usually cars or trucks (see Figure 19.9). Because terrorists desire to produce mass injuries with one attack, they typically employ high explosives. Terrorists are well versed at making IEDs (Improvised Explosive Devices) from nearly any explosive, as illustrated in Figure 19.10, which shows a bomb fashioned from military artillery rounds connected to a makeshift detonator. From recent bombing attacks with IEDs, the military-grade explosive Semtex appears to be

(a)

(a)

(b)

FIGURE 19.11 ▶ (a) Favored weaponry of transnational terrorists, the AK-47 rifle (b) armed with a 30-round "banana" magazine.

(b)

FIGURE 19.9 ▶ (a) Makeshift bedliner of a terrorist's pickup with rifles and bombs beneath it. (b) Propane canister filled with high explosives ready to be detonated.

FIGURE 19.10 ▶ Terrorists are well-versed in making powerful IEDs from military explosives such as mortar and artillery shells.

the main component of terrorist bombs, but terrorists may also use commercially available chemicals to create IEDs. Second only to explosives, firearms are terrorists' next preferred injury-producing weapon—causing about one in every five terrorism-related injuries. Firearms associated with terror attacks include handguns, assault rifles, sniper rifles, submachine guns, and machine guns (see Figures 19.11 and 19.12).

Following firearms weapon injuries are those related to military explosive devices, namely grenades and missiles or mortars. Terrorists trained in the handling of military explosives, if provided access to these devices in the United States, would not hesitate to use them against targets within U.S. borders. In past terrorist strikes occurring outside the United States, terrorists have preferred to use rocket propelled grenades (RPGs). The RPG, originally an anti-tank weapon, has been used by terrorists to destroy buildings, armored vehicles, and aircraft. Additionally, and most deadly, are mortars, often fired from tubes attached to hijacked trucks or van. These

FIGURE 19.12 ▶ Arsenal of weapons confiscated from al-Qaeda terrorists in Iraq revealing the diversity in firepower available to this and other terrorist groups.

weapons are very inaccurate and can be fired only one at a time at large targets such as buildings or large storage tanks. Last, and hopefully never a reality on American soil, are weapons of mass destruction **(WMDs)**. These include nuclear, chemical, and biological weaponry. The type of WMD posing the greatest imminent terrorist threat to civilian populations is the *dirty bomb*. These devices produce a limited explosion that releases radiological material in and around the bombing site. In most cases, these bombs produce delayed rather than immediate death from prolonged sickness caused by radiation exposure. Furthermore, the site of a dirty bomb explosion generally is uninhabitable for 4 years or more due to residual radiation. In general, within recent years the number of terror attacks interestingly has been relatively stable; however, the number of deaths has been increasing. This trend suggests that terrorists are becoming increasingly more lethal in their attacks.[16]

Victims of Terrorism

Most victims of terrorism are simply in the wrong place at the wrong time when terrorists strike a random target of opportunity. Unfortunately, most of those dying from a terror attack are civilians. Civilians account for approximately three out of every four deaths at the hands of terrorists. Second most likely to be killed in a terrorist attack are police, comprising 16 percent of terror-related deaths. Deaths of children, government workers, businesspersons, and politically affiliated individuals each represent 5 percent or less of the deaths in terror-related incidents.[17]

Locations of Terror Attacks

The most popular location for terrorist strikes is a vehicle, representing 48 percent of all known terrorist attack sites. This may be a single car bomb, but terrorists desiring to cause the most injury and death usually choose mass transit vehicles such as buses and trains. Following vehicles as popular terrorist strike locations are residences (15 percent), public locations and retail establishments (13 percent), community centers (10 percent), checkpoints (8 percent), and police facilities (6 percent).[18]

DOMESTIC TERRORISM

Domestic terrorism, as currently defined by the Patriot Act, is the same as transnational terrorism but performed within the borders of the United States. Domestic terrorism has also been defined by the FBI as "the unlawful use, or threatened use, of force or violence by a group or individual based and operating entirely within the United States or its territories without foreign direction committed against persons or property to intimidate or coerce a government, the civilian population, or any segment thereof, in furtherance of political or social objectives."[19] Although acts of domestic terror could be performed in the name of foreign terrorists (e.g., al-Qaeda) by persons born and residing in the United States, the *homegrown terrorist* seems to be the greatest threat to American security. Most homegrown terrorists are persons of nonforeign ancestry who commit terrorism in their own country against their own people. The worst act of domestic terrorism thus far in American history was committed by a homegrown terrorist, Timothy McVeigh, who killed hundreds and wounded over a thousand U.S. citizens to protest actions of U.S. law enforcement and the U.S. government. Actions like those of McVeigh have been increasing in recent years on American soil and have become the increasing concern of federal, state, and local investigators. Most of these homegrown threats come from three primary sources. The first is extremist groups formed in the United States that commit terrorist acts to draw attention to their right- or left-wing ideologies. Second are groups that commit acts of terror in the name of special causes. Last, and perhaps even most dangerous, are individual extremists known as *lone wolf terrorists*. Each of these domestic terrorist types, and their identifying characteristics, is described in the following section.

EXTREMIST DOMESTIC TERROR GROUPS

In general, an extremist group consists of individuals who share beliefs about politics, religion, social issues, special causes, and the like that are of an emotional and philosophical intensity far beyond that of mainstream society. Domestic extremist groups typically use protest, allowable under the First Amendment's freedom of expression guarantees, to express their viewpoints to American society. A small fraction of these groups, however, view legal protests as ineffective in promoting the social, political, religious, economic, or other changes they desire. These groups resort to terrorism against American citizens and targets to further their extremist agendas. Various belief systems drive extremist groups operating in the United States; however, the ones that have usually expressed their interests in the form of terrorist acts can effectively be classified as either socio-political terrorist groups or special cause terrorist groups.

Socio-Political Terrorist Groups

Socio-political terrorist groups desire to promote social and political change through violent means. Antigovernment sentiment is a common theme expressed by these groups when claiming responsibility for terrorist activities. There are generally two types of socio-political terrorist organizations: right-wing extremist groups (REGs) and left-wing extremist groups (LEGs). Obviously, because they lie at opposite ends in the socio-political belief spectrum, REG and LEG terrorists have diametrically opposed viewpoints of American society. These groups do not partake in terrorist acts against each other, however, but rather against targets outside their groups. Regardless of their ideological differences, REG and LEG terrorist groups are considered to be equally dangerous and violent.

REG EXTREMIST ORGANIZATIONS

REG terrorist organizations, for the most part, are organized around government conspiracy beliefs or ideologies of hatred directed toward specific classes of persons. Those organizing themselves on the basis of government conspiracy theories

generally believe that the U.S. government is controlled by officials attempting to destroy citizens' rights originally established by the nation's founders. Other REG themes for terror include taxation, government regulation, U.S. involvement in the United Nations, and other special interests. The groups that harbor the deepest suspicion of and hatred toward the U.S. government and government practices are most at risk of engaging in terrorist acts.

Recently, speculation has been growing that militia organizations "are to domestic terrorism what sleeper cells are to transnational terrorism." Usually, militias are paramilitary groups that espouse extremist right-wing ideologies. The typical militia member is a young, Caucasian male fascinated with firearms and other weaponry. Larger militias tend to have organizational structures with defined leaders, and their members often wear military uniforms while engaging in tactical training at privately owned compounds in remote areas. Currently, there is no known coordination among the hundreds of militia groups that operate across the nation.[20]

Next to antigovernment groups, the other most common variety of REG is ideologically focused hatred of persons and groups based on race, religion, and/or sexual orientation. Skinheads, neo-Nazis, and other white supremacists such as the Ku Klux Klan (KKK) shown in Figure 19.13, comprise the membership of these organizations. Specific identifying characteristics of these groups were discussed in detail within the "Gang Crime Scene" presented in Chapter 11. Similar to other REGs, the hundreds of hate groups currently in the United States have little or no coordination in planning joint terrorist activities. In 2009, federal, state, and local law enforcement reports to the FBI on known hate crime incidents revealed the following:

- *Victims*: Of all hate crimes, 61.1 percent were committed against persons with the other 38.1 percent being against property; African-Americans were targeted most often as victims of hate crime when the motivation for the crime

FIGURE 19.13 ▶ Hate groups, such as the KKK pictured here, along with other extremist organizations, are noted for their acts of domestic terrorism. (© Tom Kidd/Alamy)

was racial bias (71.5 percent); persons of the Jewish faith comprised the majority of hate crime victims (71.9 percent) when the criminal motivation was antireligious in nature.

- **Offenders:** The typical hate crime offender was White (62.4 percent), with the second most likely racial class of offender being African-American (18.5 percent); the majority of crimes against persons were simple assaults (40.3 percent), followed by acts of intimidation (34.6 percent), aggravated assaults (23.5 percent), and murders/rapes (1.2 percent).

- **Crime Locations:** Most hate crimes occur in or near the victims' homes (31.3 percent), with the second most likely location being highways, roads, alleys, or streets (17.2 percent).

- **Overall Motivation:** Race bias was the most frequent motivating factor for hate crime (48.7 percent), followed by religious bias (18.9 percent), sexual orientation bias (17.8 percent), ethnicity/national origin bias (13.3 percent), and bias against disabled persons (1 percent).[21]

LEG EXTREMIST ORGANIZATIONS

The ideology of **LEG terrorists** is one of anarchy and overthrow of capitalist government and business entities perceived to be rewarding the most economically and socially powerful members of society and oppressing members of society who have less power and wealth. Today, left-wing extremism often is expressed as rhetoric rather than violence, with most known LEGs choosing to express their views at protest rallies rather than orchestrate terrorist attacks. During the 1960s and 1970s, however, various high-profile LEGs were noted for their acts of violence:

- **The Weathermen (late 1960s to late 1970s):** The U.S. Capitol, the Pentagon, and various other locations associated with law enforcement were targets of random bombings by a group of American men and women calling themselves the Weathermen and aligning themselves with the Communist Party.

- **The Symbionese Liberation Army (early to mid-1970s):** To gain recognition for their antigovernment political and social ideologies, the SLA kidnapped newspaper heiress Patricia Hearst and assassinated the superintendent of the Oakland, CA school district, before being killed in a mass shootout with the Los Angeles Police Department.[22]

Special Cause Terrorist Groups

Although all terrorist groups have a special cause, those classified as **special cause terrorist** groups differ because they are motivated primarily by specific issues rather than general ideologies. Special cause terrorists are a major threat in today's society, according to recent intelligence conducted by the FBI.

Among them, a special class known as *ecoterrorists* appears to be increasing their level of terrorist activity. These groups use terrorism to bring attention to their agendas for changing present governmental and private practices that they believe to be destructive to the environment and animal life. The largest, and most active of the ecoterrorist groups are the Earth Liberation Front (E.L.F) and the Animal Liberation Front A.L.F.

EARTH LIBERATION FRONT

E.L.F. (Earth Liberation Front), or "the Elves," began in Great Britain in the early 1990s and spread its influence to the United States shortly thereafter. The group uses terror tactics to target anything that can be construed as exploiting the earth, its environment and its inhabitants. Thus far, their terror activities have been restricted to property and have not included human life. Their primary means of attack is arson through firebombing; however, the group uses additional methods of property destruction such as spray paint for committing vandalism and placing abrasives in the fuel tanks of machinery. Construction sites, luxury homes, vehicles (especially SUVs), heavy equipment, radio towers, trains, boats, and planes all have been targeted by E.L.F. The group's attacks usually are connected with locations of planned development and construction of raw land. The group is believed to operate in a cell structure, with many cells being located in the West and the Pacific Northwest. Recently, in 2008 and 2009, a group claiming responsibility for several fire bombings in Mexico and calling themselves *Frente de Liberación de la Tierra* (in English, Earth Liberation Front—E.L.F. is considered to be a Mexican cell of the U.S. E.L.F. organization. The most destructive E.L.F. attacks include the arson destruction of a $50 million condominium complex in San Diego, CA in 2003 and the 2008 burning of luxury homes in Washington state with a loss valued at $7 million. Their tell-tale crime scene signature is usually the letters "E.L.F." spray painted in red or pink on an object they have victimized or somewhere else clearly visible within the crime scene. In 2001, the FBI declared E.L.F. one of the nation's most dangerous domestic terror groups.[23]

ANIMAL LIBERATION FRONT

The **A.L.F. (Animal Liberation Front)**, founded in the United States during the early 1980s, was established as a leaderless organization that encouraged the "liberation" of animals from adverse conditions imposed by humans by any means that would not bring about physical harm to humans or nonhumans. Actions recommended to anyone who desired to become an operative for A.L.F. are as follows:

1. To inflict economic damage on those who profit from the misery and exploitation of animals.

2. To liberate animals from places of abuse, i.e., laboratories, factory farms, fur farms, etc., and place them in good homes where they may live out their natural lives, free from suffering.

3. To reveal the horror and atrocities committed against animals behind locked doors by performing nonviolent direct actions and liberations.

4. To take all necessary precautions against harming any animal, human or nonhuman.

5. Any group of people who are vegetarians or vegans and who carry out actions according to A.L.F guidelines have the right to regard themselves as part of the A.L.F.

A.L.F. terrorist operatives attack locations such as laboratories, farms, buildings, retail establishments, construction sites, commercial firms and others associated with animal storage, testing, treatment, and other animal rights issues. They use various methods of attack including explosives, firebombs, vandalism, intimidation, threats, and burglary. Many of their members share cross-over membership with E.L.F. Recently, the two terrorist groups have engaged in coordinated terrorist attacks at sites construed be harmful to both animals and the environment, leaving behind a spray-painted A.L.F/E.L.F signature. At present, a domestic terrorist suspect on the FBI's Most Wanted Terrorist list is believed to have carried out the coordinated 2003 coordinated bombings (one device being a nail-packed pipe bomb) of two commercial buildings housing animal testing sites.[24]

Lone Wolf Terrorists

Lone wolf terrorists not only carry out acts of terror by themselves, but also are inspired or motivated by the ideologies and beliefs of known terrorist groups. Many lone wolves have never had formal membership in a terrorist organization, while others have a history of current or past membership in such organizations. They may also act with or without the knowledge of the terrorist organizations by which they are inspired or from which they desire to gain recognition. In short, they are "loose cannons" that act on impulse. Most intelligence sources and the history of domestic terror activities indicate that the lone wolf is the most destructive of all terrorist types.

Timothy McVeigh's Oklahoma City bombing is a classic case of lone wolf terrorism. Emotionally distraught over the FBI's and other federal law enforcement's 1993 handling of the Branch Davidian militia seizure in Waco, Texas, McVeigh travelled to Waco to view the armed standoff in person. Exactly 2 years after the fatal Waco invasion on April 19, 1993, the Murrah Federal Building exploded on April 19, 1995, when McVeigh detonated his truck bomb. McVeigh, being a gun rights advocate, ideologically identified with the Branch Davidian militia, which provided the mental motivation to commit his horrific act of lone terrorism. Figure 19.14 shows the massive destruction to the Alfred P. Murrah Federal Building in Oklahoma City caused by McVeigh's truck bomb, and Figure 19.15 provides a timeline reconstructing his pre- and postbombing activities. Other acts of domestic terrorism committed by lone wolf terrorists include the following:

- The "Unabomber" Theodore Kaczynski, out of a fanatical desire to curb industrial innovation, conducted a reign of terror on scientists and university professors with mail bombs.

- Eric Rudolph, whose identification with the Christian Identity organization compelled him to carry out a string

FIGURE 19.14 ▶ 1995 bombing of the Alfred P. Murrah Federal Building by domestic terrorist Timothy McVeigh in which 168 people were killed. (THE DAILY OKLAHOMAN, PAUL HELLSTERN/AP Images)

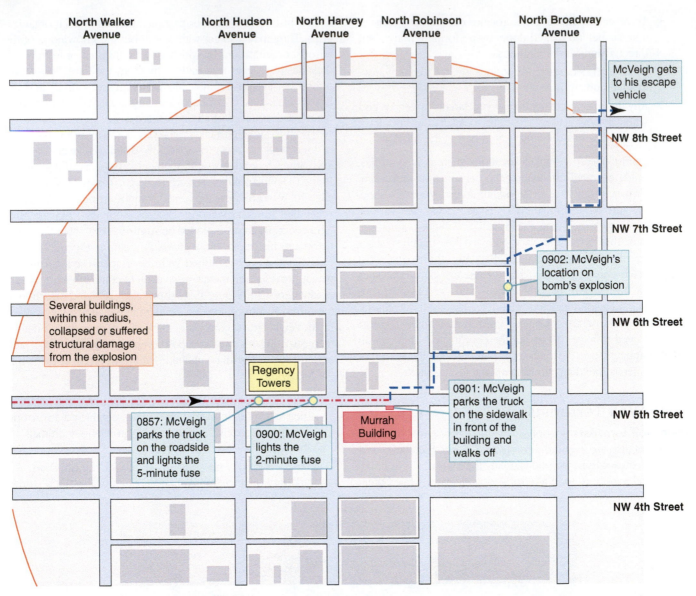

FIGURE 19.15 ▶ Timothy McVeigh's route to (red) and from (blue) the bombing site in Oklahoma City.

of bombings during the late 1990s, targeting abortion clinics, gay nightclubs, and the 1996 Atlanta Olympic games.

- Army Captain Nidal Hassan went on a shooting spree at Fort Hood in Texas, leaving 13 dead and 30 other wounded, allegedly motivated by loyalty to extremist Muslim ideals and an admiration of al-Qaeda.

- Joseph Stack III flew his plane into an IRS building in Austin, Texas on a suicide mission that injured 13 as a form of antigovernment protest terrorism.

- Jared Lee Loughner assassinated a federal judge and attempted to assassinate U.S. Representative Gabrielle Giffords in a 2011 armed assault near Tucson, Arizona—allegedly driven by his antigovernment conspiracy beliefs.

The relationship between many lone wolf terrorists and known terrorist groups is often accounted for by a phenomenon referred to *leaderless resistance*. In effect, the lone wolf terrorist belongs to a **phantom cell**—in other words, one of which a terrorist group has no knowledge. A phantom cell may consist of one person or a few individuals identifying with the ideologies and practices of a known terrorist leader or organization. Usually, members of a phantom cell gain their information from media sources and the Internet. Phantom cell members existing in different locations have no knowledge of, or communication with one another. All that they share is an allegiance to the same terrorist belief systems. Lone wolf terrorists are driven to act at times and at targets they feel are optimal for satisfying the general goals of the terrorist ideologies in which they believe. Terrorist leaders and groups generally take credit for the terrorist acts committed by members of their phantom cells.[25]

CASE CLOSE-UP 19.1

TERROR PLOT FOILED BY DOMESTIC DISPUTE
(Pinellas Park, FL)

Pinellas Park Police thought they were responding to an ordinary domestic dispute call when, after entering the home of Robert J. Goldstein (the subject of the complaint), they discovered a cache of weapons and explosives as well as plans to carry out an attack on a local Islamic center. Follow-up investigations of the incident revealed that Goldstein, along with his wife and two other men, had planned their terror attack to occur on the 1-year anniversary of the 9/11 attacks in New York City. It was further discovered that the motive for the attack was payback for Palestinian suicide bombings that had taken place in Israel.

NARCO–TERRORISM

Narco–terrorism is a hybrid term blending two words: *narco*, referring to participation in the illegal drug trade for economic profit; and *terrorism*, connoting the use of fear, intimidation, and violence for ideological purposes. Many definitions of narco–terrorism have been offered from various sources. Perhaps the most comprehensive of these is the following definition provided by the DEA:

> Narco-terrorism may be characterized by the participation of groups or associated individuals in taxing, providing security for, or otherwise aiding or abetting drug trafficking endeavors in an effort to further, or fund, terrorist activities.[26]

From a strictly investigative standpoint, however, narco–terrorism can be defined simply as terrorist acts carried out by groups directly or indirectly involved in the production, transportation, distribution, or sale of illegal drugs. Although most terrorists do use profits from illegal drug sales to fund their organizations and acts of terror, not all groups involved in the illegal drug trade employ acts of terrorism. The trend among foreign drug lords and cartels, however, has been to copy many of the violent tactics used by transnational terrorists. This is done to intimidate their enemies, government officials, and law enforcement, and to instill fear in the public so that citizens will pressure government officials to back off enforcement efforts directed at those involved in the illegal drug trade.

Many countries are safe havens for narco–terrorism due to their extreme poverty and unstable governments. For example, Afghanistan now is responsible for producing an estimated 80 to 90 percent of the world's opium that is eventually transformed to heroin and then sold illegally—despite the fact that Islam prohibits all drugs that are not medically prescribed. Most Afghan-generated heroin is eventually sold in the Middle East and in Europe. Recent intelligence reports from the CIA suggest that the Taliban receives about $70 million from their illegal drug operations, and the al-Qaeda drug profits were somewhat less. Approximately 80 percent of the world's cocaine originates from the South American country of Colombia and is shipped to the United States via Colombian drug cartels. Colombia also produces the bulk of heroin sold in the eastern U.S. states. Mexico is the largest supplier of marijuana to the continental United States, and nearly all the heroin produced in Mexico through opium poppy cultivation ends up being sold illegally in the western U.S. states. It is the Mexican drug trafficking cartels, however, that are responsible for the unprecedented amount of narco–terrorism currently evidenced along the nearly 2,000 miles of the U.S.-Mexican border.[27]

MEXICAN NARCO–TERRORISM

Although the term *narco–terrorism* is not officially recognized by the Mexican government, ample evidence suggests that drug trafficking organizations (**DTO**s) recently have resorted to tactics similar to those used by transnational terrorists operating within Middle Eastern countries. Antidrug intelligence sources indicate that three to five major DTOs currently control the major flow of drugs in and out of Mexico and all have resorted to random acts of violence to protect their illegal enterprises. DTOs' use of terror tactics is assumed to be in direct response to the Mexican government's deployment of about 27,000 military troops to various drug trafficking hot spots across the nation beginning in 1996. Since then, the DTOs have enlisted specialized enforcement and protection personnel with expertise in heavy weaponry, specialized military tactics, sophisticated communications methods, intelligence, surveillance, and countersurveillance. The main function of these personnel is to protect DTO operations and shipments of illegal drugs, most of which are received from Colombia and transported to the United States via established drug trade routes. In addition, these DTO special forces are organized and operate in a paramilitary style, deploying the following terrorist tactics:

- **Kidnapping:** DTOs are responsible for an estimated 7,000 to 10,000 kidnappings in Mexico and the United States each year. In addition to drug cartel enemies, business executives, government officials, and law enforcement are often targets of abduction. Citizens also are randomly kidnapped for intimidation purposes. Ransom demands are often received by family members and associates of the victims. About 1 in every 7 persons kidnapped is killed by the abductors.

- **Assassinations:** Political figures representing federal, state, and local governments are targeted for assassination. These persons have included police chiefs, mayors, and high-ranking government officials. Some of these victims may have been somehow connected with supported DTO activities, while others were killed merely for shock value.

- **Sniper Activity:** The creation of mass public chaos and fear through strategic sniper fire has long been a favorite terror tactic among Middle Eastern terrorist organizations. DTOs in Mexico now use it for the same purpose. Recovered weapons caches have included state-of-the-art sniper rifles (e.g., Barrett M107 .50 semiautomatic). Sniper attacks mounted by DTOs have been against military, law enforcement, and civilians.

- **Body Mutilations:** DTOs now rival, if not exceed, Middle Eastern terror groups for their public displays of mutilated bodies. Bodies that have been beheaded, dismembered, burned, and/or had their faces peeled from their skulls are prominently displayed in public for intimidation purposes. The victims usually are members of rival DTOs, but also have been citizens, women, and children. Typically, hand-scrawled messages are spray painted on walls or handwritten on placards stating the group or individual responsible for the mutilation. In addition, the killer's message often includes the victim's name and a warning to others who attempt to interfere with the DTO's drug operations.

- **Bombings:** DTOs first used explosives for purposes of terrorism in the 2008 bombing of a public plaza during a Mexican Independence Day celebration—killing 8 and injuring over 100. The bombing took place in Mexican President Felipe Calderon's home state of Morelia. It was accomplished by a lone wolf terrorist who threw grenades into the middle of a large crowd. Car bombs known as *coche bombas,* utilizing the high explosive Tovex (normally employed for excavation, similar to dynamite) and triggered by cell phone detonators, have been used against Mexican Federal Police.

- **Armed Assaults:** Coordinated, ambush-style shooting attacks are frequently used against rivals as well as nonrivals in public places using semi- and fully-automatic AK-47 and AR-15 rifles firing armor-piercing ammunition. Men, women, and children are all equally likely to be victimized during a DTO public armed assault.

- **Narcobanners: Narcobanners** often are placed in public locations created by the DTOs and denounce certain government practices or government officials. This propaganda is designed to create public distrust of officials who are attempting to interfere with the DTO's drug trafficking activities. The narcobanners often are put into place following a violent terror-style attack to persuade the intimidated public to side with the DTO so that similar future acts of violence will not occur.[28]

Human Trafficking

Narco–terrorists often combine their illegal drug trafficking activities with human trafficking. DTO members are not usually directly involved in the actual practice of trafficking persons, but rather broker out to, or hire trafficking rings (usually consisting of family members) to act as **coyotes** that actually plan and execute trafficking activities. Typically, coyotes or persons who illegally transport undocumented persons (called **pollos**) charge from $2,000 to $9,000 dollars to smuggle one person across the Mexican-U.S. border. This price can be greatly reduced if the person smuggled agrees to be a *mule* or a transporter of drugs for a DTO. In some cases, the undocumented individual can be crossed for free and receive payment of around $3,000 (often given to family members) for transporting drugs during their illegal border crossing. If crossing the border on foot, the pollo usually is given a backpack filled with 50 pounds of marijuana and has to walk several hours or days depending on the location of departure and pick-up point. These foot-style drug crossings are carried out along established routes noted for both drug and human trafficking, mainly in isolated regions of California, Arizona, and Texas. Cocaine often is transported in *body packs* consisting of kilo bricks duct tapped to the trafficker's (a woman's or child's) legs and torso beneath the clothing. Coyotes usually cross their pollos in groups of 10 to 20; but sometimes, before crossing the border, they are kidnapped or killed by bandits known as *bajadores,* who victimize these groups for their money and drugs.

After crossing the border, traffickers transport their pollos in a **load vehicle**. These usually are vans but also can be large autos or trucks specially equipped to haul large numbers of persons without being detected by law enforcement. Load vehicles generally can be identified by the following characteristics:

- **Tinted Windows:** These are used so that the number of persons contained in the vehicle cannot be readily observed from the outside.

- **Overloaded Appearance:** Some load vehicles are equipped with specially designed suspension systems so that heavy loads will not cause their bodies to sag or appear weighted down on the road. Vehicle with standard suspensions are low to the ground and have bulging tires from being overloaded with passengers.

- **Out-of-State License Plates:** Most load vehicles have license plates from states other than the one in which they are being used to create a tourist appearance and make it more difficult to conduct moving license plate checks.

Load vehicles are used to transport the pollos to a destination known as a **drop house**. These are usually apartments or houses that human traffickers rent for the sole purpose of housing pollos for 30 days until they are shipped out to their final destination—which may be anywhere in the country. Drop houses can be identified by the following:

- Large numbers of people coming and going from a residence, many of whom walk or use bicycles for transportation

- Large amounts of garbage placed outside the residence on trash pick-up days; and, if visible, the inside of the residence filled with large amounts of trash—usually in trash bags
- Little or no furniture or decorations inside the residence (if visible)
- Purchases of large amount of food at local stores near the suspected residence; usually one cook at the house, typically a female, is in charge of shopping

If a suspected drop house has been identified, and warrants cannot be obtained due to lack of probable cause, a **knock-and-talk** method whereby investigators approach residents in a consensual encounter while observing the location for the characteristics just listed is often an effective first step in establishing probable cause to secure a search warrant. Investigators who enter a suspected drop house should ask any residents for identification. Drop house residents often carry no identification or they have false identification provided to them by their traffickers. In addition, most traffickers keep one or two ledgers at the house containing the names of the pollos, the amount of money paid or owed by them, and the final destination to where they will be transported. Some drop houses may also be used as marijuana grow houses where pollos are forced to work to pay traffickers for their illegal border crossing. Females and children may be forced to engage in prostitution as a form of payment as well. In the event an arrest is made, surveillance of the drop house should be maintained to detect persons or load vehicles approaching the house. For undercover work, investigators need to be aware of any type of countersurveillance activities going on at undercover locations where contact is being made with human trafficking suspects.[29]

Transnational Terrorist Connections

Intelligence sources have suggested that a working partnership exists between Mexican narco–terrorists and operatives belonging to transnational Islamic terror groups—especially al-Qaeda and the Lebanese group Hezbollah. Some contend that drugs, guns, money, and training are being provided on a limited scale to narco–terrorists by transnational terrorists in exchange for safe havens in Mexico. Hezbollah, for example, has extensive knowledge of building underground tunnels gained from their construction of subterranean crossings beneath the Israeli border. Underground tunnels are frequently used by narco–terrorists to traffic drugs, humans, and other contraband beneath the U.S. border. Further, Islamic terrorists and other **special interest aliens** (SIAs, e.g., originating from Middle Eastern countries), often disguised as illegal Mexican immigrants, are believed to have employed narco–terrorists to smuggle them across the U.S. border along drug and human trafficking trade routes. Further evidence includes the recent discovery of cross-over tattoos on the bodies of arrested Mexican narco–terrorists styled with Farsi (Iranian) lettering and Islamic symbols.[30]

INDICATORS OF TERRORISM AND INITIAL CONTACT QUESTIONS

Following are various indicators of potential terrorists or terrorist activity and suggested lines of questioning for initial contact, as identified by the State of New York's Office of Intelligence and Homeland Security:

General Indicators

Passport history

- Recent travel overseas
- Countries of interest—Pakistan/Afghanistan/Yemen
- Multiple passports/ID documents
- Altered/falsified ID documents

Other identification

- No current/fixed address
- False ID papers (SSN)
- Multiple IDs with different name spellings/DOBs

Hotel/motel visits

- Refusal of maid service
- Asking for specific view (i.e., bridges, airports, etc.)
- Electronic surveillance equipment in room
- Suspicious or unusual items left behind
- Use of lobby or public phone instead of room phone
- Pays in cash

Thefts, purchases, or discovery of

- Weapons/explosive materials
- Camera/surveillance equipment
- Purchasing or renting vehicle under false name
- Radios, scanners
- ID documents
- Unauthorized uniforms (airport, postal, police, military)

Surveillance indicators

- Video or camera usage at nontourist sites
- Taking notes or calling on mobile phone
- Pacing off distances
- Vehicles parked without passengers
- Unusual encampments
- Ruses
- Deliberate penetration attempts
- Observing or climbing perimeter fencing

Vehicle-borne improvised explosive device (VBIED) indicators

- Vehicle riding low in the rear
- Time and Power Unit (TPU)—detonator
- Large boxes, satchels, bags, or containers in plain view
- Wires coming from front of vehicle to rear or trunk area

- Acrid smoke—indicates possible lit fuse
- Armed personnel in vehicle—may be breaching team
- Vehicle may emit a fuel-like odor
- Unattended and parked near possible target
- May have flashers on

Unusual items in vehicle/residence

- Training manuals (flight, scuba, military, or extremist)
- Blueprints of high-profile buildings
- Photos/diagrams of potential targets
- Photos/pictures or articles of known terrorists or groups
- Numerous prepaid calling cards and/or cell phones
- Global Positioning Satellite (GPS) unit
- Multiple hotel receipts
- Financial records indicating overseas wire transfers
- Rental vehicles (cash transactions on receipts, living locally but renting)

Employment

- No obvious signs of employment—but has cash
- Has student visa, but not proficient in English
- Previous military/security training or service

Suicide bomber indicators—A.L.E.R.T.

- **A**lone and nervous
- **L**oose/bulky clothing inconsistent with weather
- **E**xposed wires under clothing (possibly through the sleeve)
- **R**igid mid-section (explosive device or may be carrying a rifle)
- **T**ightened hands (may hold detonation device)
- Strange chemical odors
- Sweating, mumbling (prayers)
- Unusually calm and detached behavior
- Attempts to gain a position near crowds or VIPs
- Wears disguises appropriate to target areas to elude detection
- May be wearing military, medic, firefighter, or police uniforms
- May pose as pregnant woman
- Use of props (baby stroller, shopping cart, suspicious bag/backpack, bulky vest, or belt)

Initial Contact Questions

A. Do you have a license or any other identification?

1. Check the name on the driver's license with all other vehicle documents. Look for forgeries or copies with different physical appearances.
2. A trained terrorist is taught to produce a false document or alias.
3. Check the spelling of the individual's name. Remember, a driver's license is not proof of citizenship.

4. International drivers' licenses are called *permits*. Official international permits are valid for one year, gray in color, are not laminated, and are valid only for foreign nationals operating in the United States.
5. If driving a vehicle, ask to see any vehicle documents like title of ownership, bill of sale, or rental papers.

B. Do you have vehicle registration or insurance?

1. Verify name and address with driver's license.
2. If driving a rental car, verify name and address with rental agreement. For vehicles in general, verify authenticity of insurance documentation/carrier.

C. Where are you going or coming from?

1. Try to verify the response. This might include tickets, directions, or contact information. A terrorist is trained to provide law enforcement officers with key public points (especially tourist destinations) as an explanation for travel.
2. For example, traveling to/from Wal-Mart, grocery store, or an amusement park.
3. Try to verify the response. This might include evidence such as store bags, receipts, pamphlets, or ticket stubs.
4. Check dates, if possible.
5. If no evidence is available, ask specific questions regarding the destination; for example, Where did you park? What did you see? What did you like about the area?

D. Where do you live?

1. Try to verify the response. A potential terrorist may use a transient address (e.g., hotel, business, community center) as a permanent address.[31]

SPECIAL TERRORISM CRIME SCENE SAFETY CONCERNS

As the bombing scene at the site of the 9/11 terrorist attacks (see Figure 19.16) clearly shows, processing the crime scene of a massively destructive terror attack is a seemingly impossible task requiring countless hours and numbers of investigative personnel. When investigators encounter a terrorism crime scene, it usually is reported to the FBI and other federal authorities, who may take charge of processing the scene. When both state and federal laws are broken by terrorist actions, however, parallel investigations theoretically can be undertaken by federal, state, and local law enforcement agencies at the same crime scene. Regardless of which individuals or agencies ultimately take charge, investigators processing such crime scenes must remain aware of certain special safety concerns:

1. ***Booby Traps:*** Explosives or other devices may be placed in and around the perimeter of the crime scene. Look for items that are out of place, holes recently made in soil, or cement that appears recently poured.

FIGURE 19.16 ▶ Processing a crime scene involving mass destruction by terrorists is a daunting task for investigators, as it was for this CBP agent, who had to sift through the rubble of the 9/11 World Trade Center terrorist attack. (Courtesy of AFP/Newscom)

Trip wires used to set off an explosive device may also be present.

2. **Sniper Attacks:** Terrorists may place snipers above the crime scene at a vantage point from which they can take clear shots at investigators processing the crime scene.

3. **Secondary Explosive Devices:** Never assume that the epicenter of the bombing in an explosion scene is the only place where an explosive is located. Terrorists sometimes intentionally create an initial explosion to bait investigators toward an area around which they have planted unexploded secondary bombs. Look for trip wires at the scene. Look for suspicious persons or vehicles near the scene from which a cell phone or other electronic device could detonate an explosive.

4. **Suicide Bombers:** Keep all unauthorized persons away from the scene. Suicide bombers (sometimes women or children) have been known to fake illness or injury to lure their targets toward them before detonating a suicide bomb. There is no reliable way to tell whether a person is wearing a suicide bomb. Ensure that persons claiming to be media officials have authentic press passes.

5. **Car/Truck/Motorcycle/Boat Bombs:** Establish secure outer perimeters far enough from the crime scene to detect unauthorized approaching vehicles that may be carrying explosives.

6. **Chemical, Biological, or Radiological Agents:** Harmful chemical, biological, or radiological agents used by terrorists at the crime scene may be virtually undetectable in the short term, due to their prolonged period of onset. Some of these agents take hours, days, or even years to show their effects on the human body. Their lethality depends on the agent's intensity and the length of exposure to it. Persons complaining of sickness,

difficulty breathing, eye irritations, dizziness, disorientation, or skin rashes are a warning sign of potential toxic agents used by terrorists at the crime scene. Other signs of adverse environmental change such as dead insects, animals, discolored trees/foliage, hazy air, or oily residue dripping from surfaces or objects also indicate the possible presence of toxic agents. When in doubt, call for hazardous materials technicians who can test the crime scene area and clear it for safety before processing.

COMMON FACTORS AMONG TERRORISTS

All terrorists, whether transnational, domestic, or narco–terrorist in nature, share certain characteristics:

- **The Need for Recognition:** First, they want recognition for themselves and/or the groups they represent, sometimes before and certainly after committing a terrorist attack. Terrorists often use notes, phone calls, e-mails, or other forms of communication to inform media, authorities, and enemies who they are and what they have done or intend to do.

- **The Creation of a Signature:** Whether or not terrorists explicitly communicate their identity to outsiders, they invariably leave a terror signature at the scene that is characteristic of them and their past terrorist behavior. Using a certain type of explosive, leaving a particular sign or symbol at the scene, or staging a certain style of attack are all examples of terrorists' calling cards left for investigators to discover at the scene.

- **Selection of Targets:** The more random the target and the more injury that can be done to that target, the more terror that terrorist groups can instill in the general public.

- **Symbolism:** Unlike ordinary street offenders, terrorists use symbolism in their methods of attack and the persons, places, and things that they target with their terrorist activities. Specific days of attack may have numeric symbolism (e.g., "9/11," suggesting a state of emergency) or may commemorate the anniversary or data of an event/time of special meaning to the terrorist (e.g., the Oklahoma City bombing).

- **Extremism:** The *modus operandi* selected by terrorists generally shows violence far exceeding that necessary to carry out a particular act. Murder by dismemberment, burning, beheading, and the like are extreme methods of overkill to create shock and to instill fear.

- **Fatalism:** Many terrorists put their own life second to their cause, unlike typical offenders, who plan an escape following a crime. Their mentality is similar to that of some mass murderers who enter the crime scene knowing that although they will die there, others will die with them. Unlike the mass murderer, however, who kills for selfish reasons, terrorists believe that their own death and that of others they kill is done for a greater good.

RECONSTRUCTING A TERRORIST ATTACK CRIME SCENE

Case Example 19A presents a coordinated law enforcement response by the Los Angeles Sheriff's Department to a simulated terrorist attack at a highly populated subway station. This case illustrates that the response to an investigation of a terrorist crime scene requires not only special tactical training but specialized equipment as well. As the photos presented in Figures 19.17 to 19.29 show, officer safety and preparing for the unknown are paramount concerns for investigators and any other personnel responding to a scene involving suspected terrorist activity. After assessing these photos, consider how the standard crime scene investigative process should be applied to this mock case and to other real-life investigations of terrorist attack crime scenes.

CASE EXAMPLE 19A

LASD Simulated Terrorist Attack

FIGURE 19.17 ▶ The simulated subway terrorist attack case begins with deputies of the Los Angeles County Sheriff Department making security checks of subway riders to ensure safety and to surprise individuals planning to engage in potential terrorist activity. Why would this particular location selected as a target by terrorists? How could investigators assist security personnel in identifying possible terrorist suspects at this location? (Courtesy Jeffry Ivask, counterterrorism expert, Los Angeles County Sheriff Department)

FIGURE 19.18 ▶ In a further effort to thwart a potential terrorist attack, deputies make surprise random searches on trains throughout the day on trains. Here a search is conducted with the use of a canine unit that may detect explosives or other illegal contraband in the train or on its passengers. If an explosive is detected at this scene, what steps should be taken by investigators to determine if and/or how the explosive device is related to an act of terror or terrorist group? (Courtesy Jeffry Ivask, counterterrorism expert, Los Angeles County Sheriff Department)

FIGURE 19.19 ▶ First responding deputies wear special protective gear and a breathing apparatus to the scene of the simulated terror incident. What precautions/observations should first-responders take when approaching the scene of a suspected terrorist activity? (Courtesy Jeffry Ivask, counterterrorism expert, Los Angeles County Sheriff Department)

FIGURE 19.20 ▶ Outside the location of the scene, a secure staging area is set up using specialized DRASH (Deployable Rapid Assembly Shelter) protective shelters to house responding deputies. (Courtesy Jeffry Ivask, counterterrorism expert, Los Angeles County Sheriff Department)

(a)

(b)

FIGURE 19.21 ▶ (a) Sergeant Jeffrey Ivask, counterterrorism expert for the Los Angeles County Sheriff's Department, inside a DRASH shelter where command operations are carried out. (b) Inside the DRASH are black cases containing a HAZMAT ensemble threat suit. (Courtesy Jeffry Ivask, counterterrorism expert, Los Angeles County Sheriff Department)

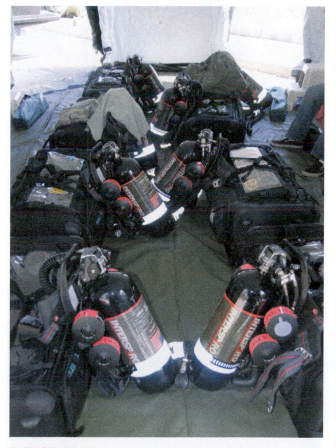

FIGURE 19.22 ▶ The inside contents of the black case containing the Hazmat ensemble threat suit. What types of precautionary intelligence information regarding terrorist groups and their activities could be provided by investigators to officers who are working the field in this scene? (Courtesy Jeffry Ivask, counterterrorism expert, Los Angeles County Sheriff Department)

FIGURE 19.23 ▶ Deputies perform a simulated secure and search operation at the location of the mock terrorist attack. (Courtesy Jeffry Ivask counterterrorism expert, Los Angeles County Sheriff Department)

FIGURE 19.24 ▶ Deputies continuing their search. What objects and/or devices should be searched for at this scene? (Courtesy Jeffry Ivask, counterterrorism expert, Los Angeles County Sheriff Department)

FIGURE 19.25 ▶ To simulate the rescue procedure during a terrorist attack, a deputy is staged as a "wounded officer down." The lead deputy will clear the tunnels in both directions before advancing to the down deputy's location. (Courtesy Jeffry Ivask, counterterrorism expert, Los Angeles County Sheriff Department)

FIGURE 19.26 ▶ Deputies locate the staged down deputy and begin to extract him from the scene. The lead deputy will clear downrange from the downed deputy to ensure suspects are clear from the location and an ambush is not awaiting them. (Courtesy Jeffry Ivask, counterterrorism expert, Los Angeles County Sheriff Department)

FIGURE 19.27 ▶ Deputies with specialized rescue gear approach the scene. (Courtesy Jeffry Ivask, counterterrorism expert, Los Angeles County Sheriff Department)

FIGURE 19.28 ▶ Deputies place the downed deputy in a gurney and begin extraction by pulling the gurney though the subway. (Courtesy Jeffry Ivask, counterterrorism expert, Los Angeles County Sheriff Department)

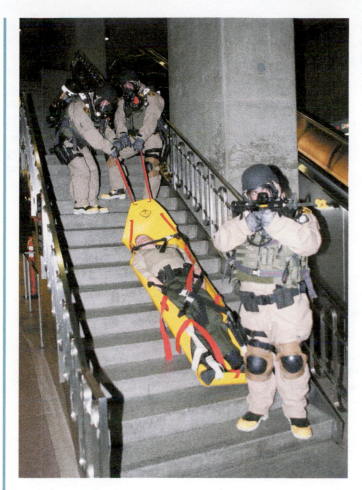

FIGURE 19.29 ▶ While one deputy provides cover, the others begin the arduous process of pulling the down deputy up a flight of stairs. After all the injured are removed and the scene is secured, local, state, and federal authorities will conduct a joint crime scene investigation. If this were a true act of terror, what types of activities should be performed by investigators in order to collect information and evidence at this scene? What types of follow-up investigative activities should be performed? (Courtesy Jeffry Ivask, counterterrorism expert, Los Angeles County Sheriff Department)

Summary

1. **Major terrorist groups.**

   The primary types of terrorism encountered are perpetrated by transnational, domestic, and narco–terrorists. Transnational terrorism, otherwise referred to as *international terrorism,* involves persons from one country perpetrating acts of terror against citizens, governments, institutions, or other entities of another country. Domestic or homegrown terrorism is restricted to terrorists acts where the offenders and victims all are of the same country. Narco–terrorists use violence, fear, and intimidation to further their illegal drug sales activities to gain personal profits and to fund their continuing criminal enterprises.

2. **Transnational terrorist organizations.**

   Major transnational terrorist groups include al-Qaeda, the Taliban, Hezbollah, and HAMAS. Members of al-Qaeda are militant Sunni rebels who believe in the expulsion of Western influence from Muslim nations by means of violence and terror. The

Taliban terrorist group, located in Afghanistan, is considered an Islamic religious sect as well as the legitimate political arm of al-Qaeda extremist ideologies. Hezbollah, aka *the party of God,* is composed of Muslim Shi'ite militants operating mainly from Lebanon but with cells established in Europe, Africa, South American, North America, and Asia. HAMAS, also known as the *Palestinian Islamic Resistance Movement,* was founded in 1987 as an extension of the longstanding Muslim Brotherhood group centered in Palestine.

3. **Domestic terrorism and domestic terrorist groups.**

   Domestic terrorism is "the unlawful use, or threatened use, of force or violence by a group or individual based and operating entirely within the United States or its territories without foreign direction committed against persons or property to intimidate or coerce a government, the civilian population, or any segment thereof, in furtherance of political or social objectives." The vast majority of these homegrown threats come from two primary sources. The first of these, domestic terrorists, are extremist groups formed in the United States that commit terrorist acts to draw attention to their right- or left-wing ideologies. The second, and perhaps even more dangerous, are individual extremists known as *lone wolf terrorists*.

4. Narco–terrorism.

Narco–terrorism is a hybrid term blending two separate words with two separate meanings: *narco*, referring to participation in the illegal drug trade for economic profit; and *terrorism*, connoting the use of fear, intimidation, and violence for ideological purposes. From a strictly investigative standpoint, the practice of narco–terrorism can be viewed as various terrorist acts carried out by groups directly or indirectly involved in the production, transportation, distribution, or sale of illegal drugs. Major drug trafficking organizations (DTOs) in Mexico now carry out most narco–terrorist activities, including the use of violence for purposes of creating public fear and intimidation as well as human trafficking across the U.S. border.

Key Terms

Patriot Act	lone wolf terrorist	narcobanners
transnational terrorism	socio-political terrorist	coyotes
Al-Qaeda	REG terrorist	pollos
jihad	LEG terrorist	load vehicle
Taliban	special cause terrorist	drop house
Hezbollah	E.L.F. (Earth Liberation Front)	car bomb
HAMAS	A.L.F. (Animal Liberation Front)	truck bomb
terrorist cell	phantom cell	walk-away bomb
WMDs	narco–terrorism	knock-and-talk
domestic terrorism	DTO	special interest aliens

Review Questions

1. Provide a general definition for the term *terrorism*.
2. When is an act of terror classified as transnational terrorism?
3. Name the major transnational terrorist groups.
4. What is a terrorist cell?
5. How are cells used as part of the organizational structure of a terrorist group?
6. Define the term *domestic terrorism*.
7. What is a lone wolf terrorist?
8. What types of terrorist groups are classified as socio-political in nature?
9. What is a special cause terrorist group?
10. Define the term *narco–terrorism*.
11. What types of terrorist behaviors do narco–terrorists engage in?
12. How do DTOs, coyotes, and pollos contribute to narco–terrorism?
13. What is a load vehicle and how is it recognized?
14. Describe the function of a drop house.
15. What are some of the factors that all terrorists share?

Internet Resources

Response to Terror	usinfo.state.gov/topical/pol/terror
Rand Corporation Terrorism Resources	www.rand.org/search
U.S. Department of State Counterterrorism	www.state.gov/www/global/terrorism/fto_info_1999.html
Hate Groups on the Internet	hatedirectory.com
Terrorism Research Center	www.terrorism.com
Student Association on Terrorism and Security Analysis	satsa.us

Applied Investigative Exercise

Suppose that you were called as a special investigator to assist in the investigation of Case Example 19A. What advice would you give your investigative colleagues? They are relying on you to inform them of relevant investigative techniques that they could use to gather physical evidence in this case of terrorism. Use any and all physical and behavioral investigative methods you have learned to help solve this case. Provide any relevant information relating to the investigation of terrorist groups that might reasonably be inferred from this crime scene.

Notes

[1] Office of the Inspector General, *A Review of the FBI's Investigations of Certain Domestic Advocacy Groups*. Oversight and Review Division, September 2010, 23.

[2] Washington Post, *The Bombing of Pan Am Flight 103*, posted at www.washingtonpost.com/wp-srv/inatl/longterm/panam103/timeline.htm.

[3] Federal Bureau of Investigation, *FBI 100: First Strike: Global Terror in America*, posted at www.fbi.gov/news/stories/2008/february/tradebom_022608.

[4] Federal Bureau of Investigation, *Terror Hits Home: The Oklahoma City Bombing*, posted at www.fbi.gov/about-us/history/famous-cases/oklahoma-city-bombing.

[5] S. USA PATRIOT Act Sunset Extension Act of 2011.

[6] Ibid.

[7] Rand Corporation, *Terrorism and Homeland Security*, posted at www.rand.org/topics/terrorism-and-homeland-security.html.

[8] Mideast Web, *Inside Al-Qaeda: The Islamist Terrorist Network*, posted at www.mideastweb.org/alqaeda.htm.

[9] Ibid.

[10] Ahmed Rashid, *Taliban: Militant Islam, Oil and Fundamentalism in Central Asia* (New Haven, CT: Yale University Press, 2000), 45–67.

[11] August Richard Norton, *Hezbollah* (Princeton, NJ: Princeton University Press, 2007).

[12] Global Security Organization, *HAMAS*, posted at www.globalsecurity.org/military/world/para/hamas.htm.

[13] Rand Corporation, *Terrorism and Homeland Security*, posted at www.rand.org/topics/terrorism-and-homeland-security.html.

[14] CBS News, *How to Form a Terrorist Cell*, posted at www.cbsnews.com/8301-502684_162-4079443-502684.html.

[15] Sue Mahan and Pamela L. Griset, *Terrorism in Perspective* (Thousand Oaks, CA: Sage, 2008), 89–112.

[16] National Counterterrorism Center, *Report on Terrorism 2009*, posted at www.nctc.gov/witsbanner/docs/2009_report_on_terrorism.pdf.

[17] Ibid.

[18] Ibid.

[19] Federal Bureau of Investigation, *Domestic Terrorism in the Post 9/11 Era*, posted at www.fbi.gov/news/stories/2009/september/domterror_090709.

[20] American Defamation League, *The Militia Movement*, posted at www.adl.org/learn/ext_us/Militia_M.asp?xpicked=4&item=mm.

[21] Federal Bureau of Investigation, *Hate Crime in the U.S. 2009*, posted at www.fbi.gov/news/stories/2010/november/hate_112210/hate_112210.

[22] Harvey W. Kushner, *Encyclopedia of Terrorism* (Thousand Oaks, CA: Sage, 2003), 66–87.

[23] Earth Liberation Front. Org , posted at earth-liberation-front.org.

[24] Animal Liberation Front.Com, posted at www.animal-liberationfront.com.

[25] COT Institute, *Lone-Wolf Terrorism*, posted at www.transnationalterrorism.eu/tekst/publications/Lone-Wolf%20Terrorism.pdf.

[26] John Holmberg, *Narcoterrorism*, posted at policy-traccc.gmu.edu/pdfs/student_research/HolmbergNarcoterrorism.pdf.

[27] Ibid.

[28] Sylvia M. Longmire and John P. Longmire, "Redefining Terrorism: Why Mexican Drug Trafficking is More Than Just Organized Crime," *Journal of Strategic Security*, Vol. 1 (1), 2008, 35–52.

[29] This discussion is drawn from the authors' experience.

[30] Sylvia M. Longmire and John P. Longmire, "Redefining Terrorism: Why Mexican Drug Trafficking is More Than Just Organized Crime," *Journal of Strategic Security*, Vol. 1 (1), 2008, 35–52.

[31] New York State Intelligence Center, *New York State Law Enforcement Terrorism Indicators Reference Card*, posted at info.publicintelligence.net/NYterroristindicators.pdf.

CHAPTER TWENTY

FROM THE CRIME SCENE TO THE COURTROOM

Learning Objectives:

After completing this chapter, you should be able to:

1. Describe the role of the investigator in court.
2. Outline the steps that investigators take to prepare for court.
3. Describe appropriate courtroom demeanor and conduct during testimony.
4. Understand the sources of proof.
5. Summarize investigator ethics and conduct.

Chapter Outline

INTRODUCTION

THROUGH THE USE OF SEVERAL steps in the court trial process, U.S. law ensures that an individual's rights are protected. The criminal process begins when a law is broken and, as mentioned in previous chapters, extends through the arrest, indictment, trial, and appeal.

There is no one single criminal court; instead, the federal system has its own court process on a national level, and each state and territory has its own set of rules that govern how the judicial process is applied. Norms and similarities do exist among all these government entities, but no two states have identical judicial systems, and nor are their systems identical to the federal system.

Each state's judicial process is not vastly different from that of any other state, nor does one state have a better chance of prosecuting a defendant than does another. There is no safe-haven state where any defendant has a better chance of avoiding justice than in another.

This process is complex and it contains several stages, along with several hearings in between. There are a number of possible resolutions of dispositions of a criminal case or charge. A case may be deferred, resulting in dismissal of the charge if the person completes a deferred prosecution agreement; or, a case may proceed to conviction and sentencing. A person can be sentenced only if convicted. A person can be convicted only on a guilty plea or by a finding of guilt after a trial by a judge or jury. A variety of sentencing possibilities is set by law. Within that range, however, the judge determines the actual sentence. An option that the court has in most cases is probation, but that depends on many variables. Additionally, courts can levy fines, community service, jail, and imprisonment.

PRIOR TO CASE FILING

When a case is investigated, there are a few different paths the suspect would have traveled. If the case has no suspect information or limited information, the suspect could not actually know they have a case pending. If a suspect has been arrested, one of three things would have occurred: The defendant has remained in custody, has bailed out, or was cited out to appear on another date. If the defendant is in custody, he or she normally is transported into a back sally port of the local courthouse that has jurisdiction on the case (see Figure 20.1). This area is often defaced by angry inmates who scratch derogatory messages in walls or other locations such as that shown in Figure 20.2. At times, these seemingly senseless acts of vandalism may contain content that may be of use to investigators.

CASE EVALUATION

Once law enforcement has concluded investigation into a criminal matter, the investigator determines whether there is enough evidence to warrant a filing of criminal charges. If the investigator chooses, there is latitude in some cases to close the case out without bringing it forward for filing. Usually, the investigator will bring a case to a filing prosecutor. The **filing district attorney** is normally a well-versed district attorney with years of experience in various aspects of the criminal court system. The filing district attorney has the discretion to decide whether or not to bring charges, and what charges to file. During this

FIGURE 20.1 ▶ Transportation bus transporting inmates to court. Once the bus pulls in, the sally port door draws down behind it. Once the inmates are removed from the bus, they are housed in lockup cells.

process the investigator and the filing district attorney engage in a discussion on what charges should be filed. Ultimately, however, the decision lies with the district attorney office. Sometimes the original charge is reduced or increased depending on a number of factors:

- Prior arrest record
- Active parole or probation
- Gang membership
- Severity of the crime

These are just some of the factors taken into account when deciding what charges, if any, to file. In minor cases, the prosecutor often decides that a particular incident, or even a particular

FIGURE 20.2 ▶ Standard display of a lack of respect for authority. Male inmates in court lockups take their aggression out on the agency that arrested them.

category of offenses, does not warrant the expenditure of resources by a criminal prosecution. These sorts of cases could include the following:

- Shoplifting with no prior record
- Misdemeanor battery
- Petty theft with no prior arrest record
- Public intoxication
- City and county ordinance violations

These are some of the crimes for which an all-out prosecution would not be worth the cost to the system. In more serious cases, the decision to withhold charges is less common. American criminal laws often contain overlapping statues bearing different penalties for the same actions. For example, an offender

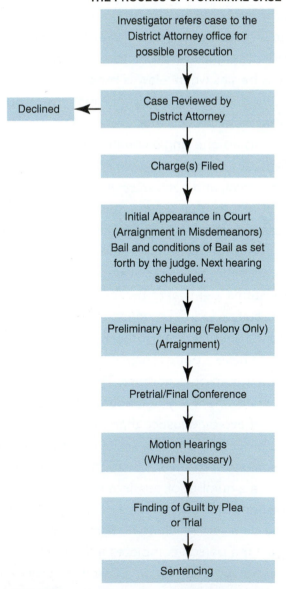

FIGURE 20.3 ▶ The typical legal path that a case takes from inception to sentencing.

FIGURE 20.4 ▶ A detective is sworn in before his testimony in a criminal trial.

who enters a convenience store, points a gun at the clerk, and demands money has committed a robbery. Technically, he has committed a theft in stealing the money; but the theft here is incorporated into the crime of robbery. Therefore, when filing a case like this, the investigator and prosecutor both understand that only one count of robbery will be filed, not robbery and theft. This discretion about what charges to file is important where some or all of the charges include mandatory minimum sentences. In these cases, the prosecutor may in effect exercise significant control over the sentence to be imposed if the defendant is convicted. By choosing to file the charge that carries the mandatory sentence, the prosecutor can guarantee that the judge cannot impose a lesser sentence.

TRIAL PROCESS

Figure 20.3 illustrates the entire criminal case process from inception to sentencing; however, this process may vary somewhat depending upon procedural differences in particular jurisdictions. Before the actual start of the trial, there will be several appearances by the defendant and/or their attorney. The first appearance for the defendant is called the **arraignment**. This is the first step in the courtroom process for the defendant. The defendant is formally read and advised of the pending charges. Additionally, the defendant is asked to enter a plea. In the United States there are three potential pleas: guilty, not guilty, and **no contest**. Guilty and not guilty pleas are self-explanatory; no contest is a plea in which the defendant accepts the sentence as if found guilty. The advantage to this plea is that most of the time it will not show the defendant as convicted of a certain crime in personal and court records. Once a plea is entered, the judge sets bail accordingly and sets a future court date. If the crime is a felony, the next appearance date is a **preliminary hearing**. If the crime is a misdemeanor, the next appearance date is set for a pretrial hearing. At a preliminary hearing, there is no jury and a judge decides whether the evidence warrants the defendant standing trial. The judge needs to

be convinced that the defendant was most likely responsible for committing the crime. Often, the defense attorney uses the preliminary hearing to have some or all of the charges dismissed. A common argument is the motion to suppress evidence based on a lack of probable cause. If a defense attorney can prove that law enforcement had no probable cause to arrest the defendant, then whether a crime was committed or not, the charges most likely will be dropped.

When the judge determines at the preliminary hearing that there are sufficient facts to believe the defendant committed the crime, the defendant will be bound over for trial. As trial nears, the prosecutor and the defense engage in various pretrial motions. These motions are used in an effort to set boundaries for trial. Typical motions are those to suppress evidence, to dismiss the case, to inspect grand jury minutes, to substitute counsel, and to produce exculpatory evidence. **Exculpatory evidence** is that which is favorable to a defendant. Normally, this type of evidence clears a defendant of any wrongdoing and ultimately leads to dismissal of that specific charge.

After all pretrial motions have been heard and ruled on, the case is prepared for trial. Technically, the trial does not begin until after the jury is seated; thus, a **jury selection** is commonly referred to as the first stage of a trial. At the beginning of a trial, the jury is chosen from the jury pool, a group of citizens randomly selected from the local community for jury duty. The judge, prosecutor, and defense attorney question each prospective juror. Jurors who for any reason are unable to judge the evidence fairly will not be able to sit on the jury. This is referred to as **challenge for cause**. A prospective juror may be challenged for conviction of serious crime, a financial interest in the outcome of the controversy, personal reasons, or professional reasons. If the case is child related, that in and of itself stirs up animosity. Many prospective jurors with children would openly admit a bias for the case. Additionally, the parties' attorneys may issue a certain number of peremptory challenges against prospective jurors. An attorney may use a peremptory challenge to keep any prospective juror off the jury, even if there is no reason to believe the prospective juror would judge the evidence unfairly. The only exception to this is race; an attorney may not exclude a juror from serving based solely on race. Active law enforcement officers are exempt from jury duty; however, a retired law enforcement officer is not. Often, the defense attorney will use a peremptory challenge to remove any prospective juror with a law enforcement background.

Once the jurors and alternate jurors have been seated, the judge usually gives the jury preliminary instructions on the law. The purpose of the preliminary instructions is to inform the jurors of the law and explain their duties. Typically, the judge summarizes the jurors' duties, instructing them on how to conduct themselves during the trial and recesses. These instructions normally last only a few minutes.

After the judge explains the preliminary instructions, the prosecutor and defense attorney give their **opening statements** to the jury. During opening statements, the lawyers outline the issues in the case and tell the jury what they expect the evidence will prove during the trial. The purpose of the opening statement is to give a general picture of the facts and issues surrounding the case—to help the jury understand the evidence and its relevance. The judge can limit the time of an opening statement.

Usually an attorney presents the opening statement as a story, trying to give a chronological sequence of the events that occurred before and during the incident. The statement is presented in the best light for the client or (if it's the prosecutor's statement) the state or federal government. The opening statement should be factual, not argumentative. The statement is not evidence, and both attorneys should not offer their opinion of the evidence. Attorneys are not permitted to make statements that cannot be supported by evidence they will present during the trial.

Once opening statements are presented, the prosecutor, who has the burden of proving his allegations, begins his **case in chief**. The case in chief is a term used to describe the actions of proving each legal claim in the indictment. Once the prosecution has concluded its case in chief, the defense attorney presents his case in chief for the defendant. The defense attorney presents evidence to refute the prosecutor's claims. During the trial, both sides will have the opportunity to call victims, witnesses, and law enforcement officers to the court to testify. As shown in Figure 20.4, all witnesses, including law enforcement officers, are required to be "sworn in" before providing testimony in a trial. In a court of law, the questioning of a witness by the party who called them to trial is referred to as **direct examination**. Once the direct examination is completed, the opposing attorney has the right to cross examine the witness. The main purpose of **cross examination** is to gain favorable facts from the witness or to impeach the witness's credibility. For example, if the prosecutor places a witness on the stand for a murder trial and the witness testifies that he or she saw the suspect commit the crime, the defense attorney can question the witness in an attempt to clarify any statements or to put doubt into the witness's testimony. The defense attorney may ask how far the witness was standing away from the crime, what time of day was it, whether the witness wears glasses, or whether the witness has any receipts or proof they were at the location. These are just a few of many questions that could be asked. As is shown in Figure 20.5, composure must always be maintained by law enforcement officers when in the courtroom, and particularly when on the witness stand while their behavior will be scrutinized by the trial judge and others in the courtroom. Once the cross examination is completed, the prosecutor may request the witness to clarify any information previously covered or yet to be. This is referred to as *redirect examination*. Once this is completed, the witness is excused.

During the trial, the prosecutor and the defense have four possible sources of evidence: witnesses, exhibits, stipulations, and judicial notices. The parties gain evidence from witnesses through examination. **Exhibits** are the next principal form of evidence in a trial. The four types of exhibits are real objects (guns, blood), items used for demonstration (diagrams, models, maps), writings (counterfeit checks, letters), and records (private business, phone, public records). Before an exhibit may be admitted as evidence in a trial, a foundation for its admissibility must be laid out. To provide this foundation, the prosecutor and defense attorney must establish what the item is and what it will show.

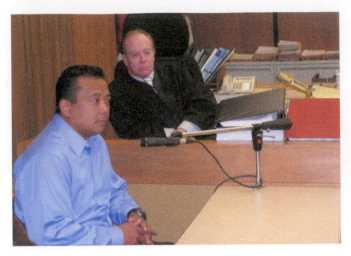

FIGURE 20.5 ▶ During the testimony the judge looks on intently in the direction of the detective.

As with witness testimony, the admissibility of exhibits is governed by rules of evidence. Rules and types of evidence were detailed in Chapter 2.

The third type of evidence that the prosecutor and defense attorneys may offer is **stipulations**. A stipulation is an agreement between the parties that certain facts exist and are not in dispute. For example, a defendant is arrested for possession of cocaine. The crime lab that tests the drug for its content may have to testify to the findings. Attorneys normally stipulate to the findings or the background of the crime lab chemist. Another common stipulation is done with expert witnesses. Attorneys may stipulate to the witnesses' credibility rather than make them spend time discussing credentials.

Judicial notice is the fourth method of offering evidence. If the judge takes judicial notice of a fact, the fact is assumed true and admitted as evidence. Judges take judicial notice of facts commonly known in the jurisdiction where the trial is held and that are easily determined and verified from a reliable source. Noting that the Denver Broncos football team is from Denver would be a simple example of taking judicial notice.

Once the defense rests its case, the prosecutor may introduce evidence that rebuts the defendant's evidence. Rebuttal evidence is usually offered to refute a specific piece of evidence introduced by the defense. The defense may then rebut evidence offered during the plaintiff's rebuttal case. Eventually both sides will rest their case and proceed to **closing arguments**. After both sides have presented their cases, the prosecutor and defense attorney present their closing arguments. During closing arguments, the attorneys attempt to persuade the jury to render a verdict in their clients' favor. Typically, the attorneys tell the jury what the evidence has proved, how it ties into the jury instructions, and why the evidence and the law require a verdict in their favor. Because closing arguments provide the attorneys with their last chance to persuade the jury, the closing arguments often provide the most dramatic moments of a trial. Closing arguments typically last 30 to 60 minutes, although they can take much longer.

After the prosecutor and defense attorney have completed their closing arguments, the judge instructs the jury on the law applicable to the case. This is referred to as *jury instructions*. In most jurisdictions, the judge both reads the instructions and provides written instructions to the jury. The jury is also given verdict forms. On the verdict forms, the jury indicates how it finds on each of the claims presented during the trial. Sometimes the jury may be given special verdict forms asking how the jury finds on a specific issue of fact or law. The jury instructions normally last 10 to 20 minutes, although they may take much longer in complex cases. In cases that involve special circumstances murder or complex white collar crimes, the instructions can take an extended amount of time. This is because the judge has to explain the various charges and what the jury can find guilt on.

Once the instructions are read, the jury is excused to the jury room for deliberations. It is up to the jury to decide how to organize itself and conduct the deliberations. The judge usually only instructs the jurors to select a foreperson to preside over the deliberations and to sign the verdict form that reflects their decisions. The judge confers with the attorneys and sends a written response to the jury. A jury might deliberate anywhere from a few minutes to several days. If a jury deliberates for under an hour, the case is either overwhelmingly for conviction or the opposite. This tells the court that there was little doubt in the decision made by the jurors. If the jury tells the judge it cannot reach a verdict, the judge usually gives the jury some further instructions and returns it to the jury room for further deliberations. If the jury still cannot reach a verdict, however, the jury is deadlocked, and a mistrial is declared. The case must then be retried.

When the jury reaches a verdict and signs the verdict forms, it notifies the judge that it has reached a decision. The attorneys, if they are not in the courtroom, are called, and everyone returns to the courtroom. The judge asks the foreperson if the jury has reached a verdict. The foreperson responds "yes," and the verdict forms are read aloud, usually by the court clerk.

CASE CLOSE-UP 20.1

INVESTIGATOR INTUITION PROMPTS SERIAL KILLER'S CONFESSION

(Atlanta, Georgia)

During the trial of the accused Atlanta child murder suspect Wayne Williams, FBI investigator and criminal profiler John Douglas used his psychological profile of Williams to help prosecutors win their case in court. Based on his behavioral assessment method, Douglas predicted that Williams was an antisocial offender type—a type of offender characterized by hypersensitivity to personal criticism and noted for hot-headed careless reactions when confronted by persons who are judgmental of them. Douglas provided his profile assessment of Williams to prosecutors, who used this information to tailor their examination of Williams on the witness stand to create a type of psychological stress that would cause him to lose his temper and say something that was self-incriminating. Following a number of cross-examination questions designed to cause William to lose his temper on the stand, the prosecutor asked, "What was it like when you wrapped your hands around their throats, Wayne? What was it? Did you panic?" No longer able to contain his temper, and in a seemingly uncontrollable manner, Williams said "NO!" At that point, the prosecutor turned to the jury stating that Williams had just confessed. In reply, Williams began screaming that he was innocent to the prosecutor and other members of the court; but at that point, it was too late. He was subsequently found guilty of first-degree murder.

TESTIMONY

The bedrock of the American judicial process is the honesty of witnesses in trial. Eyewitness testimony can make a deep impression on a jury, which is often exclusively assigned the role of sorting out credibility issues and making judgments about the truth of witness statements.[1]

When it comes to courtroom testimony, there are different types of testimony that take place. The investigator is a witness when it comes to in-court testimony. Additionally, there are witnesses to the incident who are not investigators. This kind of witness is referred to as an **outside witness**. An outside witness is a person who does not have the comfort level of experience in testifying. An experienced investigator who has testified well over a hundred times has a courtroom demeanor and ability fine-tuned over numerous court appearances. A witness without this experience can be intimidated by the courtroom, the judge, and the sheer image of everybody in the courtroom focusing their attention on them during trial. This can cause the witness to forget pertinent information and possibly cause irreparable damage to a case. The competence of a witness has to be examined before trial. This is normally done by the prosecutor and investigator as they discuss the case. An experienced investigator will know which witness is credible or whether a witness possesses characteristics that could cause him or her to be discredited on the stand.

The first responder, investigator, and those crucial to the case will be called to testify. Making a good arrest is only the initial step in getting a criminal off the street. To keep a criminal off the street, a law enforcement officer must testify in court. An officer's performance in the courtroom can largely determine what a judge or jury may decide. Courtroom testimony is one of

FIGURE 20.6 ▶ The detective and defense attorney engage in an exchange of testimony during a criminal trial. Note: The detective's hand motions depict some frustration with the line of questioning. Limited use of such body language may be appropriate as a means of adding emphasis to certain testimonial statements.

FIGURE 20.7 ▶ The detective begins his testimony. Notice the position of the hands as the detective's mouth opens. When on the witness stand, as shown here, the trial judge and other courtroom participants will analyze the body language of officers providing testimony.

the more important skills for a police officer to learn, but few officers are given any formal training regarding being a good witness. Because a case goes to trial well after the initial arrest and follow-up investigation, it is easy to understand how certain facts would naturally be forgotten. There is nothing wrong with not remembering an incident in its entirety. Many law enforcement officers cite testifying in court as one of the most stressful aspects of their job, perceiving it as an adversarial system where defense attorneys may skewer them during aggressive cross-examination. As witnesses, law enforcement officers must ensure that the facts they present communicate the complete story and that their delivery of those facts makes their testimony clear and credible.

Police officers sometimes find that their testimony straddles the domains of fact and expert witness. For example, an officer may be queried about what he did and what the defendant did and then be asked to state an opinion (like an expert witness); or, he may state an opinion that the opposing attorney challenges, and the judge must decide whether or not to admit it in the record. Officers should understand the importance of proper record keeping and always strive to develop a well-organized, standardized, and readable style for reports. This will help them clarify, organize, and remember particular points if the case goes to trial. Officers can draw pictures to illustrate their descriptions and to jog their memories in court. They can supplement standard forms and checklists with their own words and drawings to help explain a potentially confusing scenario.

PRIOR TO TRIAL

Officers should review their cases several times. The more thoroughly they know the facts and theories about the case, the more easily they can answer questions without relying on rote memory. Their knowledge and recollection will be an organic,

holistic, automatic process against cross-examination. An officer should meet with the prosecutor several times to review testimony. Together, they should clarify the officer's testimony, agree how the officer should best express himself, and discuss what the prosecution and defense sides will ask.

Officers should mentally rehearse for their case, going over the facts and testimony out loud to themselves while standing in front of a mirror or driving. Even for the seasoned witness, no substitute exists for adequate preparation. Many veteran experts have let their overconfidence lead to loose ends, inadvertently hindering their testimony.[2]

ON THE STAND

Certainly, most important aspects of courtroom demeanor cannot be programmed; witnesses bring their own unique style to the stand. Nevertheless, officers productively can apply a few principles of effective testimony. They should have a general attitude of confidence but not cockiness. To the average juror, police officers convey an air of authority and respect; therefore, they should maintain composure and dignity at all times and remember that their job is only to present the facts and evidence.

Body language is important. Officers should always sit up straight. If a microphone is present, officers should sit close enough to not have to lean over every time they speak. They should keep presentation materials neatly organized in front of them to find needed documents and exhibits. While testifying, officers should look at the attorney questioning them and then switch eye contact to the jury when answering. They should establish a connection with the jurors because juries tend to find witnesses who look straight at them more credible. Officers should remain open, friendly, and dignified and speak clearly, slowly, and concisely. They should keep sentences short and to the point and maintain a steady voice tone, as in a normal conversation. Officers' general attitude toward the jury should convey a sense of peer respect.

Officers should carefully listen to each question before they respond. If they do not fully understand the question, they should ask the attorney to repeat or rephrase it, taking a couple of seconds to compose their thoughts, if necessary. An officer who does not know the answer to the question should state plainly, "I don't know."

An officer should not try to bluff his or her way out of a difficult question. Officers should not become defensive, and, above all, they must be honest. If anyone in the courtroom detects even a somewhat dishonest answer, especially from police officers, it can ruin all the rest of the officer's testimony. Attorneys sometimes phrase questions in a way that constrains answers in a particular direction. Officers who feel they cannot honestly answer the question with a simple yes or no should respond: "Sir, if I limit my answer to yes or no, I will not be able to give factual testimony. Is that what you wish me to do?" Sometimes, the attorney voluntarily will reword the question. But, if the attorney presses for a yes-or-no answer, at that point, either the opposing attorney will voice an objection or the judge will intervene. The latter may instruct the cross-examining attorney to allow the officer more leeway in responding or to rephrase his question, or may simply order the officer to answer the question as asked.

Additionally, officers should not preface answers with such phrases as the following: "I believe...."; "I estimate...."; "To the best of my knowledge/recollection...."; "As far as I know...."; "What I was able to piece together...."; or "I'm pretty sure that...." Instead, officers should answer as definitely as possible, or honestly state that a particular piece of testimony may not be a clear perception or recollection; but they should remain firm about what they are sure about. In general, officers should try not to answer beyond the question. For example, if the attorney asks for answers phrased in precise measurements that are not relevant or that the officer cannot accurately recall, the officer should not speculate unless actually asked to do so. Speculating will open up a rugged and aggressive cross examination by the defense.

As important as the testimony is, some *nonverbal factors* also are important to the success of an investigator's testimony. First is *appearance:* Present a clean and well-kept appearance, dressing in appropriate business attire. An investigator normally will wear a suit, while the patrol officer will wear his standard street uniform. The second factor is *posture.* Present a comfortably straight posture when standing and sitting. Refrain from slouching, as this may suggest contempt or a lack of confidence or knowledge. The third factor is *gestures.* Use meaningful gestures to emphasize what is being stated (see Figure 20.6), but avoid waving and excessive hand movement. The fourth factor is *rate and tone of speech.* The rate at which the investigator speaks may affect the panel's perception of his credibility. If he gives his testimony too quickly, the panel may not hear him. The last factor is *movement.* Avoid movements that are annoying and distracting. This can be facilitated by staying consciously aware of your hand and body movements,

and keeping your hands together in your lap, in a relaxed and comfortable manner (see Figure 20.7).

Leaving the witness stand is as important as when the investigator enters the courtroom. Upon entrance and exit, the jury will follow the steps of the investigator. Jurors try to gauge what type of person the investigator may be. Jurors have had good and bad experiences with law enforcement officers, and some only know what they see on television about cops. These thoughts are racing through the jurors' minds when the investigator enters and leaves the courtroom. The impression left with the jurors will remain.[3]

ETHICAL APPLICATION IN INVESTIGATIONS AND THE COURT

More and more nowadays, law enforcement officers are accused of misconduct during courtroom trials. There really is no secret in conducting ethical investigations. The simple reality is, don't lie—tell the truth. The problem is, sometimes emotions carry an investigation and cause an investigator to alter information to sustain a conviction. In this situation the investigator can count on one of two things for sure, and maybe both. The first thing is, they will be terminated. The second thing is, depending on the egregiousness of the act, they could go to prison. Police misconduct is *procedural* when it refers violation of police department rules and regulations; *criminal* when it refers to violation of state and federal laws; and *unconstitutional* when it refers to violating a citizen's civil rights or any combination thereof. Common forms of misconduct are excessive use of physical or deadly force, discriminatory arrest, physical or verbal harassment, and selective enforcement of the law. When these sorts of arrests are made, they almost always require a follow-up investigation, and this is where the investigator could get into some trouble. When an officer uses deadly force, the investigation is done by the agency that used the deadly force and the district attorney office. Altering a report to favor the officer will result in severe misconduct issues.

Law enforcement officers are professionals; they work in a skilled occupational group whose prime consideration is providing a service that benefits the public. Because law enforcement is a profession, ethics and ethical conduct play an important role. Ethics and ethical standards involve doing the right thing, at the right time, in the right way. Law enforcement personnel must remain ethical and conduct themselves accordingly at all times, both on and off duty. The law enforcement code of ethics and the police code of conduct represent the basis for ethical behavior in law enforcement. In addition, these codes encourage law enforcement's classification as a profession. These codes are simply words, however. For them to be effective, law enforcement officials and their leaders must consider them as the bible for law enforcement. Law enforcement personnel must not only believe in the codes but also follow them and display conduct that supports them.

FIGURE 20.8 ▶ This computer-rendered illustration shows how an armed man distraught over a decision made by Judge Michael Harwin entered the judge's courtroom and opened fire.

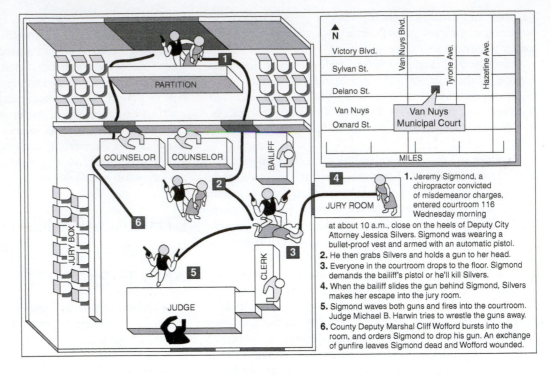

1. Jeremy Sigmond, a chiropractor convicted of misdemeanor charges, entered courtroom 116 Wednesday morning at about 10 a.m., close on the heels of Deputy City Attorney Jessica Silvers. Sigmond was wearing a bullet-proof vest and armed with an automatic pistol.
2. He then grabs Silvers and holds a gun to her head.
3. Everyone in the courtroom drops to the floor. Sigmond demands the bailiff's pistol or he'll kill Silvers.
4. When the bailiff slides the gun behind Sigmond, Silvers makes her escape into the jury room.
5. Sigmond waves both guns and fires into the courtroom. Judge Michael B. Harwin tries to wrestle the guns away.
6. County Deputy Marshal Cliff Wofford bursts into the room, and orders Sigmond to drop his gun. An exchange of gunfire leaves Sigmond dead and Wofford wounded.

COURTROOM DANGERS

Time and time again, the antics of out-of-control defendants are reported on TV in our living rooms. However, Judge Michael Harwin, shown in Figure 20.7, experienced a life-changing event in his courtroom during the early part of his career as a judge (see Figure 20.8). In 1988, he had presided over a misdemeanor trial involving evasion of police. The suspect was found wearing a bulletproof vest and a football helmet. He claimed he had been threatened by the Mafia and the police were working with the mob. At trial he claimed that a box full of audio tapes he had made contained recorded threats. The tapes ultimately were proved to have no threats on them, and the defendant was not allowed to play empty tapes to the jury. The man, Jeremy Sigmond, who had been out on bail, returned on the day of sentencing. Harwin was calling morning calendar when he heard the bailiff shout, "Drop the gun!" The judge turned to see the defendant with a gun pointed at the head of the assistant city attorney who had prosecuted the case. The defendant began yelling, "I want another trial. We're going to use my rules. Do it my way." Judge Harwin pushed the emergency button, but the alarm, although it sounded somewhere, did not tell the marshals, who were in charge of security at the time, which courtroom was in trouble. A courtroom-to-courtroom search had to be launched, with Harwin's courtroom at the end of the line. The defendant yelled to the bailiff, "Give me your gun or I'll shoot her!" The bailiff, fearing for the safety of the hostage, slid her gun away to the suspect. As the suspect reached for the bailiff's gun, the hostage was able to jerk away and run into a nearby bathroom, where she locked herself inside.

At about this time, Deputy Cliff Wofford arrived alone to see whether Harwin had pushed the emergency alarm button. Wofford opened the door, saw the gunman, and shouted, "Drop your gun!" The defendant opened fire and so did Wofford. Wofford was hit in the stomach. Incredibly, Wofford's return fire had no effect on the suspect. Wofford was able to crawl on his back out the door. The shooter then turned the gun on Harwin. Bullets slammed into Harwin's chair.

Harwin remembers feeling a rush of air as the bullets passed by his head. Realizing that the defendant was heading toward the bench, the judge was resolved not to let the gunman take control of his courtroom and hurt anybody else. With nowhere left to go, Harwin leapt off the bench and onto the gunman, who had reached the base of his steps. Both the judge and the gunman began to wrestle for control of the guns. Harwin was finally able to gain control of both guns, as several law enforcement officers ran into the court room. Harwin had the defendant's hands pinned behind him and the marshals handcuffed him without further incident. Harwin noticed that his robe was blood-stained, but his only injury was a slight cut made by one of the guns when he wrestled it away from the suspect. On examination, it became clear why Wofford's shots did not seem to affect the defendant: He had come to court with two bullet-proof vests on his back. The defendant, however, had been hit by one bullet in his back and was pronounced dead at the scene. A total of 27 shots had been fired.[4] Although situations such as this involving violence in the courtroom as rare, violent acts committed by criminal defendants are becoming more commonplace in today's courtroom. Therefore, the lesson learned in this final case study is that investigators should never let their guard down while outside or inside of the courtroom.

Summary

1. **Understand how a criminal case proceeds through the criminal justice court system.**

   Once a suspect is arrested or a police report is written, the case is transferred to a detective, who will conduct a follow-up investigation. When sufficient evidence is gathered, the investigator presents the case to the district attorney for filing. If charges are filed, the suspect, if in custody, will be arraigned. If the suspect is not in custody, a warrant will be issued for the suspect's arrest. After the suspect is arraigned, a plea will be entered and bail issues will be discussed. If the crime is a felony, a date is set for a preliminary hearing. If the crime is a misdemeanor, a pretrial date is set. If the judge finds enough evidence in the preliminary hearing that the suspect probably committed the crime, the case will be set for trial.

2. **Describe the steps in the trial process.**

   The trial process begins with jury selection. During this process the prosecutor and the defense attorney interview several perspective jurors to determine whether they would serve fairly during the trial. Once the jury is seated, the judge gives some preliminary instructions regarding the case. The prosecutor and defense engage in opening statements, discussing a general storyline of the case and what their evidence will show. Once the statements have been heard, both sides present their case to the jury. After the case has been heard, closing statements are conducted, followed by instructions from the judge. From here, the jury will deliberate and render a verdict.

3. **Assess a case for filing.**

   When an investigator finishes an investigation, a decision is made to determine whether there is enough evidence to warrant a filing. If there is, the investigator discusses it with the district attorney. Together they will take the case, characteristics, and past criminal history of the suspect into account as they determine what charges, if any, to file.

4. **Understand the sources of proof.**

   When it comes to trial, there are four sources of evidence. These are witnesses, exhibits, stipulations, and judicial notice. Witnesses provide evidence through examination and their actual involvement in the case. Exhibits are the next principal form of evidence in a trial. The four types of exhibits are real objects (guns, blood), items used for demonstration (diagrams, models, maps), writings (counterfeit checks, letters), and records (private business, phone, public records). A stipulation is an agreement between the parties that certain facts exist and are not in dispute. If the judge takes judicial notice of a fact, the fact is assumed true and admitted as evidence.

5. **Describe the role of the criminal investigator on the stand.**

   Officers should have a general attitude of confidence but not cockiness. To the average juror, police officers convey an air of authority and respect; therefore, they should maintain composure and dignity at all times and remember that their job is only to present the facts and evidence. Officers should remain open, friendly, and dignified and speak clearly, slowly, and concisely. They should keep sentences short and to the point and maintain a steady voice tone, as in a normal conversation. Officers' general attitude toward the jury should convey a sense of peer respect. Most importantly, they are there to tell the truth about an incident they have knowledge about.

Key Terms

filing district attorney
arraignment
no contest
preliminary hearing
exculpatory evidence
jury selection

challenge for cause
opening statements
case in chief
direct examination
cross examination
judicial notice

stipulations
exhibits
closing argument
outside witness

Review Questions

1. What is a district attorney who files cases called?

2. What factors are taken into account when charges are filed?

3. What is the first hearing held when a suspect is arrested?

4. Is there a preliminary hearing for a misdemeanor crime?

5. What is the judge's responsibility during a preliminary hearing?

6. In what part of the trial do the prosecutor and defense present their cases?

7. Name three things an investigator should do before the trial starts.

8. Name the four types of evidence.

9. What are nonverbal actions?

10. What is cross examination?

Notes

[1] George Fisher, "The Jury's Rise as a Lie Detector," *The Yale Law Journal* 107, 575.

[2] *FBI Law Enforcement Bulletin*, "On the Spot: Testifying in Court for Law Enforcement Officers," October 2006.

[3] Much of this information comes from the authors' practical experience in testifying in court numerous times in Los Angeles.

[4] Interview with Judge Michael Harwin.

GLOSSARY

Allan Pinkerton Founder of the Pinkerton National Detective Agency, the first private investigators in the United States. Pinkerton detectives were contracted by the U.S. government to assist federal agents in investigative and law enforcement activities such as tracking counterfeiters and providing presidential protection.

Alphonse Bertillon Creator of anthropometry, an early method of human identification designed to rival the fingerprint. Anthropometry was performed by recording body measurements such as head diameter, arm length, and foot size.

Alphonse "Scarface" Capone Infamous Chicago gangster and mob leader, dubiously designated as "Public Enemy #1" for his bootlegging activities, who was arrested and convicted on federal charges resulting from an extensive investigation carried out by Special Agent Eliot Ness of the U.S. Bureau of Prohibition.

American Board of Criminalistics One of the nation's leading professional organization that provides guidance in regard to ethics, standards, training, scientific practices and other matters affecting the field of criminalistics.

anthropometry The process of human identification through the measurement of physical body features (e.g., arms, legs, ears, nose) and their dimensions.

August Vollmer Considered the "father of modern law enforcement." While serving as Chief of Police of the Los Angeles Police Department, Vollmer created the nation's first municipal police crime lab at the LAPD.

Bow Street Runners Considered by many historians of investigation to be the world's first organized and paid plainclothes detective force. Founded in 1748 by Henry Fielding in the Bow Street area of London, "the runners" consisted of six to eight community members who carried weapons and tracked criminals throughout all of England. They are also believed to have founded the practice of bounty hunting because they routinely investigated property crimes and obtained monetary rewards upon returning stolen property to its rightful owner.

Bureau of Alcohol, Tobacco, Firearms and Explosives (ATF) Federal law enforcement agency created in 1970 to investigate violent criminals, criminal organizations, the illegal use and trafficking of firearms, the illegal use and storage of explosives, acts of arson and bombings, acts of terrorism, and the illegal diversion of alcohol and tobacco products.

Calvin Goddard Established the scientific study of ballistics and later founded the nation's first private crime lab—the Bureau of Forensic Ballistics—in New York in 1927.

Charles Appel FBI special agent who, in the 1930s, proposed the creation of the FBI crime laboratory and became its first director.

CODIS (Combined DNA Index System) Database created and administered by the FBI to house DNA genetic fingerprints of known offenders that law enforcement can access for criminal identification purposes.

criminalistics The use of scientific principles in identifying, examining, and testing physical evidence related to suspected criminal activities.

deoxyribonucleic acid (DNA) The human genetic blueprint, contained within cellular material, that is used to produce genetic fingerprints for criminal identification purposes.

Drug Enforcement Agency (DEA) Federal law enforcement agency created in 1973 by President Richard Nixon for the purpose of enforcing U.S. drug laws and codes.

Edmond Locard Founder of the world's first crime lab in Lyons, France (circa 1910) and creator of the exchange principle (every contact leaves a trace).

Eliot Ness Special agent for the U.S. Bureau of Prohibition, noted for heading investigations against Chicago area mobsters for liquor violations and credited with toppling the criminal empire of notorious gangster Alphonse "Scarface" Capone.

Eugène Vidocq Purported to be the world's first public detective and was employed by the *Sûreté* (French Undercover Police) circa 1811. He was noted for using disguises and trickery in his investigations.

Federal Bureau of Investigation (FBI) Founded in 1908 as the Bureau of Investigation, the FBI was a general investigative agency that dealt with crimes committed against the U.S. Government. The present-day mission of the FBI includes the investigation of matters relating to civil rights, counterterrorism, foreign counterintelligence, and organized crime/drugs, as well as a range of violent and financial crimes.

forensic sciences The application of science to the law, generally including the work of specialists within particular scientific fields, as opposed to criminalistics, which draws expertise from various specialized scientific disciplines.

Francis Tukey City Marshal of Boston who developed various investigative methods, including "the show-up of rogues," where police viewed known offenders for purposes of easy recognition in future crime investigations. He has also been recognized as possibly the nation's first detective.

Hans Gross Austrian attorney whose book *Criminal Investigation* introduced the idea of using scientific methods to produce physical evidence during the investigative process. He is also noted for coining the term *criminalistics* to describe the application of science to investigation.

Henry Fielding Founder of the Bow Street Runners in London circa 1748. Fielding is credited with originating the idea of thief taking, which involved private citizens responding to and investigating crimes in their own neighborhoods.

Integrated Automated Fingerprint Identification System (IAFIS) Originally known as AFIS (Automated Fingerprint Identification System), the IAFIS database contains millions of fingerprint digital images obtained from offenders and crime scenes. These can be compared to unknown or suspect fingerprints obtained in any state (or country, sometimes) to provide matches or hits for criminal identification purposes.

J. Edgar Hoover Appointed Director of the FBI in 1924 to lead and reform the FBI's crime-fighting efforts. In addition to professionalizing the standards and training of the Bureau's Special Agent force, Hoover integrated many scientific crime-fighting tools into the agency's investigative functions, including the first fingerprint classification system.

Mathieu Orfila   Spanish scientist who pioneered the field of toxicology by studying the effects of poisons first on animals and then on humans.

National Bureau of Criminal Identification   The first FBI repository of fingerprints to serve as a means of criminal identification.

National Crime Information Center (NCIC)   A nationwide system, created by the FBI in 1967, that serves as a clearinghouse of crime-related information to assist local and state law enforcement agencies with apprehending fugitives and recovering stolen property.

Paul Kirk   University professor and scientist who pioneered the method of blood spatter analysis and developed numerous advances in the study of trace evidence and arson investigation.

Pinkerton detectives   The nation's first private detective agency created by Allan Pinkerton in 1850. Pinkerton detectives, known as *Private Eyes*, provided security to the U.S. President, assisted in federal and local investigations, and captured many well-known outlaws including Jesse James, Butch Cassidy, and John Younger.

Pitchfork case   Famous murder and sexual assault case in England during the mid-1980s in which Sir Alec Jeffreys first demonstrated genetic fingerprinting by matching DNA from a crime scene to the DNA of crime suspects, resulting in the arrest and conviction of accused killer Colin Pitchfork.

Sacco-Vanzetti murder case   Early-1920s high-profile case where Calvin Goddard served as an expert witness regarding ballistics evidence. Goddard's testimony supported the guilt of the defendant's and was used to establish ballistics as a court recognized forensic examination method.

Scotland Yard Detective Branch   Assumed to be the first municipal plainclothes police detective squad, formed in London circa 1842. The public was slow to accept these out-of-uniform police officers, but eventually approved of them after their capture of notorious killer Daniel Good, who was much feared by the citizens of London.

Sherlock Holmes   Fictional detective featured in numerous novels written by Sir Arthur Conan Doyle, who based his stories on the real-life investigations of French detective Eugène-François Vidocq. The Holmes character is most noted for introducing the investigative process of deduction as a logical case solving tool—a mainstay of today's real-life investigators.

Sir Alec Jeffreys   Performed the first recognized application of DNA to a criminal case (the famed Pitchfork case) and demonstrated that genetic fingerprinting could be used as a viable investigative tool for personal identification.

Sir Francis Gaulton   Discovered that the friction ridge patterns of all human fingerprints could be classified within three general categories—arches, loops, and whorls—and theorized that each individual has a unique fingerprint pattern like that of no other person, including an identical twin.

Sir John Fielding   Younger half-brother of Henry Fielding who assumed the leadership role of the Bow Street runners in 1754 after his older brother's death that same year. He is credited with transforming the group into one of organized plainclothes detectives. A blind man, he was noted for his keen ability to apprehend criminals by recognizing their voices.

St. Valentine's Day Massacre   The 1929 murder of seven gangsters in a Chicago garage, which was orchestrated by Al "Scarface" Capone. The national media attention given to the event resulted in a large scale federal investigation against Capone and his mob, which led to their eventual arrest and conviction.

Texas Rangers   The nation's first state-level law enforcement agency, founded in Texas circa 1835 to protect the early settlers and track down wanted fugitives. One of the most notable early Texas Rangers, Frank Hamer, is credited with the ambush and killing of famed outlaws Bonnie and Clyde. The Rangers still function today as an investigative unit within the Texas Department of Public Safety.

The Untouchables   Name given to Eliot Ness and his federal law enforcement agents, who were considered to be resistant to corruption by the high-power criminals operating during the Prohibition Era such as Alphonse "Scarface" Capone and other mobsters involved in organized crime.

toxicology   The study and scientific examination of the effects of poisons on the body, including drugs and alcohol.

U.S. Department of Homeland Security (DHS)   Created in 2003 by President George W. Bush in response to the increasing threat of domestic and international terrorism. The establishment of the DHS—the largest reorganization of federal law enforcement agencies in American history—produced one umbrella organization, which includes U.S. Customs and Border Protection (CBP), Transportation Security Administration (TSA), U.S. Coast Guard (USCG), U.S. Secret Service (USSS), Officer of the Inspector General (OIG), Federal Protective Service (FPS), and U.S. Immigration and Customs Enforcement (ICE).

U.S. Immigration and Customs Enforcement (ICE)   Federal investigative agency within the Department of Homeland Security charged with the investigation of any crime connected to the American border, including weapons trafficking, child pornography, human trafficking, and drug offenses.

U.S. Marshals Service (USMS)   Originally created by President George Washington in 1789, the USMS is the oldest federal law enforcement agency in the United States. The current U.S. Marshals Service still has a general mission to protect court officers and buildings and to ensure the effective operation of the of the U.S. judicial system. In addition, U.S. Marshals assists with court security, transports prisoners, serves arrest warrants, and performs investigations leading to the capture of fugitives.

U.S. Postal Inspection Service (USPIS)   The nation's second oldest federal law enforcement agency, created in 1830, began with the mission of protecting mail and its transportation sources. Today, however, USPIS's mission is much broader—enforcing the laws that defend the nation's mail system from illegal or dangerous use, including mail fraud, mail theft, violent crimes, identity theft, bombings, child exploitation, and terrorism.

U.S. Secret Service (USSS)   The third federal law enforcement agency to be created (circa 1865) in the United States. Originally housed in the U.S. Department of Treasury, the USSS at first had a mission that included investigation of counterfeiting and protection of the U.S. President. Today, the USSS is housed within the Department of Homeland Security and investigates a broad range of crimes including fraud, computer and telecommunications fraud, false identification documents, access device fraud, advance fee fraud, electronic funds transfers, and money laundering.

actus reus An act or failure to act (omission) that results in criminal responsibility. Both *actus reus* and *mens rea* are required in most cases to prove a felony offense.

affidavit A document, generally the written part of a search warrant application, used to declare under penalty of perjury the truth of a statement made by a party involved in a legal proceeding. Affidavits are used by investigators seeking warrants and require the officer to provide a sworn statement of information that is used to establish probable cause for the judicial issuance of the warrant.

anticipatory warrant A warrant issued in anticipation of a suspect's future conduct. Probable cause may be established for this type of warrant by demonstrating that the suspect has taken significant steps toward the completion of a particular criminal act.

arrest Placing persons in legal custody or its functional equivalent based on the reasonable belief that they are committing, have committed, or are about commit a criminal offense.

arrest warrant A warrant issued by a judge or magistrate upon proper demonstration of probable cause allowing officers to take persons into legal custody.

bench hearing A court proceeding or trial that is carried out by a judge or magistrate without a jury. In trial situations, defendants effectively waive their right to a jury trial and rely on a judge to act as the trier of both the law and the facts involved in a particular case.

beyond a reasonable doubt The quantum of evidence, or legal threshold, that must be met during a court proceeding to find a criminal defendant guilty of a criminal offense. Although subjective in nature, the beyond a reasonable doubt threshold generally is considered to be met when the trier of fact (jury or judge) is 90 percent or more certain of a criminal defendant's guilt.

consensual encounter An initial contact between an officer and a citizen that does not involve words or actions on the part of the officer that would lead the citizen to believe that he or she is not free to leave the presence of the officer (i.e., being physically detained or arrested).

consent to search form A written waiver of a citizen's Fourth Amendment rights that allows an officer to conduct a search without having probable cause to do so, although such forms can be used as an added safeguard in cases where probable cause to search does exist.

corpus delicti Literally meaning "the body of the crime," this term refers to the necessary first step in the investigative process involving establishment of proof that a crime has been committed.

criminal procedural laws Laws that govern proper procedures for investigators such as arresting suspects, searching crime scenes, and seizing property as evidence.

curtilages Land areas, including structures on them, used exclusively by persons living on them, that require a warrant before they can be searched (if legal circumstances permitting a warrantless search are not present). These can be backyards, fenced grounds, storage sheds, unattached garages, dog houses, horse stables, and even tree houses.

deceptive consent Any form of coercion or trickery used by officers to gain consent from a suspect to perform a search or conduct other activities that violate the suspect's legal rights.

detention The level of contact between a citizen and officer that is more intrusive than a consensual encounter, but less intrusive than an arrest. Detention usually occurs when a reasonable person feels, through the words or actions of an officer, that they are not free to leave the officer's presence while information related to a suspected offense is being gathered.

elements of the crime Specific behaviors and/or circumstances that must be supported by facts in order for a crime to be proven. For example, a case may be tried in court on the theory that a suspect has committed burglary, but the theory must be proven by demonstrating that all of the elements of the crime of burglary are supported by the facts of the case.

exigent circumstances Emergency circumstances that permit a warrantless search to be conducted based on the assumption that taking time to secure a warrant would result in the destruction of evidence or imminent harm to individuals.

fruit of the poisonous tree The basic rule of law that specifies that all evidence obtained from an illegal search is tainted and therefore inadmissible in a court of law. This rule is based on the analogy that all fruit on a tree (i.e., all evidence from a search) will be poisonous if poison has been applied to its roots (i.e., the illegal search).

good faith exception The basic rule of law that if officers conduct a search based on a belief that they have obtained a valid warrant, evidence obtained from the search will remain admissible in court even if it is later discovered that the warrant was technically invalid when originally issued by a judge or magistrate.

inadmissible evidence Evidence that has been obtained illegally, usually through a warrantless search under circumstances that required a valid search warrant. Such evidence is barred from use during trials or other court proceedings.

inevitable discovery The basic rule of law that evidence obtained by officers during an invalid warrantless search that would inevitably be discovered during a search or other evidence gathering process is nonetheless admissible for trial purposes.

knock warrant A warrant requiring that occupants of a location that is the subject of a search or other court-authorized activity conducted by officers be notified before the location is entered.

mens rea The criminal intent, or guilty mind, on the part of an offender at the time of the offense, which is a requirement to prove most crimes that are not considered strict liability crimes.

motor vehicle exception The basic rule of law permitting officers greater discretion to search motor vehicles (including trailers and anything else that is mobile) under warrantless circumstances due to the assumption that a person's expectation of privacy is less in mobile locations than in a fixed location such as a residence.

no knock warrant A warrant that does not necessarily require that occupants of a location that is the subject of a search or other court-authorized activity conducted by officers be notified before the location is entered. Such warrants are issued when it can be demonstrated that prior notification could result in danger to persons or destruction of evidence.

open fields doctrine The legal rule that allows officers to conduct a warrantless search in open fields because in such locations there is no reasonable expectation of privacy.

plain feel exception   Evidence resembling a weapon or contraband that is felt during an officer's legally authorized pat-down search (or other legal touching) of a suspect may be seized without a warrant. Recognition of the object seized as a weapon or contraband, however, must be based on the officer's prior knowledge, experience, and training.

plain view   The legal authorization for officers to conduct warrantless searches and seizures when observing crime-related objects or activities from a location in which they are legally present.

probable cause   A reasonable belief on the part of an officer that a crime is being, has been, or is about to be committed by particular individuals or other sources capable of committing crimes (e.g., organizational entities).

reasonable suspicion   A reasonable suspicion on the part of an officer that a crime is being, has been, or is about to be committed by particular individuals or other sources capable of committing crimes (e.g., organizational entities).

search incident to arrest   The legal authorization for an officer to conduct a warrantless search of a suspect and the area of their immediate control following a lawful arrest.

search warrant return   Postsearch process that requires investigators to provide judges with a list all the items seized during a search and bring those items before a judge.

sneak and peak warrants   Search warrants that authorize law enforcement officers to enter private property without the permission or knowledge of its occupants, and to search the location for evidence in order to return with a regular search warrant.

statement of probable cause   Written statement prepared by an officer outlining all factual circumstances in support of the officer's belief that a person, place, or thing that is the target of the intended search is somehow related to a specific criminal activity.

statutes   Written laws or codes that define crimes punishable by law and the legal elements required to prove them.

stop and frisk   A type of search involving a patting down of the outside of a suspect's clothing by an officer after establishing reasonable suspicion. Such searches are for officers' protection and to prevent destruction of evidence.

strict liability offenses   Traffic violations or other minor offenses where only the act itself is required to imply guilt.

substantive criminal laws   Laws that define the legal requirements that have to be met to determine a crime has or has not been committed.

the exclusionary rule   Law prohibiting the use of evidence obtained by an illegal search in a trial or court proceeding.

totality of the circumstances   A method of judicial decision making involving consideration of all factors that are legally relevant to a particular issue. Both reasonable suspicion and probable cause decisions are made by considering the totality of the circumstances.

trier of fact   Juries are the trier of fact in a criminal trial; judges are the trier of fact in a bench hearing wherein defendants have waived their right to a jury trial.

trier of law   Judges are the trier of law in a trial or other criminal proceeding.

voluntary consent   Consent given by an individual in an informed and voluntary manner, free from coercion by authorities, to a search or other activity that normally requires a warrant.

ABFO#2   Standard measurement scale used in crime scene photographs, developed by the American Board of Forensic Odontology.

asset forfeiture laws   Laws stipulating that items of value (e.g., houses, cars, planes) acquired through illegal activities and seized in criminal investigations become the property of the law enforcement agencies seizing them.

associative evidence   Evidence that associates the suspect to the crime committed at the crime scene.

baseline coordinates   A crime scene measurement method whereby line measurements (right angles) are taken from the baseline (a straight line constructed from two fixed points) to the object of interest in the crime scene.

CIA   Acronym representing the major goals of criminal investigation standing for "C" (Crime; determining whether or not a crime was committed), "I" (Identifying suspects involved in the crime), and "A" (Associate suspects, victims, and the crime scene).

center of mass   The physical middle point of an object, such as a gun or body, that is being measured for location and distance while taking overall crime scene measurements in a crime scene investigation. For example, the location measurement of a body at a crime scene would be taken from a fixed point (e.g., wall, tree) to the body's middle torso area (i.e., the center of mass).

corpus delicti   Latin term meaning "body of the crime." As a legal principle, *corpus delicti* is the actual proof (i.e., evidence) presented in a case that demonstrates that a suspect has committed a crime.

crime scene core   The specific area of a crime scene where the criminal activity being investigated is presumed to have actually occurred, which usually contains the bulk of the physical evidence.

crime scene investigation   The systematic examination of a location, either physical or electronic, for evidence related to the commission of a crime.

crime scene photography   Photographs taken at the scene of the criminal activity being investigated to provide a visual record that can be used for investigative purposes and as courtroom evidence.

crime scene sketch   Drawings made by investigators of the overall crime scene, either in rough or finished form, that depict the relative positions and dimensions of evidence and other key objects of importance to the crime scene investigation.

crime scene storage area   A physical area at the crime scene used to temporarily store evidence until it can be transported from the crime scene.

crime scene technician   Usually civilian personnel (i.e., nonsworn officers) who perform a variety of investigative tasks such as searching for, collecting, and documenting evidence at the crime scene.

criminal investigators   Usually sworn law enforcement officers serving as specialists in the investigative process, who focus on tasks such as discovering evidence related to criminal activities, identifying and arresting crime suspects, and assisting prosecutors in preparing criminal cases.

datum point   A fixed point of reference at a crime scene from which crime scene measurements are taken.

electronic crime scenes Crime scenes involving the electronic transfer of information through cyberspace, which may or may not have an identifiable physical crime scene location.

electronic distance meter (EDM) Device used in the total station crime scene visualization method that provides 3D images used to locate and document crime scene evidence.

elevated perspective A perspective that is used most commonly to depict ground-level areas such as flooring space. It provides a two-dimensional view looking directly down from above the crime scene.

evidence collection teams Investigative personnel, sometimes consisting of both sworn and nonsworn officers as well as citizen volunteers, working together in a coordinated effort to process the same crime scene.

final walk-through The final step in processing a crime scene before releasing the scene, involving a final search for any evidence or other items that may have been overlooked during the crime scene investigation.

finished sketch A hand-drawn or computer-assisted drawing made to scale that shows the relative sizes, locations, and distances of evidence and other key components of the crime scene.

first responder Generally, police patrol units initially responding to the crime scene, but could also include emergency medical technicians (EMTs), fire, or other personnel who arrive first at a crime scene.

follow-up investigation Any further investigation of a crime that takes place after the preliminary investigation has been completed.

forensic videography Video images taken at the crime scene that are used, in addition to crime scene photographs, to document the entire scene.

grid system A crime scene search method whereby the area to be searched is broken into a series of quadrants or grids. This method is used most often in the search of large outdoor crime scenes.

hybrid search The search of a crime scene that incorporates two or more standardized search methods (e.g., combining line and zone methods).

investigative team All of the persons, including investigators, who work together in the investigative process. Teams members may include crime scene technicians, patrol officers, crime scene photographers, dispatchers, and confidential informants.

inward spiral Crime scene search method that proceeds from the outer perimeter to the innermost area of the crime scene in a spiraling motion.

lead investigators Investigators who serve in supervisory, coordinator, and liaison roles. Their duties include providing media information, requesting assistance from specialized outside personnel, interacting with the coroner's office (if necessary), obtaining search warrants, and making key decisions such as when to expand or conclude the investigation.

legal elements Specific activities outlined by law that must be proven in order for a crime to be exist; generally speaking, the elements of a crime.

logistics map Rough sketch outlining key areas of the crime scene and to plan investigative setup areas and other activities at the scene.

macroscopic scene An examination of activities that take place across the entire crime scene, as when linking criminal activities that transpire in the primary crime scene with those taking place in the secondary crime scene; for example, linking a bank robbery in one location to a getaway vehicle stolen in another location.

microscopic scene Refers to specific evidence found within a particular crime scene location; for example, a knife found in the core of a crime scene.

oblique lighting Lighting projected onto evidence from the side to cast shadows, which create greater visualization.

outer or extended area The area of a crime scene that extends beyond the core and peripheral areas of the crime scene boundaries.

outward spiral Crime scene search method that begins from the inside of the crime scene and extends to the outer perimeter of the scene.

peripheral crime scene The area extending away from the crime scene core, which may include evidence items such as shell casings, footprints, and trash discarded by the offender.

physical crime scenes Physical locations where a crime or suspected crime has been committed, as opposed to electronic crime scenes that may not necessary be confined to a specific physical location.

polar coordinates A crime scene measurement method whereby all crime scene measurements are taken from one fixed point known as a *datum point.*

preliminary investigation The investigation of the crime scene from the time a first responding police unit arrives at the scene until the crime scene is officially released.

preliminary walk-through An overall assessment of the crime scene for various factors, such as the location of evidence and potential hazards, performed before the actual processing of the crime scene.

primary crime scene The primary area where the crime being investigated took place, which includes the core, inner, and outer areas of the crime scene.

principal investigators Investigators who perform the actual leg work of the investigation, including establishing crime scene boundaries; performing a setup for the search; conducting evidence searches of the entire scene; and collecting, documenting, and packaging evidence for analysis at the crime lab.

proactive crime detection Using investigative methods to detect crime before it has been reported (e.g., conducting undercover sting operations).

reactive crime detection Using investigative methods to detect a crime after it has been reported (e.g., responding to a citizen's call for service).

rectangular coordinates Crime scene measurement method requiring the identification of two fixed, adjacent points within the crime scene that create horizontal and vertical axes, or a rectangular area, within a given location.

release of the crime scene The time at which the preliminary investigation of the crime scene is concluded and law enforcement personnel cease to control the scene.

relevant and material Referring to the legal requirement that evidence presented as proof in a court proceeding must relate to the elements of the crime for which a suspect is being charged.

report of investigation (ROI) Final investigative report containing all known aspects of a case discovered during an investigation. This report is also relied upon by prosecutors in deciding whether or not to pursue legal action against a crime suspect identified in the ROI.

rough sketch Preliminary drawing of the crime scene made by first responders and/or investigators (but not drawn to scale) for future reference.

secondary crime scene Additional locations associated with the primary crime scene, for example, a body dump site in an area located some distance away from where the victim was murdered.

secondary reference point coordinates The use of triangulation or another crime scene measurement method to establish a second set of fixed reference points (from more-distant primary fixed points), which narrow the distance needed to obtain a crime scene measurement.

smoking gun evidence Evidence at a warm crime scene (i.e., one in which the suspect has fled) that can be used to identify a suspect or indicate a suspect's whereabouts.

staging area A location within the crime scene where investigators and other personnel can store equipment or gather for consultation without disrupting evidence.

total station Crime scene imaging method involving the use of a surveyor's transit—which measures distances and elevations of selected objects and locations.

transient evidence Evidence that is highly perishable (e.g., bodily fluids containing DNA) and should be identified and collected before other types of evidence so that it can be protected and preserved.

triangulation Measurements are taken at angles from each of two fixed points and extended from the fixed points until they intersect at an object within the crime scene.

accelerant A liquid, gas, or solid that has chemical properties used to more rapidly start fires. Accelerant use is one of the most common investigative indicators of arson crimes.

alternate light source (ALS) Ultraviolet (UV), laser, infrared, and other nonstandard lighting used to illuminate crime scene evidence such as fingerprints, bodily fluids, bones, and bite marks.

backward spatter Blood projected from a wound in the direction opposite that of the moving object causing the wound. For example, backward spatter from a bullet entry wound may land on a shooter standing at close range in front of the victim.

ballistics evidence Bullets, cartridge casings, or other components of ammunition discharged from a firearm that can be used for evidentiary purposes.

bite exemplars Dental impressions taken for purposes of performing physical matches with bite mark evidence.

blood spatter Droplets of blood projected from a wound that can be examined for patterns useful to investigators in crime scene reconstruction.

C.S.I. effect The theory that superhuman investigators (usually seen on television), using crime analysis methods bordering on science fiction, have created a new generation of citizens who expect elaborate forms of physical evidence to be gathered at crime scenes and presented in court.

chain of custody Method of documenting evidence handling procedures from the time evidence is first collected until it is stored securely with the primary goal of making sure the evidence does not become destroyed, altered, or tainted.

chromogen A chemical that changes color when mixed with blood.

class characteristics Physical qualities shared by individual pieces of evidence that can be used for classification purposes. For example, grouping together firearms based on their class characteristics may include separating them into the categories of rifles, pistols, and shotguns.

coagulate The clotting of blood.

cold shock The breakage of vehicle lamp filaments after impact, suggesting that the lights were not on at the time of a collision.

comparison microscope Microscope that allows the magnification and side-by-side comparison of ballistics evidence.

concentric fracture Circular fracture lines that project away from where a bullet or other object has struck and cracked a glass surface.

control sample A sample taken from a person, place, or thing in its natural unaltered state for comparison with evidence of the same nature that has been altered. For example, a section of burnt wood that has been doused with gasoline and used to start an arson fire can be compared to an unburnt control sample of the same wood to show the extent of fire damage or to perform burn tests to prove the use of a particular accelerant.

cross-contamination A process by which evidence becomes tainted from unprotected contact with another object.

cross-transfer The process of transferring liquid or other matter from one object or person to another. For example, a shooter's bloody hand may cross-transfer blood from the victim to the steering wheel of a car.

dental fingerprinting Characteristics of teeth and dentition unique to individuals that can be used to identify offenders, crime victims, and decomposed bodies. For example, victims of a plane crash can be identified by dental records showing unique dental work and tooth patterns.

ejector marks Tool marks left on a cartridge casing expelled by the ejector of a semiautomatic firearm after firing.

electrostatic dust print lifter (EDPL) Device that uses an electromagnetic charge to capture prints in dust and other small particle matter by lifting the print from a surface.

elimination sample Samples taken from persons, places, or things that have come into contact with the crime scene or crime scene evidence to distinguish these contacts from those made by suspects. For example, elimination fingerprint samples can be taken from first responders to a crime scene to differentiate (i.e., eliminate) their prints from those left by a suspect.

exchange principle Famous theory created by Locard suggesting that every contact leaves a trace, which means that whenever an offender or object involved in a crime makes contact with the victim or an object at a crime scene there will always be some type of trace evidence to be discovered by investigators.

exemplar A known sample or example taken for purposes of comparison with evidence of an unknown origin. Exemplars can be taken from an existing source (i.e., natural exemplars) or can be created within a laboratory setting (i.e., collected exemplars).

extractor marks Tool marks left on cartridge casings pulled by the extractor of a semiautomatic firearm after firing.

firearms identification The process of identifying types of firearms by examining make, model, and type of ammunition used; not to be confused with the study of ballistics, which examines factors relating to the discharge of ammunition from firearms.

firing pin Mechanical device in a firearm that strikes the heel of a cartridge casing, causing the cartridge to fire.

fluoresce To exhibit light; for example, bodily fluids fluorescing under ultraviolet light.

foreign hair Hair that is loose or unattached to skin.

forensic odontology The forensic science concerned with classification and individualization of criminal evidence relating to human teeth and bite marks, although the analysis of impression evidence made by animal teeth may be included as well.

forward spatter Blood that is projected from a wound in the same direction as that in which the object causing the wound is travelling. For example, a bullet passing through a person's chest and exiting through their back would produce forward spatter from the exit wound.

friction ridges Raised areas on the exterior skin surface of fingers that form a fingerprint.

gel print lifter Specially designed sheets with an adhesive side used to lift prints from surfaces containing dust and other residue.

gunshot residue (GSR) Gunpowder particles, soot, ash, lead, and other residue deposited on a surface, such as a shooting victim's clothing or body, during discharge of ammunition from a firearm.

handwriting comparison The process of systematically comparing two sets of handwriting to determine whether both were written by the same individual. Handwriting samples used for this purpose are known as *handwriting exemplars.*

hot shock The directional movement of automobile lamp filaments that can indicate the direction of impact and whether lights were on at the time of a collision.

identification The ability of physical evidence to prove beyond a reasonable doubt that a specific individual committed a specific criminal act.

impression evidence Prints of objects such as tires or shoes that are found in soft substances such as dirt or sand.

individual characteristics Unique features that allow a specific piece of physical evidence to be identified as originating from a specific person, place, or thing. For example, fingerprints belonging to one individual possess unique patterns that are not the same as those belonging to any other individual.

lands/grooves Raised (lands) and lowered (grooves) surfaces on the interior surface of a gun barrel that form the rifling.

latent prints Prints (usually fingerprints) that are not visible to the unaided eye and require development by dusting or chemicals to be visualized and photographed.

minutiae Patterns and characteristics of fingerprints formed by friction ridges.

monkey wrenching The criminal act of intentionally introducing an abrasive into moving parts of machinery to cause mechanical destruction.

physical evidence Anything with tangible qualities, no matter how small, that can be measured or visualized to provide information about an actual or suspected criminal activity.

plasma The solid portion of blood.

plastic prints Prints (usually fingerprints) left in soft surfaces such as soap or putty.

point of origin The location in three-dimensional space from which a wound was inflicted, estimated through the analysis of blood spatter.

presumptive test The first test done on evidence to determine its probable nature before a second confirmatory test is performed to determine its true nature. For example, a presumptive color test is done on a drug thought to be cocaine, and a confirmatory test is performed later to verify that the drug is cocaine.

questioned evidence Physical evidence that has an unknown origin.

radial fracture Vertical and horizontal lines that radiate away from the location where a bullet or other object has struck and cracked glass.

recovery tank Apparatus used for test firing weapons that allows the recovery of bullets for ballistic comparisons.

reference sample A sample of known origin taken from people, places, or things that can be used to identify evidence of an unknown origin. For example, a carpet fiber can be taken as a reference sample from a burglary victim's residence and compared to carpet fibers found on the clothing of a serial burglary suspect.

residue print The impression of an object (e.g., shoeprint) formed by transfer of residue from an object to a surface.

serum The liquid portion of blood.

soil/botanical evidence Dirt, dust, leaves, spores, and other organic material from plants and soil that can be used as evidence in criminal cases.

striation marks Scratches or marks left on surfaces (typically metallic) that are usually unique to the weapon or other object leaving the scratches or marks. For example, firearms can often be identified (and individualized) by the unique striation marks they leave on the surface of bullets and cartridge casings.

surface tension A characteristic of liquids, such as blood, that helps them maintain their shape when placed under pressure.

tool mark evidence Impressions left by tools (including the action of firearms) on surfaces that can be used to classify or individualize the particular tool leaving the impression.

trajectory rods Pole-like objects used to identify the path of a bullet after it has struck an object; often used to illustrate which bullets traveling through surfaces (e.g., car doors) are responsible for striking shooting victims.

video spectral comparator A device used to visualize characteristics of fraudulent documents such as those created by overwriting or other methods used to alter original documentation.

visible prints Fingerprints and other prints at the crime scene that are visible with the unaided eye and are the result of some type of residue present on the surface of the object leaving the print.

void print The impression of an object (e.g., shoeprint) formed by the object making contact with and removing residue already present on a surface.

volatility A characteristic of liquids that easily evaporate and are usually explosive in nature (e.g., gasoline, turpentine, acetone).

Wallner lines or rib marks Fracture lines that indicate the direction of impact from a bullet or other objects that strike glass surfaces.

admission Statements made by a crime suspect that allow inferences of the suspect's guilt to be made, but fall short of a full confession of guilty conduct.

baiting the suspect Any tactic, including props, questions, statements, or body language, that causes deceptive suspects to trip up or tell the truth when providing false information during an interrogation.

behavior analysis interview An interrogation technique, based on concepts used in polygraph examination, that compares a suspect's behavior when telling the truth to that exhibited when suspected of not telling the truth.

brain fingerprinting A method used for deception detection whereby the brain is monitored for electronic impulses or spikes that may indicate a suspect's recognition of persons, weapons, or other evidence related to a crime.

clinical hypnosis The use of hypnosis to refresh or improve a person's memory of a criminal event.

closed-ended questions Questions that require a simple "yes/no" response or ask the witness to recall specific details of the crime.

cognitive interviewing (CI) An interviewing method based on increasing memory recall by providing cues (mental associations) between observed crime-related and non–crime-related events.

confession Verbal and/or written statement in which a person admits guilt in a particular criminal act.

credibility The ability of a witness to be perceived, especially by a jury or judge, as willing to provide accurate accounts of a criminal event.

cross-race effect The general notion that persons of the same race are better at recognizing each other's physical features.

dying declaration Statement about criminal matters, especially concerning perpetrators of crimes, made by persons when they are presumed to be near death.

eyewitness accounts Verbal or written statements made by persons who have witnessed or know about criminal activity.

false confessions Falsely claiming to have committed a crime for purposes of protecting others or seeking personal fame.

flashbulb memory A vivid and detailed memory formed within a matter of seconds as the result of viewing an extremely shocking or traumatic event such as a serious crime.

functional Magnetic Resonance Imaging (fMRI) The use of MRI technology in deception detection that examines how a person's brain reacts in different recognizable patterns when telling the truth or being deceitful.

friendly witness Witnesses who are extremely cooperative and usually go out of their way to present themselves to crime scene investigators as persons who can provide information regarding the crime.

good cop/bad cop Interrogation technique generally involving two interrogators where one (the bad cop) attempts to instill fear and discomfort in the suspect, and the other (the good cop) attempts to be understanding and provide comfort to the suspect.

hostile witness Witnesses who are not only uncooperative, but intentionally avoid or even openly express hostility toward investigators when approached for an interview.

interrogation Line of questioning that aims at determining the guilt or innocence of persons suspected of involvement in criminal activities by using specialized information gathering techniques and technology.

interrogation profiling An interrogation technique whereby a crime suspect is first profiled psychologically and the resulting profile (e.g., need or lifestyle criminal motivation) is used by interrogators to soften the suspect's resistance to telling the truth.

interview Line of questioning designed to obtain insights and observations from persons who may have personally witnessed or otherwise gained knowledge about criminal matters under investigation.

kinesics analysis The observation of a suspect's body movements during an interrogation session to distinguish truthful from deceptive statements.

mentally competent Having the mental capacity to understand one's role and rights in a legal setting.

Miranda waiver A statement, verbal or written, provided to officers by crime suspects that suggests they do not wish to invoke their Fourth Amendment rights after formal arrest or being technically placed in legal custody.

Miranda warnings Advice given by officers to suspects who have been formally arrested or are technically in custody, informing them that they have the right to remain silent and to speak to an attorney before providing information to authorities about their involvement in a criminal matter.

neuro linguistic programming (NLP) An interrogation method based on the theory that certain involuntary reactions from suspects, both verbal and nonverbal, can be used to determine when suspects are being deceptive during an interrogation session.

neutral witness Witnesses who usually cooperate with crime scene investigators; however, the information they provide will likely be limited to specific responses to questions they are asked about the crime situation.

open-ended questions Interview questions used to elicit information and details about the offense and offender in an unstructured, free-flowing dialogue.

polygraph A device that measures deception through monitoring bodily changes such as blood pressure, breathing, and electroconductivity of the skin.

post-Miranda exceptions Special laws that may permit self-incriminating statements made by individuals who have never been notified of their Miranda rights.

Reid Nine-Step Technique Method of interrogation, carried out in nine steps, that relies on a combination of targeted statements, questioning, and the analysis of the suspect's verbal and physical reactions at various stages of the interrogation process.

showup Transporting witnesses to a location where they can briefly view suspected offenders for identification purposes, usually to establish probable cause for arrest.

the third degree The use of physically coercive tactics to gain a suspect's confession to a crime.

truth serum A drug (commonly sodium pentothal) used to refresh the faded memories of witnesses or crime victims, and perhaps to gain truthful statements from crime suspects.

voice stress analysis (VSA) A lie detection method, similar to the polygraph, that detects deception through voice fluctuations.

weapon focus The general tendency of witnesses to focus on an offender's gun or other weapon during the commission of a crime, causing their inability to accurately recall other crime scene details.

5Ws & H The general line of inquiry for most investigative report: (1) Who are the parties involved? (2) What has occurred? (3) When did it happen? (4) Where did it happen? (5) Why did it happen? and (6) How did it happen?

digital audio recorder (DAR) Sound recording device that produces a digital sound data file.

FACCCT Report writing acronym standing for *Factual, Accurate, Clear, Concise, Complete,* and *Timely,* referring to all of the primary components of a well-prepared incident/crime report.

face sheet The cover sheet of an incident/crime report that contains key information and statistical data in summary form about the reported criminal incident.

field notebook Usually a small book in which hand-written notes are made regarding an officer's observations, which are typically used in the preparation of an incident/crime report.

field notes Notes taken by an officer about a crime or other incident that are used for reference later in the formal preparation of an incident/crime report.

incident/crime report An official report, consisting of a face sheet and narrative, that documents officers' observations, witness statements, and other information relating to a criminal incident.

missing person report Report documenting key information about persons whose whereabouts are unknown.

paperless reporting Electronically prepared incident/crime and other official reports that can be prepared in real time and stored as a computer data file.

private person's arrest report Report taken by an officer in response to a citizen's arrest.

report narrative The written portion of an incident/crime report containing all pertinent information about a matter investigated by officers.

supplemental report Additional reports added to the original incident/crime report. These can be the result of follow-up investigations conducted after the filing of an initial incident/crime report resulting from a preliminary investigation of a criminal activity.

"Who done it?" report A report taken on a crime-related matter where there is no workable information that would provide suspect leads in the incident/crime that has been investigated.

commodity flow analysis Crime analysis method used to document the flow of illegal goods to and from persons and/or places.

convoy Individual whose role is to detect surveillance measures directed toward the target.

countersurveillance Any efforts on the part of subjects to uncover surveillance operations.

cover story A story prepared before an investigation and told by undercover investigators, when necessary, to mask their true identity as officers (i.e., to protect themselves from being "made" and having their cover blown).

crime pattern analysis Crime analysis method that uses GPS technology to create geographic area maps illustrating patterns of criminal activity, such as hot spots for particular types of offenses and offenders.

criminal intelligence Raw information obtained from leads or other investigative sources that has been analyzed to provide specific knowledge about past, present, or future crime-related activities.

criminal profiling A behavioral investigative method involving the prediction of criminal suspect characteristics based on information obtained from the crime scene and other investigative resources.

decoy Persons used to divert the investigator from the subject under surveillance.

delusion A belief or thought with no basis in reality that may cause an individual to engage in criminal behavior.

disorganized offender Offender profile type, characterized by spontaneous commission of a criminal act, that leaves a significant amount of physical evidence at the crime scene.

event flow analysis Crime analysis method useful for showing crimes carried out in stages, the sequence of crime-planning events, or the relationship between various individuals and activities that may be connected to single or multiple criminal acts over time.

evidential intelligence The process of gathering information, derived from known specific pieces of evidence, that may lead to the discovery of other new forms of evidence.

eye The optimum vantage point for viewing the target during an undercover surveillance operation.

follow-up investigation All investigations of a criminal event taking place after the preliminary investigation has concluded.

fusion center A regional clearinghouse to store, coordinate, analyze, and disseminate intelligence information about criminal activities to local, state, and federal law enforcement agencies.

geoprofiling Crime analysis method that utilizes GPS methodology to predict the likely location of an offender's base of operations (e.g., residence, workplace, hang-outs) as well as other geographic locations frequented by offenders and their targets/victims with a high degree of regularity.

hallucination Seeing, hearing, feeling, tasting, or smelling (i.e., activity of one of the five senses) something that does not exist in reality.

informant A person who has knowledge of a criminal event and volunteers or is paid to provide such knowledge to investigators.

instrumental offenses Offenses committed for reasons directly related to the offender's need for psychological gratification.

Intelligence Cycle The six-step process used to develop intelligence in intelligence-led policing.

investigative lead Some form of information that can be obtained; persons, places, or things that may be of use for achieving investigative goals.

lifestyle/routine activity analysis (LRA) An investigative method whereby a victim's daily routines are analyzed to determine factors such as the time, place, and circumstances of a criminal victimization.

lineup A method by which crime victims and/or witnesses visually identify crime suspects presented in live or photographic form along with "fillers," or other persons similar to the suspect in physical appearance.

linkage analysis Crime analysis method used to visualize associations among offenders and offense-related factors such as crimes, individuals, groups/gangs, organizations, weapons, drugs, goods, money, and other subjects of investigative interest.

modus operandi The method of operation by which an offender carries out a crime.

NCIC (National Crime Information Center) The world's most comprehensive crime information database, operated by the FBI and accessible by all law enforcement agencies in the United States. The system includes more than 15 million active records, which are assembled into 19 files (7 for crimes against persons; 12 for crimes against property).

operative An investigator conducting surveillance activities.

operative intelligence The use of intelligence to focus on specific large-scale criminal activities over an extended time period for purposes of identifying and gathering more detailed intelligence on specific criminal activities, offenders, and their targets.

organized offender Offender profile type characterized by careful preplanning of a criminal event and leaving little, if any, physical evidence at the crime scene.

pen/trap device An electronic device used primarily to monitor incoming and outgoing communications made by telephones, cellular networks, and computer connections.

proactive investigation Situations where investigators can play a key role in addressing crime-related matters before they occur.

serial offender Persons who commit related crimes (i.e., in a series).

signature Some unique behavior exhibited by an offender during a crime that is above and beyond what is necessary to carry out the crime (i.e., the *modus operandi*).

souvenir An object taken by an offender from the victim or from the crime scene, which is later used by the offender to memorialize the criminal event.

staging Physical changes made in the crime scene by the offender after the offense has been committed, usually in an effort to cause psychological shock or to confuse investigators.

sting operation A proactive undercover operation used to lure offenders into a controlled setting (usually under electronic surveillance) and to bait offenders into carrying out crimes in the presence of investigators.

strategic intelligence Using intelligence to develop a long-term big picture of a particular crime problem.

surveillance Undercover observation of a person, place, or thing that is the target of an investigation.

surveillance plan A plan of action for conducting surveillance, which includes all present and past case background information, necessary equipment such as cameras and vehicles, surveillance objectives, warrant/other legal requirements, as well as intelligence gathered about the target.

tactical intelligence Intelligence used to identify and solve an immediate crime or security problem.

target The person, place, or thing being investigated during a surveillance operation.

telephone toll analysis An event analysis of telephone use.

theme Psychological similarities between two or more signatures of a serial offender.

threat assessment Investigative methods used to assess potential individual and group security/safety threats.

trophy An object taken from the crime scene or victim by the offender; it is similar to a souvenir, but is taken for purposes of symbolizing the offender's conquest over the victim.

undercover operative An investigator who is working an undercover assignment.

undoing A form of staging whereby the offender feels remorse after the crime and attempts to "make amends" for the harm that has occurred by altering the crime scene. For example, a murderer who has sexually assaulted his victim may redress her so that she has a more favorable appearance when her body is discovered.

victimology The investigation of offending or an offense from the victim's rather than the offender's perspective.

wiretapping Otherwise known as *electronic eavesdropping*, wiretapping involves the covert interception of communication content in the furtherance of an investigative effort.

ACE-V Fingerprint analysis method that involves a four-step identification process: "A" (analysis), determining the appropriate fingerprint classification; "C" (compare), determining specific friction ridge identification points; "E" (evaluate), determining unique ridge characteristics; and "V" (verification), having a second examiner verify conclusions drawn during the first fingerprint examination.

AFIS/ IAFIS AFIS (Automated Fingerprint Identification System) was initiated in the 1970s by the FBI as the nation's first computerized fingerprint database with search capabilities; IAFIS (Integrated Automated Fingerprint Identification System), which replaced the older FBI AFIS system in 1999, is the world's largest biometric database, housing nearly 70 million fingerprints and palm prints as well.

allele The area examined on a DNA strand to determine an individual's genetic fingerprint.

American Society of Crime Laboratory Directors (ASCLD) Provides accreditation for crime laboratories and performs site inspections of their accredited crime labs.

autoradiograph A visual graphing of results from DNA analysis showing the characteristics of an individual's genetic fingerprint.

base pairs Acid bases ("A" and "T"; "G" and "C") that join to form the nDNA genetic fingerprint.

CODIS (Combined DNA Index System) Operated by the FBI, housing nDNA information on convicted offenders and arrestees.

Daubert test Legal test used at the federal level and in some states as an alternative to the Frye test, requiring that for any given forensic science to be recognized as valid by the court, it must be based on scientifically proven evidence.

digital forensic science Digital analyses of crime scene evidence concerned with decoding, extracting, or restoring electronic documents and information contained within devices such as computers, cell phones, GPS systems, PDAs (personal data assistants), servers, video game consoles, and portable media players.

epithelial tissues Skin cells located within mucous membranes (the inner lining of the mouth, nose, and other bodily cavities) that break away and are deposited in bodily fluids—which in turn are deposited on persons, surfaces, and objects recovered as evidence.

forensic anthropology The examination of skeletal remains for purposes of discovering evidence related to a criminal investigation.

forensic entomology The examination of insects and insect activity as an indicator of time of death and factors useful for purposes of criminal investigation.

forensic pathology Medical-legal investigations performed by medical doctors specializing in the investigation of the cause of deaths.

forensic psychology and psychiatry The use of psychologists (social scientists, PhD or PsyD) and psychiatrists (medical doctors, MD) to provide expertise in crime-related matters for investigations and court proceedings.

forensic science The application of any science to the law (which must be court approved if presented as evidence at trial).

Frye test Legal test used in most states requiring that for any science to be recognized by a court as a legitimate forensic science, it must be generally accepted by a relevant scientific discipline.

Innocence Project (IP) Legal rights program with a mission to assist prisoners who can possibly be proven innocent through DNA testing.

manner of death The circumstances under which the death occurred, classified as natural, accident, suicide, homicide, or undetermined.

mtDNA DNA (deoxyribonucleic acid) stored in the mitochondria of cells (both skin and hair) that is used to create an individual's maternal genetic fingerprint.

nDNA DNA (deoxyribonucleic acid) stored in the nuclei of cells that is used to create an individual's complete genetic fingerprint.

NIBIN (National Integrated Ballistic Information Network) System operated by the ATF. It is the world's most comprehensive database for the identification of firearms and their tool marks.

PCR (polymerase chain reaction) nDNA analysis method that utilizes a small number of cells to generate a genetic fingerprint by copying selected locations of the DNA strand.

serology A crime lab section concerned with analyses of blood, blood stains, and blood testing as well as examinations of bodily fluids such as semen, sweat, and saliva.

toxicology A crime lab section concerned with the various effects, both physical and behavioral, that poisons have on the body.

abrasion ring Ripped and/or bruised appearing skin immediately surrounding the interior edges of an entry wound caused by the stretching of the skin around the bullet's point of entry.

algor mortis Changes in body temperature after death involving either warming or cooling, depending on the ambient temperature.

asphyxia A condition where the body is deprived of oxygen necessary to sustain life, leading to unconsciousness and/or death.

bullet track The path made by a bullet after it strikes and travels through the body.

bullet wipe A small dark circle on the surface of the skin surrounding the entry hole of a bullet, which is caused by the deposit of oil, soot, and other residue present on the bullet's surface.

contact wound A large torn and burnt appearing bullet entry wound produced when a firearm is discharged directly over or on the skin's surface area.

corneal clouding A condition, appearing shortly after death, that produces a thin film over the external area of the eye, creating a cloudy or glazed appearance.

defense wound Wound appearing on the fingers, hands, or forearms of victims who have used their arms to protect themselves against an attacker.

entry wound The point where a bullet or other firearm projectile enters the body; usually much smaller than an exit wound.

exit wound The point where a bullet or other firearm projectile exits the body after entry; usually much larger than an entry wound.

hilt marks Bruising or other markings left on the skin surrounding a stab wound that are produced by the handle of the knife or other sharp object producing the wound.

homicide Any death that involves the killing of one human being by the act or omission of another.

incision wound Wound produced by a knife or other sharp object capable of cutting skin.

lines of cleavage The directions, either vertical or horizontal, in which the muscles flow throughout the body.

livor mortis A bluish-purple discoloration that appears on the skin after death, produced when noncirculating blood settles to the lowest points in the body.

manslaughter An illegal homicide produced by the act or omission of another human being where the person committing the homicide does not possess malice aforethought at the time they cause the death to occur.

mass murder Four or more victims killed at one time in one location.

murder An illegal homicide produced by the act or omission of another human being where the person committing the homicide possesses malice aforethought at the time they cause the death to occur.

muzzle contusion An imprint of the gun's muzzle on the surface of skin, usually appearing on or near a contact wound.

nonhomicide A death that is not deemed to be the result of an act or omission of another human being.

pattern bruising The presence of two or more bruises in close proximity, usually caused by the fingers of offenders who tightly grip the skin of their victims.

puncture wound A wound caused by the forceful penetration of the skin with an object, sharpened only on its tip (e.g., an ice pick).

putrefaction The final stage of body decomposition, which begins approximately 24 to 36 hours after death and results in the breakdown of the body's soft tissue.

rigor mortis A stiffening of the body muscles beginning shortly after death (between 3 and 8 hours) and then dissipating approximately 36 hours after death.

serial murder Three or more separate homicidal events committed in three or more separate locations by the same killer, who experiences an emotional cooling-off period between each event.

shotgun choke Constriction placed at the muzzle end of a shotgun to control the degree to which the pellet mass spreads or scatters when it is projected.

spree murder Single homicidal event involving two or more locations and no emotional cooling-off period between the murders.

stippling/tattooing Small pepper-like spots randomly dispersed in a circular pattern on skin around the wound, caused by small particles of foreign matter and/or gunpowder that are projected onto the skin's surface by forces produced by the shooting.

wound marginal The edges of skin surrounding the opening of the wound.

autoerotic death (also known as *hypoxyphilia*) An accidental death resulting from strangulation used to heighten the victim's sexual experience by restricting blood flow to the brain.

child rape Forcible sexual relations with a victim who is considered a child by legal definition (usually someone under the age of 14 years).

criminal investigative analysis (CIA) Method developed by the FBI to investigate unidentified rapists.

domestic violence (also referred to as *intimate partner violence*) Willful intimidation, physical assault, battery, sexual assault, and/or other abusive behavior perpetrated by an intimate partner against another.

exhibitionism Intense sexual arousal caused by exposing one's genitals to strangers.

fetishism Sexual attractions to nonliving objects (e.g., shoes and underwear).

forcible rape The carnal knowledge of (i.e., sexual intercourse with) a female forcibly and against her will; however, see *sexual assault* for a more contemporary usage of this term.

frotteurism Touching and rubbing in a sexual manner against another person who is unsuspecting that such activity is occurring.

Megan's Law Federal law requiring states to register and disseminate information to the public about persons deemed to be sexual predators.

necrophilia The act of becoming sexually aroused by a corpse.

paraphilias Fantasies, behaviors, or sexual urges focusing on unusual objects, activities, or situations.

partialism Sexual arousal by interest in specific body parts (e.g., feet).

pedophile A person who obtains sexual pleasure from children.

prison rape Rape taking place in a penal institution, usually motivated by dominance of one inmate over another or as payback for unpaid gambling or drug debts.

rape kit Prepackaged kit used by medical professionals to document, collect, and preserve evidence recovered from the victim's exam.

rape trauma syndrome (RTS) A prolonged and psychologically debilitating reaction known as a form of post-traumatic stress disorder (PSD) specific to sexual assault experiences.

sado-masochism Achieving sexual pleasure by inflicting pain on oneself or on someone else.

SANE (Sexual Assault Nurse Examiner) Nursing professionals trained specifically to not only examine victims of sexually related crimes, but also to perform other investigative support functions such as follow-up counseling for victims and court testimony procedures.

serial rape A series of rapes perpetrated by the same individual over time.

sexual assault Legal term describing crimes of a sexual nature encompassing numerous contact sex crimes such as rape, attempted rape, incest, molestation, and fondling as well as various noncontact, sexually motivated acts such as sexual threats, pornography, and indecent exposure.

spousal rape Nonconsensual sexual intercourse between legally married individuals.

statutory rape Sex crime in which adults have sex with a minor under the age at which legal consent for sexual activity can be given. It is considered a lower-level felony or perhaps a misdemeanor, depending on the age difference between the victim and offender.

stranger rape Nonconsensual sexual intercourse between persons without prior knowledge of each other.

technophilia The act of engaging in computer-related sexual activities (also known as *cybersex*).

voyeurism The act of achieving sexual pleasure by viewing individuals (usually undressing or engaging in sexually related behavior) who do not suspect they are being watched.

aiding and abetting To advise, counsel, encourage, support, or similarly assist another person who is actively committing a criminal act.

associate An individual who desires to become a member of a gang and spends much time with the gang, perhaps committing criminal acts to be proved worthy of becoming a full-fledged member.

Bloods African-American street gang members, also known as *Pirus*, who are at war with members of the Crips.

body attachment A court order authorizing law enforcement to take into custody persons who have been ordered to testify in court yet refuse to appear.

cliques Smaller subsets of gang members within the same gang who share a common identity, which is usually age-related.

conspiracy Two or more persons who agree or make plans to commit a criminal act, and engage in some sort of conduct to further their offending objectives. Persons can be charged with conspiracy even though the crime that was planned never took place.

Crips African-American street gang members who are at war with members of the Bloods.

Dai Lo A term often associated with the leader of an Asian street gang.

drive-by A hit-and-run assault carried out while riding on a motorcycle or in a car.

drop-outs Gang members who are technically no longer active in the gang but still have ties to the gang.

Featherwoods A generic term referring to a female Caucasian gang member.

Folk Nation   Midwestern street gang that is at war with members of the People Nation and has a loose alliance with the Crips.

gang crime   Illegal acts that can be classified as gang motivated (e.g., establishing the reputation of a street gang) or gang related (e.g., committing a drive-by shooting).

graffiti   Writing, usually spray painted, in a public place by gang members for purposes of establishing territory, reputation, or issuing challenges.

green light   The authorization to carry out a hit on another individual or gang.

hard-core   Full members of the gang, generally considered the most streetwise, respected, and violent individuals in the gang.

hit   An order or authorization made by one person (e.g., in the case of gangs, often executed by a shot caller) to kill another.

hybrid gang   Gang having an ethnically diverse membership.

jumping in   Gang initiation process whereby an individual seeking full membership status in a street gang allows himself or herself to beaten by four or five fellow gang members for a specified period of time.

keestering   Hiding contraband in one's anal cavity for purposes of concealment from authorities.

keys   A term used by inmates referring to having control over illegal activities within a correctional institution.

Norteno   A generic term referring to a gang member or gang originating from the northern portion of California; also used as a gang identifier in various other states.

Peckerwoods   A generic term referring to a male Caucasian gang member.

People Nation   Midwestern street gang that is at war with members of the Folk Nation and has a loose alliance with the Bloods.

planned drive-by   A shooting attack by street gang members committed against their enemies or rivals at a time and in a location that (1) provides the most opportunity to cause damage and/or injury and (2) the least opportunity for apprehension by law enforcement or self-defense.

prison gang   Gangs in state- or federal-level penal institutions whose members are serving or have served sentences in such institutions.

retaliation   An act of revenge to get even or to do payback committed by one individual/gang against another.

ride-by   A hit-and-run assault carried out while riding a bicycle.

set   An individual street gang that is aligned with a larger group of gangs sharing the same name and/or identity; e.g., the 32nd Street Roller Crips are a set of the Crip gang organization.

state prison order   An order given by a prison gang to a street gang to commit a drive-by or a murder.

shot caller   Generally, the leader or spokesperson for a gang.

spontaneous drive-by   A spontaneous chance encounter between two opposing street gangs, which results in a combative situation leading to the exchange of gunfire.

Sureno   A generic term referring to a gang member or gang originating from the southern portion of California; also used as a gang identifier in various other states.

validation   Establishing the identity of individual gang members by systematic and legal means.

walk-by   A hit-and-run assault carried out while running on foot.

wannabe   Persons not considered members of the gang, but who enjoy the social aspects, status, and reputation of being a member of the gang.

amateur robber   An inexperienced robber who carries out robberies that usually are spontaneous acts that lack criminal sophistication.

armed robbery   Robbery carried out with the use of a weapon.

armored car robbery   The use of force or fear to steal money or other valuables from an armored vehicle.

ATM robbery   Robbery committed by an offender who uses force or fear against persons to obtain money that is contained within an automatic teller machine (ATM).

"C store" robbery   The robbery of a convenience store.

closing-time robbery   Robbery committed by entering a bank and obtaining cash during afternoon or evening hours shortly before the bank is closed to the general public.

cold plated   Replacing the original license plate of a vehicle with one that has been stolen from another vehicle that is usually the same make, model, and color.

customer approach   Robbery committed by an offender who enters a store or other commercial establishment pretending to be a customer and then some time later makes either an overt command or a covert demand for money from an clerk or other employee.

drug robbery   Robbery committed for purposes of stealing prescription or illegal street drugs.

false robbery report   Reporting a robbery to authorities that did not occur for reasons that may include revenge, covering up other illegal activities, or insurance fraud.

freight robbery   Robbery committed for purposes of illegally obtaining property from a transportation or storage location.

home invasion robbery   Entering of a personal residence (usually by deceit) followed by the use of force or fear to steal money and other property from its occupants.

inside job   A robbery carried out with the assistance of persons who have knowledge of the person(s) or place(s) that have been victimized.

morning glory robbery   Robbery committed by entering a bank and obtaining cash during early morning hours before the bank is open to the general public.

note pass robbery   The most common type of bank robbery, usually carried out by an offender who calmly passes a threatening note to a bank teller demanding the immediate payment of money.

professional robber   An experienced robber who carries out a robbery in a manner that usually shows some degree of planning and criminal sophistication.

robbery   The taking or attempting to take anything of value from the care, custody, or control of a person or persons by force or threat of force or violence and/or by putting the victim in fear.

stick-up robbery   Robbery committed by confronting the victim with an actual weapon (usually a handgun or knife) or something resembling a weapon (a toy or make-shift handgun or simply a hand concealed beneath clothing to fake gun possession).

straight approach Robbery committed by an offender who bursts into the store in a grand intimidating entrance and immediately demands money from the clerk—usually by pushing the weapon close to the clerk's face.

strong arm robbery Robbery committed by either using or threatening to use physical force.

take-over robbery The most dangerous and daring type of robbery, usually committed by multiple offenders who enter a bank or other establishment with weapons exposed and used to openly confront and intimidate their victims.

taxi-cab robbery The use of force or fear to obtain money and/or property from taxi cab drivers.

weapon focus A phenomenon that causes eyewitnesses of armed robbery to focus on details of the weapon that the offender is holding and thereby block out all other details of the robbery event.

addicted amateur burglar Persons who are addicted to drugs and commit burglaries (typically unsophisticated) for purposes of supporting their drug habit.

ATM burglary A form of commercial burglary involving forceful or unauthorized nonforceful access to an ATM machine for purposes of committing theft or any felony.

burglary As defined by common law, breaking and entering the dwelling of another with the intent to commit a crime.

commercial burglary Entry into a nonresidential structure to commit theft or any felony.

extra-burglary factors Behaviors carried out at the crime scene by a burglar that are unrelated to the actual taking of property (e.g., turning on lights, moving furniture).

fence An individual specializing in the sale of stolen property.

frontmen Offenders, usually part of a burglary team, who carry out the theft of property from a burglary location.

hawking Directly selling items that one has stolen during a burglary without the use of a fence.

juvenile amateur burglar Offenders who are 16 years of age or less and usually commit daytime burglaries after school or on school holidays using unsophisticated methods of entry.

point of entry The primary location used by the offender(s) to enter the residence for purposes of committing a burglary.

point of exit The primary location from which a burglar permanently flees the crime scene.

professional burglar Offenders who make their living primarily from money and valuables they obtain from committing burglaries.

residential burglary Entry into a residential structure to commit theft or any felony.

RV burglary Specific type of burglary targeting property on and within recreational vehicles.

safe burglary Forced or unauthorized nonforced entry into a safe for purposes of committing theft or any felony.

semiprofessional burglar Offenders who attempt to make a living through committing burglaries, yet are not nearly as successful or skilled as a professional burglar.

sequential search A type of search that begins with an overall survey of the burglary crime scene and proceeds to more detailed search methods such as moving and opening objects within the scene.

shouldering Using one's body, particularly shoulders and feet, to force open a locked door or other barrier in order to gain entry into a location to commit a burglary.

smash and grab Term referring to a burglary committed by aggressively breaking into a secured area (e.g., locked door, or glass display case) and stealing property located therein.

spotters Persons who are posted outside a burglary/break in location to watch for police or other persons who may be responding to the crime.

stolen property list An official list of items believed to be stolen during a burglary that is used for evidentiary purposes and for insurance claims.

vehicle burglary The unauthorized entry into a vehicle for purposes of committing theft or any felony.

wheelmen Persons who drive stolen vehicles to smash into the target location of a burglary and transport goods away for the scene, i.e., a ramraid.

young amateur burglar Offenders, usually in their late teens to early twenties, who are often associated with a semiprofessional or professional burglar and are attempting to learn "the burglary trade."

419 advance fee Messages sent by e-mail, letter, phone, fax, etc., from West African countries (most often Nigeria) promising financial fortunes to persons who furnish up-front money or an advance fee before receiving the entire fortune.

booster A professional shoplifter (alternative term for *heel*).

card trapping Fitting a loop of tape, wire, or strong thread over the ATM card reader so that when victims place their ATM card in the machine it is trapped and not returned.

cash trapping Inserting a device into the ATM machine's money dispenser that either covers or blocks bills that have been dispensed.

check kiting Writing a bad check from one bank account to deposit in another to create fraudulent balances.

chunking Persuading a group of investors to purchase a number of properties and illegally using the investors' finances and credit to purchase many more properties than promised.

churning Mortgage fraud carried out by engaging in repeated unnecessary lending services or transactions for a client to illegally obtain sales commissions and excessive fees.

counterfeiting The fraudulent manufacturing, altering, or distributing of a product of lesser value than the original product.

cramming Changes for additional goods and services added on to a victim's phone bill which are established through unauthorized, misleading or deceptive means.

crotch walk Shoplifting technique used primarily by women who place stolen items up their dress and between their thighs before walking away from the theft location.

dumpster diving Searching through trash cans and other garbage receptacles in search of documents that can be used for purposes of committing larceny-theft crimes, especially identity theft.

embezzlement The use of money (and property, in some jurisdictions) by the employee in a manner inconsistent with that specified by the employer.

heel A professional shoplifter (alternative term for *booster*).

identity (ID) theft Assuming the identity of another person for purposes of committing criminal acts.

insurance fraud   The intentional act of lying or falsifying an insurance claim to an insurance provider for purposes of illegal gain.

larceny-theft   Crimes involving the taking of anything of value without the consent of its owner, with the intent to permanently deprive him or her of the value of the property taken.

mortgage fraud   Illegally obtaining loans for the purchase of property from banks or other lending sources by intentionally misstating, forging, falsifying, or otherwise being untruthful in the loan acquisition process.

network attacks   Using a computer program (malware) to attack an ATM's information retrieval system to get access to users' card information and PIN numbers.

paperhanging   Writing checks on closed accounts or reordering checks on closed accounts for future use to commit check fraud.

pharm   The act of hijacking an entire computer domain and using it to gather information from users, who believe they are communicating with their legitimate Internet service provider.

phishing   Sending legitimate appearing e-mails directing users to phony web sites that ask for personal and financial information.

pilfering   The mishandling or theft of property.

Ponzi scheme   Fraud scheme, named for its creator Carlo Ponzi, carried out by paying investors dividends (periodic interest payments) on fake investments with cash fraudulently obtained from other investors.

property flipping   Mortgage fraud whereby loans are obtained for low-value homes at a purchase price that may be two or three times the actual value of the property.

pump and dump   Stock market scam whereby assets (stocks) are artificially inflated in value (pumped) and then deflated in value (dumped), resulting in profits to the offenders manipulating the stocks.

pyramid scheme   Fraud scheme whereby offenders provide financial rewards to earlier investors for recruiting and securing funds from later investors under the guise of legitimate business operation.

romance con   Using a false romantic relationship to lure victims into providing gifts and money, and perhaps engaging in illegal activities.

shoplifting   Theft committed at a commercial establishment; can be reclassified as commercial burglary if the intent to commit felony theft can be proven.

shoulder surfing   Looking over a person's shoulder (usually while at an ATM machine) to illegally obtain financially sensitive information such as a PIN number, which is later used for criminal activity.

skimming   Obtaining personal information from the magnetic strip of credits cards, ATM cards, ID cards, drivers licenses, etc. for purposes of committing criminal activity.

snitch   An amateur shoplifter.

straw buyer   A person who purchases a home with someone else's identity or with a false identification.

swoop and squat   Insurance fraud involving a staged auto accident whereby offenders cause an unsuspecting motorist to engage in a rear-end collision with their vehicle.

synthetic cloning   Mixing the characteristics of several cards together to form one card that represents the credit profile of a person who does not even exist.

triangulation   The use of illegally obtained financial information to purchase stolen products in the victim's name, causing investigators to focus their case on the victim rather than the offender.

unbundling   Health care fraud carried out by billing insurance companies for separate medical procedures that, in actuality, should be billed or bundled together as one complete procedure.

upcoding   Health care fraud carried out by intentionally inputting a code for a procedure costlier than the one actually performed, resulting in an illegal higher payment for medical services.

30-day special   Filing a false theft report on the vehicle and then hiding it for 30 days or so until the insurance company settles the stolen vehicle claim and issues a payment.

bait car   A vehicle that is used by police, usually equipped with surveillance video and other specialized equipment, to entice and capture auto thieves.

body switch   The entire body of a vehicle is removed from one vehicle (e.g., not stolen) and placed on the chassis of another (e.g., stolen).

bricking or stoning   Using a brick or stone to break vehicle windows.

carjacking   The act of taking a vehicle by force or fear from its owner.

check digit   A single-digit number, or the letter "X", placed in the VIN's 9th position that is created by performing a mathematical calculation that takes into consideration all of the other characters contained in the vehicle's VIN.

chop shop   A location where stolen vehicles are dismantled for their parts.

code grabbing   Using specialized software to copy electronic signals transmitted from a vehicle's RKE (Remote Keyless Entry) system to disengage door locks and/or the car's general security system.

cold plate   Stealing a license plate from another vehicle of the same year, color, model, and manufacturer as a stolen car used in a criminal activity and putting it onto the stolen car before using it to commit a second crime.

counterfeit VIN   Using a false manufactured VIN to replace VIN plates on stolen vehicle.

door wedging   Using wooden wedges or tools such as flat-end screwdrivers to pry open a small space between the vehicle's door and door frame post to gain access to locking devices.

export scam   Reporting a vehicle as stolen and then selling it to an auto theft ring for export to a foreign country.

grand theft auto (GTA)   An auto theft defined by law as a specific offense, which is distinct from crimes of theft involving other types of property.

hot wiring   Starting a vehicle's engine by performing a simple cross-wiring procedure that bypasses the normal key-operated electrical system.

Hull Identification Number (HIN)   Used to identify boats and other watercraft; affixed to the transom (the flat area at the very back of the vessel, e.g., its stern, where its motor is located).

ignition punching Inserting a screwdriver or similar-shape tool into the key area of a vehicle's ignition and applying force in a twisting motion to defeat the lock.

insurance fraud Intentionally making a false claim to an insurance provider (e.g., vehicle theft or damage) to fraudulently obtain a monetary settlement.

ISO/NICB (Insurance Service Office / National Insurance Crime Bureau) Privately operated organizations that collect and disseminate vehicle information and insurance-related data.

joyriding Stealing a car or other vehicle to have fun with.

key burglary Committing a burglary for purposes of obtaining keys, which are used to steal a vehicle.

key cloning Making a new vehicle key by decoding or duplicating the computer chip code in a transponder key.

key robbery Using physical force or a fear tactic to steal a vehicle's keys from its owner.

key theft Stealing keys to a vehicle and then using them to steal the vehicle to which they belong.

lock punching Inserting a screwdriver or similar-shape tool into the key area of a vehicle lock and applying force in a twisting motion to defeat the lock.

master keying Using a special key (i.e., master key) that fits the doors of all similar model lines to gain entry into a vehicle.

ninja rocks Small bits of porcelain (usually taken from the tops of spark plugs) used by auto thieves to break car windows to gain entry into a vehicle.

National Motor Vehicle Title Information System (NMVTIS) A nationally operated database put into service in 2009; the most comprehensive source of vehicle information available.

odometer rollback Changing the odometer reading on a vehicle so that it displays less mileage than the vehicle has actually travelled.

owner give-up Falsely reporting to insurance providers that a vehicle has been stolen to avoid making loan payments or suffering financial losses associated with continued possession of a vehicle.

phantom car A car that does not exist but has been created in official records by making a fake title and registration for purposes of committing insurance fraud.

PIN A standardized 17-digit Product Identification Number, similar to a vehicle's VIN, that is used to identify heavy equipment.

profit theft Stealing a vehicle strictly to obtain a profit, usually from cash payments provided by fences or chop shops.

salvage switching Replacing a stolen vehicle's VIN and title with the VIN and title of a similar make and model vehicle that has been salvaged.

scapegoat theft A scam (e.g., filing a false stolen vehicle report) carried out in order for a vehicle's owner to avoid detection from authorities for committing another crime in which the vehicle was involved (e.g., a hit-and-run).

Slim Jim A commercially produced device commonly used by police and tow truck drivers to open a locked vehicle without damaging windows, doors, or locks.

strip and run Stripping all valuable accessories from a vehicle immediately after it is stolen.

undercover house A specific location, usually a residential home, which is secured for purposes of conducting undercover buys of stolen cars and parts from auto thieves.

vehicle cloning Another term for VIN switching (see *VIN switching*).

VIN (vehicle identification number) A coded series of numbers and letters (17 digits beginning in 1981) that serves as a unique identification for a specific vehicle.

VIN switching Switching a stolen vehicle's identification information with that of another, unstolen vehicle of the same make, model, and other design features.

cellular phone fraud The use of a cellular phone to make unauthorized electronic bill charges and conduct other illegal financial activity.

computer as the instrumentality of the crime The use of a computer or computer technology to assist in the commission of a crime; i.e., the computer is neither the direct facilitator nor the target of a specific criminal act.

computer as the target The removal of information from computer files or databases for purposes of engaging in criminal activity; e.g., the theft of intellectual property (e.g., customer list, or pricing data) or blackmail based on information gained from computerized files (e.g., personal history data or medical information).

computer incidental to other crimes The use of a computer or computer network as a tool to enhance the commission of a crime that otherwise does not require the use of computer technology to be completed.

crimes associated with the prevalence of computers New criminal opportunities created by the development, distribution, and availability of computer technology.

cyber defamation The use of e-mails, postings, blogs, or other electronic messaging to post information that is factually inaccurate; done with malicious intent to harm someone's personal or professional reputation.

cyber stalking Using computer technology for purposes of invading the privacy of another.

cyber terrorism The use of computer resources to intimidate or coerce others.

cyber-crime Any crime that involves a computer and/or computer network.

denial of service The computer crime of flooding the Internet with several, continuous bogus requests so as to deny legitimate users access to the server or to crash the server.

digital forensics The recovery and investigation of material found in storage devices; more often than not, in computer crimes.

e-mail spoofing Forging the header of an e-mail so that the e-mail appears to originate from one source but actually has been sent from another. This practice is considered illegal when used to further criminal activity such as making an electronic threat.

hacker An individual who gains unauthorized entry into a computer or computer network by defeating an electronic security system.

hashing The process of reducing a large amount of data to a smaller amount that can be used for analytical purposes; similar to creating a data fingerprint for a given file.

logic bomb An event-dependent program designed to activate as soon as a particular event occurs, resulting in the release of a virus that causes a computer crash.

spamming Sending multiple copies of unsolicited mails or mass e-mails, which can be used to perpetrate fraud or other criminal activities.

techno-trespass Intrusion into a computer to view files or programs.

techno-vandalism Offenses involving unauthorized access to computers, computer networks, and/or electronic databases, resulting in damage to files or programs.

theft of intellectual properties Stealing information that is copyrighted, patented, or otherwise the legal intellectual property of another individual or entity.

Trojan horse An unauthorized program that functions from inside what seems to be an authorized program, thereby concealing what it is actually doing.

virus A computer program designed to disrupt the normal functioning of a computer or computer network.

virus attacks The intentional targeting of a computer or computer network with a program designed to disrupt normal function.

web jacking Using a hacking method to gain access and/or control over a website.

wire fraud Using electronic technology to commit fraudulent activities.

write blockers Devices that allow the acquisition of data from a drive without any possibility of accidentally damaging the drive's content.

accelerants Liquids, gases, or solids, usually of a volatile nature, that are used to enhance the ignition and spreading of fire. The presence of accelerants at a burning scene is an indicator of an arson fire.

alligatoring A form of charring that produces large shiny blisters on the surface of burnt wood.

backdraft A process in which oxygen necessary to feed a fire is drawn inward from external openings such as doors and windows.

blast pressure wave A wave of air traveling through space, produced by the blast of a high explosive, which can project large amounts of debris long distances from the blast site and can often be felt by eyewitnesses located near the blast.

BLEVE (Boiling Liquid Expanding Vapor Explosion) Produced by a vessel that bursts under the building pressure of expanding vapors from liquid it contains.

Bomb Disposal Unit Specialized unit used to eradicate explosive (or suspected explosive) materials from preblast or postblast bomb sites.

bomb/IED An illegal explosive device, otherwise referred to as an *improvised explosive device.*

car bomb A bomb placed in a stationary or moving vehicle.

chemical explosions Explosions caused by high-pressure gases produced by chemical reactions involving liquid, gas, or solid fuels.

containment vessel A bomb truck or other apparatus used to contain a bomb.

crater A crevice or hole left in the ground or other surface where a high explosive blast has occurred.

deflagration An explosion produced by a slow-burning detonation process, as in the case of a pipe bomb using gunpowder as an explosive agent.

detonation The most rapid form of combustion, which produces the most dramatic explosive effects; i.e., the ignition of a high explosive.

epicenter The point of origin of an explosion.

explosives Explosive materials used for a legal and legitimate purpose.

EXSPRAY A chemical agent that provides a color reaction in the presence of explosive residue; used to identify individuals who have handled explosive materials.

fire triangle The interaction of sources necessary to produce fire: heat, oxygen, and fuel.

flaming stage The stage of a fire occurring after the smoldering stage, which can cause the expansion or spreading of a blaze.

flashover An extremely dangerous situation during which entire rooms or enclosed areas burst into flames, causing total destruction and the absolute loss of human life.

heat signatures Signs of heat on surfaces of objects involved in an explosion that can be seen with the use of a thermal imaging device.

high explosives Explosives that are usually detonated by a smaller primary explosive (e.g., blasting cap) causing heat and shock that, in turn, cause a larger secondary explosive (e.g., dynamite) to explode.

ignition device Device used to produce the heat necessary to convert fuel and oxygen into fire.

incipient stage The first stage of a fire in which the fuel source is preheated by the ignition source.

inverted "V" pattern A burn pattern indicating the probable use of an accelerant.

low explosives Explosives fashioned from petroleum products, smokeless gunpowder, black powder, or some other chemical agents that are combustible through the process of deflagration (or the rapid expansion of gas by burning).

mechanical explosions Explosions caused when a vessel or container bursts as the result of internal pressure from expanding gases.

missiles Articles of debris projected from an explosion.

overhaul The inspection of a fire scene after a blaze has been extinguished to reveal unknown hazards, including areas that may cause further fires to erupt.

petaling Torn metal fragments inside the crater created by explosion of a bomb on a metal surface (such as a car floorboard) that can be used to determine the direction of the blast.

point of origin The location where a fire has started.

pour patterns Burn patterns on a surface (such as a floor) that reveal the flow of liquid accelerant used to start a fire.

puddling Burn patterns on a surface (such as a floor) that show where liquid accelerant may have collected, causing a burning puddle.

pugilist position Body position of a fourth-degree burn victim where the arms and hands are in a position that resembles the clenched fists of a boxer. This condition can indicate that the burn victim was alive at the time of exposure to the fire.

rundown burns Burn patterns that show the fire moving downward (instead of the upward direction of a naturally occurring fire), perhaps indicating the use of an accelerant.

smoldering stage The initial smoking stage of a fire, which precedes the flaming stage.

spalling Heat-induced chipping or flaking of concrete, bricks, or other masonry products.

streamers Flammable objects (e.g., paper or wood soaked in gasoline) spread throughout areas and structures and positioned to burn so that fire reaches the intended targets.

torches Professional arsonists who engage in fire setting for monetary gain.

trailers The same as a streamer (see *streamers*).

"V" burn pattern The typical burn pattern left from a naturally occurring fire (i.e., one not started using an accelerant).

amphetamine psychosis Psychotic mental symptoms—such as paranoid thoughts, hearing voices, and feeling sensations of cold bugs running over one's body—produced by the prolonged use of methamphetamine or other strong stimulant drugs.

anabolic steroids A drug used for building tissue and muscle mass.

bagging The act of inhaling fumes directly from a paper or plastic bag containing the inhalant.

barbiturates One of the oldest forms of prescription depressants, used much more infrequently nowadays because of their inherent long-term dangers to users, including high levels of tolerance leading to overdose and death.

buy-bust A one-time event where the undercover investigator purchases illegal drugs and then immediately arrests the suspect.

buy-walk An undercover drug purchase made without making an immediate arrest in hopes that the unwitting suspect will provide additional information leading to the identification and arrest of more suspects.

cannabinoids Psychoactive ingredients of marijuana that are extracted from the plant's leaves.

cathine The stimulant ingredient contained in the leaves of khat plants.

clan lab A location used for the manufacturing of methamphetamine.

cocaine Stimulant drug naturally produced from coca leaves.

codeine A narcotic prescription drug that is used as a mild pain killer as well as a cough suppressant.

crack Stimulant drug consisting of synthetically manufactured cocaine.

Controlled Substances Act (CSA) Passed in 1970; establishes federal laws regulating the manufacture and distribution of drugs in the United States.

depressants Drugs commonly known as *downers*; slow down mind and body functioning.

drug schedule Drug classification method used by the DEA (Schedules I, II, III, IV, and V), which classifies drugs according to medical and nonmedical usage and establishes criminal sanctions for drug violations.

flashbacks The recurrence of hallucinogenic effects at unplanned times during which an hallucinogenic drug has not been taken.

GHB A depressant drug, also referred to as the *date rape drug* because of its prevalent use in sexual assaults; it produces symptoms similar to those produced by alcohol, including dizziness, loss of coordination, slurred speech, and, in cases of extreme abuse, coma or death.

grow field An outdoor location used for the cultivation of illegal marijuana plants.

grow house A structure used for the indoor cultivation of illegal marijuana plants.

habituation The body's ability to develop a tolerance to a drug; a major problem encountered by narcotics users.

hallucinogens Drugs that produce an altered sensory state wherein things may be seen, felt, heard, tasted, or smelled that do not exist in reality.

hash oil Concentrated resins (i.e., cannabinoids), often resembling a sticky black liquid, extracted from marijuana plants.

hashish A concentrated resinous form of marijuana.

huffed Describes inhalant vapors inhaled directly from a rag with the mouth and nose covered.

hydrocodone A semisynthetic opiate, commonly known by its commercial name *Vicodin*, that is used for the medically legitimate purposes of cough suppression and pain management.

inhalants Vapors that, when inhaled, affect the user in a similar way to that of alcohol or other depressants that produce feelings of relaxation and inhibition.

ketamine A depressant drug normally used as an animal tranquilizer—but also approved for human use as an anesthetic.

khat A shrublike plant grown primarily in East Africa and the Arabian Peninsula that produces stimulant effects including increased energy, an elevated mood, extreme talkativeness, and increased alertness.

k-hole Symptoms caused by ketamine use including distortion of sight and sound, loss of control, lack of coordination, and extreme confusion.

MDMA Usually referred to as *ecstasy*; a stimulant that has become very popular as a club drug used by patrons of bars and nightclubs.

mescaline The primary natural psychoactive ingredient in peyote.

methamphetamine A stimulant drug made from a processed concoction of various chemical agents.

morphine A narcotic drug that is a derivative of opium, and is considered the most effective and powerful painkiller.

narcotics A general classification of drugs primarily used as pain killers or anesthetics.

oxycodone A prescription pain killer similar to morphine in its chemical composition and the effects that it produces in its users.

PCP A narcotic drug originally produced as an anesthetic for animals that produces symptoms in its users such as body numbness, rapid eye movements, slurred speech, paranoia, enhanced aggressive behavior and physical strength, and hallucinations.

peyote A hallucinogenic drug made from a small round cactus that is native to Mexico and the Southwest region of the United States.

PPC (Personal Protective Clothing)   Clothing worn to protect against exposure to hazardous materials; typically used during the investigation of clandestine drug laboratories.

precursor   A chemical or other product that is used to manufacture drugs.

psilocybin   A hallucinogenic drug found in what are usually called *magic mushrooms* that are native to Central and South America but are easily cultivated in natural or artificial environments within the United States.

reverse-buy   A situation involving an undercover officer who poses as a drug dealer and sells drugs to criminal suspects.

rock house   A location used primarily for street sales of crack cocaine, but can also serve as a manufacturing site and a safe location for users to smoke, snort, or inject the drug.

roid rage   Mood swings involving violent behavior associated with steroid use.

Schedule I   Drugs that have a high potential for abuse, no medical usage, and no established safety standards for use.

Schedule II   Drugs that have high potential for abuse, restricted medical usage, and may lead to severe psychological and/or physical dependence.

Schedule III   Drugs that have less potential for abuse than Schedule II drugs, have an accepted medical usage, and may lead to low physical dependence or high psychological dependence.

Schedule IV   Drugs that have low potential for abuse than Schedule III drugs, has an accepted medical usage, and may lead to limited physiological or psychological dependence.

Schedule V   Drugs that have the least potential for abuse, have an accepted medical usage, and may lead to limited physiological or psychological dependence.

speedballing   A combination of heroin or morphine with cocaine that is injected to produce heightened drug effects.

SSD   Sudden Sniffing Death, or sudden death by cardiac arrest minutes after breathing an inhalant.

stimulants   Drugs commonly referred to as *uppers* because persons who use them experience temporary feelings of increased physical stamina and enhanced mental awareness.

THC   The active hallucinogenic ingredient of marijuana.

A.L.F. (Animal Liberation Front)   An extremist group that encourages the "liberation" of animals from adverse conditions imposed by humans by any means that would not bring about physical harm to humans or nonhumans, but has member affiliates noted for engaging in terrorist acts to further the group's cause.

al-Qaeda   Also known as *the base*, this group is now considered one of the most dangerous and potent terrorist groups in the world; it was formerly led by the Osama bin Laden, who was killed by Navy Seals in 2011.

car bomb   An explosive device contained on or within a moving or stationary car.

coyotes   A term used for persons who smuggle illegal aliens across the U.S. border for a fee.

domestic terrorism   Acts of terror that take place within the borders of the United States or its territories.

drop house   A location used to temporarily house persons smuggled across the U.S. border.

DTO   Drug trafficking organization; may also engage in human trafficking and narco–terrorism.

E.L.F. (Earth Liberation Front)   Commonly referred to as *the Elves*, an extremist group that is known to use terror tactics to target anything that can be construed as "exploiting the earth, its environment and its inhabitants."

HAMAS   Also known as the *Palestinian Islamic Resistance Movement*, a political extremist group founded in 1987 as an extension of the longstanding Muslim Brotherhood group centered in Palestine.

Hezbollah   aka *the party of God*, an political extremist group composed of Muslim Shi'ite militants who operate mainly from Lebanon and are noted for engaging in terrorist activities directed toward the nation of Israel and countries that support the Israeli cause.

jihad   A term used to describe waging a "holy war" against another group or nation.

knock-and-talk   A method whereby investigators approach residents in a consensual encounter while observing the location for certain characteristics.

LEG terrorist   A terrorist whose actions are motivated by the desire to create anarchy and to overthrow capitalist governments and business entities.

load vehicle   A vehicle typically used to transport persons smuggled across the U.S. border to a temporary housing location (i.e., a drop house).

lone wolf terrorist   A terrorist who acts alone and may or may not belong to a formal terrorist organization.

narco–terrorism   Acts of random violence carried out by drug cartels for purposes of intimidating and creating fear among their enemies, government officials, and the public.

narcobanners   Signs placed in public locations that have been created by DTOs (drug trafficking organizations) to denounce certain government practices or government officials.

Patriot Act   Federal legislation passed by Congress in 2001 defining acts of domestic terrorism and authorizing specific law enforcement actions that may be taken to control terrorists and acts of terror.

phantom cell   Terrorist cell that may consist of one person or a small group of individuals identifying with the ideologies and practices of a known terrorist leader or organization but having no formal contact or affiliation with that terrorist organization.

pollos   A term used for persons who pay a fee to be transported illegally by coyotes across the U.S. border.

REG terrorist   A terrorist motivated by antigovernment conspiracy belief systems or ideologies of hatred directed toward specific classes of persons.

socio-political terrorist   A terrorist having the desire to promote social and political change through violent means.

special cause terrorist   A terrorist whose acts are motivated primarily by specific issues rather than by general ideologies.

special interest aliens   Persons having citizenship in countries outside the United States who may have ties with terrorist organizations.

Taliban   Sunni fundamentalist group with a strong presence in Afghanistan that is noted for cooperating with al-Qaeda in terrorist activities.

terrorist cell   A subgroup of a terrorist organization typically consisting of a leader and 3 to 10 members.

transnational terrorism Terrorist acts that originate in one country and affect the domestic security of one or more other countries.

truck bomb An explosive device contained on or within a moving or stationary truck or other vehicle used for hauling cargo.

walk-away bomb An explosive device contained on or within a moving or stationary truck or other vehicle used for hauling cargo.

WMDs Weapons of mass destruction, which are forms of nuclear, chemical, and biological weaponry.

arraignment The appearance of criminal defendants before a judge or magistrate, at which time the defendants are formally read and advised of crimes pending against them.

case in chief A term used to describe the actions of proving each legal claim outlined by the prosecution against the defendant.

challenge for cause An assertion made by trial attorneys that a juror (for any reason) is unable to judge the evidence fairly and should be excluded as a possible jury member.

closing argument The final statements made by both prosecuting and defense attorneys to a jury that typically include statements regarding what evidence has been proven, how the evidence ties into the jury instructions, and why the evidence and the law require a verdict in their favor.

cross examination Questioning of a witness by the opposing attorney; e.g., the prosecuting attorney questions a witness who has testified on behalf of the defense.

direct examination The questioning of a witness by the party who called them to trial; e.g., the defense attorney questions their own witness who is testifying on behalf of the defendant.

exculpatory evidence Evidence that is favorable to a defendant.

exhibits Types of evidence used at trial including real objects (guns, blood), items used for demonstration (diagrams, models, maps), writings (counterfeit checks, letters), and records (private business, phone, public records).

filing district attorney Prosecuting attorney who has the discretion to decide whether or not to formally charge a crime suspect with a criminal offense, and if so, what the official legal charges will be.

judicial notice A process of admitting evidence at trial whereby a judge recognizes that a particular fact is assumed to be true.

jury selection The process by which prosecuting and defense attorneys agree or disagree on which members of a jury pool should serve as jurors at trial.

no contest A plea in which the defendant accepts the sentence as if found guilty.

opening statements The beginning stage of a trial where both prosecution and defense attorneys outline the issues in a case and tell the jury what they expect the evidence will prove during the trial.

outside witness Witness testifying at trial who is not an investigator of the crime(s) of which the defendant is being charged.

preliminary hearing A court hearing in which a judge or magistrate determines whether sufficient probable cause exists to bring the defendant to trial to answer to the criminal charges that have been formally filed.

stipulations Agreements between the defense and prosecution that certain facts exist and are not in dispute, which serve as a form of evidence at trial.

NAME INDEX

SUBJECT INDEX